 ISBN 1-84356-008-9
Second Edition

First Edition Published 1982

Library of Congress Catalog Number: 6633147397

Published by The Simon Wallenberg Press

Printed in the United States of America

Warning and Disclaimer

This book is sold as is, without warranty of any kind, either express or implied. While every precaution has been taken in the preparation of this book, the authors and Simon Wallenberg Press assume no responsibility for errors or omissions. Neither is any liability assumed for damages resulting from the use of the information or instructions contained herein. It is further stated that the publisher and authors are not responsible for any damage or loss that results directly or indirectly from your use of this book.

English - Pashto
Poshto - English
Dictionary

By Gayan Chand

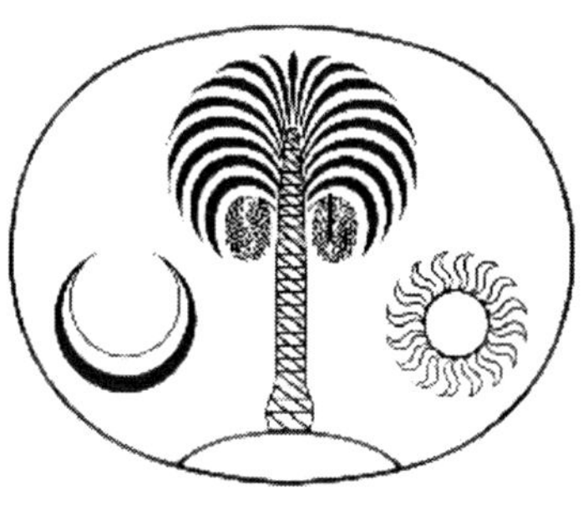

Simon Wallenberg Press

Message from Professor Dost Mohammad Gur Head of the Pashto Language Department Kabul University

I congratulate the Simon Wallenberg Press for publishing this Second edition of the Pashto - English and English - Pashto Dictionary which is bound to prove a useful resource for Pashtun students studying English at the Department.

This message gives me an opportunity to write about the Pashtun people who, unfortunately, have fared badly in much of the Western media.

The Pashtun are a proud, noble and freedom loving race with a rich culture. In a long and bloody war they defeated the Soviet invasion with weapons and training provided by the United States of America.

The thousands of Pashtun who perished during these fierce battles against the Soviet Union gave up their today for your tomorrow. The victory in Afghanistan was a key element that contributed to the eventual demise of the USSR, the subsequent fall of the Berlin Wall and freedom being gained by many millions of people. After our victory, we Pashtun were abandoned by the international community which left us destitute. Amidst grinding poverty we saw our country ravaged by warlords who were armed and encouraged by elements in neighboring countries.

Since 11 September, a bigger tragedy evolved which led to the Pashtuns becoming the most vilified ethnic group in the world. They are now an angry and frustrated people who want to reclaim their identity from being lumped with the Taliban as perpetrators of terrorism and suicide bombings. Although many Taliban are Pashtun, The Pashtun are certainly not Taliban. The tragedy for the Pashtuns has been their association with the Taliban. Only a small minority of Pashtun are responsible for the entire people to be labeled as terrorists. Pakistan's 40 million Pashtuns and Afghanistan's 10-12 million Pashtuns are like people all over the world, they want to live in peace, within the rule of law.

However the Pashtun continue to suffer in the crossfire of the war on terror and revenge for September 11. Many thousands are dead and hundreds of towns and villages have been destroyed by massive bombing.

It was the Taliban's association with Osama Bin Laden and the protection they gave Al-Qaeda after 1996 that first associated the Pashtun with terrorism in the eyes of the international community. Even then many Pashtuns resisted the Taliban. Among them was Abdul Haq - who was gunned down by the Taliban for leading a revolt in 2001 - and Hamid Karzai, who is now president of Afghanistan.

In Pakistan, secular and democratic-minded Pashtuns have long resisted the idea that the 3,000-year-old Pashtun culture and language should be Talibanised. "Around the world we are accused of being terrorists, but tolerance, taught by our elders, is in our blood. We too demand that all the world respects our values, culture and the dignity of our people."

Mr Karzai is a Pashtun who has always resisted the Taliban "Pashtuns stand united for peace, but the fire of war is burning our land and we have to find the means to extinguish it. We are caught in the middle of warmongers, extremists and militants.

The Simon Wallenberg Pashto Dictionary will prove a useful tool for both students who wish to learn Pashto and Afghans who wish to acquire a knowledge of English.

Prof Dost Mohammad Gur
Department of Poshto
University of Kabul

12 March 2007

This Dictionary is dedicated to Hamid Karzai a leading Pashtun and first President of Democratic Afghanistan.

Hamid Karzai, is an ethnic Pashtun of the influential Popalzai tribe, he was born in Kandahar, Afghanistan.

He took a postgraduate course in political science at Himachal University in Shimla, Himachal Pradesh, India from 1979 to 1983, then returned to work as a fund-raiser supporting anti-Soviet uprisings in Afghanistan during the Soviet intervention for the rest of the 1980s. After the fall of Najibullah's government in 1992, he served as a deputy foreign minister in the government of Burhanuddin Rabbani.

He married Zeenat Karzai, an obstetrician by profession in Pakistan in 1999, when she was working as a doctor with Afghan refugees and he was living there in exile. They have a son named Mirwais born on January 25th 2007 and named after a former Afghan king.

As with many other early Taliban supporters, he broke with the Taliban disgusted with their policies. Karzai refused to serve as their U.N. ambassador. And left Afghanistan to live in exile in Quetta, His father was assassinated, by Taliban agents, on July 14, 1999

After the Taliban was defeated and driven out of Kabul Afghan political leaders named Karzai Chairman of a 29-member governing committee. He was sworn-in as leader on December 22. The Loya Jirga of June 19, 2002 appointed Karzai Interim holder of the new position as President of the Afghan Transitional Administration.

Karzai was a candidate in the October 9, 2004 presidential elections. He won 21 of the 34 provinces, defeating his 22 opponents and became the first democratically elected leader of Afghanistan.

Karzai was officially sworn in as President of Afghanistan on December 7, 2004 at a formal ceremony in Kabul. Many interpreted the ceremony as a symbolically important "new start" for the war-torn nation.

Notable guests at the inauguration included the country's former King, Zahir Shah, Afghanistan's three living former presidents, and U.S. Vice President Dick Cheney.

Speakers of the Pashto Language the Pashtoon,

The PUSHTOON, PASHTUN or PAKHTOON are also known in Hindustani as PATHAN and in Persian as the AFGHAN. Pashtu-speaking people of Afghanistan and northwestern Pakistan constitute the majority of the population of Afghanistan and bore the exclusive name of Afghan before that name came to denote any native of the present land area of Afghanistan.

On the origins of the Pashtoon, most scholars believe it likely that they arose from an intermingling of ancient Aryans from the north or west with subsequent invaders. Several Pashtun clans are known to have moved from Afghanistan to Pakistan between the 13th and 16th century. Each clan, consisting of kinsmen who trace descent in the male bloodline from a common clanial ancestor, is divided into subclans, and patriarchal families. Clanial genealogies establish rights of succession and inheritance and the right to use tribal lands and to speak in tribal council.

Disputes over property, women, and personal injury often result in blood feuds between families and whole clans; these may be inherited unless settled by the intervention of clan chiefs or by council of elders.

The Pashtoon are farmers, herdsmen, and warriors. Most are sedentary farmers, combining cultivation with animal husbandry; some are migratory herdsmen and caravaners. Large numbers of them have always been attracted to military service.

There are estimated to be about 12,500,000(est. 1982) Pashtun in Afghanistan and 14,000,000 in Pakistan. They comprise about 60 clans of varying size and importance, each of which occupies a particular territory. In Afghanistan, where Pashtun are the predominant ethnic group, the main clans are the Durrani and the Ghilzay.

In Pakistan, Pashtoon predominate north of Quetta between the Sulaiman Range and the Indus River. In the hill areas the main clans are, from south to north: the Kakar, Sherani, and Ustarana south of the Gumal River; the Mahsud, Darwesh Khel, Waziri, and Bitani between the Gumal River and Thal; the Turi, Bangash, Orakzay, Afridi, and Shinwari from Thal to the Khyber Pass; and the Mohmand, Utman Khel, Tarklani, and Yusufzay north and northeast of the Khyber.

The settled areas include lowland tribes subject to direct administration by the provincial government. The main clans there are, from south to north: the Banuchi and Khatak from the Kurram River to Nowshera; and the Khalil and Mandan in the Vale of Peshawar.

Pashtunwali

Pashtunwalai, literally means the way of the Pashtuns, it's the rules and regulations and laws of the Pashtun tribes which protected the world's biggest tribal society. These rules are responsible for the survival of the Pashtun tribes for over 2000 years. Some of the rules go back to the days of Adam and eve and are still puritan today

NANEWATEI: Under Nanewatei a penitent enemy is forgiven and the feuding factions resume peaceful and friendly relations. Thus it creates a congenial atmosphere for peaceful co-existence and mutual understanding through eventual reconciliation.

TEEGA OR KANRAY: Teega or Kanray is cessation of bloodshed between contending parties. Teega (putting down of a stone) in other words means a temporary truce declared by a Jirga. The word stone is used figuratively as actually no stone is put at the time of the cessation of hostilities. Once the truce is enforced, no party dares violate it for fear of punitive measures.

BADAL: (Eye for an Eye) Self-respect and sensitivity to insult is another essential trait of Pashtun character. The poorest among them has his own sense of dignity and honor and he vehemently refuses to submit to any insult. In fact every Pashtun considers himself equal if not better than his fellow tribesmen and an insult is, therefore, taken as scurrilous reflection on his character. An insult is sure to evoke insult and murder is likely to lead to a murder.

MELMASTIA: Pashtun have been described as one of the most hospitable peoples of the world. They consider Melmastia or generous hospitality as one of the finest virtues and greet their guest warmly with a broad smile on their faces. A Pashtun feels delighted to receive a guest regardless of his past relations or acquaintance and prepares a delicious meal for him and offers up to their ability the finest meals available to them.

TOR: Pashtuns are sensitive about the honour of their women folk and slight touching of the women is at times considered a serious and an intolerable offence. The cases of adultery and illicit relations are put down with iron hand in and no quarter is given to culprits either male or female. Casting of an evil eye on woman is tantamount to imperil one's life. Both sexes, therefore, scrupulously avoid indulgence in immoral practices.

GHUNDI: Ghundi is a classic case of balance of power in tribal areas. It is derived from Pashto word Ghund, meaning a political party but it is used for an alliance. As modern states enter into bilateral agreements for promotion of trade, cultivation of friendly relations and mutual defense, similarly various sections of a tribe align themselves in blocs or Ghunds to safeguard their common interests. Ghundi is entered into defeat the aggressive and nefarious designs of a hostile neighbor. In tribal fighting the Ghundi members espouse their mutual interests against their common enemy and act as a corporate body with all the resources at their command.

LOKHAY WARKAWAL: Lokhay Warkawal literally means `giving of a pot' but it implies the protection of an individual or a tribe. A weaker tribe to a stronger one with the object of ensuring its safety and security generally gives Lokhay. It is accepted in the form of a sacrificial animal such as a goat or a sheep. When a tribe accepts a Lokhay from another tribe, it undertakes the responsibility of safeguarding the latter's interests against its enemies and protects it at all costs.

LASHKAR: Lashkar is an armed party, which goes out from a village or tribe for warlike purposes. The Lashkar may consist of a hundred to several thousand men. The Lashkar assembled for Jihad (Holy Struggle) is usually very large. The decisions of a Jirga, if violated by a party, are enforced through a tribal Lashkar. The Lashkar thus performs the functions of police in the event of a breach of tribal law.

CHIGHA: Chigha means a pursuit party. The Chigha party is formed or taken out in case armed bandits with the object of lifting cattle, looting property or abducting an inmate of the village, raid a village. Composed of armed persons, the Chigha party goes in pursuit of the raiders to affect the release of the cattle etc or recover the stolen property.

TARR: A mutual accord between two tribes or villagers themselves with regard to a certain matter is called Tarr. For instance, after sowing wheat or any other crop, the people of the village agree not to let loose their cattle to graze in the fields and thus damage the crop. The man whose cattle are found grazing in the fields in violation of this agreement has no right to claim compensation for an injury caused to his cattle by the owner of the field.

MLA TARR: Mla Tarr, which literally means `girding up of loins' denotes two things. Firstly it is used for all such members of a family who are capable of carrying and using firearms. Secondly, it means espousing the cause of a man against his enemies and providing him with an armed party. The tribesmen resort to Mla Tarr when a person belonging to their village or tribe is attacked, mal-treated or disgraced by their enemies.

BADRAGHA: An armed party escorting a fugitive or a visitor to his destination is called Badragha. Badragha is a guarantee for the safety of a man who is either hotly pursued by his enemies or there is an apprehension of his being killed on his way home. An armed party accompanies such a man as Badragha or `escort' to ensure his safe return to the place of his abode. Badragha is never attacked by the second party because of fear of reprisals and the blood feud that is sure to follow if an attack is made on it. The Badragha convoy can be depended upon only within its own geographical limits;

beyond it, the people of other tribes take the charge to convoy the traveler.

BILGA: The word Bilga is used for stolen property. A man is held responsible for theft or burglary if any of the stolen articles are recovered from his house. In such a case he is obliged to make good the loss sustained by the afflicted person. He, however, stands absolved of Bilga if he discloses the source or the persons from whom he had purchased the stolen articles.

BOTA: Bota means carrying away. It is a sort of retaliatory action against an aggressor. For instance, if a creditor fails to recover his debt from the debtor, he resorts to Bota by seizing his cattle or one of his kith and kin. The creditor keeps them as hostages till his dues are fully realized or the debtor has furnished a security to make payment within a specified period to the creditor.

BARAMTA: Baramta like Bota is resorted to when the grievances of a party are not redressed or a debtor adopts delaying tactics in respect of payment of a debt to the creditor. The word Baramta is derived from Persian word Baramad, which means recovery or restitution of property etc. Under Baramta hostages are held to ransom till the accused returns the claimed property. The Pashtuns consider it an act against their sense of honour and contrary to the principles of Pashtunwali to lay their hands on dependent classes such as blacksmiths, tailors, barbers and butchers etc belonging to the debtor's village.

BALANDRA OR ASHAR: Balandra or Ashar can be best described as a village aid program under which a particular task is accomplished on the basis of mutual cooperation and assistance. At the time of sowing or harvesting, the villagers lend a helping hand to the man who seeks their help. They take out their pair of bullocks to plough his fields at sowing time and assist him in reaping his crops at the time of harvest. The man, thus obliged, by the fellow villagers holds a feast in their honor in the evening.

MEERATA: Meerata means complete annihilation of the male members of a family by brutal assassination. This is not a custom but a criminal act. Under Meerata, the stronger member of family used to assassinate their weak but near relatives with the sole object of removing them from the line of inheritance and gaining forcible possession of their lands, houses and other property. The tribal law seriously views this kind of cold-blooded murder and persons responsible for such an inhumane and ghastly act cannot escape the wrath of Pashtuns. The Jirga immediately assembles to take suitable action against the culprits. The penalty is usually in the form of setting on fire their houses and other property and expulsion of the culprits from their area.

SAZ: The word Saz is used for blood money or compensation in lieu of killing. Under the custom of Saz a person who feels penitent after committing a deliberate murder, approaches the deceased's family through a Jirga and offers to make payment of blood money to end enmity between them. All hostilities come to an end between the parties after acceptance of Saz. Sometimes the payment of compensation takes the form of giving a girl in marriage to the aggrieved party. It is also called Swarah, which binds together the two parties in blood relations and thus helps in eradicating ill will and feelings of enmity.

ITBAR: Itbar, which means trust, or guaranteed assurance or is the arch of society, which is governed by un-written laws or conventions. All business including contracts relating to sale and mortgage or disposal of property, is transacted on the basis of trust or Itbar. Such transactions are verbal and are entered into in the presence of the village elders or a few witnesses. The violation of Itbar is considered to be dishonorable act, un-becoming of gentleman and contrary to the norms of Pashtunwali.

HAMSAYA: The word Hamsaya stands for a neighbor but in Pashto it applies to a man who abandons his home either due to poverty or blood feud and seeks protection of an elder of another village. In this way the latter becomes his client or vassal. It is, therefore, incumbent upon the protector to save his Hamsaya from insult or injury from any source.

Pushtoon Society

Islam

Islam is practised by the majority of Afghanis and governs much of their personal, political, economic and legal lives. Among certain obligations for Muslims are to pray five times a day – at dawn, noon, afternoon, sunset, and evening. Friday is the Muslim holy day.

During the holy month of Ramadan all Muslims must fast from dawn to dusk and are only permitted to work six hours per day. Fasting includes no eating, drinking, cigarette smoking, or gum chewing.
Foreigners are not required to fast; however, they must not eat, drink, smoke, or chew gum in public.

The Pushtun in Relation to Other Ethnic People in Afganistan

The Pashtun are Sunni Muslims. They constitute around 42% of the population and are concentrated in Nangrahar and Pakhtya provinces. A large population also live in neighbouring Pakistan.

Tajiks comprise roughly 27% of the population. They are Iranian in origin and speak a form of Persian found in Eastern Iran. Most are Sunni Muslim. Most reside in Kabul and Herat provinces,although some reside in the mountains north of Hindu Kush, and the Iranian border.

Hazaris make up about 9% of the population. They are descendants of the Mongols, and speak a dialect of Persian that contains many Turkish words. They are also Shiite Muslims which led to much of their persecution under Taliban rule. Most live in the Hazarajat region.

The Uzbeks live in the northern parts of the country and also comprise only 9% of the population. They are Sunni Muslims and speak a dialect of Turkish.

The Turkomen are a small minority with making only 3% of the population.
Baluchis are pastoral nomads who speak Baluchi, an Iranian language. They comprise 2% of the population.
The Family

The Role of Family Values in Pushtun Society

The family is the single most important unit in the Afghan culture. Men and women's roles are much more defined along traditional lines. Women are generally responsible for household duties, where as men will be the bread winners. In the cities professional women do exist. Families commonly arrange marriages for their children. Factors such as tribe, status, network, and wealth are the major factors forming any choice.
Families traditionally live together in the same walled compound, known as the kala. When a son gets married he and his wife begin their married lives in a room under the same roof. As with much of the Muslim world, the family is sacred and as such, is highly protected. As a result, probing about the family is not advised.

The Concepts of Honour and Shame

Honour in Afghan culture defines the reputation and worth of an individual, as well as those they are associated with. The head male of a family is responsible for protecting the honour of the family.

The issue of honour drives much of the behaviour surrounding the protection of women, modes of dress, social interaction, education and economic activity. If someone's honour has been compromised, they are shamed and will look for a way to exact revenge for themselves, their family or group.

The Role of Hospitality

Hospitality is an essential aspect of Afghan culture.

No matter who you are, if you visit a home you will be given the best the family has. This relates back to the idea of gaining honour. If you are invited for tea, which you inevitably will be, you will be offered snacks and your tea glass will be constantly filled. When you have had enough cover the glass with your hand and say "bus" (meaning 'enough').

Social Etiquette and Protocol

Meeting and Greeting When meeting someone the handshake is the most common form on greeting. You will also see people place their hands over their hearts and nod slightly. One should always enquire about things like a person's health, business, family, etc. Women and men will never shake hands let alone speak directly to one another. Eye contact should also be avoided between men and women. Between men eye contact is acceptable as long as it is not prolonged – it is best to only occasionally look someone in the eyes.

Mixing Between Genders

Free mixing between genders only takes places within families. In professional situations such as at businesses or universities, males and females may be co-workers, but are nevertheless cautious to maintain each other's honour. Foreign females must learn to read the rules and live by them. If a man speaks to you directly in a social context, he is dishonouring you. If someone speaks to you on the street, that is equally inappropriate. You should avoid looking men in the eyes, and keep your eyes lowered when you walk down the street to maintain your reputation as a proper woman.

Women must always dress properly to avoid unwanted attention. Always wear loose fitting pants under your skirts and be sure the definition of your legs is un distinguishable. It is also strongly advisable to wear a headscarf in public. On the other hand foreign men should note that it is inappropriate to initiate social conversation with a woman, and one should not ask a male about his wife or female relatives. Men and women should never be alone in the same room. If this happens you should ensure a door is left open. Men and women should never touch one another under any circumstances.

Gift Giving Etiquette

First rule of gift giving is to never give alcohol. However, if you know from first hand experience that the receiver drinks you may do so but covertly to avoid shame. The first time you go to someone's house for tea, it is appropriate to bring a small gift. If you are invited to lunch or dinner, bring fruit, sweets or pastries. Make sure the box is wrapped nicely. When bringing a gift be subtle in how it is given. Do not immediately give the present but rather discreetly place it near the door or where you sit down. When it comes to wrapping gifts there is no special protocol. Green is good for weddings.

Dining Etiquette

Dining in Afghanistan is a different experience and there are many differences in etiquette. Always remove your shoes at the door if visiting a home. If eating at someone's home, you will be seated on the floor, usually on cushions.
Food is served on plastic or vinyl tablecloths spread on the floor. Wait to be shown where to sit.
If you can, sit cross-legged. Otherwise sit as comfortably as you can. Do not site with legs outstretched and your feet facing people. Food is generally served communally and everyone will share from the same dish. Do not eat with the left hand. Always pass and receive things using your right hand too. Food is eaten with the hands. It will be a case of watch and learn. Leave food on your plate otherwise it will keep getting filled up again.

Business Etiquette, Customs and Protocol

Business Cards

Business cards are not widely used in Afghanistan. They therefore carry a sense of importance and prestige. If you are given a business card, take it respectfully and study it so that they see that you are spending time considering their credentials. Comment on it and any qualifications the giver may have. Try not to keep cards in your pocket – slip it into a holder and somewhere else respectful. There is no real protocol used for exchanging cards except to use your right hand. It may be a good idea to have your card translated into Dari or Pashtu. Make sure you don't "translate" the address.

What to Wear?

Men should wear conservative suits and shoes. If working in the country in a non-commercial capacity then wearing the traditional Afghan dress (long shirt and trousers) is best. Women must always dress modestly and conservatively. The general rule is to show as little flesh from the neck downwards. If working in business, women should wear knee-length, loose fitting business skirts with loose fitting professional trousers underneath. Wearing headscarf is advisable.

Business Meetings

Business is very much personal in Afghanistan. If you have not already invested some quality time in getting to know your counterparts, then you must use initial meetings to establish trust. Once this has been accomplished you can move on to the nitty-gritty of business. Do not be surprised or offended if during meetings people walk in and out of a room or phone calls are taken. If the meeting involves a group of people it will be led by the leader who will set the agenda, the content, and the pace of the activities.

Meetings are usually held to communicate information and decisions that have already been rather than a forum for discussion and brain storming. Meeting schedules are not very structured. Start times, points of discussion, etc are all fluid and flexible. Be prepared for a lot of tangents in the discussions.

Afghani communication style is rather indirect. It is therefore sometimes necessary to read between the lines for an answer rather than expect it to be explicitly stated. For example, if someone is asked if they can complete a job on time, you will rarely get "no" as the answer. It is therefore also important to phrase questions intelligently.
Honour and shame should always be considered. Always express yourself in a way that is not direct or pins blame on someone. Never make accusations or speak down to anyone.

The Pashto Language Family

PROTO EUROPEAN AND INDO EUROPEAN
The Indo European branched into:

- TOCHARIAN
- INDO-PERSIAN
- ANATOLIAN
- HELLENIC
- ALBANIAN

The Indo-Persian were divided to:

- INDIC
- PERSIAN
- DARDIC (Extinct)
- NURISTANI (Extinct)

The Persian Branched was Classified as:

- AWESTAN (Extinct)
- OLD PERSIAN
- Old Persian divided into 2:
- MIDDLE PERSIAN
- SOGDIAN
- PAHLAWI

Middle Persian Divided into 6 Modern Languages:

- TAJIKI
- PASHTO
- BALUCHI
- KURDISH
- FARSI
- DARI

DARI - Dari is derived from "darbari" meaning the language of the court of kings, spoken in the Central, Northern , and Western Provinces of Afghanistan
PASHTO - Pashto is spoken in the Southern , South eastern Provinces of Afghanistan, Pashtu could possibly be the ancestors all Hebrew Languages, and the language of the lost tribes of Israel. 8% of 150 million in Pakistan speak Pashto and 35% of 27 million in Afghanistan. 12 milllion in Pakistan and 9.45 million in Afghanistan with total of 21.45 million pashto speakers on each side of the Durrand Line.
UZBAKI - Uzbaki is spoken by 1 Million Turkmens and 300 thousand of those speak Turkmani
Other languages include Baluchi modern and Nooristani.

The Combined
English - Pashto
Pahsto - English
Dictionary

Introduction to the Language

Classification

Pashto is classified as an Iranian language within the Indo-Iranian branch of the Indo-European languages. Pashto belongs to the Southeastern branch of Iranian languages, along with Sarikoli, Wakhi, Munji, Shughni, and other languages. Other notable related Iranian languages include Persian, Kurdish, Gileki, and Ossetic, spoken in the Caucasus and South Asia.

Geographic distribution

Pashto is spoken by about 28 million people in the western provinces of North-West Frontier Province, Federally Administered Tribal Areas, and Balochistan of Pakistan and by over 13 million people in the south, east, west and a few northern provinces of Afghanistan.Approximately 776,000 Pashtuns speak Pashto in small pockets of India.

Smaller, modern "transplant" communities are also found in Sindh (Karachi, Hyderabad). Other smaller communities peopled by Pashtun invaders in the past centuries, exist in Northern India (Pathankot, Rampur) and northeastern Iran. It is spoken by a large part of Afghanistan's population who are of the Pashtun tribe, as well as by ethnic Pashtuns who live in Pakistan.

Official status

Pashto is an official and one of the national languages of Afghanistan as of 1936. It is one of the official languages in the western provinces of Pakistan. A related language spoken in areas of northern Afghanistan, a dialect of Persian, is Dari.

Grammar

Pashto is a S-O-V language with split ergativity. Adjectives come before nouns. Nouns and adjectives are inflected for gender (Masculine/Feminine), number (Singular/Plural) and case (Direct/Oblique). Direct case is used for subjects and direct objects in the present tense. Oblique case is used after most pre- and post-positions as well as in the past tense as the subject of transitive verbs. There is no definite article, but instead there is extensive use of the demonstratives this/that. The verb system is very intricate with the following: Simple Present, Subjunctive, Simple Past, Past Progressive, Present Perfect,and Past Perfect. In any of the past tenses (Simple Past, Past Progressive, Present Perfect and Past Perfect) Pashto is an ergative language, i.e. transitive verbs in any of the past tenses agree with the object of the sentence.

Vocabulary

Pashto, being an Indo-European language, shares many cognates with other related languages. Following the advent of Islam in Afghanistan, the Pashto language has received a significant influx of loan-words from Arabic, Persian and various Turkic languages.

Writing system

From the time of Islam's rise in South-Central Asia, Pashto has used a modified version of Perso-Arabic script called the Nasta'liq script. In recent years, however, because of the Internet, it has become increasingly popular to write Pashto in Naskh.

Pashto has several letters which do not appear in any other Perso-Arabic script which represent the retroflex versions of the consonants . The letters are written like the standard Arabic ta', dal, ra', and nun with a "pandak", "gharwandah" or also called “skarraen” attached underneath which looks like a small circle, respectively. It also has the letters ge and xin (the initial sound of which is like the German ch found in the word “ich”) which look like a ra’ and sin respectively with a dot above and beneath. Pashto also has the extra letters that Persian has added to the Arabic alphabet.

Part I

English - Pashto Dictionary

Aback, ad. *biyarta, wrusto, pastana.*

Abaisance, s. *salām, sijda, t'aẓīm.*

Abandon, v.a. *pregdal, prekkhodal, prekkhawul, preyakkhal*; *tark k.*

Abandoned, a. *prekkhodalai, preyakkhai* or *prīkkhai.*

Abandonment, s. *prekkhodana, prekkhawuna.*

Abase, v.a. *spukawul.*

Abased, v.n. *spukedal.* a. *spukawulai, spukedalai.*

Abasement, s. *spuk·wālai, spukedana.*

Abash, v.a. *sharmawul.*

Abashed, v.n. *sharmedal.* a. *sharmsār, sharmindah*; *pakkhemān*; *sharmedalai.*

Abate, v.a. *kamawul, la-ag k.* v.n. *kamedal, la-ag ked.*

Abatement, s. *kamedana, kam·wālai, kam·tiyā, la-agedana, la-ag·wālai*; *chūk.*

Abbreviate, v.a. *landawul.*

Abbreviation, s. *land·wālai.*

Abdicate, v.a. *tark k. pregdal.* (Abandon).

Abdicator, s. *tark kawūnkai, prekkhodūnkai. tārik.*

Abdomen, s. *geḍa, kheṭa.* (hypogastrium) *spokhdza, spokhz.* (hypochondrium) *ta ashai, ḍaḍa.*

Abet, v.a. *madad warkawul, pushtī k.*; *lamsawul.*

Abetment, s. *madad, pushtī, komak*; *lamsūn.*

Abettor, s. *madad-, pushtī-, komak-,* etc. *warkawūnkai*; *lamsūnai.*

Abide, v.n. *osedal, āstedal, pātedal, pātai ked. wudaredal.*

Abject, a. *khwār, dūn, sperah·kai, sperah·makh.*

Abjectness, s. *khwārī, tabāhī.*

Ability, s. *qābiliyat, ṭāqat, was, yarz*; *qābil·tob.*

Abjure, v.a. *munkiredal.*
Able, a. *qābil, tuwānā.* v.n. *shwal, tuwānedal.* v.a. *tāqat-, zor-, wāk-, was-,* etc. *laral.*
Ablution, s. *ghusl,* (ceremonial) *āwdas, wazū, taimūm* or *tebūn.*
Abode, s. *dzāe, astoga, astogana, tīkāo, mīshta, kor, makān, kilai, dera, borjal.*
Abolish, v.a. *bandawul, mauqūf-, man'a-, mansūkh-,* etc. *k.*
Abominable, a. *bad, palīt, nā-pāk, stūkh, murdār.*
Abominate, v.a. *bad manal, chinjawul, kraka ākhistal, nafrat k., ghandal, kagal.*
Abort, v.a. *geda ghurzawul, ziyān k.*
Abortion, s. *da gede ziyān.* (in animals) *piyāza.*
Abortive, a. *be-fā-ida, 'abaṣ, bāṭil, nā-kār.*
Above, p. *pās, dapāsa, bānde, dabānde, porta, pahūrta.*
Abound, *wadānedal, ziyātedal, deredal.*
About, p. *chāpera, chauper; dapāra, bābat; nizde* or *nijde, qarīb, tsakha* or *khatsa; lagiyā, mashghūl; pa andāz, pa ḥisāb.*
Abrade, v.a. *sūlawul, garawul, gargal, gasiyā k.* v.n. *sūledal, blodal, blosedal, gasiyā ked.*
Abrasion, s. *sūda, blos, gasiyā; blosedana, sūledana.*
Abreast, ad. *barābar, tsang pa tsang.*
Abroad, ad. *bahar* or *bāhir, pa pradī mulk* (or *dzāe*) *kkhke.*
Abrupt, a. *garandai, za-ar* or *zir, jalt; zig, lwār.* s. *doghal, kand, garang, kamar.*
Abruptly, ad. *nā-tsāpa, nā-gūmān, nāgāh, sam da lāsa.*
Abscess, s. *kharai, kkhanza, shīnai, nanaka-ī, kkhlūna, lūna.*
Abscond, v.n. *puṭedal, takkhtedal, firārī ked.*
Absence, s. *biyal-tūn, judā-ī, hijrān; nisht-wālai, ghair ḥāẓirī.*
Absent, a. *ghā-ib, nishtah, ghair ḥāẓir; biyal, judā; ghāfil, be-khūd, pa fikr kkhke dūb.*
Absolve, v.a. *pulawul, bakkhal* or *bakhkkhal.*
Absolved, a. *bakkhalai, pulawulai, khalāṣ, m'uāf.*
Absolute, a. *pūrah, sarāsar, amānī, tamām, ṭol, mutlaq; khpul-sar* or *khapsar, wāk-dār, mukhtār.*
Absolutely, ad. *amānī, sarāsarī, tamāmī.*
Absolution, s. *bakkhana, khalāṣī, puṭ* (or *pa-al*), *najāt.*
Absorb, v.a. *tskkhal* or *tskal* or *skal, wuchawul.*
Absorbed, v.n. *wuchedal, jaẓb ked.*
Abstain, v.a. *parhez-, pāl-,* etc. *k. lāṣ-, dzān-,* etc. *bāsal—yastal, lās-, dzān-* etc. *sātal.*
Abstemious, a. *parhez-gār, kam-khwurāk, pārsā.*
Abstinence, s. *pāl, parhez; roja; pārsā-ī.*
Abstract, s. *mujmal, khulāṣa.*
Abstract, v.a. *bāsal—yastal, kāgal—kkhkal; biyalawul, judā k.*
Abstruse, a. *bārīk, narai, puṭ; grān, mush-kil.*
Absurd, a. *'abaṣ, be-hūdah, wuch puch, yāwah, khushai, prat, harzah.*
Absurdity, s. *be-hūdagī, be-wūqūfī, kam-'aqlī.*
Abundance, s. *der-wālai, wadānī, ābādī, frewānī, ziyāt-wālai.*
Abundant, a. *der, ziyāt, frewān, ṭal.*
Abuse, s. *kkhkandzal* or *kanzal, peghor.* v.a. *kkhkandzal* or *kanzal, kanzal-, ruswā-,* etc. *k. peghor warkawul; bad sulūkī-, be-hurmatī-,* etc. *k.*
Abusive, a. *jiba-war, kanzal kawūnkai.*
Abyss, s. *garang, kanda, doghal, jawara.*
Accede, v.a. *manal, qabūlawul.*
Accent, s. *lahja, qirāt, ẓarb, ghag, makhraj.*
Accept, v.a. *manal, qabūlawul; ākhistal; khwakkhawul, pasandawul, kkhah ganral.*

Acceptable, a. *khwakkh, ghwarah.* v.n. *pasandedal, khwakkhedal, qabūledal.*
Access, s. *dakhl; rāsha darsha, nanawātah.*
Accession, s. *khātah, khatana.*
Accident, s. *āfat, wāq'ia, hādisa, balā.*
Accidental, a. *qazā-ī, qismatī.*
Acclamation, s. *zwag zūg, hāhū, chīgha; āparīn, shābāsh.*
Accommodate, v.a. *dzāyawul; khidmat k. atsanral, hawārawul.*
Accommodation, s. *dzāe; khidmat.*
Accompany, v.n. *malgarai ked; khatsa tlal.*
Accomplice, s. *mal, malgarai, sharīk, yār.*
Accomplish, v.a. *tamāmawul, pūrah k. pa dzāe rāwral; kawul, kral.*
Accomplished, a. *tamām shawai* or *-karai, pūrah; qābil, pohānd, hunar·man, kāmil.*
Accomplishment, s. *tamāmī, anjām, taiyārī; hunar, qābil·tob, kāmil·tob.*
Accord, s. *rogha, jora, pakhulā·tob, āshtī; barābarī, nisbat.* (of own-) *pa khpul.* (of one-) *yak jihat, yak dil, yo shān.* v.n. *yak sān-* or *yo shān-, barābar-,* etc. *ked. lagedal.*
According to, p. *pa—sara.* (-custom) *pa dastūr sara.*
Accordingly, ad. *la de na, dzaka.*
Accost, v.a. *pukkhtedal, salām k. pukkhtana k. wayal, khabare k. nāre wahal.*
Account, v.a. *ganral, pohedal, shmeral,* s. *hisāb, shumār; qissa, bayān, naql, tazkira; dzawāb* or *jawāb, khabara.*
Accountable, a. *zāmin; tāwān-* or *dzawāb warkawūnkai.*
Accoutre, v.a. *mlā taral, drasta-* or *wasla āghostal.*
Accrue, v.n. *hāsiledal, paidā ked.; khatal.*
Accumulate, v.a. *gatal, tolawul, yodzāe-, jam'a-, ambār-,* etc. *k.* v.n. *toledal, jam'a-, yodzāe-,* etc. *ked.*

Accuracy, s. *rikkhtīn·tob, rikkhtīnī, jukht·wālai.*
Accurate, a. *rikkhtīnai, sūchah; jukht, barābar, rikkhtiyā.*
Accusation, s. *tuhmat* or *tomat, d'awa, malāmat, peghor, tor.*
Accuse, v.a. *d'awa-, faryād-,* etc. *k. tuhmat taral* or *-wayal* or *-pore k. peghor warkawul, tor pore k.*
Accuser, s. *d'awa-* or *tor pore kawūnkai, mudda'ī.*
Accustom, v.a. *āmokhtah-, 'ādat-,* etc. *k. rugdawul.*
Ache, s. *dard, khūg, randz, zakhm.* v.n. *khūgedal, dardedal.*
Acid, a. *trīw* (f.) *tarwa.*
Acidity, s. *trīw·tob, trīw·wālai.*
Acknowledge, v.a. *manal.* v.n. *qā·iledal.*
Acknowledgment, s. *manūn, qabūl; hujjat, rasīd; shukrāna.*
Acorn, s. *kwarai.*
Acquaint, v.a. *khabarawul, pohawul, āgāh k.*
Acquaintance, s. *pejand·galī, āshnā-ī; āshnāe, pejāndah.* (f.) *āshnāya, pejandala.*
Acquainted, v.n. *khabaredal, pohedal, āgāh-, wāqif-,* etc. *ked.*
Acquire, v.a. *gatal, mūndal, paidā-, hāsil-, sagah-,* etc. *k.*
Acquit, v.a. *pulawul, bakkhal, wa-ar k.*
Acrid, a. *trīkh.* (f.) *tarkha.*
Acridity, s. *trīkh·wālai, trīkh·tob.*
Across, ad. *pore, pore ghāre.*
Act, v.a. *kawul, kral, pāzah-, 'amal-,* etc. *k.*
Action, s. *kār, krah, 'amal, harkat, pāzah, chār.*
Active, a. *chālāk, chust, takrah, tund, tez.*
Actively, ad. *pa chālākī sara.*
Activity, s. *chālākī, chustī, tund·wālai.*
Actor, s. *kawūnkai, krūnai, fā'il, 'āmil.* (in a play) *nat, pekkhe·gar, toq·mār, swāng kawūnkai* or *swāngai*

Actually, ad. *rikkhtiyā, pa wāq'i, qat'ai.*

Acute, a. *tez, terah, sakht; hokkhyār, pohānd.*

Acuteness, s. *tez·wālai, terah·tob, sakhtiyā; hokkhyār·tiyā, hokkhyārī, pohānd·wālai.*

Adage, s. *matal, misl, misāl.*

Adapt, v.a. *joṛawul, dzāyawul, hawārawul, atsanṛal, samawul, drust-, barābar-,* etc. *k.*

Add, v.a. *joṛawul, lagawul, gaḍawul.*

Addition, s. *mīzān, ḥisāb; joṛawūna, gaḍawūna.*

Additional, a. *ziyāt, nor, bul.*

Addle, a. *skhā, gandah, wrost.*

Address, v.a. *sawāl-, tapahūs* or *tapos-,* etc. *k. wayal, pukkhtedal; sar·nāma līkal* or *kāgal—kkhkal darkhwāst k. salām k.*

Adept, s. *ustāz, kārī·gar, pokh, pūrah, hunar·man.*

Adequate, a. *bas, pūrah, kāfī.*

Adhere, v.n. *lagedal, nkkhatal, chaspedal; grohedal.* v.a. *laman nīwul, tāb'i·dārī k.*

Adherent, s. *tāb'i·dār, mlā·taṛ, taraf·dār, para·dār, wābastah; charekār, hamsāyah, faqīr.* a. *slekkht·nāk, bokkht, chaspān; nkkhatai, lagedalai.*

Adhesion, s. *pewastagī; chasp; nkkhatūn.*

Adhesive, s. *slekkht·nāk, bokkht, barwai, chaspān.*

Adieu, s. *da khudāe pa amān, salām.*

Adjourn, v.a. *nāgha-, barkhwāst-, mauqūf-,* etc. *k.*

Adjust, v.a. *tartīb-, durust-, barābar-,* etc. *k. samawul, joṛawul, atsanṛal, hawārawul; pūrah-, faiṣal-, ārāstah-,* etc. *k.*

Admirable, a. *nādir, 'ajīb, gharīb.*

Admire, v.n. *grohedal.* v.a. *kkhah ganṛal, stāyal.*

Admission, s. *dakhl, nanawātah, rāsha darsha; manana, qabūledana.*

Admit, v.a. *dakhl-* or *lār warkawul; manal, qabūlawul.*

Admonish, v.a. *pand-, naṣīḥat-, tambīh-,* etc. *k. malāmatawūl, ṭaqawul, traṭal, raṭal.*

Adopt, v.a. *khwakkharwul, pasandawul, ikhtiyārawul; ākhistal.*

Adore, v.a. *parastī-, 'ibādat-, sijda-,* etc. *k.*

Adorn, v.a. *psolawul, singārawul, sāzawul, kkhewa k. kkhāyastah k. joṛawul.*

Adulation, s. *khūshāmad, chāplūsī, ḍirpalī.*

Adulator, s. *khushāmad·gar, chāplūs, ḍirpal.*

Adult, s. *dzawān, zalmai, zalmoṭai, bāligh.*

Adulterate, v.a. *gaḍawul, nāsarah k.*

Adulteration, s. *gaḍūn, qalp·wālai.*

Adulterer, s. *kāsīr, zinā·kār.*

Adultery, s. *kāsīrī, zinā.*

Advance, v.n. *wṛānde tlal* or *-ked.* s. *pór, qarz, peshagī; taraqqī; gāndah.*

Advantage, s. *kkhegaṛa, gaṭa, sūd, fā-ida, bih·būdī, naf'a; barai, ghalaba, fatḥa, wa-aṛ·wālai.*

Advantageous, a. *sūd·man, ghwarah, kkhah.*

Adventure, s. *kār, chal, chār, wāq'ia.*

Adventurer, s. *lawand, gashtai; chaṭ, lūtsak.*

Adversary, s. *dukkhman, mudda'ī.*

Adversity, s. *tangī, tangsiyā, kam·bakhtī, bad·bakhtī, sakhtī, shāmat; dukkhmani, mukhālifat, kharkhashī.*

Advice, s. *maṣlaḥat, mashwarat, pand, ṣalāḥ, naṣīḥat; khabar, iṭṭilā'a.*

Advise, v.a. *pand-, naṣīḥat-,* etc. *-warkawul; maṣlaḥat kawul; khabarawul.*

Advisable, a. *munāsib, lāzim, lā-iq, ghwarah.*

Advocate, s. *wakīl, mukhtār.*

Adze, s. *tarkkhadza, tesha, sūza.*

Afar, ad. *lire, la warāya.*

Affable, a. *ḥalīm, mihrbān, makhawar, khūsh sulūk, khūsh·goe.*

Affair, s. *kār, khabara, chār, muqaddama, mu'āmala, amr.*

Affect, v.a. *kār-, aṣr-, 'amal-, pāzah-, tāṣīr-,* etc. *k.* (feign) *bāna-, makr-,* etc., *k.*

Affectation, s. *nāz, nak͟hra, makez, nak͟hra·bāzī*; *bāna, c͟hal, fareb, makr, ḥīla.*
Affected, a. *c͟hal·bāz, makr·jan, bāna·k͟hor, farebī, ḥīla·bāz*; *nak͟hra·bāz.*
Affection, s. *mīna, muḥabbat, 'is͟hq, mihr, tapāk*; *mayan·tob, k͟hwā k͟hogī, ulfat.*
Affectionate, a. *mayan, mihrbān, k͟hwā k͟hogai.*
Affinity, s. *nisbat, 'alāqa*; *k͟hpul·walī, ris͟hta·dārī, ragai, wābastagī, sar·ris͟hta.*
Affirm, v.a. *wayal, iqrār, k. lal* or *lawdal, gawāhī lal.*
Affirmation, s. *qaul, lafẓ, qarār, iqrār, iṣbāt.*
Afflict, v.a. *āzārawul, zahīrawul, randzawul.*
Afflicted, a. *randzūr, g͟ham·jan, dard·man.*
Affliction, s. *randz, g͟ham, dard, āzār, pask͟hāk* or *pak͟hsāk, mīrtsī, sak͟htī.*
Afford, v.a. *warkawul, k͟hartsawul, da warkawulo ṭaqat laral.* v.n. *s͟hwal, kedal, tuwānedal.*
Affront, s. *k͟hwā·badī, mānrai*; *spuk·tiyā, be·izzatī.*
Afoot, a. *palai, pa kkhpo, piyādah.*
Afraid, v.n. *weredal* or *yeredal.* (in animals) *tarhedal, bugnedal.*
After, p. *pas, b'ad, wrusto.* (year after year) *kāl pa kāl.* (-to-morrow) *pas ṣabā.* (following-) *pase.* a. *wrustai, wrustanai, wrustīnai, pasīnah.*
After all, ad. *āk͟hir.*
After-birth, s. *prewān.* (caul) *obanra.*
Afternoon, s. *dwah·pahār.* (early) *pekkhīn, māspekkhīn.* (late) *dīgar, māzdīgar.*
Afterwards, ad. *pas, āk͟hir, biyā, b'ad.*
Again, ad. *biyā, dubāra, bul heṛ, bula plā, bul wār.* (-and again) *biyā biyā, wār pa wār.*
Agape, a. *c͟hīng, wīt, wāz.*
Age, s. *'umr, san.* (æra) *daur, daurān, dahr, zamāna.* (old-) *zoṛ·tiyā, zoṛ·wālai.*
Aged, a. *zoṛ, būḍā.* (-man) *spīn·gīrai.* (-woman) *spīn·sara.*
Agent, s. *pes͟hkār, nā-ib, wākīl, dīwān, kārdār.*
Aggravate, v.a. *yārawul, ṭaqawul, raṭal*; *batar k. ziyātawul.*
Aggregate, s. *ṭol, ṭol·ṭāl, jumla, wārah.*
Aghast, a. *hak·pak, ḥaq·ḥairān.*
Agile, a. *c͟hālāk, gaṛandai, tak·lāstai, jalt.*
Agility, s. *c͟hālākī, c͟hustī, sam·dastī.*
Agitate, v.a. *ts͟anḍal, k͟hwadzawul, laṛal, kk͟horawul, s͟hanawul.*
Agitated, v.n. *rapedal, k͟hwadzedal*; *es͟hedal*; *kk͟horedal.* a. *ts͟anḍalai, laṛalai.*
Agitation, s. *laṛza, rapedana*; *es͟hnā, jos͟h.*
Ago, ad. *pak͟hwā, larg͟hūne.* (long-) *lārg͟hah, lire lārg͟hah.*
Agony, s. *dzān·kandan*; *'azāb, dard.*
Agree, v.a. *manal, qabūlawul, iqrār k. rog͟ha-, joṛa-,* etc. *k. hokai wayal,* or *k.* v.n. *pak͟hulā-, rāẓī-, yo zṛah-, yo jihat-,* etc. *ked.*
Agreeable, a. *k͟hwakkh, pīrzo, k͟hwand·nāk, kkhah, kkhāg͟halai, manẓūr, g͟hwarah.*
Agreeably, ad. *pa mūjib, pa ḥukm sara*; *k͟hwand sara, k͟hwakkhī sara.*
Agreement, s. *joṛa, rog͟ha*; *s͟harṭ, wāda, lafẓ, qaul, qarār*; *neṭa, taṛa, oe.*
Agriculture, s. *kar, īwe,* or *yawe, zamīndārī, baz·garī, zirā'at, dihqānī, c͟harekārī.*
Agriculturist, s. *kar·kawūnkai, zamīndār, kikkht·gar, dihqān, c͟harekār, baz·gar.*
Ague, s. *saṛa taba, saṛa lawe* or *saṛa lare, wāreza.*
Ah! in. *wā-ī! wūe! ākhkkh! wākhkkhe! hāe! wāh! wāwailā! dareg͟ha!*
Ahead, ad. *wṛānde, pa makh kkshe.*
Aid, s. *kumak, madad, pus͟htī, yārwarī.*
Ailing, a. *randzūr, nā·joṛ, nā·rog͟h, bīmār, māndah.*
Ailment, s. *randz, nā·joṛ·tiyā, nā·rog͟h·tiyā, bīmārī, maraẓ, māndagī, dard, āzār.*
Aim, s. *niyat, maṭlab, qaṣd, g͟heraẓ, irāda*; *naẓar*; *nakkha, ts͟alai, muk͟ha.* v.a. *niyat-, qaṣd-,* etc. *k. naẓar taṛal* or *lagawul.*

Air, s. *bād, hawā.* (musical-) *badala, wazn, trang, sarod.* (assumed-) *nāz, nakhra, shokh.* (mien) *wajha, tsihra, ḍaul, chāl, chalan, ṣūrat.*

Alarm, *khof, yera* or *wera, tars, bāk*; *dagh-dagha, hāhū, ghāl-o-ghūl, shor-shaghab, zwag-zūg, hāṛa-hūṛa, chagh-chugh, ghoghā.* v.a. *werawul, tarhawul*; *baidār-, khabar-dār-*, etc. *k.* *ḍamāma-, naghāra-, ḍolkai-*, etc. *wahal.*

Alarming, a. *khof-nāk, tars-nāk, haibat-nāk.*

Alas! in. *hāe-hāe! wāe-wāe! armān dai!*

Alchemy, s. *kīmiyā.*

Alchemist, s. *kīmiyā-gar.*

Alert, a. *baidār, khabar-dār, hokkhyār*; *chā-lāk, chust, tak-lāstai.*

Alertness, s. *baidārī, hokkhyār-tiyā*; *chālākī.*

Alias, a. *nūmāndai, nūmedah, 'urf.*

Alien, a. *pradai, begānah, gharīb.*

Alight, v.n. *kūzedal, nāziledal.*

Alike, a. *gund, barābar, yo-shān, yo-rang, siyāl, makhai.*

Aliment, s. *tskkhāk-khwurāk, ṭ'aām, shūma.*

Alimentary, a. *khwurākī, da khwuṛalu.*

Alive, a. *jwandai, baidār.*

Alkali, s. *kkhora, shkār.*

All, a. *ṭol, wāṛah, amānī, kul.* (-day) *kaṛa-ī wradz.* (-night) *kara-ī shpa.* (at-) ad. *kruṭ, la sara.*

Allay, v.a. *kamawul, saṛawul, la-agawul.*

Allegiance, s. *tāb'i-dārī.*

Allegory, s. *miṣl, miṣāl, matal.*

Alliance, s. *joṛa, para, janba, joṛikkht*; *khpul-awī, khweshī.*

Alligator, s. *nahang, nāka.*

Allot, v.a. *weshal, hisk āchawul.*

Allotment, s. *wesh, brakha, hisk, wanḍ, pcṭai.*

Allow, v.a. *manal, qabūlawul*; *pregdal—pre-kkhodal*; *rawā laral*; *bakkhal, kkhandal*; *ijāzat-, ḥukm-*, etc. *warkawul.*

Allowance, s. *mawājib, tankhwāh rizq.* (in weight) *daṛa, ṭūṭankai.*

Allure, v.a. *ghulawul, darghalawul, fareftah-, mayan-*, etc. *k.*

Allurement, s. *fareftagī, ghuledana, mīna.*

Alluvium, s. *lāha, khaṭa, chīqaṛ.*

Ally, s. *mal, malgarai, yār*; *kumakī, sharīk.*

Almighty (the), *khudāe ta'ālā, ḥaqq ta'ālā.*

Almond, s. *bādām.*

Almonry, s. *langar, langar-khāna.*

Almost, ad. *nijde, qarīb.*

Alms, s. *khairāt, zakāt, ṣadqa, sarsāya, qurbānī*; *shukrāna.* (-house) *langar-khāna.*

Aloft, p. *pās, porta, bar.*

Alone, a. *yawādzai, tsaṛah, biyal, tanhā.*

Aloud, a. *pa ūchat āwāz sara.*

Alphabet, s. *paṭa-ī.*

Already, ad. *lā, os, la wṛūnbī na, larghūne.*

Also, c. *hum, aw, wa, o.*

Altar, s. *da qurbānī dzāe* or *-dunkācha.*

Alter, v.a. *badlawul, āwukkhtal.* v.n. *bad-ledal, girzedal.*

Alteration, s. *badal, tabdīl*; *girzedana.*

Altercation, s. *jagṛa, takrār, kharkhakkha, qīl-o-qāl, steza, qaẓiya, qaṭārai.*

Alternative, s. *chāra*; *wāk, ikhtiyār.*

Although, c. *agarchi, siwā la de na, ziyāt la de na, sara la de.*

Altogether, ad. *amānī, sarāsar, bilkul, ṭol-ṭāl, wāṛah, srup.* (in comp.) *tak-, ṭap-.* Ex. *tak spīn* (altogether white), *ṭap rūnd* (altogether blind).

Alum, s. *khāwra-ī, spīna khāwra.*

Always, ad. *mudām, har-kala, hamesha, tal, tar-tala.*

Amalgam, s. *qala-ī.*

Amass, v.a. *gaṭal, ṭolawul*; *yo-dzāyawul.*

Amaze, v.a. *hariyānawul, rabṛawul, sar gardān-, hekkh-, sarāsīmah-*, etc. *k.*

Ambassador, s. *āstodzai, elchī.*

Amber, s. *kah rubā.*

Ambergris, s. *'ambar.*
Ambiguous, a. *shakk·dār, shakk·man.*
Ambition, s. *himmat, zṛah, tam'a, dam.*
Amble, s. *yargha.* v.n. *pa yargho tlal.*
Ambuscade, s. } *puṭ·gana-ī, pasūnai, tsawai,*
Ambush, s. } *dakhma, kamīn.*
Amen, ad. *āmīn, hase di wī.*
Amenable, a. *eman, pos, narm*; *da qābū lāndi*; *da tāwān pīrzo.*
Amend, v.n. *raghedal, joṛedal.*
Amendment, s. *kkhegaṛa, raghedana.*
Amends, s. *tāwān, badal, nāgha, būnga.*
Amiable, a. *nek, mihrbān, ḥalīm.*
Amicable, a. *nek·khwāh, khair·khwāh.*
Amidst, p. *pa mandz kkhke.*
Amiss, a. *khaṭā, ghalat*; *bad, nā·sāz, nā·lāiq, nā·munāsib.*
Amity, s. *rogha, joṛa, dostī, āshtī.*
Ammoniac, s. (gum-) *ṣamāgh, oshāq.* (sal-) *noshādar.*
Ammunition, s. *da jang kālī, -sāmān, -asbāb*; *dārū mardak*; *golā bārūt.*
Amongst, p. *pa mandz kkshe* or *kkhke.*
Amorous, a. *mayan, 'āshiq.*
Amount, s. *mablagh, jam'a, jumla, kul, ṭol·ṭāl, wāṛah.*
Amour, s. *āshnā-ī, yārī, 'āshiqī, 'ishq·bāzī.*
Ample, a. *arat, plan, psorawar, sara·war*; *ḍer.*
Amplify, v.a. *aratawul, planawul*; *ḍerawul, ziyātawul.*
Amputate, v.a. *prekawul* or *prekṛal.*
Amulet, s. *t'awīẓ, tāwītak, amel, dawā.*
Amusement, s. *tamāsha, nandāra, loba.*
Analogy, s. *miṣāl*; *nisbat.*
Anarchy, s. *patna, balwā, yāghī·garī.*
Anathema, s. *kkhera, l'anat* or *n'alat.*
Ancestor, s. *nīkah, plār nīkah.*
Ancestry, s. *peṛa-ī, aṣl, pusht, rag, noga.*
Anchor, s. *langar.*
Anchorite, s. *zāhid, qalandar, gokkha·nishīn.*
Ancient, a. *zoṛ, pakhwānai, kuhand.*
Ancients, s. *pakhwānī 'ālam* or *-khalq.*
Anciently, ad. *pakhwā, lire larghūne.*
And, c. *aw, wa, o.*
Anecdote, s. *qiṣṣa, naql, riwāyat, khabara.*
Anew, ad. *biyā, nawi.*
Angel, s. *pirikkhtah, malak.*
Anger, s. *qahr, ghuṣṣa, ghaẓab, khapagī.*
Angle, s. *gūṭ, grut, dwa·kkhākha.*
Angry, a. *khapah, bṛoṣ.* v.n. *khapah ked.*
Anguish, s. *'aẕāb*; *swai.*
Angular, a. *kog, kṛīng, gūṭlai, kālkūchan.*
Animal, s. *dzanāwar, ḥaiwān.* a. *dzān·dār, gawai, wagaṛai.*
Animation, s. *jwand, jwandūn, dzān, sā*; *baidārī, chālākī*; *khūsh·ḥālī.*
Animosity, s. *kīna, dukkhnī, 'adāwat, badī, ṭaka, khuṣūmat, bughẓ.*
Ankle, s. *kkhangarai, kkhatgarai*; *gīṭa-ī.*
Annals, s. *tawārīkh, akhbār*; *shajara.*
Annex, v.a. *lagawul, taṛal, joṛawul*; *lāndi k. ākhistal.*
Annihilation, s. *nā·būdī, halākat, fū·fanā.*
Announce, v.a. *khabarawul, wayal*; *tsargand-, kkhkārah-,* etc. *k. munādī k. jār wahal.*
Annoy, v.a. *pārawul, zoral, rabṛawul khapaḥ k.*
Annual, a. *kālanai, har kālah.*
Annually, ad. *kāl pa kāl.*
Annul, v.a. *bandawul, man'a-, mauqūf-, mansūkh-,* etc. *k.*
Annular, a. *ghūnḍ* or *ghūnḍ·man, tsarkhan, tsalai.*
Anoint, v.a. *ghwaṛawul, mugal—mukkhal.*
Anomalous, a. *be·tartīb.*
Another, a. *bul, nor, bul·tsok, nor tsok, bul tsa, nor tsa, bul yo, nor yo.*
Answer, s. *dzawāb, pāsukh.* v.a. *dzawāb-, tāwān-,* etc. *warkawul.*
Ant, s. *megai, mor.* (black-) *tor megai.* (red-)

sūr megā. (white-) *ocnah*. (-hill) *megatūn, kkhor*.

Antagonist, s. *dukkhman, muqābil*; *raqīb, be-lak*; *dzawāb, makhai*.

Antecedent, a *pakhwānai, wṛūnbanai, pekkhīn*.

Antechamber, s. *dālān, dahlīz, manḍaw*.

Antelope, s. *osai, chikārah*.

Anterior, a. *wṛāndīnai, pakhwānai, wṛūnbanai, pekkhīn*.

Anticipation, s. *pesh·dastī, pesh·bandī*.

Antidote, s. *tiriyāk, 'ilāj*.

Antimony, s. *rānjah, surma, kuhal*. (-box) *rānjaṛūma, ranjūnūna*. (-bodkin) *salā-ī*.

Antipathy, s. *kraka*. (to food) *sekan*.

Anvil, s. *sandān, pa-alk*; *tsaṭ*.

Anxiety, s. *gham, andekkhnā, wiswās, fikr*; *gram*.

Anxious, a. *gham·jan, andekkh·man, wiswāsī, fikr·man*; *gram·nāk*.

Anus. s. *kūna, supra*. (prolapsus ani) *būra-ī* (pruritus ani) *mawekkhe*.

Any, a. *tsok, tsa*.

Apart, a. *biyal, judā, yawādzai*.

Apartment, s. *khūna, koṭa, dzāe*.

Apathetic, a. *be·parwā, be·khabar, kāhil*; *laṭ, shaṭal* or *shalaṭ, sust, ṭas mas*.

Aperture, s. *sūṛa, khula, spam* or *swam*.

Apex, s. *sar, peza, pitska, tsūka*.

Apologize, v.a. *'uzr ghokkhtal*; *minnat k*.

Apoplexy, s. *tsaṭ waṭ, sakta*.

Apostatize, v.a. *īmān-, dīn-*, etc. *bāelal*. v.n. *dīn-, īmān-*, etc. *na jārwatal*.

Apostle, s. *rasūl, astādzai, paighāmbar*.

Apothecary, s. *pansārai*.

Apparatus, s. *sāz, sāmān, kālī, asbāb*.

Apparel, s. *āghūstan, pokkhāk*; *jāme, zaṛūkī, kālī, nwarī*.

Apparent, a. *tsargand, kkhkārah, bartser, awtsār, benrah, zāhir* or *jār*.

Apparently, ad. *bartseran, pa jār, zāhiran*.

Appeal, v.a. *ghokkhtal, minnat-, sawāl-*, etc. *k*.

Appear, v.n. *tsargandedal, kkhkārah-, bartser-*, etc. *ked*.; *m'alūmedal*.

Appearance, s. *ṣūrat, wajha, tsihra, rang, shakl*.

Appease, v.a. *saṛawul, pakhulā-, razā-*, etc. *k*.

Appetite, s. *ishtihā, lwaga, khwā, liwāl·tob, zṛah*; *raghbat, shahwat, mīna*.

Applaud, v.a. *stāyal, shābāshī-, āparīn-*, etc. *k*.

Applause, s. *shābāshī, stāyana*.

Apple, s. *manṛa, seb*. (crab-) *mānṛū*. (-of eye) *lema, kasai, bātor, torai*. (Adam's-) *stūnai*.

Applicable, a. *munāsib, sazāwār, durust, jukht, joṛ*.

Application, s. *mihnat, kokkhikkh, lagiyā·tob*; *'arz, sawāl, darkhwāst*.

Apply, v.a. *lagawul, pore taṛal*; *sawāl-, 'arz-, darkhwāst-*, etc. *k*. v.n. *barābar-, jukht-*, etc. *lagedal*; *joṛedal, lagedal*.

Appoint, v.a. *kkhkenawul* or *kenawul, muqarrar k. wulāṛawul, wudrawul*. (-a time) *wāda k. neṭa taṛal*.

Appointment, s. *dzāe, 'uhda*; *lafz, sharṭ*; *wāda, neṭa, taṛa*.

Appraise, v.a. *bai'a-, qīmat-, nirkh-*, etc. *taṛal*.

Apprehend, v.a. *nīwul, giriftār k*. v.n. *pohedal, m'alūmedal*; *weredal, andekkhedal, wiswāsī ked*.

Apprehension, s. *nīwah, giriftārī, gīr*; *poha, khiyāl*; *khof, andekkhnā, wiswās, wera*.

Apprentice, s. *shāgird*.

Apprize, v.a. *khabarawul, āgāh k*.

Approach, v.n. *nijde kedal*.

Approbation, s. } *pasand, khwakkh, pīrzo,*
Approval, } *razā, manzūrī, qabūlī*.

Appropriate, v.a. *khpulawul, dzān ta ākhistal, rānīwul, lānde k*.

Approve, v.a. *khwakkhawul, manzūr-, pasand-*, etc. *k., manal, qabūlawul, kkhāghal*.

Apricot, s. *zardālū, makhranai*. (preserved-) *khubānī*. (dried-) *kishta, ashāṛai, māmū-ī*.

April, s. *wīsāk* or *baisāk*. (-shower) *wasa*.
Apropos, a. *jukkht, jor, barābar*.
Apt, a. *munāsib*; *qābil, lā-iq*; *kārī-gar*.
Aqua-fortis, s. *tez āb*.
Aquatic, a. *ābī, dariyābī*.
Aqueduct, s. *nāla, wāla, lakkhtai, nāwa, pūl*; *tarnāo*; *kārez*; *trai*.
Arable, a. *sādīn, shudiyār*; *da kar, da karalo*.
Arbitrary, a. *zorāwar, khapsar* or *khpul-sar*.
Arbitrate, v.a. *gwākkhal* or *gwākkhedal*; *gwākkh-grandai-, jirga-, munsifī-, insāf-, 'adālat-*, etc. *k*.
Arbitration, s. *gwākkh, jirga, munsifī, m'arika*.
Arbitrator, s. *jirgatū, gwākkh-grandai, munsif*.
Arbour, s. *chopāl, jūrgara, tsapar, manah, dāra, kūdala, kūda-ī*.
Arch, s. *qubba, gunbata, tāq, mihrāb, kamān*.
Archer, s. *līndai, līnda-kakkh, ghash-lāstai, rasā-līndai, kamān-kakkh, tīr-andāz, bar-kakkh*.
Archery, s. *kamān-kakkhī, tīr-andāzī*.
Architect, s. *rāj, m'imār, jorawūnkai*.
Archives, s. *daftar, shajara, tawārīkh*.
Ardent, a. *tod, garm*; *tund, tez*; *mast*.
Ardour, s. *tod-wālai, todūkha, garmī*; *tezī, tund-wālai*; *mastī, tapāk*.
Arduous, a. *sakht, grān, mushkil, drūnd*.
Area, s. *maidān, sama, zmaka*; *anganr, gholai, jawas*.
Argument, s. *bahs, hujjat, munāzara, dalīl, wāsta*.
Arid, a. *wuch, sawai, sokrah, sokhtah*; (as land) *chol, lallam*; *tosand*.
Aridity, s. *wuch-wālai, khushkī, sokhtagī*.
Arise, v.n. *pātsedal, khatal, walāredal, porta ked.*; *wudredal*.
Aristocracy, s. *khān-khwānīn, khānawādah khalq, firqa da ghato khalqo*.
Aristocrat, s. *khānawādah sarai, da ghat-*, or *da loe kor-*, etc. *sarai*.

Arm, s. *lās*. (above elbow) *gardai-lechai, tor-gharai, ma-at*. (below elbow) *tsangal, lecha* or *letsa*. (cubit bone) *linda-ī*.
Arm, v.a. *mlā taral, wasla-, drasta-*, etc. *āghostal*; *dzān sambālawul*.
Armistice, s. *rogha, jora*; *gwākkh*.
Armful, s. *ghūzai, gheg*.
Armour, s. (chain) *zghara, zira*. (steel) *juba, baktar, jaushan*. (clad in) *zghar-yālai, baktar-*, etc. *āghostai, zira-, baktar-*, etc. *pokkh*.
Armpit, s. *trakh, tkharg, arkh, baghal*.
Arms, s. *wasla, drasta, da jang kālī, -sāz, -asbāb*, or *-hatiyār*.
Army, s. *lakkhkar, fauj*.
Aromatic, a. *khūshbū-dār, bū-ī-nāk*.
Around, ad. *chāpera, khwā o shā, girdā gird, chār chāpera*.
Arouse, v.a. *wīkkhawul, pātsawul, baidārawul*.
Arrange, v.a. *sambālawul, tartīb k., tandal, atsanral, lagawul, jorawul, khundiyal*.
Arrangement, s. *tartīb, dzerma, bandobast, khundī-tob, jorikkht*.
Array, s. *para, tsīra, para-bandi, saff, qatār*; *libās, āghūstan, pokkhāk, zarūkī*. v.a. *poslal, pokkhal, āghostawul, zarūkī āgho-stal*; *para-*, etc. *taral* or *wudrawul*.
Arrears, s. *bāqī, pātī*.
Arrest, v.a. *nīwul, giriftār-, gīr-, band-, qaid-*, etc. *k*.
Arrival, s. *rātag, rātah, rasedah, dakhl, āmad, rātlana, rasedana*.
Arrive, v.n. *rātlal—rāghlal, rasedal*.
Arrogance, s. *kibr, bād, maghrūrī, khāntamā, gustākhī*.
Arrogant, a. *kibr-jan, bādī, maghrūr, gharah, gustākh*.
Arrow, s. *ghashai, tīr*. (-flight) *tīr-partāb, tīr-ras*. (wing place of-) *par-khāna*. (blunt-) *toqa, tuqqa*. (barbed-) *shata-ī*. (iron tip of-) *tūbrai*. (shaft of-) *lānga*,

tila-ī. (notch of-) *ghwākkhkai.* (wing of-) *banra, wazar.*
Arsenal, s. *silāh-khāna, jabba-khāna.*
Arsenic, s. *senkiyā, hartāl.*
Art, s. *hunar, hikmat, chal; kasb, pesha, ṣan'at, ustādī, pand, kārī-garī, dast-kārī.*
Artery, s. *rag.* (of the pulse) *nabẓ.*
Artful, a. *hikmatī, hunar-man; farebī, chal-bāz, chalwalai, hīla-bāz.*
Article, a. *kālai, shai, tsīz.*
Artifice, s. *chal, hīla, bāna, fareb, ṭagī, makr, palma, lamghara-ī, hira-ī.*
Artificer, s. *kasb-gar, kārī-gar, pesha-war.*
Artificial, a. *jūṭah, nāsarah, naqlī; kasbī, hunarī; joṛ karai, sākhtah.*
Artillery, s. *top-khāna.*
Artisan, s. See Artificer.
Artist, s. *ustād, kārī-gar, hunar-man; naqqāsh.*
Artless, a. *sādah-dil, rikkhtūnai, karah.*
As, c, *laka, hase.* (-if) *laka chi, ganre.*
Ascarides, s. *kīkkhai, chinjai.*
Ascend, v.n. *khatal, porta ked., pātsedal.*
Ascent, s. *khātah, khatana; taraqqa-ī, lwaṛa.*
Ascertain, v.a. *m'alūmawul, zdah-, taḥqīq-,* etc. *k.*
Ascetic, s. *zāhid, faqīr; malang, darwesh, qalandar.*
Ascribe, v.a. *nisbat lagawul, pore taṛal, pore k.*
Ashamed, a. *sharmindah, sharmsār, pakkhe-mān.* v.n. *sharmedal, pakkhemān ked.*
Ashes, s. *īre, khākistar.* (hot-) *skhwakkhtan, khoglan.* (cold-) *saṛe īre.*
Aside, ad. *biyal, pa ḍaḍe, pa trats.*
Ask, v.a. *pukkhtedal, ghokkhtal, sawāl-, tapos-, pukkhtana-, pursān-,* etc. *k.*
Aslant, a. *trats, tratskan, sangzan, kṛīng; shewah, sar-dzawar, sar-lwaṛ, pa rewand.*
Asleep, a. *ūdah, bīdah, khob-wṛai.*
Aspect, s. *makh, ṣūrat, tsihra, rang, shaki, rūe.*
Asperity, s. *zīg-wālai, lwāṛ-tiyā, zmokh-tiyā.*
Asperse, v.a. *peghor warkawul, tor pore k. tuhmat wayal, ghandal, kagal.*
Aspire, v.a. *tam'a, ārzū-, umed-,* etc. *laral.*
Ass, s. *khar.* (-colt) *bachrai, kūṭai, kūchai.* (wild-) *gorah khar, ghyarah.* (-load) *kharwār.* (-play) *khar-mastī, khar-khāṛai, khar-tīza.*
Assafœtida, s. *hanj, hanja.*
Assail, v.a. *halla-, dāṛa-, tsoṭ-, yūrush,* etc. *k.*
Assassin, s. *qātil, khūnī, marg kawūnkai.*
Assassinate, v.a. *wajal* or *wajlal, muṛ k., khūn-, marg-,* etc. *k.*
Assault, s. *halla, guẓār, tsoṭ, yūrush.*
Assemble, v.a. *ṭolawul, yo-dzāe-, jam'a-,* etc. *k.* v.n. *ṭoledal, yo-dzāe-, jam'a-,* etc. *ked.*
Assembly, s. *ṭolai, majlis, ḍala, jam'iyat; jirga.*
Assent, s. *raẓā, qabūl, hokai, oe.*
Assert, v.a. *wayal, lal* or *lawdal.*
Assertion, s. *wayai, wayana, khabara, lafẓ, lana, qaul, d'awa.*
Assessment, s. *kkhkewaṭ, māliya, bāj, ikhrāj.*
Assiduity, s. *kokshiksh* or *kokkhikkh, mihnat, sa'ī, tapāk.*
Assiduous, a. *mihnatī, sā'ī, kokkhikkhī.*
Assign, v.a. *neṭa taṛal, muqarrar k.; barāt warkawul.*
Assimilation, s. *gundī-tob, makhī-tob, hum-shaklī, hum-rangī.*
Assist, v.a. *komak-, madad-, mrasta-, pushtī-,* etc. *k., lās warkawul* or *nīwul.*
Assize, s. *'adālat, mahkama; nirkh, rai.*
Associate, s. *mal, malgarai, āshnāe, yār; rafīq, sharīk.* v.a. *malgīrī k.; yārī-, āshnā-ī-,* etc. *k.; kilai k.; ṣuhbat k.; sharīkī k.*
Association, s. *malgīrī, malgar-tiyā, sharīkī.*
Assort, v.a. *chunral, atsanral, tartīb k.*
Assortment, s. *tartīb, chīnda.*
Assume, v.a. *ākhistal, ikhtiyār-, d'awa-,* etc.

k. (airs) *nāz-*, *nakhra-*, etc. *k.* v.n. *nāzedal.*

Assumption, s. *khpul·sarī*, *zorāwarī*, *bādī·tob*, *kibr* ; *wāk*, *ikhtiyār* ; *ākhistana.*

Assurance, s. *bāwar*, *i'tibār*, *sā·wīsā*, *yaqīn*, *tawwakul* ; *gustākhī*, *be bākī.*

Assuredly, ad. *be·shakh*, *be shubha*, *albatta.*

Asthma, s. *sāh-* or *sā landī*, *kotāh sāhī.*

Asthmatic, a. *sāh landai*, *kotāh sāh.*

Astonish, v.a. *hariyānawul*, *rabṛawul*, *hekkh-*, *sargardān-*, *hak·pak-*, etc. *k.*

Astonishing, a. *'ajab*, *'ajībah*, *'ajūbah.*

Astonishment, s. *hariyānī* or *hairānī.*

Astray, a. *wruk*, *gumrāh*, *be lār.*

Astringent, a. *qābiẓ*, *ṭīng*, *klak*, *zmokht*, *stagh.*

Astrologer, s. *rammāl*, *najūmī.*

Astrology, s. *ramal*, *'ilm da najūm.*

Asunder, ad. *biyal*, *judā.*

Asylum, s. *āsra*, *panāh*, *nanawātah*, *aman.*

At, p. *pa*, *pa kkhke.* (-home) *pa kor kkhke.* (-least) *hargora*, *kho.* (-once) *yak lakhta*, *pa ṭakī.* (-last) *ākhir.* (-length) *bāre.* (-me) *rā bānde.* (-most) *pa hadda.* (-all times) *har wakht*, *har kala.* (-how much) *pa tsomra.* (-all) *haḍo*, *bekhī.* (-present) *pa dā sā'at* or *-wakht* or *-mahal.* (-hand) *nijde*, *khatsa* or *tsakha.* (-first) *wṛūnbe*, *awwal.* (-all events) *khwāh nā khwāh.* (-times) *kala kala.* (-sight) *pa līdah*, *pa kātah.* (-night) *pa shpe.*

Atheism, s. *ilhād*, *inkār*, *zindīqī*, *gumrāhī.*

Atheist, s. *mulhid*, *zindīq*, *munkir da khudāe.*

Athlete, s. *pahlawān*, *kaṭah.*

Athletic, a. *pahlawān*, *kaṭah*, *zor·man.*

Atmosphere, s. *bād*, *hawā.*

Atom, s. *pūṭai*, *pītsānṛai*, *ṭoṭai*, *zarra*, *chūr*, *reza*, *shama*, *daṛa.*

Atone, v.a. *tāwān-*, *badal-*, *'iwaẓ-*, etc. *warkawul*; *kafārat k.* *dzār-*, *ṣadqa-*, *qurbān-*, etc. *k.*

Atrocious, a. *bad sakht*, *bashpaṛ.*

Atrophy, s. *narci randz*, *karedana*, *wuch·klak·wālai.*

Attach, v.a. *laganul*, *taṛal*, *pore k.* *khpulawul*, *pewastah-*, *grohedah-*, etc. *k.*

Attachment, s. *pewastūn*, *taṛūn*, *band* ; *mīna*, *mayan·tob*, *muhabbat*, *grohedana.*

Attack, v.a. *halla-*, *hamla-*, *guẓār-*, *tsoṭ-*, *dāṛa dopa-*, *happa dapa-*, *yūrush-*, etc. *k.*

Attain, v.a. *mūndal*, *biyā·mūndal* ; *gaṭal*, *paidā-*, *hāṣil-*, etc. *k.* v.n. *rasedal*, *shwal.*

Attainable, a. *mūndūnai*, *shwūnai*, *da mūndalo.*

Attainment, s. *gāṭah*, *biyā·mūnd* ; *mūndana*, *rasedana.*

Attempt, s. *qaṣd*, *āzmekkht*, *zor*, *kokkhikkh*, *was*, *s'aī.*

Attend, v.a. *āwredal*, *ghwag bāsal—yastal* or *-gdal—īkkhodal*, *nghwatal*, *ghaur-*, *fikr-*, etc. *k.* ; *khabar ākhistal*, *khidmat-*, *madār-*, etc. *k.* v.n. *malgarai ked.* *hāẓir osedal.*

Attendance, s. *khidmat*, *nokrī.*

Attendant, s. *khidmat·gār*, *nokar*, *mulāzim* ; *mal*, *malgarai* ; *mlā·taṛ*, *jalaw·dār*, *nafar.*

Attention, s. *lihāẓ*, *fikr*, *s'aī*, *kokkhikkh*, *baidārī*, *khabar·dārī*, *hokkhyārī.* (to a guest) *melmastiyā*, *mezmānī*, *madār*, *makh.*

Attentive. a. *hokkhyār*, *baidār*, *khabar·dār.*

Attest, v.a. *gawāhī lal* or *lawdal*, *shāhidī warkawul* or *lal.*

Attestation, s. *gawāhī*, *shāhidī* ; *gawāhī lana* or *warkawūna.*

Attire, v.a. *zaṛūkī-*, *nwarī-*, *pokkhāk-*, *libās-*, *jāme-*, etc. *āghostal* ; *poslal*, *āghostawul.*

Attitude, s. *wajha*, *ḍaul*, *ṣūrat*, *shān*, *hāl.*

Attorney, s. *wakīl*, *mukhtār.*

Attract, v.a. *rākāgal—rākkhkal* ; *grohedah-*, *fareftah-*, etc. *k.* *ghulawul* ; *mayan k.*

Attracted, a. *rākkhkalai* ; *grohedalai*, etc. v.n. *grohedal*, *mayan ked.*

Attraction, s. *rākkhkana*, *kakkhikkh* ; *mīna*, *mayan·tob* ; *dil·barī*, *dil·farebī* ; *grohedana.*

Attribute, s. *khūe, khaṣlat, çifat, khāṣṣiyat.*
Audacious, a. *be bāk, nā·tars*; *be adab, gustākh.*
Audacity, s. *be bākī*; *be adabī.*
Audience, s. *majlis, dalbār*; *āwredūnkī, sām'iān.*
Auditor, s. *āwredūnkai, sām'i.* (of accounts) *muḥāsib, ḥisāb kawūnkai.*
Augment, v.a. *ziyātawul, ḍerawul.*
Augmentation, s. *ziyāt·wālai, ḍer·wālai*; *ziyātedana, ḍeredana.*
Augur, s. *pāl-* or *fāl katūnkai, fāl bīn, fālī, fāl yastūnkai.*
Augury, s. *fāl katana, fāl yastana, fāl bīnī.*
August, a. *ghaṭ, loe.* (the month) *bādro.*
Aunt, s. (father's or mother's sister) *tror.* (father's brother's wife) *tandor, tandyāra, kāka-ī.* (mother's brother's wife) *māma-ī.*
Auspicious, a. *iqbāl·man, bakhtawar, nek·bakht, mubārak.*
Austere, a. *sakht, zīg*; *trīw, zmokht*; *sūṭ, sūṭ·būṭ.*
Authentic, a. *rikkhtiyā, rikkhtīnai, taḥqīq.*
Author, s. *muṣannif, kitāb kkhkawūnkai*; *joṛawūnkai, kawūnkai, wayūnkai,* etc.
Authority, s. *wāk, ikhtiyār, was*; *maqdūr, zor, qudrat, ḥukūmat*; *ḥukm, farmān, sanad.*
Authorize, v.a. *ḥukm,- wāk-, ikhtiyār-,* etc. *warkawul.*
Autumn, s. *manai, khizān, kharīf.*
Auxiliary, a. *komakī, madad·gār, janba·dār.*
Avail, v.a. *fā-ida-, naf'a-,* etc. *rasawul.* v.n. *chaledal, pakār ked.* or *-rātlal.*
Avarice, s. *ḥirṣ, tam'a, bakhīlī.*
Avaricious, a. *bakhīl, ḥirṣ·nāk, ḥāriṣ, tām'i.*
Avaunt, in. *lire sha! biyarta sha!*
Avenge, v.a. *badal-, qiṣāṣ-, tāwān-,* etc. *ākh·istal.*
Averse, a. *nā·rāẓ, mukhālif, khwā bad.*
Aversion, s. *kraka, chinjedana, kagana, ghan·dana.*
Avert, v.a. *man'a-, daf'a-,* etc. *k., girzawul, jārbāsal—jāryastal.*
Avidity, s. *tam'a, lewāl·tob, shauq, raghbat.*
Avocation, s. *kār, kasb, pesha.*
Avoid, v.a. *parhez k., dzān sātal.*
Await, v.n. *muntaẓir osedal, wudredal, pātedal.*
Awake, a. *wīkkh, baidār.* v.n. *wīkkhedal, pātsedal, baidār ked.*
Aware, a. *khabar, āgāh, wāqif*; *zdah.*
Away, ad. *lire.* in. *lire sha, biyarta sha.*
Awe, s. *khof, wera* or *yera, tars, bāk, ḥaibat, tor.*
Awful, a. *khof-, tars-, sahm-,* etc. *-nāk,* etc.
Awhile, ad. *drang sā'at, la-ag sā'at.*
Awkward, a. *kāwāk*; *lwāṛ.*
Awl, s. *nīra* or *rīna.*
Awning, s. *chatrai, siwrai, shāmiyāna, sāewān*
Awry, ad. *pa trats, kṛīng pṛīng, kog wog.*
Axe, s. *tabar,* (battle-) *tabar·zīn, gurz.*
Axis, s. *quṭb, ghashai.*
Axle, s. *laṭ, tīrak, tsākkhai.*
Aye, ad. *ho, āre, kkhah.*
Azure, a. *shīn.*

B.

Babble, v.a. *bak bak-, baṛ baṛ-,* etc., *k.* v.n. *ṭaredal.*
Babbler, s. *bak bakai, baṛ baṛai, ūnai, ṭarai,*
Babe, s. *bachai, tankai, tandai, m'aṣūm* or *māshūm, tai rawai, pa-ī rawdūnkai, wṛūkai.*
Bachelor, s. *lawanḍ, tsaṛah, mujarrad.*
Back, s. *shā.* ad. *biyarta, biyā, wrusto, pastana, pas.* (behind one's-) *pase shā.*
Back, v.n. (go-), *pastana-, wrusto-, biyarta-,* etc. *ked., stūnedal* or *stanedal.* v.a. (aid) *panāh-, komak-, pushtī-,* etc. *-warkawul, ḍaḍa lagawul.*
Backbite, v.a. *chughlī-, ghībat- ghammāzī-,* etc., *k.*

Backbiter, s. *chughlkhor, ghībat kawūnkai, mawās, ghammāz.*

Backbone, s. *mlā tīr, shamdza-ī.*

Backdoor, s. *da chane war, da kor da shā war.*

Backside, s. *kunātai, kūna, ghara, dumbāla; wrustai, shā.*

Backward, a. *nā-rāz, lat, tas mas, nā-rāst; sust, pasīnah.* ad. *wrusto, pastana, bīyarta.*

Backwards, ad. *pa bīyarta, wrusto.* a. *naskor, arawulai, apūtah.*

Bad, a. *bad, nā-kārah, kharāb, nā-sarah.*

Badge, s. *nakkha* or *nakhkkha, nikkhān, togh, 'alāmat.*

Badger, s. *tor-lamai, gor-kakkh.*

Badly, ad. *pa bad shān sara.*

Badness, s. *kharābī, badī, 'aib.*

Baffle, v.a. *rabrawul, ghulawul, wār khatā k., be fā-ida-, 'abas-,* etc., *k.*

Bag, s. *taila-ī, dzola-ī.* (clothes-) *katsora, būtskha, buqcha.* (money-) *hamiyānī, badra.* (letter-) *kharīta.* (grain-) *tsata, ghūndai.* (tent-) *gharāra.* (trinket-) *butskhakai.* (leather-) *bana-ī, gūdai.* (ammunition-) *kīsa, kisbat.* (leather water-) *mashk, chāgul,* (leather air-) *shināz, zik, jai.* (baggage-) *malaw.*

Baggage, s. *asbāb, rakht, sāmān, partal.*

Bail, s. *zāminī, zamānat.* (the person) *zāmin.* (to give-) *zamānat-, zāmin warkawul.* (to take-) *zamānat-, zāmin ākhistal.*

Bailiff, s. *muhassil, patwārī, kārdār, sazāwal.*

Bait, v.a. *tsar-, wākkhah-, khwārah-,* etc. *warkawul; bāolī warkawul; nahārai-, tāmba* or *ta'ām-, khwurāk-,* etc. *warkawul.*

Bake, v.a. *pa tanūr kkhke pakhawul; karawul, wrītawul.*

Baker, s. *nānwā-ī, nān paz.*

Balance, s. *tala, tarāzū.* (the beam) *dān-da-ī.* (the scale) *pala.* (the tongue) *jiba.* (of an account) *bāqī.* v.a. *talal, jokal; bāqī pūrah k., hisāb barābar k.*

Balcony, s. *bālā-khāna.*

Bald, a. (from age) *kal.* (from disease) *ganjai, sudar, lendah, chatrai, pa-akhai.*

Bale, s. *andai, pand, petai.* (of grass) *gedai.* v.a. *sandzal, toyawul, lawastal.*

Baleful, a. *bad, muzirr, tāwānī, ziyānī.*

Balk, v.a. *wār khatā k., 'abas k., wrānawul.*

Ball, s. *pandos, pandoskai, mandos; gola-ī, mardakai; ghundūrai; nāch, gadedana.*

Ballad, s. *sandara, landa-ī, chār-bait, ghazal, tapa, misr'a, stāyana.*

Ballast, s. *langar.*

Ballot, v.a. *qur'a-, hisk-, pucha-,* etc. *āchawul.*

Bamboo, s. *bans.*

Balustrade, s. *kangura.*

Band, s. *park, tolai, tolgai, ghol, tamba; firqa, janba; khel, cham.*

Bandage, s. *pata-ī, band, tarūnai.* (for the head) *sar-pechak, sar-tarūnai, tsapūtkai, sar-basta.* (for clothes) *tanra-ī.* (a child's-) *seznī.*

Bandbox, s. *tawang.*

Banditti, s. *ghlah, shūk-mār, dār, tār, qazāk.*

Bandy, v.a. *radd badal k., qīl-o-qāl k., chaghawul.* a. *kog.* (-legged) *kage kkhpe.*

Bane, s. *zahr; nuqsān, tāwān, ziyān.*

Baneful, a. *zahr-dār; nuqsānī, muzirr, mozī,* etc.

Bang, v.a. *takawul, wahal, tak-, daz-, tas-,* etc. *wahal.*

Bangle, s. *bāhū, wakkhai, chūrā, karai, ma-atkai.*

Banish, v.a. *sharal, be watan-, jilā watan-,* etc. *k.*

Bank, s. *pūla, wand, band.* (river-) *ghāra.* (high-) *kamar.* (opposite-) *pore ghāra.* (-of clouds) *gūp, kha-at.* (for money) *khizāna, kota-ī.*

Banker, s. *sarrāf, khizānchī, set.*

Bankrupt, s. *nā-dār, dewāliyā, tabāh, khwār.*

Banner, s. *nakkha, janda, bairaq, tūgh.*

Bannock, s. (plain) *tsapata-ī, kakora.* (oiled-) *weshala.* (buttered-)*parāta, lūcha.* (sweet-) *amrasa.*

Banquet, s. *ziyāfat, melmastiyā, mihmānī.*

Banter, v.a. *toqa-, washta-, maskhara-,* etc. *k.*

Bar, s. (cross-) *hūl* (upright-) *aram, aramai.* v.a. *bandawul, hūl-, aram-,* etc. *lagawul.*

Barbarian, s. *dzangalī, jāhil, banr-mānrū.*

Barbarity, s. *be rahmī, dzangalī-tob, jāhil-tob.*

Barbarous, a. *be rahm; jāhil, dzaban, lwār.*

Barbed, a. *shata-ī-* or *biyak larūnkai.*

Barber, s. *nā-ī, gulābī.*

Barberry, s. *korai, karwara, zirishk.*

Bard, s. *mīrāsī, dum, shā'ir.*

Bare, a. *barband* or *barmand, lūts; ta-ash, khālī.* (-faced) *be makh, be hayā, be sharm, be parda.* (-footed) *abl, pkkhe-able.* (-headed) *sar-tor.* (-backed) *lūts, barband.*

Barely, ad. *surup, ta-ash, khālī, faqat, sirf.*

Bargain, s. *shart, wāda, iqrār, lafz, neta, tara, 'ahd.* v.a. *shart-,* etc. *k.* or *taral; saudā-, bai'a-* etc. *k., chana wahal.*

Barge, s. *bera-ī, kishta-ī.* (-pole) *singāwanr.*

Bark, s. (tree-) *pat, pot, potakh, postakai, khwar.* (dog's-) *ghap, ghapā, ghāp.* v.a. *pot-,* etc. *kāgal—kkhkal* or *-bāsal—yastal; ghapal, ghap wahul.* v.n. *ghapedal.*

Barley, s. *orbūshe.* (a grain of-) *orbūsha.* (husk of-) *sharhata..* (-bread) *orbūshīna.* (-gruel) *oghra.* (-grits) *dal, bata.*

Barm, s. *khamīra, toma* or *tomna, māya.*

Barn, s. *khirman, dīrmand, ambār-khāna.*

Barrack, s. *spāhī-khāna, urdū, dal.*

Barrel, s. *nal, nalī, shpela-ī.* (-bellied) *gagar, geda-war, kheta-war.*

Barren, a. (animal or tree) *shanda.* (land) *dāg, ūjār, shār.* (saline) *kkhoran.* (sandy) *shīglan.*

Barrenness, s. *shand-wālai, shand-tob.*

Barricade, s. *sangar, bāra, kūtsa-bandī.*

Barrier, s. *pūla, brīd* or *brīt, hadd.*

Barter, s. *adal-badal, plor, chana, saudā, lāgī, pīral-ploral, rākrah-warkrah.* v.a. *adal-badal-, plor-,* etc. *k., chana wahal.*

Base, a. *palīt, murdār, dūn, harāmī, bad-zāt, kam-asl, be nog.* (-coin) *nā-sarah, jūtah.*

Base, Basis, s. *āra, wekh, kūnsat, būnsat bunyād, pāya, pkkha, sar.*

Baseness, s. *dūnī, harāmī-tob, bad-zātī,* etc.

Bashful, a. *sharm-nāk, hayā-nāk* or *hayā-dār, ghairat-nāk* or *ghairat-man.*

Basin, s. (of wood) *kandai* or *kanrai, būgh.* (of pottery) *kandol, kandolai.* (kneading-) *kkhānak.* (beggar's-) *kachkol.* (wash-hand-) *tasht, lagan.* (dog's-) *chat.*

Bask, v.a. *pitāo-, nwar-, or-,* etc. *ta kkhke-nāstal.*

Basket, s. *tokra-ī.* (flat-) *shkarai* or *shkorai* or *shker, kkhkarai.* (fruit-) *kawāra, kāra.* (winnowing-) *chaj, tsap.* (safe-) *tsakai.* (clothes-)*tawang.* (bread-) *sawada.* (withy-) *kera.*

Bass, a. *bog, dad.*

Bastard, s. *harāmī, harām-zādah, khatā-zowulai.*

Baste, v.a. *wahal, takawul, kūtal, atsanral.* (sew) *gandal, pezal, bezal.*

Bastion, s. *bruj, morcha, damdama.*

Bat, s. *kkhāperak, shoparak.*

Batch, s. *gundī; nughd, zāt.*

Bath, s. (cold-) *ghusl.* (vapour-) *hammām.*

Bathe, v.a. *ghusl k., lanbal.* v n. *lanbedal.*

Baton, s. *amsā, lawar, kotak.*

Battalion, s. *paltan.*

Batter, v.a. *wahal, takawul, kūtal, narawul, dar-dar-, chūr-chūr-, kand-kapar-,* etc. *k.*

Battery, s. *morcha, damdama.*

Battle, s. *jang.* (-array) *tsīra, para-basta, saff-tarah.*

Battlement, s. *kangura.*

Bawl, v.a. *naral, chighawul, nārə-, chighe-,* etc. *wahal.*

Bay, a. *sūr*. (at-) *jah*. (to stand at-) *jah ked*.
Bayonet, s. *sīkhcha, sangīn*.
Be, v.n. *kedal, shwal, osedal*.
Beach, s. *ghāṛa*.
Beacon, s. *nakkha, nikkhān, munāra, tsalai*.
Bead, s. (stone) *mara-ī*. (glass) *mashkanra*. (jet) *shaba*.
Beak, s. *makkhūka, tsūka, shūka*.
Beam, s. *bensh, lakaṛa, lahaṛai, paṭera, barga*.
Bean, s. *lobiyā*.
Bear, s. *yag, melū, khirs*.
Bear, v.a. *wṛal, rāwṛal*; *zghamal, petsal*. v.n. *sahal, sahedal*. (-young) *zegedal, zowul*.
Beard, s. *gīra, rīsh*. (of grasses) *banbal, lasha, shoṛa*. (grey-) *spīn·gīrai*. (-less) *chaṭ*.
Bearer, s. *wṛūnkai*; *zghamūnkai*, etc.
Beast, s. *dzanāwar, ḥaiwān*. (wild-) *waḥsh* (-of prey) *dad*. (-of burthen) *bār·kakkh, sutūr*. (quadruped) *tsārwai, dāba*.
Beastliness, s. *gandagī, palītī, murdārī*; *ḥaiwān·tob, ḍangar·tob*.
Beastly, a. *gandah, palīt, murdār*.
Beat, v.a. *wahal, ṭakawul, kūṭal*; *pa-aṛ-, māt-, lāndi-*, etc. *k., barai mūndal* or *gaṭal*.
Beaten, a. *wahalai, ṭakawulai, kūṭalai*; *pa-aṛ, māt*.
Beater, s. *wahūnkai*, etc.; *pa-aṛ-*, etc. *kawūnkai, wa-aṛ, barai mūndūnkai* or *gaṭūnkai*.
Beating, s. *wahal, wahana, kūṭana, kūṭal, ṭakawul, ṭakawūna*; *pa-aṛ kawūna*, etc.
Beau, s. *ṭatai, ṭainchī, bānkiyā, ḍaulī*.
Beautiful, a. *kkhāyastah, kkhkulai, khūb ṣūrat, pa-ī-* or *pej·makhai*.
Beautify, v.a. *kkhāyastah k., kkhāyast warkawul, andzorawul*. (-oneself) *singār-, kkhewa-*, etc. *k*.
Beauty, s. *kkhāyast, kkhāyast·wālai*; *joṛāb, kṛah·wṛah, pa-ī makh·tob*.

Because, c. *dzaka, ska, la de wa, la kabla*.
Beckon, v.a. *ishārat k., lās tsanḍal*.
Become, v.n. *shwal, kedal, osedal*; *pīrzo-, lā-iq-, munāsib-*, etc. *ked*.
Bed, s. *bechānra*. (-stead) *kaṭ, pālang, manj*. (-coverlet) *bṛastan, liḥāf*. (-mattress) *tolā-ī, nihālī, taltak*. (-cushion) *bālikkht, bālīn, bālikkhtak*. (-sheet) *tsādar, pālang pokkh*. (-time) *mākhustan* or *māskhutan*. (-ridden) a. *zmol, zam·zambolai* or *zam·zmolai*.
Bee, s. *macha-ī*. (honey-) *ghlauza* or *lauza, mach·machai*. (black-) *baurā*. (-hive) *gabīna, garbīnai, kkhor*.
Beet, s. *chughandar* or *chuqandar*.
Beetle, s. *gūngaṭ, ghozai, ghozakarkai, khaaṭak, chānrī*. (mallet) *ḍabalai, baghdar, tsobāṛai*.
Befall, v.n. *nāziledal, prewatal, rasedal, wāq'i ked*.
Before, p. *pakhwā, wṛūnbe, wṛānde, qabl, dwṛānde, makh kkhke*
Beforehand, ad. *awwal, wṛūnbe, peshtar*.
Beg, v.a. *gadā-ī k., khair ghokkhtal*; *minnat-, sawāl-*, etc. *k*.
Beget, v.a. *zegawul, zowul, blārbawul, ḍakawul, paidā k., shigāra k*.
Beggar, s. *gadāe, paqīr, muflis, kangāl, nest·man, khwāṛ*.
Beggary, s. *gadā-ī, gadā·tob, paqīrī, khwārī*.
Begin, v.a. *shurū'-, ibtidā-, darak-*, etc. *k*.
Beginner, s. *shurū' kawūnkai, mubtadī*.
Begone, in. *dza! lire sha! wruk sha! chikhe!*
Behalf, s. *wāsiṭa, khāṭir, dapāra, pa ḥaqq*.
Behave, v.a. *sulūk k*. v.n. *chaledal, ramedal*.
Behaviour. s. *chāl, chalan, ṭarīqa, sulūk*.
Behind, p. *wrusto, dumbāl, pastana, pa shā*.
Behold, in. *gora! wu·gora! wu wīna!*
Behove, v.n. *lāzim-, wājib-, munāsib-*, etc. *ked*.
Belch, s. *agramai, argai, ḍakār, ṭegh*. v.a. *agramai-*, etc. *bāsal—yastal* or *-k*.
Belief, s. *bāwar, i'tibār*; *īmān, dīn*.

Believe, v.a. *bāwar-*, etc. *k.* or *laral*; *īmān-*, etc. *rāwṛal.*

Believer, s. *bāwar kawūnkai*; *īmān·dār, mūmin, m'utaqid.*

Bell, s. *zangola, zang, jaras, gingṛai, julājil.*

Belle, s. *nādira, nāznīna, pa-ī makha.*

Bellow, v.a. *naṛal, naṛā-, nāre-*, etc. *wahal.* v.n. *ghuṛunbedal, ghurchedal.*

Bellows, s. *bana-ī, pūgar.*

Belly, s. *geḍa, kheṭa*; *nas.* (-ache) *kānga.* (-fretting) *qur·qurai.*

Belong, v.n. *lagedal, nisbat ked., kedal.*

Beloved, a. *maḥbūb, mayan.*

Below, ad. *kkhkata, kkhkiya, lānde, kūz, lar.*

Belt, s. *tasmu, rog, band.* (waist-) *kamar·kīsa.* (sword-) *paṭa.* (shoulder-, ornamental) *banda-ī.*

Bench, s. *takhta, dunkācha.*

Bend, v.a. *ṭīṭawul, kagawul.* v.n. *ṭīṭedal, kagedal, kālkūch-, kaglech-*, etc. *ked.*

Beneath, p. *lānde, dalānde, kkshata, kkshiya.*

Benediction, s. *du'ā, du'ā da khair, tabarruk.*

Benefactor, s. *da n'imatūno bakkhūnkai, kkhegaṛa kawūnkai, khairāt warkawūnkai.*

Beneficent, a. *bakkhana kawūnkai, faiẓ-*, or *n'imat rasawūnkai.*

Beneficial, a. *kkhah, fā-ida-, sūd-, naf'a-*, etc. *-man.*

Benefit, s. *kkhegaṛa, gaṭa, sūd, bihbūd, fā-ida.*

Benevolent, s. *sakhī, sakhāwatī, khairātī, mihrbān.*

Bent, a. *ṭīṭ, kog.*

Benumbed, a. *qaṛqechan, maṛghechan, ūdah.*

Bequeath, v.a. *hiba-, mīrāt-*, etc. *k.*

Bequest, s. *mīrāṣ* or *mīrāt, hiba, tarka.*

Bereave, v.a. *ākhistal, shūkawul, lūts k.*

Berry, s. *dāna.*

Beseech, v.a. *minnat-, d'uā-*, etc. *k.*

Beside, ad. *tsakha* or *khatsa, nijde, pa tsang, pa aṛakh, pa ḍaḍe.*

Besides, p. *siwā, ziyāt, 'alāwa, nor.*

Besiege, v.a. *ḥiṣārawul* or *īsārawul, ger k.*

Bespeak, v.a. *numaṛ k.*

Best, a. *ghwarah, ḍer kkhah, la ṭolo na kkhah.*

Bestow, v.a. *bakkhal, warkawul, kkhandal.*

Bet, v.a. *sharṭ taṛal.*

Betimes, ad. *wakhtī.*

Betray, v.a. *ghulawul, ṭagī-, pudūli-*, etc. *k. parda porta k., khwāla wayal.*

Betroth, v.a. *kojdan k.*

Betrothal, s. *kojdan, kojdana, kojda.*

Betrothed, a. (-youth) *changhol.* (-maid) *changhala.*

Better, a. *ghwarah, awlātar, bihtar.*

Between, ad. *pa mandz* (or *myandz*) *kkshe.*

Beverage, s. *sharbat, tskkhāk.*

Bevy, s. *sail, ghol*; *peṛk, ṭolai*; *khel.*

Bewail, v.a. *wāwailā-, zārī-, faryād-*, etc. *k.* (-the dead) *wīr k., wainā wayal.*

Beware, v.n. *pohedal, khabar·dār-, hokkhyār-, baidār-, āgāh-*, etc. *osedal* or *ked.* v.a. *parhez-, pahm-*, etc. *k.*

Bewilder, v.a. *ḥariyānawul, rabṛawul, sargardānawul, hekkh-, hak·pak-, hak·ḥairān-*, etc., *k.*

Bewitch, v.a. *naẓar lagawul, siwrai āchawul, koḍ k., ghulawul, farestah-, mayan-*, etc. *k.*

Beyond, p. *pore, lire, hagha khwā, pore ghāṛa, bāhar, warā* or *warāya.*

Bias, s. *khwā, mīna, zṛah, mrasta, rujū'a.* v.a. *khwā girzawul, lamsawul, ma-il-, ma-ilān-, grohedah*, etc. *k.*

Bible, s. *kitāb.* (Pentateuch) *tauret.* (Psalms) *zabūr.* (Gospels) *anjīl.* (Muhammad's) *qurān, furqān.*

Bicker, v.a. *chighawul, raṭal, traṭal, dāṛal, qaẓiya-, jagṛa-*, etc. *k.*

Bier, s. *tābūt, da muṛī takhta.*

Biestings, s. *wargah.*

Big, s. *loe, ghaṭ, kaṭah, star.*

Bile, s. *trīkhai, zahra, ṣafrā.*

Bilious, a. *ṣafrā-ī.*

Bill, s. (bird's) *makkhūka.* (account) *ḥisāb.* (note) *ḥujjat, tamassuk,* (-of exchange) *hunḍa-ī.* (-of sale) *qibāla, bai'a·nāma.*

Bind, v.a. *taṛal, lagawul, joṛawul.* (a book) *juz·* or *jild·bandī k.*

Binder, s. *taṛūnkai, taṛūnai.* (in comp.) *-band.*

Binding, s. *taṛūn, wandanai.* (book-) *jild·bandī.*

Biography, s. *tazkira, rawāyat.*

Bird, s. *marghah, marghai.* (-catcher) *mashkār, kkhkārī.* (-lime) *slekkh.* (-net) *dām, ḍaba-ī, jāl, dwa·gaza.* (-noose) *ghunḍārai, lwīna, lūma, lūmaka.* (-springe) *laṭ, talaka, kuṛka-ī.* (-trap) *paṛka, honrā.*

Birth, s. *zowah, zowūna, zegedah, zegedana, tawallud, paidā-ish.* (-place) *waṭan, da paidā-ikkht dzāe.* (-day) *da tawallud wradz.* (-right) *ḥaqq da masharī.*

Biscuit, s. *kak, kakoṛa.* (sweet-) *amrasa.*

Bit, s. *ṭoṭa, ṭoṭai, khatsosa.* (of food) *nwaṛa-ī, ṭūk.* (of a horse) *mlūna, qā-iza, dahana.*

Bitch, s. *spa-ī.* (-in heat) *spayama* or *spa-ema.*

Bite, v.a. *chīchal, khwuṛal, dāṛal, chak lagawul.*

Bitter, a. *trīkh, talkh.*

Bittern, s. *baglai, kablai.*

Bitterness, s. *trīkh·wālai, trīkh·tob, trīkh·tiyā.*

Bitumen, s. *qafr ul yahūd.*

Black, a. *tor.* (jet-) *tak tor.*

Blacken, v.a. *torawul.* v.n. *toredal.*

Blackguard, s. *charlanḍ, chaṭ, chulur, bad·m'ash, laṛalai, ḥarāmī, lūch lawanḍ, laṛo tsaṭo, kachar.*

Blackish, a. *tor·shān.*

Blackmail, s. *būnga.*

Blacksmith, s. *lohār, āhangar.*

Bladder, s. *pūkanṛa-ī.*

Blade, s. *palka, tegh.* (of grass) *khalai.* (of scissors) *para, pal.* (of plough) *pāla, saspāra.*

Blame, s. *malāmat, 'aib, taqṣīr, quṣūr, wabāl, gunāh.* v.a. *malāmatawul, raṭal, traṭal.*

Blameable, a. *malāmatī, taqṣīrī, gunah·gār.*

Blameless, a. *be gunāh, be quṣūr, be malāmat.*

Blamelessly, ad. *nā·ḥaqq, be sabab, be gunāh,* etc.

Bland, a. *post, narm, khog, mulā-im.*

Blandishment, s. *nāz, nakhra, karashma, makez*; *kkhewa, singār, ḍaul.*

Blank, a. *ta·ash* or *t·ish, khālī, spīn, sādah.*

Blanket, s. *shaṛa-ī, krāsta.*

Blaspheme, v.a. *kufr wayal.*

Blast, s. (breath) *pūk, pūkai.* (wind) *sīla-ī, jakaṛ, chapa.* (sound) *bāng, āwāz, ghag.*

Blast, v.a. *ālwūzawul, fanā k., barbādawul, wrukawul*; *kkhere k.*

Blaze, s. *lūkhaṛa, lanba, bāmbanṛa, ḍānḍa-ī, baṛānḍa, ghaṛānḍa.* v.a. *lūkhaṛa-,* etc. *k.*

Bleach, v.a. *spīnawul, spetsal.*

Bleak, a. *soṛ, yakh.*

Blear, a, *obĵan, dund, khīran, lechan, zawlan.*

Bleat, v.a. *bregan-, me me-,* etc. *k.* v.n. *bāngedal.*

Bleed, v.n. *wīnedal, wīne bahedal.* v.a. *rag wahal, wīne bāsal—yāstal.*

Blemish, s. *'aib, quṣūr, dāgh, tor, rakhna.*

Bless, v.a. *d'uā-, tabarruk-,* etc. *k., barakat warkawul.*

Blessing, s. *d'uā da khair, barakat, tabarruk.*

Blight, s. *torka-ī, surkha-ī.*

Blind, a. *ṛūnd.* (stone-) *ṭap ṛūnd.* (night-) *shamkor* or *shokor.* v.a. *ṛandawul, nā·bīnā k.* v.n. *ṛandedal.*

Blindfold, v.a. *starge puṭawul.* (-cattle) *kholai taṛal.* (-hawks) *ṭopa-ī pasarawul.*

Blindness, s. *ṛūnd·wālai, ṛunḍ·tiyā.* (night-) *shamkor·tiyā.*

Blink, v.a. *starge wahal, dzezme rapawul, dzanbal* or *dzamal.*

Blister, s. *tanrāka, pūla-ī, maṭāka.*

Blithe, s. *kkhād, khūsh·dil, khandā·rūe.*

Bloat, v.a. *paṛsawul.* v.n. *paṛsedal.*
Block, s. *tsaṭ, mūnḍ, garga, kunda.*
Blockade, v.a. *ḥiṣārawul* or *īsārawul, bandawul.*
Blockhead, s. *gedī-khar, khar, pūhaṛ, dūzai.*
Blood, s. *wīne.* (-shed) *khūn.* (breed) *ẓāt, rag, aṣl, nog.* (-stained) *pa wino habatah.*
Bloom, v.n. *ṭūkedal, zarghūnedal, ghwaredal.*
Blossom, s. *ghūṭa-ī, gul.* v.n. *khwaredal, spaṛedal, spaṛdai ked., ghwaredal,* etc.
Blot, s. *laka, ṭakai, dāgh; 'aib, nāmūs, tor.*
Blow, s. *guẓār.* (of fist) *gasa, ḍab, sūk, ṭas.* (of breath) *pūk, pūkai.* (of wind) *sīla-ī.*
Blow, v.a. (a fire) *pūkal, pūk wahal.* (as wind) v.n. *ālwatal, chaledal.* (as a flower) *ṭūkedal, ghwaredal, spaṛedal, spaṛdai ked.* (a bugle) v.a. *ghagawul.* (-out) *muṛ-, soṛ-,* etc. *k.* (-down) *ringaṛai k.*
Bludgeon, s. *koṭak, lawaṛ, ḍāng.*
Blue, a. *shīn-, nīl-, āsmānī-,* etc., *-rang.*
Blunder, s. *khaṭā.* v.a. *khaṭā k.*
Blunderbuss, s. *gharābīn, ṣaff-shikan.*
Blunt, a. *pa-ats* or *p-uts.* (-ness) s. *pa-ats-wālai.*
Blur, s. *dāgh, 'aib, tor, laka, ṭakai.*
Blurt, v.a. *parda prānatal, khwāla wayal.*
Blush, v.n. *sharmedal.*
Bluster, v.a. *lāp wahal, ṭar-ṭar k., dam wahal.*
Blusterer, s. *lāpak, ṭarai, ḍūzak, daz.*
Boar, s. *sarkūzai, kharbishoe, khūg.* (wild-) *soḍar, matah.*
Board, s. *takhta.* (writing-) *lauḥ, paṭa-ī.* (food) *tskkhāk khwurāk.*
Boasting, s. *lāpa, lāp shāp, dam.*
Boast, v.a. *lāp-, lāpa-, dam-,* etc., *wahal* or *k.*
Boat, s. *beṛa-ī, kishta-ī.* (bridge of-) *pul, jisr.* (-man) *mānṛgai, mahanṛah, mallāḥ.*
Bodkin, s. *salā-ī, sīkhcha, stan, dūk.*
Body, s. *tan, juṣṣa, ṣūrat, wujūd, jism.* (in comp.) *andām.* (of men, etc.) *ṭolai, ṭolgai, ghol, paṛk, khel, tanba, firqa.*

Bog, s. *bokkht, bokkhtana, yala, taramna, palunda.*
Boil, v.a. *eshawul* or *yashawul, khūṭ k.* v.n. *eshedal* or *yashedal, khūṭ ked.*
Boil, s. *dāna, nanaka-ī.* (blackhead-) *tora-dāna.* (acne-) *dzwānaka.* (heat-) *garmaka.* (whitlow) *kharai, shīnai.* (carbuncle) *kkhandza.* (abscess) *kkhalūna, lūna.*
Boiler, s. *khum, kaṛahai, ḍeg, dechka.*
Boiling, s. *eshnā, khūṭkai; yashānd* or *eshānd.*
Boisterous, a. *tund, tez, mast.*
Bold, a. *maṛanai, zṛah-war, tūrzan, bahādur, dilāwar, be bāk; gustākh, chūnkai, wītak.*
Boldness, s. *maṛāna, zṛah-war-tob. tūrzan-tob, bahādurī, maṛanī-tob, be bākī; gustākhī, shokhī, chūnkī-tob, be makh-tob, be ḥayā-tob.*
Bolster, s. *bālikkht, bālīn, takiya.*
Bolt, s. *hūl, mekhchū, bala-ī, jaranda-ī, aṛamai.*
Bond, s. *band, dzolana, dzel, kaṛa-ī, zandzīr.* (note) *ḥujjat, tamassuk.* (union), *pewand, band, jorikkht.* (blood) *ragai, khpulawī, rishta, wābastagī.* (compact) *wāda, taṛūn, taṛa, bandaṇr, lafẓ.*
Bondage, s. *qaid, band, bandī-tob; bandagī, ghulāmī, mra-e-tob.*
Bondmaid, s. *wīndza, kanīza, barda.*
Bondman, s. *mra-e, ghulām.*
Bondsman, s. *ẓāmin, yarghamāl* or *yarghamal.*
Bone, s. *haḍ, haḍūkai.*
Bonfire, s. *dūna, alāo, ḍānḍa-ī.*
Bonny, a. *kkhāyastah, kkhkulai, pa-ī-makhai* or *pej-makhai, pa-ī-makh.*
Bony, a. *haḍawar.*
Booby, s. *sāduh-dil, pūhaṛ, gedī-khar, kam-'aql.*
Book, s. *kitāb.* (bound-) *jild.* (unbound-) *juz.* (-stand) *rahel.* (in comp) *-nāma.* (-binding) *juz-* or *jild-bandī.* (-boards) *kānṭa-ī.* (-binder) *jild-gar, ṣaḥḥāf.*

Boon, s. *ghanīmat, n'imat, barakat, bakht*; *in'ām, bakhkshiksh, bakkhana.* a. *khūsh-dil, kkhād, khandā-rūe. khūsh-ṭab'a.*

Boor, s. *gawār, ghundāyah, lwāṛ, pūhaṛ, dzaban.*

Boot, s. *moza, chakma.* (for women) *jista.* (to-)ad. *pa gaṭe, pa weṛiyā, pa ziyāt, junga.*

Booth, s. *tsapar, kūḍala, mana, jūngaṛa.*

Bootless, a. *'abaṣ, be fā-ida, nīma-khwā, nīmgaṛai.*

Booty, s. *lūṭ, gaṭa, shūka, tāla, ghārat.*

Borax, s. *tanrakār.*

Border, s. *ḥadd, brīd, pūla*; *ghāṛa, morga*; *tsanḍa, tselma, ja-ī, laman.*

Bore, v.a. *barma-, sūṛai-*, etc. *k., sīkhal, petsal.*

Born, a. *zowulai, zegedalai, paidā shawai,* (in comp) *-zādah, -zai, -dzoe.*

Born, v.n. *zegedal, zowul, paidā ked.*

Borrow, v.a. *por-, qarẓ-*, etc. *ākhistal.* (a thing to be returned) *'āriyat-ākhistal.*

Borrower, s. *porawuṛai, qarẓ-dār.*

Bosom, s. (embrace) *gheg, ghūzai.* (chest) *ṭaṭar.* (breast) *sīna.*

Both, a. *dwāṛah, dwah-wāṛah.*

Bottle, s. *kkhīkkha.*

Bottom, s. *wekh, tal, mūnḍ*; *kūnsaṭ, būnsaṭ.*

Bottomless, a. *be pāyān, nā-pāyāw* or *nā-pāyāb.*

Bough, s. *tsānga, khrānga, lakkhta.* (large-) *kkhākh, khanḍ, ṭāl.*

Bound, v.a. *dangal, ṭop wahal, traplal.* v.n. *trapedal, ghwurzedal.* (ricochet) v.a. *ṭīndak wahal.* (limit) v.a. *pūla-, brīd-, ḥadd-*, etc. *taṛal.*

Boundary, s. *pūla, ḥadd, brīd.*

Boundless, a. *be ḥadda, be anda, be shāna, be nihāyata, be qiyāsa.*

Bountiful, a. *sakhī, sakhāwatī, faiẓ-rasān, kkhandana-, bakkhana-*, etc. *kawūnkai.*

Bounty, s. *sakhāwat, sakhī-tob, bakkhana.*

Bow, s. *salām, adab*; *ṭīṭ-wālai.*

Bow, s. *līnda, līnda-ī, kamān.* (-string) *ĵa-ī.* (middle of-) *mūṭai.* (horn of-) *ghwagai, khām.* (notch of-) *zih-gīr.* (-for practice) *darwesha-ī.* (pellet-) *ghur-kamāna.* (pellet-cup) *pāṭa-ī.* (bar of cup) *panjakai,* (-of a fiddle) *kamāncha.* (rain-) *da būḍa-ī ṭāl, sara-shna kāsa.* (to bend a-) v.a. *ĵa-ī bānde k.* (to unbend a-) v.a. *ĵa-ī kūzawul.* (-maker) *kamān-gar.*

Bow, v.a. *ṭīṭawul.* v.n. *ṭīṭedal.*

Bowels, s. *laṛmānah, kulme.* (of ruminants) *ūjarī.*

Bower, s. *chopāl, jūngaṛa, tsapar, dzodz-khāna.*

Bowl, s. (pottery) *kanḍol, kanḍolai.* (glazed-) *zarghūn-kanḍol.* (china-) *chīna-ī* or *chīna-ī.* (wooden-) *kāsa, pīna, kunra-ī* or *kunḍa-ī.* (metal-) *kaṭorai.*

Box, s. *ṣandūq, ṣandūqcha.* (clothes-) *taunra-ī.* (band-) *tawang.* (trinket-) *haṛpa-ī.* (pill-) *dablai.* (in comp.) *-dān.* (blow) *tsapeṛa, ṭas.*

Boy, s. *halak, woṛkai.* (school-) *ĵanrai.* (plough-) *ghunḍāyah.* (dancing-) *lakkhtai, lolai.*

Boyhood, s. *halak-wālai, wṛūk-wālai, ĵanrī-tob.*

Brace, s. *taṛūn, tanra-ī, wandanai*; *lānga, piyāṛma, kakkha*; *joṛa, juft, qulba.*

Brace, v.a. *klakawul, tangawul, ṭīngawul, kāgal—kkhkal.*

Bracelet, s. (above elbow) *ma-aṭkai, bāzū-band.* (below elbow) *bāhū, bangṛai.* (at wrist) *kanganr, kaṛai, wakkhai, gajrai.*

Bracket, s. *darai, raf*; *pushta, aṛam.*

Brackish, a. *mālgīn, kkhora-nāk*; *trīw.*

Braid, v.a. *odal.*

Brain, s. *māghzah.*

Brake, s. *karkanr, jāṛ, jāmbṛa.*

Bramble, s. *karkanra, jāṛa*; *aghzai, ghana.*

Bran, s. *sūṛī*, *būṭ·sūṛī*, *gadzārī*.

Branch, s. *kkhāk͟h*, *tsānga*, *k͟hanạ*. (family-) *kor*, *naṣl*, *pus͟ht*, *alwād*.

Brand, v.a. *dāg͟hawul*, *nug͟hai gdalī—kkhodal*; *tor-*, *tuhmat-*, etc., *pore k.*, *mak͟h·torai k.*

Brandish, v.a. *tsanḍawul*.

Brass, s. *ziyaṛ*.

Brave, a. *maṛanai*, *zṛah·war*, *tūrzan*, *bahādur*, *takṛah*, *maẓbūṭ*, *dilāwar*.

Bravery, s. *maṛāna*, *mardī*, *zṛah·war·tob*, etc.

Bravo, in. *s͟hābās͟h! āprīn!*

Brawl, v.a. *jagṛa-*, *qaẓiya-*, etc. *k.*, *c͟hig͟hawul*.

Brawler, s. *jagṛāū*, *takrārī*, *jang·yālai*.

Bray, v.n. *hanṛedal*.

Breach, s. *c͟hāwd*, *tsāk*, *darz*; *kanḍaw*, *j͟ghanḍ*.

Bread, s. *ḍoḍa-ī*. (leavened-) *k͟hamīra*. (unleavened-) *patīra*. (barley-) *orbūs͟hīna*. (maize-) *sūkṛak*. (millet-) *k͟hamac͟ha*, *piyāt͟sa*. (mixed meal-) *rāṛa*, *broṛa*. (dry-) *spora ḍoḍa-ī*. (-of charity) *g͟haṛai*, *c͟haṛ*.

Breadth, s. *plan·wālai*, *arat·wālai*, *sor* or *psor*.

Break, v.a. *mātawul*. (-to atoms) *c͟har·c͟hūr-*, *daṛ·daṛ-*, *kanḍ·kapaṛ-*, *māt·guḍ-*, etc. *k.*

Breakfast, s. *nārai* or *nahārai*, *nās͟hta*, *t͟sākkhtī*. (-during Lent) *pes͟h·manai* or *·namai* or *·lamai*.

Breast, s. *sīna*. (nipple) *tai*. (-band) *tapor*.

Breastplate, s. *c͟haprās.*.

Breastwork, s. *sangar*, *mard·raw*, *faṣīl*.

Breath, s. *sā* or *sāh*, *dam* or *dama*.

Breathe, v.a. *sā-*, *dam-*, etc. *āk͟histal* or *rākāgal—rākkhkal*. (-upon) *damawul*, *dam k.*

Breeches, s. *paṛtūg*, *s͟halwār*,

Breed, s. *aṣl*, *naṣl*, *ẕāt*, *rag·rīkkha*, *nogai*, *zād·zawzāt*, *rang*.

Breed, v.a. *pālal*, *parwaral*; *zegawul*, *naṣl·paidā k.* v.n. *langedal*, *zegedal*; *blārbedal*, *warla ked.*

Breeding, s. *pālana*, *parwaris͟h*; *tarbiyat*, *t'alīm*; *langa*, *blārba*, *warla*, *ḍaka*.

Breeze, s. *hawā*, *bād*, *bādūkai*, *wagma*.

Brethren, s. *wrūnṛah*, *'azīzān*.

Brevity, s. *lanḍ·wālai*, *·lanḍ·ṭiyā*.

Bribe, s. *baḍa*, *ris͟hwat*, *mok*.

Brick, s. *k͟hakkhta*. (-bat) *ṭoṭa*, *roṛa*. (-dust) *surk͟hī*. (-kiln) *paja*. (-layer) *kullāl*.

Bridal, a. *nāweyat*.

Bride, s. *nāwe*. (bride's maid) *wrā·bānṛa-ī*, *wre-aza* or *wreyaza*, *mānja-ī*. (bride's female servant) *ĩnga*.

Bridegroom, s. *zalmai*. (bridegroom's man) *wrā·bānṛai*, *jānjī*, *mānjī*.

Bridge, s. *pul*. (-of nose) *tinḍoṛai*, *tanbeza* or *tambūzai* or *tambūzak*. (of fiddle) *ṭaṭū*, *k͟hargai*. (to make a-) v.a. *pul taṛal*.

Bridle, s. *wāga*, *mlūnz*; *jalab* or *jalaw*. (of cord) *gapī*, *pā-ī*. (camel's-) *pezwān*.

Brief, a. *lanḍ*, *kotāh*.

Brigade, s. *tuman*, *dasta*.

Brigand, s. *g͟hal*, *s͟hūk·mār*, *qaẓẓāq*.

Bright, a. *rūnṛ*, *rokk͟hān*, *tāb·nāk*; *spīn*, *s͟hīn*.

Brighten, v.a. *rūnṛawul*, *spīnawul*, *pākawul*, *rokk͟hān k.* v.n. *rūnṛedal*, *d͟zaledal* or *d͟zal ked.* *brekk͟hedal*; *spīnedal*, *s͟hīn-*, *pāk-*, etc. *ked.*

Brightness, s. *ranṛā*, *brekk͟hnā*, *rokk͟hnā-ī*.

Brim, s. *morga*, *g͟hāṛa*, *t͟sanḍa*.

Brimstone, s. *gogar* or *gogil*.

Brindled, a. *brag*, *gag*, *c͟hrag·brag*, *ablaq*.

Briny, s. *mālgīn*. (brine) *mālgīna oba*.

Bring, v.a. (-animate objects) *rāwustal*. (-inanimate objects) *rāwṛal*. (-forth young) *langedal*. (-off) *bac͟hawul*. (-up) *pālal*, *parwaral*. (-under) *lānde k.*

Brink, s. *g͟hāṛa*, *morga*, *t͟sanḍa*, *ḍaḍa*.

Brisk, a. *c͟hust*, *c͟hālāk*, *takṛah*, *tund*, *gaṛandaḍ*.

Bristle, v.a. (as the hair or skin) *wekk͟htah-*, *g͟hūnḍ-*, etc. *-zigedal* or *walāṛedal*. s. *da sarkūzī wekk͟htah*.

Brittle, a. *nāzuk*, *mātedūnai*, *narai*, *spuk*.

Broad, a. *plan*, *arat*, *sara·war* or *psora·war*.

Broadcloth, s. *banāt.*
Broadness, *plan·wālai, arat·wālai, sor* or *psor.*
Brocade, s. *kimkhwāb, zar·baft, muqqaish.*
Broil, v.a. *wrītawul, kabābawul, tcyal, talawul.*
Broken, a. *māt.* (-to bits) *māt·gud, kand·kapar, char·chār, dar·dar.*
Broker, s. *dallāl.*
Bronchocele, s. *ghur.*
Brood, s. *zawzād* or *zauzāt, alwād, bachī.*
Brood, v.n. *ghamedal, nūledal, karedal; fikr·man-, andekkh·man-, wiswāsī-,* etc. *ked.* (sit on eggs) *kurkedal, kuraka ked.*
Brook, s. *lakkhtai, nahar, arākh, wela, khwar.* (dry bed of-) *kanda, kas, shela.*
Broom, s. *jārū.*
Broth, s. *kkhorwā.*
Brother, s. *wror.* (elder-) *mashar wror.* (younger-) *kashar wror.* (middle-) *mandzwai wror.* (foster-) *da tī-* or *da to wror.* (full-) *sakah wror.* (half-) *nā·sakah wror.* (-in law) *awkkhai.* (husband's-) *lewar.* (-hood) *wrorī, wror·walī, wror·galwī, wror·wālai.*
Brow, s. *wuchwulai* or *wucharlai, tandai, kolak.* (-of a hill) *kamar, tarai.*
Brown, a. *mushkai, bor, kha-ar.* (light-) *sperah.* (dark-) *sūr·bor.*
Browse, v.a. *powul.* (tend at-) *piyāyāl.* v.n. *tsaredal.*
Bruise, v.a. *blodal, sūlawul, dzabal; kutal, takawul.* (-grain) *dal k.*
Brush, s. (weaver's-) *māla.* (fox's-) *lakai.* v.a. *jārū k.* (-clothes) *tsandal.*
Brushwood, s. *dzangal, jār, jāmbra.*
Brutal, a. *be dard, be rahm, sakht·dil, dzaban, haiwānī.*
Brute, s. *haiwān, dad, dzanāwar.*
Bubble, s. *bulbula* or *burbura, ghuiai, jakh.* v.n. *eshedal, khūt ked., khūtsedal.*
Bubo, s. *ghumba, ghundārai, stagh.*
Buck, s. *osai.* (-rabbit) *soe.*
Bucket, s. *boka, taghārai, satal; dalwa, gadhal; solāgha.*
Buckle, s. *kara-ī, gharabbai.*
Buckler, s. *dāl, spar.* (-handle) *lāstai, mūtai.* (-cushion) *gadai.* (-boss) *patrai.*
Bud, s. *ghūta-ī.* (leaf-) *ghandal.* v.n. *tūkedal, ghwaredal, zarghūnedal.* v.a. *red-, qalam-,* etc. *k.*
Buffalo, s. *mekkh, gānmekkh.* f. *mekkha.* (young-) *katai.* (two-year-old-) *jotah.* (bull-) *sandah.*
Buffoon, s. *toqī, toq·mār, washtī, washt·mār, malandai, maskharachī, pekkhe·gar.*
Buffoonery, s. *toqa, washta, malanda, maskhara.*
Bug, s. *mungarr, katmal.* (tree-) *khasak.*
Bugbear, s. *bāgū, bagalolai, bau.*
Bugle, s. *turai.* (Bugler) *turī·mār.*
Build, v.a. *jorawul.*
Building, s. *kandar, mānra-ī, kota, kor.*
Bulb, s. *ghūta, ghūta-ī.* (garlic-) *palai.*
Bulk, s. *ghat·wālai, loe·wālai.*
Bulky, a. *ghat, loe, nāpar, star, khrīs, gagar.*
Bull, s. *hīndah* or *mīndah.* (-calf) *skhai.*
Bullet, s. *mardaka* or *mardak, gola-ī.*
Bullion, s. *srah·zar, spīn·zar.*
Bullock, s. *ghwayai* or *ghwa·e ghutskai, dangar.* (steer) *zārai, skhwandarkotai, skhwandar.*
Bully, s. *zālim, zorāwar, luqah, daz, zorūnkai.*
Bulrush, s. *lūkha, kahai, nal, badagāl.*
Bump, s. *pārsob, mātūs, matāka, ghūnda, pūpaka, pund.*
Bunch, s. *ghotai, ghūncha, khosha.*
Bundle, s. *gātlai, petai, gedai, panda, pandūkai.* (-of hay) *beda, kalokkhta.*
Bung, s. *būja, dida, khulborai, shora.*
Buoyant, a. *spuk, pāyāwai.*
Bur, s. *jishai, kandala-ī.*
Burden, s. *bār.* v.a. *bār āchanul* or *k.*; *legdawul.*

Burdensome, a. *drūnd, grān, sak͟ht.*

Burglar, s. *g͟hal, kandar-,* or *gūṭ mātawūnkai.*

Burglary, s. *g͟hlā, kandar-* or *gūṭ mātawūna.* (to commit-) v.a. *kandar-* or *gūṭ mātawul* or *k., naqb-zanī k.*

Burial, s. *k͟hakk͟hawūna, k͟hakk͟hedana.* (service) *janāza.* (-ground) *goristān, qabaristān.*

Burlesque, s. *toqa, malanḍa, mazāk͟h.*

Burn, v.a. *swadzawul, sedzawul; balawul.* v.n. *swal, sedzal, baledal.*

Burning, s. *swai; sedzana; baledana; balawūna.*

Burnish, v.a. *rūnrawul, dzalkawul, rokk͟hān-, ṣaiqal-, ṣāf-, pāk-, brekk͟h-nāk-,* etc. *k.*

Burrow, v.a. *sūṛai-* or *sūṛa-, g͟hār-, surang-,* etc. *k.,* or *kanawdal,* or *kanal,* or *kanastal.*

Burst, v.n. *c͟hāwdal, pṛak c͟hāwdal, s͟hledal, ts̲īredal, c͟hāq ked.* (-into) *ḍūsa k.* (-out) *mātedal.* (-upon) *rā-māt ked.*

Bury, v.a. *k͟hakk͟hawul.*

Bush, s. *būṭai, jāṛa, ḍakai.*

Bushel, s. *ogai.* (a quarter-) *kuṛai.*

Business, s. *kār, kasb, pes͟ha, s͟hewa.*

Buskin, s. *sugul; māsa-ī.*

Bustard, s. *ts̲āṛai, k͟ha-aṛ-mor, ḥūbārah, tug͟hdarī.*

Bustle, s. *c͟hal-c͟halā, hats̲a, tag-o-dau, tagā-pū.*

Busy, a. *lagiyā, mas͟hg͟hūl.*

But, c. *lekin, mangar, wale, balki, siwā.*

Butcher, s. *qaṣṣāb.* v.a. *ḥalālawul; wajlal* or *wajal, qatl-, marg-, k͟hūn-, muṛ-,* etc. *k.*

Butt, s. *nakk͟ha, muk͟ha.* v.a. (-with the head) *ṭakar, ḍag͟hara* or *daaara, ṭakar-,* etc. *wahal.*

Butter, s. *kuc͟h.* (preserved-) *g͟hwaṛī.*

Butterfly, s. *parakai, tārūgai, kambala-ī, bāmbīlakai.*

Buttermilk, s. *s͟homle* or *s͟hlombe.* (sour-) *tarwe.*

Buttock, s. *kūnāṭai, surīn.*

Button, s. *g͟hoṭai.* (-loop) *tanra-ī, gūtma, pulg͟hwākk͟ha, g͟haṛās͟ha.*

Buttress, s. *pus͟htī, aṛam.*

Buxom, a. *takṛah, c͟hāg͟h, tāzah, k͟handā-rūe.*

Buy, v.a. *pīral* or *pīrawdal, pa bai'e āk͟histal.*

Buzz, v.n. *bonredal.*

Buzzing, s. *bonr, bonrkai, bonredana.*

By, p. *pa.* (-day) *pa wradzi.* (-thousands) *pa zargūno.* (-hundreds) *pa ṣawūno.* (-all means) *pa har s͟hān.* (-degrees) *pa ro ro, pa qalār.* (-no means) *pa hets̲ s͟hān, hec͟hare, haḍo.* (-and bye) *pa drang, drang sā'at pas.* This preposition is often followed by *sara* (with), as *pa har s͟hān sara,* by all means, etc.

C.

Cabal, s. *janba, para, gundī.*

Cabbage, s. *gobī, karamkala.*

Cabin, s. *koṭa; jūngaṛa, kuḍala, ts̲apar.*

Cable, s. *da beṛa-ī biyāstq,* or *-pa-aṛai,* or *-rasa-ī.*

Cactus, s. *ṭohaṛ, zaqūm, qūṛg͟handal.*

Cackle, v.a. *jak-jak-, c͟hag͟h-c͟hug͟h-,* etc. *k., c͟hūqa wahal.*

Cadaverous, a. *sperah.*

Cadence, s. *wazn, āwāz, g͟hag, trang, badala.*

Cage, s. *pinjra, qafas.*

Cajole, v.a. *g͟hulawul, ṭagal.*

Calamitous, a. *bad-* or *kam-bak͟ht, bad-naṣīb, balā-nāk, āfatī, g͟haẓab-nāk.*

Calamity, s. *balā, āfat, nāzila, muṣībat.*

Calcine, v.a. *kus͟htah-, īre-,* etc. *k.*

Calculate, v.a. *s͟hmāral* or *s͟hmeral, ḥisābawul, ganral.*

Calculation, s. *ḥisāb, s͟humār* or *s͟hmerah, andāza.*

Caldron, s. *k͟hum, deg, saṭal; dec͟hka, kaṛahai.*

Calendar, s. *patra, taqwīm.*
Calender, v.a. *batī-, kundī-, c̲h̲āp-*, etc. *k.*
Calf, s. *bac̲h̲ai, c̲h̲ikorai.* (bull-) *s̲k̲h̲ai.* (buffalo-) *kaṭai.* (camel-) *jūngai, botai.* (stuffed-) *spandak̲h̲.* (-of leg) *paṛkai, g̲h̲aṛai.*
Calico, s. *c̲h̲īṭ.*
Calk, v.a. *c̲h̲āwd-, darz-*, etc. *-bandī k.*
Call, s. *bāng, nāra.* (-for dogs) *tū·tū.* (-for cattle) *ṛī·ṛī.* (-for cats) *pa-as̲h̲·pa-as̲h̲.* (-for hawks) *qū·qū.* (-to drive cattle) *ta-arya·ta-arya.* (-to encourage dogs) *tap·tap.* (-to encourage fighting rams, etc.) *jig·jig, dric̲h̲·dric̲h̲.*
Call, v.a. *nāra wahal, bāng wayal, g̲h̲ag k.* (summon) *balal, ṭalab k.* (name) *wayal, nūm āk̲h̲istal*; *nūm kegdal—kek̲k̲h̲odal* or *k̲k̲h̲kegdal*, etc. (-to mind) *yādawul.* (-back) *stūnawul* or *stanawul.* (-bad names) *kanzal k., k̲k̲h̲kandzal* or *kanzal.*
Called, a. *nūmāndai, nūmedah.*
Calling, s. *kār, kasb, pes̲h̲a.*
Callous, a. *sak̲h̲t, klak*; *be dard, be parwā.*
Callousness, s. *sak̲h̲tī, klak·wālai*; *be dardī.*
Calm, a. *āsūdah, hawār, ārām, band, walāṛ.* v.a. *walāṛawul, saṛawul, ārām warkawul.* s. *qalār·tiyā-* or *walāṛ·tiyā da bād.*
Calmly, ad. *pa qalār sara, pa ro ro.*
Calmness, s. *ārām-, qalār-, walāṛ-*, etc. *-tiyā*; *rāhat, ṭāṭob.*
Calumniate, v.a. *tuhmat-* or *tūmat-, tor-*, etc. *-pore k. peg̲h̲or warkawul, g̲h̲ībat k.*
Calumny, s. *tuhmat, tor, peg̲h̲or, g̲h̲ībat.*
Camel, s. *ūk̲k̲h̲, s̲h̲utur.* (young-) *jūng* or *jūngai, botai.* (rutting-) *baṛbaṛai.* (-driver) *sarwān, ūk̲k̲h̲bah.* (-saddle) *kata, pālān.* (-litter) *kajāwa.* (-bridle) *pezwān.* (-nose peg) *nata.*
Camp, s. *ḍera, muqām*; *urdū, ḍal.*
Campaign, s. *jang, g̲h̲azā, jihād*; *sama, maidān.*

Camphor, s. *kāfūr.*
Can, v.n. *s̲h̲wal, tuwānedal.* s. *loṭkai.*
Canal, s. *nāla, wāla.* (small-) *lak̲k̲h̲tai.*
Cancel, v.a. *wrānawul, man'a k. bāṭil k.*
Cancer, s. *yaga, rasawla-ī, k̲k̲h̲andza, nāsūr.*
Candid, a. *rik̲k̲h̲tīnai, spīn, sūc̲h̲ah, ṣāf.*
Candidate, s. *umed·wār.*
Candle, s. *bāta-ī.* (-stick) *ḍīwaṭ.*
Candour, s. *rik̲k̲h̲tīn·tob, spīn·wālai, ṣafā-ī.*
Cane, s. *bet.* (sugar-) *ganna.* (-for eating) *ponḍa.* (-for the mill) *k̲h̲ū.*
Canister, s. *dablai, haṛpa-ī, ṣandūqc̲h̲a.*
Cannibal, s. *saṛī-* or *ādam·k̲h̲or, k̲h̲ūnāṛai.*
Cannon, s. *top, topa.* (-ball) *golā, gola-ī.*
Canoe, s. *kis̲h̲ta-ī.*
Canon, s. *qānūn, ā-īn, dastūr.*
Canopy, s. *c̲h̲atr, sāewān, s̲h̲āmiyāna, siwrai.*
Cant, s. *makr, riyā.* (-word) *takiya kalām.*
Canton, s. *tapa, c̲h̲am, jam, k̲h̲el.*
Cantonment, s. *urdū, ḍal, c̲h̲āwnṛa-ī.*
Canvas, s. *biyasta-ī, ṭapṛa.*
Cap, s. *ṭopa-ī, k̲h̲ola·ī.* (padded-) *ṭūk̲h̲ala-ī.* (-with ear flaps) *koṭak̲h̲a, k̲h̲ūrjīna.*
Capable, a. *qābil, tuwānā, s̲h̲wūnkai.*
Capacious, a. *arat, dzāyawar, kus̲h̲ād.*
Capacity, s. *tuwān, qābiliyat, qābil·tob, idrāk*; *arat·wālai, dzāe.*
Capital, s. *aṣl, māya, panga, saga.* a. *aṣlī, awwal, wṛūnbanai*; *da marg lā-iq* or *-sazā-wār.*
Capsicum, s. *sara·mric̲h̲.*
Caprice, s. *k̲h̲iyāl, wahm.*
Capricious, a. *k̲h̲iyālī, wahmī, nā·qalār.*
Captious, a. *ḥujjatī, takrārī, jang·yālai.*
Captivate, v.a. *g̲h̲ulawul, fareftah-, mayan-, koḍ-*, etc. *k.*
Captive, s. *qaidī, bandī.*
Captivity, s. *qaid, band.*
Capture, v.a. *nīwal, āk̲h̲istal, giriftār k.*
Caracole, v.a. *top-, k̲h̲artīza-, k̲h̲arc̲h̲aka-*, etc. *-wahal.*

Caravan, s. *kārwān, qāfila, sānga.*
Caravansary, s. *srāe, kārwān-srāe, rabāṭ.*
Caraway, s. *zīra, sperkai.*
Carbuncle, s. *kkhandza, dandārū, ghunḍārai.*
Carcass, s. *muṛai, lāsh.*
Card, s. *pāṇṛa, pata.* (playing-) *tās, ganjīfa.*
Card, v.a. *alājī-, tonbiyā-*, etc. *k.*
Cardamous, s. *ilāchī, hel.*
Carder, s. (cotton-) *alāj*; *nandāp* or *naddāf.* (his bow) *līnda.* (the beam) *ḍānḍat.* (the cord) *ja-ī.* (the beetle) *ḍabalai.* (the staff) *chūka.* (the comb) *alājī.*
Care, v.a. *fikr-, parwā-, ghaur-*, etc. *k., andekkhnā-, gham-*, etc. *k., khāṭir-, makh-, mulāḥiza-*, etc. *k., khabar-dārī-, tsoka-ī-*, etc. *k., sātana-, khundī-*, etc. *k.*
Career, s. *daur, daurān*; *manḍa, zghākkht.*
Careful, a. *khabar-dār, hokkhyār*; *fikr-man.*
Carefulness, s. *khabar-dārī, hokkhyār-tiyā.*
Careless, a. *be khabar, be parwā, be fikr, be gham, ghāfil, shārlai-wāwlai.*
Caress, v.a. *nāzawul, nāz-, mīna-, dilāsa-*, etc. *k.*
Carious, a. *chinjan, wrost, skhā, shaṛhedalai.*
Carnage, s. *qatl, marg, khūn.*
Carnal, a. *nafsānī, shahwat-nāk, mast.*
Carnivorous, a. *ghwakkha-khor.* (-animal) *dad.*
Carol, v.a. *stāyal.* s. *stāyana.*
Carouse, v.a. *bad-masti k., sharāb tskkhal* or *tskal*; *nasha k.*
Carpenter, s. *tarkāṇr, darūz-gar.*
Carpet, s. *farsh*; *ghāla-ī, ghālīcha.* (cover for a-) *chāndānī.* (praying-) *saijāda, muṣalla.*
Carriage, s. *gāḍa-ī*; *bār-bardārī, bār-kakkh*; *yūn, chāl, raftār*; *ḍaul, wajha.*
Carrier, s. *wṛūnkai*; *bār-kakkh. bār-bardār*; *harkārah, ḥammāl.*
Carrion, s. *murdār.*
Carrot, s. *gāzara, zardaka*

Carry, v.a. *wṛal, rāwṛal.*
Cart, s. *gāḍa-ī, arāba.* (-man) *gāḍa-ī-wān.*
Cartilage, s. *krachai, krachūnai, krapandūkai.* (-of the nose) *tandwai, tīndorai.*
Carve, v.a. *kanal* or *kanastal.* (-meat) *kūtal.*
Cascade, s. *tsādar, dāra, taṇdūra.*
Case s. *lifāfa, pokkh, ghilāf.* (sword-) *tekai, teka, miyān*; *kisbat, kīsa*; *ṣandūqcha, haṛpa-ī, ḥāl, ḥālat.*
Casement, s. *kaṛka-ī.*
Cash, s. *naghd* or *naqd, rok.*
Casket, s. *dabalai, haṛpa-ī, ṣandūqcha.*
Cast, v.a. *wīshtal, āchawul. ghurzawul, lawastal.*
Cast, s. *kālbūt, ghālab* or *qālib.* (at play) *daw, guzār.*
Caste, s. *rang, zāt, aṣl, qām* or *qaum, nog.*
Castle, s. *koṭ, qil'a, gaṛa-ī.*
Castor-oil, s. *da arhanḍo tel.*
Castrate, v.a. *khaṣṣī-, ākhtah-, malai-*, etc. *k.*
Casual, a. *qismatī, naṣībī, nā-gahān, nā-gūmān.*
Casualty, s. *āfat, kāna, nāzila.*
Cat, s. *pisho.* (tom-) *barghūṭ* or *narghūṭ.* (wild-) *pish-pṛāng.* (young-) *pishongaṛai.*
Catalogue, s. *siyāha.* (of men) *asāmī.*
Cataract, s *dāra, tsādar.* (of the eye) *parda, dund.*
Catarrh, s. *zukām, dūmai, sāṛa, yakhnī, nazla.*
Catastrophe, s. *balā, āfat, muṣībat, kāna.*
Catch, v.a. *nīwul, ākhistal, giriftār k.*
Catechize, v.a. *sawāl-, pukkhtana-*, etc. *k.*
Caterpillar, s. *pīsha-ī, chinjai.*
Catgut, s. *ja-ī, jaṇṛai.*
Cattle, s. *tsārwai, ḍangar, māl, dāba.*
Caudle, s. *matar, lāwaṇr, kaṛa.*
Caught, v.n. *nkkhatal.* a. *nkkhatai.*
Caul, s. *obaṇra, da bachī parda.*
Cause, s. *sabab, jihat, kabl, bā-iṣ, wāsṭa*; *muqaddama.*

Cauterize, v.a. *dāghawul, dāgh lagawul.*
Cautious, a. *khabar-dār, hokkhyār, baidār.*
Cavalcade, s. *sparlī* or *swarlī*; *jilaw.*
Cavalier, s. *spor* or *swor.*
Cavalry, s. *swārah, risāla.*
Cave, s. *smats* or *samist, ghār, kāz.*
Cavity, s. *doghal, ṭūbkai, jawara, kanda.*
Cease, v.a. *pregdal—prekkhodal—prekkhawul.* v.n. *ākhiredal, tamāmedal.*
Ceaseless, a. *mudāmī, dā-im.*
Cedar, s. *diyār.*
Cede, v.a. *pregdal, spāral, warkawul*; *manal.*
Ceiling, s. *chat, bām, tsapar.*
Celebrate, v.a. *stāyal.* (-a day) *manal.*
Celebrated, a. *nūm-war, nām-dār, nāmer, mashhūr.*
Celebration, s. *stāyana*; *manana.*
Celestial, a. *āsmānī, jannatī.*
Celibacy, s. *lawand-tob, tsaṛah-wālai.*
Cell, s. *khūna, koṭa*; *gokkha, ḥujra.*
Cellar, s. *tah-khāna.*
Cement, s. *salekkh.* (mortar) *kūnai, gach.*
Cemetery, s. *maqbara, rauẓa*; *qabristān, goristān, hadera.* (-of saints) *ziyārat, dargāh.*
Censer, s. *mujmir.*
Censor, s. *muḥtasib.*
Censure, v.a. *malāmat k., ṭaqawul, raṭal, traṭal.* (-oneself) *gram k.*
Cent, s. *sil.* (per-) *saikaṛa, pa sil, sil pase.*
Centipede, s. *zanza.*
Central, a. *miyānah, mandzai* or *mandzwai.*
Centre, s. *mandz* or *myandz.*
Centuple, a. *sil-bragh, sil-chand.*
Century, s. *sil-kāl.*
Cerate, s. *malham, paha, mom-roghan.*
Ceremony, s. *madār, khāṭir, makh, adab, taklīf, dastūr, rasm.*
Certain, a. *yaqīn, taḥqīq, ṣaḥīḥ, muqarrar.* (-one) *palānkai* or *falānai.*
Certainly, ad. *be shakk, albatta, rikkhtiyā.*
Certainty, s. *yaqīnī, zbād, taḥqīqī, iṣbāt.*
Certificate, s. *sanad, chīṭa-ī, kāghaz.*
Certify, v.a. *yaqīn-, zbād-, ṣābit-, taḥqīq-,* etc. *k.*; *khabar-, āgāh-,* etc. *k.*
Chafe, v.a. *blodal, sūlawul, mugal—mukkhal.* v.n. *blosedal, sūledal, sūdah ked.* (grieve) *ghamedal, sūledal, kaṛedal.*
Chaff, s. *būs, proṛ, sūṛī.* (of rice) *khamache.* (of corn, etc.) *drūze, gadzāre.*
Chagrin, s. *randz, khapagān, nūl, gram.*
Chain, s. *zandzīr.* (-link) *kaṛa-ī.*
Chair, s. *kursī, chaukī*; *kāṭkai, peṛa-ī.*
Chalk, s. *spīna-khāwra.*
Challenge, v.a. *jang gokkhtal*; *da'wa-,* etc. *k.* v.n. *gwākkhedal.*
Challenger, s. *mudda'a-ī*; *jang joe*; *gwākkhkai.*
Chamber, s. *koṭa, khūna.*
Chameleon, s. *karboṛai, tsarmakkhkai.*
Champ, v.a. *krapawul, chīchal.*
Champaign, s. *maidān, sama, ṣaḥrā.*
Champion, s. *pahalwān, tūrzan, bahādur.*
Chance, s. *naṣīb, qismat*; *wār, puk*; *daw.* v.n. *nāziledal, prewatal, wāqi'a ked.*
Change, v.a. *badlawul.* (-money) *mātawul.* v.n. *badledal, āwukkhtal, girzedal.*
Changeable, a. *nā-pāedār, nā-qalār*; *khūshai, nīma-khwā.*
Channel, s. *lār*; *nāla, rūd-khāna, lakkhtai.*
Chant, v.a. *sarod-, sandara-, badala-,* etc. *wayal.*
Chaos, s. *tor-tam, ẓulmat.*
Chapter, s. *bāb, faṣl.* (of Qurān) *sūra.*
Character, s. *khoe, khaṣlat*; *ṣifat, khāṣṣiyat*; *nūm, nāmūs*; *bashanj, pat.*
Charcoal, s. *skor.* (pl. *skārah*). (live-) *sarwaṭka* or *skarwaṭa.*
Charge, s. *amānat, spārah, sipurd, ḥawāla.* (order) *ḥukm, kariya, farmān.* (price) *bai'a, qīmat.* (expense) *kharts.* (onset) *halla, tsoṭ, guzār, brīd.* (advice) *maṣlaḥat.* (prohibitory) *qadaghan.*

Charge, v.a. *spāral, amānat-*, etc. *k.* (order) *farmāyal, ḥukm-*, etc. *warkawul.* (accuse) *d'awa k., tuhmat-, tor-*, etc., *-pore k.* (attack) *halla-*, etc. *k.* (load) *ḍakawul.* (enjoin) *tākīd-*, etc. *k., pohawul.* (in accounts) *kharts līkal.*

Charger, s. *jangī ās*; *tabākh, ghāb* or *qāb, tasht.*

Charitable, a. *sakhī, khairātī, sakhāwatī.*

Charity, s. *khairāt*; *zakāt, ṣadqa, sarsāya.*

Charm, s. *t'awīz.* (kind of) *mara-ī, tāwītah, amel, dawā, ṭilism.* (for snakes, etc.) *pāṛ.* (juggle) *mantar, koda, jādū, siḥr, hūda.*

Charm, v.a. *hūda-, dam-*, etc. *k.*; *pāṛawul*; *jādū-*, etc. *k., fareftah k., ghulawul.*

Charmer, s. *jādū-gar, koḍ-gar, siḥr-gar.* (snake-) *pāṛū.* (mistress) *dil-bar, dil-rubā, nāznīna.*

Charming, a. *kkhāyastah, khwakkh, khwand-nāk.*

Chart, s. *nakhkkha* or *naqsha.*

Charter, s. *sanad, 'ahd-nāma, iqrār-nāma.*

Chase, s. *kkhkār, ṣaid*; *pairawī, manḍa.* v.a. *kkhkār k., takkhtawul, zghalawul, pase manḍe-wahal.*

Chasm, s. *ḍoghal, ṭūbkai, gorhanda, gaṛang*; *kanda, chāwd, jawara.*

Chaste, a. *pāk-laman, nęko-kār, pākīzah, pāk.*

Chat, v.a. *kitī-pitī khabare k.*

Chatter, v.a. *bak-bak-, ṭar-ṭar-, chiṛ-chiṛ*, etc. *k.*

Chattels, s. *asbāb, kālī, sāmān, māl, bar-bast.*

Cheap, a. *arzān, wal* or *wel, spuk.*

Cheapness, s. *arzān-tiyā, wel-wālai.*

Cheat, s. *ṭag, farebī, darghal, sādū, makār, chal-bāz, chal-walai*; *ṭagī, droh, chal, makr.*

Cheat, v.a. *ṭagal, ṭagī-, fareb-, chal-bāzī-, darghalī-*, etc. *k., drohawul.*

Check, v.a. *hiṭālawul, ḥiṣārawul, man'a k., sambālawul, nkkhlawul, wudrawul.*

Cheek, s. *angai, anangai, koka-ī, bārkho.*

Cheer, s. *chigha, nāra*; *ārām, khwakkhī*; *'aish, khwand, maza*; *kkhādī*; *melmastiyā.*

Cheer, v.a. *chighe-*, etc. *wahal*; *tasallī-, dilāsa-*, etc. *k.*

Cheerful, a. *khwakkh, khūsh-ḥāl, kkhād, kkhādān, kkhād-man, khandā-rūe.*

Cheerless, a. *be dil, be ārām*; *khwār, lūts.*

Cheese, s. *panīr.* (soft-) *bagora, potsa.* (hard-) *qurut.*

Chequer, v.a. *brag-, gag-, rangīn-, chrag-brag-*, etc. *k.*

Cherish, v.a. *pālal, parwaral, nmāndzal*; *sātal, jghoral, khundiyal.*

Cherisher, a. *pālūnkai, parwarūnkai.* (in comp.) *parwar.*

Chess, s. *shatranj.* (-board) *bisāṭ*, (king) *shāh.* (queen) *wazīr.* (castle) *rukh.* (knight) *asp.* (bishop) *pīl.* (pawn) *piyādah.* (check) *kisht.* (checkmate) *māt.* (-player) *shatranj-bāz.*

Chest, s. *ṭaṭar, sīna.* (the cavity) *gargas, gogal.* (clothes-, etc.) *tawura-ī, ṣandūq.*

Chestnut, s. *banj, banj-pāṛ.* a. *surang.*

Chew, v.a. *chīchal, jowul, krapawul.* (the cud) *shkhwand k.*, or *-wahal*, or *-mātawul.*

Chicken, s. *chirgūrai, chūchai.* (-pox) *katsrak.*

Chide, v.a. *raṭal, traṭal, peghorawul, dāṛal.*

Chief, a. *mashar, awwal, wṛūnbai.* s. *sardār, arbāb, khān, malik, ra-is, sarghanah, rāhīṭ.*

Chiefly, ad. *akṣar, wṛūnbe, awwalan.*

Chiefship, s. *khānī, sardārī, malikī.*

Child, s. *bachai, woṛkai, wṛūkai, māshūm*; *farzand, tūng.*

Childbirth, s. *langa, lang-wālai, langa-tob.*

Childhood, s. *halak-wālai, wṛūk-wālai, halkat, halkīna.*

Childish, a. *halak-shān*; *nā-dān.*

Childless, a. *lā-walad, be zawzāt, be farzand.* (by death) *būr.*

Chill, a. *soṛ, yakh.* s. *sāṛa, yakhnī.*

Chilliness, s. *soṛ-wālai, yakhnī, sāṛa*

Chime, v.a. *tarāne wayal, trangawul, tāl wahal.* v.n. *trangedal, granjedal.* s. *trung, tāl, tarāna.*
Chimney, s. *lū-kakkh, da lūgī sūrai.*
Chin, s. *zana, zanakh, zanakh-dān.* (double-) *ghab-ghab, jajūra.*
Chink, s. *chāwd, darz, rakhna, chāq.* (sound) *shrang, granj.* v.n. *shrangedal, granjedal.*
Chintz, s. *chīt.*
Chip, s. *tota, totkai, tūtankai, tarāza.*
Chipped, a. *būrai.*
Chirp, v.a. *chanr-chanr-, chir-chir-,* etc. *k.*
Chisel, s. *tswarlai, kkhatsulai* or *shatsurlai.*
Choice, a. *ghwarah, kkhah, khāss.* s. *wāk, ikhtiyār; khwakkh, pasand, razā.*
Choke, v.a. *khapah k., mara-ī khapa k.* v.n. *khapah ked.*
Cholera, s. *wabā.*
Choose, v.a. *khwakkharwul, chunral, latawul, anrawul, kkhāghal, pasand k.*
Chop, v.a. *kūtal, warjal, tota-tota-, bja-,* etc. *k.*
Christ, s. *hazrat 'īsā, rūh-ullah.*
Christian, s. *'īsāwī, nasārā; tarsā.*
Christianity, s. *'īsāwī mazhab* or *-dīn.*
Chronic, a. *der-pā, multawī.*
Chronicle, s. *tawārīkh; akhbār; roz-nāma.*
Chuckle, v.n. *khandedal, musedal.* (over enemy) v.a. *sakha k., wiyāral.* (as a fowl) *chugh-chugh k.*
Chum, s. *mal, malgarai; hānda-ī-wāl; hujra-wāl.*
Church, s. *masjid, jumā'at.*
Churl, s. *gawār, dihqān, ghundāyah; lwār; bakhīl, shūm.*
Churn, v.a. *shā. bal.*
Churning, s. *shārbal.* (-stick) *mandānrū.* (-tie) *barangai.* (-strap) *rog, tasma.* (-dish) *donra-ī.* (-cover) *bargholai.*
Cinder, s. (cold-) *skor.* (hot-) *skarwata, khuglan, skhwakkhtan.*
Cinnabar, s. *shingrap.*
Cinnamon, s. *dārchīnī.*
Circle, s. *tsarkh, churlai, chambar, dā-ira.*
Circuit, s. *daur, daurān; gakkht.*
Circular, a. *ghūnd* or *ghūnd-man, tsarkhai.*
Circulate, v.a. *chalawul, girzawul, jārī k.* v.n. *chaledal, girzedal, jārī ked.*
Circumcision, s. *sunnat, khatna.*
Circumspect, a. *hokkhyār, baidār, khabar-dār, pokh.*
Circumstance, s. *hālat, hāl; khabara.*
Circus, s. *jaulān-gāh.*
Cistern, s. *hauz, baha-ī, talāo, dand.*
Citadel, s. *qil'a, kot, gara-ī, arg, bālā-hisār.*
Cite, v.a. *balal, talab k.; yādawal.*
Citizen, s. *kkhahr-wāl; daftarī.*
Citron, s. *nīmbū, triw nāranj.*
City, s. *kkhahr.*
Civil, a. *mulkī, dīwānī: makhawar, sulūkī, mihrbān.* (-court) *mulkī 'adālat.* (-war) *patna, khāna-jangī.* (-power) *'adālat.*
Civilian, s. *'āmmī; kasb-gar; ahl da qalam.*
Civility, s. *makhawarī, makh-tob, madār, adab, nek-sulūk, mihrbāngī.*
Civilize, v.a. *ābādawul, kkhāyastah-, ārāstah-,* etc. *k. sarī-tob chalawul.*
Claim, v.a. *d'awa-, darkhwāst-,* etc. *k.*
Claimant, s. *mudd'aī, dād-khwāh, d'awa-dār.*
Clammy, a. *bokkht, slekkht-nāk, barwai, chaspān.*
Clamour, s. *zwag-zwūg, shor-shaghab, ghoghā.*
Clamp, s. *patrai.*
Clan, s. *qām, khel, firqa, ulūs, tabar, cham.*
Clandestine, a. *put, pinham, ghalai.*
Clangour, s. *shrang, granj, trang.*
Clap, v.a. (the hands) *tāl wahal; shābāsh k.*
Clapper, s. *tak-takānrai, jiba, spai.*
Clarify, v.a. *pāk-, pākīzah-, spīn-, sāf-,* etc. *k.*
Clarion, s. *sarnāe.* (-player) *sarnāchī.*
Clash, v.a. *blodal, takar-, daka,-* etc. *khwural.* v.n. *blosedal.*

Clasp, v.a. *pa ghegi nīwul; baṛgrandī k.*
Class, s. *aṣl, ẕāt, rang, nogai; ṭolai, cham, khel; darja, pāya.*
Classification, s. *tartīb, dzerma.*
Clatter, v.a. *trangawul, shṛangawul, gṛanjawul.*
Clause, s. *faṣl; sharṭ.*
Clavicle, s. *grewa.*
Claw, s. *changul, mangul, panja, nūk.* v.a. *panja-*, etc. *wahal, nūkāra k.*
Clay, s. *maṭa-* or *maṭīna khāwra, khaṭa.*
Clayey, a. *maṭīn, khāwrīn.*
Clean, a. *pāk, pākīzah, ṣāf, spīn.* v.a. *pāk-*, etc. *k.*
Clear, a. *pāk, ṣaf; tsargand, kkhkārah, bartser, awtsār, bewrah; yalah, āzād, khalāṣ.* v.a. *spetsal, pākawul, spīn-*, etc. *k. tsargand-*, etc. *k. yalah-*, etc. *k.* (-the throat) *ghāṛa tāza k.*
Clearness, s. *pāk-wālai; tsargand-wālai*, etc.
Cleave, v.a. *chawul.* (asunder) *chaurang, k. prekawul.* (-to) v.n. *nkkhatal, lagedal, chaspedal.*
Cleaver, s. *ṭoqiyā, sātūl; prekawūnai.*
Cleft, s. *chāwd, chāq, wat, darz; kandaw, kand.*
Clemency, s. *ḥalīmī, shafaqat, raḥmat.*
Clement, a. *ḥalīm, mulā-im, raḥīm, narm.*
Clergy, s. *pādriyān, mullāyān, bāmbaṉrān.*
Clerk, s. *kātib, līkūnkaī, kkhkawūnkai.*
Clever, a. *hokkhyār, pohānd, pokh; hunrman, kārī-gar, qābil; kāgh, chirg.*
Client, s. *d'awa-gar, mudd'a-ī.*
Cliff, s. *kamar, tsaka, lākkh.*
Climate, s. *āb-o-hawā, hiwād, iqlīm.*
Climb, v.n. *khatal.*
Climber, s. *khatūnai.* (plant) *bel.*
Cling, v.n. *nkkhatal, chaspedal, lagedal.*
Clink, v.n. *shṛangedal, gṛanjedal.*
Clip, v.a. (hair, etc.) *skustal, kaṭeyal.* (cloth, etc.) *skakkhtal.* (dock) *ghūṭ k.* or *-prekawul.* (hair of head), *sar-kunḍai k.*

Cloak, s. *bārāna-ī; chogha, baraka.* (felt-) *kosai.* (fur-) *postīn.* (blanket-) *junga kiṛi shaṛa-ī.*
Clock, s. *gaṛī, sā'at.*
Clod, s. *lūṭa, chūm, gapa.*
Clog, s. *kaṉrāwa; haṭāl, nkkhata, bār.* v.a. *haṭālawul, kariyābawul, nkkhlawul.*
Close, v.a. *bandawul, joṛawul, lagawul, pewand k.; tamāmawul, khatm k.* (a door) *pore k.* (a book) *ṭapawul* or *ṭap wahal.*
Close, s. *ākhir, khatm; bāra, shpol, haḍera.*
Close, a. *nijdai; tang; pewastah; bakhīl, shūm; ṭīng, tat, gaṉr.* (as cloth) *ṭok.* (as stars) *jambaq.* (-cut) *ghūṭ, lanḍ.*
Closeness, s. *nijdekī; tang-wālai; pewastagī; bakhīlī, shūm-wālai; ṭīng-wālai.*
Closet, s. *ḥujra, khūna; gūṭ, gokkha.*
Cloth, s. *karbās, khāmtā; alwān, chīṭ*, etc. (woollen-woven-) *paṭū, baraka, shaṛa-ī, pashmīna*, etc. (woollen-unwoven-) *krāsta, lamtsai, kosai, namada*, etc. (broadcloth) *banāt.*
Clothe, v.a. *āghustawul, pokkhal, poslal; āghostal.*
Clothes, s. *zaṛūkī, nwarī* or *nmarī, pokkhāk, āghostan, libās, jāme.* (swaddling-) *oraṉrai.*
Cloud, s. *waryadz.*
Clout, s. *chīrṛa, khartsoṛai, ṭaghar.* (loin-) *lung, chotai, taṛāqa-ī.* (child's-) *kūna-starkai; taṛūnai.*
Clove, s. *lawang.* (-necklace) *lawang-hāṛ.*
Cloven, a. (cleft) *chāwd, chāq.* (-hoof) *swa.*
Clover, s. *speshtarai, shautal, speshtai.*
Clown, s. *ṭoq-mār, malanḍai, pekkhe-gar, maskharāchī; gawār, pūhaṛ, kāwāk, shāṛ.*
Cloy, v.a. *sekan k., kraka ākhistal.*
Club, s. *amsā, koṭak, lawaṛ, ḍāng.* (society) *cham, ṣuḥbat, jumā'at.*
Cluck, v.a. *kuṛ-kuṛ k.*
Clue, s. *belga* or *balga, darak.*
Clumsy, a. *kāwāk, bad-wajha, bad-ḍaul.*

Cluster, s. *wagai, khosha*; *ganr, tolai.*
Clutch, v.a. *pa mūt nīwul, ghota-, chapa-*, etc. *nīwul* or *wahal.*
Coagulate, v.a. *tīngawul, klakawul, tomna-, māya-*, etc. *k.* v.n. *kangal-, khyam-*, etc. *ked.*
Coalesce, v.n. *gadedal, yo·dzāe ked.*
Coarse, a. *lwār, ghat.*
Coast, s. *ghāra, dada, tselma.*
Coat, s. *kurta, kadā-ī, khalqa, qādara-ī, landa-ī, andraka.* (-for rain) *bārāna-ī.* (-of mail) *zghara, zira.*
Coax, v.a. *dam-, dam·dilāsa-, jāna-*, etc. *k.*, *jigī·jigī-, hāre·hāre-*, etc, *k.*
Cobbler, s. *mochī, tsamyār.*
Cobweb, s. *jāla-ī.*
Cock, s. *chirg.* (game-) *pandāw·chirg.* (of a gun) *pāe, kajak.* (-crow) *charbāng* or *chirg·bāng.*
Cockade, s. *jogha, tūgh, zunbuk.*
Code, s. *shar'a.* (Afghan-) *pukkhtūn·walī.*
Co-equal, a. *siyāl, makhai, gund.*
Coerce, v.a. *zoral, lānde k.*
Coeval, a. *hum·dzolai, hum·'umr.*
Coffer, s. *khizāna.*
Coffin, s. *tābūt.*
Cog, v.a. *chāplūsī-, dirpalī-*, etc. *k.*, *ghulawul.* (of a wheel) s. *būrai.*
Cohabit, v.a. *kilai-, kor-*, etc. *k.*, *kor·wālai k.*
Cohesive, a. *bokkht, barwai, slekkht·nāk.*
Coil, s. *pech, tāo, wal.*
Coin, s. *sika, paisa, naghd* or *naqd.* (counter-feit-) *jūtah, nā·sarah.*
Coincide, v.n. *jukht-, barābar-, jor-*, etc. *lagedal.*
Cold, a. *sor, yakh.* s. *sāra, yakhnī*; *zukām, dūmai, nuzla.*
Colic, s. *bād·gola, sūda, shwala.*
Collapse, v.n. *drabal, aluwal·prewatal.*
Collar, s. *grewān.* (-of a dress) *grewa.* (neck-) *tauq.* (dog-) *gharwandai.*

Colleague, s. *mal, malgarai.*
Collect, v.a. *tolawul, gatal, jam'a k.*, *latawul.*
College, s. *madrassa, maktab.*
Collision, s. *daka, takar*; *blos, blosedana.*
Colocynth, s. *maraghūnai, tarkha kakora.*
Colloquial, s. *da 'āmmiyāno jiba, wrāsha.*
Collusion, s. *jorikkht, tagī, sāzish.*
Collyrium, s. *rānjah, surma, kuhal.* (-case) *rānjarūma.* (-bodkin) *salā ī.*
Colonize, v.a. *ābādawul, wadānawul.*
Colony, s. *bānda, nawū-ī*; *ābādī, wadānī.*
Colour, s. *rang, laun.* v.a. *rangawul.*
Coloured, a. *rangīn, rang karai.*
Colours, s. *nakkha, janda, bairaq, togh.*
Colt, s. *bihānr.* (two-year-old-) *dwak.*
Column, s. *tsalai, munār, stan* or *sitūn.*
Comb, s. *gamanz* or *mangaz*; *shāna.* (honey-) *gabīna.* (cock's-) *chār·khwalak.* (curry-) *ghasho.*
Combat, s. *jang, muqaddama.*
Combatant, s. *jangī, mlā·tar, tūrzan.*
Combine, v.a. *jorawul*; *gadawul, laral.*
Come, v.n. *rātlal—rāghlal, rasedal.*
Comedy, s. *malanda, pekkha, toqa, swāng,*
Comely, a. *kkhkulai, kkhāyastah, pa-ī·makhai.*
Comet, s. *da jārū storai.*
Comfort, s. *ārām, mor·tiyā, ārām·tiyā*; *dilāsa, tasallī, dād, khwā·khogī.*
Coming, a. *gāndah, āyandah.*
Command, s. *hukm, kariya, farmān, amr*; *wāk, was, qābū*; *farz.* v.a. *farmāyal, hukm-*, etc. *k.*
Commander, s. *hākim, sardār, sar·guroh.*
Commence, v.a. *ibtidā-, shur'ū-, darak-*, etc. *k.*
Commend, v.a. *stāyal, sipārish k.*
Commendation, s. *stāyana, sipārish.*
Commerce, s. *saudāgarī, wapār, lāgī, rākrah·warkrah.*
Commissary, s. *dārogha*; *āstādzai.*
Commission, s. *sanad, 'uhda*; *parwāna, farmān*; *kār.*

Commit, v.a. *spāral, pāslawul, ṣumāral, ḥawāla-*, etc. *k.*; *kawul, kṛal.* (-adultery) *zinā-, kāsīrī-*, etc. *k.* (-robbery) *ghlā k.*
Committee, s. *jirga, m'arika, majlis.*
Commodious, a. *munāsib, lā-iq, pīrzo.*
Commodity, s. *māl, jins, saudā.*
Common, a. *'āmm, jārī, chalan.* s. *maidān, panḍ·ghālai, ḍāga, ṭikārkai*; *borjal.*
Commonly, ad. *akṣar, ziyātī.*
Community, s. *cham* or *jam, khel, ulūs*; *rāsha·darsha, gāwar dī·tob, malgar·tiyā.*
Compact, a. *ganr* or *gūr*; *tat, ṭīng.* (-cloth) *ṭoq.* (-crops) *ṭal.* s. *wāda, lafẓ, tāṛa, neṭa.*
Companion, s. *mal, malgarai*; *āshnāe, rafīq.*
Company, s. *majlis*; *ṭolai, paṛk, ghol*; *malgīrī, āshnā-ī*; *melmastiyā, ṣuḥbat.*
Comparison, s. *muqābala, miṣāl, nisbat.*
Compass, s. *qibla·numāe*; *chāper, gakkht*; *ḥadd, dzāe.* (reach) *partāb.* v.a. *ḥiṣārawul* or *īsārawul.*
Compasses, s. *pargār.*
Compassion, s. *dard, raḥm, zṛah·swai, tars.*
Compatible, a. *munāsib, pīrzo*; *barābar.*
Compel, v.a. *zoral, lānde k.*
Compensate, v.a. *tāwān-, nāgha-, badal-*, etc. *warkawul.*
Competence, s. *kifāyat, rozī.*
Competent, a. *qābil, lā-iq.*
Competition, s. *muqābala.*
Complacent, a. *ḥalīm, post, narm, makhawar.*
Complainant, s. *mudd'a-ī, faryādī, d'awa·gar*; *gila·man.*
Complaint, s. *nālish, māna, gila, faryād.*
Complaisance, s. *makh·tob, makhawarī, narmī, mihrbāngī.*
Complete, a. *pūrah, tamām, khatm, kāmil*; *bashpaṛ, amānī.*
Complex, a. *gaḍ·waḍ*; *grān, mushkil.*
Complexion, s. *da tsihre rang, charda, mizāj.* (dark-) *kaloṭ.*
Compliment, s. *madār, adab, salām, makh.*
Comply, v.a. *manal, qubūlawul.* v.n. *rāẓī ked.*
Compose, v.a. *joṛawul*; *tartīb-, ārāstah-*, etc. *k.*; *saṛawul*; *līkal, kāgal-kkhkal.*
Composition, s. *gaḍūn, gaḍedana, gaḍa.*
Compound, v.a. *gaḍawul.* a. *gaḍ.*
Comprehend, v.n. *pohedal.*
Comprehension, s. *poh, pahm, fikr.*
Compress, v.a. *chit k., drabawul.*
Comprise, v.a. *shāmil-, yo·dzāe-*, etc. *k.*
Compute, v.a. *ganral, shmeral, ḥisābawul.*
Comrade, s. *mal, malgarai, yār.*
Concave, a. *jawar, ḍoghal.*
Conceal, v.a. *puṭawul, pokkhal, ghalai k.*
Concealment, s. *puṭ·wālai, puṭedana, ghalī·tob.*
Concede, v.a. *manal, qabūlawul, bakkhal.*
Conceit, s. *khpul·sarī, bād, wiyāṛ, kibr.*
Conceited, a. *bādī, khpul·sar, kibr·jan.*
Conceivable, a. *shwūnkai.*
Conceive, v.n. *pohedal.* v.a. *fikr-, qiyās-*, etc. *k.*; *blārbedal, ḍakedal.*
Conception, s. *poh, pahm, fikr, qiyās, khiyāl*; *blārbedana, blārba·wālai, umed, ḍaka.*
Concern, s. *kār, m'amala*; *gham, fikr, parwā*; *andekkhnā, wiswās.*
Concerned, a. *gham·jan, fikr·man*; *wiswāsī, andekkh·nāk.*
Concerning, p. *bābat, ḥaqq.*
Concert, s. *ittipāq*; *malgar·ṭiyā*; *zamzama.*
Conciliate, v.a. *pakhulā k., gwākkhal.*
Concise, a. *lanḍ, kotāh.*
Conclude, v.a. *tamāmawul, ākhir-, khatm-*, etc. *k., khalāṣawul*; *m'alūmawul, ganral.* v.n. *pohedal.*
Concord, s. *rogha, joṛa, āshtī, ashtoka.*
Concourse, s. *ṭolai, jumā'at, ganṛ·ālam.*
Concubine, s. *wīndza, 'aurata, sūryata.*
Concupiscence, s. *nas, mastī, shahwat.*
Concur, v.n. *yo·jihat-, yo·zṛah-, rāẓī-*, etc. *ked.*

Concussion, s. *ṭakar, ḍaka.*
Condemn, v.a. *bad manal, man'a k.*; *gunāh-, wabāl-, taqṣīr*, etc., *ṣābitawul* or *dzāyawul.*
Condescend, v.a. *mihrbāngī-, makh-, mulāḥiẓa-, madār-*, etc. *k.*
Condiment, s. *masāla.*
Condition, s. *ḥāl, ḥālat, ṣūrat, yang, shān*; *wāda, neṭa, lafẓ, shart.*
Condole, v.a. *lās·nīwah k.*; *pātiḥa wayal, khwā·khogī k., pokkhal.*
Conduct, s. *chāl·chal, chalan, tarīqa*, etc.; *badraga*; *sulūk, madār, makh.*
Conduct, v.a. *badraga k., botlal—bīwul*; *rāwustal, rawānawul, chalawul.*
Confection, s. *ḥalwā, miṭiyā-ī, qanāt, shīrīnī.*
Confederacy, s. *para, janba, gundī.*
Confederate, s. *para·dār, janba·dār*; *mal.*
Conference, s. *jirga, maṣlaḥat, sawāl·dzawāb.*
Confess, v.a. *manal, khwāla wayal.* v.n. *qā-iledal.*
Confidence, s. *bāwar, yaqīn, sāwīsā, khal, i'tibār.*
Confine, v.a. *band-, qaid-, ḥiṣār* or *īsār-*, etc. *k.*
Confirm, v.a. *rikkhtiyā-, zbād-, ṣābit-, taḥqīq-*, etc. *k.*
Confiscate, v.a. *nāgha-, ẓabṭ-, qurugh-*, etc. *k.*
Confluence, s. *gaḍedana.*
Conform, v.n. *yo·shān-, yo·ḍaul-, yo·makh-, yo·zṛah-*, etc. *ked.*
Confound, v.a. *gaḍ·waḍawul, laṛal, shārbal*; *ḥariyānawul, rabṛawul, sargardānawul, pareshān-, hak·pak-, hekkh-, huts-*, etc. *k.*
Confront, v.a. *makhā·makh-, muqābala*, etc. *k.*
Confute, v.a. *lā·dzawāb-, gram-, radd-*, etc. *k.*
Congeal, v.n. *ṭīngedal, kangal ked.*; *khyam ked.*
Congratulate, v.a. *mubārakī k.* or *wayal.*
Congregation, s. *ṭolai, jamā'at, majlis.*
Conjecture, s. *gūmān, 'aql, khiyāl.*
Conjugal, a *da tsakkhtan aw da kkhadze, da wādah karai aw da wadedali.*
Conjunction, s. *pewand, joṛ, taṛūn.*
Conjuncture, s. *wakht, neṭa, nobat, ṭāng.*
Conjure, v.a. *qasam-, saugand-*, etc. *warkawul*; *jādū-, koḍa-*, etc. *k.*
Conjurer, s. *jādū·gar, koḍ·gar, siḥr·gar.*
Connect, v.a. *joṛawul, lagawul, taṛal.*
Connexion, s. *joṛ, band, taṛūn*; *nisbat*; *ragai, khpulawī, khekkhī.* (carnal-) *gho, ghowūna, kor·wālai.*
Connive, v.a. *starge puṭawul.*
Connubial, a. See Conjugal.
Conquer, v a. *barai k.*, or *-mūndal, pa-aṛ k.*, etc.
Conquest, s. *barai, wa-aṛa, wa-aṛāna.*
Conscience, s. *īmān, diyānat*; *rikkhtīn·tob.*
Conscious, a. *khabar·dār, baidār, hokkhyār.*
Consecrate, v.a. *niyāz-, khairāt-*, etc. *k.*, or *-manal.*
Consent, s. *raẓā, qabūl, hokai, oe.*
Consequence, s. *natīja*; *pāzah.*
Consequently, ad. *dzaka, tro.*
Consider, v.a. *fikr-, pahm-, qiyās-*, etc. *k.*, *andekkhnā-, hosh-*, etc. *k.*; *ganṛal.* v.n. *pohedal.*
Considerable, a. *loe, grān*; *ḍer*; *drund.*
Consign, v.a. *spāral, pāslawul, gumāral, ḥawāla k.*; *āstawul, legal.*
Consignment, s. *spārana, ḥawāla*; *asbāb, jins.*
Consist, v.n. *joṛedal, osedal, kedal, shwal.*
Consistent, a. *joṛ, sam*; *klak, ṭīng.*
Console, v.a. *tasallī-, dilāsā-, ḍāḍ-*, etc. *warkawul.*
Consort, s. *tsakkhtan, meṛah*; *kkhadza, artīna.* v.a. *kilai-, kor-, rozgār-, khasamāna-*, etc. *k.*; *yārī-, āshnā-ī-, malgīrī-*, etc. *k.*
Conspicuous, a. *tsargand, kkhkārah, mashhūr.*
Conspirator, s. *yāghī·gar, mufsid, pasātī.*
Conspire, v.a. *sāzish-, badī-*, etc. *k.*
Constant, a. *pāedār, qā-im.*
Constantly, ad. *har·wakht, har·sā'at.*

Consternation, s. *hariyānī, sargardānī*; *khof*, *yera, bāk, tor, tars, tarhara.*
Constipation, s. *qabz, qabziyat.*
Constituent, a. *aslī, zātī.*
Constitute, v.a. *joṛawul, wudrawul, paidā-, muqarrar-*, etc. *k., wulāṛawul.*
Constitution, s. *mizāj, tab'a, khwā.*
Constrain, v.a. *zoral, sambālawul, tīngawul.*
Construct, v.a. *joṛawul, binā k.*
Consul, s. *wakīl, mukhtār.*
Consult, v.a. *jirga-, maslahat-, mashwarat-*. etc. *k.*
Consume, v.a. *sarf-, talaf-, kharts-*, etc. *k.*
Consummate, a. *pūrah, pokh, kāmil.*
Consumption, s. *kharts, sarfa*; *narai-randz, diqq, sill.*
Contact, s. *joṛ, lagedana*; *blos, blosedana.* (to come in-) v.n. *blosedal, jangedal, lagedal.*
Contagion, s. *wabā*; *gazak.*
Contain, v.a. *dzāyawul.* v.n. *dzāedal.*
Contaminate, v.a. *palīt-, nā-pāk-, skhā-, kakaṛ-, gazak-*, etc. *k.*
Contemn, v.a. *spuk ganṛal.*
Contemplate, v.a. *ghaur-, fikr-*, etc. *k.*; *nandāra-, tamāsha-*, etc. *k.*
Contemporary, s. *hum-dzolai, hum-wakht, kūl.*
Contemptible, a. *spuk, dūn, khushai.*
Contemptuous, a. *kibr-jan, bādī, be makh.*
Contend, v.a. *jagṛa-, qaziya-, takrār-*, etc. *k.*
Content, a. *rāzī, moṛ.* s. *razā, moṛ-tiyā.*
Context, s. *matan, 'ibārat, mazmūn.*
Contiguous, a. *nijdai, pewastah.*
Continent, a. *parhez-gār, pāk-laman.* s. *zmaka, barr, wucha.*
Contingent, a. *mauqūf*; *'ārizī.*
Continual, a. *pāedār, jārī, dā-im, pāyandah.*
Continuance, s. *pāedārī, mudāmī, dā-imī.*
Continue, v.n. *pāedal, osedal, pātedal.*
Contortion, s. *tāo, pech, wal, kālkūchaka.*
Contour, s. *makh, gūna, tsihra, shakl, ḍaul.*
Contract, s. *wāda, neṭa, bandanṛ, lafz*; *ṭeka.*
Contract, v.a. *tangawul, kāgal—kkhkal.* (a promise) *wāda-, neṭa-*, etc. *taṛal* or *k.* (a debt) *por ākhistal.* (a marriage) *wādah k., nikāh taṛal.* v.n. *kawt ked.*
Contradict, v.a. *khilāf wayal, radd-, darogh-jan-, hoḍ-*, etc. *k.*
Contrary, a. *khilāf, mukhālif, hoḍai.* s. *'aks, hoḍ.*
Contrast, v.a. *makhā-makh-, muqābala-*, etc. *k.*
Contrite, a. *tauba-gār, pakkhemān.*
Contrive, v.a. *band-, tadbīr-, hikmat-*, etc. *taṛal.*
Control, v.a. *sambālawul, qābū-, lānde-*, etc. *k., was chalawul.*
Controversy, s. *jagṛa, qaziya, radd-badal, bahs, hujjat, steza.*
Contumacy, s. *sarkakkhī, yāghī-garī.*
Contumely, s. *peghor, kkhkandzal, spuk-tiyā.*
Contusion, s. *blos, māṭūs, pūpaka, khūg, jobal.*
Convene, v.a. *ṭolawul, yo-dzāe k., balal.*
Convenient, a. *joṛ, pīrzo, khwakkh.*
Convention, s. *jirga, majlis, m'arika*; *wāda, taṛa, bandanṛ, neṭa.*
Conversant, a. *wāqif, āmokhtah, khabar-dār.*
Converse, v.a. *khabare k., sawāl-dzawāb k.*
Convert, v.a. *badlawul*; *murīd-, mutaqid-*, etc. *k.*
Convex, a. *ghūnḍ, gunbatī.*
Convey, v.a. (things) *āstawul, wṛal, legal.* (animals) *botlal—bīwul, rāwustal.*
Convict, s. *qaidī, bandī.*
Convict, v.a. *gunāh-*, etc. *zbād k.* or *sābit k.*
Convince, v.a. *qā-il k., gram k.*
Convivial, a. *khūsh-hāl, kkhād, khandā-rūe, melmah-dost.*
Convoke, v.a. *balal, ṭalab k., ṭolawul.*
Convoy, s. *badraga* or *badraqa.*
Convulsion, s. *ghoṭa, parghaz*; *balwā.*
Cook, v.a. *pakhawul.* s. *bāwarchī* or *barchī.*
Cool, a. *soṛ, yakh*; *be parwā*; *mānṛai-gar.*

Cool, v.a. *saṛawul, yakhawul.* v.n. *saṛedal.*

Coolness, s. *sāṛa, soṛ·wālai, yakhnī.* (pique) *marawar·tiyā, marawar·tob, mānrai.*

Coop, s. (of leather) *daba.* (-maker) *dabāgh.*

Coping, s. *tsatsobai, bala-ī, parchaṭai, sarmātai, sharīfa.*

Copious, a. *ḍer, frewān.*

Copper, s. *tāmba.*

Copse, s. *jangai, darga, ghīl.*

Copulate, v.a. *ghayal—ghowul, kor·wālai-, gho-, jimā'a-,* etc. *k.*

Copy, s. *naql, namūna, nuskha; mashq.*

Coquetry, s. *nāz, nakhra, makez, karashma.*

Coral, s. *marjān.* (-diver) *marjīwanrah.*

Cord, s. (thick-) *biyāsta, pa-aṛai, rasa-ī.* (thin-) *muzai, tār, spanrsai.* (hair-) *antsa-ī, siyala-ī, wākkhkai.* (palm leaf-) *būnr.*

Core, s. *māghzah, zṛah, zaṛai.*

Coriander, s. *ḍaniya.*

Cork, s. (bung) *būja, ḍīḍa, khulborai.*

Cormorant, s. *kotān.* (glutton) *ghārai.*

Corn, s. *ghala, dāna.* (green-) *khwīd, khasīl.* (-stubble) *drūza.* (mowed-) *satrai.* (-sheaf) *geḍa-ī.* (-stack) *dala-ī.* (-bin) *kandū, koṭa-ī, khamba.* (-straw) *nāṛ.* (-broken straw) *būs.* (-treading floor) *dirmand, khirman.* (pile of trodden-) *wānra.* (of the foot) *baura-ī, rasaula-ī, kila-ī, mekh.*

Corner, s. *gūṭ, gokkha; dakhma.*

Corporeal, a. *jismānī.*

Corpse, s. *muṛai, lāsh, murdah.*

Corpulent, a. *tsorb, peraṛ, ghaṭ, punḍ.*

Correct, a. *joṛ, jukht, durust, barābar, sam, rikkhtiyā, kkhah.*

Correspond, v.n. *joṛ-, sam-, barābar-,* etc. *lagedal, makhai ked.* v.a. *chīṭa-ī-, kāghaz-,* etc. *līkal* or *kāgal—kkhkal* or *legal.*

Corroborate, v.a. *rikkhtiyā-, zbād-, ṣubūt-,* etc. *k.*

Corrode, v.a. *zang khwuṛal.* v.n. *zang ked.*

Corrupt, v.a. *bonrawul, palītawul, kakaṛawul, skhā-, wrost-,* etc *k.*

Cost, s. *bai'a, kharts, qīmat; tāwān, nuqṣān.*

Costive, a. *qābiẓ, ṭing, klak.*

Costiveness, s. *qabẓ, qabẓiyat.*

Costly, a. *qīmat·nāk, grān·bahā.*

Costume, s. *jāma, libās.*

Cot, s. *kaṭkai, kaṭolai.*

Cottage, s. *kaḍala, jūngaṛa.*

Cotton, s. *mālūch.* (-plant) *punba, kālaka.* (-seed) *pundāna.* (-stubble) *khirīz, khaṛanḍ.* (-stalks) *punbe·cho, kālak·cho.* (-pod) *ghoza.* (-picker) *panḍol·gar.* (his share) *panḍolī.* (-dresser) *naddāp, alāj.* (his mallet) *ḍabalai.* (his bow) *ḍānḍat.* (his gin) *alājī.* (carded-) *pāghunda.* (roll of-) *pūnra-ī.* (skein of-) *māshoṛa.* (-thread) *tonbiyā, aṭa.* (-reel) *aṭerān.*

Cough, s. *ṭūkhai, ṭūkha, ṭūkh·ṭūkh.* (hooping-) *pūkhalai, tora·ghāṛa, haba·ḍaba.* v.n. *ṭūkhedal.*

Council, s. *jirga, m'arika; dalbār, majlis.*

Counsel, s. *pand, naṣīhat; maṣlahat, tadbīr, mashwarat; wakīl.*

Count, v.a. *shmeral, hisāb k.; ganral.*

Countenance, s. *makh, tsihra, bashra; mihrbāngī, mrasta, mulāhiza.*

Counterfeit, a. *jūṭah, nā·sarah.* v.a. *bāna-, palma-, chal-, ṭagī-,* etc. *-k.*

Counterpane, s. *bṛastan, taltak.*

Counterpart, s. *joṛa, pala, makhai, dzawāb.*

Country, s. *mulk, hewād.* (own-) *waṭan.* (foreign-) *wilāyat.* (-man, etc.) *waṭanī.*

County, s. *pargana, tapa.*

Couple, s. *joṛa, qulba, juft; dwah.*

Courage, s. *maṛāna, mardī, zṛah, nar·tob, dilāwarī, tūrzan·tob, dzwān·mardī, himmat.*

Courageous, a. *maṛanai, zṛah·war, dilāwar, turzan, himmat·nāk.*

Courier, s. *qāṣid, chapar, āstādzai.*

Course, s. *zghākkht, manda*; *daur, daurān*; *yūn, chāl*; *lār*; *maidān.* (of-) ad. *albatta, be·shakk.*

Court, s. *dalbār, daulat·khāna.* (civil-) *'adālat, maḥkama.* (-yard) *gholai, angaur. jawas.*

Court, v.a. *ghokkhtal*; *mīna-, 'ishq·bāzī-,* etc. *-k.*

Courteous, a. *makhawar, mihrbān, nek·khoe.*

Courtesan, s. *kachana-ī, lola-ī.*

Courtesy, s. *makh,mulāḥiẓa, adab, nek·sulūk.*

Courtier, s. *dalbārī.*

Courtship, s. *'ishq·bāzī, mīna, kkhpa·ārtūn, changhal·bāzī.*

Cousin, s. (father's brother's child) m. *tarbūr*; f. *tarla.* (mother's brother's child) *da māmā dzoe* or *lūr.*

Covenant, s. *wāda, taṛa, bandaur, 'ahd, qaul.*

Cover, s. *sar·pokkh, tekai, lifāfa.* (dish-) *bargholai.* (basket-) *kāra, sawada.*

Cover, v.a. *puṭawul, pokkhal.*

Covering, s. *pokkh, pokkhikkh, libās*; *miyān.*

Covet, v.a. *ṭam'a-, ḥirṣ-,* etc. *k.*

Covetous, a. *ṭam'a·jan, ḥirṣ·nāk, liwāl.*

Covey, s. *sail, ghol.*

Cow, s. *ghwā.* (-in heat) *ghwa-ema.* (milch-) *langa-,* or *pa-ī·wara ghwā.* (dry-) *zāṛa-ī.* (-pen) *ghojal.* (herd of-) *gohār.* (-dung) *ghoshoe.* (-dung fuel) *tsapiyāka,* (-dung stack) *gohāṭa.* (-keeper) *ghobah.*

Coward, s. *nā·mard, tuzan, kaṛū, sperkai, sperah·makh, taghan.*

Coy, a. *yer·man, sharm·sār, sharm·nāk, stāra prewatai.*

Crab, s. *kūnī·kabar, changākkh.* (-louse) *baṛora.*

Crack, s. *chāwd, darz, daṛa, rakhna.* (sound) *ḍaz, ṭas, trāk, khrach, ṭaq.*

Crack, v.n. *chāwdal, darz-.* etc. *ked.* v.a. *ḍaz-,* etc. *k.,* or *wahal.*

Crackle, v.n. *tsir·tsir-, sakkhā-,* etc. *ked.*

Cradle, s. *kaṭkai*; *zāngo, gahwāra.*

Craft, s. *kār, kasb, pesha*; *fareb, chal, ḥīla.*

Craftsman, s. *kārī·gar kasb·gar, pesha·war.*

Crafty, a. *chal·bāz, ḥīla·bāz, ṭag·bāz, farebī.*

Crag, s. *tsūka, kamar, garang.*

Cram, v.a. *manḍal, ḍakawu'.*

Cramp, s. *brekkh, tāo.*

Crane, s. *ḍīng, zāṇrai, kulang.*

Crash, s. *khrach, khṛap, khṛas, drab,* v.n. *drabal, naṛedal.*

Crater, s. *garang, tortam, ḍoghal, kūhai.*

Crave, v.a. *ghokkhtal, minnat-, khwāst-,* etc. *k.*

Crawl, v.n. *tskhedal* or *tskedal, pa kharpotso tlal, ghūndzedal.*

Crazy, a. *lewanai, khushai, saudā-ī.*

Creak, v.n. *chingedal, trangedal.*

Cream, s. *perawai.*

Crease, s. *jūhaṛa, kṛaṭai, chīchaṛ, gundza.* v.a. *chunral, jung k., jūhaṛa-,* etc. *k.*

Create, v.a. *paidā k., joṛawul.*

Creation, s. *duniyā, naṛa-ī, khalq, makhlūq.*

Creator, s. *khāliq, paidā kawūnkai.*

Creature, s. *bandah, wagaṛai, ganwai*; *ḥaiwān, dzanāwar*; *makhlūq.*

Credit, s. *por, qarẓ*; *nasiyah*; *bāwar, yaqīn. i'tibār.* v.a. *bāwar-,* etc. *k.* (buy on-) *pa por-,* etc. *ākhistal.*

Creditable, a. *mu'tabar*; *nām·war.*

Creditor, s. *porawuṛai.*

Creed, s. *īmān, dīn, mazhab*; *kalima.*

Creep, v.n. See Crawl.

Creeper, s. *bel*; *dzela, juṛang.*

Crescent, s. *myāsht, hilāl.*

Cress, s. *halam, tezak, tartezak.*

Crest, s. (bird's-) *chār·khwalai* or *chār·khwalak*; *zūnḍai.* (snake's-) *chaja.* (-of a hill) *kamar, ghākkhai*; *tsūka, peza.* (-of a helmet) *ṭurra, tāj.*

Crevice, s. *sūṛai, chāwd, darz, daṛa.*

Crew, s. *ghol, ṭolai*; *ḍala.* (ship's-) *jahāzī.*

Cricket, s. *kirṛai.*
Crier, s. *jārc͟hī, munādī kawūnkai.* (-to prayers) *mu-azzin, mullā·bāng wayūnkai.*
Crime, s. *gunāh, wabāl, taqṣīr, k͟haṭā, baza. jurm.*
Crimson, a. *arg͟hawānī, lāl, sūr.*
Cringe, v.a. *c͟hāplūsī-, ḍirpali-, k͟hūs͟hāmad-,* etc. *k.*
Cripple, a. *guḍ, kaṛam, zam·zmolai. s͟hall, sukṛuk.* v.a. *guḍ-,* etc. *k.*
Crisis, s. *sā'at, ṭāng, nobat; kamāl.*
Critic, s. *ḥarf·gīr, 'aib·joe.*
Crockery, s. *lokkhī·largī, kaṭwī·kandolī.*
Crocodile, s. *magar, nahang.*
Crook, s. *kūnḍa.* (shepherd's-) *kūnṭai, aṛām-kai, mac͟hak.*
Crooked, a. *kog, kṛīng, tsoṛ, ṭīṭ, kālkūc͟h.*
Crop, s. *faṣl.* (bird's-) *jajūra, ḥauṣila.* v.a. *tsaral; s͟hūkawul; g͟hūṭ k.*
Cross, v.n. (-over) *pore watal* or *-tlal.* v.a. *lānde·bānde-, ore·pore-,* etc. *k.* (-breed) *rag gaḍawul.*
Cross, a. *sūṭ·būṭ, mānṛai·gar, marawar, k͟hapah.* (-breed) *dwah·ragah.*
Crouch, v.n. *g͟halai ked., puṭedal.* (cringe).
Crow, s. *qāg͟hah* or *qārg͟hah:*
Crow, v.a. (-over rival) *sak͟ha-, wiyāṛ-,* etc. *k.*
Crowd, s. *ganṛ·'ālam, ḍala, lakkhkar.*
Crown, s. *tāj, k͟hol.* (-of head) *ṭaṭar, ṭopal.*
Crude, a. *ūm, k͟hām, kac͟hah, nīmgaṛai, nīma·k͟hwā, ūmg͟halan.*
Cruel, a. *ẓālim, be·raḥm, kānṛai·zṛah, sak͟ht.*
Crumb, s. *ṭoṭai, pūṭai, c͟hūr, reza.*
Crupper, s. (horse's-) *dumc͟hī.* (bullock's-) *g͟hwa-e lang, piyāṛma.*
Crush, v.a. *c͟hīt·pīt-, tsaplāk-,* etc. *k., da kkhpo·lānde k., paz wahal.*
Crust, s. *ṗoṭ.* (scab) *k͟hwar, waṛ, k͟hīg.*
Crutch, s. *ṭāpoṛa.* (-of a sandal) *gaḍeka.*
Cry, v.a. *ĵaṛa'.* (-violently) *pa raṭ·raṭ ĵaṛal.* (call) *naṛal, nāre wahal, bāng wayal.*

Cry, s. *jaṛā; nāra, bāng.*
Crystal, s. *bilaur; qalam; gac͟h.*
Cubit, s. *tsangal, lec͟ha, hata.*
Cuckold, s. *dahūs, bag͟harai.*
Cucumber, s. *bādrang, tara, tarai.*
Cud, s. *s͟hk͟hwand.* (-of hawks, etc.) *par muhra.*
Cuddle, v.n. *g͟hāra·g͟haṛa-ī ked.*
Cudgel, s. *koṭak, dāng, lawaṛ.* v.a. *kūṭal, wahal, ṭakawul.*
Cuff, s. *tsapeṛa, ḍab, ṭas.* (-of a coat) *las-tūnṛai, piyāk͟hla.*
Cuirass, s. *bak͟htar, jaus͟han.*
Culinary, a. *pak͟halai.*
Cull, v.a. *s͟hūkawul; c͟hunṛal.*
Culpable, a. *malāmatī, taqṣīrī.*
Culprit, s. *gunāh·gār, taqṣīrī.*
Cultivate, v.a. *ābādawul, wadānawul; kar-, īwe* or *yawe-,* etc. *-k.*
Cultivation, s. *ābādī, wadānī; kar, īwe* or *yawe, zarā'at.*
Cultivator, s. *zamīndār, kikkht·gar.* (hired-) *dihqān, c͟harekār.*
Cumin, s. *zīra, zanka-ī.*
Cunning, a. *c͟hal·bāz, farebī; kāg͟h, c͟hirg.* s. *hunar, ḥikmat.*
Cup, s. (metal-) *kaṭorai, jām.* (pottery-) *kanḍol* or *kanḍolai.* (wooden-) *kunṛa-ī* or *kunḍa-ī, kāsa.* (china-) *piyāla, kāsa.*
Cupidity, s. *s͟hahwat, mastī, naus; ḥirṣ.*
Cupola, s. *gunbat.*
Cupping-horn, s. *kkhkar.* (to cup) v.a. *kkhkar lagawul.*
Cur, s. *spai, kūtrai; qac͟har, lawanḍ.*
Curb, s. *kaṛa, zanḍzīra.* v.a. *sambālawul, qābū k.*
Curd, s. *māstūh, c͟haka; posta, matra, k͟ha-areṛai.*
Curdle, v.a. *tomna-, māya-, ṭīng-,* etc. *k.*
Cure, v.a. *joṛawul, rag͟hawul.* s. *'ilāj, rag͟hawūna.*

Curious, a. *'ajīb, nādir ; zhwag-tsār.*
Curl, s. *wal, zulf, tsūnṛa.*
Current, a. *jārī, chalan, rawā.* s. *chalānda, dāra.*
Currier, s. *tsamyār, dabbāgh.*
Curry, v.a. *kaṛāṛa k.* (tan) *dabbāghī k.* (-favour) *chāplūsī-, ḍirpalī-,* etc. *-k.*
Curse, v.a. *kkhere-, l'anat-, bad-d'uā-,* etc. *k.* s. *kkhera,* etc. ; *balā, āfat, wabāl, ghaẓab.*
Curtain, s. *parda, satra.* (-of a fort) *shīrāza.*
Curve, s. *ṭīṭa, kālkūch, kag-lech, wal, pech.*
Cushion, s. *bālikkhtak, bālikkht-goṭai.*
Custody, s. *amānat, ḥawāla ; qaid, band ; sātana, jghorana, khundī-tob.*
Custom, s. *dastūr, rasm, chāl, 'ādat, dod, rawāj.* (tax) *māliyā, khirāj, tāwān, bāj.* (-house) *tsoka-ī, ṭānṛa.* (-collector) *muḥaṣṣil, bāj-dār.*
Cut, s. *tsīra, parhār.* (-purse) *gan-kap.* a. *tsīralai, ghwuts, jobal.*
Cut, v.a. *tsīral.* (-off) *prekawul* or *prekṛal.* (-out clothes, etc.) *skakkhtal.* (wound) *jobalawul, ghwutsawul.* (-short) *ghūṭ prekawul, lanḍ k.*
Cutler, s. *āhan-gar, ṣaiqal-gar, lohār.*
Cycle, s. *daur, daurān, tsarkh, zamāna.*
Cylinder, s. *nal, shpelai.*
Cymbal, s. *zang, zangūla, jalājal.*
Cypress, s. *sarwa, ṣanobar.*

D.

Dab, v.a. *tapal.*
Daddy s. *bābū, dādā.*
Daffodil, s. *nargis, kangas.*
Dagger, s. *chāṛa. bihbūdī, pesh-qabza.*
Daily, ad. *rozmarra, har-roza, hara-wradz.*
Dainty, a. *khūsh-khwurāk ; khwand-nāk, maza-dār, tuḥfa.*
Dale, s. *dara.*
Dalliance, s. *nāz-o-nakhra, 'ishq-bāzī, 'āshiqī-m'ashūqī ; dirang, lārghak, sustī, multawī.*
Damage, s. *tāwān, nuqṣān, ziyān, troṭ.*
Dame, s. *merman, bībī, korbana.*
Damn, v.a. *kkhere-, l'anat-, bad-d'uā-,* etc. *k., petī-mū k., gūna wrī kawul.*
Damnable, a. *l'anatī, lā-iq da kkhero.*
Damp, a. *lūnd, tar, nam-nāk, zyam-nāk, ob-jan.*
Damsel, s. *peghla, jina-ī.* (betrothed-) *changhala.*
Dance, s. *gaḍeda ; nāch ; atanṛ, jihr.* v.n. *gaḍedal.* v.a. *nāch k. atanṛ-,* etc. *-āchawul.*
Dancer, s. *gaḍedūnkai, gaḍandai.* (rope-) *bāzī-gar, naṭ.*
Dangerous, a. *khaṭar-nāk.*
Dangle, v.n. *dzwaṛandedal, awezānd ked.*
Dapple, a. *brag, gag.*
Dare, v.n. *gwākkhedal.* v.a. *jah k., gwākkhawul.*
Dark, a. *tor, tārīk.* (-complexion) *kaloṭ.*
Darkness, s. *tyāra, tārīkī ; tortam, ẓulmat.*
Darling, s. *mayan, m'ashūq, dzān.*
Darn, v.a. *bezal* or *pezal, ganḍal ; rafū k.*
Dart, s. *shalgai, barcha, bala.* (iron) *sela.*
Dash, v.a. *wīshtal.* (-in pieces) *chūr-chūr-, ṭoṭe-ṭoṭe-, pūṭī-pūṭī-,* etc. *k.* (-water) *lawastal, toyawul.*
Dastard, s. *nā-mard, tuzan, kaṛū.*
Date, s. *tārīkh.* (fruit) *khajūr.*
Daub, v.a. *lewawul, akheṛal, akhāṛa k.*
Daughter, s. *lūr.* (-in law) *ngor.* (step-) *parkaṭa-ī, ba-anza-ī.* (brother's-) *wrera.* (sister's-) *khordza.*
Dauntless, a. *be-bāk, zṛah-war.*
Day, s. *wradz.* (to-) *nan.* (of to-) *nananai.* (-by day) *wradz pa wradz.* (every-) *hara wradz.* (-book) *roznāma.* (-light) *ranṛā wradz.* (-dawn) *chirg-bāng, ṣabā, sapede.* (by-) *da wradzi.* (-star) *storga.* (all the-) *kara-ī wradz.*

Dazzle, v.n. *brekkhedal, dzaledal, dzal ked.*
Dead, a. *mur, murai.* (-as a tree) *mrām* or *mrāw.*
Deadly, a. *qātil.*
Deaf, a. *kūnr.* (-as a post) *ṭap kūnr.*
Deafness, s. *kūnr-wālai.*
Deal, v.a. *weshal, brakha k.*; *wapār-, lāgī-*, etc. *k.*; *lār-, rozgār-, lāg-*, etc. *k.* s. *da nakkhtar largai.*
Dealer, s. *wapārī, lāgī*; *saudāgar, parāchah, ṭaṭār.* (Hindu-) *banriyah, katrī, hindū.*
Dealing, s. *wapār, lāg, sūd-saudā*; *kārobār, rozgār, lār, 'alāqa.*
Dear, a. *mayan*; *grān.* (-me!) *hāe-hāe!* (my-) *dzāna, dzamā dzān!*
Dearth, s. *kākhtī, matrah, tangsiyā, ḍukāl.*
Death, s. *ajal, marg, qazā.* (early-) *dzwānī-marg.* (sudden-) *tsaṭ-waṭ*; *mafājāt.*
Debase, v.a. *spukawul, kamawul, la-agawul*; *be rūe-, be makh-*, etc. *k.*; *jūṭah-*, etc. *k.*
Debate, v.a. *bahs k.*
Debauch, s. *bad-mastī.*
Debauchee, s. *lawand, kāsīr, bad-'amalī, chaṭ.*
Debauchery, s. *lawand-tob, charcha, kāsīrī.*
Debility, s. *nā-tuwānī, kamzor-tiyā, māndagī.*
Debt, s. *por, qarz.*
Debtor, s. *porawurai, qarz-dār.*
Decant, v.a. *toyawul.* v.n. *toyedal* or *to-edal.*
Decay, v.n. *mrāmedal, wrostedal. sharhedal*; *skhā ked.*
Deceitful, a. *chal-bāz, ṭag-bāz, farebī, droh-ūnai.*
Deceive, v.a. *ṭagal, ghulawul, ṭagī-, fareb-*, etc. *k.*
December, s. *poh* or *po.*
Decent, a. *joṛ, kkhah*; *munāsib, lā-iq.*
Decide, v.a. *faiṣal k.*
Decidedly, ad. *be-shakk.*
Decisive, a. *pūrah, kāfī-shāfī.*
Declaration, s. *izhār*; *gawāhī, shāhidī.*
Declare, v.a. *wayal, lawdal* or *lal.*
Decline, v.n. *prewatal, zawāl ked.*; *lā-ag-, kam-*, etc. *ked.* v.a. *inkār k.*
Declivity, s. *jawara, tahana, rewand.*
Decompose, v.n. *wrostedal, skhā ked., sharhedal.*
Decorate, v.a. *joṛawul*; *andzorawul, singārawul, kkhāyastah-, ārāstah-*, etc. *k.*; *poslal, kkhewa k.*
Decorous, a. *joṛ, munāsib, kkhāyastah.*
Decoy, v.a. *ghulawul, ṭagawul.*
Decrease, s. *kam-tiyā, la-ag-wālai.* v.n. *kamedal, la-ag ked.*
Decree, s. *ḥukm, fatwā.*
Decrepit, a. *ṭap, khwār, zoṛ, kamzor.*
Dedicate, v.a. *niyāz-, ṣadqa-*, etc. *k.*
Deduct, v.a. *mujra ākhistal, stanawul, zwam k.*
Deed, s. *kār, kṛah, 'amal*; *sanad, qabāla.* (-of gift) *hiba-nāma.*
Deep, a. *ḍoghal, star, jawar, kand*; *pokh, hokkhyār.*
Deer, s. *osai.* (young-) *kūblai.*
Deface, v.a. *wrānawul, habata k., kharāb k.*
Defame, v.a. *ruswā-, bad-nām-*, etc. *k., ghandal*; *tuhmat-, tor-*, etc. *pore k.*
Default, s. *khaṭā, taqṣīr.*
Defeat, v.a. *māt k., pa-aṛ k.*; *man'a k.*
Defection, s. *jārwātah*; *yāghī-garī.*
Defenceless, a. *lā-chār*; *be-panāh, khushai, ḍāga-ḍagalai.*
Defend, v.a. *bachawul, panāh k., ṣātal, gālal, jghoral, khundī k., madad k.*; *'uzr-, dzawāb-*, etc. *k.*
Defendant, s. *asāmī, muddā-'alaih.*
Defender, s. *sātandoe, jghorai, bachawūnkai, panāh-, khundī-*, etc. *-kawūnkai.*
Defer, v.a. *lārghah-, dirangī-, sustī-*, etc. *k.*
Deference, s. *makh, mulāḥiza, madārā, liḥāz*; *bāwar, i'tibār.*
Deficient, a. *kam, la-ag*; *waṭah, troṭ, zwam.*
Defile, s. *tanga-ī, dara.*

Defile, v.a. *paltitawul, kakaṛawul, nā·pāk-, murdār-*, etc. *k.*
Define, v.a. *pūla-, brīd-, ḥadd-*, etc. *taṛal; m'anā bayānawul.*
Definite, a. *muqarrar.*
Deflower, v.a. *bikr shlawul*, or *mātawul.*
Deformed, a. *bad·shakl*, or *·ḍaul*, or *·rang.*
Defraud, v.a. *drohawul, ṭagal, ghulawul.*
Defray, v.a. *kharts pūrah k., khejawul.*
Defy, v.a. *jang ghokkhtal, gwākkhal, d'awa k.*
Degenerate, a. *spuk, nā·kār, khwār, kam·aṣl.*
Degrade, v.a. *spukawul, makh·tor k.*
Degree, s. *pāya, dzāe, darja, martaba; qadr, ḥadd, andāza.*
Dejected, a. *gham·jan, dil·gīr, malāl, nūl·jan.*
Deign, v.a. *manal, qabūlawul, rawā·laral.*
Deism, s. *sūfī·garī.*
Deist, s. *sūfī.*
Deity, s. *khudāe, allah, rabb.*
Delay, v.a. *drangı-, lārghah-, dzanḍ-, sustī-, multawī-*, etc. *k.*
Delegate, s. *astādzai, wakīl; nā-ib, peshkār.* v.a. *āstawul, legal, rawānawul; spāral, ḥawāla k.*
Deleterious, a. *tāwānī, nuqṣānī, muẓirr.*
Deliberate, v.a. *fikr-, ghaur-, andekkhnā-*, etc. *k., maṣlaḥat-, tadbīr-, mashwarat-*, etc. *k.*
Delicacy, s. *bārīkī, narai·wālai; nāzakī, kkhkulī·tob; khwand, maza.*
Delicate, a. *narai, bārīk; nāzak, kkhkulai.*
Delicious, a. *khwand·nāk, maza·dār.*
Delight, s. *kkhādī, khwand, khūsh·ḥālī, khwakkhī.* (-over enemy) *sakha, wiyāṛ.*
Delighted, a. *kkhād, khūsh·ḥāl, khwakkh.*
Delineate, v.a. *kāgal—kkhkal, līkal.*
Delirious, a. *be·khūd, be·hokkh.*
Delirium. s. *be·khūdī, be·hokkhī, haẕiyān.*
Deliver, v.a. *spāral, ḥawāla k.; warkawul; khalāṣawul, āzādawul, yalah k; bachawul, wurhawul; bayānawul, wayal.*
Deliverance, s. *khalāṣī, āzādī, yalah·wālai.*
Delude, v.a. *ghulawul, fareftah k.*
Deluge, s. *sailāb, nīz* or *nyūz, chala, ṭughiyānī.* v.a. *gharqawul, ḍūbawul.*
Delusion, s. *khām·khiyāl, fareb, khaṭā.*
Demand, v.a. *d'awa k., guokkhtal.*
Demeanour, s. *yūn, wajha, chāl·chalan.*
Demesne, s. *daftar, zmaka, wanḍ, ada-ī.*
Demolish, v.a. *naṛawul, wujāṛawul, wrānawul, nā·būd-, tālā-, kharāb-*, etc. *k.*
Demon, s. *dew, perai, rawai, ghūl.* (possessed of a-) *paṭ nīwulai.*
Demonstrate, v.a. *tsargandawul, bartser-, kkhkārah-*, etc. *k., kkhayal—kkhowul; zbād-, isbāt-*, etc. *k., dalīl rāwṛal.*
Demur, v.a. *drangī-, multawī-*, etc. *k.; andekkh-, shakk-, gūmān-*, etc. *laral.*
Demure, a. *ghalai, ghaṛand; drūnd, sūt.*
Den, s. *ghār, kāz; ghālai.*
Denial, s. *inkār, nahiya, munkir·tob; ibā.*
Denizen, s. *astogūnkai, osedūnkai.*
Denote, v.a. *kkhayal—kkhowul, kkhkārah k., bayānawul.*
Denounce, v.a. *ghandal, kagal, ruswā k., bad·nāmawul, malāmatawul, raṭal.*
Dense, a. *ganṛ, gūr.* (-crops) *ṭal, tat.* (-cloth) *ṭok.* (-liquids) *ṭīng.*
Dent, s. *jghanḍ, kandaw, wat.*
Denude, v.a. *barbanḍawul, poṭ-, tsarman-*, etc. *-kāgal—kkhkal* or *-bāsal—yastal.*
Deny, v.a. *inkār k.* v.n. *munkiredal.*
Depart, v.n. *tlal—lāṛal, lwukkhtal, rawānedal, drūmal; legdal—lekkhal.*
Departure, s. *tah, tlana, legdana, rawānagī, warṭag, pand.*
Depend, v.n. *dzwaṛandedal, āwezānd ked.; āsra-, umed-*, etc. *laral; mauqūf-*, etc. *ked.*
Dependence, s. *āsra, umed, takiya, bāwar; i'tibār; 'alāqa; tāb'i·dārī.*
Dependant, a. *dzwaṛanḍ; mauqūf.*
Dependent, s. *hamsāyah, tāb'i·dār.*

Deplore, v.a. *afsos-, tartāb-, gila-*, etc. *k.*
Deponent, s. *gawāhī lūnai, shāhid.*
Deportment, s. *yūn, chāl, chalan, taur.*
Depose, v.a. *gawāhī-, shāhidī-*, etc. *lal* or *lawdal*; *sharal*; *mauqūf k.*
Deposit, s. *amānat*; *graw.* v.a. *gdal* or *igdal, yakkhodal* or *ikkhodal, yakkhawul* or *ikkhawul*; *spāral*; *amānat kegdal*, etc.
Deposition, s. *gawāhī, shāhidī.*
Depository, s. *ambār-khāna, koṭī.*
Depraved, a. *bad, kharāb, nā-kār, tabāh.*
Deprecate, v.a. *minnat-, d'uā-*, etc. *k., panāh-, 'uzr-*, etc. *-ghokkhtal.*
Depreciate, v.a. *spukawul, kamawul, la-agawul*; *kagal, ghandal, spuk ganral.*
Depredation, s. *lūṭ, nātah, tālā, tākht, tārāj.*
Depress, v.a. *lānde k., ghamawul*; *ṭīṭawul.*
Depression, s. *gham, khapagān, dil-tangī, da zṛah nūl*; *doghal, jawar, tahna, jawar-tiyā.*
Deprive, v.a. *ākhistal, shūkawul, man'a k.*
Depth, s. *jawar-tiyā, star-wālai.*
Deputation, s. *jirga, m'arika, astādzī.*
Depute, v.a. *jirga-*, etc. *āstawul* or *legdal*; *wakīl wudrawul.*
Deputy, s. *nā-ib, wakīl*; *jirgatū, astādzai.*
Derision, s. *ṭoqa, khandā, pekkha.*
Derive, v.a. *mūndal, gaṭal, paidā k.*
Derogate, v.a. *ghandal, kagal, spukawul.*
Derogatory, a. *spuk, ruswā, nā-kār, nāsāz.*
Descant, v.a. *bayānawul, wayal.*
Descend, v.n. *kūzedal, nāziledal, prewatal.*
Descendant, s. *alwād, zawzād, nasl, zurriyāt.*
Descent, s. *kūzedana, prewātah, nazūl*; *jawar, tahna*; *aṣl, zāt, peṛa-ī.*
Describe, v.a. *bayānawul, kkhayal—kkhowul.*
Description, s. *bayān, naql*; *ṣūrat, shān*; *rang.*
Desert, s. *ḥaqq, qadr, sazāwārī, lā-iq-wālai.*
Desert, s. *ṣaḥrā, maidān, maira, dakkht, chol, bāyābān.* a. *wairān, wujāṛ, ta-ash, dzangal.*
Desert, v.a. *pregdal, prekkhodal, prekkhawul, prekkhal, tark k.* v.n. *takkhtedal, puṭedal.*
Deserted, a. *wairān, ghair-ābād, khushai, ṛang, sunj*; *prekkhodai, prīkkhai, tark-karai.*
Deserter, s. *takkhtedūnkai.*
Deserve, v.a. *ḥaqq laral.* v.n. *lā-iq-, wājib-, sazāwār-, qābil-*, etc. *-ked.*
Design, s. *niyat, rūkh, qaṣd, irāda*; *mudd'ā, maṭlab*; *band, chal*; *nakhkkha* or *naqsha.*
Design, v.a. *niyat-*, etc. *taṛal* or *laral*; *joṛawul.*
Desirable, a. *khwakkh, pīrzo, ghwarah.*
Desire, s. *ghokkht, armān, ārzū, murād, hanḍa, hatsa, khwakkhī.* (carnal) *naus, shahwat.*
Desire, v.a. *ghokkhtal, armān-*, etc. *laral*; *farmāyal.*
Desolate, a. *wairān, wujāṛ, ṛang, sunj, chauṛ.* v.a. *wairānawul, wujāṛawul, tālā-*, etc. *k.*
Despair, s. *nā-umedī*; *gham, nūl.*
Desperate, a. *be-bāk, lewanai.*
Despise, v.a. *spuk ganral, bad manal, kagal.*
Despot, s. *ẓālim, zorāwar, khpul-sar.*
Despotism, s. *ẓulm, zorāwarī, zabardastī.*
Destination, s. *borjal. ṭīkāo, mazal.*
Destiny, s. *naṣīb, qismat, taqdīr, bakht*; *ajal.*
Destitute, a. *khwār, lā-chār, be-kas, muflis.*
Destroy, v.a. *wrānawul, habatah-, halāk-, tālā-, kharāb-, nā-būd-, fanā-*, etc. *k.*
Destruction, s. *halākat, kharābī, wrānī*, etc.
Destructive, a. *muẓirr, ziyānī. tāwānī.*
Desultory, a. *be-tartīb, nā-qalār, be-sar.*
Detach, v.a. *biyalawul, judā k., lwuṛawul.*
Detached, v.n. *biyaledal, lwukkhtal, judā ked.*
Detachment, s. *ghol, dasta, ṭolai, ta'īnāt.*
Detail, v.a. *biyal-biyal-, judā-judā-, mufaṣṣal-*, etc. *-wayal* or *-bayānawul* or *-līkal.*
Detain, v.a. *man'a k., haṭālawul*; *khundiyal, sātal*; *stūnawul*; *bandawul, qaid k.*
Deter, v.a. *yerawul* or *werawul.*

Determination, s. *qaṣd, niyat*; *ḥukm, amr.*
Detest, v.a. *bad manal* or *ganṛal, kagal, c̲h̲injawul, kraka ākk̲h̲istal.*
Detract, v.a. *g̲h̲andal, c̲h̲ug̲h̲lī-, g̲h̲ībat-*, etc. *k. tor pore·k., spukawul*; *kamawul, la-agawul.*
Detriment, s. *tāwān, ziyān, nuqṣān, k̲h̲alal, budrī, troṭ.*
Devastate, v.a. *natal, wrānī-, lūṭ-, tālā-, paemālī-, tāk̲h̲t·tārāj-, c̲h̲auṛ-*, etc. *k.*
Develop, v.a. *ziyātawul, wadānawul.*
Deviate, v.n. *girzedal, āwukkk̲h̲tal, g̲h̲aredal, gumrāh ked.* v.a. *girzawūl.*
Device, s. *band, tadbīr, ḥikmat, c̲h̲al*; *nakk̲h̲a.*
Devil, s. *s̲h̲aiṭān*; *dew, rawai.*
Devious, a. *kag·lec̲h̲, kālkūc̲h̲an.*
Devise, v.a. *band taṛal, tadbīr-*, etc. *k.* (give) *bakk̲h̲al, hiba k.*
Devolve, v.n. *rasedal, prewatal, lāzim ked.*
Devote, v.a. *ṣadqa-, qurbān-*, etc. *k.*; *niyāz-*, etc. *manal* or *k.*; *bakk̲h̲al, wudrawul.*
Devotee, s. *zāhid, muttaqid.*
Devotion, s. *'ibādat, bandagī*; *nmūnd̲z̲*; *mas̲h̲g̲h̲ūlā s̲h̲ug̲h̲l, lagiyā.*
Devout, a. *nek, m'utakif, nmānd̲z̲·guzār.*
Dew, s. *pa-ark̲h̲a.*
Dewlap, s. *jajūra*; *g̲h̲ab·g̲h̲ab, g̲h̲uṭ·yālai, g̲h̲aṛai.*
Dexterous, a. *c̲h̲ālāk, tak·lāstai.*
Dialect, s. *jiba, wrās̲h̲a.*
Dialogue, s. *sawāl·d̲z̲awāb, k̲h̲abare.*
Diamond, s. *almās.*
Diaphragm, s. *prīnṛ, parda* (*da geḍe*).
Diarrhœa, s. *bahedana da dastūno.* (to have-) v.a. *rīk̲h̲ wahal.* (having-) a. *rīk̲h̲an.*
Diary, s. *roz·nāma.*
Dice, s. *qimār.*
Dictionary, s. *lug̲h̲at.*
Die, v.n. *mṛal, muṛ ked.*
Diet, s. *k̲h̲wurāk*; *pāl·parhez.*
Difference, s. *biyal·tūn* or *biyal·wālai, farq.*
Different, a. *biyal, bul, judā.*
Difficult, a. *sak̲h̲t, grān, mus̲h̲kil.*
Difficulty, s. *sak̲h̲tiyā, grān·tiyā, tangsiyā.*
Diffidence, s. *wiswās, andekkk̲h̲nā*; *yera, wahm*; *stāra*; *s̲h̲akk, s̲h̲ubha.*
Diffuse, v.a. *k̲h̲warawul.*
Dig, v.a. *kandal* or *kanal, konawdal, kanastal.*
Digest, v.a. *haẓm k.*
Dignity, s. *pāya, martaba*; *qadr, 'izzat.*
Dike, s. *kanda, kāha-ī*; *k̲h̲andaq*; *pūla, wand.*
Dilapidate, v.n. *naṛedal, wrānedal.*
Dilate, v.a. *planawul, arat k.*; *ūgdawul.* v.n. *g̲h̲waredal, planedal, paṛsedal.*
Dilatory, a. *sust, laṭ, drang, nā·rāst.*
Dilemma, s. *balā, nkk̲h̲atai, sāk̲h̲a.*
Diligent, a. *miḥnatī, koks̲h̲iks̲h̲ kawūnkai, sā'ī.*
Dilute, v.a. *mahīn-, narai-*, etc. *k.*
Dim, a. *dund.*
Diminish, v.a. *kamawul, lanḍawul, la-ag k.*
Diminutive, a. *pūṭai, wṛūkai, waṛkoṭai, kuc̲h̲anai, kac̲h̲oṭai, k̲h̲armandai, woṛ, la-ag.*
Dimple, s. *kwata-ī*; *ta-apai.*
Din, s. *g̲h̲āw, zwag·zūg. s̲h̲or.*
Dinner, s. *t̲s̲ākk̲h̲tī*; *ḍoḍa-ī*; *k̲h̲wurāk.*
Dint, s. *zor, quwwat.*
Dip, v.a. *ḍubawul, g̲h̲arqawul, g̲h̲oṭa-, g̲h̲ūpa-*, etc. *-warkawul -wahal* or *-k̲h̲wuṛal.* (-as bread in soup, etc.) *c̲h̲ūka k.*
Diploma, s. *sanad.*
Dire, a. *bas̲h̲paṛ, sak̲h̲t*; *haibat·nāk.*
Direct, a. *sam, neg̲h̲, barābar.*
Direct, v.a. *kkk̲h̲ayal—kkk̲h̲owul*; *farmāyal, ḥukm-c̲h̲alawul*; *naẓar lagawul*; *sar·nāma līkal*, or *-kāgal—kkk̲h̲kal.*
Direction, s. *lorai, k̲h̲wā, rūk̲h̲, mak̲h̲, palaw*; *sar·nāma, nakk̲h̲a*; *farmān, ḥukm.*
Directly, ad. *pa ṭakī, pa de sā'at, sam da lāsa.*
Director, s. *kkk̲h̲owūnkai*; *kār kawūnkai*; *pīr.*
Dirge, s. *wīr* or *vīr, wainā.*
Dirt, s. *k̲h̲īra, palītī, ras̲h̲.*
Dirty, a. *k̲h̲īran, k̲h̲ac̲h̲an, palīt.*

Dis-, the particle of negation, is expressed by the prefixes *be-*, *nā-*, *lā-*, *bad-*, etc.
Disable, v.a. *lā-chār-*, *nā-tuwān-*, *be-tāqat-*, *be-maqdūr-*, *'ājiz-*, etc. *k.*
Disadvantage, s. *tāwān*, *ziyān*, *nuqṣān*.
Disadvantageous a. *'abaṣ*, *be-fā-idah*.
Disaffected, a. *yāghī*, *sar-kakkh*, *nā-rāẓ*.
Disagree, v.n. *nā-rāẓ-*, *mukhālif-*, etc. *ked.*
Disagreeable, a. *kagalai*, *bad*, *ghāndah*.
Disagreement, s. *jagṛa*, *steza*, *poṭ*.
Disappear, v.n. *puṭedal*, *wrukedal*, *ghā-ib ked.*
Disappoint, v.a. *nā-umed k.*
Disappointed, a. *nā-umed*, *malāl*; *mīkkh-mīkkh.*
Disapprove, v.a. *bad-manal*, *kagal*, *ghandal.*
Disaster, s. *āfat*, *bad-balā*, *randz*, *muṣībat.*
Disastrous, a. *bad-* or *kam-bakht.*
Disbelieve, v.a. *na-manal*, *bāwar na-kawul.*
Discard, v.a. *sharal*; *liri k.*
Discern, v.a. *pejandal*, *m'alūmawul*; *kaṭal*, *goral*, *līdal.*
Discerning, a. *hokkhyār*, *pohānd.*
Discernment, s. *poh*, *'aql.*
Discharge, v.a. *khalāṣawul*, *ta-ashawul*; *lire-*, *biyarta-*, etc. *-k.*, *dzawāb warkawul*; *ghurzawul*, *wīshtal*; *purah k.*, *pa dzāe k.*
Discharge, s. *khalāṣī*, *dzawāb.* (explosion) *ḍaz*, *shilak.* (-from debt, etc.) *rāẓī-nāma*, *faiṣal-nāma.*
Disciple, s. *murīd*, *shāgird*, *ṭālib.* (-of Christ) *ḥawārī.*
Discipline, s. *ā-īn*, *qā'ida*, *dustūr.*
Disciplined, a. *āmokhtah*, *el.*
Disclose, v.a. *prānatal tsargandawul*, *kkhkārah-*, *bartser-*, etc. *k.*, *parda porta k.*, *khwālā wayal*, *spekkhta āṛawul*, *pudūlī k.*
Discolour, v.n. *bad-rang-*, *dāghī-*, etc. *-ked.*
Discomfit, v.a. *lānde-*, *pa-ar-*, *māt-*, etc. *k.*
Discompose, v.a. *rabṛawul*, *ḥariyānawul*; *wrānawul*, *kharāb-*, *gaḍ-waḍ-*, *be-tartīb-*, etc. *-k.*, *wār-khaṭā k.*
Disconsolate, a. *gham-nāk*, *nūl-jan*, *dil-tang*
Discontented, a. *nā-rāẓ*, *be-ṣabr.*
Discontinue, v.a. *pregdal—prekkhodal*, *prekkhawul*, *prekkhal*, *tark k.*
Discord, s. *patna*, *pasāt*; *sākha.*
Discordant, a. *nā-sāz*, *be-ṭāng.*
Discover, v.a. *m'alūmawul*, *pejandal*; *tsargandawul*, *kkhkārah-*, *bartser-*, etc. *k.*; *kkhayal—kkhowul*; *mūndal*, *biyā-mūndal.*
Discount, s. *troṭ*, *waṭa.*
Discourage, v.a. *yerawul*, *zṛah chīngawul.*
Discourse, s. *khabare*, *qīl-o-qā'*, *gangosai*, *kkhkālwa*, *wayana.*
Discreet, a. *hokkhyār*, *pohānd*, *pokh.*
Discuss, v.a. *baḥṣ k.*
Disease, s. *bīmārī*, *maraẓ*, *āzār*, *nājoṛ-tiyā*, *nārogh-tiyā*, *randz.*
Diseased, a. *bīmār*, *marīẓ*, *nājoṛ*, *nārogh*, *randzūr*, *āzārī.*
Disembark, v.a. *kūzawul.* v.n. *kūzedal.*
Disengage, v.a. *āzādawul*, *khalāṣawul*, *yalah k.*, *prānatal*, *spaṛdal.*
Disfigure, v.a. *bad rangawul*, *wrānawul.*
Disgorge, v.a. *jārbāsal—jāryastal.*
Disgrace, v.a. *bad-nām-*, *ruswā-*, *makh-tor-*, *be-nang-*, *be-makh-*, etc. *k.*, *sharmawul.*
Disgraceful, a. *bad*, *nā-kkhanai*, *nā-lā-iq.*
Disguise, s. *bāna*, *libās*, *swāng.*
Disgust, s. *kraka.*
Disgusted, v.n. *chinjedal.*
Dish, s. (wooden-) *kkhānak.* (brass-) *tālai.* (iron-) *tabakhai.* (pottery-) *taba-ī*, *taghārai.* (china-) *rikebī.* (chafing-) *majmir.* (-of stone for baking on) *shokānrai.* (-of made food) *sālan*, *qatagh*, *ngolai.*
Dishearten, v.a. *zṛah chīngawul*, *nā-umed k.*
Dishevelled, a. *spaṛdalai*; *shānlai-wānlai.*
Dishonest, a. *be-īmān*, *nā-rāst.*
Dishonour, s. *be-'izzatī*, *bad-nāmī*, *makh-torī.*
Disjoint, v.a. *kūtal*, *band prekawul*, *bja k.*
Disk, s. *chakai*, *tsarkhai*, *ṭakai*, *qurṣ.*

Dislike, v.a. *bad manal, chinjawul, kagal, kraka ākhistal, ghandal.*
Dislocate, v.a. *be·dzāe k.*
Dismal, a. *khof·nāk, andekkh·nāk, tars·nāk*; *tor, tārīk*; *gham·jan, malāl.*
Dismantle, v.a. *naṛawul, wrānawul, shūkawul, barbanḍawul, spaṛdal.*
Dismay, s. *wera* or *yera, khof, tor, bāk.*
Dismiss, v.a. *rukhṣat k., dzawāb warkawul, lire-, biyarṭa-,* etc. *k.*
Dismount, v.n. *kūzedal.*
Disobedient, a. *yāghī, sar·kakkh.*
Disoblige, v.a. *wezār-, khapah-, randzūr-,* etc. *k., kaṛawul.*
Disobliging, a. *be·makh, be·muruwwat.*
Disorder, s. *be·tartībī, gaḍ·waḍ·tob, be·bandobastī.* v.a. *gaḍ·waḍ k.*
Disown, v.n. *munkiredal.*
Disparage, v.a. *spukawul, kagal, ghandal, tor pore k., ghībat k.*
Dispatch, v.a. *astawul, legdal, legal*; *chalawul, rawānawul.*
Dispatch, s. *talwāṛ, tak·lāstai·tob, jalta-ī.*
Dispel, v.a. *khwarawul, lire k., wrukawul.*
Dispensary, s. *dawā·khāna.*
Dispense, v.a. *weshal, kkhandal.* (-with) *mu'āf k., pulawul.*
Disperse, v.a. *khwarawul, takkhtawul, tār·pa·tār k.*
Displace, v.a. *shaṛal, be·dzāe k.*
Display, v.a. *kkhkārah-, bartser-,* etc. *k.*
Display, s. *nandāra, tamāsha.*
Displease, v.a. *khapah-, marawar-,* etc. *k., kaṛawul, randzawul, wezārawul.*
Disposal, s. *wāk, qābū, rokh, ikhtiyār.*
Dispose. v.a. *tartībawul, sambālawul, gdal. īkkhodal* or *yakkhodal, īkkhawul* or *yakkhawul*; *kegdal* or *kkhkegdal, kekkhodal* or *kkhkekkhodal, khartsawul*; *warkawul, hiba k., bakkhal* or *bakhkkhal*; *kkhkenawul.*
Disposition, s. *tartīb, ḍaul*; *khwā, khoe, mizāj, lokkhai, salīqa, ṭab'a.*
Dispossess, v.a. *shaṛal, shūkawul, be·dzāe k.*
Disprove, v.a. *bāṭil-, darogh·jan k.*
Dispute, v.a. *jagṛa-, steza-, takrār-, qaẓiya-,* etc. *k.*; *baḥs k.*
Disreputable, a. *be·i'tibār, nā·lā·iq, ruswā.*
Disrespectful, a. *be·adab, be·makh.*
Dissatisfied, a. *nā·rāẓ, nā·khwakkh.*
Dissect, v.a. *tsīral, kūtal.*
Dissemble, v.a. *bāna-, lamghaṛa-ī,* etc. *k.*
Disseminate, v.a. *khwarawul, tār·pa·tār k.*
Dissension, s. *patna, jagṛa, steza, pasāt.*
Dissipate, v.a. *wrukawul, talaf-, ṣarf-, chaṛcha-,* etc. *k.*; *mastī-, nasha·khorī-,* etc. *k.*
Dissolute, a. *chaṭ, lawand, qachar.*
Dissolve, v.a. (-by fire) *wīlī k.* (-by water) *oba k.* (-an assembly) *bar·khwāst k.*
Dissuade, v.a. *man'a k., khwā girzawul.*
Distance, s. *farq.* (-of time) *mūda.* (-of place) *lār, dzāe.* (respect) *adab.*
Distant, a. *lirai, prat.*
Distend, v.a. *paṛsawul, wīṛawul.* v.n. *paṛsedal, wīṛedal.*
Distention, s. *pāṛsob, waram.*
Distil, v.a. *tsātsawul.* v.n. *tsātsedal.*
Distinct, a. *biyal, judā.*
Distinction, s. *biyal·tūn, judā-ī, farq.*
Distinguish, v.a. *pejandal*; *zdah k., m'alūmawul, nāmer-, nām·dār-, nūm·war-,* etc. *k.*
Distort, v.a. *kog k.* or *kagawul, kṛīngawul, ṭīṭawul.*
Distract, va. *rabṛawul, ḥariyānawul, sargardān-, pareshān-, lewanai-,* etc. *k.*
Distress, s. *khwārī, tangsiyā, mīrtsī, randz.*
Distress, v.a. *tangawul, rabṛawal, āzārawul, zahīrawul.*
Distribute, v.a. *weshal, wesh-, brakha-, qismat-,* etc. *k.*
District, s. *tapa, pargana.*
Distrust, s. *gumān, shakk, shubha.*

Distrustful, a. *bad-gumān, shakk-man.*
Disturb, v.a. *rabṛawul, pārawul, khwadzawul, laṛal, kkhorawul.*
Ditch, s. *kanda, kāha-ī. kaḍa-ī.*
Ditty, s. *chār-bait, ṭapa, sandara, lanḍa-ī.*
Dive, v.a. *ghūpa-, ghoṭa-*, etc. *wahal* or *k.*
Diverge, v.n. *biyaledal, girzedal, bwukkhtal.*
Diverse, a. *biyal—biyal*; *dzane.*
Diversion, s. *nandāra, tamāsha, sail, loba.*
Divert, v.a. *girzawul, āwukkhtal*; *ghulawul.*
Divest, v.a. *barbandawul*; *shūkawul.*
Divide, v.a. *prekawul* or *prekṛal, tsīral, ghwutsawul*; *weshal, brakha-, qismat-, wanḍ-*, etc. *k.*
Dividend, s. *brakha, wesh, pucha, wanḍ.*
Divination, s. *pāl katara, koḍa, 'ilm da ghā-ib.*
Divine, a. *ilāhī, rabbānī, khudā-ī.* s. *faqīh.*
Divinity, s. *khudā-ī*; *fiqha.* (the-) *khudāe.*
Division, s. *wesh, brakha, ḥiṣṣa, wanḍ,* (-of land) *paṭai, līkai, wanḍ, aḍa-ī.* (-of country) *tapa, pargana, khel.* (-of village) *kandai, mālat, cham, palaw.*
Divorce, s. *ṭalāq.* v.a. *ṭalāq k., pa kāghaz-, pa dreo kāṇro-*, etc. *ṭalāq-warkawul,*
Divulge, v.a. *tsargandawul, kkhkārah k., parda porta k., khwāla wayal, pudūlī k.*
Dizzy, a. *sargardān, akar-jan.*
Do, v.a. *kawul, kṛal, joṛawul, pa dzāe k.*
Docile, a. *el* or *īl, eman.*
Dock, s. (for vessels) *danḍ, ḥauz, ḍab.* (the plant) *shalkhai.*
Dock, v.a. (cut short) *lanḍ-, ghūṭ-*, etc. *prekawul* or *k.* (-the hair) *sar-kunḍai k.*
Doctor, s. *ḥakīm, ṭabīb.* (-of law) *faqīh.* (-of divinity) *maulawī.*
Doctrine, s. *mazhab*; *masla*; *'ilm.*
Dodge, v.a. *chal-wal-, lamghaṛa-ī-*, etc. *k.*
Doer, s. *kawūnkai, kṛūnai.*
Dog, s. *spai.* (terrier) *pishtai.* (pointer-) *khandai.* (greyhound-) *tāzī.* (mastiff-) *khaḍal.* (mongrel-) *kutah.* (-tick) *koṇr, kūnai, wradza.* (-fly) *mangaṇr-mach.* (-in heat) *spiyama* or *spe-ama.* (-platter) *chaṭ.*
Doings, s. *kār, kṛah, kṛah-wṛah.*
Doleful, a. *gham-nāk, malāl, sūṭ-būṭ.*
Doll, s. *gūda-ī, lola-ī, nāwaka-ī, nenzaka.*
Dolt, s. *pūhaṛ, gedī-khar, kawdan, kam-'aql.*
Domain, s. *mulk, daftar*; *wanḍ, aḍa-ī.*
Dome, s. *gunbat.*
Domestic, a. *āmokhtah, eman, el* or *īl.* s. *koranai*; *nokar, khāna-zād.* (-economy) *kormāna.*
Dominion, s. *ḥukūmat, sardārī, khānī.*
Donation, s. *bakhkshikkh, bakkhana, khwaṛa.*
Donor, s. *warkawūnkai, bakkhawūnkai.*
Doom, s. *ḥukm, fatwā*; *naṣīb, qismat*; *ajal.*
Door, s. *war.* (-frame) *darshal.* (-leaf) *pala, tamba.* (-heel) *chūṛ* (-keeper) *darwānchī, darwāza-wān, ghāwchī.*
Dose, s. *khwurāk.* (dry-) *paka* or *kapa.* (liquid-) *gūṭ, īnda, ghuṛap.*
Dot, s. *ṭakai, nuqta, pitsāṇrai, pūṭai.*
Double, a. *dwah-bragh, bgharg, dogānah.* (of a fox, etc.) *kālkūchaka.*
Doubt, s. *shakk, shubha, gumān.* v.a. *shakk-*, etc. *laral.*
Doubtful, a. *shakk-dār, shakk-man, gumānī.*
Doubtless, ad. *be-shakk, be-shubha, yaqīnan.*
Dough, s. *khamīra, ākkhalai.* (lump of-) *peṛa, ghunḍa.*
Dove, s. *qumrī, tatawa, spalama.* (ring-) *gūgushtū, kuṛkuṛa-ī.*
Dovetail, v.a. *ageyal.*
Dower, s. (portion) *dhadz, dūd, kulang.* (jointure) *mahr, kābīn.*
Down, p. *kkhkata, lānde, kkhke-a* or *kkhkiya.*
Down, s. *maidān, sama, maira.* (hair) *ghūna, tor-wekkhtah, zunba, waṛa-ī.* (-of beard) *khorma.*
Doze, v.a. *parnā-, khob-*, etc. *wṛal*; *ūdah-, bīdah-*, etc. *ked.*
Draft, s. *hunḍa-ī, burāt, ḥujjat.*

Drag, v.a. *rākūgal—rākkhkal, kashāla k.*
Dragon, s. *kkhā·mār, ajdahā, nihang.*
Dragoon, s. *turk·* or *chābuk·sawār, swor* or *spor.*
Drain, s. *mora-ī, nāla; lakkhtai.*
Drain, v.a. *wuchawul, rākāgal—rākkhkal.*
Dram, s. *dirham, misqāl; gūt, ghurap.*
Drama, s. *naql, swāng, pekkha.*
Draper, s. *bazzāz, parānchah.*
Drapery, s. *tūkai, zarūkai, pokkhāk.*
Draught, s. (gulp) *gūt, īnda, ghurap, qurt.* (beverage) *sharbat, tskkhāk* or *skāk.* (wind) *wo, bād; pū, tsapa.* (cattle) *bār·kakkh.* (copy) *naql.* (drawing) *nakhkkha.*
Draw, v.a. *rākāgal—rākkhkal.* (picture) *kāgal—kkhkal, līkal, kwekkhkal.*
Drawback, s. *'aib, stūnai.*
Drawers, s. *partūg, shalwār, tambān.* (hem of-) *bada.* (hole of hem) *kustīj.* (tape of-) *partūghākkh.* (leg of-) *pā-entsa.* (fork of-) *khakkhtagai.*
Drawing, s. *nakhkkha* or *naqsha; kakkhikkh, kokkha, kashāla.*
Dread, s. *yera* or *wera, bāk, khof, tars; wiswās, andekkhnā, gram.* v.n. *weredal* or *yeredal, andekkhedal.* v.a. *tars-*, etc., *laral* or *-khwural; gram k.*
Dreadful, a. *khof·nāk, haibat·nāk; bad, bashpar, sakht.*
Dreadfully, ad. *be·shāna, be·hadda.*
Dream, s. *khob.* (fancy) *khiyāl.* (nightmare) *khapasa.* v.a. *khob līdal; khiyāl k.*
Dreary, a. *wairān, wujār, khushai, sunj.*
Dredge, v.a. (flour) *bornah k.*
Dregs, s. *khatbel.* (clotted-) *matra.* (-of vegetables) *gadzārai.* (-of metals) *khīra.*
Drench, v.a. *lūndawul, khushtawul, lūnd·khusht k.* (purge) *jullāb-, jār-*, etc. *warkawul.*
Dress, s. *āghostana, pokkhāk, jāma, zarūkai, kālai, nmarai* or *nwarai.*

Dress, v.a. *āghostal, āghostawul, poslal, pokkhal.* (cook) *pakhawul.* (-a wound) *paha pore k.*
Dribble, v.n. *tsātsedal.*
Drift, s. (aim) *gharaz, matlab.* (rain and wind) *sīla-ī, jam·jakar* (-wood, etc.) *kanga·khar, niyūz·wrai.* (-mud) *laha, lāe.*
Drill, s. *barma.* (military-) *qawā'id.* v.a. *barma-, sūrai-*, etc. *k., tsekhal; qawā'id kkhayal—kkhowul.*
Drink, v.a. *tskal* or *tskkhal* or *skal.* s. *tskkhāk*, etc.
Drive, v.a. *chalawul.* (-cattle) *biyāyal—bīwul—botlal, ramawul.* (-a horse) *zoral.* (-away) *takkhtawul, sharal, ratal, lire k.* (-a nail) *wahal, tukawul, mandal.* (-into) *kkhkc·mandal, dūsa k.*
Drivel, v.a. *lāra ghurzawul* or *toyawul.*
Drizzle, v.n. *pūna-, rangai bārān-, narai bārān-*, etc. *oredal.*
Droll, a. *'ajab, khandā·nāk.* s. *toq·mār, washt·mār, maskharāchī, pekkhe·gar, malandai.*
Drollery, s. *washta, toqa, maskhara, pekkha.*
Droop, v.n. *mrāmedal, kumanredal; karedal, nūledal, ghamedal, malāl ked.; prewatal, tītedal.*
Drop, v.n. (distil) *tsātsedal.* (fall) *prewatal.* (-into) *kkhkewatal.* (slip) *khwa·edal* or *khwahedal.* (descend) *kūzedal.* v.a. (leap) *dangal.* (cease) *pregdal, prekkhodal* or *prekkhal.*
Drop, s. *tsātskai.* (a little) *chilka.*
Dropsy, s. *jahola, taghārak, istisqā.*
Dross, s. (-of metals) *khīra, mata.* (-of iron) *ospankharai.* (-of vegetables) *gadzārai, drūza.*
Drought, s. *sūkra, khushk·sālī.*
Drove, s. *tolai, park.* (-of oxen) *gohār.* (-of buffaloes) *goram.* (-of sheep, etc.) *kandak, rama, ghela.*

Drover, s. (-of oxen) *gāhū, gornān, gāharai, ghobah.* (-of buffaloes) *gūjar.* (-of sheep) *shpūn.*

Drown, v.a. *ḍūbawul, gharqawul, lāhū k.*

Drowsy, a. *khob-wṛai, parnā-wṛai.*

Drub, v.a. *wahal, ṭakawul, kūṭal.*

Drug, s. *dawā, dārū, darmān*; *būṭai.*

Druggist, s. *pansārī.*

Drum, s. *ḍol, ḍolkai, ḍamāma.* (kettle-) *ḍūmbakai, tanbal, naghāra.* v.a. *ḍol-*, etc. *wahal* or *-ghagawul.*

Drummer, s. *ḍol wahūnkai, ḍa-am* or *ḍum, naghārchī.*

Drunkard, s. *sharābī, nasha-khor, 'amalī, bangī, kaipī.*

Drunken, a. *mast*; *be-khūd, nasha-wṛai.*

Dry, a. *wuch, khushk*; *tagai, tosand.* (-bread) *spora ḍoḍa-ī.* v.a. *wuchawul.* v.n. *wuchedal.*

Dryness, s. *wūch-wālai, khushkī.*

Duck, s. *baṭa.* (wild-) *hīla-ī.*

Duck, v.a. *ghūpa-, ghoṭa-*, etc. *wahal* or *-khwuṛal*; *sar ṭīṭawul.*

Ductile, a. *narm, post* or *pos, mulā-im.*

Due, a. *bāqī*; *wājib, munāsib.* s. *ḥaqq*; *qarẓ, por*; *maḥṣūl, chūngai, dastūr.*

Dulcimer, s. *sitār, rabāb, sārinda, ghachaka, chamtāra.*

Dull, a. *pa-ats, be-dam, be-āb*; *tīrah, dund*; *kam-'aql, gedī*; *sust, laṭ, shaṭal* or *shalaṭ.*

Duly, ad. *jukht, barābaṛ.*

Dumb, a. *gung, lāl.* s. *gungai.*

Dun, v.a. *zoral, taqāẓa k.*

Dun, a. *samand.* s. *muḥaṣṣil, sazāwal.*

Dunce, s. *pūhaṛ, gūlī-khar, kam-'aql.*

Dung, s. (human-) *ghul.* (orbicular of sheep, etc.) *pucha.* (-of cows and buffaloes) *ghoshoe, ghoshāk.* (horse-) *kharshan.* (birds-) *paikhāl, rikh.* (-of kids, etc.) *poghla, pekhāṛa.* (-heap) *ḍerān, khadzala.* (mass of cow-) *sūṭa.* (fuel of cow-) *tsapiyāka.* (stack of fuel of cow-) *gohāṭa.*

Dung, v.a. *ghul k*; *khaṛal, loya baul-k., ḥājat ta kkhkenāstal.*

Dungeon, s. *qaid-khāna, zindān.*

Dupe, s. *ghulawulai*; *drohawulai, ṭīṭālai.*

Duplicate, s. *naql, joṛa.*

Duplicity, s. *palma, ṭagī, ṭīṭāl, chal-wal.*

Durable, a. *pāedār, maẓbūṭ, qā-im, ṣābit.*

Duration, s. *pāedārī, mūda.*

During, p. *tar—pore, hombra chī.*

Dusk, s. *mākkhām, shafaq.*

Dusky, a. *ṭor, mushkai, kha-aṛ, skānr.*

Dust, s. *dūṛa, khāwra, gard* or *garz, ghubār.*

Dust, v.a. *duṛawul.* (shake) *tsanḍal.* (dredge) *borṇah k.*

Dusty, a. *garz wahalai, pa dūṛo ḍak.*

Dutiful, a. *farmān-bardār, khidmatī, manūnkai.*

Duty, s. *farẓ, sharṭ.* (office) *kār.* (military) *pahra, tsoka-ī.* (tax) *malṣūl, bāj, chūngai, ḥaqq.*

Dwarf, s. *chūnai, poṭai, mandarai, tsongai.*

Dwell, v.n. *osedal, āstedal, pātedal.* v.a. *mīṇ'ta-, astoga-, kilai-, ṭīkāo-. basiyā-*, etc. *k.*

Dweller, s. *osedūnkai, āstedūnkai, astogūnkai.*

Dwelling, s. *astoga, mīshta, dzāe, kor, makān.*

Dwindle, v.n. *kamedal, la-agedal, narai-, mahīn-, bārīk-, kotāh-*, etc. *ked.*

Dye, v.a. *rangawul, rang warkawul.*

Dyer, s. *dobī, rang-rez.*

Dynasty, s. *salṭanat, khāndān, rāj.*

Dysentery, s. *ra-ama, kānga, ṛap.* (to have-) v.a. *ra-ame-, ṛap, ghurzawul, kānga niwul.*

Dyspepsia, s. *bad-haẓmī*; *agheṛana, āṭerana.* (to have-) v.a. *agheṛal, aṭeral.*

Dyspeptic. a. *āgheṛalai, aṭeralai.*

E.

Each, p. *har·yo, yo·yo.* (-other) *yo·bul, dzabla.*

Eager, a. *tez, tod, garm*; *mayan*; *liwāl.*

Eagle, s. *bātūr, gargas.*

Ear, s. *ghwag.* (-of corn) *wagai, chala-ī.* (-ring) *chala, wālai, lakkhta-ī, barghwagai, deḍa, barghoṭai, mandara-ī.* (lobe of-) *narma-ī, liraga-ī, būtska-ī.*

Earless, a. *būṛai.*

Early, a. *wakhtī.* (-crop) *mahīnah.* (-morning) *saḥār* or *saḥr, ṣubḥa.*

Earn, v.a. *gaṭal, paidā k., kamā-ī k., ḥāṣil k.*

Earnest, a. *garm, tod, sā'ī, pa jid.*

Earth, s. *khāwra*; *zmaka, zamīn*; *mulk, būm*; *duniyā, jahān, naṛa-ī.*

Earthen, a. *khāwrīn.*

Earthly, a. *jahānī, duniyā-ī.*

Earthquake, s. *zalzala, larza.*

Ease, s. *āsān·tiyā, ārām.*

East, s. *nmar·* or *nwar·khātah.*

Eastward, ad. *nwar·khātah khwā.*

Easy, a. *āsān*; *sam, spuk, halak*; *āsūdah, moṛ.*

Eat, v.a. *khwuṛal.*

Eatable, a. *khwurākī.*

Eater, s. *khwuṛūnkai, khwurindah* (in comp.) *-khor.*

Eaves, s. *bala-ī, sharīfa, sarmāta-ī, tsatsoba-ī, parchata-ī.* (-dropper) *ghwag·tsārai.* (-dropping) *ghwag·tsārana.*

Eaves-drop, v.a. *ghwag tsāral.*

Ebb, s. *zawāl, prewātah, kamedana.*

Ebullition, s. *eshnā, khūṭkai, josh.*

Eccentric, a. *pa trats*; *kāwāk, lewanai.*

Echo, s. *ghag, kāngai, anga-ī, angāza, āwāz.*

Eclat, s. *raunaq, dabdaba.*

Eclipse, s. *tandar.* v.a. *tandar nīwul.*

Economy, s. *kormāna*; *tartīb.*

Ecstacy, s. *be·khūdī, be·shāna dera kkhādī.*

Eddy, s. *ghurzai, gird·āb*; *ḍab.*

Edge, s. *ghāṛa, morga, tselma, ja-ī.* (of a blade) *dam.* (to set on-) v.a. *ghākkh ṭaghawul.*

Edge, v.a. (sharpen) *tera k.* (instigate) *lamsawul.* (fringe) *jāwja-ī lagawul.*

Edging, s. *jāwja-ī, ḷaman, palaw, trāṭa, maghzai.*

Edict, s. *sanad, raqam, farmān, jār.*

Edifice, s. *makān, māṇra-ī, mina, ḥawela-ī.*

Edify, v.a. *pohawul, kkhayal—kkhowul, t'alīm k.*

Edition, s. *chāp, tālif.*

Editor, s. *murattib, mu-allif.*

Educate, v.a. *pālal, lwalawul, tarbiyat-, t'alīm-,* etc. *k.*

Education, s. *pālana, tarbiyat, t'alīm.*

Eel, s. *mār·māhai, mār·kab.*

Efface, v.a. *wrānawul, habatah k., wrukawul.*

Effect, s. *'amal, pāzah, aṣar, kār.*

Effect, v.a. *kawul, kṛal, joṛawul, 'amal-,* etc. *k.*

Effects, s. *māl, asbāb, kālī, sāmān.* (-of deceased) *tarka, pāto.*

Effectual, a. *kārī, kāmil, pūrah, kāfī·shāfī.*

Effeminate, a. *kkhadzonak, nā·mard.*

Effervesce, v.n. *eshedal* or *yashedal, khuṭ ked.*

Effervescence, s. *eshnā, khuṭkai, josh.*

Efficient, a. *pūrah, kāmil, qābil, kār·sāz.*

Effigy, s. *but, tsera, ṣūrat.*

Effluvium, s. *būe, soṛ·bū-ī*; *bṛās.*

Effort, s. *zor, sa'ī, miḥnat, kokshiksh.*

Effrontery, s. *be·makh·tob, be·ḥayā-ī, be·sharmī.*

Effulgence, s. *raṇrā, rokkhnā-ī, brekkhnā.*

Effulgent, a. *rokkhān, dzalak·nāk, brekkh·nāk.*

Effusion, s. *rezish, toe, tvedana, bahedana.*

Egg, s. *haga-ī, hā.* (-plant) *bāṭīgaṇr.*

Egotism, s. *khpulī, khūdī, manī.*

Egregious, a. *bashpaṛ, bad, sakht, ghaṭ.*

Egress, s. *wātah, khātah, barāmad.*

Eight, a. *atah.* (eighth) a. *atam.*

Eighteen, a. *atah·las.* (18th) *atah·lasam.*
Eighty, a. *atiyā.* (eightieth) *atiyā·yam.*
Either, p. *yā.* pr. *tsok, kūm, tsa.*
Eject, v.a. *sharal, bāsal—yastal, jārbāsal—jāryastal, pore·jane k.*
Ejection, s. *sharūn, yastūn, jāryastūn.*
Elaborate, a. *narai, mahīn; mushkil, grān.*
Elapse, v.n. *teredal.*
Elastic, a. *post, narm; damdār, mulā-im.*
Elated, a. *khwakkh, kkhād, kkhād·man; bādī, kibr·jan, maghrūr.*
Elbow, s. *tsangal.*
Elder, a. *mashar.* s. *spīn·gīrai; pīr, shekh.*
Elect, v.a. *khwakkhawul, chunral.*
Elegance, s. *kkhāyast, kkhāyast·wālai, joṛāb, krah·wrah, spetsal·tob.*
Elegant, a. *kkhāyastah, nāzak.*
Elegy, s. *wīr, wainā.*
Element, s. *aṣlī shai.*
Elephant, s. *hātī, pīl.*
Elevate, v.a. *khejawul, porta k., pātsawul.*
Elevated, a. *ūchat, hask, lwaṛ.*
Elevation, s. *ūchat·wālai, bulandai, taraqqai, khātah, hask·wālai; sarfarāzī.*
Eleven, a. *yolas.* (eleventh) a. *yolasam.*
Elicit, v.a. *kāgal—kkhkal, bāsal—yastal, m'alūmawul.*
Eligible, a. *ghwarah, lā·iq, khwakkh, pīrzo.*
Elixir, s. *aksīr, 'araq.*
Elk, s. *gāwuz.*
Elocution, s. *khula·warī, khula·war·tob.*
Elope, v.n. *puṭedal, takkhtedal.* (-as a woman) *maṭīza ked.* (-with a woman) v.a. *maṭīz k.*
Eloquent, a. *khula·war, khog·zabān.*
Else, p. *yā.* pr. *bl, nor.* (any one-) *bul·tsok, nor·tsok.* (anything-) *bul·tsa, nor·tsa.*
Else, ad. *kanra, kana, ganra.*
Elsewhere, ad. *bul·charta, nor·charta.*
Elucidate, v.a. *kkhkārah k., prānatal, bayān k.*
Elude, v.n. *puṭedal, bachedal, khalāṣedal.*
Elysium, s. *jannat, bihikkht.*
Emaciate, v.n. *wuchedal, kaṛedal, zahedal.*
Emaciation, s. *ḍangar·tob, wuch·klak·tob.*
Emancipate, v.a. *āzādawul, khalāṣawul, yalah k.*
Embalm, v.a. *muṛai pa maṣālo ḍakawul.*
Embankment, s. *pūla, wand, band.*
Embark, v.n. *pa beṛa-ī sparedal* or *khatal.*
Embarrass, v.a. *rabṛawul, ḥariyānawul, tangawul, sargardānawul.*
Embarrassed, a. *ḥariyān, sargardān.*
Embassy, s. *elchī·garī.*
Embellish, v.a. *joṛawul, andzorawul, ārāstah-, kkhāyastah-,* etc. *k.*
Embellishment, s. *andzor, zeba, kkhāyast, kkhāyast·wālai, daul, kkhewa.*
Embers, s. *īre.* (hot-) *khuglan, skarwaṭa, skhwakkhtan, akhgar.* (cold-) *saṛe īre.*
Embezzle, v.a. *puṭawul, ghlā k., wrukawul.*
Emblem, s. *nakkha, nikkhān, 'alāmat.*
Embrace, s. *gheg, ghūza.*
Embrace, v.a. *ghāṛa·ghaṛa-ī-, baṛgaṛandai-, bara·gaṛa-, rogh·baṛ-,* etc. *k.*
Embrocate, v.a. *ghwaṛawul, mugal—mukkhal, tabal.*
Embrocation, s. *mālish, takoṛ, tab.*
Embroider, v.a. *bezal* or *pezal, būṭai gandal.*
Embroil, v.a. *nkkhlawul.*
Emerald, s. *zamarrud.*
Emerge, v.n. *watal, khatal.*
Emergency, s. *ẓarūrat; wāqi'a, ḥādiṣa.*
Emergent, a. *ẓarūr.*
Emery, s. *kurand.*
Emetic, s. *da bāka-ī-, da chāl-, da jāryasto-,* etc. *dawā, khwā·garzanai dārū.*
Emigrant, s. *musāfir, pradai.*
Emigrate, v.a. *kaḍa wṛal, legdal—lekkhal.*
Eminence, s. *ūchat·wālai, hask·wālai; khātah, taraqqai; ḍerai, ghunḍa-ī, kha-at, potai, rāsha, rashaka-ī; zbargī, loe·wālai; ḥaẓrat.*
Eminent, a. *ūchat; ghaṭ, loe; zbarg.*

Emissary, s. *jāsūs, tsārī, dzarai, mukhbir.*
Emollient, a. *post, narm, mulā-im.*
Emolument, s. *gaṭa, sūd, naf'a, ḥāṣil.*
Emotion, s. *eshnā, khuṭkai*; *randz, dard.*
Empale, v.a. *pa sūla-ī khejawul*; *tsekhal.*
Emperor, s. *sulṭān, bādshāh, malik.*
Emphasis, s. *tākīd*; *ẓarb*; *dranāwai, drund-wālai.*
Emphatic, a. *tākīdī*; *drūnd.*
Empire, s. *salṭanat, rāj, bādshāhī.*
Employ, v.a. *mashghūlawul, lagawul*; *chalawul*; *kharts k., sāṭal, pa kār rāwṛal.*
Employer, s. *khāwind, tsakkhtan, nāyak.*
Employment, s. *kār, khidmat, mashghūlā.*
Emporium, s. *bāzār, ganj, manḍha-ī, bandar.*
Empower, v.a. *wāk-, ikhtiyār-*, etc. *warkawul.*
Empty, a. *ta-ash, khālī, ḍaḍ.*
Emulate, v.a. *sām sorai k., ghairat laral.*
Emulation, s. *ghairat, barābarī, samsorai.*
Emulous, a. *ghairat-man, himmat-nāk.*
Enable, v.a. *quwat-, ṭāqat-, zor-, tuwān-*, etc. *warkawul.*
Enact, v.a. *farmāyal, ḥukm k.*
Enamel, s. *mīnā, jaṛāo, rang, āb.*
Enamour, v.a. *mayan-, 'āshiq-, fareftah*, etc. *k.*; *grohedah k.*
Encamp, v.a *ḍera-, muqām-*, etc. *k.*
Enchanter, s. *jādū-gar, koḍ-gar, siḥr-gar.*
Enchantment, s. *jādū, koḍa, siḥr.*
Enclose, v.a. *īsārawul* or *ḥiṣārawul, ger k.*; *shpol-, keṛa-, jal-, bāra-, pūla-*, etc. *taṛal* or *-k.*; *nghakkhtal, lifāfa k.*
Enclosure, s. *iḥāṭa, bāra, ḥiṣār, hadera.* (-for cattle) *bānḍa, shpol.* (-of a house) *jal, gholai.*
Encounter, v.a. *jang k.* v.n. *miliyā, ked. pekkhedal.*
Encourage, v.a. *dam-, dilāsa-*, etc. *warkawul.*
Encroach, v.a. *lānde k., dakhl k.*
Encroachment, s. *dakhl, gharaẓ.*
Encumber, v.a. *kariyābawul, dranawul, bār āchawul.*
End, s. *ākhir, khatm*; *anjām, tamāmī*; *ḥadd, sar-peza, tsūka.* v.a. *ākhir-, khatm-*, etc. *k.*
Endear, v.a. *mayan-, 'azīz-*, etc. *k., khpulawul.*
Endeavour, s. *miḥnat, was, sa'ī, kokshiksh, hatsa.*
Endless, a. *be-ḥadd, be-and*; *tal, mudām.*
Endorse, v.a. *ṣaḥīḥ-, dast-khaṭṭ-*, etc. *k.*
Endowment, s. *waqf, hiba*; *khairāt, niyāz, bakkhana*; *hunar.*
Endurance, s. *ṣabr, zgham, tāb, zor, ṭāqat.*
Endure, v.a. *zghamal, ṣabr k., sahal, petsal.* v.n. *pāedal, sahedal.*
Enemy, s. *dukkhman*: *mīrtsaman.*
Energetic, a. *chālāk, takṛah, maẓbūṭ.*
Energy, s. *zor, quwat, bram, tuwān.*
Enervate, v.a. *kam-zor-, kam-quwat-*, etc. *k.*
Enforce, v.a. *maẓbūṭ-, muḥkam-*, etc. *k., zoral, chalawul, rawā-, jārī-*, etc. *k.*
Engage, v.a. *mashghūlawul, lagiyā, k., sātal, lagawul, wāda-, neṭa-, sharṭ*, etc. *taṛal* or *k.*
Engaged, a. *lagiyā, mashghūl.*
Engagement, s. *iqrār, wāda, neṭa, sharṭ*; *kār, kasb, mashghūlā*; *jang, muqadamma.* (-in marriage) *koĵdan* or *koĵda.*
Engender, v.a. *paidā k., rāwṛal.*
Engine, s. *kālai, hatiyār, ālat, ṣana'at.*
Engrave, v.a. *kandal* or *kanal, kanastal.*
Engraver, s. *muhr-kan.*
Enhance, v.a. *qīmat ziyātawul, nirkh kamawul* or *-la-agawul*; *khejawul, dranawul.*
Enigma, s. *ramūz, kināya.*
Enjoin, v.a. *farmāyal, k iya-, tākīd-*, etc. *k.*
Enjoy, v.a. *khwand-, maza-*, etc. *k.*
Enjoyment, s. *khwand, maza*; *kkhādī, khwakkhī.*
Enlist, v.a. *nokar k.*; *nūm līkal*; *mal-, malgarai-*, etc. *k.*

Enmity, s. *dukkhmanī, 'inād, 'aks, mīrtsī.*
Enormous. a. *ghaṭ, bashpaṛ, loe, star, nāpaṛ.*
Enough, ad. *bas, ḍer, kāfī, kifāyat.*
Enquiry, s. *sawāl, pukkhtana, tapos* or *tafahūs, pursān, pursish, shanana.*
Ensign, s. *nakkha, nikkhān, bairaq, janḍa.*
Ensnare, v.a. *ghulawul*; *nīwul, nkkhlawul.*
Ensue, v.n. *prewatal, khatal, kedal.*
Entangle, v.a. *arjal-barjal-, aṛang-baṛang-, tsapolai-*, etc. *k.*; *nkkhlawul.*
Enter, v.n. *nanawatal, dākhiledal.*
Enterprise, s. *muhimm, grān-kār.*
Enterprising, a. *himmat-nāk, zṛah-war.*
Entertain, v.a. *pālal, sātal, nmānḍzal*; *melmastiyā-, ẓiyāfat-, mezmānī-*, etc. *k.*
Entertainer, s. *melmah-dost, korbah, sat kawūnkai.*
Entertainment, s. *melmastiyā, sat*; *tamāsha, nandāra*; *loba, sail.*
Enthusiasm, s. *sargarmi, mīna, 'ishq.*
Enthusiast, s. *saudā-ī*; *'āshiq, liwāl.*
Entice, v.a. *ghulawul, ṭagal, lamsawul, fareb-, targhīb-*, etc. *warkawul.*
Entire, a. *tamām, pūrah, ṣābat, kāmil.*
Entirely, ad. *amānī, sarāsar, surup.*
Entitle, v.a. *ḥaqq-man k.*; *nūm īgdal* or *gdal*, or *-kkhkegdal* or *-kegdal.*
Entrails, s. *laṛmānah.*
Entrance, s. *war, darwāza, khula, darak*; *nanawātah, dakhl.*
Entrance, v.a. *be-khūd-, fareftah-*, etc. *k.*, *damawul, hūda k., paṭ nīwul.*
Entrap, v.a. *nīwul, nkkhlawul, ger k.*
Entrapped, a. *nīwai, nkkhatai.* v.n. *nkkhatal* or *nkkhledal.*
Entreat, v.a. *minnat k.*; *ghokkhtal, du'ā k.*
Entreaty, s. *minnat, d'uā, darkhwāst.*
Entrenchment, s. *bāra, sangar, gaṛa-ī.*
Enumeration, s. *shmer, shumār, ḥisāb.*
Envelope, s. *lifāfa*; *poṭ, postakai.*
Envelope, v.a. *nghaṛal—nghakkhtal.*
Envious, a. *ḥāsid, ḥasad-nāk.*
Environs, s. *sawād, chār-chaper.*
Envoy, s. *elchī, wakīl, astādzai.*
Envy, s. *ḥasrat, ḥasad, rashk, wiyāṛ.*
Ephemeral, s. *fānī, teredūnai.*
Epicure, s. *geḍa-parwar, khūsh-khwurāk.*
Epidemic, s. *wabā*; *'āmm.*
Epilepsy, s. *meryai, malerga.*
Epistle, s. *nāma, chīṭa-ī, khaṭṭ, kāghaẓ.*
Epitaph, s. *da qabr kitāba.*
Epithalamium, s. *kkhādiyāna, sandara.*
Epitome, s. *khulāṣa, mukhtaṣar, lanḍa.*
Epoch, s. *tārīkh, kāl, mūda, san.*
Equal, a. *barābar, makhai, gund, yo-shān*; *sam, hawārah.* s. *samsorai, humdzolai, siyāl, sārai, twal, makhai.*
Equality, s. *barābar-wālai, makhai-tob*; *samwālai.*
Equanimity, s. *qalār-tiyā, ṣabr.*
Equestrian, a. *sparlai, sparlanai.* s. *swor* or *spor.*
Equip, v.a. *tayār k., sambālawul, mlā taṛal, wasla-, drasta-*, etc. *warkawul, dzerma k.*
Equipage, s. *sāz, sāmān, asbāb, kālī.* (retinue) *swarlī* or *sparlī, jalab.*
Equitable, a. *'ādil, rikkhtīnai, rāst-man.*
Equity, s. *inṣāf, rāstī, niyāw, 'adl.*
Equivalent. a. *barābar, twal*; *badal, 'iwaẓ.*
Equivocal, a. *shakk-man, gumānī.*
Equivocate, v.a. *palma-, hira-ī*, etc. *k.*, *aṛawale-khabare k., darogh-jane khabare k.*
Era, s. *tārīkh, kāl, san, mūda.*
Eradicate, v.a. *mūnḍ-, wekh-, būnsaṭ-*, etc. *bāsal—-y ıstal*, or *-khejawul*, or *-kāgal—kkhkal.*
Erase, v.a. *wrānawul, qalam pre-kāgal.*
Ere, ad. *wṛunbe, awwal, lā*; *pakhwā, wṛānde.* (-now) *lā tar osa.* (-while) *lā pakhwā.* (-long) *pa la-age mūde kkhke.*
Erect, a. *walāṛ, negh, lak, zīg, jig.*
Erect, v.a. *walāṛawul, wadrawul, khejawul.*

Err, v.a. *khaṭā k.*
Errand, s. *paighām.* (-boy) *harkārah.*
Erroneous, a. *ghalaṭ.*
Error, s. *khaṭā, wabāl, gunā, taqṣīr.*
Erudition, s. *'ilm, qābil·tob.*
Eruption, s. *eshnā, khuṭ, khuṭkai, josh.* (prickly heat-) *garmaka.* (acne-) *dzwānaka.* (small-pox) *nanaka-ī.* (measles-) *sharai.* (tooth-) *sara·makha.* (jet) *fawāra, dāra.*
Erysipelas, s. *surkh·bād.*
Escalade, s. *khātah pa kamandūno.* (-ladder) *kamand.*
Escape, s. *khalāṣī, tekkhta, bachāw, bach.*
Escape, v.n. *bachedal, takkhtedal, khalāṣedal, wurhedal, yalah ked.* (miss) *terwatal.*
Escheat, v.n. *lā·wāriṣ ked.*
Escort, s. *badraga*; *jalab, sparlī.*
Especially, ad. *khuṣūṣan.*
Esplanade, s. *maidān, ḍāga, panḍ·ghālai.*
Espouse, v.a. *kojdan k., wādah k., nikāḥ taṛal.* (a cause, etc.) *ākhistal, bachawul, komak warkawul.*
Essay, s. (attempt) *qaṣd.* (trial) *āzmekkht.* (endeavour) *kokshiksh, sa'ī.* (treatise) *risāla.*
Essence, s. *'araq, johar, aṣl.* (perfume) *'aṭr.*
Essential, a. *aṣlī*; *ẓarūr*; *sūchah.*
Establish, v.a. *muqarrar-, jārī-*, etc. *k., chalawul, rawānawul*; *qā-im-, maẓbūṭ-*, etc. *k., wudrawul, kkhkenawul, pāedār k.*
Estate, s. (land) *dawtar* or *daftar, wanḍ.* (fief) *jāgīr, jāedād.* (property) *māl, daulat, milk.* (hereditary) *mīrāṣ* or *mīrāt.* (deceased's) *pāto, tarka.* (rank) *pāya, martaba, darja.*
Esteem, s. *qadr, 'izzat*; *mīna, tapāk.*
Esteem, v.a. *qadr-*, etc. *pejandal*; *mu'tabar-, nek-*, etc. *gaṇṛal*; *mīna-*, etc. *k.*
Estimable, s. *'izzat·nāk, mu'tabar, nek.*
Estimate, v.a. *shmeral, gaṇṛal.*
Estimation, s. *rāe, khiyāl, poha, fikr, naẓar.*
Estrange, v.a. *marawar-, māṇṛai-*, etc. *k.*; *pradai-, begānah-*, etc. *k.*
Estrangement, s. *māṇṛai, marawar·tob*; *pradī·tob, begān·tūn, begānah·tob* or *begān·tob.*
Eternal, a. *abadī, dā-im, jāwīd* or *jāwīdān.*
Eternally, ad. *tal, tar·tala, tal·tar·tala, mudāman, hamesh.*
Eternity, s. *abad, azal, baqā.* (to all-) ad. *tar·abada, tar·azala.*
Ethereal, a. *āsmānī, hawā-ī.*
Ethics, s. *pand·nāma, naṣīḥat·nāma.*
Etiquette, s. *adab, makh, madāra.*
Etymology, s. *ṣarf*; *peza-ī, hezagī.*
Eulogy, s. *stāyana, ṣanā, t'arīf.*
Eunuch, s. *hijṛai, khunṣā.*
European, s. *farangai.* a. *farangī.*
Evacuate, v.a. *ta-ashawul, khālī-, khushai-*, etc. *k.*; *jārbāsal—jāryastal.*
Evade, v.a. *palma-, bāna-, hira-ī-*, etc. *k.*; *ṭagī-, chal·bāzī-*, etc. *k.* v.n. *bachedal, puṭedal, terwatal.*
Evanescent, a. *fānī, teredūnai.* (-colour) *om.*
Evaporate, v.n. *wuchedal.*
Evasion, s. *bāna, ḥīla*; *palma, hira-ī.*
Evasive, a. *bāna·war, ḥīla·bāz.*
Even, a. *barābar, yo·shān.* (similar) *gund.* (-in weight) *twal.* (smooth) *hawārah, sam.* (odd and-) *juft·o·tāk.*
Even, ad. *hum, lā, haḍo, yara, kho.*
Evening, s. *mākkhām, begāh.* (to-morrow-) *ṣabā begāh.* (last-) *begāh.* (of last-) *begānai, baranai.*
Evenness, a. *barābar·wālai, sam·wālai.*
Event, s. *wāqi'a, chal, khabara, qiṣṣa,* (at all-) *hargora, kām·nā·kām, khwāh·makhwāh, kho.*
Ever, ad. *kala, chare.*
Everlasting, a. *dā-im, qā-im, lā·zawal.*
Evermore, ad. *hamesh, mudām, tar·abada.*

Every, a. *har.* (-person) *har-tsok.* (-thing) *har-tsa.*
Evidence, s. *gawāhī, shāhidī*; *dallīl*; *nakkha.* (to give-) v.a. *gawāhī-* or *shāhidī lal* or *-lawdal.*
Evident, a. *tsargand, kkhkārah, bartser, awtsār.*
Evidently, ad. *zāhiran, bartseran, pa jār.*
Evil, a. *bad, kharāb.* s. *'aib, kharābī*; *balā, āfat*; *gunāh, wabāl.* (-doer) a. *bad-kirdār, gunāh-gār.*
Ewer, s. *kūza, kūza-ṛa-ī, khum-ra-ī, kunja-ī.*
Exact, a. *jukht, kaṭ-maṭ, joṛ, barābar.*
Exact, v.a. *zoral*; *taqāẓa k.*
Exaggerate, v.a. *ziyātawul, ūgdawul, mubālagha k.*
Exalt, v.a. *pāya pa porta' k.*; *khejawul, pātsawul.*
Examine, v.a. *āzmāyal, āzmekkht k.*; *imtihān ākhistal* or *k.*; *laṭawul, shanal, katal.*
Example, s. *misāl, namūna*; *'ibrat, siyāsat.*
Exasperate, v.a. *rabṛawul, zoral*; *pārawul*; *khapah k., ṭongawul, ṭongāra k., ageyal.*
Excavate, v.a. *kanal, kanawdal, kanastal.*
Excavation, s. *kanda, ḍoghal.*
Exceed, v.n. *ziyātedal.*
Excel, v.n. *pūrah-, kāmil-, ghālib-*, etc. *ked.*
Except, p. *siwā, baghair, be-la—na.*
Excess, s. *ziyātī, ḍer-wālai*; *charcha.*
Excessive, a. *ḍer, ziyāt, be-shān.*
Excessively, ad. *be-hadda, be-shāna.*
Exchange, s. *badal, 'iwaẓ*; *adal-badal*; *waṭa.*
Excise, s. *chūngai, sāw, mahṣūl.*
Excise, v.a. *tsīral, prekawul* or *prekṛal.*
Excite, v.a. *pārawul*; *lamsawul*; *pātsawul, paidā k.*; *ageyal, ṭongawul.*
Excitement, s. *eshnā*; *pārawūna*; *lamsūn.*
Exclaim, v.a. *nāra wahal, bāng wayal, shor k., chighawul.*
Exclamation, s. *nāra, sūra, chigha, ghag, zwag*; *wāwailā, faryād.*
Exclude, v.a. *sharal, lire k., raṭal.*
Excoriate, v.a. *garawul, sūlawul, nwaṛawul, sūdah k., nūkāre wahal.* v.n. *sūledal, sūdah ked.*
Excrement, s. *ghul.* (-of diarrhœa) *ka-aṛ, rīkh.* (-of dysentery) *ra-ama, ṛap.*
Excruciate, v.a. *khūgawul, 'azābawul, āzārawul.*
Exculpate, v.a. *pulawul, be-gunāh k., bakkhal.*
Excursion, s. *sail*; *gakkht.* (-foray) *dāṛa.*
Excuse, v.a. *pulawul, bakkhal*; *bāna-, hira-ī-, 'uẓr-*, etc. *k., hujjat k.*
Execrable, a. *bad, l'anatī, makrūh.*
Execrate, v.a. *kkhera k.*
Execute, v.a. *kawul, kṛal, pa-dzāe k., joṛawul, tamāmawul, pūrah k.*; *qatlawul, wajal* or *wajlal, muṛ k.*; *jārī k., chalawul.*
Execution, s. *kawūna, kṛah, joṛawuna*; *qatl.*
Executioner, s. *jallād, qātil.*
Executive, a. *kār guẓār*; *mukhtār kār.*
Executor, s. *waṣī.*
Exemplary, a. *nek, ṣawābī*; *'ibrat-nāk.*
Exemplify, v.a. *misal ākhistal*, or *-rāwṛal.*
Exempt, v.a. *pregdal—prekkhodal, āzādawul, pulawul, bakkhal, bachawul, khalāṣawul.*
Exercise, v.a. *'amal k., chalawul, jārī k., lagawul, mashghūlawul.*
Exercise, s. *'amal, ist'imāl*; *mashghulā, kār*; *sail, gakkht.* (lesson) *dars, sabaq.* (horses) *jaulān, kartab.* (hawks, dogs, etc.) *bāolī.* (troops) *qawā'id.*
Exert, v.a. *kokshiksh-, sa'ī-, zor-*, etc. *k.*; *stam wahal.*
Exhalation, s. *bṛās, bukhār, dam, lū, laṛa, piyākhla, wagma.*
Exhaust, v.a. *ta-ashawul, khālī-, khushai-*, etc. *k.*; *wrukawul, kharts-, ṣarf-*, etc. *k.*; *tamām-, pūrah-*, etc. *k.*; *staṛai-, be-dam-*, etc. *k.*
Exhaustless, a. *be-nihāyat, be-zawāl.*

Exhibit, v.a. *kkhayal—kkhowul, prānatal, kkhkārah-, bartser-, tsargand-*, etc. *k.*
Exhibition, s. *tamāsha, nandāra.*
Exhilarate, v.a. *kkhād-, khwakkh-*, etc. *k.*
Exhort, v.a. *pand, naṣīhat-*, etc. *warkawul.*
Exigency, s. *tangsiyā, lā-chārī, sakhtī, ẓarūrat.*
Exile, s. *jilā-waṭanī, be-waṭanī.* (the person) *pradai, begānah, be-waṭan.*
Exist, v.n. *shwal, kedal, osedal, maujūdedal.*
Existence, s. *shta-wālai, hastī, būd, jwand.*
Existent, a. *osan, osanai, maujūd.*
Exit, s. *wātah, watana, wartay.*
Exonerate, v.a. *pulawul, khalāṣawul.*
Exorbitant, a. *be-andāz, be-nihāyat.*
Exorcise, v.a. *damawul, hūda k., koḍ k.*
Exordium, s. *debācha, muqaddama.*
Exotic, a. *pradai, begānah, gharīb.*
Expand, v.n. *planedal, aratedal.* (swell) *paṛsedal.* (-as a flower) *ghwaredal, khwaredal.* (spread) *wīṛedal, pheledal.*
Expanse, s. *arat-wālai, plan-wālai, sor* or *psor.*
Expect, v.a. *lār katal, umed laral.*
Expectant, a. *umed-wār, muntaẓir.*
Expectation, s. *umed, āsra.*
Expedient, a. *munāsib, ghwarah, wājib.* s. *band, tadbīr, chāra, chal.*
Expedition, s. *chālākī, chustī, talwār.* (journey) *safar.* (military-) *chapāo, tākht.* (foray) *dāṛa, bota.* (against infidels) *ghazā, jihād.*
Expeditious a. *gaṛandai, tak-lāstai, chālāk, chust, za-ar* or *zir, jalt.*
Expel, v.a. *shaṛal, lire k., pore-jane k., bāsal—yastal, raṭal, traṭal.*
Expend, v.a. *kharts-, ṣarf-*, etc. *k., lagawul.*
Expense, s. *kharts*; *qīmat, bai'a.*
Expensive, a. *khartsī, tāwānī*; *grān, qīmatī, qīmat-nāk.*
Experience, s. *poha, wuqūf*; *āzmekkht.*
Experience, v.a. *tīdal, terawul, zghamal, khwuṛal, kāgal—kkhkal.*
Experienced, a. *āmokhtah, āzmūdah, pokh, wāqif, khabar-dār, zdah.*
Experiment, s. *āzmekkht, tajriba, imtiḥān.*
Expert, a. *kārī-gar, hunar-man, hokkhyār*; *chālāk, pokh.*
Expiate, v.a. *kafāra warkawul, tāwān warkawul.*
Expiration, s. *anjām, khatm, ākhirat.* (death) *dzān-kadan, marg.*
Expire, v.n. *mṛal, muṛ ked.*; *teredal*; *tamāmedal.* (breathe) *sā-, sāh-, dam-*, etc. *bāsal—yastal, -shaṛal, -pregdal—prekkhodal*, etc.
Explain, v.a. *bayānawul, pohawul, kkhayal—kkhowul, kkhkārah k.*
Explanation, s. *bayān, kkhowūna, m'anā, sharaḥ.*
Expletive, s. *takiya-kalām.*
Explicit, a. *tsargand, ṣāf, kkhkārah, ẓāhir.*
Explode, v.n. *pṛak-chāwdal, ālwatal.* v.a. *daz wahal, ālwūzawul.*
Exploit, s. *karāmat, ghaṭ-kār, zbargī.*
Explore, v.a. *laṭawul, shanal.*
Explosion, s. *ḍaz, ṭas.*
Export, v.a. *bul mulk ta āstawul* or *-legal.*
Expose, v.a. *kkhkārah-, bartser-*, etc. *k., parda porta k.*
Exposition, s. *sharaḥ, bayān.*
Expostulate, v.a. *takrār-, ḥujjat-*, etc. *k.*
Exposure, s. *kkhkārah-tob, barbanḍ-tob.*
Expound, v.a. *bayānawul, m'anā-kkhayal—kkhowul.*
Express, v.a. *wayal, lal* or *lawdal*; *nichoṛawul, nakkhtedzal, paz wahal, zbekkhal.*
Express, a. *tsargand, awtsār*; *khāṣṣ.* s. *qāṣid, chapar.*
Expression, s. *khabara, wayai, sukhan, kalām*; *nichoṛ, paz.*
Expressly, ad. *pa qaṣd, qaṣdan.*

Expulsion, s. *sharana.*
Expunge, v.a. *qalam wahal, wrānawul.*
Exquisite, a. *pākīzah, nādir, matrah, ghwarah.*
Extant, a. *osan, osanai, maujūd.*
Extempore, ad. *sam da lāsa.*
Extend, v.n. *rasedal, ūgdedal, ziyātedal.*
Extension, s. *ūgd-wālai, ziyāt-wālai.*
Extensive, a. *loe, plan, arat, ūgd, kushād.*
Extent, s. *ūgd-wālai, plan-wālai* ; *qadr, andāza,*
Extenuate, v.a. *kamawul, la-agawul.*
Exterior, a. *bāhir, wardzanai.*
Extinct, a. *wruk, ter, nā-būd, nest, nishtah.*
Extinguish, v.a. *mur-, sor-, gul-,* etc. *k.*
Extirpate, v.a. *prekawul, tsīral* ; *mund-, wekh-, būnsat-,* etc. *khejawul, -bāsal—yastal, -kāgal—kkhkal.*
Extol, v.a. *stāyal, stāyana k.* or *-wayal.*
Extort, v.a. *shūkawul, pa zor ākhistal.*
Extortion, s. *ziyātī, zulm.*
Extract, s. *'araq, jauhar.*
Extract, v.a. *bāsal—yastal, kāgal—kkhkal.*
Extraction, s. *rag, nogai, zāt, asl.*
Extraneous, a. *pradai, begānah.*
Extraordinary, a. *'ajab, nādir.*
Extravagant, a. *khartsī, tāwānī, isrāfī, be-tartīb, chakhraba kawūnkai.*
Extreme, a. *der, be-shān, be-hadd.* s. *hadd.*
Extremely, ad. *be-hadda, be-shāna.*
Extremity, s. *sar, tsūka, peza* ; *hadd, pūla, brīd* ; *rokh, dada, tselma, tsanda, palaw.* (distress) *tangsiyā, lā-chārī, mīrtsī.*
Extricate, v.a. *prānatawul, āzādawul, khalās-awul, spardal.*
Exuberance, s. *frewānī, wadānī, der-wālai.*
Exuberant, a. *frewān, wadān, der, ziyāt.*
Exudation, s. *zyam, naw* ; *khwale.*
Exude, v.a. *zyam-, naw-,* etc. *k.* v.n. *watal, khwale ked., zyam-,* etc. *ked.*
Exult, v.a. *sakha k., wiyāral, kkhādī k.*
Eye, s. *starga.* (-sight) *nazar.* (-ball) *lema, starghalai.* (-socket) *starghālai, gogil.* (-pupil) *torai, kasai, bātūr.* (-iris) *lema.* (-brow) *wrūdza.* (-lid) *dzedzma* or *dzegma.* (-lash) *bānra.* (-witness) *gawāh, shāhid.* (-of a needle) *swam* or *spam.*
Eye diseases, s. (opthalmia) *lecha.* (albugo) *gul.* (pannus) *nakhūna.* (cataract) *parda.* (sore eyes) *lechane-starge.*

F.

Fable, s. *qissa, naql, hikāyat, matal, misāl.*
Fabricate, v.a. *jorawul, tandal.*
Fabulous, a. *darogh, wahmī.*
Face, s. *makh, tsihra, bashra, mushāda, rūe gūna.* (-to face) *makhā-makh.*
Facetious, a. *toq-mār, washtai* or *washt-mār, malandai.*
Facilitate, v.a. *āsānawul.*
Facility, s. *āsān-tiyā.*
Facing, a. *makhā-makh, wrāndai.*
Fact, s. *wāq'ia, gharaz, matlab, kār, krah.*
Faction, s. *para, janba, gundī* ; *patna, pasāt.*
Factious, a. *pasātī* or *fasādī, takrārī.*
Factor, s. *kār kawūnkai, gumāshtah, dīwān.*
Factory, s. *kār-khāna, kotī.*
Faculty, s. *quwat, qudrat, tuwān* ; *khāssiyat, lokkhai, khoe, tāsīr* ; *'aql, shu'ūr.*
Fade, v.n. *mrāmedal* or *mrāwedal, kumanredal, marghechan-, pezai-, malāl-,* etc. *ked.*
Fag, v.n. *rabredal, starai ked.*
Fagot, s. *gedai, panda, bālanr.*
Fail, v.a. *khatā k.* v.n. *kamedal.*
Failing, s. *'aib, qusūr, khatā, nuqsān.*
Faint, a. *māndah, tap, nā-tuwān, za'īf.* s. *parghaz, be-khūdī,* v.n. *parghaz ked.*
Fair, a. *gorah, spīn* ; *kkhāyastah, kkhkulai, pa-ī-makhai* or *pej-makhai* ; *sāf, pāk, kkhah, jor.* (-sky) *shīn.*

Fair, s. *mela.*
Fairly, ad. *pa rāstī sara.*
Fairy, s. *parī, perai.* (the fairies) *piriyān.*
Faith, s. *īmān, dīn, khal, kesh, sāwīsā, bāwar.*
Faithful, a. *īmān·dār, wafā·dār, rikkhtīnai.*
Faithless, a. *be·īmān, be·wafā.*
Falcon, s. (Royal·) *shahīn.* (Peregrine- or Falco Sacer) *chargh, charghelai, tsarkh.* (Tercel-) *bahra-ī-bach.* See Hawk.
Falconer, s. *bāz·wān, mashkār, kkhkārī.*
Fall, v.n. *prewatal, lwedal.* (-in) *drabal.* (-into) *kkhkewatal.* (slip) *khwa-edal* or *khwahedal.*
Fall, s. *prewātah, lwedana*; *drabai*; *khwai.* (foot-) *trapai.*
Fallacy, s. *darogh, ghalat, kizb.*
Fallen, a. *prewatai, prot, lwedalai.*
Fallible, a. *gunāh·gār, quṣūr·man.*
Fallow, s. *wad, shār, banjar.*
False, a. *darogh·jan, darghal, nā·rāst, kāzib.* (-coin) *jūtah, nā·sarah.*
Falsehood, s. *darogh, kizb*; *palma, fareb.*
Falter, v.n. *taparedal*; *budrī-, tīndak-,* etc. *khwural*; *pa jibe nkkhatal.*
Fame, s. *nūm, āwāza.*
Famed, a. *nūm·war, nāmer, mashhūr.*
Familiar, a. *khamsor*; *m'alūm.* s. *āshnāe, yār, mal.*
Family, s. *kor, kada, tabar*; *khānawādah, khāndān, tabār, nasl.*
Famine, s. *grānī, kākhtī, dūkāl, qātī.*
Famish, v.n. *da lwuge mral.*
Famous, a. *mashhūr, nūm·war, nāmer.*
Fan, s. *babozai.* (-for flies) *chawra-ī.* (-for sifting grain) *chaj, tsap.*
Fanatic, s. *muta'ṣṣib, lewanai, saudā-ī.*
Fancy, s. *qiyās, khiyāl, wahm, and.*
Fang, s. *ghākkh, dāra.*
Fantasm, s. *wahm, khiyāl.*
Fantastic, a. *wahmī, khiyālī*; *washtai, malandai, swāngī.*

Far, ad. *lire* or *liri.* (as far as) *pore* or *pori, tar—pore.* (-away) *warāya.*
Farce, s. *pekkha, toqe, washta.*
Fare, s. *khwurāk, khwārah, sat*; *kreha, kirāha.* v.a. *khwural, sat k.* v.n. *teredal, chaledal, guzrānedal.*
Farewell, ad. *da khudāe pa amān, salām.*
Farm, s. *patai, wand, dawtar, zamīn, ada-ī*; *ijāra.*
Farmer, s. *zamīndār*; *ijāra·dār.*
Farrier, s. *n'al·band.*
Fart, s. *dau, ta-as, tar, tīz, pa-as, pa-aska-ī.* v.a. *aratal, tīz-,* etc. *āchawul, tar,* etc. *k.*
Farther, ad. *lire* or *liri, nor lire.*
Fascinate, v.a. *fareftah-, mayan-, kod-,* etc. *k.*
Fashion, s. *daul, shān, shakl, rang, wajha, tarkīb, chāl, rasm, dod, dastūr.*
Fashion, v.a. *jorawul, tandal.*
Fast, a. *jalt, tez, garandai, talwārī, talwār·gandai, halwāk, za-ar* or *zir*; *mahkam, mazbūt*; *tīng, klak.*
Fast, s. *roja.* v.a. *roja laral* or *-nīwul.*
Fasten, v.a. *taral, lagawul*; *tīngawul, klakawul*; *kāgal—kkhkal*; *mazbūt k.*
Fastidious, a. *bādī, kibr·jan, khāntamā.*
Fasting, a. *nahār.* (voluntary-) *nahwa, roja.*
Fat, a. *tsorb, per, perar, pund, tand, ghat, kharat.* (-as a child) *khamat,·chāgh.*
Fat, s. *spīna, wāzda.* (kidney-) *ghoz.* (melted-) *roghan, mū, ghwarī.*
Fatal, a. *qātil, kārī*; *qazā-ī.*
Fatality, s. *naṣīb, qazā, qismat, taqdīr.*
Fate, s. *ajal, marg, maut*; *qazā, qismat.*
Father, s. *plār.* (-in-law) *skhar.* (step-) *plandar.* (grand-) *nīkah.* (great grand-) *wa-ar·nīkah.* (great great grand-) *lā wa-ar·nīkah.*
Fatherless, a. *be·plār, plār·murai, yatīm.*
Fathom, s. *wāzah.*
Fatigue, v.a. *rabrawul, starai-, stomān-, tap-, haukah-, māndah-,* etc. *k.*

Fault, s. *'aib, khaṭā, taqṣīr, wabāl, gunāh, quṣūr.* (to find-) v.a. *malāmatawul, ṭaqawul, raṭal, traṭal, kagal, ghandal.*

Faultless, a. *be·gunāh, be·quṣūr, be·taqṣīr.*

Faulty, a. *'aib·nāk, quṣūr·man, gunāh·gār, taqṣīrī* ; *bad, nā·kārah.*

Favour, s. *mrasta, mihrbānī, mihrbāngī, sat, makh, sela, selwa.*

Favourable, a. *barābar, munāsib, pīrzo* ; *makhawar, mihrbān.*

Favourite, a. *khwakkh, ghwarah, kkhkulai.*

Fawn, v.a. *chāplūsī-, dirpalī-, khushāmadī-, falān dast·māl-, jig·jigī-,* etc. *k.*

Fealty, s. *wafā·dārī, tābi'·dārī, kālkhwāhī.*

Fear, s. *wera* or *yera, tars, khof, bāk, sahm, tara* ; *wiswās, andekkhnā.*

Fear, v.n. *weredal, tarhedal, bugnedal.* v.a. *tars-, tor-,* etc. *khwuṛal.*

Fearful, a. *tars·nāk, khof·nāk* ; *tarhūr, yer·man.*

Fearless, a. *be·bāk, be·ḍar.*

Feasible, a. *shwunai* or *shwūnkai.*

Feast, s. *melmastiyā, ẓiyāfat, jashn.*

Feat, s. *kār, kṛah* ; *bāzī.*

Feather, s. *banṛa, banṛaka, par.*

Feature, s. *tsihra, shakl, ṣūrat.*

February, s. *pāganṛ.*

Fee, s. *shukrāna* ; *ḥaqq, ajr, miḥnat* ; *chūngai.*

Feeble, a. *nā·tuwān, ẓa'īf, kam·ṭāqat, ṭap, kam·quwat, kam·zor, 'ājiz.*

Feed, v.a. *khwuṛawul* ; *tsarawul.* (eat) *khwuṛal.* (graze) v.n. *tsaredal* or *tsaral.* (-cattle) *wākkhah āchawul.* (-birds) *tāmba warkawul.* (nourish) *parwaral, pālal, sātal, parwarish k.*

Feel, v.a. *laṭawul, lamsawul, masa k.* (suffer) v.n. *pohedal, m'alūmedal, zghamedal, kedal.* (bear) v.a. *khwuṛal, līdal, kāgal—kkhkal.* (-pain) *khūgedal, dardedal.* (-the pulse) *nabẓ katal.* (-for others) *dil·soẓī-, gham·khwārī-, zṛah·swai-,* etc. *k.*

Feeling, s. *poh, pahm.*

Feign, v.a. *bāna-, ḥīla-, makr-,* etc. *k.* ; *palma-, hira-ī-, lamghaṛa-ī-,* etc. *k.*

Felicity, s. *kkhādī, khwakkhī, khush·ḥālī, khwand* ; *barakat, bakhtawarī, nek·bakhtī.*

Fell, v.a. *prekawul, wahal, naṛawul.*

Fell, a. *sakht, kāfir, ẓālim, khūnāṛai.*

Fellow, s. *mal, malgarai, hamdzolai, samsorai.* (match) *makhai, gund, dzawāb, jorah.* (contemptuous-) *lawanḍ, chaṭ. qachar, dahūs, chulur.* (in comp.) *ham-,*

Fellowship, s. *malgar·tiyā, sharākat* ; *rogha, joṛa.*

Felon, s. *gunāh·gār, taqṣīrī, mujrim.*

Felt, s. *lamtsa-ī, krāsta, namada.*

Female, a. *zanāna, māndīna.* s. *kkhadza, artīna.* (covert-) *maṛokkha, sohāgan.*

Feminine, a. *zanānī, māndīna, kkhadza.*

Fen, s. *jaba.*

Fence, s. *bāra, panāh.* (thorn-) *shpol, jal.* (withy or twig-) *keṛa.* v.a. *bāra-,* etc. *taṛal.*

Fence, v.a. *ḍāl·bāzī-, gatka·bāzī-,* etc. *k.*

Fennel, s. *sowa, kāgah.*

Fenugreek, s. *malkhoza.*

Ferment, s. *khamīra, tomna, māya* ; *eshnā, khuṭkai, josh* ; *balwā, patna.*

Ferment, v.n. *khamīra-,* etc. *ked.* ; *eshedal, khuṭ ked.*

Ferocious, a. *waḥshī, khūnāṛai, ẓāim.*

Ferocity, s. *waḥshat, khūn·khwārī, ẓulm.*

Ferret, s. *nolai.*

Ferrule, s. *ghamai, ṭekai.*

Ferry, s. *gudar, paṭanṛ.* (-boat) *beṛa-ī.* (-man) *mānṛgai, mahanṛah.*

Fertile, a. *zar·khez, ghala·khez, lap·tsat, barakatī.*

Fertilize, v.a. (-land) *watar k., zor-, quwat-,* etc. *warkawul.* (-animals) *dakawul, blārba k.*

Ferula, s. *bet, dira, qamchī, karoṛa.*

Fervent, a. *tod, garm.*

Fervour, s. *tod·wālai, todūkha, swai, garmī.*

Fester, v.n. *zawlan-, gazak-*, etc. *ked., khū-edal.*

Festival, s. *akhtar, 'īd.* (-after Ramazān) *wṛūkai akhtar.* (-of Abraham's sacrifice) *loe akhtar.* (-of a saint) *mela, 'urs.* (marriage-) *wādah.* (feast) *kkhādī.*

Festivity, s. *kkhādī, khūsh·hālī, khwakkhī.*

Festoon s. *laṛ, hāṛ, zunḍai, zunbak.*

Fetch, v.a. (things) *rāwṛal.* (animals) *rāwustal.*

Fetid, a. *shhā, ganḍah, bad·bū* or *bad bū-ī-dār, wrost.*

Fetter, s. *dzolana, karai, band, zandzīr.* (-for cattle) *shkel, wandar, palwākkha, ghaṛ-wandai.*

Feud, s. *patna, badī, khāna·jangī, mīrtsī.*

Fever, s. *taba.* (-and ague) *saṛa taba, saṛa lare, saṛa lawe.* (intermittent-) *wāreza taba.* (remittent-) *wāra·gara taba.* (continued-) *shebara taba.* (bilious-) *zyaṛa-ī taba.* (typhus-) *shārwa-ī taba.*

Feverish, a. *tab·jan, taba nīwulai.*

Few, a. *la-ag, kam, pūṭai, pitsānrai, tso.*

Fibre, s. *rekkha, rag, tār, pala.*

Fibrous, s. *rekkhan.*

Fickle, a. *nā·qalār, nā·pāedār, khushai.*

Fiction, s. *naql, joṛ kaṛai.*

Fictitious, a. *naqlī, nā·sarah, jūṭah.*

Fiddle, s. *sitāra, sāringai, chamtāra, sārinda,* (-string) *tār.* (-bow) *kamāncha.* (-key) *ghwaṛai.* (-bridge) *ṭaṭū, khargal.*

Fidelity, s. *īmān·dārī, rāst bāzī, wafā·dārī, namak halālī, rikkhtīn·tob.*

Fidget, v.a. *kūnāṭī khwadzawul.* v.n. *wis-wāsī ked., pa mawekkho laṛamedal.*

Fief, s. *jāedād, jāgīr, aima, dawtar.*

Field, s. *paṭai, wand.* (crop) *kikkht.* (plain) *maidān, ḍāga.*

Fiend, s. *shaiṭān*; *perai, rawai*; *dukkhman.*

Fierce, a. *tund, sakht, ẓālim, qahr·jan.*

Fiery, a. *tod, tez, garm, tāw·jan, tund, jalt.*

Fife, s. *surnāe, shpela-ī.*

Fifer, s. *surnā·chī, shpela-ī·mār.*

Fifteen, a. *pīndzah,'las.* (15th) *pīndzah-lasam.*

Fifty, a. *pindzos.* (-one) *yo·pindzos*, etc.

Fig, s. *īndzar.* (wild-) *gūlar.* (Banian-) *baṛgat.* (Sacred-) *pīpal.*

Fight, s. *jang, muqaddama.* v.a. *jangawul.*

Fighter, s. *jangī, jangawar, jang kawūnkai*; *jang·yālai.*

Figurative, a. *naqlī, shaklī, majāzī, tamṣīlī.*

Figure. s. *shakl, ḍaul, ṣūrat, rang, shān.*

Figure, v.a. *joṛawul, tanḍal*; *nakhkkha kāgal—kkhkal* or *-līkal.*

Figured, a. *būṭī·dār, rangīn.*

File, s. *sohān, chausār.* (row) *qaṭār, para.* (catalogue) *daftar, fard.*

Filings, s. *reza, chūr.*

Fill, v.a. *ḍakawul.*

Fillet, s. *paṭai, paṛūkai.* (-for the head) *sar·taṛūnai, sar·basta, tsapūṭkai.*

Fillip, s. *chūṭkī.*

Filly, s. *bihānra, biyāna.*

Film, s. *jāla-ī.* (-of the eye) *gul, nakhūna.*

Filter, s. *chānra.* v.a. *chānr k.*

Filth, s. *khīra, rash, chirk.*

Filthy, a. *khīran, palīt, nā·pāk, khachan.*

Fin, s. *wazar da kab* or *-da māhī.*

Final, a. *ākhir, wrūstai, akhīr*; *pūrah.*

Finally, ad. *ākhiran, alqiṣṣa.*

Finance, s. *mālguzārī, āmdanī.*

Find, v.a. *mūndal, biyā·mūndal, paidā k.* (-fault) *raṭal, traṭal, ṭaqawul, malāma-tawul.*

Fine, s. *nāgha, tāwān, jarīmāna.*

Fine, a. *narai, mahīn, bārīk.* (-sky) *shīn, ṣāf.*

Finger, s. *gūta.* (thumb) *baṭa-* or *ghaṭa gūṭa.* (fore-) *miswāka gūta.* (middle-) *miyandza gūta.* (ring-) *khamacha gūta.* (little-) *kacha gūta.* (-nail) *nūk.* (-quick) *awra-ī.*

Finis, s. *tam-tamām, ā<u>kh</u>ir, <u>kh</u>atm.*

Finish, v.a. *tamāmawul, pūrah-, <u>kh</u>atm-,* etc. *k.*

Fir, s. *na<u>kkh</u>tar.* (-cone) *gūjāl.* (-seed) *<u>ch</u>al<u>gh</u>ozai* or *jan<u>gh</u>oza* or *za<u>nr</u><u>gh</u>oza.*

Fire, s. *or.* (-fly) *orakai.* (-place) *n<u>gh</u>arai, or<u>gh</u>ālai.* (-wood) *bāla<u>nr</u>, <u>kh</u>a<u>sh</u>āk.* (-brand) *<u>sh</u>ū<u>sh</u>a-ī.* (-poker) *or laṛūnai.* (-stone) *<u>sh</u>okā<u>nr</u>ai.* (-works) *āta<u>sh</u>bāzī.* (-worshipper) *gabar.* (-lock) *bandū<u>kh</u>, ṭopak.*

Fire, v.a. *or pore k., balawul.* (-a gun) *<u>ch</u>alawul, <u>kh</u>alāṣawul.*

Firm, a. *maẓbūṭ, klak, ṭīng, pāedar.*

Firmament, s. *āsmān, kursī, <u>ts</u>ar<u>kh</u>.*

First, a. *awwal* or *awwulanai, wṛūnbai* or *wṛūnbanai.* (-born) *ma<u>sh</u>ar.*

Firstly, ad. *awwalan, wṛūnbe, war<u>kh</u>ata.*

Fish, s. *kab, māhai.* (-hook) *kunḍa.*

Fissure, s. *<u>ch</u>āwd. darz, daṛa, <u>ch</u>āq, ra<u>kh</u>na.*

Fist, s. *mūṭ, mūṭai; sūk.*

Fistula, s. *nāsūr.*

Fit, s. *<u>gh</u>oṭa; nobat.* (fainting-) *par<u>gh</u>az.* (hysterical-) *da piriyāno <u>gh</u>oṭa.*

Fit, a. *wājib, munāsib, lāzim, lā-iq; qābil, joṛ, barābar; pīrzo, yarzan, <u>dz</u>āe-lar.*

Five, a. *pīn<u>dz</u>ah.* (fifth) a. *pīn<u>dz</u>am.*

Fix, s. *n<u>kkh</u>atai, balā.*

Fix, v.a. *lagawul, taṛal, joṛawul, pore k.; wudrawul, walāṛawul, muqarrar-, klak-, maẓbūṭ-,* etc. *k.; <u>kh</u>a<u>kkh</u>awul, njatal; <u>kh</u>ejawul, k<u>kh</u>kenawul.*

Flabby, a. *narm, post, sust; <u>ts</u>orb.*

Flag, s. *na<u>kkh</u>a, janḍa, to<u>gh</u>, baira<u>gh</u>.*

Flag, v.n. *ṭaparedal, pāte ked., staṛai ked.*

Flagrant, a. *<u>ts</u>argand; ma<u>sh</u>hūr; bad.*

Flake, s. *<u>ts</u>apak, <u>ts</u>aparkai.*

Flame, s. *lanba, <u>sh</u>u<u>gh</u>la* (fire), *baṛānḍa, <u>gh</u>arānḍa lū<u>kh</u>aṛa, <u>gh</u>ar<u>gh</u>ara, bāmba<u>nr</u>a, ḍānḍa-ī.*

Flank, s. *ḍaḍa, aṛ<u>kh</u>, <u>ts</u>ang; <u>ts</u>elma, <u>ts</u>anḍa; ta<u>sh</u>ai.*

Flannel, s. *<u>sh</u>aṛa-ī, pa<u>sh</u>mīna, waṛīna.*

Flap, v.a. *<u>ts</u>andal, <u>kh</u>wa<u>dz</u>awul, rapawul.* v.n. *<u>ts</u>apedal, <u>ts</u>rapedal, ṭrapedal, rapedal.*

Flare, v.n. *bre<u>kkh</u>edal, rū<u>nr</u>edal, <u>dz</u>aledal.*

Flash. s. *bre<u>kkh</u>, bre<u>kkh</u>nā, <u>dz</u>alk, palwa<u>sh</u>a.*

Flask. s. *kupa-ī, kupṛa-ī; <u>kkh</u>ī<u>kkh</u>a, <u>kh</u>umra-ī.*

Flat, a. *sam, sat, hawār, barābar.* (pressed-) *<u>ts</u>aplāk, <u>ch</u>īt.* (-taste) *be-<u>kh</u>wand, be-maza, bilmagai, bilmangah.* (-on the back) *stūnī-sta<u>gh</u>.* (-footed) *<u>ch</u>apa<u>kh</u>.*

Flatten, v.a. *samawul, hawārawul; <u>ch</u>īt-,* etc. *k.*

Flatterer, s. *<u>ch</u>āplūs, <u>kh</u>ū<u>sh</u>āmad-gar, ḍirpal.*

Flattery, s. *<u>ch</u>āplūsī, <u>kh</u>ū<u>sh</u>āmadī, ḍirpalī.*

Flatulent, a. *bādī.*

Flavour, s. *<u>kh</u>wand, maza, swād, <u>ts</u>aka.*

Flaw, s. *<u>ch</u>āwd, darz, daṛa; 'aib, laka, dā<u>gh</u>,*

Flax, s. *sa<u>nr</u>.*

Flay, v.a. *<u>ts</u>arman-, poṭ-,* etc., *ā<u>kh</u>istal, -bāsal—yastal, -kāgal—k<u>kh</u>kal.*

Flea, s. *wruga.*

Fleam, s. *na<u>sh</u>tar* or *ne<u>sh</u>tar.*

Fleawort, s. *ispa<u>gh</u>ol* or *īsap<u>gh</u>ol.*

Flee, v.n. *ta<u>kkh</u>tedal, puṭedal.*

Fleece, s. *waṛa-ī, warg.*

Fleece, v.a. *<u>sh</u>ūkawul, lūṭawul.*

Fleet, a. *gaṛandai, jalt, tez, z<u>gh</u>ard, halwāk.*

Fleeting, a. *teredūnai, fānī.*

Flesh, s. *<u>gh</u>wa<u>kkh</u>a.* (body) *<u>dz</u>ān.* (lust) *naus, <u>sh</u>ahwat.* (-brush) *<u>kh</u>īsa.*

Flexible, a. *narm, post, mulā-im, ṭīṭedūnai.*

Flexure, s. *ṭīṭ-wālai, kog-wālai; kagle<u>ch</u>, kālkū<u>ch</u>; gūṭ, grut.*

Flight, s. *te<u>kkh</u>ta.* (-of birds) *sail, <u>gh</u>ol.* (-of an arrow) *partaw.*

Flighty, a. *<u>kh</u>u<u>sh</u>ai, <u>kh</u>iyālī, saudā-ī.*

Flimsy, a. *spuk, halak, narai, nā-kārah.*

Flinch, v.n. *bugnedal, weredal, haṭedal.*

Fling, v.a. *ā<u>ch</u>awul, wī<u>sh</u>tal, <u>gh</u>urzawul.*

Flint, s. *bakra-ī*. (steel) *punḍ*. (gun-) *chaq-maq*.
Flinty, a. *sakht*, *klak*, *kāṇrez*.
Flirt, s. *nakhra-bāza*, *lashmaka-ī*, *shatāha*.
Flit, v.n. *ālwatal*. v.a. *kaḍa wṛal*.
Float, s. *pāyāba* or *pāyawai*. v.n. *bahedal*, *lāhū ked.*, *lānbo ked.*
Flock, s. *ramma*. (leader of-) *nar-kakkh*, (-of sheep, goats, or deer) *kanḍak*, *ghela*. *psa*. (-of birds) *sail*, *ghol*. (-of lambs, etc.) *olah* (a crowd of men, etc.) *ṭol*. *ṭolai*, *ṭolgai*.
Flock, v.n. *ṭoledal*, *yo-dzāe-*, *jam'a-*, etc. *ked.*
Flog, v.a. *wahal*, *karoṛe-*, etc. *wahal*.
Flood, s. *sailāb*, *niyūz* or *nīz*. (-of tears) *raṭ*.
Flood, v.a. *lāhū-*, *hūk-*, etc. *k.*, *niyūz wṛal*.
Floodgate, s. *warkh*, *ghwagai*.
Floor, s. *zmaka*, *zamīn*; *takhta-bandī*.
Florid, a. *sūr*.
Florist, s. *gul-kar*.
Flounce, s. *tsanḍa*, *jānja-ī*.
Flounce, v.n. *tsrapedal*, *ghurzedal*.
Flounder, v.n. *ṭrapedal*, *tsrapedal*; *rgharedal*. v.a. *ghoṭa wahal*.
Flour, s. *oṛah*, *maidah*. (dredging-) *bornah*.
Flourish, v.n. *ābādedal*, *wadānedal*, *tāzah-*, *takṛah-*, etc. *osedal*. v.a. *tsanḍal*, *khwadza-wul*, *rapawul*.
Flow, v.n. *bahedal*, *chaledal*, *rawānedal*, *jārī ked.*
Flower, s. *gul*. (-garden) *gul-shan*. (-bed) *gul-zār*.
Flower, v.n. *khwaredal*, *ghwaredal*, *ṭūkedal*.
Fluctuate, v. *chapa-*, *chalaka-*, etc. *wahal*. v.n. *be-ārām-*, *nā-qalār-*, etc. *ked.*
Fluent, a. *jārī*, *rawān*. (in speech) *khula-war*.
Fluid, a. *wīlī*, *oba*, *ābī*, *pakhsiyāh*.
Flummery, s. *pālūda*, *oghṛa*. *atob*, *daliya*.
Flush, v.n. *sūr-makh ked.*, *sharmedal*.
Flute, s. *shpela-ī*.
Flutter, v.n. (-hover as a bird) *ṭrapedal*, *tsapedal*. (-as a leaf) *rapedal*, *shanedal*. (palpitate) *dṛazedal*, *paṛakedal*, *laṛzedal*.
Flux, s. *sailāb*; *rezish*, *nazla*; *nāstah*, *ra-ama*, *dast*.
Fly, s. *mach*. (horse-) *ghobāṛai*, *bhagaṇr*.
Fly, v.n. *ālwatal*, *wurzedal*.
Foal, s. *bihāṇr*, *biyān*.
Foam, s. *zag*, *kaf*.
Fodder, s. *wākkhah*, *giyāh*, *'alaf*. (-of corn) *khasīl*, *khwīd*. (-of maize) *ṭānṭa*. (-of rice) *palāla*. (-of pulses) *kaṭī*.
Foe, s. *dukkhman*, *khaṣam*.
Fœtus, s. *bachai*, *kachandai*.
Fog, s. *laṛa*; *ghubār*.
Foil, s. *gatka*. v.a. *wrānawul*.
Fold, s. *bāra*, *hadera*. (sheep-) *bānḍa*, *shpol*. (of a door) *tanba*, *pala*. (layer) *bragh*, *tah*. (crease) *gundza*, *chuṇra*, *kṛatai*. (-of a rope) *wal*, *tāw*, *pech*. (-on fold) ad. *pabla-*, *wabla-* or *zabla bānde*. (in comp.) *-bragh*, *-chand*.
Fold, v.a. *nghakkhtal*.
Foliage, s. *pāṇre*, *zarghūn-tob*.
Folk, s. *khalq*, *'ālam*, *makhlūq*.
Follow, v.n. *pala-pase tlal*. v.a. *pairawī-*, *murīdī-*, etc. *k.*, *manal*, *laman nīwul*.
Follower, s. *pairaw*, *murīd*, *tāb'i-dār*.
Folly, s. *nā-dānī*, *kam-'aqlī*, *nā-poha*.
Foment, v.a. *sekal*, *ṭakor k.* (stir up) *pātsa-wul*, *khejawul*, *porta k.*
Fond, a. *mayan*. (in comp.) *-dost*, *-parast*.
Fondle, v.a. *nāzawul*, *mīna k.*
Fondness, s. *mīna*, *shauq*, *zṛah*, *khwā*.
Fontanelle, s. *tandai*.
Food, s. *khwāṛah*, *khwurāk*, *shūma*, *qūt*, *ṭ'ām*. (-for a journey) *tokkha*, *tsawrai*. (-of cattle) *tsar*, *wākkhah*. (-of hawks) *tāmba*. (prepared-) *sālan*, *qatagh*, *ngholai*.
Fool, s. *nā-dān*, *kam-'aql*, *gedī-khar*, *lewanai*.
Foolish, a. *nā-dān*, *be-wuqūf*, *ka.vdan*, *pūhaṛ*, *ablah*, *palwanḍ*.

Foot, s. *pkkha* or *kkhpa*. (on-) *palai, pa kkhpo*. (-step) *qadam, manḍ, gām*. (-mark) *pal, manḍ*. (-fall) *ṭrapai*. (-stool) *moṛa*.

Footman, s. *piyādah, harkarah*; *shātar*; *mlā·taṛ*.

Footpad, s. *rāh·zan, shūk·mār, lār·wahūnkai*.

Footpath, s. *tsaṛa·lār* or *-wāṭ*.

Fop, s. *bānkā, ḍaulī, ṭaṭai, ṭainchī*.

For, p. *dapāra*; *wāsṭa, khāṭir*. (-as much) *la de na, dzaka, ska*. (-instance) *pa miṣāl, laka*. (-the most part) *akṣar*. (-what?) *tsa·la, wale*.

Forage, s. *wākkhah, gayāh, tsar*.

Foray, s. *dāṛa·dopa, hapa·dapa, bota, chapāo*.

Forbear, v.a. *zghamal, ṣabr-, pāl-, parhez-*, etc. *k*.

Forbearance, s. *ṣabr, zgham*.

Forbid, v.a. *man'a k*.

Forbidden, a. *man'a, ḥarām*.

Force, s. *zor, quwat, was, tuwān, bram, ṭāqat*; *ẓulm, ziyātī, jabr*.

Force, v.a. *zoral, tezal*.

Forceps, s. *ambūr, nūtsai*.

Ford, s. *gudar, pai*. v.n. *pore tlal* or *-watal*.

Fordable, a. *payāw*.

Fore, a. *wṛūnbai, wṛūnbanai, wṛāndīnai, pakhwānai, pekkhīn*.

Fore, ad. *wṛānde, wṛūnbe*.

Forefather, s. *nīkah*.

Forego, v.a. *pregdal—prekkhodal, tark k*.

Forehead, s. *wuchwalai* or *ucharlai, tandai*.

Foreign, a. *pradai, begānah, opṛah*.

Foreknowledge, s. *'ilm da ghā-ib*.

Foreman, s. *peshkār*.

Forementioned, a. *maẕkūr*.

Foremost, a. *wṛūnbai, wṛāndīnai, awwalanai, awwal*.

Forenoon, s. *pekkhīn, tsākkht*.

Forepart, s. *makh, sar, wṛūnbai*.

Forerunner, s. *peshraw, wṛānde tlūnai*.

Forest, s. *banṛ, dzangal, besha*.

Forestal, v.a. *pesh·dastī k*.

Foretell, v.a. *pāl-* or *fāl katal, ghā-ib wayal*.

Forethought, s. *dūr·andekkhī, pesh·fikrī*.

Forewarn, v.a. *wṛūnbe khabarawul, āgāh k*.

Forfeit, s. *nāgha, tāwān, jurīmāna, qurq*.

Forfeit, v.a. *nāgha-*, etc. *warkawul, bā-elal*.

Forge, s. *lohār·khāna, baṭ*.

Forge, v.a. *jāl·sāzī k*.

Forget, v.a. *herawul*.

Forgive, v.a. *bakkhal, pulawul*.

Forgiveness, s. *bakkhana*.

Forgotten, a. *her, ter·her*.

Fork, s. *dwa·kkhākha*. (pitch-) *panj·ghākkhai*.

Forked, a. *kkhākh·dār*.

Forlorn, a. *be·kas, khwār, yawādzai, lā·chār*.

Form, s. *ṣūrat, shakl, shān, rang, tartīb*.

Form, v.a. *joṛawul, tanḍal, tartībawul*.

Formal, a. *rasmī, chalanī, qānūnī*.

Formation, s. *tarkīb, sākht, joṛawūna*.

Former, a. *pakhwānai, wṛūnbanai*.

Formerly, ad. *pakhwā, wṛūnbe*.

Formidable, a. *tars·nāk, khof·nāk*.

Formula, s. *nuskha*; *tarkīb*; *tartīb*.

Fornication, s. *kāsīrī, zinā·kārī, ḥarām·kārī*.

Fornicator, s. *kāsīr, zinā·kār, ḥarām·kār*.

Forsake, v.a. *pregdal—prekkhodal, tark k*.

Forswear, v.a. *qasam-, saugand-*, etc. *khwuṛal*; *nā·ḥaqq qasam-*, etc, *khwuṛal*.

Fort, s. *qil'a, koṭ, gaṛa-ī, bāra, ḥiṣār*.

Forth, ad. *wṛānde*; *bāhir*.

Forthwith, ad. *os, pa ṭakī, sam da lāsa, pa de sā'at, wasīka*.

Fortify, v.a. *maẓbūṭ-, maḥkam-*, etc. *k.*; *āṛ-, ḥiṣar-, bāra-, panāh-*, etc. *k*.

Fortitude, s. *ṣabr, zgham*; *zṛah, himmat*.

Fortress, s. *koṭ, gaṛa-ī*.

Fortuitous, a. *nāgahān, ittifāqī*.

Fortunate, a. *nek·bakht, barakatī, bakhtawar, sa'ādat·man, bakhtyār*.

Fortune, s. *bakht, naṣīb, qismat*; *zamāna, rozgār*; *iqbāl, sa'ādat*; *māl, duniyā*,

daulat; *falak*, *tsarkh*. (-teller) *fāl-bīn*, *pāl-katūnkai*, *rammāl*, *d'awatī*.
Forty, a. *tsalwekkht*. (-one) *yo tsalwekkht*, etc.
Forum, s. *chauk*, *chārsū*, *bāzār*.
Forward, ad. *makhe*, *wṛānde*. a. *wṛāndai*, *makh*; *tayār*; *wīt*, *chūnkai*, *gustākh*.
Forward, v.a. *chalawul*, *rawānawul*, *āstawul*, *legal*, *rasawul*.
Foster, v.a. *pālal*, *nmāndzal*, *parwaral*. (-son) *pālalai dzoe*. (-daughter) *pālali lūr*. (-brother) *da tī* or *-to wror*. (-sister) *da ti* or *-to khor*. (-father) *plandar*, *pālūnkai plār*. (-mother) *dā-ī*, *pālūnki mor*.
Foul, a. *nā-pāk*, *palīt*, *murdār*, *kakaṛ*.
Foundation, s. *āra*, *wekh*, *bonsaṭ*, *kūnsaṭ*; *sar*, *aṣl*, *bunyād*. (pedestal) *pāya*, *asās*.
Fountain, s. *chīna*, *chashma*.
Four, a. *tsalor*. (fourth) *tsaloram*. (-fold) *tsalor-bragh*. (-footed) *chār-pā*. (-score) *tsalor shili*.
Fourteen, a. *tswārlas*.
Fowl, s. *chirg*. (water-) *hīla-ī*. (-of the air) *marghah* (p. *mārghah*), *marghai*. (Cochin-) *kulang*, *kurmang*. (game-) *panḍāw-chirg*.
Fowler, s. *kkhkārī*.
Fox, s. *lūnbaṛ*, *troṛa-ī*, *sperlam* or *spalam*.
Fraction, s. *kasr*, *ḥiṣṣa*, *ṭoṭai*, *ṭakai*.
Fracture, s. *māt*, *daṛa*, *chāwd*.
Fragile, a. *mātedūnai*, *narai*, *nāzak*.
Fragment, s. *ṭoṭa*, *reza*, *richa*, *chur*.
Fragrance, s. *'aṭr*, *khūsh-bū-ī*.
Fragrant, a. *khūsh-bū*, *bū-ī-nāk*, *khūshbū-ī-dār*.
Frail, a. *nāzak*, *nā-tuwān*, *ẓa'īf*, *kam-zor*, *nā-pāedār*, *fānī*.
Frame, s. *kināra*, *kāna*. (door-) *darshal*. (mould) *qālib*.
Frame, v.a. *joṛawul*, *taṛal*.
Frank, a. *spīn*, *ṣāf*, *sādah-dil*, *rikkhtīnai*.
Frankincense, s. *lobān*, *'ūd*.
Frantic, a. *lewanai*, *saudā-ī*.
Fraternity, s. *wrorī*, *wror-walī*.
Fraud, s. *ṭagī*, *fareb*, *droh*, *ghlā*, *chal*.
Fraudulent, a. *ṭag-bāz*, *farebī*, *chal-bāz*.
Fraught, s. *pūrah*, *ḍak*.
Fray, v.n. *sūledal*, *sūdah ked.*; *blosedal*.
Freak, s. *khiyāl*, *wahm*.
Freckle, s. *tarsarai*, *ta-apai*.
Free, a. *yalah*, *saṛah*, *wazgār*, *āzād*, *khalāṣ*. (-will) *wāk*, *ikhtiyār*, *raẓā*.
Freeze, v.n. *kangal-*, *khyam-*, etc. *ked.*, *yakhedal*.
Freight, s. *bār*; *bār-bardārī*; *kreha*, *maḥṣūl*.
Frenzy, s. *sarsām*, *lewan-tob*, *paṭ*.
Frequent, a. *ḍer*, *ziyāt*, *lagiyā*.
Frequent, v.a. *rāsha-darsha-*, *tlana-rātlana-*. etc. *k.* v.n. *osedal*, *pātedal*.
Frequently, ad. *akṣar*, *ziyātī*, *ḍer dzala*, *wār-wār*.
Fresh, a. *zarghūn*, *shīn*; *tāzah*, *takṛah*, *tayār*; *nawai*; *hosā*. (complexion) *skānr*.
Fret, v.n. *zahīredal*, *kaṛedal*, *nūledal*, *ghamedal*, *wiswāsī ked.* (-as cloth) *sūledal*. (as water) *tsapare-*, *pache-*, etc. *ked.*
Fretful, a. *khapah*, *wiswāsī*, *nā-qalār*.
Friction, s. *sūledana*, *sūda*; *mālish*, *masha*, *mukkhana*.
Friar, s. *miyā* or *mī-ā*, *paqīr*.
Friday, s. *jum'a*, *ādīna*.
Friend, s. *āshnāe*, *yār*, *dost*, *pejandgalai*.
Friendless, a. *be-kas*, *khwār*.
Friendly, a. *mihrbān*, *khair-khwāh* or *kāl-khwāh*.
Friendship, s. *āshnā-ī*, *yārī*, *yārāna*, *khpul-walī*.
Fright, s. *yera* or *wera*, *tars*, *tor*, *khof*, *tara*, *ḍār*.
Frighten, v.a. *yerawul* or *werawul*, *tarhawul*, *torawul*, *ḍārawul*.
Frightened, v.n. *weredal*, *tarhedal*, *ḍāredal*. v.a- *tor khwuṛal*.
Frightened, a. *yeredalai*, *tarhedalai*, *tor-khwuṛalai*, *ḍāredalai*.

Frightful, a. *tars-*, *khof-*, *tor-*, *haul-*, etc. *-nāk.*
Frigid, a. *sor*, *yakh*; *qarqechan*, *marghechan.*
Fringe, s. *tsanda*, *jāwja-ī*, *laman.* (frill) *sarwazana*, *zunda-ī*, *surkha-ī.*
Frisk, v.a. *traplal*, *top wahal*, *kharmastī-*, *tskhe-*, etc. *k.*
Fritter, v.n. *sharhedal.* (trifle) v.a. *jakh wahal.*
Frivolous, a. *spuk*, *halak*, *puch*, *khushai*, *nā·tsīz.*
Frock, s. *anga*, *khalqa*, *kāda-ī.* (quilted-) *andarka.* (long-) *qādara-ī.* (short-) *landa-ī.* (woman's-) *pepna-ī*, *gandola-ī.*
Frog, s. *chindakh*, *changakkh*, *shlānda.*
Frolic, s. *loba*, *mastī*, *tel·tāl*, *tskhe.*
From, p. *la*, *da*, *la—na.*
Front, s. *makh*, *wrāndai.* (in-) ad. *wrānde*, *makhā·makh*, *makh·kkhke*, *sāmure.*
Front, v.n. *wrānde-*, *makh-*, *sāmure-*, etc. *ked.*
Frontier, s. *pūla*, *brīd*, *hadd.*
Frost, s. *kangal*, *yakh.* (hoar-) *parkha*, *āsa-ī.* (-bitten) a. *qarqechan*, *marghechan*, *kaskar.*
Frosty, a. *sor*, *yakh.*
Froth, s. *zag*, *kaf.*
Frothy, a. *zag·jan*, *kaf·dār.*
Froward, a. *hodai*, *sar·kakkh*, *sar·zor*, *takaurai.*
Frown, v.a. *brandawul*, *starge brandawul.*
Frozen, a. *kangal·*, or *yakh·shawai.*
Fructify, v.a. *bārdār k.*; *blārba k.*
Frugal, a. *parhez·gār*; *kam·khwurāk.*
Fruit, s. *mewa*; *bār.*
Fruitful, a. *mewa·dār*; *bār·dār.*
Fruitless, a. *be·mewa*, *be·bār*, *shand.* (vain) *be·sūd*, *be·fā-ida*, *'abas-*, *bar·bād*, *be·būd.*
Frustrate, v.a. *bātil-*, *'abas-*, etc. *k.*, *wrānawul.*
Fry, v.a. *talawul*, *teyal*, *wrītawul*, *alwoyal.*
Frying-pan, s. *taba-ī*, *tabakhai*, *teghna.*
Fuel, s. *bālanr*, *largai*, *khāshāk*, *khadzala*, *warkhara.* (cowdung-) *ghoshoe.*
Fugitive, s. *takkhtedūnai.*

Fulfil, v.a. *tamāmawul*, *pa dzāe-*, *pūrah-*, etc. *k.*
Full, a. *dak*, *pūrah*; *mor*; *sekan.*
Fuller, s. *dobī*, *rang·rez.*
Fully, ad. *pa kkhah shān sara*, *qat'a-ī.*
Fulness, s. *tamām·tiyā*, *dak·wālai*; *mor·tiyā*; *arat·wālai*; *sekan·tob.*
Fulsome, a. *nā·khwakkh*, *kraka·nāk*; *puch.*
Fumble, v.a. *wār·khatā-k.*, *kāwākī k.*
Fumbler, s. *pūhar*, *kāwāk*, *lwār.*
Fumigate, v.a. *lū-*, *lūgai-*, *lūkhara-*, etc. *k.*
Fun, s. *loba*, *mastī*; *tamāsha*, *nandāra*; *toqa·washta*, *tel·tāl.*
Function, s. *kār*, *'amal*; *khidmat*; *'uhda.*
Fund, s. *sarmāya*, *saga*, *panga.*
Fundament, s. *būnsat*, *kūnsat*; *kūna*, *ghara*, *supra.*
Fundamental, a. *aslī*, *bunyādī*, *zātī.*
Funeral, s. *janāza.* (burial) *khakkhawūna*, *dafn.* (-service) *fātiha*, *pātā.* (-condolence) *lās·nīwah.* (-food) *shūma*, *mur·shūma.*
Funnel, s. *tsūkkhka*, *nala*; *jāba.*
Funny, a. *toq·mār*, *washtī*, *wītak.*
Fur, s. *wara-ī*, *pashm.* (-skin) *postīn.* (-coat) *nīm·tanai*, *nīmcha*, *postīncha.*
Furbish, v.a. (metals) *saiqal k.* (polish) *mugal—mukkhal.* (scrape) *togal.*
Furious, a. *qahr·nāk*, *bros*, *lewanai.*
Furl, v.a. *ngharal—nghakkhtal.*
Furnace, s. *tanūr.*
Furnish, v.a. *warkawul*, *rasawul*, *paidā k.*; *sambālawul*, *sāzawul*, *ārāstah k.*
Furniture, s. *rakht*, *asbāb*, *kālai*, *sāmān*, *sāz·sāmān*, *partal.*
Furrow, s. *līk*, *karkkha.*
Further, v.a. *madad-*, *komak-*, *mrasta-*, etc. *k.*
Fury, s. *qahr*, *ghazab*, *lewan·tob.*
Fuse, v.a. *wilī k.*, *oba k.*
Fusee, s. *bāta-ī*, *patīla* or *falīta.*
Fuss, s. *chal·chalā*, *tak·o·pū*, *rabar.*

Futile, a. *'abas, bāṭil, khushai, be fā-ida, spuk, nā-tsīz, be-sūd.*
Future, a. *gāndah, makh, rātlana, āyandah.*
Futurity, s. *ākhirat, 'āqibat.*
Fye, in. *toba! peṭī-mū!*

G.

Gabble, v.a. *bak-bak-, baq-baq-, baṛ-baṛ-, ṭar-ṭar-, char-char-,* etc. *k.*
Gabbler, s. *baq-baqai, baṛ-baṛai, ūnai, ṭarai.*
Gad, v.a. *hujra-gardī k.* v.n. *girzedal.*
Gadfly, s. *bhaganṛ, manganṛ-mach.*
Gag, v.a. *būja pa khule kkhke mandal, khula bandawul.*
Gain, s. *gaṭa, sūd, fā-ida, naf'a.*
Gain, v.a. *gaṭal, mūndal.* (-over) *grohedah k.* v.n. (win) *wa-aṛ ked.* (a victory) v.a. *barai mūndal.*
Gainer, s. *gaṭa kawūnkai, wa-aṛ, barai mūndūnkai.*
Gainful, a. *sūd-man, fā-ida-man.*
Gainsay, v.a. *khilāf wayal, radd k.*
Gait, s. *yūn, chāl, tlana, chalan, raftār.*
Gale, s. *sīla-ī, bād, ṭūpān.*
Gall, s. *trīkha, zahra, ṣafrā.* (-bladder) *trīkhai.*
Gall, v.a. *sūdah-, gasiyā-,* etc. *k., sūlawul.*
Gallant, a. *maṛanai, dzwān-mard, tūrzan.*
Gallant, s. *'ishq-bāz, kāsīr; yār, āshnāe.*
Gallantry, s. *maṛāna, zṛahwar-tob, tūrzan-tob, zmarī-tob, dzwān-mardī; kāsīrī, 'ishq-bāzī; āshnā-ī, yārāna.*
Gallery, s. *bālā-khāna, shāhnishīn, dūnkācha, aiwān.* (mine) *surang.*
Gallop, s. *poya, tākht.*
Gallop, v.a. *pa-poyo-, pa-tākht-,* etc. *zghalawul.* v.n. *pa-poyo-,* etc., *tlal* or *-zghaledal.*
Gallows, s. *dār, sūla-ī, gahwāra.* (-rope) *tezanda-ī, zanda-ī, pā-ī.*

Galls, Gallnut, s. *māzū.*
Gamble, v.a. *jū-ārī-, jū-ā-bāzī-, qimār-bāzī-,* etc. *k.*
Gambler, s. *jū-ār-gar, jū-ā-bāz.*
Gambol, s. *ṭel-ṭāl, mastī, tskhe, loba.*
Game, s. *loba, bāzī.*
Gander, s. *baṭ, qāz; pūhaṛ, gedī.*
Gang, s. *ṭolai, dāṛa, paṛk, tāmba, ghol, cham.*
Gangrene, s. *skhā, gazak.*
Gaol, s. *zindān, qaid-, bandī-,* etc. *khāna.*
Gap, s. *kanḍāw, darghol, wut, gūṭ.*
Gape, v.n. *wītedal, chīngedal, wāzedal.* v.a *khula chīngawul, -wāzawul* or *-wītawul.* (yawn) *aswelai-, .khamiyāza-,* etc. *k.* (stare) *ghaṭ-katal.*
Gaping, a. *wīt, chīng, wāz.*
Garb, s. *toga, shān, rang; jāma, pokkhāk, libās.*
Garbage, s. *ūjrai, larai.*
Garble, v.a. *latawul, chunṛal.*
Garden, s. *bāgh, bāghcha.* (flower-) *gulshan, bostān.* (-of Eden) *jannat, 'adan.*
Gardener, s. *bāghwān.*
Gardening, s. *bāghwānī, bāghwān-tob.*
Gargle, v.a. *ghar-ghaṛa k.*
Garland, s. *hār, lar, amel.*
Garlic, s. *ūga.*
Garment, s. *āghostana, jāma, zaṛūkāi, libās, nwarai.* (beggar's-) *gand* or *kind.*
Garner, s. *khamba, kandū, koṭa, ambār-khāna.*
Garnish, v.a. *joṛawul, andzorawul.*
Garrison, s. *qil'a, gaṛa-ī; da qil'e khalq.*
Garrulous, a. *baq-baqai, ṭarai, baṛ-baṛai,*
Gash, s. *parhār, tsīra, ghwuts, zakhm.* v.a. *tsīral, ghwutsawul, joblawul, zakhmī k.*
Gasp, v.a. *landa sāh-* or *sāh pa-porta ūkhistal.* v.n. *sāh khatal, sāh-landah ked.*
Gate, s. *war.* (-way) *darwāza.*
Gather, v.a. *ṭolawul, jam'a-, yo-dzāe-,* etc. *k.* (select) *anṛawul, chunṛal, laṭawul.* (pluck) *shūkawul.*

Gathering, s. *ṭol, ṭolai.* (-of cloth) *jung.*
Gaudy, a. *rangā-rang, rangīn.*
Gauge, v.a. *mech-, kach-,* etc. *k.*
Gay, a. *kkhād, kkhād-man, khūsh-hāl.*
Gaze, v.a. *katal, ghaṭ katal, dzīr k.*
Gazette, s. *akhbār.*
Gear, s. *kālī, sāz-sāmān, asbāb.*
Geld, v.a. *khaṣṣī-, ākhtah-,* etc. *k.*; *malai k.*
Gem, s. *gauhar* or *jauhar.*
Gender, s. *jins, qism.* (masculine-) *nārīnah, nar, muzakkar.* (feminine-) *māndīna, kkhadza, muwannaṣ.*
Genealogy, s. *shajra, nasal, nasab, aṣl, peṛa-ī.*
General, a. *'āmm, jārī*; *shāmil.*
General, s. *sardār, sar-guroh, mashar.*
Generally, ad. *akṣar, ziyātī.*
Generate, v.a. *paidā k.*; *zegawul.*
Generation, s. *paidā-ikkht*; *peṛa-ī, pusht*; *alwād, zāwzāt*; *zamāna, daur.*
Generosity, s. *sakhāwat, sakhī-tob, sakhā, bakkhana.*
Generous, a. *sakhī, bakkhūnai.*
Genial, a. *joṛ, khwakkh, barābar, pīrzo.*
Genitals, s. *andām-nihānī, satar, ṣūrat, 'aurat.* (hair of-) *tor-wekkhtah.*
Genius, s. *khoe, khaṣlat, ṭab'a, khwā, mizāj, lokkhai.* (evil-) *perai, parī.* (capacity) *poha, pahm, idrāk.*
Genteel, a. *makhawar, spīn-robai, satar-pokkh.*
Gentility, s. *makhawar-tob, sharāfat.*
Gentle, a. *halīm, aṣīl, ashrāf.*
Gentleman, s. *ṣāhib-* or *ashrāf-zādah.*
Gently, ad. *ro-ro, pa-qalār.*
Gentry, s. *ra-isān, ashrāfān.*
Genuine, a. *sūchah, karah, aṣīl, khāliṣ, nughd, rikkhtīnai.*
Genus, s. *rag, qūm, qism, nogai, jins.*
Germinate, v.n. *ṭūkedal, zarghūnedal.* v.a. *red k.*

Gesture, s. *harakat*; *shān.*
Get, v.a. *mūndal, gaṭal, paidā k.*
Ghastly, a. *sperah.*
Ghost, s. *rawai*; *perai.*
Giant, s. *ghaṭ-khṛīs, nāpaṛ-* or *gagar saṛai*; *dew, 'ifrīt.*
Gibbet, s. *dār, gahwāra.* v.a. *tezanda-ī warkawul*; *dzwaṛandawul.*
Giddiness, s. *sar-ghurzai, akar, sar-girzai.*
Gift, s. *bakhkshiksh, bakkhana. nazr, hiba.*
Gifted, a. *qābil, qudrat-man, zbarg.*
Gigantic, a. *khṛīs, nāpaṛ, dang-, star, ghaṭ, loe.*
Giggle, v.n. *khandedal, musedal.*
Gilding, s. *ṭilā-kārī.*
Gill, s. *wakkhkai.*
Gimlet, s. *barma, tswarla-ī.*
Gin, s. *dām, lwīna, lūma, lūmaka, paṛka, laṭ.*
Ginger, s. (green-) *adrak.* (dry-) *sūnḍ.*
Gipsey, s. *naṭ*; *kochī.*
Gird, v.a. *taṛal.*
Girder, s. *taṛūnai.* (-beam) *bensh, paṭera, tīr.*
Girdle, s. *mlā-taṛūnai, mlā-band, kamar-band.* (woman's-) *tapor.* (sash) *paṭka.*
Girl, s. *jina-ī.* (mature-) *peghla.* (betrothed-) *changhala.* (slave-) *wīndza.* (servant-) *mazdūra.* (kept-) *khidmat-gāra.* (dancing-) *lola-ī, kachana-ī.*
Girth, s. *paṭā-ī*; *tāng.*
Give, v.a. *warkawul, bakkhal, kkhandal.* (evidence) *lal* or *lawdal.*
Giver, s. *warkawūnkai, bakkhūnkai*; *lūnai.*
Gizzard, s. *shā-ṭīnga.*
Glad, a. *khwakkh, kkhād, khūsh, khūsh-hāl.*
Gladtidings, s. *zera.* (bringer of-) *zera-garai.*
Gladiator s. *tūra-bāz, shamsher-bāz.*
Gladness, s. *khwakkhī, kkhādī, khūsh-hālī.* (-over a rival) *sakha, wiyāṛ.*
Glance, v.a. *nazar pa za-ar terawul.* (shine) v.n. *dzal kedal.* (fly off) v.a. *tīndak wahal.*
Gland, s. *stagha, ghudūd, ghūnḍārai.*

Glare, s. *ranṛā, dzalah, brekkhnā.*
Glaring, a. *kkhkārah, tsargand, awtsār.*
Glass, s. *kkhīkkha.* (-cup) *piyāla.* (mirror) *ā-īna.*
Glaze, v.a. *malma-,* or *mulamm'a k., rang pore k., kāshī k.*
Glazier, s. *kāshī-gar.*
Gleam, s. *partaw, palwasha.*
Gleam, v.n. *dzalkedal, brekkhedal.*
Glean, v.a. *anṛawul, chūnṛal, drūze tolawul.*
Glee, s. *kkhādī, khwand.* (song) *ṭapa.*
Glimmer, s. *dzalak, palwasha.*
Glitter, v.n. *brekkhedal, dzalkedal, rūnṛedal.*
Globe, s. *duniyā, naṛa-ī, jahān.* (celestial) *tsarkh, falak, kursī.* (ball) *ghunḍai, manḍos, panḍos, mardak.*
Globular, a. *ghunḍ, ghunḍ-man.*
Globule, s. *gola-ī, mardakoṭai, ghunḍūrai.*
Gloom, s. *tyāra, tor-wālai, tor-tam; gham, nūl.*
Glorify, v.a. *stāyal, sanā wayal.*
Glorious, a. *mubārak; majīd; loe, jalāl; kkhah.*
Glory, s. *nang, nūm, iqbāl.*
Gloss, s. *rang.*
Glossy, a. *brekkh-nāk, dzalak-nāk.*
Glove, s. *dastāna, da lās joṛāba.* (gauntlet) *dast-gala.* (for hawking) *bela.*
Glow, v.n. *todedal, swal.*
Glow. s. *todūkkha, swai.* (-worm) *or-orakai.*
Glue, s. *slekkh; leṭa-ī.*
Glutton, s. *geḍa-war, ghārai, ghārdal, ḥirṣ-nāk, rawai.*
Gnash, v.a. *ghākkh chīchal* or *-kṛapawul.*
Gnat, s. *māshai, ghamāsha, jak* or *jakh.*
Gnaw, v.a. *chīchal, kṛapawul.*
Go, v.n. *tlal—lāṛal, drūmal* or *drūmedal, chaledal, rawānedal; kūch k., legdal.*
Goad, s. *chūka, trāṭ, konṭa-ī.*
Goal, s. *ṭīkāo, mazal, borjal.*
Goat, s. *buz* or *wuz.* (he-) *psah.* (she-) *bza.* (-in heat) *wazema.* (kid) *warghūmai, chelai.* (yearling-) *serlai.* (-hair) *wāghūne.*
Gobble, v.a. *gaṛanḍai khwuṛal.*
Goblet, s. *kaṭorai, jām, shāh-kāsa.*
Goblin, s. *bāgū, bagalola-ī; rawai.*
God, s. *khudāe, allah, rabb.* (-forbid) *khudāe di na ka* or *-kāndi.* (-preserve us) *yā khudāya-* or *yā rabba khair ka.* (-knows) *khudāe khabar* or *-zdah.* (by-!) *khudāe go.* (good-!) *allahu akbar, subḥān allah.* (my-!) *yā dzamā khudāya.* (for God's sake) *da khudāe da pāra.* (-bless thee) *khudāe di wusāta* or *-wubakkha* or *-loe ka.* (-curse thee) *peṭī mū, pa tā n'alat, khudāe di mīrāt ka.* (-grant) *khudāe di wuka* or *-wukī.* (-protect thee) *da khudāe pa amān.*
Godliness, s. *dīn-dārī, taqwā.*
Godly, a. *dīn-dār, namāndzī, nmūndz-guzār.*
Going, s. *tah, tlah, yūn, pand.*
Goitre, s. *ghur.*
Gold, s. *srah-zar, zar, ṭila.* (-smith) *zar-gar.*
Golden, a. *zarīn.*
Gonorrhœa, s. *sozāk.*
Good, a. *kkhah, nek, pakīzah, ghwarah.* s. *kkhegaṛa, fā-ida, sūd.*
Goodness, s. *kkhah-wālai, nekī.*
Goods, s. *asbāb.* (cattle) *māl.* (clothes) *rakht.* (furniture, etc.) *kālai.*
Goodwill, s. *nek-* or *khair-khwāhī.*
Goose, s. (domestic) *baṭa.* (wild-) *qāza.*
Gore, v.a. *pa kkhkar wahal.*
Gore, s. *pranṛ, jākai, malob, wīne.*
Gorge. s. *dara, tanga-ī; ghāṛa, mara-ī.*
Gormandize, v.a. *be-khrata-, be-prata-,* etc. *khwuṛal.*
Gospel s. *injīl; ḥaqq.*
Gossip, v.a. *khushe khabare k.; khabare-atare-, khabare-mabare k,*
Gourd, s. *kadū.* (-seed) *kadū-zarai.*
Gout, s. *bād, naqras.*

Govern, v.a, *hukūmat-*, *hukm-*, etc. *k.* or *chalawul.* (manage) *sambālawul.*

Government, s. *hukūmat*, *'amal*; *sarkār*, *rāj*; *sardārī*, *khānī*, *malikī*.

Governor, s. *hākim*, *sardār*, *khān*, *malik*.

Gown, s. (man's) *chapan*, *qādara-ī*. (woman's) *peshwāz*, *pepna-ī*.

Grace, s. *mihrbāngī*. (favour) *mrasta*. (pardon) *bakkhana*. (beauty) *kkhāyast*. (manner) *nāz*, *karakkhma*. (by the grace of God) *da khudāe pa mihrbāngī sara*. (-before meals) *bismillah*. (-after meals) *d'uā*, *shukur*. (a form of-) *shukur alhamdu l illah*, *rabbā ṣanā tā lara*. (title) *hazrat*.

Graceful, a. *kkhāyastah*, *kkhkulai*, *nāzak*. (in comp.) *khūsh-*.

Gracefulness, s. *kkhāyast-wālai*, *kkhāyast*, *jorāb*, *krak-wrah*.

Gracious, a. *mihrbān*.

Graciously, ad. *pa mihrbāngī sara*.

Gradation, s. *darja*, *pāya*, *wār*.

Gradually, ad. *ro-ro*, *wār pa wār*.

Graft, s. *pewand*, *band*, *qalam*.

Grain, s. *ghalla*, *dāna*. (a single-) *dāna*. (bruised-) *dal*. (ground-) *orah*. (finely ground-) *maidah*. (parched-) *nīna*, *pūlah*. (mixed-) *gādera*. (-merchant) *saudāgar*, *ghalla-farosh*, *banriyā*.

Grammar, s. *ṣarf-o-nahw*.

Granary, s. *anbār-khāna*.

Grand, a. *loe*, *ghat*, *star*.

Grandee, s. *amīr*, *arbāb*.

Grandeur, s. *loe-wālai*, *ghat-wālai*; *zbargī*.

Grant, v.a. *warkawul*, *bakkhal*; *manal*, *qabūlawul*.

Granule, s. *dāna*; *pūṭai*, *pitsānrai*.

Grape, s. *angūr*. (-vine) *tāk*. (wild-) *kwar*. (dried-) *watska*, *mewa*.

Grapple, v.a. *parzawul*, *nīwul*.

Grasp, v.a. *pa qabze-*, *pa panje-*, *pa mūṭe-*, *pa mungali-*, etc. *nīwul*.

Grass, s. *wākkhah*, *gayāh*, *'alaf*. (varieties of-) *drab*, *dūp*, *kabl*, *shama*, *shāmukha*, *dīla*, *ghūndwagai*, *sargarai*, *sarbaga*, *wīga*, *mota*, *panai*, *malai*, *manaārū*, *dadam*, etc.

Grasshopper, s. *toqā*, *kha-argai*; *mlakh*.

Grate, v.a. *taghawul*, *brekkhawul*; *zdoyal*. v.n. *gharedal*.

Grateful, a. *shukur-guzār*; *khwand-nāk*.

Gratification, s. *khwakkhī*; *khwand*. (over another's misfortunes) *sakha*, *wiyār*.

Gratify, v.a. *khāṭir k.*, *nāzawul*, *kkhāghal*.

Gratis, ad. *weriyā*, *mupt*, *hase*.

Gratitude, s. *shukur-guzārī*.

Gratuitous, a. *weriyā*, *mupt*.

Gratuity, s. *bakhkshiksh*, *in'ām*, *shukrāna*, *pekkh-kakkh*, *khwara*.

Grave, s. *gor*, *qabr*, *maqbara*. (the niche) *lahad*. (-stone) *khadza* or *khāda*. (-digger) *qabr-kan*, *gor-kan*. (-badger) *gor-kakkh*. (-clothes) *kafan*.

Grave, a. *drūnd*, *grān*; *fikr-man*, *ghalai*.

Gravel, s. *kānr*, *gghal*, *ghaṭa-shiga*.

Gravitate, v.n. *kkhkenāstal*, *prewatal*.

Gravity, s. *drūnd-wālai*, *dranāwai*.

Gravy, s. *kkhorwā*.

Gray, a. *sperah*, *kha-ar*, *khākī*. (-hair) *brag*.

Graze, v.a. *piyāyal—powul*. v.n. *tsaral*, *tsaredal*. (abrade) *blosedal*; *sūledal*.

Grazier, s. *powūnkai*. (of cows) *ghobah*. (of buffaloes) *mekkhbah*, *gūjar*. (of camels) *ūkkhbak*, *sārwān*. (of sheep, etc.) *gadbah*, *shpūn*, *shpankai*.

Grease, s. *ghwarī*, *mū*. v.a. *ghwarawul*.

Greasy, a. *ghwar*.

Great, a. *ghat*, *loe*, *star*; *zbarg*.

Greatly, ad. *nihāyat*, *der*.

Greatness, s. *star-wālai*, etc.; *zbargī*.

Greediness, s. *hirṣ*, *tam'a*, *liwāl-tob*.

Greedy, a. *hāriṣ*, *hirṣ-nāk*, *geda-war*.

Green, a. *shīn*, *zarghūn*; *ūm*, *kachah*.

Greens, s. *sāg*, *sābah*, *talkārī*, *tara*. (varieties

ot-) *panerak, shawtal, warkhārai, chalwerai, tāndola, tsārmai, jawānwān*, etc. (cultivated-) *pālak, malkhoza, āorai, mūlai, gāzara, ṭepar*, etc. (dish of-) *sāgīnrai.*

Greet, v.a. *mubārakī wayal*; *salām-'alaik-, joṛ-tāzah-*, etc. *k.*

Grief, s. *gham, randz, paskhāk* or *pakhsāk, nūl*; *gram.*

Grievance, s. *faryād*; *sakhtī, dzaur, jabr, ẓulm.*

Grieve, v.n. *nūledal, randzedal, kaṛedal, ghamedal, zahīredal.* v.a. *āzārawul, zahīrawul*, etc.

Grieved, a. *gham-jan, nūl-jan, randzūr, dil-gīr.*

Grievous, a. *gham-nāk*; *jabr-nāk, sakht, randz-nāk.*

Grill, v.a. *wrītawul, alwoyal, talawul, teyal.*

Grim, a. *sūṭ-būṭ, mushād*; *zīg, sakht, klak.*

Grimace, s. *pekkha, tsera, būṭ-urbūz.*

Grin, v.n. *musedal.* v.a. *dāṛe-, ghākkh-*, etc. *chīngawul.*

Grind, v.a. *oṛawul, anṛal, oṛah k.*

Grindstone, s. *psān.* (-wheel) *tsarkh.* (-for corn) *mechan.* (-for spices) *tīga, silāta.*

Gripe, s. *qabẓa, da mūṭī nīwah.* (belly-) *kānga, tāo, pech.*

Gripe, v.a. *pa qabẓe-, pa mūṭī-*, etc. *nīwul.* (as birds and beasts) *pa panje-, pa manguli-*, etc. *nīwul.* (as the belly) v.n. *kānga-, tāo-*, etc. *ked.*

Gristle, s. *krachai, krachūnai, krachandūkai.*

Grit, s. *kānṛ, shiga*; *dal, drūza, gadzārai.*

Gritty, a. *shiglan, kānṛan, kānṛez.*

Groan, v.a. *zwergai* or *zgerwai-, angahār* or *hengahar-*, etc. *k.*

Grocer, s. *pansārī, banṛiyā.*

Groin, s. *mghāna.*

Groom, s. *shātar, jalau-dār, nafar.*

Groove, s. *kīla, karkkha.*

Grope, v.n. *ṭaparedal.* v.a. *laṭawul.*

Gross, a. *tsorb, peraṛ*; *ghaṭ, lwāṛ*; *nāpaṛ, star.*

Gross, s. *ṭol, ṭol-ṭāl, tamām, kull.*

Ground, s. *zmaka* or *mzaka, zamīn.*

Groundless, a. *be-mūjib, nā-ḥaqq.*

Group, s. *ṭolgai, tamba, tsīṛa, paṛk, jam.*

Grouse, s. *kha-aṛārai, kha-aṛai-kauntar, kha-aṛgaṭ.*

Grove, s. *jangai, banṛ.*

Grovel, v.n. *rghaṛedal—rghakkhtal.*

Grow, v.n. (increase) *ghaṭedal, ziyātedal, loe ked.* (vegetate) *ṭūkedal, zarghūnedal.* (-old) *zaṛedal.* (become) *kedal.*

Growl, v.n. *ghuṛunbedal, gṛanjedal.*

Grudge, v.a. *daregh k.* (owe a-) *dukkhmanī-, badī-, khwā-badī-, 'inād-, kīna-*, etc. *laral.*

Gruel, s. *atob, oghṛa, daliya*; *āsh, shīra.*

Gruff, a. *sakht, tursh-rūe, suṭ-būṭ, qahr-jan.*

Grumble, v.a. *gila-, māna-*, etc. *k.* v.n. *gṛanjedal, ghuṛunbedal.* (as the bowels) *qur-qur ked.*

Guarantee, s. *ẓamānat.* (person) *ẓāmin.*

Guard, s. *pahra, tsoka-ī*; *pāswān, kashak*; *pahra-dār, tsoka-ī-dār.* (over crops and cattle) *kakkhai.* (protector) *sātūnkai, sātandoe, jghorai, pāslawūnai.*

Guard, v.a. *pahra-*, etc. *k.*; *pāswānī-*, etc. *k.*, *gālal*; *kakkhī-tob k.*; *sātal, jghoral, pāslawul, khundī k.*, or *khundiyal.*

Guess, v.a. *qiyās-, khiyāl-, aṭkal-*, etc. *k.*, *pejandal, m'alūmawul.*

Guest, s. *melmah, mezmān.*

Guidance, s. *kkhowuna, hidāyat, murshidī.*

Guide, s. *balad, lār-kkhowūnkai, būmiyā.* (spiritual) *pīr, murshid, hādī, peshwā.*

Guile, s. *ṭag-bāzī, chal-bāzī, lamghaṛa-ī-tob. ṭagī, ḥīla, fareb.*

Guilt, s. *gunāh, taqṣīr*; *wabāl, baza.*

Guiltless, a. *be-gunāh, be-quṣūr, be-taqṣīr.*

Guilty, a. *gunāh-gār, taqṣīr, quṣūr-man.*

Guise, s. *ṣūrat, shakl, shān*; *bāna, libās*; *parda.*

Guitar, s. *sitāra, chamtāra.* (Fiddle).
Gullet, s. *mara-ī, sra·ghāṛa.*
Gulp, s. *ghurap, gūṭ, īnda.* v.a. *nghardal.*
Gum, s. *chīṛ, jāwla.* (of teeth) *ūra-ī* or *awra-ī.*
Gun, s. *bandūkh, ṭopak.* (-barrel) *nala.* (-stock) *kundāgh.* (-sight) *mach, zarai, dīdwān, ghūṭa-ī* (-match) *bāta-ī, patīla.* (-cock) *pāya.* (-trigger) *chajak.* (-priming pan) *kandol, māsha, ātash·khāna.* (-chamber) *khizana.* (-priming powder) *ranjak.* (-cleaning rod) *bargho, margholai.* (ramrod) *gaz, sīkh.* (-aiming rest) *sipāwa* or *sipāya.* (-powder) *dārū.* (-ball) *mardaka.*
Gunner, s. *ṭopak·chī, bandūkh·chī*; *top·chī.*
Gush, v.n. *pa·dāro watal* or *-bahedal.* v.a. *dāra wahal.*
Gust, s. *chapa, jakaṛ, sīla-ī.*
Gut, s. *kulma, laṛmūn*; *larai, ūjrai.*
Gutter, s. *nāwa, lakkhta-ī, wāla, tarnāo.*
Guttural, a. *ḥalqī.*
Gymnastic, a. *kushtī, pahalwānī.*
Gyves, s. *dzolana, pakhwandai, pāekara, pāela.*

H.

Haberdasher, s. *banjārī.*
Habit, s. *'ādat, yūn, 'amal*; *khoe, khaslat*; *mizāj, ṭabī'at.*
Habitation, s. *astoga, kor*; *dzāe, meshta, borjal.*
Habitual, a. *'ādatī, āmokhtah.*
Habituate, v.a. *'ādatī-*, etc. *k.*, *rūgdawul.*
Hack, v.a. *kūtal, ṭoṭa·ṭoṭa-, chūr·chūr-*, etc. *k.*
Hag, s. *zaṛa-ī, jāḍa-ī.*
Haggard, a. *tap, ḍangar, wuch·klak, tsoṛ.*
Hail, s. *jāla, gala-ī.* v.n. *jāle-*, etc. *oredal.*
Hail, v.a. *salām·'alaik-, joṛ·tāzah-*, etc. *k.*
Hair, s. *wekkhtah.* (dressed) *sar·kunḍai.* (lock or curl of-) *tsūnra, tsunraka, zulf, wal.* (braid or plait of-) *orbal, kontsa-ī, nghakkhai.* (top knot of-) *tsaṛai.* (-of pubes) *tor·wekkhtah.* (-of the body) *zunba, ghūna.* (goat's-) *ūjghūne.* (ribbon or braid for the-) *bachawai, pekawai, peyawai.*
Hairy, a. *babar, waṛan.*
Hale, a. *takṛah·tāzah, rogh·mot, joṛ, tandurust.*
Half, a. *nīm.* (-done) *nīmgaṛai.* s. *nīmai, nīmāyah.*
Hall, s. *dālān, khūna.* (public-) *ḥujra.* (-of audience) *dalbār, bārgāh.*
Halloo, v.a. *chigha-, nāra-*, etc. *wahal.*
Hallowed, a. *pāk, muqaddas.*
Halo, s. *hāla, shpol.*
Halt, v.n. *wudredal*; *guḍedal*; *jah ked.* v.a. *dera-, muqām-, ṭikāo-*, etc. *k.*
Halter, s. *khapī* or *gapī, pā-ī, bāḍgol.* (headstall) *ter·sarai.* (hangman's-) *tezanda-ī, zanda-ī, pā-ī.*
Halve, v.a. *nīmawul, dwah·nīm k.*
Ham, s. (thigh) *wrūn, patūn.*
Hamlet, s. *bānḍa, kaloṭai.*
Hammer, s. *pa-alk, tsaṭak.* (wooden-) *baghdar, ḍabalai.* (washerman's-) *tsobāṛai.*
Hammer, v.a. *wahal, ṭakawul, trakawul, ṭak wahal.*
Hamper, s. *khalta, kawāra, ṭokra-ī, kāra, sawada.*
Hamper, v.a. *kariyābawul, haṭālawul.*
Hamstring, v.a. *pai k.*, or *-wahal.*
Hand, s. *lās*; *chaka, panja, mangul.* (-ful) *lapa* or *lapaka, paka* or *kapa.* (palm of-) *warghawai, khapaṛ.* (-breadth) *tsapak.* (closed-) *mūṭ.* (-in hand) *chak·pa·chak.* (-cuff) *karai.* (-held to receive) *mangul, changul.* (-held to take or seize) *panja.*

Handful, s. *chung, qawda.* (double-) *lapakai.*
Handkerchief, s. *rumāl, dast·māl.* (-for head) *sar·basta, sar·pechak, sar·taṛūnai, tsapoṭkai.*
Handle, s. *mūṭai, lāstai, dasta.*
Handle, v.a. *lās lagawul, -warwṛal, -wahal,* etc., *laṭawul, nīwul*; *chalawul.*
Handmaid, s. *mazdūra, khidmat·gāra sahela-ī.* (brides-) *īnga.*
Handmill, s. *mechan.* (lower stone) *kkhkatanai pal.* (upper stone) *portanai pal.* (-handle) *lāstai.* (pivot or axle) *tīrak.* (axle bar) *ḍīḍa, kkhārag.* (-cup) *ghāṛa.* (-hopper) *ḍol, ganḍ.*
Handsome, a. *kkhāyastah, kkhkulai, pa·ī·makhai* or *pej·makhai.*
Handsomely, ad. *pa kkhah shān sara.*
Handsomeness, s. *kkhāyast, kkhāyast·wālai, kkhkulai·wālai, kkhkulī·tob, pej·makh·tob.*
Handy, a. *tak·lāstai*; *tayār*; *nijdai.*
Hang, v.n. *dzwaṛandedal, āwezānd . ked.* v.a. *āwezānd k., dzwaṛandawul.* (a criminal) *tezanda-ī warkawul, pa dār khejawul.*
Hangman, s. *jallāt, tezanda-ī warkawūnkai, dār·kash.*
Hank, s. *tranjūkai.* (ring) *karai.*
Hanker, v.n. *liwāl-, mayan-*, etc. *ked.* v.a. *mīna-, raghbat-, shauq-*, etc. *laral.*
Hapless, a. *kam·bakht, be·qismat, be·naṣīb.*
Haply, ad. *kkhā-ī, gunde*; *wī ba.*
Happen, v.n. *kedal, shwal, nāziledal, prewatal, teředal, waqi'a ked., pekkhedal.*
Happily, ad. *pa khair sara, pa kkhādī sara.*
Happy, a. *khwakkh, kkhād, kkhād·man.*
Harangue, v.a. *w'aẓ k., kalām wayal.*
Harass, v.a. *rabṛawul, āzārawul, tangawul, tongawul, ṭongāra k.*
Harbinger, s. *peshraw, astādzai.*
Harbour, s. *bandar*; *panāh.*
Hard, a. *klak, sakht*; *grān, mushkil*; *pokh, takṛah.*
Hard-hearted, a. *nā·tars, kāṇrai·zṛah, be·dard.*
Hardiness, s. *klak·wālai, maẓbūṭ·tiyā, takṛah·wālai*; *zṛah·war·tob.*
Hardly, ad. *pa mushkil sara, pa rabaṛ sara*; *kamtar, mushkila, hīla.*
Hardness, s. *klak·wālai, sakht·wālai.*
Hardship, s. *tangsiyā, rabaṛ, sakhtī.*
Hardware, s. *da ospane kālī.*
Hardy, a. *klak, maẓbūṭ, zṛah·war, maṛanai, takṛah, ṭīng.*
Hare, s. *soe.* (hare's form) *soghālai.*
Harebrained, a. *khushai, lewanai.*
Hark, in. *wāwra! ghwag bāsa!* or *-nīsa!* or *-kega da!*
Harlot, s. *kāsīra, shatāha*; *lola-ī, kachana-ī.*
Harm, s. *tāwān, ziyān, nuqṣān.*
Harmful, a. *tāwānī, nuqṣānī, ziyānī.*
Harmonious, a. *barābar, yo·shān*; *khog.*
Harmony, s. *rogha, joṛa, āshtī*; *sarod, tarāna.*
Harness, s. *da ās kālī*; *sāz·sāmān.*
Harp, s. *barbaṭ.*
Harpoon, s. *biyak.*
Harrow, s. *ghākkhawar.*
Harsh, a. *trīw, trīkh*; *zīg, lwāṛ.*
Harvest, s. *faṣl.* (reaped-) *lau.* (gathered-) *khirman, dirmand.* (spring-) *oṛai.* (autumn-) *manai.*
Hash, v.a. *qīma k., ṭoṭe k.*
Haste, s. *talwār, talwal, jaltī, shitābī.* (to make-) *talwār-*, etc. *k.*
Hasty, a. *talwārī, talwalai, jalt.*
Hat, s. *ṭopa-ī, khola-ī.*
Hatch, v.n. *kuṛaka ked.*; *pa hago kkhkenāstal, bachī bāsal—yastal.*
Hatchet, s. *tabar.*
Hate, v.a. *bad manal, kagal, chinjawul, ghandal, kraka ākhistal.*
Hateful, a. *bad, kagalai, kraka·nāk, ghāndah.*
Hatred, s. *badī, khwā·badī, dukkhnī, kīna, khuṣūmat, ṭaka, ghach.*

Haughtiness, s. *kibr, bād, maghrūrī, khpul-sarī.*

Haughty, a. *kibr-jan, bādī, khāntamā.*

Haul, v.a. *rākāgal—rākkhkal.*

Haunch, s *kūnātai; ṭūṭa, dūḍa, patūn.*

Haunt, s. *borjal, meshta, astoga.*

Haunt, v.n. *osedal, āstedal.*

Hautboy, s. *sarnāe, tūrai.*

Have, v.a. *laral, darlal.*

Haven, s. *bandar, panāh.*

Havock, s. *takht-tārāj, tālā, kharābi, wrānī.*

Hawk, s. *bāz.* (goshawk) *bāz, kaṭah-bāz, jurrah.* m. (varieties of-) *turmatai, bākkha, shaindai, lagar, jagar, regai, shikrai.* (-of the first year) *chūz.* (-of the second year) *khāna-kurīz.* (old-) *terīnāk.* (-from the nest) *shānī.* (caught-) *dāmī.* (-perch) *chakas.* (-bells) *gīngrai.* (-jessies) *tasme.* (-hood) *ṭopa-ī.* (-lure) *dalba.* (-drag) *bāolī.* (-glove) *bela.*

Hawk, v.a. *da bāz-* or *da chargh kkhkār k.*; (expectorate) *ghāṛa tāza k.* (sell) *banjārī k.*

Hay, s. *wuch wākkhah, wuch-giyāh, pashkālai.* (-of pulses) *kaṭī.* (coil of-) *beda.*

Hazard, s. *khaṭra, bāk, muhimm, andekkhnā.* (stroke) *daw, guzār.* (chance) *gumān.*

Haze, s. *dund, ghubār, dūp, laṛa, tyāra.*

He, pr. *haghah, dā, dah, de, di.*

Head, s. *sar, kala, koṭai.* (-band) *sar-pechak, sar-taṛūnai.* (-piece) *paṭkai, lūnga-ī.* (-stall) *ter sarai.* (-and tail) *shīr-khaṭ.* (crown of-) *ṭopal, ṭaṭar.*

Headlong, a. *aluwal; talwalai; naskor.*

Headstrong, a. *zorāwar, sar-zor, sar-kakkh, ṭakanṛai, khpul-sar, hoḍai.*

Heal, v.a. *joṛawul, raghawul.* v.n. *joṛedal. raghedal.*

Health, s. *rogh-wālai, joṛ-wālai, rogh-tiyā, joṛ-tiyā, tandrustī.*

Healthy, a. *rogh, joṛ, tandrust.*

Heap, s. *ṭop, kat, rāsha, rash.* (all of a-) *sūṭ-būṭ, aluwal, yak-lakhta.*

Heap, v.a. *tapal, ṭolawul, ḍera-ī-, kat-, etc. k.*

Hear, v.a. *āwredal; ghwag bāsal—yastdl, -nīwul,* or *-kegdal—kekkhodal.* (attend) *nghwatal.* (over-) *ghwag tsāral.*

Hearer, s. *āwredūnkai, sām'i.*

Hearing, s. *āwredana, sim'a.*

Hearsay, s. *āwredali khabara, afwāh.*

Heart, s. *zṛah, dil.* (-string) *māndara.* (-ache) *zṛah-swai, zṛah-nūl.* (-burning) *mānṛai, mīrtsī.*

Heartily, ad. *pa dwāṛo stargo.*

Hearty, a. *takṛah, tāzah, rogh-joṛ; zrah-war.*

Heat, s. *tod-wālai, todūkha, garmī, tāw.*

Heat, v.a. *todawul.* (warm) *taṛam k.*

Heathen, s. *but parast, kāfir.*

Heave, v.a. *khejawul; āchawul, ghurzawul, wīshtal.*

Heaven, s. *āsmān, falak; jannat, bihikkht.*

Heaviness, s. *drūnd-wālai, dranāwai.*

Heavy, a. *drūnd.*

Hedge, s. *bāra, shpol, keṛa, jal.*

Hedgehog, s. *shīshkai, zigkai.*

Heed, s. *parwā, fikr, poh, pahm, khabar.*

Heedful, a. *khabar-dār, baidār, hokkhyār.*

Heel, s. *pūnda* or *pūnḍa-ī.* (-of a door) *chūṛ.*

Heifer, s. *skhwandāra, skhwandarkoṭa-ī.*

Height, s. *ūchat-wālai, hask-wālai.*

Heighten, v.a. *ūchatawul; ziyātawul.*

Heinous, a. *bad-sakht, bad-balā.*

Heir, s. *wāris, ḥaqq-dār.* (-less) *lā-wāris.*

Hell, s. *doghakkh* or *dozakh, jahannum, saqar.*

Hellebore, s. *kūtkī.*

Helm, s. *sīngāwanṛ, chapa.*

Helmet, s. *khol.*

Help, s. *madad, komak, pushtī, mrasta; tsāra, 'ilāj.* v.a. *madad-, etc. k.* or *-war-kawul; tsāra-, etc. laral.*

Helper, s. *madad-gār, komakī, yār, mal.*

Helpless, a. *lā-tsār, nā-tuwān, 'ājiz.* (-from wounds) *zmol, zam-zmolai, kand-kapaṛ.*
Helter-skelter, a. *gaḍ-waḍ, lānde-bānde.*
Hem, s. *laman, jānja-ī; trāṭa, maghzai.* (corner of a dress) *pitskai.*
Hem, v.a. *ganḍal, bezal.*
Hemp, s. *sanr.*
Hen, s. *chirga.*
Hence, ad. *la de na, dzaka; la de dzāya.* in. *lire! lire sha!*
Henceforth, ad. *wṛānde.*
Her, pr. *hagha, dā, da, de, di.*
Herald, s. *jār-chī, munadī kawūnkai.*
Herb, s. *būṭai.* (pot-) *sāg.*
Herbage, s. *wākkhah, giyāh.*
Herd, s. *ramma, ṭol, ṭolai, ṭolgai, paṛk.* (-of cows) *gāhar, gohār.* (-of buffaloes) *goram.*
Herdsman, s. (-of oxen) *gāhū, ghobah.* (-of buffaloes) *gūjar, mekkhbah.* (-of sheep, etc.) *gaḍbah, shpūn.*
Here, ad. *dalta, dale, hīsta.*
Hereafter, ad. *la de na wrusto, biyā.*
Hereby, ad. *pa de, la de na.*
Hereditary, a. *mīrāṣī.* (-tenant) *mīrāṣ khor.*
Herein, ad. *pa de kkhke.*
Heresy, s. *rāfiẓī-tob, darogh.*
Heretic, s. *rāfiẓī, khārijī, darogh-jan.*
Herewith, ad. *de sara.*
Heritage, s. *mīrāṣ* or *mīrāt.*
Hermaphrodite, s. *kkhadzūnak, khunṣā, hijṛai.*
Hermit, s. *gokkha nishīn.*
Hernia, s. *tsūhṛa, khoṭa bād.*
Hero, s. *bahādur, maṛanai, turzan.*
Heroism, s. *maṛanī-tob, tūrzan-tob.*
Heron, s. *baglai.*
Hesitate, v.n. *wṛānde-wrusto ked., stāra pre-watal, shakk-man-, wiswāsī-, andekkh-man-,* etc. *ked.*
Heterodox, a. *khārijī; mukhālif.*
Heterogeneous, a. *gaḍ-waḍ, argajah; mu-khālif, 'aks, nā-munāfiq.*
Hew, v.a. *prekawul* or *prekṛal, kūtal; tsau-rang k.*
Hiccough, s. *haṭkai.*
Hidden, a. *puṭ, pinham.*
Hide, v.n. *puṭedal.* v.a. *puṭawul.*
Hide, s. *tsarman, poṭ, tsarm.*
Hideous, a. *bad, nā-kārah, haul-nāk.*
Hie, v.n. *drūmal, za-ar* or *zir-, gaṛandai-,* etc. *tlal—lāṛal.*
High, a. *ūchat, hask; lwaṛ; dang.*
Highlander, s. *rohīlai, kohistānai, da ghra saṛai, ghartsanai.*
Highly, ad. *ḍer, nihāyat, be-shāna.*
Highminded, a. *kibr-jan, bādī.*
Highness, s. *ūchat-wālai, hask-wālai; lwaṛ-tiyā; dang-wālai.* (title) *ḥaẓrat.*
Highway, s. *bādshāhī lār, saṛak.*
Highwayman, s. *lār wahūnkai, shūk-mār, rāh-zan, ghal.*
Hilarity, s. *kkhādī, khūsh-ḥālī, khandā, mastī.*
Hill, s. *ghar, koh.* (low spur of-) *pukkhta, kha-aṭ.*
Hillock, s. *ghunḍa-ī, ḍera-ī, taraqqa-ī, pota-ī.*
Hilt, s. *mūṭai, lāstai, qabẓa.*
Hinder, v.a. *haṭālawul, kariyābawul, man'a k.*
Hinderance, s. *haṭāl, kariyāb, āṛ, ḥarakat.*
Hindermost, a. *wrustai, wrustanai, akhīr, pastanai, ākhirīn.*
Hinge, s. *qabẓa, chūṛ.*
Hint, s. *ishārat, kināyat.*
Hip, s. *ṭuṭa, ḍūḍa.* (-bone) *kkhna.*
Hire, s. *ajr, ujrat, miḥnat, mazdūrī, kreha.*
Hireling, s. *mazdūr.*
Hiss, v.a. (as snake, etc.) *pakh wahal.* (as meat on the fire) *sakkha-, dzadz-,* etc. *wahal.*
History, s. *tawārīkh, rawāyat, taẓkira.*
Hit, v.a. *wahal, lagawul.* v.n. *jangedal, lagedal.*
Hither, ad. *dalta, rāhīsta, de khwā, de palaw.*
Hitherto, ad. *tar osa, tar osa pore.*

Hive, s. *kor, khūna.* (bees-) *gabīna, garbīnai.* (wasps-) *kkhor.* (ants-) *megatūn.*
Hoar, a. *sperah, brag, spīn.*
Hoard, v.a. *tolawul, gatal, ambār-, jam'a-,* etc. *k.*
Hoard, s. *jam'a, panga, saga, anbār, māya.*
Hoarse, a. *bog, dad.*
Hobble, v.n. *gudedal, pa kharpotso tal—lāral; taparedal.*
Hocus-pocus, s. *chal·wal, jādū, kod.*
Hodge-podge, a. *gad·wad, arang·barang argajah.*
Hodiernal, a. *nananai.*
Hoe, s. *kodāla-ī, saspor, sakkhsora, kasha-ī.* (small) *rambai.*
Hog, s. *kharbīshoe, sarkūzai.* (wild-) *sodar, matah.*
Hoist, v.a. *khejawul, ūchatawul, porta k.*
Hold, v.a. *nīwul.* (take) *ākhistal.* (-fast) *klak nīwul, tīngawul.* (contain) *dzāyawul.* (consider) *ganral.* (keep-) *sātal, sambālāwul, khundī k.* v.n. (remain) *osedal, pātedal.* (cling) *nkkhatal.* (contain) *dzā-edal.* (connect) *lagedal.*
Holder, s. *ākhistūnai; sātandoe, sātūnkai; dzāyūnkai, larūnkai.* (in comp.) *-dār, -gīr, -khor.*
Hole, s. *sūra, sūrai.* (pit) *doghal, tūbkai* or *tublai, kanda.* (opening) *khula, swam* or *spam.*
Holiday, s. *akhtar, 'īd.*
Hollo, in. *o! ai! yā! yāe!* v.a. *nāra wahal.*
Hollow, a. *ta-ash* or *t-ish, khālī; dad, kāwāk; khushai.*
Hollow, s. *tahana, jawara; kanda, kas.*
Holy, a. *pāk; nek, pārsā.*
Holy Ghost, s. *rūhu-l-quds, ruh·ullah.*
Homage, s. *tāb'i·dārī, salāmī.*
Home, s. *borjal, kor, dzāe, astoga, mīshta, tikāo.* (country) *watan, mulk, wilāyat, dzāe·dzāegai.* (-made) *koranai, khānagī.*

Homeless, a. *be·kor, dar·ba·dar, khāwre·pa·sar.*
Homely, a. *khamsor, sādah; lwār.*
Homogeneous, a. *barābar, yo shān, yo jins.*
Hone, s. *belāw, belho, barjo, psān.*
Honest, a. *rikkhtīnai, nek, karah, sam.*
Honesty, s. *rikkhtīn·tob, nekī, rāstī.*
Honey, s. *shāt* or *shahad.* (-comb) *gabīna.*
Honeycombed, a. *zang wahalai, chinjī khwuralai.*
Honour, s. *nang, nūm, 'izzat, makh, abrū.*
Honourable, a. *nang·yālai, 'izzat·nāk; nūm·war; makharwar.*
Hood, s. *topa·ī, khola-ī, kulāh.* (woman's-) *parūnai, oranai.* (snake's-) *chaja.*
Hoof, s. *sum.* (cloven-) *swa, kkhongarai.*
Hook, s. *kunda.* (flesh-) *nukhakkh.*
Hoop, s. *chambar, chak.*
Hoot, v.a. *chighawul.*
Hop, v.a. *tskharwul, tskhe k., tīndak-, top-,* etc. *wahal.*
Hope, s. *umed, āsra; khal.* v.a. *umed-,* etc *laral.*
Hopeful, a. *umed·wār.*
Hopeless, a. *nā·umed.*
Horde, s. *ulas, tapa.*
Horizon, s. *ufuq.*
Horizontal, a. *prot, mlāst, sam.*
Horn, s. *kkhkar, kkhākh.*
Horned, a. *kkhkarawar, kkhākh·dār.*
Hornet, s. *danbara, dandāra, ghālbūza.*
Horrible, a. *bad sakht; kagalai, ghāndah; khof-, haul-, tars-,* etc. *-nāk.*
Horripilate, v.n. *ghūna zīgedal.*
Horror, s. *wera* or *yera, tor, tars.*
Horse, s. *ās.* (pack-) *yābū, tatū.* (ambling-) *yarghah.* (-dealer) *dallāl.* (-breaker) *chābuk sawār.* (-man) *spor* or *swor.* (-shoe) *nāl.*
Horticulture, s. *bāghwānī, gul karana.*
Hose, s. *jorāba, moza.* (leather) *mūsa-ī.*

Hospitable, a. *melmah·dost, ḍoḍa-ī·mār.*
Hospital, s. *bīmār·khāna ; langar·khāna.*
Hospitality, s. *melmastiyā.*
Host, s. *korbah, melmah·dost ; meṛah, tsakkh-tan ; lakkhkar, ganr·khalq.*
Hostage, s. *yarghamāl.*
Hostess, s. *korbana, merman.*
Hostile, a. *dukkhman, mukhālif.*
Hostility, s. *dukkhmanī, badī, 'adāwat.*
Hot, a. *tod, garm.*
Hound, s. *tāzī-* or *kkhkārī spai.* v.a. *spī pase k.*
Hour, s. *sā'at, gaṛai.*
Hourly, ad. *har sā'at, sā'at pa sā'at.*
House, s. *kor, khāna.* (storied-) *mānṛa-ī, angaṛ.* (premises) *ḥawela-ī, mena.* (-holder) *korbah, dawtarī.* (-wife) *korbana, merman.* (-keeping) *kormāna.* (-hold) *ṭabaṛ, kor, khāndān, khān·o·mān, kaḍa.* (-tax) *lūgī·tāwān.* (-ruins) *kanḍar.* (-rent) *kreha, tāwān.* (-breaker) *ghal, gūṭ mātawūnkai, kanḍar kawūnkai.* (court of a-) *gholai.* (side of a-) *chana.*
Hovel, s. *jūngaṛa, kaḍala, manah.*
Hover, v.n. *tsrapedal, rapedal ; girzedal.*
How, ad. *tsanga? tsa ranga? pa tsa shān?*
However, ad. *walekin, wale, mangar.*
Howl, v.a. *ghapal, angolā k., nāra wahal.*
Hubbub, s. *zwag·zwūg, chagh·chugh, nārc·sūre, hāṛa·hūṛa, dagh·dagha.*
Hue, s. *rang, laun.* (-and cry) *hūhā.*
Hug, v.a. *ghāṛa·ghaṛa-ī k.*
Huge, a. *loe, ghaṭ, star ; nāpaṛ, khṛīs.*
Hum, v.n. *bonṛedal.* v.a. *zwag k.*
Hum, s. *bonṛa.* (conversation) *gangosai, skālwah* or *kkhkālwah.*
Human, a. *basharī, insānī, nāsūt.* (-being) s. *wagaṛai, gawai ; bashar, insān.*
Humane, a. *nek·khoe, mulā-im, raḥm·dil.*
Humanity, s. *saṛī·tob, ādmiyat, insāniyat ; nek·khaṣlatī, mom·dilī.*
Humble, a. *'ājiz, nā·tsīz, gharīb, kamīn.*
Humbly, ad. *'ājizī sara.*
Humbug, s. *allam·ghallam, shkhaṛā.*
Humid, a. *lūnd ; nam·nāk, zyam·nāk, naw-jan.*
Humidity, s. *lūnd·wālai ; zyam, nam, naw.*
Humiliation, s. *'ājizī; gharībī, nā·tsīzī ; spuk·tiyā, makh·torī.*
Humility, s. *'ājizī, gharībī, nā·tsīzī, kamīn·tob.*
Humorous, a. *ṭoqī, washtī, khandā·bāz.*
Humour, s. *khwā, khoe, mizāj.* (matter) *ziwa, zahūb, khīrai, rīm.* (fun) *washta, ṭoqa.* (moisture) *zyam, nam, naw.*
Humour, v.a. *nāzawul, nāz wṛal, khāṭir k.*
Hump, s. *kūb* or *kwab.* (-backed) *kūbai, chūghai.*
Hundred, s. *sal* or *sil.* (more than one-) *saw.* (one hundred) *sil.* (two, three, four, etc. hundred) *dwah-, dre-, tsalor-,* etc., *-sawa.*
Hunger, s. *lwaga, liwāl·tob.*
Hungry, a. *wagai, liwāl, naghlānd.*
Hunt, v.a. *kkhkār k.* (search) *laṭawul, shanal.*
Hurl, v.a. *ghurzawul, wīshtal, āchawul.*
Hurrah, in. *shābāsh! āparīn!*
Hurricane, s. *sīla-ī, ṭūfān.*
Hurry, v.a. *talwār-, talwal-, jaltī-, gaṛandai-,* etc. *k.*
Hurt, s. *khūg, zakhm, parhār ; tāwān, nuqṣān, ziyān.* a. *zakhmī, parhār·jalai, jobal.* v.a. *khūgawul, jobalawul, zahīrawul ; tā-wān-, nuqṣān-,* etc. *k.*
Hurtful, a. *tāwānī, ziyān·kār, nuqṣānī ; muzirr, wrān·kār, stūkh.*
Husband, s. *meṛah, tsakkhtan, khāwand.*
Husbandman, s. *zamīndār, kikkht·gar.* (hired-) *charekār, dihqān.*
Husbandry, s. *kar, kikkht·garī, zamīndārī.* (thrift) *kormāna, khāna·darī ; sātana, bachawūna.*

Hush, in. *chip! chup!*
Husk, s. *būr, poṭ, baṭ; sūṛī, būṭ·sūṛī.*
Hut, s. *jūngaṛa, kuḍalī, tsapar, manah.*
Hyacinth, s. *nargis, kangas.* (colour) *sausan.*
Hyena, s. *kog, sar·ṭīṭai, kaftār.*
Hypochondriasis, s. *khapaqān, saudā-ī.*
Hypocrisy, s. *makr, riyā.*
Hypocrite, s. *makrai, makr·jan, riyā·kār.*
Hypothesis, s. *qiyās, rāe, andāza, gumān.*
Hysterics, s. *pariyān, da pariyāno ghoṭa.*

I.

I, pr. *zah, khpul; mā.*
Ice, s. *kangal, yakh.*
Idea, s. *khiyāl, rāe, fikr, poh, and.*
Identical, a. *be·dū, hūbahū, kaṭ·maṭ, pa ṭakī.*
Identity, s. *ṣūrat, shān; pejandgalī; yo·wālai.*
Idiom, s. *iṣṭilāḥ, iṣṭilāḥī khabara, chalana.*
Idiomatic, a. *iṣṭilāḥī, chalanī, rawājī.*
Idiot, s. *gedī, kam·'aql, nā·dān, nā·poh.*
Idle, a. *wazgār, khālī, be·kār.* (lazy) *nā·rāst, sust, laṭ.* (useless) *'abaṣ, be·fā-ida.* (trifling) *be·hūdah, wuch·puch, nā·kārah.*
Idleness, s. *nā·rāstī, sustī, laṭ·wālai.*
Idol, s. *būt, tsera.*
Idolater, s. *but parast, mushrik.*
Idolatry, s. *but parastī, shirk.*
Idolize, v.a. *parastī k.* (admire) v.n. *gro-hedal.*
If, c. *ki, agar.* (as-) *laka chī, ghūnde, ganṛa, goyā.*
Ignite, v.n. *baledal, swal.* v.a. *balawul, sedzal, or pōre k., swadzawul.*
Ignoble, a. *lānde·zāt, kam·aṣl, bad·aṣl, spuk, pāsū, bad·zāt.*
Ignominious, a. *ruswā, bad·nūm, nā·kārah, bad.*
Ignominy, s. *bad·namūsī, sharmindagī, ruswā-ī, makh·torī.*
Ignorance, s. *nā·dānī, be·khabarī, nā·pohī, jel.*
Ignorant, a. *nā·dān, nā·poh, jāhil; be·khabar.*
Ignorantly, ad. *nā·dānista, be·khabara.*
Ill, a. *bad, nā·kārah, nā·sāz, nā·kkhanai, kharāb.* (sick) *nā·rogh, nā·joṛ, randzūr, bīmār.*
Illegal, a. *nā·rawā, ḥarām.*
Illegitimate, a. *ḥarāmī, ḥarāmūnai, ḥarām zādah.*
Illiberal, a. *shūm, shūm·shaghāl, bakhīl.*
Illiterate, a. *nā·lwustai, jāhil, ummī.*
Ill-natured, a. *bad·khoe, bakhīl, sūṭ·būṭ.*
Illness, s. *nā·joṛ·tiyā, nā·rogh·tiyā, āzār, bīmārī.*
Illtimed, a. *be·wakht, be·ṭāng.*
Illumination, s. *rokkhnā-ī, raṇrā-ī; chirāgh·dān.*
Illuminate, v.a. *rokkhān-, raṇrā-,* etc. *k., chirāgh·dān k.*
Illusion, s. *khām khiyāl, ghulatī, fareb.*
Illustrate, v.a. *kkhayal—kkhowul, tsargandawul, kkhkārah k., bayānawul, tamṣīl k.*
Illustration, s. *bayān, kkhowūna, miṣāl.*
Illustrious, a. *nūm·war, nāmdār, nāmar.*
Im-, negative prefix. (in comp.) *be-, nā-, kam-.*
Image, s. *but, tsera; ṣūrat, shakl.*
Imaginary, a. *khiyālī, wahmī, gumānī.*
Imagination, s. *khiyāl, qiyās, fikr, gumān, rāe.*
Imagine, v.a. *qiyās-, fikr-,* etc. *k.*
Imbecile, a. *kam·'aql, nā·tuwān, palwanḍ.*
Imbibe, v.a. *tskkhal* or *skal, dzbekkhal, rawdal; wuchawul.*
Imbue, v.a. *rangawul; khaṛob k.; ḍakawul.*
Imitate, v.a. *pairawī k., naql k., swāng k.*
Imitator, s. *pairaw; nāqil; swāngai.*
Immaculate, a. *be·gunāh, be·'aib, pāk ṣāf, spīn·spetsalai, nog.*
Immaterial, a. *be·wujūd, nābūd; khushai, nā·kār.*
Immature, a. *ūm, khām, kachah, umghalan, nīma·khwā, nīmgaṛai.*

Immediately, ad. *os, pa de sā'at, sam da lāsa, pa ṭakī, dam dar ḥāl.*
Immemorial, a. *la yād na bāhir, da yāda ter.*
Immense, a. *be-ḥadd, be-nihāyat, be-shān*; *loe, ghaṭ, star, bashpaṛ, nāpaṛ.*
Immensely, ad. *be-qiyāsa, be-shāna, be-kacha,* etc.
Immerse, v.a. *ḍūbawul, gharqawul, ghūpa-, ghoṭa-,* etc. *narkawul.*
Imminent, a. *nijdai, rātlūnai, prewatūnai.*
Immoderate, a. *be-ḥisāb, be-kach, be-andāzah*; *nā-parhez-gār.*
Immodest, a. *be-sharm, be-ḥayā, be-makh.*
Immodesty, s. *be-sharmi, be-ḥayā-tob, be-makh-tob.*
Immolate, v.a. *qurbān-, ṣadqa-, zār-,* etc. *k.* (-oneself) v.n. *qurbān-,* etc. *ked.*
Immoral, a. *bad-kār, bad-kirdār, ḥarām-kār.*
Immortal, a. *be-marg, jāwīdān.*
Immortality, s. *baqā, jāwīdānī.*
Immortalize, v.a. *jāwīdān k., pātai k.* v.n. *pāedal, jāwīdān ked., pātai ked.*
Immoveable, a. *maẓbūṭ, qā-im, pāedūnai.*
Immunity, s. *khalāṣī, āzādī, najāt.*
Immutable, a. *be-tabdīl.*
Impair, v.a. *kamawul, spukawul, wrānawul.*
Impart, v.a. *pohawul, khabarawul*; *warkawul.*
Impartial, a. *rāst-kār, 'ādil, rikkhtīnai, ṣādiq, niyāw kawūnkai, be-mrasta.*
Impassable, a. *be-lār, be-gūdar, band.*
Impatient, a. *be-ṣabr, be-zgham*; *jalt, tund, tez.*
Impeach, v.a. *d'awa k., tuhmat pore k.*
Impede, v.a. *haṭālawul, kariyābawul, nkkhlawul, man'a k.*
Impediment, s. *haṭāl, kariyāb, āṛ, nkkhatai.*
Impel, v.a. *zoral, tezal, zghalawul, chalawul.*
Impend, v.n. *dzwaṛandedal, nijdai rasedal.*
Impending, a. *nijdai*; *dzwaṛand.*
Impenitent, a. *nā-toba-gār, nā-pakkhemān.*
Imperative, a. *ḥukmī, farẓī*; *amr.*
Imperceptible, a. *puṭ, nā-m'alūm.*
Imperfect, a. *nīmgaṛai, ūm, nīma-khwā.*
Imperial, a. *bādshāhī*: (hair on chin) *charekār.*
Imperious, a. *kibr-jan, khāntamā, khpul-sar.*
Imperishable, a. *pāedār, qā-im, lā-zawāl, pātedūnai, be-marg.*
Impertinent, a. *be-dzāe, be-adab, wītakai.*
Impervious, a. *klak*; *ṭing*; *be-lār, band.*
Impetuous, a. *tund, tez, gaṛandai, jalt.*
Impetus, s. *zor, quwat.*
Impious, a. *be-dīn, kāfir.*
Implacable, a. *be-raḥm, sakht-dil, kāṇrai-zṛah, nā-pīrzo da pakhulā, bad-dukkhman.*
Implant, v.a. *khakkhawul, njatal.*
Implement, s. *kālai, hatiyār, sāz.*
Implicate, v.a. *nkkhlawul, gaḍawul*; *malgarai-, sharīk-,* etc., *k.*
Implicit, a. *kāmil, pūrah, tamām.*
Implore, v.a. *minnat-, d'uā-,* etc. *k.*
Imply, v.a. *m'anā-, dalīl-,* etc. *laral, nakkha-, ishārat-,* etc. *k.*
Import, s. *m'anā*; *da pradī mulk māl.*
Import, v.a. *da pradī mulk māl khpul waṭan ta rāwṛal.*
Important, a. *drūnd, grān, ẓarūr.*
Importune, v.a. *taqāẓā k., lagiyā ghokkhtal.*
Impose, v.a. *āchawul, lagawul, kegdal.* (upon) *ghulawul, ṭagal, fareb-,* etc. *warkawul.*
Impost, s. *tāwān, sāw, bāj*; *maḥṣūl, nāgha.*
Impostor, s. *ṭag, chal-bāz, bāna-khor, farebī, darghal, sādū, ḥīla-bāz.*
Imposture, s. *ṭagī, ghulat, fareb, droh.*
Impotent, a. *nā-tuwān, 'ājiz*; *nā-mard.*
Impoverish, v.a. *khwār-, gharīb-,* etc. *k.*
Impracticable, a. *na-kedana, na-shwūnkai.*
Imprecate, v.a. *kkhera-, n'alat-, bad-d'uā-,* etc. *k.*
Impregnate, v.a. *ḍakawul*; *blārba k.*
Impress, v.a. *ṭāpa-, chāpa-,* etc. *k.,* or *-wahal*; *kkhke-manḍal.* (-on the mind) *tākīd k.*

Impression, s. *ṭāpa, chāpa*; *nakkha, dāgh*; *gumān, khiyāl, fikr*.
Imprint, v.a. *ṭāpa-, chāpa-*, etc. *k.*; *dāghawul*.
Imprison, v.a. *qaid-, band-*, etc. *k*.
Improbable, a. *la 'aqla lire* or *-bāhir*.
Improper, a. *nā·munāsib, na·kkhanai, nā·sāz, nā·rawā, nā·kār, kānah*.
Improve, v.a. *joṛawul, raghawul*. v.n. *joṛedal, raghedal*.
Improvement, s. *kkhegaṛa, joṛ·tiya*.
Improvident, a. *be·tadbīr, kotāh·andesh*.
Imprudent, a. *be·khabar, be·fikr*.
Impudent, a. *be·adab, gustākh*; *be·ḥayā*.
Impulse, s. *zor, quwat, ḥarakat*.
Impulsive, a. *tund, tez, gaṛandai, talwalai*.
Impure, a. *nā·pāk, palīt, murdār*.
Impute, v.a. *lagawul, pore k*.
In, p. *danana, kkhke, pa kkhke*.
In-, negative prefix. (in comp.) *be-, lā-, nā-*.
Inability, s. *nā·tuwānī, lā·tsārī, 'ājizī*.
Inaccessible, a. *nā·mūndanai*.
Inaccurate, a. *ghalaṭ, nā·durust*.
Inactive, a. *sust, laṭ, shadal*; *be·kār*; *proṭ*.
Inadequate, a. *kam, la-ag*; *nā·qābil*.
Inadmissible, a. *nā·qabūl, band, man'ah*.
Inadvertent, a. *be·khabar, be·fikr*.
Inanimate, a. *be·dzān, be·sāh, muṛ*.
Inapplicable, a. *nā·munāsib, nā·sāz*.
Inattentive, a. *be·parwā, be·khabar*.
Inaugurate, v.a. *kkhkenawul, wudrawul*.
Inauspicious, a. *bad·bakht shūm·bakht, asī*.
Incalculable, a. *be·shumār, be·ḥisāb, be·kach*.
Incantation, s. *jādū, koḍa, siḥr, dam, hūda, pāṛ, mantar, du'ā, t'awīz*.
Incapable, a. *nā·qābil, nā·tuwān, be·was*.
Incautious, a. *be·tadbīr, nā·khabar·dār*.
Incendiary, s. *shūsha-ī mār*, or *lagawūnkai*, or *pore kawūnkai*.
Incense, s. *'ūd*. (-dish) *majmir*.
Incense, v.a. *khapah k., kaṛawul*.
Incentive, s. *sabab, bā'is*; *lamsūn*.

Incessant, a. *lagiyā, mudām, hamesh*.
Incessantly, ad. *har sā'at, sā'at pa sā'at*.
Incest, s. *mor-, khor-, lūr-*, etc. *ghodī*.
Incident, s. *wāqi'a, ḥādiṣa, chal, wārida*.
Incidentally, ad. *nā·gumāna, nā·gahāna*.
Incision. s. *tsīra, zakhm, parhār*.
Incite, v.a. *lamsawul*; *pārawul*; *agayal*.
Inclination, s. *khwā, mīna, zṛah, shauq*.
Incline, v.a. *khwā ta k., mayan k, zṛah lagawul*; *ṭīṭawul*. v.n. *khwā ta ked.*, etc.
Include, v.a. *shāmil-, yo·dzāe-, dākhil-*, etc. *k.*; *dzāyawul*.
Incog, ad. *pa puṭa*.
Incoherent, a. *be·joṛ, be·hūdah, be·khūd*.
Income, s, *āmad, ḥāṣil*.
Incommode, v.a. *taklīf warkawul*.
Incomparable, a. *be·siyāl, lā·ṣānī, be·miṣāl*.
Incompatible, a. *mukhālif*.
Incompetent, a. *nā·qābil, nā·tuwān*.
Incomplete, a. *nīmgaṛai, nā·tamām*.
Incomprehensible, **Inconceivable**. a. } *be·qiyās, shandah, la 'aqla lire* or *-bāhir*.
Inconclusive, a. *be·iṣbāt, be·dallīl*; *nā·zbād, nā·ṣābit*.
Incongruous, a. *be·joṛ, nā·sāz, be·ṭikānah, be·hūdah, bar·khilāf, nā·muwāfiq*.
Inconsiderate, a. *be·liḥāẓ, be·parwā, be·ghaur. be·fikr, be·tadbīr, ghāfil*.
Inconsistent, a. *be·jor*, etc. (*v.* Incongruous).
Inconsolable, a. *gham·jan, nūl·jan, be·tasallī*.
Inconstant, a. *nā·pāedār, nā·qalār, be·wafā*.
Incontestible, a. *ṣābit, zbād, lā·dzawāb, qaṭ'a-ī*.
Incontinent, a. *be·parhez, bad·laman, bad·parhez*.
Incontrovertible, a. *zbād*, etc. (*v.* Incontestible).
Inconvenience, s. *be·ārāmī, rabaṛ, taklīf, harj*.
Inconvenient, a. *be·dzāe, nā·kārah, nā·munāsib*.

Incorporate, v.a. *gaḍawul, yo·dzāe k., laṛal.*
Incorrect, a. *nā·durust, ghalaṭ, darogh·jan.*
Incorrigible, a. *bad·sakht, hets da kkhah, lā·'ilāj.*
Incorruptible, a. *be·fanā, pāedār.*
Increase, v.a. *ziyātawul, wadānawul, ḍerawul.* v.n. *ziyātedal, wadānedal, ḍeredal.*
Increase, s. *ziyāt·wālai, wadānī, ḍer·wālai.*
Incredible, a. *bē·i'tibār, shandah.*
Incrust, v.a. *lewawul.*
Incubate, v.n. *kuṛaka kkhkenāstal; pakhedal.*
Inculcate, v.a. *pohawul, pahmawul, tākīd k.; kkhayal—kkhowul.*
Incumbent, a. *farẓ, lāzim, wājib, ẓarūr.*
Incur, v.n. *pīrzo-, lā-iq-,* etc. *ked.* v.a. *rāwṛal, lagawul, āchawul, ākhistal.*
Incurable, a. *lā·'ilāj, lā·dawā, lā·tsār.*
Incursion, a. *chapāo, dāṛa·dopa, hapa·dapa, tākht·tārāj, halla.*
Indebted, a. *qarẓ·dār, porawuṛai.*
Indecent, a. *pūch, chūnkai; be·ḥayā, be·nang; nā·lā-iq, nā·munāsib; be·adab, be·pardah.*
Indeed, in. *rikkhtiyā! khudāe·go! āyā! he!* ad. *haḍo, yara, kho.*
Indefatigable, a. *miḥnatī, sā'ī, kokshikshī.*
Indefinite, a. *be·ṭikānah, be·kach.*
Indemnity, s. *badal, tāwān, nāgha.* (-for blood) *diyat.* (-for abduction) *swara.*
Indenture, s. *iqrār·nāma, 'ahd·nāma.*
Independent, a. *khpul·sar, da khpul wāk khāwand; yāghī, sar·kakkh.*
Indescribable, a. *lā·bayān.*
Index, s. *nakkha, nikkhān; dalīl.* (-of a book) *fihrist.* (-finger) *kkhowūnai; mis·wāka gūta.*
India, s. *hind, hindūstān.* (language of-) *hindko.* (Mussalmān native of-) *hindkai.* (Pagan native of-) *hindū.*
Indian-corn, s. *jwār, ghaṭ jwār, maka-ī.*
Indicate, v.a. *kkhayal—kkhowul.*
Indication, s. *kkhowūna; nakkha; dalīl.*
Indifferent, a. *be·parwā, be·khabar; khushai.*
Indifferently, ad. *hase, be·parwā-ī sara.*
Indigent, a. *khwār, ḥājat·man, muḥtāj, muflis.*
Indigestion, s. *bad·haẓmī, agheṛ, aṭer.*
Indignant, a. *khapah, qahr·jan, qahr·nāk.*
Indignity, s. *spuk·tiyā, makh·torī, sharmin·dagī.*
Indigo, s. (-plant) *wasma.* (-dye) *nīl.* (-maker) *nīl·gar.*
Indirect, a. *kog, natskan, girzedalai.*
Indirectly, ad. *pa trats; pa chal sara; pa wasīle sara.*
Indiscreet, a. *be·tadbīr, be·sha'ūr, kam·'aql.*
Indiscriminate, a. *gaḍ·waḍ, aluwal.*
Indispensable, a. *ẓarūr, lāzim, wājib; farẓ.*
Indisposed, a. *nā·khwakkh, nā·rāẓ; nā·rogh, nā·joṛ.*
Indisputable, a. *lā·radd, qaṭ'a-ī, yaqīnī.*
Indistinct, a. *dund; puṭ; nā·sāf.*
Individual, a. *biyal, judā, mufrid, yawādzai.* s. *tan, kas, saṛai, wagaṛai, gawai.*
Individuality, s. *nātka-ī, yawādzai·wālai, yo·wālai, biyal·wālai.*
Individually, a. *biyal·biyal, yo·yo, judā·judā.*
Indolent, a. *sust, laṭ, nā·rāst, shalaṭ.*
Indubitable, a. *be·shakk, be·shubha, be·gumān.*
Induce, v.a. *lamsawul, targhīb warkawul.* (bring on) *rāwṛal, paidā k., khejawul, porta k.; 'amal-, pāzah-,* etc. *k.*
Indulge, v.a. *nāzawul, khāṭir k.; pālal, nmāndzal; bakkhal, mihrbāngī k.*
Indulgent, a. *mihrbān, khāṭir·dār, nāz wṛūnkai, narm, bakkhūnkai.*
Indurate, v.n. *klakedal, ṭīngedal.*
Industrious, a. *miḥnatī, kokshikshī.*
Industry, s. *miḥnat, kokshiksh, mushaqqat.*
Inebriate, v.a. *nasha warkawul, be·khūd-, be·hokkh-,* etc. *k.; mast k.*
Ineffable, a. *lā·bayān, be·bayān.*

Inefficacious, a. *be·pāzah, nā·kārah, 'abas, be·tāsīr, be·asr, khushai, spuk.*
Inequality, s. *lwaṛ·jawar·tiyā, zīg·wālai, nā·hawār·tiyā.*
Inert, a. *be·ḥarakat; be·pāzah; sust, laṭ.*
Inestimable, a. *be·bahā, be·qīmat; grān.*
Inevitable, a. *muqarrar, qaṭ'a·ī.*
Inexcusable, a. *be·'uzr, be·ḥujjat, lā·dzawāb.*
Inexhaustible, a. *be·pāyān, be·ḥadd, be·nihāyat. be·and, be·ḥisāb.*
Inexorable, a. *sakht, nā·tars, kāṇrai·zṛah.*
Inexpedient, a. *be·dzāe, nā·munāsib, nā·kkhanai, nā·sāz.*
Inexperienced, a. *nā·wāqif, nā·āmokhtah, nā·'ādat, nā·āshnā, nā·balad.*
Inexpert, a. *kam·ustāz, be·hunar, kachah.*
Inexplicable, a. *lā·bayān, nā·m'alūm.*
Infallible, a. *nā·khaṭā, qādir, nā·ghalaṭ.*
Infamous, a. *bad, bad·namūs, makh·tor.*
Infamy, s. *bad·namūsī, makh·torī, ruswā-ī.*
Infancy, s. *māshūm-,* or *m'aṣūm·wālai, bachai-, tandai-,* etc. *-tob.*
Infant, s. *māshūm, tandai, bachai, kachoṭai, waṛkoṭai, kamkoṭai, wṛūkai, pa-ī·rawai.*
Infantry, s. *piyādah, mlā·taṛ; palṭan.*
Infatuated, a. *lewanai, fareftah, khushai.*
Infatuation, s. *lewantob, fareftagī, khushī·tob.*
Infect, v.a. *bangawul, boṇrawul, gazak k., wahal, lagawul.*
Infer, v.n. *pohedal.* v.a. *gaṇral.*
Inference, s. *khulāṣa, ḥāṣil, natīja.*
Inferior, a. *kam·pāyah, kam·aṣl, kamtar, spuk, adnā; lāndai, kūz, lar, kkhkatanai.*
Infernal, a. *doghakkhī, jahannamī.*
Infidel, s. *kāfir, be·dīn, be·īmān, be·islām.*
Infidelity, s. *kufr, be·dīnī, be·īmānī.*
Infinite, a. *be·nihāyat, be·ḥadd, be·and, be·shān, be·pāyān, be·kach, be·shumār.*
Infirm, a. *ṭap, nā·tawān, kamzor, ẓa'īf.*
Inflame, v.a. *balawul, swadzawul.* v.n. *baledal, sedzal, swal.*
Inflammation, s. *swai.*
Inflate, v.a. *pūkal, paṛsawul.* v.n. *paṛsedal.*
Inflect, v.a. *ṭīṭawul, kagawul, aṛawul, girzawul.*
Inflexible, a. *klak, sakht, zīg, krosand; khpul·sar, sar·kakkh, ṭakaṇrai, hoḍai.*
Inflict, v.a. *pore k., āchawul, rasawul, lagawul, warkawul, kawul, kṛal.*
Influence, s. *pāzah, 'amal, asr tāsīr.*
Influenza, s. *dūmai, nuzla, zukām, sāṛa, yakhnī.* (to have-) *sāṛa-, yakhnī-,* etc. *wahal.*
Inform, v.a. *khabarawul, āgāh k.; pohawul, kkhayal—kkhowul.*
Information, s. *khabar; āgāhī.*
Informer, s. *mukhbir, tsārai.*
Infringe, v.a. *mātawul.*
Infuse, v.a. *āchawul, gaḍawul; lamdawul; damawul, dam warkawul.*
Ingenious, a. *ḥikmatī, hunar·man, pohānd.*
Ingenuous, a. *rikkhtūnai, nek, karah, sādah, spīn, rāst, sam, pāk·ṣāf.*
Inglorious, a. *spuk, halak, be·nām, be·nang.*
Ingraft, v.a. *pewand-, qalam-,* etc. *lagawul; kkhke·manḍal, khakkhawul, lagawul.*
Ingrate, a. *namak·ḥarām, nā·shukr·guzār.*
Ingratiate, v.a. *lār ākhistal* or *-mūndal.*
Ingredient, s. *juz, shai; gaḍa.*
Ingress, s. *nanawātah, dakhl.* (-and egress) *wātah·nanawātah, rāshah·darshah.*
Inhabit, v.a. *astoga-, mīshta-,* etc. *k.* v.n. *osedal, āstedal.* (colonize) v.a. *ābādawul.*
Inhabitant, s. *osedūnkai, astogūnkai.*
Inhale, v.a. *sāh-, dam-,* etc. *pa·porta ākhistal* or *-rākāgal—rākkhkal.*
Inherent, a. *ẕātī, aṣlī, jibillī.*
Inherit, v.a. *mīrāṣ-* or *mīrāt ākhistal* or *-mūndal.* v.n. *mīrāt·khor ked.*
Inheritance, s. *mīrāṣ* or *mīrāt.*
Inheritor, s. *mīrāt khor, wāriṣ.*
Inhospitable, a. *bakhīl, shūm, be·makh.*

Inhuman, a. *nā-insān, nā-tars, be-dard.*

Inimical, a. *mukhālif, bad-niyat, dukkhman, khwā bad.*

Inimitable, a. *be-nazīr, be-miṣāl.*

Iniquitous, a. *bad, nā-ḥaqq, be-inṣāf.*

Iniquity, s. *badī, be-inṣāfī, nā-ḥaqqī, zulm, gunāh, pasāt, wabāl, baza.*

Initial, a. *wṛūnbanai, awwalanai.*

Initiate, v.a. *jārī k., chalawul, rawānawul; āmokhtah k., lagawul, lwalawul; bāolī warkawul.*

Injection, s. *nanayastah; ḥuqna.*

Injudicious, a. *be-tadbīr, be-shu'ūr, nā-lā-iq, nā-kkhanai, nā-kkhāyastah.*

Injunction, s. *ḥukm, amr, kariya, tākīd.* (prohibition) *qadaghan.*

Injure, v.a. *tāwān-, ziyān-,* etc. *rasawul; āzārawul, khūgawul; wrānawul, habatah k.*

Injurious, a. *mozī, muzirr; ziyān-kār, nuqṣānī, tāwānī; randz rasawūnkai, stūkh.*

Injury, s. *nuqṣān, ziyān, tāwān, īzā, zarar.*

Injustice, s. *be-inṣāfī, nā-ḥaqqī, zulm.*

Ink, s. *siyāhī.* (red-) *shangrip.* (-stand) *mashwāṇra-ī.*

Inlaid, a. *jaṛāo.*

Inmate, s. *osedunkai, astogūnkai; hamsāyah, kilai-wāl.*

Inn, s. *srāe, rab...*

Innate, a. *zātī, aṣlī, jibillī.*

Innocent, s. *māshūm* or *m'aṣūm, be-gunāh, pāk ṣāf, spīn, nek, be-quṣūr, be-taqṣīr.*

Innovation, s. *nawai dastūr, -chalan,* etc.

Innumerable, a. *be-shumār, be-ḥisāb.*

Inoculate, v.a. *rag wahal.*

Inoffensive, a. *be-gunāh, be-quṣūr; gharīb.*

Inordinate, a. *be-andāzah, be-kach, be-ḥadd.*

Inquietude, s. *nā-qalār-tiyā, be-ārām-tiyā.*

Inquire, v.a. *pukkhtedal, pukkhtana-, tapos-* or *tapakus-, sawāl-,* etc. *k.* (-into) *laṭawul, [illegible]*

Inquirer, s. *ṭālib, pukkhtana-, pursān-, ṭalab-,* etc. *kawūnkai.*

Inquiry, s. *tapos, pursān, tālāsh, taḥqīqāt.*

Inroad, s. *ḍūsa, ḍāṛa-dopa, chapāo, halla.*

Insane, a. *lewanai, saudā-ī, khushai.*

Insanity, s. *lewantob, saudā.*

Insatiable, a. *ḥirṣ-nāk, ghārai, bad-liwāl.*

Inscribe, v.a. *līkal, kāgal—kkhkal.*

Inscription, s. *līk; sar-nāma.*

Insect, s. *chinjai, khazanda.*

Insensible, a. *be-hokkh, be-khūd, be-khabar, be-ḥiss; be-parwā, be-dard.*

Insert, v.a. *nanabāsal—nanayastal, kkhke-bāsal—kkhke-yastal, manḍal, kkhke-manḍal; gayayal; khakkhawul, njatal.* (write) *kāgal—kkhkal, līkal.*

Inside, s. *danana; bāṭin; laṛmūn.*

Insidious, a. *darghal, drohai, ṭag-bāz, farebī, ḥīla-bāz.*

Insight, s. *wuqūf, shnākht, pejāndah, poh, līdah, kātah, m'arifat.*

Insignia, s. *nakkhe, 'alāme, nikkhānūna.*

Insignificant, a. *nā-tsīz, spuk, khushai.*

Insincere, a. *nā-rāst, makar, be-īmān, be-wafā, nā-khāliṣ, dwah-rangai.*

Insinuate, v.a. *nana-* or *kkhke-bāsal—yastal; ishārat k., gumān rāwṛal.*

Insipid, a. *be-khwand, balmangah* or *balmagai.*

Insist, v.a. *zoral, tākīd k.; jah k.*

Insolent, a. *be-adab, gustākh, sar-kakkh.*

Insolvent, a. *nā-dār, diwālī.*

Inspect, v.a. *katal, līdal, goral, tamāsha-, nandāra-, mulāḥaza-,* etc. *k.*

Inspection, s. *katana, līdah, tamāsha,* etc.

Inspector, s. *nāzir, dāroghah, katūnkai.*

Inspiration, s. *ilhām, ladūn, waḥī; sāh. dam, rākkhkalai sāh* or *-dam.*

Inspire, v.a. *ilhām k.; sāh ākhistal* or *-rāhāgal—rākkhkal.*

Instal, v.a. *kkhkenawul, wudrawul, muqarrar k., walāṛawul.*

Instalment, s. *qisṭ, ūgṛā-ī.*
Instance, s. *wāqi'a*; *nakkha*; *misāl.* (for-) *pa misāl.*
Instant, s. *laḥza, dam, drang.* a. *ḥāẓir*; *ḥāl.*
Instantly, ad. *pa ṭakī, os, pa de sā'at, sam da lāsa, dam dar ḥāl.*
Instead, ad. *pa dzāe, pa badal, pa 'iwaẓ.*
Instigate, v.a. *lamsawul, lamsūn k.*
Instigation, s. *lamsūn, targhīb.*
Instigator, s. *lamsūnai.*
Instinct, s. *shu'ūr, 'aql, hokkh, sud.*
Institute, v.a. *wudrawul, muqarrar k., taṛal. jārī k., walāṛawul.*
Instruct, v.a. *lwalawul, kkhayal—kkhowul, tarbiyat-, kkhowuna-,* etc. *k.*; *pohawul.*
Instruction, s. *kkhowuna, sabaq, t'alīm,* etc.
Instructor, s. *ākhūn, ustāẓ, mu'allim.*
Instrument, s. *kālai, hatiyār, ālat.* (agent) *waṣīla, wāsiṭa.* (cause) *bā'is, 'illat, sabab.* (deed) *sanad, qibāla.*
Instrumental, a. *komakī, madad·gār.*
Insufficient, a. *kam, la-ag*; *nāqiṣ, nā·qābil.*
Insult, v.a. *spuk wayal, kanzal* or *kkhkandzal, be·'izzat-, be·makh-,* etc. *k.*
Insuperable, a. *mushkil, grān, na·shwūnai.*
Insurgent, s. *balwā·gar, yāghī·gar, pasātī.*
Insurrection, s. *balwā, pasāt, patna.*
Integral, a. *pūrah, amānī, sābat.*
Integrity, s. *rikkhtīn·tob, nekokārī, rāstī.*
Integument, s. *tsarman, postakai, poṭ*; *paṭ, khwar.*
Intellect, s. *'aql, hokkh, poha, pahm.*
Intelligence, s. *khabar*; *poh, hokkhyār·tiyā.*
Intelligent, a. *pohānd, pahm·nāk, 'aql·man, hokkhyār, khabar·dār.*
Intemperance, s. *bad·parhezī, bad·pālī*; *bad·mastī, bad·'amalī.*
Intemperate, a. *bad·parhez·gār, sharābī, nasha·khor, bad·'amal, bad·kār.*
Intend, v.a. *niyat-, qaṣd-, irāda-,* etc. *k.*
Intense, a. *ḍer, nihāyat, sakht, bad.*

Intensity, s. *ḍer·wālai, zor, ziyātī,* etc.
Intent, a. *lagiyā, mashghūl.* s. *maṭlab, niyat, qaṣd, muda'ā, murād.*
Intention, s. *niyat,* etc. (*v.* Intent).
Intentionally, ad. *pa qaṣd.*
Inter, v.a. *khakkhawul.*
Intercede, v.a. *bakkhana-, khalāṣī-,* etc. *ghokkhtal, shafā'at k.*; *gwākkh-* or *gwākkh·grandai k.*
Intercept, v.a. *nīwul, lānde k., stūnawul*; *nkkhlawul, hiṭālawul.*
Intercessor, s. *sipārish-, shafā'at-,* etc. *ka-wūnkai*; *gwākkh·grandai, mandz·garai.*
Interchange, s. *badal, adal·badal, len·den.*
Intercourse, s. *'ilāqa, lār, suḥbat, rāshah·darshah.*
Interdict, v.a. *qadaghan-, man'a-,* etc. *k.*
Interest, s. *kār, gharaẓ, maṭlab*; *kkhegaṛa, sūd, gaṭa, naf'a, fā-ida*; *brakha, wesh, ḥiṣṣa.*
Interested, a. *gharaẓ·man, khpul·maṭlab, gharaẓī.* (self-) *khpul·gharaẓ.*
Interesting, a. *khwand·nāk, maza·dār, dil·chasp.*
Interfere, v.a. *gharaẓ k., lās lagawul, -āch-awul, -waṛwṛal,* or *-pa kkhke khwadzawul.*
Interim, s. *mandz, miyān, miyandz.*
Interior, a. *danananai, darūnī, bāṭinī.*
Interlace, v.a. *agayal, lānde·bānde k., gayayal.*
Interlude, s. *tamāsha, nandāra, swāng.*
Intermeddle, v.a. *lās lagawul,* etc., *dast·andāzī k., dakhl-, gharaẓ-,* etc. *k.* (*v.* Interfere).
Intermediate, a. *mandzwai.*
Interminable, *be·sar, be·and, be·ḥadd.*
Intermission, s. *nobat, wār*; *nāgha*; *furṣat.*
Intermit, v.n. *pa·nobat-, pa·wār-,* etc. *rātlal.*
Intermittent, a. *wārī.* (-fever) *wareza.*
Internal, a. *bāṭinī, darūnī, dananānai.*
Internals, s. *laṛmānah.*
Interpose, v.n. *pa·mandz rātlal—rāghlal.*

v.a. *pa·mandz kegdal*, or *kkhkegdal—kekkhodal*, or *kkhkekkhodal*, etc.; *gwākkh-* or *gwākkh·grandī k.*

Interpret, v.a. *tarjuma k.*, *pohawul*, *kkhayal—kkhowul*, *m'anā kkhkārah k.*

Interrogate, v.a. *pukkhtedal*, *sawāl·dzawāb-*, *tapos-*, etc. *k.*

Interrupt, v.a. *kariyābawul*, *hitālawul*, *bandawul*, *nkkhlawul*, *harakat k.*

Interruption, s. *kariyāb*, *hitāl*, *harj*, *khalal*, *nkkhatai*, *harakat*.

Interstice, s. *darz*, *rakhna*; *khūna*; *grut*.

Interval, s. *mandz*, *miyān*; *wār*.

Intervene, v.n. *pa·mandz rātlal—rāghlal*; *gwākkh-* or *gwākkh·grandī k.*

Intervention, s. *pa·mandz rātlana*; *gwākkh*.

Interview, s. *dīdan*, *līdah*, *kātah*, *mulāqāt*.

Intestate, a. *be·wasīyat*.

Intestine, s. (large-) *kulma*, *larmūn*. (small-) *larai*, *ūjarai*.

Intimate, a. *khamsor*, *gad*; *wāqif*; *balad*. s. *yār*, *āshnāe*, *mal*, *rafīq*.

Intimate, v.a. *khabarawul*; *wayal*.

Intimately, ad. *pa kkhah shān sara*.

Intimation, s. *khabar*; *nakkha*, *ishārat*.

Intimidate, v.a. *yerawul* or *werawul*.

Into, p. *pa kkhke*, *kkhke*, *pa mandz kkhke*.

Intolerant, a. *be·sabr*, *be·zgham*.

Intoxicate, v.a. *be·khūd k.*, *nasha warkawul*; *mast k.*, *kaipī k.*

Intoxication, s. *nasha*, *kaip*; *be·khūdī*, *mastī*.

Intractable, a. *sar·kakkh*, *sar·zor*, *khpul·sar*, *takanrai*, *hodai*.

Intrenchment, s. *sangar*, *bāra*, *morcha*.

Intrepid, a. *maranai*, *tūrzan*, *zrah·war*, *be·bāk*, *dilāwar*, *bahādur*.

Intricate, a. *grān*, *mushkil*; *kog·wog*, *pech·dār*; *arjal·barjal*, *tsapolai*.

Intrigue, s. *jorikkht*, *sāzish*, *kār·sāzī*; *lār*, *'alāqa*, *rāz·o·niyāz*, *yārāna*.

Intrinsic, a. *zātī*, *aslī*.

Introduce, v.a. *nana-* or *kkhke bāsal—yastal*. (-a person) *pekkhawul*. (a custom) *chalawul*, *jārī k.* (to a place) *rāwustal*.

Introduction, s. *nanayastah*; *mulāqāt*; *debācha*.

Intrude, v.a. *dūsa k.*, *nanawatal*, *lās lagawul*, *-āchawul*, etc.

Intrust, v.a. *spāral*, *pāslawul*, *hawāla k.*

Intuition, s. *ilhām*, *ladūn*; *m'arifat*, *poh*, *pahm*.

Intwine, v.a. *agayal*, *gayayal*, *ngharal—nghakkhtal*.

Inundate, v.a. *hūk-*, *lāhū-*, etc. *k.*, *niyūz-*, *nīz-*, etc. *wral*. (-a field) *kharob k.*

Inundation, s. *sailāb*, *nīz* or *niyūz*, *tughiyānī*, etc.

Inure, v.a. *āmokhtah-*, *'ādat-*, etc. *k.*, *rugdawul*.

Invade, v.a. *halla-*, *dāra-*, *chapāo-*, *dūsa-*, etc. *k.* v.n. *khatal*, *prewatal*, *pre·mātedal*.

In vain, ad. *'abas*, *be·fā-ida*.

Invalid, a. *bātil*, *'abas*, *nā·kārah*, *nāqis*. s. *nā·jor*, *nā·rogh*, *randzūr*, *za'īf*.

Invaluable, a. *be·bahā*, *grān·bahā*, *be·qīmat*.

Invariable, a. *be·tabdīl*, *be·biyal·tūn*, *pāedār*.

Invariably, ad. *har·kala*, *mudāman*, *hamesha*.

Invasion, s. *halla*, *chapāo*, *tākht*, *dūsa*, *dāra*.

Invective, s. *peghor*, *kanzal* or *kkhkandzal kkhera*, *malāmat*, *tuhmat*, *tor*.

Inveigle, v.a. *ghulawul*, *tagal*, *damawul*, *dam-*, *fareb-*, etc. *warkawul*.

Invent, v.a. *jorawul*, *nawai·hikmat bāsal—yastal*, *nawai paidā k.*

Invention, s. *hikmat*, *chal*.

Inventory, s. *siyāha*, *daftar*, *fard*.

Inverse, a. *arawul*, *naskor*, *wājgūn*, *'aks*, *apūtah*, *chapah*.

Invert, v.a. *arawul*, *naskorawul*, *'aks-*, etc. *k.*

Invest, v.a. *warkawul*, *bakkhal*; *poslawul*, *āghūstawul*; *īsārawul* or *hisārawul*, *ger k.*

Investigate, v.a. *tapahus* or *tapos-*, *pukkhtana-*, *pursān-*, *taḥqīq-*, etc. *k.*, *pukkhtedal*, *laṭawul*, *shanal*.
Inveterate, a. *kuhand*, *pakhwānai*, *zoṛana i*; *pokh*, *klak*, *sakht*.
Invidious, a. *ḥasad·nāk*, *kīna·war*, *wiyāṛ·jan*.
Invigorate, v.a. *quwat warkawul*, *quwat·nāk-*, *maẓbūṭ-*, *takṛah-*, *tāzah-*, etc. *k.*
Invisible, a. *puṭ*, *ghā-ib*; *wruk*.
Invite, v.a. *sat k.*, *balal*.
Inviting, a. *dil·kakkh*, *dil·chasp*, *dil·rubā*; *maza·dār*, *khwand·nāk*. s. *sat kawuna*.
Invocation, s. *d'uā*; *d'awat*; *ghokkht*.
Invoice, s. *siyāha*, *bījak*, *chalān*.
Invoke, v.a. *d'uā k.*, *balal*, *nūm ākhistal*, *ghokkhtal*.
Involuntary, a. *be·ikhtiyār*, *be·was*, *be·wāk*.
Involve, v.a. *āchawul*, *nkkhlawul*, *nīwul*.
Inward, a. *danananai*, *darūnī*, *bāṭinī*.
Inwrought, a. *jaṛāo*; *kūṭalai*.
Irascible, a. *qahr·nāk*, *ghuṣṣa·nāk*, *tund*.
Ire, s. *ghuṣṣa*, *ghaẓab*, *qahr*, *bṛos·wālai*.
Irksome, a. *sakht*, *grān*, *drūnd*, *rabaṛ·jan*.
Iron, s. *ospana*. (-slag) *ospankhaṛai*. (bar-) *kashai*. (-monger) *lohār*, *āhan·gar*.
Iron-gray, a. *nīlai*.
Irony, a. *ṭoqa*, *khandā*, *pekkha*.
Irradiate, v.n. *dzalakedal*, *rūnredal*.
Irrational, a. *be·hūdah*, *nā·poh*, *be·'aql*.
Irregular, a. *be·tartīb*, *be·ā-īn*, *be·qā'ida*; *nā·lā-iq*.
Irrelevant, a. *be·dzāe*, *be·nisbat*, *nā·kārah*.
Irreligious, a. *be·dīn*, *bilmāz*, *be·maẓhab*.
Irremediable, a. *lā'ilāj*, *lā·chār*, *lā·dawā*.
Irreproachable, a. *be·gunāh*, *be·malāmat*.
Irresistible, a. *zorāwar*, *maẓbūṭ*, *be·band*.
Irresolute, a. *be·himmat*, *nā·qalār*, *nā·mard*.
Irretrievable, a. *ter*, *wruk*, *lāṛ*; *lā·'ilāj*.
Irreverent, a. *be·adab*, *be·makh*.
Irrigate, v.a. *ɔba-*, *watar-*, *khaṛob-*, *lūnd-*, etc. *k.*
Irritable, a. *khapah·nāk*, *bṛos*, *khaṛ*.
Irritate, v.a. *pārawul*, *ṭongawul*, *agayal*, *rabṛawul*, *ṭongāra k.*
Irritation, s. *khapagī*; *ṭongāra*; *pārawūna*; *dard*, *pasāt*, *swai*.
Irruption, s. *halla*, *tākht*, *ḍūsa*, *dāṛa*; *khuṭ*, *eshnā*; *dāra*, *fawāra*.
Island, s. *bela*, *jazīra*. (sandbank) *chara*.
Isolated, a. *biyal*, *yawādzai*, *judā*.
Issue, s. *anjām*, *natīja*, *ḥāṣil*; *pūzah*; *gaṭa*; *alwād*, *zawzāt*; *lār*, *wātah*; *war*, *khula*.
Issue, v.n. *watal*, *bahedul*, *chaledal*, *prewatal*. (-an order) v.a. *chalawul*, *jārī k.*
It, pr. *haghah*, *dā*, *dah*, *de*, *di*, *e*.
Itch, s. *khārikkht*, *koe*, *kaha*; *pishak*, *spūnrai*. v.n. *khārikkhtedal*, *kaha-*, etc. *ked.*
Item, s. *shai*, *tsīz*, *kālai*.
Itinerate, v.n. *girzedal*. v.a. *gakkht-*, *sail-*, etc. *k.*
Itself, pr. *khpul*, *khpul dzān*.

J.

Jackal, s. *gīdaṛ*, *sūrlanḍ*, *shaghāl*.
Jackdaw, s. *qāghah*.
Jacket, s. *kurta*, *nīm·tana-ī*.
Jade, s. (horse) *tap·dangar ās*. (woman) *pūhaṛa-*, *shalata-*, etc. *-kkhadza*, *gashta-ī*, *baghara-ī*.
Jagged, a. *zig*, *lwāṛ*.
Jail, s. *qaid khāna*, *bandī·khāna*, *zindān*.
Jailer, s. *da qaid·khāne dārogha*.
Jam, s. *zokkha*, *khog·pakhalai*, *murabba*. v.a. *bandawul*, *ṭīngawul*, *klakawul*.
January, s. *māh*.
Jar, s. *loṭkai*, *mangai*, *khum*, *maṭkai*, *batakai*. (-of leather) *daba*, *kupa-ī*, *jāba*.
Jargon, s. *wucha·pucha-*, *gaḍa·waḍa-*, *aṛa·baṛa-*, etc. *-khabara*, or *-wrāsha*.

Jasmine, s. *rāmbel-chāmbel.*
Jaundice, s. *ziyaṛai.*
Jaunt, s. *sail, gakkht.*
Javelin, s. *bala, barcha, neza, shalgai.*
Jaw, s. *jāma.* (upper-) *portana-ī jāma.* (lower-) *kkhkatana-ī jāma.* (-angle) *kaj.*
Jay, s. *shīn-tagh.*
Jealous, a. *bad-gumān, wiyaṛ-jan, sūndah.*
Jealousy, s. *bad-gumānī, wiyāṛ, rashk.*
Jeer, v.a. *khandā pore k.*
Jehovah, s. *allah, yāhū, khudāe ta'ālā.*
Jelly, s. *zokkha*; *māya.*
Jeopardy, s. *khaṭra, wera, muhimm.*
Jerk, v.a. *pṛakawul*; *ṭel wahal.*
Jest, s. *ṭoqa, washta, malanḍa, maskhara.*
Jester, s. *ṭoq-mār, washtai, malanḍai, maskharā-chī, pekkhe-gar.*
Jesus, s. *īsā.* (-Christ) *ḥaẓrat īsā.*
Jet, s. *dāra, fuwāra, shutraka.* (-bead) *shaba.* (-black) a. *tak-tor.*
Jew, s. *jahūd.*
Jewel, s. *gāṇra, kālai, zewar.*
Jeweller, s. *zar-gar.*
Jingle, s. *shṛang, gṛanj, krach.* v.n. *shṛang-edal, gṛanjedal.*
Job, s. *kār.* (a little-) *kārgoṭai.*
Jockey, s. *chābuk-sawār.*
Jocose, a. *ṭoqī, washtī, khandā-bāz* or *-rūe.*
Jocularity, s. *washta-ṭoqa, khandā-bāzī.*
Jocund, a. *khūsh-rūe, kkhād, khūsh-ḥāl.*
Jog, v.a. *ṭakaṛ-, ṭel-, gasa-,* etc. *wahal.* v.n. *ṭaparedal.*
Join, v.a. *joṛawul, lagawul, pewand k., gaḍ-awul.* v.n. *gaḍedal, yo dzāe ked.*
Joint, s. *joṛ*; *band, pewand*; *ghūṭa.*
Jointure, s. *mahr, dahadz, dod.*
Joke, s. *ṭoqa, washta, malanḍa.*
Jollity, s. *kkhādī, khūsh-ḥālī.*
Jolly, a. *kkhād, kkhād-man, khwakkh*; *rogh-moṭ.*
Jolt, s. *ṭakaṛa, ḍaka, ṭel*; *tīndak, budrī.*
Jot, s. *ṭakai, pūṭai, batsarai, ṭoṭa, ẕarra.*
Jovial, a. *khwakkh,* etc.. (*v.* Jolly).
Journal, s. *roz-nāmcha.*
Journey, s. *safar, pand.* (a day's-) *mazal* or *manzil.*
Joy, s. *kkhādī, khūsh-ḥālī.* (over rival) *sakha.*
Joyful, a. *kkhād-man, khūsh-ḥāl.*
Joyfully, ad. *pa kkhādī sara, khūsh-ḥālī-, khwakkhī-,* etc. *-sara.*
Jubilee, s. *akhtar,'īd*; *kkhādī, mela.*
Judge, s. *ḥākim, qāẓī, munṣif.*
Judge, v.a. *'adālat-, inṣāf-, niyāw-,* etc. *k.*; *qiyās-, fikr-,* etc. *k.*; *gaṇral.*
Judgment, s. *ḥukm, fatwā*; *'aql, poha.* (opinion) *fikr, rāe, qiyās.* (-seat) *maḥ-kama.* (-day) *ḥashr, ākhirat, qiyāmat.*
Judicature, s. *ḥukm, qaẓā.*
Judicial, a. *shara'ī.*
Judicious, a. *hokkhyār, pohānd, 'aql-man.*
Jug, s. *kūza, kūza-ṛa-ī, khumra-ī, kanja-ī.*
Juggler, s. *bāzī-gar, jādū-gar, koḍ-gar.*
Juice, s. *oba, pa-ī, ras, gūṛa-ī, rub*; *naw, zyam, nam.*
July, s. *pashakāl, sāwaṇr.*
Jumble, v.a. *gaḍ-waḍ k.*
Jump, v.a. *ṭop-, trap-,* etc. *wahal, dangal.*
Juncture, s. *joṛ, band, pewand*; *wakht, tāng.*
June, s. *hāṛ.*
Junior, a. *kishar.*
Jurisdiction, s. *ḥukūmat, 'amaldārī, wāk.*
Jurisprudence, s. *fiqha.*
Jury, s. *jirga m'arika.* (-man) *jirgatū.*
Just, a. *'ādil, munṣif, rikkhtīnai, rāst*; *jukht, barābar, sam.* ad. *surup, faqaṭ.*
Justice, s. *inṣāf, 'adālat, niyāw, dād.*
Justifiable, a. *rawā, wājib.*
Justification, s. *ḥujjat.*
Justify, v.a. *'uẕr-, ḥujjat-,* etc. *rāwṛal.*
Justly, ad. *pa ḥaqqa, pa rikkhtiyā.*
Justness, s. *rikkhtīn-tob, rāstī, nekī.*

Juvenile, a. *kishar, dzwān.* s. *janrai, zalmai, halak, workai.*

Juvenility, s. *janrī·tob, halak·wālai, dzwānī, zalmī·tob.*

K.

Keen, a. *terah, dam·dār*; *jalt, tez, tund.* (acid) *brekkhan.* (eager) *garm, tod, liwāl.*

Keenness, s. *terah·wālai*; *tund·wālai*, etc.

Keep, v.a. *sātal, jghoral, khundiyal, khundī k.*; *pālal, parwaral, nmāndzal.* (-watch) *gālal.* (observe) *manal.* (-back) *pātai k., pātawul, stūnawul.* (possess) *laral.* (-an engagement) *pūrah-, adā-*, etc. *k.*

Keep, v.n. *pātedal, pātai ked., pāedal, osedal.*

Keeper, s. *sātandoe, sātūnkai, jghorai, pālūnkai, khundī kawūnkai.*

Keeping, s. *sātana, pālana, jghorana, khundī kawūna*; *pāedana, osedana, pātedana.*

Keepsake, s. *yād·gār, yād·dāsht.*

Kernel, s. *chaka-ī, maghzai, zarai.*

Kettle, s. *dechka, deg, khum.* (earthen-) *katwa-ī.*

Kettledrum, s. *naghāra, damāma, dūkāra, dūmbakai, tambal.*

Key, s. *kunja-ī.* (-hole) *da jandre khula.*

Kick, v.a. *lata-, laghata-*, etc. *wahal.*

Kid, s. *warghūmai, chelai, serlai, psharlai, wuzgarai.*

Kidnap, v.a. *botlal—bīwul, bota k., takkhtawul.*

Kidney, s. *pukkhtawarga.* (-bean) *lobiyā.*

Kill, v.a. *wajal* or *wajlal, mur k., qatlawul.* (for food) *hallālawul.*

Killed, a. *maqtūl, wajalai, mur karai*; *hallāl karai.*

Killer, a. *qātil, wajlūnai, khūnī, mur-* or *marg kawūnkai.* (in comp.) *-kush.*

Killing, s. *khūn-, mur-, marg-, qatl-*, etc. *-kawūna, wajlana.*

Kiln, s. *paja*; *bat.*

Kin, s. *ragai, khpul, khekkh, 'azīz.*

Kind, a. *mihrbān*; *makhawar.*

Kind, s. *zāt, asl, rang, nog, qism, shān.*

Kindle, v.a. *balawul, pūkal, swadzawul.* v.n. *baledal, swal, sedzal.*

Kindly, ad. *pa mihrbāngī sara.*

Kindness, s. *mihrbānī* or *mihrbāngī.*

Kindred, s. *khpul·walī, khekkhī.* a. *yo·shān, ragai, hum·rang, hum·jins.*

King, s. *bādshāh, shāh, sultān.*

Kingdom, s. *bādshāhat, sultanat, rāj.*

Kingfisher, s. *māhī·khwurak, babozai.*

Kinsman, s. *khpul, khekkh.* (paternal-) *plār·ganai.* (maternal-) *mor·ganai.*

Kiss, s. *kkhkul, macha, chapa-ī.* v.a. *kkhkulawul, machawul, chapa-ī-, kkhkul-*, etc. *k., koka-ī-, khula-*, etc. *-ākhistal.*

Kitchen, s. *langar, jal·nāna-ī, ngharai.*

Kite, s. *tapūts.* (paper-) *godā, patang.*

Kitten, s. *pishongarai.*

Klick, v.a. *tak wahal.*

Knack, s. *hikmat, chal, pech, kārī·garī.*

Knapsack, s. *dzola-ī, gūdai, bana-ī, butskha.*

Knave, s. *tag, darghal, charland, farebī, be·īmān, chal·bāz, chal·walai.*

Knavery, s. *tagī, tag·bāzī, chal·bāzī*, etc.

Knavish, a. *tag·bāz, be·īmān, farebī.*

Knead, v.a. *aghagal—ākkhal.* (-the limbs) *mandal, kkhke·mandal, chāpī k.*

Knee, s. *zangūn, doga.* (-cap) *zangānah·starga.*

Kneel, v.a. *doga-, zangūn-*, etc. *-lagawul.* v.n. *pa dogo-, zangāno-*, etc. *-kkhkenāstal.*

Knife, s. *chāra.* (pen-) *charūka-ī, chāqū.*

Knit, v.a. *gayayal, agayal*; *dūr k.* (-the brows) *starge brandawul.*

Knitting, s. *dūr.* (-needle) *dūk.*

Knob, s. *ghūtai, pūtai, ghūndai*; *pārsob, mātus, pūpaka*; *rasaula-ī, ghundārai.*

Knock, v.a. *traq-, tap-, tak-*, etc. *-wahal.*

(-up against) *ṭakaṛ-, ḍaka-*, etc. *-khwuṛal*. v.n. *blosedal, lagedal, jangedal.*

Knot, s. *ghūṭa, taṛa, bandaṇr.*

Know, v.a. *m'alūmawul, pejandal, gaṇral, zdah k.* v.n. *khabaredal, pohedal, zdah ked.*

Knowing, a. *zdah, khabar·dār, hokkhyār, pokh, wāqif.*

Knowingly, ad. *pa 'aql sara, pa khabar sara.*

Knowledge, s. *poha, 'aql, khabar, 'ilm.*

Known, a. *zdah, pejāndah, m'alūm.*

Knuckle, s. *band, da gūṭe band.* (-bone) *bujal, ṭaka, arghund.*

L.

Label, s. *sar·nāma, ṭīka.*

Laboratory, s. *kār·khāna.*

Laborious, a. *miḥnatī, kokshikshī*; *mushkil, grān, sakht.*

Labour, s. *miḥnat, kokshiksh, sa'ī, mushaqqat, mazdūrī*; *rabaṛ*; *kār, kasb, pesha.* (childbirth) *langa, langedana.* (-pain) *stam.*

Labour, v.a. *miḥnat-, mazdūrī-*, etc. *k.* (be in-) v.n. *langedal.* (worry oneself) v.n. *rabṛedal.* (to strain) v.a. *stam·wahal.*

Labourer, s. *mazdūr*; *kasb·gar.*

Labyrinth, s. *kaga·waga, warṭa, mār·pech.*

Lac, s. (gum) *da pala-ī chīṛ.* (dye) *lāk.* (100,000) *lak.*

Lace, s. *jālaka-ī, jāla-ī, muqaish.*

Lacerate, v.a. *shlawul, wrarawul, chāk k.*; *mātawal, ghwutsawul.*

Laceration, s. *shledah, wraredah, chāwd*; *tsīra, parhār, zakhm.*

Lack, v.n. *muḥtāj-, ḥājat·man-*, etc. *ked.* v.a. *ghokkhtal.*

Lad, s. *halak, zaṇrai, ghunḍāyah, zalmai.*

Ladder, s. *andarpāya, pawṛa-ī, pārchang.*

Lade, v.a. *bār āchawul, legdal—lekkhal, ḍakawul.*

Ladle, s. *kaṛecha-ī, harkāra.* (small-) *kāchogha, tsontsa-ī, chamcha-ī* or *tsamtsa-ī.*

Lady, s. *bībī, merman, ṣāḥiba.* (-fly) *bībī·pāto bakhmaṇa-ī.*

Lag, v.n. *pātedal, ṭaparedal.*

Laity, s. *'āmmiyān.* (one of the-) *'āmmī.*

Lake, s. *loe ḍanḍ, tālāw* or *tālāb.*

Lamb, s. *wrai, ga-aḍūrai.* (wether-) *wuch·kūl.*

Lame, a. *guḍ, khūg, kaṛam.*

Lameness, s. *guḍ·wālai.*

Lament, v.a. *afsos-, gham-, wāwailā-*, etc. *k.*, *jaṛal, wīr-, hāe·hāe-, hāe·hūe-, jaṛā-*, etc. *k.*, *wainā wayal.*

Lamentation, s. *afsos, jaṛā, wīr, sānda, faryād*, etc.

Lamenter, s. *wīṛa·jalai, wainā wayūnkai*, etc.

Lamp, s. *chirāgh, ḍīwa.* (-stand) *ḍīwat.* (-black) *kajal, lūgai.* (-black cup) *masa.* (-wick) *bāta-ī.*

Lance, s. *neza, bala, barcha.*

Lance, v.a. *tsīral*; *tsīkhal, tetsal.*

Lancet, s. *nashtar* or *nekkhtar.*

Land, s. *mzaka* or *zmaka, zamīn.* (country-) *mulk, hewād.* (own-) *waṭan, būm.* (table-) *bāwra-ī, būṛa, steza.* (ploughed-) *sādīn.* (sown-) *shudyāra.* (bare-) *ḍāga, ṭikārkai.* (fallow-) *waḍ.* (waste-) *shāṛ.* (patch of-) *paṭai*; *pāra.* (irrigated-) *watar, ābī.* (unirrigated-) *lalamī.* (inundated-) *khaṛob.* (marsh-) *jaba.* (village-) *ada-ī, wanḍ.* (church-) *sīra-ī, bogarai.*

Land, v.n. *kūzedal.* v.a. *kūzawul.*

Landholder, s. *dawtarī* or *daftarī, jāgīr·dār, zamīn·dār, brakha·khor.*

Landlord, s. *dawtarī, zamīn·dār, nāyak*; *korbah, meṛah, khāwand, tsakkhtan, māl·dār.*

Landmark, s. *tsalai, pūla.*

Lane, s. *kūtsa.*

Language, s. *jiba, wrāsha.*

Languid, a. *ṭap, staṛai, stomān, māndah, haukah*; *sust, laṭ, shalat, kāṛai·wāṛai.*

Languish, v.n. *mṛāwedal* or *mṛāmedal, wuc̲h̲edal, kamaṉredal*; *kaṛedal, nūledal, zahedal*; *staṛai-, stomān-, zahīr-*, etc. *ked.*

Languor, s. *sustī, stomānī, māndagī.*

Lantern, s. *fānūs.*

Lap, s. *g̲h̲eg, g̲h̲ūzai*; *laman, pitskai, dzola-ī.*

Lap, v.a. *tsaṭal.* (wrap) *ng̲h̲aṛal—ng̲h̲akk̲h̲tal.*

Lapidary, s. *muhr·kan.*

Lapse, v.n. *teredal, g̲h̲uzāredal, ter watal.*

Large, a. *loe, star, g̲h̲aṭ, 'aẓīm.*

Largeness, *loe-, star-*, etc., *-wālai.*

Largesse, s. *bak̲h̲kshiksh, bakk̲h̲ana, in'ām, k̲h̲airāt.*

Lark, s. *k̲h̲a·aṛāra, kopla, agan.*

Larynx, s. *ḥalq, wuc̲h̲a·g̲h̲āṛa*; *stūnai.*

Lascivious, a. *mast, s̲h̲ok̲h̲ī, s̲h̲ahwatī, hawas·nāk.*

Lasciviousness, s. *mastī, s̲h̲ahwat, naus, hawas.*

Lash, s. *bac̲h̲awai, bac̲h̲okai, bac̲h̲akarai*; *karoṛa.*

Lash, v.a. *karoṛa wahal*; *taṛal.*

Lass, s. *jina-ī, peg̲h̲la, lūr, k̲h̲oraka-ī.*

Lassitude, s. *sustī, stomānī.*

Last, a. *wrustai, wrustanai, āk̲h̲ir, pasīn.*

Last, v.n. *pāedal, c̲h̲aledal, pātedal, osedal.*

Lasting, a. *pāedār, qā-im, maẓbūṭ.*

Lastly, ad. *wrusto, āk̲h̲ir.*

Latch, s. *hūl, aṛam, aṛamai.*

Latchet, s. *rog, tasma.*

Late, a. *nā·wak̲h̲t, pasīn*; *osanai*; *mutawaffī.*

Lately, ad. *osan, nan wrad̲z̲, da la-ago wrad̲z̲o.*

Lateness, s. *nā·wak̲h̲tī*; *lārg̲h̲ah, drang.*

Latent, a. *puṭ, g̲h̲alai.*

Later, a. *nawai.*

Lather, s. *zag, kaf.*

Latitude, s. *plan·wālai, arat·wālai, sor* or *psor.*

Latitudinarian, s. *be·s̲h̲ar'a, āzād·ṭab'a saṛai.*

Latter, a. *wrustanai, pasanai.*

Lattice, s. *jālakai, s̲h̲abaka, j'afarī.*

Laud, v.a. *stāyal, stāyana k.*, or *-wayal.*

Laugh, v.a. *k̲h̲andal, k̲h̲andā k.*

Laughter, s. *k̲h̲andā, qah·qaha, haṉr·haṉr.*

Launch, v.a. *obo ta kūzawul*; *g̲h̲wurzawul, c̲h̲alawul, āc̲h̲awul, wīs̲h̲tal.*

Lave, v.a. *wīnd̲z̲al* or *mīnd̲z̲al, wlal, lambawul.*

Lavish, a. *k̲h̲arts̲ī, isrāfī, musrif.*

Lavish, v.a. *k̲h̲arts̲-, tāwān-, isrāf-*, etc. *k.*

Law, s. *fiqha.* (divine-) *s̲h̲ar'a, s̲h̲arī'at.* (rule) *qā'ida, qānūn, ā-īn, rasm.* (justice) *'adālat, inṣāf, niyāw.* (right) *ḥaqq, rawā.* (Afghan-) *puk̲k̲h̲tūn·walī.*

Lawful, a. *rawā, ḥallāl.*

Lawsuit, s. *muqaddama, d'awa, qaẓiya.*

Lawyer, s. *qāẓī, faqīḥ.*

Lax, a. *sust, prānatai, spaṛdalai, arat.*

Laxative, a. *pos-, narm-*, etc. *-kawūnkai.* s. *pos·jāṛ, narm·jullāb, mūnzij.*

Lay, v.a. *gdal* or *īgdal, yak̲k̲h̲odal* or *īk̲k̲h̲odal, yak̲k̲h̲al* or *īk̲k̲h̲al, kegdal* or *k̲k̲h̲kegdal, kek̲k̲h̲odal* or *k̲k̲h̲kek̲k̲h̲odal, kek̲k̲h̲al* or *k̲k̲h̲kek̲k̲h̲al.* (-hold of) *āk̲h̲istal, nīwul.* (-down) *ts̲amlawul.* (-on) *āc̲h̲awul, lagawul.* (-in) *ṭolawul, gaṭal.* (-out) *gazawul* or *g̲h̲azawul.*

Lay, s. *g̲h̲azal.*

Layer, s. *brag̲h̲, tah.* (-of bricks) *rada.*

Layman, s. *'āmmī.*

Laziness, s. *sustī, nā·rāstī, laṭ·wālai.*

Lazy, a. *sust, nā·rāst, laṭ, s̲h̲aṭal* or *s̲h̲alaṭ.*

Lead, s. *sīka, sīsa*; *mas.* (red-) *sendūr.* (white-) *sapeda.*

Lead, v.a. *rāwustal, biyāyal—bīwul, botlal—bīwul.*

Leader, s. *sardār, nāyak, sar·guroh, pes̲h̲wā.*

Leaf, s. *pāṉra.* (of a book) *waraq.* (-of a door) *pala, tanba.*

League, s. *para, janba, gundi*; *bandaṉr,*

wāda, lafẓ, taṛa, jorikkht, qaul. (measure) *farsakh.*
Leak, v.n. *tsātsedal.*
Leaky, a. *tsātsedūnai, māt.*
Lean, a. *narai, ḍangar, khwār, lāghar.*
Lean, v.n. *takiya k., ḍaḍa lagawul.*
Leanness, s. *ḍangar-tob, narai-wālai.*
Leap, v.a. *dangal, traplal, ṭop wahal.*
Leap, s. *ṭop, dang, trap.*
Learn, v.a. *zdah k., yādawul.*
Learned, a. *zdah, yād, āmokhtah* ; *'ālim, pohānd.*
Learner, s. *shāgird, ṭālib, sabaq lwustūnai.*
Learning, s. *'ilm.*
Lease, s. *gānṛa, ijāra.*
Least, a. *kisharīn, kamtarīn, la ṭolo na la-ag* or *-wūṛ.* (at-) ad. *bāre, kho, ākhir.*
Leather, s. *tsarman.* (-dresser) *dabbāgh.* (-worker) *tsamyār, mochī.* (-strop) *rog, tasma.* (-bottle) *chāgul, ĵa-ī, batak.* (-scraper) *zarbiyāng.*
Leave, v.a. *pregdal, prekkhodal, prekkhal* ; *rukhṣat ākhistal.* v.n. *rawānedal, tlal—lāṛal.*
Leave, s. *rukhṣat, ijāzat, ḥukm, izan.*
Leaven, s. *khamīra, māya, tomna.*
Leavings, s. *jūṭa, pāte, pas-khurdah.*
Lecher, s. *kāsīr, lawanḍ, qachar, chaṭ.*
Lecture, s. *sabaq, dars.* v.a. *sabaq wayal.*
Ledge, s. *ghāṛa, morga, ĵa-ī, ḍaḍa* ; *kamar.*
Leech, s. *ĵawara.*
Leek, s. *gandana.*
Leer, v.a. *pa-trats katal* ; *pa-zarana-ī katal.*
Lees, s. *khaṭbel, matra.*
Left, a. *pātai, bāqī.* (not right) *kīṇr, gats.* (-handed) *gatsai.* v.n. *pātai ked.*
Leg, s. (whole-) *kkhānga.* (below knee) *paṛkai, lengai.* (-of a table, etc.) *pāya, kkhpa* or *pkkha.* (-of drawers) *pāentsa.* (-of mutton, fowl, etc.) *patūn.*
Legacy, s. *mīrāt, waṣīyat, hiba.*
Legal, a. *shara'ī, rawā.*
Legate, s. *astādzai, wakīl, elchī.*
Legation, s. *elchī-garī* ; *jirga, m'arika.*
Legend, s. *rawāyat, qiṣṣa, tazkira.*
Legerdemain, s. *bāzī-garī, jādū-garī, naẓar-bandī.*
Legion, s. *ḍala, ganṛ 'ālam* ; *tuman, dasta, ulus.*
Legislate, v.a. *ḥukm-, ā-īn-, qānūn-,* etc. *chalawul.*
Legislator, s. *ḥākim, shari'yat-jārī kawūnkai.*
Legislature, s. *sarkār, 'adālat.*
Legitimate, a. *rawā, ḥallāl.*
Legume, s. *palai.*
Leisure, s. *wazgār-tiyā, furṣat.*
Lemon, s. *nībū, tursh nāranj,*
Lend, v.a. *por warkawul, qarẓ warkawul.* (a thing itself to be returned) *'āriyatī warkawul.*
Lender, s. *qarẓ-, por-,* etc. *-warkawūnai.*
Length, s. *ūgd-wālai.*
Lengthen, v.a. *ūgdawul.*
Lenient. a. *mulā-im, narm, ḥalīm.*
Lenity, s. *mulā-im-tob, narm-wālai, raḥm.*
Lent, s. *roĵa.* (Muhammadan) *ramẓān.*
Lentils, s. *moṭ, mahe* ; *chanṛa* ; *ma-ī* ; *lobiyā.* (cooked-) *paitī, rāṛa.*
Leopard, s. *pṛāng, baur, baurgai, yūz.*
Leper, s. *koṛī, bragai, pesai.*
Leprosy, s. *koṛ, brag, pes.*
Less, a. *la-ag, kam, lāndai.*
Lessen, v.a. *la-agawul, kamawul.* v.n. *la-agedal, kamedal.*
Lesson, s. *dars, sabaq* ; *pand, naṣīḥat.*
Lest, c, *mabādā, hase di na wī, kkhā-ī.*
Let, v.a. *pregdal, prekkhodal, prekkhal, prekkhawul.* (-go) *yalah-, khalāṣ-, āzād-,* etc. *k.* (hire) *karīh* or *kreha-,* etc. *warkawul.* (allow) *izan-, ḥukm-, rukhṣat-,* etc. *warkawul.*

Let, s. *āṛ, kariyāb, hiṭāl.*
Lethargy, s. *sustī, laṭ·wālai.*
Letter, s. *ḥarf; khaṭṭ, chīṭa-ī, rawāna.*
Levee, s. *dalbār.*
Level, a. *sam, hawār, barābar, sat.* v.a. *samawul, naṛawul, hawārawul.*
Lever, s. *aṛām, dah·marda.* (-for water) *dīngara-ī.*
Levity, s. *spuk·wālai, halak·wālai.*
Levy, v.a. *ṭolawul, yo dzāe-, jam'a-,* etc. *k.*
Lewd, a. *bad·mast, shahwat·nāk.* (-woman) *lashmaka-ī, shatāha.*
Lewdness, s. *mastī, shahwat.*
Lexicon, s. *lughat.*
Liable, a. *shwūnkai, pīrzo.*
Liar, s. *darogh·jan, durghal.*
Libel, s. *peghor, tor, tuhmat, bad·namūsī, ruswā-ī, malāmat.*
Liberal, s. *sakhī, bakkhūnkai, warkawūnai.*
Liberate, v.a. *āzādawul, khalāṣawul, pregdal, wurhawul, yalah k.*
Liberated, a. *yalah, āzād, khalāṣ.*
Libertine, s. *lawanḍ, chaṭ, lūtsak, qachar.*
Liberty, s. *yalah·tob, khalāṣī, āzādī; wāk, ikhtiyār; rukhṣat, ijāzat.*
Libidinous, a. *bad·mast, shahwat·nāk.*
Library, s. *kitāb·khāna.*
License, s. *izan, ḥukm, parwāna, sanad.*
Licentious, a. *bad·laman, bad·parhez·gār, bad·kār, ḥarām·kār; sar·kakkh.*
Lick, v.a. *tsaṭal.* (beat) *wahal, ṭakawul.*
Lid, s. *bargholai, sar·pokkh.*
Lie, s. *darogh.* v.a. *darogh wayal.*
Lie-down, v.n. *mlāstal, tsamlāstal, gazedal* or *ghazedal.* (-concealed) *ghalai kedal.*
Lieutenant, s. *nā-ib, qā-im muqām, jam'a·dār.*
Life, s. *dzān, jwāk, jwand; jwandūn, rozgār, zindagānī, hayāt.*
Lifeless, a. *be·dzān, be·sāh, muṛ.*
Lifetime, s. *'umr, jwandūn, hayāt.*
Lift, v.a. *porta k., khejawul, ūchatawul.*

Ligament, s. *pala, rag.* (-of the heel) *kūchai, spīna.* (-of horse's leg) *pai.*
Ligature, s. *taṛūn, taṛa, band, paṭa-ī, skoe.*
Light, s. *raṇrā, rokkhnā-ī.* a. *rokkhān, rūṇr; spuk, halak.* v.a. *rūṇrawul, rokkhān k.* (-a fire) *balawul.* v.n. *rūṇredal, rokkhān ked.* (-as fire) *baledal.* (descend) *kūzedal, prewatal, nāziledal.*
Lighten, v.a. *spukawul, kamawul.* v.n. *rūṇr-edal, brekkhedal, dzalkedal.*
Lightness, s. *spuk·wālai.*
Lightning, s. *brekkhnā, barq.*
Like, a. *gund, miṣāl, ghūndai, rang, shān.* ad. *laka, pa shān, ghūndi, hase.* s. *pasand, khwakkh.*
Like, v.a. *khwakkh-, pasand-, qabūl-,* etc. *k.* v.n. *khwā·ta ked.*
Likelihood, s. *shān, shakl, ṣūrat, gumān.*
Likely, a *shwūnai.* ad. *kkhā-ī, ghūnde.* (most-) *aghlab, ghāliba.*
Liken, v.a. *miṣāl-, tamṣīl-,* etc. *k., barābar-awul, joṛawul.*
Likeness, s. *tsera, ṣūrat, taṣwīr, miṣāl, tamṣīl.*
Likewise, ad. *hum, 'alāwa, ziyāt la de na.*
Liking, s. *mīna, shauq, khwā.*
Lily, s. *sausan.* (water-) *nīlofar.*
Limb, s. *band, andām.* (-of a tree) *kkhākh, khṛand.*
Lime, s. *chūna; kūnai.* (-kiln) *paja.*
Limestone, s. *da chūne kāṇrai.* (nodulated-) *qurut·kāṇrai.*
Limit, s. *ḥadd, brīd, pūla, ṭikāna.* v.a. *ḥadd-,* etc. *taṛal.*
Limp, v.n. *guḍedal, ṭaparedal, ṭapal.*
Limpid, a. *spīn, pāk, ṣāf, narai.*
Line, s. *līk, līka, karkkha, khaṭṭ.* (rope) *pa-aṛai, biyāsta, rasa-ī.* (row) *qaṭār, para, tsīṛa.* (clothes-) *tsakai, paikal, saha, tanāw.* (-of a book) *jadwal.*
Lineage, s. *aṣl, nasal, mūnḍ, nasab.*
Lineament, s. *ṣūrat, khāl·o·khaṭṭ, rang, ḍaul.*

Linen, s. *khāmtā, karbās.* (-draper) *bazzāz.*
Linger, v.n. *kaṛedal, zahīredal, nūledal.* (delay) v.a. *drang-, lārghah-, dzanḍ-,* etc. *k.* v.n. *pātedal, ṭaparedal, pātai ked.*
Linguist, s. *pa jibo āmokhtah* or *-maṛanai.*
Lining, s. *astar, zerāstar.*
Link, s. *kara-ī.* (torch) *mash'al, shonṭa-ī.*
Linseed, s. *alsī, da saṇr zaṛai* or *-tukhm.*
Lintel, s. *darshal, sarāna.*
Lion, s. *zmarai* or *mzarai, babar·zmarai, sher.*
Lip, s. *shūnḍa.* (-of a cup) *morga.* (hare-) *shūnḍ·pārah kanḍā.*
Liquid, a. *narai, oblan.* (melted) *wilī.*
Liquidate, v.a. *pūrah-, adā-,* etc. *k.*
Liquor, s. *oba*; *'araq*; *sharāb.*
Liquorice, s. *khwaga·wala.*
Lisp, v.a. *ṭataṛai-, gāngūra-, nkkhati jiba-,* etc. *wayal.*
List, v.a. *ghokkhtal*; *āwredal* or *ārwedal.*
List, s. *siyāhī, fard, fihrist*; *jāwja-ī.*
Listen, v.a. *āwredal, nghwatal, ghwag bāsal—yastal, -kegdal—kekkhodal, -nīwul,* etc. (spy) *ghwag tsāral.*
Listless, a. *be·dzān, be·sāh, be·dam, sust, laṭ.*
Literal, a. *lughawī*; *aṣlī*; *rikkhtīnai, jukht.*
Literary, a. *'ilmī*; *kitābī.*
Literati, s. *mullāyān.*
Literature, s. *'ilm, 'ilm·o·fazal.*
Litigate, v.a. *d'awa-, qaẓiya-,* etc. *k.*
Litigious, a. *jagṛāū, qaẓiya·kār, tākrārī.*
Litter, s. *ḍola-ī, anbāla-ī.* (camel-) *kajāwa.* (grass) *wākkhah.* (refuse) *khazala, khāshāk.*
Little, a. *la-ag, kam.* (small) *wor, wuṛūkai, pūṭai.* ad. *la-ag·kūṭī* or *lakūṭī, pitsāṇrai, khāsha, ẓarra.*
Littleness, s. *la-ag·wālai, wuṛūk·wālai.*
Live, v.a. *jwand-, jwāk-, rozgār-,* etc. *k., jwandūn-, 'umr-,* etc. *terawul.* v.n. *jwandai ked., osedal.*
Livelihood, s. *rozī, rozgār, rizq, guẓrān.*
Lively, a. *chālāk, chust*; *khūsh·ṭab'a, shokhīn.*
Liver, s. *īna, dzigar.*
Livery, s. *jāma, libās, bāna.*
Livid, a. *sperah, ziyaṛ, shīn.*
Living, a. *jwandai*; *jān·dār,* s. *rozgār, rozī, guẓrān, rizq.*
Lizard, s. *samsara, tsarmal·khkai, khādama-ī, karborai.* (iguana) *ghārandūnai.*
Lo, in. *gora! wāh!*
Load, s. *bār, poṭai.* (half-) *anḍa-ī.* (for head) *panḍa, panḍūkai.*
Load, v.a. *bārawul, legdal—lekkhal*; *ḍakawul*
Loadstone, s. *āhan·rubā.*
Loam, s. *maṭa·khāwra, maṭīna·zmaka.*
Loan, s. *qarẓ, por.* (of a thing itself to be returned) *'āriyat.*
Loath, a. *nā·rāẓ, nā·khwakkh, daregh·man.*
Loathe, v.a. *bad manal, kagal, ghandal, kraka ākhistal, chinjawul.*
Loathsome, a *kraka·nāk, kagalai, chinjan, makrūh, ghāndah.*
Loathing, s. *kraka, kagah, ghandana, chinjana.*
Local, a. *makānī, khāṣṣ.*
Lock, s. *jandra, qulf.* (-of hair) *zulf, tsūṇra, tsuṇraka, kajak, wal.* (-plaited) *kontsa-ī, orbal.* (-of wool) *waṛa-ī.* (-of goat's hair) *ojghūna.* (-of a gun) *chaq·maq.*
Lock, v.a. *jandra lagawul* or *-band k.* (stick) v.n. *nkkhatal, jangedal.*
Locker, s. *ṣandūq, tauṇra-ī, kandū·ṛai.*
Locket, s. *t'awīz.*
Locomotion, s. *ḥarakat*; *sail, girzedūn.*
Locust, s. *mlakh.*
Lodge, s. *jūngaṛa, takiya, dzāe, āstāna, kor.*
Lodge, v.n. *osedal, āstedal.* v.a. *ṭikāo-, astoga-, kilai-,* etc. *k., dzāe nīwul.* (place) *gdal,* etc.
Lodger, s. *osedūnkai, āstedūnkai, astogūnkai.*
Lodging, s. *ṭīkāo, dera, dzāe.*
Loft, s. *koṭa, bām, chat.*
Lofty, a. *ūchat, hask, dang, buland, lwaṛ*

Log, s. *garya, mūnḍ, tsaṭ.*
Logic, s. *manṭiq, da munāẓire 'ilm.*
Loins, s. *mlā, shā-lanḍa, ḍūḍa;* (side of-) *ta-ashai.*
Loiter, v.a. *drang-, lārghah-, dzanḍ-,* etc. *k.* v.n. *ṭapal, ṭaparedal, pātedal, pātai ked.*
Loll, v.a. *takiya-, ārām-,* etc. *k., loṭ-pot k.* v.n. *tsamlāstal, rghaṛedal—rghakkhtal.* (hang out) *watalai dzwaṛandedal.*
Lonely, a. *yawādzai, tsaṛah, biyal, tanhā.*
Long, a. *ūgd.* (duration) *ḍer-pā.* (distance) *ḍer, lire* or *liri.* (-ago) ad. *lire-lārghah, larghūne.* (as long as) ad. *hombra chi, tso chi, tar haghah pore chi.*
Long, v.n. *liwāl-, ūgai-, mayan-,* etc. *ked.* v.a. *ghokkhtal.*
Longevity, s. *zoṛ-tiyā, zoṛ-wālai.*
Longing, s. *liwāl-tob; mīna, armān, shauq, raghbat, khwā.*
Look, s. *katal, līdal, goral, kasal, naẓar k.*
Look, s. *kātah, līdah, naẓar, nigāh.*
Looking, s. *katana, līdana.* (-glass) *āhīna.* (-for the thumb) *ārsa-ī, shast.*
Looks, s. *ṣūrat, shakl.*
Loom, s. *rach, shāna.*
Loop, s. *pulwākkha, gharwandai, ghuryāsha.*
Loose, a. *prānatai, arat, āzād, yalah, khushai, gharand; spaṛdalai.*
Loose, v.a. *pregdal, prekkhodal; khalāṣawul, āzādawul, yalah k.; spaṛdal, prānatal; arat k.*
Looseness, s. *arat-wālai.* (-of bowels) *nāstah*
Lop, v.a. *prekawul* or *prekṛal, ghūṭ-, lanḍ-,* etc. *k.*
Lord, s. (God) *khudāe, rabb.* (master) *mālik, tsakkhtan, meṛah.* (owner) *khāwand, ṣāḥib.* (spiritual-) *sayad, pīr, ḥaẓrat.* (temporal) *sardār, khān, malik.*
Lordly, a. *khāntamā, kibr-jan.*
Lordship, s. *sardārī, khānī, malikī.* (your-) *ḥaẓrat.*

Lose, v.a. *wrukawul.* (at play, etc.) *bāelal* v.n. *pa-aṛ ked.* (-in trade) *ziyān-, tāwān-* etc. *k.*
Loser, s. *pa-aṛ, bāelūnai.*
Loss, s. *ziyān, tāwān, nuqṣān, troṭa, talaf.*
Lost, a. *wruk, puṭ; bāelalai.*
Lot, s. *qismat, naṣīb, bakht.* (share) *brakha, wesh, wanḍ.* (die) *hisk, pucha, qur'a.*
Lottery, s. *qur'a-bāzī, shartī.*
Loud, a. *ūchat-āwāz, shor-nāk, tāo.*
Loudly, ad. *pa tāo sara.*
Lounger, s. *nā-rāst; hujrai.*
Louse, s. *spaga.* (-nit) *richa.* (crab-) *broṛa.* (cattle-) *koṛr, kūnai, kāna, wrādza.*
Lousy, a. *spagan.* (mean) *gandah.*
Love, v.n. *mayan-, 'āshiq-,* etc. *ked.* v.a. *mīna-, muḥabbat-, 'ishq-,* etc. *laral* or *k.*
Love, s. *mīna, muḥabbat, 'ishq; mayan-tob, 'ishq-bāzī, āshnā-ī, yārī.*
Lovely, a. *kkhkulai, kkhāyastah, pej-makhai* or *pa-ī-makhai.*
Lover, s. *yār, āshnāe, mayan, 'āshiq, m'ashūq.*
Low, a. *kūz, lānḍai, kkhkatah, lar, past.* (mean) *spuk, dūn, gandah.* (-stature) *mandarai.* (-price) *wel, arzān.* (-spirited) *malūl, zahīr.* (-breed) *kam-aṣl, lānḍai-ẓāt, pāsū.*
Low, v.n. *ghurchedal, ghuṛunbedal.* v.a. *naṛal, nāra-, ḍarān-,* etc. *wahal.*
Lower, a. *kkhkatanai, kūz, lar, lānḍai.*
Lower, v.a. *kūzawul, kkhkatah-, lānḍai-,* etc. *k.; ṭīṭawul.* (lessen) v.a. *spukawul, kamawul.* (as the sky) v.n. *toredal, ṭīṭedal.* (frown) v.a. *brandawul, brand katal.*
Lowland, s. *sama, maidān; tahana.*
Lowly, a. *gharīb, kamīn, ḥalīm.*
Lowness, s. *kūz-, kkhkatah-,* etc. *-wālai.*
Loyal, a. *khair-khwāh, wafā-dāṛ, namak-ḥallāl.*
Lucid, a. *ṣāf, spīn; tsargand, kkhkārah.*

Luck, s. *ba**kh**t, qismat, naṣīb.*
Lucky, a. *ba**kh**tāwar, barakatī, nek·ba**kh**t.*
Lucrative, a. *sūd·man, fā-ida·man, naf'a·nāk.*
Lucre, s. *duniyā, daulat, māl, sūd,*
Ludicrous, a. ***kh**andā·nāk, wa**sh**tī, ṭoqī.*
Lug, v.a. *rākāgal—rā**kkh**kal, ka**sh**āla k.*
Luggage, s. *asbāb, partal; balā·batar.*
Lukewarm, a. *taṛam.*
Lull, v.a. *lala-ī-, lalo-, ṭāṭa-ī-, ḍīng·ḍīnga-ī-,* etc. *k.*; ***kh**ob-, ārām-,* etc. *rāwṛal; damawul, ūdah k.*; *saṛawul, kamawul.*
Lumbago, s. ***ts**ak.*
Lumber, s. *balā·batar, be·**kkh**ai, nā·pakār.*
Luminous, a. *ro**kkh**ān, rū**ṇ**r.*
Lump, s. ***gh**aṭai, **gh**ūnḍūrai, peṛa, **ch**aka-ī, **ch**akṛa-ī.* (all of a-) *sūṭ·būṭ, aluwal.*
Lunacy, s. *lewan·tob, saudā.*
Lunatic, s. *lewanai, saudā-ī.*
Luncheon, s. *nihārai, nwaṛa-ī, da paste ḍoḍa-ī.*
Lungs, s. *sagai, parpūs.*
Lurch, v.n. ***ts**angzan ked.*
Lure, v.a. ***gh**ulawul, ṭagal; pa dalbe nīwul, pa ṭam'e-* or *pa ṭāmbe-,* etc. *nīwul.*
Lurk, v.n. ***gh**alai **kkh**kenāstal, puṭedal.* v.a. *pasūnai-, **ts**awai-,* etc. *nīwul.*
Lurking-place, s. *pasūnai, **ts**awai, puṭgana-ī.*
Luscious, a. ***kh**og, **kh**wand·nāk, maza·dār.*
Lust, s. ***sh**ahwat, mastī, nas, naus.*
Lustful, a. ***sh**ahwat·nāk, mast.*
Lustre, s. *ra**ṇ**rā, **dz**alak, bre**kkh**nā.*
Lustrous, a. *rū**ṇ**r, bre**kkh**·nāk, **dz**alak·nāk.*
Lusty, a. *zorāwar, tuwānā, quwat·nāk, tandrust; ma**gh**zan, gagar, kaṭah, peṛ, **ch**ā**gh**.*
Lute, s. ***sh**pela-ī, bindla-ī.*
Luxuriance, s. *prewānī, ziyātī, wadānī, ḍer·wālai, ābādī.*
Luxuriant, a. *prewān, ziyāt, wadān, ḍer.*
Luxurious, a. *nafs·parast, ārām·ṭalab.*
Luxury, s. *moṛ·tiyā, ārām·tiyā.*
Lynx, s. *pṛāng·pī**sh**, yūz.*

M.

Mace, s. *amsā, lawaṛ, ḍāng, ḍāngora-ī, gruz, koṭak.*
Macerate, v.a. ***kh**uṛīnawul, pastawul, **kh**u**sh**tawul, lūnd sātal.*
Machination, s. *band, taṛa, joṛi**kkh**t.*
Machine, s. *kālai, hatiyār.*
Mad, a. *lewanai, saudā-ī, **kh**u**sh**ai.*
Madam, s. *bībī, merman.*
Madder, s. *rodang, majīt.*
Madness, s. *lewan·tob, saudā.*
Magazine, s. *za**kh**īra, **kh**izāna, ganj.*
Maggot, s. ***ch**injai, kī**kkh**ai.*
Magic, s. *jādū, koḍa, siḥr.*
Magician, s. *jādū·gar, koḍ·gar, siḥr·gar.*
Magistrate, s. *ḥākim, 'amal·dār.*
Magnanimity, s. *himmat, zṛah.*
Magnanimous, a. *himmat·nāk, zṛah·war.*
Magnet, s. *āhan·rubā, **ch**umbak·kā**ṇ**rai.*
Magnificence, s. *raunaq, dabdaba, tamtarāq.*
Magnificent, a. *raunaq·dār.*
Magnify, v.a. *ziyātawul, **gh**aṭ-, loe-,* etc. *k.* (praise) *stāyal, ṡanā wayal.*
Magnitude, s. *loe-, **gh**aṭ-, star-,* etc. *-wālai.*
Maid, s. *jina-ī, pe**gh**la.* (bond-) *wīn**dz**a, kanīza.* (servant-) *mazdūra, **ch**ūra-ī, sahela-ī.* (bride's-) *wreyaza* or *wre-aza, wrā·bā**ṇ**ra-ī, mānja-ī, īnga.*
Mail, s. *z**gh**ara; **ch**alqat, zira.* (a man in-) *z**gh**ar·yālai.*
Maim, v.a. *guḍawul, **kh**ūgawul, kaṛam k.*; *jobalawul, **gh**wu**ts**awul, zam·zmolai k.*
Maimed, a. *guḍ, **kh**ug, jobal, **gh**wu**ts**, kaṛam, zam·zmolai, za**kh**mī, parhār·jalai, parhār·jan, māt·guḍ, sukṛuk.*
Main, a. *wṛūnbanai, awwalanai, wṛūnbai.*
Mainly, ad. *akṡar, ziyāt, ḍer, **gh**āliban, a**gh**lab.*
Maintain, v.a. *iqrār-, d'awa-,* etc. *k.*; *wayal.*

(defend) *jghoral, khundi k.* (support) *parwaral, pālal, sātal.*

Maintenance, s. *rozī, khwurāk, parwarish.*

Maize, s. *jwār, ghaṭ-jwār.* (ear of-) *wagai.* (ear cone of-) *shata-ī.*

Majestic, a. *shāhī, bādshāhī; loe, ghaṭ,'aẓīm.*

Majesty, s. *dabdaba, raunaq, jalāl; ḥaẓrat; salṭanat.*

Major, a. *loe, mashar; ziyāt, akṣar.*

Make, v.a. *joṛawul, kawul, paidā k.* (-amends) *tāwān warkawul.* (-away with) *wrukawul, puṭawul; wajlal, muṛ kawul.* (-good) *pūrah-, adā-,* etc. *k.* (-known) *khabarawul.* (-of, or understand) *pohedal.* (-out) *tsargandawul, kkhkārah-, daryāft-,* etc. *k.* (-over) *spāral, pāslawul, gumāral.* (-sure of) *yaqīn gaṇṛal.* (mix) *gaḍawul.* (-up, as a quarrel, etc.) *pakhulā k., gwākkhal, gwākkh-grandī k.* (collect) *ṭolawul.* (-towards) *khwā-ta-, lorī-ta-,* etc. *tlal—lāṛal.* (-much of) *nāzawul, nmāndzal.*

Make, s. *shakl, ḍaul, ṣūrat.*

Maker, s. *joṛawūnkai.* (in comp.) *-gar, -sāz, -kār.*

Making, s. *joṛawūna, sākht.*

Malady, s. *maraẓ, āzār, bīmārī, randz, nā-joṛ-tiyā, nā-rogh-tiyā.*

Male, a. *nar, nārīnah.* (-of cattle for breeding) s. *mīndah* or *hīndah.* (stallion) *turum.*

Malediction, s. *kkhera, bad-d'uā, l'anat.*

Malefactor, s. *gunāh-gār, bad-kār.*

Malevolence, s. *khwā-badī, kīna, badī.*

Malevolent, a. *khwā-bad, kīna-war.*

Malice, s. *kīna, badī, bughẓ.*

Malignant, a. *kīna-waṛ, bad.*

Malinger, v.a. *bāna-, lamghaṛa-ī-,* etc. *k.*

Mallet, s. *molai, ḍabalai, baghdar.* (washerman's-) *tsobāṛai.*

Maltreat, v.a. *bad-sulūk k., be-makh k., wahal.*

Mamma, s. *aba-ī, ada-ī, mor.*

Mammon, s. *daulat, duniyā, nafs.*

Man, s. *saṛai, wagaṛai, gawai; bashar, insān, bandah.* (wild-) *baṇṛ-mānū.*

Manacles, s. *da lās karī.*

Manage, v.a. *chalawul, kawul, sambālawul, tadbīr k., band taṛal.*

Manageable, a. *da kawulu, da sambālawulu,* etc. *pa qābū, gharīb; spuk, āsān.*

Management, s. *kār-sāzī, tadbīr, intiẓām.*

Manager, s. *kār-sāz, pesh-kār, dārogha h.*

Mandate, s. *ḥukm, farmān, farmā-ikkht.*

Mane, s. *wraṣ, yāl, okkhī, orī.*

Mange, s. *khārikkht, pam, pūn, garg, pa-akh.*

Manger, s. *ākhor.*

Mangle, v.a. *māṭawul, kanḍ-kapaṛ-, ṭoṭe-ṭoṭe-, chūr-laṭ-, char-chūr-, daṛ-daṛ-,* etc. *k.*

Mango, s. *am.* (-tree) *da am wana.*

Mangy, a. *paman, pa-akhai, gargai.*

Manhood, s. *dzwānī, zalmī-tob; mardī.*

Maniac, s. *lewanai, saudā-ī.*

Manifest, a. *tsargand, kkhkārah, bartser, ẓāhir.* v.a. *tsargandawul, kkhkārah-,* etc. *k., kkhayal—kkhowul.*

Manifestly, ad. *bartseran, pa jār* or *-ẓāhir.*

Manifestation, s. *tsargand-tob, kkhkārah-wālai; iẓhār, jār.*

Manifesto, s. *ishtihār, jār, iẓhār-nāma.*

Manifold, a. *ḍer, bragh-bragh, braghan.*

Mankind, s. *sarai, wagaṛai, gawai, insān, bashar.*

Manliness, s. *saṛī-tob, maṛanī-tob, nārīn-tob.*

Manly, a. *maṛanai, nārīnah.*

Manner, s. *shān, ṭaur, toga, rang, yang, wajha; ḍaul. chāl-chal, ṭaraḥ.*

Mannerly, a. *sulūkī, makhawar, adabī.*

Manners, s. *chāl, ādāb, khoe-khaṣlat, makh.*

Manœuvre, s. *chal, ḥikmat; tadbīr, band; fareb, lamghaṛa-ī.*

Manor, s. *dawtar, jāgīr, mulk; wanḍ, ada-ī.*

Mansion, s. *koṭa, mena.* (storied) *mānra-ī, ḥawela-ī.*

Manslaughter, s. *marg, khūn, qatl.*

Manslayer, s. *qātil, khūnī, marg kawūnkai.*
Mantle, s. (man's-) *chogha, kosai, junga-kaṛi shaṛa-ī; lūnga-ī, shamla, shāl.* (woman's-) *tsādar, paṛūnai, pachorai, chāyal, oḍana-ī, yaklā-ī.*
Manual, a. *dastī, da lās.* s. *kitāb.* (in comp.) *-nāma.*
Manufacture, s. *ḍast-kārī, joṛikkht, sākht.*
Manufacturer, s. *joṛawūnkai, kārī-gar.*
Manufactory, s. *kār-khāna.*
Manure, s. *sara, sarā.*
Manuscript, s. *dast-khaṭṭ; qalamī kitāb.*
Many, a. *ḍer, gaṇr.* (too-) *ziyāt.* (how-) *tso, tsomra.* (so-) *hombra, daghombra.* (as many as) *hombra chi.* (-coloured) *rangā-rang.* (-times) *ḍer dzala, wār-wār.*
Map, s. *nakhkkha, naqsha,*
Mar, v.a. *wrānawul, kharāb-, habatah-,* etc. *k.*
Marble, s. *mardaka.* (-stone) *marmar.*
March, s. *kūch, safar, pand.* (month) *chetar.*
Mare, s. *āspa, mādyān.*
Margin, s. *ghāṛa, morga, tselma, tsanḍa, ja-ī, laman.* (-of a book) *ḥāshiya.*
Marine, a. *daryābī.*
Mark, s. *nakkha; dāgh.* v.a. *nakkha lagawul; dāghawul; naẓar-, fikr-,* etc. *k.*
Marked, a. *nakkha-dār; dāghī; mashhūr.*
Market, s. *bāzār, ganj, haṭa-ī, manḍha-ī.*
Marketable, a. *bāzārī; chalanī.*
Marl, s. *maṭa-khāwra, maṭīna-zmaka.*
Marquee, s. *khaima, dera.*
Marriage, s. *wādah, nikāḥ.* (-feast) *kkhādī.* (-procession) *janj, wrā.* (-male guest) *jānjī, wrā-bāṇrai, mānjī.* (-female guest) *wrā-bāṇra-ī, wre-aza, mānja-ī.* (-gift) *belak.*
Married, a. (-man) *wādah-kaṛai.* (-woman) *wādah-shawī.* (under coverture) *maṛokkha.* v.n. *wadedal.*
Marrow, s. *māghzah, maghz.*
Marry, v.a. *wadawul, nikāḥ taṛal.* (-a husband) *tsakkhtan-, meṛah-,* etc. *k.* (-a wife) *kkhadza k.*
Marsh, s. *jaba.*
Marshy, a. *jaba-nāk, lūnd, zyam-nāk.*
Mart, s. *bāzār, ganj, haṭa-ī.*
Martial, a. *jangī, lakkhkarī.*
Martyr, s. *shahīd.*
Martyrdom, s. *shahādat.*
Marvel, v.n. *hariyānedal, hariyān* or *ḥairān ked., rabṛedal.*
Marvellous, a. *'ajab, 'ajīb, 'ajūbah, badī'a.*
Masculine, a. *nar, nārīnah, saṛai.*
Mash, s. *oghṛa, atūb, daliya.* v.a. *paz wahal.*
Mask, s. *parda, tsera; libās, swāng; fareb, bāna, chal.* v.a. *parda-,* etc. *k.*; *puṭawul, pokkhal.*
Mason, s. *rāj, m'imār.*
Mass, s. *ghunḍa, peṛa, chakṛa-ī; dala-ī, ḍera-ī.*
Massacre, s. *qatl, qatli-'āmm.* v.a. *qatlawul.*
Massive, a. *loe, ghaṭ, star; drūnd.* (-person) *khṛīs, nāpaṛ, punḍ, gagar.*
Mast, s. *tīr, loe stan da jahāz.*
Master, s. *khāwand, tsakkhtan, meṛah, nāyak, mālik.* (-of a house) *korbah.* (tutor) *ākhūn. ustād.* (school-) *mullā, mu'allim.*
Master, v.a. *lānde k., sambālawul. barai mūndal.*
Mastery, s. *barai; ḥukūmat.*
Masticate, v.a. *jowul* or *joyal, chīchal, kṛapawul.*
Mastiff, s. *khaḍal, ghaṭ ghartsanai-spai.*
Mat, s. *pūzai, pūhaṛ, anḍerai.*
Match, s. (contest) *bāzī, sharṭ.* (equal) *makhai, joṛah, gund, siyāl; sārai, samsorai, hum-dzolai.* (gun-) *patīla, bāta-ī.* (fire-) *shonṭa-ī; shūsha-ī.* (marriage) *kojdan.* (-maker) *rebār, dallāl, mandz-garai.*
Match. v.a. *barābarawul, joṛawul, lagawul; jangawul.* v.n. *barābaredal, joṛedal, lagedal.*

Matchless, a. *be-misāl, be-siyāl, be-nazīr, lā-sānī.*
Mate, s. *mal, mal-garai, joṛah, yār.*
Material, a. *jismī, tan-dār ; zarūr, grān.*
Materials, s. *kālī, haṭyār, asbāb, sāmān.*
Materially, ad. *ḍer, ziyāt, nihāyat.*
Maternal, a. *morunai.* (-relation) s. *mor-ganai.*
Mathematics, s. *'ilm da riyāzī.*
Matrix, s. *qālib, sāncha.*
Matrimony, s. *wādah.* (state of-) *wādah-tūn.*
Matron, s. *mor; merman, bībī, spīn-sara.* (-of a house) *korbana.* (-under coverture) *maṛokkha.*
Matted, a. *arjal-barjal, tsapolai, nkkhatai.*
Matter, s. *jism, māda, jauhar.* (affair) *kār, khabara.* (thing) *tsīz, shai.* (pus) *ziwa* or *zawa, zahūb, rash.* (dirt) *khīra, chirk, chikhai.* (concern) *gharaz.*
Mattock, s. *kodāla-ī, sakkhsora, saspor, kasha-ī.*
Mattress, s. *tolā-ī, nihālī, toshak, taltak.*
Mature, a. *pokh, pūrah, kāmil.*
Maturely, ad. *pa fikr-, ghaur-*, etc. *-sara.*
Maturity, s. *pokh-wālai, kamāl.*
Maul, v.a. *wahal, ṭakawul, kūṭal, mātawul.*
Maund, s. *man, las daṛa-ī.*
Maw, s. *jajūra.*
Mawkish, a. *balmangah* or *balmagai, be-khwand.*
Maxim, s. *matal, wayai, qānūn, masla.*
May, s. *jeṭ.*
Maze, s. *kaga-waga, pech-o-kham.*
Meadow, s. *warsho, chaman, kurūgh.*
Meagre, a. *ḍangar, narai, rangai, mahīn.*
Meal, s. *oṛah.* (fine-) *maidah.* (coarse-) *dal.* (rice-) *khamacha.* (pulse-) *rāṛa.*
Mean, a. *bakhīl, shūm ; spuk, dūn ; handai-zāt, kam-asl ; mandzwai, āwsaṭ.* s. *mandz.*
Mean, v.a. *m'anī-, maṭlab-*, etc. *laral ; qasd k.*

Meander, v.n. *girzedal, pechedal.*
Meaning, s. *m'anī, maṭlab ; qasd, mudd'ā.*
Meanness. s. *bakhīlī, shūm-wālai, spuk-tiyā.*
Means, s. *m'arifat, wasīla, wāsiṭa ; kabl.* (property) *panga, saga, māya ; māl, kharts.* (manner) *wajha, shān, rang, ṭaur.* (by no-) *hets-chare, kruṭ.* (by what-) *pa tsa shān.*
Meantime, } ad. *pa de mandz kkhke.*
Meanwhile, }
Measles, s. *sharai, sara-makha.*
Measure, v.a. *mech-, kach-*, etc. *k.* (weigh) *jokal, talal.* (divide) *weshal.*
Measure, s. *mech, kach ; tol, andāza, joka ; wesh.* (action) *kār, chal, band, tarkīb.* (grain-) *kuṛai, ogai, daṛa-ī.* (verse) *wazn.* (-in music) *tāl, tāng.* (-for land) *pa-aṛai.* (beyond-) ad. *la hadda ter.*
Measureless, a. *be-kach, be-andāzah, be-hadd, be-shān, be-qiyās.*
Meat, s. *ghwakkha.* (food) *khwurāk, ḍoḍa-ī, ghiza.*
Mechanic, s. *kasb-gar, pesha-war.*
Mechanism, s. *tarkīb, joṛikkht, sākhtagī.*
Medal, s. *tughma ; nakkha.*
Meddle, v.a. *gharaz k., lās lagawul, -āchawul, -war-wṛal*, etc.
Medial, a. *mandzwai, miyānah.*
Mediate, v a. *gwākkhal, gwākkh-grandī k.*
Mediation, s. *gwākh ; sipārish.*
Mediator, s. *gwākkh-grandai ; mandz-garai.*
Medical, a. *ṭibbī.* (-man) s. *ṭabīb.*
Medicine, s. *dawā, dārū, darmān.* (science of-) *ṭibb.* (practice of-) *ṭibābat, ṭabībī.*
Mediocrity, s. *nīmgarī-tob, ausaṭ.*
Meditate, v.a. *fikr-, ghaur-, andekkhnā-*, etc. *k.*
Medium, a. *mandzwai, miyānah.* s. *wasīla, wāsiṭa, m'arifat.*
Medley, s. *gāḍera, argajah, gaḍ-waḍ.*
Meek, a. *halīm, gharīb, pos, narm.*
Meekness, s. *halīm-tob, gharībi, pos-wālai.*
Meet, a. *pīrzo, wājib, munāsib, lā-iq.*

Meet, v.n. *pekkhedal, wrānde-, miliyā-*, etc. *ked.*; *jangedal, lagedal, yo·dzāe ked.* (find) v.a. *mūndal.*

Meeting, s. *majlis, tolai*; *mulāqāt, dīdan*; *jirga, jumā'at.* (-place) *borjal, tīkāo.*

Meetness, s. *pīrzowuna, pīrzo·wālai, lā-iq·wālai, munāsibat.*

Melancholy, a. *gham·jan, malāl*; *saudā-ī.* s. *nūl, gham*; *saudā.*

Mellow, a. *pokh, khurīn, pos*; *patakh.*

Melodious, a. *khush·āwāz, khūsh·bāng.*

Melody, s. *sarod, badala. tarāna.*

Melon, s. (water) *hindwāna, tarbūza.* (musk) *kharbūza*; *dastambol.* (sweet-) *khatakai, sarda, hand·yālai.* (wild-) *kākora, hāl-kūnda-ī.* (bitter-) *tarkha kākora.*

Melt, v.a. *wīlī k.*; *oba k.* v.n. *wīlī ked.*; *oba ked.*

Member, s. (-of the body) *andām, band.* (partner) *sharīk, brakha·khor.* (-of an assembly) *majlisī, jirgatū.* (clause) *juz, fasl.*

Membrane, s. *parda, jāla-ī.* (-of belly) *spekkhta.* (-of the heart) *dzān·khwal.*

Memoir, s. *tazkira, tawārīkh.*

Memorable, a. *qābil-* or *lā·iq da yād.*

Memorandum, s. *yād·dāsht, yād·gārī.*

Memorial, s. *yād·gār*; *'arzī, darkhwāst.*

Memory, s. *yād, hifz.*

Menace, v.a. *ratal, tratal, dabawul, dāral.*

Mend, v.a. *jorawul, raghawul.* (-clothes) *bezal, pezal.* v.n. *joredal, raghedal.*

Mendicant, s. *faqīr, gadāe*; *tālib.*

Menial, s. *nokar, chūrai, mazdūr.*

Menses, s. *haiz, zarūkī.*

Menstrual, a. *haizī.* (-woman) *haiz·dāra, haiza, bilmāza.* (-cloth) *derān.*

Mensuration, s. *mech, kach.*

Mental, a. *bātinī, qalbī.*

Mention, v.a. *yādawul*; *wayal, khabarawul.*

Mercantile, a. *da saudāgarī, tijāratī.*

Mercenary, a. *khpul·gharaz, duniyā·parast, zar·āshnāe.* (-soldier) *mlā·tar.*

Merchandise, s. *māl, jins, saudā*; *saudāgarī, banj, bipār* or *wapār, tijārat.*

Merchant, s. *saudā·gar, wapārī, banjārī*; *set*; *parāchah.*

Merciful, a. *mom·dil, rahm·dil.* (-God) *rahīm, rahmān, karīm.*

Merciless, a. *be·rahm, be·dard.*

Mercury, s. *pārā, sīmāb.*

Mercy, s. *rahm, rahmat, khwā·khūgī.*

Merely, ad. *sirp, surup, ta-ash, khālī, faqat.*

Meridian, s. *gharma, takanra·gharma.*

Merit, s. *haqq, qadr, yarz*; *sawāb.*

Meritorious, a. *wājib, lā-iq*; *sawābī.*

Merriment, s. *kkhādī, khūsh-hālī, khandā, washta·toqa.*

Merry, a. *kkhād, kkhād·man, khūsh·hāl, khandā·rūe.*

Mesh, s. *tor, jāla-ī. shabaka.*

Mess, s. *qatagh, ngolai.* (-of herbs) *sāgīnrai.* v.a. *hānda-ī-wālī k.*; *chūka k.*

Message, s. *khabar, paighām, karya.*

Messenger, s. *astādzai, qāsid, harkārah.*

Messmate, s. *hānda·ī·wāl.*

Metallic, a. *kānī.*

Metaphor, s. *misāl, majāz, kināyat.*

Metaphysics, s. *'ilm da maujūdāt.*

Mete, v.a. *weshal*; *mech-, kach-*, etc. *k.*

Metempsychosis, s. *tanāsukh.*

Meteor, s. *lūk, laka-ī, shughla.*

Method, s. *tartīb, shān, rang, daul, hikmat, toga, yang*; *taur, tarīqa.*

Methodise, v.a. *tartībawul.*

Metre, s. *wazn, mech, mīzān.*

Metropolis, s. *pāe·takht, dāru·l·mulk.*

Mettle, s. *garand·wālai, tund·wālai*; *marāna*

Mettlesome, a. *garandai, tund, tez*; *maranai*

Mew, v.a. *miyāw k.*

Midday, s. *gharma, takanra·gharma, nīma wradz.*

Middle, a. *mandzwai, miyānah.* s. *mandz* or *miyandz.* (-finger) *mandza·gūta.*
Middling, a. *nīmgaṛai, hase.*
Midge, s. *māshai, ghamāsha.* (water) *jak, jakh.*
Midnight, s. *nīma·shpa, shūma.*
Midst, a. *mandzwai, miyānah.*
Midway, s. *nīma·lār, pa lāri.*
Midwife, s. *qābila, dā-ī.*
Mien, s. *tsihra, ṣūrat*; *rang, ḍaul*; *chāl, yūn.*
Might, s. *quwat, zor, was, tuwān, bram, qudrat.*
Mighty, a. *zorāwar, maẓbūṭ, tuwānā, qawī.*
Mitigate, v.a. *kaḍa wṛal, legdal—lekkhal, kūch-, naql-,* etc. *k.*
Milch, a. *langa, pa-ī·wara.*
Mild, a. *ḥalīm, narm, pos, khog*; *emaṇ.*
Mildew, s. *chaṇrāsa, chata-ī.*
Mildness, s. *ḥalīm·tob, narmī, pos·wālai,* etc.
Military, a. *jangī, lakkhkarī.*
Milk, s. *pa-ī, shaudah.* (sour-) *khaidak, praṇr.* (curdled-) *māstah.* (butter-) *shomle* or *shlonbe, kha-areṛai.* (whey) *tarwe.* (candle-) *matar* or *matra, kaṛa.* (-pail) *doṇra-ī, lawaghūna.* (-maid) *ghobana.* (-man) *ghobah.* (-and water) *lassī.* (first-) *wargah.*
Milk, v.a. *lwashal.*
Milkless, a. *wucha, zāṛa-ī.*
Mill, s. (hand-) *mechan.* (water-) *jaranda, āsiyā.* (oil-) *gāṇra-ī.* (-stone) *da mechani gaṭa.*
Miller, s. *jarand·garai, muẓd·garai, āsiyā·wān.*
Millet, s. *ghokkht, gdan, kārah.*
Million, s. *las laka.*
Mimic, s. *pekkhe·gar, malanḍai, swāngai.*
Mimicry, s. *pekkha, malanḍa, swāng.*
Mince, v.a. *qīma-, ṭoṭe·ṭoṭe-, reze·reze-,* etc. *k., warjal.*
Mind, s. *zṛah, dil, dzān*; *'aql, poha, pahm, hokkh*; *khwā*; *gharaẓ*; *fikr, rāe*; *yād.* (presence of-) *ausān, baidārī.* (out of one's-) *ausān·tlalai.*
Mind, v.a. *yād laral, manal, fikr-,* etc. *k.*
Mindful, a. *yādawar, khabar·dār, hokkhyār.*
Mine, s. *kān*; *surang, naqab.* pr. *dzamā, khpul.*
Mine, v.a. *kān·kanal, -kanaudal,* or *-kanastal, surang wahal.* (-a house) *kanḍar māṭawul* or *k.*
Miner, s. *kān·kanūnkai*; *surang wahūnkai, naqab·zan*; *kanḍar kawūnkai.*
Mingle, v.a. *gaḍawul, laṛal, ṛaqawul.*
Minister, s. (-of state) *wazīr.* (agent) *wakīl, nāẓir, nā-ib, gumāshtah, dīwān.*
Minister, v.a. *khidmat k.*; *warkawul.*
Ministry, s. *khidmat.*
Minor, a. *kashar* or *kishar*; *la-ag, kam.*
Minority, s. *kishar·tob, wuṛūk·wālai*; *la-ag, kam.*
Minstrel, s. *muṭrib, sandar·bol, sarodī, mīrāṣī, ḍum.*
Mint, s. *ṭaksāl, ẓarb·khāna.* (the plant) *n'anā, pūdīna.*
Minute, s. *laḥẓa, sā'at, dam.* (note) *yād·gār.*
Minute, a. *narai, mahīn, bārīk*; *pūṭai, pitsāṇrai.*
Minutely, ad. *pa kkhah shān sara.*
Miracle, s. *karāmat, m'ujaza.*
Miraculous, a. *'ajab, 'ajīb, karāmatī.*
Mirage, s. *sarāb.*
Mire, s. *khaṭa, chikaṛ, chakṛaba.*
Mirror, s. *ā-īna, shīsha, hindāra.* (-for the thumb) *shasht, ārsā-ī.*
Mirth, s. *kkhādi, khūsh·hālī. khwakkhī, khandā.*
Miry, a. *chikṛan, khaṭolan.*
Misapply, v.a. *be·dzāe lagawul, 'abaṣ k.*
Misapprehension, s. *nā·pohī, khaṭā.*
Misbegotten, a. *ḥarāmī, pa khaṭā paidā,* or *ghalaṭ·paidā.*

Misbehaviour, s. *bad-chāl, bad-sulūkī, nā-rāstī.*
Miscarry, v.n. *wrukedal.* (abort) v.a. *geḍa ghurzawul, ziyān-, tāwān-,* etc. *k.*
Miscellaneous, a. *biyal, judā ; be-tartīb, gaḍ-waḍ.*
Miscellany, s. *jung, gāḍera, aṛgaja.*
Mischief, s. *tāwān, nuqṣān, ziyān ; dukkh-manī, badī ; pasāt; shar, sharārat ; wīta, shokhī.*
Mischievous, a. *moẕī, muzirr, ziyān-kār, ta-wānī ; bad, kharāb, sharīr.* (-boy) *wītakai.*
Misconduct, s. *bad 'amalī, -kārī, -chalan,* etc.
Miscreant, s. *kāfir, bad-ẕāt, mardūd.*
Misdeed, s. *gunāh, quṣūr, taqṣīr, wabāl.*
Miser, s. *shūm, bakhīl, tang-dast.*
Miserable, a. *khwār, tabāh, kharāb-khastah.* (worthless) *nā-kārah, nā-tsīz, nā-kas.*
Misery, s. *khwārī, tabāhī, khasgī* or *khastagī, nā-kasī, tangsiyā, nā-chārī, muflisī.*
Misfortune, s. *āfat, balā, bad-, kam-, tor-,* etc. *-bakhtī, nāzila, muṣībat.*
Mislay, v.a. *wrukawul, be-dzāe keḍal* or *kkhkeḍal.*
Mislead, v.a. *ghulawul, gumrāh k.*
Mismanage, v.a. *be-tadbīrī k., wrānawul, kharābawul.*
Miss, v.a. *khaṭā k.* v.n. *ter watal.*
Missing, a. *puṭ, wruk.*
Mission, s. *āstawuna, risālat.*
Missionary, s. *āstādzai.*
Misspell, v.a. *peẓa-ī-, hezgī-, hijgī-,* etc. *pa khaṭā wayal* or *-k.*
Mist, s. *laṛa, dund, gard, ghubār.*
Mistake, s. *khaṭā, būlāwa, ghalaṭ.*
Mistress, s. *merman, korbana ; m'ashūqa, yāra, āshnāya, 'aurata.*
Mistrust, s. *shakk, bad-gumān, wiswās.* v.n. *shakk-,* etc. *laral.*
Mistrustful, a. *shakk-man, bad-gumānī, wis-wāsī, be-i'tibār, stāra-prewatai.*

Misty, a. *dund, gard-jan, ghubārī.*
Misunderstanding, s. *nā-pohī, nā-pahmī ; mānṛai, marawar-tiyā ; mīrtsī, badī.*
Mite, s. *pūṭai, batsarai, pitsāṇrai ; richa.*
Mitigate, v.a. *la-agawul ; kamawul, saṛawul.*
Mix, v.a. *gaḍawul ; laṛal, ṛaqawul.*
Mixed, a. *gaḍ ; laṛalai.*
Mixture, s. *gaḍa, gāḍera ; murakkab.*
Moan, s. *zwergai* or *zgerwai, bilāṇra, heng, angahār.* v.a. *zwergai-,* etc. *k.*
Moat, s. *kanda, kāha-ī, khandaq.*
Mob, s. *paṛk, ṭolai, ḍala, ghol, gaṇr.*
Mob, v.a. *ger k., isārawul* or *ḥiṣārawul.*
Mock, v.a. *pekkhe k., khandā pore k.*
Mockery, s. *pekkha, khandā, ṭoqa.*
Mode, s. *shān, rang, toga, ṣūrat, wajha ; chāl, chalan, ṭaur, dastūr, rasm, ṭarīqa.*
Model, s. *naqsha, namūna ; nakkha, ḍaul ; qālib, kālbūt.* v.a. *pa nakkhe-,* etc. *joṛa-wul.*
Moderate, v.a. *sambālawul, kamawul.*
Moderate, a. *mandzwai, miyānah, muwāfiq.*
Moderation, s. *ṣabr, zgham, parhez.*
Modern, a. *nawai, osanai, osan.*
Modest, a. *sharm-, ḥayā-, ghairat-,* etc. *-nāk, sharm-sār ; nek, pāk-laman.*
Modesty, s. *sharm, ḥayā,* etc.
Modify, v.a. *ṣūrat-,* etc. *warkawul ; bad-lawul.*
Modulate, v.a. *āwāz joṛawul, sarod k., tarāna-, sandara-, zamzama-,* etc. *wayal.*
Moiety, s. *nīm, nīmai, nīmāyah.*
Moist, a. *lūnd, zyam-nāk, nam-nāk, naw-jan.*
Moisten, v.a. *lūndawul* or *lambdawul.*
Moisture, s. *lūnd-wālai, zyam, naw, nam.*
Mole, s. *potai, ghunḍa-ī, ḍera-ī, kha-aṭ ; dam-dama.* (-of the skin) *ta-apai, khāl.*
Molest, v.a. *pārawul, rabṛawul, zoral.*
Molestation, s. *āzār, rabaṛ, ṭongāṛa, blos,* etc.
Mollify, v.a. *narmawul, pastawul, saṛawul.*

Molten, a. *wīlī, wīlī shawai.*
Moment, s. *lahza, dam, sā'at, drang*; *parwā, fikr, gharaz.*
Momentary, a. *teredūnai, nā-pāedār.*
Momentous, a. *drūnd, grān, mushkil*; *zarūr, muhimm.*
Monarch, s. *bādshāh, amīr, sultān.*
Monarchy, s. *bādshāhī, saltanat.*
Monday, s. *pīr, gul.*
Money, s. *rok, tanga, naghd* or *naqd, paisa, rūpa-ī.* (-changer) *sarrāf.*
Moneyed, a. *daulat-man, duniyā-dār, māl-dār, da rūpo paiso khāwand.*
Moneyless, a. *ta-ash lās, be-daulat, muflis.*
Mongoose, s. *nolai.*
Mongrel, a. *nīmchah, dwah-ragah.*
Monitifn, s. *nasīhat, pand.*
Monitor, s. *nāsih, pand warkawūnkai.*
Monkey, s. *bīzo, shādo.*
Monopoly, s. *khāss saudā, ijāra.*
Monotonous, a. *yo-shān, yo-wazn.*
Monsoon, s. *parshakāl.*
Monster, s. *dew, dad, rawai*; *banr-mānū.*
Monstrous, a. *haul-nāk, 'azīm, 'ajīb.*
Month, s. *myāsht.* (solar-, used with reference to agriculture and the seasons, commencing at April) *wīsāk, jet, hār, pashakāl, bādro, asū, kātak, mangar, poh, māh, paganr, chaitr.* (lunar-, used with reference to dates, festivals, etc.) *hasan husen, safara, wrūnba-ī khor, dwayama khor, driyama khor, tsalorama khor, da khudāe myāsht, da sho qadr* or *da barāt myāsht, da roje myāsht, da wurūkī akhtar myāsht, khālī* or *miyāna, da loe akhtar myāsht.*
Monthly, ad. *myāsht pa myāsht, māh-wārī.*
Monument, s. *tsalai, nikkhān, nakkha.* (tomb) *maqbara, qabr, khāda.*
Mood, s. *hāl, shān*; *rang, khoe.*
Moody, a. *khapah, malāl, sūt-būt.*
Moon, s. *spogma-ī.* (new-) *myāsht.* (-less) *torogma-ī.* (-light) *spogma-ī, rabanra.* (-stroke) *bar.* (-struck) *bar-wahalai.*
Moor, s. *habshī, zangī.* (marsh) *jaba.*
Moor, v.a. *langar achawul, lagawul, taral.*
Mope, v.n. *ghamedal, nūledal*; *malāl kedal.*
Mopish, a. *gham-jan, nūl-jan, malāl.*
Moral, a. *pāk, pākīzah, nekokār.* s. *nasīhat, pand*; *hāsil, gharaz.*
Morality, s. *nekī, nekokārī, rikkhtīn-tob.*
Moralize, v.a. *pand wayal, nasīhat wayal.*
Morals, s. *nek-chalan, nekokārī, sīrat.*
Morally, ad. *pa haqq, pa rikkhtiyā.*
Morass, s. *jaba, bokkhtana, taramna, yala.*
Morbid, a. *kharāb, wrān*; *nā-jor, nā-rogh.*
More, a. *ziyāt, nor.* (-and more) *nor ziyāt.* (-or less) *la-ag ziyāt.*
Moreover, ad. *bal, balki, wale, nor, siwā la de na.*
Morning, s. *sahr* or *sahār.* (-star) *starga.* (to-morrow-) *sabā* or *subha.*
Morose, a. *sūt-būt, bad-khoe, trīw-makh, tursh-rūe, bakhīl.*
Morrow, s. *sabā, subha.* (day after-) *bul-sabā.*
Morsel, s. *nwara-ī, gola*; *pitsānrai, pūtai.*
Mortal, a. *fānī, tlūnai, teredūnai.* (human) *insānī, basharī, wagarai.* (deadly) *qātil, kārī, halākil.*
Mortal, s. *sarai, wagarai, gawai, insān, bashar.*
Mortality, s. *ajal, marg, maut*; *sarī-tob, bashriyat, insāniyat.*
Mortar, s. *baghara-ī.* (cement) *kūnai, gach.*
Mortgage, v.a. *gānra-, graw-*, etc. *k.*
Mortification, s. *gazak, skhā-wālai*; *randz, da zrah nūl, paskhāk.*
Mortify, v.n. *gazak-, skhā-*, etc. *ked.*, *wrost-edal.* v.a. *karawul, sedzal, āzārawul.*
Mosque, s. *jumā'at, masjid.*
Moss, s. *da wano waran khwar*; *babar wākkhah chi da wano pa pot bānde tūkegī.*
Most, a. *aksar, ziyāt, nihāyat.*

Mostly, ad. *aksar, ziyātī, aghlab, ghāliban.*

Mote, s. *khas, khasanrai, khāsha.*

Moth, s. *or-pukkht, patang*; *da zarūko chinjai.*

Mother, s.' *mor, aba-ī, ada-ī.* (-in-law) *khwākkha.* (grand-) *nyā, anā.* (great grand-) *warla-anā, da nyā mor.* (great great grand-) *lā-warla-anā, da nyā nyā.* (step-) *ba-an-mor, maira-mor.* (-less) *yasīr, be-mor, mor-murai.* (-of pearl) *sīpa-ī.*

Motion, s. *harakat, khwadzedana.*

Motive, s. *sabab, bā'is, matlab, mūjib, kabl.*

Motley, a. *brag, gag, chrag-brag, brag-yālai*; *gad-wad*; *rangīn.*

Motto, s. *'alāma, nakkha.*

Mould, s. *qālib, kālbūt, sāncha.* (mildew) *zang, chanrāsha.* (earth) *khāwra.* (manure) *sara.*

Mould, v.a. *jorawul, tandal, sūrat-, daul-,* etc. *warkawul.*

Moulder, v.n. *sharhedal, wrostedal, khāwre ked.*

Mouldy, a. *zang-jan, chanreshan.*

Moult, v.a. *kurīz k., rajawul.* v.n. *rajedal.*

Mound, s. *dera-ī, ghunda-ī, potai, kha-at, rāsha, rashaka, tall.*

Mount, v.n. *khatal.* (-upon) *sparedal.* v.a. *khejawul.* (-a jewel) *jarāo k.*

Mountain, s. *ghar, koh.* (-ridge) *ghākkhai, kamar.* a. *ghartsanai, kohistānī.* (-goat) s. *ghartsah.*

Mountaineer, s. *kohistānai, rohilai, ghartsanai.*

Mountainous, a. *ghartsan, kohistān.*

Mourn, v.a. *jaral, wīr k., wainā wayal.* v.n. *karedal, nūledal, ghamedal.*

Mourner, s. *wīr-jalai, gham-khor.*

Mournful, a. *wīr-nāk, gham-nāk.*

Mourning, s. *wīr, jarā*; *gham, nūl*; *wainā wayana.*

Mouse, s. *mayakūrai.* (-hole) *sūra.*

Mouth, s. *khula.* (small-) *khulga-ī.*

Mouthful, s. *nwara-i, mara-ī, gola.*

Move, v.a. *khwadzawul.* v.n. *khwadzedal.*

Movement, s. *harakat, khwadzedana.*

Mow, v.a. *lau k., rawdal, rebal.*

Mower, s. *lau-garai.*

Much, a. *der, prewān.* s. *prewānī, der-wālai.* (how-) *tsomre.* (so-) *hombra.* (so much so) *tar daghah pore.*

Mucilage, s. *chīr, salekkh, leta-ī, l'uāb.*

Mucilaginous, a. *salekkh-nāk, laha-jan, l'uāb-dār, chīran.*

Mucus, s. *laha, l'uāb.* (-of nose) *karmeza, kanr, kharmat, grang.* (-of bowels) *rama, rap.* (-of urethra, etc.) *maza-ī.*

Muck, s. *sara, derān, khīrai, rash.*

Mud, s. *lāha, khata, chīkar.* (-for building) *paskha.*

Muddy, a. *khatolan, kha-ar, chikran.*

Muffle, v.a. *ngharal—nghakkhtal, putawul, pokkhal.*

Mug, s. *piyāla, kandolotai.*

Mulberry, s. *tūt.* (royal-) *shāh-tūt.* (seedless-) *be-dāna tūt.* (black-) *tor-tūt.* (white-) *spīn-tūt.* (grey-) *bor-tūt.*

Mulct, v.a. *tāwān-, nāgha-,* etc. *ākhistal.*

Mule, s. *khachar* or *kachar, qātar.*

Multiform, a. *rangā-rang.*

Multiplication, s. *bragh, zarb, jor.*

Multiplicity, s. *prewānī, der-wālai, ziyāt-wālai.*

Multiply, v.a. *zarb-, bragh-,* etc. *k., hisāb-jorawul.* (increase) v.a. *ziyātawul, wadānawul, derawul.* v.n. *ziyātedal, wadānedal, deredal.*

Multitude, s. *lakkhkar, pauz* or *fauj, dala, ganr khalq* or *-'ālam.*

Mumble, v.a. *bar-bar-, pus-pus-, gūn-gūn,* etc. *k.*

Mummy, s. *momiyāe.*

Munch, v.a. *krapawul, jowul* or *joyal, chīchal.*

Mundane, a. *duniyā-ī.*

Munificence, s. *sakhī-tob, sakhāwat, bakkhan-tob.*

Munificent, a. *sakhī, sakhāwatī, bakkhana kawūnkai.*

Murder, s. *marg, khūn, qatl.* (price of-) *diyat.* v.a. *khūn-*, etc. *k., muṛ k., wajal* or *wajlal.*

Murderer, s. *khūnī, qātil, marg kawūnkai.*

Murderous, a. *khūn-khwār, khūnāṛai.*

Murky, a. *tor, dund, tīrah, gard-jan.*

Murmur, v.a. *baṛ-baṛ-, ṭar-ṭar-*, etc. *k.* (complain) *māna-, gila-*, etc. *k.* (-as a brook) *juṛ-juṛ k.* (-as the belly) *quṛ-quṛ k.* s. (-of conversation) *gungosai, pus-pus, zwag-zwūg, kkhkālwa.*

Murrain, s. *ṭak, ṭak-sarai.*

Muscle, s. *ghwakkha, līnda-ī.*

Muscular, a. *ghwakkha-war, gagar, mazai. khrīs.*

Muse, v.a. *fikr k.* v.n. *fikr-man ked.*

Museum, s. *'ajā-ib-khāna.*

Mushroom, s. *kha-areṛai, gūmāndū, samārūgh.*

Music, s. *sarod, zamzama, tarāna.*

Musical, a. *sarodī, khūsh-āwāz.*

Musician, s. *sarod-gar, muṭrib, ḍum, mīrāṣī.*

Musk, s. *mukkhk.* (-pod) *mush-kunḍa-ī.* (-rat) *mukkhkai mayak. mukkhkīn mayak.*

Musket, s. *ṭopak, bandūkh.*

Muslin, s. *malmal.*

Must, v. imp. *boya chi, zarūr* or *lāzim dai chi.* (he must do it) *boya chi wu e kawī* or *kī.* Must is also expressed by using the past participle of the verb with *boya.* Ex. (it must be done) *kaṛalai boya.* Or it is expressed by using the infinitive alone with the third person singular present tense, of the auxiliary *yam.* Ex. (we must go) *mūnga ta tlal dai.*

Mustard, s. *sharsham.* (wild-) *awrai.* (-tops) *ghandal.* (-seed) *mandaw.* (-threshed stalks) *kāmbūra.*

Muster, v.a. *shmeral, shmāral, sān nīwul.*

Musty, a. *wr st, skhā; chanreshan.*

Mutable, a. *nā pāe-dār, be-qalār.*

Mute, a. *gung, lal; chip, ghalai.*

Mutilate, v.a. *māṭawul, prekawul, kharāb k.; jobalawul, ghwutsawul, kaṛam k.*

Mutineer, s. *yāghī-gar, pasātī.*

Mutinous, a. *yāghī, sar-kakkh.*

Mutiny, s. *yāghī-garī, balwā, pasāt.*

Mutter, v.a. *baṛ-baṛ-, ṭar-ṭar-, pus-pus-*, etc. *k.*

Mutton, s. *da ga-ade ghwakkha.* (shoulder of-) *walai.* (leg of-) *patūn.*

Mutual, a. *da dwāṛo palo* or *-lorīo* or *-khwāo; ṭarafain, jānibain.*

Mutually, ad. *yo bul sara, dzabla.*

Muzzle, s. *poza, ūrbūz, tambeza.* (-for the mouth) *tambūzak, tambezai, korai.* v.a. *khula bandawul, tambūzak*, etc. *ṭaṛal* or *-lagawul.*

Myriad, s. *las zara; tūmān.*

Myself, pr. *zah khpul, khpul-dzān.*

Mysterious, a. *puṭ, nā-m'alūm, ghā-ib.*

Mystery, s. *ghā-ib, puṭa-khabara.*

N.

Nail, s. *mekh, mogai.* (-of finger, etc.) *nūk.*

Nail, v.a. *ṭakawul.* (pay cash) *rok warkawul.*

Naked, a. *barbanḍ* or *barmanḍ, lūts.* (stark-) *lūts-pūts, lūts-lapaṛ, lūts-laghaṛ.*

Nakedness, s. *barbanḍ-tob, laghaṛ-tob, lūts-wālai.*

Name, s. *nūm, nām.* v.a. *nūm kegdal* or *kkhkegdal.* (mention) *nūm ākhistal, yādawul.*

Named, a. *nūmedah, nūmāndai.*

Namely, ad. *y'ane, maṣlan, ganre.*

Namesake, s. *hum·nām, pa nāmah sharīk.*
Nap, s. *ṭūk.* (sleep) *khob, parnā, churt.*
Nap, v.a. *khob-, parnā-,* etc. *wṛal.* v.n. *khob zangedal.*
Nape, s. *tsaṭ; waja.*
Napkin, s. *rūe·māl, dast·māl.*
Narration, s. *bayān; qiṣṣa, rawāyat, naql.*
Narrator, s. *nāqil, qiṣṣa kawūnkai.*
Narrow, a. *tang.* v.a. *tangawul.* v.n. *tangedal.*
Narrowly, ad. *pa sakhtī sara; pa fikr sara.*
Narrowness, s. *tang·wālai; tangsiyā; bakhīl·tob.*
Nasty, a. *nā·kārah, makrūh, kagalai; nā·pāk, palīt, khīran, murdār.*
Nation, s. *qām, ulūs, tabār, firqa.*
National, a. *qāmī; waṭan·dost.*
Native, a. *aṣlī, ẕātī; waṭanī, mulkī, wilāyatī.* s. *waṭanī, wilāyatī, balad.* (-country) *waṭan, wilāyat.*
Nativity, s. *paidā-ikkht, zegedah.*
Natural, a. *ẕātī, ṭab'a-ī.* (-son) *ḥarāmī.*
Naturalize, v.a. *khpulawul, sharīk k.*
Naturally, ad. *pa·khpula.*
Nature, s. *khoe, khaṣlat, lokkhai, mizāj, ṭab'a, ṭabī'at.* (world) *naṛa-ī, duniyā, 'ālam.*
Naught, s. *hets.*
Naughty, a. *bad, kharāb, nā·kārah.*
Nausea, s. *mīkkh·mīkkhai, kaha, koe, bāka-ī, kraka, kūz·kātah.*
Nauseate, v.a. *chinjawul, kūz katal* or *-goral.* v.n. *chinjedal, mīkkh·mīkkh ked.*
Nauseous, a. *chinjan, kraka·nāk, bad·khwand.*
Naval, ad. *jahāzī, dariyābī.*
Navel, s. *nū* or *nūm.*
Navigate, v.a. *jahāz chalawul.*
Nay, ad. *nah, yah, āyā.*
Near, a. *nijdai.*
Nearness, s *nijdekī,*
Neat, a. *pākīzah* or *pāzīkah, sādah, spetsalai.*
Neatness, s. *pākīzagī, spetsal·tob, joṛāb.*

Necessarily, ad. *kkhā-ī, boya, khwāh·makhwāh.*
Necessary, a. *lāzim, ẓarūr, bāedah, wājib.* (it is-) *boya chi, lāzim dai.* s. *chār·choba.* (to go to the-) *awdas k.*
Necessitous, a. *ḥājat·man, muḥtāj, darmāndah.*
Necessity, s. *ḥājat, ẓarūrat.*
Neck, s. *mara-ī, ghāṛa, markanḍa-ī.* (nape) *ormeg.*
Necklace, s. *amel, kār, psol.* (-ring) *oga-ī.*
Necromancer, s. *siḥr·gar, koḍ·gar, jādū·gar.*
Necromancy, s. *siḥr, koḍa, jādū.*
Nectar, s. *āb da ḥayāt, da kawṣar oba.*
Need, s. *ḥājat, ghokkht, ẓarūrat.* v.a. *ḥājat-,* etc. *laral, ghokkhtal.*
Needful, a. *ḥājat·man; lāzim, ẓarūr, pa·kār.*
Needle, s. *stan.* (eye of-) *swam* or *spam.* (packing-) *sparkhai.* (knitting-) *dūk, sīmak.* (-work) *ganḍal, skoe.*
Needless, a. *'abaṣ, be·fā-ida, nā pakār, be·kkhai.*
Needy, a. *muḥtāj, ḥājat·man.*
Nefarious, a. *bad, nā·kārah, nakkhanai.*
Negative, a. *nahī, nafī.* v.a. *man'a-, nahiya-,* etc. *k.*
Neglect s. *ghaflat, be·fikrī, be·khabarī, be·parwā-ī.*
Negligent. a. *ghāfil, be·khabar, be·parwā.*
Negotiate, v.a. *sawāl·dzawāb-, m'amala-, jirga-, kār·rozgār-, khabara-,* etc. *k.*
Negotiator, s. *dallāl, rebār, mandz·garai.*
Negro, s. *ḥabshī, zangī.*
Neigh, s. *shashnrai, hanr.* v.n. *shashnredal, hanredal.*
Neighbour, s. *gāwanḍai, hamsāyah.*
Neighbourhood, s. *gāwanḍ, cham.*
Neither, c. *na yo na bul.*
Nephew, s. (sister's son) *khora-e.* (brother's son) *wrārah.* (clansman's son) *'azīz.*
Nerve, s. *pla, rag, wuja; himmat, zṛah, quwat.*

Nerveless, a. *be·himmat, be·zṛah, nā·mard.*
Nervous, a. *yer·man, harānd, yeredūnkai.*
Nest, s. *jāla, āshiyānc.*
Net, s. (fish-) *jāla.* (bird-) *jāl.* (-for hay, etc.) *trangaṛ, koṛai, lad, shalīta.*
Nether, a. *lar, lāndai, kūz.*
Nettle, v.a. *pārarul, ṭongarwul, khapah k.* s. *jalbang.* (-rash) *laṛama.*
Never, ad. *hechare, hado, kets·kala, la·sara.*
Nevertheless, ad. *walekin, magar, sara la de.*
Neuter, a. *hijrai.* (-verb) *lāzimī.*
Neutral, a. *biyal, judā.*
New, a. *nawai, tāzah, osanai.* (-cloth) *kora, shaḍala, batī ḍaka.*
News, s. *khabar.* (good-) *zerai, sār.* (-paper) *akhbār.*
Next, a. *nijdai.* (the-) *bul.* (-time) *biyā.*
Nib, s. *tsūka, peza.* (beak) *makkhūka.*
Nibble, v.a. *chīchal.*
Nice, a. *khwand·nāk, maza-dār.* (accurate) *jukht, barābar, joṛ.* (fine) *narai, bārīk.* (delicate) *nāzuk.*
Nicely, ad. *pa maze sara, pa kkhah shān sara.*
Niche, s. *ṭāq, ṭāqcha, darai, rap.*
Nick, s. *barghanḍ, jghanḍ, kandaw.* (-of time) *ṭāng, neṭa, puk, mūda.*
Nickname, s. *laqab.*
Niece, s. (brother's daughter) *wrera.* (sister's daughter) *khordza.* (clanswoman's daughter) *khor·lanṛa.*
Niggard, a. *bakhīl, shūm, tang·dast.*
Nigh, a. *nijde, tsakha* or *khatsa.*
Night, s. *shpa.* (all-) *kara-ī·shpa.* (last-) *begāh, barāyah, begana-ī-, parūna-ī-, barana-ī-,* etc. *shpa.* (to-) *nan·shpa, mākkhām, begāh.* (dark-) *tora·shpa, taro-gma-ī.* (moonlight-) *spogma-ī, ranṛā·shpa.* (-blind) a. *sho·kor* or *shom·kor.* (-blindness) *sham·kor·tiyā.* (-attack) *sho·khūn.* (-watching) *sho·gīrī.*
Nightingale, s. *bulbul, kastūra.*

Nightmare, s. *khapasa* or *khapaskai, rawai.*
Nimble, a. *gaṛandai, chust, chālāk, tak·lāstai, jalt, tez, zghard.*
Nine, a. *nuh.* (ninth) *nuham.* (-fold) *nuh·bragh, nuh·chand.*
Nineteen, a. *nuh·las.* (nineteenth) *nuh·lasam.*
Ninety, a. *nawe.* (ninetieth) *nawiyam.*
Nip, v.a. *shūkawul.* (pinch) *skūnḍal.* (-with cold) *sedzal, wahal.*
Nippers, s. *ambūr, nūtsai.*
Nipple, s. *tai.*
Nitre, s. *kkhora.* (nitrous) a. *kkhoran.*
No, ad. *na, yah, āyā.* (-one) *hets·tsok.*
Nobility, s. *amīr·tob, sāwū·tob, sharāfat.*
Noble, a. *aṣīl, sāwū, ashrāf; loe, ghaṭ, zbarg.* s. *amīr, arbāb, khān.*
Nobly, a. *amīr·shān.*
Nobody, s. *hets tsok, hets kas; nā·tsīz, nā·kas, lā shai.*
Nocturnal, a. *da shpe.* (-pollution) *shaiṭān khaṭā.*
Nod, v.a. *sar ṭīṭawul.* v.n. *khob zangedal.*
Node, s. *pāṛsob, stagh, ghunḍārai, margharai.*
Noise, s. *ghag, zwag, ghāw, shor, chagh, bāng,* etc. (to make a-) *ghagawul, chaghawul, zwag-,* etc. *k.* v.n. *ghagedal, chaghedal.*
Noisome, a. *kagalai, gandah, kraka·nāk, bad.*
Noisy, a. *shor·mār, ghag·mār, shor·pusht, ghāw·nāk, zwag·nāk.*
Nominal, a. *khiyālī, nāmī.*
Nominate, v.a. *muqarrar k., wudrawul, kkhkenawul; nūm akhistal* or *-kkhayal—kkhowul.*
Nomination, s. *muqarrar kawuna, wudrawuna.*
None, a. *hets.*
Nonexistence, s. *nisht·wālai, nestī.*
Nonexistent, a. *nishtah, nest.*
Nonplus, v.a. *hariyānawul, rabṛawul lā·dzawāb-, lā·chār-, band-,* etc. *k.*

Nonsense, s. *wucha-pucha-, be-hūda-, ḍūza-,* etc. *-khabara, qatāra, shkhaṛa, kitī-pītī,* etc.

Nonsuit, v.a. *bāelawul, pa-aṛ k.*

Nook, s. *gūṭ, gokkha.*

Noon, s. *gharma, ṭakanṛa-* or *ṭakanḍa-gharma.*

Noose, s. *pulwākkha, ghaṛwandai, ghaṛāsha, pakhwandai, kamand, zanda-ī.* (-of hair) *lūma, lūmaka.*

Nor, c. *na.* (nor one nor the other) *na yo na bul.*

North, s. *shamāl, quṭb, kkhai ṭaraf.* (-star) *quṭb storai.*

Northward, a. *quṭb khwā* or *-lorai* or *-ḍaḍa,* etc.

Nose, s. *poza.* (-bag) *tobra.*

Nosegay, s. *gul-dasta.*

Nostril, s. *spegma, spenga.*

Not, ad. *na.* imp. *ma.* (-at all) *la sara, haḍo.*

Notable, a. *mashhūr, nūm-war*; *lā-iq da yād.*

Notch, s. *barghanḍ, ĵghand, wut.*

Note, s. *nakkha, 'alāmat.* (letter) *khaṭṭ, chīṭa-ī.* (bond) *ḥujjat, tamassuk.* (voice) *tarāna, bāng, āwāz.* (musical-) *zīr, trang, wazn.* (memo.) *yād-dāsht.* (marginal-) *ḥāshiya.*

Note, v.a. *qiyās-, fikr-, ghaur-,* etc. *k.* (write) *līkal, kāgal—kkhkal, darj k.* (look) *katal, goral, līdal, naẓar k.*

Noted, a. *mashhūr, nūm-war, nām-dār.*

Nothing, s. *hets, hets shai*; *nā-tsīz.*

Notice, s. *naẓar, liḥāẓ, mulāḥiẓa*; *khabar, iṭṭilā'a, jār.* v.a. *naẓar-,* etc. *k.*

Notify, v.a. *khabarawul, jār wahal.*

Notion, s. *khiyāl, gumān, fikr, wahm.*

Notoriety, s. *zwag, shuhrat, āwāza.*

Notorious, a. *mashhūr, m'alūm, tsargand.*

Notwithstanding, c. *walekīn, magar, sara la de, har tsomra, bā-wujūd.*

Noun, s. *ism, nūm.*

Nourish, v.a. *sātal, pālal, nmānḍzal, parwaral.*

Nourisher, s. *pālūnkai, sātūnkai,* etc.

Nourishing, s. *pālana, sātana.* a. *quwat-nāk.*

Nourishment, s. *parwarish, pālana*; *khwurāk.*

Novel, a. *nawai.* s. *qiṣṣa, naql.*

November, s. *magar.*

Novice, s. *shāgird, nawai āmokhtah, kachah.*

Now, ad. *os, dā sā'at.* (-adays) *nan-wradzi.*

Nowhere, ad. *hets-charta, hets-dzāe.*

Nowise, ad. *hets-shān, hets-rang.*

Noxious, a. *ziyānī, nuqṣānī, tāwānī, mozī, muẓirr.*

Nudity, s. *barbanḍ-tob, lūts-wālai.*

Nugatory, s. *'abaṣ, nā kārah, lā ḥāṣil, be-fā-ida.*

Nuisance, s. *wabāl, moẓī, muẓirr.*

Null, a. *'abaṣ, bāṭil, spuk, khushai.*

Numb, a. *ūdah, be-ḥiss.* (with cold) *qaṛqe-chan, marghechan.*

Number, s. *shumār* or *shmer, ḥisāb, 'adad.* v.a. *shmeral* or *shmāral, ḥisāb k.*

Numberless, a. *be-shumār, be-ḥisāb.*

Numeration, s. *shumār* or *shmer, ḥisāb.*

Numerous, a. *ḍer, gaṇr, frewān, wadān.*

Nuptial, a. *nikāḥī.* (-ceremony) *wādah.* (-knot) *nikāḥ.* (-song) *kkhādiyāna.* (-feast) *kkhādī.*

Nurse, s. *dā-ī.* v.a. *pālal, tai warkawul.*

Nurture, s. *parwarish, pālana.* v.a. *pālal, parwaral.*

Nut, s. *jauz.* (Nutmeg) *jauza.*

Nutriment, } s. *khwurāk, khwāṛah, ghiẓā,*
Nutrition, } *parwarish.*

Nutritious, a. *quwat-nāk, quwat bakkhūnkai.*

Nymph, s. *ḥūra, parī.*

O.

O (sign of vocative), *o, wo, ai, yā.* in. *āh, e, eh, he, hāe.* (in pain) *wāe, wā-ī.*

Oak, s. *balūṭ.* (-apple) *māzū.*

Oakum, s. *saṇr, paṭ.*

Oar, s. *chapa.*
Oath, s. *qasam, saugand, ḥalaf.*
Obdurate, a. *sakht, be-dard, be-raḥm; ṭakanrai, hoḍai, khpul-sar, sar-kakkh.*
Obedient, a. *farmān-wṛūnkai, ḥukm-manūnkai, tābi'a-dār.*
Obeisance, s. *salām, ādāb; sijda.*
Obelisk, s. *munāra, tsalai, stan; khaza* or *khāda.*
Obese, a. *peraṛ, tsorb, ghaṭ, punḍ, lwāṛ, peṛ.*
Obey, v.a. *manal, ḥukm pa-dzāe rāwṛal, tābi'a-dārī k.*
Object, s. *shai, tsīz; gharaẓ, niyat, maṭlab.*
Object, v.a. *'uẕr-, takrār-, ḥujjat-,* etc. *k.; daregh k.*
Objection, s. *'uẕr, ḥujjat, takrār; daregh.*
Oblation, s. *qurbān, ṣadqa, dzār; naẕr, niyāz.*
Obligation, s. *farẓ, sharṭ, wājib; neṭa, wāda, taṛa, bandanṛ, lafẓ, qaul; minnat, khāṭir-dārī.*
Oblige, v.a. *minnat-dār-, khāṭir-dār-,* etc. *k.* (force) *zoral, be-was k.*
Obliged, a. *minnat-dār, iḥsān-man.*
Obliging, a. *khāṭir-dār, makhawar, mihrbān.*
Oblique, a. *tratskan, koẓ, kṛīng.*
Obliterate, v.a. *wrānawul, wrukawul, wahal.*
Oblivion, s. *her-wālai, nisiyān.*
Oblivious, a. *her-man, be-fikr, nisiyān-kawūnkai.*
Oblong, a. *ūgd.*
Obloquy, s. *peghor, tuhmat, tor, malāmat.*
Obnoxious, a. *moẓī, muẓirr, be-kkhai.* (liable) *shwūnkai, lāndai, maghlūb.*
Obscene, a. *pūch, palīt, murdār, pūhaṛ, nā-pāk.*
Obscure, a. *tor, tīrah; dund, kha-aṛ, gard-man, gard-jan; puṭ, nā m'alūm; kam ẕāt* or *-aṣl,* or *-nogai,* etc.
Obscurity, s. *tyāra, tor-tam, ẓulmat.*
Obsequies, s. *fātiḥa* or *pātā, lās-nīwah, d'uā.*
Obsequious, a. *khūshāmad-gar, ḍirpalai, jig-jigiyā.*

Observance, s. *makh, adab, khidmat: 'amal, ist'imāl; dastūr, rasm, ṭarīqa.*
Observation, s. *naẓar, mulāḥiẓa; līdah, kātah; khabara, wayai.*
Observe, v.a. *katal, goral, līdal, naẓar k.; manal; wayal, khabara k.*
Obsolete, a. *ghair ist 'imāl, -chalan, -riwāj,* etc. *mansūkh, band, bāṭil.*
Obstacle, s. *aṛ, band, nkkhatai, kariyāb.*
Obstinate, a. *sar-kakkh, khpul-sar, hoḍai, haṭai.*
Obstreperous, a. *jang-yālai, shorī, takanṛai, pasātī.*
Obstruct, v.a. *haṭālawul, kariyābawul, nkkhla wul, bandawul, man'a k.*
Obstruction, s. *aṛ, band, nkkhatai.*
Obtain, v.a. *mūndal, gaṭal, biyā-mūndal.* v.n. *jārī ked.; chaledal, lagedal.*
Obtrude, v.a. *dūsa k.* v.n. *be-dzāe nanawatal, -rāghlal, -prewatal,* etc.
Obtuse, s. *pa-ats* or *p-uts.* (stupid) *pūhaṛ, kawdan.* (not pointed) *lwāṛ, ghaṭ.*
Obviate, v.a. *girzawul, man'a k., lār nīwul.*
Obvious, a. *tsargand, kkhkārah, ẓāhir, bartser..*
Occasion, s. *heṛ, plā, dzal, guẕār; nobat, neṭa, mūda, wakht.* (cause) *bā'iṡ, sabab.* (need) *pa-kār, ẓarūr, gharaẓ.*
Occasion, v.a. *paidā k., rāwṛal, khejawul, kawul, kṛal.*
Occasionally, ad. *kala-kala, kala-nā-kala.*
Occupation, s. *kār, kasb, mashghulā, chār.*
Occupy, v.a. *mashghūlawul, lagawul, dzāyawul; dzāe nīwul, ākhistal, lānde k.; 'amal k.*
Occur, v.n. *kedal, prewatal, nāziledal, wāqi'a ked.* (-to the mind) *yādedal.*
Occurrence, s. *wāqi'a, chal, ḥādiṡa, ittifāq.*
Ocean, s. *baḥr, qālī-* or *qārī dariyāb.*
Ochre, s. *ziyaṛa-khāwra.* (red-) *bagwa, sara-khāwra.*
October, s. *kātah.*

Odd, a. *'ajab, 'ajīb.* (not even) *tāk* or *ṭāq.* (-and even) *tāk·o·juft.*

Odds, s. *farq, biyal·tūn, biyal·wālai, tafāwat.* (strife) *patna, steza.* (gain) *zor, aghlab.* (-and ends) *balāe·batar.*

Ode, s. *ghazal, landa-ī, sandara, chār·bait.*

Odious, a. *makrūh, kaṛalai, ghāndah, kharāb, nā·khwakkh, nā·pasand, khwā·bad.*

Odium, s. *malāmat, peghor, tor, tuhmat; kīna, badī, khwā·badī.*

Odoriferous, a. *khūsh·bū-ī·dār, bū-ī·nāk.*

Odour, s. *bū-ī, bo* or *boe.* (sweet-) *khūsh·bū-ī* or *khūsh·boe.*

Œsophagus, s. *sara·ghāṛa, ḥalq.*

Of, p. *da.* (on account-) *dapāra da.*

Off, ad. *lire* or *liri.* (-hand) *sam da lāsa.* (to go-, come-, etc.) v.n. *lire ked.* (to go off, as a gun, etc.) v.n. *khalāṣedal, chaledal.* (well-) a. *mor.* (-and on) ad. *kkhkata·porta.*

Offal, s. *ūjarai, larai; murdār; jūṭa, pas·khurda.*

Offence, s. *gunāh, taqṣīr, wabāl.* (pique) *mānrai, marawar·tiyā; randz, khapagī.*

Offend, v.a. *gunāh-,* etc. *k., marawar-,* etc. *k., khapah-,* etc. *k.*

Offended, a. *marawar, khapah, bezār.*

Offender, s. *gunāh·gār, taqṣīrī.*

Offensive, a. *bad, nā·pasand, kharāb; moẓī, muẓirr.*

Offer, v.a. *warkawul.* (sacrifice) *qurbān-, ṣadqa-,* etc. *k.* (devotō) *nazr-, niyāz-,* etc. *gdal* or *īgdal.* (present) *nazrāna-, pekkh·kakkh-,* etc. *warkawul.* (attempt) *qaṣd-, niyat-,* etc. *k.* (propose) *wayal, pukkkhtedal.*

Offering, s. *qurbān, ṣadqa, dzār; nazr, niyāz.*

Office, s. *kār, khidmat; dzāe, 'uhda, manṣab.* (-room) *daftar·khāna.* (good-) *sulūk, mrasta.* (bad-) *bad·sulūk, badī.*

Officer, s. *sardār, 'uhda·dār, manṣab·dār.*

Official, a. *sarkārī, khidmatī.*

Officiate, v.a. *khidmat k., nā-ib·garī-, qā-im·muqāmī-,* etc. *k.*

Officious, a. *harbaṛai, 'alwalai; khidmatī.*

Offspring, s. *alwād, zāwzād, farzand, tūng.*

Often, ad. *wār·wār, bār·bār, ḍer·dzala.*

Ogle, v.a. *zarana-ī-, dzīr-,* etc. *k., pa·zarana-ī katal, starge wahal, pa·trats katal.*

Oh, in. *āh! eh! he! hāe! wāe! wāh!*

Oil, s. *tel.* (-man) *telai.* (-press) *gānra-ī.* (-cake) *kal.* (-jar) *daba.* (hair-) *pulel* or *fulel.*

Oily, a. *ghwaṛ, tel·jan.*

Ointment, s. *malham, paha, tab.*

Old, a. *zoṛ, kuhand.* (-man) *spīn·gīrai, būḍā.* (-woman) *spīn·sara, būḍa-ī.* (-age) *zoṛ·tiyā, zoṛ·wālai.*

Olive, s. *kkhona* or *kkhawana, zaitūna.*

Omelet, s. *khāgīna.*

Omen, s. *pāl.* (good-) *akhtar.*

Ominous, a. *bad·pāl, bad·shugun.*

Omission, s. *khaṭā, quṣūr, ter·wātah.*

Omit, v.a. *terawul, herawul, pregdal.*

Omnipotent, a. *qādir, kirdigār.*

Omnipresent, a. *ḥāẓir·o·nāẓir, har dzāe.*

On, p. *pa, bānde, pre, par, da bānde, da pāsa, pre·bānde.* (in front) *wṛānde, makh·kkhke.*

Once, ad. *yo dzal, -heṛ, -wār, -guzār,* etc., *yawa·plā.* (-before) *pakhwā, wṛānde.* (at-) *os, pa ṭakī, pa de sā'at.* (all at-) *yak·lakhta, nātsāpa, tsaṭ·waṭ.*

One, a. *yo.* (in comp.) *yak.* (every-) *har·yo.*

Oneness, s. *yo·wālai, yaktā-ī.*

One's-self, pr. *dzān, khpul·dzān; nafs.*

Onerous, a. *drūnd, grān, mushkil, sakht.*

Onion, s. *piyāz.*

Only, ad. *sirp* or *surup, faqaṭ, khālī, ta-ash.* a. *yawādzai, tsaṛah, biyal.*

Onset, s. *halla, tsot, guzār, brīd.*

Onward, ad. *wrānde, makh·kkhke.*

Ooze, v.n. *tsātsedal, watal.* s. *lāha, khaṭa.* (green-) *ūbṛa-ī.* (moisture) *zyam, naw.*

Opaque, a. *dund, kha-ar, ganr, gūr.*

Open, a. *prānatai, wāz, arat.* (clear) *ṣāf, spīn.* (apparent) *tsargand, kkhkārah.* (-as a door) *lire* or *liri.*

Open, v.a. *prānatal, aratawul.* (undo) *spardal.* (spread-) *khwarawul, ghwarawul.* (-as a flower) v.n. *khwaredal, ghwaredal.* (as a door) v.a. *lire k.*

Opening, s. *prānatana; sparakkhtana; khwaredana,* etc. (orifice) *khula, sūra.*

Openly, ad. *pa tsargand, pa jār* or *-ẓāhir.*

Openness, s. *arat·wālai; tsargand·tob.*

Operate, v.a. *kār-, 'amal-, pāzah-, aṣar-,* etc. *k.*

Operator, s. *kār·kawūnkai, fā'il; kār·guẓār.*

Opinion, s. *fikr, rāe, tadbīr, khiyāl, gumān, qiyās.*

Opiniative, a. *khpul·rāe, khpul·sar, kibr·jan.*

Opium, s. *apīm, afiyūn, tiriyāq.*

Opponent, s. *mudda'ī, mukhālif, ẓidd; dukkhman.*

Opportune, a. *munāsib, jukht, pa·dzāe, pa·wakht.*

Opportunity, s. *wakht, tāng, neta, nobat, sā'at, puk.*

Oppose, v.a. *man'a k., haṭālawul, bandawul, lār nīwul, jangawul, muqābala k.* v.n. *makhā·makh-,* etc. *ked., jangedal.*

Opposite, a. *makhā·makh, wrāndai; mukhālif, aks.*

Opposition, s. *ẓidd, hod; jang, dukkhmanī, badī.*

Oppress, v.a. *zoral, ẓulm-, jafā-,* etc. *k., āzārawul.*

Oppression, s. *ẓulm, jafā, dzaur, zorāwarī, zabardastī, zor, ziyātī.*

Oppressor, s. *ẓālim, jafā·kār, zorāwar.*

Opprobrious, a. *bad, nā·kārah, bad·nāmūs, ruswā-ī.*

Option, s. *wuk, ikhtiyār, khwakkh, pasand, raẓā.*

Opulent, a. *daulat·man, māl·dār, duniyā·dār.*

Or, c. *yā.* (-else) *ki·na, kanra; ganre.*

Orach, s. *sārma.*

Oracle, s. *kalām.* (person) *zbarg.*

Oral, a. *zabānī, wayai.*

Orange, s. *nāranj.* (colour) *sūr·bor.*

Oration, s. *w'aẓ, khabara, taqrīr.*

Orator, s. *w'aẓ kawūnkai, taqrīrī, sukhan·sāz.*

Orb, s. *tsarkh.* (-of sun, etc.) *kakorai, ṭakai, chakla-ī; qurṣ.*

Orbicular, a. *ghund, ghund·man.*

Orbit, s. *daur, daurān.*

Orchard, s. *bāgh.*

Ordain, v.a. *muqarrar k., wudrawul, farmāyal, wayal.*

Ordeal, s. *āzmekkht, imtiḥān.*

Order, s. *tartīb, tadbīr; ḥukm, farmā-ikkht, farmān, amr; qām, ẓāt, nog, rang; dastūr, ṭarīqa, rasm.* (in order that) *tso chi.*

Order, v.a. *farmāyal, ḥukm k.*

Orderly, a. *ārāstah, pa tartīb, pa qā'ida.*

Ordinance, s. *ḥukm, amr; shar'a, qānūn; sunnat; qā'ida, ā-īn.*

Ordinary, a. *'āmm, jārī, chalanī; spuk, halak.*

Ordnance, s, *top, top·khāna.*

Ordure, s. *ghul, murdār, khīra.*

Ore, s. *khāwra, kānrai.* (copper-) *da tāmbe kānrai.* (iron-) *da ospane khāwra.*

Organ, s. *ālat, 'aẓū.* (musical-) *bāja.*

Organize, v.a. *jorawul, tarkīb k., tandal.*

Orifice, s. *khula, sūra.* (small-) *swam* or *spam.*

Origin, s. *aṣl, nogai, mund, wekh, būnsaṭ.*

Original, a. *aṣlī, awwal, nog.*

Originally, ad. *wrūnbe, pa aṣl, pa awwal.*

Originate, v.a. *paidā-, jārī-,* etc. *k., chalawul, bāsal—yastal, kāgal—kkhkal.*

Ornament, s. *zewar, kālai, gānra* or *gahana; zeb, zīnat; andzor, kkhewa, singār.* (-for the head) *t'awīẓ, gul, dāra-ī, tīk.* (-for the ear) *lakkhta-ī, wāla-ī.* (-for the nose) *pezwān, natka-ī, chār·gul, pīsha-ī.* (-for the neck) *amel, ūga-ī, baḍa-ī.* (-for the arm) *kara, wakkhai, kanganr, bangrai, gūjra-ī, bāhū, ma-aṭkai.* (-for the feet) *pāekara, pakhwandai, pāenzeb.* (-for the finger) *tsalai, gūṭa, anrwat, shasht, ārsā-ī.*

Ornament, v.a. *joṛawul, andzorawul, dzān-, ḍaul-,* etc. *joṛawul, kkhewa-, singār-,* etc. *k.*

Orphan, s. *yatīm, yasīr, plār·muṛai, mor·muṛai.*

Orpiment, s. *hartāl, zarnīkh.*

Orthodox, a. *momin, sunnī, īmān·dār, chār·yārī; sūchah, rikkhtīnai, rāst·man.*

Oscillate, v.n. *dzwaṛandedal, zangedal, rapedal.* v.a. *ṭāl khwuṛal* or *-wahal.*

Oscillation, s. *zangedana, ṭāl, zāngo.*

Ostensible, a. *tsargand, kkhkārah, jār* or *ẓāhir.*

Ostentation, s. *lāpa, dzān kkhkārah·kawūna, dzān stāyana.*

Ostentatious, a. *lāpai, ṭatai, dzān kkhkārah kawūnkai, dzān stāyūnkai* or *-stāyana kawūnkai.*

Ostler, s. *ṭeliyā, nokar, nafar.*

Other, pr. *nor, bul.* (-wise) ad. *nor·shān, būl·shān; ka·na, ganra, kanra.*

Otter, s. *saglāo* or *sanglāo, sīndlāo.*

Ought, v. imp. *boya chi, kkhā-ī chī.*

Ounce, s. *nīma·chiṭāka-ī.*

Our, ours, pr. *dzamūnga* or *dzamūga.*

Ourselves, pr. *mūng·* or *mūg·khpul.*

Out, ad. *bāhir, warchane* or *wardzane.* (expelled) a. *sharaṭai.* (expended) a. *pūrah, tamām.* (extinguished) a. *muṛ, soṛ.* (get out!) in. *lire sha, biyarta sha.*

Outcast, s. *sharaṛalai, sharūnai, pradai.*

Outer, a. *bāhir; pradai, begānah, oprah.*

Outlaw, s. *farārī ghal, yāghī·gar, sharūnai.*

Outlet, s. *khula, lār; warkh; ghwagai.*

Outline, s. *nakhkkha* or *naqsha, kīl, karkkha.*

Outlive, v.n. *pāedal, pātedal, bachedal.*

Outrage, s. *zor, ẓulm, ziyātī, jafā, be·satrī.*

Outright, ad. *sam da lāsa, tsaṭ·waṭ; amānī, pūrah, pāk·ṣāf.*

Outside, s. *bāhir, makh.* (without) p. *warchane* or *wardzane.* (on the-) p. *pās, dapāsa, bānde.*

Outstrip, v.a. *pa zghākkht-* or *pa daw-,* etc. *lānde k.,* or *-wrusto prejdal.*

Outward, a. *bāhir, bartser, oprah.*

Outwardly, ad. *bartseran, pa jār, ẓāhiran.*

Outwit, v.a. *ṭagal, ghulawul.*

Oval, a. *ūgd, ghunḍ·man,*

Oven, s. *tanūr.*

Over, p. *pās, bānde, da bānde.* (across) *pore.* (above) *da pāsa.* (more-) *ziyāt, ḍer.*

Overbalance, v.n. *dranedal, sangzan ked.*

Overbearing, a. *zabardast, zorāwar, ẓālim; kibr·jan, maghrūr, khpul·sar, khpul·rāe.*

Overcast, a. *ganr, gūr, puṭ, tor, siwrai·kaṛai.*

Overcome, v.a. *lānde k., pa-aṛ k., barai mūndal, wahal, mātawul.*

Overflow, v.n. *toyedal* or *toe ked., lāhū ked.*

Overhaul, v.a. *laṭawul, atsanral, shanal.*

Overhear, v.a. *āwredal, ghwag tsāral.*

Overleap, v.a. *pore dangal.*

Overlook, v.a. *katal, līdal, goral.* (forgive) *bakkhal, pulawul.* (pass over) v.n. *ter watal.*

Overplus, s. *ziyātī, bāqī, junga.*

Overpower, v.a. *lānde k., pa-aṛ k.*

Overrate, v.a. *ziyāt ganral* or *-shmeral.*

Overrule, v.a. *ḥukm mātawul* or *-wahal.*

Overrun, v.a. *tākht·tārāj-, lūṭ-, tālā-, wairān-,* etc. *k.* (spread) v.n. *khwaredal, ghwaredal, wīṛedal.*

Overseer, s. *peshkār, dārogha.* (of crops) *kakkhai.*

Overset, v.a. *naskorawul, aṛawul.*

Oversight, s. *khaṭā, ter·wat.*

Overt, a. *tsargand, kkhkārah, prānatai, ẓāhir.*

Overtake, v.a. *lānde k., nīwul.*

Overthrow, v.a. *mātawul, wahal, pa-aṛ-*

lānde-, etc. *k.*; *naṛawul*, *ghūrzawul.* (ruin) *pāe-māl-*, etc. *k.*, *latārawul.* (in wrestling) *parzawul.*

Overthrow, s. *māt*, *shikast*, *pa-aṛ.*

Overture, s. *sawāl*, *pukkhtana*, *khabara.*

Overturn, v.a. *naskorawul*, *aṛawul*, *pa-aṛ-makh k.*

Overwhelm, v.a. *ḍūbawul*, *gharqawul.*

Owe, v.n. *porawuṛai-*, *qarẓ-dār-*, etc. *ked.*

Owl, s. *gūngai*, *chagharū.*

Own, pr. *khpul.*

Own, v.a. *khpulawul*, *laral*; *manal*, *gaṇral*; *qabūlawul*, *iqrār k.* v.n. *qā-il ked.*

Owner, s. *khāwand*, *meṛah*, *tsakkhtan*, *mālik.*

Ox, s. *ḍangar*; *ghwāe* or *ghwayai*, *ghutskai.*

Oxymel, s. *sikanjabīn*, *turanjabīn.*

Oyster, s. *kastūra.*

P.

Pace, s. *qadam*, *yūn*, *gām*; *chāl*, *tag*, *raftār.*

Pacify, v.a. *pakhulā k.*, *saṛawul*, *rogha-joṛa-*, etc. *k.*; *tasallī-*, *dilāsa-*, etc. *warkawul.*

Pack, s. *bār*, *peṭai*, *panḍ*, *laḍ.* (half-) *anḍai.* (-ropes) *wākkhkai*, *siyala-ī.* (-sack) *malaw*, *ghundai*, *tsaṭa.* (-net) *trangaṛ*, *korai*, *laḍ*, *shalīta.* (-saddle) *kata*, *pālān.* (party) *paṛk*, *ṭolai.*

Pack, v.a. *dzāyawul*, *taṛal*, *ṭolawul*, *nghaṛal* —*nghakkhtal.*

Packet, s. *gāṭla-ī*, *panḍūkai*, *panḍa*, *geḍai.*

Packthread, s. *natsai*, *muzai.*

Pad, s. *manjala* or *manjīla*; *bālikkhtak*, *bālikkhtgoṭai*, *moṛa.*

Paddle, v.a. *chape wahal.* (in water) *lānbo k.*

Padlock, s. *jandra*, *qulf.*

Pagan, s. *but-parast*, *kāfir*, *gabr.*

Paganism, s. *but-parastī*, *kāfir-tob.*

Page, s. *ṭeliyā*, *nokar*, *jilaw-dār*; *mra-e*, *ghulām.* (-of a book) *safḥa.*

Pageant, s. *tamāsha*, *nandāra.*

Pail, s. *taghār*, *gaḍhal*, *ḍol*, *satal*, *maṭkai.* (milk-) *doṇra-ī*, *lawaghūna.*

Pain, s. *khūg*, *daṛd*, *zakhm*, *'azāb*, *swai.* v.a. *khūgawul*, *daṛdawul*, *zahīrawul.* v.n. *khūgedal*, *daṛdedal*, *zahīredal*, *swal.*

Painful, a. *dard-man*, *zakhmī*, *khūg-man.*

Pains, s. *kokshiksh*, *miḥnat*, *sa'ī.* (-of child-birth) *da langedo dard.*

Paint, v.a. *rangawul*, *rang lagawul.*

Painting, s. *rangawūna*; *tsera*, *taṣwīr*, *naqsha.*

Pair, s. *bragh*, *qulba*, *joṛa.*

Palace, s. *dargāh*, *bārgāh*, *daulat-khāna.*

Palatable, a. *khwand-nāk*, *maza-dār.*

Palate, s. *tālū.* (soft-) *kūmal.*

Pale, s. *sperah*, *sperchan*, *be-rang*; *ziyaṛ*, *shīn*, *spīn*; *kha-aṛ*, *īro-rang.* (stake) s. *mogai.*

Palisade, s. *keṛ*, *bāra.*

Pall, s. *tsādar*, *kapan* or *kafan.*

Palliate, v.a. *spukawul*, *kamawul*, *la-agawul.*

Pallid, a. *sperah*, *sperchan*, *ziyaṛ*, *shīn*, *kha-ar.*

Palm, s. *warghawai*, *khapar*, *lapa.* (-measure) *tsapak.* (-tree) *khajūr.*

Palpable, a. *tsargand*, *kkhkārah*, *bartser.*

Palpitate, v.n. *rapedal*, *laṛzedal*, *dṛakedal.*

Palpitation, s. *laṛza*, *dradzedana*, *dṛakedana*, *rapedana.* (-of heart) *khafqān.*

Palsied, a. *shall*, *guzan wahalai.*

Palsy, s. *guzan.*

Paltry, a. *spuk*, *khushai*, *nā-kārah.*

Pamper, v.a. *nāzawul*; *maṛawul.*

Pamphlet, s. *risāla*, *woṛ* or *wūṛ kitāb*, *juz.*

Pan, s. (metal) *tabakhai*, *dechka*, *kaṛahai*, *baṭ.* (pottery) *lokkhai*, *kaṭwa-ī*, *taba-ī*, *maṭkai.* (of wood) *kkhānak*, *kachkol.*

Panacea, s. *aksīr.*

Pancake, s. *paṛāta*, *weshala*, *kāk*, *kakoṛai.*

Pander, s. *baṛwā*, *dallāl.* v.a. *dallālī k.*

Pane, s. (-of glass) *ā-īna.*

Panegyric, s. *stāyana, ṣanā, t'arīf.*

Panegyrist, s. *stāyana-, ṣanā-*, etc. *goe* or *-wayūnkai.*

Pang, s. *tsiṛīka, brekkh, dard.* (death-) *dzān·kandan.*

Pangolin, s. *kishor.*

Panic, s. *tor, tara, haibat, wera, khof* (-struck) *tor khwūṛalai, weredalai.*

Pannier, s. *kawāra, kāra, kajāwa.*

Pant, v.a. *sā pa lanḍa ākhistal.*

Pantaloons, s. *paṛtūg, tambān, shalwār.* (the string) *paṛtūghākkh.* (the hem) *baḍa.* (the leg) *pāentsa.* (the fork) *khakkhtag.*

Panther, s. *pṛāng, baur, baurgai.*

Pantry, s. *ambār·khāna.*

Pap, s. (teat) *tai.* (paste) *leṭa-ī, oghṛa, atob.*

Papa, s. *bābā, bābū; plār.*

Paper, s. *kāghaẕ.*

Par, s. *barābar·wālai, twal, gundī.*

Parable, s. *matal, miṣāl.*

Parade, s. *dab'daba, tamtarāq.* (military) *qawā'id, sān.* (-ground) *qawā'id·gāh, maidān.*

Paradise, s. *jannat, bihikkht.*

Paradox, s. *da 'aqla līre, aṛawuli khabara.*

Paragraph, s. *juz, qiṭ'a.*

Parallel, a. *sam, barābar, sara sam.*

Paralysis, s. *guzan, shall.* (-of face) *laqwa.*

Paralytic, a. *shall, guzan·wahalai.*

Paramount, a. *mashar, ghaṭ, loe.*

Paramour, s. *yār, āshnāe, m'ashūq.*

Parapet, s. *mard·rau, kangūra; sangar, bāra, panāh.*

Paraphrase, s. *tarjūma, sharaḥ.*

Parasite, s. *khūshāmad·gar, ḍirpal; ṭufailī, lwegand, taghārai.*

Parboil, v.a. *nīm·josh k., nīma·khwā eshawul.*

Parcel, s. *gāṭla-ī, butskha, butskhaka.* (-of land) *bakhra, wesh, paṭai.*

Parch, v.a. *wrītawul, talawul, alwoyal, teyal, kaṛawul.* v.n. *wuchedal, wrītedal, kaṛedal.*

Parched, a. *wrīt, teyalai, alwoyalai*, etc. (-grain) s. *nīna, pūlah.*

Parchment, s. *raqq.*

Pardon, s. *bakkhal, m'uāf k.*

Pare, v.a. *khriyal, togal, tarāshal.* (-the nails) *nūkūna ākhistal.* (a tree) *lakkhte prekawul* or *-shūkawul.*

Parent, s. *mor, plār.*

Parentage, s. *aṣl, kor, nogai, khāndān, khūna, nasal, nasab.*

Paring, s. *tarāza, chūr.*

Parish, s. *tapa, kandai, cham, mālat, wanḍ.*

Parity, s. *barābarī, samsor·tiyā. siyālī, gundī.*

Park, s. *kkhkār·gāh.* (artillery-) *top·khāna.*

Parley, v.a. *sawāl·dzawāb-, khabare-*, etc. *k.*

Parliament, s. *da ulus jirga, da qām majlis.*

Parlour, s. *dar·dālān.*

Paroxysm, s. *ghoṭa, nobat, bārī.*

Parrot, s. *totā, totī.*

Parry, v.a. *girzawul, bachawul, daf'a-, lire-*, etc. *k., bandawul, man'a k.*

Parsimonious, a. *kam·kharts, tang·dast, bakhīl.*

Parson, s. (moslem-) *imām.* (pagan-) *bām-baṇr.* (christian) *pādrī.*

Part, s. *brakha, ḥiṣṣa, wesh.* (-of debt) *ūgrā-ī, qisṭ.* (place) *dzāe, zmaka.* (piece) *ṭoṭa.* (side) *janba, para, ṭaraf.* (-of speech) *kalima.* (for the most-) *akṣar.* (own-) *khpul·dzān.* (a small-) *la-ag·shān.* (to take in ill-) *bad manal.* (to take in good-) *kkhah manal.*

Part, v.a. *biyalawul, dwah·dzāe k., judā k.* (share) *weshal.* (-with) *pregdal, prekkho-dal, prekkhawul, prekkhal, tark k.* v.n. *biyaledal, dwah·dzāe-, judā-*, etc. *ked., lwukkhtal.* (take leave) *rukhṣatedal.*

Partake, v.a. *brakha ākhistal.* v.n. *malgarai-, sharīk-, brakha·khor-*, etc. *ked.*

Partaker, s. *brakha·khor, sharīk; malgarai, mal.*

Partial, a. *taraf-dār, janba-dār*; *mayan*; *nīmgarai.*
Partiality, s. *taraf-, janba-*, etc. *-dārī, mrasta, pās-wālai*; *mīna, sela*; *khwā.*
Participate, v.n. *malgarai-, sharīk-, gad-*, etc. *ked.*
Participle, s. (active-) *ismi-fā'il.* (passive-) *ismi-mafa'ūl.*
Particle, s. *takai, pitsānrai, pūtai, zarra, reza.*
Particular, a. *khāṣṣ.* s. *khabara*; *tafṣīl*; *juz-o-kul.* (in-) ad. *khuṣūṣan, pa takī.*
Partisan, s. *para-, janba-, gundī-*, etc. *-dār*; *malgarai, mal, sharīk*; *yār, komakī.*
Partition, s. *wesh, taqsīm*; *parda, dīwāl.*
Partly, ad. *la-ag-shān, nīme-nīme, yo la-ag tsa.*
Partner, s. *mal, malgarai, sharīk, brakha-khor, ambāz.*
Partnership, s. *malgīrī, malgar-tiyā, shirākat, ambāzī.*
Partridge, s. (black-) *tārū.* (grey-) *tang-zarai* or *tangzarai.* (Greek-) *zarkah.*
Parts, s. (talents) *'aql, poha, sha'ūr, dānish.* (regions) *hewād, zmaka, mulk.* (districts) *tapa, pargana.* (private-) *ṣūrat, tor-wekkh-tah, andām-nihānī, da parde dzāe.*
Parturition, s. *lang-wālai, langedana.* (delivery) *khalāṣī.*
Party, s. *tolai, park.* (person) *kas, tan.* (meeting) *majlis.* (convivial-) *suhbat.* (side) *para, janba, gundī, taraf.* (family-) *cham, firqa, khel, qām.*
Pass, v.n. *teredal, chaledal, tlal—lāral.* (-over) *pore watal.* (-by) *ter watal.*
Pass, s. (ford) *gūdar.* (ferry) *patanr, gūdar.* (hill-) *ghākkhai, kotal.* (defile) *tanga-ī, darra.* (road) *lār.* (permit) *parwāna.* (state) *hāl, nobat.* (stroke) *guzār, dūw, wār.*
Passage, s. *lār, darak, gūdar*; *safar.*
Passenger, s. *musāfir, rāh-rau.*
Passion, s. *qahar, ghuṣṣa.* (lust) *nafs, hawas, shahwat.* (love) *mīna, 'ishq.* (suffering) *quwat, zgham, ṣabr.* (ardour) *tāo.*
Passionate, a. *qahar-jan, ghazab-nāk*, etc. *bros, khīr, tund-, tod-, tez-*, etc. *mizāj* or *-khoe.*
Passive, a. *be-harakat, prot, walār.* (in grammar) *mafa'ūl, majhūl.*
Passport, s. *rawāna, parwāna.*
Past, a. *ter, tilai, tlalai.* (-and forgotten) *ter-o-her.*
Paste, s. *batī, leta-ī*; *atob.* (-board) *kāntī.*
Pastern, s. *lās, kkhpa.* (-leathers) *pakh-wandai.* (-joint) *gīta-ī.*
Pastime, s. *tamāsha, loba, bāzī, mashghulā.*
Pastor, s. *shpūn, gūjar.* (spiritual-) *imām, hādī, shekh, pīr.*
Pastry, s. *weshala, parāta, ghunzākkha.*
Pasture, s. *wākkhah, giyāh, 'alaf, tsar.* (-ground) *tsarā-gāh, maira, warsho.* v.n. *tsaredal.* v.a. *tsarawul, piyāyal, powul.*
Pasturing, s. *tsar, piyāyana, powuna.*
Pat, a. *jukht, jor, sam, barābar, drust.* s. *tas, taq, trak.* v.a. *lās wahal pa chā bānde, dilāsa warkawul k.* (slap) *tas*, etc. *wahal, taqawul.*
Patch, v.a. *jorawul.* (-cloth) *bezal* or *pezal, gandal, tūkai-, khakkhtagai-*, etc. *pore gandal.* s. *tūkai, marīnra, pīna, jor, pewand*, etc.
Patent, s. *sanad, parwāna, farmān.*
Paternal, a. *plāranai.* (-relation) *plār-ganai.*
Path, s. *lār, wāt.* (bye or foot-) *tsara lār* or *-wāt.*
Pathetic, a. *zrah-swai, khwā-khūgai, dzigar-swai.*
Patience, s. *ṣabr, zgham, sah.* (to have) v.a. *ṣabr-*, etc. *laral*, or *k.*
Patient, a. *ṣābir, zgham-, ṣabr-*, etc. *-nāk.* s. *bīmār, marīz, nā-jor, randzūr, nā-rogh.*
Patriarch, s. *mashar, spīn-gīrai*; *nīkah, zbarg.*
Patrimony, s. *mīrāt, dawtar, milk.*

Patriot, s. *watan·dost.*
Patrol, s. *shab·gakkht*; *qarāwal.*
Patron, s. *murabbī, pushtī, nāyak.* (-saint) *pīr.*
Patten, s. *kanrāwa.*
Patter, v.a. (as rain) *darahār-, shirahār-*, etc. *k.*, or *-wahal.*
Pattern, s. *nakkha, namūna*; *qālib.*
Paucity, s. *kam·tiyā, tangsiyā, qīmatī, kākhtī, qātī.*
Pauper, s. *gadāe, faqīr, nā·dār, nā·kas.*
Pause, v.a. *dama k., fikr k.* v.n. *wudredal.*
Pave, v.a. *farsh·bandī k.*
Pavilion, s. *khaima.*
Paw, s. *mangul, panja, changul.*
Pawn, v.a. *graw-, gānra-*, etc. *k.*
Pay, s. *talab, tankhwāh, mawājib*; *kharts, mazdūrī, shukrāna.* (-master) *bakhshī, khizānchī.*
Pay, v.a. *talab-*, etc. *warkawul.* (discharge) *adā-, pūrah-*, etc. *k.*
Pea, s. *matar, krāk.* (chick-) *chanra.*
Peace, s. *rogha, jora, āshtī, khair, khairiyat, aman, ārām·tiyā, āsūdagī.*
Peaceable, a. *eman, gharīb, kam·sharr.*
Peaceful, a. *āsūdah, ārām, be·patna, be·pasāt.*
Peach, s. *shaftālū.*
Peacock, s. *tāūs, mor.*
Peak, s. *tsūka, peza, sar.*
Peal, s. *daz, ghurunb.*
Pear, s. *tāngū, nāk, nāshpātai.*
Pearl, s. *marghalara, marwārīd, durr.* (mother of-) *māhī·ghwag, sadaf.* (-diver) *marjīwanrah.*
Peasant, s. *zamīndar, dihqān, charekār.*
Pease, s. *chanra, mot, mahe, ma-ī* or *mayī, māsh.* (split-) *dāl.* (ground-) *rāra, gir·gira.* (-pod) *palai.* (-husks) *sūrī, būt·sūrī.* (cooked-) *paitī.*
Pebble, s. *gīta-ī, dabara, kānrota.*

Peck, v.a. *tongawul, tongāra k., makkhūka wahal.*
Peculiar, a. *khāss*; *matrah*; *ajīb.*
Peculiarity, s. *khāssiyat, lokkhai, khoe, khaslat.*
Pecuniary, a. *naghdī* or *naqdī.*
Pedagogue, s. *ustād, mullā, ākhūn.*
Pedestal, s. *pāya, āra, asās, wekh, dunkācha, kkhpa.*
Pedigree, s. *pera-ī, pusht, asl, nasab.*
Pedlar, s. *banjārī.*
Peel, v.a. *pot-, khwar-*, etc. *bāsal—yasta* or *-kāgal—kkhkal.* v.n. *nwaredal.*
Peep, v.a. *pa·puta-, pa·zarana-ī-*, etc. *katal*
Peep, s. *put·nazar, zarana-ī, dzīr.*
Peer, s. *sārai, makhai, samsorai, siyāl, gund arbāb, sardār, khān, malik.*
Peerage, s. *kursī·nāma*; *shajara.*
Peerless, a. *be·misāl, lā·sānī, be·siyāl, nādir*, etc.
Peevish, a. *sūt·būt, būt·ūrbūz, trīkh·rūe, khapah.*
Peg, s. *mogai, mekh, sparkhai.*
Pelf, s. *tanga, taka, paisa*; *duniyā, daulat, māl.*
Pelican, s. *kotān.*
Pellet, s. *ghundoskai, pandoskai, mardaka, gola-ī.* (-of goat's, etc. dung) *pucha.*
Pellicle, s. *tsaparkai.*
Pelt, v.a. *wīshtal, lawastal, āchawul, ghur·zawul.*
Pelvis, s. *tabakhai, spokhadza.*
Pen, s. (writing-) *qalam.* (cattle-) *bānda, shpol.*
Penalty, s. *tāwān, nāgha, jarīmāna, sazā.*
Penance, s. *kafārat.*
Pencil, s. *salā-ī, sīkh, dūk.*
Pendant, a. *dzwarand, āwezānd.* s. *zundai, zunbak.*
Penetrate, v.n. *nanawatal, ore pore watal.*
Penetration, s. *nanawātah, dakhl*; ***poh, 'aql.***

Penis, s. *tsūkkhai, ḍaga, ẓakar.* (virilis) *ghenr.* (child's-) *tsakkhkūṛai, cholak.*

Penitence, s. *toba, pakkhemānī, istighfār.*

Penitent, a. *toba·gār, pakkhemān.*

Penknife, s. *chāqū, chaṛūka-ī.*

Penman, s. *kātib, kkhkūnkai.*

Pennant. s. *janḍa, bairagh, nakkha.*

Penny, s. *paisa, ṭanga, ḍāng, damṛa-ī.* (-weight) *sharshā-ī, dwa rata-ī.*

Pension, s. *waẓīfa ; jāgīr.*

Pensioner, s. *waẓīfa·khor, jāgīr·dār.*

Pensive, s. *fikr·man, andekkh·man.*

Pentateuch, s. *tauret, kitāb da ḥaẓrat mūsā.*

Penurious, a. *shūm, bakhīl, tang·dast.*

Penury, s. *tabāhī, khwārī, tangsiyā.*

People, s. *'ālam, khalq, wagaṛī, mardum.* (tribe) *ulus, qām, khel.* v.a. *ābādawul, wadānawul.*

Pepper, s. *mrich.* (red-) *sra·mrich.* (cubeb-) *ḍanbara.*

Perambulate, v.n. *girzedal.* v.a. *gakkht k.*

Perceive, v.a. *līdal, m'alūmawul.* v.n. *pahedal, rasedal, pejandal.*

Perception, s. *fikr, poha, hokkh, wuqūf.*

Perch, s. (-for birds) *chakas.* v.n. *kkhkenāstal.*

Perchance, ad. *gora, gunde, ganre, kkhā-ī.*

Percolate, v.a. *chanṛal, ghalbelawul.*

Percussion, s. *ṭaq, ṭakar.*

Perdition, s. *kharābī, halākī, tabāhī.*

Peremptory, a. *qaṭa'ī, pūrah, kāfī shāfī.*

Perennial, a. *pāedār, dā-im ; yo·kālanai, kālanai.*

Perfect, a. *pūrah, tamām, kāmil ; pāk, be·aib.*

Perfection, s. *kamāl, kāmil·tob, tamāmī, pūrah·wālai.*

Perfectly, ad. *amānī, sarāsar.*

Perfidious, a. *be·wafā, be·īmān, namak·ḥarām.*

Perfidy, s. *be·īmānī, be·wafā-ī, namak·ḥarāmī.*

Perforate, v.a. *sūṛai k., tetsal, sīkhal.*

Perform, v.a. *kawul, kṛal, pūrah-, adā-,* etc. *k., guẓāral, tamāmawul, pa dzāe rāwṛal.*

Performance, s. *kār, kṛah, kawūna, adā.*

Perfume, s. *khūshbūī, 'aṭr.* (oil-) *fulel.*

Perfumer, s. *'aṭṭār.*

Perhaps, ad. *gunde, wī ba,* etc. (*v.* Perchance.)

Peril, s. *khaṭra, wera, khof, muhimm.*

Perilous, a. *khaṭar·nāk, wera·nāk, khof·nāk.*

Period, s. *wakht, ṭāng, nobat, mūda, neṭa, maḥal, wār, plā, heṛ.*

Periodical, a. *wārī, nobatī.*

Perish, v.n. *mṛal, muṛ-, halāk-, fū·fanā-,* etc. *ked.*

Perishable, a. *fānī, nā·pāedār, teredūnai.*

Perjure, v.a. *nā·ḥaqq-,* or *darogh qasam-,* or *nā·ḥaqq saugand-,* etc. *khwṛal.*

Permanent, a. *pāedār, maẓbūṭ, qā-im, lā·zawāl.*

Permanently, ad. *pāedārī sara, tar·tala.*

Permission, s. *iẓn, ḥukm, ijāzat.*

Permit, s. *parwāna.* v.a. *rawā laral ; ḥukm-, iẓn-,* etc. *warkawul.*

Pernicious, a. *tāwānī, nuqṣānī, ziyānī ; moẓī, muẓirr.*

Perpendicular, a. *negh, walāṛ, lak, jig.*

Perpetrate, v.a. *kawul, kṛal.*

Perpetual, a. *dā-imī, mudāmī, jāwīdān.*

Perpetually, ad. *har·kala, tal, tar·tala, ham·esha.*

Perplex, v.a. *rabṛawul, hariyānawul, sargar·dānawul, hak·pak-, hekkh-, huts-,* etc. *k.*

Perplexity, s. *rabaṛ, hariyānī, sargardānī,* etc

Perquisite, s. *gaṭa, shukrāna, dastūrī.*

Persecute, v.a. *āzārawul, zoral, tangawul, khūgawul, ẓulm-,* etc. *k.*

Persecution, s. *zor, ẓulm, ziyātī ; taqāẓa.*

Persecutor, s. *ẓālim, jafā·kār, zorūnkai.*

Perseverance, s. *himmat, sa'ī, kokshiksh.*

Persevere, v.a. *himmat-,* etc. *k.* v.n. *lagiyā osedal.*

Persist, v.a. *ḥujjat-, takrār-,* etc. *k.* v.n. *lagiyā osedal, qā-im-,* etc. *osedal.*

Person, s. *sarai, wagaṛai, ganrai, kas, tan.*

(self) *khpul, dzān.* (body) *ṣūrat, andām, tan.*
Personal, a. *khpul, khāṣṣ.*
Personality, s. *ṣūrat, nātka-ī, peṛandgalī.*
Personally, ad. *pa khpula, pa dzān.*
Personate, v.a. *ṣūrat-, libās-, swāng-,* etc. *k.,* or *-ākhistal* or *-joṛawul.*
Perspiration, s. *khwala.*
Perspire, v.n. *khwale ked.*
Persuade, v.a. *rāwustal, raẓā k., tasallī,* etc. *warkawul; lamsawul; ma-ilān-,* etc. *k.*
Persuasion, s. *tasallī, dilāsa; targhīb, lamsūn.*
Pert, a. *shokh, wītak, be·makh, be·adab.*
Pertinacious, a. *ḥujjatī, takrārī, hoḍai, ṭakanṛai.*
Pertinent, a. *joṛ, munāsib, wājib, juḳht, lā-iq.*
Perturbation, s. *nā·qalār·tiyā, wiswās; gram.*
Perusal, s. *lwustana; katana, mulāḥiẓa.*
Peruse, v.a. *lwustal; katal, naẓar-,* etc. *k.*
Pervade, v.n. *pheledal, khwaredal, wīṛedal.*
Perverse, a. *hoḍai, khpul·sar, ṭakanṛai, haṭ.*
Pervert, v.a. *girzawul, aṛawul, be·lār k.*
Pest, s. *balā, wabāl, janjāl; wabā.*
Pester, v.a. *tangawul, zoral, janjālī k.*
Pestiferous, a. *moẕī, muẓirr, ziyān·kār.*
Pestilence, s. *wabā, tāwūn* or *ṭa'ūn.*
Pestle, s. *molai, pācho, hokla-ī.*
Pet, s. *marawar·tiyā, mānṛai; maṛana.*
Petition, v.a. *'arẓ-, sawāl-, darkhwāst-,* etc. *k.,* or *-laral,* or *-ghokkhtal; 'arẓī āchawul.*
Pettish, a. *khapah, mānṛī·gar, marawar.*
Petty, a. *woṛ, kachoṭai; spuk, nā·tsīz.*
Petulant, a. *shokh, be·adab; wītak, chūnkai.*
Pewter, s. *qal'a-ī, jas.*
Phalanx, s. *palṭan, ghol, ṭol, paṛk, tamba.*
Phantom, s. *wahm, khiyāl, siwrai; rawai.*
Phenomenon, s. *awtsār; 'ajab·kār* or *·chal.*
Phial, s. *kkhīkkha.*
Philanthropist, s. *khair·khwāh, insān·dost.*
Philology, s. *'ilm da ṣarf·o·naḥw.*
Philosopher, s. *ḥakīm, ṣūfī, 'ālim, failsūf.*
Philosopher's stone, s. *kīmiyā, aksīr, pāras.*
Philosophy, s. *'ilm da maujūdāt.*
Philter, s. *ṭoṭka, t'awīẕ, mantar.*
Phlegm, s. *balgham, khrāshkai, grolbai.*
Phlegmatic, a. *balghamī, soṛ·mizāj.*
Phlogistic, a. *khushk, wuch, tod, garm.*
Phœnix, s. *'unqāc, humāc, quqnūs.*
Phrase, s. *khabara, wayai; lughat, 'ibārat.*
Phraseology, s. *'ibārat, maḥāwara.*
Phthisis, s. *narai·randz, diqq, sill.*
Physic, s. *dawā, dārū, darmān.* (science) *ṭibb.* (practice) *ṭibābat, ṭabībī.*
Physical, a. *ẕātī, jibillī, ṭaba'ī.*
Physician, s. *ṭabīb, ḥakīm.*
Physics, s. *'ilm da maujūdāt, ḥikmat.*
Pick, v.a. (pluck) *shūkawul, laṭawul, ṭolawul.* (select) *chunṛal, anṛawul, chīndah k., khwakkhawul.* (-up) *ākhistal, porta k.* (teeth, etc.) *ṭunbal.* (-knot, etc.) *spaṛdal, prānatal.* (-a quarrel) *gwākkhal, gwākkhedal.*
Pickaxe, s. *kodāla-ī, kaha-ī.*
Pickle, s. *āchār.*
Pickpocket, s. *gan·kap, uchakkah·ghal.*
Picture, s. *tsera, taṣwīr, nakhkkha, ṣūrat.*
Piebald, a. *ablaq, chrag·brag, brag·yālai.*
Piece, s. *ṭoṭa, reza, ṭūk.* (patch) *ṭūkai, pīna, marīnṛa.* (land) *paṭai, wanḍ.* (joint) *joṛ, pewand.*
Piecemeal, a. *biyal, judā, yo·yo.* ad. *ṭoṭe·ṭoṭe, chūr·chūr, daṛ·daṛ.*
Pier, s. *pushtu, band; pāya, stan.*
Pierce, v.a. *sūṛai k., sīkhal, tetsal, zanal, tsarkh k.; ore·pore-, pore·rāpore-,* etc. *bāsal—yastal.*
Piety, s. *taqwā, zuhd, dīn·dārī, īmān·dārī.*
Pig, s. *kharbishoe, kharbishkatai, sarkūzai.* (-of iron) *sala.*
Pigeon, s. *kauntar,* or *kotar,* or *kawtar.*
Pigmy, s. *lweshtīnak, chūnai, ṗotai.*
Pike, s. *neza, balla, barcha, shalgai.*

Pile, s. *ḍera-ī, kat, ṭop, rashaka* ; *mogai.*
Pile, v.a. *ḍera-ī-, tūda-, dalai-, rāsha-*, etc. *k.*
Piles, s. *bawāsīr, manekkhī.*
Pilfer, v.a. *puṭawul, ghlā k.*
Pilgrim, s. *ḥājī, ḥajj kawūnkai, ziyārat kawūnkai.*
Pilgrimage, s. *ḥajj, ziyārat.*
Pill, s. *gola-ī, mardakai.*
Pillage, s. *lūṭ, tālān, tākht-o-tārāj, chawr.*
Pillage, v.n. *lūṭawul, lūṭal, natal, nātārawul.*
Pillar, s. *stan* ; *tsalai.*
Pillory, s. *shikanja, kāṭ, tsarkh.*
Pillow, s. *bālikkht, takiya.* (small-) *bālikkht-goṭai.*
Pimp, s. *baṛwā, dallāl, dahūs.*
Pimple, s. *nanaka-ī, dāna.* (on face) *dzwānaka.*
Pin, s. *stan* ; *salā-ī.*
Pincers, s. *ambūr.* (small) *nūtsai.*
Pinch, s. *skūnḍāra* ; *pūṭai, pitsānṛai, chūndai.*
Pinch, v.a. *skūnḍal* or *tskūnḍal.*
Pine, s. *nakkhtar, sanobar.* (-torch) *shonṭa-ī.*
Pine, v.n. *kaṛedal, nūledal, dzawredal, ghamedal, pakhsedal, zahīredal, zahedal.*
Pinion, s. *wazar, tsāng* ; *banṛa, kkhāh-par.* (fetter) *dzolana, kara-ī.*
Pinion, v.a. *sūṭ-būṭ taṛal.*
Pinnacle, s. *tsūka, peza, sar* ; *kangūra.*
Pioneer, s. *bel-dār.*
Pious, a. *taqwā-, īmān-, dīn-*, etc. *-dār*, or *-larūnkai, nmāndzī, nmūndz kawūnkai*, or *-guẕār.*
Pipe, s. *shpela-ī, nala.* v.a. *shpela-ī ghagawul.*
Pique, s. *mānṛai, marawar-tiyā, khwā-badī, zṛah-badāwai.*
Piss, v.a. *baul-, wāṛa baul-, mutiyāze-*, etc. *k.*
Pistol, s. *tamāncha.*
Pit, s. *ḍoghal, ṭublai, jwar-ghālai.* v.a. *jangawul.*
Pitch, s. *rānāẕaṛah.* (degree) *ḥadd, nobat.*
Pitch, v.a. *wudrawul, walāṛawul, khejawul.* (cast) *āchawul, wīshtal, lawastal, ghurzawul.*
Pitcher, s. *loṭkai, mangai, maṭ, maṭkai.*
Pitchfork, s. *kkhākha-ī, dre-kkhākha-ī, sānga-ī.*
Pith, s. *māghzoh, zaṛai.*
Pitiful, a. *khwā-khūgai.* (paltry) *spuk.*
Pitiless, a. *be-dard, be-raḥm.*
Pittance, s. *ṭukṛa, nwaṛa-ī, rozī.*
Pity, s. *zṛah-swai, khwā-khūgī, dard, raḥm, gham* ; *afsos, daregh.*
Pivot, s. *tīrak, salā-ī* ; *ḍīḍa, khulborai.*
Place, s. *dzāe, zmaka, makān.* (stead) *'iwaẓ, badal.* (rank) *pāya, martaba.* (office) *'uhda.* (residence) *astoga, meshta.*
Place, v.a. *gdal* or *īgdal, yakkhodal, yakkhal, yakkhawul, kegdal* or *kkhkegdal, kekkhodal*, etc.
Placenta, a. *prewān.*
Placid, a. *khog, narm, pos* or *post.*
Plague, s. *wabā, tāwūn* ; *āfat, balā* ; *wabāl* ; *janjāl.* v.a. *rabṛawul, āzārawul, pa balā ākhtah k.*
Plain, a. *sam, hawār, barābar, sat.* (simple) *sādah, ṣāf, spīn.* (unmixed) *torai, spor* ; *karah, sūchah.* s. *maidān, sama.*
Plainly, ad. *spīn, ṣāf, rikkhtiyā.*
Plaint, s. *gila, māna, mānṛai* ; *faryād, wāwailā.*
Plaintiff, s. *mudda'ī, faryādī.*
Plaintive, a. *gila-man, mānṛī-gar, māna kawūnkai.*
Plait, s. *tā, taha, wal, bragh* ; *jūhaṛa, kṛaṭai, gundza, chīchaṛ.* v.a. *odal* ; *āgayal, chunṛal.*
Plan, s. *tadbīr, ḥikmat, band, chal* ; *nakhkkha* or *naqsha, namūna.* v.a. *joṛawul, band taṛal, chal k.*
Plane, s. *randa.* (-tree) *chinār.*
Plane, v.a. *togal, khrayal* or *khriyal, randa k.*
Planet, s. *storai.*
Plank, s. *takhta.*

Plant, s. *būṭai, ḍakai.*

Plant, v.a. *lagawul, khakkhawul; wudrawul, lakawul, wulāṛawul.*

Plantain, s. *kela.* (herb-) *isapghol* or *spaghol.*

Plantation, s. *jangai, baṉr.*

Plaster, s. *lew, akhāṛah, gach, khaṭa; malham, paha, tab, ẓamād.* v.a. *lewawul, akheṛal, tapal, khaṭa k.*

Plat, s. (-of ground) *paṭai, pāṛa, ḍāga.*

Plate, s. *rikeba-ī, raghai, pashqāb.* (-of iron for baking on) *tabakhai, teghna.* (earthen ditto) *taba-ī.*

Plated, a. *mulamma.*

Platform, s. *dunkācha, gaṛwanj; manah.*

Platter, s. *kkhānak, taghārai, tabakhai, tālai.*

Plaudit, s. *shāhbāshī, āparīn.*

Plausible, a. *khog-khulai, chalwalai, khula-war.*

Play, s. *loba, bāzī; nandāra, tamāsha; jūārī.*

Play, v.a. *lobe k.* (gamble) *jūārī k.* (-the fool) *malande k.* (act) *pekkhe k.* (music) *sarod-, tarāne-,* etc. *ghagawul.* (in comp.) *-kawul, -kṛal.*

Playfellow, s. *hum-dzolai.*

Playful, a. *mast, shokhīn.*

Plaything, s. *da lobe kālai.*

Plea, s. *ḥujjat, dalīl, 'uẕr, d'awa, hira-ī.*

Plead, v.a. *wayal, lal, lawdal, 'uẕr-,* etc. *k.*

Pleasant, a. *khwand-nāk, kkhah.*

Pleasantness, s. *khwand, maza, kkhādī.*

Pleasantry, s. *khandā, washla, ṭoqa.*

Please, v.a. *rāẓī-, khwakkh-, kkhād-,* etc. *k.*; *khwand warkawul.*

Pleased, a. *khwakkh, khūsh-ḥāl, kkhād, kkhād-man.*

Pleasure, s. *khwakkhī, kkhādī, khūsh-ḥālī, khwand.* (will) *raẓā, marzī.* (spiteful-) *sakha, wiyāṛ.*

Plebeian, a. *'āmm, adnā, kam-ẕāt.* s. *'āmmī.*

Pledge, s. *graw, gāṉra.* (word) *wāda, lafẓ, bandaṉr, taṛa.* (token) *nakkha, yād-gār.*

Pleiades, s. *perūne, jambaq storī.*

Plenary, a. *pūrah, tamām, amānī.*

Plenipotentiary, s. *kul mukhtār, wāk-dār.*

Plenitude, s. *pūrah-wālai; ḍer-wālai.*

Plentiful, a. *ḍer, ziyāt, prewān, wadān.*

Plenty, s. *ḍer-wālai, prewānī, ziyāt-wālai, ābādī, wadānī.*

Pliable, } a. *narm, post, mulā-im.*
Pliant, }

Plight, s. *ḥāl, ḥālat, chal.* v.a. *graw-, gāṉra-,* etc. *k.*; *wāda-, neṭa-, lafẓ-,* etc. *taṛal.*

Plod, v.a. *miḥnat-, kokshiksh-,* etc. *k.* v.n. *ṭaparedal.*

Plot, s. *band, sāzish, joṛikkht.* (-of land) *paṭai, wanḍ.* (stratagem) *chal, lamghaṛa-ī.*

Plot, v.a. *joṛawul, band taṛal, sāzish-,* etc. *k.*

Plough, s. *yiwa* or *īwa, yoya, qulba.* v.a. *īwe* or *yiwe k.*

Ploughshare, s. *pāla, saspār, spāra.*

Plover, s. *ṭīṭārai.*

Pluck, v.a. *shūkawul.* (-out) *kāgal—kkhkal, bāsal—yastal.*

Plug, s. *būja, shoṛa, mūṉrai, ḍīḍa, khulborai.*

Plum, s. *bera, baḍa bera, sāwū bera, makhranai.*

Plumage, s. *baṉre, nazar.*

Plume, s. *zunḍai.* (-head) *qarqara.*

Plume, v.a. *baṉre joṛawul, dzān joṛawul.*

Plummet, s. *sahūl, chāwul.*

Plump, a. *tsorb, chāgh, ghaṭ, punḍ.*

Plunder, v.n. *lūṭ-, tālā-, nātār-,* etc. *k., natal.*

Plunge, v.a. *ḍūbkai-, ghoṭa-, ghūpa-,* etc. *warkawul* or *-wahal* or *-khwuṛal.*

Plural, a. *jam'a.*

Ply, s. *tā, bragh, chūṉra, chīchar, gundza.*

Ply, v.a. *chalawul, lagawul, kawul, kṛal.*

Pocket, s. *jeb*; *kīsa, dzola-ī.*

Pock-mark, s. *ta-ap, ta-apai.*

Pod, s. *palai, ghoza.*

Poem, s. *ghazal, chār bait, sandara.*

Poet, s. *shā'ir, qaṣīda go,e, sandar go,e.*
Poetry, s. *sh'ir, bait, naẓm.*
Poignant, a. *tez, tunā, sakht.*
Point, s. *peza, tsūka, sar.* (dot) *ṭakai, dāna, nuqta.* (spot) *dāgh, tsirīka, laka.*
Point, v.a. *terah k., peza-,* etc. *joṛawul; naẓar lagawul.* (-out) *kkhayal—kkhowul.*
Pointed, a. *peza dār* or *-larūnkai.*
Poise, v.a. *talal, jokal, barābarawul.*
Poison, s. *zahr.* v.a. *zahr warkawul.*
Poisonous, a. *zahr·nāk.*
Poke, v.a. *negh wahal; laṭawul.*
Poker, s. (fire-) *or laṛūnai.* (goad) *ch̤ūka.*
Pole, s. *lakaṛa.* (barge-) *bala-ī.* (balance-) *ḍānḍa-ī.* (North-) *quṭb.* (-star) *da quṭb storai.*
Police, s. *band·o·bast, intiẓām.* (superintendent of-) *koṭwal.* (-office) *tānṛa.* (-man) *tsoka-ī dār.*
Policy, s. *intiẓām, tadbīr, ḥikmat 'amalī.*
Polish, v.a. *mugal—mukkhal, togal, ṣaiqal k.*
Polite, a. *makhawar, sulūkī, mihrbān; dalbārī.*
Politeness, s. *makh, makhawarī, sulūk.*
Politic, a. *ḥikmatī, tadbīrī.*
Political, a. *mulkī; 'amalī, tadbīrī.*
Politician, s. *tadbīrī, jirgatū.*
Politics, s. *tadbīr da mulk* or *-salṭanat,* etc.
Poll, s. *sar, koṭai.* (-tax) *jaziya.* v.a. *lanḍ-, ghūṭ-,* etc. *prekawul.*
Pollute, v.a. *nā·pāk-, palīt-, murdār-, kakaṛ-,* etc. *k.* (-oneself) *mūṭak wahal.* (-oneself in sleep) *āwdas awukkhtal, shaiṭān khaṭā k.*
Pollution, s. *nā·pākī, palītī,* etc.; *shaiṭānī khaṭā.*
Polytheism, s. *but parastī, shirk.*
Polytheist, s. *but parast, mushrik.*
Pomegranate, s. *anangai, anangūṛai, anār.* (wild-) *narsawai.*
Pommel, v.a. *wahal, ṭakawul, kūṭal.*
Pomp, s. *dabdaba, tamtarāq, sāmāna.*

Pompous, a. *khāntamā, sar hawā.*
Pond, s. *ḍanḍ, nāwar, wasta, wangara.*
Ponder, v.a. *fikr-, ghaur-,* etc. *k.*
Ponderous, a. *drūnd, grān.*
Pony, s. *ṭaṭū, yābū.*
Pool, s. *ḍanḍūkai; ḍab, kol.*
Poor, a. *khwār, gharīb, muflis, nā·kas.*
Poorly, a. *nājoṛ, nārogh, bīmār.* ad. *nīmgaṛai.*
Pop, s. *ṭas, ṭak, ḍaz, ṭar,* etc. v.a. *ṭas-,* etc. *wahal.*
Poppy, s. *koknār, khāsh khāsh.* (wild-) *redai.*
Populace, s. *ulus, 'āmmiyān, 'awām.*
Popular, a. *'āmm, jārī, chalanī, riwāj.*
Population, s. *ābādī, wadānī; 'ālam, khalq, ulus.*
Populous, a. *ābād, wadān.*
Porch, s. *manḍaw, dahlīz.*
Porcupine, s. *shkūnr.*
Pore, s. (-of the skin) *ghūna.* (to roughen or erect the-) v.n. *ghūna zīgedal.* (aperture) *sūṛa.*
Pore, v.a. *lagiyā katal* or *-goral—līdal, dzīr'k.*
Porous, a. *sūṛa·war.*
Porpoise, s. *tsūtsa, sūs.*
Port, s. *bandar.* (door) *war, darwāza.* (mien) *yūn, chāl.* (aperture) *darbacha, karka-ī.*
Portable, a. *spuk, halak, da wṛalo.*
Portal, s. *darwāza, āstāna.*
Portend, v.a. *dallīl k., āgāhī k., pāl kkhayal—kkhowul.*
Portent, s. *dallīl, āgāhī, pāl* or *fāl; bad fāl, bad shugun.*
Porter, s. *ḥammāl, mazdūr.* (gate-) *darwāza·wān, ghāw·chī.*
Portico, s. *manḍaw, dahlīz, jilau khāna.*
Portion, s. *brakha, ḥiṣṣa, wesh, nanḍ, qismat.*
Portly, a. *ghaṭ, juṣṣa·war, jasīm, khṛīs, gagar, star.*

Portmanteau, s. *khurjīn, yakhdān, rakht-dān, dzola-ī, gūdai.*

Portrait, s. *tsera, taṣwīr, ṣūrat.*

Pose, v.a. *pa-ar k., lā dzawāb k., hariyānawul.*

Position, s. *shān, wajha, ḥāl, ṣūrat.*

Positive, a. *yaqīn, qaṭa'ī, be-shakk, be-shubha.* (stubborn) *khpul rāe, khpul-sar.* (real) *aṣlī, sūchah.*

Possess, v.a. *laral, darlal.*

Possession, s. *qābū, qabẓa.* (to take-) v.a. *qābū-*, etc. *k., khpulawul, ākhistal, lānde k.* (to give-) *bakkhal* or *bakhkkhal, warkawul, kkhandal.*

Possessor, s. *meṛah, tsakkhtan, mālik, khāwand.* (in comp.) *-larūnkai, -dār, -man, -war*, etc.

Possibility, s. *imkān, kedana, shwah.*

Possible, a. *mumkin, shwūnkai, kedūnkai.* (to be-) v.a. *imkān laral, shwal.*

Possibly, ad. *gunde, kkhā-ī, bā-īda, wī ba.*

Post, s. (office) *kār, khidmat, 'uhda.* (station) *dzāe, makān.* (military-) *tsoka-ī, tānra.* (pillar) *stan, tsalai.* (mail-) *ḍāk.* (-man) *qāṣid, dāk-wālā.* (express-) *chapar.*

Post, v.a. (station) *wudrawul, kkhkenawul, walāṛawul.*

Posterior, a. *wrustai, wrustanai, pastanai.*

Posteriors, s. *kūnāṭī.*

Posterity, s. *alwād, zurriyāt, nasl.* (to the latest-) *naslan b'ad naslan.*

Postpone, v.a. *drang-, lārghah-, multawī-*, etc. *k., mu'aṭṭal-, barkhwāst-, nāgha-*, etc. *k.*

Postscript, s. *tatimma.*

Posture, s. *shān, wajha, ṣūrat, ṭaur.*

Pot, s. *lokkhai.* (metal-) *kaṛahai, deg, dechka, khumṛa-ī.* (earthen-) *hānḍa-ī, kaṭwa-ī, kawdīk.* (water-) *mangai, maṭkai, loṭkai.* (-lid) *bargholai, sar-pokkh.* (-herb) *sāg, sabzī, nākkhah.*

Potato, s. *ālū.*

Potent, a. *zorāwar, maẓbūṭ, quwat-nāk, tuwānā.*

Potentate, s. *bādshāh, amīr, sardār, malik.*

Potion, s. *sharbat, nosh, tskkhāk* or *skāk.*

Potsherd, s. *kaudai, kaudarai.*

Pottage, s. *sāgīnrai, sāg, āsh.* (-of meat, etc.) *qatagh, ngolai, sālan.*

Potter, s. *kulāl, kumhār.*

Pottery, s. *kaṭwa-ī lokkhai.* (glazed-) *kāshīn.*

Pouch, s. *jeb, kīsa*; *dzola-ī, bana-ī, gūdai*; *toshdān.*

Poultice, s. *leṭa-ī, paha, tab.*

Poultry, s. *chirg, chirgūṛī.*

Pounce, v.a. *pa panjo wahal.*

Pound, s. *nīm ser.*

Pound, v.a. *ṭakawul, kūṭal, dzabal, daṛ daṛ-, chūr chūr-*, etc. *k.*

Pour, v.a. *toyawul, āchawul.* (-out) *sandzal.* (-as rain) v.n. *oredal, tsātsedal.* (-over) v.n. *toyedal* or *to-edal.*

Pout, v.a. *būṭ ūrbūz nīwul.*

Poverty, s. *khwārī, tabāhī, muplisī, iplās, tangsiyā.*

Powder, s. *oṛah, maidah, chūr.* (gun-) *dārū.* (-horn) *kkhkar.* (medicine) *paka, kapa, kharpaṭ.*

Powder, v.a. *oṛawul, maidah-, oṛah-*, etc. *k.* (dust) *bornah k.*

Power, s. *zor, quwat*; *was, ṭāqat*; *tuwān, bram.* (authority) *wāk, majāl, ikhtiyār, ḥukm.* (possession) *qābū, qabẓa.*

Powerful, a. *zorāwar, tuwānā, maẓbuṭ, zabardast.*

Pox, s. *bād da farang, garmī, juẓām.* (small-) *nanaka-ī.*

Practicable, a. *shwūnkai, mumkin, da kawulo.*

Practical, a. *'amalī, ist'imālī, kṛūnai.*

Practice, s. *'ādat, 'amal, yūn, dastūr, chāl chal.*

Practise, v.a. *kawul, 'ādat-*, etc. *k., mashq k.*

Praise, s. *stāyana, ṣanā, ṣifat, t'arīf.* v.a. *stāyal, stāyana-*, etc. *wayal* or *k.*

Prance, v.a. *traplal, ṭop wahal, kharmastī k., tskhe k.*

Prank, s. *kharmastī, ṭel ṭāl, laṭah per.*

Pray, v.a. *nmūndz k.*, or *-guzāral* ; *du'a-, minnat-*, etc. *k., darkhwāst k., ghokkhtal.*

Prayer, s. *nmūndz* ; *du'ā.* (-for Lent) *tarāwe.*

Preach, v.a. *w'az k.* ; *khuṭba lwustal.*

Preamble, s. *debācha, muqadamma.*

Precarious, a. *nā-pāedār, teredūnai, zawālī.*

Precaution, s. *dūr andeshī, wṛānde katana.*

Precede, v.n. *wṛānde tlal.*

Precedent, a. *wṛāndīnai.* s. *miṣāl, nakkha.*

Preceding, a. *pakhwānai, wṛūnbanai.*

Precept, s. *matal, miṣāl* ; *ḥukm, kariya* ; *pand, naṣīḥat.*

Preceptor, s. *ākhūn, ustāz* ; *nāṣiḥ, pand war-kawūnkai.*

Precinct, s. *ḥadd, pūla, brīd.*

Precious, a. *qīmat-nāk, grān-bahā, matrah* ; *'azīz.*

Precipice, s. *kamar, kanda, gaṛang, tāk.*

Precipitate, a. *jalt, tez, jalt-bāz, talwār-gandai, talwalai, haṛbaṛai.*

Precipitate, v.a. *āchawul, wīshtal, ghurzawul. lawastal* ; *dangawul* ; *jaltī-, talwār-, z-ir-* or *za-ar-*, etc. *k.* v.n. *ghurzedal, prewatal, kkhkenāstal.*

Precipitation, s. *jaltī, talwār, be-ṣabrī.*

Precise, a. *jukht, drust, joṛ, pūrah.*

Precisely, ad. *jukht, joṛ, rikkhtiyā, bedū.*

Precision, s. *barābar-wālai, jukht-wālai, taḥqīq.*

Preclude, v.a. *man'a-, band-, pore jane-.* etc. *k., stanawul, shaṛal.*

Precursor, s. }
Predecessor, s. } *peshrau, wṛānde tlūnai.*

Predestination, s. *taqdīr, qaẓā.*

Predicament, s. *ḥāl* ; *nobat, chal.*

Predicate, s. *khabar, ṣifat, m'aqūl.*

Predict, v.a. *pesh khabarī-, khabar da ghā-ib-*, etc. *wayal, fāl nīwul, fāl katana k.*

Predominate, v.n. *ghālib-, ghalaba-, ziyāt-, ganṛ-, ḍer-*, etc. *ked.*

Preface, s. *debācha, muqadamma.*

Prefer, v.a. *khwakkhawul, ghwarah k., kkhah ganṛal, kkhāghal* ; *sar buland-, sar farāz-, sar bālā-*, etc. *k.*

Preferable, a. *ghwarah, kkhah.*

Preference, s. *khwakkh* ; *mrasta.*

Preferment, s. *sar farāzī, pāya pa porta.*

Prefix, v.a. *wṛānde-, pa makh-*, etc. *lagawul.*

Pregnant, a. *brālba* or *blārba, ḍaka, warla, shigāra, bār-dāra.* (full) *ḍak, pūrah.* (to make-) v.a. *blārba-*, etc. *k.*

Prejudice, s. *ṭarafdārī, mrasta* ; *mīna, khwā, mā-ilān* ; *bad gumānī, khwā badāwai* ; *tāwān, ziyān.*

Prejudicial, a. *tāwānī, ziyānī, nuqṣānī, bad, muẓirr.*

Prelate, s. *imām, mujtahid.*

Preliminary, a. *wṛūnbanai, awwalanai.*

Premature, a. *be-wakht, be-ṭāng* ; *nīma khwā, kachandai, nīmgaṛai.*

Premeditate, v.a. *pesh fikrī-, pesh bandī-*, etc. *k.* ; *qaṣd-, niyat-*, etc. *taṛal*, or *k.*

Premier, a. *mashar.* s. *wazīr* ; *sarghanah.*

Premium, s. *sūd, naf'a* ; *in'ām, bakhkshiksh* ; *shukrāna, muzd.*

Preparation, s. *tayārī, dzerma, tadbīr.*

Prepare, v.a. *tayārī-*, etc. *k., joṛawul, tayār-awul.*

Preponderate, v.n. *dranedal, drūnd ked., ziyātedal, ḍeredal.*

Preponderation, s. *dranāwai, ḍer-wālai*, etc.

Preposition, s. *ḥarf.*

Prepossess, v.a. *mayan-, mā-ilān-*, etc. *k.*

Prepossession, s. *mayan-tob, mīna.*

Preposterous, a. *be-hūdah, abtar, wūch pūch* ; *naskor, aṛawulai.*

Prepuce, s. *chīchaṛa, da tsūkkha-ī tsarman.*

Prerogative, s. *ḥaqq, wāk, ikhtiyār.*

Presage, s. *pāl, dalālat, āgāhī, nakkha.*

Prescience, s. *khabar da ghā-ib, ghā-ib·dānī.*

Prescribe, v.a. *wayal, farmāyal, hukm k., kkhayal—kkhowul.* (medically) *nuskha līkal, -kāgal—kkhkal.* (fix) *taṛal, muqarrar k.*

Presence, s. *huẓūr, khidmat.* (-of mind) *baidārī, ausān, hokkhyār·tiyā.*

Present, a. *hāẓir, maujūd*; *osan, osanai.* (at-) ad. *dā sā'at, os.* s. *bakhkshiksh, naẓr, pekkhkakkh, naẓrāna, shukrāna.*

Present, v.a. *bakhkkhal* or *bakkhal, kkhandal, warkawul.* (show) *bartser-, kkhkārah-, ẓāhir-,* etc. *k.* (-a gun) *naẓar lagawul.* (introduce) *pekkhawul, wṛānde-, makhā makh-,* etc. *k.*

Presently, ad. *os, dastī, pa de sā'at.*

Preservation, s. *sātana, jghorana, khundī·tob, bachawūna.*

Preservative, a. *sātūnai, sātandoe, jghorai, bachawūnkai.*

Preserve, v.a. *sātal, jghoral, khundiyal, khundī k., bachawul.*

Preserver, s. *sātandoe, jghorai, khundī·kawūnkai, bachawūnkai.*

Preside, v.a. *sardārī-, mīr majlisī-, masharī·tob-,* etc. *k.*

President, s. *sardār, mashar*; *mīr majlis.*

Press, v.a. (squeeze) *nachoṛawul, paz wahal, nakkhtedzal.* (-down) *drabal.* (-into) *kkhke·manḍal.* (knead the limbs) *manḍal.* (urge) *zoral, tezal.* (vex) *tangawul, dabawul.* (-to the bosom) *baṛgaṛandī k.*

Press, s. (oil-) *gāṉra-ī.* (book-) *shikanja.* (a crowd) *ḍala, gaṉr 'ālam.*

Pressure, s. *zoṛ*; *bār*; *tangsiyā, grān·tiyā.*

Presume, v.a. *gaṉṛal, qiyās-, khiyāl-, gumān-,* etc. *k.*; *dam wahal, gustākhī k.*

Presumptuous, a. *kibr·jan, shokh, gustākh.*

Pretend, v.a. *bāna-, chal-, hīla-, lamghaṛa-ī-, ṭagī-, hira-ī-,* etc. *k.*

Pretender, s. *bāna·khor, chal·bāz.* (claimant) *d'awa·dār, mudda'ī.* (boaster) *lāpai.*

Pretension, s. *d'awa*; *hujjat.*

Preternatural, a. *karāmatī, zbarg.*

Pretext, s. *bāna, chal, hira-ī, palma, 'uẓr.*

Pretty, a. *kkhāyastah, kkhkulai, pej·makhai* or *pa-ī·makhai.* ad. *tsı la-ag* or *la-ag tsa, nijde.*

Prevail, v.a. *barai mūndal, lānde-, pa-aṛ-,* etc. *k.* v.n. *ziyātedal*; *jārī ked., chaledal.*

Prevalence, s. *zor, ziyātī, ghalba.*

Prevalent, a. *ziyāt*; *jārī*; *zorāwar, wa-aṛ*; *ghālib.*

Prevaricate, v.a. *palma-, hira-ī-, guzmuzai-,* etc. *k.*

Prevent, v.a. *man'a k., kariyābawul, haṭālawul, bandawul, āṛawul.*

Preventer, s. *mān'i, man'a kawūnkai.*

Prevention, s. *man'a, haṭāl, kariyāb, āṛ, band.*

Previous, a. *pakhwānai, wṛūnbanai, wṛāndīnai, awwalanai.*

Previously, ad. *pakhwā, wṛūnbe, wṛānde, qabl, awwal.*

Prey, s. *kkhkār, māta.* (booty) *lūṭ.* (beast of-) *dad, wahsh.*

Price, s. *bai'a, baya, bahā, qīmat.* (-current) *nirkh.*

Prick, v.a, *tsekhal, sīkhal, stan-, chūka-,* etc. *wahal, sūṛai k.*

Prickle, s. *āzghai* or *āghzai, khār.*

Prickly, a. *āzghan* or *āghzan.*

Pride, s. *kibr, mastī, wiyāṛ.* (proper-) *nang, ghairat.*

Priest, s. *imām, shekh, pīr, mullā.*

Priestcraft, s. *mullā·tob.*

Priesthood, s. *imāmat, pīr khāna.*

Primarily, ad. *wṛūnbe, awwal.*

Primary, a. *wṛūnbanai, awwalanai.*

Prime, a. *awwal, aṣlī, khāṣṣ, sāwū, karah, sūchah.*

Prime, v.a. *ranjak āchawul.*

Primitive, a. *zoṛ, pa<u>kh</u>wānai, awwalanai; aṣlī, ẕātī.*
Primogeniture, s. *ma<u>sh</u>ar·tob, loe·wālai, loyat.*
Prince s. *<u>sh</u>āh·zādah, malik.*
Princess, s. *<u>sh</u>āh·zāda-ī, malika.*
Principal, a. *ma<u>sh</u>ar, awwal, sardār; sar, loe, <u>gh</u>aṭ.* s. *panga, saga, māya, aṣl; sardār, sar, sar<u>gh</u>anah, ma<u>sh</u>ar.*
Principality, s. *ṣūba, rāj, qalam·rau.*
Principally, ad. *akṣar, awwalan, <u>kh</u>uṣūṣan.*
Principle, s. *aṣl, awwal sabab, jauhar; bā'iṣ, jihat; maẕhab, dīn; qānūn, ā-īn.*
Print, v.a. *<u>ch</u>āp k., <u>ch</u>āpa wahal.*
Prior, a. *wṛūnbanai, wṛāndīnai, pa<u>kh</u>wānai, awwalanai.*
Privity, s. *awwaliyat, wṛāndīn·tob.*
Prison, s. *qaid-* or *bandī <u>kh</u>āna, zindān.*
Prisoner, s. *qaidī, bandī, asīr; naẕar·band.*
Privacy, s. *<u>kh</u>ilwat, parda, parda·po<u>kkh</u>ī, puṭ·wālai, yawā<u>dz</u>ī·tob, biyal·wālai.*
Private, a. *puṭ, yawā<u>dz</u>ai, tanhā, <u>ts</u>aṛah, biyal.*
Privately, ad. *pa puṭa, pa parde.*
Privation, s. *ni<u>sh</u>t·wālai, nābūdī.*
Privilege, s. *ḥaqq; <u>kh</u>alāṣī, āzādī.*
Privities, s. *ṣūrat, satr, tor·we<u>kkh</u>tah, andām nihānī, da <u>sh</u>arm <u>dz</u>āe.*
Privy, a. *<u>kh</u>abar·dār, baidār, wāqif, āgāh.* s. *<u>ch</u>ār <u>ch</u>oba, jāe·ẕarūr.*
Prize, s. *in'ām; bāzī, <u>sh</u>arṭ, daw; lūṭ, gaṭa, tālā.* (-fighter) *pahlawān.*
Prize, v.a. *<u>kkh</u>ah-, 'azīz-, grān-,* etc. *ga<u>n</u>ral.*
Probability, s. *ṣūrat, <u>sh</u>akl; kedana.*
Probable, a. *<u>sh</u>wūnkai, kedūnkai.*
Probably, ad. *gunde, <u>kkh</u>ā-ī, wī ba* or *ba wī.*
Probation, s. *āzme<u>kkh</u>t; umed·wārī.*
Probationer, s. *umed·wār.*
Probe, v.a. *sī<u>kh</u>-, salā-ī-,* etc. *wahal, <u>ts</u>e<u>kh</u>al, sī<u>kh</u>al, sū<u>gh</u>awul.*
Probity, s. *nekī, ri<u>kkh</u>tīn·tob, rāstī.*
Problem, s. *masla, sawāl.*

Problematical. a. *<u>sh</u>akk·man, <u>sh</u>akk·dār.*
Proboscis, s. *<u>kh</u>arṭam* or *<u>kh</u>arṭūm, sūnḍak.*
Proceed, v.n. *tlal—lāṛal, <u>ch</u>aledal, rawānedal, drūmedal, teredal; watal, paidā ked.* v.a. *kawul, kṛal.*
Proceeding, s. *kār, kṛah, 'amal, mu'amala, <u>ch</u>al.*
Proceeds, s. *gaṭa, sūd, paidā-i<u>kkh</u>t.*
Process, s. *tarkīb, <u>ch</u>alan, <u>sh</u>ān, ṭaur, rang; jagṛa, mu'amala, muqadamma.*
Procession, s. *swarlī; tamā<u>sh</u>a.*
Proclaim, v.a. *munādī k., ḍamāme-, jār-,* etc. *wahal, ma<u>sh</u>hūr-, jārī-,* etc. *k.*
Procrastinate, v.a. *drangī-, <u>dz</u>anḍ-, lār<u>gh</u>ah-, multawī-,* etc. *k.*
Procreate, v.a. *zegawul, rāwṛal, paidā k.*
Procurable, a. *muyassar, da mūndalo, da paidā kawulo, mūndūnai.*
Procure, v.a. *mūndal, paidā k., rāwṛal, rasawul.*
Procurer, s. *dallāl, rebār.*
Prodigal, a. *<u>kh</u>ar<u>ts</u>ī, iṣrāfī, tāwān kawūnkai.*
Prodigality, s. *<u>kh</u>ar<u>ts</u>, tāwān, iṣrāf, <u>ch</u>a<u>kh</u>ṛaba.*
Prodigious, a. *'ajīb, 'aẕīm, loe, <u>gh</u>aṭ, nāpaṛ.*
Prodigy, s. *'ajab, <u>sh</u>anda; subḥān allah.*
Produce, v.a. *rāwṛal, paidā k.*
Produce, s. *ḥāṣil, paidā-i<u>kkh</u>t; sūd, gaṭa, naf'a.*
Productive, a. *rāwṛūnkai, paidā kawūnkai.* (-land) *<u>gh</u>ala·<u>kh</u>eza, <u>gh</u>ala·būda, zorāwara, lap·<u>ts</u>aṭa.* (-cattle) *pa-ī·wara.* (-tree) *mewa·dāra.* (-animal) *zeganda-ī.*
Profane, v.a. *nāpāk-, palīt-, murdār-, bilmāz-,* etc. *k.*
Profane, a. *bilmāz, ḥarām, nā·rawā,* etc.
Profess, v.a. *manal, wayal, iqrār k., lal, lawdal.*
Professedly, ad. *pa <u>ts</u>argand, pa jār* or *ẕāhir.*
Profession, s. *iqrār, qaul; kār, kasb.*
Professor, s. *ustād, mullā, mu'allim.*

Proffer, v.a. *nazr-, nazrāna-, pekkhkakkh-*, etc. *warkawul*; *wrānde-, pekkh-*, etc. *k.*; *'uzr k.*

Proficient, a. *pokh, hokkhyār, kārī-gar, khabar-dār.*

Profile, s. *tratskan ṣūrat, tratskana tsihra.*

Profit, s. *sūd, gaṭa, kkhegaṛa, fā-ida, naf'a, būd.* v.a. *gaṭal, sūd-*, etc. *mundal.*

Profitable, a. *sūd-man, fā-ida-man.*

Profligate, a. *lawanḍ, bad-kār, chaṭ. qachar.*

Profound, a. *jawar, star*; *ghaṭ, loe*; *narai, bārīk.*

Profundity, s. *jawar-tiyā, star-wālai*; *loeyat*, etc.

Profuse, a. *tāwānī, khartsī*; *ḍer, frewān, wadān.*

Profusion, s. *tāwān, kharts*; *frewānī, wadānī*, etc.

Progenitor, s. *nīkah, plār-nīkah.*

Progeny, s. *alwād, zāwzād, farzand, nasl, tūng.*

Prognostic, s. *nakkha, 'alāmat, dalīl.*

Prognosticate, v.a. *pesh khabarī k., fāl katal.*

Progress, v.n. *tlal—lāṛal, chaledal, rawān-edal.* s. *tlana, chalan, rawānagī.*

Progression, s. *chāl, tah, yūn, raftār.*

Progressive, a. *chaland, rawān.*

Prohibit, v.a. *man'a-, qadaghan- kariya-*, etc. *k.*

Project, s. *tadbīr, band, ḥikmat, tajwīz.*

Projection, s. *tsūka, peza*; *ghunḍa*; *pāṛsob.*

Prolapsus ani, s. *būṛa-ī, watana da kulme.*

Prolific, a. *zeganda-ī*; *mewa-dāra*; *tukhm-reza.*

Prolix, a. *ūgd, ṭūland* or *ṭūlānd.*

Prolong, v.a. *ūgdawul, ṭūl k.*; *ziyātawul.*

Prominent, a. *ūchat, khatalai*; *tsargand, kkhkārah.*

Promiscuous, a. *gaḍ waḍ, laṛalai, aṛgajah.*

Promise, s. *wāda, lafz, qaul, bandanr, oe, neta.* v a. *wāda-*, etc. *taṛal* or *k.*

Promising, a. *shwūnai, kkhah, nek bakht, kkhāyastah, joṛ.*

Promissory, a. *sharṭī, qarārī.* (-note) *tamassuk.*

Promontory, s. *khatali zmaka, peza, sar.*

Promote, v.a. *ziyātawul, khejawul*; *sar farāz-, sar buland-, pāya pa porta-*, etc. *k.*

Promotion, s. *sar farāzī, sar bulandī.*

Prompt, a. *chust, chālāk, tayār, gaṛandai.*

Prompt, v.a. *kkhayal—kkhowul*; *yād warkawul*; *lamsawul.*

Promptitude, s. *chālākī, chustī, tayārī.*

Promulgate, v.a. *munādī k., ḍamāme-, jār-*, etc. *wahal, mashhūr k.*

Prone, a. *pa-aṛ-makh*; *prot*; *ṭīṭ*; *mā-ilān, tayār.*

Prong, s. *kkhākha-ī, dwa kkhākha-ī.*

Pronoun, s. *zamīr.*

Pronounce, v.a. *wayal*; *ḥukm-, fatwā-*, etc. *k.*

Proof, s. *dalīl, ḥujjat, zbād* or *iṣbāt.* a. *āzmayalai, pokh, āzmūdah.*

Prop, s. *pusht, pushtībān, aṛam, aṛamkai.*

Propagate, v.a. *zegawul, paidā-, jārī-*, etc. *k.*

Propel, v.a. *zghalawul, chalawul, rawānawul*; *āchawul, wīshtal, ghurzawul.*

Propensity, s. *shauq, raghbat, khwā, mīna, mā-il.*

Proper, a. *khāṣṣ*; *rawā*; *kkhah, kkhāyastah. joṛ, wājib, munāsib, pīrzo, drust.*

Properly, ad. *aṣlan* or *pa aṣl*; *pa kkhah shān sara, pa rikkhtiyā.*

Property, s. *māl, milk*; *khoe, khaṣlat, lokkhai, khāṣṣiyat, ṣifat.*

Prophecy, s. *ghā-ib go-ī, da ghā-ib khabara.* v.a. *ghā-ib wayal, da ghā-ib khabarawul.*

Prophet, s. *paighāmbar, nabī, rasūl.*

Propitiate, v.a. *khwā saṛawul* or *-kkhah k., mihrbān k., pakhulā k.*; *kafārat-, ṣadqa-, qurbān-*, etc. *k.*

Propitious, a. *mubārak, nek, mihrbān.*

Proportion, s. *brakha, andāza, qadr, wesh.* v.a. *barābar-*, etc. *k., samawul; weshal.*

Propose, v.a. *'arz-, sawāl-, darkhwāst-*, etc. *k.*; *tapos* or *tapahus-, pukkhtana-*, etc. *k.*

Proprietor, s. *meṛah, tsakkhtan khāwand, mālik, nāyak, khaṣam.*

Propriety, s. *kkhāyast-wālai, drust-wālai, nek chalan, munāsibat, lā-iqat, pīrzo-wālai.*

Prorogue, v.a. *barkhwāst-, mauqūf-, nāgha-*, etc. *k.*

Prose, s. *naṣr.* (-writer) *naṣr nawīs.*

Prosecute, v.a. *chalawul, kawul, lagiyā k.* v.n. *lagedal, mashghūledal, lagiyā osedal.* (sue) v.a. *d'awa-, faryād-*, etc. *k., ghāṛa-, grewa-*, etc. *nīwul.* v.n. *pase prewatal, pase lagedal.*

Prosecutor, s. *mudda'-ī, laman-, ghāṛa-*, etc. *nīwūnkai, d'awa-*, etc. *kawūnkai.*

Proselyte, s. *murīd, m'utaqid.*

Prospect, s. *nandāra, līdah, naẓar,* (likelihood) *ṣūrat.* (hope) *umed.*

Prosper, v.n. *barakatī-, bakhtawar-*, etc. *osedal* or *-ked.*; *wadānedal, ābādedal, maṛedal.*

Prosperity, s. *barakat, bakht, nek bakhtī; ābādī, wadānī, moṛ-tiyā.*

Prosperous, a. *barakatī, iqbāl-man, sa'ādat-man, bakhtawar; moṛ, ābād, wadān.*

Prostitute, s. *kachana-ī, lola-ī.*

Prostitution, s. *kachana-ī-tob, lola-ī-tob.*

Prostrate, a. *pa-aṛmakh, prot.* v.n. *pa-aṛmakh prewatal.* v.a. *sijda k.*; *naṛawul, ghuzārawul; parzawul.*

Prostration, s. *pa-aṛmakh-tob*; *sijda*; *kamzor-tiyā.*

Protect, v.a. *bachawul, panāh k., nanawātah manal, sātal, jghoral, khundī-, khaṣamāna-*, etc. *k.*; *pālal, nmāndzal.*

Protection, s. *panāh*; *sātana*, etc. (asylum) *nanawātah.*

Protector, s. *sātandoe, jghorai*; *pālankai*; *nāyak.*

Protest, v.a. *iqrār k., lal, lawdal; raṭal, traṭal; nāre-, faryād-*, etc. *k.*

Protract, v.a. *ūgdawul; drang-, lārghah-*, etc. *k.*

Protrude, v.n. *bāhar watal, khatal.*

Protuberance, s. *ghunḍakai, pāṛsob, pūpaka.*

Proud, a. *kibr-jan, bādī, mast, khāntamā, maghrūr.*

Prove, v.a. *ṣābit-, ṣubūt-, zbād-, rikkhtiyā-*, etc. *k.* (try) *āzmāyal, āzmekkht k.* (happen) v.n. *kedal, shwal, prewatal, khatal.*

Provender, s. *wuch wākkhah dapāra da tsārwo.*

Proverb, s. *matal, miṣāl, maṣal.*

Proverbial, a. *matalī*; *mashhūr.*

Provide, v.a. *rāwṛal, paidā k., tadbīr-, tayār-, dzerma-*, etc. *k., khabar ākhistal, khabar gīrī k.*; *warkawul*; *shart taṛal.* (-against) *pesh-fikrī k.*

Provided, c. *pa shart, pa ṣūrat, pa ḥāl.*

Providence, s. *khudāe, rabb, razzāq.* (foresight) *dūr andeshī, pesh-fikrī.*

Provident, a. *dūr andesh, khabar-dār.*

Providentially, ad. *da khudāe pa ḥukm sara, da rabb pa mihrbāngī sara.*

Province, s. *ṣūba, pargana, tapa*; *kār, khidmat*; *gharaẓ.*

Provision, s. *tadbīr, fikr*; *dzerma, tayārī.*

Provisions, s. *khwurāk, khwāṛah, ṭa'ām, ghiẓā.* (-for a journey, etc.) *azūqa, tokkha, tantosh, tsawrai.* (-for an army, etc.) *rasad, zakhīra, sūrsāt.*

Provisional, a. *shartī.*

Proviso, s. *shart.*

Provocation, s. *pārawuna, ṭongāra*; *gwākkh.*

Provoke, v.a. *pārawul, zoral, āgayal, gwākkhal, khapah k.*

Prowess, s. *maṛāna, maṛanī-tob, tūrzan-tob, bahādūrī, dzwānmardī.*

Prowl, v.n. *ghalai girzedal, gakkht k.*

Proximate, a. *nijde, nizd, rātlūnai.*
Proximity, s. *nijdekī* or *nizdekī.*
Proxy, s. *badalī, 'iwazī*; *nā-ib.*
Prudent, a. *khabardār, pokh, hokkhyār.*
Prune, v.a. *prekawul, tarāshal, shūkawul.* (-as birds) *baṉre joṛawul, waza-ar tsanḍal.* s. *ashāṛai, kishta.*
Pry, v.a. *zarana-ī-, tsār-, jāsūsī-, dzīr-*, etc. *k.*
Psalm, s. *zabūr*; *stāyai.*
Puberty, s. *dzwānī, bulūghat, zalmī·tob.*
Public, a. *'āmm, mashhūr*; *tsargand, kkhkārah.* s. *khalq, 'āmmiyān, ūlas* or *ulūs.*
Publicity, s. *shuhrat, gada.*
Publicly, a. *pa tsargand, pa jār* or *pa ẓāhir.*
Publish, v.a. *mashhūr-, ẓāhir-, gaḍ-*, etc. *k.*
Pucker, s. *jung, gundza, chunr, kṛatai, chīchaṛ.*
Puddle, s. *tsaparai, ḍanḍūkai.*
Puff, s. *pū, pūk.* (-of wind) *tsapa.* v.a. *pūkal, pūk wahal*; *paṛsawul, tyak k.*
Pugilist, s. *mūka-ī-* or *sūk wahūnkai, musht·zan.*
Puisne, a. *kashar, kachoṭai.*
Puissant, a. *zorāwar, quwat·nāk.*
Pull, v.a. *rākāgal—rākkhkal.* (-out) *kāgal—kkhkal, bāsal—yastal.* (-along) *kashāla k.* (-down) *naṛawul.* s. *kakkh, rākkhkah.*
Pullet, s. *chirgūṛai, chūchai.*
Pulley, s. *tsarkha-ī.*
Pulp, s. *māghzah.*
Pulpit, s. *mimbar.*
Pulsate, v.n. *dṛazedal.* v.a. *tsiṛīke wahal.*
Pulsation, s. *dṛaz, tsiṛīka.*
Pulse, s. *nabẓ, rag.* (to feel the-) *nabẓ kat'al.* (pea) s. *chanṛa, moṭ, māhe, māsh, ma-ī* or *mayī.*
Pulverize, v.a. *oṛawul, oṛah-, maidah-*, etc. *k.*
Pump, v.a. *oba pa nalo rākāgal—rākkhkal* or *-bāsal—yastal*; *matlab-, rāz-*, etc. *bāsal—yastal.*
Pumpkin, s. *kadū.* (-seed) *kadū zaṛai.*
Pun, s. *laṭīfa, dwa ma'nī khabara.*

Punch, v.a. *sūṛai k.*; *sūk wahal.*
Punctual, a. *pūrah, sūchah, rikkhtīnai.*
Punctuality, s. *rikkhtīn·tob, rāstī.*
Punctually, ad. *jukht-pa neṭe* or *-wakht.*
Puncture, s. *sūṛa, tsīra.*
Pungent, a. *tez, tund.*
Punish, v.a. *sazā warkawul, wahal, tāwān ākhistal.*
Punishment, s. *sazā, 'uqūbat, siyāsat.*
Puny, a. *kachoṭai, kuchinai, kharmandai, poṭai, woṛ, khamachah, woṛūkai.*
Pupil, s. *shāgird, murīd, chelah.* (-of eye) *torai, bātor, kasai, lema, ṭagh.*
Puppet, s. *godā, goda-ī, nāwaka-ī, nenzaka, nāzaka.*
Puppy, s. *kūtrai, kungarai.*
Purchase, v.a. *pa bai'e ākhistal, pīral, pīrodal.*
Purchaser, s. *pa bai'e ākhistūnkai, pīrūnkai.*
Pure, a. *pāk, ṣāf, karah, sūchah, khāliṣ, torai, kkhah*; *pāk laman, nek, pākīzah* or *pāzīkah*; *pūrah.*
Purely, ad. *surup, ta-ash, khālī.*
Purgative, a. *mushil, jullābī.*
Purgatory, s. *i'raf.*
Purge, s. *jullāb, jāṛ.* v.a. *jullāb-*, etc. *warkawul.* v.n. *nāstah lagedal, pa dastūno kkhkenāstal.*
Purification, s. *pākawuna.* (ceremonial) *awdas, tebūn,* or *temūn,* or *tayammum, ṭahārat.*
Purify, v.a. *pākawul, pāk-, pākīzah-, ṣāf*, etc. *k., spetsal* or *spedzal.*
Purity, s. *pākī, pakīzagī, pāk-, ṣāf-*, etc. *-wālai, spetsal·tob*; *rikkhtīn·tob.*
Purple, a. *arghawānī, tor sūr.*
Purport, s. *ma'nī, ma'nā, maṭlab.*
Purpose, s. *niyat, qaṣd, irāda, murād, gharaẓ.* (on-) ad. *pa qasd.* (to what-?) *tsa la, tsa dapāra, wale.* (to the-) *ṣawāb, joṛ, jukht.* v.a. *niyat-*, etc. *taṛal,* or *lagal,* or *k.*
Purr, v.a. *khur wahal, khur khur k.*

Purse, s. *hamiyānī, kīsa, būtskhaka.*
Purslain, s. *warkhāṛai, khulfa* or *khurfa.*
Pursuant, a. *muwāfiq.* (-to) ad. *pa mūjib.*
Pursue, v.n. *pase zghaledal—zghākkhtal*; *pase tlal, -lagedal, -ked.*, etc.
Pursuit, s. *zghākkht, tekkhta*; *mashghūlā, kār*; *kokshiksh, tapos, talāsh.*
Purulent, a. *zawlan.*
Purvey, v.a. *khwurāk-, rasad-, sūrsāt-, zakhīra-*, etc. *ṭolawul.*
Pus, s. *zawa* or *ziwa, ra-ash, zahūb, khīrai.*
Push, v.a. *ṭel-, ḍakka-*, etc. *wahal.*
Pusillanimous, a. *nāmard, yer-man.*
Pustule, s. *nanaka-ī, dāna*; *kharai.*
Put, v.a. *gdal* or *īgdal, īkkhodal, īkkhawul, īkkhal, kkhkegdal*, etc., *lagawul.* (-away) *lire k., sharal.* (-off) *mu'aṭṭal-, drang-*, etc. *k.* (-on) *āghostal, pa dzān-*, etc. *k.* (-out) *muṛ k.* (-together) *joṛawul, yo dzāe k., ṭolawul.* (-up with) *wṛal, zghamal.*
Putrefy, v.n. *wrostedal, pūdah-, skhā-*, etc. *ked.*; *sharhedal.*
Putrid, a. *wrost, skhā, pūdah.*
Puzzle, v.a. *hariyānawul, rabrawul, hak pak k., hairān* or *hariyān-, sarāsīmah-*, etc. *k.* s. *pech, ghūṭai, kaga waga.*

Q.

Quack, s. *lāpai, nīmgaṛai ṭabīb, -mullā*, etc.
Quack, v.a. *qā qā k.*
Quadrilateral, a. *chār gūṭlai.*
Quadruped, s. *tsārwai, dāba, sutūr.*
Quadruple, s. *tsalor bragh, tsalor chand.*
Quaff, v.a. *skal, tskal* or *tskkhal.*
Quagmire, s. *bokkhtana, khaṭa, palanda, taramna.*
Quail, s. *mṛaz, nwaṛaz.*
Quaint, a. *'ajīb*; *laṭīf, nāzak, bārīk.*
Quake, v.n. *laṛzedal, rapedal, pṛakedal.*

Qualification, s. *lā-iqat, qābilyat.*
Qualified, a. *lā-iq, qābil, yarzan.*
Quality, s. *khoe, khaṣlat, ṣifat, ṭab'a, lokkhai.* (rank) *martaba, pāya, darja, kor.*
Qualm, s. *bāka-ī, chāl.* (-of conscience) *gram.* (to have a-) *bāka-ī-*, etc. *k.*; *gram ked.*
Quantity, s. *qadr, andāza, wazn.*
Quarrel, v.a. *jang-, jagaṛa-, qaẓiya-*, etc. *k.*
Quarrelsome, a. *jang-yālai, jagṛāū, bādī.*
Quarry, s. (game) *kkhkār.* (stone-) *da kāṇro kān.*
Quart, s. *ser.*
Quarter, s. *pāo, tsalorama brakha.* (side) *khwā, lorai, tselma, rokh*; *aṛakh, tsang, dada.* (district) *palaw, cham, khel, kandai, mahalla.* (asylum) *panāh, nanawātah, āmān, amn.* (lodging) *dzāe, astoga, bor-jal, ṭikāo.*
Quash, v.a. *māṭawul.* (annul) *bāṭil k.*
Quaver, v.n. *trangedal*; *laṛzedal, rapedal, pṛakedal.*
Quay, s. *pushta, dunkācha.*
Queen, s. *malika.* (-at chess, etc.) *wazīr.*
Queer, a. *'ajab, 'ajīb.*
Quell, v.a. *kkhkenawul, saṛawul, māṭawul, lānde-, man'a-*, etc. *k.*
Quench, v.a. *saṛawul, muṛ k.*
Query, s. *sawāl, tapos* or *tafaḥus.*
Quest, s. *talāsh, ṭalab, tagā pū.*
Question, s. *sawāl, tapos, pukkhtana*; *gumān, shakk, shubha.* v.a. *pukkhtedal, sawāl-*, etc. *k., gumān-*, etc. *laral.*
Questionable, a. *shakk-man, gumānī.*
Quibble, s. *hira-ī, palma, lamghaṛa-ī, ḥīla, chal.*
Quick, a. *za-ar* or *zir, jalt, gaṛandai, chālāk, zghard, tez, talwār-gandai.* (alive) *jwandai.* s. *ūra-ī, jwanda-ī ghwakkha.*
Quicken, v.a. *jwandai k.*; *za-ar* or *zir-*, etc. *k.*
Quickly, ad. *zir zir, pa talwār, pa gaṛandī.*

Quickness, s. *talwār, garand-wālai.*
Quicksand, s. *bokkhtana, ghal shiga.*
Quicksilver, s. *pārā, sīmāb.*
Quiet, a. *chup, ghalai; qalār, ārām.* s. *qalār-tiyā, ārām-tiyā, āsūdagī.*
Quietly, ad. *ro ro, pa qalār sara.*
Quietness, s. *ghalī-tob; ārām-tiyā; gharībī.*
Quill, s. *banra, shāh par* or *kkhāh par.*
Quilt, s. *brastan; nihālī, tolā-ī, toshak.*
Quince, s. *biha-ī* or *bī.* (-seed) *bī dāna.*
Quinsy, s. *haspa, khunāq.*
Quintessence, s. *jauhar, aṣl; khulāṣa.*
Quit, v.a. *pregdal, prekkhodal, prekkhal, tark k.*
Quite, a. *pūrah, amānī, sarāsar, tamām, wārah, tol tāl.* (in comp.) *tak-, tap-,* etc.
Quiver, s. *larza, parak.* (-for arrows) *shkkhwalai, tar kakkh.*
Quiver, v.n. *larzedal, rapedal, parakedal.*
Quota, s. *brakha, wesh, ḥiṣṣa.*
Quote, v.a. *sanad rāwral, da bul chā khabara* (or *wayai*) *yādawul.*

R.

Rabbit, s. *khargosh, koranai soe.*
Rabble, s. *dala, park, ganr khalq.*
Race, s. *manda, zghākkht.* (generation) *aṣl, nasl, zāt, khāndān, kor, noga.*
Rack, s. *shikanja, tsarkh, pāna, kāt.* v.a. *pa shikanjo-,* etc. *khejawul, 'azābawul.*
Radiance, s. *brekkhnā, ranrā, palwasha.*
Radiant, a. *brekkh-nāk, rūnr, dzalkan.*
Radiate, v.n. *brekkhedal, dzalkedal, rūnredal.*
Radical, a. *aṣlī, zātī.*
Radish, s. *mūla-ī, turp.*
Raffle, v.a. *pa hisk-, pa pucho-, pa qur'o-,* etc. *khartsawul.*
Raft, s. *jāla, bera.*

Rafter, s. *bensh, lakara, patera.*
Rag, s. *chirra, parūkai, pārcha, purza, khartsorai.*
Rage, s. *qahr, ghuṣṣa, ghazab, tāo; saudā.*
Ragged, a. *tūkī tūkī.* (in rags) *gand* or *kind- poksh.* (uneven) *zig, lwār jawar, kandai kaudarai.*
Raging, a. *ghazab-nāk, qahr-jan, khapah, eshānd.*
Rail, v.a. *ker-, bāra-, shpol-,* etc. *taral* or *-lagawul.* (abuse) *peghor warkawul, kanzal* or *kkhkandzal.* (blame) *malāmatawul, ratal, tratal.*
Raiment, s. *āghostan, zarūkai, nwarai, jāma, pokkhāk, libās.*
Rain, s. *bārān.* (slight-) *rangai bārān, pūna.* (heavy-) *ganr bārān, shebah.* (spring shower) *hakkhma, wasa.* (hot weather-) *parshakāl.* (-bow) *shna kāsa, sara kāsa, da būda-ī tāl.*
Rain, v.n. *oredal, tsātsedal, bāranedal.*
Raise, v.a. *pātsawul, khejawul, porta k.* (erect) *walārawul, wudrawul, lakawul.* (educate) *pālal, nmāndzal, parwaral.*
Raisin, s. *watska, mewa.*
Rake, s. *pāra, ghākkhawar, panj-gakkhai; lawand, chat, kāsīr, lūtsak.*
Rake, v.a. *ghākkhawar girzawul, panj-gakkhai wahal; kāsīrī-,* etc. *k.* (search) *latawul.* (collect) *tolawul.*
Rally, v.a. *tīngawul, sambālawul, jorawul, mazbūt k., komak rasawul.* (jeer) *khandā-, toqa-,* etc. *k.*
Ram, s. *mag, ga-ad.* (fighting) *ghūch.*
Ram, v.a. *mandal, kkhke mandal.*
Ramble, v.n. *girzedal, sail k.*
Rambler, s. *gashtai, āwārah, lawand.*
Ramify, v.n. *khwaredal, wīredal, pheledal.*
Rammer, s. *pāeko, dabalai, bargho.*
Rampant, a. *mast, shokhīn.*
Rampart, s. *kkhahr panāh, bāra, sangar.*

Rancid, a. *skhā, wrost, trīw, trīkh.*
Rancour, s. *kīna, bughz, khwā badī, 'inād.*
Random, a. *tawakkulī, qismatī.* (at-) ad. *hase.*
Range, v.a. *sail-, gakkht-*, etc. *k.* v.n. *girzedal.* (set) *tartībawul, sambālawul.*
Rank, s. *martaba, pāya, dzāe, darja; para, saff, qatār.* a. *wrost, skhā, bad·būī·dār.* v.a. *para-*, etc. *taral; ganral, shmeral.*
Rankle, v.n. *baledal, eshedal, khūyedal* or *khū-edal, swal.*
Ransack, v.a. *latawul, shanal; tālā-, lūt-*, etc. *k.*
Ransom, s. *būnga.*
Rant, v.a. *lāpe shāpe wahal; baq baq-, bar bar-*, etc. *k.*
Rap, v.a. *wahal, trakawul, tak wahal, takawul.*
Rapacious, a. *lūt·bāz, ghārat·gar; khūnārai.*
Rape, v.a. *bikr mātawul, pa zabardastī ghowul.* (-seed) *awrai.*
Rapid, a. *garandai, za-ar* or *zir, jalt, tez, tund.*
Rapidity, s. *jaltī, talwār, tundī, tezī.*
Rapine, s. *lūt, ghārat, tālān, tākht tārāj.*
Rapture, s. *dera khūsh·hālī, josh, eshnā.*
Rare, a. *nādir, matrah, kam paidā.* (thin) *narai.*
Rarify, v.a. *narai-, mahīn-, bārīk-*, etc. *k.*
Rarely, ad. *kamtar, la-ag.*
Rascal, s. *harāmī, laralai, badm'āsh, charland.*
Rash, a. *talwalai, talwār·gandai, jalt, be·tadbīr, zir.* (-on the skin) *garmaka, larama, sra makha, jarmora, nanaka-ī, dzwānaka.*
Rasp, v.a. *sohān-, chausār-*, etc. *wahal*, or *k.*; *sūlawul, zīgawul, zdoyal.*
Rat, s. *magak, magah, samandai.* (musk-) *mukkhkai magak.*
Rate, s. *bai'a, qīmat, nirkh; andāza, hisāb; shān, taur.* v.a. *bai'a-*, etc. *taral; andāza-*, etc. *k., ganral.* (scold) *ratal, tratal, dāral.*

Rather, ad. *wrūnbe, awwal, lā.*
Ratify, v.a. *qabūlawul, muqarrar k.*
Ratio, s. *andāza, wazn.*
Rational, a. *'aql·man, pohānd; munāsib.*
Rationality, s. *'aql, poh, pahm, sha'ūr.*
Rattle, v.a. *shrangawul, granjawul, ga·arahār k.* s. *chanr chanrai, granjāū.*
Ravage, v.a. *tālā-, wairān-, ūjār-, kkhpo lānde-*, etc. *k., latārawul, natal.*
Rave, v.a. *be·khūdī khabare k., bar bar k.*
Raven, s. *kāgh.*
Ravenous, a. *liwāl, wagai, naghlānd.*
Ravine, s. *khwar, kandą, kas.*
Ravish, v.a. *bikr shlawul* or *-mātawul; pa zor ākhistal; satr ākhistal.*
Raw, a. *ūm* or *om, nīma·khwā, nīm·pokh, kachah.* (abraded) *sūdah, sūlawulai.* (-cold) *sor.*
Rawness, s. *om·wālai; sāra.*
Ray, s. *palwasha, partaw, dzalak, shughla.*
Raze, v.a. *narawul, kkhpo lānde-, latārah-*, etc. *k.*
Razor, s. *ustura, pāka-ī.* (-strap) *pataka.*
Reach, v.n. *rasedal, rātlal, rāghlal.* (touch) *lagedal, jangedal.* (-out) *ghazedal* or *gazedal.* (fetch) v.a. *rāwral.*
Reaction, s. *zor, quwat.*
Read, v.a. *lwustal, kitāb katal.*
Readiness, s. *tayārī, chālākī.*
Reading, s. *lwustūn.* (-the Qurān) *qirāt.*
Ready, a. *tayār, chālāk, hāzir.*
Real, a. *rikkhtīnai, aslī, sūchah, karah.*
Reality, s. *rikkhtiyā, rikkhtīn·tob, haqīqat.*
Realize, v.a. *mūndal, gatal; paidā-, hāzir-*, etc. *k.*
Really, ad. *rikkhtiyā, khudāe go.*
Realm, s. *mulk, rāj, bādshāhī; hiwād.*
Reap, v.a. *lau k., rebal, rawdal; mūndal, gatal.*
Reaper, s. *lau·garai; gatūnkai.*

Rear, s. *wrūstai, shā, dumbāl.* (in the-) ad. *wrūsto, pa shā, pastana.*

Rear, v.a. *khejawul, pātsawul, walāṛawul.* v.n. *walāṛedal, pātsedal, khatal.* (-up) *negh-, lak-, jig-,* etc. *walāṛedal* or *-ked.* (nourish) *parwaral, pālal, nmāndzal.*

Reason, s. *'aql, poh, pahm.* (cause) *sabab, kabl, bā'is; mūjib, wāsiṭa, jihat.* (proof) *dalīl, ḥujjat.* (right) *ḥaqq, inṣāf.* v.a. *baḥs-,* etc. *k.*

Reasonable, a. *wājib, munāsib, kkhāyastah, kkhah.*

Rebel, s. *yāghī-gar. sar-kakkh.* v.a. *yāghī-garī-, sar-kakkhī-,* etc. *k.* v.n. *yāghī-,* etc. *ked.*

Rebellious, a. *yāghī, ṭughiyān.*

Rebound, v.a. *tīndak wahal, ṭop wahal.*

Rebuke, v.a. *malāmatawul, raṭal, dāṛal;* (-oneself) *gram k.*

Recall, v.a. *biyā balal, stūnawul* or *stanawul; yādawul.*

Recant, v.a. *rāe badlawul.* v.n. *girzedal, jārwatal, stūnedal* or *stanedal; munkiredal.*

Recapitulate, v.a. *biyā bayānawul.*

Recede, v.n. *wrusto ked., stanedal, haṭedal, pastana ked., jārwatal.*

Receipt, s. *rasīd, ḥujjat, tamassuk.*

Receive, v.a. *ākhistal; manal.*

Recent, a. *nawai, osanai, nan wradzanai.*

Recently, ad. *os, pa zir mūde.*

Receptacle, s. *khūna, dzāe, kor, makān.*

Reception, s. *ākhistah; manana; istiqbāl; melmastiyā.*

Recess, s. *ṭāq, ṭāqcha, rap, dara-ī; gūṭ, gokkha.* (suspension) *barkhwāst, wazgār-tiyā, t'aṭīl.*

Recipe, s. *nuskha.*

Reciprocal, a. *da dwāṛo paṛo, -loro, -ḍaḍo,* etc., *ṭarfain, jānibain.*

Recite, v.a. *bayānawul, yādawul, naql k.*

Reckon, v.a. *shmeral, shumāral, ḥisābawul; gaṇṛal.* v.n. *pohedal, pahmedal.*

Reclaim, v.a. *joṛawul, sambālawul, ābādawul, wadānawul.*

Recline, v.n. *tsamlāstal, tsamlal, mlāstal. ghazedal* or *gazedal.*

Recluse, s. *gokkha-nishīn.*

Recognisance, s. *iqrār-nāma.*

Recognition, s. *pejāndah, pejandgalī.*

Recognize, v.a. *pejandal.*

Recoil, v.a. *tīndak wahal.* v.n. *stanedal, pa biyarta jārwatal.*

Recollect, v.a. *yādawul; zdah k.*

Recollected, s. *yād, zdah.*

Recommend, v.a. *sipārish k., spāral.*

Recompense, v.a. *tāwān-, badal-,* etc. *warkawul.*

Reconcile, v.a. *pakhulā k., rogha joṛa k., khwā saṛawul; manal, barābarawul.*

Record, s. *daftar, tawārīkh.* v.a. *līkal, darj k.*

Recorder, s. *qānūn-goe, sarishta-dār.*

Recount, v.a. *bayānawul.*

Recover, v.n. *raghedal, joṛedal.* v.a. *biyā-mūndal.*

Recovery, s. *raghedana, joṛedana; biyā-mūndah.*

Recreation, s. *sail, tamāsha, loba, wazgār-tiyā.*

Recriminate, v.a. *chighawul, sara kanzal k., lagiyā sara peghorūna warkawul.*

Recruit, v.a. *hosā-,* etc. *k., dama warkawul; pūrah-,* etc. *k., nawai nokar k.*

Rectify, v.a. *joṛawul, sam-, drust-,* etc. *k.*

Rectitude, s. *rikkhtīn-tob, nekī, rāstī, ṣawāb.*

Rectum, s. *chustai, kulma.*

Recumbent, a. *mlāst, prot, ghazedalai.*

Recur, v.n. *rātlal, rāghlal; yādedal.*

Red, a. *sūr, lāl, surkh, rat.*

Redeem, v.a. *khalāṣawul, āzādawul, bachawul.*

Redress, v.a. *tāwān warkawul, dādrasī, niyāw-,* etc. *k.*

Reduce, v.a. *kamawul, lundawul, sarawul*; *rāwral.*
Reduction, s. *kam·tiyā, la-ag·wālai*; *trot, zwam.*
Redundant, a. *ziyāt, der.*
Reed, s. *dūrma, darwai, nal, shpelai, lūkha.*
Reel, s. *aterān, tsarkhai.* (-of thread) *ata* or *ateha.* (dance) *atanr.*
Refer, v.a. *pukkhtedal, spāral, lidal—goral, katal, lagawul, nisbat laral.* v.n. *lagedal.*
Reference, s. *nisbat, 'alāqa, ta'alluq, lār.*
Referee, s. *munsif.*
Refine, v.a. *pāk-, sāf-, spīn-,* etc. *k., narai-,* etc. *k.*
Refit, v.a. *jorawul.*
Reflect, v.a. *fikr-, ghaur-,* etc. *k.*; *siwrai-, 'aks-,* etc. *āchawul.*
Reflux, s. *jārwātah, stūnedah.*
Reform, v.a. *nawai jorawul, ārāstah k.*
Refractory, a. *yāghī, sar·kakkh, takanrai.*
Refrain, v.a. *parhez k., dzān sātal.* v.n. *dada ked.*
Refresh, v.a. *hosā-, tāzah-,* etc. *k., dama warkawul, khwā sarawul.*
Refreshment, s. *khwūrāk, naharai, ta'ām*; *ārām, dama.*
Refuge, s. *āsra, panāh*; *nanawātah, amn.*
Refugee, s. *nanawātai, panāh·gīr.*
Refulgent, a. *rūnr, rokkhān, brekkh·nāk.*
Refund, v.a. *stūnawul* or *stanawul, biyarta-, pastana-,* etc. *warkawul*; *tāwān warkawul.*
Refuse, v.a. *namanal, naqabūlawul, daregh-, ibā-,* etc. *k.,* or *-rāwral.*
Refute, v.a. *bātil-, radd-,* etc. *k.*; *gram k.*
Regain, v.a. *biyā mūndal.*
Regal, a. *bādshāhī.*
Regard, v.a. *nazar-, nigāh-,* etc. *k., katal*; *manal*; *fikr-,* etc. *k., khabar ākhistal*; *ganral.*
Regardless, a. *be·khabar, be·parwā.*
Regent, s. *qā-im muqām, nā-ib.*
Regimen, s. *pāl, parhez, tīmār.*
Regiment, s. *paltan.* (-of horse) *risāla.*
Region, s. *zmaka, mulk, hiwād.*
Register, s. *daftar, sijill, shajara.*
Regret, s. *afsos, daregh, armān, tartāb, stomānī, pakkhemānī.* v.a. *afsos-,* etc. *k.* v.n. *stomānedal, pakkhemān ked.*
Regular, a. *barābar, sam, hawār, drust*; *qānūnī, ā-īnī, intizāmī.*
Regulation, s. *ā-īn, qānūn*; *tartīb.*
Reject, v.a. *lire k., sharal*; *jārbāsal—jāryastal*; *nā·qabūl*; *nā·khwakkh-,* etc. *k.*
Reign, v.a. *bādshāhī-, rāj-, hukm-,* etc. *k.*
Reimburse, v.a. *warkawul, tāwān-, badal-, 'iwaz-,* etc. *warkawul, stūnawul, pūrah-,* etc. *k.*
Rein, s. *wāga, mlūna*; *jalab, bādgol.*
Reinstate, v.a. *pa dzāe kkhkenawul* or *-muqarrar k.*
Rejoice, v.a. *kkhādī-, khūsh·hālī-,* etc. *k.* v.n. *kkhādedal, khūsh·hāledal, kkhād·man ked.* (spitefully) v.a. *sakha-, wiyār-,* etc. *k.*
Rejoin, v.a. *jorawul, lagawul.* v.n. *gadedal.*
Reiterate, v.a. *dubāra-, biyā biyā-, wār wār-,* etc. *wayal.*
Relate, v.a. *bayānawul, wayal, qissa k.*; *nisbat-, 'alāqa-,* etc. *laral.* v.n. *lagedal.*
Relation, s. *bayān, qissa*; *nisbat-, 'alāqa-, khpul, khekkh, 'azīz.* (paternal-) *plār·ganai.* (maternal-) *mor·ganai,* etc.
Relationship, s. *khpul·walī, khpulawī, 'azīz·walī* or *'azīz·galwī, khekkhī*; *ragai, had.*
Relative, s. *khpul, khekkh,* etc. (*v.* Relation) a. *nisbatī.*
Relax, v.a. *arat-, sust-,* etc. *k.*
Relaxation, s. *arat·wālai, sust·wālai*; *sustī*; *wazgār·tiyā.*
Release, v.a. *āzādawul, khalāsawul, wurhawul, yalah k., pregdal, prekkhodal, prekkhal.*
Relent, v.n. *narmedal, mulā-im ked.*

Relentless, a. *be-raḥm, sang-dil, kāṉṟai zrah.*
Reliance, s. *bāwar, umed, takiya, tawakkul.*
Relief, s. *madad, komak*; *ārām*; *badlī.*
Relieve, v.a. *madad-, komak-,* etc. *rasawul*; *ārām warkawul*; *badlī k.*
Religion, s. *dīn, īmān, mazhab, kesh.*
Religious, a. *dīn-dār, īmān-dār, nmāndzī, nmāndz-guzār*; *dīnī, mazhabī.*
Relinquish, v.a. *pregdal, prekkhodal, prekkhal, tark k.*
Relish, v.a. *khwand-, maza-,* etc. *warkawul, maza-dār-, khwand-nāk-,* etc. *k.*
Reluctance, s. *daregh, stomānī.*
Reluctant, a. *nārāz, stomān.*
Rely, v.a. *bāwar-, takiya-, tawakkul-,* etc. *k.*
Remain, v.n. *pātedal, pāedal, osedal, pātai ked.*
Remainder, s. *bāqī, pātai.*
Remains, s. *pas-khurda, jūṭa.* (mortal-) *muṟai.*
Remark, v.a, *nazar-, nigāh-,* etc. *k., yādawul, wayal.*
Remarkable, a. *'ajīb, 'ajab*; *mashhūr.*
Remedy, s. *'ilāj, dawā, tsāra, darmān, tadbīr.* v.a. *'ilāj-,* etc. *k., joṟawul, raghawul.*
Remember, v.a. *yādawul, yād laral, pejandal*; *zdah k.*
Remembrance, s. *yād*; *pejāndah.*
Remind, v.a. *yād warkawul.*
Remiss, a. *sust, ghāfil, soṟ, narm.*
Remit, v.a. *bakkhal, pulāwul, mu'āf k.* (send) *āstawul, legal.* (lessen) *kamawul, la-agawul.*
Remittance, s. *bakkhana*; *āstawūna*; *kamawūna.*
Remnant, a. *bāqī, pātai.*
Remonstrance, s. *'arẓī*; *takrār*; *gila.*
Remorse, s. *paskhāk* or *pakhsāk, pakkhemānī.*
Remote, a. *liri* or *lire, prat.*
Remove, v.a. *liri k., khejawul*; *kaḍa wṟal, legdal—lekkhal, kūch k.*

Remunerate, v.a. *ajr-, ujrat-, miḥnat-,* etc. *warkawul*; *tāwān-, shukrāna-,* etc. *warkawul.*
Rend, v.a. *shlawul, tsiral, tsāk k., mātawul, wrarawul.*
Render, v.a. *kawul, kṟal, rāwṟal.*
Rendezvous, s. *borjal.* v.n. *ṭoledal, yo dzāe ked.*
Renew, v.a. *biyā kawul, -rāwṟal, -ākhistai,* etc. *nawai-, tāzah-,* etc. *k.*
Rennet, s. *tomna, māya*; *siyalai.*
Renounce, v.n. *munkiredal, jārwatal.* v.a. *inkār-,* etc, *k., pregdal, prekkhodal, prekkhal.*
Renowned, a. *nāmwar, mashhūr.*
Rent, a. *shledalai, tsīralai.* s. *tsāk, tsīra, darz.* (hire) *kreha, kirāha*; *ijāra.*
Rent, v.n. *shledal* or *tsīredal*; *wraredal.*
Renunciation, s. *inkār, tark.*
Repair, v.a. *joṟawul, pewand-, marammat-,* etc. *k.*
Repartee, s. *ḥāẓir dzawābī.*
Repast, s. *naharai, nāshta, ḍoḍa-ī.*
Repay, v.a. *badal-, tāwān-,* etc. *warkawul*; *qarẓ-, por-,* etc. *khejawul*; *pūrah-, adā-,* etc. *k.*
Repeal, v.a. *bāṭil-, radd-,* etc. *k.*
Repeat, v.a. *biyā-, dubāra-,* etc. *wayal, bayānawul, mukarrar wayal.*
Repeatedly, ad. *biyā qa biyā, daf'atan.*
Repel, v.a. *liri k., shaṟal, raṭal, haṭālawul.*
Repent, v.a. *toba bāsal—yastal.* v.n. *stomānedal, pakkhemān ked.*
Repentance, s. *toba, stomānī, pakkhemānī.*
Repentant, a. *toba-gār, stomān, pakkhemān.*
Repine, v.n. *kaṟedal, nūledal, ghamedal.*
Replete, a. *pūrah, ḍak, moṟ.*
Reply, v.a. *dzawāb-, pāsukh-,* etc. *warkawul.*
Report, s. *khabar, āwāza*; *bāng, ḍaz, ghag.* v.a. *khabarawul, khabar warkawul*; *bāng wayal*; *ḍaz wahal, ghagawul.*

Repose, v.n. *tsamlāstal, mlāstal, ghazedal*; *ūdah ked.* v.a. *khob-, ārām-*, etc. *k.*
Reprehensible, a. *malāmatī, nākārah.*
Represent, v.a. *'arz k.*; *kkhayal—kkhowul.*
Representation, s. *'arzī*; *tsera, ṣūrat*; *tamāsha.*
Representative, s. *wakīl, nā-ib, qā-im muqām.*
Reprimand, v.a. *malāmat k., ṭaqawul, raṭal.*
Reprisal, s. *bota, bramta.*
Reproach, v.a. *peghor warkawul*; *gila k.*
Reprobate, s. *gumrāh, mardūd, wruk lāṛ.*
Reprove, v.a. *malāmatawul, traṭal, raṭal, dāṛal.*
Reptile, s. *chinjai, khazanda.*
Republic, s. *da ulas* or *ulūs jirga*; *da jirgo ḥukūmat.*
Repudiate, v.a. *inkār k., sharal, kkhayal.*
Repugnance, s. *kraka*; *daregh.*
Repugnant. a. *mukhālif, kagalai.*
Repulse, v.a. *mātawul, takkhtawul, haṭālawul.*
Reputable, a. *mu'atabar, i'tibārī.*
Reputation, s. *nūm, nang, abrū, i'tibār.*
Request, v.a. *darkhwāst-, 'arz-, sawāl-*, etc. *k., ghokkhtal, pukkhtedal.*
Require, v.a. *ghokkhtal, ḥājat laral.*
Requisite, a. *pakār, lāzim, zarūr.*
Rescue, v.a. *khalāṣawul, wurhawul, bachawul.*
Resemblance, s. *barābarī, mushābihat.*
Resembling, a. *ghondi, pa shān, pa rang.*
Resent, v.a. *bad manal.*
Resentment, s. *kīna, badī, dukkhmanī.*
Reserve, v.a. *sātal, khundiyal, khundī k.*
Reservoir, s. *ḥauz, baha-ī, ḍanḍ, tālāw.*
Reside, v.n. *āstedal, osedal, pātedal.* v.a. *astoga-, meshta-* etc. *k.*
Resident, s. *osedūnkai, astogūnkai, āstedūnkai.*
Residue, s. *bāqī, pātai*; *tarka.*
Resign, v.a. *pregdal, prekkhodal, prekkhal*; *tark k.*; *spāral, pāslawul*; *bakkhal.*
Resignation, s. *tark, prekkhodana*; *spārana, spārakkhtana*; *tawakkul*; *ist'ifā.*
Resin, s. *rāndzaṛah, chūṛel*; *jāwla.*
Resist, v.a. *mazbūṭī-, barābarī-, jang-*, etc. *k.* v.n. *ṭīng-, klak-, mazbūṭ-*, etc. *wudredal*, or *ked., haṭedal.*
Resolute, a. *mazbūṭ, klak, ṭīng, zṛah-war.*
Resolution, s. *qaṣd, niyat.*
Resolve, v.a. *qaṣd k., niyat taṛal.*
Resort, v.a. *rāsha darsha k.*
Resound, v.n. *ghagedal, ghuṛunbedal.*
Resource, s. *chāra, 'ilāj*; *chal, ḥikmat.*
Respect, s. *'izzat, adab*; *nisbat, 'alāqa.* (with respect to) *pa ḥaqq kkhke.* (in many respects) *pa ḍero khabaro kkhke.* (in every respect) *pa hare khabare.* v.n. *grohedal*; *manal.*
Respectable, a. *mu'atabar, 'izzat-nāk.*
Respectful, a. *adab kawūnkai.*
Respective, a. *khāṣṣ*; *khpul khpul.*
Respire, v.a. *sāh ākhistal.*
Respite, s. *furṣat*; *wazgār-tiyā*; *nāgha.*
Response, s. *dzawāb, pāsukh.*
Responsibility, s. *zimma*; *tāwān.*
Responsible, a. *zimma-dār, tāwān warkawūnkai.*
Rest, s. *ārām-tiyā, qalār-tiyā*; *ārām, qalār* or *qarār, furṣat.* (pause) *wār, dama.* (sleep) *khob.* (prop) *aṛam.*
Rest, a. *bāqī, pātai*; *nor, nor ṭol.*
Restive, a. *sar-kakkh, sar-zor, ṭakanrai.*
Restless, a. *be-ārām, nā-qalār.*
Restore, v.a. *biyā pa dzāe walāṛawul, pa biyarta warkawul.*
Restrain, v.a. *sambālawul, bandawul, man'a k., īsārawul, haṭālawul.*
Result, s. *ḥāṣil*; *'amal*; *khatah*; *pāzah.*
Resume, v.a. *biyā ākhistal.*
Resurrection, s. *ākhirat, ḥashr, qiyāmat.* (day of-) *wradz da ḥashr*, etc.
Retail, v.a. *bel bel-, la-ag la-ag-*, etc. *khartsawul, lāgī k.*
Retain, v.a. *sātal, laral, khundī k.*

Retaliate, v.a. *badal-, jazā-, qiṣāṣ-,* etc. *ā<u>kh</u>istal; bota-, bramta-,* etc. *k.*
Retard, v.a. *haṭālawul, kariyābawul; drang-, lār<u>gh</u>ah-, multawī-,* etc. *k.*
Retch, v.a. *bāka-ī-, qai-, <u>ch</u>āl-,* etc. *k., jārbāsal—jāryastal, kūz katal, zmake ta goral.*
Reticular, a. *jāl·dār, jālī.*
Retinue, s. *swarlī; jalab.*
Retire, v.n. *wrusto-, biyarta-,* etc. *ked., haṭāledal, pastana jārwatal* or *-tlal—lāṛal pā<u>ts</u>edal; puṭedal.°*
Retired, a. *puṭ, yawā<u>dz</u>ai, bel* or *biyal.*
Retirement, s. *yawā<u>dz</u>ī·tūn, bel·tūn.*
Retract, v.n. *girzedal, landedal.* v.a. *inkār-, bāṭil-,* etc. *k., jārbāsal—jāryastal.*
Retreat, v.n. *ta<u>kkh</u>tedal, haṭāledal, biyarta-,* etc. *ked.* s. *te<u>kkh</u>ta, māt.* (cover) *puṭgana-ī, psūnai, <u>ts</u>awai.* (asylum) *panāh, nanawātah.*
Retrench, v.a. *kamawul, la-agawul, landawul.*
Retribution, s. *sazā, siyāsat, badal, jazā.*
Retrieve, v.a. *sambālawul, biyā mūndal.*
Return, v.n. *girzedal, jārwatal, stūnedal, āwu<u>kkh</u>tal, pastana rātlal—rā<u>gh</u>lal.* v.a. *pa biyarta āstawul, stūnawul.*
Return, s. *jarwātah; badal.* (profit) *sūd, gaṭa.* (answer) *<u>dz</u>awāb.* (form) *ṣūrat ḥāl.*
Reveal, v.a. *<u>ts</u>argandawul. <u>kkh</u>kārah k., parda porta k., wayal.*
Revel, v.a. *mastī-, bad mastī k.*
Revenge, v.a. *badal-, qiṣāṣ-,* etc. *ā<u>kh</u>istal.*
Revengeful, a. *kīna·war.*
Revenue, s. *bāj, <u>kh</u>irāj, maḥṣūl, sāw.*
Revere, v.a. *zbarg ganral* or *-manal.* v.n. *grohedal.*
Reverence, s. *grohedana, manana; sat, adab; salām, sijda.*
Reverse, v.a. *naskorawul, aṛawul, apūṭah k.*
Reverse, a. *naskor, aṛawulai; apūṭah.* s. *āfat, balā, bad-* or *tor ba<u>kh</u>tī.*

Review, v.a. *nandāra-, tamā<u>sh</u>a-, <u>dz</u>er-,* etc. *k.*
Revile, v.a. *kanzal, kanzal k., <u>kkh</u>kan<u>dz</u>al, pe<u>gh</u>or warkawul.*
Revolution, s. *<u>ts</u>ar<u>kh</u>, daur; balwā, pasāt.*
Revolve, v.n. *<u>ch</u>urledal, <u>ts</u>ar<u>kh</u>edal, girzedal.* v.a. *fikr-, <u>gh</u>aur-,* etc. *k.*
Reward, s. *ujrat, miḥnat; ba<u>kkh</u>ana, in'ām ṣawāb, barakat.*
Rheumatism, s. *bād, wo.*
Rhinoceros, s. *genḍai.*
Rhubarb, s. *rewand.* (fresh) *rawā<u>sh</u>.*
Rhyme, s. *radīf, naẓm.*
Rib, s. *pu<u>kkh</u>ta-ī.*
Riband, s. *paṭa-ī, re<u>kkh</u>a; pekawai.*
Rice, s. *wrīja.* (-in the husk) *<u>sh</u>ola.* (broken-) *<u>kh</u>ama<u>ch</u>a.* (boiled-) *kamoda, <u>ch</u>alāū.* (-straw) *palāla.* (-field) *<u>sh</u>ol·gara, <u>sh</u>ālī·zāra, kadhal.* (-planting) *nihālī.*
Rich, a. *māl·dār, duniyā·dār, daulat·man.*
Riches, s. *māl, duniyā, daulat.*
Rick, s. *dala-ī, ḍera-ī.*
Rid, v.a. *liri k., jārū k., ta-a<u>sh</u>awul, <u>kh</u>alāṣawul, āzādawul, wurhawul, rihā k.*
Riddle, s. *mu'amma.* (sieve) *<u>gh</u>albel.*
Ride, v.n. *swaredal* or *sparedal.* v.a. *swarlī k.*
Rider, s. *swor* or *spor; sparlanai.*
Ridge, s. *kamar, pu<u>sh</u>ta* or *pu<u>kkh</u>ta, <u>gh</u>ā<u>kkh</u>ai.*
Ridicule, s. *<u>kh</u>andā, ṭoqa, pe<u>kkh</u>a, malanḍa.*
Ridiculous, a. *<u>kh</u>andā·nāk, ṭoqī, malanḍai.*
Rifle, v.a. *<u>sh</u>ūkawul, natal, lūṭawul.*
Rig, v.a. *joṛawul. tartībawul.*
Right, a. *ri<u>kkh</u>tiyā, drust, ju<u>kh</u>t, rāst, joṛ, wājib, rawā, barābar, <u>kkh</u>āyastah, <u>kkh</u>ah.* (-hand) *<u>kkh</u>ai.* in. *ju<u>kh</u>t! joṛ! drust!* etc. s. *ḥaqq; wāk, i<u>kh</u>tiyār; māl, milk; 'adl, inṣāf; <u>kkh</u>ai.* v.a. *joṛawul, samawul,* etc.
Righteous, a. *nek, nekokār, ri<u>kkh</u>tīnai, rāst·bāz, pāk, ṣawābī.*
Righteousness, s. *nekī, rāstī, ri<u>kkh</u>tīn·tob, ṣawāb.*

Rightful, a. *ḥaqq·dār, haqq·man.*

Rigid, a. *klak, lak, zīg, negh, sakht, tsak, ṭing.*

Rigidity, s. *klak·wālai, zīg·wālai,* etc.

Rigour, s. *sakhti; sāṛah, yakhnī; laṛza.*

Rigorous, a. *sakht, zīg; soṛ, yakh.*

Rim, s. *ghāṛa, morga, tsanda, ja-ī.* (wheel-) *kīra-ī, garda-ī; drakaṛ.*

Rind, s. *baṭ, paṭ, poṭ, khwar, postakai.*

Ring, s. *kara-ī.* (finger-) *tsalai.* (nose-) *pezwān, natka-ī.* (ear-) *chala, wālai.* (neck-) *oga-ī.*

Ring, v.n. *trangedal, shṛangedal, gṛanjedal.*

Ringdove, s. *gūgushtū, qumrī, spalama, tatawa, kur·kura-ī.*

Ringleader, s. *sarguroh, sarghanah, nāyak.*

Ringlet, s. *tsūnṛa, tsunṛaka, zulfa, gesū.*

Ringworm, s. *pishak, spūnṛai.*

Rinse, v.a. *wīndzal* or *mīndzal, wlal.*

Riot, s. *balwā, pasāt, kharkhakkha.* (revel) *khar mastī, bad·mastī, ṭel ṭāl.*

Riotous, a. *balwā·gar, pasātī, sar·kakkh; mast.*

Rip, v.a. *tsīral, tsāk k., shlawul.*

Ripe, a. *pokh, khuṛīn.*

Ripple, s. *tsaparkai, pacha.*

Rise, v.n. *pātsedal, porta ked., walāṛedal, khatal.*

Rise, s. *khātah, taraqqa-ī.*

Risk, s. *khaṭra, muhimm, bāk, yera.*

Rite, s. *ṭarīqa, rasm; mazhab, sunnat.*

Rival, s. *dukkhman, raqīb.* (-wife) *ba-an.*

Rivalry, s. *dukkhmanī, raqībī.*

River, s. *sīnd, dariyāb, nahar.*

Rivulet, s. *lakkhtai, aṛākh, wela.*

Road, s. *lār, rāh, wāṭ.*

Roam, v.n. *girzedal, rammedal, khushai girzedal.*

Roan, a. *samand.*

Roar, v.a. *nāra-, tanṛ-, ḍerān-,* etc. *wahal.* v.n. *gharedal, ghuṛunbedal.*

Roast, v.a. *wrītawul, kabābawul, talawul, teyal.*

Rob, v.a. *shūkawul, lūṭawul, natal, ghlā k., lār wahal.*

Robber, s. *ghal, shūk·mār, lār wahūnkai.*

Robbery, s. *ghlā.* (highway-) *shūka.*

Robe, s. *jāma, āghostan, libās.* (-of honour) *khalāt* or *khil'at.*

Robust, a. *mazbūṭ, takṛah, mazai, gagar.*

Rock, s. *tīga, gaṭ.*

Rock, v.a. *khwadzawul, ṭāl wahal, jūṭa·ī warkawul, zangawul, shanawul.* v.n. *zangal, zangedal, khwadzedal, shanedal.*

Rocky, a. *kānṛedz, sanglākh, gaṭīn.*

Rod, s. *lakkhta, hamsā* or *amsā.*

Rogue, s. *ṭag, ṭag·bāz, chal·bāz, farebī.*

Roguery, s. *ṭagī, ṭag·bāzī, chal·bāzī, fareb.*

Roll, v.a. *ngharal—nghakkhtal.* (-on the ground) v.n. *rgharedal—rghakkhtal, lots pots ked.*

Roll, s. *nghakkht; wal, pech, tāo.* (-of paper) *dasta, fard.* (list) *daftar, sijill.* (plait) *bragh.*

Roller, s. *māla, mandānṛo.* (bandage) *paṭa-ī.*

Romance, s. *qissa; darogh·jana khabara.*

Romantic, s. *'ajab, 'ajīb; khiyālī.*

Romp, v.a. *ṭel ṭāl-, khar mastī-, laṭah per-,* etc. *k., khajūnko-, tskhe* or *tske-,* etc. *k.*

Roof, s. *chat, tsapar, bām, koṭa.* (of mouth-) *tālū.*

Rook, s. *qāghah.*

Room, s. *khūna, dzāe, koṭa.* (public-) *ḥujra.*

Roomy, a. *araṭ, prānatai.*

Roost, s. *chakas, basera.* v.a. *basera k.*

Root, s. *wekh, wula, mūnḍ; bonsaṭ, kūnsaṭ, bunyād.*

Root up, v.a. *wekh-, mūnḍ-,* etc. *bāsal—yastal, -kāgal—kkhkal; mūnḍ-, bonsaṭ-,* etc. *kheja-wul.*

Rooted, a. *khakkh, mazbūṭ, njatai.*

Rope, s. *pa-aṛui, rasa-ī.* (hair-) *wākkhkai, siyala-ī.* (palm-leaf-) *būnṛ, biyāsta.*
Rosary, s. *tasbīḥ, tasbe.* (one bead of-) *tasba.*
Rose, s. *gul.* (wild white-) *phulwāṛai.*
Rosin, s. *rāndzaṛah.*
Rot, v.n. *wrostedal, sharhedal, skhā ked., bonṛedal.*
Rotate, v.n. *tsarkhedal, churledal, girzedal.*
Rotation, s. *tsarkh; daur.* (in-) ad. *wār pa wār sara.*
Rotten, a. *wrost, skhā, sharhedalai, bonṛedalai.*
Rough, a. *lwāṛ, zīg, klak; zmokht, trīkh, brekkhan.*
Round, a. *ghunḍ, ghunḍ-man.* s. *gakkht; guzār.* p. *chāpera.* (to turn-) v.n. *girzedal; churledal.*
Roundness, s. *ghunḍ-wālai.*
Rouse, v.a. *pātsawul, wīkkhawul, baidār k.*
Rout, v.a. *takkhtawul; mātawul, tār pa tārawul.* s. *tekkhta, māt, tār pa tār, shikast.*
Route, s. *lār, rāh.*
Rove, v.n. *girzedal.* v.a. *sail-, gakkht-,* etc. *k.*
Row, s. *para, kat, qaṭār, tsīṛa, ṣaff.*
Row, v.a. *chape wahal.*
Royal, a. *bādshāhī.*
Rub, v.a. *mugal—mukkhal, mālish k.*
Rubber, s. *māla, muhra.* (flesh-) *khīsa.*
Rubbish, s. *khadzala, khāshāk, waṛkhara.*
Ruby, s. *l'al, yāqūt.*
Rudder, s. *singāwanṛ, sukkān.*
Ruddy, a. *sūr, l'al* or *lāl.*
Rude, a. *be-adab; nā-dān; lwāṛ.*
Rudiment, s. *aṣl, wekh, mūnḍ.*
Rue, v.n. *toba-gār-, pakkhemān-, stomān-,* etc. *ked.*
Rue, s. (wild) *spelanai, spānda, sipand.*
Rueful, a. *toba-gār, stomān; gham-jan, malūl.*
Ruffian, s. *ṭag, ḥarāmī, khūnāṛai, ghal.*
Ruffle, v.a. (-the feathers) *banṛe tārawul.* (-the skin) *ghūne zīgawul.* (crumple) *jungawul.* (disturb) *pārawul.*
Rug, s. *ghālīcha* or *qālīcha; namad, lamtsa-ī; krāsta, kosai, shaṛa-ī.*
Rugged, a. *zīg, lwāṛ, klak; kānṛedz, sanglākh.*
Ruin, v.a. *wrānawul, kharābawul, ujāṛawul, latāṛawul, habatah-, abtar-, chauṛ-, ṛang-,* etc. *k.*
Ruination, s. *wrānī, kharābī.*
Ruinous, a. *wrān, wujāṛ, māt guḍ,* etc.; *tāwānī, ziyānī, nuqṣānī.*
Ruins, s. *kanḍar, kharāba.*
Rule, s. *qānūn, qā'ida, ṭarīqa, ā-īn, lār; 'amal, ḥukm, ḥukūmat.*
Ruler, s. *ḥākim, sardār, khān, amīr; misṭar, saṭar-* or *jadwal kakkh, lauḥa.*
Rumble, v.a. *juṛ juṛ-, qur qur-,* etc. *k.* v.n. *ghaṛedal, ga-aredal, ghuṛunbedal.*
Ruminate, v.a. *shkhwand wahal* or *k.*; *fikr k.*
Rummage, v.a. *laṭawul, shanal.*
Rumour, s. *āwāza, khabara, afwāh.*
Rump, s. *kūnāṭai, surīn; ḍuḍa* or *or ṭūṭa.*
Rumple, v.a. *jungawul, mātawul, kraṭī-,* etc. *k.*
Run, v.n. *zghaledal—zghākkhtal, drūmedal.* v.a. *manḍe wahal.* (-away) v.n. *takkhtedal.* (-on) *chaledal.* (flow) *bahedal, rawānedal.* (-after) *pase zghaledal* or *-prewatal.* (-over) *toyedal* or *to-edal.* (-out) *watal; tamāmedal.* (-down) *lāndi k.; kagal, ghandal.* (-up) *khatal.* v.a. *khejawul.* (-away with) *takkhtawul.*
Runaway, s. *takkhtedūnai.*
Rupee, s. *rupa-ī.*
Rupture, s. *māt.* (disagreement) *wrānī.* (hernia) *tsūḥṛa.*
Rural, a. *dihātī, dzangalī.*
Rush, v.a. *halla-, ḍūsa-,* etc. *k.* v.n. *khatal; watal.*
Rust, s. *zang.*

Rustic, a. *dihqānī, gawār, lwāṛ.* s. *kilī·wāl, dihqān, ghunḍāyah.*
Rustle, v.a. *shirahār-, ga-arahār-,* etc. *k.*
Rut, s. *kīla, līk, karkkha.* (heat) *mastī.*
Ruthless, a. *be·raḥm, be·dard, kāṇrai zṛah.*
Ruttish, s. *shahwat·nāk, mast.* (-female) *tera, sema.* (in comp.) *-ema* or *-yama.*

S.

Sable, a. *tor*; *mushkai.* (-fur) *samūr, postīn.*
Sabre, s. *shamsher, tūra, tegh.*
Sack, s. *tsaṭa, ghundai, juwāl.*
Sack, v.a. *tālā·, lūṭ-, nātār-,* etc. *k., natal.*
Sacred, a. *pāk, majīd, muqaddas.*
Sacrifice, s. *qurbān, ṣadqa, dzār.*
Sad, a. *gham·jan, dil·gīr, āzurdah, malūl.*
Saddle, s. *zīn, kātī.* (-pad) *ṭogham* or *toghal, kejam, qajarī.* (-cloth) *zīn·pokkh.* (-girth) *tātang, tāng.* (-pad) *kho·gīr.* (-bag) *khūrjīn.* (-pommel) *ngūbai, kāsh, āna.* (-straps) *kānjogha.* v.a. *zīn taṛal.*
Saddler, s. *sarrāj, zīn sāz.*
Sadness, s. *gham, nūl, dil·gīrī*; *saudā.*
Safe, a. *salāmat, amn amān, khair ṣalāḥ.* (-guard) *panāh, pushta.* (meat-) *tsakai.*
Saffron, s. *gūngū, kangū, z'afarān.*
Sagacious, a. *hokkhyār, pohānd, 'aql·man.*
Sagacity, s. *poh, pahm, sha'ūr.*
Sage, s. *'āqil, dānā, 'aql·man.* s. *ḥakīm, zbarg.*
Sail, s. *bādwān.*
Sailor, s. *mallāḥ, jahāzī.*
Saint, s. *walī, abdāl, zbarg, pīr.* (the saints) *auliyā, āstāna·dārān.*
Sake, p. *dapāra, wāsṭa*; *la kabla.*
Salacious, a. *mast, shahwat·nāk.*
Salamander, s. *samandar.*
Salary, s. *ṭalab, muwājib, tankhwāh.*
Sale, s. *plor, prolana, prowuna, kharts, bai'a.*
Saline, a. *mālgīn, kkhora·nāk, kkhoran.*
Saliva, s. *lāṛa* or *lāṇṛa, tūk, tūkai.*
Salivate, v.a. *khula rāwṛal.*
Sallow, a. *ziyaṛ*; *skāṇṛ.*
Sally, v.n. *tākht-, tsoṭ-, halla-,* etc. *k.*
Salt, s. *mālga.* (-collector) *mālgbah.* (-meat) *lāndai.* a. *mālgīn, namkīn.* (-less) *balmagai, balmangah.*
Saltpetre, s. *kkhora.*
Salubrious, a. *kkhah muwāfiq.*
Salutary, a. *sūd·man, fā-ida·man.*
Salutation, a. *d'uā, salām.*
Salute, v.a. *salām-, salāmī-,* etc. *k.*
Salvation, s. *khalāṣī, najāt, rihā-ī.*
Salve, s. *malham, paha, tab.*
Same, a. *haghah, daghah.* (in comp.) *yo-, hum-.* (the-) ad. *bedū.*
Sameness, s. *yo shānī, yoyat, barābarī.*
Sample, s. *namūna, nakkha.*
Sanctify, v.a. *pāk-,* etc. *k.*; *muqaddas gaṇṛal.*
Sanction, s. *ḥukm, izn, ijāzat.* v.a. *ḥukm-,* etc. *k.*
Sanctuary, s. *dargāh*; *panāh.*
Sand, s. *shiga, reg.* (-bank) *char.*
Sandal, s. *tsapla-ī, gāwlai.* (-wood) *chandaṇṛ.*
Sandy, a. *shiglan.*
Sane, a. *hokkhyār, hokkh·man, khabar·dār.*
Sanguinary, a. *khūnāṛai, khūn khwār.*
Sanguine, a. *sūr*; *qawī*; *umed·wār.*
Sap, s. *pa-ī, oba, gūṛa-ī, rub.*
Sap, v.a. *surang wahal*; *mūnḍ bāsal—yastal.*
Sapient, a. *'aql·man, dānā.*
Sapling, s. *khalai, buzghalai*; *nihāl*; *keṛa.*
Sarcasm, s. *tarkha khabara, l'an ṭ'an.*
Sash, s. *paṭka, lūnga-ī, mlā wastanai*; *jāl.*
Satan, s. *shaiṭān, iblīs.*
Satiate, v.a. *maṛawul, ḍakawul.*
Satiety, s. *moṛ·wālai, moṛ·tiyā, maṛa khwā.*
Satin, s. *aṭlas, dariyā-ī.*
Satire, s. *ṭoqa, pekkha.*
Satisfaction, s. *raẓā·mandī, khāṭir khwāhī.*
Satisfactory, a. *khāṭir khwāh, joṛ, ghwarah.*

Satisfy, v.a. *rāẓī-, khāṭir jam'a-,* etc. *k.*; *maṛawul, saṛawul*; *pohawul.*

Saturate, v.a. *kharob-, serāb-,* etc. *k.*; *khusht k.*

Saturday, s. *khālī, shamba.*

Sauce, s. *chāshnī*; *kkhorwā.*

Saucepan, s. (metal) *dechka, kaṛahai.* (pottery) *kaṭwa-ī, kodai.*

Saucy, a. *be-adab, shokhīn, wītak, chāwdīnak.*

Sausage, s. *kulma.*

Savage, a. *dzangalī, waḥshī*; *ẓālim, khūnāṛai.*

Save, v.a. *bachawul, sātal, khundī-, sarfa-,* etc. *k.*

Saving, s. *sūd, gaṭa, sarfa.* ad. *siwā, baghair.*

Saviour, s. *bachawūnkai, shafī.*

Savour, s. *khwand, maza, tsaka.*

Saw, s. *ara.* (-dust) *chūr.*

Say, v.a. *wayal, khabare k.*; *lal* or *lawdal.*

Sayer, s. *wayūnkai*; *lūnai* or *lūnkai.*

Saying, a. *wayana*; *khabara, wayai.*

Scab, s. *khīg, waṛ, khwaṛ.*

Scabbard, s. *teka, kāṭī, miyān.* (-mounting) *pāenak, mūnāl, tahnāl.*

Scaffold, s. *manā*; *garwanj*; *dunkācha.*

Scald, v.a. *swadzawul.* v.n. *swal, sedzal.* (-head) s. *ganja.*

Scaldheaded, a. *ganjai, suḍar, lenḍah.*

Scale, s. *tala.* (-cup) *pala.* (fish-) *khwar, tsaparkai.* (gradation) *kach, mech.* (skin) *khwar, poṭ.*

Scales, s. *tala, tarāzū, mīzān.* (beam) *ḍānḍa-ī.*

Scale, v.n. *khatal.* (peel) *lwaṛedal, nwaṛedal.*

Scan, v.a. (verse) *wazn k., jokal, talal.* (examine) *katal, āzmāyal, shanal, laṭawul.*

Scandal, s. *tuhmat* or *tūmat, tor, peghor, ruswā-ī.*

Scanty, a. *la-ag, kam, rangai, pitsāṇrai.*

Scar, s. *dāgh*; *ta-apai*; *ṭakai*; *nughai.*

Scarce, a. *la-ag, kam, matrah, pitsāṇrai.*

Scarcely, ad. *kamtar, pa mushkil sara, hīla.*

Scarcity, s. *kam-tiyā, tangsiyā, kākhti* or *qaḥṭī.*

Scare, v.a. *yerawul, tarhawul, bugnawul.*

Scarecrow, s. *tsera.* (bogie) *bau, bagalola-ī.*

Scarf, s. *paṭka, lūnga-ī*; *oḍana-ī, dū-paṭa.*

Scarify, v.a. *kkhkar lagawul, wīne bāsal—yastal.*

Scarlet, a. *sūr, lāl.*

Scatter, v.a. *khwarawul, tār pa tārawul,*

Scavenger, s. *jārū kakkh.* (at shrines, etc.) *mīnjawar.*

Scene, s. *nandāra, tamāsha.* (place) *dzāe.*

Scent, s. *bo, bū-e* or *bū-ī.* v.a. *bū-ī k., bū-ī ākhistal.*

Scheme, s. *tadbīr, ḥikmat, band*; *chal, lamghaṛa-ī*; *maṭlab, niyat.*

Schism, s. *khalal, pasāt, mīrtsī*; *rifẓ.*

Schismatic, a. *rāfiẓī, khārijī*; *pasātī.*

Scholar, s. *shāgird, ṭālib*; *'ālim, mullā.*

School, s. *maktab, madrasa.* (-boy) *dzaṇrai.* (-master) *ākhūn, mullā, ustād, mu'allim.* (-fellow) *hum dars, hum sabaq, hum dzolai.*

Science, s. *'ilm, ḥikmat, hunar.*

Scirrhus, s. *yaga.*

Scissors, s. *biyātī, qainchī, ghachī.*

Scoff, v.a. *kanzal-, ṭoqe-, pekkhe,* etc. *k.*

Scold, v.a. *raṭal, traṭal, dāṛal, ṭaqawul, malāmatawul, peghorawul.*

Scope, s. *niyat*; *gharaẓ*; *arat-wālai*; *dzāe.*

Scorch, v.a. *kaṛawul, alwoyal, lūghaṛan-, lūlapah-, kaskar-, sūngaṭ-, saṭkūrai-,* etc. *k.*

Score, v.a. *shmeral, shumāral, ḥisābawul*; *līkal, karkkha kāgal—kkhkal, -bāsal—yastal.* (scratch) *ġargal, garawul.*

Score, s. *karkkha, khaṭṭ*; *ḥisāb*; *shil*; *sabab.*

Scorn, v.a. *spuk ganral.*

Scorpion, s. *laṛam.*

Scoundrel, s. *bad ẓāt, ḥarāmī.*

Scour, v.a. *mugal—mukkhal, togal, skoyal, zdoyal.*

Scourge, v.a. *karora-, qamchī-, dira-*, etc. *wahal.*
Scout, s. *dzarai, tsārī, jāsūs, yalah·dār.* v.a. *tsāral, tsār-, zarana-ī-*, etc. *k.*
Scowl, v.a. *starge brandawul.*
Scramble, v.a. *lūṭ māt k.*
Scrap, s. *ṭoṭa, reza· pūṭai, pitsāṇrai.*
Scrape, v.a. *garawul, togal, khriyal, gargal.*
Scrapings, s. *tarāshe.* (pot-) *koyanai, koela.*
Scratch, v.a. *garawul, gargal, skoyal.*
Scream, v.a. *chigha-, nāra-, sūra-*, etc. *wahal.*
Screen, v.a. *parda-, panāh-*, etc. *k., puṭawul, pokkhal; bachawul.*
Screw, s. *pech, marwat.*
Scribe, s. *kātib, līkūnkai, kkhkawūnkai.*
Scrip, s. *bana-ī, gūdai, dzola-ī.*
Scripture, s. *kitāb da majīd.* (C.) *tauret, zabūr, injīl.* (H.) *shāstar.* (M.) *qurān, furqān.*
Scrofula, s. *anjīr.*
Scroll, s. *daftar, fard, ṭomār; nghakkhtai kāghaz.*
Scrotum, s. *khoṭa, da khoṭo pūkanṛa-ī.*
Scrub, v.a. *mugal—mukkhal, togal.*
Scruple, v.a. *shakk-, shubha-, gumān-*, etc. *laral.*
Scrupulous, a. *wahmī, wiswāsī, shakkī.*
Scrutinize, v.a. *āzmāyal, laṭawul, shaṇal, talal.*
Scrutiny, s. *āzmekkht, shanana, imtiḥān.*
Scuffle, v.a. *parzawul, ṭel wahal, sara nkkhlawul.*
Sculk, v.n. *ghalai ked., puṭedal.*
Sculptor, s. *naqqāsh, but sāz, sang tarāsh.*
Scum, s. *jakh, rag, kaf.*
Scurf, s. *pa-akh, poṭakai, khig.*
Scurrilous, a. *jiba·war, kanzal kawūnkai.*
Sea, s. *dariyāb, qālī dariyāb, baḥr.*
Seal, s. *muhr.* (-stone) *ghamai.* (-cutter) *muhr kan.* v.a. *muhr layawul.*
Seam, s. *joṛ, skoe, ganḍal, darz.*

Sear, v.a. *dāghawul.*
Search, v.a. *laṭawul, shanal, talāsh k.*
Season, s. *wakht* or *waqt, mūda, neṭa; mausam* or *mosim, faṣl.*
Season, v.a. *namkīn-, maza·dār-*, etc. *k., maṣālah-*, etc. *warkawul* or *-āchawul; pokh-, maẓbūṭ-*, etc. *k.*
Seasonable, a. *joṛ, jukht, barābar.*
Seasonably, ad. *pa wakht, pa neṭe, pa mūde.*
Seasoning, s. *maṣālah* or *masāla; mālga.*
Seat, s. *kursī, da nāst dzāe; dzāe, muqām.* v.a. *kkhkenawul* or *kenawul.*
Secede, v.n. *jārwatal, stūnedal.*
Seclude, v.a. *belawul, yawādzai-, judā-*, etc. *k.*
Seclusion, s. *tanhā-ī, bel·tūn; ghalī·tob.*
Second, a. *dwayam, ṣānī, bul.* s. *pal, laḥẓa; mal, yār, komakī, pushtī, madad·gār.* v.a. *madad k., pushtī-, komak-*, etc. *warkawul.*
Secondly, ad. *ṣānī-an, biyā, bul.*
Secresy, s. *parda, parda pokkhī, ghalī·tob, tara-ī, puṭ·wālai.*
Secret, a. *puṭ, pinham.* (in-) ad. *pa puṭa, pa tara-ī, pa parde.* s. *rāz, sirr, puṭa khabara.*
Secretary, s. *munshī.*
Secrete, v.a. *puṭawul, pokkhal; paidā k.*
Secretion, s. *rezish.*
Secretly, ad. *pa puṭa, pa parde, pa tara-ī.*
Sect, s. *firqa, mazhab, ummat; ẓāt, noga.*
Sectary, s. *rāfiẓī, khārijī.*
Section, s. *juz, faṣal, sipāra; para, janba, gundī.*
Secular, a. *duniyā-ī, 'āmmī.*
Secure, a. *salāmat, amn, amān; maẓbūṭ, qā-im, ṭīng,* v.a. *sambālawul, maẓbūṭ-*, etc. *k., sāṭal, khundī k.*
Security, s. *salāmatī, panāh, amānat.* (bail) *ẓāmin.* (bond) *ẓamānat.* (false-) *be·khabarī.*
Sedan, s. *ḍola-ī, anbāla-ī.* (camel-) *kajāwa.*
Sedate, a. *qalār, ghalai.*
Sedentary, a. *be·ḥarakat, nāst.*

Sediment, s. *khaṭbel, matar.*
Sedition, s. *yāghī-garī, balwā-tob, patna, pasāt.*
Seditious, a. *pasātī, balwā-sāz, balwā-gar, yāghī-gar, yāghī, mufsid, sar-kakkh.*
Seduce, v.a. *ghulawul, darghalawul, be-lāri k.*
Sensation, s. *darghal-tob, ghulawuna, fareb.*
See, v.a. *katal* or *kasal, goral—līdal, naẓar k.* (perceive) v.n. *pohedal, rasedal.* in. *gora!*
Seed, s. *tukhm. dāna.* (-of stone fruit, melons, etc.) *zaṛai.* (progeny) *alwād, zāwzad* or *zawzāt, tūng.* (sperm) *manī, mardī.*
Seeing, s. *līdah, kātah, naẓar.* a. *bīnā.* (-that) ad. *dzaka.*
Seek, v.a. *laṭawul, talāsh k.*; *ghokkhtal, d'uā-*, etc. *k.*
Seem, v.n. *kkhkāredal, m'alūmedal.*
Seemingly, ad. *pa kkhkārah, pa līdah, pa kātah.*
Seemly, a. *munāsib, kkhāyastah, joṛ, lā-iq.*
Seize, v.a. *nīwul, ākhistal, qabẓ-, giriftār-*, etc. *k.*
Seldom, ad. *kamtar, kala nā kala.*
Select, v.a. *khwakkhawul, chunral, anrawul, pasand-, qabūl-, chīndah-, ghwarah-*, etc. *k.*
Self, pr. *dzān, khpul.*
Selfish, a. *khpul gharaẓ, khpul maṭlab, gharaẓī, gharaẓ-man, khpul nafs.*
Sell, v.a. *khartsawul, prowul, ploral* or *prolal, pa bai'e warkawul.*
Seller, s. *khartsawūnkai, prowūnkai*, etc.
Semen, s. *mardī, manī.*
Senate, s. *jirga*; *majlis*; *dīwān.*
Senator, s. *jirgatū, majlisī.*
Send, v.a. *āstawul, legdal* or *legal.* (-for) *rābalal, balal, ghokkhtal, ṭalab k.*
Senior, a. *mashar, loe.*
Senna, s. *sana makī.*
Sensation, s. *ḥiss, dzān, sāh, sud.* (to have-) v.n. *pa dzān pohedal.* v.a. *ḥiss-*, etc. *laral.*
Sense, s. *'aql, poha, pahm*; *m'anī*; *hokkh, sud, khabar.* (to have-) v.a. *'aql-*, etc. *laral.*

Senseless, a. *be-ḥiss*, etc.; *be-hūdah, be-m'anī.*
Sensible, a. *baidār, hokkhyār, khabar-dār.*
Sensitive, a. *dzān-dār, jwandai.*
Sensual, a. *nafsānī, shahwatī, mast.*
Sensuality, s. *nafs parastī*; *mastī*; *shahwat, nafs.*
Sentence, s. *ḥukm, fatwā.* (of Quran) *āyat.* v.a. *ḥukm-*, etc. *k.*
Sentiment, s. *fikr, rāe, poha.*
Sentinel, s. *pāsbān, pahra-dār, tsoka-ī-dār.*
Separate, v.a. *biyalawul* or *belawul, judā k.* v.n. *biyaledal, lwukkhtal, lwaṛedal.* a. *bel* or *biyal, judā.*
Separately, ad. *biyal biyal, judā-judā.*
Separation, s. *biyal-tūn, judā-ī, biyal-wālai.*
September, s. *asū.*
Sepulchre, s. *gor, qabr*; *laḥd.*
Sequel, s. *'āqibat, ākhir*; *khatm.*
Sequester, v.a. *biyalawul*; *qurq k.*
Seraglio, s. *zanāna, ḥaram srāe.*
Serene, a. *qalār, ārām*; *spīn, shīn, ṣāf.*
Series, s. *qaṭār*; *hār, laṛ*; *silsila.*
Serious, a. *drūnd, grān, muhimm.*
Sermon, s. *w'aẓ*; *khuṭba*; *pand, naṣīḥat.*
Serpent, s. *mār.* (python) *kkhāh mār.* (viper) *mangor, mangarai.* (amphisbœna) *laṭka, landa-ī.*
Serpentine, a. *mār pech, walandai, kog wog, kālkūchan.*
Servant, s. *nokar, khidmat-gār, mazdūr.*
Serve, v.a. *nokarī-, khidmat-, mazdūrī-*, etc. *k.* v.n. *kedal, lagedal, chaledal.*
Serviceable, a. *pa-kār, fā-ida-man, sūd-man.*
Servile, a. *khūshāmad-gar, chāplūs, ḍirpal.*
Servility, s. *khūshāmad-garī, chāplūsī*, etc.
Sesamum, s. *kunzala.*
Session, s. *majlis, jalsa, maḥkama.*
Set, s. *joṛa*; *firqa*; *para, gundī.* a. *jaṛāo.* v.a. *gdal* or *īgdal, īkkhodal, īkkhal, kegdal* or *kkhkegdal*, etc., *laga.vul, joṛawul, khejawul, kkhkenawul* or *kenawul.* v.n.

kūzedal, prewatal. (-out) *rawānedal, drūmal, drūmedal, tlal—lāṛal.*

Settle, v.a. *astoga k., dzāe nīwul, ābādawul.* (fix) *muqarrar k., wudrawul, kkhkenawul.* (arrange) *tartībawul, atsawral, samawul, barābarawul.* (compose) *saṛawul.* (-an account) *pūrah-, adā-,* etc. *k.* (-a difference) *pakhulā k., gwākkh-grandī k.* (-down) v.n. *kenāstal* or *kkhkenāstal.*

Settled, a. *qalār, ārām; nāst, prot; pūrah, adā.*

Settlement, s. *bandobast.* (colony) *ābādī.* (marriage-) *kābīn.* (-of dispute) *rogha, joṛa, faiṣal.*

Seven, a *owah.* (seventh) *owam.*

Seventeen, a. *owah-las.*

Seventy, a. *awwyā.* (seventieth) *awwyāyam.*

Sever, v.a. *prekawul, biyalawul; lwaṛawul.*

Several, a. *dzani, b'aẓi, tso, ḍer.*

Severally, ad. *yo yo, biyal biyal, judā judā.*

Severe, a. *sakht, tez, tund, klak.*

Sew, v.a. *gandal, skoe k.* (darn) *bezal, pezal.* (-up) *agayal.*

Sex, s. *jins, ẓāt.*

Sexton, s. *mūaẓẓin; mīnjawar* or *mujāwir.*

Shabby, a. *spuk, khwār; pūhaṛ; khushai.*

Shade, s. *sorai, siwrai.*

Shadow, s. *sorai; 'aks; panāh.*

Shaft, s. *tīr, ḍānḍa-ī, stan.* (-of a well) *koṭa.* (-of a carriage) *bāzū, gānḍa-ī.*

Shaggy, a. *babar, waṛan.*

Shagreen, s. *kīmukht.*

Shake, v.a. *khwadzawul, tsanḍal, kkhorawul, rapawul.* (-down) *drabal.* v.n. *khwadzedal, rapedal, laṛzedal, kkhoredal.*

Shallow, a. *pāyāo* or *pāyāb; nādān, nīmgaṛai.*

Sham, s. *bāna* or *bahāna, lamghaṛa-ī, chal, ṭagī.* a. *jūṭah, nāsarah, darogh-jan.* v.a. *bāna-,* etc. *k.*

Shame, s. *sharm, hayā; sharmindagī; makh, ghairat.*

Shameful, a. *ruswā, bad; sharmsār, sharmnāk; ghairat-man* or *ghairat-nāk.*

Shameless, a. *be-sharm, be-hayā, be-nang, be-makh,* etc.

Shampoo, v.a. *chāpī k., manḍal.*

Shank, s. *kkhānga; tsānga; kkhākh; lasta.*

Shape, s. *shakl, ṣūrat, ḍaul, rang.*

Share, s. *brakha, wesh, ḥiṣṣa, wanḍa.* (plough-) *pāla, saspār.*

Share, v.a. *weshal.* v.n. *sharīk ked.*

Sharer, s. *brakha-khor, sharīk.*

Sharp, a. *terah, tez.* (sour or acid) *trīw, trīkh, brekkhan.* (active) *chālāk.* (clever) *pohānd.*

Sharpen, v.a. *terah-,* etc. *k.*

Sharper, s. *ṭag, ṭag-bāz, darghal.*

Shatter, v.a. *chūr chūr-, daṛ daṛ-, ṭoṭe ṭoṭe-, reze reze-, kanḍ kapaṛ-,* etc. *k.*

Shave, v.a. *khriyal* or *khrayal; togal.*

Shaving, s. *ṭoṭkai, tarāza, tūtankai.*

Shawl, s. *shāl.* (-for waist) *abra.*

She, pr. *hagha, dā, de, da, e.*

Sheaf, s. *geḍa-ī.*

Shear, v.a. *skūstal, skūl-* or *skwal k., kaṭeyal.*

Shears, s. *biyātī, khorkhal, kāz, skūlai.*

Sheath, s. *teka, miyān; kāṭī.*

Shed, s. *chopāṛ, jūngaṛa, kaḍala, manḍaw, kūḍa-ī.*

Shed, v.n. *rejedal; to-edal* or *toyedal.* v.a. *āchawul, ghurzawul, toyawul.*

Sheep, s. *ga-aḍ, ga-aḍūrai.* (long-tailed-) *herṛai, berṛai, barra.* (-owner) *ga-aḍbah.* (-cot) *shpol, bānḍa.* (ewe-) *ga-aḍa, meg.* (ram) *mag, ga-aḍ.* (wether) *wuch-kūl.*

Sheer, a. *ṣāf, pāk.*

Sheet, s. *tsādar, dū-paṭa.*

Shelf, s. *ṭāq, ṭāqcha, darāi, rap.*

Shell, s. *gūjai, sīpa-ī.* (cowrie) *kunjaka, kawḍa-ī.* (fruit) *poṭ, postakai.*

Shelter, s. *panāh, amn* or *aman; nanawātah.*

v.a. *panāh-.* etc. *warkawul*; *pokkhal, puṭawul.*

Shepherd, s. *shpūn.* (-boy) *shpankai.*

Sherbet, s. *guṛobai, sharbat.*

Shield, s. *spar, ḍāl, salaṭ.* (-handle) *dastmāya, da guda-ī laṛ.* (boss) *patrai.*

Shield, v.a. *bachawul, jghoral, sātal, panāh-,* etc. *k.*

Shift, s. *ḥikmat, chal, band, chāra.* (evasion) *hira-ī, lamghaṛa-ī, ḥīla, bāna.* (shirt) *ganḍolai, pepna-ī, khata, qamīṣ.*

Shift, v.a. *khwadzawul, badalawul, girzawul.* v.n. *khwadzedal, girzedal, āwukkhtal.*

Shine, v.n. *brekkhedal, dzalkedal* or *dzaledal, rūnredal, rokkhānedal.*

Shining, a. *brekkh-nāk, rokkhān, rūnr, dzalkān.*

Ship, s. *jahāz, beṛa-ī.*

Shirt, s. *qamīṣ, khata, ganḍolai, pepna-ī.*

Shiver, v.n. *rapedal, regdedal, larzedal.* s. *larza.* (break) *mātawul.* (*v.* Shatter.)

Shoal, s. *ṭolai, sail, ghol, pāyāo*; *char.*

Shock, s. *ḍaka, ṭakar.*

Shocking, a *makrūh, kraka-war* or *-nāk.*

Shoe, s. *panra, pāezār, jūṭa-ī*; *mochanra, kokkha, jisṭa.* (-maker) *mochī, tsamyār.* (horse-) *na'l.* (to put on-) v.a. *pa kkhpo k., na'l k.* or *-lagawul.*

Shoot, v.a. *wīshtal, ṭopak-,* etc. *khalāṣawul* or *chalawul.* v.n. *ṭūkedal, zarghūnedal.*

Shop, s. *dūkān, haṭa-ī*; *kār-khāna.* (-keeper) *dūkān-dār, banriyā, kaṭrī.*

Shore, s. *ghāṛa.* (near-) *rā-pori ghāṛa.* (far-) *pori ghāṛa.*

Short, a. *lanḍ, kotāh.* (less) *kam, la-ag.* (size) *mandarai, khamachah.*

Shorten, v.a. *lanḍawul*; *kamawul.* v.n. *lanḍedal*; *kamedal.*

Shortly, ad. *pa lanḍa, za-ar* or *zir, pa drang sā'at.*

Shot, s. (small) *chara.* (bullet) *mardakai.* (cannon-) *gola-ī.* (stroke) *guzār.* *awīshtai.*

Shoulder, s. *oga.* (-blade) *walai.*

Shout, v.a. *nāra-, chigha-,* etc. *wahal, bāng wayal.*

Shove, v.a. *ṭel-, ḍaka-, ṭakar-, ṭāl-,* etc. *wahal.*

Shovel, s. (iron) *yūm* or *yīm, kara.* (wooden) *rāshbel.*

Show, s. *nandāra, tamāsha.* v.a. *kkhayal—kkhowul, kkhkārah-, bartser-,* etc. *k., tsargandawul*; *pohawul, pahmawul.*

Shower, a. *jaṛa-ī, bārān.* (spring-) *wasa.* (heavy-) *shebah.* (slight-) *pūna.* v.n. *oredal, bārānedal, tsātsedal.*

Showy, a. *raunaq-dār, kkhāyastah, ḍaulī.*

Shred, s. *rekkha, paṛūkai, reza, purza.*

Shrewd, a. *pokh, hokkhyār, chirg, kāgh.*

Shriek, v.a. *nāra-, sūra-, chigha-,* etc. *wahal.*

Shrine, s. *ziyārat, āstāna, dargāh.*

Shrink, v.n. *haṭedal*; *stanedal*; *bugnedal*; *jārwatal.* (as the belly) *wuchedal, kawt ked.*

Shrivel, v.n. *wuchedal, kawt ked., chichar ked.*

Shroud, s. *kafan, tsādar.*

Shrub, s. *būṭai, jāṛa, ḍakai.* (thorny-) *karkanra.*

Shrubbery, s. *janga-ī, jāṛ.*

Shudder, v.n. *laṛzedal, ghūne zīgedal, regdedal.* v.a. *ḍagaṛodze nīwul*; *kraka ākhistal.*

Shuffle, v.a. *ṛaqawul, laṛal, gaḍ-waḍawul.* (equivocate) *janra-, hira-ī-, lamghaṛa-ī-,* etc. *k., palma wayal.* (in gait) v.n. *ṭaparedal.*

Shun, v.a. *parhez k., ḍaḍa ākhistal.* v.n. *bugnedal, takkhtedal, ḍaḍa ked.*

Shut, v.a. *bandawul, lagawul.* (as a door) *pori k.* (as the eyes) *puṭawul.* (as a book) *ṭap wahal.*

Shutter, s. *parda, takhta.* (-of a door) *tamba, pale.*

Shy, a. *yer-man, harānd*; *sharmsār.* v.n. *bugnedal.*

Sick, a. *nā-rogh, nā-joṛ, bīmār, randzūr*

(-of) *bezār, starai stomān.* (-of food, etc.) *sekan.* (-at stomach) *mīkkh mīkkh, chinjedalai.*

Sickle, s. *lor, lawa* or *lawāor.*

Sickly, a. *marazī, za'īf, nā-rogh.*

Sickness, s. *nā-jor-tiyā, bīmārī, āzār, randz.*

Side, s. *palaw, tselma, rokh, khwā, lorai; arkh, dada, tsang; ghāra; taraf, para, janba.* (-piece) *bāzū.*

Sideways, ad. *pa trats.*

Sieve, s. *ghalbel, parwezai; chaj, tsap.*

Sift, v.a. *ghalbelawul, chaj-,* etc. *wahal; chunral, chānrawul; latawul, shanal.*

Sigh, v.a. *aswelai k.*

Sight, s. *nazar; līdah, kātah; tamāsha, nandāra.*

Sign, s. *nakkha, alāma.* v.a. *dast khatt k.*

Signal, s. *nakkha, ishārat, nikkhānī.*

Signet, s. *muhr, ghamai.*

Significant, a. *m'anī-dār, m'anawī.*

Signification, s. *m'anī, matlab.*

Signify, v.a. *m'anī laral.*

Silence, s. *ghalī-tob.* in. *chup!*

Silent, a. *ghalai, chip.*

Silently, ad. *ro ro, ghalai ghalai.*

Silk, s. *rekkham.* (-worm) *da rekkham chinjai.* (-cocoon) *pela, ghoza.*

Silken, a. *rekkhmīn.*

Silly, a. *sādah, kawdan, nādān.*

Silver, s. *spīn zar.* (-smith) *zar-gar.*

Similar, a. *barābar, ghondai, gund, yo shān.*

Simile, s. *matal, misāl, tashbīh.*

Simper, v.n. *musedal.*

Simple, a. *sādah, sarah, karah; spor, torci.*

Simpleton, s. *pūhar, kawdan, gedī khar.*

Simply, ad. *sirp* or *surup, khālī, ta-ash.*

Sin, s. *gunāh, wabāl, taqsīr, khatā, baza.*

Since, ad. *laka chi; pas, dzaka chi.* (-when?) *kala, la kūma.*

Sincere, a. *ril-khtīnai, rāst-bāz, karah, sādah.*

Sinew, s. *pai, pla, rag, wuja.*

Sinful, a. *gunāh-gār, taqsīrī.*

Sing, v.a. *sarod-, sandare-,* etc. *wayal.*

Singe, v.a. *swadzawul.* v.n. *swal, sedzal.*

Singer, s. *sarodī, mutrib, sandar-goe.*

Single, a. *yo, yawādzai, witar, tsarah, tāk.* (-fold) *yawastawai, yak-tā.* (unmarried) *lawand.*

Singly, ad. *yo yo.*

Singular, a. *wāhid; 'ajab.*

Sinister, a. *nā-rāst, bad, kog, tratskan.*

Sink, v.a. *dūbawul, gharqawul.* v.n. *dūbedal, gharqedal.*

Sinner, s. *gunāh-gār, bad kār, taqsīrī.*

Sip, v.a. *skal* or *tskal* or *tskkhal, chūpal, zbekkhal.* (taste) *tsatal, tsakal.*

Sir, s. *sāhib, jī, bābū, lālā.*

Sire, s. *plār; hazrat.*

Sister, s. *khor.* (husband's) *ndror.* (by brother) *bābī, wrandār, wandyār.* (by husband's brother) *yor.* (wife's) *kkhīna, khwakkhīna.* (foster-) *da to khor.* (tribal-) *khoringa.* (-hood) *khoringa-ī.*

Sit, v.n. *kenāstal* or *kkhkenāstal.*

Site, s. *dzāe, zmaka.*

Sitting, s. *nāstah* or *kkhkenāstah.*

Situation, s. *dzāe; 'uhda, darja; khidmat, kār.*

Six, a. *shpag.* (sixth) *shpagam.*

Sixteen, a. *shpāras.* (sixteenth) *shpārasam.*

Sixty, a. *shpetah.* (sixtieth) *shpetam.* (-one) *yo shpetah.* (-two) *dwah shpetah,* etc.

Size, s. *qadr, andāza; slekkht; batī.*

Skein, s. *tranjai, tranjūkai, ata* or *ateha.*

Sketch, s. *naqsha* or *nakhkkha, taswīr.* v.a. *naqsha-,* etc. *kāgal—kkhkal,* or *-līkal,* or *-bāsal—yastal.*

Skewer, s. *sīkh, sīkhcha, salā-ī, sparkhai.*

Skilful, a. *qābil, pokh, kārīgar, hunar-man.*

Skill, s. *hunar, kārī-garī, qābiliyat.*

Skim, v.a. *zag liri k.* or *-ākhistal.* (-over) *nazar pa zir terawul.*

Skin, s. *tsarman, poṭ.* v.a. *tsarman-*, etc. *liri k.*, or *-bāsal—yastal* or *-kāgal—kkhkal.*

Skip, v.a. *trapa-, ṭop-*, etc. *wahal, khajūnko-, tskhe-*, etc. *k.*

Skirmish, s. *ṭas ṭūs, dandūkār.*

Skirt, s. *laman, ja-ī, pītskai* ; *ghāṛa, tselma.*

Skittish, a. *be·qalār, yer·man* ; *mast, shokhīn.*

Skull, s. *kapara-ī, kakara-ī.*

Sky, s. *āsmān.* (clear-) *shīn āsmān.* (dark-) *gaṉr* or *gūr·āsmān.*

Slab, s. *takhta.* (stone-) *tīga, siyādza.*

Slack, a. *sust, arat, prānatai* ; *laṭ, nā·rāst.*

Slake, v.a. *saṛawul.*

Slander, s. *tuhmat* or *tūmat, tor, peghor palma.* v.a. *tūmat-, tor-*, etc. *pori k.*, *peghor warkawul, palma wayal.*

Slanting, a. *tratskan, sar jawar, rewand.*

Slap, v.a. *ṭas-, tsāpeṛa-, kṛap-*, etc. *wahal.*

Slash, v.a. *ghwutsawul, tsīral* ; *wahal* ; *tsanḍal.*

Slattern, a. *pūhaṛ, shaṭal* or *shalaṭ, shāwlai wāwlai.*

Slaughter, s. *qatl, khūn, qatli'āmm.*

Slave, s. *mra-e, ghulām, agar* (f.) *wīndza, barda, agara.*

Slavery, s. *mra-e·tob, ghulāmī.*

Slay, v.a. *qatlawul, muṛ k.*, *wajal* or *wajlal.* (-for food) *ḥallālawul.*

Slayer, s. *qātil, khūnī.*

Sleek, a. *tsorb, chāgh* ; *ghwaṛ* ; *ṣāf, spetsalai, spīn.*

Sleep, s. *khob.* v.a. *khob k.* v.n. *ūdah-, bīdah-*, etc. *ked.* (to put to-) v.a. *ūdah k.*, *tsamlawul.*

Sleepy, a. *khob·nāk, parnā-, khob-*, etc. *-wṛai* ; *drane starge.*

Sleeve, s. *lastūnrai, āstīn.*

Slender, a. *narai, trandz, nāzak, nīahīn, bārīk.*

Slice, s. *tarāza, ṭoṭkai.*

Slide, v.n. *kkhwahedal* or *kkhwa-edal, kkhakedal, laghzedal.*

Slight, a. *la-ag, kam* ; *spuk, halak.* (*v.* Slender) v.a. *spuk gaṉral, spuk naẓar k.*

Slim, a. *narai, trandz.* (*v.* Slender).

Slime, s. *chiqaṛ, khaṭa, lāha.* (vegetable-) *ubṛa-ī.*

Slimy, a. *chiqran, kkhwai.*

Sling, s. *machoghna* or *machaloghza, trankūtsa.* (the cup of a-) *gāṭa-ī.* (cradle) *zāngo, gahwāra, amel* or *ḥamā-il.* v.a. *wīshtal.*

Slip, v.n. *kkhwahedal.* (*v.* Slide). (-away) *teredal.* (-from the memory) *heredal.* (-from sight) *puṭedal.* (-from the hand) *khalāṣedal, yalah ked.*

Slip, s. *kkhwaheduna, laghz* ; *khaṭā, ter wat* ; *ṭoṭa, rekkha paṭa-ī* ; *qalam.*

Slipper, s. *panra, kokkha, paizār* or *pāezār, jista.*

Slippery, a. *kkhwai, laghzan, chiqran.*

Slit, v.a. *tsīral, shlawul, chawul, chāk k.* s. *tsīra, chāwd, daṛa, chāk* or *chāq.*

Sloping, a. *tratskan, rewand, sar jawar, sar lwaṛ.*

Slothful, v.a. *sust, laṭ, nā·rāst, kāhil, shaḍal.*

Slough, s. *chiqaṛ* or *qīchaṛ, bokkhtana* ; *khwar, postakai, tsarman.*

Sloven, a. *pūhaṛ, palīt, shalaṭ* or *shaṭal.*

Slow, a. *sust, laṭ, ro, qalār.*

Slowly, ad. *ro ro, qalār qalār.*

Sluggard, a. *shaḍal, laṭ, ārām ṭalab.*

Sluice, s. *warkh, ghwagai* ; *mūra-ī.*

Slur, s. *dāgh, laka* ; *tor, peghor.* v.a. *dāghawul, wrānawul.*

Slut, s. *pūhaṛa, shalaṭa* ; *hujra-ī, gashta-ī* ; *spa-ī.*

Sly, a. *chalwalai, chal·bāẓ.*

Smack, v.a. *ṭas-, ṭaq-, tsāpeṛa-*, etc. *wahal.* (taste) *tsaka, khwand, maza.*

Small, a. *woṛ, la-ag, warūkai, wūṛkoṭai, pūṭai, mandarai, kachoṭai, kuchinai, kharmandai.*

Smallness, s. *la-ag·walai, wuṛūk·wālai.*

Smallpox, s. *nanaka-ī.* (scar) *ta-apai.* (chicken) *katswak.*

Smart, a. *chālāk, chust, tez, tund.* v.a. *swai k.* v.n. *swal, sedzal.*

Smear, v.a. *lewawul, tabal, ghwaṛ k.*; *akheṛal.*

Smell, s. *bū, bū-ī.* v.n. *bū-ī tlal.* v.a. *bū-ī k.*

Smile, v.n. *musedal.* v.a. *muskai k.*

Smite, v.a. *wahal.*

Smith, s. *lohār, āhan·gar.* (gold-) *zar·gar.*

Smoke, v.a. *lū-, lūgai-*, etc. *k.* (as tobacco) v.a. *skal* or *tskkhal.*

Smoky, a. *lūghaṛan.*

Smooth, a. *sam, hawār, barābar*; *narm.* v.a. *samawul, atsauṛal, hawārawul*, etc.

Smother, v.a. *sāh bandawul, ghāṛa-, mara-ī-*, etc. *-khapa k., sāh ḍūbawul.*

Smut, s. *pūch go-ī.* (mildew) *tor, chauṛāṣha.*

Snail, s. *shāpeṭai, gūjai, da kārghah paaska-ī.*

Snake, s. *mār.* (-charmer) *pāṛū.*

Snap, v.a. *chīchal*; *mātawul*; *chuṭkī k.* (-as a dog) *ghapul, dāṛal.*

Snare, s. *dām.* (different kinds) *lūma, lūmaka, lwīna, jāl, ghūnḍārai, paṛka, talaka, laṭ, kuṛka-ī, hoṇrā.*

Snarl, v.a. *ghapal, dāṛal.*

Snatch, v.a. *pa ḥamle ākhistal, shūkawul, ghoṭa k., tsapa wahal.*

Sneak, v.n. *ghalai ked., puṭ girzedal.*

Sneer, v.a. *spuk naẓar k., poza-* or *ūrbūz būṭawul.*

Sneeze, v.n. *pranjedal, prachedal.* v.a. *ngai k., ngal.*

Snipe, s. *karak, ṭamṭīl.*

Sniff, v.n. *sūṛredal, sūghedal.*

Snore, v.a. *kha-ar wahal, kha-arkai k.*

Snort, v.n. *prashedal, sūṛredal.*

Snot, s. *kaṛbeza* or *kaṛmeza.*

Snout, s. *poza, ūrbūz, tambūza.*

Snow, s. *wāwra.* v.n. *wāwre oredal* or *-prewatal.*

Snub, v.a. *dāṛal, raṭal, ṭaqawul.*

Snuff, s. *sūṛr.* (tobacco) *nās, naswār.* v.n. *sūṛredal.* v.a. *naswār k.*

Snug, a. *puṭ, ghalai*; *khwakkh, moṛ.*

So, ad. *hase, dā·hase, dā rang, hase shān, laka.* (-much) *hombra, tsombra.* (-much so) *tar de ḥadda pori.* (-long as) *tso chi, hombra chi.* (-be it) *wī di, hase di wī.* (it may be-) *wi ba, hase ba wī.* (-that) *tso chi.* (-often as) *har kala chi.* (-and so) *palānkai.*

Soak, v.a. *lūndawul, khushtawal.* (-up) v.a. *wuchawul, tskhal.*

Soap, s. *ṣābūn.* v.a. *ṣābūn lagawul.*

Sob, v.a. *zgerwai* or *zwergai-, salga-ī* or *sugala-ī-, ārkhakkh-, alhang-*, etc. *k., kūk wahal, jaṛal, pa raṭo raṭo jaṛal.*

Sober, a. *parhez·gār, parhezī*; *hokkhyār, baidār.*

Sociable, a. *majlisī, ṣuḥbatī, melmah·dost.*

Society, s. *ṣuḥbat, majlis*; *shirākat, malgar·tiyā, malgīrī, malgar·tob.*

Sod, s. *chūm, lūṭa.*

Sodden, a. *khuṛīn, post, oblan.*

Sodomite, s. *kūnī, kūnīgai.*

Sodomy, s. *kūnī·tob. bachī·bāzī, halak·bāzī, lawāṭat, ighlām.*

Soft, a. *pos* or *post, narm, mulā im.*

Softly, ad. *ro ro, pa qalār.*

Soil, s. *mzaka* or *zmaka, khāwra.* (country) *waṭan, wilāyat*; *mulk, hiwād.* (manure) *sara.* v.a. *palīt-, khīran-, kakaṛ-*, etc. *k.*

Sojourn, v.n. *āstedal, osedal.* v.a. *astoga, mesht-, ṭikāo-*, etc. *k., dzāe nīwul*; *musāfiri k.*

Sojourner, s. *osedūnkai, astogūnkai*; *musāfir.*

Solace, s. *tasallī, ārām*; *khwakkhi.* v.a. *tasallī-*, etc. *warkawul, pokkhal.*
Solder, v.a. *qala'ī k., joṛawul.*
Soldier, s. *spāhī, lakkhkarī.* (heavy armed-) *puṭ spāhī.* (light armed-) *tsaṛah spāhī.* (irregular) *mlā taṛ, jazāelchī.*
Soldiership, s. *spāhī-garī*; *spāhī-tob.*
Soldiery, s. *lakkhkar, fauj* or *pauj, ḍal.*
Sole, a. *yawādzai, tsaṛah*; *yak-tā.* s. *khapaṛ, tala, warghawai.* (-of a shoe) *talai.*
Solely, ad. *sirp* or *surup, ta-ash, faqaṭ.*
Solemn, a. *grāň, drūnd*; *'ibrat-nāk.*
Solemnize, v.a. *manal*; *'urs-, 'īd-, 'ibādat-*, etc. *k., qā-im-, rawā-*, etc. *laral.*
Solicit, v.a. *ghokkhtan, minnat-*, etc. *k.*
Solicitation, s. *ghokkht, minnat, darkhwāst, sawāl.*
Solicitous, a. *andekkh-man, wiswāsī, fikr-man.*
Solicitude, s. *andekkhnā, wiswās, fikr, gham.*
Solid, a. *klak, ṭīng, sakht, drūnd, gaṇr, pokh, khyam.*
Solidity, s. *klak-*, etc. *-wālai, dranāwai.*
Solitary, a. *yawādzai, tanhā, biyal, tsaṛah.*
Solitude, s. *tanhā-ī, biyal-tūn*; *dzangal, bayābān*; *gokkha, khilwat.*
Solve, v.a. *prānatal, tsargandawul*; *wīlī k.*
Solvent, a. *zar-dār, māl-dār*; *wīlī kawūnkai.*
Some, a. *la-ag, la-ag ḍer*; *dzane, tsok, kūm, tsa.*
Somebody, s. *palānkai, tsok, kūm, kas, tan.*
Somehow, ad. *yo shān sara, tsa chal sara.*
Something, s. *shai, tsīz.* a. *la-ag ḍer, pitsānrai.*
Sometimes, ad. *kala kala.*
Somewhat, a. *la-ag, kam, pitsāṇrai.* ad. *la-ag-kūṭī* or *lakūṭī, tsakho, la-ag shān.*
Somewhere, ad. *chare.*
Son, s. *dzoe.* (-in law) *zūm, zūmgai.* (grand-) *nwasai.* (great grand-) *kaṛwasai.* (step-, by father) *parkaṭai.* (step-, by mother) *ba-anzai.* (brother's) *wrārah.* (sister's-) *khora-e* or *khoraye.* (only-) *kashai.*

Song, s. *sandara, sarod, badala, ṭapa, tarāna.*
Sonnet, s. *chār bait, ghazal, lanḍa-ī, sandara.*
Soon, ad. *zir, pa zir mūde, pa la-ag sā'at kkhke.*
Sooner, ad. *wṛūnbe, awwal.*
Soot, s. *lūgai, mas, ḍūna*; *koyina.*
Soothe, v.a. *tasallī warkawul, khwā saṛawul, pokkhal.*
Soothsayer, s. *pāl-* or *fāl-goe*, or *-katūnkai.*
Sooty, a. *lūghaṛan.*
Sop, s. *nwaṛa-ī.* v.a. *chūka k., khushtawul.*
Sorcerer, s. *jādū-gar, koḍ-gar, siḥr-gar.*
Sorcery, s. *jādū, koḍa, siḥr.*
Sordid, a. *shūm, bakhīl, tang-dast, stagh.*
Sore, s. *parhār, zakhm.* a. *zakhmī, khūg.*
Sorrel, s. *tarūkai.*
Sorrow, s. *gham, nūl*; *randz, afsos*; *pakkhemānī, stomānī*; *armān, tartāb.* v.n. *ghamedal, nūledal, randzedal, pakkhemānedal, stomānedal.* v.a. *afsos-, armān-*, etc. *k.*
Sorrowful, a. *gham-jan, gham-nak, nūl-jan, dil-gīr.*
Sorry, a. *toba-gār, pakkhemān, stomān.* (vile) *nā-kārah, khushai, hets shai.*
Sort, s. *qism, rang, shān, noga.* v.a. *chunral, atsanral, tartībawul, chīndah k.*
Sot, s. *bangī, sharābī, nasha-khor.*
Soul, s. *rūḥ, nafs, dzān.* (souls) *arwāḥ.*
Sound, a. (honest) *sūchah, karah, rikkhtīnai.* (healthy) *joṛ, rogh moṭ, tandrust.* (safe) *salāmat, pūrah, ṣābit, amānī.* (right) *jukht, barābar, sam.*
Sound, s. *ghag, zwag, bāng, ḍaz.* v.a. *ghagawul, zwag k., bāng wayal, ḍaz wahal.*
Soundly, ad. *pa kkhah shān sara.*
Soundness, s. *tandrustī, salāmatī*; *ṣiḥhat.*
Soup, s. *kkhorwā.*
Sour, a. *trīw.*
Source, s. *munḍ, wekh, aṣl, sar, bonsaṭ.*
Souse, v.a. *lūndawul, khushtawul*; *ḍūbawul.*
South, s. *suhel, kīṇr-ṭaraf.*

Sovereign, s. *bādshāh, sultan, amīr.*
Sow, v.a. *karal, kar k.* (-for another) *bogarai k.*
Space, s. *dzāe.* (-of time) *mūda, wakht, 'arṣa.*
Spacious, a. *arat, prānatai, dzāe-war.*
Spade, s. *yūm* or *yīm, kara.*
Span, s. *lwesht, langor, anang, gadozai.*
Spar, s. *bensh, tīr, largai.* (small-) *chanra; aram, aramkai.*
Spar, v.a. *jang k., sūkūna sara wahal, lāsuna sara tsandal.*
Spare, v.a. (save) *bachawul, bakkhal, pulawul.* (forego) *pregdal, prekkhodal, prekkhal.* (give) *warkawul.*
Spare, a. (scanty) *kam, la-ag, rangai.* (slender) *narai, trandz.* (short) *land, tang.* (unoccupied) *khālī, wazgār.* (superfluous) *ziyāt, pāltū.*
Sparing, a. *kam-kharts, tang-dast.*
Spark, s. *batsarai, batsarkai, ghurutskai.*
Sparkle, v.n *brekkhedal, dzalkedal, rūnredal.*
Sparkling, a. *brekkh-nāk, dzalkān, rūnr.*
Sparrow, s. *chanr chanr, chughuk.*
Spasm, s. *ghota, tāo, pech.*
Spatter, v.a. *tsirīke wahal; dāghawul, palītawul.*
Spawn, s. *hadai, oba.*
Speak, v.a. *wayal, khabare k., lal.*
Spear, s. *neza, balla, barcha, shalgai.*
Special, a. *khāṣṣ.*
Specie, s. *zar, naghd* or *naqd.*
Species, s. *zāt, rang, qism, noga.*
Specific, a. *zātī, nogai,* s. *mujarrab.*
Specimen, s. *namūna, nakkha, miṣāl.*
Spec, s. *takai, laka, tsirīka, dāgh.*
Speckled, a. *tak-yālai, brag-yālai.*
Spectacle, s. *tamāsha, nandāra.*
Spectacles, s. *chashme, chashmake.*
Spectator, s. *nandārchī, tamāsha-bīn.*
Spectre, s. *rawai, khapaskai; sirwai.*
Speculate, v.a. *fikr-, qiyās-, khiyāl-,* etc. *k.*
Speculative, a. *fikr-man, khiyālī, atkalī.*
Speculator, s. *atkal-bāz, saudāgar.*
Speech, s. *jiba, wayai, wayana, khabara, wrāsha, sukhun.*
Speechless, a. *gūng, lāl, lā dzawāb.*
Speed, s. *talwār, talwal, jaltī, garandī-tob.*
Speedily, ad. *pa talwār, pa garandī, pa jaltī.*
Speedy, a. *garandai, za-ar* or *zir, jalt, tez.*
Spell, s. *jādū, kod, mantar.*
Spell, v.a. *paiza-ī-, pakkhoya-, hijgī-,* etc. *k.*
Spend, v.a. *kharts-, ṣarf-,* etc. *k., lagawul.* (pass) *terawul.* (emit) *khalāṣawul, chalawul.* v.n. *chaledal, kamedal, teredal, khalāṣedal.*
Spendthrift, s. *khartsī, tāwānī, iṣrāfī.*
Sphere, s. *tsarkh; ghūndai.*
Spherical, a. *ghūnd, ghūnd-man.*
Spice, s. *maṣālah* or *masāla.*
Spider, s. *jolā.* (tarantula-) *ghanra.*
Spigot, s. *būja, khulborai, dida.*
Spike, s. *wagai, khosha.* (nail) *mogai.*
Spill, v.a. *toyawul, ghurzawul, āchawul.* v.n. *toyedal* or *to-edal, prewatal, bahedal.*
Spin, v.a. *tsarkha k.; tsarkhawul, churlawul, girzawul.* v.n. *tsarkhedal, churledal, girzedal.*
Spinach, s. *pālak.*
Spindle, s. *dūk, barandai, jalak, tsarkhai, tsarkhalgai, girzandai, tsūkkhai.* (stalk) *tīla-ī, nāra.*
Spinning, s. *tsarkhawuna.* (-wheel) *tsarkha.*
Spire, s. *munāra.*
Spirit, s. *rūh, nafs, dzān; dam, sāh; zrah, dil; himmat, marāna; nang, ghairat; khoe, mizāj; 'araq, jauhar.*
Spirited, a. *zrah-war, maranai, himmat-nāk, nang-yālai, ghairat-nāk* or *ghairat-man.*
Spiritual, a. *rūhānī, bātinī.*
Spit, v.a. *tūkal, tū-, tūkānrai-,* etc. *ghurzawul.*

Spit, s. *sīkh, sīkhcha.*
Spite, s. *kīna, ẓidd, khwā badī, 'adāwat, 'inād, 'aks, rakha, droh, ghach.* (in spite of) *par 'aks, par khilāf.*
Spiteful, a. *kīna-war, khwā bad, 'inādī.*
Spittle, s. *tū, tūk, tūkānrai, lāṛa, lānra.*
Splash, v.a. *tsiṛīke-, charaq-,* etc. *wahal, lawastal.*
Spleen, s. *torai.* (spite) *kīna, khwā badī.*
Splendid, a. *rokkhān, dzalkān; loe, ghaṭ.*
Splendour, s. *raunaq, dabdaba, tamtarāq.*
Splice, s. *joṛ, pewand.* v.a. *joṛawul, pewand k.*
Splint, s. *tūtankai.* (-in horses) *haḍai.* (surgical) *takhta, kalokkhta, kalola. skanḍa.*
Splinter, s. *ṭoṭkai, daṛa, kak, tarāza.*
Split, v.n. *chāwdal, shledal.* v.a. *chawul, shlawul.* (peas, grain, etc.) *dal k., dalawul.*
Spoil, v.a. *wrānawul, kharābawul, habatah-, 'abaṣ-, ṛang-, abtar-,* etc. *k.* (plunder) *lūṭawul, shūkawul, natal, tālā-,* etc. *k.* s. *lūṭ, tālā, shūka, ghārat, gaṭa.*
Spontaneously, ad. *pakhpula.*
Spoon, s. *chamcha-ī* or *tsamtsa-ī* or *tsontsa-ī, kāchogha.* (large) *kaṛcha-ī, harkāra.*
Sport, s. *loba; khandā, ṭoqa washta; kkhkār.* v.a. *lobe k.; khandā-,* etc. *k.; kkhkār k.*
Sportsman, s. *kkhkārī.*
Spot, s. *ṭakai, laka; dāgh, 'aib, tsiṛīka; dzāe.*
Spotted, a. *chrag brag, gaḍ, ṭak-yālai, brag-yālai.*
Spout, s. *tsūkkhka, tsakkhkūṛai.* (of water, etc.) *dāra, fawāra; charaq.* v.n. *pa dāro-,* etc. *watal* or *-bahedal.* v.a. *dāra-,* etc. *wahal.*
Sprain, s. *wal, tāo, pech.* v.a. *wal-,* etc. *khwuṛal.*
Sprawl, v.n. *rghaṛedal—rghakkhtal, lots poṭs hed.*
Spread, v.a. *khwarawul, wīṛawul, phelawul.* v.n. *khwaredal, wīṛedal, pheledal.*
Sprig, s. *lakkhta, kkhākhcha.*

Sprightly, a. *chust, chālāk; kkhād, kkhād-man; mast, shokhīn.*
Spring, s. (season) *sparlai, bahār.* (source) *chīna, chashma.* (leap) *ṭop, trapa, dang. ghurzang.* (elasticity) *dam.* (instrument) *kamāncha.* (bound) *tīndak, khachūnai.*
Spring, v.a. (leap) *ṭop-,* etc. *wahal, dangal, traplal.* (bound) *tīndak-,* etc. *wahal.* (germinate) v.n. *ṭūkedal, zarghūnedal.* (issue) v.n. *khatal, watal, jārī ked.*
Sprinkle. v.a. *charqāo k., tsātsawul, tsiṛīk-awul.* (-from mouth) *pūg wahal.*
Sprout, s. *khalai, buzghalai, ghandal, tegh.* v.n. *ṭūkedal, zarghūnedal, ghundzedal.*
Spruce, a. *daulī, joṛābī, spīn spetsalai, kṛah wṛah, kkhāyastah, pāk ṣāf.*
Spruceness, s. *joṛāb, kkhāyast, kkhāyast-wālai.*
Spur, s. *mamrez* or *mahmeza.* (cock's-) *khāro.* v.a. *tezal, pūnḍa-* or *pūnḍa-ī-mamrez-,* etc. *wahal.*
Spurious, a. *jūṭah, nā-sarah, nā-karah.*
Sputter, s. *tsir, sakkhā, dzaz.* v.a. *tsir-,* etc *wahal.*
Spy, s. *tsārī, jāsūs, zarai, mukhbir.* v.a *tsāral, tsār-, zarana-ī-, jāsūsī-,* etc. *k.*
Squabble, v.a. *jagṛa-, qaẓiya-, steza,* etc. *k.*
Squalid, a. *palīt, gandah, khīran, murdār.*
Squall, s. (wind) *sīla-ī, jakaṛ, jam jakaṛ* (cry) *chigha, jaṛā.* v.a. *chighawul, jaṛal*
Squander, v.a. *iṣrāf-, talaf-,* etc. *k., wru-kawul.*
Square, a. *chār gūṭlai, chār kunjai, murabb'ah.*
Squash, v.a. *chīt pīt k., paz wahal.*
Squeamish, a. *mekkh mekkh.*
Squeeze, v.a. *nichoṛawul.* (-out) *nakkhtedzal.* (press) *manḍal.* (flatten) *chīt k.*
Squint, v.a. *pa kago-, pa kṛīngo-, pa chapako-,* etc. *stargo katal.*
Squirrel, s. *bilūngaṛai, gidaṛai, bilawṛai.*

Squirt, s. *pichkāra-ī.* v.a. *pichkāra-ī wahal.* (-from the mouth) *pūg wahal*; *mazmaza k.*
Stab, v.a. *pa chāṛe-*, etc. *negh wahal, sūk wahal.*
Stable, a. *pāedār, qā-im, mazbūṭ.* s. *ṭabela.*
Stack, s. *dala-ī, ṭap, ḍera-ī.*
Staff, s. *lakaṛa*; *amsā*; *ḍānḍa-ī.* (shepherd's) *aṛamkai, konṭai.* (stem) *chaṛ.*
Stage, s. *mazal* or *manzil.* (degree) *darja.* (platform) *manā*; *dunkācha*; *gaṛwanj.*
Stagger, v.n. *rapedal, laṛzedal*; *gaḍ waḍ tlal, ṭaparedal*; *hak pak ked., hariyānedal.*
Stagnant, a. *band, walāṛ.* (-water) *ḍab.*
Stain, s. *dāgh, laka, tsiṛīka.*
Stair, s. *pārchang, pawṛa-ī, andarpāya.*
Stake, s. (peg) *mogai.* (post) *dār, sūla-ī.* (at play) *daw, sharṭ.*
Stale, a. *zoṛ, begānai, baranai.*
Stalk, s. *nāṛa, tila-ī*; *mūnḍ, ḍakai.*
Stall, s. *dzāe, khūna*; *ākhor.*
Stallion, s. *sānr, turum.*
Stammer, v.n. *tartaredal.* v.a. *guzmuzai k.*
Stammerer, s. *tartarai, chāṛā, tatai.*
Stamp, s. *chāp*; *muhr*; *manḍa*; *rang.* v.a. *chāp wahal*; *muhr lagawul*; *manḍal, manḍa wahal.*
Stampede, s. *ghwa-e·manḍ.*
Stand, v.n. *wudredal, walāṛedal, pātsedal.* (-fast) *tam ked.* (-at bay) *haṭedal*; *jah-* or *jig ked.* (erect) *neghedal, lak ked.*
Standard, s. *nakkha, nikkhān, togh, janḍa, bairaq* or *bairagh.*
Standing, a. *walāṛ, negh*; *lak*; *jig*; *pāedār.*
Staple, s. *saudā.* (lock-) *hūl, aṛam.* (hook) *kunḍa.*
Star, s. *storai.* (planet) *starga.*
Starch, s. *batī.* v.a. *batī ḍakawul.*
Stare, v.a. *ghaṭ katal.*
Starling, s. *sarkhaka.*
Start, v.n. *rawānedal, tlal—lāṛal, drūmedal, drūmal.* (fear) *bugnedal, tarhedal.*

Startle, v.a. *bugnawul, tarhawul, yerawul.*
Starve, v.n. *da lwuge mṛal* or (v.a.) *-muṛ k.*
State, v.a. *bayānawul, wayal, lal, lawdal.*
State, s. *ḥāl, ḥālat*; *shān, shauqat*; *rāj, mulk.*
Statement, s. *ṣūrat ḥāl, bayān, wayai*; *ḥisāb.*
Station, s. *dzāe*; *mazal*; *darja, martaba.* v.a. *wudrawul, kkhkenawul, walāṛawul.*
Statue, s. *but, tsera.*
Stature, s. *qadd, qāmat.* (tall) *dang.* (short) *mandarai.*
Statute, s. *qānūn, qā'ida, ā-īn.*
Stay, v.n. *osedal, pātedal, pātai-, tam-*, etc. *ked., āstedal.* (prevent) *man'a k., haṭālawul, kariyābawul.*
Stead, s. *dzāe, badal, 'iwaẓ.*
Steadfast, Steady, a. } *mazbūṭ, qā-im, pāedār, qalār.*
Steal, v.a. *ghlā k., puṭawul.* (-upon) *chapāo k.* (-away) v.n. *puṭedal.*
Stealth, s. *ghalī·tob, puṭ·wālai*; *ghlā.* (by-) *ghalai ghalai, puṭ puṭ.*
Steam, s. *bukhār, bṛās.*
Steep, a. *ūchat, husk*; *jawar*; *lwaṛ, kamar.*
Steep, v.a. *khushtawul, lūndawul.*
Steer, s. *skhwandar, skhwandarkai.*
Steer, v.a. *chalawul, kkhayal—kkhowul.*
Stem, s. *kkhākh, kharand, ṭanga, ḍanḍara, mūnḍ.* (of grasses, etc.) *nal, nāṛa.*
Stem, v.a. *bandawul, man'a k., haṭālawul.*
Stench, s. *bad·bū-ī, skhā·bū-ī, soṛ·bū-ī.*
Step, s. *qadam, gām*; *chāl, yūn*; *pāya, darja.*
Sterile, a. *shanḍ.* (as land) *kkhora·nāk.*
Stern, a. *trīkh, sakht, klak.* s. *shā, wrusta.*
Stew, s. *pulāo, qorma, dam pukht.*
Steward, s. *dīwān, kārdār.*
Stick, s. *largai, hamsā*; *lawaṛ, ḍāng, koṭak.*
Stick, v.n. *nkkhatal, nkkhledal, chaspedal, lagedal.* (pierce) v.a. *sīkhal, tetsal.* (-into) *njatal, kkhke·manḍal, khakkhawul, kkhke·bāsal—kkhke·yastal.*

Stickle, v.a. *takrār-, ḥujjat-*, etc. *k.*

Stiff, a. *ṭīng, klak*; *lak, negh*; *zīg, lwāṛ*; *tsak.*

Stifle, v.a. *sāh bandawul.*

Stigma, s. *tor, tuhmat, peghor*; *dāgh, laka.*

Stigmatize, v.a. *tor-, tuhmat-*, etc., *pori kawul, peghor warkawul.*

Still, a. *ghalai, chup*; *walāṛ, qalār*; *band, be-ḥarakat.* (water) *dab.* ad. *tar osa, os hum, lā.* s. *khum.*

Stimulate, v.a. *zoral, tezal*; *wīkkhawul, pātsawul, baidār k.*; *lamsawul.*

Sting, s. *nekkh*; *lasha.* v.a. *nekkh wahal.*

Stingy, a. *shūm, bakhīl, tang-dast, sakht.*

Stink, v.n. *bad-, skhā-, soṛ-*, etc. *bū-ī tlal.*

Stipulate, v.a. *wāda-, bandanr-, neṭa-*, etc. *k.*, or *-taṛal.*

Stir, v.a. *khwadzedal, kkhoredal.* v.n. *laṛal, ṛaqawul, khwadzawul, kkhorawul.*

Stirrup, s. *rikāb.* (-leather) *dawāl, tasma.*

Stitch, s. *skoe.* v.a. *gandal, skoe k., skoyal, agayal.*

Stock, s. *tsaṭ.* (tree) *mūnḍ, gharand.* (-for legs) *kāṭ.* (source) *aṣl, noga.* (gun-) *kundāgh.* (store) *panga, saga, māya.*

Stocking, s. *jorāba, moza.* (leather-) *māsa-ī.*

Stocks, s. *kāṭ.* (torture-) *pāna, kunda.* (to put in the-) *pa kāṭ khejawul, pāna ṭakawul.*

Stomach, s. *geḍa, kheṭa*; *ūjrai.* (crop) *jajūra.*

Stone, s. *kānrai, gaṭ, tīga, giṭai,* (-of the bladder) *gīṭa-ī.* (grave-) *khāda* or *khaza.* (ring-) *ghamai.* (-of fruit) *haḍ.* v.a. *pa kānro-, pa gaṭo-*, etc. *wīshtal* or *-muṛ k., sangsār k.*

Stony, a. *kānredz, sanglākh, tarāṛah.*

Stool, s. *peṛa-ī, moṛa.* (purge) *dast, nāstah.*

Stoop, v.n. *ṭīṭedal.* v.a. *sar ṭīṭawul.*

Stop, v.a. *pātawul, pātai k., man'a k., bandawul, īsārawul*; *wudrawul, walāṛawul*; *hiṭālawul, kariyābawul*; *nkkhlawul.* v.n. *pātedal, pātai ked., osedal*; *bandedal*; *īsāredal*; *wudredal, walāṛedal*; *nkkhledal, nkkhatal.*

Stopper, s. *būja, shoṛa*; *mūnrai*; *khulborai, ḍīḍa.*

Store, s. *ambār, ganj, ḍerai*; *saga, panga, māya.* (-house) *koṭa, ambār khāna, khazāna.* v.a. *ṭolawul, jam'a k., yo dzāe k.*

Stores, s. *zakhīra, sūrsat, rasad*; *tokkha, tsawrai*; *asbāb, sāmān*; *hatiyār, kālī.*

Stork, s. *ḍīng.*

Storm, s. *sīla-ī, tūpān* or *ṭūfān.* v.a. *halla-, ḥamla-*, etc. *k.* (-by night) *sho-khūn k.*

Story, s. *qiṣṣa, naql.* (stage) *mazal, maḥal.*

Stout, a. *maẓbūṭ, ghaṭ, kaṭah*; *gagar, khṛīs, nāpaṛ*; *lwāṛ, punḍ, ṭanḍ.*

Stow, v.a. *dzāyawul, kkhke-mandal, kkhkegdal, kkhekkhodal, kkhekkhal.*

Straddle, v.n. *chīnge kkhpe tlal—lāṛal.*

Straggle, v.n. *khor khor-*, or *khwarai khwarai-, tār pa tār-*, etc. *girzedal.*

Straight, a. *sam, negh, sat.*

Straightway, ad. *sam da lāsa.*

Strain, v.a. *ghalbelawul, chānrawul.* (labour) *stam wahal.* (endeavour) *ḥadd k.*

Strainer, s. *chānra, ghalbel, parwezai.*

Strait, s. *tanga-ī*; *tangsiyā, tangī, sakhtī.*

Strange, a. *pradai, begānah*; *'ajab.*

Stranger, s. *nā-āshnāe, nā-balad, pradai.*

Strangle, v.a. *mara-ī-, ghāṛa-*, etc. *khapa k.*

Strap, s. *tasma, rog.* (-of churning staff) *baṛangai.* (shoulder-) *paṭa.*

Stratagem, s. *chal, ḥīla, fareb, lamghaṛa-ī.*

Stratum, s. *bragh, tā.*

Straw, s. *khas, khasanrai, kāna-ī.* (Maize-) *ṭānṭa.* (Rice-) *palāla.* (Mustard-) *kāmbūra.* (Pulse-) *kaṭī.* (broken-) *būs* or *būsī.*

Stray, v.n. *wrukedal, gumrāh-, be-lār-, khaṭā-*, etc. *ked., khushai girzedal.*

Streak, s. *kīl, līka, karkkha.* (-of light) *partaw, palwasha.*

Stream, s. *dāra, sailāb, chala, chalānda.* v.n. *bahedal, chaledal, jārī ked.*
Street, s. *lār, kūtsa.*
Strength, s. *zor, quwat, bram, tuwān, tāqat.*
Strengthen, v.a. *zor-*, etc. *warkawul, mazbūt-, klak-*, etc. *k.*
Strenuous, a. *sargcrm, mazbūt, klak.*
Stress, s. *zor, quwat*; *dranāwai, bār.*
Stretch, v.a. *rākāgal—rākkhkal, ūgdawul.* (-out) *ghazawul.* v.n. *ūgdedal*; *ghazedal.*
Strew, v.a. *khwarawul, rejawul* or *rejdawul, satrai watrai-, tār pa tār-, khwarai-*, etc. *k.*
Strict, a. *sakht, klak, ting, tang*; *jukht, jor.*
Strictly, ad. *pa rikkhtiyā.*
Stride, s. *tūlānd.* v.n. *pa tūlānd tlal—lāral.*
Strife, s. *patna, steza, mīrtsī, jagra, 'adāwat.*
Strike, v.a. *wahal, jangawul.*
String, s. *mazai.* (tie) *tanra-ī.* (-of beads) *lar, hār.* (-of cattle) *qatār.* v.a. *pewdal.*
Stringy, a. *rekkha-dār.*
Strip, s. *pata-ī, pāra, tarāza, rikkhkai, parūkai.*
Strip, v.a. *barbandawul*; *shūkawul.*
Stripe, s. *karkkha.* (blow) *guzār.* (whip) *karora.*
Stripling, s. *halak, janrai*; *zalmai, ghundāyah.*
Strive, v.a. *mihnat-, kokshiksh-*, etc. *k.*; *zidd-, qasd-*, etc. *k.*
Stroke, s. *guzār.* (at play) *daw.* v.a. *-lās wahal* or *-girzawul*, etc.
Stroll, v.n. *girzedal.* v.a. *sail-, gakkht-*, etc. *k.*
Strong, a. *mazbūt, klak, mazai, zorāwar.*
Structure, s. *tarkīb, jorawūna*; *shakl, sūrat.*
Struggle, v.a. *parzawul*; *jang k.*; *mihnat k.*
Strumpet, s. *gashta-ī, baghara-ī, hujra-ī, kāsīra, kūtsa gashta, kachana-ī, lola-ī.*
Strut, v n. *pa daul tlal—lāral*, or *-girzedal.*
Stubble, s. *drūza, khariz, nār, tānta.*
Stubborn, a. *takanrai, khpul-sar, hod, jah, sar-kakkh, khpul-rāe.*

Stud, s. *ghūta-ī, gul-mekh.* (-of horses) *galla.*
Student, s. *shāgird, tālib da 'ilm.*
Study, v.a. *fikr k.*; *zdah k.*
Stuff, s. *tsīz, shai*; *asbāb, sāmān, kālai*; *rakht, zarūkai, tūkai*; *be-hūda-, khusha-ī-, pūcha-, dūza-*, etc. *khabara.*
Stuff, v.a. *mandal, kkhke-mandal.*
Stumble, v.a. *tīndak-, takar-, budrī-, kangas-, skandarī-*, etc. *khwural.*
Stump, s. *mūnd, kharand, tsat.* (-of a tooth) *dara, wekh.*
Stun, v.a. *parghazī-, gans-, dap-, sar-kawdan-, be-hokkh-*, etc. *k.*
Stupid, a. *kawdan, palwand, gedī khar, nā-poh, kam 'aql.*
Stupefy, v.a. *be-hokkh-, be-khūd-*, etc. *k.*
Sturdy, a. *mazai, mazbūt, gagar, nāpar, ghat, khrīs.*
Stutter, v.n. *tartaredal.*
Sty, s. (in the eyelid) *gholawunkai.*
Style, s. *inshā, 'ibārat*; *nūm, laqab.* v.a. *wayal, balal* or *bolal, nūm ākhistal* or *-warkawul, -lagawul.*
Subdue, v.a. *lāndi k., qābū k., wahal.*
Subject, s. *r'ayat, tābi'a-dār*; *khabara, matlab, mazmūn.* (in grammar) *fā'il.* v.a. *lāndi k., r'ayat-*, etc. *k.*
Sublime, a. *ūchat, buland*; *ghat, loe.*
Submissive, a. *tābi'a-dār, farmān wrūnkai.*
Submit, v.a. *farmān wral, hukm manal, tābi'a-dārī k.*; *pekkhawul, wrāndi gdal* or *-kkhkegdal*, etc.
Subordinate, a. *kashar*; *kkhkatanai, lāndīnai.*
Suborn, v.a. *pa mok-* or *pa bade gatal* or *-mūndal, -paidā k.*, etc. *bada-*, etc. *warkawul.*
Subscribe, v.a. *manal, qabūlawul, nūm līkal, dast khatt k.*
Subscription, s. *manana, dast khatt*; *bakkhana, bakhkshiksh.*

Subsequent, a. *wrustai, wrustanai, pasanai, akhīr.*
Subsequently, ad. *wrusto, pas, ākhir.*
Subservient, a. *madad·gār, komakī, madad-,* etc. *warkawūnkai.*
Subside, v.n. *kamedal, la-agedal*; *kkhkenāstal, prewatal.*
Subsidy, s. *pekkh·kakkh, khirāj, n'al·bandī.*
Subsist, v.n. *pāedal, osedal, pātedal, pātai ked.* v.a. *rozgār-, guzrān-,* etc. *k.*; *pālal, nmāndzal.*
Subsistence, s. *rozī, rozgār, guzrān, jwand, jwandūn.*
Substance, s. *shai, tsīz*; *māl, duniyā, daulat*; *sar, aṣl*; *khulāṣa, jauhar*; *māya, saga.*
Substantial, a. *pāedār, mazbūṭ*; *maujūd, aṣlī*; *māl·dār, daulat·man.*
Substantiate, v.a. *rikkhtiyā-, rikkhtīnai-, ṣābit-, zbād-,* etc. *k.*
Substantive, s. *shai, nūm*; *aṣl.*
Substitute, s. *badal, 'iwazī.*
Subterfuge, s. *hira-ī, bāna, lamghara-ī, palma.*
Subtile, a. *narai, bārīk, mahīn.*
Subtle, a. *hokkhyār, pokh*; *chal·bāz, ḥīla·bāz.*
Subtract, v.a. *ākhistal, prekawul, bāsal—yastal.*
Subvert, v.a. *wrānawul, naskorawul, naṛawul.*
Succeed, v.a. (follow) *pairawī k.* v.n. *pase lagedal, pase rātlal—rāghlal.* (prosper) v.a. *was chalawul, bakht mūndal, kār gaṭal.* (conquer) v.a. *pa-aṛ k., barai mūndal.* v.n. *wa-aṛ ked., was chaledal.*
Success, s. *wa-aṛāna, barai, bakht, barakat, gaṭa.*
Successful, a. *wa-aṛ, barakatī, bakhtāwar.*
Succession, s. *wār, dzāe nīwah.*
Successive, a. *wārī, pa wār rātlūnai.*
Successively, ad. *wār pa wār, pala pase.*
Successor, s. *pairaw, qā-im muqām.*
Succour, s. *mrasta, madad, komak.*
Succulent, a. *objan, pa obo ḍak, serāb.*
Succumb, v.n. *la brama prewatal, lāndi ked.*
Such, p. *hase, dā·hase, done.* (-a one) *palānkai, tsok.*
Suck, v.a. *chūpal, zbekkhal.* (-the breast) *rawdal.*
Suckle, v.a. *tai warkawul.*
Suckling, s. *tai rawdūnkai, tandai* or *tankai.*
Suction, s. *chūpana*; *rākkhkana.*
Sudden, a. *nāgahān, nā·gumān, tsaṭ waṭ.*
Suddenly, ad. *nāgāh, nātsāpa, nā·gumāna.*
Sudorific, a. *khwale rāwṛūnkai, da khwalo dawā.*
Sue, v.a. *d'awa-, muqaddama-,* etc. *k.*; *ghokkhtal, minnat k.*
Suffer, v.a. *zghamal, wṛal, khwuṛal, rākāgal—rākkhkal.* v.n. *zghamedal, petsal, sahal, sahedal.* (allow) *pregdal, prekkhodal, prekkhal*; *ijāzat-, izn-, ḥukm-, rukhṣat-,* etc. *warkawul.*
Sufferer, a. *khūg·man, dard·man, randzūr.* (in comp.) *-khor, -kakkh, -man,* etc.
Suffering, a. *khūg*; *zgham·nāk, ṣabr·nāk.*
Sufficient, a. *bas, kāfī, ḍer*; *lā-iq, qābil.*
Suffocate, v.a. *sāh-, dam-,* etc. *bandawul.*
Sugar, s. *shakara, tarī, nabāt.* (raw-) *gūṛa.* (-candy) *qand.* (-cane) *ganna, ponḍa, khū.*
Suggest, v.a. *ishārat-, 'arz-, kkhowuna-,* etc. *k., wayal.*
Suit, v.a. *joṛawul, barābarawul, samawul, lagawul, dzāe laral, pīrzowul.* v.n. *barābaredal, lagedal, pīrzo ked., pa·kār rātlal—rāghlal.*
Suit, s. (-of clothes) *joṛa.* (-of cards) *rang.* (law-) *d'awa, muqaddama, jagṛa.* (petition) *'arz, sawāl.* (retinue) *swarlī, jalab.* (wish) *ghokkht, darkhwāst.*
Suitable, a. *joṛ, barābar, munāsib, wājib, pīrzo, kkhāyastah, kkhah, yarzan.*
Suitor, s. *mudd'aī*; *ṭalab·gār.*
Sulky, a. *marawar, mānṛī·gar, khapah.*
Sulphur, s. *gogaṛ, gogird.*

Sultry, a. *dūp, garm.*
Sum, s. *ṭol ṭāl, jam'a, mablagh, kull.* v.a. *ḥisāb k.*
Summary, s. *mujmal, khulāṣa.* a. *land.*
Summer, s. *oṛai, dubai, tābistān.* (-house) *chopāṛ.*
Summit, s. *sar, peza, tsūka.*
Summon, v.a. *balal, rābalal, ṭalab k.*
Summons, s. *ṭalab nāma*; *bālah, balana.*
Sumptuous, a. *grān qīmat, be-bahā*; *shāh kharts.*
Sun, s. *nwar* or *nmar.* (-beam) *partaw.* (-shine) *pitāo, gharma.* (-rise) *nwar khātah.* (-set) *nwar prewātah.* (-dial) *da siwrī tsalai.* (-flower) *gul da nwar parast.*
Sunday, s. *itwār, yak shamba.*
Sundry, a. *aṛgajah, balāe batar, dzane, b'aẓe, biyal.*
Superabundant, a. *ḍer, ziyāt, frewān.*
Superb, a. *'aẓīm, be bahā, be siyāl, lā ṣānī.*
Supercilious, a. *kibr-jan, maghrūr, khāntamā.*
Superficial, a. *nīmgaṛai, kachah*; *bāhir, wardzane.*
Superficies, s. *makh, zmaka, maidān, zamīn.*
Superintendent, s. *nāẓir, kār kawūnkai, dāroghah, sardār, mīr majlis.*
Superior, a. *mashar*; *ghwarah*; *loe, ghaṭ, star*; *bar, pāsanai, portanai.*
Supernatural, a. *la 'aqla bāhir, khilāf la 'ādata.*
Superscription, s. *sar-nāma.*
Supersede, v.a. *bāṭil k., lāndi k.*
Superstition, s. *wahm, bāṭil īmān.*
Supine, a. *sat, stūnī-stagh.* (careless) *be parwā, sust*; *laṭ, nā-rāst.*
Supper, s. *da māskhutan ḍoḍa-ī*; *shūma.*
Supplant, v.a. *shaṛal, pa-chal sara be dzāyawul.*
Supple, a. *narm, mulā-im, pos* or *post.*
Suppliant, a. *riyāẓ-man, minnat-dār.*
Supplication, s. *minnat, du'ā.*

Supply, v.a. *warkawul, rasawul, rāwṛal, paidā k.*
Support, v.a. *wṛal, zghamal, petsal.* (nourish) *pālal, nmāndzal.* (keep) *sātal, jghoral, khundī k.* (assist) *pushtī-, komak-, āṛ-, mrasta-,* etc. *k.*
Support, s. *āṛ, pushta*; *komak, mrasta*; *parwarish.*
Supporter, s. *pushtībān, takiya*; *pālūnkai, sātūnkai, sātandoe, jghorai.*
Suppose, v.a. *gaṇṛal, angeral, qiyās-, fikr-, khiyāl-,* etc. *k.* v.n. *pohedal.*
Suppress, v.a. *kkhkenawul, lāndi k., man'a k., mātawul, bandawul.* (conceal) *puṭawul.*
Suppurate, v.n. *zawlan ked., khūyedal, pakhedal.*
Supreme, a. *ṣadar*; *kull mukhtār, loe, ghaṭ.*
Sure, a. *yaqīn, rikkhtīnai, wāq'ī*; *maẓbūṭ, pokh.*
Surely, ad. *rikkhtiyā, yara, be shakka.*
Surety, s. *ẓāmin.* (the thing) *ẓamānat.*
Surface, s. *makh, zmaka, maidān, zamīn.*
Surfeit, s. *agheṛ, ateṛ, sekan.* v.a. *agheṛal, ateṛal, be prate-, be-khrate-,* etc. *khwuṛal.* v.n. *sekan ked.*
Surge, v.n. *ghurzedal.* v.a. *chape wahal.*
Surgeon, s. *jarrāḥ, ṭabīb.*
Surly, a. *bakhīl, trīkh-* or *tursh rūe, sūṭ būṭ.*
Surname, s. *da qām-, da khel-, da khāndān-,* etc. *nūm* or *nāma*; *laqab, nūm.*
Surplus, s. *pātai, ziyātī, bāqī.*
Surprise, v.a. *hariyānawul, rabṛawul*; *chapāo k.* v.n. *be-khabar rasedal, nātsāpa prewatal.*
Surrender, v.a. *pāslawul, spāral.*
Surround, v.a. *īsārawul, gerawul.*
Survey, v.a. *mech-, kach-,* etc. *k.*; *katal, kasal, goral—līdal, naẓar-,* etc. *k.*
Survive, v.n. *pāedal, jwandūi pātai ked.*
Suspect, v.a. *shakk-, shubha-, gumān-,* etc. *laral.*

Suspend, v.a. *dzwaṛandawul, āwezānd k.* (-from office) *mu'attal-, man'a-, band-,* etc. *k.*

Suspense, s. *shakk, shubha, wiswās, andekkhnā.*

Suspicion, s. *gumān, shubha, shakk*; *tuhmat, tor, peghor, sigāl.*

Sustain, v.a. *wṛal, zghamal, petsal, khwuṛal, kāgal—kkhkal.* (aid) *madad-, pushtī-, komak-,* etc. *warkawul.* (keep) *sātal, jghoral, khundī k.* (cherish) *pālal, nmāndzal.*

Sustenance, s. *rozī, khwuṛāk, parwarish.*

Swagger, v.a. *ḍūze-, lāpe-, lāpe shāpe-,* etc. *wahal.*

Swallow, s. *totakarai.* (swift) *totakai.* (sand martin) *totakarkai.*

Swallow, v.a. *nghaṛdal, terawul.*

Swallow-wort, s. *spalma-ī.*

Swamp, s. *jaba.*

Swan, s. *qāz.*

Swarm, s. *ṭol, paṛk, lakkhkar, ganra gūnra.* (-of bees) *ghubār.* (-of locusts) *lakkhkar.*

Swarthy, a. *skānr*; *ghanum rang.*

Swathe, v.a. *nghaṛal — nghakkhtal, paṭa-ī taṛal.* (a babe) *seznī taṛal, blegdal.*

Sway, v.a. *ḥukm chalawul, ḥukūmat k.* (bias) *mā-il-, mā-ilān-,* etc. *k., rāwustal.*

Swear, v.a. *qasam-, saugand-,* etc. *khwuṛal.* (-falsely) *darogh-, nāḥaqq-,* etc. *qasam khwuṛal.*

Sweat, v.n. *khwale ked.*

Sweep, v.a. *jārū k.*

Sweeper, s. *jārū·kakkh, shāhī khel, muṣallī, chūrai.* (-of a mosque, etc.) *mīnjawar.*

Sweepings, s. *khāshāk, khadzala, kharshan, warkhaṛa.*

Sweet, a. *khog, shīrīn, khwand·nāk.*

Sweetheart, s. *yār, yāra*; *mayan, mayana*; *'āshiq, 'āshiqa*; *m'ashūq, m'ashūqa*; *āshnāe, āshnāya.*

Sweetish, a. *khog·nāk, khog·loṛai.*

Sweetmeat, s. *qanāt, mityā-ī, shīrīnī.* (varieties) *amrasa, ghunzākkhai, dzalobai, rewṛa-ī, laṭū, batāsa, ḥalwā, pāpar,* etc. etc. (-seller) *ḥalwā-ī.*

Sweetness, s. *khog·wālai, khog·loṛ.*

Swell, v.n. *paṛsedal, punḍedal, tyak ked.*

Swelling, s. *pāṛsob.*

Swift, a. *gaṛandai, jalt, tez, zir.*

Swim, v.a. *lānbo wahal* or *k.* v.n. *pa lānbo tlal—lāṛal, rawānedal, chaledal.*

Swimmer, s. *lānbo·zan.*

Swindler, s. *darghal, ṭag, sādū.*

Swing, s. *ṭāl, gahwāral.* (cradle) *zāngo.* (whirligig) *banre·chagh.* v.a. *ṭāl wahal, zangawul.* v.n. *zangal, zangedal.*

Switch, s. *lakkhta, keṛa.*

Swivel, s. *zambūrak, shāhīn.*

Swoon, s. *parghaz.* v.n. *parghazī prewatal.*

Swoop, v.a. *pa chape-, pa ghoṭe-, pa guzār-,* etc. *wahal* or *-nīwul.*

Sword, s. *tūra, tegh.* (-spear) *sela.* (-knot) *zunḍai, kīlak.*

Swordsman, s. *tūrzan, tūra·bāz.*

Sycophant, s. *khūshāmad·gar, ḍirpal.*

Sylvan, a. *dzangalī, dashtī.* s. (satyr) *banr mānū.*

Symbol, s. *nakkha, nikkhān, 'alāmat.*

Sympathy, s. *khwā·khūgī, zṛah swai.*

Symptom, s. *nakkha,* etc. (*v.* Symbol).

Synod, s. *jirga-* or *majlis da shekhāno* or *-da imāmāno* or *-da mullāyāno.*

Syntax, s. *naḥw.*

Syringe, s. *pichkāra-ī, ḥuqna.*

Syrup, s. *gūṛa-ī, qiwām, zokkha, rub.*

System, s. *qānūn, ā-īn, qā'ida, ṭarīqa.*

T

Table, s. *mez, takhta*; *naqsha.* (-cloth) *dastar·khwān.* (-cover) *chāndanī.*

Tablet, s. *lauḥ, takhta.*
Tacit, a. *ghalai, chup.*
Tactics, s. *da jang ḥikmat.*
Tail, s. *lama, laka-ī.* (-bone) *laka lamai.* (-less) *landai.* (fat tailed) a. *lamarar.*
Tailor, s. *darzī, khaiyāṭ.*
Taint, v.a. *bonrawul, wrost-, skhā-,* etc. *k.*
Take, v.a. *ākhistal, nīwul, lāndi k.* (-in) *dzāyawul.* (suppose) *ganral.* (effect) *pāzah k.* (carry) *yosal, wṛal.* (lead) *botlal—bīwul.* (-off) *bāsal—yastal.* (-out) *kāgal—kkhkal.* (-care of) *sātal, jghoral, khundī k.* (-down) *kūzawul.* (-care) *pahm k.*
Talc, s. *abraq, da shige gul, zarbarakh.*
Tale, s. *qiṣṣa, naql, rawāyat.* (-bearer) *chughl-khor, mawās.*
Talent, s. *'aql, sha'ūr, poh, hunar.*
Talk, v.a. *wayal, khabare k.* s. *wayana, khabara*; *wrāsha, wayai*; *gangosai.*
Tall, a. *ūchat, hask, dang, lwaṛ.*
Tallow, s. *ghwaṛ, spīna, mū.*
Talon, s. *nūk, mangul, changul, panja.*
Tambourine, s. *tambal, ḍūmbakai, ḍūmkai.*
Tame, a. *āmokhtah, el, koranai.* v.a. *āmokhtah k., elawul.*
Tamper, v.a. *lās lagawul, lamsawul, lamsūn k.*
Tan, v.a. *dabbāghī k., tsarman joṛawul* or *-pakha k.* (-by the sun) v.n. *swal, sedzal.*
Tank, s. *ḍanḍ, ḥauẓ, tālāo, nāwar.*
Tanner, s. *dabbāgh, tsamyār.*
Tantalize, v.a. *pa umed nā umed k.*
Tap, v.a. *ṭak-, ṭrak-,* etc. *wahal.* (pierce) *tsīkhal, sūṛai k.*
Tape, s. *paṭa-ī*; *niwāṛ.*
Taper, s. *bāta-ī, patīla.* a. *gāo dum, trandz.*
Tar, s. *rāndzaṛah, chūṛel.*
Tardy, a. *sust, laṭ, drangai.*
Tardiness, s. *sust-wālai, drang, dzanḍ.*
Target, s. *mūkha, nakkha, kuhāṛa*; *ḍāl, spar.*
Tarnish, v.a. *khīran-, kakaṛ-, murdār-,* etc. *k.*
Tarry, v.n. *osedal, pātedal*; *walāṛedal, wudredal*; *lārghah-, dzanḍ-, drang-,* etc. *k.*
Task, s. *kār, mashghūlā*; *dars, sabaq*; *miḥnat.*
Tassel, s. *zunḍai, zunbak.*
Taste, s. *khwand, maza, tsaka*; *tsakindan.* v.a. *khwand-,* etc. *-wahal, ākhistal,* or *-k., tsakal.*
Tattle, v.a. *bak bak-, buṛ baṛ-, ṭar ṭar-,* etc. *k.*
Taunt, v.a. *pekkhe-, ṭoqe-, khandā-,* etc. *pore k.*
Tawny, a. *skānr, ghanum rang.*
Tax, v.a. *bāj-, khirāj-, sāw-, maḥṣūl-,* etc. *lagawul* or *-taṛal.* (cattle-) s. *sargalla, goshī.* (land-) *kulang, sarghala, sar-sabzī.* (house-) *lūgī-tāwān, khāna-shumārī.* (poll-) *jaziya.*
Tea, s. *chāe.* (-cup) *piyāla.*
Teach, v.a. *kkhayal—kkhowul, pohawul*; *lwalawul, tarbiyat-, t'alīm-,* etc. *k., āmokhtah-, 'ādat-, zdah-,* etc. *k.*
Teacher, s. *ākhūn, ustād, mu'allim.*
Tear, v.a. *shlawul, tsīral, wrarawul, chāk k.* v.n. *shledal, tsīredal, wraredal.* (-out) *kāgal—kkhkal, bāsal—yastal.*
Tear, s. *okkha.* (-ful) a. *okkhan.*
Tease, v.a. *pārawul, tangawul, ṭongawul.*
Tedious, a. *drūnd, grān, sakht.*
Teem, v.n. *ganr ked., ḍeredal, wadānedal.*
Tell, v.a. *wayal, khabarawul*; *bayānawul*; *kkhayal—kkhowul.* (-tales) *chughlī k.*
Temerity, s. *be-adabī*; *be-tadbīrī*; *be-bākī.*
Temper, s. *khoe, khaṣlat, lokkhai, mizāj, ṭab'iyat.* (-of metals) *āb, dam.*
Temperate, a. *barābar, joṛ, muwāfiq*; *parhez-gār*; *m'utadil, na tod na soṛ.*
Tempest, s. *sīla-ī, tūpān* or *ṭūfān.*
Temple, s. *'ibādat-gāh, masjid, jumā'at.* (-of Mecca) *qibla, k'aba.* (-of Jerusalem) *bait ul muqaddas.* (-of the head) *lweganda, ṭek.*
Temporal, a. *duniyā-ī, fānī, jahānī.*
Temporary, a. *teredūnai, la-ag wradzanai.*

Temporize, v.a. *drang-, lārghah-, multawī-,* etc. *k.*

Tempt, v.a. *ghulawul, darghalawul, lamsawul, targhīb-,* etc. *warkawul.*

Ten, a. *las.* (tenth) a. *lasam.* (-fold) *las bragh; las pa yo.* (-times) *las heṛa, las dzala.*

Tenable, a. *klak, ṭing, maḥkam, mazbūṭ.*

Tenacious, a. *klak, ṭing, sakht; bokkht, slekkht-nāk; shūm, bakhīl; khpul rāe.*

Tenant, s. *hamsāyah, faqīr, ijāra-dār, āsāmī.*

Tend, v.a. *sātal, jghoral; khabar ākhistal, khidmat k.* (-flocks) *shpanī k.* v.n. *girzedal, mā-il-, ma-ilān-,* etc. *ked.*

Tendency, s. *mā-il-, khwā; gharaz; maṭlab, mudd'ā.*

Tender, a. *nāzak, narm, mulā-im, post.*

Tendon, s. *pala, rag, wuja.* (-of horse's leg) *pai.* (-of the heel) *spīna, kūchai.*

Tendril, s. *zela, bela.*

Tenesmus. s. *kānga, tāo, pech.*

Tenet, s. *masla; bāwar, īmān; ṭarīqa.*

Tenor, s. *m'anī; yūn, chalan.* (in music) *dzīr.*

Tense, a. *rākkhkalai, klak, ṭing.*

Tent, s. *ḍera, tambū, khaima.* (nomad's) *kigda-ī.* (-in surgery) *bāta-ī.* (-rope) *māndara, mazai.*

Tenth, a. *lasam.* (-part) s. *lasama brakha.*

Tepid, a. *taṛam, nīm garm.*

Term, s. *khabara, wayai, lafz.* (time) *neṭa, mūda.* (stipulation) *sharṭ, taṛa, wāda, bandanr.* (limit) *ḥadd.* (phrase) *'ibārat.* (good terms) *rogha joṛa, pakhulā.*

Termagant, s. *jiba-wara, jang-yāla-ī.*

Terminate, v.n. *tamāmedal, pūrah ked., anjāmedal.* v.a. *tamāmawul,* etc.

Terrace, s. *dunkācha.* (-of a house) *chat, bām.*

Terrible, a. *haul-nāk, khof-nāk.*

Terrify, v.a. *yerawul, tarhawul.*

Territory, s. *mulk, zmaka, hiwād.*

Terror, s. *yera* or *wera, tor, khof.* (-struck) *tor khwuṛalai.*

Test, v.a. *āzmāyal* or *āzmoyal, āzmekkht k.*

Testament, s. (Old) *tauret.* (New) *injīl,* (will) *waṣiyat nāma.*

Testicle, s. *and, haga-ī, khoṭa.*

Testify, v.a. *shāhidī-, gawāhī-,*etc. *lal* or *lawdal,* or *-warkawul.*

Testimonial, s. *rāzī-nāma; gawāhī-nāma.*

Testimony, s. *gawāhī, shāhidī.*

Tether, v.a. *taṛal.* s. *shkal* or *shkel, wandar.*

Text, s. *matan, aṣl.* (of Qurān) *āyat.*

Texture, s. *tarkīb, joṛawuna, sākht.*

Than, ad. *la—na.*

Thank, v.a. *shukr k., -bāsal—yastal, -guzāral, -pa dzāe rāwṛal,* etc.

Thankful, a. *shukr guzār.*

That, pr. *haghah, e, kūm, dā.* c. *tso chi, dapāra da.*

Thatch, s. *tsapar, chat.*

Thaw, v.n. *oba ked.; wīlī ked.*

The, art. *haghah, daghah, dā.*

Theft, s. *ghlā.*

Theme, s. *masawda* or *musawadda; manshā.*

Then, ad. *hāla, pas; tro, bāre; nor, biyā.*

Thence, ad. *dzaka, la haghe na.* (-forth) *pas, pas la haghe na.*

Theology, s. *fiqha.*

Theory, s. *'ilm, qiyās, khiyāl.*

There, ad. *halta, hore, horta, hagha khwā.*

Thereabout, ad. *la-ag ḍer* or *la-ag ziyāt, nijde, takhmīnan.*

Therefore, ad. *pas, dzaka, tro.*

Thick, a. *ghaṭ, ṭing, lwāṛ; ganr, tat, ṭal* (-as the voice) *bog, ḍaḍ.*

Thicket, s. *jangai, jāṛ, jāmbṛa, karkanr.*

Thief, s. *ghal, uchakah, chakah ghal.*

Thigh, s. *wrūn, patūn, kkhānga.*

Thimble, s. *gūtma.*

Thin, a. *narai, mahīn, bārīk, trandz, nāzak.* (lean) *ḍangar, khwār.* (scanty) *rangai.*

Thing, s. *shai, tsīz, kālai.*

Think, v.a. *fikr-, qiyās-, khiyāl-*, etc. *k.*; *gumān-, andekkhnā-*, etc. *k.*; *ghaur-, parwā-*, etc. *k.*; *ganral, angeral.* v.n. *pohedal.*

Third, a. *driyam* or *dre-am.* (-part) s. *driyama brakha.*

Thirst, v.n. *tagai ked.* s. *tanda, tagai·wālai.*

Thirsty, a. *tagai.*

Thirteen, a. *diyārlas.*

Thirty, a. *dersh.* (thirtieth) *dersham.* (thirty-one) *yo dersh.* (-two) *dwah dersh*, etc.

This, pr. *dā, daghah, dah, de, hāyah.* (-very one) *bedū, pa ṭakī.*

Thistle, s. *āzghakai, kārīza.*

Thither, ad. *halta, hore, horta, warhīsta, hagha khwā.*

Thong, s. *tasma, rog.*

Thorax, s. *taṭar, gargas, gogal, sīna.*

Thorn, s. *āzghai* or *āghzai, khār.* (-bush) *ghana, karkanra.* (-apple) *dātūra.* (-apple seed) *tora dāna.* (thorns) *ghane.*

Thorny, a. *āzghan* or *āghzan, khār·dār*

Thorough, a. *pūrah, pokh, bashpaṛ, amānī.*

Thou, pr. *tah, tā, de, di.*

Though, c. *agarchi, siwā la de na.* (as-) *laka chi.*

Thought, s. *fikr, qiyās, khiyāl*; *ghaur, khabar, parwā*; *gumān, sigāl*; *andekkhnā.*

Thoughtful, a. *fikr·man, andekkh·man.*

Thoughtless, a. *be·fikr, be·parwā, be·khabar.*

Thousand, a. *zar.* (two-) *dwah zara*, etc.

Thraldom, s. *qaid, band, nkkhatai.*

Thrash, v.a. *wahal, ṭakawul, kūṭal,* (-corn) *ghobal k.*

Thrashing-floor, s. *khirman, dirmand.*

Thread, s. *spanrsai, tār, mazai.* v.a. *pewdal, peyal.*

Threaten, v.a. *ḍabawul, ḍabka k.*

Three, a. *dre* or *dri.* (-fold) *dre bragh*; *dre pa yo.*

Threshold, s. *āstān, dargāh*; *dahlīz.*

Thrice, ad. *dre heṛa, -dzala, -plā, -guzāra,* etc.

Thrifty, a. *kam kharts, kam tāwān kawūnkai, bachāū, kifāyat kawūnkai.*

Thrive, v.n. *wadānedal, ābādedal, maṛedal.*

Throat, s. *mara-ī, markanḍai, ghara-ī.* (fauces) *ghāṛa, ḥalq.*

Throb, v.a. *tsiṛīka wahal.* v.n. *ḍrazedal.*

Throne, s. *takht, masnad, gadda-ī.*

Throng, s. *ṭol, paṛk, ḍala, ganra gūnra.*

Through, p. *pore, pa mandz kkhke.* (-and through) *pore ore, ore rāpore.* (by means of) *pa m'arifat, la kabla.*

Throughout, ad. *amānī, sarāsar.*

Throw, v.a. *wīshtal, āchawul, ghurzawul, lawastal.* (-up) *jārbāsal—jāryastal*; *pregdal, prekkhodal, prekkhal, tark k.*

Thrust, v.a. *negh wahal*; *ṭel-, ḍaka-, sūk-,* etc. *wahal.* (-into) *manḍal, kkhke·manḍal*; *nana-,* or *kkhke·bāsal—nana-,* or *kkhke·yastal.*

Thumb, s. *ghaṭa-gūta.*

Thump, v.a. *ḍab-, ṭak-, sūk-, gasa-,* etc. *wahal.*

Thunder, s. *tālanda, tanrā.* (-bolt) *tandar, ṭaka.* v.n. *ghuṛunbedal, ghaṛedal.*

Thursday, s. *pānshamba, da ziyārat wradz.*

Thus, ad. *hase, dā·hase, hase shān, dā shān, dā rang.* (-much) *done, hombra, daghombra.*

Thwart, v.a. *wār khaṭā k., wrānawul, aṛawul, 'aks-, zidd-,* etc. *k.*

Thyself, pr. *tah khpul.*

Tick, s. (sound) *ṭak, ṭas.* (louse) *kūnai, kana, konr, wrādza.*

Ticket, s. *chīṭa-ī*; *sar·nāma.*

Tickle, s. *takha.* v.a. *takhawul, takhnawul.* v.n. *takhedal, takhnedal.*

Tidings, s. *khabar.* (good-) *zera, zerai.* (the bearer of good-) *zera·garai.*

Tidy, a. *ḍaulī, spīn spetsalai.*

Tie, s. *taṛūn, tanra-ī, wandanai.* v.a. *taṛal, lagawul.*

Tiffin, s. *nāshta, nahārai.*

Tiger, s. *zmarai* or *mzarai.*

Tight, a. *tang, chust, rākkhkalai, klak.*

Tighten, v.a. *tangawul, klakawul, rākāgal—rākkhkal.*

Till, p. *tar haghah pore.* (when?) *tar kala pore.* (-now) *tar osa pore.*

Till, v.a. *kar-, īwe-,* or *yawe-,* etc. *k., zmaka aṛawul.*

Tillage, s. *kar, īwe,* or *yiwe,* or *yawe.*

Timber, s. *largai*; *bensh.*

Time, s. *wakht* or *waqt.* (season) *neṭa, mūda, nobat, ṭāng.* (age) *'umr, kāl*; *zamāna, daur.* (turn) *wār, heṛ, plā, dzal, guzār.* (leisure) *wazgār·tiyā, furṣat.* (-in music) *tāl, wazn.* (at all times) *har wakht, har kala.*

Timid, a. *yer·man, harānd, wiswāsī, yere-dūnkai.*

Tin, s. *qal'aī.* (-man) *qal'aī·gar.*

Tinder, s. *khū, khpah, baḍagāl.*

Tinge, s. *rang.* v.a. *rangawul.*

Tingle, v.n. *shṛangedal.* (tickle) *takhnedal.* (with pain) *swal, brekkhedal.*

Tiny, a. *woṛ, woṛkoṭai, pūṭai, kharmandai.*

Tip, s. *sar, peza, tsūka, nūka.*

Tire, v.n. *staṛai-, stomān-, haukah-, māndah-,* etc. *ked.* v.a. *staṛai-,* etc. *k.*

Tiresome, a. *drūnd, grān, rabaṛ·nāk.*

Tithe, s. *'ushr.* (-to servants) *chūngai.*

Titillate, v.n. *takhnedal, koe-, kaha-,* etc. *ked.*

Titillation, s. *takhai, koe, kaha, megī megī.*

Title, s. *nūm, nāma, laqab, khitāb.* (right) *ḥaqq.*

Titter, s. *muskai.* v.n. *musedal.*

Tittle, s. *zarra, khas, pitsānrai, pūṭai, ṭakai.*

Tittle-tattle, s. *gap shap, bak bak, lāp shāp, zwag pak.*

To, p. *ta.* (-day) *nan.* (-morrow) *sabā* or *ṣabāḥ.* (-night) *nan begā, mākkhām.* (-morrow night) *sabā begā.* (-me) *rā ta.* (-thee) *dar ta.* (-him, etc.) *war ta.*

Toad, s. *chīndakh.* (-stool) *kha-areṛai, gū-māndū.*

Toast, v.a. *wrītawul, alwoyal, teyal, talawul.*

Tobacco, s. *tambākū.* (-pipe) *chilam.*

Toe, s. *da kkhpe* or *pkkhe gūta.*

Together, ad. *yo dzāe, dzabla, sara.*

Toil, v.a. *miḥnat-, kokshiksh-, tagāpū-,* etc. *k.*

Toilette, s. *kkhewa, singār.*

Token, s. *nakkha, nikkhān, 'alāmat.*

Tolerate, v.a. *wṛal, zghamal*; *rawā ganral, pregdal, prekkhodal, prekkhal.*

Toll, s. *maḥṣūl, chūngai, tāwān.*

Tomb, s. *qabr, gor, maqbara.* (the niche) *laḥd.* (the tablet) *khaza* or *khāda.*

Tone, s. *zwag, ghag, āwāz, bāng.* (elasticity) *dam.*

Tongs, s. *ambūr.*

Tongue, s. *jiba.*

Tonsil, s. *da jibe laṛ, haḍ.*

Too, ad. *hum, lā.* (-much) *ḍer, ziyāt.*

Tool, s. *kālai, hatiyār, ālat.*

Tooth, s. *ghākkh.* (molar-) *dāṛa, da jāme ghākkh.* (decayed-) *chinjo khwuṛalai ghākkh.* (-pick) *ghākkh ṭanbūnai* or *sūṛa-yūnkai* or *skoyūnkai, khilāl.* (-brush) *miswāk.* (-ache) *ghākkh khūgai, da ghākkh dard.* (-less) *kaṛshap, kanḍās.*

Top, s. *sar, tsūka, peza.* (on-) *dapāsa, da-bāndi, pa porta.* (toy) *tsarkhandūkai, chalkha-ī, churlanda-ī, lāḍū, bahna.*

Topic, s. *mazmūn, manshā, mudd'ā.*

Topknot, s. *tsanra-ī.*

Topsyturvy, a. *naskor, aṛawulai, pa-aṛ·makh.*

Torch, s. *shūsha-ī*; *mashāl.* (-of pine wood) *shonṭa-ī.*

Torment, s. *'azāb, āzār.* v.a. *'azābawul, āzārawul, khūgawul, kaṛawul.*

Torpid, a. *susṯ, laṯ.* (-with cold) *maṟg̠heċ̠han, qaṟqeċ̠han.*

Torrent, s. *dāra, sailāb, nīz* or *niyūz, ċ̠halānda.*

Tortoise, s. *s̱ẖamṣ̱ẖata-ī, kaṣ̱ẖap.*

Torture, s. *'azāb.* (instruments of-) *ṣ̱ẖikanja, pāna, kāṯ, ṯsarkh.* v.a. *'azābawul; pāna warkawul, pa ṣ̱ẖikanjo-, pa kāṯ-, pa ṯsarkh-,* etc. *kheȷawul.*

Toss, v.a. *g̠hurzawul, āċ̠hawul, lawastal.* v.n. *g̠hurzedal.* (-money) v.a. *ṣ̱ẖīr k̠haṯ k.*

Total, a. *ṯol, amānī, pūrah, tamām, wāṟah.* s. *ṯol ṯāl, jam'a.*

Totally, ad. *amānī, sarāsar.* (in comp.) *tak-, ṯap-,* etc.

Totter, v.n. *ṯaparedal.*

Touch, v.a. *lās lagawul* or *-warwṟal; masa-, lams-,* etc. *k.* v.n. *lagedal, jangedal, blodal, blosedal.*

Touchy, a. *tod-,* or *tund mizāj.*

Tough, a. *klak, sak̠ht, ṯīng.*

Tour, s. *daur, safar, gakkht; sail.*

Tow, s. *saṉr, da saṉro paṯ.*

Towards, p. *k̠hwā ta, lorī ta, mak̠h ta, ḏaḏe ta, palaw ta,* etc. (-me) *rāhīsta.* (-thee) *dar hīsta.* (-him, her, it, them) *war hīsta.*

Towel, s. *dast·māl, rūmāl.*

Tower, s. *bruj* or *burj.*

Town, s. *kkhahr, kilai, dih.*

Townsman, s. *kkhahr·wāl, kilī·wāl, da kkhahr-, da kilī-,* etc. *saṟai.*

Toy, s. *da lobe kālai.* v.a. *lobe k.; nāz k.*

Trace, s. *nakkha, darak, belga.* v.a. *belga bāsal—yastal; nakhkkha* or *naqs̱ẖa kāyal —kkhkal* or *līkal.*

Track, s. *pal, manḏ, darak; lār, rakkh.* v.a. *pal-,* etc. *goral—līdal-, -mūndal, -laṯawul,* etc.

Tract, s. *maidān, zmaka; mulk, hiwād.* (treatise) *risāla, nāma.*

Tractable, a. *narm, g̠harīb, mulā-im.*

Trade, s. *saudāgarī, warkṟah rākṟah, lāgī, saudā; kasb, kār.* v.a. *saudāgarī-,* etc. *k.*

Trader, s. *saudāgar, wapārī, banjārī, parānċ̠hah.* (travelling-) *rawānī, lohānī.*

Tradesman, s. *kasb·gar, peṣ̱ẖa·war.*

Tradition, s. *ḥadīṣ, k̠habara, naql, wayai.*

Traditional, a. } *wayali* or *rāg̠hlali k̠habara,*
Traditionary, } *da peṟe pa peṟo k̠habara.*

Traduce, v.a. *tor-, tuhmat-,* etc. *pore k., peg̠hor warkawul, bad·nāmawul, kagal, g̠handal.*

Traffic, v.a. (*v.* Trade.)

Tragical, a. *g̠ham·nāk, haibat·nāk, haul·nāk.*

Trail, v.a. *rākāgal—rākkhkal, kaṣ̱ẖāla k.*

Train, v.a. *āmokhtah k.; bāolī warkawul; kkhayal—kkhowul, lwalawul; pālal.*

Train, s. (escort) *swarlī, jalab.* (-of a dress) *laman.* (series) *qaṯār.*

Trait, s. *'ādat; nakkha; karkkha.*

Traitor, s. *namak ḥarām, ṯag, darg̠hal.*

Trammel, s. *jāl, lūma, dām; paikaṟa.*

Trample, v.a. *laṯāṟawul, kkhpo lāndi-, pāċmāl-, g̠hwa-emanḏ-,* etc. *k., g̠hobalawul.*

Trance, s. *parg̠haz, da periyāno g̠hoṯa, bek̠hūdī.*

Tranquil, a. *qalār, walāṟ, ārām.*

Tranquilize, v.a. *ārāmawul, qalārawul, saṟawul, walāṟawul.*

Transact, v.a. *mu'āmala-, kār-, rozgār-,* etc. *k., ċ̠halawul, lagawul, jārī k., rawānawul.*

Transaction, s. *kār, rozgār, m'uāmala, k̠habara.*

Transfer, v.a. *wṟal, rasawul; spāral, pāslawul.*

Transfix, v.a. *ore pore tetsal* or *-sīk̠hal, pewdal.*

Transgress, v.a. *mātawul; k̠hatā k.*

Transient, a. *teredūnai, nā·pāedār, fānī.*

Translate, v.a. *tarjuma k., naql k.*

Transmit, v.a. *āstawul, legal, rasawul.*

Transparent, a. *ṣāf, s̱ẖaffāf; bārīk.*

Transpire, v.n. *tsargandedal, kkhkārah ked., watal, khatal, m'alūmedal.*
Transport, v.a. *wral, yosal; botlal—bīwul; legdal—lekkhal; jalā-watan k.*
Transpose, v.a. *arawul, badlawul, gadwad-awul.*
Transverse, a. *tratskan, kog.*
Trap, s. *dām.* (net-) *jāl, dwah gaza.* (noose-) *lūma, lūmaka, ghundārai.* (springe) *lat, talaka, qurqa-ī.* (catch-) *park, honrā.* (ambush) *psūnai, tsawai, putgana-ī.* v.a. *nīwul, nkkhlawul.*
Trappings, s. *kālī, asbāb,* (armour) *drasta, wasla.* (horse-) *bargastawān,*
Trash, s. *balāe batar, khadzala, khāshāk.*
Travel, v.a. *safar-, sail-, musāfirī-,* etc. *k.*
Traveller, s. *musāfir.*
Tray, s. *khwān, khwāncha, sīnī.*
Treacherous, a. *be-īmān, be-wafā, darghal-bāz.*
Treachery, s. *be-īmānī, darghal-tob.*
Treacle, s. *gūra, awlū, kak; tiriyāq.*
Tread, v.a. *kkhpa-* or *pkkha-, qadam-,* etc. *gdal,* or *-īgdal,* or *-kkhkegdal.* (-upon) *latārah-, lat pat-, kkhpo lāndi-,* etc. *k.* (as birds) v.n. *khatal.* (-corn) v.a. *ghobal k.* (after one) *pala pase tlal.*
Treason, s. *namak harāmī, pasāt, darghal-bāzī, ghadr,*
Treasure, s. *khazāna, ganj, daulat.*
Treasurer, s. *khazānchī.*
Treasury, s. *khazāna, tūng; makhzan.*
Treat, v.a. (parley) *sawāl dzawāb-, khabara-,* etc. *k.* (use) *sulūk-, mu'āmala-,* etc. *k.* (guest) *ziyāfat-, melmastiyā-, sat-,* etc. *k.* (-well) *kkhah sulūk k.* (-badly) *bad sulūk k.* (-a disease) *chāra-, 'ilāj-,* etc. *k* (manage) *jorawul, chalawul.* (mention) *yādawul, bayānawul.*
Treaty, s. *'ahad, qaul-qarār, tara, bandanr.*
Treble, a. *dre bragh, dre chand.* (in music) *dzīr* or *zīl.*

Tree, s. *wana, drakhta.* (small-) *dakai.* (Mulberry-) *tūt.* (Sissoo-) *shewa.* (Acacia modesta) *palosa.* (Acacia Arabica) *kīkar.* (Pine-) *nakkhtar.* (Cedar-) *diyār.* (Plane-) *chinār.* (Melia sempervirens) *shanda-ī, bukāyanra.* (Seris-) *srīkh.* (Willow-) *wala.* (Olive-) *kkhona.* (Tamarisk-) *ghaz.* (Bauhinia variegata) *koliyār,* etc. etc.
Tremble, v.n. *rapedal, regdedal, larzedal.*
Tremendous, a. *haibat-nāk; bashpar, loe.*
Tremor, s. *larza, gagarodza.*
Trembling, s. *rapedūn, larzedana.*
Trench, s. *kanda, kaha-ī.*
Trencher, s. *kkhānak, pīna, taghār.*
Trepidation, s. *larza, rapedana, gagarodza.*
Trespass, s. *gunāh, wabāl, taqsīr, khatā.*
Trial, s. *āzmekkht, imtihān.*
Triangle, s. *dre gokkha, musallas.*
Tribe, s. *qām* or *qaum, firqa, tabār, khel.*
Tribulation, s. *gham, randz, mīrtsī, paskhāk, āfat, balā.*
Tribunal, s. *mahkam, 'adālat.*
Tribute, s. *pekkh-kakkh, khirāj, bāj, 'ushr.*
Trice, s. *pal, lahza.*
Trick, s. *fareb, lamghara-ī, ghulat, tagī, chal.* (habit) *'ādat, khoe.* v.a. *tagal, ghulawul.*
Trickle, v.n. *tsātsedal.*
Triennial, a. *dre kālanai.*
Trifle, s. *khasanrai, nā-tsīz, lā shai, hets.*
Trifle, v.a. *lobe k., 'abas k., jakh wahal.*
Trifling, a. *spuk, khushai, be-hūdah, pūch.*
Trim, v.a. *jorawul, atsanral, drust k.*
Trinity, s. *taslīs, salāsa.*
Trinket, s. *kālai, zewar, gānra.*
Trip, v.a. *tīndak-, takar-, budrī-, kangas-, skandarī-,* etc. *khwural.*
Tripe, s. *ūjarai, kulma.*
Triple, a. *dre bragh, dre chand, dre tarafah.*
Tripod, s. *dre pāya, darbala-ī.*
Trite, a. *zor, pakhwānai, mashhūr.*

Triturate, v.a. *oṛawul, oṛah-, maidah-*, etc. *k. dalawul, dzabal.*

Trivial, a. *spuk, khushai, adnā.*

Triumph, v.a. *barai mūndal*, or *-gaṭal.* (joy over enemy) *wiyāṛ-, sakha-*, etc. *k.*

Troop, s. *paṛk, ghol, galla, tanba, ṭol, ṭolgai.* (-of horse) *risāla.*

Trooper, s. *bār-gīr, turk sawār.*

Trophy, s. *ghanīmat, lūṭ, shūka, yzṭa.*

Trot, v.a. *pa ḍugland-, pa dachko-*, etc. *tlal.*

Trouble, s. *rabaṛ, mihnat, diqq-dārī, randz, āzār, dzaur.* v.a. *rabṛawul, āzārawul, diqq k.*

Troublesome, a. *rabṛūnai, rabaṛ-nāk, diqq-dār, janjālī.*

Trough, s. *pūl, nāwa, tarnāo.*

Trowel, s. *karanḍa-ī.*

Trowsers, s. *paṛtūg, shalwār, tambān.* (-band) *paṛtūghākkh.* (-hem) *baḍa.* (-fork) *khakkhtag.* (-leg) *pāentsa.*

Truant, a. *gashtai, khushai, hujrai.*

Truce, s. *m'arika, rogha joṛa, ṣulha.*

Trudge, v.n. *ṭaparedal, ro ro tlal.*

True, a. *rikkhtiyā, rikkhtīnai, sūchah, karah, rāst, pokh, pūrah.*

Truly, ad. *pa rikkhtiyā ; yara.*

Trumpet, s. *tūrai, būq.*

Trunk, s. (box) *ṣandūq, tauṛra-ī.* (tree) *mūnd, tanga, garga.* (body) *ṣūrat, tan.* (snout) *khaṛtam, sūnḍak.*

Trust, s. *bāwar, i'tibār, sā-wīsā, khal ; umed, takiya, āsra, tawakkul ; amānat, hawāla ; por, qarz, nasiyah.*

Trust, v.a. *bāwar-*, etc. *k.* or *laral ; amānat-*, etc. *ydal* or *īydal, spāral, pāslawul ; por-*, etc. *warkawul.*

Trustee, s. *zimma-dār, amānat-dār.*

Trusty, a. *i'tibārī, īmān-dār, wafā-dār.*

Truth, s. *rikkhtiyā, rāstī.*

Try, v.a. *āzmāyal* or *āzmoyal, āzmekkht k., s'aī-, kokshiksh-*, etc. *k., was chalawul ; 'adālat k.*

Tub, s. *taghār, ḍol, satal, gaḍhal.*

Tube, s. *shpela-ī, nala, tsūkkhka.*

Tuesday, s. *naha, sih shamba.*

Tuft, s. *zunḍa-ī, ghūncha.* (-of hair) *tsaṛa-ī* or *tsauṛa-ī ; parcham* or *parkham.* (bird's) *chār khwalak.* (-of grass, etc.) *kalokkhta.*

Tug, v.a. *rākāgal—rākkhkal.*

Tuition, s. *tarbiyat, t'alīm ; parwarish.*

Tumble, v.n. *prewatal, lwedal,* (roll on the ground) *rghaṛedal—rghakkhtal, lots pots k.* v.a. *bāzī-garī-, naṭ-bāzī-*, etc. *k.*

Tumour, s. *pāṛsob, ghumba, ghunḍārai, stagh.*

Tumult, s. *balwā, ghulghula, zwag-zūg, shor, shor-shaghab.*

Tune, s. *sarod, tarāna, badala, wazn.*

Turban, s. *pagṛa-ī, paṭkai, dastār, manḍos.* (end of-) *shaklai, shamla.*

Turbid, a. *kha-aṛ, lāha-jan, khaṭolai.*

Turbulence, s. *pasāt, shor.*

Turbulent, a. *pasātī, shor-nāk.*

Turf, s. *chūm, lūṭa, kulūkh.*

Turmeric, s. *korkamān.*

Turn, s. *tsarkh, daur.* (twist) *tāo, wal, pech. marwat.* (time) *wār, guzār ; heṛ, plā, dzal.* (walk) *sail, gakkht.* (bend) *kaglech, hālkūch.*

Turn, v.n. *girzedal, tsarkhedal, churledal, āwukkhtal, badledal.* (-back) *jārwatal, stūnedal*, or *stanedal, pastanah ked.* (become) *kedal, shwal.* v.a. *girzawul, tsarkhawul, churlawul.* (-back) *stūnawul.* (-over) *arawul.* (-out) *sharal.* (-from) *shā k., pregdal.*

Turnip, s. *ṭepaṛ, shalgham.*

Turpentine, s. *rāndzaṛah.*

Turret, s. *b:uj ; kangūra.*

Tutor, s. *ākhūn, ustād, mu'allim.*

Twang, s. *ṭang, trang.* v.n. *ṭangedal, trangedal.*

Tweezers, s. *nūtsai.*

Twelve, a. *dwah·las.* (twelfth) *dwah·lasam.* (-month) *kāl, dwah·las myāshti.*

Twenty, a. *shil.* (twentieth) *shilam.* (-one) *yo·wīsht.* (-two) *dwah·wīsht,* etc.

Twice, ad. *dwah hera, -guzāra, -dzala, -wāra,* etc.

Twig, s. *lakkhta.*

Twilight, s. *shafaq; sapede.*

Twins, s. *jora, bragh.* (one of-) *braghūnai.*

Twine, s. *mazai, tār.*

Twine, v.a. *pech-, tāo-, wal-,* etc. *khwural.*

Twinkle, s. (of time) *pal, lahza.* (-of a star) *palwasha.* v.n. *dzalkedal* or *dzaledal.*

Twirl, v.a. *churlawul, tsarkhawul, tsandal* or *tsandawul.*

Twist, s. *pech, wal, tāo, marwat.* v.a. *pech-,* etc. *warkawul.* (fold) *nghakkhtal.* (bend) *ṭīṭawul, krīngawul.*

Twitter, v.a. *chaur chaur-,* etc. *k.*

Two, a. *dwah, dwe.*

Type, s. *nakkha, 'alāmat, noga, misāl.*

Tyrannize, v.a. *jabr-, zulm-,* etc. *k.*

Tyranny, s. *zulm, zor, ziyātī, zabardastī, jafā.*

Tyrant, s. *zālim, jābir, jafā·kār.*

Tyro, s. *shāgird, mubtadī, nawai āmokhtah.*

U.

Udder, s. *ghulāndza.*

Ugly, a. *bad·sūrat, bad·shakal, mushād.*

Ulcer, s. *nāsūr; yaga.*

Ultimate, a. *ākhir, wrustanai, pasīn.*

Ultimately, ad. *ākhir, wrusto, pas.*

Umbrage, s. *sorai* or *siwrai, gūr, gaur, chatr.* (offence) *marawar·tiyā, mānrai; mīrtsī.*

Umbrella, s. *chatra-ī.*

Umpire, s. *mandz·garai, munsif.*

Un-, neg. prefix. (in comp.) *be-, nā-, lā-,* etc.

Unable, a. *nā·turān, nā·qābil.*

Unanimous, a. *yo zrah, yo jihat, yo ittifāq, pa yawe khule* or *-jibe.*

Unavailing, a. *'abas, be·fā,ida, nā·pakār.*

Unawares, ad. *nātsāpa, nāgāh, yak lakhta.*

Unbecoming, a. *nā·lā-iq, nā·munāsib, na-kkhanai, nā·kkhandah.*

Unbelief, s. *kufr, be·īmānī, kāfir·tob.*

Unbeliever, s. *kāfir, be·dīn, be·īmān.*

Unbosom, v.a. *prānatal, wayal, parda liri-,* or *porta k., tsargandawul.*

Unbroken, a. *amānī, pūrah, salāmat.*

Unbutton, v.a. *tanra-ī-, palwākkha-, ghūṭa-ī-, gharāsha-,* etc. *prānatal* or *spardal.*

Unceremonious, a. *khamsor, be·takalluf.*

Uncertain, a. *nā·m'alūm, be·ṭikānā.*

Unchaste, a. *bad laman, shatāh, nā·pāk.*

Uncircumcised, a. *nā·solat* or *nā·sunnat, shopā.*

Uncivil, a. *be·adab, be·makh, lwār, dzaban.*

Uncivilized, a. *lwār, pūhar, shār.*

Uncle, s. (paternal) *trah, kākā, ākā.* (maternal) *māmā, nūc.*

Unclean, a. *palīt, nā·pāk, khiran, murdār.*

Unclouded, a. *shīn, sāf.*

Uncomfortable, a. *be·ārām, nā·khwakkh.*

Uncommon, a. *nādir, matrah, kamtar.*

Unconcerned, a. *be·parwā, be·khabar, be·gham, be·fikr.*

Uncouth, a. *lwār, pūhar, shār, dzaban.*

Uncover, v.a. *barbandawul, bargholai-, sar·pokkh-,* etc. *liri k.* (the head) *sar tor k.* (the face) *be·satr-, be·parde-,* etc. *k.* (a roof) *spardal.*

Unction, s. *mālish, mukkhana.*

Unctuous, a. *ghwar.*

Uncultivated, a. *ghair ābād, shār, wujār, wairān.*

Undecided, a. *wiswāsī, andekkh·man; nā·tamām, nīmgarai, nīma·khwā.*

Undefiled, a. *pāk, pākīzah, sāf.*

Undeniable, a. *lā·radd, qat'a-ī.*

Under, ad. and p. *lāndi, dalāndi, kkhkata, kkhkiya.* (-part) s. *talai, lāndi khwā.* (-most) a. *lāndīnai, kkhatanai.*
Undergo, v.a. *wṛal, zghamal, khwuṛal.*
Underhand, ad. *pa puṭa, pa tara-ī, pa parde.*
Undermine, v.a. *surang wahal; naṛawul; wekh-, mūnḍ-,* etc. *wahal* or *khejawul.*
Underneath, ad. *dalāndi, kkhkata, kkhkiya.*
Underrate, v.a. *lāndi-, spuk-, nā-tsīz-,* etc. *ganṛal, ghandal, kagal.*
Understand, v.a. *pohedal, pahmedal, rasedal.*
Understanding, s. *poha, pahm, 'aql; joṛikkht, maṣlaḥat.*
Undertake, v.a. *ākhistal, porta k., khejawul, kawul, chalawul, lās lagawul.*
Undertaking, s. *kār, mu'āmala.*
Undervalue, v.a. *spuk-, kam-, nā-tsīz-,* etc. *ganṛal.*
Underwood, s. *jangai, dzangal, jāṛ, karkanṛ.*
Undivided, a. *pūrah, tamām, amānī.*
Undo, v.a. *spaṛdal, prānatal, khwarawul.*
Undone, a. *spaṛdalai* or *spaṛai; wrān, kharāb.*
Undoubted, a. *yaqīn, be-shakk aw shubha.*
Undress, v.a. *jāme-,* etc. *bāsal—yastal.*
Undulate, v.n. *laharedal, ghurzedal.*
Uneasy, a. *be-ārām, nā-qalār; andekkh-man, wiswāsī.*
Unemployed, a. *kariyāb, khushai, be-kār, aṭāl, wazgār.*
Uneven, a. *lwaṛ jawar, kandai kawdarai, kkhkata porta, nā-hawār.*
Unexampled, a. *be-siyāl, lā-sānī, be-miṣāl.*
Unexpected, a. *nā-gahān, nā-gumān.*
Unexpectedly, ad. *nā-tsāpa, nāgāh.*
Unfair, a. *nā-rāst, nā-ṣāf.*
Unfaithful, a. *be-īmān, be-wafā.*
Unfeeling, a. *be-dard, kānṛai zṛah, be-raḥm.*
Unfit, a. *nā-lā-iq, nā-qābil.*
Unfold, v.a. *prānatal, spaṛdal, tsargandawul, kkhkārah k* v.n. *khwaredal, ghwaredal, ṭūkedal.*

Unforeseen, a. *nā-m'alūm, nā-līdah.*
Unfortified, a. *be-panāh, khushai.*
Unfortunate, a. *kam-bakht, bad-naṣīb, lā-chār, stāra prewatai.*
Unfounded, a. *bāṭil, be-hūdah.*
Unfruitful, a. *shanḍ, be-mewa, nā-mewa-dār.*
Unfurnished, a. *khushai, be-sāz, be da kālo.*
Ungird, v.a. *mlā prānatal.*
Ungodly, a. *be-dīn, nā-khudā-tars.*
Ungovernable, a. *sar-zor, sar-kakkh, yāghī.*
Ungrateful, a. *namak ḥarām, nā-shukr-guzār, nā-ḥaqq-shinās.*
Unguarded, a. *be-khabar, ghāfil.*
Unhappy, a. *khapah, malūl, dil-tang, nā-khwakkh, nā-kkhād.*
Unhealthy, a. *nā-joṛ; nā-muwāfiq.*
Unheard, a. *nā-āwredah.*
Unholy, a. *ḥarām, nā-pāk, bilmāz, nā-rawā.*
Uniform, a. *barābar, sam, hawār, yo-shān.* s. *jāma, joṛa, libās.*
Unimaginable, a. *be-qiyās.*
Uninhabited, a. *ghair-ābād, wairān, wujāṛ.*
Union, s. *joṛ, pewastūn, taṛūn; rogha, joṛa, ittipāq; joṛikkht, malgar-tiyā.*
Unit, s. *yo.* (Unity) s. *yo-wālai, yak-tā-ī.*
Unite, v.a. *joṛawul, lagawul, pewand k.*
United, a. *pewastah; yo zṛah, yo jihat.*
Unitedly, ad. *pa ittipāq sara.*
Universal, a. *kullī, amānī, muṭlaq.*
Universally, ad. *bil-kull, sarāsar, tamāmī.*
Universe, s. *duniyā, jahān, naṛa-ī.*
Unjust, a. *be-inṣāf; nā-ḥaqq.*
Unknowingly, ad. *pa nā-dānī sara, nā-pohī sara, be-khabarī sara.*
Unlawful, a. *ḥarām, nā rawā, nā-ḥaqq.*
Unlearned, a. *jāhil, nā-lwustai, ammī.*
Unless, ad. *magar* or *mangar, ganṛa* or *kanṛa* or *ka na.*
Unload, v.a. *bār-kūzawul, ta-ashawul.*
Unlucky, a. *kam-bakht, be-naṣīb, shūm-bakht, bad-bakht, stāra prewatai.*

Unmarried, a. *lawand, nā·wādah karai.* (f.) *peghla, nā·wādah·shiwi.*
Unmeaning, a. *a. be·m'anī, be·hūdah.*
Unmoved, a. *pāedār, qā-im, mazbūt, ting.*
Unoccupied, a. *khālī, khushai*; *wazgār.*
Unpack, v.a. *prānatal, spardal, ghwarawul.*
Unprotected, a. *khushai, be·panāh, be·wasīla.*
Unravel, v.a. *prānatal, spardal, ghwarawul, khwarawul, wīrawul.*
Unreasonable, a. *be·dzāyah, nā·munāsib.*
Unripe, a. *om, nīma·khwā, nīm·pukhtah, nīmgarai, kachah, khām.*
Unrivalled, a. *be·siyāl, lā·sānī, be·misāl.*
Unroll, v.a. *prānatal, spardal, ghwarawul, khwarawul, wīrawul.* v.n. *ghwaredal, wīredal, khwaredal.*
Unruly, a. *sar·zor, sar·kakkh.*
Unsafe, a. *khatr·nāk, be·amn.*
Unsatisfied, a. *nā·rāz, nā·khwakkh.*
Unsatisfactory, a. *nā·sāz, nā·pīrzo.*
Unseasonable, a. *be·dzāe, be·tāng, be·khratai, be·wakht.*
Unseen, a. *put, ghā-ib, nā·līdah.*
Unserviceable, a. *nā·pakār, nākārah.*
Unsheltered, a. *khushai, be·panāh.*
Unshod, a. *abl, kkhpa·* or *pkkha·abla.*
Unsuccessful, a. *pa-ar, bāelūnkai.*
Untamed, a. *dzangalī, wahshī*; *lwār, dzaban.*
Untidy, a. *shadal, pūhar, shārwlai·wārwlai.*
Untie, v.a. *prānatal, spardal.*
Until, ad. *tar—pore, tso chi.* (-when?) *tar kala pore.* (-now) *tar osa pore.*
Untimely, a. *be·tāng, be·wakht, be·khratai.*
Unto, p. *ta, la, lara, wa—ta,* etc. (-me) *rā ta, rā lara, lā la, lā lara, mā ta,* etc. (-thee) *dar ta, da la, dar lara, tā ta, wa tā ta, tā wa tā,* etc. (-him, her, it, them) *war ta, wa la, war lara, haghah ta, hagho ta,* or *-la,* or *-lara.*
Untold, a. *be·hisāb, be·shumār*; *nā·wayalai, nā·guftah.*
Untoward, a. *nā·kārah*; *arawulai*; *bad.*
Untrue, a. *darogh·jan, jūtah, nā·rāst.*
Untruth, s. *darogh, kizb, nā·rāstī.*
Untwist, v.a. *spardal, prānatal, khwurawul.*
Unusual, a. *kam·ist'imāl, kam·chalan, shāzz.*
Unveil, v.a. *be·satr-, be·parde-,* etc. *k., bar·bandawul.*
Unwary, a. *be·khabar, ghāfil.*
Unwearied, a. *tāzah, nā·starai, hosā.*
Unwell, a. *nā·jor, nā·rogh.*
Unwieldy, a. *loe, ghat, star, drūnd.*
Unwilling, a. *nā·rāz, daregh·man.*
Unworthy, a. *nā·lā-iq, nā·pīrzo.*
Up, p. *bāndi, porta, pās.* (-on) *pa-, par-, pri-,* etc. *bāndi.* (-to) *-ta, -la, -lara, -pore.* (-and down) *lar bar, kūz pās, kkhkata porta, lāndi bāndi, lwar jawar.*
Upbraid, v.a. *malāmatawul, peghorawul, taqawul, ratal, tratal, dāral.*
Uphold, v.a. *sambālawul, khejawul, porta nīwul, pushtī-, komak-,* etc. *warkawul.*
Uplift, v.a. *khejawul, porta ākhistal* or *k.*
Upon, ad. *bāndi, dapāsa, dabāndi, pa·bāndi, pri·bāndi.*
Upper, a. *bar, pāsanai, portanai.*
Upright, a. *walār, negh, jig, lak*; *rikkhtīnai, rāst·man, nek.*
Uprightness, s. *walār·tiyā, negh·wālai,* etc.; *nekī, rikkhtīn·tob, rāstī.*
Uproar, s. *balwā, ghāl·o·ghūl, shor·shaghab.*
Upset, v.a. *naskorawul, arawul, narawul, āchawul, ghurzawul*; *toyawul, sandzal.* v.n. *naskoredal, naredal, lwedal, prewatal*; *toedal.*
Upshot, s. *anjām, gata. hāsil.*
Upside-down, a. *naskor, arawulai.*
Upwards, ad. *pās, porta, bar*; *ziyāt.*
Urbanity, s. *makhawarī, nek sulūkī.*
Urge, v.a. *zoral, tezal, chalawul, rawānawul*; *tākīd-, taqāza-,* etc. *k.*; *lamsawul.*
Urgent, a. *zarūr, tang, sakht.*

Urine, s. *baul, mitiyāza, peshāb.*
Usage, s. *sulūk.* (custom) *rasm, dastūr.* (habit) *'ādat, chalan.* (rule) *ā-īn, qā'ida.*
Use, s. *kār, fā-ida*; *'amal, ist'imāl.*
Use, v.a. *pa·kār rāwṛal, lagawul, chalawul*; *'amal-*, etc. *k.*; *sulūk-*, etc. *k.*
Useful, a. *fā-ida·man, sūd·man, pa·kār.*
Useless, a. *nā·kārah, 'abaṣ, khushai, be·fā-ida.*
Usual, a. *ist'imālī, jārī, chalanī.* (as-) *pa·dastūr.*
Usually, ad. *akṣar, aghlab.*
Usurer, s. *sūd·khor, ribā·khor.*
Usurp, v.a. *shūkawul, nā·ḥaqq ākhistal, pa·zor-, pa·zabardastī-*, etc. *-lāndi k., -dzān ta ākhistal.*
Usurpation, s. *shūka, pa·zor-*, etc. *ākhistana.*
Usury, s. *sūd, ribā.*
Utmost, a. *nihāyat, ḥadd.*
Utter, a. *nihāyat, bashpaṛ, amānī.*
Utter, v.a. *wayal, lal, lawdal*; *chalawul, jārī k.*
Utterly, ad. *sarāsar, amānī, tamāmī.*
Uvula, s. *kūmai, laṛ.*
Uxorious, a. *kkhadza·dost* or *·parast.*

V.

Vacant, a. *ta-ash, khālī, khushai.*
Vacate, v.a. *ta-ashawul, khālī-*, etc. *k.*
Vacation, s. *t'aṭīl, farāghat, wazgār·tiyā, furṣat.*
Vagabond, s. *lawanḍ, lūtsak, chaṭ, kūtsa·gard, hujrai, awārah, qachar.*
Vagary, s. *khiyāl, wahm.*
Vague, a. *nā·m'alūm, khushai.*
Vain, a. *'abaṣ, bāṭil, be·fā-ida*; *wiyāṛ·jan, bādī, khpul·rāe, khāntamā, bād·hawā.*
Vainly, ad. *'abaṣ, be·fā-ida.*
Valiant, a. *maṛanai, tūrzan, zṛah·war, bātor. dilāwar, bahādur, zmarai.*
Valid, a. *maẓbūṭ, maḥkam, qā-im*; *joṛ, drust, rikkhtīnai, zbād.*
Valley, s. *dara, sama, maidān.*
Valour, s. *maṛāna, tūrzan·tob, zṛah·war·tob, maṛanī·tob, zmarī·tob, bahādurī.*
Valuable, a. *qīmat·nāk, grān bahā.*
Value, v.a. *bai'a-, qīmat-*, etc. *taṛal* or *-lagawul* or *k.*; *qadr-, 'izzat-*, etc. *pejandal, ganṛal.*
Valve, s. *ghwagai, warkha*; *war, tamba, pala.*
Van, s. *pesh·khaima*; *harāwul, qarāwul.*
Vanish, v.n. *puṭedal, lwukkhtal—lwuṛedal, wrukedal*; *ālwatal*; *wuchedal.*
Vanity, s. *wiyāṛ, dam, lāpa shāpā*; *be·hūdagī, spuk·tiyā*; *khpul·sarī, bād hawā-ī.*
Vanquish, v.a. *pa-aṛ-, māt-, lar-, lāndi-*, etc. *k., barai mūndal.*
Vapid, a. *be·khwand, balmagai, balmangah.*
Vapour, s. *bukhār, bṛās*; *laṛa*; *lūgai*; *ghubār.*
Variable, a. *nā·qalār, nā·pāedār, nīma khwā.*
Variance, s. *dukkhmanī, mīrtsī, kharkhakkha*; *patna, pasāt, 'aks*; *gwākkh*; *ẓidd.*
Variation, s. *biyal·wālai, farq.*
Variegated, a. *rangā·rang, brag·yālai.*
Variety, s. *rang pa rang, raqam pa raqam*, etc.
Various, a. *biyal·biyal, rangā·rang, shānā·shān, judā·judā, dzane.*
Varnish, v.a. *rangawul, rang lagawul, baṭī ḍakawul. lāk-, slekkh-*, etc. *lagawul.*
Vary, v.n. *badledal, āwukkhtal, girzedal, biyaledal.* v.a. *badlawul, āwukkhtal*, etc.
Vassal, s. *humsāyah, faqīr, r'aīyat.*
Vast, a. *loe, ghaṭ, star, 'aẓīm.*
Vastly, ad. *nihāyata, be·shāna.*
Vat, s. *ḥauẓ.*
Vault, s. *gunbata, qubba.* (cellar) *tah khāna.* (cave) *smats, ghār.* (tomb) *qabar, laḥad.*
Vault, v.a. *ghurzang-, tīndak-, ṭop-, khachānai-*, etc. *wahal, dāngal*; *gunbata-*, etc. *joṛawul.*

Vegetable, s. *wākkhah, ḍakai, būṭai.* (greens) *sāg, sabzī.*
Vegetate, v.n. *ṭūkedal, zarghūnedal.*
Vehement, a. *sakht, tod, tund, tez.*
Vehicle, s. *gāḍa-ī*; *swarī* or *sparī.* (means) *m'arifat, wasīla, wāsiṭa.* (in medicine) *badragha* or *badraga.*
Veil, v.a. *parda-, maizar-, oḍana-ī-, bolqa* or *burq'a-*, etc. *pa-sarawul, satr pokkhal* or *k.*, *puṭawul, pokkhal.*
Vein, s. *rag, nas.* (jugular) *kkhāh rag.*
Velocity, s. *garand-wālai, za-ar-* or *zir-tiyā, jaltiyā.*
Velvet, s. *bakhmal, makhmal.*
Venal, a. *zar dost, zar parast.*
Vend, v.a. *khartsawul, ploral* or *prolal, prowul.*
Venerable, a. *zbarg, loe.*
Venerate, v.a. *manal, zbarg ganral.* v.n. *grohedal.*
Venery, s. *gho, ghowuna, kor-wālai.* *jimā'a, sūhbat.* (chase) *kkhkār.*
Venesection, s. *rag wahana.*
Venetian, s. *kaṛka-ī.*
Vengeance, s. *badal, qiṣāṣ*; *qahr, qiyāmat, balāe.* (to take-) v.a. *badal-*, etc. *ākhistal.* (with-) *pa qahr.*
Venial, a. *da bukkhalo, da pulawulo*; *rawā.*
Venom, s. *zahr.*
Venomous, a. *zahr-nāk, zahr-dār.*
Vent, s. *sūṛa, khula, lār, war.* (-of a chimney) *dūd-* or *lū-kakkh.* (-of a canal) *warkh, ghwayai.* (to give-) v.a. *khalāṣawul, pregdal, prekkhodal, prekkhal.*
Ventilator, s. *bād-kakkh, bād-rau.*
Venture, s. *khaṭra.* (chance) *daw.* (fate) *naṣīb.* (at a-) *pa tawakkul.* v.a. *himmat-, qaṣd-*, etc. *k.*; *daw k.*
Venturesome, a. *himmatī, himmat-nāk, bakhtbāz.*
Venus, s. (star) *gūp, da melmana starga, zuhra.*
Veracity, s. *rikkhtīn-tob, rāstī, ḥaqq.*
Verb, s. *f'il.* (active-) *f'il i mut'addī.* (passive-) *f'il i majhūl.* (neuter-) *f'il i lāzimī.*
Verbal, a. *zabānī, wayalai.* (-noun, active participle) *ism i fā'il.* (-gerund) *ism i maṣdar.* (present participle) *ḥāṣil bil maṣdar.*
Verbatim, ad. *khabara pa khabare, ḥarf pa ḥarf, ṭakai pa ṭakī, ḥarfan ḥarfan.*
Verdant, a. *shīn, zarghūn, tar o tāzah.*
Verdict, s. *ḥukm, fatwā, faiṣal.*
Verdigris, s. *zangār.*
Verdure, s. *shīn-wālai, shīn wākkhah, sabzī.*
Verge, s. *ghāṛa, morga, tsanḍa, laman, ja-ī.*
Verge, v.n. *girzedal, ma-ilān ked.*, *rasedal, lagedal, jārwatal, āwukkhtal.*
Verify, v.a. *rikkhtīnai-, zbād-, taḥqīq-*, etc. *k.*
Verily, ad. *rikkhtiyā, yara.*
Verity, s. *rikkhtiyā, rikkhtīn-tob, rāstī.*
Vermicelli, s. *māeche.*
Vermin, s. *mozī dzanāwar, chinjī-minjī, khazande-mazande, mlakh-magak*, etc.
Vernacular, s. *mulkī, waṭanī, wilāyatī*; *da waṭan wrāsha* or *-jiba.*
Verse, s. *naẓm, sh'ir, bait.* (-of Quran) *āyat.*
Version, s. *naql, tarjuma.*
Vertigo, s. *girzedana da sar, akar, pa stargo tyāra, sar churlāi* or *-girzai.*
Very, ad. *ḍer, ziyāt.* (this-) *bedū, pa ṭakī.*
Vesicle, s. *tanrāka.*
Vespers, s. *nmākkhām.*
Vessel, s. *lokkhai, kaṭwa-ī.* (blood-) *rag.* (boat) *beṛa-ī, jahāz.*
Vestibule, s. *manḍaw, dahlīz.*
Vestige, s. *nakkha, pal, ṭakai.*
Vesture, s. *aghostan, nwarai, pokkhāk, jāma.*
Vetch, s. *chanra, moṭ, kṛāk.*
Veteran, a. *zoṛ, pokh, pūrah.*
Vex, v.a. *pūrawul, ṭongawul, rabṛawul, kaṛawul.*
Vexation, s. *ṭongāṛa, rabaṛ, khapagī, diqqat.*

Vexatious, a. *rabaṛ-nāk, khūg-nāk, janjālī, āzār rasawūnkai.*
Vial, s. *kkhīkkha.*
Vibrate, v.n. *rapedal, regdedal, pṛakedal; zangal, zangedal, kkhoredal.*
Vice, s. *badī, 'aib, sharārat.* (instrument) *zambūr.*
Viceroy, s. *qā-im muqām, nā-ib; nāẓim, nawwāb.*
Vicinity, s. *nijdekī, gāwanḍ.*
Vicious, a. *bad, nākārah, bakhīl, 'aib-nāk.*
Vicissitude, s. *wār, nobat, wakht, ṭāng.*
Victim, s. *qurbān, jār* or *dzār, ṣadqa.*
Victor, s. *bar, wa-aṛ, ghālib, pa-aṛ kawūnkai.*
Victorious, a. *wa-aṛ, bar, barai mūndūnkai,* or *-mūndalai,* or *-gaṭalai.*
Victory, s. *barāī, wa-aṛāna.*
Victuals, s. *khwurāk, khwāṛah, qūt, ṭa'ām, ghiẓā.*
Vie, v.a. *barābarī k., was chalawul, ḥadd k.*
View, s. *naẓar, nandāra, tamāsha, līdah, kātah, dzīr, mulāḥiẓa; niyat, maṭlab, gharaẓ.* v.a. *goral, līdal, katal, kasal, naẓar-,* etc. *k.* (to have in-) v.a. *niyat-,* etc. *laral.* (to consider) v.a. *ganṛal.*
Vigil, s. *sho-gīrī, tsoka-ī.*
Vigilance, s. *baidārī, khabar-dārī, hokkhyār-tiyā.*
Vigilant, a. *baidār, khabar-dār, hokkhyār, wīkkh.*
Vigorous, a. *zorāwar, quwat-nāk, tawānā, qawī.*
Vigour, s. *zor, quwat, barm* or *bram, tuwān, ṭāqat, tāo.*
Vile, a. *bad, kharāb, nā-kārah, dūn, khwār, spuk, palīt, murdār.*
Vilify, v.a. *tor-, tuhmat-,* etc. *pore k., peghor warkawul, kanzal* or *kkhkandzal, ghandal, kagal, bad nāmawul, ruswā k.*
Village, s. *kilai, dih.*
Villager, s. *kilī-wāl, da kilī saṛai.*
Villain, s. *bad-m'ash, bad-zāt, ḥarāmī. chulur, charlanḍ.* (farm servant) *dihqān, charekār.*
Villanous, a. *bad, nā-kārah, ḥarām-kār.*
Villany, s. *sharārat, pasāt, bad-zātī, ṭagī, namak-ḥarāmī.*
Vindicate, v.a. *ṣābitawul, pūrah-, zbād-, rikkhtiyā-, qā-im-,* etc. *k.; 'uẓr rāwṛal.*
Vindication, s. *iṣbāt, zbād; 'uẓr.*
Vindictive, a. *kīna-war.*
Vine, s. *tāk, kwar.* (-yard) *raz.*
Vinegar, s. *sirka.*
Violate, v.a. *mātawul; wrānawul.*
Violence, s. *zor, ẓulm, jabar, zabardastī, jafā; sakhtī, tūndī; qahr, ghaẓab.*
Violent, a. *sakht, tund, tez; qahr-nāk, ghaẓab-nāk.*
Violin, s. *rabāb, sārinda, ghachaka.*
Viper, s. *mangor, mangarai.*
Virgin, s. *peghla, ja-an, jūna-ī, jina-ī, bākira.*
Virility, s. *mardī, quwat da bāh.*
Virtually, ad. *pa wāq'ī, pa aṣl, pa rikkhtiyā.*
Virtue, s. *nekī, nekokārī, ṣawāb.* (quality) *lokkhai, ṣifat, khoe, khaṣlat, khāṣṣiyat.*
Virtuous, a. *nek, nekokār, ṣawābī, pāk, pāk-laman, nek-khoe, -khaṣlat, -bakht,* etc.
Virulent, a. *sakht, tund, tez, jābir, qātil.*
Visage, s. *makh, tsihra, rūe, gūna, bashra, ṣūrat.*
Viscid, a. *barwai, bokkht, slekkht-nāk, chaspān.*
Visible, a. *kkhkārah, tsargand, bartser, awtsār, ẓāhir.*
Vision, s. *naẓar, līdah, kātah.* (dream) *khob, khiyāl.*
Visionary, s. *khiyālī, wahmī.*
Visit, v.a. *līdah-, kātah-, dīdan-, mulāqāt-,* etc. *k.* (a shrine) *ziyārat k.*
Vital, a. *jwandai; da marg aw jwāk.*
Vitality, s. *dzān, jwandūn, jwāk.*
Vitals, s. *laṛmānah, dzigar, īna.*
Vitiate, v.a. *spukawul, habatah k., wrānawul, kharābawul, tabāh k.*

Vitriol, s. *totā*. (blue-) *nīla·totā*. (green-) *shna·*, or *sabza·totā*.
Vituperation, s. *malāmat, peghor, tor, tuhmat, kanzal*, or *kkhkandzal*.
Vivacious, a. *kkhād, khūsh·hāl, khandā·rūe*.
Vivid, a. *rūnr, rokkhān, brekkh·nāk*; *jwandai*.
Vocabulary, s. *lughat, da kalimo kitāb*.
Vocation, s. *kār, kasb, pesha*.
Vocative, s. *nidā, bāng, ghag*.
Vociferate, v.n. *bāng wayal, nāra-, chigha-, sūra-*, etc. *wahal, chighawul*.
Vogue, s. *chāl, chalan, dastūr*. (in-) *rawā*.
Voice, s. *āwāz, bāng, zwag, ghag*. (active-) *sīgha i m'arūf*. (passive-) *sīgha i majhūl*.
Void, a. *ta-ash, khālī, khushai*; *'abas, bātil*.
Void, v.a. *jārbāsal—jāryastal, ghurzawul*. (-at stool) *ghul k., kharal*.
Volition, s. *wāk, ikhtiyār, ghokkht*.
Volley, s. *shilak, bār, dandūkār*.
Voluble, a. *jiba·war*; *chālāk*.
Volume, s. *kitāb, jild*; *qadr, andāza*.
Voluntarily, ad. *pa khpula*.
Voluntary, a. *khpul·wāk, khpul·ikhtiyār*.
Voluptuary, s. *geda·parast, shahwat·parast*.
Voluptuous, a. *geda-* or *kheta-, shahwat-, nafs-*, etc. *parast*.
Vomit, v.a. *jārbāsal—jāryastal, qai-, bāka-ī-, chāl-*, etc. *k., kūz katal, zmake ta katal, -goral*, etc.
Voracious, a. *liwāl, wayai*.
Vortex, s. *ghurzai, gharq·āb, gird·āb*.
Votary, s. *ghulām, mra-e*; *hājat·man, niyāz·man*; *parastār, manūnkai*.
Vote, s. *lafz, qaul, khabara, wayai*. v.a. *khwakkhawul, qabūlawul, pasandawul*.
Vouch, v.a. *gawāhī-, shāhidī-*, etc. *warkawul*, or *-lal*, or *-lawdal*; *dalīl-, hujjat-*, etc. *-warkawul*; *wayal*.
Voucher, s. *hujjat, dalīl, sanad*; *gawāh, shāhid*.
Vouchsafe, v.a. *bakkhal, warkawul, mihrbāngī k*.
Vow, s. *neta, wāda, shart, qaul, lafz*; *nazr, niyāz*. v.a. *neta-*, etc. *k.* or *-taral*; *nazr-*, etc. *warkawul, -warwral*.
Vulgar, a. *'āmm*. (mean) *spuk, nā·kārah*. (the-) *'āmmiyān, 'awāmm*.
Vulture, s. *ganjai, gargas*.
Vulva, s. *kus*.

W.

Wabble, v.n. *khwadzedal, zangedal*.
Wad. s. *būja, dīda, shora*; *manjīla*.
Waddle, v.n. *arate-* or *chīnge kkhpe tlal—lāral*.
Wade, v.n. *pa obo kkhke girzedal*.
Wafer, s. *tika-ī, chaka-ī, tsaparkai*.
Waft, v.a. *rasawul, ālwūzawul, āstawul*.
Wag, s. *pekkhe·gar, toq·mār, malandai, maskharāchī, washtai*.
Wag, v.a. *khwadzawul, tsandal, rapawul*.
Wage, v.a. *kawul, kral, chalawul, ākhistal*.
Wager, v.a. *shart taral, daw k*.
Wages, s. *talab, tankhwāh, mihnat, kharts, muzd, mazdūrī*; *muwājib*.
Wagon, s. *gāda-ī, 'arāba*.
Wagtail, s. *māmūlaka, shīn·topa-ī, ziyarānaka*.
Wail, s. *wīr, wainā, wāwailā, jarā, sānda*.
Wailing, a. *wīra·jalai, jarānd*.
Waist, s. *mlā, landa*.
Wait, v.n. *osedal, pātedal, pātai ked., wudredal*; *hāzir osedal*. (-upon) v.a. *khidmat k*.
Waiter, s. *khidmat·gār*.
Waive, v.a. *pregdal*, etc. *tark k*.
Wake, v.n. *wīkkhedal, pātsedal, baidār ked*. v.a. *wīkkhawul, pātsawul, baidār k*.
Wakeful, a. *wīkkh, baidār, khabar·dār*.

Walk, v.n. *tlal—lāṛal, drūmal* or *drūmedal, chaledal, girzedal, pa kkhpo tlal.*

Walk, s. *sail, gakkht; chāl, yūn; lār.*

Wall, s. *dīwāl.* (side wall of a house) *chana.* (-eyed) a. *chaghar.* (to build a-) v.a. *dīwāl wahal* or *-khejawul.*

Wallet, s. *bana-ī, gūḍai, dzola-ī, chamta.*

Wallow, v.n. *rgharedal—rghakkhtal, lots-pots ked.*

Walnut, s. *akoṛ, ūghz.* (soft-) *chaghza-ī.* (hard-) *maṭāk.*

Wan, a. *ṭap, ziyaṛ, sperah.*

Wand, s. *amsā, lakkhta.*

Wander, v.n. *khushai-, dar ba dar-,* etc. *girzedal, rammedal; be-lār-, gumrāh-,* etc. *ked.*

Wane, v.n. *kamedal, zahedal, la-ag-, zawāl-,* etc. *ked., prewatal.*

Want, s. *ghokkht, ḥājat, darkhwāst.* (penury) *tangsiyā, khwārī.* (deficiency) *troṭa, waṭa.*

Want, v.a. *ghokkhtal, ḥājat laral; pukkhtedal. sawāl-, darkhwāst-,* etc. *k.*

Wanting, a. *kam, nāqiṣ, nīmgaṛai, ḥājat-man.*

Wanton, a. *mast, shokh, shahwat-nāk, bad-laman, shatāh, lashmakai, be-ḥayā.*

War, s. *jang, jadal; patna, kharkhakkha.* (civil-) *khāna-jangī.* (religious-) *ghazā, jihād.*

Warble, v.a. *chanṛ-chanṛ-, chighāra-, bul-ghāk-,* etc. *k.*

Ward, v.a. *sātal, jghoral, khundī k.* (-off) *raf'a-daf'a k., bachawul.*

Ward, s. *kandai, mālat, maḥalla, cham.*

Ware, s. *māl, jins, saudā, asbāb, shai, tsīz.* (-house) *kār-khāna, māl-khāna, ambār.* (hard-) *da ospane kāli.* (crockery-) *kaṭwī lokkhī.*

Warily, ad. *pa hokkhyār-tiyā-, pa baidārī-, pa pahm-, pa khabar-dārī-,* etc. *-sara.*

Warlike, a. *jangī.*

Warm, a. *tod, garm.* (luke-) *taṛam.*

Warmth, s, *tod-wālai, todūkha, garmī.*

Warning, s. *khabar, āgāhī.* (example) *'ibrat.* (to give-) v.a. *khabar-,* etc. *k.*; *'ibrat war-kawul.* (to take-) v.a. *'ibrat ākhistal.*

Warp, v.a. *pech-, tāo-,* etc. *warkawul.* v.n. *kagedal.*

Warp, s. *pūda, tār; tanasta, kanṛai.*

Warrant, s. *parwāna, sanad, barāt, ḥukm-nāma.*

Warrant, v.a. *wayal; wāk-, ikhtiyār-,* etc. *warkawul; rawā-, rikkhtiyā-, sūchah-,* etc. *ganṛal* or *k.*; *pushtī-, madad-,* etc. *war-kawul.*

Warrantable, a. *rawā, lāzim, shara'ī.*

Warranted, a. *sharṭī, qarārī.*

Warrior, s. *ghāzī, jangī, mujāhid.*

Wart, s. *zakha.*

Wary, a. *hokkhyār, pokh, chirg, kāgh, gharand.*

Wash, v.a. *wīndzal* or *mīndzal, wlal.* (-one-self) *lambal, ghusl k.* (-for prayers) *awdas-, wazū-,* etc. *k.*

Washerman, s. *dobī.* (-woman) *dobanṛa.* (-of the dead) *ghāsil.* (-his boiler) *khūm.* (-mallet) *tsobāṛai.*

Wasp, s. *ḍanḍāra, ḍanbara, sra macha-ī, ghālboza.*

Waste, v.a. *'abaṣ kharts k., iṣrāf-, tāwān-, talaf-,* etc. *k., wrukawul.* v.n. *wuchedal, kaṛedal, zahedal.*

Waste, a. *wairān, wujāṛ, kharāb, shāṛ.* s. *maira, shāṛa; tāwān, iṣrāf, talaf.*

Wasteful, a. *muṣrif, iṣrāfī, talaf kawūnkai.*

Watch, v.a. *tsoka-ī-, pahra-, pāswānī-,* etc. *k.*; *sho-gīrī-, baidārī-,* etc. *k., kashak gālal, jghoral.*

Watch, s. *gaṛa-ī, sā'at.* (-maker) *gaṛa-ī-,* etc. *-sāz* or *-joṛawūnkai.* (-house) *tānṛa.* (-tower) *bruj.* (-man) *pāswān, tsoka-ī-dār, pahra-dār.* (-man over fields, cattle, etc.) *kakkhai.* (-word) *nakkha, lafẓ.*

Watchful, a. *khabar·dār, baidār, hokkhyār.*

Water, s. *oba, āb.* (-carrier) *mashkī, saqāo.* (-bag) *mashk, ja-ī; palānra.* (-course) *khwar, kanda, kas, shela.* (-closet) *chār·choba.* (-cresses) *tartezak, halam.* (-fall) *dāra, tsādar.* (-fowl) *hīla-ī.* (-lily) *nīlofar.* (-man) *mahanrah, mānrgai.* (-melon) *hind·wāna, tarbūza.* (-mill) *jaranda, āsiyā.* (-pot) *loṭkai, mangai.*

Watery, a. *ob·lan, ob·jan, abī; lūnd khūsht, zyam·nāk.*

Wattle, s. (hedge) *keṛ.* (bird's-) *jajūra, ghuṭ·yālai.*

Wattle, v.a. *agayal, gayayal* or *gayawul.*

Wave, s. *chapa, mauj, lahar.*

Wave, v.n. *zangal* or *zangedal; laharedal.* v.a. *tsanḍal, kkhorawul, hanawul.*

Waver, v.n. *rapedal, tsrapedal; wrāndi wrusto-, be·qalār-, be·ārām·,* etc. *ked.*

Wavering, a. *nā·qalār.*

Wax, s. *mūm.* (-cloth) *mūm·jāma.* (sealing-) *lāk.*

Way, s. *lār; ṭaur, shān, toga, rang; ṭarīqa, dastūr, chalan.*

Waylay, v.a. *lār nīwul, psūnai k.*

Wayward, a. *sar·kakkh, khpul·sar; wītak, shokh.*

We, pr. *mūng, mūg, mū.*

Weak, a. *nā·tuwān, kam·zor, 'ājiz, ẓa'īf, zahīr, kam·quwat, kam·ṭāqat, māndah.* (low) *spuk, khwār, nā·tsīz.* (as tea, etc.) *narai, mahīn.*

Weakness, s. *kamzor·tiyā, na·tuwānī, 'ājizī.*

Wealth, s. *duniyā, daulat, māl, zar.*

Wealthy, a. *duniyā·dār, daulat·man, zar·dār, tuwān·gar.*

Wean, v.a. *la to na ghūṭ k.*

Weanling, s. *zāṛai, ghūṭkai, būhārai.*

Weapon, s. *wasla, drasta, hatiyār, kālai.*

Wear, v.a. *āghostal, pa dzān k.,* or *-āchawul.* (rub) v.n. *sūledal.* (waste) *zaṛedal.* (last) *chaledal, teredal, pāedal.*

Wearisome, a. *drūnd, grān, staṛai kawūnkai.*

Weary, a. *staṛai, stomān, haukah.*

Weather, s. *āsmān, bād, hawā, mosam, wradz.* (-cock) *bād numāe* or *-kkhowūnkai.*

Weave, v.a. *ūdal* or *odal.*

Weaver, s. *jolāh, dāhor.* (-loom) *shāna, rach.* (-beam) *paleṭanr* or *paṭelanr.* (shuttle) *mākū.* (-brush) *māla.* (-paste) *batī.* (-yarn) *tanasta.* (-yarn beam) *hata.* (-web) *būda* or *pūda.* (-reeds) *nala, dūrma.* (-spindle) *garzanai.* (-reel) *nicha.*

Web, s. *tanasta, kanrai, būda.* (spider's-) *jāla-ī.*

Wed, v.a. *wadawul, wādah k., nikāḥ taṛal.* v.n. (applied to the woman) *wadedal, wādah ked.*

Wedding, s. *wādah, nikāḥ.* (-party) m. *janj.* f. *wrā.* (-guest) m. *jānjī, mānjī, wrā·bānrai.* f. *wre-aza* or *wreyaza, wrā·bānra-ī, mānja-ī.*

Wedge, s. *pāna, shpetai.*

Wednesday, s. *chār shamba.*

Weed, s. *wākkhah.* v.a. *lalūn-, goḍ-,* etc. *k.*

Weeding, s. *lalūn, goḍ, pūjī.* (-hoe) *rambai.*

Week, s. *hafta.*

Weekly, ad. *hafta pa hafte.*

Weep, v.a. *jaṛal, okkhe toyawul.* (mourn) *wīr-, wāwailā-,* etc. *k., wainā wayal.*

Weeper, s. *wīra·jalai, wainā wayūnkai; jaṛānd.*

Weeping, s. *jaṛā; wīr, wāwailā.*

Weevil, s. *gūnr, buza.*

Weigh, v.a. *talal, tol k., jokal.*

Weight, s. *tol, jok; wazn, andāza; dranāwai, drūnd·wālai; bār.* Bazar weights (two lbs.) *ser,* (oke = 7 sers) *ogai.* (quarter oke) *kuṛhai.* (4 sers) *daṛa-ī.* (10 daṛa-ī or maund) *man.* (8 maunds) *kharwār.* (¼ ser) *pāo.* (½ ser) *dwah·pāwa.* (¾ ser) *dre pāwa.* (1¼ ser) *pīndzah pāwa.* (1½ ser) *yo·nīm ser.* (1¾ ser) *pāo kam dwah sera.*

(2 sers) *dwah sera*. (2¼ sers) *pāo bāndi-* or *pāo dapāsa—dwah sera*. (2½ sers) *dwah-nīm sera*, etc. (2 oz.) *chīṭāka-ī*. (1 oz.) *nīma chīṭāka-ī*. (½ oz.) *sharshā-ī*. (¼ oz.) *nīma sharshā-ī*. (2 drs.) *paisa*. Jeweller's weights. *rata-ī* = 1·8 gr.; *māsa* = 8 *rata-ī*; *misqāl* = 4 *māsa* + 3½ *rata-ī*; *tola* = 12½ *māsa* or 180 grs.

Weighty, a. *drūnd, grān*.

Welcome, a. *mubārak, kkhah, khwakkh, khair*. s. *mubārakī, du'ā da khair, rogh-baṛ, bara-gaṛa, bar-gaṛandī*. in. *har-kala har-kala! pa khaira-* or *pa khair sara rāghlai ye! khairāt di rāwuṛ!* v.a. *joṛ tāzah sara k., mubārakī warkawul*. (to be-) v.n. *pa khaira-*, or *pa khair sara rāghlal*.

Welfare, s. *khairiyat, tandrust-wālai, kkhegaṛa, bihbūdī, bihtarī*; *wadān-wālai, ābād-wālai*.

Well, s. *kūhai, chāh*. (-with lever) *dingara-ī, yak-langa*. (-with steps) *baha-ī*. (-with wheels) *arhaṭ*.

Well, a. *kkhah, joṛ, rogh*; *nek, khwakkh, mubārak*. ad. *kkhah, pa kkhah shān sara*. (very-) *ḍer kkhah*. (-done!) *ākh* or *ākhkkh, ākhkkhai*. (-then) *biyā, nor*. (as-) *hum*. (as well as) *laka chi*. (-nigh) *nijde*. (-born) a. *sāwū, aṣīl*. (-wisher) *khair-khwāh, du'ā-goe*.

Wen, s. *baura-ī, kala-ī, rasaula-ī, ghumba*.

Wench, s. *wīndza, mazdūra, khidmat-gāra, suhela-ī*; *ja-an, jina-ī, peghla, kkhadza*; *kachana-ī, lola-ī*.

West, s. *nwar prewātah, qibla, maghrab*. (-ward) *nwar prewātah khwā*.

Wet, a. *lūnd, khusht, naw-jan, nam-nāk*.

Wether, s. *wuch-kūl*.

Wetness, s. *lūnd-wālai, khusht-wālai*; *nau, zyam*.

Wetnurse, s. *dā-ī*.

What, pr. *kūm, tsok, tsa*. (-else?) *nor tsa*. (-ther?) *biyā*.

Whatever, pr. *har kūm, har tsok*, etc.; *kūm chi, har chi*.

Wheat, s. *ghanum*.

Wheedle, v.a. *ghulawul, darghalawul, dam warkawul*. (coax) *jigī-, hāṛe-, jāna-*, etc. *k*.

Wheel, s. *tsarkh*. (-spoke) *tīrai, palai, shpeshtai*.

Wheel, v.n. *girzedal, churledal, tsarkhedal*.

Wheeze, v.a. *sāh pa ūchata ākhistal, sāh shranganwul*.

Whelp, s. *bachai, kūtrai*.

When, ad. *kala, kūm wakht*.

Whenever, ad. *har kala chi, har-*, or *kūm wakht chi*.

Where, ad. *charta, kūm dzāe, kūma khwā*. (no-) *hets charta, hets dzāe*.

Whereas, ad. *dzaka chi, la de na, balki, wale*.

Whereat, ad. *pas, biyā, nor, pa de*.

Wherefore, ad. *pas, dzaka, la kabla*.

Wherever, ad. *har charta chi, har-*, or *kūm dzāe chi*.

Whet, v.a. *terah-, tez-*, etc. *k*.

Whether, c. *ki, yā, khwāh*.

Whetstone, s. *psān, belho* or *belāo, barjo, tsarkh*.

Whey, s. *tarwe, lassī*; *mājūban* or *mā ul joban*.

Which, pr. *kūm, kūm yo*.

While, s. *wakht* or *waqt, mūda*.

Whilst, ad. *tso chi, hombra chi, tar haghah pore chi*.

Whim, s. *wahm, khiyāl*.

Whine, v.a. *pṛang-, rangaṭ-, kūk-*, etc. *wahal*.

Whip, s. *karoṛa, dura, tāziyāna, qamchīna*. v.a. *karoṛa-*, etc. *wahal* or *-lagawul*.

Whirl, v.a. *girzawul, churlawul, tsarkhawul*. v.n. *girzedal, churledal, tsarkhedal*.

Whirligig, s. *baṛen-chagh, jalandarai, churla-ī, bāmbūra*.

Whirlpool, s. *ghurzai, gird·āb, gharq·āb.*
Whirlwind, s. *borbūka-ī.*
Whiskers, s. *kāna-ī.*
Whisper, v.a. *pus pus k., ro ro pa ghwag kkhke wayal.*
Whistle, v.a. *shpela-ī wahal* or *-ghagawul.*
Whit, s. *ṭakai, khasanrai, pūṭai, pitsānrai, zarra.*
White, a. *spīn, saped* or *safed.*
White-ant, s. *oenah.*
Whiteness, s. *spīn·wālai.*
Whither, ad. *charta, kūma khwā.*
Whitlow, s. *kharai, shīnai.*
Whizz, s. *sagh.* v.a. *sagh k.*
Who, pr. *tsok, kum.* (-ever) *har tsok chi.*
Whole, a. *pūrah, amānī, tamām; drust, salāmat.* s. *ṭol, wāṛah.* (-sale) *ṭālah.*
Wholesome, a. *kkhah, ghwarah, joṛ, muwāfiq.*
Wholly, ad. *amānī, sarāsar, bil·kull, muṭlaq.*
Whore, s. *kachana-ī, lola-ī, kāsīra, shatāha.*
Whoremonger, s. *kāsīr, zinā·kār.*
Why, ad. *wale? tsa la?*
Wick, s. *bātai, patīla.*
Wicked, a. *bad, bad·kār, gunāh·gār, sharīr.*
Wickedness, s. *badī, bad·kārī, sharārat, gunāh.*
Wicket, s. *kaṛka-ī, tambaṛa-ī.*
Wide, a. *plan, arat, psōrawar* or *sarah·war.* (-open) *chīng, wīt.* (-as a door) *liri.*
Widen, v.a. *planawul, aratawul; chīngawul, wītawul.*
Widow, s. *kūnda.* (-hood) *kūnḍ·tūn.*
Widower, s. *kūnd.*
Width, s. *plan·wālai, arat·wālai, psor, sor.*
Wield, v.a. *chalawul, girzawul.*
Wife, s. *kkhadza, artīna, merman, kor, ṭabar.* (cotemporary-) *ba-an.* (under coverture) *maṛokkha.* (brother's-) *wrandār* or *wandyār, bābī.* (son's-) *ngor.* (husband's brother's-) *yor.*
Wild, a. *dzangalī, wahshī, dashtī, ṣaḥrānai; khiyālī, wahmī; be·tartīb, nā·parhez·gār; be·qaid, sar·kakkh.* s. *dzangal, maira, ṣaḥrā.* (-beast) *dad, waḥsh.*
Wilderness, s. *dzangal, dakkht, ṣaḥrā, maira.*
Wile, s. *bāna, chal, lamghaṛa-ī, ḥīla, fareb.*
Wilful, a. *khpul·sar, khpul·rāe, sar·kakkh.*
Wilfully, ad. *pa qaṣd.*
Will, s. *marẓī, raẓā; wāk, ikhtiyār; khwakkhī, kāl·khwāhī; was, ḥukm.* (testament) *waṣiyat·nāma.* (good-) *nek·khwāhī, khair·khwāhī, nek·sigālī.* (bad-) *bad·khwāhī, bad·sigālī.*
Will, v.a. *ghokkhtal, khwakkhawul; farmāyal.*
Willing, a. *rāẓī, raẓā·man, khwakkh.* (God-) *da khudāe pa ḥukm sara, inshā allahu ta'ālā.*
Willingly, ad. *pa khwakkhī sara, pa dwāṛo stargo.*
Wily, a. *chal·bāz, farebī, bāna·khor, ḥīla·bāz.*
Win, v.a. *gaṭal, mūndal, wṛal, pa-aṛ k.* v.n. *ghālib-, wa-aṛ-,* etc. *ked.* (-a battle) *barai mūndal.* (-over) *rāwustal, grohedah k.*
Wind, s. *bād, wo, hawā.* (breath) *sāh, dam.* (to take-) v.a. *dama k.,* or *-nīwul, sāh ākhistal.* (hot-) s. *lū, paro, tod bād.* (cold-) *sūla-ī, soṛ bād.*
Wind, v.a. *tsarkhawul.* (envelope) *ngharal—nghakkhtal.* (twist) *tāwawul, tāo-, pech-, wal-,* etc. *warkawul; tāo-, kālkūch-,* etc. *khwuṛal.* v.n. *girzedal, kagedal.*
Winding, a. *pech·dār, wahlandai, kog·wog.* s. *tāo, pech, kalkūchaka, kag·lech.* (-sheet) *kafan, tsādar.*
Window, s. *darbacha* or *darīcha, kaṛka-ī.*
Windpipe, s. *wucha ghāṛa, ḥalq.*
Windy, s. *bādī, hawā·dār.*
Wine, s. *sharāb.* (-bibber) *sharāb·khor.*
Wing, s. *wazar, tsānga, banra; bāzū.*
Wink, P. *chashmak, ghamza.* v.a. *ẓegma-* or *zezma-, starga-,* etc. *wahal.* (blink) *dzumbal, brandzawul.* (-at faults) *starge puṭawul.* (hint) *ishāra k.*

Winner, s. *gaṭūnkai, wa-aṛ, pa-aṛ kawūnkai.*
Winning, s. *gaṭana, wa-aṛāna.*
Winnow, v.a. *chaj-, tsap-*, etc. *k.* or *-wahal, ālwūzawul.*
Winter, s. *jamai* or *jimai, sāṛa.*
Wipe, v.a. *masḥa k., pāk-, ṣāf-*, etc. *k., mugal—mukkhal. jārū k.*
Wire, s. *tār.* (-drawer) *jandra, tār·kakkh, rākkhko.* (to draw-) v.a. *tār kāgal—kkhkal.*
Wisdom, s. *'aql, poha, pahm, sha'ūr, wuqūf.*
Wise, a. *'aql·man, pohānd, dānā, hokkhyār, 'āqil.* s. *shān, rang, ṭaur, toga.*
Wisely, ad. *pa 'aql-*, etc. *-sara.*
Wish, s. *ghokkht, ārzū, mudd'ā, hanḍa, shauq.* v.a. *ghokkhtal, ārzū-*, etc. *laral.*
Wishful, a. *ārzū·man, rāghib, liwāl.*
Wisp, s. *kalokkhta.*
Wit, s. *zīrakī.*
Witch, s. *jādū·gara, koḍ-, siḥr-*, etc. *-gara.* (-craft) *jādū-*, etc. *-garī.*
With, p. *sara, khatsa* or *tsakha.*
Withal, ad. *sara la de, ziyāt la de na.*
Withdraw, v.a. *stanawul, pa biyarta ākhistal.* v.n. *jārwatal, stanedal, biyarta ked.*
Wither, v.n. *mṛāmedal* or *mṛāwedal, wuchedal, kamanṛedal, pezai-, maṛghechan-*, etc. *ked.*
Withers, s. *mandaw, wulai.*
Withhold, v.a. *stanawul*; *khundī k.*
Within, p. *danana, pa kkhke.*
Without, p. *bāhir, warchani* or *wardzani.* (not possessed of) *be-, lā-, nā-, ghair-*, etc.
Withstand, v.a. *āṛ-, man'a-*, etc. *k.* v.n. *wudredal, teredal, pāedal, ṭīng ked., walāṛedal.*
Witness, s. *gawāh, shāhid*; *gawāhī, shāhidī*; *gawāhī-*, etc. *-lūnai* or *-lūnkai*, or *-warkawūnkai.* v.a. *katal, goral—lidal.* (to give-) v.a. *gawāhī-*, etc. *lal* or *-lawdal*, or *-warkawul.* (to be-) v.n. *gawāh-*, etc. *ked.*

Wittol, s. *dahūs, bagharai.*
Witty, a. *zīrak, tez·pahm.*
Wits, s. *'aql, hokkh, ausān.* (out of his-) *ausān·tlalai.*
Wizard, s. *jādū·gar, bāzī-, koḍ-, siḥr-*, etc. *-gar.*
Woe, s. *gham, randz*; *afsos, daregh.*
Woeful, a. *gham·jan, gham·nāk, andekkh·man.*
Wolf, s. *sharmakkh, lewah.*
Woman, s. *kkhadza, artīna, arwata, 'aurata, zanāna.* (lying in-) *langa, zarghāla, tsalwekkhta-ī.*
Womb, s. *riḥam, gaṇranai.*
Wonder, v.a. *'ajab k.* v.n. *hariyānedal.*
Wonder, s. *hariyānī* or *ḥairānī.* (-struck) *hak·pak, hak·hariyān.*
Wonderful, a. *'ajab, 'ajīb, badī'ah.*
Wont (to be), v. imp. Is expressed by the continuative past tense of verbs Ex. *rātah ba* or *ba rātah*, he used to come or was wont to come.
Wont, s. *'ādat, dastūr.*
Wood, s. *largai.* (forest) *baṇr.* (grove) *jangai.* (fire-) *bālaṇr, khāshāk.*
Wool, s. *waṛa-ī, pashm.*
Woollen, a. *waṛīnah, pashmīnah.*
Woolly, a. *waṛan, babar.*
Word, s. *khabara, wayai, lafẓ, wayana.* (news) *khabar.* (-of honour) *qaul.* (in a-) *gharaẓ.*
Work, s. *kār, kasb*; *khidmat, miḥnat*; *shughl, mashghūlā.* (effect) *pāzah, 'amal.*
Work, v.a. *kār-*, etc. *k., kawul, kral.*
Workman, s. *kār kawūnkai, kasb·gar, kārī·gar.*
Workmanship, s. *kārī·garī.*
World, s. *duniyā, jahān, naṛa-ī, 'ālam.*
Worldly, a. *duniyā-ī*; *duniyā parast.*
Worm, s. *chinjai, khazanda.* (Guinea-) *nārū.* (Tape-) *kadū zaṛai.* (intestinal) *wagha.* (Ascarides) *kīkkha.* (-of a still) *marwat.*

Wormwood, s. *tarkha, mastiyāra.*

Worn, a. *zoṛ; be-dzān, be-ḥāl.* (frayed) *sūdah, sūledalai.* (exhausted) *ṭap, staṛai.*

Worry, v.a. *pārawul, ṭongawul, kaṛawul, zoral.*

Worse, a. *nor bad.* (-than he) *la haghah na bad.*

Worship, s. *'ibādat, sijda.* (title) *ḥaẓrat.* v.a. *parastī-, 'ibādat-,* etc. *k.*

Worsted, a. *pa-aṛ, māt, bāelalai.* s. *ojghūnai, waṛa-ī; natsa-ī* or *antsa-ī, wākkhkai.* (ball of-) *spandakh.*

Worth, s. *bai'a, bahā, qīmat; qadr; kkhegaṛa.* v.n. *arzedal.*

Worthless, a. *be-fā-ida, nā-kārah, 'abaṣ, khushai, nā-tsīz, habatah, hets da kkhah.*

Worthy, a. *kkhāyastah, kkhah, lā-iq, wājib, yarzan, pīrzo.*

Wound, s. *parhār, zakhm.* v.a. *jobalawul, ghwutsawul, zakhmī k.*

Wounded, a. *parhār-jalai, jobal, ghwuts, zakhmī, zam-zmolai.* v.n. *jobaledal, ghwuts-,* etc. *ked.*

Wrangle, v.a. *jagṛa-, qaẓiya-, steza-,* etc. *k.*

Wrangler, s. *jagṛāū, jang-yālai, qaẓiya-kār, ḥujjatī, takrārī.*

Wrap, v.a. *nghaṛal—nghakkhtal.*

Wrapper, s. *lifāfa.*

Wrath, s. *qahr, ghaẓab, broṣ-wālai.*

Wrathful, a. *qahr-jan, ghaẓab-nāk, bros, khīr.*

Wreak, v.a. *āchawul; ghurzawul, khalāṣawul, chalawul, mātawul, lagawul.*

Wreath, s. *tāo, wal, pech; hār, laṛ.*

Wreck, s. *tālān, tabāhī, kharābī, halākat.*

Wrench, v.a. *tāo-, pech-,* etc. *warkawul; kāgal—kkhkal, bāsal—yastal; shūkawul.*

Wrest, v.a. See preceding word.

Wrestle, v.a. *parzawul k.*

Wrestler, s. *pahalwān, parzawul kawūnkai.*

Wretch, s. *kam-bakht, bad-naṣīb, khāna kharāb.*

Wretched, a. *khwār, tabāh, be-kas, lā-chār.*

Wretchedness, s. *khwārī, tabāhī, tor-bakhtī.*

Wright, s. *darūzgar, tarkāṇr.* (in comp.) *-gar.*

Wring, v.a. *tāwawul; nichoṛawul.*

Wrinkle, s. *chīchaṛ, jūhaṛa, gundza.*

Wrist, s. *maṛwand, band.*

Write, v.a. *likal, kāgal—kkhkal.*

Writer, s. *kātib, likūnkai, kkhkūnkai.*

Writing, s. *likal, kkhkal, khaṭṭ.*

Writhe, v.n. *pechedal, lamghaṛa-ī ked.*

Wrong, a. *nā-rawā, nā-ḥaqq, nā-kkhanai, be-inṣāf; ghalaṭ, khaṭā, bad.* s. *ẓulm, zabardastī, jafā, nā-ḥaqqī, nuqṣān, nā-rawā-ī, ẓarar.* (right or-) *ḥaqq nā-ḥaqq.*

Wry, a. *krīng, kog, tsoṛ.*

Y.

Yard, s. *gholai, angaṇr, hadera; gaz.*

Yarn, s. *spaṇrsai, mazai.*

Yawn, v.a. *aswelai k., argamai k.*

Yea, ad. *ho, āre.*

Year, s. *kāl.* (this-) *sag-* or *saganai kāl,* or *sakh-* or *sakhanai kāl.* (next-) *rātlūnai-* or *makhai kāl.* (last-) *paṛos-,* or *paṛosag-,* or *paṛosganai kāl.* (-before last) *waṛam kāl.* (three years ago) *lā waṛam kāl.* (-by year) *kāl pa kāl.* (every-) *har kāl.* (whole-) *kāl-o-ṣlīn, wāṛah kāl, kāl-o-sar.* (-old, in comp.) *-kālah, -kālanai.*

Yearn, v.n. *kaṛedal, nūledal, liwāl ked., pechedal, pakhsedal.*

Yeast, s. *khamīra, tomna, māya.*

Yell, v.a. *chigha-, sūra-, nāra-,* etc. *wahal.*

Yellow, a. *ziyaṛ.*

Yelp, v.a. *ghapal.*

Yes, ad. *ho, āre; āyā!*

Yester, ad. *parūnai, begānai.* (-day) *parūn, parūna-ī wradz.* (day before-) *waṛama wradz.* (two days before-) *lā waṛama wradz*. (-night) *begāh*, *begāna-ī-* or *parūna-ī-shpa*. (night before-) *warama shpa*.

Yet, c. *wale*, *walekin*, *lekin*, *magar*. (beside) *'alāwa*, *siwā*, *lā*. (still) *os hum*, *tar osa*. (again) *biyā*.

Yield, v.a. *rāwṛal*, *warkawul*, *paidā k*. (consign) *spāral*, *pāslawul*. (consent) *manal*, *qabūlawul*. (give way) v.n. *kamedal*.

Yoke, s. *jugh*, *ṭauq*. (fastening rope) *sarbānḍa*. (-peg) *jaghūnḍai*. (couple) *qulba*, *joṛa*, *juft*.

Yonder, ad. *halta*, *hori* or *hūri*, *hūrita*, *horta*.

You, pr. *tāsū*, *mo*.

Young, a. *dzwān*. s. *bachai*.

Youngster, s. *halak*, *jaṉrai*, *zalmai*.

Youth, s. *dzwān*, *zalmai*, *ghunḍāyah* ; *dzwānī*, *zalmī-tob*.

Z.

Zeal, s. *garmī*, *shauq*, *ghairat*, *tapāk*.

Zealot, s. *zāhid*, *shekh*, *ghairat-man*.

Zealous, a. *garm*, *tund*, *tez*.

Zephyr, s. *bād da ṣabā*, *nasīm* ; *narai wo* or *-bād*.

Zest, s. *khwand*, *maza*.

Zigzag, s. *kaga waga*, *kṛīng pṛīng*.

Zinc, s. *jas*, *jasta*.

Part II

Pashto - English Dictionary

A

DICTIONARY;

PUKKHTO OR PUKSHTO AND ENGLISH.

ABBREVIATIONS.

a. adjective; ad. adverb; c. conjunction; in. interjection; pl. plural; s.m. substantive masculine: s.f. substantive feminine; v.a. verb active; v.n. verb neuter; p. preposition; pr. pronoun; part. particle; Irr. irregular; Def. defective.

A. Arabic; P. Persian; S. Sanskrit; H. Hindi; T. Turki.

N.B. The letters ځ *dz* and ج *j*, څ *ts* and چ *ch*, ج *j* and ژ *z*, or ږ, ق *q* and ک *k* are sometimes used the one for the other. The long vowels ا *ā*, و *o* or *ū*, and ي *e* or *ī* are often replaced by their corresponding short vowels َ *a*, ُ *u*, and ِ *i*. The letter م *m* preceding ب *b* in a word is often changed to ن *n*.

The letter ږ *ǵ* has the sound of *z* in *azure* amongst the Western Afghans, and of *j* in *just* amongst the Eastern Afghans. ږ *g* has the same sound as ږ *ǵ* amongst the Western tribes, and the sound of ګ *g*, for which it is often changed, amongst the Eastern tribes. ښ has the sound of *kkh* amongst the Eastern Afghans, and of *ksh* amongst the Western Afghans, by whom it is often changed to ش *sh*.

ابل

ا *alif*, The first letter of the Pukkhto alphabet; is often interchanged with the short vowel *zabar*, especially in the vocative case; is sometimes added as the initial letter to words commencing with و or ي, as in اورور *oror* for ورور *wror*, ايواځي *īwādzai* for يواځي *yawādzai*.

آب *āb*, s.m. Water; lustre; reputation, honour. P.

ابا *abā*, in. Father! A. *ibā*, s.f. Denial, refusal. A.

آباد *ābād*, a. Cultivated, peopled, prosperous. P.

آبادي *ābādī*, s.f. Cultivation, prosperity. P.

اباسين *abāsīn*, s.m. The father of rivers. The Indus. Also written *obāsīnd*.

ابتدا *ibtidā*, s.f. Beginning, commencement. A.

ابد *abad*, s.m. Eternity. A. *abadan*, a. Eternal.

ابدال *abdāl*, s.m. A saint. A.

ابدالي *abdālī*, s.m. Name of an Afghan clan in the country between Kandahar and Herat. *abdālai*, s.m. A man of the tribe.

آبرو *ābrū*, s.m. Honour, reputation, name, renown. P. *abrū*, s.m. The eyebrow. P.

ابره *abra*, s.f. The outer cloth of a garment; a sash for the waist. P.

آبرېښم *ābrekkham* or *ābreksham*, s.m. New silk, floss silk. P. (*ābresham*).

ابل *abl*, a. Barefooted, unshod; powerless, weak. S. (*abal*). *kkhpa-abla*, a. Barefooted, unshod.

ابله *ablah*, a. Foolish, silly, stupid. A.

ابي *aba-ī*, s.f. A mother.

آپرين *āparīn*, in. Bravo! well done! P. (*āfarīn*).

اپريدي *aprīdī*, s.m. Name of a tribe of Pathans in the Kohat hills. Also written *afrīdī*.

اپس دندي *apas-ḍunḍa-ī*, s.f. Name of a game; tip-cat; bat and ball.

اپلت *aplat*, a. Obscene, dirty, filthy.

اپوټه *apūṭah*, a. Inverted, reversed, inside-out. H.

اترنګ *atrang*, s.m. Name of a plant, used in dyeing and medicine (*asclepias echinata*). H.

آتش *ātash*, s.m. Fire (in comp. only). P.

اتفاق *ittifāq*, s.m. Agreement, concord. A.

اتفاقي *ittifāqī*, a. Accidental. A.

اتم *atam*, a. The eighth.

اتنړ or اتڼ *ataṇr*, s.m. A kind of dance, a jig, a reel, round dance.

اتوار *itwār*, s.m. Sunday. S.

اتوب *atob*, s.m. Gruel, pap.

اته *atah*, a. Eight. *atah-las*, a. Eighteen.

اتيا *atiyā*, a. Eighty. *atiyāyam*, a. Eightieth.

اټال *aṭāl*, a. Idle, unemployed, out of work.

اټکل *aṭkal*, s.m. Conjecture, guess. H.

اټه *aṭa*, s.f. A ball, reel, or skein of thread. H. (*aṭṭī*).

اټيران *aṭerān*, s.m. A reel for thread. H.

اټيرل *aṭeral*, v.n. To be dyspeptic.

اټيرنه *aṭerana*, s.f. Indigestion, dyspepsia.

اټيه *aṭiya*, } s.f. See اټه.
اټيهه *aṭeha*, }

اثبات *iṣbāt*, s.m. Confirmation, proof. A.

اثر *aṣr*, s.m. Effect, mark, sign. A.

اجاره *ijāra*, s.f. Farm, hire, rent. A.

اجازت *ijāzat*, s.m. Leave, permission, order. A.

اجر *ajar*, } s.m. Hire, wages, reward. A.
اجرت *ujrat*, }

اجل *ajal*, s.m. Fate, death. A.

اڅنړل *atsaṇral*, v.a. To arrange, harmonize, level, smooth.

اچت *uchat*, a. Elevated, high, lofty. S. (*unchā*).

اچرلي *ucharlai*, s.m. The forehead, brow.

آچو *āchū*, s.f. A raspberry; the bush and fruit.

آچول *āchawul*, v.a. To cast, throw, fling.

آخ *ākh*, in. Ah! Good! Well! How good! A.

اخاړه *akhāṛah*, s.m. Plaster; daubing, plastering.

اخبار *akhbār*, s.m. Intelligence, news; a newspaper (pl. of خبر A.).

اختر *akhtar*, s.m. A star; good omen, good fortune; a festival. *loe-akhtar*, the great festival; name of a month corresponding with *zī-hijja*. *wṛūkai-akhtar*, the little festival, or the month corresponding with *shawāl*. P.

آخته *ākhtah*, a. Castrated; involved, caught, entangled, trammeled. P.

اختيار *ikhtiyār*, s.m. Authority, power; option, choice. A.

آخر *ākhir*, s.m. Conclusion, end. ad. At last, finally. A.

آخرت *ākhirat*, s.m. Futurity. A.

آخستل *ākhistal*, v.a. To accept, take; appropriate, seize, capture. A. (*akhaz*)?

آخښ *ākhkkh* or *ākhksh*, in. Alas! Heigho! See آخ.

اخګر *akhgar*, s.m. Live coal, hot ember. P.

اخلاص *ikhlāṣ*, s.m. Sincerity, kindness, affection. A.

آخون *ākhūn*, s.m. A tutor, teacher, master. Also written *ākhūnd*. P.

اخيړل *akheṛal*, v.a. To daub, plaster, smear.

ادا *adā*, s.f. Payment, performance. A.

ادب *adab*, s.m. Courtesy, politeness, respect. A.

ادنا *adnā*, a. Inferior, mean, small. A.

ادوبدو *adūbadū*, a. Distended, tumefied, blown, swelled.

اديته *adīna*, s.f. Friday; Sabbath. P.

ادئي *ada-ī*, s.f. Fields, plots of land round a village. Mother.

اذان *azān*, s.m. Call to prayer. A.

اذن *izn*, s.m. Leave, permission, order. A.

اذوقه *azūqa*, s.f. Food, provisions, victuals. A.

اراخ *arākh*, s.m. A brook, rivulet, water-course.

اراده *irāda*, s.f. Design, desire, wish. A.

آراسته *ārāstah*, a. Adorned, arranged, composed. P.

آرام *ārām*, s.m. Comfort, ease, rest. P.

ارباب *arbāb*, s.m. A noble, chief, lord (pl. of رب A.).

اربوز *urbūz*, s.m. The snout, muzzle.

ارت *arat*, a. Loose, open, wide. *aratawul*, v.a. To loosen.

ارتاو *artāw*, s.m. See پرتاب.

ارتل *aratal*, v.a. To break wind; widen.

آرته *ārta* or ښپه آرته *kkhpa-ārta*, s.f. Name of a wedding ceremony; the first visit of a lover at the house of his affianced, on the third day after betrothal; he takes some present for his affianced bride and is in return regaled with sherbet and cakes. After this ceremony, but not before, he can visit at the bride's house whenever convenient. S. (*ārtā*). *kkhpa-ārtūn*, s.m. Courtship.

ارتينه *artīna*, s.f. A woman, wife; female. A. (*'aurat*).

ارجل برجل *arjal-barjal*, a. Entangled, noosed, trapped.

آرخښ *ārkhakkh*, s.m. A gasp, gurgle.

اردو *urdū*, s.m. A camp, cantonment. T.

ارز *arz*, s.m. Price, alue. P.

ارزان *arzān*, a. Cheap, inexpensive. P.

آرزو *ārzū*, s.m. Desire, want, wish. P.

ارزيدل *arzedal*, v n. To be worth, fetch.

ارومي *argamai*, s.m. A belch, eructation.

ارري *argai*, s.m. See preceding. P. (*āroqh*).

آرسئي *ārsa-ī*, s.f. A small mirror worn on the thumb by women. H.

ارغند *arghund*, s.m. A knuckle bone.

ارگ *arg*, s.m. A citadel, palace. P.

ارگجه *argajah*, a. Mixed, miscellaneous. H.

ارمان *armān*, s.m. Regret, sorrow; desire, wish. in. Woe! Alas!

اروته *arwata*, s.f. A woman, wife, female. A. (*'aurat*).

آرويدل *ārwedal*, v.a. To hear, listen.

آره *āra*, s.f. A base, foundation. *ara*, s.f. A saw. P.

ارهټ *arhaṭ*, s.m. An irrigation well worked by wheels. H.

ارهر *arhar*, s.m. Name of a pulse, "pigeon pea" (*Cytisus cajan*). H.

ارهنډ *arhanḍ*, s.m. The castor oil tree (*Ricinus communis*). S.

آري *āre*, ad. Yea, yes, verily, aye. P.

آړ *āṛ*, s.m. Difficulty, obstruction; a screen, shelter; a fetter, bond. H.

اړامکي *aṛāmkai*, s.m. A shepherd's crook.

اړخ *aṛkh*, s.m. Armpit; flank, side.

اړم *aṛam*, s.m. A buttress, prop, support.

اړمي *aṛamai*, s.m. A small prop, a bar; the bar of a door.

اړنگ بړنگ *aṛang-baṛang*, a. Confused, entangled.

اړول *aṛawul*, v.a. To overturn, upset, invert, turn over.

اړيړئي *aṛeṛa-ī*, s.f. A stop, catch, bolt; the small cross-bars to which the waterpots of an irrigation wheel are fastened.

اړيکي *aṛekai*, s.m. The bar or bolt of a door or window; a small prop or support; hindrance, obstacle.

آزاد *āzād*, a. Free, liberated, loose. P.

آزار *āzār*, s.m. Affliction, distress. P. *izār*, s.m. Trowsers, drawers. P.

آزرده *āzurdah*, a. Sad, sorrowful, grieved. P.

ازغن *azghan*, a. Thorny, prickly.

ازغي *azghai*, s.m. A thorn, prickle.

آزمايښت *āzmāyikkht* or آزميښت *āzmekkht*, s.m. Proof, trial, test. P. (*āzmā-īsh*).

آزمايل *āzmāyal* or آزمويل *āzmoyal*, v.a. To examine, proof, test, try. P. (*āzmūdan*).

اړيل *agayal*, v.a. To wattle, net; stitch, sew; to provoke, urge, incite, instigate.

آس *ās*, s.m. A horse. P. (*asp*).

اسامي *asāmī*, s.m. A tenant, client; defendant. A.

آسان *āsān*, a. Easy, facile. P.

اسباب *asbāb*, s.m. Chattels, goods (pl. of سبب A.).

اسپغول *ispag̲h̲ol*, s.m. Name of a herb (*Plantago ispaghula*). The seeds are used in medicine. P.

اسپند *ispand*, s.m. Name of a plant; the Syrian rue (*Peganum harmala*). The seeds are used in medicine, and the dried herb as incense to drive away evil spirits. P.

آسپه *āspa*, s.f. A mare. *aspa*, s.f. Quinsy; scurvy.

استاځي *astād̲z̲ai*, s.m. A messenger, delegate, apostle.

استاذ *ustāẕ*, s,m. A master, teacher. P. (*ustād*).

آستان *āstān*, s.m. A threshold; shrine of a saint; family, house. P.

استر *astar*, s.m. The lining of a dress. P.

استره *astura*, s.f. A razor. P.

استوژه *astoǰa*, } s.f. Abode, dwelling, residence.
استوګه *astoga*, } Also *astogana*.

استوګونکي *astogūnkai*, s.m. Resident, dweller.

استيفا *istīfā*, s.f. Renouncing; resignation. A.

آستين *āstīn*, s.m. A sleeve. P.

آستول *āstawul*, v.a. To send, transmit, despatch, depute. P. (*firistādan*).

آستيدل *āstedal*, v.n. To abide, dwell, reside. P. (*istādan*). See *osedal*.

اسراف *isrāf*, s.m. Extravagance, prodigality, waste. A. (*iṣrāf*).

آسره *āsra*, s.f. Hope, refuge, trust, reliance. S. (*āsrā*).

اسلام *islām*, s.m. The Muhammadan religion. A.

آسمان *āsmān*, s.m. The sky, heaven. P.

اسو *asū*, s.m. Name of the sixth Hindu month. September-October. S. (*āsin*)

آسوده *āsūdah*, a. Contented, tranquil, quiet. P.

اسويلي *aswelai*, s.m. A gape, sigh, yawn.

اسي *asī*, a. Unfortunate, unlucky. *asa-ī*, s.f. Hoar-frost.

آسيا *āsiyā*, s.f. A water-mill. P.

اسير *asīr*, s.m. A captive, prisoner. P.

اشارت *is̲h̲ārat*, s.m. A hint, nod, sign, wink. A.

اشاري *as̲h̲ārai*, s.m. A dried apricot.

اشر *as̲h̲arr*, a. Abusive, wicked, vicious, obscene. A.

اشتوکه *as̲h̲toka*, s.f. Concord, peace. P. (*ās̲h̲tī*).

اشتها *is̲h̲tihā*, s.f. Appetite, desire. A.

آشناي *ās̲h̲nāe*, s.m. A friend, lover. P. (*ās̲h̲nā*). *ās̲h̲nā-ī*, s.f. Friendship, intimacy.

آښل *āk̲k̲h̲al*, v.a. To knead or mix dough. Def. in pres. ten. See آغړل.

آښلي *āk̲k̲h̲alai*, s.m. Dough. a. Kneaded.

اصل *aṣl*, s.m. Lineage, origin, source; capital. A.

اصلي *aṣlī*, a. Genuine, original. A.

اصيل *aṣīl*, a. Noble, well bred. A.

اطلاع *iṭṭilā'* s.f. Notice, information. A.

اعتبار *i'tibār*, s.m. Credit, trust, reliance. A.

اعجوبه *a'jūbah*, s.m. A miracle, prodigy, wonder. A.

اغ دغ *ag̲h̲·dug̲h̲*, s.m. Fraud, deceit, imposture.

اغر *ag̲h̲ar*, s.m. Fixing the arrow on the bowstring preparatory to shooting.

آغزکي *āg̲h̲zakai*, s.m. Name of a thorny plant.

آغزن *āg̲h̲zan*, a. Thorny, prickly.

آغزي *āg̲h̲zai*, s.m. A thorn, prickle.

آغړل *āg̲h̲agal*, v.a. To knead or mix dough. Def. in past ten. See آښل. P. (*āg̲h̲is̲h̲tan*).

اغلب *ag̲h̲lab*, ad. Most likely, most probably. A.

آغله *āg̲h̲alah*, a. Mixed, kneaded; good, pleasing.

آغوستل *āghūstal*, v.a. To dress, put on clothes, attire. P. (*āghastan, āghandan*).

آغوستن *āghoston*, s.m. Apparel, dress, raiment, clothing.

آغوستول *āghostawul*, v.a. To attire, clothe, dress.

اغيرل *agheral*, v.a. s. (*ajtran*). See اثيرل.

آفت *āfat*, s.m. Calamity, misfortune. A.

افسوس *afsos*, s.m. Grief, sorrow, regret. in. Alas! pity! ah! P.

افغان *afghān*, s.m. An Afghān.

افيم *afīm*, s.m. Opium. A. (*afiyūn*).

اقبال *iqbāl*, s.m. Good fortune, prestige, good auspices. A.

اقرار *iqrār*, s.m. Argument, assurance, confession. A.

اقليم *iqlīm*, s.m. Country, climate, region. A.

اكا *akā*, s.m. A paternal uncle.

اكثر *aksar*, a. Most. ad. Mostly, generally. A.

اكر *akar*, s.m. Giddiness, vertigo.

اكوبكو *akū-bakū*, s.m. Name of a bird; name of a game; it is played with cakes of moist clay of a globular shape, hollowed out, and made to explode by being dashed on a hard surface with the opening downwards.

اكوړ *akoṛ*, s.m. A walnut; the tree.

اكوړي *akoṛai*, s.m. A kind of leather, tanned red.

آگاه *āgāh*, a. Apprized, aware, informed. P.

اگر *agar*, s.m. A captive, slave, bondsman. P. c. If. P.

اگرچه *agarchi*, c. Although, though. P.

اگرمي *agramai*, s.m. See اررمي.

اگن *agan*, s.m. Name of a bird; the skylark. H.

اگئي *aga-ī*, s.f. An egg.

آل *āl*, s.m. Children, progeny. A.

الاج *alāj*, s.m. A carder or comber of cotton. A. (*ḥallāj*).

الاجي *alājī*, s.f. A comb for clearing cotton of its seeds.

الاستي *alāstī*, a. Absent, invisible.

البته *albatta*, ad. Certainly, undoubtedly, of course. A.

الجه *ulja*, s.f. Booty, plunder.

السي *alsī*, s.f. Linseed. H.

الفت *ulfat*, s.m. Familiarity, friendship, intimacy, kindness. A.

آلفته *āluftah*, a. Vexed, troubled, distressed. P.

القصه *alqiṣṣa*, ad. In fine, in short. A.

الله *allah*, s.m. God. in. Good God! My God! Oh God! A. *allah-bāsh*, s.m. Greeting, shaking hands.

آلو *ālū*, s.m. A kind of plum; a plum. P.

الوان *alwān*, s.m. A kind of cotton cloth dyed red; coloured cloth. A.

آلوتل *ālwatal*, v.n. To fly, float in the air.

الوچه *alūcha*, s.f. A kind of plum. P.

آلوده *ālūdah*, a. Soiled, stained, spattered. P.

آلوزول *ālwuzawul*, v.a. To make fly; to sift or winnow corn, etc., by throwing it up in the air against the wind.

الوس *ulūs*, s.m. A clan, people, tribe. T.

الول *aluwal*, a. All of a heap, by the run, all in a lump.

الوويل *alwoyal*, v.a. To parch, roast, scorch, burn.

الوي *alawai*, a. Parched, roasted, scorched, burnt.

الهنگ *alhang*, s.m. Crying, sobbing, blubbering.

امام *imām*, s.m. The chief priest of a mosque; the large bead of a rosary. A.

امان *amān*, s.m. Protection, quarter, safety. A.

امانت *amānat*, s.m. Deposit, trust. A.

اماني *amānī*, a. All, entire, whole. ad. Entirely, wholly. s.f. Deposit, security, trust. A.

امبار *ambār*, s.m. A heap, a store of grain, etc. P.

امبور *ambūr*, s.m. Forceps, pincers, pliers. P.

آمدني *āmadanī*, s.f. Income, revenue; import. P.

آمدرفت *āmad-raft*, s.m. Coming and going, intercourse, thoroughfare. P.

امر *amr*, s.m. Command, order; affair, business. A.

امرسه *amrasa*, s.f A kind of sweetmeat.

امسا *amsā*, s.f. A staff, stick. A. (*'aṣā*).

امكان *imkān*, s.m. Possibility. A.

امل *amal*, s.m. Intoxication; habitude.

املي *amalī*, s.m. A man addicted to intoxicating drugs.

املوك *amlūk*, s.m. Name of a tree that bears an edible fruit (*Diospyros sp.*).

امن *aman*, s.m. Safety, security, asylum. A.

آموخته *āmokhtah*, a. Learned, taught; experienced, habituated, accustomed. P.

اميد *umed*, s.m. Expectation, hope; pregnancy. P.

امير *amīr*, s.m. A noble, grandee, ruler. A.

اميل *amel*, s.m. An ornament for the neck; a necklace of charms, etc. A. (*ḥimā-il*).

آمين *āmīn*, ad. Amen, so be it. A. *amīn*, s.m. A guardian, umpire, trustee. a. Constant, faithful, trusty. A.

انا *anā*, s.f. A grandmother, paternal or maternal. *warla-anā*, s.f. A great grandmother.

انار *anār*, s.m. A pomegranate. P.

انبالئ *anbāla-ī*, s.f. A howdah; a sedan or litter for women, carried on a pole by men. A. (*'amārī*).

انجام *anjām*, s.m. Accomplishment, end. P.

انجير *anjīr*, s.m. Scrofula; diseased glands in the neck.

انځئ *antsa-ī*, s.f. Cord, string, twine. H. (*āns*).

انت *and*, s.m. An age, cycle of five hundred years; idea, thought, fancy; testicle, egg. S.

اندازه *andāza*, s.f. Measure, quantity; guess. P.

اندرپايه *andarpāya*, s.f. A ladder, steps, stairs.

اندركه *andarka*, s.f. A coat, doublet. S. (*angarkhā*).

اندرور *andror*, s.f. A husband's sister. See ندرور.

آنده *inda*, s.f. A sip, gulp, mouthful.

انديښ *andekkh* or *andeksh*, s.m. Meditating, cogitating, thinking. P. (*andesh*).

انديښنه *andekkhna*, s.f. Anxiety, care, thought, dread. Also *andekkhnā*.

انډوخر *andokhar*, s.m. Name of a game; baste the bear. Called also *swara-ḍabala-ī*, The basters riding on the backs of other boys round the bear.

انډئ *anḍai*, s.m. A bundle, package.

انډيري *anḍerai*, s.m. A mat made of palm leaves.

انذور *anzor* or انځور *andzor*, s.m. Ornament, decoration, embellishment.

انسان *insān*, s.m. Man, mankind. A.

انسټ *ansiṭ*, s.m. Name of a plant.

انصاف *inṣāf*, s.m. Equity, justice. A.

انعام *in'ām*, s.m. A favour, gift, present. A.

انكار *inkār*, s.m. Denial, negation. A.

انګازه *angāza*, s.f. Echo, resonance, reverberation.

انګبين *angabīn*, s.m. Honey; the comb. P.

انګړ *angaṛ*, s.m. A house, mansion.

انګڼر *angaṇr*, s.m. An area, court, yard. S. (*āngan*).

انګولا *angolā*, s.f. The howl of a wild animal.

انګه *inga*, s.f. A bride's maid or attendant for the first few days after marriage. *anga*, s.f. A frock, coat. S. (*angā*).

انګئ *anga-ī*, s.f. Name of a game; prisoners' bars.

انګيټئ *angeṭa-ī*, s.f. A chafing dish. H. (*angeṭhī*).

انګيرل *angeral*, v.a. To fancy, imagine, suppose, think. P. (*ingārdan*).

اننګ *anang*, s.m. A pomegranate; the space between the thumb and fore-finger; a short span.

اننګوړي *anangūṛai*, s.m. A small pomegranate.

اننګي *anangai*, s.m. The cheek.

آنه *āna*, s.f. The pommel of a saddle.

انی *ana-ī*, s.f. A woman's name; Annie.

انړل *anṟal*, v.a. To grind, powder, triturate.

انړول *anṟawul*, v.a. To choose, gather, pick, select, separate, sort.

انوټ *anwaṭ*, s.m. A ring for the thumb or great toe. H.

او *aw*, c. And, also. *ao*, ad. Aye, yes. *o*, in. Oh! Halloa! Hie!

اوار *awār*, s.m. Booty, plunder, spoil; injustice, delay, tyranny. P.

آواره *āwārah*, a. Dissolute, vagabond; spiritless, mean.

آواز *āwāz*, s.m. Voice, sound, report. P.

آوازه *āwāza*, s.f. Rumour, report, fame, celebrity.

اوبال *obāl*, s.m. A crime, fault, sin. A.

اوبړي *obṟa-ī*, s.f. The green vegetation in ponds, etc. Confervæ; duckweed.

اوبنړه *obanṟa*, s.f. The caul; the membrane enveloping the fœtus.

اوبه *oba*, s.f. Water, liquid, fluid. P. (*āb*). A splint in the leg of a horse, etc. *oblan*, a. Watery, sodden.

اوپره *ūprah*, a. Foreign, strange.

اوتر *awtar*, a. Ruined, spoiled; dissolute, wanton, deranged. A. (*abtar*).

اوجاړ *ūjāṟ*, a. Desert, waste, desolated, ruined. S.

اوجري *ūjrai*, s.m. An entrail, gut; tripe. H. (*ūjh*).

اوڅار *awtsār*, a. Clear, evident, manifest. s.m. symptom, sign; evidence, mark. H. (*ūjāl*).

اوچت *ūchat*, a. High, lofty, raised, elevated. S. (*ūnchā*).

اودرول *ūdarawul*, v.a. To fix, set up, pitch (as a tent); to halt, stop, stay (as a boat, cattle, etc.); to make stand.

اودریدل *ūdaredal*, v.n. To abide, halt, stop, stay, stand up, stand still.

اودس *awdas*, s.m. Washing the hands, a form of ablution before prayers; purification. P. (*āb·dast*).

اودل *ūdal*, v.a. To weave, braid, net. P. (*āwīdan*).

اوده *ūdah*, a. Asleep, sleeping. *ūda*, s.f. A charm, blowing, breathing upon by way of charm; mesmerism. (The power is supposed to be acquired by direct commission from above, or by inheritance). Also written *hūda*. A. (*'uhda*).

اوډني *oḍana-ī*, s.f. A woman's veil or mantle. S. (*oṟhnā*).

اور *or*, s.m. Fire. S. (*āg*).

اوراوره کي *or·orahkai*, s.m. Name of a plant; the wild onion or leek; it is used as a condiment.

اوربوشه *orbūsha*, s.f. A barley corn. *orbūshe*, pl. Barley.

اوربوشینه *orbūshīna*, s.f. Barley-meal, barley-bread.

اوربل *orbal*, s.m. A curl, ringlet, or lock of hair on the forehead.

اورپښت *orpukkht*, s.m. A moth.

اورلړوني *or·laṟūnai*, s.m. A fire-poker.

اورمیږ *ormeg*, s.m. The neck, throat.

اورنړي *oranṟai*, s.m. A swaddling-cloth, a baby's winding sheet. S. (*oṟhnī*).

آوررول *āwrawul*, v.a. To cause to hear.

اوره *orah*, s.m. A cloud, the clouds. P. (*abr*).

اوره کي *orahkai*, s.m. A firefly, glow-worm.

آوري *āwrai*, s.m. Mustard seed; name of a herb; wild mustard.

اوري *ora-ī*, s.f. The gums; quick of the nails.

اوريځ *oryadz*, اوريځه *oryadza*, s.f. A cloud.

آوريدل *āwredal*, v.a. To hear, listen, P. (*āwrīdan*).

اوريدل *oredal*, v.n. To rain, drizzle. P. (*bārīdan*).

اوړ *oṟ*, s.m. A weaver's tool; the web through which the woof passes.

اورنبي oṛunbe, ad. Firstly, first, formerly, previously. Also written wṛūnbe. oṛunbanai or wṛunbanai, a. Former, previous.

اورنئي oṛana-ī, s.f. See اونئي.

اورول oṛawul, v.a. To powder, grind, pulverize.

اوره oṛah, s.m. Flour, meal, powder.

اوري oṛai, s.m. Summer.

اوژغونه oʐ̌ghūna, s.f. A goat's hair. oʐ̌ghune, pl. Goat's hair.

اوږد ūgd, a. Long, extended.

اوږمكئي ugmaka-ī, s.f. The moon; moonlight.

اوږه ūga, s.f. Garlic. oga, s.f. The shoulder.

اوږي ogai, s.m. A measure of grain, etc. equal to 14lbs. oga-ī, s.f. An ornament for the neck; a necklet or collar of silver or gold.

اوس os, ad. Now, at this time.

اوسپنخړي ospankhaṛai, s.m. Iron slag or dross.

اوسپنه ospana, s.f. Iron.

اوسط awsaṭ, a. Medium, mean, middling. A.

اوسن osan, a. Existing, present.

اوسني osanai, a. Modern, late, recent.

اوسي osai, s.m. A deer, gazelle.

اوسيدل osedal, v.n. To abide, exist, remain, dwell, reside, stay. See āstedal.

اوښ ūkkh, s.m. A camel. P. (ūshtur).

اوښبه ūkkhbah or ūkshbah, s.m. A camel-man, an owner of camels.

آوښتل āwukkhtal, v.a. To change, turn, alter. P. (bāz-gashtan).

اوښه okkha, s.f. A tear. P. (ashk).

اوښي awkkhai, s.m. A brother-in-law; wife's brother; sister's husband. A. (akh, brother). okkhī, s.m. The mane of a horse.

اوغان awghān, s.m. An Afghan.

اوغز ūghz, s.m. A walnut.

اوگره ogra, s.f. Porridge, pap, gruel. P. (oghrā).

اوگرائي ūgrā-ī, s.f. A portion, part, instalment; a debt paid at different times. H.

اول awwal, a. First, foremost. A.

اولاد awlād, s.m. Progeny, issue, children. A. Also written alwād.

اولو awlū, s.m. Treacle, molasses.

اوله olah, s.m. A flock of lambs kept separate from their mothers.

اوم om or ūm, a. Crude, raw, uncooked, unripe, immature. P. (khūm). awam, a. The seventh.

اومه omah, s.m. Name of a plant. It is used in tanning, and is added to snuff to increase its pungency.

اونگئي ūnga-ī, s.f. The moon.

اوني ūnai, s.m. A babbler, chatterer.

اووم owam, a. The seventh.

اووه owah, a. Seven.

اووي owī, s.m. A cock's comb; a horse's mane.

اوه awah, a. Seven. awa, s.f. A pimple, pustule, vesicle.

اوي oe, s.m. Consent, promise, pledge.

اويا awiyā, a. Seventy.

اويزاند awezānd, a. Hanging, pendant, suspended. P. (āwez).

اوينه oenah, s.m. The white ant.

اهاړ ahāṛ, s.m. Name of the third Hindu month. June-July.

اي ai, in. Oh! Halloa! sign of the vocative case. P.

آيا āyā, in. No! Is it! Really! How odd! P. ad. No, not at all, never.

ايړي erṛai, s.m. The long-tailed sheep. S. (bheṛī).

ايره īra, s.f. Ash. īre, pl. Ashes.

ايړي eṛai, s.m. See ايړي.

ايسار īsār, a. Hindered, stopped, surrounded. s.m. A castle, fort; embarrassment; perplexity. A. (ḥiṣār).

ايستل estal, v.a. To draw out, extract, expel. Also yastal. Def. in. pres. ten. See باسل.

ايشنه eshana, s.f. Agitation, ferment, ebullition, effervescence. P. (josh).

ايشول eshawul v.a. To boil, heat, make boil. P. (joshandan).

ايشيدل eshedal, v.n. To boil, bubble, effervesce. P. (joshīdan).

ايښهل ekkhal or īkkhal, v.a. To lay, put, place, set. Also yakkhal. Def. in pres. ten. See ږدل. P. (nishāndan).

ايښودل ekkhodal, or īkkhodal, } v.a. See ايښهل.
ايښول ekkhawul, or īkkhawul, }

ايل el or īl, a. Domestic, tame, not wild.

ايله elah, a. Free, liberated. P. (yalah).

ايمان īmān, s.m. Faith, religious belief. A.

ايمن eman, a. Calm, gentle, patient.

ايمنه emna, s.f. A woman's name.

اينځر īndzar, s.m. A fig; the tree. P. (anjīr).

آئين ā-īn, s.m. Law, rule, regulation. P.

آئينه ā-īna, s.f. A mirror, looking-glass; the liver, the gall bladder.

اينه īna, s.f. The gall bladder, the liver, lungs and heart, the vitals.

ايوه īwa, s.f. A plough, ploughing.

ب

ب be. The second letter of the Pukkhto alphabet. It is often changed for و in words adopted from the Persian and Sanscrit.

بَ ba or به ba, part. The sign of the future and continuative past tenses of verbs.

با bā, p. With, by. Only used in comp. with words from the Persian. P.

باب bāb, s.m. Account, business, matter; chapter or section of a book; door, gate. A.

بابا bābā, in. Father! Sire! A term of affection and respect used towards old men, and by children to a grandfather. T.

بابت bābat, s.m. Affair, business; item, article; account, on account of. A.

بابړ bābaṛ, s.m. Name of an Afghan clan.

بابکو bābako, in. Dear child! A term of affectionate address to a child.

بابو bābū, in. Father! Sire! A term of affection or esteem used towards a father or old man.

بابي bābī, s.f. A brother's wife, sister-in-law. in. Mother! Granny dear! s.m. Name of an Afghan clan.

باتور bātūr, s.m. An eagle; brave, valiant (corrupt: of P. bahādur). bātor, s.m. The pupil of the eye.

باتئ bāta-ī, s.f. A wick, match, candle, spile; bougie, a tent for a wound. S. (battī).

باټ bāṭ, s.m. A hone, grindstone.

باټينګڼړ bāṭīnganṛ, s.m. The egg-plant (solanum longum). P. (baingan).

باج bāj, s.m. Tax, toll, impost, duty. P.

باجره bājra, s.f. Indian corn, spiked millet (Holcus spicatus). P. (bājrā).

باجه bājah, s.m. Wife's sister's husband, brother-in-law.

باد bād, s.m. Air, wind; rheumatism. P.

بادام bādām, s.m. An almond. P.

بادخور bād·khor, s.m. A disease of horses; œdema. Name of a kind of hawk. P.

بادخورک bād·khorak, s.m. The sparrow-hawk. P.

بادرنګ bādrang, s.m. A cucumber. P.

بادرو bādro, s.m. Name of the fifth Hindu month. August-September. S. (bhādon). bādraw, s.m. An air-hole, ventilator. Also bād·khāna. P.

بادشاه bādshāh, s.m. Monarch, sovereign, king. P.

بادکښ bād·kakkh, s.m. A ventilator, chimney. P. (bād·kash).

بادګوله bād·gola, s.f. Colic, flatulent colic. P.

بادوان bād·wān, s.m. A sail, wing; a shade or screen for a lamp. P.

بادهوا bād·hawā, s.f. A paper kite. P.

بادي *bādī*, a. Flatulent, windy ; haughty, proud.

باڈگول *bāḍgol*, s.m. A leading string, rein, head rope of a horse. H. (*bāgḍor*).

بار *bār*. s.m. A burden, load ; time, occasion, turn, place. P.

باران *bārān*, s.m. Rain ; a shower, downpour. P.

بارخو *bārkho*, s.f. The cheek, side of the face.

بارک *bārak*, s.m. A man's name, Barak. *bārakzī*, s.m. The clan Barak. *bārakzai*, s.m. A man of the clan Barak. *bārakza-ī*, s.f. A woman of the clan Barak. The late Amir Dost Muhammad Khan was the head of this now famous clan.

بارکښ *bār-kakkh*, s.m. A rope, cord, etc. for tying up baggage ; a beast of burthen. a. burthen-bearing ; meek, humble. P. (*bār-kash*).

باره *bāra*, s.f. A rampart, fortification, enclosure, ditch, entrenchment, fence. P.

باريک *bārīk*, a. Fine, narrow, slender, subtile. P.

باري *bāre*, ad. Once ; at length ; then.

باړ *bāṛ*, s.m. A volley of musketry. An iron dish for roasting grain. S.

باړه *bāṛa*, s.f. An enclosure, sheepfold. S. (*bāṛā*).

باز *bāz*, s.f. A female falcon. P. See جرّه

بازار *bāzār*, s.m. A market, mart. P.

بازو *bāzū*, s.m. The arm ; side of a bedstead ; fold of a door ; the flank, side of anything. P.

بازوبند *bāzū-band*, s.m. An ornament for the arm. P.

بازي *bāzī*, s.f. Cheat, trick, deception, stratagem ; play, sport, game. P.

بازيگر *bāzī-gar*, s.m. A tumbler, rope-dancer, juggler ; cheat, impostor.

باس *bās*, s.m. A privy, necessary ; odour, smell. S.

باسل *bāsal*, v.a. To extract, draw out, pull out. Def. in past tense. See ايستل.

باښه *bākkha*, s.f. A sparrow-hawk. P. (*bāsha*).

باښين *bākkhīn*, s.m. A sparrow-hawk. P. (*bāshīn*).

باطل *bāṭil*, a. Futile, useless, vain. A

باطن *bāṭin*, a. Concealed, internal. A

باعث *bā'is*, s.m. Account, cause, reason. A.

باغ *bāgh*, s.m. A garden, grove, orchard. P.

باغوان *bāghwān*, s.m. A gardener.

باقي *bāqī*, s.m. Arrears, balance, remnant ; existing, remaining. A.

باک *bāk*, s.m. Anxiety, dread, fear. P.

باکي *bāka-ī*, s.f. Nausea, sickness. H. (*ūbkā-ī*).

باګو *bāgū*, or
باګولي *bāgola-ī*, s.f. } A bogy, goblin, ghost.

بالښت *bālikkht*, s.m. A bolster, pillow. P. (*bālish*). *bālikkht-goṭai*, s.m. A cushion.

بالښتک *bālikkhtak*, s.m. A cushion, pad.

بالغ *bāligh*, a. Adult, mature, full-grown. A.

بالڼر *bālanr*, s.m. Fuel, fire-wood.

بالين *bālīn*, s.m. A bolster, pillow, cushion, pad. P.

بام *bām*, s.m. The roof of a house. P.

بامبڼر *bāmbanr*, s.m. A Brahmin. S. (*bāmhan*).

بامبڼره *bāmbanra*, s.f. A blaze, conflagration. A Brahmin woman.

بامبيلکي *bāmbī-lakai*, s.m. A kind of butterfly.

باندِ *bāndi*,
باندي *bānde*, } p. Above, atop, on, upon.

بانډه *bānḍa*, s.f. A cattle or sheep-pen ; a hamlet. S. (*bāṛā*).

باڼر *bānr*, s.m. Cordage made of palm-leaves.

باڼره *bānra*, s.f. The eyelash.

بانکيا *bānkiyā*, s.m. A fop, beau. H. (*bānkā*).

بانګ *bāng*, s.m. A call, cry, shout. P.

بانګيدل *bāngedal*, v.n. To low, bleat, bellow.

بانه *bāna*, s.f. An excuse, pretence, sham, pretext. P. (*bahāna*).

باور *bāwar*, s.m. Belief, faith, credit, trust. P.

باوسير *bāwsīr*, s.m. Hemorrhoids, piles. A. (*bawāsīr*).

باولي *bāolī*, s.f. The drag on which hawks, dogs, etc. are trained and taught to hunt. A well, with steps to the water. H. *bāolī-warkawul*, v.a. To initiate, train, teach.

باهر *bāhar*, ad. Outside, without, beyond, foreign. S.

باهو *bāhū*, s.m. An ornament for the arm.

بائيده *bā-īdah*, a. Fit, proper, necessary, suitable. ad. Necessarily, of necessity, it behoves.

بائيكر *bā-īkar*, s.m. Name of a shrub (*Adhatoda vasica*). H. (*bākar*).

بائِلل *bā-elal*, v.a. To fail, forfeit, lose. P. (*bākhtan*).

ببر *babar*, a. Hairy, shaggy. P.

ببوزي *babozai*, s.m. A fan made of palm leaves, a fan. Name of a bird, the kingfisher.

ببۍ *baba-ī*, s.f. Name of a bird. An affectionate term for "mother."

بت *but*, s.m. An image, idol, figure, form, model. One of the walls that supports the cross-beam of a Persian wheel.

بتان *batān*, s.m. See پتان.

بتر *batar*, a. Worse, very bad. P. (*badtar*).

بتک *batak*, s.m. A water cruse, in the shape of a double convex disc, made of leather or pottery.

بتکي *batakai*, s.m. Dimin. of preceding.

بته *bata*, s.f. A heron, crane.

بتي *batī*, s.f. Glue, paste, starch, size.

بټ *baṭ*, s.m. A furnace, kiln; an iron pot or dish for roasting grain; bark, rind, husk; prosperity, good luck.

بټه *baṭa*, s.f. Husked or pounded barley.

بجز *bajuz*, p. Except, besides, save, without. P.

بجل *bujal*, s.m. Ankle-joint, knuckle-bone. F.

بڅخه *butskha*, s.f. A clothes-bag, bundle of clothes. T. (*buqcha*).

بڅخکۍ *butskhaka-ī*, s.f. A reticule, small bag for collyrium, needles, etc.

بڅري *batsarai*, }
بڅرکي *batsarkai*, } s.m. A spark, scintillation.

بچاو *bachāo*, s.m. Escape, protection, shelter, H. *bachawul*, v.a. To save, shelter, etc.

بچري *bachrai*, s.m. An ass's colt, young donkey.

بچکري *bachakarai*, s.m. The lash of a whip; end of a sling.

بچو *bachū*, in. Dear babe! Baby dear! Baby! A term of affectionate address to a child.

بچونګړي *bachūngarai*, s.m. A babe, infant, a very young animal.

بچوي *bachawai*, s.m. The lash of a whip; end of a sling; a band or ribbon for fastening women's hair; a tassel of braided cords attached to the back hair of women.

بچي *bachai*, s.m. A babe, infant, child, young one. P. (*bacha*).

بحث *bahs*, s.m. Argument, discussion, controversy. A.

بحر *bahr*, s.m. The ocean, sea. A.

بخت *bakht*, s.m. Fate, fortune, luck. P.

بخره *bakhra*, s.f. Lot, portion, share. P.

بخښ *bakhksh*, s.m. Lot, share, portion; bestowing, giving; forgiveness. P. (*bakhsh*).

بخښښ *bakhkshiksh*, s.m. Donation, gift, grant. P. (*bakhshish*).

بخښل *bakhkkhal* or *bakhkshal*, v.a. See بښل. P. (*bakhshīdan*).

بخښنه *bakhkkhana*, s.f. Pardon, forgiveness, forgiving; giving, bestowing.

بخملۍ *bakhmala-ī*, s.f. Name of an insect of a scarlet colour, the scarlet lady; called also *bībī-pāto*. (From A. *makhmal*).

بخيل *bakhīl*, s.m. A miser, niggard. a. Vicious, ill-tempered, spiteful, stingy. A.

بخيلي *ba<u>kh</u>īlī*, s.f. Avarice, stinginess; obstinacy, vice, ill-temper, spite.

بد *bad*, a. Bad, evil, vicious. P.

بدر *badar*, s.m. The silky cotton tree (*Bombax heptaphyllum*). *badar-kand*, or *badar-kā<u>n</u>rai*, s.m. The gum resin of the tree: used in medicine. The silky cotton is used as a stuffing for pillows.

بدرگه *badraga*, s.f. A convoy, escort, guide. A. (*badraqa*).

بدري *badra-ī*, s.f. A woman's name. *budrī*, s.f. A stumble, trip; loss, injury, damage.

بدعا *bad'uā*, s.f. A curse, malediction. P. (*bad d'uā*).

بدل *badal*, s.m. Exchange; revenge, retaliation. A. *badalawul*, v.a. To exchange, etc.

بدلمن *bad-laman*, a. Wanton, dissolute, unchaste.

بدله *badala*, s.f. Melody, music, tune.

بدن *badan*, s.m. The body. A.

بدي *badī*, s.f. Enmity, evil, mischief.

بڈائي *baḍā-ī*, s.f. Dignity, rank; magnitude, greatness. S. (*baṛā-ī*).

بڈگال *baḍagāl*, s.m. The silky down on the flower spike of the bullrush. H. (*baṛā gālā*). See لوخه.

بڈه *baḍa*, s.f. A bribe, douceur; the upper hem of a pair of trousers, through which passes the fastening band.

بر *bar*, a. High, upper, top; victorious, successful. s.m. A stroke of the moon, moon-blast. *bar wahalai*, a. Moon-struck.

برابر *barābar*, a. Abreast, equal, even, level, alike, smooth, straight.

برایه *barāya*, ad. Last night, yesternight.

برباد *barbād*, a. Ruined, wasted, thrown away. P.

بربره *burbura*, s.f. A bubble. P. (*bulbulā*).

بربست *barbast*, s.m. Chattels, effects, goods. P.

بربنډ *barbanḍ*, a. Bare, naked, uncovered. P. (*barahna*).

برپا *barpā*, a. Raised, set on foot, commenced. P.

برج *bruj*, s.m. A turret, tower, bastion. P. (*burj*).

برجو *barjo*, s.f. A hone, whetstone. Also *barjo kā<u>n</u>rai*.

برڅير *bar<u>ts</u>er*, a. Clear, manifest, evident, visible.

برڅيرن *bar<u>ts</u>eran*, ad. Apparently, manifestly, visibly, clearly.

برخه *bra<u>kh</u>a*, s.f. See بخره.

برړه *baraṛa*, s.f. Name of a shrub (*Periploca aphylla*).

برطرف *bartaraf*, a. Apart, aside, dismissed, turned off, discharged. A.

برغ *bra<u>gh</u>*, s.m. A fold, layer, plait; duplication, multiplication, fold.

برغټ *bar<u>gh</u>uṭ*, s.m. A wild cat.

برغنډ *bar<u>gh</u>anḍ*, s.m. A notch, dent, nick.

برغو *bar<u>gh</u>o*, s.m. The cleaning rod of a gun.

برغوټي *bar<u>gh</u>oṭa-ī*, s.f. A disease of the parotid gland, mumps.

برغوږ *bar<u>gh</u>wag*, s.m. An ear-drop, pendant, or ring.

برغولي *bar<u>gh</u>olai*, s.m. A dish-cover, lid.

برغوني *bra<u>gh</u>ūnai*, s.m. A twin, one of twins.

برکت *barakat*, s.m. Blessing, prosperity, fortune. A.

برکتي *barakatī*, a. Blessed, fortunate, prosperous.

برگ *brag*, a. Spotted, speckled, streaked. s.m. A leper.

برگړندي *bargaṛandai*, s.m. Embracing, hugging, cuddling.

برگستوان *bargastawān*, s.m. Mail armour for a horse; sword proof trappings. P. (*bargastān*).

برگويټ *bargweṭ*, s.m. A man's name. One of the great ancestors of <u>Kh</u>aṭak clan.

برگه *barga*, s.f. A beam, rafter. H. (*bargā*).

برگي *bragai*, s.m. Leprosy; a leper.

برم *bram*, s.m. Force, power, strength; guard, protection. P. (*barm*).

برمته *baramta*, s.f. Reprisal, seizing the property or persons of an offending tribe or family in retaliation for injuries done, and as pledges or hostages for restitution or settlement.

برمند *barmand*, a. See بربند.

برمه *barma*, s.f. An auger, gimlet, centre-bit or borer, worked with a bow and string. H. (*barmā*).

برند *brand*, a. Frowning, scowling, staring. P. (*barham*).

برندول *brandawul*, v.a. To frown, scowl.

برندي *barandai*, s.m. A spindle for twisting thread. A teetotum, spun by two strings pulled in opposite directions.

برني *baranai*, a. Stale, old, yesterday's.

بروړه *baroṛa*, s.f. A wood-louse; crab-louse; name of a venomous insect. Nettlerash, hives. *broṛah*, s.m. Mixed meal of pulses and cereals. See راړه.

برونړۍ *barwaṉṛa-ī*, s.f. The socket in which the pivot of an irrigation wheel works.

بروي *barwai*, a. Viscid, glutinous, sticky, starchy.

بره *barrah*, s.m. A kid, lamb, sheep. P.

بره‌ګړه *bara-gaṛa*, s.f. Embrace, hug.

برهم *barham*, a. Confused, disconcerted, vexed. P.

بري *barai*, s.m. Victory, success, triumph.

بريت *bret*, s.m. The mustache. P. (*burut*). *brīt*, s.m. Boundary, limit, separation. P. (*burīd*).

بريګن *bregan*, s.m. The bleat of a goat or sheep.

بريښ *brekkh*, s.m. Piercing, lancing, pricking or stabbing pain; a throb, spasm, cramp, stitch; a cutting pain. P. (*burrish*).

بريښنا *brekkhnā*, s.f. brilliancy, lustre, splendour; lightning.

بريښيدل *brekkhedal*, v.n. To glitter, shine; lighten. A. (*baraq*).

بړاس *bṛās*, s.m. Heat, steam, vapour.

بړانډه *baṛānḍa*, s.f. A conflagation, blaze.

بړبړ *baṛbaṛ*, ad. Often, repeatedly, frequently. P. (*bārbār*).

بړبړي *baṛbaṛai*, s.m. A prattler, gabbler, chatterbox.

بړبوکۍ *baṛbūka-ī*, s.f. A dust devil, whirlwind.

بړستن *bṛastan*, s.f. Coverlet, quilt, counterpane.

بړني *baṛanai*, s.m. Name of a tree.

بړوا *baṛwā*, s.m. A pimp. H. (*bhaṛwā*).

بړوټ *bṛūṭ*, s.m. Name of a grass (*Cyperus verticillatus*).

بړوس *bṛūs*, a. Angry, furious, savage, enraged. *bṛūs-wālai*, s.m. Anger, rage, wrath.

بړينچغ *baṛenchagh*, s.m. A whirligig; a cross bar balanced on the top of an upright post, on which as a pivot it is made to revolve by the riders, who sit in chairs attached to the ends of the cross bar.

بز *buz*, s.m. A he-goat. P.

بزاز *bazāz*, s.m. Cloth-merchant, draper, mercer. P.

بزغاله *buzghālah*, s.m. A kid. P.

بزغلي *buzghalai*, s.m. A bud, sprout, young shoot.

بزه *baza*, s.f. Sin, crime. P. Name of a shrub. See بائيکر. *bza*, s.f. A she-goat; a curlew. P.

بژه *bjah*, a. Chopped, minced, cut up.

بس *bas*, a. Enough, plenty, sufficient.

بساط *bisāt*, s.m. A display, show, or spread of things, as furniture, merchandize, etc. bedding, sheeting, flooring. A.

بسمه *basma*, s.f. Indigo. S.

بسمل *bismil*, a. Sacrificed. *bismil kawul*, v.a. To sacrifice.

بسم‌الله *bismillah*, In the name of God. *bismillah kawul*, v.a. To commence, begin.

بسيا *basiyā*, a. Cultivated, peopled, inhabited. S.

بشپړ *ba<u>sh</u>paṛ*, a. Complete, entire, perfect.

بشر *ba<u>sh</u>ar*, s.m. Man, mankind. A.

بشره *ba<u>sh</u>ra*, s.f. Face, visage, countenance.

بشري *ba<u>sh</u>arī*, a. Human, of man.

بشكه *bu<u>sh</u>ka*, s.f. Name of a plant, used as a pot-herb; goosefoot (*Chenopodium album*).

بشنج *ba<u>sh</u>anj*, s.m. Character, reputation, name.

ببښل *ba<u>kkh</u>al*, v.a. To give, pardon, forgive, excuse. See بخښل

ببښنه *ba<u>kkh</u>ana*, s.f. A gift, pardon, forgiveness.

بط *bat*, s.m. A duck. A.

بعد *b'ad*, ad. After, subsequently. A.

بعيد *b'aīd*, a. Far, remote. A.

بغارګ *b<u>gh</u>ārg*, a. Double, duplex, two-fold.

بغاره *ba<u>gh</u>āra*, s.f. A scream, shriek.

بغبغو *ba<u>gh</u>ba<u>gh</u>o*, s.m. The rice bird (*Ardea torra*).

بغدر *ba<u>gh</u>dar*, s.m. Hammer, mallet. s. (*mugdar*).

بغرږ *ba<u>gh</u>arg*, s.m. Rebound, recoil, return. Double, duplex.

بغرګه *b<u>gh</u>arga*, s.f. A breach, gap; a deep wound. P. (*bu<u>gh</u>āra*).

بغري *ba<u>gh</u>arai*, s.m. A pimp; term of abuse. *ba<u>gh</u>ara-ī*, s.f. A mortar; *vulva*; a term of abuse. P. (*<u>gh</u>ubāra*).

بغض *bu<u>gh</u>z*, s.m. Hatred, malice, rancour, spite. A.

بغل *ba<u>gh</u>al*, s.m. The armpit, side; embrace. P.

بغير *ba<u>gh</u>air*, ad. Besides, except, without. A.

بقا *baqā*, s.f. Eternity, perpetuity. A.

بقال *baqāl*, s.m. A corn chandler, grocer, A.

بک *bak*, s.m. Jabber, gabble, prattle, talk. S.

بک بکي *bak·bakai*, s.m. A gabbler, prattler, chatterbox.

بکاره *bakārah*, s.m. Courier, messenger. H. (*bakārā*).

بکاول *bakāwul*, s.m. A cook, victualler. P.

بکاينړ *bakāyanṛ*, s.m. Name of a tree (*Melia sempervirens*). H. (*bakāyan*).

بکري *bakra-ī*, s.f. A flint, quartz.

بګلولي *bagalola-ī*, s.f. A bogy, goblin, scarecrow, hag.

بګلي *baglai*, s.m. A crane, heron; the rice bird. H. (*baglā*).

بګنيدل *bugnedal*, v.n. To shy, start, fear. *bugnawul*, v.a. To frighten, scare, start.

بګوړه *bagoṛa*, s.f. A kind of cheese; dry curds; the Persian *qurūt*.

بګوه *bagwa*, s.f. Red ochre, red clay.

بل *bul*, a. Another, other, different. *bal*, a. Burnt, fired, ignited, kindled, lighted.

بلا *balā*, s.f. Affliction, calamity, misfortune.

بلابتر *balā·batar*, s.m. Lumber, trash, rubbish.

بلاربه *blārba*, a. Pregnant, with young.

بلاربيدل *blārbedal*, v.n. To conceive, become pregnant. *blārbawul*, v.a. To make pregnant.

بلاغند *balā<u>gh</u>und*, s.m. Name of a tree and its fruit (*Ægle marmelos*).

بلانړه *bilāṇrah*, s.m. A moan, groan, wail.

بلاوه *bulāwa*, s.f. Mistake, error. H. (*bhūl*).

بلبل *bulbul*, s.m. A nightingale; a shrike. A kind of dance, a reel. P.

بلد *balad*, s.m. A guide, resident. a. Acquainted, familiar. P.

بلغاک *bul<u>gh</u>āk*, s.m. The twitter of birds.

بلغم *bal<u>gh</u>am*, s.m. Phlegm, mucus. P.

بلکه *balki*, ad. But, nay, rather. A.

بلګه *balga*, s.f. A clue, trace, track, etc. of stolen goods.

بلل *balal*, v.a. To call, summon, convoke. H. (*bulānā*).

بلماز *bilmāz*, a. Prayerless, profane, unholy, impure, corrupt. P. (*be·namāz*).

بلمګي *bilmagai*, } a. Saltless, tasteless, with-
بلمنګي *bilmangai*, } out flavour. (Corrupt: of *be·mālga*).

بلند *buland*, a. High, lofty, tall. P.

بلندي *bulandai*, s.m. An eminence, height, elevation.

بلو *balaw*, s.m. A hone, razor-strop, whetstone.

بلوا *balwā*, s.f. Mutiny, riot, tumult. A.

بلوڅ *balots*, s.m. A Baloch; the tribe.

بلودل *blodal*, v.a. To chafe, fret, abrade, graze, rub, touch; to vex, annoy, worry. P. (*burīdan.*)

بلور *bilaur*, s.m. Crystal, glass. P.

بلوس *blos*, s.m. A rub, graze, touch; annoyance, vexation.

بلوسيدل *blosedal*, v.a. See بلودل.

بلوغت *bulūghat*, s.m. Puberty, adolescence, youth. A.

بلول *balawul*, v.a. To burn, kindle, set alight, fire, ignite.

بلونګړي *bilūngaṛai*, s.m. A squirrel.

بله *bala*, s.f. A javelin, dart, pike. H. (*ballā*).

بلئ *bala-ī*, s.f. The edge of a roof, eaves; door-bolt, boat-hook, barge-pole. H. (*ballī*).

بليدل *baledal*, v.n. To burn, blaze, take fire, ignite. H. (*balnā.*)

بليږدل *blegdal*, v.a. To swaddle, swathe.

بم *bam*, s.m. A bass, deep, or hollow sound. A.

بمبره *bambara*, s.f. A wasp, hornet.

بُن *ba-an*, s.f. A cotemporary or rival wife; each of a man's several wives is *ba-an* to the other. The children by one wife are *ba-anzī* to those by the others. See بُنزي.

بنا *binā*, s.f. Preparation; foundation, building, edifice. A.

بنات *banāt*, s.m. Broad-cloth, woollen cloth. H.

بنبل *banbal*, s.m. The beard of grasses, etc.

بنبوله *banbola*, s.f. A wicker box coated with clay for the storing of grain.

بنج *banj*, s.m. The horse chestnut tree, the fruit. *banaj*, s.m. Trade, merchandise. S.

بنجاري *banjārī*, s.m. A trader, peddler, grain merchant. S. (*banjārā*).

بانجخ *banjakh*, s.m. Name of a plant, the seed of which contains cowitch.

بنجئ *banja-ī*, s.f. The Cassia tree.

بند *band*, s.m. A band, fastening, knot, tie; a joint, knuckle; arrest, captivity, imprisonment; artifice, dodge, trick. P.

بندر *bandar*, s.m. An emporium, sea port. P.

بندلئ *bindla-ī*, s.f. A flute, fife, whistle.

بندنړ *bandanr*, s.m. Promise, covenant. S. (*bandhan*).

بندوخ *bandūkh*, s.m. A gun, matchlock. T. (*bandūq*).

بندوبست *bandobust*, s.m. Arrangement, management, settlement. P.

بنده *bandah*, s.m. A servant, slave, bondsman; a creature. P.

بندي *bandī*, s.m. A captive, prisoner. S. *banda-ī*, s.f. An ornament for the neck; an ornamental shoulder sling worn by women. S.

بُنزي *ba-anzai*, s.m. Step-son; son of the husband by another wife. (See پرکټي). *ba-anza-ī*, s.f. Step-daughter; a former or other wife's daughter.

بنګ *bang*, s.m. The hemp plant (*Cannabis Indicus*). H. (*bhang*).

بنګي *bangī*, s.m. One addicted to the use of bang, or any other intoxicating drug; a drunkard.

بنګښ *bangakkh*, s.m. Name of a Pathan tribe located about Kohat.

بنګول *bangawul*, v.a. To taint, corrupt, pollute.

بنئ *bana-ī*, s.f. A wallet or bag made of an entire kid's skin; bellows made of a pair of such skins attached to one nozzle.

بنياد *bunyād*, s.m. Base, origin, foundation. A.

بنړ *banr*, s.m. A wood, forest. S. (*ban*).

بنړمانو *banr-mānū*, s.m. A wild man, man of the woods. S. (*ban-manukh*).

بنړه *banṛa*, s.f. A quill, large feather; a feather.

بنړکه *banṛaka*, s.f. A feather, small feather.

بنړۍ *banṛa-ī*, s.f. Name of a tree; mistletoe. *banṛai*, a. Red-haired, rufus; shock-headed.

بنړیه *banṛiyah*, s.m. A Hindu shopkeeper. s. (*banniyā*).

بنفشه *binafsha*, s.f. A violet, the plant. P.

بو *bū* or *bo*, s.m. Odour, scent, smell. P. *baw*, s.m. A goblin, scare-crow.

بوتکي *būtkī*, s.f. Name of a gold coin; Belgian ducat.

بوتلل *botlal*, v.a. To carry away, conduct, lead, convey. Only applied to animate objects. See بیول.

بوته *bota*, s.f. Carrying away, leading off, etc. See برمته.

بوتي *botai*, s.m. A young camel. P.

بوټ *būṭ*, a. Surly, cross, sullen, ill-tempered. Also *sūṭ·būṭ*.

بوټسوړي *būṭsūṛī*, s.m. Chaff, bran, husks, shell, etc.

بوټي *būṭai*, s.m. A plant, herb, bush, shrub. *būṭī*, pl. Drugs, vegetable medicines; flowers embroidered, painted, or carved. H. (*būṭā*).

بوجه *būja*, s.f. A bung, cork, stopper, plug.

بوڅکۍ *būtska-ī*, s.f. The lobe of the ear.

بود *būd*, s.m. Existence, being; profit, gain.

بوده *būda*, s.f. (In weaving) the woof of the web. P.

بوډاګي *būḍāgai*, s.m. A decrepid old man. H. (*būṛhā*).

بور *baur*, s.m. A panther, leopard. *bor*, s.m. A dent, chip, flaw, fracture. a. grey, brown; a grey horse. H. (*bhūrā*). *būr*, s.m. Husk, skin, chaff; the linear leaves of the pine, tamarisk, and similar trees. A father who has lost a child by death.

بورا *baurā*, s.m. A large black bee. S. (*bhaunṛā*).

بورجل *borjal*, s.f. An abode, home, house, resort; a place of resort, assignment, or meeting. A. (*marja'*).

بورګي *baurgai*, s.m. A panther, small leopard.

بورنه *bornah*, s.m. Dredging, flour, meal, etc. used to sprinkle upon meat, dough, etc. Also بورنړه.

بوره *būra*, s.f. A woman who has lost her child by death.

بورۍ *baura-ī*, s.f. A bunion, corn.

بوړه *bauṛa*, s.f. An elevated plateau, table-land, or flat bit of land on a hill side.

بوړي *būṛai*, s.m. The cog of a Persian wheel. a. Chipped, cracked (as a cup); clipped, slit, split (as the nose or ears). *būṛa·ī*, s.f. Name of a disease (*prolapsus ani*).

بوزه *boza*, s.f. Fermented liquor, beer. P.

بوزينه *bozīna*, s.f. Leather of a red colour, prepared from goat skins. P.

بوږ *bog*, a. Hoarse, rough, husky voice. s.m. A sore throat, aphonia, loss of voice.

بوس *būs*, s.m. Chaff, chopped straw. H. (*bhūs*).

بوساړه *būsāṛa*, s.f. A stack of būs.

بوستان *bostān*, s.m. A flower-garden. P.

بوښت *bokkht*, a. Sticky, adhesive. s.m. A quicksand, bog, quagmire.

بوښتنه *bokkhtana*, s.f. A bog, quicksand.

بوغ *būgh*, s.m. A wooden bowl or cup.

بوق *būq*, A bugle, clarion. A.

بوکه *boka*, s.f. A water-bucket. H.

بوکي *bokī*, s.m. Name of an Afghan clan.

بوګري *bogarai*, s.m. Church land, glebe; land given to priests and holy men free of rent; ploughing and sowing, free of cost, for priests, etc. or for one another.

بول *baul*, s.f. Urine. A. *waṛa·baul kawul*, v.a. To make water, urinate. *loya·baul kawul*, v.a. To go to stool, ease oneself.

بولاق *bolāq*, s.m. An ornament for the nose. H.

بولقه *bolqa*, s.f. A sheet or mantle with eyelets to see through: it is a woman's outdoor dress, and covers the whole body from head to foot: it is only used by women living in cities or large towns. A. (*burqa'*).

بوم *būm*, s.m. A country; an owl; a native or home-bred person; a guide. a. Acquainted, familiar, habituated. P.

بوميا *būmiyā*, s.m. A conductor, guide, resident.

بونست *bonsaṭ*, s.m. Foundation, origin, root; name of a plant.

بونگه *būnga*, s.f. Black-mail, ransom.

بونړ *būnr*, s.m. A disease of the nose, ozœna; one afflicted with the disease. Cordage made of palm leaves, and used for netting of beds, etc. H. (*bān*). *bonr*, s.m. A buzz, hum (as of a bee or fly).

بونړيدل *bonredal*, v.n. To buzz, hum; putrefy, rot, become fly-blown, tainted, etc. *bonrawul*, v.a. To taint, fly-blow, pollute, etc.

بوهار *būhār*, s.m. Spring. P. (*bahār*).

بوهاري *būhārai*, s.m. A weanling, an animal newly weaned from its mother.

بويه *boyah*, a. Necessary, proper, indispensable. ad. Necessarily, properly, fitly.

به *ba*, A particle used as the sign of the future and continuative past tenses. Also written بَ.

بها *bahā*, s.f. Cost, price, value. A.

بهادر *bahādur*, s.m. A champion, hero. a. Courageous, brave. P.

بهادري *bahādurī*, s.f. Bravery, courage. *bahādurai*, s.m. A little hero, a coward.

بهانړ *bihānr*, s.m. A colt, young horse.

بهانيه *bahāniyah*, a. Costly, expensive, valuable, precious.

بهبود *bihbūd*, a. Advantageous, profitable. P.

بهبودي *bihbūdī*, s.f. Advantage, profit, gain, good. A large knife, dagger.

بهتان *buhtān*, s.m. Calumny, defamation; lying. A.

بهتر *bihtar*, a. Better, preferable, well. P.

بهتري *bihtarī*, s.f. Advantage, welfare.

بهره *bahra*, s.f. Lot, share; gain, profit. P.

بهښت *bihikkht*, s.m. Heaven, paradise. P. (*bihisht*).

بهگنړ *bhaganr*, s.m. A fly, gadfly.

بهم *baham*, ad. Together, one with another. P.

بهنه *bahna*, s.f. A top, whip-top. P.

بهي *baha-ī*, s.f. A masonry tank or reservoir, with steps leading down to the water. *bihī*, s.f. A quince, the tree. P.

بهيدل *bahedal*, v.n. To float, flow, stream, pass, rush, gush. S. (*bahnā*).

بي *be*, p. Without, void of. Used in composition as a privative particle, and equivalent to the English prefixes *in-*, *im-*, *ir-*, *un-*, etc., and the affix *-less*. Ex. *be-hokkh*, insensible; *be-ṣabr*, impatient; *be-adab*, irreverent; *be-wafā*, unfaithful; *be-shakk*, doubtless, etc. P.

بيا *biyā*, ad. Again, afresh, once more. P. (*bāz*).

بيابان *bayābān*, s.m. A desert, waste, wilderness. P.

بياتي *biyātī*, s.m. Scissors, shears, clippers.

بياسته *biyāsta*, s.f. Cable, cord, rope; the rope of a Persian wheel, to which the water-pots are fastened.

بياموندل *biyāmūndal*, v.a. To acquire, gain, get, find, recover, regain, obtain.

بيان *bayān*, s.m. Explanation, recital, relation. P.

بيانول *bayānawul*, v.a. To explain, recite, relate, tell, say, describe.

بيايل *biyāyal*, v.a. Def. in past ten. See بيول.

بيبي *bībī*, s.f. A lady, married woman. H. *bebe*, in. Sister dear! (to an elder sister).

بيپرتي *be-partai* or *be-pratai*, a. Gormandizing, surfeiting; gluttonous, greedy.

بيت *bait*, s.m. A couplet, verse; house, temple. A. *bet*, s.m. A cane, rattan. S.

بيټ *baiṭ*, s.m. The name of one of the three sons of Kais. He is also called بټن *baṭan*, and the tribe descended from him بټني *baṭanī*. See کيس.

بيخ *bekh*, s.m. A root; origin, foundation. P.

بېخرتي *be-khratai*, a. Excessive, much, very much; unseasonable, inopportune, out of time; unbounded, without limit.

بيد *bed*, s.m. A willow tree. P.

بيدار *baidār*, a. Awake, vigilant, alert, watchful; conscious, sensible. P. (*bedār*).

بيداري *baidārī*, s.f. Wakefulness, sleeplessness; vigilance, alertness, watching. P.

بيدو *bedū*, ad. Identical, the same, exactly.

بيده *beda*, s.f. The coil or twist into which lucerne, vetches, etc. are rolled, preparatory to storing for winter use. *bīdah*, a. Asleep, sleeping.

بيديا *bediyā*, s.f. A desert, wilderness. A. (*bādiyā*).

بيرته *biyarta*, ad. Back, back again, return; aside, apart, away.

بيرغ *bairagh*, s.m. Banner, standard. A. (*bairaq*).

بيرنړ *beranṛ*, s.m. A kind of grass.

بيره *bera*, s.f. Name of a thorny bush (*zizyphus jujuba*); the berry. S. (*ber*). A fetter, manacle. H.

بيړه *beṛa*, s.f. A float, raft. S. (*beṛā*).

بيړۍ *beṛa-ī*, s.f. A boat, barge.

بيزل *bezal*, v.a. To darn, hem, baste.

بيزار *bezār*, a. Annoyed, vexed; disgusted, sick of. P.

بيزو *bīzo*, s.m. A monkey.

بيساک *baisāk*, s.m. Name of the first Hindu month. April-May. S. (*baisākh*).

بيستۍ *biyasta-ī*, s.f. Coarse cloth, canvass, baize.

بيسر *bīsar*, s.m. A small nose-ring, worn as an ornament by women. H.

بيش *besh*, a. More; superior (in comp. only). P.

بيشه *besha*, s.f. A forest, wood. P.

بيعه *bai'a*, s.f. Barter, exchange. trade. A. (*bai'*).

بيعانه *bai'āna*, s.f. Deposit, security, earnest-money.

بيک *biyak*, s.m. Harpoon, five-pronged fork.

بيګا *begā*, s.f. See بيګاه.

بيګار *begār* or *bīgār*, s.m. A pressed labourer (with or without pay). H.

بيګاري *bīgārī*, s.f. Forced labour. s.m. A pressed labourer. H.

بيګانه *begānah*, a. Foreign, strange, unknown. P.

بيګانګي *begānagī*, s.f. Strangeness, being foreign, not of the same house, not domestic. P.

بيګاني *begānai*, a. Last preceding, last past, preceding, stale, last night's, yesterday's.

بيګاه *begāh*, s.m. The evening. Also بيګا *begā*.

بيل *biyal* or *bel*, a. Apart, distinct, separate. H. (*byorā*). *bel*, s.m. Name of a tree and its fruit (*Ægle marmelos*); a creeper, climbing plant.

بيلاو *belāw*, s.m. A hone, razor strop.

بيلتون *biyaltūn*, s.m. Absence, separation; difference, distinction.

بيلچه *belcha*, s.f. A mattock, hoe. P.

بيلک *belak*, s.m. A wedding-gift from bridegroom to the bride; an enemy, rival, guardian; an arrow tip. P.

بيلګه *belga*, s.f. See بلګه.

بيله *bela*, s.f. An island, delta, sandbank.

بيم *bīm*, s.m. Awe, fear, dread. P.

بيمار *bīmār*, a. Sick, ill. s.m. A sick man. P.

بيماري *bīmārī*, s.f. Disease, sickness. P.

بينا *bīnā*, a. Seeing, having sight. P.

بيند *bend*, s.m. See بيده *beda*.

بينش **bensh**, s.m. A beam, rafter.

بيوره *bewrah*, a. Clear, manifest, simple, plain.

بيول *bīwul*, v.t. To conduct, lead, take along, convey. Applied only to animate objects. See بوتلل. P. (*bi·bur*)?

بيوه *bewa*, s.f. A widow. P.

بيه *baia*, s.f. Price, value. A. (*bai'*).

بيهودگي *behūdagī*, s.f. Absurdity, nonsense, folly.

بيهوده *behūdah*, a. Absurd, idle, foolish, frivolous. P.

پ

پ *pe*, The third letter of the Pukkhto alphabet. It is frequently used for ف. Ex. آپرين *āparīn* for آفرين *āfarīn*, etc.

پَ *pa*, p. By, with, for; in, into, within; above, on, upon. Also written به. P. (*bā*).

پا *pā*, s.m. The foot, leg. Used in comp. only. Ex. *pā·band*, s.m. A hobble, fetter. a. Bound, clogged, fettered, tethered. P.

پاپړه *pāpra*, s.f. The herb fumatory (*Fumaria officinalis*). H. (*phāphrī*).

پاتو *pāto*, s.f. Name of a scarlet insect. See بخملي.

پاتي *pātai*, a. Left, remaining; abiding, staying.

پاتيدل *pātedal*, v.n. To remain, survive, be left. Also *pātai·kedal*.

پاټئ *pāṭa-ī*, s.f. The cup or pan of a sling or pellet bow.

پاڅول *pātsawul*, v.a. To arouse, awaken, stir up; raise, set up, elevate.

پاڅيدل *pātsedal*, v.n. To arise, rise, get up, sit up.

پاداش *pādāsh*, s.m. Revenge, requital, retaliation. P.

پادشاه *pādshāh*, s.m. Sovereign, king, emperor. P.

پادشاهي *pādshāhī*, s.f. Royal, regal; empire, kingdom. P.

پارا *pārā*, s.f. Mercury, quicksilver. S.

پارچنګ *pārchang*, s.m. A ladder, steps, stairs.

پارچه *pārcha*, s.f. A bit, fragment, scrap, shred; the water trough of an irrigation well. P.

پارو *pārū*, s.m. A kind of rake.

پارول *pārawul*, v.a. To annoy, vex, disturb, irritate, excite, stir up.

پاره *pāra*, s.f. A bit, scrap, slip, shred. P.

پاړبنج *pāṛbanj*, s.m. Name of a tree, horse chesnut.

پاړو *pāṛū*, s.m. A snake charmer. *pāṛū·k.*, v.a. To charm.

پاړه *pāṛa*, s.f. A patch of unploughed land in a field; unfinished work, incomplete action; a kind of rake.

پاړي *pāṛai*, s.m. The hog deer (*cervus porcinus*). H. (*pāṛhā*).

پازه *pāzah*, s.m. Action, effect, operation, result.

پازيکه *pāzīkah*, a. See پاکيزه

پاس *pās*, p. Above, aloft, on, upon. s.m. Attention, observation, watch. P. An ointment made of oil and lime, and used as a remedy for mangy camels.

پاسخ *pāsukh*, s.m. Answer, reply. P.

پاسلول *pāslawul*, v.a. To entrust, commit, recommend.

پاسنګ *pāsang*, s.m. Balance, weight. P.

پاسني *pāsanai*, a. Upper, higher, high, superior.

پاسو *pāsū*, a. Ill-bred, vulgar, low, mean.

پاسوان *pāswān*, s.m. A shepherd, watchman, guard, sentinel. P. (*pāsbān*).

پاسواني *pāswānī*, s.f. Guarding, watching, keeping; protection; occupation of a shepherd.

پاشنه *pāshna*, s.f. The heel of a door; the socket in which it revolves; the heel. P. (*pāshnā*).

پاښ *pākkh*, s.m. Name of a mountain near the Kasıghar hill in the Takhti-Sulaimān range. It is described as the spot first colonized by the Pukkhtūn nation on their arrival from the West.

پاغنده *pāghunda*, s.f. A ball or roll of carded cotton ready for spinning. P.

پاک *pāk*, a. Clean, pure; holy, innocent. P.

پاکلمن *pāk·laman*, a. Chaste, modest; holy, pure. P. (*pāk·dāman*).

پاکول *pākawul*, v.a. To cleanse, purify, wash.

پاکي *pākī*, s.f. Cleanliness, purity; cleaning, purifying; chastity, innocence; a razor. P.

پاکيزه *pākīzah*, a. Chaste, clean, pure, holy. P.

پال *pāl*, s.m. Abstinence, diet, regimen; augury, omen, presage. A. (*fāl*).

پالان *pālān*, s.m. A pack saddle. P.

پالک *pālak*, s.m. Garden spinach. H.

پالل *pālal*, v.a. To cherish, rear, educate, protect. S. (*pālnā*).

پالنگ *pālang*, s.m. A bedstead, bed. S. (*palang*).

پالوده *pālūda*, s.f. A kind of vermicelli. P. (*fālūda*). A kind of wild plum.

پاله *pāla*, s.f. A ploughshare. S. (*phāl*).

پالهنگ *pālhang*, s.m. A tether; a log tied to the neck of an ox, etc. to prevent its straying. P.

پاليز *pālez*, s.m. A melon field. P. (*fālez*).

پانشنبه *pānshamba*, s.f. Friday. P. (*panj·shamba*).

پانه *pāna*, s.f. A wedge for splitting wood; thumbscrew, mode of torture. H. (*phanī*).

پانړ *pānr*, s.m. A cliff, precipice, steep bank.

پانړه *pānra*, s.f. A leaf, leaf of a tree or book. S. (*pannā*).

پاو *pāo*, s.m. A fourth, quarter. S.

پاي *pā-ī*, s.f. A halter, leading string; pins used by weavers in weaving. H. *pāe*, s.m. The foot. P.

پاياب *pāyāb*, } a. Fordable, within depth. P.
پاياو *pāyāo*, }

پايابه *pāyāba*, s.f. A float, a buoy.

پائيدل *pa-edal*, v.n. To endure, last, remain, tarry, survive. P. (*pā-īdan*).

پائيکو *pa-eko*, s.f. A crusher, pounder, thresher, flail, roller.

پائيله *pā-ela*, s.f. An anklet with bells; an ornament for the feet.

پائيمال *pā-emāl*, a. Trampled, ruined, crushed.

پاينده *pāyandah*, a. Constant, durable, lasting.

پائينڅه *pā-entsa*, s.f. The leg of a pair of drawers. P. (*pā-encha*).

پائينک *pā-enak*, s.m. The mounting at the end of a sword scabbard.

پايه *pāya*, s.f. A step; dignity, rank; foundation. P.

پپئي *pupa-ī*, s.f. A kiss on the cheek.

پت *pat*, s.m. Character, reputation, honour. S.

پتاو *pitāo*, s.m. Sunshine, sun's rays. P. (*partau*).

پتري *patrai*, s.m. A clamp, metal binding; the boss of a shield. H. (*pattar*).

پتنگ *patang*, s.m. A moth; paper kite. S.

پتنه *patna*, s.f. Anarchy, civil war, strife; sedition, rebellion. P. (*fitna*).

پتنړ *patanr*, s.m. The stand of a spinning wheel; a ferry, passage across a river. H. (*pātan*).

پتون *patūn*, s.m. The thigh, shank.

پته *pata*, s.f. A card, ticket.

پتيره *patīra*, s.f. Unleavened bread.

پټ *paṭ*, s.m. Delirium, madness; bark of a tree. *puṭ*, a. Concealed, secret, hidden, covered.

پټ‌پټانړي *puṭ·puṭānrai*, s.m. Name of a game; hide and seek.

پټخ *paṭakh*, a. Hard, tough; decayed, worn. s.m. A razor strop.

پټکه *paṭka*, s.f. A girdle, sash, waist-cloth. s. (*paṭkā.*)

پټکي *paṭkai*, s.m. A small turban. *paṭakī*, ad. Immediately, instantly, on the spot; the same, very same, identical.

پټګني *puṭgana-ī*, s.f. Ambuscade, ambush, lair, cover.

پټو *paṭū*, s.m. A kind of woollen cloth. s.

پټوار *paṭwār*, s.m. Bailiff, land steward, village accountant. H.

پټوسکي *paṭūskai*, a. A little, very little, some, few.

پټول *puṭawul*, v.a. To conceal, cover, hide, veil.

پټه *paṭa*, s.f. A shoulder belt, sword belt.

پټي *paṭai*, s.m. A field, patch of cultivated land. *paṭa-ī*, s.f. The alphabet; writing tablet; bandage, plaister.

پټيدل *puṭedal*, v.n. To abscond, hide.

پټيره *paṭera*, s.f. A beam, rafter, large timber.

پټيلړ *paṭelaṛ*, s.m. See پليتړ. H. (*paṭelā*).

پجه *paja*, s.f. A furnace, kiln. H. (*pajāwā*).

پڅ *pa-aṯs* or *p-uṯs*, a. Blunt, dull, obtuse.

پڅاڼړي *piṯsāṇṛai*, a. Small, little, few, some.

پڅکه *piṯska*, s.f. Corner, end, nib, point.

پڅيدل *pa-aṯsedal* or *p-uṯsedal*, v.n. To become blunt, obtuse, dull.

پچنه *pac̱hana*, s.f. A scratch, prick, prod, cut; a scarifier, cupping instrument.

پچني *pac̱hanai*, a. Scarified, cupped, pricked.

پچواړي *pac̱hwāṛa-ī*, s.f. Heel ropes for a horse. H.

پچه *puc̱ha*, s.f. Orbicular dung (as of camels, deer, etc); a lot or share of land; a ripple or catspaw on the surface of water.

پخ *pa-akh* or *p-ukh*, s.m. Scurf, dandriff, scab, scale. *pakh*, s.m. A hiss, spit (as of a cat, etc.). *pakh-wahal*, v.a. To hiss, spit (as a cat).

پخپله *pakhpula*, ad. Spontaneously, voluntarily, of own accord.

پخته *pukhtah*, a. Baked, cooked, dressed, ripe; shrewd, expert, knowing; firm, solid, strong. P.

پخساک *pakhsāk*, s.m. Distress, grief, sorrow, solicitude. P. (*pakhshā*).

پخسول *pakhsawul*, v.a. To distress, annoy, trouble, worry.

پخسه *pakhsa*, s.f. Stiff clay or mud, used to build walls; mire, mud, slush.

پخسيدل *pakhsedal*, v.n. To desire, fret, pine, yearn, long.

پخلا *pakhulā*, a. Appeased, conciliated, pacified, reconciled, on speaking terms.

پخلي *pakhalai*, a. Cooked, prepared, dressed; cooking, dressing, preparing (food); firm, solid, sound; experience, maturity, ripeness. *pukhalai*, s.m. the hooping cough.

پخوا *pakhwā*, a. Former, previous, prior. ad. Before, ere now, previously.

پخواني *pakhwānai*, a. Ancient, former, preceding.

پخول *pakhawul*, v.a. To cook, dress, prepare.

پخوندي *pakhwandai*, s.m. A button hole, loop; an ornament for the feet, anklet.

پخه *pa-akha* or *p-ukha*, s.f. Chaff, husk, skin; leafy covering of the ear of Indian corn.

پخي *pa-akhai* or *p-ukhai*, a. Scabby, scurfy.

پخيدل *pakhedal*, v.n. To ripen, mature; boil; suppurate.

پخيل *pakhiyal*, s.m. Perspiring, sweating.

پدود *padod*, ad. As if, just as, like, similarly. P.

پديد *padīd*, a. Clear, evident, manifest. P.

پده *pada*, s.f. A species of willow.

پر *par*, s.m. A feather, quill; wing; the flat board of a water or other wheel. s. *pur*, a. Complete, full, loaded (in comp. only). P. *parr*, s.m. The whirr of a snipe, quail, etc. taking wing. H. (*phurr*). *pri*, p. On, upon, atop (in comp.). See پري

پراټه *parāṭa*, s.f. A kind of bread made in thin layers of pastry. H. (*parāṭhā*).

پراچه *parāc̲h̲ah*, s.m. A pedlar, hawker, travelling merchant; mule driver; descendant of a Hindu converted to Islam.

پراچګۍ *parāc̲h̲aga-ī*, s.f. A female of the preceding.

پراګنده *parāgandah*, a. Dispersed, scattered. P.

پرانتل *prānatal*, v.a. To loose, open, undo, untie. P. (*farāk̲h̲tan, farāzīdan*).

پرت *prat*, a. Absurd, fruitless, idle, vain; distant, far, remote.

پرتاب *partāb*, s.m. Bowshot, gunshot, range of an arrow, etc. P.

پرتل *partal*, s.m. Baggage for a journey, baggage of an army. H. Name of a game, marbles.

پرتوړ *partūṛ*, s.m. See پرتوګ

پرتوغاښ *partūg̲h̲āk̲k̲h̲*, s.m. The band or string for tying the *partūṛ*.

پرتوګ *partūg*, s.m. Loose trowsers, drawers.

پرچټۍ *parc̲h̲aṭa-ī*, s.f. Thatch or coping of a mud wall, eaves. H. (*parc̲h̲hatī*).

پرخم *park̲h̲am*, s.m. A tassel, tuft; the tuft at the end of a cow's tail. P. (*parc̲h̲am*).

پُرخه *pa-ark̲h̲a*, s.f. Dew, hoar frost. *park̲h̲a*, s.f. A boulder, rock.

پرداخت *pardāk̲h̲t*, s.m. Attention, service, care. P.

پرداز *pardāz*, s.m. Finishing, performing (in comp.). P.

پرده *parda*, s.f. A veil, curtain, screen; secrecy, privacy. P.

پردي *pradai*, a. Foreign, strange. H. (*pardes*).

پرزو *pirzo*, a. Becoming, fit, proper, suitable; inclined, partial, longing. P. (*paz̲īr*).

پرزول *parzawul*, v.a. To overthrow, floor; struggle, wrestle.

پرزوه *pirzawa*, s.f. Desire, wish, bent, fancy.

پرزيدل *parzedal*, v.n. To be floored, thrown, upset, prostrated, etc. in wrestling.

پرسان *pursān*, s.m. Asking, enquiry. P.

پرست *parast*, s.m. Adorer, worshipper (in comp.). P.

پرستي *parastī*, s.f. Worship, devotion, adoration. P.

پرسش *pursis̲h̲*, s.m. Inquiry, interrogation. P.

پرش *pras̲h̲*, s.m. A snort, sniff; sneeze.

پړشکال *pars̲h̲akāl*, s.m. The hot weather rains; rainy season; name of the fourth Hindu month. July-August. S. (*bars̲h̲akāl*).

پرغز *parg̲h̲az*, s.m. Convulsion, fainting fit, hysterics.

پرغزي *parg̲h̲azī*, a. Stunned, faint, senseless, convulsed.

پرکار *purkār*, a. Coarse, thick, fat; well made. P.

پرکټي *parkaṭai*, s.m. A step-son: wife's son by a former husband.

پرکي *parkai*, s.m. A butterfly.

پرګار *pargār*, s.m. A pair of compasses. P.

پرګنه *pargana*, s.f. A district, province, shire. P.

پرنا *parnā*, s.f. A doze, nap; nodding, sleeping. *parnā-wṛal*, v.a. To doze, nap, nod, sleep.

پرناله *parnāla*, s.f. A gutter, drain, scupper. H.

پرنج *pranj*, پرنجي *pranjai*, } s.m. A sneeze.

پرنجيدل *pranjedal*, v.n. To sneeze.

پرنړ *pranṛ*, s.m. Curdled, sour, or turned milk. a. Clotted, curdled (as blood, etc.).

پرو *paro*, s.m. A hot wind. S. (*purwā*).

پروا *parwā*, s.f. Anxiety, care, concern; dread, fear; wish, desire. P.

پروانه *parwāna*, s.f. An order, license, pass, warrant. P.

پروت *prot*, a. Prostrate, fallen, lying down.

پرور *parwar*, a. Cherisher, protector (in comp. only). P.

پروردګار *parwardagār*, s.m. The nourisher, God. P.

پروردہ *parwardah*, a. Cherished, nourished, bred. s.m. Dependent, protegé. P.

پرورش *parwarish*, s.m. Maintenance, support, patronage; cherishing, nourishing. P.

پرورل *parwaral*, v.a. To cherish, foster, feed, support. P. (*parwardan*).

پروړ *proṛ*, s.m. Chaff; husk of Indian corn.

پروړه *proṛa*, s.f. Chaff; husk of rice, millet, etc.

پروسکال *paroskāl*, ad. Last year.

پروسکني *parosganai*, a. Last year's, of last season.

پرولل *prolal*, } v.a. To barter, exchange, sell,
پرورل *prowul*, } trade. P. (*farokhtan*).

پرون *parūn*, ad. Yesterday.

پروني *parūnai*, a. Yesterday's, last, last past, yester.

پرويزي *parwezaī*, s.m. A sieve. P. (*parwezah*).

پره *para*, s.f. The plate, or board of a water, or spinning wheel; a row, rank, line, file; faction, party, set. H. (*parā*).

پرهار *parhār*, } s.m. A cut, laceration, wound.
پرهر *parhar*, } H. (*prahār*).

پرهرژلي *parhar-jalai*, a. Wounded, cut.

پرهيز *parhez*, s.m. Abstinence, continence; sobriety, regimen. P.

پرهيزگار *parhezgār*, a. Abstemious, continent, sober, frugal. P.

پرهيزگاري *parhezgārī*, s.f. Abstinence, sobriety.

پري *pre*, p. On, upon, above, atop. *parī*, s.f. A fairy. P.

پريباسل *prebāsal*, v.a. To cast upon, fling, throw, discharge upon. Def. See پريبستل

پريدل *predal*, } v.a. To abandon, desert,
پريږدل *pregdal*, } give up; cease, desist, leave off; relinquish, let go, set free. Def. See پريښول. P. (*farohīdan*).

پريشان *pareshān*, a. Confused, perplexed. P.

پريشاني *pareshānī*, s.f. Perplexity, confusion. P.

پريښودل *prekkhodal*, } v.a. To abandon, desert;
پريښول *prekkhawul*, } let go, etc. See پريږدل P. (*faroshāndan*).

پريکول *prekawul*, v.a. To cut, sever, divide, lop off.

پريو *paryo*, s.m. A follower, pursuer. P. (*pairau*).

پريوان *prewān*, s.m. The after-birth, placenta. H. (*puren*). a. Copious, abundant, much. P. (*farāwān*.)

پريواني *prewānī*, s.f. Abundance, plenty.

پريوتل *prewatal*, v.n. To drop, fall down, tumble; to alight, fall upon, come upon. P. (*faro uftan*).

پريوتي *prewatai*, a. Fallen, s.m. Name of a plant.

پريوستل *prewastal*, } v.a. To cast, throw, fling,
پريبستل *preyastal*, } etc. upon. Def. See پريباسل.

پريښل *preyakkhal*, v.a. See پريښودل.

پړ *paṛ*, s.m. A gaming house, where dice are played. H. (*phaṛ*). *pa-aṛ* or *p-ūṛ*, a. Beaten, conquered, overcome; losing, unsuccessful. *p-uṛ* or *pa-aṛ-kawul*, v.a. To conquer, subdue, overcome. *pa-aṛ* or *p-uṛ-kedal*, v.n. To lose, be beaten, overcome, subdued.

پړانګ *pṛāng*, s.m. A leopard, panther. P. (*palang*).

پړانګ پيش *pṛāng-pīsh*, s.m. A wild cat, lynx.

پړانه وړانه *pa-aṛāna wa-aṛāna*, s.f. Loss and gain; betting, gambling, wagering.

پړپوس *paṛpūs*, s.m. The lungs. H. (*phephṛā*).

پړسوب *paṛsob*, s.m. Tumour, swelling, inflation.

پړسول *paṛsawul*, v.a. To dilate, distend, expand. H. (*pasārnā*).

پړسيدل *paṛsedal*, v.n. To swell, tumefy, dilate.

پړق *paṛaq*, s.m. A razor strop.

پړک *paṛak*, s.m. Agitation, flutter. H. (*phaṛak*). *paṛh*, s.m. A crowd, mob, bevy, herd.

پړکول *paṛakawul*, v.a. To agitate, shake, stir.

پړکه *paṛka*, s.f. A kind of bird trap, gin.

پړکي *paṛkai*, s.m. The leg below the knee, the calf.

پړکيدل *paṛakedal*, v.n. To flutter, quiver, hover.

پړمخ *pa-aṛmakh*, a. Prone, face-downwards, upset.

پړنګ *pṛang*, s.m. A cry, whimper, whine.

پړوکي *paṛūkai*, s.m. A riband, shred, strip, tatter.

پړوني *paṛūnai*, s.m. A woman's mantle, or veil.

پړه *pa-aṛa*, s.f. Defeat, failure, loss at play.

پړي *puṛai*, s.m. A cable, rope, cord.

پړين *pṛīn*, s.m. Diaphragm, hypogastrium.

پس *pas*, ad. After, behind; then, next, therefore, at length. P. *pa-as*, s.m. Flatus, wind from the bowels. *pus-pus*, s.m. Whispering H. (*phus*).

پسات *pasāt*, s.m. Mutiny, rebellion, sedition; depravity, iniquity, mischief. A. (*fasād*).

پساتي *pasātī*, a. Mischievous, quarrelsome, seditious.

پسان *psān*, s.m. A grindstone, whetstone. S. (*sān*).

پست *past*, a. Low, below; abject, mean. P.

پستنه *pastana*, ad. After, behind, back, in rear; since, subsequently.

پستو *pastu*, s.m. An inner room, cell.

پستوني *pastawunai*, s.m. Name of a tree (*Grewia Asiatica*).

پسخاک *paskhāk*, s.m. See بخساک P.

پسخه *paskha*, s.f. Stiff mud or clay, used to build walls.

پسرلي *psarlai*, s.m. The spring.

پسکي *pa-aska-ī*, s.f. Flatus, wind from the bowels. *pa-aska-ī-āchawul*, v.a. To break wind.

پسند *pasand*, s.m. Approbation, choice. a. chosen, approved. P.

پسندول *pasandawul*, v.a. To choose, approve.

پسنديدل *pasandedal*, v.n. To be chosen, approved. P. (*pasandīdan*).

پسوز *psor*, a. Broad, wide.

پسول *psol*, s.m. A necklace of coins; ornament.

پسولول *psolawul*, v.a. To adorn, decorate, ornament.

پسوني *pasūnai*, s.m. Ambush, cover, lair.

پسه *psah*, s.m. Goats, sheep; goat species

پسينه *pasīnah*, a. Late, last, late sown crops. P.

پش *pa-ash*, s.m. A wheeze, sound of air forced from a bag; a blacksmith. *pash-pash*, in. Call to a cat, puss! puss!

پشت *pusht*, s.m. Ancestry; a generation of progenitors; the back; a ridge; a prop, support, help; an assistant; reservoir of a canal. P.

پشته *pushta*, s.f. A buttress, prop, support. in. A word used to drive away a cat—away puss!

پشتي *pushtī*, s.f. A prop, buttress, support; aid, succour, help. P. *pishtai*, s.m. A terrier dog.

پشرلي *psharlai*, s.m. A yearling kid.

پشقاب *pashqāb*, s.m. A salver, tray, platter.

پشک *pishak*, s.m. A disease of the skin; ringworm; the bald-headed vulture.

پشکالي *pashkālai*, s.m. Hay, dry fodder.

پشم *pashm*, s.m. Wool, down, fur, hair. P.

پشمي *pashmī*, a. Woolly, downy.

پشمينه *pashmīnah*, a. Woollen. *pashmīna*, s.f. A kind of woollen cloth. P.

پشو *pisho*, s.m. and f. A cat.

پشوخت *pishokhuṭ*, s.m. Tonquin bean; the

seed of a climbing plant, the seed pod of which is covered with cowhage; the bean is used as a charm against evil eye, etc.

پشه *pasha*, s.f. A musquito, gnat. in. A word used to drive away a cat. P.

پښ *pakkh*, s.m. See پاښ.

پښت *pukkht*, s.m. Ancestry, lineage; back, ridge; a mountain range. P. (*pusht*).

پښتنه *pukkhtana*, s.f. Enquiry, investigation, interrogation, questioning. An Afghan or Pathan woman, a female Pukkhtūn.

پښتو *pukkhto*, s.f. The Afghan language.

پښتورګه *pukkhtawarga*, s.f. A kidney.

پښتون *pukkhtūn*, s.m. An Afghan, a Pathan; one whose language is the Pukkhto. *bar-pukkhtūn*, s.m. An upper or highland Afghan. *lar-pukkhtūn*, s.m. A lower or lowland Afghan.

پښتونخوا *pukkhtūn-khwā*, s.f. Afghanistan, the country of the Afghans, or Pathans.

پښتونوالي *pukkhtūnwālai*, پښتونولي *pukkhtūnwalī*, s.m. The Afghan constitution, Pukkhtūn code, the manners and customs of the Pathans.

پښته *pukkhta*, s.f. A small hill. P. (*pushta*).

پښتي *pukkhta-ī*, s.f. A rib, the ribs. *pukkhtī*, s.f. Enquiry, investigation, questioning.

پښتيدل *pukkhtedal*, v.a. To ask, question, interrogate, enquire. S. (*pūchhnā*).

پښويه *pakkhwaya*, or *pakkhoya*, s.f. Orthography, spelling, naming or forming words.

پښه *pksha* or *pkkha*, s.f. The foot.

پښيمان *pakkhemān*, a. Penitent, repentant, sorry. P. (*pashemān*).

پښيماني *pakkhemānī*, s.f. Penitence, regret, sorrow.

پقير *paqīr*, s.m. A beggar, mendicant; hermit, recluse. A. (*faqīr*).

پک *puk*, s.m. Chance, opportunity, turn, time.

پکار *pakār*, a. Effective, useful, serviceable. Also په کار.

پکل *pakal*, v.a. To chuck, or jerk anything into the mouth from the palm of the hand. H. (*phānknā*). s.m. A railing, fence, screen, lattice of reeds, etc.

پکو *pako*, a. Bothered, confused, amazed.

پکه *paka*, s.f. A palm full, enough to fill the palm for a chuck into the mouth. H. (*phankā*). *paka-wahal*, v.a. To chuck into the mouth (as grain, etc.).

پګړۍ *pagṛa-ī*, s.f. A turband. H. (*pagṛī*).

پګڼر *paganṛ*, s.m. Name of the eleventh Hindu month. February-March. S. (*phāgan*).

پل *pal*, s.m. A mill stone; potter's wheel; footprint, trace; wheel, truck-wheel; one side of a pair of scales. P. (*pallā*). *pul*, s.m. A bridge, ridge, bank, embankment. P. *pul*, a. Let off, excused, acquitted, absolved.

پلا *plā*, s.f. Period, turn, time, round.

پلار *plār*, s.m. A father. P. (*padur*).

پلارګني *plārganai*, s.m. Paternal relation; father's family, connexions, household, etc.

پلاله *palāla*, s.f. Rice straw, straw of millet, corn, etc. (unbroken). S. (*parāl*). P. (*pulāl*).

پلانړه *palānṛa*, s.f. A pack-saddle. P. (*pālān*). Mule load of water; water skins.

پلاو *pulāo*, s.m. A kind of dish made of rice, meat, fruits, spices, etc. cooked together. P.

پلټن *palṭan*, s.f. A battalion, regiment, peloton. H.

پلټل *palaṭal*, v.a. To return, turn back, retreat; to overturn; turn, wind. H. (*palaṭnā*).

پلغت *palaghat*, ad. Quickly. P.

پلک *palak*, s.m. The eyelid; an instant, moment; a wink. P. *pa-alk*, s.m. A sledge hammer; a ploughshare.

پلکه *palka*, s.f. The blade of a sword.

پلمه *palma*, s.f. Calumny, slander; deception, falsehood, prevarication. P.

پلن *plan*, a. Broad, wide, spacious. P. (*pahan*).

پلندر *plandar*, s.m. Step-father: father to wife's children by a former husband. P. (*padandar*).

پلنده *palanda*, s.f. A bog, quagmire.

پلنول *planawul*, v.a. To widen, make broad.

پلو *palau*, s.m. Border, hem, skirt of a dress; side, direction, quarter; margin, edge, verge. P. (*pahlū*). H. (*pallā*).

پلواښه *pulwākkha*, s.f. Button-hole, loop, noose, slip-knot, lasso.

پلور *plor*, s.m. Buying and selling, trade.

پلورل *ploral*, v.a. To sell, vend. See پرولل.

پلوسه *palosa*, s.f. Name of a tree (*Acacia modesta*).

پلوشه *palwasha*, s.f. A ray of light, glitter of a star, radiance of the moon; light, glitter.

پلول *pulawul*, v.a. To acquit, absolve, excuse.

پلوند *palwand*, a. Foolish, stupid.

پله *pala*, s.f. Nerve, sinew, tendon; direction, quarter, side.

پلي *palai*, s.m. A pod, legume. S. (*phalī*). *pala-ī*, s.f. The spoke of a wheel. Name of a tree (*Butea frondosa*). S. (*palās*). *palai*, a. Afoot, on foot.

پليت *palīt*, a. Defiled, polluted, unclean. P. (*palīd*).

پليته *palīta*, s.f. A wick, match, torch. P. (*falīta*).

پليتي *palītī*, s.f. Impurity, pollution.

پليټنړ *paleṭanṛ*, s.m. A weaver's beam. See پټيلنړ.

پلينه *plenah*, | پليون *plewan*, } s.m. Name of a tree (*Salvadora Persica*), the root of which is used as a tooth-brush. S. (*pīlū*).

پم *pam*, s.m. Mange, itch.

پماني *pamānai*, s.m. Name of a tree (*Vitex negundo*).

پمبه *pumba*, s.f. The cotton plant. P.

پمبچو *pumbechū*, s.f. A cotton pod; the withered stalks of the plant.

پمن *paman*, a. Mangy, scabby.

پنا | پناه } *panā*, s.f. Refuge, shelter, protection, aid. P.

پنبه *punba*, s.f. See پمبه.

پنځوس *pandzos*, a. Fifty.

پنځه *pindzah*, a. Five. P. (*panj*). *pindzah-binā*, s.f. The five foundations (of religion), viz. The belief, prayer, fasting, pilgrimage, and alms.

پنجره *pinjra*, s.f. A cage; lattice. S. (*pinjrā*).

پنجکي *panjakai*, s.m. The cross bar between the strings of a pellet-bow; a latch, catch, stop.

پنجه *panja*, s.f. A claw, hand, paw. P.

پند *pand*, s.m. Advice, counsel. P. Distance, journey. S. (*pend*).

پندانه *pundāna*, s.f. Cotton seed.

پندوک *pandūk*, s.m. A bud, blossom.

پنده *punda*, s.f. The heel.

پندئي *punda-ī*, s.f. The iron top of a spear; a disease of the fetlock, the grease.

پنډ *panḍ*, s.m. A package, bundle, load for the head. *punḍ*, s.m. A steel for striking fire from a flint. *punḍ-bakra-ī*, flint and steel. *punḍ*, s.m. A band, herd, flock; tumour, bump, swelling; *vulva*. a. Corpulent, fat, stout. P.

پنډاوچرګ *panḍāw-chirg*, s.m. A game cock; fowl of a large breed with big bones and few feathers.

پنډغالي *panḍ-ghālai*, s.m. A common or open space outside a village on which the cattle are collected on going to and returning from pasture.

پنډوس *panḍos*, s.m. | پنډوسکي *panḍoskai*, } A ball, a play ball, a cricket ball.

پنډوکي *panḍūkai*, s.m. A bundle, parcel, package.

پندولي *pandolī*, s.f. A portion or share of a cotton crop allotted to the women who pick it, by way of perquisite or hire for their labour. *pandol·gara*, s.f. A woman who picks the cotton crop.

پنده *panda*, s.f. A small load, bundle.

پندۍ *panda-ī*, s.f. The calf of the leg. H. (*pindlī*). *punda-ī*, s.f. The heel; iron tip of a spear.

پنديدل *pundedal*, v.n. To swell, expand, distend, tumefy. P. (*pundīdan*).

پنګه *panga*, s.f. Capital, reserve, stock. S. (*punjī*)).

پنهم *pinham*, a. Concealed, hidden, secret. P. (*pinhān*).

پني *panai*, s.m. Name of a scented grass (*Andropogon muricatum*). *pannī*, s.m. Name of a Pathan tribe.

پنير *panīr*, s.m. Cheese. P.

پنيرک *panīrak*, s.m. Name of a potherb (*Malva parviflora*). The seeds and root are used in medicine.

پنړه *panra*, s.f. A shoe, slipper. S. (*panhī*).

پو *pū*, a. Light, smooth, slight. s.m. Enquiry, search; a puff, blast, blow, breath. P.

پوپکه *pūpaka*, s.f. A bump, swelling, tumour.

پوتي *pūtai*, s.m. A heap, mound, lump, mass.

پوټ *pot*, s.m. Bark, rind, shell, crust, skin. P. (*post*).

پوټسوړي *pot·sūṛī*, s.m. Bran, chaff, husk.

پوټکي *potakai*, s.m. Scurf, dandriff, scab.

پوټوسکي *potūskai*, a. Diminutive, wee, tiny, small. s.m. An atom, jot, tittle, bit.

پوټي *pūtai*, a. Small, puny, wee, tiny. s.m. A bit, pinch, crumb, little bit; a dwarf, pigmy.

پوجي *pūjī*, s.f. Weeding, thinning, pruning.

پوڅکۍ *potsaka-ī*, s.f. A mushroom, fungus. *pūtsaka-ī*, s.f. The lobe of the ear.

پوڅه *potsa*, s.f. Curds, cream-cheese, dry curds.

پوڅۍ *pūtsa-ī*, s.f. The lobe of the ear.

پوچ *pūch*, a. Obscene, absurd, useless, foolish. P.

پوچګوئي *pūch·goī*, s.f. Obscenity, nonsense, rigmarole. *pūch·goe*, s.m. A talker of nonsense, smut, bosh, etc.

پوخ *pokh*, a. Ripe, mature; cooked, dressed; firm, strong; expert, shrewd, knowing.

پوخلي *pukhalai*, s.m. Hooping-cough; croup.

پوده *pūda*, s.f. Cloth in the loom; the warp or web. P. (*pud*). *pūdah*, a. Crumbling, decayed, rotten, mildewed. P.

پور *por*, s.m. A loan, advance; debt. *pori*, ad. To, up to; till, whilst; over, across, beyond; at, upon; as far as, near, close to. H. (*par*). See پوري.

پورتني *portanai*, a. Upper, superior, upmost.

پورته *porta*, ad. Above, atop, on, upon, over, up. a. More, greater, superior. *porta·kawul*, v.a. To raise, erect, lift, exalt. *porta·kedal*, v.n. To ascend, arise, rise.

پوروړي *poranwṛai*, s.m. A debtor; creditor; avenger.

پوره *pūrah*, a. Complete, entire, full, perfect. S. (*pūrā*).

پوري *pore*, ad. To, up to; as far as, near, close to; upon, at; till, whilst; over, across, beyond. H. (*par*). *pore·ore* or *pore·rā·pore*, Through and through, in and out, right through, from end to end, etc. *pore·kawul*, v.a. To apply, attach, fix, shut, set, place, etc.

پوري ژني *pore·ǰanai*, a. Ejected, expelled, cast out. Also پوري جني *pore·janai*.

پوړ *poṛ*, a. Half cooked (as food), half ripe (as fruit), half grown, or near puberty (as an animal). *pauṛ*, s.m. Cord, cable, rope, hobble, tether.

پوړه *poṛa*, s.f. A rake, shovel for removing stable litter. s. (*phāorī*).

پوړئ *pauṛa-ī*, s.f. A ladder. H. (*pauṛī*).

پوزه *poza*, s.f. The nose, snout. P.

بوزي *pūzai*, s.m. A small mat made of palm leaves.

پوږ *pūg*, s.m. A blow, puff, squirt, a bellows. *pūg-wahal*, v.a. To puff, blow (as on fire); to squirt, sprinkle from the mouth (as water on cloth, etc.).

پوس *pos*, } a. Soft, supple, pliant, ductile,
پوست *post*, } elastic, tender, tractable.

پوست *post*, s.m. Bark, crust, hide, shell, skin, etc.; poppy-head or capsule. P. *post-bāsal* or *kāgal*, v.a. To flay, skin, peel, bark, shell, etc.

پوستکي *postakai*, s.m. Crust, scab, bark, rind; an untanned hide.

پوستي *postī*, s.m. A drunkard, sot; one addicted to the use of the intoxicating liquor prepared from the fresh poppy-head. P.

پوستين *postīn*, s.m. A fur coat; sheep-skin coat. P.

پوسل *poslal*, v.a. To attire, clothe, dress.

پوش *posh*, in. Look out! Clear the way! Stand by! Have a care! H. (*poesh*) or for *poh sha* (imperative). *posh* (in comp.), covering, wearing. P.

پوښ *pokkh*, s.m. Apparel, clothing, dress. P. (*posh*).

پوښاک *pokkhāk*, s.m. Clothes, garments. P. (*poshāk*).

پوښښ *pokkhikkh*, s.m. Covering, dress, vestment. P. (*poshish*).

پوښل *pokkhal*, v.a. To clothe, cover, dress, hide, screen; to cheer, console, sympathize, etc. P. (*poshīdan*).

پوغله *poghla*, s.f. Dung of young animals, of kids and lambs before it becomes orbicular.

پوک *pūk*, s.m. A puff, blow, squirt, etc. from the mouth. H. (*phūnk*).

پوکل *pūkal*, v.a. } To blow puff, breathe on,
پوکول *pūkawul*, } inflate; to squirt from the mouth.

پوکنړئ *pukanṛa-ī*, s.f. A bladder, the urinary bladder. H. (*phuknā*).

پوکي *pūkai*, s.m. A puff, blow, whiff.

پول *pūl*, s.m. An aqueduct; gutter, trough. P. *pūl*, s.mf. A film over the eye, albugo. s. (*phūlī*).

پولاد *polād*, s.m. Fine steel. P. (*fūlād*).

پولک *pūlak*, s.m. A clamp, bit, or wedge to fix the share to the plough.

پوله *pūla*, s.f. A ridge, bank, hedge; limit, boundary, or division line or mark. *pūlah*, s.m. Parched grain. s.

پولئ *pūla-ī*, s.f. A vesicle, blister, bleb. H. (*pholā*).

پون *pūn*, s.m. The mange.

پونه *pūna*, s.f. Drizzle, mist, small rain. H. (*phūnhī*).

پونړئ *pūṇra-ī*, s.f. A ball or roll of cotton prepared for spinning. H. (*pūnī*).

پوول *powul*, v.a. To graze; lead cattle to pasture. Def. in pres. ten. See پيايل.

پوه *poh*, a. Clever, intelligent, knowing, wise.

پوهاند *pohānd*, a. Clever, intelligent, learned, wise.

پوهړ *pūhaṛ*, a. Careless, untidy, slovenly, dirty; foolish, stupid, sottish. H. (*phūhar*). *pohuṛ*, s.m. A large mat made of palm leaves. H.

پوهول *pohawul*, v.a. To acquaint, inform, explain, etc.

پوهه *poha*, s.f. Judgment, intellect, understanding. P. (*fahm*).

پوهيدل *pohedal*, v.n. To understand, appreciate, perceive, know. P. (*fahmīdan*).

پويه *poya*, s.f. A canter, gallop. P.

په *pa*, p. See پ.

په *pah*, / پها *phā*, } in. Pooh! pooh! bosh! fudge!

پهار *pahār*, s.m. A measure of time; about three hours. s. (*pahar*).

پهره *pahra*, s.f. A watch, vigil; tour of watch; guard, sentinel. s. (*pahrā*).

پهلواړي *phulwāṛai*, s.m. A white rose; strips of clean straw, used by women to plait with the back hair (as an ornament).

پهلوان *pahlawān*, s.m. An athlete, champion, wrestler, hero, gladiator. P.

پهلواني *pahlwānī*, s.f. Heroism, athletics, wrestling.

پهم *pahm*, s.m. Intellect, mind, reason, sense, P. (*fahm*).

پهمول *pahmawul*, v.a. To acquaint, inform, etc. P. (*fahmāndan*).

پهميدل *pahmedal*, v.n. To understand, perceive, know. P. (*fahmīdan*).

پهورته *pahorta*, ad. See پورته.

پهه *paha*, s.f. A poultice, ointment, plaister.

پئ *pa-ī*, s.f. Milk; the sap of trees. s. (*pai*). *pai*, s.m. The foot; a sinew; tendon of the leg; footing, basis; track, trace; a ford. P. *pai·oba*, fordable, within depth. *pai·kawul*, v.a. To hamstring; cut a tree close to the roots. *pai·wṛal*, v.a. To know, follow, catch at the meaning, etc. *pai*, ad. After, behind, following. *pai·ā·pai*, In succession, one after another. P.

پياڅه *piyātsa*, s.m. Bread made from millet or rye.

پياخله *piyākhla*, s.f. Collar, cuff, wristband. Exhaling, perspiring, sweating.

پيادة *piyādah*, s.m. A footman; foot soldier. a. On foot, afoot. P.

پياړمه *piyāṛma*, s.f. A brace for tightening the netting of a bedstead; the crupper of a saddle; the strap of a spinning wheel, etc.

پياز *piyāz*, s.m. An onion. P.

پيازكي *piyāzakai*, s.m. Wild onion; squill.

پيازه *piyāza*, s.f. Abortion; aborting, miscarrying; clearing, dividing, splitting.

پياله *piyāla*, s.f. A cup, goblet; fire-pan of a gun. P.

پياوي *payāwai*, s.m. A float, buoy, angler's float.

پيايل *piyāyal*, v.a. To graze or pasture cattle, to tend flocks. See پيول.

پيپنۍ *pepna-ī*, s.f. A chemise, shift, shirt.

پيتي *paitī*, s.f. Cooked peas or pulse.

پيټ *peṭ*, s.m. / پيټی *peṭai*, } A bundle, load, package, burden; tumbril, box, parcel. H. (*peṭī*).

پيټي مو *peṭī·mo*, in. Fie on thee! A curse on you! The devil seize thee! H. (*phiṭī·munh*).

پيجمخي *pejmakhai*, a. Handsome; beardless, smooth-faced; light or fair complexioned.

پيڅل *petsal*, v.a. To bear, endure, suffer, undergo. P. (*pechīdan*).

پيچ *pech*, s.m. A coil, twist; screw; complication, deceit, difficulty. P.

پيچش *pechish*, s.m. Contortion, twist, gripes. P.

پيچك *pechak*, s.m. A skein or hank of thread; a reel. P.

پيچومه *pechūma*, s.f. Zigzag; elevation, rise.

پيچيدل *pechedal*, v.n. To wind, twist, writhe, coil, etc. P. (*pechīdan*).

پيخاره *paikhāra*, s.f. See پوغله.

پيخال *paikhāl*, s.m. Dung of birds. P.

پيخل *paikhal*, s.m. See پخيل.

پيدا *paidā*, a. Born, created, produced. P.

پير *pīr*, s.m. A saint; spiritual guide; descendant of a saint; old man; Monday. P. *per*, s.m. Bend, curve, turn, wind, twist. H. (*pher*).

پيرامن *pairāman*, s.m. Circumference. ad. Around, about, roundabout. P.

پيراهن *pairāhan*, s.m. A frock, long shirt. P.
پيړ *peraṛ*, a. Corpulent, fat, bulky, large.
پيرزو *pīrzo*, a. See پرزو.
پيرل *pīral*, v.a. See پيرودل.
پيروان *perwān*, s.m. See پريوان.
پيروي *pairawai*, s.m. Cream; a suckling.
پيرودل *pīrodal*, v.a. To buy, purchase. P. (*farokhtan*).
پيروني *perone*, s.f. The Pleiades.
پيري *pere*, s.m. A demon, evil spirit, one of the genii; a devil. *periyān*, pl. (*met.*) Hysterics.
پيرياني *periyānai*, s.m. A demoniac, one possessed with a devil. *periyāna-ī*, s.f. A hysterical woman.
پيړ *peṛ*, a. Fat, obese, gross; coarse, thick; bulky.
پيړزه *peṛza*, s.f. A mound, hillock, detached hill.
پيړه *peṛa*, s.f. A lump of dough; a kind of sweetmeat. S. (*peṛā*).
پيړۍ *peṛa-ī*, s.f. A chair, settle, ottoman; a generation of ancestors. S. (*pīṛhī*).
پيزار *paizār*, s.m. A shoe, slipper, sandal. P.
پيزل *pezal*, v.a. To darn, repair, mend, stitch.
پيزنه *pezna*, s.f. A sieve. P.
پيزوان *pezwān*, s.m. A nose-ring. An ornament worn in the nose by women.
پيزواني *pezwānai*, s.m. A bullock with its nose bored for a ring or bridle.
پيزه *peza*, s.f. Apex, tip, summit, top, peak.
پيزي *pezai*, a. Faded, decayed, withered. *peza-ī*, s.f. Spelling, forming syllables, joining letters. The name of a woman.
پيژانده *pejāndah*, a. Recognized, known, familiar. s.m. Recognition, remembrance.
پيژندګلي *pejandgalī*, s.f. Acquaintance, knowledge, recognition, familiarity.
پيژندل *pejandal*, v.a. To distinguish, recognize, know, recollect. H. (*pahchānnā*).

پيس *pes*, s.m. Leprosy; a leper. P.
پيساڼري *pīsāṇrai*, s.m. A little, bit, fraction, atom, pinch, jot, etc.
پيسه *paisa*, s.f. Name of a copper coin. H. (*paisā*).
پيسي *pesai*, a. Leprous. s.m. A leper.
پيش *pesh*, a. Before, in front. The vowel point ـُ *u*. P.
پيشاب *peshāb*, s.m. Urine. P.
پيشتر *peshtar*, ad. Before, formerly. P.
پيشكار *peshkār*, s.m. An agent, deputy, manager. P.
پيشګي *peshagī*, s.m. Advance of money or wages, etc. P.
پيشلمي *peshlamai*, } s.m. The meal before
پيشمني *peshmanai*, } sunrise during the month Ramazān; an early breakfast.
پيشوا *peshwā*, s.m. A guide, leader. P.
پيشواز *peshwāz*, s.m. A gown; an open frock worn by dancing women. P.
پيشه *pesha*, s.f. Calling, trade, profession; habit, custom. P.
پيشه ور *pesha-war*, s.m. A mechanic, artificer.
پيشۍ *pīsha-ī*, s.f. A caterpillar; a small nose-ring worn as an ornament by women; a leather bag or wallet.
پيښ *pekkh*, a. Before, in front, advanced. P. (*pesh*).
پيښاور *pekkhāwar*, s.m. Name of a city and province: Peshawar.
پيښكښ *pekkh-kakkh*, s.m. Offering, present, tribute. P. (*pesh-kash*).
پيښول *pekkhawul*, v.a. To bring forward, introduce, bring together, cause to meet.
پيښه *pekkha*, s.f. Mockery, ridicule, caricature. H. (*pekhnā*). *pekkhe-kawul*, v.a. To make faces, ridicule, ape, mock.
پيښيدل *pekkhedal*, v.n. To happen, occur, befall; to meet, encounter. P. (*peshīdan*).
پيښين *pekkhīn*, a. Ancient, prior, former. s.m. Noon, afternoon. P. (*peshīn*).

پيغام *paighām*, s.m. A message. P.

پيغامبر *paighāmbar*, s.m. A messenger, prophet. P.

پيغله *peghla*, s.f. A damsel, maid, virgin.

پيغور *peghor*, s.m. Reproach, abuse, raillery; calumny, slander. P. (*peghāra*). *peghor-warkawul*, v.a. To reproach, rail at, abuse; calumniate, slander.

پيک *paik*, s.m. A messenger, porter, runner. P.

پيکار *paikār*, s.m. Contest, battle, war. P. A pedlar.

پيکان *paikān*, s.m. The head of an arrow. P.

پيکر *paikar*, s.m. Countenance, face, form; likeness, portrait. P.

پيکړه *paikaṛa*, s.f. An anklet, ornament for the ankle; fetter, hobble.

پيکل *pekal*, s.m. A clothes-line, rope to hang clothes upon.

پيکوي *pekawai*, s.m. See پييوي.

پيل *pīl*, s.m. An elephant. P.

پيله *pela*, s.f. Silkworm's cocoon; silkworm. P.

پيمان *paimān*, s.m. Promise, oath, contract. P.

پيمانه *paimāna*, s.f. A goblet; a dry measure. P.

پيمايش *paimā-ish*, s.m. Measure, limit. P.

پيمخي *paimakhai*, a. See پاجمخي. Also پي مخي *pa-ī-makhai*.

پينځه *pīndzah*, a. Five.

پينڅه *paintsa*, s.f. The leg of a pair of trousers. P. (*pāencha*).

پينل *pīnal*, v.a. To chuck into the mouth from the hand.

پينه *pīna*, s.f. A trencher, wooden bowl, kneading trough.

پيودل *pewdal*, v.a. To thread, file, string, spit. H. (*pironā*).

پيودلي *pewdalai*, a. Filed, strung, threaded.

پيوره *paiwara*, a. Milky, milk-giving, milch, full of milk. Also پي وره *pa-ī-wara*.

پيوست *pewast* or *paiwast*, s.m. Connection, junction; relationship, friendship. P.

پيوستون *pewastūn*, s.m. Adhesion, connection, attachment; contiguity, proximity, relationship.

پيوسته *pewastah*, a. Connected, joined, attached. P.

پيوند *pewand*, s.m. A joint, patch, fastening; bud, graft. P.

پييوي *peyawai*, s.m. A band for the hair; the bunch of braids plaited with the hair of young women and allowed to hang down the back.

ت

ت *te*, The fourth letter of the Pukkhto alphabet.

تَ *ta*, or ته *tah*, pr. The second personal pronoun, thou. part. The sign of the dative case, to, unto. It always follows its noun.

تا *tā*, ad. As far as, to, till, whilst, so that. P. s.f. A fold, sheet, layer, plait. P. (*tah*). pr. The inflected form of the second personal pronoun in the oblique cases singular, thee, by thee, thou.

تاب *tāb*, s.m. Heat, fury, rage; endurance, suffering; power, strength; coil, twist; light, splendour. P.

تابدان *tābdān*, s.m. A sky-light, lattice. P.

تابژن *tābjan*, a. Glittering, shining. P. (*tābān*). Also written تابجن *tābjan*.

تابستان *tābistān*, s.m. The hot weather, summer. P.

تابع *tābi'*, s.m. A dependant, subject. A.

تابعدار *tābi'dār*, a. Obedient, submissive, subject. s.m. A subject; follower, dependant.

تابعداري *tābi'dārī*, s.f. Obedience, allegiance, fidelity.

تابوت *tābūt*, s.m. A coffin, bier. *tābūt-i-sakīna*, s.f. The ark of the covenant given to Adam from heaven. A.

تابين *tābīn*, s.m. A subject, follower, dependent.

تابه *tāba*, s.f. A frying-pan. P.

تاثير *tāsīr*, s.m. Effect, operation, impression. A.

تاج *tāj*, s.m. A crown, diadem; crest of a bird. P.

تاجر *tājir*, s.m. A merchant, trader. A.

تاجک *tājik*, s.m. A cultivator, peasant; mechanic. The name of a tribe; they are settled about the large cities of Afghanistan, and form the bulk of the population on the western borders of the country; their language is the Persian, and they are supposed to be descendants of the ancient Persians.

تاخت *tākht*, s.m. A gallop, run; foray, raid; attack, invasion; plunder, ravage. P.

تاخير *tākhīr*, s.m. Delay, procrastination. A.

تار *tār*, s.m. Wire; cord, thread. P. *tār-tār* or *tār-patār*, a. Confused, dispersed, scattered.

تاراج *tārāj*, s.m. Plunder, spoil, booty. P.

تارک *tārik*, s.m. Leaving, forsaking; a deserter. A.

تارو *tārū*, s.m. A black partridge; a drone, humble bee; a kind of wasp without a sting. A kind of saddle cloth.

تاروګي *tārūgai*, s.m. A kind of butterfly.

تارول *tārawul*, v.a. To scatter, disperse.

تاريخ *tārīkh*, s.m. Era, date; annals, history. A.

تاريک *tārīk*, a. Dark, obscure. P.

تاريکي *tārīkī*, s.f. Darkness, obscurity. P.

تاړ *tāṛ*, s.m. Plunder, spoil; a gang of robbers.

تاړه *tāṛah*, a. Spoiled, ruined, sacked.

تاړي *tāṛī*, s.m. Clapping the hands to express approbation, or in time to music. H. (*tārī*).

تازه *tāzah*, a. Fresh, new; green, verdant; young, robust; happy, pleased. P.

تازي *tāzi*, s.m. A greyhound; an Arab horse; a hunting dog, hound. P.

تازيانه *tāziyāna*, s.f. A whip, scourge, birch. P.

تاس *tās*, s.m. A goblet or cup of brass; a platter or tray of copper. P. Cards; a game at cards. H.

تاسو *tāsū*, pr. Plural form of the second personal pronoun: ye, you. Also written تاسُ *tāsu*.

تاغه *tāghah*, s.m. Name of a tree, the wood of which is used to make charms against the evil eye; the white poplar (*Populus albus*). H. (*tāgh*).

تافته *tāfta*, s.f. A kind of silk, taffeta; a colour of horses, cream colour. P.

تاک *tāk*, s.m. A vine. P. A precipice, cliff; mountain side. a. Odd, single, unique. A. (*ṭāq*).

تاکيد *tākīd*, s.m. Emphasis, injunction; confirmation. A. *tākīd-kawul*, v.a. To enjoin, insist, urge, press.

تاکيدي *tākīdī*, a. Emphatic, decided, confirmed.

تال *tāl*, s.m. Clapping the hands to music; chime. S.

تالاب *tālāb*, } s.m. A pond, tank, reservoir.
تالاو *tālāo*, } P.

تالاش *tālāsh*, s.m. Investigation, inquiry, search. P. (*talāsh*). Name of a valley between Bajawar and Swat.

تالنده *tālanda*, s.f. Thunder.

تالو *tālū*, s.m. The palate; a disease of the palate in cattle. S.

تاله *tāla*, s.f. Booty, spoil, pillage, plunder, ruin; a kind of fine spring grass.

تالي *tālai*, s.m. A metal platter or tray. S. (*thālī*).

تامبه *tāmba*, } s.f. Copper. S. (*tāmbā*).
تانبه *tānba*, }

تامّل *tā-ammul*, s.m. Hesitation, meditation. A.

تان *tān*, s.m. A note in music, tone, tune. S.

تاندوله *tāndola*, s.f. Name of a potherb.

تانده *tāndah*, a. Fresh, green, verdant.

تانسته *tānasta*, s.f. The warp or threads stretched lengthwise on the loom. P.

تانگ *tāng*, s.m. A band, brace, saddle-girth. P. (*tang*),

تانړه *tā<u>n</u>ra*, s.f. A guard, picket; police station. S. (*thānā*).

تاو *tāo*, s.m. See تاب.

تاوان *tāwān*, s.m. Amends, recompense; retaliation; debt, fine, mulct. P. Used in opposition to *qiṣāṣ*, which means actual revenge,—blood for blood,—injury for injury, etc. *tāwān-ā<u>kh</u>istal*, v.a. To fine, mulct; take the responsibility. *tāwān-kedal*, v.n. To suffer loss, injury, etc. *tāwān-warkawul*, v.a. To make amends, compensate, pay a fine. *tāwān-kawul*, v.a. To expend, incur, etc.

تاواني *tāwānī*, a. Injurious, incurring loss, noxious.

تاوس *tāos*, s.m. A peacock. A. (*ṭāūs*).

تاوون *tāwūn*, s.m. The plague. A. (*ṭā'ūn*).

تاووني *tāwūnai*, s.m. A man afflicted with the plague.

تاويتک *tāwītak*, s.m. An ornamental charm worn on the bosom by women.

تب *tab*, s.m. A poultice, epithem.

تباخ *tabā<u>kh</u>*, s.m. A charger, plate, dish. A. (*ṭabāq*).

تبار *tabār*, s.m. Race, family, tribe, people. P.

تباه *tabāh*, a. Ruined, spoiled; abject, wretched. P.

تباهي *tabāhī*, s.f. Ruin, wreck; depravity, wretchedness.

تبخي *taba<u>kh</u>ai*, s.m. An iron platter for baking cakes on. A. (*ṭabāq*). The pelvis.

تبديل *tabdīl*, s.m. Alteration, change. A.

تبر *tabar*, s.m. An axe, hatchet, cleaver. P. *tabar-zīn*, s.m. A horseman's battle-axe.

تبرّک *tabarruk*, s.m. Blessing, benediction. A.

تبړه *tabaṛa*, s.f. A slate, slab of stone.

تبسم *tabassum*, s.m. A smile, simper. A.

تبق *tabaq*, }
تبخ *taba<u>kh</u>*, } s.m. A disease of cattle, the glanders.

تبه *taba*, s.f. Fever; heat, fervour. P. S. (*tap*).

تبئ *taba-ī*, s.f. A flat dish of pottery for baking cakes on.

تپ *tap*, s.m. A mole, freckle; scar or pit of small-pox. *tap-tap*, in. A call to encourage dogs to go into a hole.

تپاس *tapās*, s.m. Labour, toil, search, enquiry. S.

تپاک *tapāk*, s.m. Esteem, regard, affection, love. S.

تپړا *tapṛā*, s.f. A potter's tool; a wooden tapper or mallet; tapping. H. (*thāpī*).

تپک *tapak*, s.m. The roll or sound of a drum. A sledge hammer. P.

تپل *tapal*, v.a. To dab, stick against; daub, smear; heap, mass, pile. H. (*thāpnā*).

تپنړئ *tapa<u>n</u>ra-ī*, s.f. See تپړا.

تپور *tapor*, s.m. An ornamental breast-band worn by young women; a stomacher.

تپوس *tapos*, s.m. Enquiry, search. A. (*tafaḥuṣ*).

تپه *tapa*, s.f. A district, parish; a clan, tribe. H.

تپي *tapai*, a. Freckled, pitted, scarred, spotted. s.m. A mole, freckle, scar, pit of small-pox.

تت *tat*, a. Close, compact, dense, thick. H. (*ṭhaṭh*).

تتړي *tataṛai*, a. Lisping, stammering. s.m. A lisper, stammerer.

تتمه *tatimma*, s.f. Appendix, supplement. A.

تتوه *tatawa*, s.f. A ring-dove.

تجارت *tajārat*, s.m. Commerce, trade. A.

تجربه *tajriba*, s.f. Experiment, proof, trial, test. A.

تجويز *tajwīz*, s.m. Contrivance, plan, scheme;

enquiry, consideration ; determination, judgment. A.

تخ tich, s.m. The scabbard of a sword, sheath of a dagger.

تحرير tahrīr, s.m. Writing correctly ; written ; dated. A.

تحصيل tahsīl, s.m. Acquisition, acquirement; profit, gain ; collection ; collectorate. A.

تحفه tuhfah, a. Curious, rare, choice, excellent. A.

تحقيق tahqīq, a. Authentic, verified, ascertained. ad. Indeed, really, truly. s.m. Precision, exactness. A.

تحقيقات tahqīqāt, s.m. Inquiry, investigation. A.

تحمل tahammul, s.m. Endurance, forbearance. A.

تخت takht, s.m. A throne. P.

تخته takhta, s.f. A board, plank ; sheet of paper ; bench, form ; bier. *takhta·bandī*, s.f. Boarding, planking, wainscot. *takhta·pokkh*, s.m. A stage, platform, flooring. *takhta·nard*, s.m. Backgammon. P.

تخرگ takharg, or tkharg, s.m. The armpit.

تخرگي takhargai, s.m. The fillet or patch in the armpit of a dress.

تخفيف takhfīf, s.m. Abatement, mitigation, relief. A.

تخم tukhm, s.m. Seed, sperm ; an egg ; a testicle. P.

تخمخ takhmakh, in. Fie ! shame !

تخمه tukhma, s.f. Origin, principle. P. Indigestion. A.

تخميناً takhmīnan, ad. About, nearly, by guess. A.

تخنول takhnawul, } v.a. To tickle. P. (tākht, assault, etc.).
تخول takhawul, }

تخنيدل takhnedal, } v.n. To tickle, titillate.
تخيدل takhedal, }

تخه takha, s.f. } **Tickling, titillation.**
تخي takhai, s.m. }

تدارک tadāruk, s.m. Chastisement, retaliation ; medy, precaution ; provision, preparation. A.

تدبير tadbīr, s.m. Advice, counsel, deliberation ; contrivance, management, policy ; arrangement, order. A.

تدريج tadrīj, s.m. Gradation, scale. A.

تذکره tazkira, s.f. Biography, memoir. A.

تر tar, a. Damp, moist. P. ad. As far as, to, until, up to, etc. It is generally followed by the adverb *pore* or *pori*. Ex. *tar·osa·pore*, until now. *tar·kala·pore*, till when ? *tar·kūma·pore*, as long as, etc. *tri*, p. See تري.

تراټ trāṭ, s.m. A whip, goad.

تراټه trāṭa, s.f. Piping, or edging of a dress.

تراړه tarāṛa, s.f. Gravel, shingle.

ترازو tarāzū, s.m. A balance, scale. P.

ترازه tarāza, s.f. A slice, shaving, bit. P. (*tarāsha*).

تراش tarāsh, s.m. Cutting, clipping ; cut, form, shape ; (in comp.) -cutter, -carver. P.

تراغ tarāgh, s.m. A coil, plait, twist.

تراک trāk, s.m. A crack, fissure ; slit, rent, tear. A. Also تراق trāq.

ترانه tarāna, s.f. Melody, music, song ; symphony, tune. P. *tarāne·wayal*, v.a. To sing.

تراوي tarāwe, s.f. A prayer comprising twenty genuflexions, performed at bedtime every night during the month of Ramazān.

ترب turb, s.m. A radish. P.

تربت turbat, s.m. A tomb, sepulchre. A.

تربور tarbūr, s.m. A cousin : father's brother's son.

تربوزه tarbūza, s.f. A water melon. P.

تربيت tarbiyat, s.m. Education, instruction, tuition. A.

ترپ trap, s.m. A leap, bound, jump ; hop, skip.

ترپلل *traplal*, v.a. To jump, vault, bound, etc.
ترپه *trapa*, s.f. See ترپ.
ترپي *trapai*, s.m. A footfall, sound of steps.
ترتاب *tartāb*, s.m. Remorse, sorrow, regret.
ترتړي *tartaṛai*, s.m. See تتړي.
ترتله *tartala*, ad. Always, ever, continually.
ترتيب *tartīb*, s.m. Arrangement, disposition, order, method. A.
ترتيزک *tartezak*, s.m. Water-cress. P. (*tezak*).
ترټل *traṭal*, v.a. To scold, reprimand, taunt; drive away, repel. See رټل *raṭal*.
ترجمه *tarjuma*, s.f. Translation, interpretation. A.
ترجمان *tarjumān*, s.m. An interpreter. A.
ترڅ *tra*ts, a. Slanting, sloping, aside, wry, crooked. H. (*tirchhā*).
ترخ *trakh*, s.m. The armpit.
ترخان *tarkhān*, s.m. Free, exempted from taxation; name of a tribe of Turks; wormwood.
ترخه *tarkha*, s.f. The herb wormwood, absinth (*Artemisia Judaica*).
ترخئ *tarkha-ī*, s.f. Name of a plant, wild camomile (*Anthemis nobilis*).
تردد *taraddud*, s.m. Hesitation, suspense. A.
ترس *tars*, s.m. Fear, dread, terror. P.
ترسا *tarsā*, s.m. A heretic, infidel, idolator, pagan. P.
ترسان *tarsān*, ترسناک *tarsnāk*, a. Timid, fearful, cowardly. P.
ترسري *tarsarai*, ترسيري *tarserai*, s.m. A headstall, halter for a horse; a freckle, spot in the skin.
ترش *tursh*, a. Acid, sour; austere, crabbed, cross. P.
ترشي *turshī*, s.f. Acidity, sourness; acids; ill-temper, austerity. P.
ترښځ *tarkkhadz*, ترښځه *tarkkhadza*, s.f. An adze; a band, fillet, or strip of cloth let into the side of a dress.

ترغيب *targhīb*, s.m. Incitement, instigation. A.
ترقي *taraqqī*, s.f. A rise, elevation, ascent; promotion, advancement; increase; proficiency. A.
ترک *turk*, s.m. A Turk; a soldier; a robber; (in poetry) a handsome youth. P. *tark*, s.m. Desertion, forsaking. A. *trak*, s.m. A crack, cleft, split; sand-crack, a disease of the hoof in cattle; a crack, the sound of splitting, bursting, tearing, etc.
ترکاڼړ *tarkāṉṛ*, s.m. A carpenter,
ترکښ *tarkakkh*, s.m. A quiver. P. (*tarkash*).
ترکلاڼړي *tarkalāṉṛī*, s.m. Name of a Pathan tribe settled in Bajawur,
ترکه *tarka*, s.f. Legacy, bequest; effects or estate of a deceased person. A.
ترکيب *tarkīb*, s.m. Composition, mixture; make, form. A.
ترګمئ *tarugma-ī*, s.f. A dark, moonless night; obscurity, darkness.
ترله *tarla*, s.f. A cousin: father's brother's daughter.
ترم *turum*, s.m. A stallion, kept only for covering. P.
ترمنه *taramna*, s.f. A bog, quagmire, quicksand.
ترمي ترمي *tarmai-tarmai*, a. Dispersed, scattered, dispelled.
ترناو *tarnāo*, s.m. An aqueduct, trough, gutter.
ترنځ *trandz*, a. Slim, compressed, slight, spare. P. (*taranj*).
ترنج *turanj*, s.m. A citron, lime, lemon. *taranj*, s.m. Name of several plants of the orders *Euphorbia* and *Asclepias*, containing milky sap. *tranj*, s.m. A skein or roll of thread.
ترنجوکي *tranjūkai*, ترنجي *tranjai*, s.m. Small skein of thread.
ترنکوڅه *trankūtsa*, s.f. A sling.

ترنگ *trang*, s.m. Twang, jar, vibration, sound.

ترنگبين *tarangabīn*, } s.m. Manna produced
ترنجبين *taranjabīn*, } from the camel's thorn (*Hedysarum alhagi*). Oxymel, honey and limejuice. s. p.

ترنگړ *trangaṛ*, s.m. A net for carrying grass, etc.

ترو *tro*, ad. Consequently, therefore, then, for that; at length, afterwards, at that time.

تروټ *troṭ*, s.m. Damage, injury; loss, deficiency.

تروټه *troṭa*, s.f. Detriment, discount.

ترور *tror*, s.f. Aunt: father's or mother's sister.

ترورۍ *trora-ī*, s.f. A fox.

تروکه *tarūka*, s.f. Sorrel (*Rumex vesicarius*). Wood-sorrel (*Oxalis corniculata*).

تروه *tarwa*, a. See تريو.

تروی *tarwai*, s.m. Name of a purgative plant (*Ipomœa turpethum*). H. (*teorī*). *tarwe*, s.f. (pl. of *tarwa*) Sour milk, whey, curds and whey.

تره *trah*, s.m. Uncle: father's or mother's brother. *tara*, s.f. Greens, vegetables, potherbs. P. A kind of cucumber (*Cucumis acutangulus*). H. (*tura-ī*). Alarm, dread, fear.

ترهاو *tirhāo*, s.m. The third part of an oke. See اوري.

ترهر *tarhar*, a. Timid, fearful, nervous. s.m. Fear, alarm, dismay. Also ترهور *tarhūr*.

ترهول *tarhawul*, v.a. To alarm, frighten, start, etc. (as game).

ترهيدل *tarhedal*, v.n. To start, fear, shy, etc. (as animals). P. (*tarīdan*).

تري *tarī*, s.f. Moisture; water in opposition to land; moist or brown sugar. ad. By water. P. *tarai*, s.m. An aqueduct or canal on the side of a hill. *turai*, s.m. A kind of cucumber (*Cucumis utilissimus*).

tara-ī, ad. Clandestinely, confidentially, secretly. *tura-ī*, s.f. A bugle. H. (*turhī*).

تري *tre*, p. From, by, than, with.

ترياك *tariyāk*, s.m. Opium. A. (*tiriyāq*).

تريز *tarīz*, s.m. A patch, piece sewed on to a dress or garment. P.

تريج *tarīj*, a. Strong, violent, rough. A.

تريخ *trīkh*, a. Bitter, nauseous; sour, austere, cross, ill-tempered. *f.* *tarkha*.

تريخي *ṭrīkhai*, s.m. Bitterness; gall, bile; the gall-bladder; anger, malice, ill-feeling.

تريو *trīw*, a. Acid, sharp, sour; austere, crabbed, morose, cross. *f.* *tarwa*.

تريه *tariyah*, in. A shepherd's call to drive sheep, etc.

تړاق *tṛāq*, s.m. A knock, rap, tap. H. (*taṛākā*).

تړاقي *taṛāqa-ī*, s.f. A loin clout; a cord tied round the waist, and used as a fastening for the clout covering the privates. H. (*taṛāgī*).

تړپ *tṛap*, s.m. Haste, hurry; flutter; leap. H. (*taṛap*).

تړپول *tṛapawul*, v.a. To agitate, disturb, flurry. H. (*taṛpānā*).

تړپيدل *tṛapedal*, v.n. To flutter, palpitate, writhe. H. (*taṛapnā*).

تړق *tṛaq* , s.m. A pat, tap, rap, knock, slap.

تړل *taṛal*, v.a. To tie, fasten, bind, lash. P. (*tār*, thread, cord).

تړم *taṛam*, a. Lukewarm, tepid.

تړون *taṛūn*, s.m. Binding, fastening, lashing; agreement, bargain, compact, treaty.

تړنه *taṛana*, } s.f. See preceding.
تړه *taṛa*, }

تړی *taṛai*, s.m, Lisping; a lisper.

تزن *tuzun*, a. Base, cowardly.

تږی *tagai*, a. Thirsty. P. (*tishna*).

تسبه *tasba*, s.f. The bead of a rosary. A. (*tasbīḥ*). *tasbe*, p. A rosary, chaplet of beads.

تسخير *taskhīr*, s.m. Capture, subjection. A.
تسكين *taskīn*, s.m. Comfort, consolation. A.
تسلي *tasallī*, s.m. Comfort, solace, consolation. A.
تسليم *taslīm*, s.m. Resignation, obedience; obeisance, salutation; health, safety. A.
تسمه *tasma*, s.f. A thong, leather strap. H.
تش *ta-ash*, a. Empty, void, hollow. ad. Only, merely, simply. P. (*tihī*).
تشبيه *tashbīh*, s.m. Comparison, simile. A.
تشت *tasht*, s.m. A basin used to wash the hands over. P. A platter, salver, tray.
تشخانه *tashkhāna*, s.f. The fire pan of a gun. P. (*ātash-khāna*).
تشخيص *tashkhīṣ*, s.m. Ascertaining, distinguishing; valuation, assessment. A.
تشويش *tashwīsh*, s.m. Anxiety, disquietude. A.
تشي *ta-ashai*, s.m. The flank, side, hypochondrium.
تښتن *takkhtan*, s.m. See ښتن.
تښتول *takkhtawul*, / تښول *takkhawul*, v.a. To put to flight, run away with, carry off, elope with, etc. P. (*tākhtāndan*).
تښتيدل *takkhtedal*, / تښل *takkhal*, v.n. To flee, decamp, retire, retreat, run away. P. (*tākhtan*).
تصديق *taṣdīq*, s.m. Attestation, verification. A.
تصرف *taṣarruf*, s.m. Disposal, use; expenditure, extravagance. A.
تصنيف *taṣnīf*, s.m. Composition, authorship. A.
تصوير *taṣwīr*, s.m. Image, picture, portrait. A.
تعجب *t'ajjub*, s.m. Wonder, surprise, astonishment. A.
تعريف *t'arīf*, s.m. Explaining, praising. A.
تعطيل *ta'ṭīl*, s.m. Vacation; neglecting, abandoning. A.
تعظيم *t'aẓīm*, s.m. Honour, reverence, respect. A.
تعلق *t'alluq*, s.m. Relation, connection; dependence; correspondence, commerce. A.
تعليم *t'alīm*, s.m. Teaching, tuition. A.
تعويذ *t'awīz*, s.m. An amulet, charm. A.
تغار *taghār*, s.m. A bread-tray; a bucket, pail. P.
تغارك *taghārak*, s.m. Dropsy; a small pail. P.
تغاري *taghārai*, s.m. A bread-basket; an earthenware dish or platter; a small bucket or pail. A. a. A glutton.
تغمه *taghma*, s.f. A mark, weal, welt; a medal. A.
تغير *taghīr*, s.m. / تغيري *taghīrī*, s.f. / تغيير *taghaiyur*, s.m. Change, alteration. A.
تف *taf*, s.m. Vapour, steam. P. *tuf*, s.m. Saliva. P.
تفاوت *tafāwat*, s.m. Difference, distinction: distance. A.
تفرقه *tafriqa*, s.f. / تفريق *tafrīq*, s.m. Division, separation. A.
تفسير *tafsīr*, s.m. Commentary, explanation. A.
تفصيل *tafṣīl*, s.m. Detail, explanation, separation. A.
تفنگ *tufang*, s.m. A musket. P.
تقاضا *taqāẓā*, s.f. Exacting, dunning; importunity. A.
تقدير *taqdīr*, s.m. Destiny, fate, lot. A.
تقرير *taqrīr*, s.m. Detail, relation, recital. A.
تقسيم *taqsīm*, s.m. Dividing, division, distribution. A.
تقصير *taqṣīr*, s.m. Crime, error, fault. A.
تقليد *taqlīd*, s.m. Imitation; forging; copying; believing without enquiry. A.
تقوي *taqwā*, s.f. Piety, the fear of God. A.
تك *tak*, ad. Altogether, wholly, utterly; only used with respect to colour. Ex. *tak-tor-saṛai*, a jet-black man. *taka-spīna-kkhadza*, a snow-white woman.
تكبير *takbīr*, s.m. Repeating the creed, or saying "God is great" (*allahu-akbar*). A.

تکرار *takrār*, s.m. Altercation, contention, dispute. A.

تکراري *takrārī*, s.m. A wrangler, caviller. a. Disputing, importuning, wrangling. A.

تکړه *takṛah*, a. Active, vigorous, strong, robust, healthy. *takaṛa*, s.f. A pebble; boulder.

تکل *takal*, s.m. Attempt, effort, endeavour. See کټل.

تکلاستي *taklāstai*, a. Agile, nimble, smart, active, alert.

تکليف *taklīf*, s.m. Ceremony; difficulty, inconvenience, trouble, ailment, distress, annoyance. A.

تکمه *tukma*, s.f. A button loop; the sac or tubercle of piles. P.

تکيه *takiya*, s.f. A bolster, pillow; a faqīr's stand or hut. *takiya-kalām*, s.m. An expletive, cant phrase. P.

تګ *tag*, s.m. Departure; toiling, running about.

تګاپو *tagāpū*, s.m. Bustle, toil, labour, search. P.

تل *tal*, ad. Always, ever, perpetually. *til*, s.m. Sesamum, the seed. S. *tal*, s.m. The base, bottom, foot, sole. S. (*talā*). *tall*, s.m. A hillock, mound, heap. A.

تلاش *talāsh*, s.m. Enquiry, study, search. P.

تلب *talab*, s.m. Salary, wages, hire, pay. A. (*ṭalab*).

تلتک *taltak*, s.m. Coverlet, counterpane; mattress.

تلخ *talkh*, a. Acrid, bitter, rancid. P.

تلخان *talkhān*, s.m. Meal of parched grain, made into a paste for food on a journey. P.

تلف *talaf*, s.m. Destruction, loss, ruin; prodigality, waste. A.

تلکه *talaka*, s.f. A kind of snare for catching birds, a springe.

تلل *tlal*, v.n. To go, depart, set out, leave. H. (*chalnā*). See لاړل *lāṛal*. *talal*, v.a. To balance, weigh. H. (*tolnā*).

تلوار *talwār*, s.m. Haste, speed, quickness.

تلوسه *talwasa*, s.f. Commotion, distraction. P. (*talwāsa*).

تلول *talwal*, s.m. Dispatch, haste, speed, quickness. *talawul*, v.a. To fry, grill, broil.

تلولي *talwalai*, a. Precipitate, rash, hasty, quick. *talawalai*, a. Broiled, fried, grilled.

تله *tlah*, s.m. Exit, exodus, departure, setting out. *tala*, s.f. Balance, scale; the sole of the foot.

تلي *talai*, s.m. The sole of a shoe; under surface of a thing; sole of the foot: palm of the hand. S. (*talī*). *tilai*, s.m. Form, figure, shape. *tila-ī*, s.f. The shaft of an arrow, stalks of corn, reeds, grasses, etc.; a straw, straw. H. (*tīl*).

تم *tam*, s.m. Continuance, permanence, rest. a. Staying, abiding, tarrying.

تماچه *tamācha*, s.f. A pistol; a blow, cuff, slap. A. (*ṭamāncha*).

تماشا *tamāshā*, / تماشه *tamāsha*, s.f. A show, sight, spectacle, amusement, entertainment. A.

تماکو *tamākū*, / تمباکو *tambākū*, s.m. Tobacco.

تمام *tamām*, a. Complete, entire, perfect. A.

تمامي *tamāmī*, s.f. Completion, end; perfection.

تمبل *tambal*, s.m. A kettle-drum, tambourine. A. (*ṭabal*).

تمبو *tambū*, s.m. A tent. H.

تمبوزک *tambūzak*, s.m. A muzzle; a muzzle of spikes fastened on the nose of a calf to prevent its sucking.

تمبوزي *tambūzai*, s.m. The muzzle, snout; bridge of the nose.

تمبه *tamba*, s.f. The leaf of a door; prop of a door; a group, party, herd.

تمبګي *tambaga-ī*, s.f. The leaf of a window or shutter.

تمبيزه *tambeza*, s.f. } The muzzle, snout.
تمبيزي *tambezai*, s.m. }

تمتراق *tamtarāq*, s.m. Grandeur, magnificence, pomp. A. (*tamṭarāq*).

تمسك *tamassuk*, s.m. Note of hand, bond, receipt. A.

تمن *tuman*, s.m. A crowd, troop, party; brotherhood, connection; a score, twenty. P.

تموز *tamūz*, s.m. Heat, warmth; name of a month, July. P.

تمه *tama*, s.f. Avarice, avidity; covetousness, greediness. A. (*ṭama'*).

تميز *tamīz*, s.m. Discretion, sense, judgment. A.

تن *tan*, s.m. Body, person; individual. P.

تنا *tanā*, s.f. Thunder.

تناو *tanāo*, s.m. A cord, rope; strap.

تنبيه *tanbīh*, s.m. Admonition, advice, correction. A.

تنتنا *tantanā*, s.f. Fame, sound, rumour; dignity, pomp. A. (*ṭanṭanā*).

تنخواه *tankhwāh*, s.m. Salary, wages, pay. P.

تند *tund*, a. Active, fast, quick; hot, spirited, rash; acrid, pungent. P.

تندار *tandār*, s.f. Uncle's wife. See تندور.

تندر *tandar*, s.m. Thunder; a thunder-bolt; eclipse. P.

تندور *tandor*, s.f. Paternal aunt, father's brother's wife. *tandūr*, s.m. An oven. P.

تندوره *tandūra*, s.f. A cascade, waterfall.

تندوړي *tindoṛai*, s.m. The cartilage of the nose.

تندوي *tandwai*, s.m. Cartilage, gristle.

تنده *tanda*, s.f. Thirst.

تندي *tundī*, a. Acrimony; impetuosity, fierceness. P. *tandai*, s.m. An infant, babe, suckling; sprout, shoot, young plant; the forehead; the crown of the head, vertex.

تنديار *tandyāra*, s.f. Father's brother's wife. See تندار.

تندل *tandal*, v.a. To make, form, mend, repair.

تنذري *tanzarai*, } s.m. A grey partridge.
تنزري *tanzarai*, }

تنکي *tankai*, s.m. A babe, suckling; sprout, shoot, young plant. a. Young, tender, unripe.

تنگ *tang*, a. Confined, narrow, tight; scarce, wanting, barren; distressed, in want; dejected, sad. P. *tung*, s.m. An ewer, vase, long-necked jar. P.

تنگسه *tangsa*, } s.f. Distress, poverty; scarcity, want; narrowness, tightness.
تنگسيا *tangsiyā*, }

تنگه *tanga*, s.f. The stock or stem of a tree; body or centre width of a garment; name of a coin equal to one-third of a rupee. H.

تنگي *tangai*, s.m. A defile, gorge, hill pass. *tangī*, s.f. Distress, poverty, want; avarice, parsimony, stinginess; narrowness, tightness. P.

تنور *tanūr*, s.m. A furnace; oven. P.

تنومند *tanomand*, a. Corpulent, robust. P.

تنها *tanhā*, a. Alone, solitary; single; apart. ad. Merely, only, singly. P.

تنهائي *tanhā-ī*, s.f. Solitude, loneliness, privacy. P.

تنړا *tanṛā*, s.f. Thunder; roar of a wild animal.

تنړاکه *tanṛāka*, s.f. A bleb, vesicle, blister.

تنړکار *tanṛakār*, s.m. Borax. P. (*tinkār*).

تنړئي *tanṛa-ī*, s.f. Button loop; strings of a dress; cord, pack thread, etc. used to tie bundles.

تو *tū*, s.m. Spittle, saliva. H. (*thūk*). *tū-tū*, in. Call to a dog. H.

توا *tawā*, s.f. A frying pan. P.

تواريخ *tawārīkh*, s.m. Annals, dates; history. A.

توان *tuwān*, s.m. Force, power, strength. P.

توانا *tuwānā*, a. Able, powerful, strong. P.

توانگر *tuwāngar*, a. Rich, wealthy; powerful, able. P.

توانګري *tuwāngarī*, s.f. Opulence, wealth; ability, power. P.

توانيدل *tuwānedal*, v.n. To be able. P. (*tuwānīdan*).

توب *tob*, A particle affixed to nouns and adjectives to denote state, pursuit, or quality. Ex. *tang*, a. Tight. *tang-tob*, s.m. Tightness. *spāhī*, s.m. Soldier. *spāhī-tob*, s.m. soldiering, profession of a soldier. *saṛī*, s.m. Men. *saṛī-tob*, s.m. The state of men, humanity. A. (*tab'a*). See تيا.

توبړه *tobṛa*, s.f. A nose bag (for a horse); saddle bag; a beggar's wallet. H. (*tobṛā*).

توبري *tobrai*, s.m. The head of an arrow, dart, etc.

توبه *toba*, s.f. Contrition, penitence, remorse. in. Fie! shame! A.

توبه ګار *toba-gār*, a. Penitent, contrite. A.

توپ *top*, s.m. A cannon, gun. T.

توپان *tūpān*, s.m. A hurricane, storm; deluge. A. (*tufān*).

توپک *topak*, s.m. A matchlock, musket. T.

توپنګچه *tūpangcha*, s.f. A pistol. P. (*tufangcha*).

توت *tūt*, s.m. The mulberry, tree and fruit. A.

توتا *totā*, s.m. } A parrot; the cock or hammer
توتي *totī*, s.f. } of a gun. H.

توتکي *totakai*, s.m. A swift, swallow.

توتکرکي *totakarkai*, s.m. A sand martin, swallow.

توتکري *totakarai*, s.m. A swift, swallow.

توتنکي *totankai*, s.m. A chip, filing, shaving, fragment. H. (*tūtan*).

توتيا *totiyā*, or نيله توتيا *nīla-totiyā*, s.f. Blue vitriol, sulphate of copper. s.

توجه *tawajja*, s.f. Attention, regard; favour. A.

توخي *tokhī*, s.m. Name of a section of the Ghilzai tribe.

تود *tod*, a. Hot, warm. P. (*tūnd*). H. (*tāt*).

تودوخه *todūkha*, s.f. Sultriness, heat, warmth.

تور *tor*, a. Black, dark. P. (*tār*). s.m. Fright, panic; slander, calumny; a net, snare. *tor-pore-kawul*, v.a. To calumniate, blacken, slander.

تورغړي *torghaṛai*, s.m. The arm above the elbow.

تورلمي *torlamai*, s.m. A badger.

توره *tūra*, s.f. A sword. *tora*, s.f. A copper coin, equal to half an anna.

توره آنه *tora-āna*, s.f. Name of a black coloured bird with a forked tail; the king-crow or tyrant fly-catcher. Called also *ḍāng-luka-ī*, club tail.

توره غاړه *tora-ghāṛa*, s.f. Hooping cough.

توري *torai*, s.m. The spleen; pupil of the eye. a. Simple, plain, pure, unmixed. *tora-ī*, s.f. A kind of cucumber (*cucumis acutangulus*). H. (*torī*).

توريت *tauret*, s.m. The Pentateuch, Old Testament. A. (*torāt*).

تورل *togal*, v.a. To plane, shave; polish, smooth.

توسن *tausan*, s.m. A war horse; high spirited horse. P.

توسند *tosand*, a. Dry, parched, withered. H. (*tūsā*).

توشدان *toshdān*, s.m. A pouch, cartridge-box. P.

توشک *toshak*, s.m. A mattress, quilt. P.

توښه *tokkha*, s.f. Necessaries, provisions, supplies for a journey. P. (*tosha*).

توغ *togh*, s.m. A banner, ensign, standard. P.

توغل *toghal*, } s.m. A saddle cloth of felt.
توغم *togham*, }

توقه *tūqa*, s.f. A blunt arrow; a small hill. P. (*tukka*).

توک *tūk*, s.m. Spittle. H. (*thūk*).

توکل *tūkal*, v.a. To spit. *tawakkul*, s.m. Faith, hope, reliance, trust in God. A.

توګه *toga*, s.f. Manner, method, way, mode.

تول *tol*, s.m. Gravity, weight. s. *tūl*, s.m. A crop or field ready for reaping. *twal*, a. Equal, even, same weight, six of one and half a dozen of the other.

تولاند *tūlānd*, s.m. A stride, long step; gait of a bird.

تولائي *tolā-ī*, s.f. A mattress, quilted bed.

توله *tola*, s.f. Name of a weight equal to 180 grs. (troy). s. (*tolā*).

تومان *tomān*, s.m. A sum equal to twenty rupees; a myriad; 10,000. P. See تمن.

تومت *tomat*, s.m. See تهمت.

تومنه *tomna*, } s.f. Rennet; ferment, yeast;
تومه *toma*, } essence, origin.

تونبيا *tonbiyā*, s.f. Carded cotton; thread made from carded cotton. H. (*tūmiyā*).

تونګ *tawang*, s.m. A band-box; a reed-basket for the clothes of women. *tuwang*, s.m. Magazine, store, treasury. P. *tūng*, s.f. A maiden, damsel, girl.

تونګي *tawangai*, s.m. A band-box; a small basket made of reeds, and used by women to keep jewelry, ornaments, clothes, etc. in.

تونړئي *taunṟa-ī*, s.f. A clothes chest, locker, safe.

توهړ *tohaṟ*, s.m. Cactus, prickly pear. H. (*thūhar*).

توي *toe*, a. Spilt, shed, overflowed, upset (as water from a bowl).

تويول *toyawul*, v.a. To pour out, upset, spill, shed.

توييدل *toyedal*, v.n. To overflow, flow out, be spilt.

ته *tah*, a. Going; walking, proceeding. pr. The second personal pronoun, thou. *ta*, s.f. Fold, layer, plait; the bottom, under surface. P. *ta-k͟hāna*, s.f. A cellar, vault. P. *tih*, a. Void, empty. P.

تهان *thān*, s.m. A piece, length of cloth; manger, stall for cattle. H.

تهمت *tuhmat*, s.m. Calumny, slander, suspicion, false accusation. A.

تهنال *tahnāl*, s.m. The mounting at the end of a scabbard. P.

تهنه *tahana*, s.f. A hollow, dip in the ground.

تي *tai*, s.m. A teat, nipple.

تيا *tiyā*, A particle added to adjectives in forming nouns denoting possession of their quality. Ex. *ārām*, a. Easy. *ārāmtiyā*, s.f. Easiness. *k͟hamsor*, a. Familiar. *k͟hamsortiyā*, s.f. Familiarity. *grān*, a. Dear. *grāntiyā*, s.f. Dearness.

تيار *tayār* or *taiyār*, a. Ready, complete, prepared, finished.

تياره *tyāra*, s.f. Darkness, gloom, obscurity (pl. of *tor*, black).

تياري *tayārī*, s.f. Readiness; preparation. P.

تيبون *taibūn*, s.m. See تيمم.

تيڅل *tetsal*, v.a. To perforate, pierce; to cram, stuff. H. (*tīsnā*).

تير *ter*, a. Lapsed, passed, gone by. *tīr*, s.m. An arrow; beam, ridge-pole. P.

تيرک *tīrak*, s.m. The iron axle on which the stone of a mill revolves; an axle.

تيرول *terawul*, v.a. To give the male to the female; to cause to pass.

تيره *terah*, a. Acute, keen, sharp. *tera*, a. Ready for the male, in heat. *tīrah*, a. Dark, obscure. P.

تيري *terai*, s.m. Excess; passing, lapsing; excellence, superiority.

تيريدل *teredal*, v.n. To pass, lapse, go by.

تيز *tez*, a. Acute, sharp, keen. P. *tīz*, s.m. Wind from the bowels, flatus. *tīz-āc͟hawul*, v.a. To break wind.

تيزل *tezal*, v.a. To hasten, urge, press.

تيزندئي *tezanda-ī*, s.f. A slip knot; hangman's noose, halter, rope.

تيږه *tīga*, s.f. A boulder, rock; pebble, stone, slab.

تيشه *tesha*, s.f. A carpenter's adze. P.

تيښته *tekkhta*, s.f. Defeat, flight, retreat.

تيغ *tegh*, s.m. A scimitar, sword. P. A sprout, shoot, blade of grass.

تيغنه *teghna*, s.f. An iron plate for baking on.

تيک *tyak*, a. Distended, inflated, expanded.

تيکه *teka*, s.f. }
تيکي *tekai*, s.m. } A scabbard, sheath.

تيل *tel*, s.m. Oil. S.

تيلي *telī*, s.m. An oilman. (f.) (*telanra*).

تيمم *tayammum*, s.m. The ceremonial purification before prayers, with dust or sand, when water is not at hand. A.

تينبوزک *tīnbūzak*, s.m. The muzzle, snout,

تينبوزي *tīnbūzai*, s.m. A muzzle.

تيندک *tīndak*, s.m. A trip, stumble; ricochet, bound.

تييل *teyal*, v.a. To broil, fry, grill, roast.

تييني *teyanai*, s.m. A broil, grill, fry.

ټ

ټ *ṭa*, The fifth letter of the Pukkhto alphabet. It corresponds with the Sanskrit ट, represented by ٹ in the Hindūstānī, and exactly resembles it in sound.

ټاپ *ṭāp*, s.m. An impression; stamp, die, seal. H. (*thāp*).

ټاپو *ṭāpū*, s.m. An island. H.

ټاپوړه *ṭāpoṛa*, s.f. A crutch, a stilt; washerman's board or plank.

ټاپه *ṭāpa*, s.f. A stamp, die, seal, print. H. (*thāpa*).

ټاټ *ṭāṭ*, s.m. Canvas, sackcloth. H. Conceit, vanity, swagger. H. (*ṭhāṭh*).

ټاټوب *ṭāṭob*, s.m. Calmness, composure, rest, repose.

ټاټوکه *ṭāṭūka*, s.f. Name of an edible ground nut.

ټاټۍ *ṭāṭa-ī*, s.f. Lullaby, rocking, swinging. *ṭāṭī*, s.m. A dandy, fop, beau.

ټاس *ṭās*, s.m. An explosion, pop, snap. bang.

ټاق *ṭāq*, s.m. A bang, explosion, discharge.

ټاقر *ṭāqar*, s.m. A decrepid old man. S. (*ṭhākur*).

ټاک *ṭāk*, s.m. The fruit of the bael tree (*Ægle marmelos*). A bang, rap, knock.

ټاکو *ṭākū*, s.m. A robber, highwayman, pirate. H. (*ḍākū*). Name of a disease in buffaloes.

ټال *ṭāl*, s.m. A swing; the branch of a tree. H. (*ṭhāl*).

ټاله *ṭāla*, s.f. Wholesale, by the lump (pl. of *ṭol*).

ټانټه *ṭānṭa*, s.f. Stalk of Indian corn. H. (*ḍānṭhī*).

ټانګ *ṭāng*, s.m. A period, season, time, term.

ټانګو *ṭāngū*, s.m. }
ټانګۍ *ṭānga-ī*, s.f. } Name of a tree and its fruit; a kind of pear tree.

ټبر *ṭabar*, s.f. A wife. s.m. Family, household. H.

ټبړ *ṭabaṛ*, s.m. Family, household.

ټبکي *ṭubkai*, }
ټبلي *ṭublai*, } s.m. A pit, hole, cavity.

ټبي *ṭabai*, s.m. A flat stone, slate, slab of pottery, etc. used to bake cakes upon.

ټپ *ṭap*, a. Weak, haggard, worn, exhausted. s.m. A slap, hit, whack, rap; smack, thud, concussion. ad. Altogether, entirely, totally; used with adjectives to denote intensity. Ex. *ṭap·ṛūnd·saṛai*, s.m. A perfectly blind man. *ṭapa·kanṛa·kkhadza*, s.f. A completely deaf woman.

ټپټپانړي *tapṭapānṛai*, s.m. Name of a game played by children.

ټپريدل *ṭaparedal*, v.n. To totter, plod, stagger, creep, etc. (as an old man). P. (*tapīdan*).

ټپړ *ṭapaṛ*, }
ټپنړ *ṭapanṛ*, } s.m. Canvas, sackcloth. H.

ټپل *ṭapal*, v.n. See ټپريدل.

ټپوڅ *ṭapūts*, s.m. A kite (*Milvus sp.*).

ټپي *ṭapai*, s.m. A spot, blotch, or patch of colour on the hide of an animal.

ټپيدل *ṭapedal*, v.n. See ټپل.

ټټ *ṭaṭ*, s.m. Conceit, vanity.

ټټي *ṭaṭai*, s.m. A fop, beau, coxcomb; braggart.

ټټر *ṭaṭar*, s.m. The breast, chest, thorax. Vertex, poll. H. (*ṭaṭrī*).

ټټو *ṭaṭū*, s.m. A pony. H. Bridge of a fiddle.

ټټوګي *ṭaṭūgai*, s.m. A small pony.

ټټۍ *ṭaṭa-ī*, s.f. A matted screen; privy. H. (*ṭaṭī*).

ټچ *ṭach*, s.m. See ټاس.

ټخ *ṭukh*, s.m. See ټوخ.

ټر *ṭar*, s.m. Flatus, explosion of wind from behind; bosh, fudge, humbug.

ټرټر *ṭarṭar*, s.m, Gabble, chatter, jabber.

ټرق *ṭraq*, } s.m. See ټق.
ټرک *ṭrak*, }

ټري *ṭarai*, s.m. Gabbler, chatterbox, prattler.

ټريدل *ṭaredal*, v.n. To break wind; to gabble, jabber.

ټز *ṭaz*, } s.m. A pop, puff; flatus. H. (*ṭhas*).
ټس *ṭas*, } A slap, cuff, whack.

ټسټوس *ṭasṭūs*, s.m. Cracking, popping; discharge of firearms (as in a skirmish).

ټسمس *ṭasmas*, a. Apathetic, dull, lazy.

ټغ *ṭagh*, s.m. The pupil of the eye; the blue jay (*Coracias Bengalensis*). A creak, croak, grating sound.

ټغر *ṭaghar*, s.m. A woollen carpet; felt; felt saddle cloth; old rag, clout, etc.

ټغن *ṭaghan*, s.m. A coward, poltroon.

ټغول *ṭaghawul*, v.a. To jar, grate, set on edge (as the teeth or nails).

ټق *ṭaq*, s.m. A blow, rap, knock, whack, thump, etc. *ṭaq·kawul*, v.a. To bump, clash. *ṭaq·wahal*, v.a. To hit, strike, knock (as a nail, etc.).

ټقول *ṭaqawul*, v.a. To censure, scold, reprove; to beat, batter, baste.

ټک *ṭak*, s.m. Murrain, disease of cattle; a bang, slam; blow, thump, rap; a footfall, sound of feet.

ټکا *ṭakā*, s.f. A footfall, sound of footsteps; explosion, sound of firearms.

ټکارکي *ṭikārkai*, s.m. A plot of clear, hard, and level ground.

ټکانه *ṭikāna*, s.f. Abode, lodging, residence, dwelling; boundary, limit, extent. H. (*ṭhikānā*).

ټکاو *ṭikāo*, s.m. See ټکانه.

ټکټکانړي *ṭakṭakānṛai*, s.m. Name of a game played by children; the clapper of a mill; a woodpecker.

ټکر *ṭakar*, s.m. A jolt, push, shove. H.

ټکړ *ṭukṛ*, s.m. A bit, morsel, piece. H. (*ṭukṛā*).

ټکسري *ṭaksarai*, a. Mangy; a term of abuse. s.m. Murrain.

ټککه *ṭakaka*, s.f. A cross bar of wood placed above the blade of a spade for the foot to rest upon.

ټکلاستي *ṭaklāstai*, a. Active, nimble, smart, handy.

ټکنده غرمه *ṭakanda·gharma*, } s.f. Noon; mid-
ټکنړه غرمه *ṭakanṛa·gharma*, } day; heat of noon or midday.

ټکنړي *ṭakanṛai*, a. Obstinate, stubborn, restive.

ټکور *ṭakor*, s.m. Fomentation, poultice. H.

ټکول *ṭakawul*, v.a. To beat, bruise, hammer.

ټکه *ṭaka*, s.f. Animosity, jealousy, hatred; thunderbolt; knuckle-bone. *ṭakah*, s.m. A species of ibex, or mountain goat.

ټکي *ṭakai*, s.m. A dot, spot, spec; mark, streak; a bullock, horse, etc. with a spot on the forehead; appointed time or place; an atom, drop, molecule. *ṭika-ī*, s.f. A biscuit; wafer. H. (*tikiyā*); an orb, disk (as of the sun, etc.); a mark or butt for arrows; a loud laugh, guffaw. *pa-ṭakī*, ad. On the spot, at once, this minute.

تګ *ṭag*, s.m. A cheat, impostor; assassin, robber. H. (*ṭhag*).

تګي *ṭagī*, s.f. Cheating, deceiving, robbery, theft.

تل *ṭal*, a. Close, dense, thick; full, replete, satiated. s.m. Division of a town or village; cluster of houses; a field, bed of flowers; closeness, denseness.

تم *ṭam*, s.m. Bark of a dog, growl of a wild beast.

تمتيل *ṭamṭīl*, s.m. A sandpiper, snippet.

تمک *ṭimak*, s.m. The crosspole of a tent.

تنبل *ṭunbal*, v.a. To clean, pick (as the teeth); pluck, pick out (as thorns, etc.).

تند *ṭanḍ*, a. Corpulent, fat, stout.

تنګ *ṭang*, s.m. A creak, jar, twang, jingle. H. (*ṭankā*).

تنګ تونګ *ṭang-ṭūng*, s.m. Ding-dong, chime, notes of musical instruments.

تنګول *ṭangawul*, v.a. To jingle, clank, sound.

تنګه *ṭanga*, s.f. Name of a copper coin. H. (*ṭakā*). Money, wealth.

تنګيدل *ṭangedal*, v.n. To creak, jar, grate, twang.

توپ *ṭop*, s.m. A bound, jump, leap. H. (*ṭap*). A heap, pile, stack; excess, surplus.

توپک *ṭopak*, s.m. A musket, matchlock.

توپل *ṭopal*, s.m. The vertex, crown of the head.

توپۍ *ṭopa-ī*, s.f. A cap, hat, helmet; bowl or cup of a pipe. H. (*ṭopī*).

توټه *ṭoṭa*, s.f. A bit, chip, fragment. A beggar's cup or tray. *ṭūṭa*, s.f. The hip, haunch. H. (*pūṭhā*).

توخ *ṭūkh*, s.m. Saliva, spittle.

توخه *ṭūkha*, s.f. } Cough, expectoration.
توخي *ṭūkhai*, s.m. }

توخلي *ṭūkhalai*, s.m. Hooping cough; croup. *ṭūkhala-ī*, s.f. Cap, head covering, bonnet.

توخيدل *ṭūkhedal*, v.n. To cough, expectorate, spit.

توغ *ṭūgh*, a. Bent, bowed, stooping.

توقا *ṭoqā*, s.m. A grasshopper.

توقمار *ṭoqmār*, s.m. A buffoon, jester, clown.

توقه *ṭoqa*, s.f. Jest, joke, pleasantry, ridicule. A. (*ẓuḥka*).

توقي *ṭoqī*, s.m. A jester, buffoon, clown.

توک *ṭok*, a. Closely woven (as cloth). *ṭūk*, s.m. An atom, bit, particle. H.

توکيا *ṭokiyā*, s.f. A cleaver, bill-hook.

توکيدل *ṭūkedal*, v.n. To bud, grow, germinate, sprout. S. (*ṭūknā*).

توکرۍ *ṭokra-ī*, s.f. A basket. H. (*ṭokrī*).

توکي *ṭūkai*, s.m. A piece of cloth, length of cloth; piece, patch, repair. H.

تول *ṭol*, a. All, the whole, total. s.m. A party, flock, gang, drove.

تولتال *ṭolṭāl*, a. All, the whole, sum total.

تولګي *ṭolgai*, s.m. A party, small herd or flock.

تولول *ṭolawul*, v.a. To collect, gather, bring together.

تولي *ṭolai*, s.m. An assembly, party, company.

توليدل *ṭoledal*, v.n. To assemble, congregate, flock, herd or crowd together.

تونګ *ṭong*, s.m. Irritation, provocation.

تونګاره *ṭongāra*, s.f. Insult, abuse, provocation, pecking. H. (*ṭungār*).

تيپر *ṭīpar*, s.m. A turnip.

تيت *ṭīṭ*, a. Bent, curved, crooked, bowed. *ṭīṭawul*, v.a. To bend, bow. *ṭīṭedal*, v.n. To be bent, bowed, inclined.

تيتاري *ṭīṭārai*, s.m. A plover, pewit, lapwing. H. (*ṭaṭirī*).

تيتال *ṭīṭāl*, s.m. Cheat, imposture, fraud; evasion. P. (*ṭīṭāl*).

تيغ *ṭegh*, s.m. A belch, eructation.

څنبيدل *dzanbedal*, v.n. To shake, totter, quiver; move, wag, writhe. P. (*junbīdan*).

څند *dzand*, s.m. Delay, procrastination.

څنګل *dzangal*, s.m. A wood; wilderness. S. (*jangal*).

څنړي *dzanṛai*, s.m. A boy, youth, school-boy.

څني *dzane*, or *dzine*, pr. The indefinite pronoun; any, some, certain, few. Also څنِ *dzani* or *dzini*.

څوان *dzwān*, s.m. An adult, young man. a. Adolescent, youthful. S. (*jawān*).

څواني *dzwānī*, s.f. Youth, adolescence.

څواني مرګ *dzwānī-marg*, s.m. A form of curse; early or untimely death. P. (*jawānā-marg*).

څور *dzaur*, s.m. Oppression, violence; trouble, pain; grief, sorrow. A. (*jaur*).

څوړند *dzwaṛand*, a. Hanging, pendant.

څوز *dzoz*, s.m. Name of a plant, the camel's thorn (*Hedysarum alhagī*). P. (*jāj*).

څوزخانه *dzoz-khāna*, s.f. A hut made of camel's thorn, and used as a cool retreat in the hot weather.

څولنه *dzolana*, s.f. A chain, fetter. P. (*zanlānah*).

څولي *dzola-ī*, s.f. Havresack, bag, wallet. H. (*jholī*).

څوم *dzūm*, s.m. A son-in-law. S. (*jamāī*).

څومګي *dzūmgai*, s.m. A young son-in-law.

څوي *dzoe*, s.m. A son. P. (*zāe*).

څي *dzai*, s.m. Child, son, descendant. See زي

څير *dzīr*, s.m. Contemplation, regard; look, survey, glance; a shrill sound, the highest note in music. P. (*jīl*). A kind of soft leather.

څيرمه *dzerma*, s.f. See زيرمه.

څيزمه *dzezma*, s.f. The eyelid.

څيل *dzel*, s.m. Ignorance, stupidity; obstinacy, perversity. A. (*jahl*). A line or string of buckets, etc. H. (*jel*).

ج

ج *jīm*, The eighth letter of the Pukkhto alphabet. It is sometimes substituted for the letters ز, ژ, and ش.

جابر *jābir*, s.m. A despot, oppressor, tyrant. A.

جابه *jāba*, s.f. A leathern jar or pot with a spout, used by grocers to pour out oil, etc. H. (*jhābā*).

جادو *jādū*, s.m. Magic, conjuring. P.

جادوګر *jādū-gar*, s.m. A conjuror, juggler, magician.

جادوګري *jādū-garī*, s.f. Conjuring, sorcery, magic.

جاډي *jāḍa-ī*, s.f. A worn out old camel; a hag.

جار *jār*, s.m. Announcement, proclamation, notice. A. (*iẓhār*); a sacrifice, oblation, victim, offering. Evident, manifest. A. (*ẓāhir*).

جارباسل *jārbāsal*, v.a. To divert, turn aside, turn back; to vomit, spew. Def. See جاريستل.

جارچي *jārchī*, s.m. A crier, herald.

جارو *jārū*, s.m. A besom, broom, brush. H. (*jhāṛū*).

جاروتل *jārwatal*, v.n. To go back, return, revert.

جارول *jārawul*, v.a. To arrange or collect together the threads of the warp preparatory to weaving; to brush, sweep. H. (*jhāṛnā*).

جاري *jārī*, a. Current, flowing, proceeding. A.

جاريستل *jāryastal*, v.a. To vomit, spew; return, turn back. Def. See جارباسل.

جاړ *jāṛ*, s.m. Brambles, bushes, underwood; a brake, thicket; a purge, stool. H. (*jhāṛ*).

جاړه *jāṛa*, s.f. A bramble, bush, thorny bush.

جاسوس *jāsūs*, s.m. A detective, spy, emissary. A.

جاسوسي *jāsūsī*, s.f. Spying, duty of a detective.

ٹيک *ṭek*, s.m. The temple, side of the head.

ٹيک *ṭīk*, s.m. } An ornament for the forehead;
ٹيکه *ṭīka*, s.f. } a wafer of silver or gilt paper worn on the forehead. H. (*ṭīkā*).

ٹيکاو *ṭīkāo*, s.m. Abode, lodging, residence. H. (*ṭhikānā*).

ٹيل *ṭel*, s.m. A jostle, shove, push. H. (*ṭhel*).

ٹيل ټال *ṭel·ṭāl*, s.m. Jostling; romping; dalliance.

ٹينچي *ṭainchī*, s.m. A fop, beau, coxcomb, puppy.

ٹينګ *ṭīng*, a. Close, compact, thick; coagulated, curdled; stiff, firm; tight, strong.

ث

ث *ṣe*, The fourth letter of the Arabic alphabet, and the sixth of the Pukkhto. It is only found in words adopted from the Arabic. It is sometimes pronounced *th* as in the English *think*.

ثابت *ṣābit*, a. Proved, confirmed, established; firm, durable, stable. A.

ثاني *ṣānī*, a. Second, the second. A.

ثبوت *ṣabūt*, s.m. Conviction, proof; firmness, stability. A.

ثنا *ṣanā*, s.f. Applause, praise, eulogium. A.

ثواب *ṣawāb*, s.m. A virtuous action; future reward of virtue. A.

څ

څ *dze*, or *dzīm*, The seventh letter of the Pukkhto alphabet. It is a soft form of ج, and is used instead of that letter in some words derived from the Persian and Hindī. It is also sometimes substituted for ز and س

څار *dzār*, s.m. An offering, sacrifice, victim.

څاله *dzāla*, s.f. A spider's web; bird's nest. S. (*jālā*).

څان *dzān*, s.m. Soul, life; mind, spirit; self; the privates; a lover, loved one. a. Beloved, dear. P. (*jān*).

څاندار *dzāndār*, s.m. Having life, an animal.

څانکندن *dzān·kandan*, s.m. Agony of death, the death-struggle. P. (*jān·kandan*).

څاي *dzāe*, s.m. Place, site, situation, station. P. (*jāe*). *dzāe·laral*, v.a. To fit, suit, become. *dzāe·nīwul*, v.a. To take up place or position, locate oneself; inhabit, colonize; take effect.

څبله *dzabla*, ad. Together, in company, one with another. *dzabla·bānde*, Fold on fold, etc.

څز *dzaz*, s.m. A fizz, hiss, sputter.

څکه *dzaka*, ad. Because, hence, consequently, therefore, on this account. P. (*zirāki*).

څګر *dzigar*, s.m. The liver; heart, vitals; courage, mind, pluck. P. (*jigar*).

څل *dzal*, ad. Once, one time. *yo·dzal*, once. *dwah·dzala*, twice. *dre·dzala*, thrice. *las·dzala*, ten times, etc. *dzul*, s.m. Body clothes for a horse, or for cattle. H. (*jhul*).

څلوبي *dzaloba-ī*, s.f. A kind of sweetmeat. H. (*jalebī*).

څله *dzala*, s.f. Perplexity, distraction, hesitation.

څلکيدل *dzalkedal*, } v.n. To glitter, shine,
څليدل *dzaledal*, } sparkle, lighten. H. (*jhalak*).

څما *dzamā*, The genitive case singular of the first personal pronoun زه *zah*: Mine, of me.

څمل *dzamal*, v.a. To blink, wink (as in sunlight).

څمونږ *dzamūg*, } The genitive plural of the
څمونګ *dzamūng*, } first personal pronoun: Ours, of us.

څناور *dzanāwar*, s.m. An animal. P. (*jānwar*).

څنبل *dzanbal*, v.a. See څمل.

څنبول *dzanbawul*, v.a. To wag, shake; wink.

جاكي *jākai*, a. Curdled, coagulated, clotted (as blood).

جاگير *jāgīr*, s.m. Land held in fief, a pension in land, land granted by government as a reward for military service, etc. P.

جال *jāl*, s.m. A net, sash. S. a. Counterfeit, forged. A. (*j'al*).

جاله *jāla*, s.f. A raft of timber or inflated hides; a bird's nest.

جالي *jāla-ī*, s.f. A cobweb; the green vegetation in pools and watercourses; duckweed. S. (*jālā*).

جام *jām*, s.m. A bowl, cup, goblet. P.

جامبړه *jāmbṛa*, s.f. A coppice, brake, thicket.

جامه *jāma*, s.f. Garment, dress, robe; the jaw, the upper or lower jaw bone. P.

جان *jān*, s.m. See ځان.

جانب *jānib*, s.m. Part, side. ad. Towards. A.

جانجي *jānjī*, s.m. A bridegroom's wedding guest or attendant.

جانور *jānwar*, s.m. See ځناور.

جاوجي *jāwja-ī*, s.f. The hem, skirt, border, edging, etc. of a dress.

جاوله *jāwla*, s.f. Bees' wax, fresh resin, gluten of wheat, milky sap of plants, etc.

جاويد *jāwīd*, s.m. }
جاويدان *jāwīdān*, } Endless, eternal. P.

جاويداني *jāwīdānī*, s.f. Eternity, immortality.

جاه *jāh*, s.m. Dignity, pomp, rank. P.

جاهل *jāhil*, a. Ignorant, barbarous, brutal. s.m. Fool, blockhead, ignoramus. A.

جاهلي *jāhilī*, s.f. Ignorance, stupidity.

جاي *jāe*, s.m. See ځاي.

جائداد *jā-edād*, s.m. Assets, effects, property. An assignment of land for the maintenance of troops. P.

جبر *jabr*, s.m. Force, oppression, violence. A.

جبه *jaba*, s.f. A bog, mere, marsh. H. (*jhābar*). *juba*, s.f. A frock, shirt; coat of mail. A.

جبين *jabīn*, s.m. The forehead. P.

جت *jat*, s.m. Name of a tribe located in the western parts of Afghanistan; they are largely engaged in trade.

جټ *jaṭ*, s.m. Name of a clan of Rajpūts, settled in the Panjāb; they are entirely occupied in agriculture.

جثه *jus̤s̤a*, s.f. Body, figure. A.

ججوره *jajūra*, s.f. The crop of a bird, maw, the first stomach of ruminants; double chin, dewlap. H. (*jhojh*).

ججوي *jajū-ī*, s.f. Name of a plant, Anemone.

جخ *jakh*, s.m. Froth, foam. H. (*jhāg*). A midge, water-fly.

جخت *jukht*, a. Accurate, even, exact. P. (*juft*).

جد *jadd*, s.m. An ancestor, grandfather. A.

جدا *judā*, s.f. Apart, separate, distinct, different. P.

جدل *jadal*, s.f. Altercation, battle, strife. A.

جدول *jadwal*, s.m. Lines drawn on the sides of a page: marginal lines in a book. A.

جديد *jadīd*, a. Fresh, new. A.

جذام *juẕām*, s.m. Leprosy. A.

جذب *jaẕb*, s.m. Absorption; imbibing, absorbing. A.

جذبه *jaẕba*, s.f. Fury, passion, rage. A.

جر *jar*, s.m. A gutter, drain; crack, fissure, cleft, etc. in the ground. P.

جراح *jarrāḥ*, s.m. A surgeon. A.

جرس *jaras*, s.m. A bell. A.

جرکاڼړي *jur-kāṉṟai*, s m. To boot, surplus, over and above, into the bargain, profit, gain.

جرگتو *jirgatū*, s.m. Member of a Jirga.

جرگه *jirga*, s.f. An assembly, council, meeting, etc. of the heads of a village community, or the representatives of a clan, for consultation and deliberation on matters affecting the interests of the people they represent; a consultation.

جرم *jurm* or *jirm*, s.m. Crime, fault, sin. A.

جرمانه *jurmāna*, s.f. A fine, penalty.

جرموړه *jarmoṛa*, s.f. Name of an eruption of the skin; hives, nettlerash.

جرندګري *jaranḍ·garai*, s.m. A miller.

جرنده *jaranda*, s.f. A mill for grinding corn, whether worked by cattle or water.

جرندئي *jaranda-ī*, s.f. A door bolt.

جره *jurrah*, s.m. A male falcon. A. See باز.

جريب *jarīb*, s.m. A measure of land equal to four kanāl. See کنال.

جريده *jarīdah*, a. Alone, solitary, unattended, unencumbered, travelling post-haste. A.

جړ *jaṛ*, s.m. Bubbling, oozing, trickling with a murmur (as water from a spring head). H. (*jhir·jhir*).

جړانګو *jaṛāngū*, s.m. Name of a tree (*Cassia fistula*).

جړاو *jaṛāo*, a. Jewelled. S.

جړجوري *juṛ·jūṛai*, a. Trickling, murmuring, bubbling.

جړنګ *juṛang*, s.m. A creeping plant (as melons, etc).

جړئي *jaṛa-ī*, s.f. Continued rain, shower, wet weather. H. (*jhaṛī*). The root of a herb used as a remedy for snake bites. S. (*jaṛī*).

جز *juz*, s.m. A part, portion, section; division of a book containing eight leaves. A. *juz*, p. Besides, except. P.

جزا *jazā*, s.f. Retaliation, requital, return; compensation, reward. A.

جزائيل *jazā·el*, s.m. A rifle; long gun; swivel, wall piece, camel-gun. A.

جزايلچي *jazā-elchī*, s.m. A sharpshooter, marksman, rifleman.

جزبز *jizbiz*, s.m. A game played with knuckle bones. P.

جزبندي *juzbandī*, s.f. Binding of a book.

جزدان *juzdān*, s.m. Book-cover, bag for books.

جزيره *jazīra*, s.f. An island. A.

جزيه *jaziya*, s.f. A poll tax, capitation tax, levied by the Afghans on their subjects of another race and creed. A.

جس *jas*, s.m. Pewter. H. (*jast*).

جست *jast*, s.m. A bound, jump, leap, spring. P.

جست وجوي *just·o·jūe*, s.m. Enquiry, investigation, search. P.

جسته *jista*, s.f. A kind of boot with high narrow heels. P.

جسر *jasr*, s.m. A large, strong camel. A. *jisr*, s.m. A bridge. A.

جسم *jism*, s.m. The body, living body. A.

جسه *jussa*, s.f. The human body. See جثه.

جشي *jas͟hai*, s.m. Name of a prickly plant: the prickle of some kinds of grass.

جغ *jug͟h*, s.m. Yoke of a plough; yoke for oxen; a pair of oxen, S. (*jug*).

جغاغه *jag͟hāg͟ha*, s.f. Name of a herb, caper spurge.

جغندر *jug͟handar*, s m. Beetroot. P. (*c͟huqandar*).

جفا *jafā*, s.f. Oppression, violence, injustice. P.

جفاکار *jafākār*, s.m. A tyrant, oppressor.

جفاکاري *jafākārī*, s.f. Tyranny, oppression.

جفت *juft*, s.m. A couple, match, pair. P.

جفتک *juftak*, s.f. A kick with both hind legs.

جق جق *jaq·jaq*, s.m. Cackle of fowls; chatter, gabble.

جک *jak*, s.m. See جګ.

جکړ *jakaṛ*, s.m. Gust of wind, wind and rain, drift of wind. H. (*jhakkar*).

جګړه *jagaṛa*, s.f. Altercation, strife, contention, wrangling. H. (*jhagṛa*).

جګناتي *jagnāta-ī*, s.f. A kind of fine cloth, muslin.

جل *jal*, s.m. A hedge of thorns round a house. A skylark. *j-il* or *ja-al*, s.f. A damsel, maid, virgin.

جلا *jilā*, s.f. Exile, separation. A. *jilā-watan*, s.m. Banishment, exile, emigration.

جلاب *julāb*, s.m. Cathartic, purge. A.

جلات *jallāt*, s.m. An executioner. A. (*jallād*).

جلاجل *jalājil*, s.m. A small bell: strings of them are fastened on the necks of cattle and the ankles of women.

جلار *jalār*, s.m. An irrigation wheel worked on the bank of a stream.

جلال *jalāl*, s.m. Majesty, splendour, glory, dignity, grandeur, state. A.

جلب *jalab*, s.m. A rein; attendance, retinue, escort. A. (*jilaw*).

جلبنگ *jalbang*, s.m. The stinging nettle (*Urtica interrupta*).

جلت *jalt*, a. Quick, active, brisk, fast; hasty, rash. P. (*jald*).

جلته *jalata*, s.f. A hamper, tall wicker basket.

جلتيا *jaltiyā*, s.f. Haste, speed, hurry, etc.

جلد *jald*, a. See جلت. *jild*, s.m. A book, volume, edition. A.

جلک *jalak*, s.m. A spindle, spinning reel.

جلنانی *jalnāna-ī*, s.f. A kitchen, cook-house. P.

جلندري *jalandara-ī*, s.f. A whirligig.

جلوه *jilwa*, s.f. Adornment, splendour; nuptial meeting or feast; blandishment, coquetry. A.

جلي *jala-ī*, s.f. A scream, shriek.

جم *jam*, s.m. A cluster, group; clan, tribe; faction, party, society.

جماعت *jamā'at*, s.m. Assembly, congregation, crowd; mosque, house of prayer, meeting house. A.

جمال *jamāl*, s.m. Beauty, elegance. A.

جمالگوټه *jamālgoṭa*, s.f. A purgative nut, seed of *Croton tiglium*. A.

جمدر *jamdar*, s.m. Darnel, tares, wild oats. P.

جمعه *jama'a*, s.f. Assembly, congregation; sum total, amount, whole; plural number. A. (*jama'*). *juma'a*, s.f. Friday. A.

جمله *jumla*, s.f. Aggregate, whole, sum total. A.

جن *j-in* or *ja-an*, s.f. A damsel, maid. See جل. *jinn*, s.m. A demon, devil, one of the genii. A.

جناب *janāb*, s.m. Excellency, highness, majesty; dignity, power; margin, side; threshold. A.

جنازه *janāza*, s.f. A funeral. A.

جنبان *junbān*, a. Moving, stirring, shaking. P.

جنبش *junbish*, s.m. Agitation, movement. P.

جنبق *junbaq*, a. Close, clustered, massed.

جنبه *janba*, s.f. Party, faction, clan. A. (*jānib*).

جنت *jannat*, s.m. Paradise. A.

جنج *janj*, s.m. Bridegroom's party in a marriage procession or feast: party of men who accompany the bridegroom to fetch the bride home.

جنجال *janjāl*, s.m. Difficulty, bother, trouble; contention, strife, wrangling. S.

جنجنړ *janjanṛ*, s.m. Name of a kind of vetch.

جندره *jandra*, s.f. A padlock, instrument for drawing wire.

جنډه *janḍa*, s.f. Banner, ensign, standard, flag. H. (*jhanḍā*).

جنس *jins*, s.m. Genus, kind, species; gender; merchandise, goods, etc. A.

جنگ *jang*, s.m. Battle, combat, fight, war. P. *jung*, a. Collected, gathered, crumpled. s.m. A young camel. A collection, miscellany, assembly, gathering.

جنگه *junga*, s.f. Excess, surplus, boot, profit.

جنگي *jangī*, a. Warlike, brave. *jangai*, s.m. A grove, plantation, coppice. *jungai*, a. Collected, gathered (as cloth). s.m. A young camel.

جنوب *junūb*, s.m. The South. A.

جنون *junūn*, s.m. A madman, maniac; insanity, madness. A.

جني *jina-ī*, s.f. A girl, daughter (not arrived at puberty); a virgin; a spinster.

جو *jau*, s.m. Barley. P.

جواب *jawāb*, s.m. Answer, reply; dismissal. A.

جوار *jwār*, s.m. Maize, Indian corn (*Zea mays*). H. (*joār*). *narī·jwār*, s.m. Indian millet (*Holcus sorghum*).

جوارگر *jūār·gar*, s.m. A gambler, gamester.

جواري *jūārī*, s.m. A gambler, gamester. H. s.f. Gambling, gaming. *jwārī*, s.m. See جوار.

جوال *jowāl*, s.m. A sack, bag. P.

جوانوان *janwāwān*, s.m. A kind of mustard or rape; the seeds yield an acrid oil, used as a cattle medicine, etc.

جواهر *jawāhir*, s.m. A gem, jewel. A.

جوبه *joba*, s.f. Emporium, market, mart. P.

جوټه *jūṭa*, s.f. Leavings, refuse (as of food, etc.); base, false (as coins, gems, etc.). S. (*jhūṭhā*). *joṭah*, s.m. A buffalo calf.

جوټي *jūṭa-ī*, s.f. Nodding, rocking (as in sleep); swaying, vibrating, swinging.

جودر *jawdar*, s.m. See جمدر.

جور *jaur*, s.m. See ځور.

جوړ *joṛ*, a. Healthy, strong, vigorous; prepared, arranged; right, correct. P. ad. Exactly, precisely, well.

جوړاب *joṛāb*, s.m. Beauty, elegance, grace.

جوړښت *joṛikkht*, s.m. Alliance, confederation, union; combination, junction.

جوړه *joṛa*, s.f. A couple, set, pair; suit of clothes. H. (*joṛā*). Peace, amity, concord, truce.

جوز *jauz*, s.m. A nut, kernel. A.

جوزه *jauza*, s.f. A nutmeg.

جوس *jawas*, s.m. Area, courtyard.

جوش *josh*, s.m. Effervescence, ebullition; heat, rage; passion, lust. P.

جوکل *jokal*, v.a. To weigh, measure. H. (*jokhnā*).

جولا *jolā*, s.m. A weaver; spider. P. (*julāh*).

جولان *jaulān*, s.m. Moving, wandering; capering, springing, lunging. P.

جولانگري *jaulāngarī*, s.m. Cantering, galloping; exercising, lunging (a horse).

جوله *jola*, s.f. See جهوله.

جولي *jola-ī*, s.f. See ځولي.

جونگړه *jūngaṛa*, s.f. A hut, hovel, cabin, shed; hamlet. H. (*jhompṛā*).

جوني *jūna-ī*, s.f. See جني.

جووه *jowa*, s.f. A gutter, drain, water channel (for irrigating a field, etc.). P. (*jūe*).

جوهر *jauhar*, s.m. A jewel, gem; essence, matter; virtue, work; the water or wavy marks on some kinds of steel.

جوهړه *jūhaṛa*, s.f. A crease, pucker, wrinkle, furrow. H. (*jhūrī*).

جه *jah*, a. Stubborn, refractory (as an animal); at bay, resisting. *ja·ja*, in. Words used to drive cattle.

جهاد *jihād*, s.m. Crescentade, war with infidels. A.

جهاز *jahāz*, s.m. A ship. P.

جهان *jahān*, s.m. The world, universe; people. P.

جهت *jihat*, s.m. Account, cause, reason; side, surface; form, manner, mode. A.

جهر *jihr*, s.m. A kind of dance performed by men.

جهل *jahl*, s.m. Ignorance, stupidity. A.

جهم جکړ *jham·jakaṛ*, s.m. Wind and rain in gusts, drifts of wind and rain. H

جهوله *jahola*, s.f. Name of a disease; chlorosis, anœmia, splenitis.

جي *jai*, s.m. A leather bag for water.

جيب *jeb*, s.m. A pocket. S.

جيټ *jeṭ*, s.m. Name of the second Hindu month, May-June; name of a tree, Egyptian Sesbania.

جينکي *jīnaka-ī*, s.f. A little girl, female child.

څ

څ *tse*, The ninth letter of the Pukkhto alphabet. It is a softened form of چ for which it is substituted in many words adopted from the Persian and Hindī. It is sometimes used instead of س and ش.

څاپېړه *tsāpeṛa*, s.f. A slap, blow, cuff. S. (*chapeṭā*).

څاڅکي *tsātskai*, s.m. A drop, minim, sprinkle.

څادر *tsādar*, s.m. A sheet, veil, mantle. H. (*chādar*).

څار *tsār*, s.m. Spying, scouting.

څارل *tsāral*, v.a. To spy, scout.

څاروی *tsārwai*, s.m. Cattle; a quadruped, beast, grazing animal. P. (*chārwā*).

څاره *tsāra*, s.f. Aid, help; cure, remedy. P. (*chāra*).

څاري *tsārī*, s.m. A scout, spy.

څاښت *tsākkht*, s.m. Forenoon, midtime between sunrise and noon; a meal taken at that time, breakfast. P. (*chāsht*).

څاښتي *tsākkhtī*. s.f. Breakfast, forenoon meal.

څاښکه *tsākkhaka*, s.f. A starling.

څاښي *tsākkhai*, s.m. Spinning rod, spindle.

څاک *tsāk*, s.m. Fissure, rent, slit; opening of a pocket; skirt or corner of a dress. P. (*chāk*).

څانګ *tsāng*, s.m. } څانګه *tsānga*, s.f. } Wing of a bird; branch of a tree; pang, sharp pain.

څپ *tsap*, s.m. A winnowing tray made of reeds; winnowing. *tsap-wahal*, v.a. To winnow.

څپر *tsapar*, s.m. A thatch, thatched roof. H. (*chhappar*). A wooden frame used as a crusher to separate grain from husk.

څپرکي *tsaparkai*, s.m. A film, flake, pellicle, scale; thin sheet of water (as after rain).

څپري *tsaparai*, s.m. A puddle, pool. H. (*chhaprī*).

څپړ *tsapaṛ*, s.f. Pad of a camel's or elephant's foot; sound of soft footsteps. H. (*chhap*).

څپک *tsapak*, s.m. A hand's breadth, hand, palm. H. (*chappā*). A flake, pellicle, scale.

څپلاک *tsaplāk*, a. Crushed, squashed, pressed, squeezed. H. (*chhapākā*).

څپلۍ *tsapla-ī*, s.f. A sandal (of leather or grass. H. (*chappal*).

څپوټکي *tsapūṭkai*, s.m. An old cloth, kerchief, or duster tied over the head by women when grinding corn, sweeping the house, etc. H. (*chapoṭī*).

څپولي *tsapolai*, a. Entangled, knotted, matted (as the hair). H. (*chipatā*).

څپه *tsapah*, a. Inverted, upside down. *tsapa*, s.f, A wave, billow; blast, gust, puff, etc. of wind. H. (*chhappā*).

څپياکه *tsapiyāka*, s.f. A cow-dung cake (flat and dry), used as fuel.

څپېړه *tsapeṛah*, a. Grey, ash-coloured; pale. in. Coward! dastard! term of abuse. *tsapeṛa*, s.f. A slap with the open hand.

څپېدل *tsapedal*, v.n. To flutter, hover, flap the wings.

څټ *tsaṭ*, s.m. Nape, back of the neck.

څټک *tsaṭak*, s.m. A sledge hammer.

څټکي *tsaṭakai*, s.m. A small sledge hammer.

څټل *tsaṭal*, v.a. To lick, lap. H. (*chāṭnā*). *tsaṭal*, v.n. To be accumulated, collected, massed. s.m. Heap, mass; wholesale, by the lump. P. (*chastan*).

څټوټ *tsaṭwaṭ*, s.m. Apoplexy, sudden death.

ad. All at once, suddenly, instanter. H. (*chaṭ-paṭ*).

څټه *tsaṭa*, s.f. A sack; a sackful. H. (*chaṭ*).

څڅوبي *tsatsobai*, s.m. The coping or eaves of a roof or wall; a leaking or dropping of water.

څڅول *tsatsawul*, v.a. To pour by drops, drop, distil.

څڅيدل *tsatsedal*, v.n. To leak, trickle, drop, distil. P. (*shāshīdan*).

څخو *tsakho*, a. Some, few, somewhat, more or less. ad. Slightly, in some degree, somewhat.

څخه *tsakhah*, p. About, near, with, beside. ad. Together, altogether. P. (*chakh*).

څخيدل *tskhedal*, v.n. To crawl, creep, go on all fours (as a child). P. (*chakhīdan*).

څخيکول *tskhe-kawul*, v.a. To hop, skip.

څر *tsar*, s.m. Food, forage, pasture. S. (*char*).

څرپ *tsrap*, s.m. A flutter, flap; whirr.

څرپول *tsrapawul*, v.a. To flutter, flap the wings.

څرپيدل *tsrapedal*, v.n. To flounder, flap about (as a fish in shallow water).

څرخ *tsarkh*, s.m. A wheel; grindstone; revolution, turn, spin; chance, fortune; the heavens; a kind of falcon; a stab, puncture, prick. P. (*charkh*).

څرخه *tsarkha*, s.f. A reel; spinning wheel. P. (*charkha*).

څرخندوکي *tsarkhandūkai*, s.m. A teetotum, a boy's top.

څرخول *tsarkhawul*, v.a. To spin, reel, twirl, turn.

څرخيدل *tsarkhedal*, v.n. To revolve, spin, etc.

څرګند *tsargand*, a. Clear, evident, apparent, manifest, plain.

څرل *tsaral*, v.n. See څريدل.

څرمن *tsarman*, s.f. Hide, skin; leather. P. (*charm*).

څرمه *tsarma*, s.f. See څيلمه.

څروټکه *tsarwaṭka*, s.f. An ember, burning coal, live ashes.

څرول *tsarawul*, v.a. To graze, pasture cattle. P. (*charāndan* or *charānīdan*).

څريدل *tsaredal*, v.n. To graze, browse, crop. P. (*charīdan*).

څريکه *tsirīka*, s.f. A prick, throb, lancing or shooting pain (as of a boil, etc.). P. (*charkh*). A spot, splash, stain (as of mud, etc.).

څړه *tsaṛah*, a. Alone, solitary; unmarried, single; light, unencumbered; simple, S. (*chhaṛā*). *tsaṛa-lār*, s.f. A footpath, bye road, track, etc. only practicable for one man at a time.

څړي *tsaṛa-ī*, s.f. A top knot, tuft or lock of hair on the crown of a shaven head.

څږي *tsagai*, s.m. The lungs, a lung.

څښاک *tskkhāk* or *tsakshāk*, s.m. Beverage, drink, liquor. *khwurāk-o-tskkhāk*, s.m. Aliment, food, victuals, meat and drink.

څښتن *tsakkhtan*, s.m. Owner, proprietor, lord, master, husband.

څښکو *tsakkhkū*, s.f. Name of a plant (*Cassia absus*): the seeds are used as a remedy in ophthalmia. P. (*chāksū* or *chākshū*).

څښکوري *tsakkhkūrai*, s.m. A small pipe, tube, nozzle, spout, etc.; child's penis.

څښل *tskkhal*, *tsakkhal*, or *tsakshal*, v.a. To drink, absorb, imbibe. P. (*chashīdan* or *chakānīdan*).

څک *tsak*, a. Stiff, unpliant, rigid. s.m. Lumbago. H. (*chik*).

څکل *tsakal*, v.a. To taste. S. (*chakhnā*) or P. (*chashīdan*).

څکنتون *tsakintūn*, } s.m. Flavour, taste,
څکندن *tsakindan*, } savour.

څکول *tskawul*, v.a. To cause to drink water (as cattle); to draw, lengthen, stretch.

څکوندل *tskūndal*, v.a. To pinch, tweak; squeeze, wring. P. (*chakāndan*).

څکه *tsaka*, s.f. Flavour, taste, relish; a precipice, cliff. *tsaka* or *tska*, ad. Then, therefore, thus.

څکي *tsakai*, s.m. A basket or safe suspended from the roof, to preserve the contents from cats, insects, etc. s. (*chhīkā*).

څکيدل *tskedal*, v.n. See څخيدل.

څلور *tsalor*, a. Four. P. (*chahār*).

څلورم *tsaloram*, a. Fourth.

څلويښت *tsalwekkht* or *tsalwekśht*, a. Forty. P. (*chahār·bīst*).

څلويښتي *tsalwekkhtī*, s.f. The forty days of purification after childbirth; the fortieth day after the death of a person, when the relatives visit the grave, and feed the poor, etc.

څله *tsala*, ad. Why? wherefore? what for? P. (*charā*).

څلي *tsalai*, s.m. A ring for the finger or toe. H. (*chhallā*); a pile or heap of stones on the grave of a martyr (generally somebody murdered on the way side); a pillar of mud or masonry, as a boundary mark; a mound or platform from which to watch a field; a butt or mark for arrows; a temporary platform or shed.

څليښ *tsalekkh*, } s.m. Glue. P. (*saresh*).
څليښت *tsalekkht*, }

څليښناک *tsalekkhnāk*, a. Adhesive, glutinous, cohesive, clammy, viscous.

څم *tsam*, a. Flat, smooth, level, even.

څمڅئ *tsamtsa-ī*, s.f. A spoon, ladle. P. (*chamcha*).

څملاستل *tsamlāstal*, } v.n. To lie down, recline,
څملل *tsamlal*, } repose, lie flat.

څملول *tsamlawul*, v.a. To put to bed, put to rest.

څنډل *tsandal*, v.a. To agitate, shake, dust (as clothes), wave (as a sword). H. (*chhānṭnā*).

څنډه *tsanda*, s.f. Brim, margin, edge; fringe, rim, verge, side.

څنګ *tsang*, s.m. The side, flank. *tsang·pa·tsang*, ad. Abreast, side by side.

څنګزن *tsangzan*, a. Top-heavy, tilted, lurched over.

څنګل *tsangal*, } s.f. The elbow; elbow joint;
څنګله *tsangala*, } the forearm, cubit.

څنګه *tsanga*, ad. How? In what manner?

څو *tso*, a. Any, some, somewhat. P. (*chand*). ad. Till, until. P. (*chūn*). How many? how much? P. (*chand*).

څوارلس *tswārlas*, a. Fourteen.

څوباړي *tsobāṛai*, s.m. A flat piece of wood used to beat clothes in the process of washing. P. (*chobah*).

څوټ *tsoṭ*, s.m. Attack, onset, foray, sortie; a blow, contusion, hurt. s. (*choṭ*).

څوڅ *tsūts*, s.m. A porpoise. s. (*sūs*).

څورب *tsorb*, a. Fat, corpulent, stout. P. (*ch..b*).

څورلي *tswarlai*, s.m. A chisel; a burglar's instrument for digging through a mud wall.

څور *tsor*, a. Crooked, wry, crumpled; emaciated, thin, withered (as a child badly nourished).

څوري *tsoṛai*, s.m. A bullock, etc. with crumpled horns,

څوښئ *tsūkkha-ī*, s.f. The penis of a boy; a nozzle, spout. P. (*choshak*).

څوک *tsok*, pr. Who? Which? Some, certain. Used only with reference to human beings.

څوکه *tsūka*, s.f. Apex, peak, tip, point, beak.

څوکئ *tsoka-ī*, s.f. A guard, watch; place or station of a guard; tour of watching. H. (*chaukī*).

څول *tswal*; a. Tattered, torn, rent, worm-eaten. *tswal·tswal*, a. In rags, in tatters, in shreds.

څومبره tsombra,
څومره tsomra, } ad. How much?
څونبره tsonbra,

څونڅئ tsontsa-ī, s.f. See څمڅئ.

څونړکه tsūnṛaka, } s.f. The tuft or curl of hair
څونړه tsunṛa, } left on the crown or temples of a shaven head. H. (chonḍā).

څوني tsone, ad. How much?

څوهره tsūhra, s.f. Hernia, rupture. H. (chūhrā).

څوي tsawai, s.m. Ambush, cover, ambuscade.

څه tsah, pr. What, any, some: what? P. (chi).

څهره tsihra, s.f. Face, countenance, visage. H. (chihrā).

څيخل tsekhal, v.a. To probe, prick, stab; cram, stuff. P. (sīkh, a probe).

څير tser, a. Like, similar, resembling.

څيره tsera, s.f. Picture, portrait, image, idol; effigy, scarecrow, grimace. P. (chehr).

څيريدل tsīredal, v.n. See شليدل.

څيړه tsīṛa, s.f. A line, file, row; party, knot, troop.

څيز tsīz, s.m. A thing, item, article, object. P. (chīz).

څيلمه tselma, s.f. Border, margin, edge, side.

چ

چ che, or chīm, is the tenth letter of the Pukkhto alphabet. It is sounded like the ch in chair.

چابک chābuk, a. Active, quick, alert. s.m. A whip. P.

چابکي chābukī, s.f. Activity, dispatch, celerity.

چاپ chāp, s.m. Impression, stamp, print; a seal; an edition; flint lock (of a gun, etc.). H. (chāmp). a. Printed, stamped. H. (chhāp).

چاپلوس chālpūs, s.m. A flatterer, wheedler, toady. P. (chālpos).

چاپلوسي chāplūsī, s.f. Flattery, toadyism.

چاپه chāpa, s.f. A stamp, die, seal; a bundle of thorns of the ber bush, after the leaves have been shaken off. H. (chāp).

چاپي chāpī, s.f. Shampooing, pressing or squeezing the limbs. H. (chāmpī).

چاپير chāper, ad. All round, roundabout, around, on all sides. H. (chaupher).

چار chār, a. Four. P. s.m. Affair, business; remedy, cure. P.

چارخولک chār-khwalak, s.m. A cock's comb, wattle.

چاره chāra, s.f. Cure, help, remedy. P.

چاړا chāṛā, a. Stammering, stuttering; dumb, mute.

چاړه chāṛa, s.f. A long knife. H. (chhurā).

چاغ chāgh, a. Healthy, plump, vigorous; fat, stout, corpulent. P. (chāq).

چاک chāk, s.m. A fissure, rent, slit, chāk-kawul, v.a. To rend, split open, disembowel. Also چاق.

چاکر chākar, s.m. Servant, help, retainer. P.

چاکري chākarī, s.f. Attendance, service. P.

چاکو chākū, } s.m. A penknife. P.
چاقو chāqū, }

چاګل chāgul, s.m. A leather bottle for water. P. (chaghal).

چال chāl, s.m. Gait, motion, pace; bound, spring; custom, habit; manner, way; artifice, deceit, trick. S. Vomiting, spewing. H. (chhāl). chāl-kawul, v.a. To vomit, spew.

چالاک chālāk, a. Active, clever; dexterous, expert. P.

چالاکي chālākī, s.f. Activity, dexterity. P.

چاڼ chāṇr, a. Filtered, sifted, strained. H. (chhānā).

چاڼره chāṇra, s.f. Thatch, roofing of reeds,

twigs, etc. as a flooring for the earth of the roof. H. (c͟hhān).

چانړي c͟hāṉrī, s.m. A dung-beetle.

چاود c͟hāwd, a. Cracked, split. s.m. A fissure, rent.

چاودل c͟hāwdal, v.n. To crack, split.

چاودينک c͟hāwdīnak, a. Bold, pert, saucy (as a child).

چاول c͟hāwul, s.m. A plummet. H. (sāhūl).

چاه c͟hāh, s.m. A well. P.

چايل c͟hāyal, s.m. A mantle, veil of chintz.

چپ c͟hap, a. The left hand, left side. P. c͟hip, or c͟hup, a. Silent. in. Silence! Hush! H.

چپاو c͟hapāo, s.m. A foray, raid, surprise.

چپاول c͟hapāwul, s.m. An advance guard of cavalry.

چپړدخ c͟hapaṛdak͟h, s.m. A game played by boys: ducks and drakes, pitch and toss.

چپړوس c͟hapṛūs, a. See چاپلوس.

چپک c͟hapak, a. Squint-eyed, squinting, askew. c͟hapake·starge, Squinting eyes.

چپن c͟hapan, s.m. A coat, frock. H. (c͟hapkan).

چپه c͟hapah, a. Inverted. P. c͟hapa, s.f. A billow, wave; blast, puff, gust of wind; swoop of a hawk; height or crisis of a disease; an oar, paddle. H. See څپه.

چپي c͟hapa-ī, s.f. A kiss. H. (pac͟hc͟hī).

چت c͟hit, a. Flattened, pressed, crushed, squashed, H. c͟hat, s.m. Ceiling, roof. H. (c͟hhat).

چتر c͟hatr, s.m. Scar of a wound, bald spot on the head. H. (c͟hittī).

چتري c͟hatrai, a. Scarred, bald. s.m. Awning, canopy; umbrella. S. (c͟hhattar).

چتي c͟hita-ī, s.f. A titmouse. H. (c͟hiṭṭī).

چټ c͟haṭ, a. Bald-faced, beardless. s.m. A rake, debauchee, profligate, vagabond; thief, robber. P. (c͟hattah).

چټ پټ c͟haṭ·paṭ, ad. Hastily, quickly. H.

چټاکي c͟hiṭāka-ī, s.f. Name of a weight equal to two ounces (Avoirdupois). H. (c͟hhaṭāṉk).

چټکه c͟hiṭka, s.f. A kind of red cotton cloth.

چټي c͟haṭī, s.f. Debauchery, profligacy.

چج c͟haj, s.m. A tray for winnowing corn, etc. P. (c͟hac͟h).

چجک c͟hajak, s.m. The trigger of a gun.

چجه c͟haja, s.f. The poles projecting from the roof of a house; the side ribs of an ox, etc.; the crest or hood of a snake; stakes driven into the ground for catching fish. H. (c͟hhujjā).

چخړبه c͟hak͟hṛaba, s.f. Mud, slime, ground saturated with rain.

چخړه c͟hik͟hṛa, s.f. See چخي.

چخن c͟hik͟han, a. Rheumy, mattery; filthy, dirty. P. (c͟hirk).

چخه c͟hik͟ha, in. Away! Begone! Get out! P. (c͟hak͟he).

چخي c͟hik͟hai, s.m. Mucus, rheum, matter from the nose or eyes, etc.

چر c͟har, s.m. Chirp, twitter of a bird; chatter, prattle of children. A sand bank, mud deposited by a flood. H. c͟hur, s.m. A gutter, furrow made by running water. c͟hari, ad. See چري.

چراغ c͟hirāg͟h, s.m. A light, lamp. P. Illumination.

چرب c͟harb, a. See څورب.

چربي c͟harbī, s.f. Fat, tallow, suet. P.

چرت c͟hurt, s.m. A doze, nap; nodding. H.

چرته c͟harta, ad. Where; anywhere; ever.

چرچري c͟har·c͟hara-ī, s.f. A cracker, squib, firework.

چرخ c͟harkh, s.m. See څرخ.

چرړه c͟hirṛa, s.f. A rag, shred, tatter. H. (c͟hithṛā).

چرس c͟hars, s.m. A resinous product obtained from the flowers of the Indian hemp, and used as an intoxicating drug. H. (c͟harras).

چرسي *c̲h̲arsī*, s.m. One addicted to the use of c̲h̲ars.

چرغ *c̲h̲arg̲h̲*, s.m. Name of a kind of hawk (*Falco sacer*). P. (*c̲h̲ark̲h̲*).

چرک *c̲h̲irk*, s.m. Dirt, filth; pus, matter. P.

چرکين *c̲h̲irkīn*, a. Dirty, filthy; purulent, mattery. P.

چرګ *c̲h̲irg*, s.m. A cock. a. Clever, shrewd, canny. Dappled, pied, spotted, mottled.

چرګ بانګ *c̲h̲irg·bāng*, s.m. Cock-crow, day-break. Also *c̲h̲ir·bāng*, or *c̲h̲ar·bāng*.

چرګ برګ *c̲h̲rag·brag*, a. Piebald, spotted, streaked.

چرګک *c̲h̲irgak*, s.m. The hoopoe. Also called *mullā·c̲h̲argak*.

چرګوړي *c̲h̲irgūṛai*, s.m. A chicken, pullet.

چرګي *c̲h̲argai*, s.m. An animal with a white face, or with a spot on the forehead. S. (*c̲h̲arkā*).

چرلندۍ *c̲h̲urlanda-ī*, s.f. A humming-top.

چرلنډ *c̲h̲urlanḍ*, s.m. A blackguard, knave, rascal.

چرلول *c̲h̲urlawul*, v.a. To spin, turn, make revolve.

چرلۍ *c̲h̲urla-ī*, s.f. A whirligig: a child's game in which walnuts are made to spin.

چرليدل *c̲h̲urledal*, v.n. To spin, revolve, whirl.

چرمباز *c̲h̲arambāz*, s.m. The outside bullock of two or more treading corn.

چرمينه *c̲h̲armīna*, s.f. Rope made of strips of raw hide. P.

چرې *c̲h̲are*, ad. Ever, at any time: anywhere; where. *c̲h̲are·c̲h̲are*, ad. Occasionally, sometimes, at times.

چريکار *c̲h̲arekār*, s.m. A farm servant, ploughman. The hair above the chin, imperial.

چړ *c̲h̲aṛ*, s.m. A sandbank or deposit left by a flood, bar in a river; a cascade, waterfall; a foot soldier's pike or staff; the bread of charity collected from house to house for the poor. *c̲h̲uṛ*, s.m. The heel of a door, the peg on which it revolves.

چړچه *c̲h̲aṛc̲h̲a*, s.f. Dissipation, luxury, excess.

چړق *c̲h̲aṛaq*, s.m. A waterspout: sound of water splashing on the ground, splash, smash, crash.

چړقاو *c̲h̲aṛqāo*, s.m. Sprinkling. H. (*c̲h̲hirkāo*).

چړوکۍ *c̲h̲aṛūka-ī*, s.f. A small knife, penknife.

چړي *c̲h̲aṛī*, s.m. A collector of the bread of charity.

چسپ *c̲h̲asp*, s.m. Cohesion, viscidity, stickiness. P.

چسپان *c̲h̲aspān*, a. Adhesive, sticky, viscous.

چسپول *c̲h̲aspawul*, v.a. To cement, glue, stick.

چسپيدل *c̲h̲aspedal*, v.n. To adhere, cleave to, stick. P. (*c̲h̲aspīdan*).

چست *c̲h̲ust*, a. Active, quick; narrow, straight; tight, close fitting (as a dress). P.

چستي *c̲h̲ustī*, s.f. Agility, activity, fleetness. P. *c̲h̲ustai*, s.m. Gut, tripe; rectum. P. (*c̲h̲ustā*).

چشم *c̲h̲as̲h̲m*, s.m. The eye. P. (In comp. only).

چشمک *c̲h̲as̲h̲mak*, s.m. A wink, winking. P.

چشمکه *c̲h̲as̲h̲maka*, s.f. An eye-glass. *c̲h̲as̲h̲make*, pl. A pair of spectacles.

چشمه *c̲h̲as̲h̲ma*, s.f. A spring, fountain; eye-glass. P.

چشي *c̲h̲is̲h̲ai*, s.m. Name of a plant, the seed of which sticks to the fleece of sheep, etc., burdock.

چغ *c̲h̲ag̲h̲* or *c̲h̲ig̲h̲*, s.m. Altercation, dispute; clamour, noise; shout, yell, scream. *c̲h̲ig̲h̲·c̲h̲ig̲h̲*, s.m. The cackle of fowls. *c̲h̲ag̲h̲·c̲h̲ug̲h̲*, s.m. Clamour, noise, tumult.

چغار *c̲h̲ug̲h̲ār*, s.m. Noise or song of birds; sound of a musical instrument.

چغاره chighāra, s.f. Clamour, outcry, noise.

چغر chaghar, s.m. A wall-eyed horse. P.

چغرو chagharū, s.m. An owl.

چغول chaghawul, v.a. To make a row, disturbance, noise.

چغيدل chaghedal, v.n. To dispute, haggle, wrangle.

چغزئ chaghza-ī, s.f. A kind of soft walnut. chaghzī, s.m. Whizz of an arrow passing through the air; crackling of wood when split.

چغک chughuk, s.m. A sparrow. P.

چغل chughal, s.m. Tell-tale, backbiter, sneak. P.

چغلي chughlī, s.f. Backbiting, tale-telling. P.

چغي chughai, s.m. A blinkard; seeing with the eyes half closed.

چف chuf, s.m. A breath, puff, blow (as of a charmer).

چقمق chaqmaq, s.m. The flint lock of a gun. T.

چقه chuqa, s... The cackle of fowls when angry; pecking, picking up grain, etc.

چک chak, s.m. A circular frame of wood or masonry, used as a foundation for wells; a disk. chik, s.m. Ropes used to yoke bullocks to a Persian wheel, traces.

چکچکه chakchaka, s.f. Clapping the hands by way of applause.

چکړ chikaṛ, s.m. Mire, mud, slosh. H. (chīkaṛ).

چکس chakas, s.m. A perch, roost for birds (hawks particularly). H.

چکله chikla, s.f. A drop, dash, sprinkling, thimbleful.

چکلئ chakla-ī, s.f. The cog-wheel of a Persian irrigation wheel; a whirligig.

چکمه chakma, s.f. A stocking; boot. H.

چکورئ chikorai, s.m. A newly-born calf.

چکه chakā, s.f. The palm, the hand; coagulated milk, curds. H. (chakkā). chakah, a. Practised, expert (as a thief). H. (uchakkā).

چکئ chaka-ī, s.f. Wafer, disk; biscuit, cake; lump, mass, clot; tail of the dumbah sheep.

چل chal, s.m. Artifice, deception, subterfuge, trick. S.

چلان chalān, s.m. Invoice, remittance, advice of despatch. S.

چلاو chalāo, s.m. Boiled rice. P.

چلباز chalbāz, s.m. A cheat, impostor, rogue.

چل چل chal-chal, s.m. Bustle, hurry, stir. S.

چل چلا chal-chalā, s.f. Bustle, stir, preparation of setting out on a journey. S.

چلر chulur, s.m. Blackguard, vagabond, rogue.

چلغوزي chalghozai, s.m. The pistachio nut; kernels of the pine seed. P.

چلقت chalqat, s.m. A thick padded coat for soldiers, a coat of mail.

چلکه chalaka, s.f. A wave, ripple, undulation.

چلم chilam, s.m. A tobacco bowl, smoking apparatus. H.

چلن chalan, s.m. Behaviour, custom, habit; currency. a. Current. S.

چلول chalawul, v.a. To start, set agoing; fire, shoot. H. (chalānā).

چله chala, s.f. A deluge, flood, stream, torrent. An ear-ring. H. (chhaṛā).

چلئ chala-ī, s.f. An ear of corn.

چليدل chaledal, v.n. To move, proceed, go, elapse, pass (as coin, etc.); flow; blow; stand, avail, succeed; walk, etc. H. (chalnā).

چم cham, s.m. See جم.

چمتاره chamtāra, s.f. A violin. H. (chautārā).

چم وخم cham-o-kham, s.m. A graceful gait, strut, waddle. P.

چمن chaman, s.m. A meadow, lawn, grassplot. P.

چميار chamyār, s.m. A currier, tanner. P.

چنار chinār, s.m. Name of a tree, the plane tree (*Platanus orientalis*). P.

چنبيل chanbel, s.m. The jasmine. H.
چنجي chinjai, s.m. An insect, worm. H. (chunna). chinjawul, v.a. To disgust,
چنجيدل chinjedal, v.n. To be disgusted, nauseated, feel squeamish.
چند chand, a. Few, some, various, several; (in comp.) -times, -fold. ad. How many? How much? P.
چندنړ chandanr, s.m. Sandal wood. S.
چندنړهار chandanr-hār, s.m. A kind of necklace made of sandal-wood beads. S.
چنډال chanḍāl, s.m. An abject, low, mean, or worthless fellow. S.
چنډاول chanḍāwal, s.m. A rear guard of cavalry; the rear guard of an army; name of the Kazilbash troopers of Kabul. P.
چنغله changhala, s.f. A betrothed girl, bride elect.
چنغول changhol, s.m. A betrothed youth.
چنګ chang, s.m. A guitar, harp; a claw, the expanded hand. P.
چنګاښ changākkh, s.m. A crab, cray-fish. P. (changār).
چنګال changāl, | s.m. Claw, talon of bird,
چنګل changul, | the hand; the fingers. P.
changal, s.m. A measure of land equal to fifteen jarīb.
چنه chana, s.f. The short side of a house; mud wall of a house; side of a room. Barter, bargaining, haggling.
چنړابه chanrāsa, | s.f. Mildew, mould.
چنړاشه chanrāsha, |
چنړچنړ chanr-chanr, | s.m. A sparrow,
چنړچنړک chanr-chanrak, | cock-sparrow.
چنړکاو chanrkāw, s.m. Sprinkling. H. (chhirkāo).
چنړل chunral, v.a. To crease, fold, plait; to select, sift, separate, pick. H. (chunnā).
چنړه chanra, s.f. Chick pea, vetch (*Cicer arietinum*). H. (channā). chunra, s.f. A fold, crease, pucker.

چوپاړ chopāṛ, | s.m. A summer-house,
چوپال chopāl, | arbour, temporary shed. S. (chaupāṛ).
چوپل chūpal, v.a. To suck, chew (as mangoes, sugar-cane, etc.). S. (chuhnā).
چوتي chotai, s.m. A clout or cloth worn between the legs to conceal the privates; ropes used in fastening a camel's load.
چوټي choṭī, s.m. A peak, mountain top; top-knot or crown-tuft (left on a shaven head). a. Dishevelled, unplaited, loose (as hair). H.
چوچي chuchai, s.m. A chicken, pullet. P.
چور chūr, a. Broken, bruised, shattered. S. s.m. Bit, atom, scrap; powder, filings, sawdust; sack, ruin, plunder. S.
چورنګ chaurang, s.m. Cutting off the four legs of an animal at one blow. S.
چوري chūrai, s.m. A menial servant, sweeper. H. (chūhṛā). chaura-ī, s.f. A fly flapper, generally made of horse-hair or the tail of the Tibet ox. H. (chaunrī).
چوړ chawṛ, a. Desolate, deserted, ruined. H. chūṛ, s.m. The heel or pivot on which a door revolves.
چوړه chūṛa, s.f. A bangle, bracelet. S. (chūṛā).
چوړيل chūṛel, s.m. Tar, pitch.
چوز chūz, s.m. A young or first year's hawk. P.
چوسار chausār, s.m. A file, rasp. H.
چوغي chūghai, a. Bowbacked, bent (from age or debility).
چوک chūk, s.m. Abatement, diminution, mitigation (as of anger, etc.); damage, loss, waste; error, miss, fault. H. chauk, s.m. A market, courtyard. H. chok, a. Seated, or squatted on all fours (as a camel, etc.).
چوکه chūka, s.f. A goad, prod, prick. H. (chonkā). A sharp, pricking, or stinging pain; dipping, moistening, sopping (as bread in milk, etc. at meals.)

چوکي chauka-ī, s.f. A chair, stool; guard, watch; guard-house, station. H. (chaukī).

چوکیدار chaukīdār, s.m. Guard, watchman. H.

چول chawul, v.a. To split, rend, cleave asunder. chol, s.m. An arid tract, desert, waste. P. (chūl).

چولک cholak, s.m. Penis of a boy till circumcised. P.

چوم chūm or chom, s.m. A turf; clod of earth.

چونکي chūnkai, a. Indecent, obscene, shameless; impudent, bold, saucy.

چونګي chūngai, s.m. Duty, fee, tax, toll. H. (chūngī).

چونه chūna, s.f. Lime, mortar. S. (chūnā).

چوني chūnai, s.m. A dwarf, elf, pigmy; glazing on pottery, china; a gem, jewel, spark or bead.

چه chi, c. That, which; as, whereas; so, so that; whether, because. P.

چیتر chetar, s.m. Name of the twelfth Hindu month, March-April. S. (chait).

چیټي chīṭa-ī, s.f. A letter, note. H. (chiṭṭhī).

چیچړ chīchaṛ, s.m. A fold, crease, furrow, pucker, wrinkle.

چیچل chīchal, v.a. To bite, masticate, gnaw.

چیخل chīkhal, v.a. To goad, poke, punch.

چیرته cherta, ad. Where? • See چرته.

چیره chīra, s.f. A turban with narrow twisted folds; maidenhead. S.

چیړ chīṛ, s.m. Gum, mucilage.

چیغه chīgha, s.f. A shout, scream, yell; clamour, noise, uproar. P. (chīkh).

چیلو chīlū, s.m. Name of a potherb.

چیلي chelai or chīlai, s.m. A kid, young goat. H. (chherī).

چیندخ chīndakh, s.m. A frog; bull frog.

چینګ chīng, a. Gaping, open, wide; straddled.

چینه chīna, s.f. A spring, fountain.

ح

ح he or ḥā, is the eleventh letter of the Pukkhto alphabet, and the sixth of the Arabic. It is only found in words adopted from the Arabic. It is sometimes replaced by ه, than which letter it has a different sound, being pronounced in the throat, and strongly aspirated.

حاجت ḥājat, s.m. Want, necessity, need. A.

حاجتمن ḥājatman, } a. Needy, indigent. P.
حاجتمند ḥājatmand, }

حاجي ḥājī, s.m. A pilgrim to Mecca: one who has made the pilgrimage to Mecca. A.

حاصل ḥāṣil, s.m. Produce, profit, result; corn, crops; duty, revenue; acquiring, collecting. A. ḥāṣil-laral, v.a. To produce, yield, give.

حاصلول ḥāṣilawul, v.a. To collect, acquire, gain.

حاصلیدل ḥāṣiledal, v.n. To accrue, result, be gathered.

حاضر ḥāẓir, a. Present, ready, willing. A.

حاطه ḥāṭa, s.f. Enclosure, premises. A.

حافظ ḥāfiẓ, s.m. A blind man who has learnt the Quran by heart. Name of a Persian poet.

حاکم ḥākim, s.m. Commander, judge, master, ruler, governor. A.

حال ḥāl, s.m. Case, condition, state; affair, business, matter; now, present time. A.

حالت ḥālat, s.m. Case, condition, state.

حالي ḥālī, a. Modern, new, existent.

حامله ḥāmila, a. Pregnant, with young. A.

حبس ḥabs, s.m. Retention, imprisonment; prison; a prisoner. A.

حبشي ḥabshī, s.m. A Caffre, negro. A.

حبیب ḥabīb, s.m. A lover, friend. a. Beloved, dear. A.

حج ḥaj, s.m. Pilgrimage to Mecca. A.

حجاب *ḥijāb*, s.m. Bashfulness, modesty; curtain, veil. A.

حجام *ḥajjām*, s.m. A barber; cupper, phlebotomist. A.

حجامت *ḥajjāmat*, s.m. Shaving, cupping.

حجت *ḥujjat*, s.m. Argument, proof, reason; dispute, altercation. A.

حجتي *ḥujjatī*, a. Litigious, argumentative, quarrelsome. s.m. Wrangler, caviller, arguer.

حجره *ḥujra*, s.f. A cell, chamber, closet. A. A public room or house in each quarter of a village, for the use of travellers and visitors, hostelry. A vestry, ward.

حد *ḥadd*, s.m. Boundary, limit; extent, extremity, degree; impediment; definition; starting post. A.

حديث *ḥadīs*, s.m. A tradition; the traditions and sayings of Muḥammad. A.

حذر *ḥazr*, s.m. Caution, prudence, fear. A.

حرارت *ḥarārat*, s.m. Fervour, heat, warmth. A.

حراست *ḥirāsat*, s.m. Care, watching, guarding. A.

حرام *ḥarām*, a. Forbidden, unlawful, wrong; sacred. A.

حرامي *ḥarāmī*, s.m. A bastard; robber, cheat; rogue, rascal. A.

حرص *ḥirṣ*, s.m. Greediness, ambition, avarice. A.

حرصناك *ḥirṣnāk*, a. Greedy, ambitious, covetous.

حرف *ḥarf*, s.m. A letter, particle, word. A.

حركت *ḥarkat*, s.m. A short vowel. *ḥarakat*, s.m. Action, gesture, movement; impediment, obstacle, hindrance, prevention. A.

حرم *ḥaram*, a. Forbidden, sacred. s.m. The temple at Mecca; a sanctuary. *ḥarama*, s.f. A seraglio; concubine, wife. A.

حرمت *ḥurmat*, s.m. Chastity, honour; dignity, esteem, reverence. A.

حريان *ḥariyān*, a. See حيران.

حريف *ḥarīf*, s.m. A rival, enemy; partner, associate, friend. a. Clever, cunning; pleasant, agreeable. A.

حساب *ḥisāb*, s.m. Accounts; calculation, reckoning, account. A.

حسد *ḥasad*, s.m. Envy, jealousy, malice; emulation, ambition. A.

حسرت *ḥasrat*, s.m. Grief, sorrow, regret; desire, longing, yearning. A.

حسن *ḥasan*, a. Beautiful, good; a man's name. *ḥusn*, s.m. Beauty, elegance; goodness. A.

حسن حسين *ḥasan-ḥusen*, s.m. Name of a month, the Muḥarram.

حشر *ḥashr*, s.m. A concourse, meeting; resurrection of the dead. A.

حشمت *ḥashmat*, s.m. Dignity, pomp, state; train, retinue. A.

حصار *ḥiṣṣār*, s.m. Citadel, fortress. A. Enclosure, fence; besieging, surrounding.

حصه *ḥiṣṣa*, s.f. Division, part; lot, portion, share. A.

حضرت *ḥazrat*, s.m. Dignity, presence; highness, majesty, reverence, etc. (title of respect). A.

حضور *ḥuzūr*, s.m. Appearance, attendance, presence; your worship, etc. A.

حفاظت *ḥifāzat*, s.m. Care, custody; keeping, protection. A.

حق *ḥaqq*, s.m. Truth, right; equity, justice; portion, lot; the Deity. A. *ḥuq*, s.m. The sound of retching, vomiting.

حقا *ḥaqqā*, in. By God! Really! True! Indeed! A.

حقنه *ḥuqna*, s.f. A clyster; syringe. A.

حقير *ḥaqīr*, a. Contemptible, vile; lean, thin. A.

حقيقت *ḥaqīqat*, s.m. Truth; sincerity; explanation, narration, account. A.

حقيقي *ḥaqīqī*, a. Accurate, certain, real, true; own; just. A.

حکاك *ḥukāk*, s.m. A lapidary. A.

حکايت *ḥikāyat*, s.m. History, story, tale; narration. A.

حکم *ḥukm*, s.m. Command, decree, order, sentence; permission. A.

حکمت *ḥikmat*, s.m. Knowledge, wisdom; art, skill, cleverness; mystery, principle. A.

حکمتي *ḥikmatī*, a. Artful, clever, wise, skilful.

حکومت *ḥukūmat*, s.m. Authority, dominion, government, sovereignty. A.

حکيم *ḥakīm*, s.m. A doctor, physician; philosopher, sage. A.

حلال *ḥalāl*, a. Lawful, legal, right; clean, pure. A.

حلف *ḥalaf*, s.m. An oath. A.

حلق *ḥalq*, s.m. The throat, windpipe. A.

حلقه *ḥalqa*, s.f. A circle, ring; knocker for a door; a fraternity, society. A.

حلوا *ḥalwā*, s.f. A kind of sweetmeat made of flour, butter and sugar. A.

حلواي *ḥalwā-ī*, s.m. A confectioner.

حليم *ḥalīm*, a. Affable, gentle, tractable, mild. A.

حماقت *ḥimāqat*, s.m. Folly, ignorance, stupidity. A.

حمال *ḥammāl*, s.m. A porter, carrier. A.

حمام *ḥammām*, s.m. A Turkish bath, vapour bath. A.

حمايت *ḥimāyat*, s.m. Countenance, protection, support, defence, help, assistance. A.

حمايتي *ḥimāyatī*, s.m. Protector, patron, deliverer.

حمل *ḥaml*, s.m. A burden, load; pregnancy. A.

حمله *ḥamla*, s.f. Assault, attack, onset, charge. A.

حنا *ḥinnā*, s.f. See نکريزي.

حنظل *ḥanẓal*, s.m. See مرغوني.

حواله *ḥawāla*, s.f. Care, charge, custody, trust. A.

حور *ḥūr*, s.m. A boy of Paradise. A.

حوره *ḥūra*, s.f. A virgin of Paradise; black-eyed nymph. A.

حوصله *ḥauṣila*, s.f. Ambition, spirit, mettle; crop, maw, stomach. A.

حوض *ḥauẓ*, s.m. A cistern, tank, reservoir, vat. A.

حويلي *ḥawelai*, s.m. A dwelling, habitation, house; tenement, premises. A. Also *ḥawela-ī*, s.f.

حيا *ḥayā*, s.f. Bashfulness, modesty, shame. A.

حيات *ḥayāt*, s.m. Life. A.

حيران *ḥairān*, a. Astonished, amazed; perplexed, confounded. A.

حيراني *ḥairānī*, s.f. Amazement, confusion; perplexity, perturbation. A.

حيض *ḥaiẓ*, s.m. Menses, catamenia. A.

حيضه *ḥaiẓa*, s.f. A menstruous woman.

حيف *ḥaif*, s.m. Iniquity, oppression. a. Futile, useless. in. Alas! Ah! A.

حيله *ḥīla*, s.f. Artifice, pretence, deceit, trick. A.

حين *ḥīn*, s.m. Time, interval. A.

حيوان *ḥaiwān*, s.m. An animal, brute. A.

حيوانتوب *ḥaiwān-tob*, s.m. Brutality, savageness.

خ

خ *khe* is the twelfth letter of the Pukkhto alphabet, and the seventh of the Arabic. It is a guttural letter, and pronounced like the *ch* in the Scotch *loch*.

خاتم *khātim*, s.m. A seal; finger ring. A.

خاتمه *khātima*, s.f. Conclusion, end, finis. A.

خاته *khātah*, s.m. Ascent, rise; rising, ascending.

خادمه *khādama*, } s.f. Name of a kind of
خادمي *khādama-ī*, } lizard with a bristly back.

خاده *khāda*, s.f. A grave-stone, tombstone; a pole or wooden tablet at the head of a grave.

خار *khār*, s.m. A thorn, bramble, prickle, thistle; a spike; the spur of a cock. P.

خارج *khārij*, a. Excluded, outcast, expelled. A.

خارجي *khārijī*, s.m. Name of a heretical sect amongst Moslems.

خاربهت *khārikkht*, s.m. Itch, mange. P. (*khārisht*).

خارو *khāro*, s.f. A cock's comb, wattle. P. (*khār*).

خاشاک *khāshāk*, s.m. Rubbish, litter, refuse. P. Firewood, fuel. P.

خاش خاش *khāsh-khāsh*, s.m. Poppy seed. P.

خارک *khārak*, s.m. See بهارک.

خازه *khāza*, s.f. See خاده.

خاشه *khāsha*, s.f. A straw, splinter, bit, chip, etc.; name of a disease of the eye; mote in the eye.

خاشه کبں *khāsha-kakkh*, s.m. One who extracts motes from the eye; curer of the khasha.

خاص *khāṣṣ*, a. Excellent, noble, pure; special, private, particular; peculiar, single, sole. A.

خاصه *khāṣṣa*, s.f. A kind of bread; a kind of muslin.

خاصيت *khāṣṣiyat*, s.m. Attribute, quality, temper, disposition, nature, property. A.

خاطر *khāṭir*, s.m. Heart, soul; inclination, propensity; account, sake; will, choice. A.

خاک *khāk*, s.m. Ashes, earth, dust. P.

خاکستر *khākistar*, s.f. Ashes. P.

خاکه *khāka*, s.f. Broken rice, etc. unfit for use; a fragment, particle of gems, etc.

خاگينه *khāgīna*, s.f. Omelet, dish of fried eggs. P.

خال *khāl*, s.m. A black spot, or mole on the skin; an artificial spot for ornament on the face, breasts, etc.

خالص *khāliṣ*, a. Genuine, pure, simple. A.

خالصه *khāliṣa*, s.f. Fallow land.

خالي *khālī*, a. Empty, vacant; unmixed, pure; mere, only; idle, unemployed. s.f. Saturday; the eleventh Afghan month corresponding with *zī-qa'da*. P.

خام *khām*, s.m. The horn end of a bow. A. See اوم.

خامتا *khāmtā*, s.f. A kind of coarse cotton cloth.

خاموش *khāmosh*, a. Mute, silent, still. P.

خان *khān*, s.m. A lord, prince; a title used by all Afghans and Pathans. T.

خانتما *khāntamā*, a. Proud, arrogant, vain.

خانه *khāna*, s.f. House, room, place. P.

خاندان *khāndān*, s.m. Family, household.

خانواده *khānawāda*, s.f. Family, house, tribe.

خانومان *khānomān*, s.m. Household (as house, family, servants, cattle, furniture, goods, chattels, fixings, etc.).

خاوره *khānwra*, s.f. Dust, earth, clay.

خاورين *khānwrīn*, a. Clayey, earthy, dusty.

خاوند *khāwand*, s.m. Master, owner, husband. lord, proprietor. P.

خايه *khāya*, s.f. Testicle. P.

خبث *khubṣ*, s.m. Envy, malice. A.

خبر *khabar*, s.m. Advice, intelligence, news, report, rumour. A.

خبردار *khabar-dār*, a. Careful, cautious; aware, informed. A.

خبرگير *khabar-gīr*, s.m. A spy, informer; patron, protector.

خبرلوڅ *khabar-lots*, a. Eloquent, talkative.

خبرول *khabarawul*, v.a. To report, inform.

خبره *khabara*, s.f. Language, speech; affair, matter, thing.

خبريدل *khabaredal*, v.n. To be aware, acquainted, informed, etc.

خبيث *khabīṣ*, a. Impure, malignant, wicked. s.m. An evil spirit. A.

خپر *khapar*, s.f. Palm of the hand; sole of the foot.

خپسکي *khapaskai*, s.m. } The nightmare. A. خپسه *khapasa*, s.f. } (*kābūs*).

خپل *khpul*, pr. Self, own. P. (*khūd*). *pa-khpul*, or *pa-khpula*, ad. Spontaneously, of own accord. P. (*bā-khūd*).

خپل سر *khpul-sar*, a. Obstinate, self-opinionated.

خپلوالي *khpul-wālai*, s.m. Connection, relationship.

خپلول *khpulawul*, v.a. To adopt, appropriate, make one's own; win over, bias, sway, predispose.

خپلوي *khpulawī*, s.f. Connection, relationship, family, kindred, friendship.

خپليدل *khpuledal*, v.n. To be related, connected; to be biassed, influenced.

خپور *khpor*, a. Blown, blossomed, expanded (as a flower): dispersed, loose, scattered.

خپه *khapah*, a. Angry, offended, displeased, vexed. *khapa*, s.f. Suffocation, strangulation. P. (*khafa*). *khpah*, s.m. Tinder, touchwood.

خپگان *khapagān*, s.m. } Anger, rage, vexa- خپگي *khapagī*, s.f. } tion.

خپي *khapī*, s.f. See کپي.

ختر *khatar*, s.m. See خطر.

ختل *khatal*, v.n. To ascend, mount, rise; issue. P. (*khāstan*, *khez-*).

ختم *khatm*, s.m. Conclusion, end; seal. a. Done, completed. A.

ختنه *khatna*, s.f. Circumcision. A. *khatana*, s.f. Rising, mounting, ascending.

خته *khata*, s.f. A shirt, shift.

خټ *khat*, s.m. A hillock, knoll, mound; a low hill; bank of clouds. *kha-aṭ* or *khaṭ*, a. Muddy, turbid, miry. *khuṭ*, s.m. Effervescence, boiling, bubbling.

خټکيدل *khuṭkedal*, v.n. To bubble, boil, effervesce; to boil with rage, etc. H. (*khaṭaknā*).

خټبيل *khaṭbel* or *kha-aṭbel*, s.m. Dregs, lees, sediment, dross, precipitate.

خټک *khaṭak*, s.m. A kind of black beetle. An unripe water melon used to make pickles. Name of a Pathan tribe settled in the low hills on the south of the Kabul river, between Peshawar and Attak.

خټکي *khaṭakai*, s.m. A kind of melon of a green colour (peculiar to Afghanistan). *khuṭkai*, s.m. Ebullition, effervescence.

خټوله *khaṭola* or *kha-atola*, a. Muddy, turbid (as water).

خټه *khaṭa* or *kha-aṭa*, s.f. Mire, mud, slush, slime. *khuṭa*, s.f. Clay, marl.

خجل *khijil*, a. Bashful, modest. A. (*khajal*).

خجونکو *khajūnko*, a. Capering, frisky, prancing; rebounding, skipping (as a ball or stone over the surface of water).

خڅوزه *khatsoza*, s.f. A bit, fragment, chip, shred.

خڅه *khatsa*, p. See خټه.

خچر *khachar*, s.m. A mule. H. (*khachchar*).

خچن *khachan*, a. Dirty, rheumy. See چخن.

خچه *khacha*, s.f. The little finger; a bound, ricochet, rebound.

خداي *khudāe*, s.m. God, The Deity. P. (*khudā*). *khudā-ī*, s.f. Divinity, Godhead. P.

خدايا *khudāyā*, in. Oh God! P.

خدمت *khidmat*, s.m. Attendance, duty, service. A.

خدمتي *khidmatī*, a. Attentive, diligent, heedful.

خدمتگار *khidmat-gār*, s.m. A servant, attendant.

خدنگ *khadang*, s.m. Name of a tree, from the wood of which bows are made. A poplar tree. P.

خدل *khaḍal*, s.m. A large dog in good condition; a mastiff. a. Stout, burly, muscular.

خر *khar*, s.m. An ass, donkey. P. *kha-ar*, s m. A snore. A.

خراب *kharāb*, a. Bad, depraved; spoiled, ruined; deserted, waste; abandoned, lost. A.

خرابي *kharābī*, s.f. Evil, mischief; destruction, ruin; waste.

خراج *khirāj*, s.m. Duty, revenue, rent, tax. A.

خراړه *kharāṛa*, s.f. Name of a bird; the sand grouse; a kind of sky-lark.

خراسان *khurāsān*, s.m. Name of a country. Afghanistan.

خراشكي *kharāshkai*, s.m. Phlegm, expectorated mucus, sputum. P. (*kharāsh*).

خربشوي *kharbishoe*, s.m. A boar, hog, pig.

خربوزه *kharbūza*, s.f. A musk melon. P.

خرپټ *kharpaṭ*, s.m. A powder; a palmful to chuck into the mouth.

خرپوڅه *kharpotsa*, s.f. Crawling on all fours (as a child).

خرټ *kharaṭ*, a. Fat, stout, plump.

خرټه *kharaṭah*, s.m. Cheat, hypocrite, knave.

خرجدال *kharjadāl*, s.m. See خردجال.

خرجگجگلي *kharjagjagalai*, s.m. Name of a game played by boys.

خرجين *khurjīn*, s.m. A bag, wallet, reticule. P.

خرڅ *kharts*, s.m. Expense, outlay; expenditure, means; price, fee, duty. A. (*kharch*).

خرڅوړي *khartsoṛai*, s.m. A rag, shred, tatter.

خرڅي *khartsī*, a. Extravagant, prodigal, lavish.

خرچ *khrach*, s.m. A crack, creak, crash, split; sound of splitting wood.

خرخاري *kharkhārai*, s.m. Ass's play, foolishness, nonsense; romping, boistering.

خرخښه *kharkhakkha*, s.f. Noise, tumult, discord, wrangling; a crowd, mob. P (*kharkhasha*).

خرد *khurd*, a. Little, small. P.

خردجال *khardajāl*, s.m. Antichrist.

خردگ *khardag*, s.m. Name of a plant (*Salvia pumila*).

خرس *khirs*, s.m. A bear. P.

خرسند *khursand*, a. Contented, pleased, satisfied. P.

خرشن *kharshan*, s.m. Horse dung.

خرطوم *kharṭūm*, s.m. Proboscis of an elephant; dewlap of bulls, etc. A.

خرغيڼري *khar·gheṇrai*, s.m. A toadstool, mushroom.

خرفه *khurfa*, s.f. Purslain. A.

خرقه *khirqa*, s.f. A patched garment, a kind of dress (worn by dervishes). A.

خُركي *kha-arkai*, s.m. A snore, purr.

خرگي *khargai*, s.m. A young ass. *kha-argai*, s.m. A kind of grasshopper.

خرّم *khurram*, a. Cheerful, merry, joyful. P.

خرمن *khirman*, s.m. Harvest. P. Threshing-floor.

خرمندي *kharmandai*, a. Tiny, small, wee, little.

خرمه *khurma*, s.f. A date (fruit and tree). P. (*khurmā*).

خرنار *kharnār*, s.m. Name of a plant, mullein (*Verbascum thapsus*).

خروار *kharwār*, s.m. An ass-load. P.

خروسک *kharosak*, s.m. A disease of the throat, quinsy.

خروش *kharosh*, s.m. Bustle, stir, tumult, noise. P.

خري *kharai*, s.m. A whitlow.

خريد *kharīd*, s.m. Purchase. P.

خريدار *kharīdār*, s.m. A purchaser. P.

خريړي *khareṛai*, s.m. Curds and whey; junket. *kha-areṛai*, s.m. A kind of edible mushroom.

خريز *khirīz*, s.m. Cotton stalks or stubble.

خريطه *kharīta*, s.f. Bag, packet, purse; letter bag, mail. P.

خريل *khrayal*, v.a. To shave. P. (*kharāshīdan*).

خړ *kha-ar*, a. Muddy, turbid; cloudy, obscure; drab, dust-coloured. *khur*, s.m. Sound of vomiting or retching, hawking. *khar*, s.m. A ravine, dry water course. See خوړ.

خړانګه *khrānga*, s.f. Bough or stem of a tree.

خړپ *khrap*, s.m. A crunch, crush, squash, smash.

خړتم *khartam*, s.m. See خرطوم.

خړس *khras*, s.m. Blow, clash, crash, slam.

خړل *kharal*, v.a. To dung, ease one's self, stool.

خړمت *kha-armat*, s.m. Snot, snivel, mucus of nose.

خړمور *kha-armor*, s.m. A kind of bustard, obārah.

خړند *kharand*, s.m. Stump of a tree, stubble.

خړوب *kharob*, a. Watered, saturated, irrigated (as a field).

خړيس *khrīs*, a. Big, burly, great; stupid, heavy, dull. s.m. A lout, lubber.

خړين *khurīn*, a. Soft, sodden (as victuals), ripe, rotten (as fruit), festered (as a sore).

خزان *khizān*, s.m. Autumn. P.

خزانه *khizāna*, s.f. Treasury, store; magazine, granary; chamber of a gun.

خزله *khazala*, s.f. Litter, refuse, sweepings, etc.

خزنده *khazanda*, s.f. A reptile, insect, creeping thing. P.

خږ *khug*, a. Bruised, hurt, injured, pained. s.m. A bruise, cut, injury, wound; ailment, malady, disease. *khag*, s.m. Death rattle, gurgle in the throat.

خس *khass*, s.m. Litter, straw, dry grass, twigs, etc. P.

خسا *khsā*, a. See سخا.

خسمانه *khasmāna*, s.f. Protection, support; custody, ownership; housewifery, domestic economy. A. (*khaṣmāna*).

خسنړي *khasanrai*, s.m. A straw, mote, dry twig, etc.

خسي *khasī*, a. Castrated, gelt. s.m. A gelding, any castrated animal. A. (*khuṣṣī*). *khsai*, s.m. See سخي.

خسيل *khasīl*, s.m. Green corn used as fodder.

خشاک *khashāk*, s.m. Refuse, litter, rubbish; dry twigs, leaves, etc. P.

خشاوزه *khashāwza*, s.f. Orris root; root of the Iris or sweet flag. See سخاوره.

خشت *khisht* or *khusht*, a. Damp, humid, moist, wet; drenched, dripping, reeking. *khusht-pusht*, a. Drenched to the skin, wet through, etc.

خشک *khushk*, a. Dry, arid, withered. P.

خشکه *khushka*, s.f. Plain boiled rice. P.

خشکي *khushkī*, s.f. Dryness, aridity; drought, dearth; dry land, travelling by land. P.

خشنود *khushnūd*, a. Contented, pleased. P.

خشي *khushai*, a. Crazy, demented, flighty; open, defenceless; unguarded, unprotected; without friends, etc. P. (*khushk* or *khush*).

خښ *khakkh*, a. Buried, interred, embedded.

خښتګ *khakkhtag*, } s.m. A piece of cloth
خښتګي *khakkhtagai*, } sewn into the fork of a pair of drawers or armpit of a coat. P. (*khash*, armpit).

خښته *khakkhta*, s.f. A brick. P. (*khisht*)

خښي *khakkhī*, s.m. Name applied to the Yusufzai tribe of Afghans. *khakkhai*, s.m. A male of the tribe. *khakkha-ī*, s.f. A female of the tribe.

خصلت *khaṣlat*, s.m. Nature, disposition; quality, virtue; custom, habit. A.

خصم *khaṣam*, s.m. A husband. A.

خصوصا *khuṣūṣan*, ad. Especially, particularly. A.

خضر *khizr*, s.m. The prophet Elias. A.

خط *khaṭṭ*, s.m. Epistle, letter, note; writing; a line, lineament; down on the face, youthful beard. A.

خطا *khaṭā*, s.f. Error, fault, crime; mistake, miss. A.

خطاب *khiṭāb*, s.m. Address, title. A.

خطبه *khutba*, s.f. A sermon preached on Fridays in Muhammadan places of worship for the welfare and prosperity of the reigning sovereign. A.

خطر *khaṭar*, s.m. } Danger, fear, hazard, risk.
خطره *khaṭra*, s.f. } A.

خطرناک *khaṭar-nāk*, a. Dangerous, hazardous.

خطيب *khaṭīb*, s.m. A preacher. A.

خفقان *khafaqān*, s.m. Palpitation of the heart, breast-pang; vexation. A.

خګلن *khuglan*, s.m. Embers, hot ashes, hot cinders.

خل *khal*, s.m. Faith, hope, trust, belief.

خلات *khilāt*, s.m. A dress of honour, reward, present. A. (*khil'at*).

خلاص *khalāṣ*, a. Free, liberated; discharged, done. A.

خلاصه *khulāṣa*, s.f. Conclusion, inference, moral; abstract, summary. A.

خلاصي *khalāṣī*, s.f. Deliverance, freedom, release.

خلاف *khilāf*, s.m. Contradiction, opposition. a. Contrary, false. A.

خلاملا *khalā-malā*, a. Candid, frank, sincere.

خلبوري *khulborai*, s.m. A bung, cork, plug, spigot.

خلته *khalta*, s.f. A hamper (used by hill men). P. (*khalīta*). See جلته.

خلش *khalish*, s.m. Interruption, hindrance; doubt, solicitude; suspicion. P.

خلط *khalṭ*, s.m. Confusion, mixture. *khilṭ*, s.m. One of the four humours of the human body. A.

خلق *khalq*, s.m. Creation, universe; mankind, people, the world. A. *khulq*, s.m. Nature, disposition, civility, politeness. A.

خلقت *khalqat*, s.m. Creation, people, the world. A.

خلقه *khalqa*, s.f. A coat, frock, gown. A.

خلل *khalal*, s.m. Defect, injury; interruption; prejudice. A.

خلوت *khilwat*, s.m. Privacy, retirement; closet, private chamber; private conference. A.

خله *khula*, s.f. The mouth; orifice, entrance.

خلي *khalai*, s.m. Bud, shoot, sprout. S. (*kalī*).

خم *kham*, s.m. A coil, twist; curl, ringlet. *khum*, s.m. An alembic, still, retort; jar, vase; boiler. P.

خمار *khumār*, a. Drunken, intoxicated; intoxicating, languishing (as the eyes). s.m. Headache, sickness after a debauch. P.

خمبه *khamba*, s.f. A kind of corn bin made of wattles, and plastered over with clay.

خمټ *khamaṭ*, a. Plump, chubby (as a baby).

خمچه *khamachah*, a. Little, short, small. *khamacha-guṭa*, s.f. The little finger. *khamache-pukkhta-ī*, s.f. The short ribs.

خمچي *khamache*, s.f. Coarsely ground millet or rice, broken rice; millet bread. H. (*kamāch*).

خمرئ *khumra-ī*, s.f. A drinking flask or cup; a small drum carried by beggars; a small mat of palm leaves used to pray upon. A.

خمسور *khamsor*, a. Familiar, free, unceremonious.

خمزري *khumazarai*, s.m. See شاپيانګه.

خمن *khaman*, a. Bent, curved, crooked. P. (*kham*).

خمير *khamīr*, a. Fermented, leavened. A.

خميره *khamīra*, s.f. Dough, leaven, yeast, ferment.

خنجاړه *khanjāṛa*, s.f. A kind of millet grain.

خنجر *khanjar*, s.m. A dagger. A.

خنجک *khinjak*, s.m. The mastic tree and fruit (*Pista Cabulica*).

خند *khand*, s.m. Name of a boy's game played with knuckle bones; marbles.

خندا *khandā*, s.f. A laugh; laughter. P. (*khandah*).

خندق *khandaq*, s.m. A ditch, moat, fosse. A.

خندل *khandal*, v.a. To laugh at, scoff, ridicule.

خندول *khandawul*, v.a. To cause to laugh.

خنده *khandah*, s.m. A pointer dog. Also *khandai*.

خندي *khundī*, a. Preserved, protected, kept; arranged, settled. *khundī-kawul*, v.a. To keep, preserve, take care of.

خنديدل *khandedal*, v.n. To giggle, laugh, titter. P. (*khandīdan*).

خنديل *khundiyal*, v.a. To keep, guard, protect, etc.

خنډ *khanḍ*, s.m. Stump of a tree.

خنډن *khanḍan*, s.m. Zedoary (*Curcuma zerunbet*).

خنک *khunuk*, a. Cold, cool, chilly; temperate. P.

خنکي *khunukī*, s.f. Coldness, chilliness. P.

خو *khū*, s.m. Tinder, touchwood; a kind of sugar cane. H. *kho*, ad. Certainly, surely; then, at least.

خوا *khwā*, s.f. Margin, side, direction, quarter; nature, temperament; constitution, health; desire, wish.

خوار *khwār*, a. Poor, wretched; abject, mean; lean, thin; friendless, ruined. P.

خواري *khwārī*, s.f. Poverty, beggary, ruin; distress, etc.

خواړه *khwāṛah* s.m. Food, victuals.

خواست *khwāst*, s.m. Desire, wish; want, request. P.

خواښه *khwākkha*, s.f. Mother-in-law. P. (*khwāsh*).

خواله *khwāla*, s.f. Disclosing, revealing. *khwāla-wayal*, v.a. To disclose, reveal.

خوان *khwān*, s.m. } A tray, salver, platter.
خوانچه *khwāncha*, s.f. } P. A small tray.
dastar-khwān, s.m. A table cloth, table-cover. P.

خواهش *khwāhish*, s.m. Desire, inclination, wish. P.

خوب *khob*, s.m. Sleep, slumber; a dream. P. (*khwāb*). *khūb*, a. Good, excellent; amiable, pleasant; fair, beautiful. P.

خوبي *khūbī*, s.f. Excellence, beauty, goodness, etc. P.

خوټه *khoṭa*, s.f. A testicle.

خوځول *khwadzawul*, v.a. To move, shift, remove, shake, agitate, wag.

خوځيدل *khwadzedal*, v.n. To move, shake, wag, stir.

خود *khūd*, pr. Self (in comp. only). P. *khod*, ad. See خو.

خودله *khūdala*, s.f. Bulrush, reed; the flower spike and down: the down is used as tinder.

خور *khor*, s.f. A sister. pl. *khwainde*. P. (*khwāhar*). *khor*, a. Open, expanded, blown (as a flower); dispersed, scattered; loose, dishevelled. *khwa-ar*, s.m. Scurf, scab, crust; bark, peel, rind, husk.

خوراک *khwurāk*, s.m. Food, victuals, diet, eatables. P.

خوراکي *khwurākī*, a. Edible, eatable, esculent.

خورځه *khordza*, s.f. Sister's daughter, niece.

خورجين *khūrjīn*, } s.m. Portmanteau, carpet-
خورجي *khūrjai*, } bag; a wallet, reticule. P.

خورجينه *khūrjīna*, s.f. A travelling-cap with flaps to cover the ears.

خورخل *khorkhal*, s.m. } Shears for shearing
خورخول *khorkhwal*, } sheep.

خورلنړه *khor·lanra*, s.f. A sister's daughter (used by a clan or tribe to designate the daughter of any member after marriage).

خورمه *khorma*, s.f. Incipient beard, down on the face.

خورنده *khwurindah*, a. Gluttonous, gormandizer. P.

خوروړل *khwararawul*, v.a. To open, expand, loose, dishevel, spread out, disperse, scatter. *khūrawul*, v.a. To feed, supply with food.

خوري *khaura-ī*, s.f. Alum. *khawrai*, s.m. See خاوره.

خوريدل *khwaredal*, v.n. To expand; blossom, blow; to disperse, spread, scatter.

خورينگه *khorīnga*, s.f. Adopted sister, female friend.

خورينگي *khorīngai*, s.m. Sisterly love, friendship among women.

خوري *khora-e*, s.m. Sister's son, nephew.

خوړ *khwaṛ*, s.m. A ravine, watercourse, dry bed of a river.

خوړل *khwuṛal*, v.a. To eat, feed; bite. P. (*khurdan*).

خوړول *khūṛawul* or *khwuṛawul*, v.a. To feed, victual, supply with food.

خوړه *khwaṛa*, s.f. Donation, gratuity, subscription; sandy bed of a ravine or dry watercourse.

خوږ *khog*, a. Sweet. *khūg*, a. See خش. P. (*khūsh*).

خوږلوري *khog·lorai*, a. Sweetish, pleasant.

خوږه وله *khwaga·wala*, s.f. Liquorice root.

خوش *khūsh*, a. Agreeable, pleasant. P.

خشوي *khashoe*, s.m. See غشوي.

خوشه *khosha*, s.f. An ear of corn, bunch of grapes, spike of flowers, etc. P.

خوښ *khwakkh*, a. Delighted, pleased; pleasant, agreeable; charming, attractive. P. (*khūsh*).

خوښي *khwakkhī*, s.f. Will, pleasure, choice; delight, joy, gladness. P. (*khūshī*).

خوښينه *khwakkhīna*, s.f. See ښينه.

خوف *khof*, s.m. Fear, fright, alarm. A. (*khauf*).

خوګ *khūg*, s.m. A pig, hog. P. (*khūk*).

خول *khol*, s.m. A helmet, steel cap; case, sheath. H.

خوله *khwula*, s.f. A divorced wife who is taken back and received by the husband.

خولي *khwale*, s.f. (sing. obsolete) Perspiration, sweat. P. (*khwae*).

خولۍ *khola-ī*, s.f. A cap, skull-cap,

خون *khūn*, s.m. Murder, manslaughter; blood. P.

خوني *khūnī*, s.m. A murderer.

خوناق *khonāq*, s.m. A disease of the throat, quinsy. A. (*khunāq*).

خوند *khwand*, s.m. Flavour, taste; pleasure delight.

خوندناک *khwand·nāk*, a. Agreeable, pleasant.

خونه *khūna*, s.f. Chamber, room; court, hall, house; family, tribe. P. (*khāna*). *khawana*, s.f. Olive tree.

خوي *khoe*, s.m. Temper, disposition, nature; custom, habit, manner. P. (*kho*).

خويد *khwīd* or *khīd*, s.m. Green corn (used as fodder). P.

خوئيدل *khwa-edal*, v.n. To slip, slide, fall.

خيابان *khayābān*, s.m. An avenue; flower bed. P.

خيار *khiyār*, s.m. Choice, selection, trial. A.

خياط *khiyāṭ*, s.m. A tailor. A.

خيال *khiyāl*, s.m. Fancy, idea, thought; opinion, suspicion; delusion, vision. A.

خيانت *khiyānat*, s.m. Embezzlement, robbery of entrusted property; perfidy, treachery. A.

خيټه *kheṭa*, s.f. See ګېډه.

خيدک *khaidak*, s.m. Sour milk.

خير *khīr*, a. Enraged, angry; sorry, vexed. P. (*khīra*). *khair*, a. Good, well. s.m. Happiness, welfare; health, goodness; alms, charity. A.

خيرات *khairāt*, s.m. Alms, charity. A.

خيره *khīra*, s.f. Dirt, filth, pollution, ordure.

خيرن *khīran*, / خيري *khīrai*, a. Dirty, soiled, filthy, polluted.

خيز *khez*, s.m. Bounding, leaping, rising. P.

خيژول *khejawul*, v.a. To lift, elevate, raise, erect. P. (*khezāndan*).

خيږ *khīg*, s.m. The scab of a sore. S. (*khāj*).

خيښ *khekkh*, s.m. A kinsman, relation; wife's relations. P. (*khwesh*).

خيښي *khekkhī*, s.f. Relationship by marriage.

خيک *khīk*, s.m. A large inflated hide (used to cross rivers upon).

خيل *khel*, s.m. A clan, tribe; division of a clan, family. A.

خيل‌خانه *khel-khāna*, s.f. Clan, kindred.

خيم *khyam*, a. Coagulated, solidified, hardened (as the chest, milk, etc.). A. (*qiyām*).

خيمه *khaima*, s.f. A tent, marquee. A.

د *dāl* is the thirteeenth letter of the Pukkhto alphabet; it has a soft dental sound, and is often changed to ل in words derived from the Persian and Sanskrit.

د *da*; A particle, the sign of the Genitive case; it always precedes the word it governs, and is not affected by gender or number. It is sometimes used as the sign of the Ablative case instead of the particle له. Ex. دَ کلي نه *da kilī na*, for له کلي نه *la kilī na*, from the village.

دِ *di*, pr. 1. A form of the Genitive and Instrumental cases singular of the second personal pronoun ته *tah*, thou. Also written دي *de*. 2. A form of the Oblique cases singular of the proximate third personal pronoun دي *de*, he, she, it. 3. The sign of the third person in both numbers of the Imperative Mood.

دا *dā*, pr. One of the proximate demonstrative pronouns; this; that.

داب *dāb*, s.m. The large wooden axle of a Persian wheel; custom, manner; condition, situation. A.

دابه *dāba*, s.f. A quadruped, beast, brute; cattle. A.

داتکي *dātkai*, s.m. A plant used in dyeing (*Grislea tomentosa*). H. (*dhārī*).

داتوره *dātūra*, s.f. The thorn apple (*Datura fastuosa*). H. (*dhatūrā*).

داج *dāj*, s.m. Darkness, obscurity. A marriage portion: all that a wife takes with her to her husband. A. (*dahez*).

داخل *dākhil*, a. Entered, arrived. s.m. Arriving, entering. A.

داد *dād*, s.m. Equity, justice, law; revenge; (in comp.) given, bestowed. P.

دادا *dādā*, in. A term of affectionate address to a father or elder brother. Dear father! dear brother! H.

دار *dār*, s.m. Gallows, gibbet, stake. P. Dwelling, mansion. A. Master, owner, possessor, etc. (in comp.). P. A current, jet, spirt, stream. S. (*dhār*).

دارو *dārū*, s.m. Medicine, physic; gunpowder. H.

داروغه *dāroghah*, s.m. Overseer, superintendent, manager. P.

داره *dāra*, s.f. A stream, jet, spirt; cascade. S. (*dhār*).

داريال *dāryāl*, s.m. A tambourine.

داړ *dāṛ*, s.m. A band, company, gang (of

robbers). s. (ḍāṛ). A jaw tooth, grinder, molar. s. (ḍāṛh).

داړل dāṛal, v.a. To bite, lacerate, tear with the teeth (as a dog, etc.). To scold, reprove, snap at.

داړه dāṛa, s.f. A foray, raid, surprise; cattle lifting; band, gang (of robbers); molar tooth.

داستان dāstān, s.m. A fable, story, tale. P.

داښت dākkht, s.m. A potter's furnace or oven. Durability, strength, endurance. P. (dāsht).

داغ dāgh, s.m. A spot, stain, blemish, mark; scar, cicatrix; brand, cautery. P.

داغي dāghī, a. Spotted, stained; scarred; cauterized; branded; blemished. P.

دال dāl, s.m. Pulse, lentils, vetches. S. a. Expressive, significant, typical (in comp.) A.

دالان dālān, s.m. Anteroom, hall, vestibule. P.

دام dām, s.m. A net, snare, trap. P.

دامن dāman, s.m. Border, skirt (of a garment, etc.); base or foot of a mountain. P.

دانا dānā, a. Learned, wise. s.m. A wise man. P.

داناي dānā-ī, s.f. Wisdom, knowledge. P.

دانست dānist, s.m. Knowledge, opinion. P.

دانش dānish, s.m. Intelligence, learning, science. P.

دانگ dāng, s.m. Name of a small coin; the sixth part of a دينار (dīnār).

دانه dāna, s.f. A berry; corn; grain, seed; pimple, boil; speck, granule. P. dāna-dār, a. Granular. tora-dāna, s.f. A boil, black head, furuncle; name of a black seed used in medicine.

داو dāw, s.m. Ambuscade, ambush; opportunity, power; time, turn, stroke (at play); stake, wager; cast or throw at dice, etc. P. H.

داي dā-ī, s.f. Nurse, midwife. P.

دائره dā-ira, s.f. A circle, orbit, ring; emblems, lines, symbols (used as amulets and charms). A.

دائم dā-im, a. Always, continual, perpetual. A.

دباره dubāra, ad. Again, second time. P.

دباغ dabbāgh, s.m. Currier, tanner. A.

دباغي dabbāghī, s.f. Business of a tanner.

دبانِد dabāndi, } ad. Outside, upon, on top,
دباندي dabānde, } above, over.

دباو dabāw, s.m. Authority, power, strength; subjection, pressure. H.

دبدبه dabdaba, s.m. Dignity, pomp, state. A.

دبلي dablai, s.m. A box, casket. H. (ḍibbī).

دبه daba, s.f. A jar or flagon made of untanned hide, and used to hold oil, butter, etc. H. (ḍabbā).

دبي dabī, s.f. Fruit ripened in straw or leaves, etc.

دپ dap, a. Deafened, stunned, stupefied.

دپاړ dapāra, } p. For, for the sake of, on
دپاره dapāra, } account of.

دپټه dupaṭṭa, s.f. A sheet of two breadths, used as a mantle or shawl. H.

دجاج dujāj, s.m. Domestic fowl. A.

دختر dukhtar, s.f. Daughter, girl, virgin. P.

دخل dakhl, s.m. Access, entrance; intrusion, interference; produce, profit, advantage. A.

دخمه dakhma, s.f. Ambush, lair, cover.

دد dad, s.m. A beast of prey, rapacious animal. P.

در dar, s.m. A door. P. durr, s.m. A pearl. A. dar, A particle used as a pronominal dative prefix of the second person with verbs and adverbs, without change for gender or number. Ex. dar dzam (I come to thee), dar bāndi (upon thee), etc.

دراز darāz, a. Extended, long. P.

درامد darāmad, s.m. Entrance. P.

درانی *durānī*, s.m. Name applied collectively to the western tribes of Afghans. P.

درائي *darā-ī*, s.f. A kind of red silk cloth. P.

درب *drab*, s.m. A bang, crash; roll, rumble. Name of a grass (*Agrostis linearis*). H. (*dāb*).

دربار *darbār*, s.m. A court, audience hall; levee. P.

درباري *darbārī*, a. Courtly. s.m. A courtier. P.

دربچه *darbacha*, s.f. See دریچه.

دربل *drabal*, v.a. To shake, press down (as flour, etc.). *drabal*, v.n. To subside, settle, sink, fall in, break down (as a roof, etc.); to crash, crumble.

دربلئ *darbala-ī*, s.f. A tripod.

دربي *drabai*, s.m. A bang, crash, crumble, roll, rumble.

درپري *draparai*, s.m. Nettlerash, hives.

درج *darj*, s.m. A place for writing; written; a volume. A.

درجه *darja*, s.f. Degree, rank; step, stair. A.

درخته *drakhta*, s.f. A tree, shrub. P. (*darakht*).

درخواست *darkhwāst*, s.m. Appeal, demand; entreaty, request; desire, wish; proposal. P.

درد *dard*, s.m. Pain, ache, affliction; compassion, pity, sympathy. P. *durd*, s.m. Dregs, sediment. P.

دردمن *dardman*, a. Pained, afflicted, distressed. P.

درز *darz*, s.m. A crack, split, flaw; seam, suture; a rag, slip, strip, shred, etc. (of cloth). P.

درزي *darzī*, s.m. A tailor. P.

درس *dars*, s.m. A lesson, reading; lecture. A.

درست *drast*, a. All, whole, entire; fit, proper; just, true. ad. Entirely, wholly. P. (*durust*).

درسته *darasta*, s.f. Arms, armour, weapons.

درشت *durusht*, a. Rough, hard, harsh, stiff, rigid; fierce, surly, morose, stern. P.

درشتي *durushtī*, s.f. Asperity, roughness, severity, sternness, fierceness. P.

درشل *darshal*, s.f. The frame of a door.

درغل *darghal*, a. False, base (as coin, etc.). s.m. Cheat, liar, hypocrite. Depravity, treachery, vice.

درغلول *darghalawul*, v.a. To cheat, deceive, mislead. H. (*warghalānā*).

درغول *darghol*, s.m. A gap, vent, sluice (as in a canal) to carry off the water of floods, etc.

درک *darak*, s.m. Mark, sign, trace; abode, place; entrance, passage; commencement; knowledge, understanding. A.

درکړ *drakaṛ*, s.f. Main spoke of a wheel; rim or felloe of a wheel.

درگاه *dargāh*, s.m. Court, palace; threshold; throne (divine); a shrine, sanctuary, mosque. P.

درگه *darga*, s.f. A copse, brake, thicket.

درلل *darlal*, v.a. } To have, own, possess, maintain, keep, retain.
درلول *darlawul*, } See لرل.

درم *diram*, s.m. Money, specie; name of a coin; name of a weight. P. See درهم.

درمان *darmān*, s.m. Drug, medicine, remedy. P.

درمانده *darmāndah*, a. Distressed, destitute. P.

درماندگي *darmāndagī*, s.f. Adversity, distress; poverty, penury, misery. P.

درمند *dirmand*, s.m. A threshing floor; garner; harvest heap. P. (*khirman*).

درميان *darmiyān*, a. Between, amidst, among. P.

درناوي *daranāwai*, s.m. Heaviness, solidity, weight; steadiness, constancy; courtesy, politeness, respect (to a superior).

درنده *darindah*, a. Rapacious, savage, fierce. P.

درنګ *drang*, s.m. Delay, procrastination, hesitation. P. (*dirang*).

درو *diraw*, s.m. Reaping, mowing, harvesting. P.

دروازه *darwāza*, s.f. Gate, entrance, door. P.

دروان *darwān*, s.m. A gate-keeper, porter. P.

درود *darūd*, s.m. Benediction, blessing. P.

دروزګر *darūz·gar*, s.m. A carpenter. P. (*darūd·gar*).

دروزه *drūza*, s.m. Stubble; shavings; chaff.

دروړ *darwaṛ*, } s.m. A cut, slit, or mark
درغوړ *darghwaṛ*, } in the ears of cattle (for recognition).

دروغ *darogh*, s.m. A lie, falsehood, untruth. P.

دروغجن *daroghjan*, } a. False, lying. s.m.
دروغژن *daroghǰan*, } A liar.

درومل *drūmal*, v.n. To go, depart, set out, run, start.

درون *darūn*, ad. In, within. P.

دروند *drūnd*, a. Heavy, weighty, ponderous.

دروه *droh*, s.m. Artifice, deceit, evasion, fraud; stratagem, feint (in war); hatred, malice, spite. S.

دروي *darwai*, s.m. Name of a reed from which mats are made (*Arundo karka*).

درويزګر *darwez·gar*, s.m. A beggar, mendicant.

درويزه *darweza*, s.f. Beggary, mendicancy. P. (*daryūza*).

درويشت *darwisht*, a. Twenty-three.

دره *dura*, s.f. A birch, scourge, cat of three tails. A. *dara*, s.f. A glen, valley; defile, gorge, hill pass. P.

درهم *dirham*, s.m. A drachm; name of a coin equal to the twentieth of a *dīnār*. A.

درهيسته *dar·hīsta*, ad. Towards or near thee or you.

درِ *dri*, } a. Three. S. (*tirī*).
دري *dre*, }

دري *dara-ī*, s.f. A carpet. H. (*darī*).

درياب *daryāb*, s.m. River, sea, ocean. P. (*daryā*).

دريابي *daryābī*, a. Aquatic, of the sea.

دريافت *daryāft*, s.m. Enquiry, investigation; discovery, comprehension, understanding. P.

دريچه *darīcha*, s.f. A window, ventilator; air hole in a wall. P.

دريدل *daredal*, v.n. See ودريدل.

دريښاخي *dre-kkhākhai*, s.m. A three-pronged pitchfork used to winnow corn.

دريغ *dregh*, s.m. Disinclination, repugnance; sigh, sorrow. P. (*daregh*).

دريغه *dregha*, s.m. Alas! Heigh ho! P. (*dareghā*).

دريه *darya*, s.f. See داريال.

دړزيدل *dṛazedal*, } v.n. To flutter, palpitate,
دړکيدل *dṛakedal*, } bound, quiver. H. (*dhaṛaknā*).

دړه *daṛe*, s.f. A chip, splinter, fragment. H. *daṛe·daṛe*, a. Shattered, in atoms, bits, etc. *daṛa*, s.f. A stone or weight fixed to the lighter scale of a balance to equalize both sides. H. (*dhaṛā*). A ridge or bank of earth, high land, crest of a hill.

دړي *daṛa-ī*, s.f. A dry measure equal to four *ser* or eight pounds. H. (*dhaṛī*). A frontlet, ornament worn on the forehead by women. *daṛai*, s.m. A shelf, cupboard.

دزد *duzd*, s.m. A robber, thief. P.

دست *dast*, s.m. Purge, stool. Cubit, hand. P.

دستار *dastār*, s.m. A turband. P.

دستک *dastak*, s.m. Account book; passport, pass; summons, warrant. P.

دستکي *dastakai*, s.m. A small rafter placed over the large beams in a roof.

دستګله *dastgala*, s.f. A glove, mitten; gauntlet.

دنبل *dunbal*, s.m. A boil, bubo. P.

دنبه *dunba*, دمبه *dumba*, } s.f. The fat-tailed sheep. P.

دند *dund*, s.m. Haze, mist, smoke; obscurity, darkness, gloom.

دندارو *dandārū*, s.m. A boil, carbuncle.

دندانه *dandāna*, s.f. Tooth of a saw or comb; a cascade, waterfall. P.

دندوکار *dandūkār*, s.m. Noise of thunder, roar of artillery, tumult; haze, smoke, etc.

دنکاچه *dunkācha*, s.f. See دوکانچه.

دنګ *dang*, a. Tall, high (in stature). s.m. A tall man; a jump, leap, vault, bound.

دنګل *dangal*, v.a. To jump, leap, bound.

دنګول *dangawul*, v.a. To make jump, leap, etc. (as a horse over a fence); to throw one off a wall, horse, etc.

دننه *danana*, p. In, within, inside. P. (*andarūn*).

دنیا *duniyā*, s.f. The world; people; wealth. A.

دو *dwa* or *do*, a. Two (in comp.). P. *daw*, s.m. See داو. *dau*, s.m. A run, race. *dau-kawul*, v.a. To run. P. (*daw*).

دوا *dawā*, s.f. Medicine, remedy; amulet, charm. A.

دوات *dawāt*, s.m. An inkstand. A.

دواړه *dwāṛah*, a. Both. Corr. of *dwah-wāṛah*.

دوبي *dūbai*, s.m. Summer, hot weather. *dobī*, s.m. A dyer, washerman. H. (*dhobī*).

دوپ *dūp*, s.m. Sunshine, glare, haze. S. (*dhūp*).

دوتر *dawtar*, s.m. Estate, hereditary, possession in land, fief. P. (*daftar*).

دود *dod*, s.m. Custom, fashion, way; dowry, property given with a bride; entertainment of a guest. a. Similar, like. ad. Likewise, similarly. *dūd*, s.m. Vapour, smoke. P.

دور *dūr*, a. Far, distant, remote. P. *davr*, s.m. Revolution, circular motion; age, cycle, period; time, turn. A.

دوران *daurān*, s.m. Time, age, cycle; vicissitude, fortune; turn, period, revolution. A.

دورمه *dūrma*, s.f. See دروي. H. (*durmā*). Pens for writing the oriental character are made from the reed stalk.

دوړه *dūṛa*, s.f. Dust, dry earth. S. (*dhūr*).

دوزخ *dozak͟h*, s.m. Hell. P.

دوزخي *dozak͟hī*, a. Infernal, hellish.

دوزه *dūza*, s.f. Bosh, folly, nonsense.

دوزي *dūzai*, s.m. A blockhead, booby, fool, simpleton, twaddler.

دوست *dost*, s.m. A friend; lover. P.

دوسه *dūsa*, s.f. A rush, forcible entry. H. (*dhasā*). *dusa-kawul*, v.a. To invade, rush into, force through, etc.

دوش *dos͟h*, s.m. The shoulder, back. ad. Last night. P.

دوشاله *dos͟hāla*, s.f. A mantle or plaid made of two breadths of cloth sewn together. P.

دوشخانه *dos͟hk͟hāna*, s.f. A vessel in which skins are placed preparatory to tanning. P.

دوشرل *dos͟haral*, s.m. A two-year-old goat, etc.

دوشنبه *dos͟hanba*, s.f. Monday. P.

دوغ *dog͟h*, s.m. Butter-milk. P.

دوغبس *dog͟hak͟kh*, s.m. See دوزخ.

دوک *dwak*, a. A two-year-old (colt, sheep, etc.). H. (*dok*). *dūk*, s.m. A bodkin, knitting pin; spindle. P.

دوکان *dūkān*, s.m. A shop, workshop. P.

دوکانچه *dūkānc͟ha*, s.f. A platform, terrace; form, bench, settle (before a door or shop); seat or raised earth round a tree, etc.

دوکړه *dūkṛa*, s.f. A kind of kettle-drum.

دوګانه *dogānah*, a. Double, twofold; a prayer with two genuflexions. P.

دولت *daulat*, s.m. Riches, wealth; fortune, property; empire, state; cause, effect, means. A.

دستمايه *dastmāya*, s.f. The handle strap of a shield.

دستمبول *dastambol*, s.m. A musk melon.

دستور *dastūr*, s.m. Custom, fashion, usage; mode, manner, regulation. A clyster, enema. P.

دسته *dasta*, s.f. A handle; pestle; quire of paper; nosegay; bundle of 24 arrows; a bundle, handful; skein of thread or silk; division, brigade, etc. of an army. P.

دستي *dastī*, a. Manual, of the hand. ad. Quickly, immediately, sharply.

دسخط *daskhat*, s.m. Signature. P. (*dast-khatt*).

دښت *dakkht*, s.m. Desert, wild, waste. P. (*dasht*).

دښمن *dukkhman*, s.m. An enemy, foe. P. (*dushman*).

دښمني *dukkhmanī*, } s.f. Enmity, hostility,
دښني *dukkhnī*, } hatred.

دعا *du'ā*, s.f. Benediction, blessing; prayer; imprecation, invocation. A.

دعوت *da'wat*, s.m. Convocation, invitation; entertainment, feast. A.

دعوه *da'wa*, s.f. Claim, plaint; accusation, action at law. A.

دغا *daghā*, s.f. Deceit, imposture, treachery. P.

دغدغه *daghdagha*, s.f. Alarm, call to arms; tumult. A.

دغمه *daghma*, s.f. A welt, weal, mark of a stripe.

دغه *daghah*, pr. The proximate demonstrative pronoun, this, these. A. (*dikhah* or *dak*).

دف *daf*, s.m. A tambourine. P.

دفتر *daftar*, s.m. Record, register, roll; archives; a book; land, estate, registered share of land. P.

دفعه *daf'a*, s.f. Averting, repelling; time, turn; moment. A. (*dafa'*).

دفن *dafan*, s.m. Burial; funeral. A.

دق *diqq*, s.m. Trouble, vexation; hectic fever. A.

دقيقه *daqīqa*, s.f. A minute, moment; anything minute or subtle; a trifle, unimportant matter. A.

دل *dal*, s.m. Bruised or coarsely ground grain, grits. S. (*daliyā*). *dil*, s.m. The heart, soul; courage. P.

دلازاك *dalāzāk*, s.m. Name of a tribe who formerly held the Peshawar valley, whence they were ejected by the Afghans.

دلال *dallāl*, s.m. A broker, agent, salesman; a pimp, go-between; horse dealer. A.

دلاور *dilāwar*, a. Brave, gallant, courageous. P.

دلاوري *dilāwarī*, s.f. Bravery, courage. P.

دلبار *dalbār*, s.m. See دربار.

دلبه *dalba*, s.f. A lure for hawks. A. (*ṭalaba*).

دلته *dalta*, ad. Here, hither. P. (*dar īn jā*).

دلدل *daldal*, s.m. A quagmire, quicksand. H.

دلوه *dalwa*, s.f. A bucket water-pail. A.

دلي *dala-ī*, s.f. A corn stack or rick. *dale*, ad. See دلته.

دليل *dalīl*, s.m. Demonstration, proof; director, guide. A.

دم *dam*, s.m. Breath, life; ambition, pride; moment, minute; edge of a sword; stewing over a slow fire. P. *dum*, s.m. Tail, end, extremity. P.

دماغ *dimāgh*, s.m. The brain. A.

دمامه *damāma*, s.f. A kettle-drum. P.

دمبال *dumbāl*, ad. After, behind, in rear. P.

دمباله *dumbāla*, s.f. A rear guard. P.

دمچي *dumchī*, s.f. A crupper. P.

دمدمه *damdama*, s.f. A mound, bastion, redoubt. A.

دمړي *damṛa-ī*, s.f. The eighth part of a paisa. H.

دمه *dama*, s.f. Breath, respiration; rest, repose, ease; asthma; a pair of bellows. P.

دولتي *dolata-ī*, s.f. A kick with both hind legs.

دومي *dūmai*, s.m. } Cold, catarrh, influenza.
دومه *dūma*, s.f. }

دون *dūn*, a. Abject, base, ignoble, mean, vile. A.

دوند *dūnd*, s.m. See دند. H. (*dhundh*).

دونه *dūna*, s.f. A bonfire. H. (*dhūnī*).

دوني *dūne* or *dūnī*, ad. This much, to this extent.

دونړي *do<u>n</u>ra-ī* or *dau<u>n</u>ra-ī*, s.f. A milk pail. H. (*dohnī*).

دوه *dwah*, a. Two.

دوهي *dūha-ī*, s.f. Fire-place, chimney. H. (*dūhiyā*).

دوي *doe*, s.m. Custom, fashion, usage. *dwī*, pr. plural of دي *dai*, or *de*, this.

ده *dah*, pr. This. See دي. *dih*, s.m. A village. P. *dah*, in. A word used to drive or urge a horse.

دهات *dihāt*, s.m. The country. P.

دهان *dahān*, s.m. The mouth; orifice, aperture. P.

دهانه *dahāna*, s.f. Bridle bit, mouth piece. P.

دهځ *daha<u>dz</u>*, s.m. Dowry, marriage portion, the property the wife carries with her to her husband. A. (*dahez*).

دهړه *dahṛa*, s.f. A jaw tooth, grinder, tusk.

دهشت *dah<u>sh</u>at*, s.m. Alarm, fear, dread, terror. A.

دهقان *dihqān*, s.m. Peasant, villager; ploughman, farm servant. P.

دهليدل *dahaledal*, v.n. To fear, quake, tremble. H. (*dahalna*).

دهمرده *dahmardah*, a. Bold, brave, strong. *dahmarda*, s.f. A lever.

دهور *dahor*, s.m. A weaver.

دهوس *dahūs*, s.m. Cuckold, term of abuse. A. (*daiyūs*).

دهه *daha*, s.f. The first ten days of Muḥarram; models of the tombs of Hasan and Husen carried about in procession during that time. P. (*dahā*).

دي *dai* or *de*, pr. This. Also written ده *dah*, دَ *da*, and د *di*. A. (*de* or *dī*).

ديار *diyār*, s.m. The cedar tree (*Cedrus deodara*).

ديارلس *diyārlas*, a. Thirteen.

ديانت *diyānat*, s.m. Honesty, probity; piety, virtue. A.

ديبا *debā*, s.f. Brocade. P.

ديباجه *debāja*, } s.f. Exordium, introduc-
ديباچه *dībā<u>ch</u>a*, } tion, preface. A.

ديت *diyat*, s.m. Law of retaliation; price of blood; fine paid for murder, wounding, etc. A.

ديچکه *de<u>ch</u>ka*, s.f. A cauldron, stewpan, cooking pot. P. (*deg<u>ch</u>a*).

ديد *dīd*, s.m. Sight, show, spectacle. P.

ديدار *dīdār*, } s.m. Interview, sight, seeing. P.
ديدن *dīdan*, }

ديده *dīdah*, a. Seen, observed. *dīda*, s.f. The eye. P.

ديرش *der<u>sh</u>*, a. Thirty.

ديره *dera*, s.f. A dwelling, tent. H. (*derā*).

ديگ *deg*, s.m. A cauldron, boiler. P.

ديگچه *deg<u>ch</u>a*, s.f. Stewpan, saucepan. P.

دين *dīn*, s.m. Religion, faith. A.

دينار *dīnār*, s.m. Name of a coin, a ducat. The tenth part of a pice. A.

ديني *dīnī*, a. Religious; spiritual. A.

ديو *deo*, s.m. A demon, devil. P.

ديوال *dīwāl*, s.m. A wall. P. (*dīwār*).

ديوان *dīwān*, s.m. Divan, tribunal; steward, custodian; a book of poems, the rhymes of which end successively with every letter of the alphabet. P.

ديوانه *dīwānah*, a. Mad. See ليوني.

د

د *ḍāl* or *ḍe* is the fourteenth letter of the Pukkhto alphabet. It is similar in sound to the Sanskrit ड, and corresponds to the ڈ *ḍa* of the Hindūstānī.

داد *ḍāḍ*, s.m. Comfort, consolation.

داده *ḍāḍa*, s.f. An unripe ear of corn; the ear of Indian corn roasted for food.

دار *ḍār*, s.m. Anxiety, fear; fright, terror. H. (*ḍar*).

داره *ḍāra*, s.f. Arbour, shed, hut of branches, etc.

داګ *ḍāg*, s.m. } Clear, dry and level ground;
داګه *ḍāga*, s.f. } a patch of hard and bare ground.

دال *ḍāl*, s.m. A shield, buckler. H. (*ḍhāl*).

داندت *ḍānḍat*, s.m. A cotton carder's bow.

داندي *ḍānḍa-ī*, s.f. The beam of a balance; a pair of scales. H. (*ḍanḍī*). A blaze, conflagration.

دانګ *ḍāng*, s.m. A club, bludgeon, stick. H. Name of a copper coin, a penny.

دانګ لکي *ḍāng-laka-ī*, s.f. See توره آنه.

دانګوري *ḍāngora-ī*, s.f. A small club, baton.

دانګي *ḍānga-ī*, s.f. See تانګو.

دب *ḍab*, s.m. A slap, blow, thump. H. (*dhap*). An eddy, whirlpool; backwater, still water. Power, authority, strength. H. Fashion, shape; breeding, manners; mode, way. H. (*ḍhab*).

دبدبني *ḍabḍabanai*, a. Anxious, irresolute, wavering.

دبدوب *ḍabḍūb*, a. Apathetic, paralyzed, senseless.

دبره *ḍabara*, s.f. A pebble, stone, boulder.

دبلي *ḍabala-ī*, s.f. A mallet, pestle.

دبول *ḍabawul*, v.a. To beat, thrash, pommel.

دټي *ḍaṭai*, s.m. A brag, boaster, bully; term of abuse.

دچکه *ḍachka*, s.f. A trot; amble; jolt.

دد *ḍaḍ*, a. Empty, vacant, void; deep, bass, hoarse (sound).

ددوزه *ḍaḍūza*, s.f. Haze, smoke; flame and smoke.

دده *ḍaḍa*, s.f. The flank, side; edge, border; direction.

دران *ḍarān*, s.m. A bellow, low, bray (as of ox, ass, etc.).

درپل *ḍirpal*, s.m. A flatterer, parasite, toady.

درپلي *ḍirpalī*, s.f. Flattery, toadyism.

دره *ḍara*, s.f. Chip, splinter, fragment, shred, bit.

دز *ḍaz*, s.m. Bang, burst, explosion, report. A braggart, bully, blusterer.

دزدوز *ḍaz-ḍūz*, s.m. Report of firearms; a skirmish.

دغره *ḍaghara*, } s.f. Butting, shoving, pushing; a butt, shove, push.
دقره *ḍaqara*, } H. (*ṭakkar*).

دک *ḍak*, a. Full, replete.

دکال *ḍukāl*, s.m. Dearth, famine, scarcity. H.

دکه *ḍaka*, s.f. A thrust, jolt, shove, push. H. (*dhakkā*). A clutch, grab, pounce, swoop. a. Pregnant, with young; full.

دکي *ḍakai* or *ḍikai*, s.m. A sapling, young tree; a dry stump or stalk; a twig, switch, stick, dry bush.

دګلاند *ḍuglānd*, s.m. Amble, jog, trot; ambling horse.

دګه *ḍaga*, s.f. The penis.

دګي *ḍagai*, s.m. A thin, lean, bony ox or horse, a rosinante. H. (*ḍaggā*).

دل *ḍal*, s.m. A kind of rake; cantonment, camp.

دله *ḍala*, s.f. Assembly, crowd, mob. S. (*ḍal*).

دم *ḍum*, s.m. Name of a tribe or caste of musicians and dancers. H. (*ḍom*).

دمامه *ḍamāma*, s.m. A drum; drumming. *ḍamāme-rahal*, v.a. To drum.

ډمډوم *ḍamḍūm*, s.m. Rattle, roll, sound of a drum.

ډنبره *ḍanbara*, s.f. Hornet, wasp. Name of a tree with thorny stems and dotted leaves; the black berries are used as pepper, and sticks are made from the branches.

ډنډ *ḍanḍ*, s.m. A pool, pond, tank.

ډنډاره *ḍanḍāra*, s.f. A hornet, wasp; a stem, stalk, sprout (of herbs); stalk of leaves.

ډنډوکي *ḍanḍūkai*, s.m. A puddle, pool, tank.

ډنګ *ḍang*, s.m. Melody, tune, modulation. H.

ډنګر *ḍangar*, a. Thin, lean, scraggy. s.m. Cattle; a bullock, buffalo. H. (*ḍāngar*).

ډنګرۍ *ḍingara-ī*, ډنګلۍ *ḍingala-ī*, s.f. A machine for drawing water from wells (by means of a lever pole, which is supported on a post, and has a bucket slung at one end and a weight fixed at the other). H. (*ḍhenklī*).

ډو *ḍaw*, s.m. Flatus, emission of wind from behind.

ډوب *ḍūb*, a. Drowned, immersed, sunk. H.

ډوډه *ḍūḍa* or *ḍiwḍa*, s.f. The hip, haunch; hip joint.

ډوډۍ *ḍoḍa-ī*, s.f. Bread; food. S. (*roṭī*).

ډور *ḍūr*, s.m. Knitting. *ḍūr-kawul*, v.a. To knit. H. (*ḍor*).

ډوزک *ḍūzak*, s.m. A brag, bully.

ډوزه *ḍūza*, s.f. Chatter, prattle, nonsense; boasting, bragging, bluster, swagger.

ډوغ *ḍūgh*, s.m. Expectoration, hawking, clearing the throat of phlegm.

ډوغل *ḍoghal*, s.m. A cavity, hole, pit.

ډول *ḍaul*, s.m. Manner, mode; dress, fashion. H. *ḍol*, s.m. A large drum; the cog-wheel of a Persian irrigation wheel; hopper, rim of a hand- or other mill. H. (*ḍhol*).

ډولکي *ḍolkai*, s.m. A small drum.

ډوله *ḍola*, s.f. A small bowl or basin; a cup, jar.

ډولۍ *ḍola-ī*, s.f. A sedan chair or litter (carried by two men). H.

ډومبک *ḍūmbak*, s.m. The rattle or roll of a drum.

ډومبکي *ḍūmbakai*, s.m. A kettle-drum, tambourine, gong, small drum.

ډيډه *ḍīḍa*, s.f. A bung, plug, stopper; the piece of wood let into the hole of the lower stone of a handmill (to hold the iron pivot on which the upper one turns). *ḍeḍa*, s.f. A kind of ear-ring. H.

ډير *ḍer*, a. Abundant, plenty, enough; many, much. H. (*ḍher*). *ḍer-wālai*, s.m. Abundance, plenty.

ډيران *ḍerān*, s.m. A dunghill; a cloth worn by women during the menses.

ډيره *ḍera*, s.f. A camp, tent, temporary lodging. H. (*ḍerā*).

ډيرۍ *ḍera-ī*, s.f. A hillock, mound, heap, pile. H. (*ḍherī*). *ḍerai*, s.m. A crowd, mob, multitude.

ډيل *ḍīl*, s.m. Dress, mode, fashion; form, manner, shape; body, bulk, size. H. *ḍīl-ḍaul*, s.m. Appearance, dress, costume, fashion.

ډينګ *ḍīng*, s.m. A crane, stork (*Ardea sp.*).

ډينګ ډينګي *ḍīng-ḍīngai*, s.m. Ding-dong, lullaby, song, chime, nursery rhyme.

ډيوالي *ḍīwālai*, s.m. A bankrupt. H. (*dewāliyā*).

ډيوټ *ḍīwaṭ*, s.m. A candlestick, lamp-stand. S.

ډيود *ḍīwad*, s.m. A kind of perfumed candle used at weddings; a lamp-stand.

ډيوه *ḍīwa*, s.f. A lamp. S. (*dīwā*).

ذ

ذ *ẕāl* is the fifteenth letter of the Pukkhto alphabet, and the ninth of the Arabic. It is only found in words adopted from the latter language.

ذات *z̤āt*, s.m. Essence, nature, soul; body, person, substance; breed, caste, race. A.

ذبحه *z̤abḥa*, s.f. Sacrifice, slaughter. A.

ذخيره *z̤aḵẖīra*, s.f. Store, treasure; provisions, victuals. A.

ذره *z̤arra*, s.f. An atom, bit, jot, particle, little. A.

ذكر *z̤akar*, s.m. Membrum virile. A. *z̤ikr*, s.m. Memory, recital, mention, relation. A.

ذلت *z̤illat*, s.m. Baseness, vileness, meanness. A.

ذليل *z̤alīl*, a. Abject, base, mean. A.

ذم *z̤am*, s.m. Blame, reproach. A.

ذمه *z̤imma*, s.f. Charge, trust; duty, responsibility, obligation. A.

ذوق *z̤auq*, s.m. Taste; delight, joy, pleasure. A.

ذهن *z̤ihn*, s.m. Acumen, mind, sagacity, genius. A.

ذهين *z̤ahīn*, a. Acute, sagacious, witty. A.

ر

ر *re* is the sixteenth letter of the Pukkhto alphabet; it has a soft, but clear and distinct, sound as the *r* in the word *rain*.

را *rā*, A particle used with verbs and adverbs as a pronominal dative prefix for the first person; me, us, to me, to us. Ex. *rākawul*, to give me; *rāṭsakẖa*, with me, etc.

راب *rāb*, s.m. Syrup. H.

رابري *rābrī*, s.f. Caudle, gruel, pap. H.

رابطه *rābiṭa*, s.f. Bond, connection, link. A.

رابيا *rābiyā*, s.f. A pair of leather sacks or bags for carrying water upon bullocks, camels, etc.

راپور *rāpori*, راپوري *rāpore*, } ad. On this side, here, hitherward, near me, us, etc.; up to me, or us.

راتگ *rātag*, s.m. Arrival, coming.

راتلل *rātlal*, v.n. To arrive, come. See راغلل.

راج *rāj*, s.m. Government, kingdom, reign, sway. S. A mason, builder, bricklayer. P.

راجا *rājā*, s.m. A title of Hindu potentates; king, prince, duke. S.

راحت *rāḥat*, s.m. Ease, quiet, repose, tranquility. A.

راړه *rāṛa*, s.f. See بروړه.

راز *rāz*, s.m. A secret, mystery. P.

رازدار *rāz-dār*, a. Trusty, faithful. s.m. A confidant.

رازق *rāziq*, s.m. The Deity; provider of daily wants. A.

راس *rās*, s.m. A bridle, leading-string, reins. H. Head; head of cattle. A.

راست *rāst*, a. Right, just, true; straight, level; right, right hand. P.

راستي *rāstī*, s.f. Fidelity, justice, loyalty. ad. Truly, indeed, really. P.

راشبيل *rāshbel*, s.m. A wooden shovel (used to winnow corn).

راشتلي *rāshtalai*, s.m. Refuse grain left on the ground after removal of the corn from the threshing floor.

راشكي *rāshakai*, s.m. A heap, lump, small mound.

راشه *rāsha*, s.f. A heap of grain, provisions, supplies; eminence, hillock, mound. *rāsha-darsha*, s.f. Visiting, acquaintance, intercourse.

راښكو *rākkhko*, s.m. A wire drawer; puller, drawer, strainer.

راضي *rāẓī*, a. Agreed, content, willing, satisfied. A.

راغ *rāgh*, s.m. A meadow, lawn; villa, summer-house; hill-side, declivity. P.

راغلل *rāghlal*, v.n. To arrive, come. See راتلل.

راغه *rāghah*, s.m. Mountain skirt, hill side.

رافضي *rāfiẓī*, s.m. A heretic. A.

راقي *rāqī*, s.f. Cornelian, red agate.

راكس *rākis*, s.m. The centre one of a bevy of oxen treading out corn. *rākas*, s.m. Demon, devil. S.

راكول *rākawul*, v.a. To give me, or us.

راګ *rāg*, s.m. Music, song, tune. S.

رامزدګي *rāmzadagī*, s.f. A crowbar, lever; roller.

راموسي *rāmūsai*, s.m. The musk deer.

رانجونوني *rānjūnūnai*, s.m. A box or case for rānjah.

رانجه *rānjah*, s.m. Powdered antimony (applied to the edges of the eyelids as an ornament, and as a protection from excessive glare), collyrium.

رانده *rāndah*, a. Driven out, rejected, expelled. P.

رانيول *rānīwul*, v.a. To capture, seize, take.

راوړل *rāwṛal*, v.a. To bear, bring, carry, fetch, etc. (only applied to inanimate objects). To bear, produce, bring forth, yield (as young fruit, etc.). P. (*āwurdan*).

راوستل *rāwustal*, v.a. To lead, conduct, bring, fetch, etc. (only applied to animate objects). P. (*firistādan*).

راه *rāh*, s.m. Road, way; manner. (in comp.). P.

راهيت *rāhīt*, s.m. Head man of a village.

راهيسته *rāhīsta*, ad. Here, hither, this way, near me, etc.

راي *rāe*, s.m. Opinion, thought; counsel. P.

رب *rabb*, s.m. The Deity. A. *rub*, s.m. Juice, syrup. P.

ربا *ribā*, s.f. Usury. A. *ribā-khor*, s.m. An usurer.

رباب *rabāb*, s.m. A rebeck, violin. P.

رباط *rabāṭ*, s.m. Hostelry, inn, caravansary. A.

ربړ *rabaṛ*, s.m. Bother, trouble, toil, labour. H.

ربړول *rabṛawul*, v.a. To bother, worry, fatigue, drive about.

ربړيدل *rabṛedal*, v.n. To labour, toil, trudge about, fatigue oneself, etc.

ربنړه *rabanṛa*, s.f. Moonlight.

رپ *rap*, s.m. A shelf, cupboard. P. (*raf*).

رپک *rapak*, s.m. A small shelf, bracket.

رپيدل *rapedal*, v.n. To flutter, palpitate, quake, quiver, tremble, writhe, etc.

رت *rat*, A particle used with adjectives to denote intensity (mostly of colour). Ex. *rat-tor*, a. Jet black. *rat-shīn*, a. Bright green.

رتي *rata-ī*, s.f. Name of a seed used as a weight (*Abrus precatorius*). S. (*rattī*).

رټ *ra-aṭ*, s.m. A gush of tears, violent crying. a. Ample, capacious; loose, open, expanded.

رټل *raṭal*, v.a. To reject, turn away, repel (as a visitor). To abuse, scold, taunt, reprove. H. (*raṭnā*).

رجوع *rujū'*, s.f. Turning towards, return; bent, bias. A.

رچ *rach*, s.m. A weaver's loom. H. (*rāchh*). *ruch*, s.m. Avidity, desire, pleasure (in eating). S. An ox that wounds itself by crossing the feet in walking.

رحلت *riḥlat*, s.m. Departure; death. A.

رحم *raḥm*, s.m. Compassion, kindness, mercy, pity. A. *riḥam*, s.m. The womb. A.

رحمان *raḥmān*, s.m. The Deity. a. Merciful. A.

رحمت *raḥmat*, s.m. Compassion, mercy, pity. A.

رخت *rakht*, s.m. Apparel, furniture, goods, implements; a plough; tanned leather. P.

رخسار *rukhsār*, s.m. The cheek, face. P.

رخصت *rukhṣat*, s.m. Discharge, leave, permission. A.

رخنه *rakhna*, s.f. A cleft, fissure; hole, notch, fracture, flaw. P. See نخره.

رخه *rakha*, s.f. Hatred, malice, spite.

رد *radd*, s.m. Refutation, rejection; rejoinder. A.

رده *radda*, s.f. A layer, series, row; layer of bricks in a wall; work of a day (mason's). H. (*raddā*).

رديف *radīf*, s.m. Following in regular succession (as the letters of the alphabet), the rhyming word of a poem, a man riding behind another on the same horse, etc. A.

رډ *raḍ*, a. Ajar, open, wide open; amazed, confounded, petrified, stunned.

رړئي *raṛa-ī*, s.f. Seed of a tree (*Melia sempervirens*).

رز *raz*, s.m. A vineyard. P.

رزق *rizq*, s.m. See روزي.

رژيدل *raǰedal*, v.n. To cast off, moult, shed (as hair, horns, feathers, leaves, etc.); to be dispersed, shed, dropped, scattered. P. (*re<u>kh</u>tan*, *rez-*).

رس *ras*, s.m. Extract, juice, sap. S. Arriving (in comp. only). P.

رساله *risāla*, s.f. Mission; book; essay, letter; troop of horse. A.

رسالينديي *rasālīndai*, s.m. An archer, bowman.

رسد *rasad*, s.m. Grain, provision, stores; supplies collected for an army. P.

رسم *rasam*, s.m. Custom, law; model, plan. A.

رسوا *ruswā*, a. Disgraced, dishonoured. P.

رسواي *ruswā-ī*, s.f. Ignominy, disgrace, dishonour.

رسول *rasul*, s.m. A messenger, apostle; the prophet Muḥammad. A. *rasawul*, v.a. To send to, to convey to, conduct or lead to, etc.; make arrive. P. (*rasāndan*).

رسولئي *rasawla-ī*, s.f. Bunion, corn, gall, wen; a cancer, diseased gland.

رسئي *rasa-ī*, s.f. A cord, rope, string. S. (*rassī*).

رسيد *rasīd*, s.m. Arrival; acknowledgement, receipt. P.

رسيدل *rasedal*, v.n. To arrive, attain, reach, come up to, etc. P. (*rasīdan*).

رشته *ri<u>sh</u>ta*, s.f. Line, series; connexion, relation. *ri<u>sh</u>ta-dār*, s.m. Relation, kinsman. P.

رشک *ra<u>sh</u>k*, s.m. Envy, jealousy; malice, spite. P.

رشکي *ra<u>sh</u>akai*, s.m. A small mound, tumulus; heap, pile.

رشوت *ri<u>sh</u>wat*, s.m. A bribe. A.

رښتيا *ri<u>kkh</u>tiyā*, a. True. s.f. Truth, veracity, reality. P. (*rāstī*).

رښتينتوب *ri<u>kkh</u>tīn-tob*, s.m. Truthfulness, honesty, probity, righteousness.

رښتيني *ri<u>kkh</u>tīnai*, } a. True, truthful, veracious; honest, upright, righteous.
رښتوني *ri<u>kkh</u>tūnai*, }

رښکئي *ri<u>kkh</u>ka-ī*, s.f. A band, fillet, ribbon, shred, slip, strip, fibre. P. (*re<u>sh</u>a*).

رضا *raẓā*, s.f. Assent, consent; pleasure, will. A.

رطوبت *ruṭūbat*, s.m. Humidity, wetness. A.

رعايت *ri'āyat*, s.m. Attention, favour; protection, kindness; indulgence, remission; honour, respect. A.

رعيت *ra'yat*, s.m. A subject, tenant. A.

رغبت *ra<u>gh</u>bat*, s.m. Avidity, desire, wish; pleasure; affection, esteem. A.

رغړول *r<u>gh</u>aṛawul*, v.a. To trundle, roll (as a hoop, etc.). P. (*<u>gh</u>altānīdan*).

رغړيدل *r<u>gh</u>aṛedal*, v.n. To roll, wallow, tumble, toss (as an animal on the ground); to roll, trundle (as a stone down a slope). Def. in past ten. P. (*<u>gh</u>altīdan*).

رغښتل *r<u>gh</u>a<u>kkh</u>tal*, v.n. See preceding word.

رغي *ra<u>gh</u>ai*, s.m. A bowl, deep plate (as a soup plate); a deep and flat basket (in opposition to a shallow one).

رفتار *raftār*, s.m. Going, motion; gait, pace. P.

رفعه *raf'a*, s.f. Removing, repelling. A. *raf'a-daf'a*, s.f. Deciding, settling, finishing. A.

رفو *rafū*, s.m. Darning, mending clothes; a darn. A.

رفيق *rafīq*, s.m. Associate, comrade, friend. A.

رقص *raqṣ*, s.m. A dance, dancing. A.

رقعه *ruq'a*, s.f. A letter, note; bit, patch, piece. A.

رقم *raqam*, s.m. A royal edict; kind, sort; mode, method; mark, sign. A.

رقيب *raqīb*, s.m. Rival, enemy. A.

رکاب *rikāb*, s.m. Stirrup; escort, train. A. A platter, salver, tray. P.

رکابي *rikābī*, s.f. A plate, dish. P.

رکات *rakāt*, s.m. A genuflexion, prostration (in prayer). A. (*rak'at*).

رکښ *rakkkh*, s.m. Furrow, groove (as of a rifle); line, rut, track, scratch. P. (*rakh*).

رکن *rukn*, s.m. A pillar, prop, support. A.

رکوع *rukū'*, s.f. Bowing the head or body (in prayer). A.

رکيب *rikeb*, s.m. A stirrup iron. P. (*rakīb*).

رکيبي *rikebī*, s.f. See رکابي.

رګ *rag*, s.m. A vein; tendon; nerve. P. *rag-wahal*, v.a. To inoculate; to bleed, let blood.

رګړي *rigaṛai*, a. A child stinted in milk.

رګي *ragai*, s.m. Consanguinity, blood-relation; congenital or hereditary trait.

رمباړه *rambāṛa*, s.f. A bellow, low (as of oxen).

رمبکي *rambakai*, s.m. The bellow of a bull.

رمبه *ramba*, s.f. A borer, centre-bit, auger. H. (*barmā*).

رمبي *rambai*, s.m. A hoe, instrument for weeding; a cobbler's knife for cutting leather. H. (*ramba*).

رمز *ramaz*, s.m. A hint, nod, sign, wink. A.

رموز *ramūz*, s.m. Enigma, riddle. A.

رمول *ramawul*, v.a. To frighten, scare, terrify; to conduct or lead cattle (out to graze). H. (*ramnā*).

رمه *ra-ama*, s.f. Mucus; muco-purulent matter from the bowels; any mucous discharge; dysentery. Also *r-ima*, and mostly used in the plural as *ra-ame* or *r-ime*. P. (*rīm*). *ramma*, s.f. A herd, drove, or flock of cattle, sheep, etc.). P.

رمي *ra-amai* or *r-imai*, s.m. Dysentery, bowel complaint.

رميدل *ramedal*, v.n. To be alarmed, terrified; to flock, herd together. P. (*ramīdan*).

رنځ *randz*, s.m. Affliction, grief, pain; disgust, offence, vexation. P. (*ranj*).

رنځور *randzūr*, a. Afflicted, sick, pained; distressed, grieved; offended, vexed. P. (*ranjūr*).

رنځول *randzawul*, v.a. To afflict, pain, vex, etc.

رنځيدل *randzedal*, v.n. To fret, grieve, be hurt, pained, distressed. P. (*ranjīdan*).

رنجړومه *ranjaṛūma*, s.f. A collyrium box, case for powdered antimony. See رانجه.

رنجک *ranjak*, s.m. Priming powder. H.

رند *rind*, s m. Debauchee, blackguard, rake. P.

رندار *rundār*, s.f. See وروندار.

رنده *randa*, s.f. A plane; carpenter's tool. P.

رنګ *rang*, s.m. Colour; paint; kind, sort; manner, method, way. P.

رنګټ *rangaṭ*, s.m. Crying, blubbering, weeping. H. (*rohaṭ*).

رنګړ *ringaṛ*, a. } Beaten down; laid low,
رنګړي *ringaṛai*, } levelled (as crops by wind and rain).

رنګي *rangai*, a. Scanty, thin (as hair, crops, rain, etc.).

رنګين *rangīn*, a. Coloured, painted; variegated, etc. P.

رڼا *raṇā*, s.f. Light, daylight, brilliancy, lustre, etc.

رو *ro*, a. Easy, slow, soft, quiet. *ro-ro*, ad. Gently, slowly. *rū*, s.m. Face, surface. P.

روا *rawā*, a. Allowable, lawful, right, current, proper, etc. P. *rwā*, s.f. See ورا.

رواج *rawāj*, s.m. Custom, usage, fashion. a. Customary, current, fashionable, saleable. A.

رواش *rawāsh*, s.m. Rhubarb; blanched leaf-stalk of the plant. P.

روان *rawān*, a. Current, flowing, moving, going. P. *ruwān*, a. See وران.

روانه *rawānah*, a. Despatched, departed. P. *rawāna*, s.f. A pass, passport. P.

رواني *rawānī*, s.m. Course, proceeding. P. *ruwānī*, s.f. See ورانى.

روايت *riwāyat*, s.m. Fable, fiction, tale; history. A.

روبرو *rūbarū*, ad. Face to face, in front, opposite. P.

روپئي *rūpa-ī*, s.f. Name of a silver coin, rupee. S. (*rupiyā*).

روځ *rwadz*, s.f. A day, day, daytime. P. (*roz*).

روح *rūh*, s.m. Soul, spirit. A.

روخ *rokh* or *rūkh*, a. Fit, proper, ready; side, direction. P. (*rukh*).

روخي *rokhai*, s.m. Part, side (as of opponents).

رود *rod*, s.m. A river, stream. P.

رودل *rawdal*, v.a. To suck (as a child the breast). To mow, reap, cut (as corn, etc.).

رودنگ *rodang*, s.m. Madder (*Rubia tinctoria*). P.

روز *roz*, s.m. Day, daytime. (in comp). P.

روزگار *rozgār*, s.m. Employment, service; time, world. P.

روزمره *rozmarra*, ad. Always, daily, continually. P.

روزي *rozī*, s.f. Daily food, sustenance. P.

روژتي *rojatai*, s.m. A faster, keeper of Lent.

روژه *roja*, s.f. Fast, Lent. P. (*roza*).

روږد *rūgd*, a. Habituated, accustomed; affluent, comfortable. A. (*raghd*).

روست *rost*, a. Decayed, carious, corrupt, rotten; fetid, putrid, stinking. Also وروست.

روستو *rūsto* or *rwusto*, ad. See ورستو.

روښان *rokkhān*, a. Bright, light, luminous; clear, manifest, conspicuous; glittering, radiant, refulgent. P. (*roshān*).

روښن *rokkhan*, a. Bright, light, shining. P. (*roshan*).

روښنائي *rokkhnā-ī*, s.f. Brightness, light. P. (*roshnā-ī*).

روضه *rauza*, s.f. Mausoleum, tomb, garden. A.

روغ *rogh*, a. Hale, healthy, sound, vigorous, well.

روغبړ *roghbar*, s.m. Shaking hands, asking after health; embracing.

روغن *roghan*, s.m. Grease, fat, tallow. P.

روغه *rogha*, s.f. Amity, peace; harmony, intercourse, friendship.

روک *rok*, s.m. Cash, ready money. S.

روګ *rog*, s.m. A strap, thong of a sandal, strap of a churning stick, etc.

روګه *rwuga*, s.f. See وروږه.

رومال *rūmāl*, s.m. A handkerchief; towel, napkin. P.

رون *rūn*, s.m. The thigh. H. (*rān*).

رونق *raunaq*, s.m. Beauty, elegance; order, symmetry; ornament, splendour. A.

رونړ *rūnr*, a. Bright, lustrous, radiant, shining.

روه *roh*, s.m. Name of an extensive tract occupied by the Eastern highlands of Afghanistan, between Kandahar on the west and the Indus on the east, Badakhshan on the north and Sind on the south.

روهلي *rohilai*, s.m. A Rohilla, native of Roh, so called by the people of Hindūstān; a highlander.

روي *rawai* or *riwai*, s.m. A ghost, goblin, demon; nightmare. *rūe*, s.m. Face, countenance, surface; cause, reason, sake. P.

رويت *rūyat*, s.m. Appearance, shape, etc. A.

روېدل *rū-edal,* v.n. To cavil, dispute, wrangle.

رهته *rahata,* s.f. Content, ease, tranquility. A. (*rāhat*).

رهټ *rahaṭ,* s.m. A wheel for drawing water, an irrigation wheel. H.

رهيل *rahel,* s.m. Reading desk, support for a book. P. (*rahl*).

ري *rai,* s.m. Price current, rate, tariff.

ريا *riyā,* s.f. Dissimulation, evasion, hypocrisy. A. *rayā,* s.f. Braying of an ass.

رياست *riyāsat,* s.m. Command, dominion. A.

رياضت *riyāẓat,* s.m. Temperance, continence. A.

رياكار *riyā-kār,* s.m. A hypocrite. A.

ريبار *rebār,* s.m. A go-between, match-maker (between lovers or betrothed couples).

ريباري *rebārī,* s.f. Match-making, etc.

ريبدون *rebdūn,* s.m. Name of a tree (*Tecoma undulata*).

ريبل *rebal,* v.a. To mow, reap, cut (as corn, etc.).

ريچه *rīcha,* s.f. Young louse, nit, egg of a louse; a particle, jot, tittle. *rīche-rīche,* p. Atoms, particles, bits, etc.

ريخ *rīkh,* s.m. Dung of birds; loose stool, watery excrement of man or animals (as in diarrhœa). P.

ريخان *rīkhān,* a. Loose in the bowels, affected with diarrhœa, purged.

ريخي *rīkhai,* s.m. Dysentery, diarrhœa (in cattle). Tear, rent, slit (in clothes); a hole in a reservoir to let out the water.

ريدوان *redwān,* s.m. See ريبدون.

ريدي *redai,* s.m. Wild poppy; ragged robin; wild tulip.

ريزه *reza,* s.f. A bit, chip, filing, scrap, shred, etc. P.

ريږدول *regdawul,* v.a. To agitate, shake, move, etc.

ريږديدل *regdedal,* v.n. To flutter, shake, quiver vibrate.

رئيس *ra-īs,* s.m. A chief, prince, lord. A.

ريش *rīsh,* s.m. The beard (in comp.). P.

ريشل *reshal,* v.a. To spin, twist. P. (*resha,* fibre).

ريښم *rekkham,* s.m. Silk. P. (*resham*).

ريښمين *rekkhmīn,* a. Silken, silky. P. (*reshmīn*).

ريښه *rekkha,* s.f. A fibre, shred, thread, yarn, strip, etc. P. (*resha*).

ريګ *reg,* s.m. Sand (in comp.). P.

ريم *rīm,* s.m. Matter, pus, rheum; dregs, dross. P.

ريمن *rīman,* a. Purulent, mattery, filthy, etc.

رينه *rīna,* s.f. A cobbler's awl. Also *nīra.*

ريودل *riyawdal,* v.a. To raise, elevate, lift.

ريوړئ *rewṛa-ī,* s.f. A kind of sweetmeat. H. (*rewṛī*).

ريوند *rewand,* a. Sloping, slanting.

ړ

ړ *ṛe* or *ṛa* is the seventeenth letter of the Pukkhto alphabet. It has the same sound as the Sanskrit ड़ *ṛa,* or the Hindūstānī ڑ *ṛa,* with which it corresponds.

ړانځړه *ṛāndzaṛah,* s.m. Pitch, tar; crude turpentine.

ړپ *ṛap,* s.m. Mucus, slimy discharge from the bowels (as in dysentery).

ړپول *ṛapawul,* v.a. To agitate, shake.

ړپيدل *ṛapedal,* v.n. To palpitate, writhe, quiver, tremble, wag, wave, move, etc.

ړت *ṛat,* a. Red, reddish. S. (*rat*). *ṛat-ghwāye,* s.m. A red bull. *ṛata-gīra,* s.f. A red beard.

ړقول *ṛaqawul,* v.a. To mix, mingle, stir up; to jostle, shove, shake; punch, thump.

ړنبي *ṛunbai,* a. See وړنبي.

ړندول *ṛandawul,* v.a. To blind, deprive of sight.

رنديدل *ṛandedal*, v.n. To grow blind, become blind.

رنګ *ṛang*, a. Broken up, destroyed, spoiled, razed; desolate, ruined, deserted.

روانډي *ṛwānde*, p. See وړاندي.

روند *ṛūnd*, a. Blind, sightless; dark, obscure.

ري *ṛī*, in. A word used in driving cattle. *ṛai*, m. and *ṛa-ī*, f. A particle affixed to nouns as a sign of diminution. Ex. *khas*, s.m. A dry stick or straw. *khasaṛai*, s.m. A straw, splinter (such as gets blown into the eye). *kūza*, s.f. A water jar or guglet. *kūza·ṛa-ī*, s.f. A small gugglet.

ز

ز *ze* is the eighteenth letter of the Pukkhto alphabet, and eleventh of the Arabic. It has no corresponding letter in the Sanskrit. It is often used instead of the letters ځ and ج, and sometimes also for ژ and ږ.

زاد *zād*, s.m. Food, provisions. A. a. Born (in comp.). P.

زار *zār*, a. Afflicted, lamenting. s.m. Lament, groan, complaint. P. See ځار *dzār*.

زاري *zārī*, s.f. Crying, lamenting, groaning. P.

زاړي *zāṛai*, s.m. A weanling, young of cattle, etc. after being weaned. a. Late, former; old, worn out. *zāṛa-ī*, s.f. A woman, cow, etc. whose milk has run dry; an animal out of milk.

زامن *zāman*, s.m. pl. of ځوي *dzoe*.

زانګو *zāngo*, s.f. A cradle, rocking chair, swing; rocking, swinging.

زانو *zānū*, s.m. The knee. P.

زانړه *zānṛa*, s.f. A crane, the Coolan (*Ardea courlan*).

زاهد *zāhid*, s.m. Hermit, monk, recluse. a. Religious, devout. A.

زاي *zāe*, s.m. See ځوي *dzoe*.

زباد *zbād*, a. Proved, tested, tried, verified. A. (*isbāt*).

زبان *zabān*, s.m. Dialect language, speech; tongue. P.

زبر *zabar*, a. Above, superior; the vowel mark ـَ *a*. A.

زبردست *zabar·dast*, a. Oppressive, powerful, violent. P.

زبرګ *zburg*, s.m. Ancestor, elder; saint. a. Venerable, saintlike, reverend; great, large. P. (*buzurg*).

زبرګي *zburgī*, s.f. Eminence, greatness, superiority, etc.

زبون *zabūn*, a. Bad, evil, wicked; faulty, unlucky. P.

زبيښل *zbekkhal*, v.a. To suck, inhale, imbibe; to crumble, squash with the fingers (as bread, etc.).

زحمت *zaḥmat*, s.m. Affliction, trouble, pain. A.

زخم *zakhm*, s.m. A cut, wound, injury, sore, pain. A.

زخمي *zakhmī*, a. Wounded, hurt, pained, injured.

زخه *zakha*, s.f. A wart; excrescence on the bark of a tree. P.

زخيره *zakhīra*, s.f. See ذخيره.

زد *zad*, s.m. A blow, striking (in comp). P.

زدايت *zdāyat*, s.m. Descent, family, race.

زدويل *zdoyal*, v.a. To grate, pare, rub, wear away; polish, scour, etc. P. (*zidāyīdan*).

زده *zdah*, a. Acquired, known, learned; remembered, recognized. P. (*āzmūdah*). *zadah*, a. Struck, beaten (in comp.); decayed, withered (as wood, etc.). P.

زر *zar*, s.m. Gold, money, riches. P. *spīn·zar*, s.m. Silver. *srah·zar*, s.m. Gold, pure gold. a. A thousand. P. (*hazār*). *za-ar* or *z-ir*, ad. Quickly, speedily, sharply. P. (*zūd*)

زراعت *zarā'at*, s.m. Agriculture, husbandry; crops, cultivation. A.

زربرخ *zarbarakh*, s.m. Talc, mica. A. (*abraq*).

زربيانګ *zarbiyāng*, s.m. Name of a currier's tool; a wooden scraper or muller for cleaning leather.

زردالو *zardālū*, s.m. An apricot. P.

زردکه *zardaka*, s.f. A carrot; name of a bird, yellow-hammer. P. (*zardak*).

زرغاله *zarghāla*, s.f. A lying-in or puerperal woman; the forty days after childbirth, puerperal state.

زرغون *zarghūn*, a. Green, verdant; sprouted, grown, germinated, fresh, new.

زرکه *zarka*, s.f. Red-legged partridge, chikor.

زرګر *zar·gar*, s.m. A goldsmith. P.

زرګير *zar·gīr*, s.m. A thumbstall of leather (worn by archers, etc.).

زرني *zaranai*, s.m. A spy, scout, detective. *zarana-ī*, s.f. Peeping, spying; scouting, watching.

زرنيخ *zarnīkh*, s.m. Arsenic. P.

زرنړه *zaranra*, s.f. Mud, slime, ooze (as at bottom of pools, etc.). *zaranrah*, s.m. See زالخړه.

زري *zarai*, s.m. A spy, scout; the sight (at the muzzle) of a gun. *zarī*, a. Golden, worked or woven with gold. P. *zare·zare*, a. Shattered, broken to atoms, etc. See ذره.

زرين *zarīn*, a. Golden. P.

زړوکي *zaṛūkai*, s.m. A dress, garment; apparel, clothes; old rags, old clothes, etc.

زړه *zṛah*, s.m. Heart, mind, soul; courage, spirit; the heart. P. (*zahra*).

زړي *zaṛai*, } s.m. A flat seed (as of melons, زنړي *zanrai*, } etc.) in opposition to round ones (called tukhm).

زږګي *ziggai*, s.m. See شيشکي.

زښت *zikkht*, a. Ugly, deformed; stern, severe. P. (*zisht*).

زعفران *z'afarān*, s.m. Saffron. A.

زغ *zagh*, s.m. See زغ.

زغاښتل *zghākkhtal*, v.n. To run, flee. Def. in. pres. ten. See زغليدل.

زغرد *zghard*, a. Fast, quick. ad. Quickly, fleetly.

زغره *zghara*, s.f. Chain armour, mail. P. (*zira*).

زغلول *zghalawul*, v.a. To drive, put to flight, make run, urge (as a horse).

زغليدل *zghaledal*, v.n. To run, flee. See زغاښتل. P. (*gurekhtan*).

زغمل *zghamal*, v.a. To bear, endure, undergo, sustain, suffer.

زغن *zaghan*, s.m. A kite. P.

زقوم *zaqūm*, s.m. Name of a plant, Indian cactus; it is said to form the diet of those condemned to hell. A.

زک *zik*, s.m. An inflated hide for crossing over rivers.

زکات } زکاة } *zakāt*, s.m. Alms distributed according to the rules laid down in the Qurān. A. زکوت }

زکام *zukām*, s.m. Catarrh, influenza, cold. A.

زکه *zaka*, c. See څکه. P. (*zirā ki*).

زکي *zakī*, a. Pious, continent. A.

زګ *zag*, s.m. Foam, froth, scum. H. (*jhāg*).

زګيروي *zgerwai*, s.m. A groan, moan, wail, whine.

زلزله *zalzala*, s.f. An earthquake. A.

زلفه *zulfa*, s.f. A curl, ringlet, lock of hair. P. (*zulf*).

زلفي *zulfa-ī*, s.f. A sword knot, tassel; door chain, staple, hook. P.

زلل *zalal*, s.m. Injury, loss, deficiency; blundering, erring; falling, stumbling. P.

زلمي *zalmai*, s.m. A youth, young man. A. (*talmīz*).

زلو *zallū*, s.m. A leech. P.

زلچه *zalīcha*, s.f. A rug, woollen carpet. P. (*qālīcha*).

زم *zam*, s.m. Hurt, injury, wound. P. (*za<u>kh</u>m*). *zam·zmolai*, a. Halt, helpless, crippled, maimed. Also *zam·zambolai.*

زمانه *zamāna*, s.f. Age, time; fortune; the world; the heavens. A. *zamāna·sāz*, s.m. A time server. P.

زمبور *zambūr*, s.m. See امبور.

زمرد *zumurrud*, s.m. An emerald. P.

زمري *zmarai*, s.m. A tiger. Name of a plant, Dwarf palm (*Chamærops Richiana*).

زمزم *zamzam*, s.m. Hagar's well at Mecca. A.

زمزمه *zamzama*, s.f. A concert; singing. A.

زمستان *zamistān*, s.m. Winter. P.

زمکه *zmaka*, s.f. Land, ground, earth, soil; the earth.

زموخ *zmo<u>kh</u>*, a. } Astringent, binding, dry,
زموخت *zmo<u>kh</u>t*, } rough (to the taste). P. (*zamu<u>kh</u>t*).

زمول *zmol*, a. } Helpless, crippled, maimed,
زمبول *zambol*, } wounded, unable to move from wounds.

زمولي *zmolai*, a. } Carried by the hands and
زمبولي *zambolai*, } legs (as a wounded man). See زم. (For *zam·bīwulai*).

زمي *zma-ī*, s.f. Name of a plant that is burnt for the potash it yields (*Suæda fruticosa*).

زمين *zamīn*, s.m. The earth; ground, soil. land. P.

زميندار *zamīn·dār*, s.m. A farmer; peasant. P.

زميندارى *zamīn·dārī*, s.f. Agriculture, husbandry; an estate, farm.

زن *zan*, s.f. A woman, wife. P.

زنا *zinā*, s.m. Adultery, fornication. P.

زناکار *zinā·kār*, s.m. An adulterer, fornicator.

زنانه *zanāna*, s.f. A woman, female; wife; the women's apartments. a. Feminine. P.

زنبق *zanbaq*, s.m. The tuberose (*Polianthes tuberosa*). Flowers embroidered on a dress. P.

زنبک *zunbuk*, s.m. Tassel, knot, rosette, flower.

زنبه *zunba*, s.f. Down or hair on the body.

زنځير *zan<u>dz</u>īr*, s.m. A chain. P. (*zanjīr*).

زندان *zindān*, s.m. A prison, jail. P.

زندګاني *zindagānī*, } s.f. Existence, life; liv-
زندګي *zindagī*, } ing, livelihood. P.

زنده *zindah*, a. Alive, living. P.

زندئ *zunda-ī*, s.f. A halter, hangman's rope.

زنډي *zuṇḍai*, s.m. A tassel, pendent. H. (*jhuṇḍ*).

زنزه *zanza*, s.f. A centipede.

زنکئ *zanka-ī*, s.f. Cummin seed.

زنګ *zang*, s.m. Mould, rust. P. (*zangār*). Cymbal, bell (for the feet of dancing women). Name of a country, Zanguebar.

زنګل *zangal*, v.n. To hang, swing, wave, sway, etc. s.m. A forest, wood; wilderness. S. (*jangal*).

زنګول *zangawul*, v.a. To rock, swing, wave, etc.

زنګوله *zangūla*, s.f. A small bell, cymbal. P.

زنګون *zangūn*, s.m. The knee. P. (*zānū*). *zangānah·starga*, s.f. The knee cap, knee pan.

زنګي *zangī*, s.m. An African, negro. P.

زنګيدل *zangedal*, v.n. To hang, swing, wave, vibrate.

زنل *zanal*, v.a. To imbed, insert, implant; strike, thrust, hit; stab, prick, impale. P. (*zadan, zan-*).

زنه *zana*, s.f. The chin; pit of the chin. P. (*zana<u>kh</u>*).

زنړغوزه *za<u>nr</u><u>gh</u>oza*, s.f. A pine cone, fir cone; pine tree; seed of the edible pine. P. (*<u>ch</u>al<u>gh</u>oza*).

زنړي *za<u>nr</u>ai*, s.m. A flat seed (as of melons, etc.). A boy under the age of puberty; a school-boy.

زوال *zawāl*, s.m. Decline, wane, setting. A.

زوانکه *zawānaka*, s.f. Acne, pimples on the face of youths.

زود *zūd*, ad. Quick, quickly. P.

زودي *zūdī*, s.f. Alacrity, haste, quickness.

زور *zor*, s.m. Force, power, strength; effort, violence, vigour; weight. P. *zaur*, s.m. Anxiety, grief, sorrow, pain, trouble. A. (*jaur*). *zwar*, s.m. The vowel-point zabar.

زوراور *zorawar*, a. Powerful, violent, strong. P.

زورل *zoral*, v.a. To vex, irritate; compel, force, coerce; to digest.

زوړ *zoṛ*, a. Aged, ancient, old, worn out. P. (*zāl*).

زوزات *zauzāt*, } s.m. Children, issue, progeny, offspring. P. (*zah-*
زوزاد *zauzād*, } *wa-zād*).

زوږ *zwag*, s.m. Clamour, din, noise, sound.

زوښه *zūkkha*, s.f, A syrup or jelly prepared from ber or jujube berries.

زوغال *zūghāl*, s.m. Charcoal. P. (*zughāl*).

زولن *zawlan* or *ziwlan*, a. Purulent, suppurating, mattery.

زوم *zum*, s.m. A son-in-law. S. (*jamā-ī*). *zwam*, a. Deficient, less, little; deducted, subtracted. ad. Rarely, seldom.

زومګي *zūmgai*, s.m. A son-in-law. S. (*jamā-ī*).

زومنه *zwamna*, s.f. Deficiency, loss.

زوول *zowul*, v.a. To bear, bring forth (as young). P. (*zādan*).

زوولي *zowulai*, a. Born, brought forth.

زوه *ziwa* or *zawa*, s.f. Matter, pus, ichor.

زوي *zoe*, s.m. A son.

زويرګي *zwergai*, s.m. See زګيروي.

زه *zah*, pr. I, the first person.

زهر *zahar*, s.m. Poison. P.

زهره *zahra*, s.f. Bile; the gall bladder; courage, heart, pluck. P.

زهګير *zahgīr*, s.m. The catch or notch at the end of a bow (to hold the bow-string).

زهوب *zahūb*, s.m. Matter, discharge (of a sore), pus.

زهي *zahe*, in. Bravo! Well done! Lo! P.

زهيدل *zahedal*, v.n. To decrease, waste, grow thin.

زهير *zahīr*, a. Reduced, weakened, thin (from sickness); melancholy, sad. A.

زي *zai*, s.m. Son, child, descendant (in comp.). P. Added to Afghan surnames it denotes the clan or tribe. Ex. *Yūsufzai*, s.m. A man of clan Yusuf. *Yūsufza-ī*, s.f. A Yusufzai woman. *Yūsufzī*, s.m. pl. The Yusufzais.

زيات *ziyāt*, a. Excessive, surplus, too much; more. A. (*ziyād*).

زياتي *ziyātī*, a. Excessive, great, more. (*ziyādatī*).

زيارت *ziyārat*, s.m. A shrine; tomb of a saint; visiting a shrine. A.

زيان *ziyān*, s.m. Damage, deficiency, loss; miscarriage, abortion. P.

زيانکار *ziyān-kār*, } a. Injurious, pernicious,
زياني *ziyānī*, } noxious. P.

زيب *zeb*, s.m. Beauty, elegance, ornament. P.

زيتونه *zaitūna*, s.f. The olive tree. A. (*zaitūn*).

زير *zer*, a. Below, under. The vowel point ـِ *i*. P.

زيراستر *zerāstar*, s.m. The lining of a dress. P.

زيرک *zīrak*, a. Acute, sagacious, penetrating, witty. P.

زيرکي *zīrakī*, s.f. Acumen, discernment, wit. P.

زيرمه *zerma*, s.f. Arrangement, preparation, disposal, setting in order.

زيري *zerai*, s.m. Glad tidings, good news.

زيريګر *zerai-gar*, } s.m. Bearer of glad
زيري ګري *zerai-garai*, } tidings.

زيړ *ziyaṛ*, a. Yellow. P. (*zard*). s.m. Brass.

زيړانکه *ziyaṛānaka*, s.f. The yellow wagtail.

زيړګله *ziyaṛgula*, s.f. Name of a herb (*Calendula officinalis*).

زيړي *ziyaṛai*, s.m. Jaundice, icterus; yellowness.

زيږ *zīg*, a. Hard, rough, harsh, rigid, stiff; stern, austere, severe. P. (*zisht*).

زيږول *zegawul*, v.a. To beget, procreate, produce.

زيږيدل *zegedal*, v.n. To be born, begotten, brought forth. P. (*zā-īdan*).

زيست *zīst*, s.m. Existence, life; employment. P.

زيله *zela*, s.f. A creeping plant; creeper, tendril.

زيم *zyam*, s.m. Humidity, moisture, dampness.

زيمناك *zyam-nāk*, a. Damp, humid, moist.

زين *zīn*, s.m. A saddle. P.

زينت *zīnat*, s.m. Beauty, elegance; dress, ornament. A.

زينه *zīna*, s.f. A ladder, steps. P.

زيور *zewar*, s.m. Jewels, ornaments. P.

ژ

ژ *ĵe* is the nineteenth letter of the Pukkhto alphabet, and the fourteenth of the Persian, from which it is adopted. It has the sound of *s* in the word *pleasure*. By the Eastern Afghans it is sometimes used for ج or ږ, and by the Western tribes for ز.

ژامه *ĵāma*, s.f. The jaw, jaw-bone. P.

ژانه *ĵāna*, s.f. Adulation, flattery; coaxing.

ژاوله *ĵāwla*, s.f. Resin, pitch, wax, gum.

ژبه *ĵiba*, s.f. The tongue; language, speech; dialect. S. (*jībh*).

ژبونكي *ĵabūnkai*, s.m. Collar, cuff, frill etc. (of a garment).

ژر *ĵ-ir* or *ĵa-ar*, ad. Quickly, speedily. See زر *zir*.

ژرنده *ĵaranda*, s.f. A water mill. See جرنده.

ژړا *ĵaṛā*, s.f. Crying, sobbing, weeping. P. (*giriya*).

ژړل *ĵaṛal*, v.n. To weep, cry, sob, wail.

ژغند *ĵghand*, s.m. A notch, nick, dent.

ژغ *ĵagh*, s.m. See جغ.

ژغورل *ĵghoral*, v.a. To keep, preserve, protect, guard, defend, nourish, support.

ژغوري *ĵghorai*, s.m. Protector, guardian, etc.

ژغونډي *ĵaghūnḍai*, s.m. The peg in a yoke (to prevent its slipping from the ox's neck).

ژلئ *ĵala-ī*, s.f. Hail. P. (*ĵāla*).

ژمي *ĵimai*, s.m. Winter, cold weather.

ژړي *ĵaṛrai*, s.m. Catgut, bow-string, fiddle-string. A boy, lad, school boy.

ژواك *ĵwāk*, s.m. Life, existence, being.

ژوبل *ĵobal*, a. Bruised, wounded, hurt.

ژور *ĵawar*, a. Deep, depressed, sunk.

ژورغالي *ĵawar-ghālai*, s.m. A pit or trench dug round the root of a tree (for water); a small pit made to hold a plant or sapling.

ژوره *ĵawara*, s.f. A leech.

ژوژ *ĵwaĵ*, s.m. See زوږ.

ژوند *ĵwand*, s.m. }
ژوندون *ĵwandūn*, } Being, life, existence.

ژوندي *ĵwandai*, a. Alive, living. P. (*zinda*).

ژوول *ĵowul*, }
ژويل *ĵoyal*, } v.a. To chew, masticate; chew the cud. P. (*ĵāwīdan*).

ژئ *ĵa-ī*, s.f. Catgut, string of a bow or violin, etc. A water bag made of hide.

ږ

ږ *ge* is the twentieth letter of the Pukkhto alphabet, and peculiar to the Afghan language. By the Western tribes it is sounded like ژ, with which it is often interchanged. By the Eastern tribes it is pronounced as گ, for which it is generally changed. In words introduced from Persian or Sanskrit, where this letter replaces ج, it has the sound of that letter or of *z* in *azure*.

ږدل *gdal*, v.a. To fix, place, put, set, lay. Def. in past ten. See کیښول. P. (*hīdan*).

ږدن *gdan*, s.m. A kind of millet. H. (*kodon*).

ږغ *gagh*, s.m. Noise, sound; accent, voice.

ږغورل *gghoral*, v.a. See ژغورل.

ږلۍ *gala-ī*, s.f. Hail. See ژلۍ.

ږمنځ *gamandz*, ږمنز *gamanz*, } s.f. A comb, hair comb.

ږو *go*, ad. A word used in comp. to denote oath or affirmation. Ex. *khudāe-go*, in. By God!

ږوند *gwand*, s.m. See ژوند.

ږوږ *gwag*, s.m. Noise, clamour, din, etc.

ږوی *gawai*, s.m. A being, creature, person. See وګړي.

ږیره *gīra*, s.f. The beard. P. (*rīsh*).

ږیري *gīrai*, a. Bearded, having a beard. *spīn-gīrai*, s.m. A white beard, grey beard, old man, elder. *rat-gīrai*, s.m. A red beard, one who dyes the beard with *nakrīza* (henna).

س

س *sīn* is the twenty-first letter of the Pukkhto alphabet, and the twelfth of the Arabic. It has the same sound as the English *s* in the word *song*, and in Pukkhto is sometimes, though wrongly, changed for the letters خ and ح.

سا *sā*, s.f. Breath, life, respiration, vital spark. S. (*sāns*).

سابق *sābiq*, a. Former, preceding. A.

سابون *sābūn*, s.m. Soap. A.

سابو *sābū*, s.m. Name of a grass from which mats are made (*Panicum Colonum*).

سابه *sābah*, s.m. Name of a grass (see preceding). Vegetables, greens.

ساپټ *sāpaṭ*, ad. Completely, entirely, wholly.

ساتل *sātal*, v.a. To keep, preserve; defend, protect, shelter; nourish, support.

ساتندوی *sātandoe*, ساتونکی *sātūnkai*, } s.m. Guardian, keeper, protector, etc.

ساتول *sātūl*, s.m. A chopper, cleaver; bill-hook.

ساحر *sāḥir*, s.m. Magician, juggler, conjurer. A.

ساخت *sākht*, s.m. Make, construction; fabrication, pretence. P. A kind of leather, morocco leather.

ساختګي *sākhtagī*, s.f. Fabrication, pretence, sham.

ساخه *sākha*, s.f. A grating sound; calamity; judgment day. A. (*ṣākhat*).

ساد *sād*, a. Honest, good, trustworthy. S. (*sādh*).

سادو *sādū*, s.m. Impostor, knave, cheat.

ساده *sādah*, a. Plain, simple, unadorned; artless, candid, sincere; beardless; white. P.

سادین *sādīn*, s.m. Newly ploughed land, land prepared for sowing.

سار *sār*, s.m. Good news, glad tidings.

سارمه *sārma*, s.f. Name of a potherb.

سارنده *sārinda*, سارنګۍ *sāringa-ī*, } s.f. A violin, guitar.

ساروان *sārwān*, s.m. A camel driver. P. (*sārbān*).

ساري *sārai*, a. Equal, par. s.m. A match, compeer, peer. P. (*sār*).

سړه *sāṛa*, s.f. Cold weather; cold, frigidity.

ساز *sāz*, s.m. Accoutrements; apparatus, furniture; a musical instrument. P.

سازش *sāzish*, s.m. Confederacy, combination; plot, conspiracy. P.

سازنده *sāzindah*, s.m. Maker, peformer. P.

ساعت *sā'at*, s.m. A minute, moment, hour. A.

ساعي *sā'ī*, s.m. Enthusiasm, zeal. a. Eager, earnest, zealous. A.

ساغر *sāghar*, s.m. A bowl, goblet. P.
ساغری *sāgharī*, s.m. The space between the tail and *anus* of a horse; a kind of leather, shagreen. P.
ساکن *sākin*, a. Quiet, tranquil, at rest. s.m. Resident, inhabitant. A.
ساگ *sāg*, s.m. Greens, potherbs, vegetables. S.
ساگینړي *sāgīnṛai*, s.m. A dish of rice and greens.
سالن *sālan*, s.m. Mixed or spiced food; flesh, fish, etc. eaten with rice or bread. H.
سالو *sālū*, s.m. A kind of red cloth of cotton. S.
ساله *sālah*, a. Aged (in comp. only); added to numeral adjectives denotes age or years. Ex. *chār-sālah*, a. Four years old. P.
سالیانه *sāliyānah*, a. Annual, yearly. P.
سامان *sāmān*, s.m. Apparatus, furniture, tools; arms, accoutrements. P.
سامانه *sāmāna*, s.f. Parade, pomp, state.
سامع *sāmi'*, s.m. A hearer. A.
سان *sān*, s.m. Muster, review of an army; calico; a grindstone, whetstone. P.
سانده *sānda*, s.f. Lament, wail.
ساندا *sānḍā*, s.m. Name of a kind of lizard with a thick tail. H.
سانګه *sānga*, s.f. A travelling party; a spear. S. A lament, wail; a bough, branch.
سانګۍ *sānga-ī*, s.f. A pitchfork.
سانړ *sāṇr*, s.m. A stallion, bull. S.
ساو *sāw*, s.m. Tax, tribute. *sāū*, a. Noble, well bred. P. (*shāhū*).
ساونړ *sāwaṇr*, s.m. Name of the fourth Hindu month, July-August. S. (*sāwan*).
ساه *sāh*, s.m. Breath, vital spark, life. S. (*sāns*).
ساه‌لنډي *sāh-lanḍai*, a. Asthmatic. *sāh-lanḍī*, s.m Asthma, dyspnœa, shortness of breath.
ساه‌ویسا *sāh-wīsā*, s.f. Belief, faith, trust, hope.
سایل *sāyil*, s.m. Asker, petitioner. A.
سایه *sāya*, s.f. Shade, shadow; apparition, spectre; shelter, protection; awning, canopy. P.
سب *sibb*, s.m. Reproach, reviling. A.
سبا *sabā*, s.m. Dawn, morning; morrow. A. (*ṣabāḥ*).
سبب *sabab*, s.m. Cause, motive, reason; means, instrument; affinity, connexion, relationship. A.
سبحان *subḥān*, s.m. Praising (God); the Deity. A. *subḥān-allah*, in. Good God! Oh God! A.
سبزه *sabza*, s.f. Herbage, verdure; incipient beard, bloom. *sabzah*, a. Grey, iron grey; sallow. P.
سبزي *sabzī*, s.f. Greens, vegetables. P.
سبق *sabaq*, s.m. A lecture, lesson, reading. A.
سبک *subuk*, a. See سپک.
سبوس *sabūs*, s.m. Bran, chaff. P.
سپارش *sipārish*, s.m. Recommendation, intercession. P. (*sifārish*).
سپارل *spāral*, v.a. To commit, consign, give in charge, intrust; recommend, etc. P. (*sipārīdan* or *sipurdan*).
سپاره *sipāra*, s.f. Name of a chapter in the Qurān (for *sīpāra*, thirty sections). P. *spāra*, s.f. An iron ploughshare.
سپاه *sipāh*, s.m. An army; a soldier. P.
سپاهي *spāhī*, s.m. A soldier. P.
سپر *spar*, s.m. A shield, buckler. P. (*sipar*).
سپرخي *sparkhai*, s.m. A packing needle, skewer, pin.
سپرد *sipurd*, s.m. Care, charge, keeping, trust. P.
سپرغه *spaghra*, s.f. A well. (Raverty).
سپرلني *sparlanai*, s.m. Cavalier, horseman, rider.
سپرلي *sparlai*, s.m. The spring. *sparlī*, s.f. Riding, horse riding, equitation.
سپره *sapara*, s.f. Name of the second month of the Muḥammadan calendar. A. (*ṣafar*).

supra, s.f. The anus; a napkin, table-cloth. P. (*sufra*).

سپړل *spaṛal*, سپړدل *spaṛdal*, v.a. To undo, unclose, unfold, unravel, open out, etc.

سپږن *spaẓan*, a. Lousy, full of vermin, filthy.

سپږه *spaga*, s.f. A louse. P. (*sapash*).

سپک *spuk*, a. Light, flimsy; cheap; mean, trifling. P. (*subuk*).

سپلم *spalam*, s.m. See سپیرلم.

سپلمه *spalama*, s.f. A ring-dove.

سپلمي *spalma-ī*, s.f. Name of a plant (*Calotropis procera, Asclepias gigantea*), the mudar plant.

سپم *spam*, s.m. The eye of a needle; aperture, orifice, perforation. A. (*famm*).

سپند *sipand*, s.m. See سپیلني.

سپندخ *spandakh*, s.m. A large ball of worsted or cotton; a stuffed calf placed near a cow deprived of her own (to make her give milk).

سپنړسی *spanṛsai*, s.m. Cord, thread, twine, string.

سپوږمځ *spokhadz*, سپوږمځه *spokhadza*, s.f. Hypogastrium, belly below the navel, pubes, pelvis.

سپور *spor*, a. Dry, plain, unmixed, stale (as food). *spora-doḍa-ī*, s.f. Dry bread. *spor*, a. Riding, mounted, seated upon. s.m. A horseman, cavalier. P. (*sawār*).

سپوږمي *spogma-ī*, s.f. Moon, moonlight.

سپونړي *spūnṛai*, s.m. Ringworm, porrigo.

سپه *sipah*, s.m. See سپاه.

سپهر *sipahr*, s.m. Celestial sphere, sky; fortune, time; the world. P. *sipahar*, s.m. Afternoon, the third watch. P.

سپي *spai*, s.m. A dog, hound.

سپیازه *spiyāza*, s.f. Abortion, miscarrying, dropping the young prematurely (applied to brutes only). a. Raw, unripe; useless, foolish.

سپیټه *sapeṭa*, ad. Never, positively, not a bit.

سپېڅل *spedzal* or *spetsal*, v.a. To clean, clear, purify.

سپېڅلي *spetsalai*, a. Spotless, clean, neat, spick-span.

سپید *saped*, a. White. P. (*safed*).

سپیدار *spedār*, s.m. The white poplar tree. P. (*sefedār*).

سپیده *sapeda*, s.f. White lead; dawn, day-break. P. (*safeda*).

سپیدي *sapedī*, s.f. Whiteness; dawn. P. (*safedī*).

سپیرکۍ *sperka-ī*, s.f. Lovage (the plant and seed). (*Ligusticum ajowan*).

سپیرلم *sperlam*, s.m. The grey-tailed fox; any quadruped (cattle) with a grey or white tail.

سپیره *sperah*, a. Grey, ashy, hoary; pale, colourless, ghastly.

سپیره کی *sperah-kai*, a. Pale, ashy, ghastly; coward.

سپیږمه *spegma*, s.f. The nostril.

سپیښته *spekkhta*, s.f. Membrane covering the stomach or heart; peritoneum, pericardium.

سپیلني *spelanai*, s.m. Name of a plant, Syrian rue (*Peganum harmala*).

سپیمه *spiyama*, s.f. A bitch in heat seeking the dog.

سپین *spīn*, a. White, pure, fair, spotless.

سپینګه *spenga*, s.f. See سپیږمه.

سپینه *spīna*, s.f. The tendon of the heel (*tendo Achillis*). Fat, suet, tallow.

ست *sat*, s.m. Invitation (to dinner), hospitality; civility, politeness. a. Flat, level; supine, straight on the back. H. (*chit*).

ستا *stā*, The genitive case singular of the second personal pronoun تهٔ *tah*; of thee, thine.

ستار *sitār*, s.m. A guitar (of three strings), violin. P.

ستاره *stāra*, s.f. A star; a kind of firework. P. (*sitāra*). *stāra-prewatal*, v.n. To be unlucky, to have one's star in the descendant.

ستاسُ *stāsu*, } pl. of ستا. Yours, of you.
ستاسو *stāso*, }

ستانه *stāna*, s.f. A threshold; house, family, race (of saints particularly). P. (*āstāna*).

ستايل *stāyal*, v.a. To laud, praise, glorify, extol. P. (*sitūdan*).

ستر *satr*, s.m. Veiling, covering, concealing; privates. A. *star*, a. Big, bulky, great, huge, strapping, etc.; deep, profound (as a well). P. (*saturg*).

سترغلي *starghalai*, s.m. The orbit; eyeball.

ستركه *starga*, s.f. The eye; a planet. (Diminutive of P. *sitāra*).

ستره *satra*, s.f. A curtain, mantle, veil.

ستري *satrai*, s.m. A cut crop as it lies on the field; pile of corn sheaves; heap, pile, mass. H. (*sathrāw*). *satrai-watrai*, a. Scattered, lying about (as leaves on the ground).

ستړي *staṛai*, a. Fatigued, weary, tired, fagged. P. (*siturdah*).

ستغ *stagh*, s.m. A bot, worm in the skin of cattle; a boil or abscess produced by the worm. a. Astringent, binding, rough to the taste; mean, sordid, avaricious.

ستل *satal*, s.m. A copper pail or bucket, cauldron. P.

ستم *sitam*, s.m. Oppression, violence, tyranny. P. *stam*, s.m. Forcing, straining; labour, travail. *stam-wahal*, v.a. To force, strain (as at stool, etc.).

ستن *stan*, s.f. A needle, pin; pillar, post. P. (*sitūn*).

ستنه *stana*, s.f. Return, retreat; retrenchment.

ستنول *stanawul*, v.a. To send back, return; to take back, retrench.

ستنيدل *stanedal*, v.n. To return, go back, retire.

ستوان *satwān*, s.m. Peasemeal, meal of parched corn, pulse, etc. S. (*sattū*).

ستوخ *stokh*, } a. Straight, difficult; bad, hateful. P. (*satakh*).
ستوغ *stogh*, }

ستور *sutūr*, s.m. Cattle, beast of burden. P.

ستوري *storai*, s.m. A star. P. (*sitāra*).

ستوكه *stoga*, s.f. See استوكه.

ستومان *stomān*, a. Disgusted, vexed; repentant, sorry; fatigued, tired, fagged, weary.

ستون *stūn*, a. Returned, sent back; retrenched, withdrawn.

ستونول *stūnawul*, v.a. To send back, call back, recall; withdraw, retrench, subtract.

ستونيدل *stūnedal*, v.n. To return, come back; retire, etc.

ستوني *stūnai*, s.m. The larynx, *pomum Adami*.

ستوني ستغ *stūnī-stagh*, a. Supine; flat on the back.

ستيزه *steza*, s.f. Argument, controversy, dispute; quarrel, battle, conflict. P. (*siteza*). *sateza*, s.f. Table-land, flat ground on a hill side.

سټ *saṭ*, s.m. A cutler's block, a block of wood for fixing an anvil; a log, stump, root of a tree. An assault, sudden attack. The nape, back of the neck.

سټكوري *saṭkūrai*, a. Burnt, scorched, parched; dried up, withered, shrivelled; frost-bitten.

سجده *sijda*, s.f. Bowing the head and touch. the ground with the forehead, prostration, adoration. A.

سجل *sijjil*, s.m. Bond, deed, register; decree of a judge; seal of a judge. The recording angel. A.

سچ *such*, a. Pure genuine, real; candid, honest. S. Also سچه *suchah*.

سحار *sahār*, } s.m. Dawn, daybreak; morning, forenoon; morrow, to-morrow. A.
سحر *sahr*, }

سحر *siḥr*, s.m. Sorcery, magic, jugglery. A.

سحرگر *siḥr·gar*, s.m. Magician, conjurer, sorcerer.

سخ *sakh*, in. Excellent! Good! ad. The present year.

سخا *sakhā*, s.f. } Munificence, generosity, liberality. A.
سخاوت *sakhāwat*, s.m. }

سخا *skhā*, a. Putrid, rotten, stinking. H. (*ubsā*).

سخاوره *skhāwaga*, s.f. Name of a medicinal root (*Kæmpferia galanga*); orris root, root of the Iris (*Iris Persica*).

سخت *sakht*, a. Hard, strong; difficult, troublesome; obdurate, violent; austere, stingy; cruel, harsh; painful, rigid, severe. P.

سختي *sakhtī*, s.f. Difficulty, trouble; violence, cruelty; austerity, severity, etc. P.

سخر *skhar*, s.m. A father-in-law. P. (*khusar*). *sakhar*, s.m. A rock, boulder, stone.

سخره *sakhara*, s.f. A rock, boulder, stone.

سخن *sukhun*, s.m. Word, speech; affair, matter. P.

سخوښتن *skhwakkhtan*, s.m. Cinders, hot ashes.

سخوند *skhwand*, s.m. The cud. *skhwand·wahal*, v.a. To chew the cud.

سخوندر *skhwandar*, s.m. A young bullock, steer.

سخه *sakha*, s.f. Joy, delight, gladness, etc. (at the misfortune of another), crowing over an enemy.

سخي *sakhī*, a. Munificent, generous, liberal. A. *skhai*, s.m. A calf, yearling calf.

سد *sud*, s.m. Consciousness, intelligence; sensation, sense; memory. S. (*sudh*). *sadd*, s.m. A barrier, wall. A.

سر *sar*, s.m. The head; point, apex, summit, top. P. *sirr*, s.m. A mystery, secret. A.

سراب *sarāb*, s.m. Mirage, glare, vapour resembling water at a distance (seen on desert plains). A. Mica, talc. A.

سراج *sarrāj*, s.m. A saddler. A.

سراسر *sarāsar*, a. All, the whole. ad. Wholly, entirely. P.

سراسري *sarāsarī*, a. Brief, short, concise. P.

سراسيمه *sarāsīmah*, a. Amazed, confounded. P.

سراغ *surāgh*, s.m. Enquiry, search; mark, trace. P.

سرانه *sarāna*, s.f. The upper bar of a doorway or frame.

سرانجام *sarānjām*, s.m. Apparatus, utensils, materials; chattels, furniture, goods; ingredients, requisites; conclusion, accomplishment, end. P.

سرانداز *sarāndāz*, s.m. The head piece of a bed; a carpet spread at the head of a room. P.

سراي *srāe*, s.m. A caravansary, hospice, inn, hostelry; house. P. (*sarāe*).

سربانده *sarbānda*, s.f. A patch of land, or portion of a field left unploughed or uncut. A rope used to fix the yoke of a plough.

سربانډه *sarbānḍa*, s.f. Rope made of slips of raw hide; a rope for fastening the yoke of a plough.

سربسته *sarbasta*, s.f. A cloth tied round the head by women when occupied with household duties, etc. P.

سرپ *surup*, s.m. Lead. P. (*surb*). *sirp* or *srup*, ad. Simply, purely, altogether, out and out, merely, etc. P. (*ṣirf*).

سرپوښ *sarpokkh*, s.m. A cover, lid. P. (*sarposh*).

سرچشمه *sarchashma*, s.f. A fountain, spring. P.

سرحد *sarḥadd*. s.m. Boundary, frontier, limit. P.

سرخ *surkh*, a. Red (in comp.). P. *surkh·bād*, s.m. Name of a disease, erysipelas. P.

سرخچه *surkhcha*, s.f. A red apricot. P.

سرخکه *sarkhaka*, s.f. A starling; a kind of Mina (*Graculus roseus*).

سرخي *surkhī*, s.f. Blight in corn, mildew; jaundice; brick dust; redness. P. *surkha-ī*, s.f. A frill or fillet of cloth sewn on to the legs of women's trousers.

سرد *sard*, a. Cold (in comp.). P.

سردار *sardār*, s.m. Chief, principal, head. P.

سررشته *sar-rishta*, s.f. Affinity, connection; office, employment; cord, rope. P.

سرژه *sarja*, s.f. A species of mountain deer.

سرسام *sarsām*, s.m, Delirium, frenzy. P.

سرسايه *sarsāya*, s.f. Alms distributed on the conclusion of the Ramazān fast. A veil given by the father to a bride on the last day of the marriage festivities. P.

سرسري *sarsarī*, a. Easy, facile. P.

سرشاهي *sarshāhī*, s.f. Name of a weight equal to half an ounce.

سرشت *sarisht*, s.m. Intellect, nature; temperament, disposition; complexion. P.

سرغنه *sarghanah*, s.m. A chief, head man. P.

سرغوند *sarghūnd*, s.m. A glandular tumour of the neck.

سرفه *sarfa*, s.f. Advantage, gain, profit; frugal, sparing in expense; deficiency, default; forbearance. A. (*sarf*). *surfa*, s.f. A cough. P.

سركار *sarkār*, s.m. Government, court; province, district; superintendent. P.

سركښ *sarkakkh*, a. Obstinate, rebellious, disobedient, perverse, etc. P. (*sarkash*).

سركښي *sarkakkhī*, s.f. Obstinacy, rebellion, etc.

سركنډه *sarkunda*, s.f. A cropped, cut, or trimmed head of hair; the hair cut short.

سركنډي *sarkundai*, s.m. A man or boy with the hair trimmed or cut short.

سركوزي *sarkūzai*, s.m. A pig, hog, swine.

سركول *sarkol*, s.m. A mill-dam weir.

سركه *sirka*, s.f. Vinegar. P.

سركۍ *sirka-ī*, s.f. Name of a scarlet insect, the scarlet fly.

سرگردان *sargardān*, a. Bothered, confused, perplexed; wandering, at a loss, etc. P.

سرگرداني *sargardānī*, s.f. Perplexity, trouble, worry.

سرگړي *sargarai*, s.m. Name of a grass (*Apluda aristata*).

سرگشته *sargashtah*, a. Amazed, astonished; giddy, flighty, wandering. P.

سرگله *sargala*, s.f. A grazing tax, tax on cattle. P.

سرگين *sargīn*, s.m. Cow-dung. P.

سرما *sarmā*, s.f. Winter. P.

سرماتي *sarmātai*, s.m. Coping, eaves of a wall.

سرمال *sarmāl*, s.m. A rope used to fasten together the two halves of a bullock or camel load.

سرمايه *sarmāya*, s.f. Capital, stock, store. P.

سرمه *surma*, s.f. P. See رانجه.

سرنا *sarnā*, } s.f. A clarion, flageolet. P.
سرنائي *sarnā-ī*, }

سرناچي *surnāchī*, s.m. A flageolet player.

سرنامه *sarnāma*, s.f. Superscription, address, title. P.

سرنګ *surang*, s.m. A mine, tunnel, subterranean passage. S.

سرنګي *surangai*, s.m. A burrow, little tunnel, etc. Diminutive of preceding word.

سرواښ *sarwākkh*, s.m. A rope made of hair, and used to fasten cattle; a tether.

سرووټکه *sarwatka*, s.f. See سکروټه.

سرود *sarod*, s.m. A song; music, melody. P.

سرودگر *sarod-gar*, } s.m. A singer, musician. P.
سرودي *sarodī*, }

سرور *sarwar*, s.m. A chief, leader. P.

سروزنه *sarwazana*, s.f. The hem in trousers, through which the waistband passes; a frill or fillet of cloth added to a pair of trousers.

سروه *sarwa*, s.f. The cypress tree. P. (*sarw*).

سره *sara*, s.f. Manure, offal, dung. *sara*, ad. With, along with, together, in company.

سره ور *sarah-war*, a. Ample, broad, wide. See سور.

سریخ *srīkh*, s.m. Name of a tree (*Mimosa seris*). S. (*siris*).

سریښ *sarekkh*, s.m. See سلیښ.

سرین *surīn*, s.m. The buttock. P.

سړبنړ *saṛbanṛ*, s.m. Name of the eldest son of Kais (the great ancestor of the Afghans). His tribe. *saṛbanṛai*, s.m. A male of the tribe.

سړپ *sṛap*, s.m. The sound of splashing water; squash, smash, dash, etc. H. (*suṛap*).

سړه *saṛah*, a. Done, finished; free, liberated; alone, solitary; genuine, pure.

سړه بنړ *saṛah-banṛ*, s.m. See سړبنړ.

سړه لري *saṛa-lire*, } s.f. Fever and ague.
سړه لوي *saṛa-lawe*, }

سړي *saṛai*, s.m. A man, human being. *saṛī-tob*, s.m. Human nature, humanity.

سزا *sazā*, s.f. Correction, punishment, retribution. P.

سزاوار *sazāwār*, a. Deserving, fit, worthy; suitable, proper. P.

سزاول *sazāwal*, s.m. Bailiff, tax-gatherer.

سږ *sag*, ad. } This year, the current year.
سږکال *sag-kāl*, }

سږمه *sagma*, s.f. The nostril.

سږني *saganai*, a. This year's, of the present year.

سږي *sagai*, s.m. The lung. P. (*shush*).

سسپار *saspār*, s.m. A plough-share.

سسپور *saspor*, s.m. A mattock, hoe.

سست *sust*, a. Indolent, lazy, negligent; feeble, slow, languid; loose, relaxed. P.

سستي *sustī*, s.f. Idleness, laziness, etc. P.

سښا *sakkha*, s.f. Fizz, sputter, etc. (as of roasting meat).

سښسوره *sakkhsora*, s.f. See سسپور.

سطح *saṭah*, s.m. A surface, flat surface. A.

سعادت *sa'ādat*, s.m. Felicity, happiness, good fortune. A.

سعیه *sa'ya*, s.f. Endeavour, effort, purpose. A. (*sa'ī*).

سغ *sagh*, s.m. See شغ.

سفر *safar*, s.m. A journey, voyage. A.

سفوف *safūf*, s.m. A powder. A.

سقاو *saqqāw*, s.m. A water carrier. A.

سک *sak*, a. Stiff, rigid. s.m. Lumbago, rheumatism. H. (*chik*).

سکاروي *skārwai*, s.m. Pleurisy; rheumatism, sciatica.

سکالوه *skālwah*, s.m. Conversation, discourse, talk, hum, buzz, murmur (of conversation).

سکانړ *skāṇr*, a. Dark complexioned, ruddy, healthy, fresh, or agreeable complexion. s.m. A horse of a light bay colour.

سکروټه *skarwaṭa*, s.f. Embers, live coal.

سکړک *sukṛuk*, a. Numbed, chilled, paralyzed with cold. *sukṛak*, s.m. Bread made of Indian corn or maize meal.

سکستل *skustal*, v.a. To shear, clip (as sheep, etc).

سکښتل *skakkhtal*, v.a. To cut, shape, design, cut out (as clothes). To clip, shear.

سکل *skal*, v.a. See څښل.

سکنجبین *sikanjabīn*, s.m. Oxymel; a drink made of lime-juice, honey and water. P.

سکندري *skandara-ī*, s.f. A stumble, trip.

سکور *skor*, s.m. Charcoal.

سکول *skwal*, s.m. Shearing, clipping. *skwal-kawul*, v.a. To shear, clip.

سکونت *sukūnat*, s.m. Habitation, residence; quiet, rest, tranquility. A.

سکونډاره *skūnḍāṛa*, s.f. A pinch; pinching.

سکونډل *skūnḍal*, v.a. To pinch, tweak.

سکوي *skoe*, s.m. A stitch; sewing. Anxiety,

solicitude. *skoe·kawul*, v.a. To stitch, hem, sew.

سکويل *skoyal*, v.a. To rub, scrape, scratch (as the skin).

سکه *sika*, s.f. Lead; coin, impression, stamp; sterling, current. A. P. *sakah*, a. Related (of the same parents), full, own. S. (*saga*). *ska*, ad. Because, therefore, then; as if, as it were.

سگ *sag*, s.m. A dog. P. *sag*, ad. See سر.

سگال *sigāl*, s.m. Suspicion. thought; calumny. P.

سگل *sugul*, s.f. A kind of buskin made of untanned leather, and worn by mountaineers as a protection for the legs from the snow.

سگلاو *sagalāw*, s.m. An otter. P. (*sagulāb*).

سگلئي *sagala-ī*, s.f. See سلگئي.

سگه *saga*, s.f. Capital, stock, store.

سل *sal* or *sil*, a. A hundred, one hundred, centum. P. (*ṣad*). *sill*, s.m. Consumption, phthisis, hectic fever. A.

سلاره *silāra*, s.f. A kind of striped cloth.

سلام *salām*, s.m. Salutation; peace, safety. A.

سلامت *salāmat*, s.m. Health, recovery; safety, salvation. A.

سلائي *salā-ī*, s.f. A bodkin, pin, skewer, pencil, etc. S. The upright pillar of a Persian wheel; a steel bodkin for applying antimony to the eyelids, etc.

سلت *salaṭ*, s.m. A shield, buckler.

سلسله *silsila*, s.f. Chain, series, succession; descent, lineage. A.

سلطان *sulṭān*, s.m. Emperor, sovereign, king. A.

سلطاني *sulṭānī*, a. Princely, royal. A.

سلطنت *sulṭanat*, s.m. Empire, sovereignty. A.

سلگئي *salga-ī*, s.f. A sob, sigh, hiccough, sobbing cry.

سلوک *sulūk*, s.m. Behaviour, conduct, manner; intercourse, treatment, usage; attention, civility. A.

سله *sala*, s.f. A pig or mass of iron. H. (*sarī*).

سلي *salai*, s.m. An iron ring for the finger (worn as a charm against all kinds of calamities).

سليخ *salekh*, } s.m. Glue; birdlime; adhesiveness, cohesion, viscidity. P. (*saresh*).
سليښ *salekkh*, }

سليقه *salīqa*, s.f. Disposition, nature; address, dexterity, method, etc. A.

سم *sum*, s.m. A hoof, whole hoof (as of a horse, etc.). *sam*, a. Even, flat, level, plane, straight. *samm*, s.m. Poison, venom. A. *sam*, s.m. An arrow. A. (*sahm*).

سماع *simā'*, s.f. Hearing, listening; a song, singing. A.

سمبالول *sambālawul*, v.a. To control, manage, moderate; to prop, support; protect, preserve; arrange, settle, put in order, etc. S. (*sambhālnā*).

سمت *simt*, s.m. Path, road, way; direction, quarter. A.

سمڅ *smats*, s.f. A cavern, cave. P. (*sumuj*).

سم دَلاسه *sam da lāsa*, ad. Straight from the hand, out of hand, forthwith, etc.

سمساره *samsāra*, s.f. A kind of lizard, iguana.

سمست *samist*, s.f. See سمڅ.

سمسور *samsor*, a. } Come out, ripened, matured (as corn when in ear). s.m. A peer, equal, match, compeer.
سمسوري *samsorai*, }

سمن *saman*, s.m. Jasmine, lily of the valley. P.

سمند *samand*, a. Dun-coloured (horse). P.

سمندر *samandar*, s.m. A salamander. P.

سمندي *samandai*, s.m. A rat of a dun colour.

سمور *samūr*, s.m. A marten, sable; sable skin. P.

سمه *sama*, s.f. A plateau, plain. Name of the Yūsufzai plain.

سن *san*, s.m. Age, year. A.

سنار *sunār*, s.m. A goldsmith. S.

سنبل *sunbul*, s.m. Hyacinth. P. Maiden-hair fern.

سنت *sunnat*, s.m. Circumcision; the traditions of Muḥammad; ordinance. A.

سنځل *sandzal*, v.a. To empty, bale, pour out. P. (*sanjīdan*).

سنج *sanj* (in comp.). A weigher. P. *sunj*, a. Empty, void, desolate, waste, deserted.

سنجاب *sanjāb*, s.m. Ermine. P.

سند *sannad*, s.m. Certificate, deed, diploma, document, grant, etc. A. *sind*, s.m. A river. The name of a country. S. (*sindh*).

سندان *sandān*, s.m. An anvil. P.

سندره *sandara*, s.f. A song; melody, song.

سنډا *sanḍā*, a. Burly, powerful, strong, stout. S.

سنډاسي *sanḍāsī*, s.m. A Hindu ascetic, devotee. S. (*sunyāsī*).

سنډه *sanḍah*, s.m. A bull buffalo. S. (*sānḍ*).

سنکیا *sankiyā*, s.f. Arsenic. S. (*sankhiyā*).

سنګ *sang*, s.m. A stone (in comp.). P.

سنګار *singār*, s.m. Decoration, dress, ornament, toilet. S.

سنګاونړ *singāwaṉṛ*, s.m. A rudder, helm; barge pole, boat hook. A. (*sukkān*).

سنګر *sangar*, s.m. Barricade, stockade. S.

سنګزن *sangzan*, a. Lop-sided, top-heavy, lurched over, over-balanced.

سنګلاخ *sanglākh*, a. Stony, rocky; difficult, arduous. P.

سنګين *sangīn*, a. Heavy, weighty; solid, hard; important, serious, difficult; stony. s.m. A bayonet. P.

سنه مکي *sanah-makī*, s.m. Senna leaves (*Cassia lanceolata*). Name of a stone, serpentine, porphyry. H.

سني *sunnī*, s.m. An orthodox Muḥammadan; one who believes in the equality of the four successors of Muḥammad. a. Catholic, orthodox, true. A. *sunnī-tob*, s.m. Orthodoxy.

سنړ *saṉṛ*, The hemp plant (*Crotalaria juncea*); hemp. S. (*san*).

سو *sau*, a. A hundred. Only used with reference to more than one hundred. Ex. *sal* or *sil*, One hundred. *dre-sawa*, Three hundred. S.

سوا *siwā*, p. Except, besides, without. A.

سوال *sawāl*, s.m. Question, interrogation, proposition. A.

سوانګ *swāng*, s.m. Disguise, imitation, sham. S.

سوانګي *swāngai*, s.m. An actor, imitator.

سوټبوټ *sūṭ-būṭ*, a. Cross, surly, ill-natured; withered, dry; pure, simple; disagreeable, ugly; pinioned, tightened; all of a heap, by the run, etc.

سوټه *sūṭa*, s.f. Dung of cattle (as found on pastures), scybala. A. (*sudda*).

سوځول *swadzawul*, v.a. To burn, set on fire. P. (*sokhtāndan*, *sozān-*).

سوچه *sūchah*, a. Genuine, pure, prime, real. S.

سوخته *sokhtah*, a. Burnt (in comp.). P.

سود *sūd*, s.m. Gain, advantage; interest, profit. P.

سودا *saudā*, s.f. Commerce, trade, marketing, etc. P. Hypochondriasis, melancholy, madness; desire, love, ambition. A.

سوداګر *saudāgar*, s.m. A merchant, trader. P.

سودائي *saudā-ī*, a. Mad, melancholy, insane. A.

سوده *sūdah*, a. Abraded, frayed, rubbed, galled. P. Genuine, pure, simple; artless. S. (*sūdhā*). *sūda*, s.f. A stoppage, obstruction (of the bowels). A. (*sudda*). *sawda*, s.f. A basket, hamper; a wicker frame used as a dish cover, meat safe, etc.

سوډر *soḍar*, s.m. A boar, wild boar. S. (*sūkar*). a. Bald, barepated.

سور *sor*, s.m. Breadth, expanse, width. H. (*chauṛ*). *sor*, a. Riding, mounted. s.m. A cavalier, horseman. P. (*sawār*). *sūr*,

a. Red. f. *sra.* P. (*surkh*). *sūr*, s.m. Name of a tribe of Afghans.

سوراغزي *sūr-āghzai*, s.m. Name of a plant with red thorns (*Catha edulis*).

سورپلي *sūr-palai*, s.m. Name of a plant, the seed pod of which is covered with red prickles; cowitch (*Mucuna pruriens*); a kind of stinging nettle; a kind of grass with barbed spikes in the beard.

سورت *sūrat*, s.m. A chapter (of the Qurān). A.

سورسات *sūrsāt*, s.m. Provisions, stores, supplies, etc. (collected for a king, or an army on the march). P.

سورلكي *sūr-lakai*, s.m. Name of a bird with a red tail; stonechat, wheatear.

سورلنډ *sūrlanḍ*, s.m. A jackal.

سورلي *swarlī*, s.f. Riding; cavalcade, suite. P. (*sawārī*). *swarlai*, s.m. A chisel; burglar's tool, jemmy, pick.

سورمل *sūrmal*, s.m. Name of a grass with barbed spikes in the beard (*Apluda aristata*).

سورمېږي *sūr-megai*, s.m. The red ant.

سوره *swara*, s.f. A daughter or slave girl given as the price of murder or blood, or in exchange for a wife or girl eloped with or abducted.

سوري *sūrai*, s.m. Aperture, orifice, hole, passage. P. (*sūrākh*). *sorai* or *siwrai*, s.m. Shadow, shade. *sūre*, s.f. (pl. of *sūra*, obsolete). A bawl, bellow, shout, scream.

سوريته *sūryata*, s.f. A female slave or bondwoman who has borne a child to her master; a concubine.

سوړ *soṛ*, a. Cold, frigid, frosty. P. (*sard*).

سوړبوئي *soṛ-bū-ī*, s.f. Stink, fœtor, stench.

سوړه *sūṛa*, s.f. A burrow, hole; aperture, orifice. P. (*sūrākh*).

سوړي *sūṛai*, s.m. A fissure, crack, cleft.

سوز *soz* (in comp.). Burning. P.

سوزاك *sozāk*, s.m. Gonorrhœa. P.

سوزش *sozish*, s.m. Burning, heat, fervour; inflammation; vexation.

سوزن *sozan*, s.m. A needle; pricker, pin. P.

سوزني *sozanī*, s.f. A quilt, counterpane, coverlet. P.

سوزه *sūza*, s.f. A fillet, patch, etc. in a dress; an adze.

سوسر *sūsar*, s.m. A porpoise. S. (*sūs*).

سوسن *sausan* or *sosan*, s.m. Name of a plant, the Chinese Iris, Daurian Lily; a purple or violet colour. A.

سوغ *sogh*, s.m. A sniff, snort, snuff; sound of blowing the nose. S. (*sūngh*). *sūgh*, s.m. A pinch of snuff, or anything taken between the finger and thumb.

سوغات *saughāt*, s.m. A curiosity, rarity, present. P.

سوغالي *soghālai*, s.m. A hare's form.

سوغن *sūghan*, a. Sniffling, snorting, snuffing. s.m. A sniveller.

سوغول *sūghawul*, v.a. To prod, poke, thrust.

سوغيدل *sūghedal*, v.n. To be pierced, stabbed, etc.

سوك *sūk*, s.m. The fist; a blow, cuff (with the fist); the stump of a tree.

سوكړ *sūkaṛ*, s.m. A tall, gaunt, thin, etc. man; a thin wiry beard.

سوكړك *sūkṛuk*, s.m. Bread made of Indian corn or maize.

سوكړه *sokṛah*, a. Dry, parched, withered. S. (*sūkhā*).

سوګند *saugand*, s.m. An oath. P.

سول *swal*, v.n. To burn, catch fire, ignite. Pr. *swadzī*. P. (*sokhtan, soz-*).

سولاغ *sūlāgh*, s.m. A hole, aperture, etc. P. (*sūrākh*).

سولاغه *sūlāgha*, s.f. A water bucket; a strainer, colander.

سولول *sūlawul*, v.a. To rub, file, rasp, grate, abrade.

سولي *sūla-ī*, s.f. A gibbet, stake; a pole, juggler's pole. s. (*sūlī*).

سوليدل *sūledal*, v.n. To fray, chafe, fret, abrade, etc.

سوم *swam*, s.m. See سپم.

سونبه *sūnba*, s.m. A socket; heel of an arrow, axe, lance, etc.; a blacksmith's punch; a sponge staff, ramrod. H. (*sumbā*).

سوندر *swandar*, s.m. See سخوندر.

سونده *sūnda*, s.f. Jealousy, suspicion.

سونډ *sūnḍ*, s.m. Dry ginger. s. (*sonṭh*). See شونډ.

سونډک *sūnḍak*, s.m. The trunk or proboscis of an elephant. s. (*sūnḍ*).

سونګټ *sūngaṭ*, a. Burnt, scorched; withered.

سونګي *ṣongai*, s.m. A pigmy, dwarf.

سونړ *sūnṟ*, s.m. See سوغ.

سونړول *sūnṟawul*, v.a. To blow the nose, snuff, snort.

سونړيدل *sūnṟedal*, v.n. To sniff, snuff, smell, etc.

سوور *swor*, a. Riding, mounted. s.m. A cavalier, horseman. P. (*sawār*).

سووه *sowa*, s.f. Name of a plant, sweet fennel (*Anethum sowa*). s. (*soā*).

سوه *swa*, s.f. A cloven hoof (as of oxen, sheep, etc.).

سوهاګن *sohāgan*, s.f. A favourite wife. s. See مروبهه.

سوهان *sohān*, s.m. A file, rasp. P.

سوي *sawai*, a. Consumed; burnt. *swai*, s.m. Burning, ardour; pain; compassion, pity.

سويشل *sweshal*, v.a. To milk. See لوشل.

سويه *soya*, s.f. } A hare. s. (*sasā*).
سوني *so-e*, s.m. }

سه *sih*, a. Three (in comp.). P.

سهل *sahl*, a. Easy, facile, ad. Easily. A. *sahal*, v.n. To bear, endure, suffer. s. (*sahnā*).

سهم *sahm*, s.f. Dread, awe, terror, fear. P.

سهوه *sahwa*, s.f. Mistake, error. A. (*sahw*).

سهه *saha*, s.f. Breath, life; respiration. Clothes line, clothes horse.

سهيدل *sahedal*, v.n. To endure, suffer. See سهل.

سهيل *suhel*, s.m. The star Canopus; the south. A.

سهيلي *sahelī*, s.f. A lady's maid, housemaid; a concubine, handmaid. s.

سياځه *siyādza*, s.f. A slab for grinding spices on; a cobbler's lapstone.

سياست *siyāsat*, s.m. Government; punishment. A.

سيال *siyāl*, s.m. An equal, peer; clansman, kin; like, resembling.

سيالي *siyālī*, s.f. Equality, purity, resemblance.

سياه *siyāh*, a. Black (in comp.). P.

سياهه *siyāha*, s.f. Muster, catalogue, register, etc.

سياهي *siyāhī*, s.f. Ink; blackness; register, list. P.

سيب *seb*, s.m. An apple. P.

سيپي *sīpa-ī*, s.f. A shell. H. (*sīpī*).

سيټ *seṭ*, s.m. A banker, merchant. s. (*seṭh*).

سيځل *sedzal*, v.n. To burn, catch fire. See سول *swal*.

سيخ *sīkh*, s.m. A skewer, spit, ramrod. P.

سيخچه *sīkhcha*, s.f. A small skewer, etc.; a prong or bayonet fixed to a matchlock. P.

سيد *sayad*, s.m. A prince, lord; a descendant of Husain, the grandson of Muḥammad. A.

سير *sair*, s.m. Excursion, jaunt, picnic, recreation, walk. A. *ser*, s.m. Name of a weight equal to two pounds. H. *ser*, a. Satiated, full, replete, etc. (in comp.). P.

سيراب *serāb*, a. P. See خړوب.

سيرت *sīrat*, s.m. Manners, morals, conduct. A.

سيرلي *serlai*, s.m. A yearling kid.

سيرۍ *sera-ī*, s.f. Rent free land given to men of the religious classes, glebe; an estate, pension in land, fief.

سيزل *sezal*, } v.n. To burn, consume, kindle, catch fire. P. (*sokhtan*, *soz-*).
سيځل *sedzal*, }

سيسه *sīsa*, s.f. Lead. S. (*sīsā*).

سيکړه *saikṛa*, s.f. A hundred; a centum. S.

سيکل *sekal*, v.a. To foment, toast, warm. H. (*senknā*).

سيکن *sekan*, s.m. Aversion, antipathy, disgust; dislike, loathing (of food, etc.).

سيل *sail*, s.m. Walking, rambling; flowing, current; flood; flock of birds; shoal of fishes. A.

سيلاب *sailāb*, s.m. A current, torrent, flood; deluge, inundation. a. Abounding in water. P.

سيله *sela*, s.f. Partiality, friendship, affection. A. A javelin, pike; rapier, long sword. S.

سيلي *siyalai*, s.m. Rennet; the prepared stomach of a kid or lamb filled with coagulated milk. *siyala-ī*, s.f. Rope made of goat's hair, etc. *sīla-ī*, s.f. A slap, blow with the open hands. P. (*selī*). A dust storm, whirlwind; hurricane, tempest.

سيم *sīm*, s.m. Silver. P. Wire of any kind.

سيماب *sīmāb*, s.m. Quicksilver, mercury. P.

سيمرغ *sīmurgh*, s.m. A fabulous bird, griffin. P.

سيمک *sīmak*, s.m. A weaver's bodkin; knitting needle. P.

سيمه *sema*, s.f. A mare or ass in heat (seeking the male). *sīma*, s.f. Path, way, road; quarter, side, part.

سيميا *sīmiyā*, s.f. Vermicelli. H. (*senwiyā*).

سيند *sīnd*, s.m. A river, sea. S. (*sindh*).

سينګار *singār*, s.m. See سنګار.

سينه *sīna*, s.f. Bosom, breast. P.

سيني *sīnī*, s.m. A tray, salver. P.

سيو *sew*, s.m. An apple. P.

سيوري *sewrai*, s.m. Shadow, shade.

ش

ش *shīn*, is the twenty-second letter of the Pukkhto alphabet. It has the sound of *sh* in English, and in Persian words introduced into Pukkhto is often changed to ښ.

شا *shā*, s.f. The back; the shoulders. P. (*shāna*).

شاباز *shābāz*, s.m. The bass string of a musical instrument; a royal falcon. P.

شاباش *shābāsh*, in. Bravo! well done! P.

شاپيانګه *shāpiyānga*, s.f. Name of a plant (*Withiana coagulans*).

شاپيټي *shāpeṭai*, s.m. A small shell found in hill streams, and on mountain sides; a snail (*Achatina acicula*).

شاتر *shātar*, s.m. A groom, running footman.

شاټينګه *shā·ṭinga*, s.f. The gizzard (of a fowl, etc.).

شادو *shādo*, s.m. A monkey.

شاربل *shārbal*, v.a. To churn, stir about, etc. P. (*shor dādan* or *shorīdan*).

شاړ *shāṛ*, a. Rude, unmannered, boorish. Idle, out of work, unemployed; fallow, waste, uncultivated. s.m. A boor, bumpkin, clown, clodhopper.

شاش *shāsh*, s.m. Urine. P.

شاعر *shā'ir*, s.m. A poet. A.

شاګرد *shāgird*, s.m. An apprentice, pupil, disciple. P.

شال *shāl*, s.m. A shawl. S.

شالۍ *shāla-ī*, s.f. Rice plant, rice crop. S. (*shālī*).

شامت *shāmat*, s.m. Adversity, bad fortune. A.

شامل *shāmil*, a. Blended, comprised, united;

included, contained. ad. Together, along with. A.

شامي *s͟hāma-ī*, s.f. A sepulchre, tomb, vault for dead bodies.

شاميانه *s͟hāmiyāna*, s.f. Awning, canopy. P.

شان *s͟hān*, s.m. Affair, business; condition, degree; dignity, state; constitution, nature. a. Like, resembling; used as an adjunct of similitude. Ex. *tor·s͟hān*, a. Blackish; *spin·s͟hān*, a. Whitish. ad. Like, as, similar, etc. P. (*sān*).

شانه *s͟hāna*, s.f. A weaver's comb. P.

شاول *s͟hāwul*, s.m. A plummet, plumb-line. H. (*sāhūl*). P. (*s͟hāqul*).

شاولي واولي *s͟hāwlai·wāwlai*, a. Careless, untidy; foolish, indiscreet; loose, dishevelled.

شاه *s͟hāh*, s.m. A king; a title assumed by men of the *pīr* class. P.

شاهتره *s͟hāhtara*, s.f. Name of a herb, common fumitory (*Fumaria officinalis.*). P.

شاهد *s͟hāhid*, s.m. A witness. A.

شاهده *s͟hāhida*, s.f. A sweetheart, mistress. P.

شاهدي *s͟hāhidī*, s.f. Evidence, testimony. A.

شاهزاده *s͟hāh·zādah*, s.m. A prince, king's son. P.

شاهزادئ *s͟hāh·zāda-ī*, s.f. A princess. P.

شاهي *s͟hāhī*, a. Kingly, royal. s.f. Sovereignty, reign. P.

شاهين *s͟hāhīn*, s.m. A kind of falcon. P.

شايان *s͟hāyān*, a. Legal, worthy, suitable. P.

شايد *s͟hāyad*, ad. Perhaps, possibly, perchance. P.

شب *s͟hab*, s.m. Night (in comp.). P.

شب‌بو *s͟hab·bo*, s.m. The tuberose lily (*Polianthes tuberosa*). P.

شبكه *s͟habaka*, s.f. A lattice, latticed window; a net, reticulated veil. P.

شبنم *s͟hab·nam*, s.m. Dew; hoar frost. P.

شبه *s͟hiba*, s.f. Agate, coral; a bead. P.

شبهه *s͟hubha*, s.f. Uncertainty, doubt; suspicion; hesitation. A.

شپاړس *s͟hpāṛas*, a. Sixteen.

شپږ *s͟hpag̱*, a. Six. P. (*s͟has͟h*).

شپشتي *s͟hpis͟htai*, s.m. The spoke of a wheel.

شپنغوده *s͟hpan·g͟hoda*, s.f. Name of a bird, the shepherd's deceiver, lapwing, pewit.

شپنكي *s͟hpankai*, s.m. A shepherd-boy.

شپني *s͟hpanī*, s.f. Shepherd life, tending sheep.

شپول *s͟hpol*, s.m. A sheep cot, sheep pen, or fold; a thorn hedge; halo round the moon.

شپون *s͟hpūn*, s.m. A shepherd. P. (*s͟hubān*).

شپه *s͟hpa*, s.f. Night. P. (*s͟hab*).

شپيته *s͟hpetah*, a. Sixty.

شپيتي *s͟hpetai*, s.m. A wedge to cleave wood with.

شپيشتي *s͟hpes͟htai*, s.m. A wedge; a kind of clover. P. (*supust*).

شپيشتري *s͟hpes͟htarai*, s.m. A kind of trefoil or vetch (*Medicago denticulata*).

شپيلئ *s͟hpela-ī*, s.f. A tube, pipe, barrel of a gun; fife, flute, whistle; hollow reed; blow-pipe. *s͟hpelai*, s.m. Whistling, a whistle. *s͟hpelai g͟hag̱awul*, v.a. To whistle.

شتاب *s͟hitāb*, s.m. Haste, quickness, speed. a. Hasty, quick, rash. P.

شتاه *s͟hatāh*, a. Artful, cunning; immodest, lewd. A.

شتاهه *s͟hatāha*, s.f. A lewd, wanton, etc. woman.

شترلړ *s͟huturlaṛ*, s.m. The bar or beam that prevents the ropes of a Persian wheel (on which are fastened the water pots) from coming in contact with each other.

شتركه *s͟huturaka*, s.f. A cascade; spurt, jet, gush (of water).

شتري *s͟huturī*, s.f. Name of a kind of cloth made of camel's hair. P.

شته *s͟hta*, A form of the third person singular and plural, present tense of the auxiliary verb يم yam, I am; there is, there are. P. (hast).

شتي shata-ī, s.f. A barbed arrow; the spike or ear of maize after the grain has been removed; the green mould on old walls; the green scum on stagnant pools.

شتل shaṭal, a. Lazy, indolent. See شدل.

شجاع shujā', a. Brave, bold, courageous. A.

شجاعت shujā'at, s.m. Bravery, courage. A.

شجره shajara, s.f. List of saints; genealogical table. A.

شځرلي shatsurlai, s.m. A chisel.

شخ shakh, a. Hard, rough, tough, rigid, stiff. P.

شخړه shkhaṛa, s.f. Gibberish, nonsense, twaddle, trash; crowd, mob, multitude.

شخوده shakhūdah, a. Clawed, scratched. P.

شخول shkhwal, s.m. Din, tumult, noise; rumble, murmur, rustle.

شخولي shkhwalai, s.m. A quiver for arrows.

شخوند shkhwand, s.m. The cud. shkhwand-wahana, s.f. Chewing the cud, ruminating. shkhwand-wahunkai, s.m. A ruminant, an animal that chews the cud. See سخوندر skhwandar.

شدت shiddat, s.m. Force, violence, vehemence. A.

شدني shudanī, a. Possible, practicable, probable. P.

شدياره shudyāra, s.f. Land ploughed and made ready for sowing. P. (shudkār).

شديد shadīd, a. Difficult; acute, intense; vehement, violent. A.

شدل shaḍal, a. Indolent, lazy, slow; unbleached or unwashed cloth.

شر sharr, s.m. Villany, wickedness, depravity, evil. A. shir, s.m. Pitter-patter, sound of falling rain; the whizz of an arrow passing through the air.

شراب sharāb, s.m. Wine, spirits. A.

شرارت sharārat, s.m. Depravity, villany, wickedness. A.

شراکت shirākat, s.m. Partnership, fellowship. A.

شربت sharbat, s.m. Sherbet, beverage, drink. P.

شرحه sharḥa, s.f. Commentary, explanation; allowance, pay, rate. A.

شرشاي sharshā-ī, s.f. See سرشاهي.

شرط sharṭ, s.m. Agreement, bargain; stipulation, condition; bet, wager; mark, sign. A.

شرطي sharṭī, a. Conditional; a bargainer, better. A.

شرعه shar'a, s.f. Muḥammadan law; equity, law. A.

شرعي shar'a-ī, a. According to law, legal. A.

شرغشي sharghashai, s.m. Name of a reed from the stalks of which stools, baskets, etc. are made (*Saccharum sara*, and *S. spontaneum*).

شرغه sharghah, a. A horse with a white forehead, or with white eyes.

شرك shirk, s.m. Infidelity, paganism; company, society, partnership. A.

شرکت shirkat, s.m. Partnership. A.

شرم sharm, s.m. Bashfulness, modesty, shame. P.

شرمښ sharmakkh, s.m. A wolf.

شرمناك sharm-nāk, a. Bashful, modest, unassuming. P.

شرمنده sharmindah, a. Ashamed, disgraced, shamed. P.

شرمندگي sharmindagī, s.f. Disgrace, shame. P.

شرمول sharmawul, v.a. To disgrace, shame, dishonor; to rape, ravish.

شرميدل sharmedal, v.n. To blush, be modest, be abashed, ashamed, etc.

شروع shurū', s.f. Beginning, commencement. A.

شري sharai, s.m. The measles; a rash on the body of infants; tooth-rash. A. (sharā).

شرير sharīr, a. Wicked, depraved, vicious. A.

شريعت sharī'at, s.m. Muḥammadan law; equity, justice, law. A.

شريف sharīf, a. Noble, eminent. A.

شريفه sharīfa, s.f. The eave of a roof; projecting ledge of a wall.

شريک sharīk, s.m. Accomplice, ally; comrade, partner. A.

شړته sharata, s.f. See شړهته.

شړشم sharsham, s.m. Mustard (the plant and seed). P. (sarshaf). S. (sarson).

شړل sharal, v.a. To eject, depose, turn out, drive away. A. (shārid).

شرنګ shrang, s.m. A jingle, clink, chink; chime, ring, echo,

شرنګول shranganul, v.a. To jingle, ring, etc.

شرنګيدل shrangedal, v.n. To chime, jingle, ring, tinkle, etc. P. (charangīdan).

شړونکي sharūnkai, } a. Deposed, expelled,
شړوني sharūnai, } ejected.

شړهته sharhata, s.f. A barleycorn, grain of barley; a particle, bit, small quantity.

شړهيدل sharhedal, v.n. To crumble, decay, decompose, rot, become sodden, etc. H. (sarnā).

شړئ shara-ī, s.f. A blanket. A. (sh'ar).

شست shast, s.m. The space between the thumb and forefinger; a thumbstall (used by archers); aim, sight (as of a gun or arrow). P.

شستئ shasta-ī, s.f. Name of a plant (*Chrysanthemum Indicum*).

ششت shasht, s.m. A mirror attached to a ring, and worn on the thumb by women.

ششني shashanai, } s.m. The neigh of a
ششڼري shashanrai, } horse.

ششڼريدل shashanredal, v.n. To neigh.

شعر shi'r, s.m. Poetry, verse. A.

شعله shu'la, s.f. A blaze, flame. A.

شعور shu'ūr, s.m. Intellect, reason, knowledge. A.

شغ shagh, s.m. Whizz, whirr (as of a bullet or bird passing through the air), etc.

شغال shaghāl, s.m. A jackal. P.

شغرب‌مغرب shaghrib-maghrib, s.m. East and west. A. (mashriq-maghrib).

شغل shughl, s.m. Employment, occupation. A.

شغله shughla, s.f. See شعله.

شفا shifā, s.f. Cure, recovery; remedy. A.

شفاعت shafā'at, s.m. Entreaty, intercession, recommendation. A.

شفتالو shaftālū, s.m. A peach. P.

شفق shafaq, s.m. Twilight, dusk. A.

شفقت shafaqat, s.m. Clemency, compassion, kindness, mercy. A.

شک shakk, s.m. Doubt, suspicion; hesitation, uncertainty. A.

شکار shkār, s.m. Alkali, potash.

شکال shkāl, s.m. Hobbles for the fore feet of a horse. See شکيل.

شکايت shikāyat, s.m. Complaint, accusation. A.

شکر shukr, s.m. Gratitude, thanks. A.

شکرانه shukrāna, s.f. Gratitude, thanks; premium, fee, payment for service done. P.

شکره shakara, s.f. Sugar. P. (shakar).

شکري shikrai, s.m. A kind of falcon or hawk. P. (shikrah). shkarai, s.m. A flat basket of a circular shape. H. (sikhar).

شکست shikast, a. Broken, fractured; dispersed, worsted, beaten. P.

شکل shakl, s.m. Appearance, figure, form, etc. A.

شکلي shaklai, s.m. The end or tail of a turband.

شکم shikam, s.m. The belly (in comp.). P.

شکمن shakk-man, a. Doubtful, dubious, suspicious.

شکنجه shikandza, s.f. A press, vice; bookbinder's press; stocks for the legs; rack, pillory; torture. P. (*shikanja*).

شکور *shkor*, } s.m. A flat basket. H. (*sikhar*).
شکير *shker*, }

شکونړ *shkūṛ*, s.m. A porcupine.

شکيل *shkel*, s.m. P. (*shikīl* or *shiyil*). See شکال.

شګاره *shigāra*, s.f. A pregnant woman or animal.

شګري *shigrai*, s.m. A priming horn, powder horn.

شګلن *shiglan*, a. Sandy, gravelly.

شګوفه *shigūfa*, s.f. A bud, blossom. P.

شګه *shiga*, s.f. Sand, gravel.

شل *shall*, a. Paralyzed, palsied. P. *shal*, s.m. A pike, javelin, spear. P. *shil*, a. Twenty, a score.

شلانده *shlānda*, s.f. A toad, frog.

شلټ *shalaṭ*, a. See شتل.

شلخي *shalkhai*, s.m. Name of a pot-herb; common dock (*Rumex acutus*).

شلغم *shalgham*, s.m. A turnip. P.

شلک *shilik*, s.m. A discharge, salvo, round, volley, salute, boom of a gun. A. (*shalakh*).

شلم *shilam*, a. Twentieth.

شلوار *shalwār*, s.m. Trowsers, pants. P.

شلول *shlawul*, v.a. To tear, rend, split, break, burst. H. (*chīrānā*).

شلوم *shlom*, s.m. } See شوملي.
شلونبي *shlonbe*, s.f. }

شليته *shalīta*, s.f. A large sack or net for baggage, etc. (when loaded on cattle). P.

شلېدل *shledal*, v.n. To burst, tear, split, break, etc. H. (*chīrnā*).

شمار *shumār*, s.m. Counting, reckoning. P.

شمارل *shmāral*, v.a. To count. See شميرل.

شمال *shamāl*, s.m. The North; North wind. A.

شمځۍ *shamdza-ī*, s.f. Spine, back-bone.

شمشتۍ *shamshata-ī*, s.f. A tortoise.

شمشير *shamsher*, s.m. A sword. P.

شمعه *sham'a*, s.f. A candle, lamp. A.

شمکلي *shamkalai*, s.m. The unwoven end of a web or warp (used as a duster, etc.).

شمکور *shamkor*, a. Night-blind, nyctalopic. s.m. One who is subject to night-blindness. P. (*shab-kor*).

شمکوري *shamkorī*, s.f. Night-blindness, nyctalopia.

شمکي *shamkai*, s.m. Name of a plant used in medicine; vervain.

شمله *shamla*, s.f. The end of a turband; a shawl or sash for the waist.

شموخه *shamūkha*, s.f. Name of a grass and its seed (*Panicum frumentaceum*). P. (*shāmākh*).

شمه *shama*, s.m. An atom, jot, particle; odour, perfume. A.

شميرل *shmeral*, v.a. To count, compute, reckon. P. (*shumārīdan*).

شناخت *shnākht*, s.m. Acquaintance, recognition, knowledge. P. (*shinākht*).

شناز *shināz*, s.m. An inflated hide, used to cross rivers upon. P. (*shinā*, swimming).

شنبه *shanbah*, s.m. Saturday. P.

شنده *shandah*, a. Desperate, inconceivable, incredible, impossible.

شنډ *shanḍ*, a. Barren, sterile, unproductive, unfruitful. H. (*sanḍhar*).

شنديۍ *shanda-ī*, s.f. Name of a tree (*Melia sempervirens*); evergreen bead-tree.

شنګرپ *shingrip*, s.m. Cinnabar, vermillion. P. (*shangarf*).

شنګرۍ *shingra-ī*, s.f. Tower, keep, hornwork of a fort; a mould for casting pottery, etc.

شنل *shanal*, v.a. To explore, look, search, try, sound, etc. P. (*shāndan*, to comb).

شنوا *shinwā*, a. Hearing. P. (*shinudan*).

شنه *shna*, Feminine of شين, which see.

شني shnai, s.m. Name of a tree and its fruit (*Pistacia Kabulica*), the mastic tree.

شنيدل shanedal, v.n. To flutter, writhe, quiver, wriggle, shake, etc.

شو sho or shaw, s.m. See شب.

شو پا shopā, a. Uncircumcised; term of abuse.

شوپرک sho·parak, s.m. A bat. P. (shab·para).

شوتل shotal, s.m. Name of a trefoil (*Trifolium repens*). P. (shaftal). Name of a potherb (*Malva parviflora*), marsh mallow.

شوخ shokh, a. Cheerful, humorous; playful, mischievous; insolent, pert; wanton, saucy. P.

شوخون sho·khūn, s.m. A night attack, surprise. P. (shab·khūn).

شوخي shokhī, s.f. Fun, mischief, frolic; coquetry, lewdness, wantonness. P.

شوده shaudah, s.m. Milk.

شور shor, s.m. Cry, noise, riot. P.

شوړه shoṛa, s.f. The beard of grasses; a wisp of grass or straw used as a plug or bung.

شوشک shūshk, s.m. The curve of an arch.

شوشئ shūsha-ī, s.f. A firebrand, torch. P. (shūsha).

شوق shauq, s.m. Desire, inclination; fondness, love; gaiety, cheerfulness; curiosity. A.

شوقدر sho·qadar, s.m. Name of a festival on the 14th of the month sh'abān (shabi·barāt). P. (shab·qadr).

شوک shūk, a. Plucked, robbed, stripped, etc. shūk·pūk, a. Plucked bare, bare as a bone.

شوکاڼړي shokāṇṛai, s.m. A flat stone used to bake cakes upon; soapstone, firestone, (used for the vent hole of a furnace, etc.).

شوکت shaukat, s.m. Dignity, pomp, state. A.

شوکور sho·kor, a. See شمکور.

شوکول shūkawul, v.a. To pluck, pick, cull; to rob, strip, tear off, etc. P. (shukhūdan).

شوکه shūkı, s.f. Plundering, robbing, stripping (as passengers on the roads). The beak of a bird.

شوګه shūga, s.f. A kind of rice.

شوګير sho·gīr, a. Watching by night, vigilant; a night watch, vigil. P. (shab·gīr).

شوګيري sho·gīrī, s.f. Watching at night, awake all night, etc.

شول shwal, v.n. To be, become, exist. P. (shudan).

شولخ sholakh, s.m. The skin of the tongue.

شولګره sholgara, s.f. A rice field, a rice swamp.

شوله shola, s.f. The rice plant. P. (shālī). shūla, s.f. The colic. S. (sūl).

شوم shūm, a. Miserly, stingy; unfortunate, vile; hungry, faint. A.

شوملې shomle, s.f. (pl. of shomla, obsolete). Butter milk, curds, and whey.

شومه shūma, s.f. The watch between midnight and daylight; food taken at that hour; food given to the friends of a deceased person on the night of the funeral. P.

شومي shūmī, s.f. Hunger, faintness; stingyness, niggardliness; misfortune, etc. A.

شونټئ shonṭa-ī, s.f. A pine torch, slips of resinous pine wood used as torches, matches, etc.

شونډ shūnḍ, s.m. The lip. S. (honṭh).

شونډپاره shūnḍ·pāra, s.f. Hare lip.

شونډک shūnḍak, s.m. The proboscis of an elephant.

شونډه shūnḍa, s.f. The lip.

شوه shawa, s.f. Name of a tree, the sisoo (*Dalbergia sisoo*).

شوي shoe, s.m. Coarse cotton cloth.

شها shahā, s.f. A mistress, sweetheart. A.

شهاب shihāb, s.m. A meteor, falling star. A. shahāb, s.m. Milk and water. A.

شهتير shahtīr, s.m. A rafter, beam. P.

شهد shahd, s.m. Honey. P.

شهده <u>sh</u>uhdah, s.m. A blackguard, debauchee, rake, libertine, profligate. H. (<u>sh</u>uhdā).

شهرت <u>sh</u>uhrat, s.m. Fame, renown; divulging, celebrating, publishing. A.

شهلا <u>sh</u>ahlā, a. Hazel-eyed. A.

شهند <u>sh</u>ahand, s.m. A kind of falcon.

شهوت <u>sh</u>ahwat, s.m. Lust, concupiscence. A.

شهوتناک <u>sh</u>ahwat·nāk, } a. Lascivious, lewd,
شهوتي <u>sh</u>ahwatī, } lustful; lust exciting. A.

شهيد <u>sh</u>ahīd, s.m. A martyr, witness. a. Killed. A.

شهين <u>sh</u>ahīn, s.m. A kind of falcon; a camel gun, a wall piece, carronade. P. The beam of a balance.

شي <u>sh</u>ai, s.m. An article, item, thing. A.

شهيبره <u>sh</u>ebara, s.f. A continued fever.

شيبه <u>sh</u>ebah, s.m. A downpour, heavy shower (of rain).

شيخ <u>sh</u>ekh, s.m. A chief, prelate; venerable old man; a title given to converts to Islam. A.

شيدا <u>sh</u>aidā, a. Love mad; in love. P.

شير <u>sh</u>er, s.m. A lion, tiger. P. <u>sh</u>īr, s.m. Milk (in comp.). P.

شيرازه <u>sh</u>īrāza, s.f. The stitching at the back of a book; the curtain or wall of a fort. P.

شيرخشت <u>sh</u>īr·<u>kh</u>i<u>sh</u>t, s.m. A kind of manna. P.

شيرخط <u>sh</u>īr·<u>kh</u>aṭ, s.m. Heads and tails, pitch and toss, tossing money for play. (<u>sh</u>īr, head; <u>kh</u>aṭ, tail).

شيره <u>sh</u>īra, s.f. Batter, pap. P.

شيرين <u>sh</u>īrīn, a. Sweet; affable, gentle, pleasant, etc. (in comp.). P.

شيشک <u>sh</u>ī<u>sh</u>k, s.m. Name of a plant (*Lithospermum arvense*).

شيشکي <u>sh</u>ī<u>sh</u>kai, s.m. A hedgehog. P. (<u>ch</u>izak).

شيشه <u>sh</u>ī<u>sh</u>a, s.f. A mirror, looking glass. P.

شيطان <u>sh</u>aiṭān, s.m. The devil, Satan. A.

شيطاني <u>sh</u>aiṭānī, s.f. Devilry, wickedness.

شيعه <u>sh</u>ī'ah, s.m. A follower of the sect of 'Ali; a heretic, infidel; sectarian. A.

شيله <u>sh</u>ela, s.f. A ravine, gully, watercourse; dry bed of a river.

شين <u>sh</u>īn, a. Green, verdant; fresh, clear; blue, azure (as the sky). f. <u>sh</u>na.

شيني <u>sh</u>īnai, s.m. A whitlow; a tick, dog-louse.

شيوه <u>sh</u>ewa, s.f. Declivity, slope, slant. P. (<u>sh</u>eba). Business, profession, trade; custom, habit; toilet, decoration; coquetry.

ښ

ښ kk<u>h</u>īn or ks<u>h</u>īn, called also <u>kh</u>e<u>sh</u>īn, is the twenty-third letter of the Pu<u>kkh</u>to alphabet. It is a combined form of خ and ش and corresponds in sound with the Hindi ष or ख. By the Yusufzais and Eastern Afghans generally, it is pronounced as kk<u>h</u>, and by the <u>Kh</u>aṭaks and Western tribes as ks<u>h</u>. It is very often substituted for ش in words introduced from the Persian.

ښاپيرک kk<u>h</u>āperak, s.m. A bat. P. (<u>sh</u>ab·parak).

ښاپيري kk<u>h</u>āperai, s.m. A fairy; the king of the fairies. P. (<u>sh</u>āh·parī).

ښاخ kk<u>h</u>ā<u>kh</u>, s.m. Branch or bough of a tree; the branch or arm of a river, etc. P. (<u>sh</u>ā<u>kh</u>).

ښاخي kk<u>h</u>ā<u>kh</u>a-ī, s.f. A pitchfork, prong.

ښاد kk<u>h</u>ād, a. Delighted, happy, pleased, gay, etc. P. (<u>sh</u>ād).

ښادان kk<u>h</u>ādān, } a. Joyous, happy, gay.
ښادمن kk<u>h</u>ād·man, }

ښادي kk<u>h</u>ādī, s.f. Delight, joy, happiness, pleasure, etc. P. (<u>sh</u>ādī).

ښاديانه kk<u>h</u>ādiyāna, s.f. Festivity, music, song; rejoicing. P. (<u>sh</u>ādiyāna).

ښارک kk<u>h</u>ārak, s.m. The piece of wood (in the mouth of the upper millstone) through which the iron axle of a hand-mill passes; a piece of wood in the mouth of a churning jar or bottle for the passage of the churn stick.

ښرګ *kkhārag*, s.m. The jugular vein. P. (*shāh·rag*).

ښاروني *kkhārūna-ī*, s.f. A starling.

ښاغل *kkhāghal*, v.a. To gratify, please, content; to choose, like, prefer.

ښامار *kkhāmār*, s.m. King of serpents, a dragon. P. (*shāh·mār*).

ښانک *kkhānak*, s.m. A kneading dish, trencher, a wooden platter. P. (*shānak*).

ښانګه *kkhānga*, s.f. The lower limb, thigh and leg, inferior extremity.

ښانګه ور *kkhānga·war*, a. Long-legged, spindle-shanked.

ښايست *kkhāyast*, s.m. Beauty, comeliness, elegance, grace; worthiness, propriety, fitness. Also *kkhāyast·wālai*.

ښايسته *kkhāyastah*, a. Handsome, beautiful, comely; worthy, fit, proper; well, good. P. (*shā-īstah*).

ښائي *kkhā-ī*, ad. May be, perhaps, possibly, probably. P. (*shāyad*).

ښپه *kkhpa*, s.f. The foot.

ښتري *kkhatrī*, s.m. A Hindu trader or shop-keeper. S. (*khatrī* or *kshatri*).

ښتګري *kkhatgarai*, s.m. The ankle, ankle joint; fetlock, fetlock joint.

ښځونک *kkhadzonak*, s.m. Hermaphrodite, effeminate man.

ښځه *kkhadza* or *kkhidza*, s.f. Woman, wife. a. Female, feminine, feminine gender. A. (*zauja*).

ښخ *kkhakh*, a. Hard, rigid, inflexible, stiff. P. (*shakh*). a. Buried, etc. See خښ.

ښرا *kkharā*, s.f. A curse. See ښيره.

ښروه *kkhorawa*, s.f. The yew tree (*Taxus baccata*). The castor oil tree (*Ricinus communis*). A (*khuroa'*).

ښکار *kkhkār*, s.m. Chase, hunting, sport; game, prey; plunder. P. (*shikār*).

ښکاره *kkhkārah*, a. Clear, manifest, apparent, visible, evident. P. (*āshkār*).

ښکاري *kkhkārī*, s.m. A hunter, fowler, sportsman; a robber. P. (*shikārī*).

ښکالوه *kkhkālwah*, s.m. Conversation, discussion; buzz, hum, murmur (of talking).

ښکته *kkhkata*, ad. Down, below, under. *kkhkatanai*, a. Inferior, lower, under.

ښکر *kkhkar*, s.m. A horn, antler; powder horn.

ښکري *kkhkarai*, s.m. A flat round basket. See شکري *shkarai*.

ښکل *kkhkul*, s.m. A kiss. *kkhkul·kawul*, v.a. To kiss. *kkhkal*, v.a. To draw, pull, tighten; to pen, write; endure, suffer; flay, remove, strip. See کښل.

ښکلول *kkhkulawul*, v.a. To kiss.

ښکلي *kkhkulai*, a. Kissed; handsome, pretty; comely, elegant; agreeable, pleasant. *kkhkalai*, a. Drawn, tight, tense; written; suffered, endured, etc.

ښکنځل *kkhkandzal*, s.m. Abuse, vituperation. P. *kkhkandzal* or *kkhkandzal·kawul*, v.a. To abuse, call bad names, etc. P. (*shikanjīdan*).

ښکول *kkhakawul*, v.a. To move, shake, loosen; slide, slip; push, thrust. *kkhkawul*, v.a. To cause to draw, extract, etc. See ښکل *kkhkal*.

ښکېدل *kkhakedal*, v.n. To fall, glide, slip, slide.

ښکيل *kkhkel*, s.m. A hobble, tether, fetter for the feet of cattle (to prevent their straying); cheat, fraud, imposition, trick. See شکيل.

ښکيه *kkhkiya*, ad. See ښکته.

ښلونه *kkhalūna*, s.f. A whitlow, abscess, boil.

ښندل *kkhandal*, v.a. To bestow, contribute, give, dispense, spend, etc.

ښنزه *kkhanza*, s.f. A boil, abscess, pustule.

ښنګری *kkhangarai*, s.m. Ankle, ankle-joint; fetlock; a cloven hoof.

ښنه *kkhna*, s.f. The hip bone (*os ilium*).

ښوڅه *kkhūtsa*, s.f. Nettlerash, hives.

ښور *kkhor*, s.m. Nest or hive of ants, bees, or wasps, etc.

ښورن *kkhoran*, a. Barren, sterile; nitrous, saline (as land).

ښوروا *kkhorwā*, s.f. Soup, broth. P. (*shorbā*).

ښورول *kkhorawul*, v.a. To move, agitate, rock, wave to and fro, etc.

ښوره *kkhora*, s.f. Nitre, saltpetre. P. (*shora*). *kkhora-nāk*, a. Barren, sterile, full of nitre.

ښوریدل *kkhoredal*, v.n. To move, undulate, vibrate, wave, swing. P. (*shorīdan*).

ښونه *kkhona*, s.f. The olive tree.

ښوول *kkhowul*, v.a. To show, indicate. See ښيل.

ښوی *kkhwai*, a. Slippery, smooth.

ښوهول *kkhwahawul*, } v.a. To slide, slip, or
ښويول *kkhwayawul*, } push along (on a smooth surface).

ښوئیدل *kkhwa-edal*, v.n. To slip, slide, glide, fall down. Also ښوهیدل, *kkhwahedal*. P. (*shāfīdan*).

ښه *kkhah* or *kshah*, a. Good, proper, well; healthy, sound; fair, pleasant, etc. in. Well! Good! P. (*khūb*).

ښهر *kkhahr*, s.m. A town, city. P. (*shahr*).

ښي *kkhai* or *kshai*, a. Right, right hand, etc.

ښیره *kkhera* or *kshera*, s.f. Curse, malediction, imprecation, denunciation.

ښیښه *kkhīkkha*, s.f. A bottle, glass, phial. P. (*shīsha*).

ښیګړه *kkhegaṛa*, s.f. Excellence, goodness; value, worth; profit, advantage, benefit.

ښيل *kkhayal*, v.a. To show, point out; teach, instruct. P. (*nishāndan*). Def. in past ten. See ښوول. *kkhayal*, v.a. To reject, repudiate, turn off (as a disobedient son, etc.); to arm, equip oneself. P. (*shāyīdan*).

ښینه *kkhīna*, s.f. Sister-in-law, wife's sister.

ص

ص *swād* is the fourteenth letter of the Arabic and the twenty-fourth of the Pukkhto alphabet. It is generally pronounced like س, and is only found in words adopted from the Arabic.

صاحب *ṣāhib*, s.m. Master, lord; owner, possessor. A.

صادر *ṣādir*, a. Happened, issued, produced, passed, etc. A.

صاف *ṣāf*, a. Clean, pure, candid, frank, etc. A.

صافي *ṣāfī*, s.f. A filter, strainer.

صبا *ṣabā*, s.m. Morning, dawn; to-morrow; the morning breeze. A. (*ṣabāḥ*).

صبح *ṣubḥ*, s.f. Morning, daybreak, dawn. A.

صبر *ṣabr*, s.m. Endurance, patience. A.

صحاف *ṣaḥḥāf*, s.m. A bookbinder; bookseller. A.

صحبت *ṣuḥbat*, s.m. Companionship, society; picnic, dinner party, company; cohabitation; coition. A.

صحت *ṣiḥḥat*, s.m. Health, integrity, perfection. A.

صحرا *ṣaḥrā*, s.f. A desert, wilderness. A.

صحي *ṣaḥī*, a. Accurate, true, just, certain, perfect, entire. A. (*ṣaḥīḥ*).

صداقت *ṣadāqat*, s.m. Sincerity, truthfulness, candour, friendship. A.

صدقه *ṣadqa*, s.f. Alms, propitiatory offerings, sacrifice. A.

صديق *ṣadīq*, a. Faithful, true, sincere, just. A.

صراف *ṣarrāf*, s.m. A banker, money lender. A.

صرف *ṣirf*, ad. Only, alone; simply, merely,

etc. A. *ṣarf*, s.m. Excess, gain, increase; expense, expenditure, waste. A.

صرفه *ṣarfa*, s.f. Expense, expending; profit, profusion; surplus; waste. A.

صف *ṣaff*, s.m. A line, file, rank, row; series, order, etc. A.

صفا *ṣafā*, a. Clean, clear, pure. A.

صفائي *ṣafā-ī*, s.f. Purity, cleanness; innocence. A.

صفت *ṣifat*, s.m. Attribute, quality; commendation, praise; description; an adjective. A.

صفحه *ṣafḥa*, s.f. Page of a book; face, surface. A.

صفره *ṣafara*, s.f. Name of the second month of the Muḥammadan calendar. A. (*ṣafar*).

صلحه *ṣulḥa*, s.f. Concord, peace; reconciliation, truce, treaty, armistice. A. (*ṣulḥ*).

صلوة *ṣalāt*, } s.m. Benediction, prayer; صلات *ṣalāt*, } mercy or compassion of God. A.

صندل *ṣandal*, s.m. Sandal wood. A.

صندوق *ṣandūq*, s.m. A box, trunk, chest, casket. A.

صندوقچه *ṣandūqcha*, s.f. Casket, small box.

صنوبر *ṣanobar*, s.m. A fir, pine, conifer. A.

صواب *ṣawāb*, s.m. Virtuous action; rectitude, right. A.

صوبه *ṣūba*, s.f. A province, division of a country. A. *ṣūba·dār*, s.m. Viceroy, provincial governor.

صورت *ṣūrat*, s.m. Appearance, form, face; portrait, countenance; manner; case, condition, state; body, person; the privates. A.

صوفي *ṣūfī*, a. Pious, devout; intelligent, wise. s.m. A philosopher, members of the Sūfī sect. A.

صياد *ṣayād*, s.m. A hunter, fowler, sportsman A.

صيد *ṣaid*, s.m. Game, prey. A.

صيقل *ṣaiqal*, s.m. Cleaning, polishing, scouring, furbishing; a polisher, etc. A.

صيقلگر *ṣaiqal·gar*, s.m. A polisher of swords, knives, etc.

ض

ض *dwād* or *ẕād*, is the fifteenth letter of the Arabic, and the twenty-fifth of the Pukkhto alphabet. It is pronounced like ز, and is only found in words from the Arabic, in which language it has the sound of *d* or *dh*.

ضابط *ẕābiṭ*, s.m. Master, ruler, governor. A.

ضابطه *ẕābiṭa*, s.f. Canon law, rule, regulation. A.

ضامن *ẕāmin*, s.m. Security, sponsor, bail, bond. A.

ضامني *ẕāminī*, s.f. Surety, bail, security.

ضايعه *ẕāy'a*, s.f. Loss, detriment, injury. *ẕāy'ah*, a. Lost, destroyed, spoiled, perished; fruitless, abortive. A. (*ẕāī'*).

ضبط *ẕabṭ*, s.m. Confiscation; check, control. a. Confiscated, seized. A.

ضحا *ẕuḥā*, s.m. Forenoon, between sunrise and noon; a prayer repeated at that time. A.

ضد *ẕidd*, s.m. Contrary, opposite; enemy, rival; opposition, contrariety. A.

ضرب *ẕarb*, s.m. A blow, thump; coining; stamp; violence; emphasis (in speech). A.

ضرر *ẕarar*, s.m. Damage, detriment, injury; loss, ruin; affliction, distress. A.

ضرور *ẕarūr*, a. Expedient, necessary; urgent, unavoidable. A.

ضرورت *ẕarūrat*, s.m. Necessity, exigence, want; compulsion, force. A.

ضعف *ẕu'f*, s.m. Debility, weakness. A.

ضعيف *ẕa'īf*, a. Weak, feeble, infirm. A.

ضلعه *ẕil'a*, s.f. A district, division of a province. A.

ضماد *ẕamād*, s.m. Embrocation, plaister, A.
ضمانت *ẕamānat*, s.m. Security, bail, surety. A.
ضيافت *ẕiyāfat*, s.m. Banquet, entertainment, feast; invitation, hospitality. A.

ط

ط *ṯoe* is the sixteenth letter of the Arabic and the twenty-sixth of the Pukkhto alphabet. It is only found in words adopted from the Arabic, and has a sound stronger than ت, for which it sometimes changed.
طابوت *ṯābūt*, s.m. A coffin, bier. A.
طاعت *ṯā'at*, s.m. Obedience, devotion. A.
طاق *ṯāq*, s.m. An arch, cupola; alcove, shelf. a. Odd, singular, unique, not even. A. *juft-o-ṯāq*, s.m. Odd and even (the game).
طاقچه *ṯāqcha*, s.f. A niche, recess, shelf.
طاقت *ṯāqat*, s.m. Ability, force, power, strength. A.
طاقي *ṯāqī*, a. Arched, arching.
طالب *ṯālib*, s.m. An enquirer, seeker; student. Asking, demanding. A.
طالع *ṯāli'*, s.m. Appearing, rising (as the sun). A. *ṯāli'-man*, a. Fortunate, prosperous.
طائفه *ṯā-ifa*, s.f. People, nation, race, tribe; party, band, troop; suite, equipage. A.
طب *ṯibb*, s.m. Medicine, magic. A.
طبابت *ṯibābat*, s.m. The practice of medicine. A.
طباق *ṯabāq*, s.m. A kneading dish or platter. A.
طبعه *ṯab'a*, s.f. Disposition, temperament, nature, quality. A. (*ṯab'*).
طبق *ṯabaq*, s.m. A dish, plate; leaf; disk; cover; a layer; gold leaf. A.
طبقه *ṯabqa*, s.f. A floor, stage, story; class, order; degree, rank; a shelf, recess. A.
طبل *ṯabl*, s.m. A drum. A.
طبله *ṯabla*, s.f. A small tambourine, small drum; a wooden platter or tray for fruit, etc. A.
طبيب *ṯabīb*, s.m. A physician. A
طبيبي *ṯabībī*, s.f. Profession of a physician, physic. A.
طبيعت *ṯabī'at*, s.m. Nature, disposition, temper; constitution, health; property, quality, essence. A.
طبيله *ṯabela*, s.f. A stable. A.
طرب *ṯrab*, s.m. Hilarity, mirth, joy. A.
طرحه *ṯarḥa*, s.f. Manner, mode. A. (*ṯaraḥ*).
طرز *ṯarz*, s.m. Fashion, mode, manner. A.
طرف *ṯaraf*, s.m. Side, direction, quarter. A. *ṯaraf-dār*, s.m. A follower, partizan. a. Partial, prejudicial. *ṯaraf-dārī*, s.f. Favour, assistance; prejudice.
طرفين *ṯarafain*, s.m. Both sides, both parties. A.
طريقه *ṯarīqa*, s.f. Path, way; manner, mode; religion, rite; sect, party; custom, habit. A.
طعام *ṯa'ām*, s.m. Food, victuals; eating. A.
طعامبه *ṯa'āmba*, s.f. Food, victuals.
طعنه *ṯa'na*, s.f. Reproach, disgrace, reproof; scoffing, reviling, taunting. A. (*ṯa'n*).
طغيان *ṯug͟hiyān*, s.m. Rebellion, sedition; perverseness, insolence. *ṯug͟hiyānī*, s.f. Excess, overflowing, flood. A.
طفل *ṯifl*, s.m. Babe, infant. A. *ṯiflī* or *ṯufūliyat*, s.m. Infancy, childhood. A.
طفيل *ṯufail*, s.m. Sponger, parasite, glutton. A. ad. Through, by means of, by agency of. A.
طلا *ṯilā*, s.f. Gold; name of a gold coin, ducat. A.
طلاق *ṯilāq*, s.m. Divorce, repudiation. A.
طلاي *ṯilā-ī*, a. Golden, covered with gold. A.
طلب *ṯalab*, s.m. Demand, desire, request; call, summons; enquiry, search; pay, salary, A. *ṯalab-dār*, s.m. A credit dunning, demanding. *ṯalab-gār*, s.m. A seeker,

enquirer. a. Desirous. *ṭalab-nāma*, s.f. A summons, citation.

طلبه *ṭalaba*, s.f. A lure, call, etc. for hawks, etc.

طلسم *ṭilism*, s.m. Amulet, charm, spell, talisman; marvel, wonder, prodigy. A.

طمعه *ṭam'a*, s.f. Avidity; desire, longing; avarice, greediness, covetousness. A. (*ṭam'*).

طناب *ṭanāb*, s.m. Tent rope, clothes line, cord, etc. A.

طور *ṭaur*, s.m. Manner, mode; condition, state. A.

طوفان *ṭūfān*, s.m. Deluge, inundation; tempest, storm, hurricane. A. *ṭūfānī*, a. Boisterous, stormy; quarrelsome.

طوق *ṭauq*, s.m. Yoke, collar; necklace; ring for the neck. A.

طول *ṭūl*, s.m. Length. a. Long, lasting. A.

طومار *ṭūmār*, s.m. A book, volume. A.

طهارت *ṭahārat*, s.m. Purity, cleanliness; sancity; purification. A.

طي *ṭai*, s.m. Folding, rolling up. A.

ظ

ظ *z̤oe* is the seventeenth letter of the Arabic and the twenty-seventh of the Pukkhto alphabet. It is only found in words from the Arabic.

ظالم *z̤ālim*, s.m. Oppressor, tyrant. a. Cruel, oppressive, tyrannical. A.

ظاهر *z̤āhir*, a. Manifest, apparent, evident, clear; outward appearance.

ظاهرا *z̤āhirā*, ظاهراً *z̤āhiran*, } ad. Outwardly, apparently, publicly, openly, evidently. A.

ظاهري *z̤āhirī*, a. Outward, external, apparent. A.

ظرافت *z̤arāfat*, s.m. Elegance; politeness; wit, humour; polish. A.

ظرف *z̤arf*, s.m. A vase, vessel, jar. a. Witty, ingenious. A.

ظريف *z̤arīf*, a. Witty, jocose; ingenious, clever; elegant, polished, polite. A.

ظفر *z̤afar*, s.m. Victory, triumph. A.

ظلم *z̤ulm*, s.m. Oppression, injustice, cruelty, tyranny. A.

ظلمت *z̤ulmat*, s.m. Obscurity, darkness. A.

ظن *z̤ann*, s.m. Idea, thought, opinion; suspicion, jealousy. A.

ظنّي *z̤annī*, a. Supposed; suspected. A.

ظهر *z̤uhr*, s.m. Mid-day; the time just after the sun has passed the meridian. A.

ع

ع *'ain* is the eighteenth letter of the Arabic and the twenty-eighth of the Pukkhto alphabet. It is a very weak guttural aspirate, articulated by compression of the muscles of the fauces. It varies in sound according to the vowel point by which it is "moved," and in this work is represented by ' placed above and before the vowel by which it is "moved," as *'a*, *'i*, *'u*, etc. It is only found in words derived from the Arabic, and is sometime replaced by ا.

عابد *'ābid*, s.m. A devotee, votary. A.

عاجز *'ājiz*, a. Humble, helpless; hopeless, dejected; exhausted, weak; impotent, powerless. A.

عاجزي *'ājizī*, s.m. Weakness; helplessness; humility.

عادت *'ādat*, s.m. Custom, usage, habit. A. *'ādatī*, a. Habituated, accustomed, inured, addicted.

عادل *'ādil*, a. Just; upright, impartial. A.

عارف *'ārif*, a. Devout, holy; wise, ingenious. A.

عاريت *'āriyat*, s.m. Borrowing, lending (what is itself to be returned). A. *'āriyatī*, a. Borrowed; lent.

عاشق *'āshiq*, s.m. A lover. A. *'āshiqī*, s.f. Amour, love, courtship.

عاشوره *'āshora*, s.f. The first ten days of the month Muharram. A.

عاصي *'āṣī*, s.m. A sinner, rebel. A.

عافيت *'āfiyat*, s.m. Health, safety. A.

عاقبت *'āqibat*, s.m. Conclusion, end; futurity, the future. ad. After all, finally, at last. A.

عاقل *'āqil*, a. Sensible, wise. A.

عالم *'ālam*, s.m. The world, universe; people, mankind, creation; time, state. A. *'ālim*, a. Learned, knowing, wise. A.

عالي *'ālī*, a. Eminent, high, sublime. A.

عام *'āmm*, a. Common, general, public. s.m. The vulgar, public, common people. A.

عامّي *'āmmī*, s.m. A layman; one of the public.

عامل *'āmil*, s.m. Revenue collector, governor, ruler, finance minister. A.

عائد *'ā-id*, a. Happening, occurring; reverting, returning (as money, etc.). A.

عبادت *'ibādat*, s.m. Adoration, divine worship. A.

عبارت *'ibārat*, s.m. Meaning, signification; phrase, style, speech. A.

عبث *'abaṣ*, a. Vain, useless, absurd, idle. ad. In vain, uselessly. A.

عبرت *'ibrat*, s.m. Example, warning. A.

عبور *'ubūr*, s.m. A ferry, ford; crossing, passing over. A.

عتاب *'itāb*, s.m. Anger, displeasure, rebuke, reproach, reprimand. A.

عجائب *'ajā-ib*, a. Wonderful, astonishing. s.m. Wonders, curiosities. A.

عجب *'ajab*, عجيب *'ajīb*, } a. Wonderful, rare, curious. A.

عجز *'ajz*, s.m. Impotence, weakness, helplessness; meekness, humility, submission. A.

عدالت *'adālat*, s.m. A court of justice; equity, justice; law. A.

عداوت *'adāwat*, s.m. Animosity, enmity, hostility, hatred, strife. A.

عدد *'adad*, s.m. Number; item. A.

عدل *'adl*, s.m. Justice, equity. A.

عدم *'adam*, s.m. Nonexistence, nonentity; nothing; privation. A.

عدول *'udūl*, s.m. Refusing, declining. A.

عذاب *'azāb*, s.m. Anguish, torment, pain; torture, punishment. A.

عذر *'uzr*, s.m. Apology, excuse. A. *'uzr-khwāh*, s.m. Apologist; condoler, sympathizer. P. *'uzr-khwāhī*, s.f. Apology, excuse; condolence, sympathy. P.

عرس *'urs*, s.m. Oblations, offerings (to a saint); a marriage feast. A.

عرش *'arsh*, s.m. Firmament; roof; throne. A.

عرصه *'arṣa*, s.f. Area, space; interval, while, time; a plain. A.

عرض *'arẓ*, s.m. Petition, request, representation. A. *'arẓ-begī*, s.m. An officer who presents petitions, letters, etc. (in native courts). T. *'arẓ-dāsht*, s.m. Statement, written petition. P. *'arz-dār*, s.m. A petitioner. P. *'araẓ*, s.m. An accident, casualty; muster of troops. A.

عرضي *'arẓī*, s.f. A memorial, petition; letter from an inferior. A.

عرف *'urf*, a. Known as, alias, commonly called; the late; proper, equitable; goodness, merit; confession. A.

عرفي *'urfī*, a. Notorious, well-known, public. A.

عرق *'arq*, s.m. Essence, juice; spirit; sap; sweat. A.

عروس *'arūs*, s.m. Bridegroom, spouse. A. *'arūsa*, s.f. Bride. *'arūsī*, s.f. Marriage, wedding. A.

عزت *'izzat*, s.m. Grandeur, power; glory; honour, respect. A.

عزلت *'azlat*, s.m. Retirement (from office), dismissal, discharge. A.

عزلتي *'azlatī*, s.m. A hermit, recluse. A.

عزلي *'azlī*, s.f. Abdication, retirement. A.

عزم *'azm*, s.m. Purpose, intention, design. A.

عزيز *'azīz*, a. Dear, beloved, precious. s.m. An esteemed or honoured friend; great man, saint; a nephew; a king of Egypt (the title). A.

عزيزگلوي *'azīz·galwī*, عزيزولي *'azīz·walī*, s.m. Relationship between nephew and uncles.

عزيزي *'azīzī*, s.f. Esteem, respect, friendship.

عسل *'asl*, s.m. Honey. A.

عشر *'ushr*, s.m. Tithe, tenth part. A.

عشرت *'ashrat*, s.m. Enjoyment, pleasure, delight; society, pleasant intercourse, etc. A.

عشق *'ishq*, s.m. Affection, love. A. *'ishq·bāz*, a. Amorous, gallant. P. *'ishq·bāzī*, s.f. Love-making, gallantry. P.

عصا *'aṣā*, s.f. A club, mace, baton, staff. A.

عطا *'aṭā*, s.f. A gift, present; giving. A.

عطار *'aṭṭār*, s.m. A perfumer. A.

عطر *'aṭr*, s.m. Perfume, fragrance, essence. A.

عظيم *'aẓīm*, a. Great, huge, immense; high in dignity. A.

عفريت *'ifrīt*, s.m. Demon, spectre, ghost. A.

عقب *aqab*, ad. After, behind, in rear. A.

عقد *'aqd*, s.m. Agreement, compact, contract; knot; marriage knot; necklace, collar. A.

عقل *'aql*, s.m. Reason, sense; intellect, wisdom; opinion, understanding. A. *'aql·man*, a. Intelligent, wise. P. *'aql·manī*, s.f. Wisdom, intelligence. P.

عقلي *'aqlī*, a. Judicious, rational, sensible, reasonable. A.

عقوبت *'uqūbat*, s.m. Punishment, torture. A.

عقيده *'aqīda*, s.f. Belief, faith, tenet. A.

عكس *'aks*, s.m. Contrary, opposite; reflection, inversion; image, shadow. A.

علاج *'ilāj*, s.m. Cure, remedy; medicine. A.

علاقه *'ilāqa*, s.f. Relation, connection, interest; commerce, correspondence, intercourse. A.

علامت *'alāmat*, s.m. Mark, sign, symptom; emblem, ensign, escutcheon. A.

علاوه *'alāwa*, ad. Besides, in addition. A.

علت *'illat*, s.m. Cause, pretence; dirt, filth; defect, disease. A.

علف *'alaf*, s.m. Grass, hay, fodder. A.

علم *'ilm*, s.m. Knowledge, science. A.

علما *'ulamā*, s.m. The learned, scholars, wise. A.

علمي *'ilmī*, a. Learned, scientific. A.

علي *'alī*, a. Eminent, high, noble. A. *'alī bau·bau*, s.m. A bogy, goblin, scarecrow.

عليحده *'alaiḥidah*, a. Apart, separate, distinct. A.

عليم *'alīm*, a. Learned, wise. A.

عمارت *'imārat*, s.m. Building, edifice; habitation, fortification. A.

عمده *'umdah*, a. Great, noble; choice, excellent. A.

عمر *'umr*, s.m. Age, lifetime. A.

عمل *'amal*, s.m. Action, operation, effect; work, practice. A.

عمله *'amala*, s.f. Officials, staff, subordinates. A.

عملي *'amalī*, a. Practical, artificial. A.

عناب *'unnāb*, s.m. Jujube fruit and tree. A.

عناد *'inād*, s.m. Obstinacy, perverseness, stubbornness. A. *'inādī*, a. Stubborn, obstinate, etc.

عنايت *'ināyat*, s.m. Favour, gift, present. A.

عنقا *'unqā*, s.f. The phœnix. A.

عنقريب *'anqarīb*, ad. Nearly, shortly, soon. A.

عنكبوت *'ankabūt*, s.m. A spider. A.

عود *'ūd*, s.m. Aloes wood; incense. A.

عورت *'aurat*, s.m. The private parts. A.

عورته *'aurata*, s.f. A woman, wife.

عوض *'iwaẓ*, s.m. Retribution, recompense, reward; exchange. A.

عهد *'ahd*, s.m. Compact, contract; promise, treaty; conjuncture, season, time; reign, life-time; oath, vow. A.

عهده *'uhda*, s.f. Commission, obligation, agreement; appointment, office, post. A.

عيال *'ayāl*, s.m. Family, children; household, domestics, etc. A.

عيان *'ayān*, a. Clear, visible, manifest. A.

عيب *'aib*, s.m. Blemish, defect, vice; disgrace, fault, sin. A. *'aib-nāk*, a. Defective, faulty.

عيد *'īd*, s.m. Festival, holy day; Easter. A.

عيش *'aish*, s.m. Enjoyment, delight, pleasure. A. *'aish-o-'ashrat*, s.m. Jollity, enjoyment. A.

عين *'ain*, a. Exact, just, very, real, etc. s.m. The eye; sight; essence. A.

عينكه *'ainaka*, s.f. An eyeglass, spectacles. A. (*'ainak*).

غ

غ *ghain*, is the nineteenth letter of the Arabic, and the twenty-ninth of the Pukkhto alphabet. It is a guttural letter, and is pronounced by a compression of the fauces at the time of articulation. It is sometimes used instead of ق, and is itself sometimes replaced by ګ.

غاب *ghāb*, s.m. A dish, plate. A. (*qāb*).

غار *ghār*, s.m. A cave, cavern, pit. A.

غارت *ghārat*, s.m. Devastation, plunder, sack. A.

غارمه *ghārmah*, s.m. Sun's rays; heat of the sun; noonday heat. P. (*garma*).

غارندوني *ghārandūnai*, s.m. A kind of lizard, the iguana.

غاري *ghārai*, s.m. A glutton.

غاړه *ghāṛa*, s.f. The throat, fauces; coast, shore; border, bank, margin; neck of a bottle or jar; joke, pleasantry, fun. *ghāṛa-ghara-ī*, s.f. Embracing, hugging. a. Connected, joined together.

غازي *ghāzī*, s.m. Champion, hero, warrior (for the faith), crescentader. A.

غاښ *ghākkh*, s.m. A tooth.

غاښور *ghākkhawar*, s.m. Having large teeth; a kind of harrow or rake.

غاښي *ghākkhai*, s.m. A prong, pitchfork; crest or ridge of a mountain, pass over a mountain.

غافل *ghāfil*, a. Careless, negligent, thoughtless. A.

غالب *ghālab*, s.m. A form, mould. A. (*qālib*). *ghālib*, a. Excelling, overcoming, superior. ad. Most likely.

غالبوزه *ghālbūza*, s.f. A hornet, wasp.

غال وبول *ghāl-o-būl*, غال وغول *ghāl-o-ghūl*, } s.m. Clamour, uproar, noise, din.

غالي *ghāla-ī*, غاليچه *ghālīcha*, } s.f. A rug, small carpet. A.

غانده *ghāndah*, a. Disagreeable, offensive, loathsome, stinking. P. (*gandah*).

غاو *ghāw*, s.m. Noise, din, uproar, tumult.

غاوچي *ghāwchī*, s.m. Doorkeeper, porter.

غائب *ghā-ib*, a. Absent, invisible, concealed. A

غايت *ghāyat*, a. Very, chiefly, extremely. s.m. Extremity, end; filth, ordure, dirt. A.

غبار *ghubār*, s.m. Dust, haze, obscurity, vapour; impurity, foulness. A.

غبرګ *ghbarg*, a. Double, duplex, twofold.

غبغب *ghab-ghab*, s.m. Dewlap, double-chin. P.

غپ *ghap*, s.m. Bark, yelp, snap (of a dog).

غپل *ghapal*, v.a. To bark, snap, yelp, etc.

غپه *ghupa*, s.f. A dip, dive, plunge.

غټ *ghaṭ*, a. Big, bulky, large, stout, great, etc.; great in rank, power, etc. H. (*kaṭṭā*).

غټي *ghaṭai*, s.m. A block, lump, mass, etc.

غڅکي *ghutskai*, s.m. A bullock, ox, bull.

غچ *ghach*, s.m. Hatred, malice, spite, envy. Noise, sound of walking in mud, etc. H.

غچي *ghachī*, s.f. Scissors. See بياتي.

غدر *ghadar*, s.m. Villany, deceit, perfidy. A.

غذا *ghizā*, s.m. Aliment, food, diet. A.

غر *ghar*, s.m. Mountain, hill. S. (*gir*). *ghur*, s.m. Bronchocele, goitre. *gha-ar*, s.m. Leap, bound, jump. Rattle (as of wheels).

غرا *gharā*, s.f. Peal, roar, boom, thunder; roaring, thundering (noise).

غراره *gharāra*, s.f. A large sack. A.

غرانډه *gharānḍa*, s.f. A blaze, flame.

غربت *ghurbat*, s.m. Emigration, travelling; exile, separation from friends. A.

غربه *gharaba*, s.f. A cannon, gun.

غربي *gharabbai*, s.m. Boom, report (of a cannon). A buckle, breastplate, clasp.

غرپ *ghurap*, s.m. A gulp. P.

غرپش *ghurpish*, s.m. Din, clamour, noise, row.

غرڅني *ghartsanai*, a. Mountain, highland, of the hills.

غرڅه *ghartsah*, a. A hill goat; inhabitant of the hills, highland (animal).

غرزنگ *ghurzang*, s.m. A bound, leap. P.

غرض *gharaz*, s.m. Aim, object, design, purpose; business, meaning, interest, occasion, use, want; spite, selfishness, hatred. ad. In fine, in short, in a word.

غرغړه *gharghaṛa*, s.f. Gurgling, a gurgle. A. A blaze, flame, fire.

غرغشت *gharghusht*, s.m. Romping, frolic, fun, sport; a play amongst women. *ghurghusht*, s.m. Name of the third son of Kais. *ghurghushtī*, s.m. The Ghurghushtis, clan or tribe of Ghurghusht.

غرغشتي *gharghashtī*, s.f. A kind of peach (*Amygdalus Persicus*).

غرق *gharq*, a. Drowned, sunk, immersed. A.

غرقاب *gharqāb*, s.m. A whirlpool, vortex. P.

غرکمانه *ghur-kamāna*, s.f. A pellet bow. P. (*golā*). P. (*kamān*).

غرگي *ghargai*, s.m. Boulder, rock; stone, pebble; hillock, mound.

غرمه *gharma*, s.f. Noon, mid-day, hottest part of the day. *ṭakanḍa-*, *ṭakanṛa-*, or *ṭakana-ī-gharma*, s.f. Exactly noon, hottest time of the day.

غرند *ghrand*, s.m. The neck, throat, windpipe. P. (*gardan*).

غرندي *ghrandai*, s.m. The hollow over the collar bone.

غرنگ *gharang*, s.m. The creaking of a wheel.

غرنيکه *ghar-nīkah*, s.m. A great grandfather.

غروب *ghurūb*, s.m. The west; setting (of the sun). A.

غرور *ghurūr*, s.m. Pride, vanity. A.

غروري *ghurūrai*, s.m. A node, tumour.

غره *gharah*, a. Haughty, arrogant, proud, vain: deceived, misled; cross, stern. A. *ghara*, s.f. Backside, podex. *ghurra*, s.f. First day of the moon; whiteness. A.

غري *gharai*, s.m. The throat. See غرند.

غرياښه *ghuryākkha*, s.f. } A buttonhole, loop.
غرياښي *ghuryākkhai*, s.m. } See پلواښه.

غريب *gharīb*, a. Meek, humble; poor; foreign, strange. A.

غريدل *gharedal*, v.n. To chatter, gabble, jabber; to bellow, roar; peal, boom, thunder.

غريز *gharīz*, s.m. Clemency, forbearance. P.

غريو *gharew*, s.m. Noise, hum, murmur; lamentation, groaning, weeping. P.

غړانگه *ghaṛānga*, s.f. A shout, scream, yell; a long neck. *ghaṛānga-war*, a. Long-necked.

غړڅکي *ghuṛutskai*, s.m. A spark. See بڅري.

غرل *gharal*, v.a. To plait, spin, twist, roll; to fold, roll up, envelop. See غښتل.

غرنب. *ghurunb*, s.m. Boom, peal, roar, thunder, etc.

غرنبل *ghranbal*, v.n. } To bellow, roar, low; غرنبېدل *ghranbedal*, } to peal, thunder, boom.

غرند *gharand*, a. Lax, loose; frail, soft, weak; idle, lazy, negligent; tardy, slow; cautious, stealthy, sly.

غروندي *gharwandai*, s.f. A dog collar, halter, tether for horses; a loop, slip knot; the loop in the letters ټ, ډ, ړ.

غري *gharai*, s.m. A kind of coarse bread given to the poor; the calf of the leg.

غرېدل *gharedal*, v.n. To growl, snarl; to grate, jar (upon the ear); to blow, wheeze, breathe roughly.

غز *ghaz*, s.m. The Tamarisk tree (*Tamarix Indica*).

غزا *ghazā*, s.f. War against infidels, crescentade. in. Astonishing! A.

غزار *ghuzār*, a. Dropped, fallen, upset.

غزل *ghazal*, s.m. An ode, love song. A.

غزول *ghazawul*, v.a. To lay flat, lay down, prostrate, stretch out (as the arm, leg, etc.).

غزيدل *ghazedal*, v.n. To lie down, lie flat, recline, etc. Also *gazedal*.

غږ *ghag*, s.m. Noise, sound, voice, etc.

غږول *ghagawul*, v.a. To sound, make a noise, etc.

غږيدل *ghagedal*, v.n. To sound, resound, vibrate, etc.

غسل *ghusl*, s.m. Ablution, bathing. A.

غشايه *ghushāyah*, s.m. pl. of غشوئي.

غشو *ghasho*, s.m. A curry comb.

غشوئي *ghushoe*, s.m. Dung of cows and buffaloes.

غشي *ghashai*, s.m. An arrow; spoke of a wheel; pole or shaft of a cart, plough, etc. a. Direct, swift, straight.

غښتل *ghakkhtal*, v.a. To plait, twist; roll, fold, envelop. Def. in pres. ten. See غرل.

غصب *ghasab*, } s.m. Compulsion, force; oppression, violence; plunder; passion, vengeance, wrath. A.
غضب *ghazab*, }

غصه *ghussa*, s.f. Anger, passion. A.

غفلت *ghaflat*, s.m. Negligence, carelessness. A.

غفور *ghafūr*, a. Merciful, forgiving. A.

غل *ghal*, s.m. A thief, robber. *ghul*, s.m. Dung, excrement, fæces.

غلا *ghlā*, s.f. Robbery, theft.

غلاف *ghilāf*, s.m. A case, cover, sheath. A.

غلام *ghulām*, s.m. A slave. A.

غلانزه *ghulānza*, s.f. Udder, mammary gland.

غلبله *ghalbala*, s.f. Noise, uproar, tumult.

غلبه *ghalaba*, s.f. Advantage, superiority assault; prevalence; strength. A.

غلبيل *ghalbel*, s.m. A colander, sieve; sifting winnowing. P. (*ghirbāl*).

غلت *ghulat*, s.m. Cheat, trick, deceit (a. play). *ghulatī*, s.f. Swindling, cheating.

غلط *ghalat*, s.m. Error, mistake. a. Wrong, mistaken. A.

غلغله *ghulghula*, s.f. Tumult, row, disturbance, etc. P.

غلوزه *ghlawza*, s.f. A honey bee. See لوزه.

غلول *ghulawul*, v.a. To deceive, dupe, mislead. H. (*ghūlānā*).

غله *ghalla*, s.f. Corn, grain. A.

غلي *ghalai*, a. Concealed, hidden; silent, still; sneaking, stealthy. *ghulai*, s.m. A whirlpool, eddy, vortex; a bubble.

غليم *ghalīm*, s.m. A robber; enemy. A. (*ghanīm*). *ghalīmī*, s.f. Animosity, hatred, enmity.

غم *gham*, s.m. Anxiety, sorrow, grief. A. *gham-jan*, a. Grieved, sorrowful.

غمّاز *ghammāz*, s.m. Informer, tale-bearer. A.
ghammāzī, s.f. Backbiting, tale-bearing.

غماشه *ghamāsha*, s f. A gnat, musquito.

غمبه *ghumba*, s.f. A gland, bubo, tumour.

غمزه *ghamza*, s.f. A wink, glance; ogling. A.

غمي *ghamai*, s.m. The stone of a ring; a seal; ferule of a knife handle, etc.

غميدل *ghamedal*, v.n. To fret, chafe, worry; to be overcome, subdued, conquered.

غنا *ghanā*, s.f. Riches, wealth. A.

غنچه *ghuncha*, s.f. A bud, sprout; a bunch. P.

غندِ *ghundi*, a. See غوندِ.

غندل *ghandal*, s.f. A sprout, shoot; young shoots of mustard and other plants used as potherbs. *ghandal*, v.a. To disparage, run down, find fault with; to dislike, disapprove, disrelish.

غنداړي *ghundārai*, s.m. A noose, snare for birds (formed of a hair loop fixed to a lump of clay); a phlegmon, carbuncle; a disease in cows, etc.

غندايه *ghundāyah*, s.m. A lad, youth, stripling; a boor, clodhopper, country bumpkin.

غندهاري *ghundhārai*, s.m. See غنداړي.

غنزاښه *ghunzākkha*, s.f. A kind of sweet cake made of flour and sugar, fried in butter.

غنزاښي *ghunzākkhai*, s.m. An instrument for separating the seeds of cotton from the fibre.

غنم *ghanum*, s.m. Wheat. P. (*gandum*).

غنه *ghana*, s.f. A thorny bush, branch of a thorny tree. pl. *ghane*, thorns, bramble.

غني *ghanī*, a. Wealthy, rich. A.

غنيمت *ghanīmat*, s.m. Plunder; abundance; good fortune, boon. A.

غنړه *ghanra*, s.f. A kind of spider, the tarantula (*Lycosa tarantula*).

غو *gho*, s.m. Copulation, coition.

غوا *ghwā*, s.f. A cow. S. and P. (*gāw*).

غواښكي *ghwākkhkai*, s.m. The notch in the head of an arrow.

غوباړي *ghobārai*, s.m. A horsefly, gadfly.

غوبل *ghobal*, s.m. Treading out corn by driving cattle over it; threshing.

غوبني *ghobanī*, s.f. Cowherding, tending cattle.

غوبه *ghobah*, s.m. A cowherd, grazier of cows.

غوپه *ghopa*, s.f. A dive, dip, plunge; dipping, submersion, immersion.

غوټ *ghūṭ*, a. Docked, clipped, cut short.

غوټه *ghoṭa*, s.f. A dip, dive, plunge; dipping, immersion; a clutch, snatch, swoop; a fit, paroxysm, convulsion. A. (*ghoṭā*). *ghūṭa*, s.f. An articulation, joint, knot; band, strap; group, party (of horsemen.)

غوټي *ghūṭai*, a. Docked, cropped, cut short. s.m. A horse with a docked tail, dog with cut ears, man with an amputated limb, tree with the boughs cut off, etc. *ghūṭa-ī*, s.f. A rose-bud, a bud; a globule, drop, bubble; a button, knot, jewelled flower, etc.

غوجل *ghojal*, s.f. A cow-shed, cow-pen.

غوڅ *ghwats*, a. Cut, divided, incised.

غوچه *ghūcha*, in. Ho! Hallo! I say!

غور *ghaur*, s.m. Reflection, thought, meditation, care, attention. A.

غوراسكي *ghwarāskai*, s.m. Name of a shrub (*Dodonœa Burmanniana*).

غورزول *ghwarzawul*, v.a. To fling, pitch, project; to cast off, throw away.

غورزيدل *ghwarzedal*, v.n. To palpitate, toss, flutter, bound, etc.

غوره *ghūrah*, s.m. A cotton pod; unripe dates or grapes. P. *ghwarah*, a. Choice, good, excellent, preferable. P. (*gawārah*).

غوړ *ghwaṛ*, s.m. Fat, grease, suet. a. Oily, greasy, fatty, unctuous.

غوړپكه *ghoṛpaka*, s.f. Calamity, accident; event, occurrence; cry of distress.

غوړول *ghwaṛawul*, v.a. To unclose, open (the

eyes); distend, inflate, spread. *ghwaṛawul*, v.a. To anoint, grease, oil, lubricate, etc.

غوړي *ghwaṛī*, s.m. Butter, grease, tallow, *ghī*.

غوړيدل *ghwaṛedal*, v.n. To germinate, sprout, grow, expand, spread, open, unfold, etc.

غوړيژه *ghwaṛeja*, s.f. Name of a plant (*Indigofera Gerardiana*).

غوز *ghoz*, s.m. The fat of the kidneys; flatus, wind from the belly. P.

غوزکرکي *ghozakurkai*, s.m. A dung beetle.

غوزه *ghoza*, s.f. Pod, capsule, cocoon, shell, etc. P. (*ghoja*).

غوزي *ghūzai*, s.m. Bosom, embrace, arms; armful; lap. P. (*āghosh*). *ghozai*, s.m. A kind of black beetle.

غوږ *ghwag*, s.m. The ear; screw of a violin. P. (*gosh*).

غوږي *ghwagai*, s.m. A floodgate, lock, sluice; the horn end of a bow; key of a violin; streak of sunlight through clouds.

غوشاك *ghoshāk*, s.m. Fresh cowdung.

غوښت *ghokkht*, s.m. Italian millet (*Panicum Italicum*). Desire, request, want, wish. P. (*khwāst*).

غوښتل *ghokkhtal*, v.a. To solicit, request, desire, wish, want. P. (*khwāstan*, *khwāh-*).

غوښه *ghwakkha*, s.f. Flesh, meat. P. (*gosht*). *ghwakkha-war*, a. Fleshy, stout, plump.

غوښي *ghokkhai*, s.m. See غوږي.

غوغا *ghoghā*, s.f. Clamour, din, noise, etc. P.

غول *ghūl*, s.m. An imaginary demon of the woods, man-wolf, loup-garou. A. *ghol*, s.m. Party, crowd, gang; corps, troop, company; flock, flight (of birds). H. (*gol*).

غولونكي *gholawunkai*, s.m. A stye on the eyelid.

غوله‌كمانه *ghola-kamāna*, s.f. See غركمانه.

غولي *gholai*, s.m. Area, yard, court. *ghola-ī*, s.f. A small party, gang; small flock (of birds).

غوند *ghūnd*, a. Alike, similar.

غوندې *ghūndi*, غوندي *ghūnde*, ad. As if, as it were, just as, etc.

غوندي *ghūndai*, s.m. A bag, pannier or sack of goat's hair (for carrying loads upon camels, bullocks, etc.). S. (*gon*).

غونډ *ghūnḍ*, a. Round, globular, circular; plump, squat; lumpy. s.m. A bubo.

غونډري *ghūnḍurai*, s.m. A ball, globe, anything circular or round, a lump.

غونډكئ *ghūnḍaka-ī*, s.f. Any round projection, knob, or mass; *mons veneris*.

غونډه *ghūnḍa*, s.f. A hillock, small detached hill, a mound; lump of dough; boulder, pebble, etc.

غونډهاري *ghūnḍhārai*, s.m. See غنډاري.

غونډي *ghūnḍai*, a. Dumpy, low, squat, dwarf, short; a venomous spider, tarantula. *ghūnḍa-ī*, s.f. A low mound, hillock; a dumpy or short woman, etc.

غونزيدل *ghūnzedal*, v.n. To creep, crawl.

غونه *ghūna*, s.f. The hair of the skin; pores of the skin; colour of the skin. *ghūna-zīgedal*, v.n. To roughen (as the skin from from cold, etc.), to stand on end (as the hair, etc.), to horripilate.

غوول *ghowul*, v.a. To copulate, have sexual intercourse. P. (*gādan*). Def. in pres. ten. See غيل.

غوئيلنك *ghwa-e-lang*, s.m. The rope passed between the hind legs of a bullock to fix the packsaddle; a crupper.

غوئيمنډ *ghwa-e-manḍ*, s.m. Stampede of oxen or cattle; footmarks of a herd of cattle; a rush, bolt, stampede. a. Trodden, trampled, crushed (under foot).

غوئيمه *ghwa-ema*, s.f. A cow or buffalo ready for, or seeking the male.

غوئي *ghwa-e*, s.m. A bull; bullock, ox.

غه *ghah*, pr. See هغه.

غيب *ghaib*, a. Absent, invisible, concealed. A.

غيبت *ghībat*, s.m. Slander, detraction, calumny. A. *ghaibat*, s.m. Absence, invisibility. A.

غير *ghair*, a. Different, strange, foreign. ad. except, unless. s.m. A stranger. In composition it denotes negation. A.

غيرت *ghairat*, s.m. Modesty, bashfulness; self-respect; honour, courage; emulation, jealousy, enmity. A. *ghairat-man*, a. or *ghairat-nāk*, a. Bashful; jealous; emulous, etc.

غيره *ghyara*, s.f. The wild donkey, wild ass.

غيږ *gheg*, s.m. The arms, embrace, bosom; an armful; the lap; a wallet. P. (*āghosh*).

غيل *ghayal*, v.a. To copulate. Def. in past ten. See غوول. P. (*gā-īdan*). *ghīl*, s.m. A grove, wood, forest. A.

غيله *ghela*, s.f. A herd or flock of goats and sheep. P. (*galla*).

غيړ *gheṛ*, s.m. The penis of a man or beast; *membrum virile*. P. (*ker*).

ف

ف *fe* is the twentieth letter of the Arabic, and thirtieth of the Pukkhto alphabet. It is frequently changed for پ.

فاتحه *fātiha*, s.f. Commencement, exordium; the beginning of the first chapter of the Qurān; it is repeated when praying for the souls of the dead. A.

فاجر *fājir*, s.m. Adulterer, fornicator. A.

فاحش *fāhish*, a. Indecent, obscene. A.

فارسي *fārsī*, a. Persian. P.

فارغ *fārigh*, a Disengaged, at leisure. A.

فاسد *fāsid*, a. Depraved, vicious. A.

فاسق *fāsiq*, a. Impious, sinful; fornicator. A.

فاش *fāsh*, a. Apparent, manifest. P.

فاصله *fāṣila*, s.f. Interval, space. A.

فاضل *fāẓil*, a. Abundant; excellent; learned. A.

فاعل *fā'il*, s.m. Agent, actor; doing, making. A.

فاقه *fāqa*, s.f. Starvation; poverty, want. A.

فال *fāl*, s.m. Augury, omen; diet, regimen. A.

فالتو *fāltū*, a. Spare, surplus. H.

فالوده *fālūda*, s f. Name of a sweetmeat; a kind of flummery. P.

فانوس *fānūs*, s.m. A lantern; shade for a lamp. P.

فاني *fānī*, a. Transitory, inconstant. A.

فائده *fā-ida*, s.f. Advantage, benefit, profit. A.

فتحه *fatha*, s.f. Conquest, victory. A.

فتراك *fitrāk*, s.m. Saddle straps; cords fixed to a saddle and used to tie game, etc., to. P.

فتنه *fitna*, s.f. Disturbance, hostility; sedition, strife. A.

فتور *futūr*, s.m. Anarchy, strife, quarrel. A.

فتوى *fatwā*, s.f. Decree, sentence, judgment. A.

فتيله *fatīla*, s.f. A match, wick. A.

فدا *fidā*, s.f. Ransom, sacrifice. A.

فراخ *farākh*, a. Ample, spacious; abundant, cheap; wide, expanded. P.

فرار *farār*, a. Absconding, flight. *farārī*, s.m. A deserter, runaway. A.

فراست *firāsat*, s.m. Sagacity, penetration. A.

فراش *farāsh*, s.m. Valet, bed-maker, chamberlain; carpet spreader. A.

فراغت *firāghat*, s.m. Ease, leisure, repose. A.

فراق *firāq*, s.m. Absence, separation. A.

فراموش *farāmosh*, a. Forgotten. P.

فراوان *farāwān*, a. Abundant, much. P.

فرحت *farhat*, s.m. Pleasure, joy. A.

فرد *fard*, s.m. A list, catalogue, roll; sheet (of paper); individual, one, single. A.

فردا *fardā*, s.f. Morrow, to-morrow. A.

فرزند *farzand*, s.m. A child, issue, progeny. P.

فرسخ *farsakh*, } s.m. A league, parasang;
فرسنگ *farsang*, } four miles. P.

فرش *farsh*, s.m. Flooring, pavement; carpeting; bedding; matting, etc. A.

فرښته *firikkhta*, s.m. An angel. P. (*firishta*).

فرصت *furṣat*, s.m. Ease, convenience, leisure; occasion, opportunity, rest. A.

فرض *farẓ*, s.m. Divine command; obligation, duty, indispensable duty. A.

فرق *farq*, s.m. Difference, distinction. A.

فرقه *firqa*, s.f. A class, tribe, set, sect. A.

فرمان *farmān*, s.m. Command, order; edict, grant, patent. P.

فرمايل *farmāyal*, v.a. To command, order, direct. P. (*farmūdan*).

فرنګي *farangī*, a. European, Frank. P. *farangai*, s.m. A European.

فرياد *faryād*, s.m. Complaint, cry for redress, exclamation, lament. P.

فريب *fareb*, s.m. Deception, trick; fraud, deceit. P.

فريبي *farebī*, a. Impostor, cheat. P.

فريفته *fareftah*, a. Infatuated, charmed, enamoured. P.

فريوان *frewān*, a. See فراوان.

فساد *fasād*, s.m. Mutiny, rebellion; disturbance, tumult, riot. A. *fasādī*, a. Rebellious, mutinous, seditious, etc.

فسق *fisq*, s.m. Adultery; obscenity; iniquity, sin. A.

فصل *faṣl*, s.m. Crop, harvest; time, season; section, chapter. A.

فصيح *faṣīḥ*, a. Eloquent, fluent (in speech). A.

فصيل *faṣīl*, s.m. Breastwork, parapet. A.

فضل *faẓl*, s.m. Excellence, virtue; increase, gain; favour, gift, grace. A.

فضول *fuẓūl*, a. Redundant, exuberant; excessive, extravagant. A. *fuẓūlī*, s.f. Excess, redundance, extravagance.

فطر *fiṭr*, s.m. Breaking (a fast). A. *'īdu-l-fiṭr*, s.m. The festival held on the termination of the Ramaẓān. A.

فطرت *fiṭrat*, s.m. Cunning, sagacity; alms distributed on the *'īdu-l-fiṭr*. A.

فعل *f'il*, s.m. Operation, action, work; a verb. A.

فغان *fighān*, s.m. Complaint, lament, wail. in. Alas! P.

فقر *fuqr*, s.m. Poverty, beggary. A.

فقط *faqaṭ*, ad. Merely, simply, only. A.

فقهه *fiqha*, s.f. Theology, jurisprudence. A. (*fiqh*).

فقيه *faqīh*, s.m. A thelogian. A.

فقير *faqīr*, s.m. A beggar, mendicant (religious). A. *faqīrī*, s.f. Beggary, poverty; life of a faqīr.

فکر *fikr*, s.m. Reflection, thought; idea, notion; care, concern; anxiety, solicitude. A.

فلان *falān*, s.m. Penis, *membrum virile*. P.

فلانکي *falānkai*, } s.m. A certain one, so and
فلاني *falānai*, } so, such a thing, etc. A. (*falāna*).

فلک *falak*, s.m. The heavens, sky; destiny, fate, fortune. A.

فليته *falīta*, s.f. See فتيله.

فليل *fulel*, s.m. A kind of scented hair oil.

فن *fann*, s.m. Science, skill, art. A.

فنا *fanā*, s.f. Frailty, mortality. a. Frail, mortal. A.

فواره *fawāra*, s.f. A jet, spout, fountain, spring. A.

فوت *faut*, s.m. Death. A. *fautī*, a. Dead.

فوج *fauj*, s.m. An army. A.

فوفنا *fū-fanā*, a. Annihilated, destroyed, utterly destroyed, exterminated.

فهرست *fihrist*, s.m. Index; list, inventory. P.

فيصله *faiṣala*, s.f. Decision, decree; sentence, settlement. A. *faiṣal*, a. Decided, settled.

فيض *faiẓ*, s.m. Abundance, plenty; bounty, favour, grace. A.

فيل *fīl*, s.m. An elephant. P

ق

ق *qāf*, is the twenty-first letter of the Arabic, and the thirty-first of the Pu<u>kkh</u>to alphabet. With few exceptions it is only found in words from the Arabic.

قاب *qāb*, s.m. A kneading trough; platter, dish, salver. A.

قابض *qābiẓ*, a. Astringent; seizing, taking. A.

قابل *qābil*, a. Able, clever, skilful, worthy; possible, sufficient. A.

قابله *qābila*, s.f. A midwife.

قابو *qābū*, s.m. Authority, command; will, power; opportunity, possession. T.

قاتر *qātar*, s.m. A mule. P.

قاتل *qātil*, a. Deadly, killing, mortal. s.m. An assassin, murderer. A.

قاتي *qātī*, s.f. See قحط.

قادر *qādir*, a. Powerful, potent. A.

قادري *qādarai*, a. Curtailed, docked, cut off. *qādara-ī*, s.f. A kind of frock or gown worn by the Afghans.

قارغه *qār<u>gh</u>ah*, s.m. A crow, rook.

قاري *qārī*, s.m. A reader of the Qurān. A.

قاري‌درياب *qārī-dariyāb*, } s.m. The ocean, sea.
قالي‌درياب *qalī-dariyāb*, } A. (*q'ari-daryā*).

قاشوغه *qā<u>sh</u>o<u>gh</u>a*, s.f. A ladle, spoon. P.

قاصد *qāṣid*, s.m. Courier, messenger, postman. A.

قاصر *qāṣir*, a. Defective, impotent; deficient, failing. A.

قاضي *qāẓī*, s.m. A judge, lawgiver. A.

قاعده *qā'ida*, s.f. Rule, system; custom, manner. A.

قاغه *qā<u>gh</u>a*, s.f. A crow, jackdaw, chough. S. (*kāgā*).

قافله *qāfila*, s.f. A caravan, travelling party. A.

قال *qāl*, s.m. A word, saying, speech. A. *qīl-o-qāl*, s.m. Dispute, altercation, controversy.

قالب *qālib*, s.m. A mould, cast; form, figure, bust, model; the body. A.

قالي *qālī*, s.f. } A carpet, woollen carpet. P.
قالين *qālīn*, s.m. }

قاليچه *qālī<u>ch</u>a*, s.f. A rug, drugget, small carpet. P.

قام *qām*, s.m. Family, tribe. See قوم.

قامت *qāmat*, s.m. Stature; figure, form. A.

قانع *qān'i*, a. Satisfied, contented. A.

قانون *qānūn*, s.m. Canon, regulation, statute, rule. A.

قائزه *qā-iza*, s.f. A watering bridle; bit of a bridle. A. (*qā-izī*).

قائل *qā-il*, a. Convinced, acknowledging. A.

قائم *qā-im*, a. Firm, fixed, stable, erect. A.

قبا *qabā*, s.f. A frock, gown, jacket; a quilted coat; cover for a book. A.

قباحت *qabāḥat*, a. Deformity; dishonesty, wrong. A.

قبر *qabar*, s.m. A grave, tomb. A.

قبض *qabẓ*, s.m. Contraction; costiveness; astringency; receipt; tax, tribute. A.

قبضه *qabẓa*, s.f. Handle (of a sword, etc.); grip, grasp; possession. A.

قبل *qabl*, First, foremost. ad. Previously, before. A. *qabal*, a. Besieged, invested, surrounded. A. *qibal*, s.m. Power; plenty; presence; on the part of, in respect of. A.

قبله *qibla*, s.f. In front, opposite; altar, temple; worship; father. A.

قبول *qabūl*, s.m. Assent, consent; approbation, favourable reception. a. Accepted, approved, consented. A. A holster.

قبولي *qabūlai*, s.m. A holster, pistol case for saddle. A. (*qubūr*).

قبه *qubba*, s.f. An arch, dome, vault. A.

قبيله *qabīla*, s.f. A family; tribe; wife. A.

قت *qat*, s.m. A fold, layer, plait. *qat-pa-qat*, Fold on fold, layer on layer.

قتار *qatār*, s.m. A line, file, rank, row, series, order. A. (*qaṭār*).

قتاري *qatārai*, s.m. Contention, squabble, foolish talk; a wrangler.

قتره *qatra*, s.f. A drop, minim. A. (*qaṭra*).

قتغ *qata<u>gh</u>*, s.m. Meat, fish, soup, etc., eaten with bread to give it a relish; made dish, entrée. P.

قتال *qitāl*, s.m. Battle, slaughter. A.

قتل *qatl*, s.m. Slaughter, homicide, murder. A.

قتي *qutai*, s.m. A ball for play (made of leather or cotton). *quta-ī*, s.f. A dimple on the cheek. *qutta-ī*, s.f. A powder flask (made of untanned leather). S. (*kuppī*).

قجري *qajarī*, s.f. A kind of saddle cloth made of thick felt (it covers the saddle and the horse's fore and hind quarters as well). P.

قچر *qa<u>ch</u>ar*, s.m. A mule. a. Obstinate, perverse. H. (*kha<u>ch</u><u>ch</u>ar*). s.m. A sneak, knave, rogue, cheat. H. (*kam<u>ch</u>or*).

قچي *qi<u>ch</u>ai*, s.m. A band, gang, party.

قحط *qaḥṭ*, s.m. Famine, scarcity, dearth. A.

قد *qadd*, s.m. Height, stature. A.

قدر *qadr*, s.m. Value, worth, price; dignity, importance; degree, measure; quantity, size; destiny, fate. A.

قدرت *qudrat*, s.m. Authority, power; omnipotence. A.

قدرتي *qudratī*, a. Divine. A.

قدغن *qada<u>gh</u>an*, } s.m. Prohibition, injunc-
قتغن *qata<u>gh</u>an*, } tion. P.

قدم *qadam*, s.m. Footstep, pace. A.

قديم *qadīm*, a. Ancient, old. A.

قر *qur*, s.m. Rumbling sound in the bowels. *qur-qur*, s.m. Borborygmus. A. (*qarāqar*).

قرابت *qarābat*, s.m. Affinity, kinship, relationship; vicinity, proximity. A.

قرات *qirāt*, s.m. Reading, pronunciation. A.

قرار *qarār*, s.m. Rest, quiet, tranquility; stability, firmness; agreement, engagement; patience, waiting. a. Firm, stable; quiet, tranquil. A.

قراري *qarārī*, s.f. Firmness, stability; rest, ease. a. Firm, stable; quiet, etc.

قران *qurān*, s.m. Name of the book of the Arabian prophet Muḥammad; also called *furqān*.

قراول *qarāwal*, s.m. Advance guard of an army; picquet, vidette, sentinel. T.

قربان *qurbān*, s.m. Sacrifice, oblation, victim; a quiver. A.

قربت *qurbat*, s.m. Relationship; proximity. A.

قرت *qurut*, s.m. A kind of very hard cheese; a ball of compressed and dried curds. *qurut-kā<u>n</u>rai*, s.m. A pebble of nodular limestone (so named from the resemblance to a nodule or ball of *qurut*), *kankar*.

قرص *qurṣ*, s.m. An orb, disc; the sun; name of an ornament for the neck (of women).

قرض *qarẓ*, s.m. A debt; loan. A.

قرط *qurṭ*, s.m. A gulp, draught. A.

قرعه *qur'a*, s.f. Lot, wager, drawing lots. A.

قرق *qurq*, s.m. Confiscation, embargo, seizure. A.

قرقره *qarqara*, s.f. A plume of feathers for the head (generally of crane's feathers). A. (*qarqarā*, a crane).

قرقري *qarqarai*, s.m. The gripes in a horse.

قرغيچن *qar<u>gh</u>e<u>ch</u>an*, } a. Benumbed, chilled,
قرقيچن *qarqe<u>ch</u>an*, } doubled up with cold, etc.

قرمساق *qurramsāq*, s.m. Cuckold; pimp; a term of abuse. P.

قرن *qarn*, s.m. A conjunction of the planets; a century. A.

قرنا *qarnā*, s.f. Clarion, trumpet, horn. A.

قريب *qarīb*, a. Close, near; akin, relative. A.

قلا *qalā*, s.f. See قلعه.

قلاب *qullāb*, s.m. A hood for the head of a hawk. A.

قلابه *qulāba*, s.f. A hook, hinge, staple. A.

قلار *qalār*, a. Resting, quiet. See قرار.

قلاش *qalāsh*, a. Cunning, crafty, shrewd.

قلبه *qulba*, s.f. A plough. A.

قلپ *qalp*, a. Adulterated, alloyed; counterfeit (as coin, etc.). A. (*qalb*).

قلعه *qil'a*, s.f. Castle, fort; royal residence. A.

قلعي *qil'aī*, s.f. Tin; sodder. A.

قلف *qulf*, s.m. A lock; bolt. A.

قلم *qalam*, s.m. A pen, reed; graft; cutting of a plant. A.

قلنج *qulinj*, s.m. The colic. A.

قلندر *qalandar*, s.m. A hermit, anchorite, ascetic; a monk who has abandoned the world, family, friends, etc. A.

قلنګ *qulang*, s.m. Revenue, tax.

قمار *qimār*, s.m. Dice, gambling with dice. A. *qimār-bāz*, s.m. A gambler.

قماش *qamāsh*, s.m Manners, foibles; goods, chattels. A.

قمچي *qamchī*, s.f. A horsewhip. T.

قمر *qamar*, s.m. The moon. A.

قمري *qumrī*, s.f. A turtle dove. A.

قميص *qamīṣ*, s.m. Chemise, shirt. A.

قنات *qanāt*, s.m. Walls of a tent; canvas walls used to enclose a space about a tent. A. *qanāt*, s.m. Confectionary, sweetmeats. A. (*qanād*).

قناعت *qanā'at*, s.m. Contentment, tranquility; abstinence. A.

قنج *qanj*, s.m. Deceit, imposture, trick. A.

قند *qand*, s.m. Sugar candy, sugar. A.

قنديل *qandīl*, s.m. Chandelier, lamp. A.

قواعد *quwā'id*, s.m. Regulations, rules; military exercise, drill. A.

قوام *qiwām*, s.m. Essence, extract, syrup. A. *qiwāmī*, a. Ropy, thick, syrupy.

قرينه *qarīna*, s.f. Analogy, context, likeness, similarity, tenour. A.

قز *qaz*, s.m. Raw silk. P.

قسب *qasab*, s.m. Red silk; small turban.

قسط *qist*, s.m. Instalment, portion, tax. A.

قسم *qism*, s.m. Kind, species, sort; division, part. A. *qasam*, s.m. An oath. A.

قسمت *qismat*, s.m. Destiny, fate, lot; distribution, share; division, portion. A.

قشلاق *qishlāq*, s.m. A hamlet, village; winter quarters of the nomade tribes of western and northern Afghanistan. T. The summer quarters are termed *īlāq*. T.

قصاب *qaṣṣāb*, s.m. A butcher. A.

قصاص *qiṣāṣ*, s.m. The law of retaliation (as eye for eye, blood for blood, etc.). A.

قصد *qaṣd*, s.m. Intention, purpose, aim, wish. A.

قصداً *qaṣdan*, ad. Purposely, intentionally. A.

قصر *qaṣr*, s.m. Defect, diminution. A.

قصور *quṣūr*, s.m. Defect, failure, omission, want; error, fault; crime, sin. A.

قصه *qiṣṣa*, s.f. Story, tale; relation, narration; dispute, quarrel. A.

قصيده *qaṣīda*, s.f. An ode, poem. A.

قضا *qaẓā*, s.f. Fate, destiny; death, fatality; order, decree, judgment; praying at the appointed time; saying a prayer after the appointed time has passed. A.

قضاق *qaẓẓāq*, s.m. A cossack, robber. T.

قضيه *qaẓiya*, s.f. Contention, litigation, quarrel; calamity, misfortune; death; declaration, proposition. A.

قطب *quṭb*, s.m. North pole; Polar star; axis or spindle of a mill-stone; axis. A.

قطعي *qaṭ'aī*, a. Incontestible, true, fact. ad, Really, truly, fully. A.

قفس *qafas*, قفص *qafaṣ*, s.m. A cage; latticework. E.

قفل *qufl*, s.m. See قلف.

قوت *qūt*, Victuals, aliment, food; subsistence, livelihood. A. *qūt-lā-yamūt*, s.m. Sufficient to sustain life. A. *quwat*, s.m. Strength, vigour; power, authority; faculty, virtue. A.

قوج *qūj*, s.m. A fighting ram. P.

قوچق *qūchaq*, a. Fat, stout, lusty. T.

قوده *qawda*, s.f. A handful, a gripful.

قورمه *qorma*, s.f. A dish of meat stewed up with spices and fruits. P.

قول *qaul*, s.m. Word, saying; contract, promise; agreement, consent. A.

قوم *qaum*, s.m. Nation, people, family, sect, tribe. A.

قوي *qawwī*, a. Powerful, strong, vigorous; solid, firm, stable. A.

قهر *qahr*, s.m. Anger, passion, rage; vengeance, fury; severity, punishment. A.

قهرژن *qahr-jan*, } a. Irascible, passionate,
قهرناک *qahr-nāk*, } wrathful, furious.

قهقهه *qahqaha*, s.f. Loud laughter. A.

قي *qai*, s.m. Spewing, vomiting. A.

قياس *qiyās*, s.m. Consideration, judgment, opinion, thought; guess, supposition. A.

قيامت *qiyāmat*, s.m. The last day; resurrection; calamity. a. Wonderful, marvellous. A.

قيد *qaid*, s.m. Bondage, imprisonment; fetter, obstacle; obligation, compact. A.

قيدي *qaidī*, s.m. Prisoner, captive.

قيزه *qaiza*, s.f. See قائزه.

قيل *qīl*, s.m. A word, speech, saying. A.

قيمت *qīmat*, s.m. Price, value. A. *qīmatī*, a. High-priced, expensive: valuable.

قيمه *qīma*, s.f. Minced meat. A.

قينچي *qainchī*, s.f. Scissors. H.

ک

ک *kāf* is the twenty-second letter of the Arabic and the thirty-second of the Pukkhto alphabet. It is pronounced like the English *k*, and is sometimes interchanged with ق.

کَ *ka* is a form of the third person singular and plural of the present tense of the verb کول *kawul*, to do. It is also used as an abbreviated form for کړ *ka*, and وُ کړ *wu ka*, which are forms of the imperfect and past tenses, and the imperative mood of that verb. See following word.

کا *kā* is a form of the third person singular and plural of the present tenses, and imperative mood of the verb کول *kawul*, to do.

کابين *kābīn*, s.m. A marriage portion or settlement, wife's portion, dowry. P.

کاتک *kātak*, s.m. Name of the seventh Hindu month: October-November. S. (*kātik*).

کاته *kātah*, s.m. A glance, look; looking.

کاپور *kāpūr*, s.m. Camphor. A. (*kāfūr*).

کاتب *kātib*, s.m. A scribe, writer. A.

کاټي *kāṭī*, s.f. A wooden saddle; stocks for criminals. S. (*kāṭhī*).

کاختي *kākhtī*, s.f. Famine, scarcity, dearth. A. (*qaḥt*).

کاذب *kāzib*, s.m. A liar. a. False. A.

کار *kār*, s.m. Business, profession; action, affair; labour, work. P. *pa-kār*, a. Necessary, useful; required, wanted.

کارد *kārd*, s.m. A knife. P.

کارښت *kārikkht*, s.m. A wine-press; a vat in which grapes are pressed.

کاروان *kārwān*, s.m. Caravan, travelling party. P.

کاره *kāra*, s.f. A deep basket made of cane or reeds; a kind of millet. (*Paspalum kora*).

کاري *kārī*, a. Effectual, efficacious. P.

کاريز *kārez*, s.m. An aqueduct; subterranean canal for irrigating fields. P.

کاريزه *kārīza*, s.f. Name of a plant, safflower (*Carthamus oxyacantha*). P. (*khārīza*).

کاريگر *kārī·gar*, s.m. Artificer, mechanic, workman; skilful workman. P.

کاړ *kāṛ*, کانړ *kāṉṛ*, } s.m. Coarse sand, gravel, shingle.

کاړه *kāṛa*, s.f. Caudle, posset, curdled milk.

کاز *kāz*, s.m. Shears, scissors; den of a wild beast; a cavern or cave used by shepherds as a shelter for their flocks. P. *kāz*, s.m. A wild goose. T. (*qāz*).

کاږل *kāg̠al*, v.a. To draw, extract, pull out; to write, delineate, sketch. Def. in past ten. See کښل.

کاسب *kāsib*, s.m. Mechanic, artist, artificer. A.

کاسه *kāsa*, s.f. A bowl, cup, goblet. A. *shna·kāsa*, s.f. A rainbow.

کاسير *kāsīr*, s.m. Adulterer, fornicator. *kāsīrī*, s.f. Adultery, fornication.

کاش *kāsh*, s.m. Pommel or bow of a saddle; a small holster or saddle bag.

کاشکي *kāshke*, in. God grant! Would to God! P.

کاشي *kāshī*, s.m. A glazed tile or brick. P. *kāshī·gar*, s.m. Maker of glazed pottery. P. *kāshīn*, s.m. Glazed pottery. P.

کاغ *kāẕh*, a. Cunning, clever, acute.

کاغذ *kāg̠haz*, s.m. Paper. P. *kāg̠hāzī*, s.f. A kind of thin skinned lime. a. Delicate, soft, thin; written, printed; documentary.

کافر *kāfir*, s.m. Unbeliever, infidel. A. *kāfirī*, Name of a people inhabiting Kafiristan, a country of Hindu Kush to the north of Kabul. *kāfirai*, s.m. A man Kafir. *kāfira-ī*, s.f. A Kafir woman.

کافي *kāfī*, a. Enough, sufficient; competent, able. A.

کاک *kāk*, s.m. A biscuit, a hard cake of bread, etc. baked upon heated stones. P.

کاکا *kākā*, s.m. Paternal uncle; term of respectful address to a senior. H. Elder brother. P.

کاکړ *kākaṛ*, s.m. Name of an Afghan clan.

کاکل *kākul*, s.m. A curl, lock, ringlet. P.

کاکنج *kākanj*, s.m. Name of a kind of millet (*Panicum Italicum*).

کاکئ *kāka-ī*, s.f. Paternal uncle's wife. H.

کال *kāl*, s.m. A year. P. (*sāl*). *sag·kāl*, This year. *paros·kāl*, or *parosag·kāl*, Last year. *waṛam·kāl*, Year before last. *lā·waṛam·kāl*, Three years ago.

کالبوت *kālbūt*, s.m. Human body; heart; form, figure, mould, model. P. (*kālbud*).

کالخواهي *kālkhwāhī*, s.f. Good will, good wishes; approbation, choice. P. (*khair·khwāhī*).

کالکوچ *kālkūch*, s.m. A bend, turn, curve, twist.

کالکوچن *kālkūchan*, a. Bent, curved, distorted.

کالکوچکه *kālkūchaka*, s.f. A bend, turn, swerve (as of a hunted hare, fox, etc.).

کالکنډي *kālkunḍai*, s.m. A kind of small edible melon that grows wild.

کالکه *kālaka*, s.f. Cotton in the pod; the cotton plant. *kālak·cho*, s.m. Dry stalks of the cotton plant (used as fuel).

کالي *kālai*, s.m. Article, instrument, tool; garment, dress; ornament, jewel. pl. *kālī*, Apparatus, tools; furniture, clothes, jewelry, etc. P. (*kālā*).

کام *kām*, s.m. Desire, wish. P. *kām·nā·kām*, ad. Willing or unwilling, nolens volens.

کامبوري *kāmbūrai*, s.m. Dry mustard stalks after threshing out the seed.

کامبيله *kāmbela*, s.f. Name of a tree (*Rottlera tinctoria*). H. (*kamīla*).

کامل *kāmil*, a. Complete, perfect; learned. A.

کامياب *kāmyāb*, a. Prosperous, successful. P. *kāmyābī*, s.f. Prosperity, success.

کان *kān*, s.m. A mine, quarry. P. *kān*, s.m. Reed, rush, bullrush (*Panicum spicatum* and *Juncus effusus*).

کانټۍ *kānṭa-ī*, s. f. Book-board, pasteboard.

کانجنړ *kānjanṟ*, s.m. Part of a Persian wheel; the large beam that rests on the side walls, and fixes the central upright pillar of the wheel.

کانډِ *kāndi*, } A form of the third person
کاندي *kānde*, } singular and plural of the present tense of the verb کول *kawul*, to do.

کانگه *kānga*, s.f. Gripes, tenesmus, tormina; violent straining at stool without ejection of matter. H. (*kānkhā*).

کانگي *kāngai*, s.m. Echo, reverberation.

کانه *kāna*, s.f. Calamity, disaster; business, affair; border, margin; frame, edging; a quill feather; upper part of the face. *kānah*, a. Stupid, ignorant, foolish; decayed, rotten at the core. S. (*kānā*).

کاني *kānī*, a. Mineral, fossil. P. *kānai*, a. Blind of one eye. S. (*kānā*). *kānaī*, s.f. Whiskers, hair at the temples; a reed, straw, cane, etc. (used by weavers to spread the warp upon).

کانړي *kānṟai*, s.m. A stone. P. (*kān*).

کاواک *kāwāk*, a. Demented, insane; awkward, clumsy; hollow, useless; thoughtless; acting as one deprived of self control.

کاه *kāh*, s.m. Straw, stubble. P. *kāh-gil*, s.m. Plaster of mud and straw for walls. P.

کاهښت *kāhakkht*, s.m. Mange, itch; grating, or setting the teeth on edge.

کاهل *kāhil*, a. Indolent, lazy, slow. A. *kāhilī*, s.f. Apathy, indolence, neglect.

کاهن *kāhin*, s.m. Astrologer, magician. A. *kāhinī*, s.f. Astrology, magic, sorcery.

کب *kab*, s.m. A fish.

کباب *kabāb*, s.m. Roasted meat. P. *kabābī*, s.m. A cook.

کبر *kibr*, s.m. Arrogance, pride. A. *kibr-jan*, a. Arrogant, haughty, proud.

کبره *kbara*, s.f. Name of a plant (*Capparis spinosa*). H. (*kabar*).

کبک *kabk*, s.m. A partridge. P.

کبل *kabal*, s.m. Cause, motive, reason. *kabl*, s.m. Name of a grass (*Agrostis linearis*).

کبلي *kablai*, s.m. A fawn, young gazelle; sandpiper, snippet; curlew.

کبي *kabī*, s.f. A halter for a horse; a rope passed over the head and through the mouth, instead of a headstall and bit.

کبير *kabīr*, a. Great, large; senior, full-grown. A.

کپري *kaparai*, s.m. The skull. S. (*khoprī*).

کپړۍ *kupṟa-ī*, s.f. A powder flask of leather; a leathern jar or bottle. S. (*kuppī*).

کپي *kapī*, s.f. See کبي. *kupa-ī*, s.f. See کپړۍ.

کت *kat*, s.m. Catechu. H. (*kath*). *kat*, s.m. A pile, heap; line, series, row.

کتاب *kitāb*, s.m. A book. A. *kitābī*, a. Written; learned, well read.

کتل *katal*, v.a. To look, see, view. H. (*taknā*).

کته *kata*, s.f. A pack-saddle or pad for bullocks, donkeys, etc.

کتي پتي *kitī-pitī*, s.f. Gibberish, nonsense. a. Confused, jumbled (as speech).

کتي لعل *kuti-l'al*, s.m. Name of a plant (*Withiana somniferum*).

کټ *kaṭ*, s.m. A cot, bed, bedstead. S. (*khaṭ*). *kaṭ-kai*, s.m. A small bed, settle, cot. *kaṭ-oṭai*, s.m. A child's bed, cradle.

کټ‌وټ *kaṭ-waṭ*, a. See کړ.

کټوري *kaṭorai*, s.m. A brass bowl, metal cup. H. (*kaṭorā*).

کټوۍ *kaṭwa-ī*, s.f. An earthenware cooking pot.

کټه *kaṭah*, a. Big, bulky, large. H. (*kaṭṭā*).

کټي *kaṭai*, s.m. A buffalo calf; the straw of pulse (used as fodder).

كثرت *kas̤rat*, s.m. Abundance, excess. A.

كثير *kas̤īr*, a. Abundant, excessive. A.

كځوړه *kat͟soṛa*, s.f. A bag, purse, reticule, wallet.

كځوك *kat͟swak*, s.m. Mild small-pox, chicken-pox.

كجاوه *kajāwa*, s.f. A camel-litter. P.

كجك *kajuk*, s.m. Hammer or cock of a gun; a curl or lock of hair worn on the forehead by females.

كجل *kajal*, s.m. Soot, lamp-black. S.

كچ *kac͟h*, s.m. Measurement; fault, flaw, error. a. Diminutive, small, less, little. H. (*kac͟hc͟hā*). *kuc͟h*, s.m. Butter.

كچكول *kac͟hkol*, s.m. A bowl or trough of wood used by mendicants to collect contributions in. P.

كچماچو *kac͟hmāc͟hū*, s.m. Name of a plant (*Solanum nigrum*), deadly nightshade.

كچني *kac͟hana-ī*, s.f. Courtezan, whore, dancing girl. H. (*kanc͟hanī*). *kuc͟hinai*, a. Small, diminutive, puny.

كچوټي *kac͟hoṭai*, a. Diminutive, tiny, wee.

كچه *kac͟hah*, a. Crude, immature, raw; silly, inexperienced; clay-built, slight. H. (*kac͟hc͟hā*).

كداي *kadā-ī*, s.f. A kind of frock, long coat, gown.

كدخدا *kad-k͟hudā*, s.m. Head man of a village or family; married man, master. P. *kad-k͟hudā-ī*, s.f. Marriage, the office of *kad-k͟hudā*.

كدو *kadū*, s.m. Pumpkin, bottle gourd. H.

كډله *kaḍala*, s.f. A cabin, hut, hovel (of reeds, etc.); a hole, pit.

كډه *kaḍa*, s.f. Family, household; migration, flitting, change of residence.

كډهل *kaḍhal*, s.m. Land prepared for sowing rice in.

كډئ *kaḍa-ī*, s.f. A pit, hole; ditch, trench; the hole under a loom for the weaver's feet when at work.

كر *kar*, s.m. Agriculture, farming; tilling, ploughing, and sowing. P. *ka-ar*, s.m. Thin, watery excrement, looseness of the bowels.

كراسته *krāsta*, s.f. Felt, a thick woollen fabric (unwoven).

كرام *kirām*, a. Venerable, noble, great. A.

كرامت *kirāmat*, s.m. Excellence, nobleness; miracle. A.

كراهت *kirāhat*, s.m. Aversion, disgust. A.

كراهه *kirāha*, s.f. Hire, rent, fare. P. (*kirāya*).

كربوړي *karboṛai*, s.m. A kind of lizard; chameleon.

كرپ *krap*, s.m. A munch, crunch.

كرپندوكي *krapandūkai*, } s.m. Cartilage, gristle.
كرپندي *krapandai*, }

كرپول *krapawul*, v.a. To crunch, munch; bite, champ, gnaw.

كرت *karat*, s.m. One time, stroke, turn, go. A. *yo-karat*, once. *dre-karata*, thrice, etc. *karāt-marāt*, often, frequently, etc. A.

كرتب *kartab*, s.m. Action, business; practice, exercise; skill; horse exercise. S.

كرتوت *kartūt*, s.m. Work, business, action. S.

كرته *kurta*, s.f. A coat, jacket, tunic. P.

كرټ *kruṭ*, ad. At all, not at all, never, by no means, not in the least.

كرچ *krac͟h*, s.m. An old hawk or falcon (one fully trained). *krac͟h*, s.m. Sound of a crunch, crash, squash, etc.

كرچوني *krac͟hūnai*, } s.m. Cartilage, gristle.
كرچي *krac͟hai*, }

كرچي *kric͟hī*, s.f. Name of a plant (*Anthemis nobilis*).

كرخت *karak͟ht*, a. Austere, rigid, rough, hard. P.

کردار *kirdār*, s.m. Conduct, action, deed. P.

کرري *kirṛai*, s.m. A cricket. *kariṛī*, s.m. Name of an Afghan tribe, also called كرلانړي.

كرسي *kursī*, s.f. Chair, seat, throne; firmament, heaven. P. *kursī-nāma*, s.f. Genealogical tree; list of precedence.

كرښمه *karakkhma*, s.f. Amorous look, wink, ogle, leer. P. (*karashma*).

كرښنه *karakkhna*, s.f. Carving, drawing, painting, engraving.

كرښه *karkkha*, s.f. A line, streak, scrawl. scratch, furrow.

كرغ *kurugh*, s.m. A meadow, pasture.

كرك *karak*, s.m. A snipe, woodcock. P. *kark*, s.m. Rhinoceros, rhinoceros hide. P. (*karg*). *krak*, s.m. A furrow, rut, scratch.

كركنډه *karkanḍa*, s.f. A rolling stone; landslip on a hill-side; rock or stone hurled down a hill upon an enemy.

كركڼړ *karkanṛ*, s.m. A brake, copse, thicket.

كركڼړه *karkanṛa*, s.f. A bramble, brier, thorny bush; the jujube tree (*Zizyphus vulgaris*).

كركه *kraka*, s.f. Aversion, disgust. A. (*ikrāh*).

كرل *karal*, v.a. To till, plough and sow. P. (*kāshtan-kār*).

كرلانړي *karlānṛī*, s.m. Name of a tribe of Afghans located in Bājawar.

كرم *karam*, s.m. Clemency, kindness. A. *kirm*, s.m. A worm. P.

كرمنك *kurmang*, s.m. Pheasant, wild fowl.

كرنډي *karanḍa-ī*, s.f. A trowel. H. (*karnī*).

كروړ *karoṛ*, a. Ten millions; a crore. S.

كروړه *karoṛa*, s.f. A whip, scourge. H. (*koṛā*). *karwaṛa*, s.f. Blackberry bush and fruit (*Rubus vulgaris*).

كروسند *krosand*, a. Dry, withered (as wood).

كروه *kroh*, s.m. A coss; a measure of distance nearly equal to two miles. P.

كره *karah*, a. Genuine, pure; candid, sincere. S. (*kharā*). *kara*, s.f. Spade, hoe. *kara*, ad. With, along with. See سره.

كرهړ *kurhaḍ*, s.m. Name of a plant used as a potherb (*Chenopedium album*).

كړئ *kara-ī*, s.f. A fetter, ring, buckle, link, staple; beam, rafter. H. (*kaṛī*). *kara-ī*, ad. All, the whole, the entire (day or night). *kara-ī-wradz*, All day. *kara-ī-shpa*, All night. *kure*, in. Begone! Get out! away (to a dog).

كرياب *kariyāb*, a. Disengaged, idle, unused; clogged, hampered, hindered, obstructed; distressed, helpless, tired.

كريابي *kariyābī*, s.f. Obstruction, hindrance, impediment, bar, hitch, etc.

كريړه *kirīṛa*, s.f. Name of a plant (*Capparis aphylla*). S. (*karīl*). Weeds, grass, etc., collected from a ploughed field.

كريړي *kirīṛai*, s.m. Name of a tree (*Salvadora Persica*).

كريز *kurīz*, s.m. Moulting (of birds). P.

كريم *karīm*, a. Merciful, gracious, bountiful. A.

كريهه *kreha*, s.f. See كراهه.

كريه *karīh*, a. Abominable, detestable; dirty, filthy. A. *karya*, s.f. Injunction, charge, command.

كړ *kuṛ*, s.m. A gurgle, bubbling sound; cackle or cluck of a hen.

كړاونه *kaṛāwna*, s.f. See كنړاوه.

كربيزن *karbezan*, a. Snotty-nosed, sniveller.

كربيزي *karbeze*, s.f. (pl. of *karbeza*, obsolete) Snot, mucus from the nose.

كړپ *kṛap*, s.m. See كرپ.

كړتي *kṛaṭai*, s.m. A crease, furrow, crumple, pucker, wrinkle.

كړشپ *kaṛshap*, a. Toothless, old. *kaṛshapai*, s.m. A toothless old man.

كړكړي *kuṛkuṛai*, s.m. A turtle dove.

كړكه *kuṛaka*, s.f. A clucking hen; a sitting or hatching hen.

کړکۍ *kuṛka-ī*, s.f. A kind of bird trap made of a horn bow and catgut, a gin, springe. *kaṛka-ī*, s.f. A wicket, window, loophole; gate. H. (*khiṛkī*).

کړل *kṛal*, v.a. To do, perform, execute, etc. P. (*kardan*).

کړم *kaṛam*, a. Maimed, halt, crippled, lame.

کړميزې *kaṛmeze*, s.f. Snot. See کربيزې.

کړوسي *kaṛwasai*, s.m. A great grandson.

کړه *kṛah*, s.m. Act, deed; doing, making.

کړه وړه *kṛah·wṛah*, s.m. Beauty, grace; neatness, tidiness, spruceness; arrangement, order.

کړهي *kaṛahai*, s.m. A caldron, boiler (metal); an iron cooking pot. S. (*kaṛāhī*). *kuṛhai*, s.m. Name of a corn measure, the fourth part of an اوړي *ogai*.

کړيڅۍ *kaṛetsa-ī*, s.f. A ladle, iron spoon. H. (*karc͟hhī*).

کړيدل *kaṛedal*, v.n. To be parched, scorched, dried; to be reduced, emaciated; to waste, wither, pine, droop (through sickness or grief). H. (*kuṛhnā*).

کړينګ *kṛīng*, a. Awry, distorted, crooked, twisted. *kṛīng·pṛīng*, a. All awry, all askew.

کږدۍ *kigda-ī*, s.f. A tent made of coarse camlet, or goat's hair cloth (used by nomad Afghans).

کږل *kagal*, v.a. To disapprove, to dislike; find fault with, disparage, run down. P. (*kaj*).

کږلي *kagalai*, a. Calamitous, unlucky; unwelcome.

کږليچ *kaglec͟h*, s.m. A bend, crook, turn.

کس *kas*, s.m. Human being, individual, person; anyone, a man. P. *kas*, s.m. A ravine, gully, dry course of a torrent, passage cut by floods. H. *kus*, s.m. Vulva, vagina. P.

کسب *kasb*, s.m. Trade, occupation, employment. A.

کسبت *kisbat*, s.m. An instrument case; huntsman's bag for balls, powder, etc., etc.; a bag or case in which barbers, surgeons, etc., keep their tools. A.

کستيج *kustīj*, s.m. The hole in the hem of a pair of drawers, etc., through which the string passes.

کسکر *kaskar*, a. Burnt, dry, arid, scorched; contracted, shrivelled; withered, frost bitten.

کسل *kasal*, v.a. To see, look. See کتل.

کسوري *kasūrai*, a. Broken spirited, distressed, unequal to, impotent.

کسي *kasai*, s.m. The pupil of the eye.

کشاله *kas͟hāla*, s.f. Dragging, trailing, pulling, etc.

کشپ *kas͟hp*, s.m. A tortoise. P. (*kas͟haf*).

کشته *kis͟hta*, s.f. A kind of dried plum, used in medicine, and by goldsmiths to clean their metals with. P. *kus͟hta*, s.f. A sublimate of mercury. P. *kus͟htah*, a. Killed, slain; slaked (as lime, etc.). P.

کشر *kas͟hr*, a. Junior, younger; cadet, subaltern; less, minor.

کشک *kas͟hak*, s.m. Watchman, guard, porter. P.

کشمالو *kas͟hmālū*, s.m. Name of a plant, holy basil (*Ocymum sanctum*).

کشور *kis͟hor*, s.m. The manis or pangolin, scaly ant-eater (*Manis crassicaudata*). *kis͟hwar*, s.m. Country, region, climate. P.

کشي *kas͟hai*, s.m. An only son. *kas͟ha-ī*, s.f. Bar or pig iron; a hoe, mattock. H. (*kasī*).

کښ *kak͟hh*, s.m. A draw, pull; inhalation, whiff, inspiration; suck. P. (*kas͟h*).

کښت *kik͟hht*, s.m. A crop, sown field, growing crop. P. (*kis͟ht*). *kuk͟hht*, s.m. A defile, gorge, gap in the hills. (Raverty.)

کښل *kakshal* or *kkshal*, v.a. To draw out, extricate, extract, pull, pluck out; to write, draw, sketch, etc. Def. in pres. ten. See کارل. P. (*kashīdan*). *kkshul*, s.m. A kiss.

کښلول *kkshulawul*, v.a. To kiss.

کښلي *kkshulai*, a. Comely, fair, handsome, pretty; kissed.

کښول *kakshawul* or *kkshawul*, v.a. To cause to extract, draw, etc. To cause to write, etc. See کښل.

کښه *kakkha*, s.f. Brace, tightener, puller.

کښي *kakkhai*, s.m. A watchman, guard (over cattle, crops, etc.). P. (*kashak*). *kkshe*, p. In, within. *pa·kkshe*, ad. Inside, within.

کښيباسل *kkshebāsal*, v.a. To insert, introduce, implant, stick in, stuff in, etc. Def. in past ten. See کښيېستل *kksheyastal*.

کښيده *kakkheda*, s.f. A kind of needlework, embroidery. P. (*kashīda*).

کښيږدل *kkshegdal*, v.a. To place, set, put down, arrange, dispose, etc. Def. in past ten. See کښيښول.

کښيکښل *kkshekkshal*, v.a. To shampoo (or ښکيښکل *kkhkekkhkal*).

کښيناستل *kkshenāstal*, v.n. To sit, settle, be seated. P. (*nishastan*).

کښينول *kkshenawul*, v.a. To seat, settle, instal, fix, set down, etc.

کښيوتل *kkshewatal*, v.n. To fall into, drop into, enter, descend into, etc.

کښيېستل *kksheyastal*, v.a. To insert, introduce, etc. Def. in pres. ten. See کښيباسل *kkshebāsal*.

کعبه *k'aba*, s.f. The temple at Mecca. A.

کفارت *kifārat*, s.m. Expiation, atonement, penance. A.

کفايت *kifāyat*, s.m. Enough, sufficiency; economy, thrift. A.

کفر *kufr*, s.m. Blasphemy, infidelity, paganism. A.

کفن *kafan*, s.m. Winding sheet, shroud. A.

کک *kak*, s.m. A splinter, straw; treacle, syrup.

ککري *kakara-ī*, s.f. The skull. *kakārai*, s.m. A pup, puppy dog.

ککړ *kakaṛ*, a. Defiled, polluted, stained; a spiritless man. f. *kakaṛa*, Raped, ravished; a whore, strumpet.

ککوي *kakawai*, s.m. Name of a bird.

ککوړه *kakoṛa*, s.f. Name of a plant, bitter gourd.

ککوړي *kakoṛai*, s.m. A kind of biscuit, round cake baked on heated stones; a disk.

کل *kal*, a. Bald, scald headed. P. *kal*, s.m. oil-cake. S. (*khal*). *kull*, a. All, universal; amount, total. A.

کلال *kulāl*, s.m. A potter. P.

کلام *kalām*, s.m. A word, speech; conversation, talk. A.

کلان *kalān*, a. Elder, great; large. P.

کلت *kulat*, s.m. Name of a grain, seed of (*Dolichos biflorus*). S. (*kulthī*).

کلک *klak*, a. Firm, hard; stiff, rigid, etc. P. (*karakht*).

کلکل *kalkal*, s.m. Wrangling, quarrelling. H.

کلمه *kulma*, s.f. An entrail, gut; sausage. A. (*qulmā*). *kalima*, s.f. A word, speech; the Muḥammadan belief or creed. A.

کلنګ *kulang*, s.m. A long-legged fowl; a crane, heron. P. A pick, pickaxe; a bow; hammer of a gun; dower, furniture of every description which a bride brings to her husband.

کلني *kalanai*, Added to words in composition, denotes the age. Ex. *pīndzah·kalanai*, a. Five years old.

کلوټ *kaloṭ*, a. Dark, dark-complexioned.

کلوښته *kalokkhta*, s.f. A wisp of straw, floss of silk, curl, tuft, bundle, etc.

کله *kala*, ad. Ever, at any time, sometime;

when? since when? *kala·kala*, Now and then, occasionally, sometimes. *kala·shū·lā·kala*, Since when? how long? *kala*, s.f. The head. P.

كلي *kilai*, s.m. A village. A. (*qil'a*). *kalai*, a. Short-horned, without horns. P. (*kal*). *kala-ī*, s.f. Bunion, callosity, corn. *killī*, s.f. A key. H. *kullī*, s.f. A gargle, gargling. H.

كم *kam*, a. Deficient, less, little, seldom. scanty (in comp.). P. *kum* or *kam*, pr. What? which? See كوم.

كمال *kamāl*, s.m. Perfection, excellence; completion. a. Complete, perfect. A.

كمان *kamān*, s.m. A bow. *kamān·gar*, s.m. A bow-maker. P.

كمانچه *kamāncha*, s.f. Bow of a violin. P.

كماني *kamā-ī*, s.f. Earning, gain, profit, wages. H.

كمبلئ *kambala-ī*, s.f. A butterfly.

كمر *kamar*, s.f. A cliff, precipice; steep bank; ridge of a hill, etc.; the waist, loins. P. *kamar·kīsa*, s.f. A waist belt with powder flask, etc., etc. *kamar·band*, s.m. A girdle, waist-belt. P.

كمري *kamarī*, a. Relating to the loins, lumbar; weak in the loins (as a horse).

كمک *kumak*, s.m. Aid, help; reserve of an army. P. *kumakī*, a. Auxiliary. s.m, Assistant, helper.

كمند *kamand*, s.m. A ladder of ropes; halter, lasso, noose; a tethering rope; ringlet or long curl. P.

كمنړ *kamanr*, a. Faded, withered, decayed.

كمنړيدل *kamanredal*, v.n. To droop, decay, wither, fade, etc. H. (*kumhlānā*).

كموده *kamoda*, s.f. A dish of rice boiled with ghee, and flavoured with spices.

كميس *kamīs*, s.m. A shirt. See قميص.

كمين *kamīn*, a. Mean; defective; humble, poor. s.m. A village serf. P.; an ambuscade. A.

كمينه *kamīnah*, a. Humble, meek; abject, base; mean, ignoble. P. *kamīnī*, s.f. Humility, meekness; baseness.

كن *kan* (in comp.), Digger, digging. P. *kun* (in comp.), Actor, doer; doing, acting. P.

كناټي *kunāṭai*, s.m, Buttock, rump. *kunāṭa-war*, a. Broad-buttocked, large rumped.

كنار *kinār*, s.m. Side, edge; bosom, embrace. P.

كنال *kanāl*, s.m. A land measure equal to twenty *marla*; the fourth part of a *jarīb*.

كنايت *kināyat*, s.m. } Allusion, hint, metaphor, sign. A.
كنايه *kināya*, s.f. }

كنټكين *kanṭkīn*, a. Made of thread.

كنج *kunj*, s.m. A corner, nook; grove, bower. P.

كنجک *kunjak*, s.m. } A cowrie, small shell (used as money). (*Cypræa moneta*).
كنجكه *kunjaka*, s.f. }

كنجوغه *kanjogha*, s.f. Saddle straps, cords attached to a saddle (used to tie game, etc.).

كنجئ *kunja-ī*, s.f. A key. S. (*kunjī*). A small water jar or ewer (of pottery).

كند *kand*, s.m. A gorge, ravine, dry water-course, excavation. P. *kind*, s.m. A tattered and patched garment worn by dervishes. *kund*, a. Blunt. P.

كنداغ *kundāgh*, s.m. The stock of a gun. P. (*kunda*).

كندره *kandara*, s.f. A fissure, chasm; gully, watercourse, ravine; broken or ravine cut ground. S. (*kandarā*).

كندل *kandal*, v.a. To dig, excavate. P. (*kandan*).

كندو *kandū*, s.m. A corn bin.

كنده *kanda*, s.f. A gully, ravine, watercourse, (cut by floods). P. *kunda*, s.f. Block, log; stock of a gun, ploughshare, etc. P.

كندي *kandai*, s.m. A potsherd, bit of broken pottery; a division, or quarter of a village, parish ward. s. (*khanḍ*). *kundī*, s.f. Calendering (cloth). H.

کند *kanḍ*, s.m. Sugar candy. s. (*khanḍ*). Gum. s. (*gond*). *kunḍ*, s.m. A widower.

کندا *kunḍā*, a. Harelipped, having a broken horn.

کنداس *kunḍās*, s.m. A man who has lost, or broken his front teeth; a toothless old man.

کندال *kanḍāl*, s.m. A cup, bowl, basin, etc. (of pottery).

کندتون *kunḍtūn*, s.m. Widowhood.

کندر *kanḍar*, s.m. Ruins of a house or village, broken and decayed walls, ruins; a place haunted by demons. H. (*khanḍar*).

کندک *kanḍak*, s.m. A herd of deer, flock of goats or sheep; a piece of bread.

کندکپړ *kanḍ-kapaṛ*, a. Shattered, smashed, broken to bits, cut to pieces, etc.

کندلي *kanḍala-ī*, s.f. Name of a plant (*Bryonia grandis*). A prickly seed that sticks to the fleece of sheep.

کندو *kanḍaw*, s.m. A notch, dent, gap; dip in a hill, gap in a wall, notch in wood, etc. a. Dented, notched. H. (*khanḍā*).

کندول *kanḍol*, } s.m. See کندال.
کندولي *kanḍolai*, }

کنده *kanḍa*, s.f. The spring or source of a river. *kunḍa*, s.f. A widow. A hook, fish hook, hook of a door, etc. H. (*kunḍā*).

کندئي *kanḍa-ī*, s.f. See کنړي.

کنزل *kanzal*, v.a. See سکنځل.

کنزله *kunzala*, s.f. Sesame, the plant and seed (*Sesamum orientale*). P. (*kuṇjad*).

کنزه‌گوته *kanza-gūta*, s.f. The third or ring finger.

کنستل *kanastal*, v.a. To dig, excavate.

کنف *kanaf*, s.m. Brink, edge, margin. A.

کنګال *kangāl*, a. Poor, friendless. s.

کنګښړ *kangakhaṛ*, s.m. Rubbish, sticks, straw, etc. carried down by floods, drift wood.

کنګر *kangar*, s.m. Pumice stone. H. (*khangaṛ*).

کنګره *kangura*, s.f. A pinnacle, turret; battlement, parapet; niched or loopholed wall; porthole; the plume of a helmet; ornaments on a crown. P.

کنګري *kangarai*, s.m. A puppy. See کوتري.

کنګس *kangas*, s.m. A trip, stumble.

کنګل *kangal*, a. Congealed, frozen; compact, solid, dense. s.m. Ice.

کنګو *kangū*, s.m. Saffron.

کنل *kanal*, v.a. } To dig. See کندل.
کنودل *kanawdal*, }

کنه *kana*, s.f. A dog tick, sheep louse, large tick. The border of a garment, edge of a shawl. P.

کنيزه *kanīza*, s.f. A female servant, housemaid; a concubine. P. (*kanīz*).

کنړ *kaṉr*, s.m. Mucus from the nose, snot.

کنړاوه *kaṉrāwa*, s.f. A clog, patten. H. (*khaṛāṅw*).

کنړه *kaṉra*, c. If not, of course, otherwise, then.

کنړي *kaṉrai*, s.m. The warp (in weaving). *kaṉra-ī*, s.f. A wooden cup or bowl.

کواره *kawāra*, s.f. A pannier or basket, used to carry fruit, etc. in. H. (*gaṅwārā*).

کوب *kūb*, s.m. A hump, hunch. a. Humped. s. (*kub*).

کوبي *kūbai*, s.m. A hunch-back, humped ox or camel, etc. One of the pieces or stops of wood, in the horizontal wheel of a Persian wheel, which catches the cogs of the smaller wheel.

کوپ *kūp*, a. Bowed, stooping, bent, crooked in the back (as from old age).

کوپله *kopla*, s.f. A lark, skylark.

کوت *kawt*, a. Contracted, drawn in, pinched, tucked in, shrunk (as the belly from hunger).

کوتان *kotān*, s.m. A pelican.

کوتاه *kotāh*, a. Brief, short (in comp.). P.

کوتر *kautar*, s.m. A pigeon. P. (*kabūtar*).

کوتري *kūtrai*, s.m. A pup, puppy dog. H. (*kutrū*).

کوتل *kotal*, s.m. A pass over a mountain. P. A led horse. H. *kūtal*, v.a. To cut up, disjoint, divide. H. (*kāṭnā*).

کوتي *kwatai*, s.m. A dimple on the cheek or chin.

کوتي لال *kūtī-lāl*, s.m. See کتي لعل.

کوټ *koṭ*, s.m. A castle, fort, stronghold, hill fort. S.

کوټخه *koṭakha*, s.f. A cap made to cover the forehead and ears, a travelling cap; a mouth-piece or nosebag for cattle.

کوټک *koṭak*, s.m. Bludgeon, club; a pestle. H. (*kūtak*). The back of the head, occiput.

کوټل *kūṭal*, v.a. To pound, bruise; cudgel, beat, thrash, wallop. H. (*kūṭnā*).

کوټوال *koṭwāl*, s.m. The chief constable of a village or town. H.

کوټه *koṭa*, s.f. A mansion, large house; a chamber room. H. (*koṭhā*). *kūṭah*, s.m. A dog. H. (*kuttā*).

کوټئ *koṭa-ī*, s.f. A factory, warehouse, bank. H. (*koṭhī*). *koṭai*, s.m. The head. *kūtai*, s.m. An ass colt, a young donkey. H. (*khotrā*).

کوثر *kauṣar*, s.m. Name of a well in Paradise. Name of a disease, tetanus, lockjaw; stroke of the wind, or of cold.

کوڅه *kūtsa*, s.f. A lane, street. P. (*kūcha*).

کوڅئ *kotsa-ī*, s.f. See کونځئ.

کوچ *kūch* or *koch*, s.m. Migration, a march. P. *kochi*, s.m. A nomade.

کوچټ *kūchaṭ*, a. Small, little, young. P. (*kachak*). *kūchaṭ-wālai*, s.m. Smallness; childhood.

کوچمال *kūchmāl*, s.m. The leader of a march; conductor of a caravan.

کوچي *kūchai*, s.m. The tendon of the heel (*Tendo Achillis*). H. (*khūnch*). *kūchai*, s.m. An ass colt. *kocha-ī*, s.f. A cloak made of felt. *kochī*, s.m. A nomade.

کودالي *kūdāla-ī*, s.f. A hoe, mattock. S. (*kudālī*).

کودري *kawdarai*, s.m. A potsherd.

کودک *kodak*, s.m. A boy, youth. P.

کودله *kodala*, s.f. Hut, cabin, hovel.

کودن *kawdan*, a. Silly, foolish, imbecile. A.

کودي *kodai*, s.m. A pot, pipkin; potsherd.

کوديک *kawdīk*, s.m. A cooking pot, earthen pot.

کوډ *koḍ*, s.m. A shell, charm. S. (*gadh*).

کوډه *koḍa*, s.f. Sorcery, enchantment; jugglery. *koḍ-gar*, s.m. A sorcerer, magician, conjurer.

کوډئ *kawḍa-ī*, s.f. A cowrie. S. (*kauṛī*). *kūḍa-ī*, s.f. A shed, arbor, temporary hut made of boughs and leaves. S. (*kūṭī*).

کور *kor*, s.m. A house, dwelling, habitation; wife, family. H. (*ghar*). *kwar*, s.m. A wild grape tree, vine. *kor*, a. Blind. P. Border, margin, side. H.

کوربه *korbah*, s.m. Landlord, master of house; host, paterfamilias.

کورته *kūrta*, s.f. A coat, jacket, frock. P.

کورغنډل *korghunḍal*, s.m. Indian cactus, prickly pear.

کورکمان *kūrkamān*, s.m. Turmeric.

کورمانه *kormāna*, s.f. Domestic economy, housewifery, keeping house.

کوروالي *kor-wālai*, s.m. Marital duty, intercourse between husband and wife.

کوره *korah*, a. New, unused. H. (*korā*).

کوري *korai*, s.m. Net for carrying grass, forage, etc. H. (*khārā*). *kūrī*, in. Away! Get out!

کوړ *koṛ*, s.m. Leprosy. S. (*koṛh*).

کوړمه *koṛma*, s.f. Family, household, wife.

کوړه *koṛa*, s.f. A hole made in the ground for playing at marbles. H.

کوړي *kūṛai*, s.m. A measure of corn equal to the fourth part of an اوري *ogai*. H. (*kuṛā*). *koṛī*, s.m. A leper. a. Leprous. S. (*koṛhī*).

کوز *kūz*, a. Below, under; low, lower.

کوزکتل *kūz-katal*, v.a. To look down, be sick at stomach, feel nausea.

کوزغالي *kūz-ghālai*, s.m. A dog's basin or eating dish.

کوزه *kūza*, s.f. A guglet, long-necked water jar.

کوژدن *kojdan*, کوژدنه *kojdana*, s.f. Betrothal, marriage engagement. See غوښتل.

کوژه *koja*, s.f. Eating the fast, not keeping the روژه.

کوږ *kog*, a. Bent, crooked, askew. P. (*kaj*).

کوږل *kwagal*, v.a. To endeavour, strive.

کوږووږ *kog-wog*, a. Very crooked, all awry.

کوس *kūs*, s.m. A large drum. P.

کوښښ *kokkhikkh*, s.m. Endeavour, application, zeal. P. (*koshish*).

کوښلي *kūkkhalai*, a. See کښلي *kkshulai*.

کوښه *kokkha*, s.f. A kind of slipper. P. (*kaush*).

کوک *kūk*, s.m. Crying, sobbing. S.

کوکري *kūkarai*, s.m. A puppy dog. S.

کوکړي *kokaṛai*, s.m. A biscuit, bun. See ککوري.

کوکنار *koknār*, s.m. The poppy plant; the capsule. P.

کوکه *kūka*, s.f. See کوک.

کوکوري *kokoṛai*, s.m. A large bannock or cake of bread baked upon heated stones.

کوکي *kūka-ī*, s.f. Name of a tree (*Rhamnus virgatus*). *kokai*, s.m. A boy, lad, child. H. (*khokhā*). *koka-ī*, s.f. The cheek, side of the face; a little girl, female child.

کول *kawul*, v.a. To do, act, perform. *kūl*, a. Cotemporary, peer, of the same age. *kol*, s.m. A pond; a ford, shallow water. A. (*qūl*). *kol*, s.m. See کهول.

کولک *kolak*, s.m. The brow above the forehead; a hole in the roof by way of chimney.

کولنډ *koland*, s.m. A piece of stick used to tether cattle, etc. by the neck or foot; a log of wood attached to the neck of cattle to prevent their straying.

کولي *kolai*, s.m. A helmet, hat. P. (*kulāh*).

کوليار *koliyāṛ*, s.m. Name of a tree (*Bauhinea variegata*). H. (*kachnār*).

کوم *kūm*, pr. What? which? that which. P. (*kudām*).

کومک *komak*, s.m. Aid, help. See کمک.

کومي *kūmai*, s.m. The palate; cleft in the palate.

کونتر *kawntar*, s.m. A pigeon. See کوتر.

کونټي *kūnṭai*, s.m. A shepherd's crook; a stick with a crook at the end.

کونځي *kontsa-ī*, s.f. The braided or plaited hair at the back of the head of women.

کونسټ *kūnsaṭ*, a. Contracted, shrunk, shrivelled. s.m. Foundation, base, root; stock or stump (as of a tree).

کونکي *kawunkai*, s.m. Actor, agent, doer, performer. *konkai*, a. (for *kamkai*), Diminutive, small.

کونګړي *kūngaṛai*, s.m. A puppy dog.

کونه *kūna*, s.f. Backside, podex, anus. P. (*kūn*). *kūna-starkai*, s.m. A clout, child's napkin.

کوني *kūnī*, s.m., کونيګي *kūnīgai*, A catamite.

کوني *kūnai*, s.m. A dog louse, dog tick. Mortar, lime, whitewash.

کوني کبر *kūnī-kabar*, s.m. A crab.

کوڼ *kūṇr*, a. Deaf. P. (*kar*). *koṇr*, s.m. A tick, dog-louse.

کوه *koh*, s.m. Mountain, hill (in comp.). P.

کوهستان *kohistān*, s.m. Mountain country,

highlands. P. Name of the highland tract north of Swat.

کوهي *kūhai*, s.m. A well. S. (*kūā*).

کوئ *koe*, s.m. Itching, titillation.

کويښل *kwekkhal*, v.a. To write. Def. in pres. ten. See کاږل.

کوئ‌کبر *koe-kabar*, s.m. See کوني‌کبر.

کويلي *koyilai*, کويني *koyinai*, s.m. Pot-scrapings, burnt part of victuals at the bottom of a pot. H. (*khoyā*).

که *ki*, c. If, as, that. P.

کهاره *kahāra*, s.f. A pannier. See کواره.

کهاړه *kahāṛa*, s.f. A ring of rope, straw, etc. used as a target for arrows.

کهالي *kahālī*, s.f. Indolence, laziness; yawning, gaping, stretching. A. (*kāhilī*).

کهتر *kihtar*, a. Junior, minor, less, small. P.

کهربا *kahrubā*, s.f. Amber. P.

کهند *kuhand*, a. Ancient, old. P. (*kuhan*).

کهول *kahol*, s.m. Family, house, tribe.

کهه *kaha*, s.f. Itching; nausea.

کهي *kahai*, s.m. A reed, rush; a kind of clay, ochre. *kaha-ī*, s.f. A pickaxe; axle of a water mill; a ditch, trench.

کيجم *kejam*, s.m. A saddle cloth of felt.

کيدل *kedal*, v.n. To be, to become.

کير *kīr*, s.m. Rice and milk cooked together. S. (*khīr*). *ker*, s.m. *Penis virilis*. P.

کيرړي *kīrṛai*, s.m. A mole cricket.

کيرئ *kīra-ī*, s.f. The felloe or rim of a wheel.

کيړ *keṛ*, s.m. A screen or wattling made of the twigs of the tamarisk tree; a hedge, paling, etc. of tamarisk twigs.

کيړه *keṛa*, s.f. An iron ring in a plough; twigs or saplings (generally of the tamarisk tree) used in forming the roof of a house. H. (*keṛā*).

کيږدل *kegdal*, v.a. (For کښيږدل or بهکيږدل.) To set, place, put, etc. Def. in past ten. See کيښوں.

کيس *kais*, s.m. The name of the great ancestor of the Afghans. He had three sons named Saṛabanṟ, Batanṟ, and Ghurghusht, to whom are traced in three great divisions all the different tribes of Afghans.

کيش *kesh*, s.m. Faith, religion, belief; manner, quality. P. Damask, diaper. H. (*khīs*).

کيښودل *kekkhodal*, کيښول *kekkhawul*, کيښوول *kekkhowul*, v.a. To place, put, set, etc. Def. in pres. ten. See کيږدل.

کيښئ *kīkkha-ī*, s.f. A worm, mite, insect.

کيف *kaif*, s.m. Intoxication. A. *kaifī*, a. Intoxicated; intoxicating. s.m. A drunkard, sot.

کيفيت *kaifiyat*, s.m. Condition, state; statement, account; description, remark. A.

کيک *kaik*, s.m. A flea. P.

کيکړ *kīkaṛ*, s.m. Acacia tree. H.

کيل *kīl*, s.m. Furrow, rut, track, scratch. H. (*līk*).

کيلک *kīlak*, s.m. A hobble or fetter for the feet of a horse; a cord or tassel used to tie the scabbard to the sword handle.

کيمخت *kīmukht*, s.m. Shagreen; leather prepared from the hide of the horse or ass.

کيميا *kīmiyā*, s.f. Alchemy, chemistry. A.

کيناستل *kenāstal*, v.n. To sit, sit down, settle, subside. (For بهکيناستل or کښيناستل.)

کيند *kīnd*, s.m. A tattered and patched garment worn by dervishes.

کينول *kenawul*, v.a. To seat, instal, set. (For کښينول or بهکينول.)

کينه *kīna*, s.f. Malice, spite, rancour. P. *kīnawar*, a. Spiteful, revengeful, malicious.

کينړ *kīnṟ*, a. The left hand, left side, left.

گ

گ *gāf*. This letter being unknown in the Arabic is called the Persian kāf. It is the twenty-sixth letter of the Persian, and the thirty-third of the Pukkhto alphabet. It always has the sound of *g* hard as in *gun*. By the Yusufzais and Eastern Afghans it is very generally substituted for ږ *g*.

گاټلۍ *gāṭla-ī*, s.f. A bundle, package. H. (*gaṭhrī*).

گاټۍ *gāṭa-ī*, s.f. A small flat pebble, or bit of pottery set at the bottom of a pipe bowl, to prevent the tobacco getting into the stem. *gāṭai*, s.m. A round pebble, or pallet of dried clay, used to shoot from a sling.

گاډۍ *gāḍa-ī*, s.f. A cart, waggon. H. (*gāṛī*).

گاډېره *gāḍera*, s.f. Mixed grain, meal of pulses, corn, etc. mixed together; bread of mixed meal.

گازره *gāzara*, s.f. A carrot. S. (*gājar*).

گاګره *gāgra*, s.f. Granite, amygdaloid, trap-rock.

گالل *gālal*, v.a. To keep, preserve; watch over, care for; to finish, complete.

گام *gām*, s.m. A pace, step. P.

گانده *gāndah*, s.m. Future, coming time. P. (*āyanda*).

گانډۍ *gānḍa-ī*, s.f. The pole or shaft by which a Persian wheel is set in motion, and to which the bullocks are yoked.

گانګوړه *gāngūṛa*, s.f. Snivelling, snuffling, speaking through the nose.

گاڼره *gānṛa*, s.f. Pawn, pledge; jewel, ornament, trinket. S. (*gahnā*).

گاڼرۍ *gānṛa-ī*, s.f. An oil press. H. (*ghānī*).

گاودم *gāwdum*, a. Tapering, like a cow's tail. P.

گاوز *gāwuz*, s.m. Stag, elk. P. (*gawaz*).

گاولي *gāwlai*, s.m. A kind of sandal or slipper made of leather.

گاومېښ *gāwmekkh*, s.m. A buffalo. P. (*gāw-mesh*).

گاونډ *gāwanḍ*, a. Neighbouring, next door.

گاونډي *gāwanḍai*, s.m. A neighbour, parishioner, fellow townsman. S. (*gāonṭī*).

گاه *gāh*, s.m. Time; place (in comp.). P.

گاهر *gāhar*, s.m. A drove of oxen, herd of cows.

گاهو *gāhū*, s.m. Drover, cattle driver.

گاهي *gāhe*, ad. Ever, anytime; once, sometime. P. *gāhe-gāhe*, ad. At times, sometimes, occasionally. P. *gāhī*, s.f. A deep wound or sore.

گايل *gāyal*, a. Wounded. H. (*ghāyal*).

گبر *gabr*, s.m. A fire worshipper, Zoroastrian. P.

گبينه *gabīna*, s.f. Honey; honeycomb. P. (*angabīn*).

گپه *gapa*, s.f. Chatter, prattle, talk. H. (*gap*). A lump or handful of mud.

گپي *gapī*, s.f. A cord used as halter, bit and bridle of rope.

گتکه *gatka*, s.f. Fencing foil. H. (*gadkā*).

گتمه *gutma*, s.f. A button hole or loop; a thimble, thumbstall of leather.

گټ *gaṭ*, s.m. A boulder, rock, stone; a dark and heavy cloud. *guṭ*, s.m. A corner, angle, recess; a hole dug in a wall by burglars.

گټل *gaṭal*, v.a. To acquire, realize, gain; to win, succeed, gain the victory, etc. P. (*yāftan*).

گټمۍ *guṭma-ī*, s.f. A thimble.

گټه *gaṭa*, s.f. A pebble, stone; advantage, gain, profit.

گټۍ *giṭa-ī*, s.f. A potsherd, bit of stone; gravel, shingle; urinary calculus, stone in the bladder. *giṭai*, s.m. Pebble, small stone.

گټين *giṭīn*, a. Stony, pebbly, gravelly, shingly.

گځاري *gadzārai*, s.m. Refuse, chaff, stubble.

گڅ *gats*, a. Left, the left side.

گڅي *gatsai*, a. Left-handed.

گچ *gech*, s.m. Lime, cement, mortar. H.

ګداي *gadāe*, s.m. A beggar, mendicant. P. (*gadā*). *gadā-ī*, s.f. Begging; beggary, poverty. P.

ګدل *gdal*, v.a. To place, set. P. (*hīdan*). See ږدل.

ګډ *ga-aḍ*, s.m. A ram, sheep. H. (*gāḍar*). *gaḍ*, a. Mixed, compounded, blended. *guḍ*, a. Halt, lame, crippled, maimed.

ګدړ *gidaṛ*, s.m. A jackal. H. (*gīdaṛ*).

ګډندي *gaḍandai*, s.m. A dancer.

ګډوډ *gaḍ-waḍ*, a. Higgledy-piggledy, confused, entangled, jumbled. H. (*gaḍ-baḍ*).

ګډوري *gaḍūrai*, s.m. A lamb.

ګډوزي *gaḍozai*, s.m. A span, the space between thumb and forefinger.

ګډول *gaḍawul*, v.a. To mix, compound, combine, etc.; to make dance.

ګډون *gaḍūn*, s.m. Intercourse; mixture. Name of a Pathan tribe located on the southern slopes of the Mahaban mountain.

ګډه *ga-aḍa*, s.f. An ewe, sheep.

ګډهل *gaḍhal*, s.m. A bucket, tub, pail.

ګډي *guḍa-ī*, s.f. A lame woman; a doll. H. (*guḍ'ā*). *guḍai*, s.m. A lame man, etc. *gaḍa-ī*, s.f, A cushion, pad. H. (*gaddī*).

ګډيدل *gaḍedal*, v.n. To dance; to be mixed, confused, blended, etc.

ګډيدنه *gaḍedana*, s.f. Dancing; mixing, blending.

ګډيدونکي *gaḍedūnkai*, } s.m. A dancer;
ګډيدوني *gaḍedūnai*, } mixer.

ګډيره *gaḍera*, s.f. Mixture; intercourse.

ګډيکه *gaḍeka*, s.f. The support of a spinning wheel; the crutch at the side of a sandal.

ګذار *guẕār*, s.m. A blow, stroke; pass, turn, round, etc. P.

ګذر *guẕar*, s.m. A ferry, ford, passage. P.

ګذران *guẕrān*, s.m. Employment, living, livelihood. I.

ګړ *ga-aṛ*, s.m. Rumble, rattle, clatter, etc. (as of wheels).

ګر *gar* (in comp.), added to words denotes -doer, -maker, -performer. P.

ګران *grān*, a. Important, momentous; heavy, weighty; dear, precious; difficult, hard. P. (*girān*). *grānī*, s.f. Dearth, scarcity, dearness of provisions, etc.

ګرت *grut*, s.m. Interdigital space (hand or foot); angle between the trunk and branch of a tree. *grut-niwul*, v.a. To hold between the finger and thumb (as a pen, arrow, etc.).

ګرد *gird*, a. Circular, round. P. *girdāgird*, a. Round about, all round, on all sides. P. *gard*, s.m. Dust; the globe; fortune. P.

ګرداب *girdāb*, s.m. A whirlpool. P.

ګردن *gardan*, s.m. The neck. P.

ګردني *gardanī*, s.f. A horse cloth. P.

ګردون *gardūn*, s.m. A wheel; firmament, heavens; destiny, fortune; a chariot. P.

ګردي ليچي *gardai-lechai*, s.m. The arm above the elbow; humerus.

ګرز *garz*, s.m. Dust. P. (*gard*). *gurz*, or *gruz*, s.m. A battle-axe, club, mace. P.

ګړزندي *ga-arzandai*, } s.m. A reel, spindle;
ګړزني *ga-arzanai*, } whirligig.

ګړزول *ga-arzawul* or *girzawul*, v.a. To turn, change about, turn round, wheel, twirl, etc.

ګړزيدل *ga-arzedal* or *girzedal*, v.n. To revolve, spin, turn about, wander, meander, walk about, etc. P. (*gardīdan*).

ګرګل *gargal*, v.a. To scratch, claw, scrape (with the nails).

ګرکنډه *garkanḍa*, s.f. See کرکنډه.

ګړکي *ga-arkai*, s.m. The rattle or rumble of wheels.

ګرګ *garg*, s.m. Mange, itch, scab. *gurg*, s.m. A wolf. P.

ګرګره *gurgura*, s.f. Name of a tree yielding an edible fruit or berry (*Reptonia buxifolia*).

گرگس *gargas*, s.m. A vulture. P. (*kargas*). *gargas*, s.m. The cavity of the chest, thorax.

گرگه *garga*, s.f. A log, block, stump of a tree.

گرم *garm*, a. Hot, warm; active, zealous; fiery, virulent; eager, intent; crowded, thronged. P. *gram*, a. Confuted, convicted; censured, rebuked. *guram*, s.m. A clump of trees; anxiety, mental distress, perturbation.

گرمکه *garmaka*, s.f. A heat spot, vesicle, pustule. pl. *garmake*, Prickly heat (*Lichen tropicus*).

گرمه *garmah*, s.m. A kind of melon. P.

گرمي *garmī*, s.f. Heat, warmth, etc.; the venereal disease. P.

گرنډه *garanḍa*, s.f. Name of a shrub and its fruit (*Carissa spinarum*). H. (*karaundā*).

گرو *graw*, s.m. Pawn, pledge. P. (*girau*).

گرول *garawul*, v.a. To scratch, claw, scrape (with the nails).

گرولبي *grolbai*, s.m. Phlegm, mucus or pus from the lungs.

گروه *griwa*, s.f. The collar bone, neck above the collar bone; collar of a garment; button-loop. P. (*girebān*). *guroh*, s.m. A band, troop; people, tribe; party, sect. P.

گروهيدل *grohedal*, To admire, follow; be attracted, captivated; flock to; to fear, respect, revere. P. (*girwīdan*).

گريوان *girewān*, s.m. Collar of a garment; the neck. P. (*girebān*).

گريوه *grewa*, s.f. See گروه *griwa*.

گړ *gaṛ*, A castle, fort. S. (*gaṛh*).

گړدۍ *gaṛda-ī*, s.f. The whirl of a spindle.

گړنج *gṛanj*, s.m. A clink, jingle, ring (of money), tinkle (of a bell), etc. *guṛanj*, s.m. A low voice, whisper.

گړندي *gaṛandai*, a. Quick, hasty, precipitate, rash; nimble, swift, fast.

گړنګ *gaṛang*, s.m. Abyss, crater; cavity, shaft, pit. *gṛang*, s.m. Mucus from the nose, snot.

گړوبي *guṛobai*, s.m. Sherbet, eau sucré, sugar and water.

گړونج *gaṛwanj*, s.m. A frame or stand for water jars; a stand, stage, platform. S. (*ghaṛwanchā*).

گړه *guṛa*, s.f. Raw sugar, brown sugar. S. (*guṛ*).

گړۍ *gaṛa-ī*, s.f. A measure of time, about twenty-four minutes; a clock, watch. S. (*ghaṛī*). A pond, pool. H. (*gaṛhaī*). A fort, castle. S. (*gaṛhī*).

گز *gaz*, s.m. A yard measure; a ramrod. P.

گزك *gazak*, a. Festered, sloughed, suppurated, mortified (a wound); nipped with cold. P. s.m. Corruption, decay.

گزن *guzan*, s.m. Palsy, paralysis. *guzan-wahalai*, a. Palsied, paralysed.

گږ *gag*, a. Dappled, mottled; hybrid, mongrel.

گستاخ *gustā̱kh*, a. Insolent, impertinent, rude, saucy, pert. P. *gustā̱kẖī*, s.f. Impertinence, assurance, pertness, etc.

گسه *gasa*, s.f. Rebound, recoil, ricochet; blow, dig, stroke, poke.

گسيا *gasiyā*, a. Abraded, rubbed, frayed. S. (*ghasā*).

گښت *ga̱kkht*, s.m. Patrolling, walking round, strolling, wandering. P. (*ga̱sẖt*).

گفتار *guftār*, s.m. Discourse, conversation. P.

گفتگوي *guft-goe*, s.m. Conversation, talk, etc. P.

ګګر *gagar*, a. Brawny, muscular, stout, strong.

ګګروڅه *gagaṛo̱dza*, s.f. A shiver, tremble.

ګګشتو *gugu̱sẖtū*, s.m. A turtle dove, ring-dove. H. (*ghūghū*).

گل *gul*, s.m. A rose; a flower in general. P. A disease of the eye, albugo. Monday. *gil*, s.m. Clay, earth. P.

گلاب *gulāb*, s.m. Rosewater. P. *gulābī*, s.m. A barber.

گلخن *guḻkẖan*, s.m. A flat slab of stone used

for the flooring of a Turkish bath; a furnace, stove. P.

گلستان *gulistān,* } s.m. A rose bed, flower
گلشن *gulshan,* } garden. P.

گلو *gulū,* s.m. The throat, neck. P. *gilau,* s.m. Name of a plant, called also *kulma·walai* (*Mimosa scandens*). H. (*gīlā*).

گله *gila,* s.f. Complaint, lament, grumble. P. *gila·man,* a. Complaining, grumbling. P. *galla,* s.f. A herd, flock. P.

گلئ *gala-ī,* s.f. Hail. See ږلئ.

گم *gum,* a. Lost, missing, wanting. P.

گمارل *gumāral,* v.a. To consign, entrust, give in charge, commit. P. (*gumārīdan, gumāsh-tan*).

گماشته *gumāshtah,* s.m. Agent, factor. P.

گمان *gumān,* s.m. Doubt, suspicion; imagination, fancy; thought, supposition. P.

گمراه *gumrāh,* a. Erring, astray. P.

گمنز *gamanz,* s.f. A comb. See ږمنز.

گناه *gunāh,* s.m. Crime, fault, sin. P.

گنبته *gunbata,* s.f. An arch, dome, cupola, vault. P. (*gumbad*).

گنج *ganj,* s.m. A granary, market; treasure, store. P.

گنجي *ganjai,* a. Bald, scald headed; a vulture. H. (*ganjā*).

گنجيفه *ganjīfa,* s.f. A pack of cards; game at cards. P.

گند *gand,* s.m. A patchwork garment worn by dervishes. *gind,* s.m. A ball for play. S. (*gend*). *gund,* a. Equal, level, even, on a par; peer, compeer, match. *gundi,* ad. By chance, perhaps, possibly.

گندنه *gandana,* s.f. A leek (*Allium porrum*). P.

گنده *gandah,* a. Fœtid, stinking. P. *gundah,* a. Coarse, thick. P.

گنډ *ganḍ,* s.m. Edging of a garment; an ornamental collar worn by women; edging of clay round a millstone. S. (*ganḍā*). A patchwork coat worn by dervishes.

گنډل *ganḍal,* v.a. To hem, sew, stitch, baste, etc. P. (*nigandan*).

گنډولي *ganḍolai,* s.m. A short sleeved shift or jacket worn by women.

گنډهير *ganḍher,* s.m. Name of a plant (*Rhazzia stricta*).

گنډهيرئ *ganḍhera-ī,* s.f. A joint or segment of sugar cane (cut for convenience of chewing). S. (*ganḍerī*).

گنډي *gunḍī,* s.f. Collar of a dress; edging of a garment; a button loop, button. H. (*ghunḍī*). *gunḍai,* s.m. Refuse ears of corn, straw, etc. left on the threshing-floor. *gunḍe,* ad. By chance, possibly, perhaps.

گنډيري *ganḍerai,* s.m. The oleander or rose-bay (*Nerium odorum*).

گنزه *gunza,* s.f. A crease, crumple, pucker, wrinkle; a comb.

گنس *gans,* a. Stunned, stupefied, deafened. P.

گنکپ *gankap,* s.m. A cut-purse, pickpocket. H. (*gaṭh·kaṭā*).

گنگ *gung,* a. Dumb, mute. P.

گنګري *gungrī,* s.m. Boiled grain of pulse, wheat, etc. Grain steeped in water. S. (*ghūngnī*).

گنګړي *gingaṛai,* s.m. A small bell for the feet of pigeons, hawks, etc. H. (*ghūngrū*).

گنګس *gangas,* s.m. A bend, swerve, turn, twist; narcissus, daffodil.

گنګوسي *gangosai,* s.m. Rumour, report; hum, murmur, whisper; sound of footsteps, talking, etc.

گنه *gunah,* s.m. Sin, crime, fault. P. *gunah·gār,* s.m. A sinner, culprit. *gunah·gārī,* s.f. Sinfulness, guiltiness, criminality. P. *ganna,* s.f. The sugar cane. H. (*gannā*).

گنهر *gunhar,* s.m. Name of a potherb (*Amarantus polygamus*).

گنړ *ganṛ*, a. Close, dense, thick, crowded; cloudy. S. (*ghan*).

گنړل *ganṛal*, v.a. To count, reckon; to consider, know. P. (*angārdan*).

گنړني *ganṛanai*, s.m. The womb.

گنړه *ganṛa*, ad. As if, as though; know, reckon.

گواښ *gwākkh*, s.m. Arbitration, mediation; compromise, settlement.

گواښگرندي *gwākkh·grandai*, s.m. Intercessor, mediator; negotiator, arbitrator.

گواښل *gwākkhal*, } v.n. To pick a quarrel, گواښيدل *gwākkhedal*, } peck at, irritate, prepare to quarrel; chide, reproach, blame. To mediate, parley, compromise, settle a quarrel. P. (*gawājidan*).

گواندي *gawānḍai*, s.m. A neighbour.

گواه *gawāh*, s.m. A witness. P.

گواهي *gawāhī*, s.f. Evidence, testimony. P. *gawāhī·lal*, v.a. To testify, give evidence. *gawāhī·lūnai*, s.m. A witness, testifier.

گوپ *gūp*, s.m. The evening star, Venus; a bank of clouds.

گوته *gūta*, s.f. A finger, toe.

گوټ *gūṭ*, s.m. A corner, angle, nook; a hole dug in a wall by burglars. *gūṭ·mātanul*, v.a. To break into a house through a hole in the wall (as burglars).

گوجر *gūjar*, s.m. A grazier, cowherd. Name of a tribe of Rājpūts dwelling amongst the Eastern Afghans, and mostly occupied as cattle breeders and graziers. S.

گوجي *gūjai*, s.m. A small fresh-water shell; a fir cone.

گودر *gūdar*, s.f. Ford, ferry, passage. P. (*guzar*).

گوډ *goḍ*, s.m. Weeding, thinning plants. S. (*khod*). *goḍ·kawul*, v.a. To weed.

گوډا *gūḍā*, s.m. A doll, puppet. H.

گوډي *gūḍai*, s.m. A pouch; ear of Indian corn before the grain is formed. *gūḍa-ī*, s.f. A doll, puppet.

گور *gor*, s.m. A grave, tomb. P. *gor·kan*, s.m. A grave-digger. P. *gūr*, a. See گنړ.

گوراگور *gorāgor*, a. Fast, quick.

گورستان *goristān*, s.m. A graveyard. P.

گورکښ *gor·kakkh*, s.m. Name of an animal found in graveyards, Indian badger.

گورل *goral*, v.a. To see, look, inspect, view, etc. P. (*girāndan*). Def in past tenses. See کتل.

گورم *goram*, s.m. A drove of buffaloes.

گوروان *gorwān*, s.m. A drover, grazier, cattle driver.

گوره‌خر *gorah·khar*, s.m. The wild ass. P. (*gorkhar*).

گورهنده *gorhanda*, s.f. Rough uneven ground; ravine, chasm, pit, fissure.

گوړئ *gūṛa-ī*, s.f. Juice or sap of trees.

گوشي *goshī*, s.f. Capitation tax on cattle.

گوښه *gokkha*, s.f. Corner, angle, nook; privacy, retirement; aside, side; cell, closet. P. (*gosha*).

گوګړ *gogaṛ*, s.m. Sulphur. P. (*gogird*). *gūgaṛ*, a. Aged, old, worn out (man or beast).

گوګل *gogal*, s.m. Cavity of the chest, thorax. *gūgal*, s.m. Name of a gum resin, Indian bdellium. S. *gogil*, s.m. Sulphur. P. (*gogird*).

گوله *gola*, s.f. A mouthful, morsel.

گولئ *gola-ī*, s.f. A ball, bullet, pill. P. (*golī*).

گوماندو *gūmānḍū*, s.m. Mushroom, toadstool.

گونځه *gūndza*, s.f. A crease, wrinkle. See گنزه.

گونګټ *gūngaṭ*, s.m. A dung beetle.

گونګو *gūngū*, s.m. The yellow crocus, saffron.

گونګي *gūngai*, s.m. An owl.

گونه *gūna*, s.f. Colour, face, figure, form; kind, species. P.

گونړ *gūnṛ*, s.m. A weevil, insect in corn. H. (*ghūn*).

گوهاټه *gohāṭa*, A stack of cowdung (dried and stored for use as fuel).

گوهار *gūhār*, s.m. A drove of oxen or buffaloes.

گوهر *gauhar* or *gūhar*, s.m. A pearl, gem; essence, nature, substance, disposition; intellect, wisdom; lustre of a gem or metal. P.

گوي *goe*, s.m. Dry cowdung; a ball. P.

گويا *goyā*, ad. As if, thus, as one would say, etc. P.

گه *gah*, s.m. Time, place. See گاه.

گهواره *gahwāra*, s.f. A cradle, swing. P.

گهور *gahūr*, a. Dense, shady, umbrageous.

گهي *gahe*, ad. Ever. See گاهي.

گهيځ *gahīdz*, s.m. Dawn, morning.

گياه *giyāh*, s.m. Grass, herbage, weeds. P.

گيدي *gedī*, a. Stupid. P. *gedī-khar*, s.m. Stupid ass.

گيډه *geḍa*, s.f. Belly, abdomen.

گيډي *geḍai*, s.m. A load of wood, grass, etc., for the head. *geḍa-ī*, s.f. A small sheaf of corn, a bundle of grass, faggot of sticks, etc.

گير *gīr*, a. Caught, seized, captured, taken; (in comp.) conqueror, taker, seizer. P. *ger*, a. Surrounded, besieged, enclosed. H. (*gher*).

گيړکه *gīṛaka*, s.f. A magpie.

گيسو *gesū*, s.m. A curl, ringlet. P.

گينډي *genḍai*, s.m. A rhinoceros; a shield of rhinoceros hide. S. (*gainḍā*).

گينړني *genṛanai*, s.m. The womb. H. (*ghaṛiyā*).

گيول *gayawul*, } v.a. To interlace, intertwine,
گييل *gayayal*, } wattle, net.

ل

ل *lām* is the twenty-third letter of the Arabic, and the thirty-fourth of the Pukkhto alphabet. It is often substituted for the letters د and ر in words from the Hindi and Persian.

لا *lā*, ad. Even, yet, still, hitherto, otherwise, unless. A particle prefixed to words to denote privation or negation, and equivalent to the English prefixes *im-*, *in-*, *un-*, etc., and the affix *-less*. A.

لابه *lāba*, s.f. Jest, irony, ridicule. P.

لاپه *lāpa*, s.f. Boasting, bragging. P. (*lāf*). *lāp-shap*, a. Proud, arrogant; bragging, boasting.

لات *lāt*, s.m. Name of an idol of the ancient Arabians.

لاټو *lāṭū*, s.m. A shrike, butcher bird; a humming-top; a whip-top. H.

لاجبر *lājbar*, s.m. Lapis lazuli. P. (*lājward*).

لاچي *lāchī*, s.f. Cardamums. H. (*ilāchī*).

لاډو *lāḍū*, s.m. A kind of sweetmeat. H. (*laḍḍū*). A humming-top. H. (*lāṭṭū*).

لار *lār*, s.f. A road, way, path. P. (*rāh*).

لارغه *lārghah*, s.m. Delay, procrastination; lateness, slowness. ad. Ago, formerly. *lire-lārghah*, ad. Long ago, of yore, long since.

لاړل *lāṛal*, v.n. To go, depart, set out. Def. in pres. ten. See تلل *tlal*. P. (*rāh-raftan*.)

لاړه *lāṛa*, s.f. Saliva, spittle. S. (*lār*).

لازم *lāzim*, a. Necessary, urgent; proper, suitable. A.

لاس *lās*, s.m. The hand; the arm. P. (*dast*).

لاسته *lāsta*, s.f. Direction, side, quarter.

لاستي *lāstai*, s.m. Handle, haft, hilt.

لاشوړه *lāshoṛa*, s.f. Name of a tree and its fruit (*Cordia Myxa*). H. (*lāsoṛa*).

لاښ *lāksh*, s.m. A corpse, carcase. P. (*lāsh*).

لاغر *lāghar*, a. Weak, thin, lean. P.

لافه *lāfa*, s.f. See لاپه.

لاک *lāk*, s.m. Gum lac; sealing wax. S. (*lākh*).

لاکن *lākan*, a. Waxed; covered with wax. *lākin*, c. But, etc. See ليکن.

لاګ *lāg*, s.m. Dealings on credit with a tradesman.

لاگي *lāgī*, s.f. Trade, commerce. s.m. A dealer, customer.

لال *lāl*, a. Red; dumb. P. s.m. A ruby. P. (*l'al*).

لالا *lālā*, in. Master! Sir! H.

لالن *lālan*, s.m. A lover, sweetheart. S.

لاله *lāla*, s.f. A tulip. P. *lāla·gul*, s.m. The corn-poppy.

لالي *lālai*, a. Dear, beloved, darling.

لانبو *lānbo*, s.f. Swimming. *lānbo·zan*, s.m. A swimmer.

لاندِ *lāndi*, } ad. Below, under, beneath,
لاندي *lānde*, } down. *lānde·bānde*, ad. Upside down, topsyturvy, tumbled, jumbled.

لاندي *lāndai*, s.m. Salt meat, sun-dried meat.

لانډۍ *lānḍa-ī*, s.f. A kind of snake, *amphisbœna*.

لانډيس *lānḍes*, s.m. Name of a tree and its fruit (*Cassia fistula*).

لانگه *lānga*, s.f. The cord at the foot of a bed, which is used to brace up or tighten the netting. The name of a tree from the wood of which arrows are made.

لانړه *lānṟa*, s.f. Name of a plant (*Salsola kali*); it is burnt for the potash it yields: Spittle, saliva. See لاړه.

لانوده *lānwdah*, a. Wet, damp. Pl. of لوند.

لاونړ *lāwanṟ*, s.m. Caudle, posset.

لاهو *lāhū*, a. Flooded, swept away by a flood, floated down by a river, etc.

لاهه *lāha*, s.f. Alluvium, mud, mire, muddy deposit left by floods.

لاي *lāe*, s.m. Mire, mud. See preceding word.

لائق *lā-iq*, a. Becoming, fit, suitable; proper, deserving, worthy; capable, qualified, expedient. A.

لب *lab*, s.m. The lip; brim, edge; bank, margin; coast, shore. P.

لباس *libās*, s.m. Apparel, clothes, dress; garb. A.

لب‌څټ *lap·tsaṭ*, a. Fertile, fruitful (as land).

لپړ *lapaṟ*, a. Coarsely ground, gritty, unevenly mixed, clogged, clotty, lumpy (as food); thick stalks, stringy fibres, etc. mixed with potherbs; stiff, stark.

لپه *lapa*, s.f. The palm held to receive a thing; a handful, palmful. *lapakai*, s.m. The quantity containable in both hands held together. H. (*lapkā*).

لت‌پت *lat·pat*, a. Soiled, polluted, splashed; trampled, trodden down. etc.

لتاړه *latāṟah*, a. Trodden, trampled; spoiled, ruined.

لته *lata*, s.f. A kick. H. (*lāt*).

لټ *laṭ*, s.m. An axle; axle of a Persian wheel, weaver's loom, etc. A fishing stake, bird springe. a. Dull, indolent, lazy, listless. s.m. A lubber, lazy brute.

لټ‌پټ *laṭ·paṭ*, a. Tangled, tumbled, confused; soiled, stained; trampled, trodden.

لټول *laṭawul*, v.a. To examine, seek, search, rummage, turn over, investigate, look into, etc. H. (*ṭaṭolnā*).

لټه‌پير *laṭa·per*, s.m. Romping, frolicking, playing pranks, playing roughly, boisterous play.

لحاف *liḥāf*, s.f. A coverlet, quilt. A.

لحد *laḥad*, s.m. The niche in the side of a grave for the reception of a dead body. A.

لحظه *laḥza*, s.f. A moment; glance, look. A.

لد *lid*, s.m. Horse dung. H. (*līd*).

لدن *ladan*, } s.m. Inspiration. *'ilmi·ladūn*,
لدون *ladūn*, } s.m. Inspired knowledge, inherent wisdom. A.

لډر *laḍar*, s.m. A dealer in old clothes, rags, etc. a. Imbecile, foolish, stupid.

لذت *lizzat*, s.m. Flavour, taste; delight, enjoyment. A.

لذيذ *lazīz*, a. Pleasant, savoury. A.

لر *lar*, a. Lower, inferior; subordinate, minor;

conquered, subdued. p. Under, below, beneath. *lar·taraf*, s.m. The losing side, lower side. *liri*, ad. Far, far off, off, away. P. (*dūr*).

لرغونِ *larghūni*, ad. Already, ere now, before, long since, long ago.

لرغوني *larghūnai*, a. Former, pristine, old. *larghūne*, ad. Long ago, formerly, anciently, of old.

لرگي *largai*, s.m. A stick, staff; timber, wood. H. (*lakṛī*). *liragai*, s.m. The lobe of the ear.

لرل *laral*, v.a. To own, have, possess. P. (*dāshtan*, *dār-*).

لره *lara*, A particle used as the sign of the dative case; to, unto, near, with, at; for, for the sake of.

لري *larai*, s.m. The small intestines; bowel, gut. Defeat, discomfiture, loss. *lire*, ad. Off, away; far, far off, distant.

لړ *laṛ*, s.m. A row, bead, string, thread (as of beads, pearls, pots, etc.), H.

لړزه *laṛza*, s.f. A shake, tremor, quiver. P.

لړزيدل *laṛzedal*, v.n. To tremble, shake, shiver, quiver. P. (*larzīdan*).

لړل *laṛal*, v.a. To mix, stir, stir up, combine, stir about. H. (*lahrānā*).

لړم *laṛam*, s.m. A scorpion.

لړمون *laṛmūn*, s.m. The bowels, the internals, the heart, liver, lungs, etc. P. (*darūn*).

لړمه *laṛama*, s.f. Nettlerash, hives, urticaria.

لړوڅتو *laṛo·tsaṭo*, a. Mean, low, vulgar. s.m. A rascal, blackguard, scoundrel, vagabond.

لړه *laṛa* or *la-aṛa*, s.f. Fog, mist, vapour.

لږ *la-ag* or *lag*, a. Small, little, less; few, scarce. *la-ag·der*, a. More or less, somewhat, a little, few, some.

لږکوټي *la-agkūṭī*, ad. Little; somewhat, few; scantily, slightly.

لس *las*, a. Ten. S. (*das*). *lasam*, a. Tenth.

لستونړي *lastūnṛa'*, s.m. Sleeve of a dress.

لسته *lasta*, s.f. Handle, hilt. P. (*dasta*).

لسره *lasara*, ad. Never, not at all, not a bit.

لشمکه *lashmaka*, } s.f. Artful, intriguing,
لشمکي *lashmaka-ī*, } cunning, deceitful (woman); wanton, lewd, shameless (woman).

لشه *lasha*, s.f. Spike, prickle, bristle; sting of an insect; beard or spike of corn, grasses, etc. P. (*nesh*).

لښته *lakkhta*, s.f. A twig, switch, rod, cane.

لښتي *lakkhtai*, s.m. A brook, rivulet, linn, stream. *lakkhta-ī*, s.f. A dancing girl; ear-drop, pendant (of gold or silver). Name of a plant, the root of which is used as a charm by wounded persons to protect them from the evil wishes of their enemies, who, it is believed, by eating some of the root and then breathing upon a wounded man can prevent the healing of his wound, until some of their own spittle be applied to it; visitors to a wounded man are therefore requested to spit on a bit of the root, which is then passed over the wounds. The root is commonly found mixed with those of the madder plant (*majīṭ* or *rodang*) as sold in the shops.

لښکر *lakkhkar*, s.m. An army, multitude. P. (*lashkar*).

لښکي *lakkhke*, ad. Little. See لکوټي.

لطافت *laṭāfat*, s.m. Delicacy, elegance; humour, wit, facetiousness. A.

لطف *luṭf*, s.m. Courtesy, gentleness, kindness. A.

لطيف *laṭīf*, a. Elegant, delicate; agreeable, pleasant; courteous, kind, gracious. A.

لطيفه *laṭīfa*, s.f. A joke, witticism. A.

لعاب *lu'āb*, s.m. Mucilage. A.

لعل *l'al*, s.m. A ruby. P.

لعن *l'an*, s.m. Cursing, damning. A.

لعنت *l'anat*, s.m. Anathema, curse, malediction. A. *l'anatī*, a. Damned, cursed, execrated. A.

لغت *lughat*, s.m. Dialect, phraseology; dictionary; word. A.

لغته *laghata*, s.f. A kick. P. (*lagad*).

لغړ *laghaṛ*, a. Bare, stripped, naked; poor, destitute. *lūts-laghaṛ*, a. Bare as a bone, stark naked.

لغز *laghz*, s.m. A slip, slide, stumble. A. *lughz*, s.m. Enigma, riddle. A.

لغوي *lughawī*, a. Linguistic, literal meaning of a word. A.

لفافه *lifāfa*, s.f. Cover, envelope, wrapper. A.

لفظ *lafẓ*, s.m. A word, saying. A.

لقب *laqab*, s.m. Surname, title; nickname. A.

لقمه *luqma*, s.f. A morsel, mouthful. A.

لقوه *laqwa*, s.f. Spasmodic distortion of the face; paralysis of the facial nerve. A.

لقه *luqah*, s.m. A bully, brag.

لک *lak*, a. Stiff, rigid, straight; punctured, bored, pierced. s.m. A lac, a hundred thousand. S.

لکړه *lakaṛa*, s.f. A beam, rafter; pole, staff; barge pole; boat hook. H. (*lakāṛ*).

لکوټي *lakūṭe*, or *lakūṭī*, ad. A little, somewhat, slightly, not much. See لږکوټي

لکوړي *lakoṛai*, s.m. Name of a fruit.

لکه *laka*, s.f. A blemish, blot, spot, stain; the tail (of bird or beast). ad. Like, so, as, thus.

لکه‌لمي *laka-lamai*, s.m. The rump bone, tail bone, coccyx.

لکۍ *laka-ī*, s.f. The tail (of bird or beast); a meteor, falling or shooting star.

لګړ *lagaṛ*, s.m. A kind of hawk. H.

لګنړ *lagaṉṛ*, s.m. A washing basin. P. (*lagan*).

لګول *lagawul*, v.a. To attach, fix, join; ascribe, impose, add; place, put, set; employ, engage, use; set to work, etc. S. (*lagānā*).

لګيا *lagiyā*, a. Applied, attached, placed; employed, occupied; intent.

لګيدل *lagedal*, v.n. To adjoin, reach, touch, apply; happen, befall, occur, begin; be occupied, employed etc. H. (*lagnā*.)

لال *lal*, a. Dumb, mute, speechless. P. (*lāl*).

لل *lal*, v.a. To utter, pronounce, say, express. Only used with a few words as, *ganāhī-lal*, v.a. To give evidence, testify, bear witness, etc. *salām-lal*, v.a. To say salām, pay respects.

للم *lalam*, a. Arid, dry, unirrigated (land).

للمي *lalamī*, s.m. Crops entirely dependent on the rains for water, unirrigated crops.

للۍ *lala-ī*, s.f. Lullaby, hushaby. *lala-ī-lalosha*, Hushaby baby, words intoned to put a child to sleep.

للون *lalūn*, s.m. Weeding, thinning (a field or garden).

لم *lam*, s.m. Tail, end, extremity; fat tail of the Afghan sheep. P. (*dum*). *lamawar*, a. Fat tailed, having a fat tail.

لمبړ *lumbaṛ*, s.m. A fox. H. (*lambar*).

لمبل *lambal*, v.a. To bathe, wash, clean, purify.

لمبه *lamba*, s.f. A blaze, flame.

لمبيدل *lambedal*, v.n. To wash, bathe.

لمڅي *lamtsai*, s.m. Felt. P. (*namad*)

لمسول *lamsawul*, v.a. To incite, instigate, urge, prompt, tempt. A. (*lams*).

لمسون *lamsūn*, s.m. Instigation, prompting.

لمغړۍ *lamghaṛa-ī*, s.f. Contortion, writhe, twist; device, trick, wile; shamming, malingering.

لمن *laman*, s.m. Border, hem, skirt; margin, edge, verge. P. (*dāman*).

لمور *lamawar*, a. Fat tailed (as Afghan sheep).

لنبل *lanbal*, v.a. To bathe. See لمبل.

لنده *linda*, s.f. A bow.

لندي *lindai*, s.m. An archer, bowman. *linda-ī*, s.f. A small bow used by carpenters to work a drill or *barma*; the bow of a fiddle; one of the bones of the forearm; the outer bone of the leg; the hamstrings; any bent or arched twig; guard of a sword; a jet, spout, spurt of water.

لند *lanḍ*, a. Brief, short.

لنډه *lanḍa*, s.f. Lower end of the spine, sacrum.

لنډئي *lanḍa-ī*, s.f. A kind of poetry or verse, with seven or eight syllables to the line. A kind of snake, the head and tail of which are like each other (*amphisbæna*).

لنگ *lang*, a. Lame, crippled. P. *lung*, s.m. A cloth worn over the loins and hips when bathing; a clout worn between the thighs. P.

لنگټئي *lingaṭa-ī*, s.f. Name of a herb (*Heliotropum orientale*).

لنگر *langar*, s.m. An anchor; almshouse; kitchen. P.

لنگري *langarai*, s.m. A shallow metal dish, in which dough is kneaded; a deep bowl of metal or pottery in which snuff, spices, etc. are pounded; mortar. H. (*langrī*).

لنگور *langor*, s.m. A span between the thumb and fore finger.

لنگه *langa*, a. Puerperal, childbed; a puerperal woman, a woman for forty days after childbirth; an animal about to drop its young; an animal suckling its young; a bird hatching or sitting on eggs; with young, breeding, pregnant. *langa·kkhadza*, a puerperal woman. *langa·ghwā*, a milch cow *langa·chirga*, a brood hen. *langa*, s.f. A brace. See لانگه.

لنگئي *lunga-ī*, s.f. A scarf, sash (used as a head dress, or waist band, or worn as a sash over the shoulders). P. (*lūngī*).

لنگيدل *langedal*, v.n. To litter, drop young. P. (*langīdan*).

لو *lū*, s.m. Smoke. P. (*dūd*). *lau*, s.m. Reaping, mowing. P. (*dirau*).

لوړ *lwāṛ*, a. Coarse, thick; rough, uneven; boorish, clownish; rude, unpolished.

لواطت *lawāṭat*, s.m. Sodomy. A.

لوال *liwāl*, a. Hungry, peckish; longing, yearning; inclined, hankering. A. (*lunwāh*).

لواور *lawā·or*, s.m. A sickle, scythe. See لور *lor*.

لوبان *lobān*, s.m. Benzoin. A.

لوبه *loba*, s.f. Play, fun, frolic, game. A. (*l'ab*).

لوبيا *lobiyā*, A kind of bean (*Dolichos sinensis*).

لوټ *lūṭ*, s.m. Booty, plunder, spoil. S.

لوټه *lūṭa*, s.f. A clod, clod of earth. H. (*londā*).

لوټکي *loṭkai*, s.m. A pot, pipkin (of the kind used on Persian wheels). H. (*loṭā*). A small pillar of baked clay, three of which are used to form a tripod for the support of the iron dish on which cakes of bread are baked.

لوڅ *lūts*, a. Bare, naked, nude. P. (*lūch*). *lūts·lapaṛ*, or *lūts·pūts*, a. Stark naked, bare as a bone, without a shred.

لوڅک *lūtsak*, } a. Alone, destitute, friendless;
لوچک *lūchak*, } profligate, vagabond, libertine; having little hair on the body (as a dog, etc.).

لوڅه پوڅه *lotsa·potsa*, s.f. Rolling and tumbling (as a baby on its back); rolling on the ground (as a dog, horse, etc.). H. (*loṭ·poṭ*).

لوح *lauḥ*, s.m. A board or tablet used by school-boys to write upon. A.

لوحه *loḥa*, s.f. A ruler, or scale of iron for drawing lines.

لوخړه *lūkhaṛa*, s.f. A blaze, flame. S. (*lūkh*).

لوخه *lūkha*, s.f. Bulrush (*Pencillaria spicata*); soft rush (*Juncus effusus*). P.

لودل *lawdal*, v.a. To say, express. See ل. Particularly applied to giving evidence, paying respects, etc. P. (*lāwīdan*).

لودي *lodī*, s.m. Name of an Afghan tribe, famous as having furnished emperors of Hindostan.

لور *lor*, s.m. A sickle, scythe. Direction, side. *lūr*, s.f. A daughter. P. (*dukhtar*).

لورايه *lawarāya*, ad. From afar, a long way off. (For له وَرايه *la warāya*).

لوري *lorai*, s.m. Direction, quarter, side.

لوړ *lawaṛ*, s.m. A bludgeon, club, baton; a wooden pestle. s. (*loṛhā*). *lwaṛ*, a. Elevated, raised, high; upland, rising, hilly, etc. (ground). *lwaṛa·jawaṛa·zmaka*, High and low-, up and down-, undulating-, uneven-, or broken ground.

لوړول *lwaṛawul*, v.a. To detach, divide, separate, part, sever.

لوړيدل *lwaṛedal*, v.n. To part, separate, fall away.

لوزه *lauza*, s.f. A honey bee.

لوږه *lwuga*, s.f. Hunger. s. (*bhūkh*).

لوږي *lwugai*, a. Hungry, famished. s. (*bhūkhā*).

لوستل *lwustal* or *lūstal*, v.a. To read, learn. P. (*nabistan*, to write).

لوستل *lawastal*, v.a. To bale, empty; disperse, scatter, strew, daub, dash, besmear. Irr. pres. *lawanī*. Past. *lawast:*

لوشل *lwashal*, v.a. To milk (as a cow, etc.) P. (*doshīdan*).

لوښتل *lwukkhtal*, v.n. To part, separate, diverge, fall away, abscond. Def. in pres. ten. See لوړيدل.

لوښي *lokkhai*, s.m. A basin, pan, pot, etc. s. (*lokhar*). Nature, temperament, quality.

لوغزه *lwaghza*, s.f. A milch cow, goat, etc.

لوغړن *lūghaṛan*, a. Charred, smoked, smoke stained.

لوغونه *lawaghūna*, s.f. A milk pail.

لوګري *lau·garai*, s.m. A reaper, mower.

لوګي *lūgai*, s.m. Smoke, vapour, steam.

لوليه *lūlapah*, a. Burnt to ashes, scorched.

لولو *lolo*, s.m. An ornament for the arm or turban.

لولول *lwulawul*, v.a. To cause to read, to teach or learn by reading.

لوله *lola*, s.f. A ball or skein of thread; roll of paper, cloth, etc. P.

لولي *lolai*, s.m. A dancing boy. *lola-ī*, s.f. A dancing girl, prostitute. P. (*lūlī*).

لوم *lūm*, s.m. A net, noose, snare. P. (*dām*). s. (*lūm*),

لومکه *lūmaka*, } s.f. A noose, snare; a bird
لومه *lūma*, } trap of horse-hair nooses.

لون *laun*, s.m. Colour, hue; kind, species. s.

لونبړ *lūnbaṛ*, s.m. A fox. See لمبړ.

لوند *lūnd*, a. (f. *lamda*) Damp, moist, wet. P. (*nam*).

لونډ *lawanḍ*, s.m. A bachelor; widower; adventurer, vagabond, rake. P. (*lawind*).

لونګ *lawang*, s.m. A clove. s. (*laung*). *laung*, s.m. Posset, caudle, boiled milk and sugar.

لونه *lūna*, s.f. An abscess, boil.

لوهار *lohār*, s.m. A blacksmith. s.

لوهاني *lohānī*, s.m. Name of an Afghan tribe, principally occupied as carriers of merchandise between Hindustan and Turkistan. (For *rawānī*, by which name they are sometimes called.)

لوی *loe*, a. Great, large; corpulent, stout; chief, superior; full grown: great in office, rank, etc.

لويدل *lwedal*, v.n. To fall, slip, slide; drop down, fall down, tumble down, etc.

لويشت *lwesht*, s.f. A span between the thumb and little finger. P. (*bilisht*).

لويشتنک *lweshtinak*, } s.m. A pigmy, dwarf;
لويشتينک *lweshtīnak*, } small span; precocious child.

لويګنده *lweganda*, s.f. The temple, space between the ear and eye; fontanelle of an infant.

لوينه *lwīna*, s.f. A net or snare for birds.

لويږند *lwegand*, s.m. A sponger, parasite, toady.

له *la*, A preposition governing the ablative

case; from. A preposition or affix governing the dative case; to, unto.

لهري *lahaṛai*, s.m. A beam, rafter.

لهلپاند *lahlapānd*, a. Scorched, charred. See لولپه.

لياقت *liyāqat*, s.m. Capacity, fitness; ability, skill; merit, worth. A.

ليټي *leṭa-ī*, s.f. Batter, paste, pap. H. (*leṭī*). *leṭai*, s.m. Hard clay, marl.

ليڅ *leċh*, s.m. Ophthalmia, disease of the eyes.

ليڅن *leċhan*, a. Blear-eyed.

ليڅه *leċha*, s.f. The cubit, forearm.

ليڅي *leċha-ī*, s.f. The trotters of a sheep, etc.

ليدل *līdal*, v.a. To see, look, perceive. P. (*dīdan*). Irr. Pres. *wīnī*. Past, *līdah*.

ليده *līdah*, s.m. Seeing, sight, vision. P. (*dīdah*).

ليره *līra*, s.f. A shred or strip of cloth. H. (*līr*).

ليري *lera-ī*, s.f. Narrow ridge or edge of a hill.

ليزم *lezam*, a. Confuted, abashed.

ليږل *legdal*, v.a. To march, set out, pack up and depart.

ليږدول *legdawul*, v.a. To load and move off, march.

ليږل *legal*, v.a. To send, despatch, transmit.

ليښل *lekkhal*, v.a. To load, lade; march, set out. Def. in pres. ten. See ليږدل.

ليک *līk*, s.m. A line, mark, ruled line; furrow, rut, scrawl, wheel track. H.

ليکل *līkal*, v.a. To write. S. (*likhnā*).

ليکن *lekin*, c. But, yet, moreover. A.

ليکه *līka*, s.f. A line, furrow. See ليک.

ليمه *lema*, s.f. The pupil of the eye; the eye.

لينده *līnda*, s.f. A bow.

ليندي *līndai*, s.m. A bow. See لندي.

ليڼده *lenḍah*, a. Bald; scald headed.

لينګي *lengai*, s.m. The leg.

ليو *lew*, s.m. Plaster, mud plaster. H.

ليوال *lewāl*, a. Hungry. s.m. Appetite, hunger. See لوال.

ليور *lewar*, s.m. Husband's brother. S. (*dewar*).

ليوني *lewanai*, a. Demented, mad. P. (*dīwānah*).

ليوول *lewawul*, v.a. To plaster, daub, smear.

ليوه *lewah*, s.m. A wolf.

ليه *liyah*, a. Useless, worthless; uncontrolled, dissolute; wanton, lewd. Covered, veiled; noble, exalted. A. *liya*, s.f. The Tamarisk tree. ad. Merely, simply, only.

mīm is the twenty-fourth letter of the Arabic, and the thirty-fifth of the Pukkhto alphabet. It is a labial letter, and is sounded like the English *m*. In words where it is followed by ب it is sometimes changed to ن, as لنبه *lanba*, for لمبه *lamba*, flame. Prefixed to the imperative of a verb it denotes prohibition, being in place of the particle مه *ma*, as مکوه for مه‌کوه *makawā*, don't. It is added to the cardinal numbers to form the ordinals, as لس *las*, ten—لسم *lasam*, tenth.

م *mi*, a form of the genitive and instrumental cases, singular number, of the first personal pronoun زه *zah*, I. Also written مي *me*.

ما *mā*, The instrumental case and inflected form of the first personal pronoun زه.

مابوب *mābūb*, a. Beloved. See محبوب.

ماپښين *māpakkhīn*, or *māpakshīn*, s.m. Afternoon; afternoon prayers. P. (*namāz-peshīn*).

مات *māt*, a. Broken, cracked; beaten, dispersed; torn, lacerated. P.

ماتول *mātawul*, v.a. To break, burst open, smash; to break in upon, disperse, beat, etc.

ماته *māta*, s.f. Prey, quarry. S. (*mārā*).

ماتيدل *mātedal*, v.n. To break, burst, crack.

ماتس *māṭus*, s.m. A bump, swelling (from a blow).

ماچي *māche*, s.f. (pl. of *mācha*) Vermicelli.

ماخستن *mā<u>kh</u>ustan*, s.m. Bedtime, evening; bedtime prayers. P. (*namāz·<u>kh</u>uftan*).

مادہ *māda*, s.f. Article, clause; matter, subject. A. (*mādda*). *māda*, s.f. Female. a. Feminine. P.

ماديان *mādiyān*, s.f. A mare. P.

مادين *mādīn*, s.f. A female. P.

مار *mār*, s.m. A serpent, snake. P.

مارج *mārij*, s.m. A flame of fire. A.

مارجړي *mār·jaṛai*, s.m. Name of a bulbous root used as a remedy for snake bites.

مارغه *mār<u>gh</u>ah*, s.m. Pl. of مرغه which see.

ماړي هاړي *māṛe·hāṛe*, in. Exclamation of complaint, dear me! oh dear!

مازدگر *māzdigar*, s.m. Afternoon; evening; afternoon prayers. P. (*namāz dīgar*).

مازو *māzū*, s.m. A gallnut. P.

ماسپښين *māspakkhīn*, s.m. See ماپښين.

ماسته *māstah*, s.m. Curds, curds and whey.

ماسختن *māsk<u>h</u>utan*, s.m. See ماخستن.

ماسوا *mā·siwā*, ad. Besides, moreover. A.

ماسه *māsa*, s.f. Name of a weight equal to twelve grains. H.

ماسئ *māsa-ī*, s.f. Leather socks worn inside the shoes, and not removed in the house.

ماش *mā<u>sh</u>*, s.m. Name of a kind of pulse or bean (*Phaseolus Max*). S. *girgirah·mā<u>sh</u>*, s.m. Bean meal.

ماشله *mā<u>sh</u>ala*, } s.f. A skein, hank of thread
ماشوړه *mā<u>sh</u>oṛa*, } or silk.

ماشوق *mā<u>sh</u>ūq*, s.m. A lover. See معشوق.

ماشوم *mā<u>sh</u>ūm*, s.m. An infant. See معصوم.

ماشي *mā<u>sh</u>ai*, s.m. A musquito, gnat.

ماښام *mā<u>kkh</u>ām* or *mā<u>ksh</u>ām*, s.m. Evening. P. (*namāz <u>sh</u>ām*).

ماغزه *mā<u>gh</u>zah*, s.m. The brains (pl. of مغز which see).

ماکو *mākū*, s.m. A weaver's shuttle. S. (*mākho*). Name of an Afghan clan.

مال *māl*, s.m. Property, wealth; effects, goods; cattle, merchandise. A. *māl* (in comp.), Rubbing, rubber. P. *ma-āl*, s.m. End, issue. A. *<u>kh</u>air·ma-āl*, s.m. A happy issue.

مالدار *māl·dār*, a. Wealthy, rich in cattle, etc. Owner of cattle; cattle grazier.

مالت *mālat*, s.m. A division, quarter, parish, ward. A. (*muḥalla*).

مالش *māli<u>sh</u>*, s.m. Polishing, rubbing, friction. P.

مالک *mālik*, s.m. Master, owner, proprietor. P.

مالکنډئ *mālkunḍa-ī*, } s.f. Name of a plant,
مالکنړئ *mālku<u>n</u>ra-ī*, } caltrops (*Tribulus terrestris*).

مالگه *mālga*, s.f. Salt.

مالگبه *mālgbah*, s.m. Collector of salt, dry salter.

مالگين *mālgīn*, a. Salt, saline.

مالگينړي *mālgī<u>n</u>rai*, s.m. A game played by boys.

مالوچ *mālū<u>ch</u>*, s.m. Picked cotton, carded cotton.

ماله *māla*, s.f. A weaver's brush; clod crusher; rubber. P.

ماما *māmā*, s.m. Maternal uncle. S.

مامن *māman*, Place of security, asylum. P.

مامور *māmūr*, a. Established, ordered, fixed. S.

ماموله که *māmūlaka*, s.f. A water-wagtail. A. (*māmolā*).

مامويِ *māmū-ī*, s.f. A dried apricot, with the kernel preserved inside it.

مامي *māmī*, s.f. Aunt, maternal uncle's wife.

مانجي *mānjī*, s.m. A marriage guest of the bridegroom. H. (*mānjhā*, wedding feast).

ماندره *māndara*, s.f. A tent rope; a heart string, one of the *cordæ tendineæ*.

مانده *māndah*, a. Weary, fatigued, tired. P. *mānda*, s.f. A heart string, tendinous cord of the heart.

ماندينه *māndīna*, s.f. A female. P (*mādīn*).

مانع *mān'i*, s.m. Forbidder, preventor; obstacle, hindrance. A.

مانګي *māngai*, } s.m. A boatman, sailor. H.
مانړګي *mān̲rgai*, } (*mānjhī*).

مانموله *mānmola*, s.f. Name of a potherb.

مانه *māna*, } s.f. Blame, complaint; mur-
مانړه *mān̲ra*, } mur, lament.

مانړو *mān̲rū*, s.m. A kind of wild sloe or plum; the name of a herb used in medicine.

مانړي *mān̲rai*, s.m. Estrangement, misunderstanding; umbrage, pique. *mān̲ra-ī*, s.f. Edifice, building; pile, storied house.

مانړيګر *mān̲rī-gar*, a. Annoyed, piqued, displeased, estranged.

ماولي *māwlai*, s.m. The piece of wood, in the centre of the upper millstone, through which the pivot of the lower one passes.

ماه *māh*, s.m. The moon (in comp.); month. P.

ماهي *māhai*, s.m. A fish. P. (*māhī*).

مائچي *mā-iche*, s.f. Vermicelli. See ماچي.

مائل *mā-il*, s.m. Propensity, inclination, tendency. A.

مائلان *mā-ilān*, a. Partial, biassed, inclined. A.

مايه *māya*, s.f. Capital, stock; leaven, ferment; rennet. P. *māyah*, s.m. A double humped camel. P.

مباح *mubāh*, s.m. An indifferent action, an action neither ordained nor prohibited in the law. A.

مباد *mabādā*, in. God forbid! lest! be it not! P.

مبارک *mubārak*, a. Fortunate, happy; holy. in. Hail! welcome! A. *mubārakī*, s.f. Congratulation, happiness. A.

مبالغه *mubālig̲ha*, s.f. Hyperbole, exaggeration. A.

مبتدي *mubtadī*, s.m. Tyro, novice, beginner; beginning. A.

مبتلا *mubtilā*, a. Captivated, fascinated; involved in trouble, distracted. A.

مبلغ *mublag̲h*, s.m. A sum, ready money; much, many. A.

مبهم *mubham*, a. Ambiguous, occult, unknown, secret. A.

مترٖه *matra*, s.f. Posset, sillabub, curdled milk; dregs, sediment, refuse. *matrah*, a. Rare, scarce.

متصل *mutassil*, a. Contiguous, close, adjoining. A.

متعلق *mut'alliq*, a. Concerning, relative; belonging to. A.

متفرق *mutafarriq*, a. Separate, distinct; dispersed. A.

متفق *mutaffiq*, a. United, agreeing; accomplice. A.

متل *matal*, s.m. Proverb, adage; fable, saying. A. (*masal*).

متن *matan*, s.m. Middle or text of a book. A.

متوجه *mutawajjah*, a. Facing, turning; attending, favouring. A.

متولي *mutawallī*, s.m. Superintendent or treasurer (of a mosque). A.

مته *matah*, s.m. A wild boar.

متيازه *mitiyāza*, s.f. Urine. S. (*mūt*).

مټ *ma-aṭ*, s.m. The arm; fore limb of an animal.

مټ *maṭ*, s.m. Celerity, dispatch; deep dust on a road; a kind of earthenware pot. *muṭ*, s.m. The fist, closed hand. H. (*muṭh*).

مټاک *maṭāk*, s.f. A walnut with a hard shell.

مټاکه *maṭāka*, s.f. A bump, swelling from the sting of a bee, etc.; nettlerash; ball of a pellet-bow; kind of hard walnut.

مټر *muṭar*, s.m. Dolt, fool, piss-a-bed. S. (*mūtr*).

مټکي *maṭkai*, s.m. Bracelet, ornament for the arm. A large earthen jar. H. (*maṭkā*).

مټه *maṭa*, s.f. Clay, marl, greasy earth. S. (*maṭṭī*). *maṭah*, a. Lazy, stubborn, obstinate.

مټي *muṭai*, s.m. The fist; handle, hilt. s. (*muṭhī*). *muṭa-ī*, s.f. A bow for cleaning cotton; the club with which it is worked. Handle of a plough, hilt of a sword, etc.

مټیائي *miṭiyā-ī*, s.f. A sweetmeat; confectionary. H. (*miṭhā-ī*),

مټیز *maṭīz*, s.m. A man who has eloped with another's wife or daughter.

مټیزه *maṭīza*, s.f. A woman who has eloped with a man to whom she is not married; elopement, running away (of lovers).

مثال *miṣāl*, s.m. Metaphor, allegory; likeness, simile; parable, saying. A.

مثقال *miṣqāl*, s.m. Name of a weight equal to fifty-four grains (Troy). A.

مثل *maṣal*, s.m. A proverb. See متل.

مثلاً *maṣlan*, ad. For example; *e.g.*; *i.e.*; *viz.* A.

مجاور *majāwar*, s.m. A verger, sweeper at a mosque or shrine. A.

مجرا *mujrā*, s.f. Premium, allowance; deduction, retrenchment. A.

مجرب *mujarrab*, a. Proved, tried; skilled, expert. A.

مجرد *mujarrad*, a. Alone, single; unmarried. A.

مجرم *mujrim*, a. Sinful, criminal. s.m. culprit. A.

مجلس *majlis*, s.m. Assembly, congregation; meeting, party. A.

مجمر *majmir*, s.m. A chafing dish, incense dish. A.

مجمل *mujmal*, s.m. Abstract, summary. A.

مجنون *majnūn*, a. Insane, love mad, P.

مڅوڅکي *matsotskai*, s.m. See مچچکي.

مچ *mac͟h*, s.m. A fly; the sight at the muzzle of a gun.

مچچکي *mac͟hic͟hkai*, s.m. Name of a plant used in medicine.

مچک *mac͟hak*, s.m. A shepherd's crook.

مچمچي *mac͟hmac͟hai*, s.m. A honey bee.

مچلوغزه *mac͟halog͟hza*, مچوغنه *mac͟hog͟hana*, } s.f. A sling (for throwing stones).

مچه *mac͟ha*, s.f. A kiss. H. (*mac͟hhī*).

مچي *mac͟ha-ī*, s.f. A bee.

محافظت *muḥāfiẓat*, s.m. Custody, care, protection. A.

محال *maḥāl*, a. Absurd, impossible. A.

محبت *muḥabbat*, s.m. Affection, love. A.

محبوب *maḥbūb*, a. Loved, beloved. A.

محتاج *muḥtāj*, a. Needy, indigent, necessitous. A.

محتسب *muḥtassib*, s.m. A censor. A. An official who parades the streets armed with a thong, sees that the faithful duly perform their prayers and repeat the belief, etc. A.

محراب *miḥrāb*, s.m. The alcove or closet in a mosque, in which the priest, facing Mecca, performs prayers before the congregation. A.

محرم *muḥarram*, a. Sacred, forbidden. A.

محرمه *muḥarrama*, s.f. Name of the first month of the Muḥammadan calendar.

محروم *maḥrūm*, a. Forbidden, prohibited; deprived, excluded. A.

محصول *maḥṣūl*, s.m. Custom, excise, duty, tax.

محض *maḥẓ*, a. Pure, simple. ad. Purely, solely. A.

محفوظ *maḥfūẓ*, a. Secure, protected. A.

محکم *muḥkam*, a. Firm, strong. secure. ad. Firmly. A.

محکمه *muḥkama*, s.f. A court of justice. A.

محل *maḥall*, s.m. Place, house, abode; time. A.

محله *muḥalla*, s.f. A district, parish, ward; place, building, edifice. A.

محمد *muḥammad*, a. Praised. s.m. Name of the Arabian prophet. A.

محنت *miḥnat*, s.m. Labour, toil, trouble; wages, hire; affliction, difficulty, misfortune. A.

مخ *makh*, s.m. Face, front, surface; civility, kindness, courtesy. s. (*mukh*). *makhā-makh*, ad. Face to face, opposite.

مخالف *mukhālif*, a. Adverse, opposed, contrary. A.

مخالفت *mukhālifat*, s.m. Opposition, contrariety. A.

مخبر *mukhbir*, s.m. A spy, reporter, informer. A.

مختار *mukhtār*, s.m. A free agent, attorney. a. Absolute, independent; chosen, selected. A.

مختصر *mukhtaṣir*, a. Abridged. s.m. Compendium, abstract, epitome. A.

مختلف *mukhtalif*, a. Discordant, diverse. A.

مخسره *makhsara*, s.f. Jesting, joking. See مسخره.

مخرني *makhranai*, s.m. A kind of plum, apricot.

مخفي *makhfī*, a. Secret, concealed, hidden. A.

مخلص *mukhliṣ*, a. Sincere, true (friend). A. *mukhlaṣ*, s.m. Asylum, refuge. A.

مخلوت *makhlūt*, a. Mixed, combined, confused. A.

مخلوق *makhlūq*, s.m. Creature, created being. a. Created. A.

مخور *makhawar*, a. Polite, courteous, civil, kind.

مخه *mukha*, s.f. A butt for arrows, archery butt. *makha*, s.f. Direction, side, way.

مخي *makhai*, a. Equal, even, par. s.m. compeer, peer, equal, clansman.

مدار *madār*, s.m. Affability, complaisance, favour, politeness, kindness. A. (*mudārā*).

مدام *mudām*, ad. Always, continually, ever. A.

مدت *muddat*, s.m. Time, space, long time. A.

مدد *madad*, s.m. Aid, help, succour. A.

مدرس *mudarris*, s.m. Professor, teacher, head of a college. A.

مدرسه *madrassa*, s.f. College, university, school. A.

مدعا *mudd'ī*, s.f. Desire, wish; object, view. A.

مدعي *mudda'ī*, s.m. A plaintiff, claimant, prosecutor; enemy. A. *mudda'ī-alaihi*, s.m. A defendant. A.

مذكور *mazkūr*, a. Aforesaid, mentioned. s.m. Discourse, mention, conversation. A.

مذمت *mazamat*, s.m. Abuse, contempt. A.

مذهب *mazhab*, s.m. Religion, sect. A.

مذي *maza-ī*, s.f. Mucus from urethra or vagina. A.

مراد *murād*, s.m. Desire, wish; purport, design. A.

مرانده *marānda*, s.f. A tent rope. See مانده.

مراوه *mrāwa*, s.f. The part of a Persian wheel which supports one of the troughs.

مربي *murabbī*, s.m. Tutor; guardian; patron. A.

مرت *murt*, s.m. A kind of wormwood; a powder applied to the private parts of infants.

مرتبه *martaba*, s.f. Degree, office, rank; class, order; time, turn. A.

مرتد *murtadd*, s.m. Apostate, renegade. A.

مرجان *marjān*, s.m. Coral. P.

مرجيونړه *marjīwaṉṟah*, s.m. Coral diver, pearl diver. s. (*marjīyā*).

مرچ *mrach*, s.f. Pepper. s. (*mirch*). *sra-mrach*, s.f. Red pepper, capsicum.

مرد *mard*, s.m. A man; a male. P.

مردار *murdār*, a. Polluted, filthy, foul; ugly. s.m. Carrion, offal, pollution. P.

مردانه *mardānah*, a. Manly, brave. P.

مردرو *mard-rau*, s.m. Parapet, breastwork. P.

مردك *mardak*, s.m. A ball, cannon ball.

مردكه *mardaka*, s.f. } A bullet, pellet, bolus;
مردكي *mardakai*, s.m. } a marble, pebble.

مردم *mardum*, s.m. Man, mankind; people, the world. P.

مردود *mardūd*, a. Outcast, reprobate, rejected. A.

مرده *murdah*, a. Dead. s.m. A corpse. P.

مردي *mardī*, s.f. Manliness, bravery; virility, semen. P.

مرسته *mrasta*, s.f. Partiality, favour; help, aid, assistance.

مرسل *mursal*, s.m. Messenger; prophet. A.

مرسله *mursila*, s.f. Epistle, missive. A.

مرشد *murshid*, s.m. Guide, teacher, director (religious); monitor, instructor. A.

مرصع *muraṣṣa'*, a. Jewelled, gilt. A.

مرض *maraẓ*, s.m. Disease, sickness. A.

مرضي *marẓī*, s.f. Will, pleasure. A. *maraẓī*, a. Sick, diseased. A.

مرغ *mragh*, s.m. A large stone used in the exercise of "putting the stone."

مرغچچي *marghachichai*, s.m. Name of a grain used to make necklaces, etc.; Job's tears, seeds of *Coix lachryma*.

مرغړي *margharai*, s.m. A tumour, glandular swelling.

مرغلره *marghalara*, s.f. A pearl.

مرغمي *marghumai*, s.m. A kid. See ورغومي.

مرغه *marghah* (pl. *mārghah*), s.m. A bird. P. (*murgh*). *margha*, s.f. A kind of grass (*Milium filiforme*). P. (*margh*).

مرغي *margha-ī*, s.f. A little bird, any small bird.

مرکنډي *markanda-ī*, s.f. The throat, neck; windpipe and gullet.

مرګ *marg*, s.m. Death, decease, demise. P.

مرګوټي *margoṭai*, s.m. Paroxysm of death, death struggle, death.

مرله *marla*, s.f. A land measure equal to four and a half yards square.

مروت *marwat*, s.m. A coil, twist; screw. *marwat*, s.m. Name of a district between the Indus and Sulaiman mountains; name of the tribe inhabiting Marwat. *muruvvat*, s.m. Urbanity, generosity; fortitude, manliness. A.

مرور *marawar*, a. Displeased, offended, piqued.

مروري *marorī*, s.f. Name of a plant (*Helicteres isora*). H.

مروړ *maroṛ*, s.m. Convolution, turn, twist. H.

مرهم *marham*, s.m. A plaister, ointment, salve. A.

مرئ *mara-ī*, s.f. The neck, throat, gullet and windpipe; a bead; a charm.

مريد *murīd*, s.m. Disciple, follower. A.

مريض *marīẓ*, a. Diseased, sick. A.

مرينړه *marīnṛa*, s.f. Patch of a field left uncut, work left unfinished.

مرئي *mra-e*, s.m. A slave, bondsman.

مړ *muṛ*, a. Dead, lifeless, defunct. P. (*murd*). *muṛ-kawul*, v.a. To kill, deprive of life, put out (as fire, etc.).

مړام *mṛām*,
مړاو *mṛāw*, } a. Decayed, withered, faded.

مړانه *maṛāna*, s.f. Bravery, heroism, manliness. P. (*mardānah*).

مړځپن *maṛtsapan*, a. Faded, withered, decayed.

مړد *maṛd*, s.m. A saint, religious guide.

مړشومه *muṛ-shūma*, s.f. Food sent by friends and relatives to the house of a deceased person on the day of death.

مړز *mṛaz*, s.f. A quail.

مړغونه *maṛaghūna*, s.f. Bitter apple, colocynth (*Citrullus Colocynthis*).

مړغيچن *maṛghechan*, a. Faded, withered; frost bitten, nipped by cold. See مړځپن.

مړل *mṛal*, v.n. To die. P. (*murdan*).

مړني *maṛanai*, a. Brave, daring, manly. s.m. A hero. P. (*mardānah*).

مړوښه *maṛokkha*, s.f. A married woman, woman under coverture, wife.

مړوند *maṛwand*, s.m. The wrist, wrist joint.

مړونډي *maṛwanda-ī*, s.m. Name of a shrub (*Vitex negundo*).

مړه *maṛah*,
مړي *maṛai*, } in. Man! Sir! Master! Sirree! P. (*mard*).

مړي *muṛai*, a. Dead, lifeless. s.m. A corpse,

dead body. *maṛa-ī*, s.f. A morsel, mouthful.

مزاج *mizāj*, s.m. Constitution, temperament, habit, disposition, temper, nature. A.

مزاخ *mazākh*, s.m. A joke, jest; ridicule. A.

مزد *muzd*, s.m. Hire, salary, wages; perquisite, premium; corn taken by a miller as the price of grinding. P. *mazdah*, s.m. A miller.

مزدگري *muzd-garai*, s.m. A miller.

مزدور *mazdūr*, s.m. A labourer, workman. P, *mazdūrī*, s.f. Labour, work; hire, wages. P.

مزري *mzarai*, s.m. A leopard, panther; tiger.

مزكه *mzaka*, s.f. Earth, ground, land, soil.

مزل *mazal*, s.m. A stage. See منزل.

مزه *maza*, s.f. Flavour, relish, taste; delight, enjoyment, pleasure. P. (*mazā*).

مزي *mazai*, a. Powerful, strong. s.m. Cord, twine, thread, string; edging or piping of a dress.

مږ *mag*, s.m. A ram. s. (*mekh*).

مږك *magak*, s.m. A rat.

مږكوري *magakūṛai*, s.m. A mouse, young rat.

مږل *mugal*, v.a. To rub. Def. in past ten. See مښل.

مږه *magah*, s.m. A rat. P. (*mūsh*).

مس *mis*, s.m. Copper. P. *mas*, s.m. A cup for collecting lamp-black.

مسافر *musāfir*, s.m. A traveller, stranger. A.

مست *mast*, a. Drunk, intoxicated; proud, wayward; wanton, sensual. P.

مستك *mastak*, s.m. Name of a weed, darnel, tares. Name of a resin, mastick. A. (*maṣṭakī*).

مسجد *masjid*, s.m. A mosque, house of prayer. A.

مسحه *masḥa*, s.f. Anointing; wiping. A. (*masḥ*).

مسخراچي *maskharāchī*, s.m. A buffoon, jester, clown. P.

مسخره *maskhara*, s.f. Drollery, jesting. P.

مسرف *musrif*, a. Prodigal, extravagant. A.

مسكن *maskan*, s.m. Abode, dwelling. A.

مسكي *muskai*, s.m. Laughing, smiling; simper, smile. H. (*muskān*).

مسل *musal*, v.n. To simper, smile.

مسله *masala*, s.f. Proposition, question; a precept of Muhammad. A.

مسند *masnad*, s.m. A throne. A.

مسواك *miswāk*, s.m. A toothbrush. A.

مسي *masa-ī*, s.f. An ornament for the head.

مسيدل *musedal*, v.n. To simper, smirk, smile.

مسين *misīn*, a. Made of copper or brass, brazen. P.

مسينه *misīna*, s.f. A set of copper pots and pans.

مشابه *mushābih*, a. Resembling, like. A.

مشابهت *mushābihat*, s.m. Resemblance, likeness, conformity. A.

مشاته *mushāta*, s.f. An ugly face, cross look.

مشاد *mushād*, a. Ugly, cross-looking.

مشال *mashāl*, s.m. A torch. A. (*mash'al*).

مشت *musht*, s.m. A fist, closed hand. P.

مشته *mushta*, s.f. A cotton carder's beetle or club.

مشر *mashar*, a. Elder, senior, chief,

مشرف *musharraf*, a. Honoured, exalted, A.

مشرق *mushriq*, s.m. The east. A.

مشرك *mushrik*, s.m. An infidel. A.

مشغول *mashghūl*, a. Busy, occupied, employed. A.

مشغولا *mashghūlā*, s.f. Business, occupation; pastime, recreation.

مشفق *mushfiq*, s.m. Friend, companion. a. Kind, merciful, obliging. A.

مشق *mashq*, s.m. Copy, exercise, example. A.

مشقاب *mashqāb*, s.m. A trencher, kneading dish. T.

مشقت *mushaqqat*, s.m. Labour, pains, trouble, toil. A.

مشک *ma<u>sh</u>k*, s.m. A leather sac for holding water. P. *mu<u>sh</u>k*, s.m. Musk. P.

مشکار *mu<u>sh</u>kār*, s.m. A falconer; chief huntsman. P. (*mīr-<u>sh</u>ikār*).

مشکل *mu<u>sh</u>kil*, a. Difficult. A.

مشکنډۍ *mu<u>sh</u>kunḍa-ī*, s.f. A pod or bag of musk.

مشکنړه *ma<u>sh</u>kaṉra*, s.f. A glass bead.

مشکی *mu<u>sh</u>kai*, a. Musk-coloured, dark brown.

مشکین *mu<u>sh</u>kīn*, a. Musky, smelling of musk.

مشوانړۍ *ma<u>sh</u>wāṉra-ī*, s.f. An inkstand. H. (*mīsiyānī*). *ma<u>sh</u>wāṉrī*, s.m. Name of an Afghan clan.

مشورت *ma<u>sh</u>warat*, s.m. Consultation, counsel, advice. A.

مشه *ma<u>sh</u>a*, s.f. The priming pan of a gun.

مشهور *ma<u>sh</u>hūr*, a. Notorious, celebrated, famous, well known, published. A.

مښل *mu<u>kh</u>hal*, v.a. To rub, polish; anoint, lubricate. Irr. Pres. *mugi*. Past. *mu<u>kh</u>hah*. P. (*mu<u>sh</u>tan*).

مښوکه *ma<u>kh</u>hūka*, s.f. Beak, bill of a bird.

مصاله *maṣāla*, s.f. Spice, seasoning. A. (*maṣālaḥ*).

مصرف *maṣraf*, s.m. Cost, expenditure. A. *muṣrif*, a. Prodigal, extravagant. A.

مصروف *maṣrūf*, a. Expended; changed. A.

مصلحت *maṣlaḥat*, s.m. Advice, consultation, counsel; convenience, expedience. A.

مصله *maṣalla*, s.f. A carpet used to pray on. A.

مصیبت *muṣībat*, s.m. Adversity, calamity, disaster, misfortune. A.

مضبوط *maẓbūṭ*, a. Firm, fixed, strong. A.

مضر *muẓirr*, a. Hurtful, pernicious. A.

مضمون *maẓmūn*, s.m. Meaning, sense. A.

مطابق *muṭābiq*, a. Agreeable, conformable, suitable. A.

مطالعه *muṭāl'a*, s.f. Contemplation, consideration; reading, study. A.

مطبوع *maṭbū'*, a. Acceptable, worthy; innate, natural. A.

مطرب *muṭrib*, s.m. A musician. A.

مطلب *maṭlab*, s.m. Desire, wish; aim, object; meaning, purport. A.

مطلق *muṭlaq*, a. Absolute, supreme. ad. Entirely, wholly, altogether. A.

مطلوب *maṭlūb*, a. Wanted, required. A.

مظلوم *maẓlūm*, a. Injured, oppressed; mild, gentle. A.

معاش *m'ā<u>sh</u>*, s.m. Living, livelihood, subsistence. A. *m'ā<u>sh</u>arat*, s.m. Conversation, society, living together. A.

معاف *mu'āf*, a. Absolved, exempted, forgiven. A. *mu'āfī*, s.f. Exemption, immunity; rent free lands A.

معالجه *mu'ālija*, s.f. Cure, remedy; healing. A.

معاملت *mu'āmalat*, s.m. } Affair, transaction,
معامله *mu'āmala*, s.f. } business. A.

معتبر *mu'tabar*, a. Trustworthy, reputable, confidential, respectable. A.

معتدل *mu'tadil*, a. Temperate, moderate. A.

معتقد *m'utaqid*, s.m. A believer, faithful person. a. Confiding, believing, trusting. A.

معتقف *m'utaqqif*, a. Devout, pious. A.

معجزه *m'ujiza*, s.f. A miracle. A. (*m'ujiz*).

معجون *m'ajūn*, s.m. Confection, electuary. A.

معدوم *m'adūm*, a. Abolished, non-existent. A.

معده *m'ida*, s.f. Stomach. A.

معذور *m'aẕūr*, a. Excused, disappointed. A.

معرفت *m'arifat*, s.m. Knowledge; account, cause, reason. p. By, through, by means of. A.

معرکه *m'arika*, s.f. Assembly or convocation of arbitrators to settle disputes between warring tribes. A.

معروف *m'arūf*, a. Known. A.

معشوق *m'a<u>sh</u>ūq*, s.m. A loved man; lover. A. *m'a<u>sh</u>ūqa*, s.f. A mistress, sweetheart.

معصوم *m'aṣūm*, s.m. An infant, babe. a. Innocent, simple; defended, preserved. A.

معطل *m'aṭṭal*, a. Idle, neglected, unemployed; suspended from office, disengaged. A.

معقول *m'aqūl*, a. Just, proper, reasonable. A.

معلوم *m'alūm*, a. Known; notorious, distinguished; apparent, evident. A.

معمار *m'imār*, s.m. A builder; mason. A.

معمور *m'amūr*, a. Full, stocked; cultivated; happy. A.

معمول *m'amūl*, a. Customary, practised. A.

معنا *m'anā*, } s.f. Meaning, signification,
معني *m'anī*, } sense. A.

معهود *m'ahūd*, a. Agreed, determined, fixed, promised. A.

معين *mu'aiyan*, a. Appointed, established, certified, fixed. A.

مغاك *mughāk*, s.m. A pit. P.

مغانه *mghāna*, s.f. The groin, inside of thigh.

مغرب *maghrib*, s.m. The west. A.

مغرور *maghrūr*, a. Arrogant, proud, haughty. A.

مغز *maghz*, s.m. Brain, marrow, pith. P.

مغزن *maghzan*, a. Powerful, strong.

مغزي *maghzī*, s.f. Border, edging. P.

مغلوب *maghlūb*, a. Conquered, overcome. A.

مغيلان *mughīlān*, s.m. Acacia tree. A.

مفاجات *mafājāt*, s.m. Sudden death. A.

مفارقت *mufāriqat*, s.m. Absence, separation. A.

مفاصله *mafāṣila*, s.f. Interval, distance. A.

مفت *muft*, ad. Gratis, for nothing. A.

مفتاح *miftāḥ*, s.m. A key. A.

مفتي *muftī*, s.m. A lawgiver, chief justice. A.

مفرد *mufrad*, a. Alone, solitary, single. s.m. The singular number. A.

مفسد *mufsid*, s.m. Rebel, seditious person; evil-doer, michief maker. A.

مفصل *mufaṣṣal*, a. Detailed, distinct; full, ample. ad. Fully, distinctly. A.

مفلس *muflis*, a. Destitute, poor.

مفيد *mufīd*, a. Profitable, salutary. A.

مقابل *muqābil*, a. Confronting, opposite; comparing, matching, equalling. A.

مقابله *muqābala*, s.f. Comparison, matching; opposition, contending. A.

مقاتله *muqātila*, s.f. Slaughter, carnage. A.

مقال *maqāl*, s.m. Speech, discourse, talk. A.

مقام *muqām*, s.m. Abode, dwelling; mansion, place; stage, resting place. A.

مقبره *maqbara*, s.f. A tomb, sepulchre, mausoleum. A.

مقبول *maqbūl*, a. Acceptable, agreeable; accepted. A.

مقتدي *muqtadī*, s.m. Imitator, follower. A.

مقتول *maqtūl*, a. Killed, slain. A.

مقدار *miqdār*, s.m. Measure, quantity. A.

مقدس *muqaddas*, a. Consecrated, holy. A.

مقدم *muqaddam*, a. Prior, antecedent; chief, leader. A.

مقدمه *muqaddama*, s.f. Preamble, preface; affair, matter business; cause (in law). A.

مقدور *maqdūr*, s.m. Ability, power, possibility. A.

مقرر *muqarrar*, a. Fixed, established, certain; unquestionable, infallible. ad. Certainly, positively. A.

مقسوم *maqsūm*, a. Distributed, divided. A.

مقصد *maqṣad*, s.m. Design, purpose, wish, aim. A.

مقعد *muq'ad*, s.m. The hips; anus, podex. A.

مقل *muql*, s.m. Fruit of the dwarf palm. A.

مقوي *muqawwī*, a. Strengthening, tonic. A.

مقيش *muqqaish*, s.m. Brocade. A.

مقيم *muqīm*, a. Constant, fixed, stable. s.m. Resident, dweller, lodger. A.

مكار *makkār*, a. Deceitful, insidious. s.m. Cheat, hypocrite, impostor. A.

مكاري *makkārī*, s.f. Hypocrisy, imposture, roguery. A.

مكان *makān*, s.m. Place, station. A.

مكتب *maktab*, s.m. A school. A.

مکر *makr*, s.m. Deceit, evasion, fraud. A.

مکرر *mukarrar*, a. Repeated, reiterated. A.

مکروه *makrūh*, a. Odious, hateful, disgusting. A.

مکنړه *makanra*, s.f. The wooden catch which fixes the upright pillar of a Persian wheel to the cross-beam.

مکيز *makez*, s.m. Pretence, coquetry.

مګر *magar*, c. Except, but, otherwise, only, moreover, unless. P. s.m. A crocodile, alligator. S.

مګهر *maghar*, s.m. A stone used in a game like pitch and toss, ducks and drakes, etc.; a stone used in the exercise of "putting the stone."

مل *mal*, s.m. Associate, comrade, chum. S. (*mel*).

ملا *mlā*, s.f. The loins, waist. *mullā*, s.m. Schoolmaster, doctor, scholar, learned man. A.

ملاتړ *mlā·taṛ*, s.m. Armed retainer, henchman; mercenary soldier; reserve of an army; aid, succour, support. a. Armed, accoutred, having the loins girded.

ملاچرګک *mullā·chargak*, s.m. The hoopoe.

ملاح *mallāḥ*, s.m. Boatman, sailor. A.

ملاحظه *mulāḥiẓa*, s.f. Consideration, contemplation, notice, regard; looking at, A.

ملازم *mulāzim*, s.m. Attendant, servant. a. Attentive, diligent. A.

ملاست *mlāst*, a. Reclining, lying down.

ملاستل *mlāstal*, v.n. To recline. See څملاستل.

ملاقات *mulāqāt*, s.m. Interview, meeting; visiting. A.

ملال *malāl*, a. Dejected, sad; drooping, faded. s.m. Languor; grief, sadness. A.

ملامت *malāmat*, s.m. Blame, censure, rebuke. a. Reproved, censured. A. *mulāmatī*, a. Reprehensible, blameable. A.

ملتوي *multawī*, a. Protracted, delayed. s.f. Delay, procrastination. A.

ملخ *mlakh*, s.m. A locust. P. (*malakh*).

ملعون *mala'ūn*, a. Cursed, execrated. A.

ملخوزه *malkhoza*, s.f. Name of a potherb, fenugreek (*Trigonella fœnugræcum*).

ملک *mulk*, s.m. Country, kingdom, region. A. *malik*, s.m. Chief, master, king. A. *milk*, s.m. Possession, property, right. A. *malak*, s.m. An angel. A.

ملکه *malaka*, s.f. An angel. *malika*, s.f. Queen, empress, mistress, wife of a *malik*.

ملکي *malikī*, s.f. Office or duty of malik. *mulkī*, a. Civil, political, relating to the country or empire. *milkī*, s.m. A farmer, land-holder. A.

ملګري *mal·garai*, s.m. Associate, comrade, chum.

ملګرتيا *malgar·tiyā*, | ملګيري *malgīrī*, } s.f. Friendship, companionship association, etc.

ململ *malmal*, s.m. Muslin. H.

ملمه *malmah*, a. Enamelled, glazed, gilded; coated, covered. A. (*mulamm'ā*).

ملنده *malanda*, s.f. A joke, jest.

ملندي *malandai*, s.m. Buffoon, jester, clown.

ملنګ *malang*, s.m. An ascetic, hermit. H.

ملنګان *malangān*, s.m. Name of a grass (*Cyperus elatus*). H. (*malanga*).

ملو *malaw*, s.m. A sac or bag in which loads are packed previous to loading.

ملوب *malob*, s.m. Blood and water.

ملوک *malūk*, a. Delicate, handsome.

ملول *malūl*, a. Faded; sad. See ملال.

ملونه *mlūna*, s.f. Bridle, reins and bit. P. (*dahāna*).

مله *mala*, s.f. Name of a grass.

ملهم *malham*, s.m. Ointment, salve. P.

ملي *malai*, a. Emasculated, castrated (by crushing the testicles). H. (*malā*).

مليا *miliyā*, a. Encountering, meeting. S. (*milā*).

ممانعت *mumāni'at*, s.m. Prohibition, hindrance. A.

ممانړه *mamāṉra*, s.f. Name of a tree (*Sageretia oppositifolia*).

ممتاز *mumtāz*, a. Eminent, illustrious, exalted. A.

ممريز *mamrez*, s.m. A spur. P. (*mahmez*).

ممكن *mumkin*, a. Possible. A.

مملكت *mumlakat*, s.m. Empire, dominion. A.

مملوک *mamlūk*, a. Possessed, in one's power. s.m. A Mameluke, captive, slave. A.

من *man*, s.m. Name of a weight. The *man* of Tabriz, used in Western Afghanistan, is equal to eight pounds (avoirdupois); that of Peshawur is equal to eighty pounds. A.

منا *manā*, s.f. A raised platform or stage for watching a field from.

منات *manāt*, s.m. Name of an idol of the ancient Arabians. A.

مناجات *munājāt*, s.m. Prayers, supplications. A.

منادي *munādī*, s.f. Proclamation. A.

مناره *munāra*, s.f. A minaret, turret. A.

مناسب *munāsib*, a. Convenient, proper, fit. A.

مناسبت *munāsibat*, s.m. Expediency, propriety, fitness; comparison, connexion, relation. A.

منافق *munāfiq*, s.m. Atheist, heretic; hypocrite; enemy. A.

منال *manāl*, s.m. Substance, wealth. A.

منبر *minbar*, } s.m. A pulpit. A.
ممبر *mimbar*, }

منت *minnat*, s.m. Entreaty, supplication, obligation, favour. A.

منتر *mantar*, s.m. Charm, spell, philter. S.

منتظر *muntaz̤ir*, a. Expecting, looking for. A.

منځ *manḏz*, s.m. Centre, middle. ad. Between, atwixt.

منځگري *manḏz·garai*, s.m. Mediator, go-between.

منځوي *manḏzwai*, a. Central, medial.

منج *manj*, s.m. A bed, bedstead. S. (*manjā*). *munj*, s.m. Name of a grass from which ropes are made (*Saccharum munja*). S. (*mūnj*).

منجقي *manjaqai*, s.m. Clitoris.

منجله *manjala*, } s.f. A ring of grass or rags,
منجيله *manjīla*, } used as a stand for round bottomed vessels, or as a pad for the head to support a load, etc.

منحصر *munḥaṣir*, a. Besieged, surrounded. A.

من *man*, } m. A possessive particle added to
مند *mand*, } nouns and adjectives to denote endowment or possession. P.

منډانړو *manḍāṉrū*, s.m. A churning stick; rolling pin. H. (*manthanī*). Name of a plant.

منډري *manḍrai*, a. Short, squat, little. H. (*mandarā*). *mundarai*, s.m. An ear-ring. H. (*mundrā*).

منډو *manḍaw*, s.m. The withers of a horse, etc. H. (*mondhā*). Mustard seed.

منډ *manḍ*, s.m. Footprint, footmark; footstep; the stump of a tree.

منډر *munḍar*, s.m. The stump of a tree.

منډر *manḍar*, } s.m. Name of one of the
منډن *manḍan*, } two great divisions of the
منډنړ *manḍaṉr*, } Yūsufzai tribe, located on the Sama or Yūsufzai plain.

منډل *manḍal*, v.a. To cram, stuff, thrust, or force in; to knead the limbs, shampoo.

منډو *manḍaw*, s.m. An arbour; porch, verandah, shed. H. (*manḍwā*).

منډوس *manḍos*, s.m. A play ball. A cloth tied over the head and under the chin; a small turban. H. (*munḍāsā*).

منډه *manḍa*, s.f. A pace, step; race, run, course. *manḍa·wahal*, v.a. To stamp with the foot. *manḍe·wahal*, v.a. To run, race.

منډهي *manḍha-ī*, s.f. A market. H. (*manḍī*).

منډي *munḍai*, s.m. The innermost of two

bullocks treading corn, or working a Persian wheel. A pollard, or lopped tree; a man who has lost a limb; a short, squat person.

منزل *manzil*, s.m. A day's journey, stage. A.

منزلت *manzilat*, s.m. Dignity, rank. A.

منسوخ *mansūkh*, a. Abolished, cancelled. A.

منشا *manshā*, s.f. Beginning, origin, source. A. *munshā*, s.f. Intention, meaning, wish. A.

منشي *munshī*, s.m. Secretary, writer, clerk. A.

منصب *manṣab*, s.m. Dignity, office. A.

منصف *munṣif*, s.m. Arbitrator, judge, umpire. a. Equitable, just. A. *munṣifī*, s.f. Arbitration, judgment; decision, justice. A.

منظور *manẓūr*, a. Approved, accepted, chosen; seen, looked at. A.

منعه *man'a*, s.f. Refusal, prohibition. A. (*mana'*).

منكر *munkir*, s.m. Denying, rejecting. A.

منګ *mung*, pr. We. See مونږ.

منګار *mangār*, s.m. A viper. See منګور.

منګاره *mangāra*, s.f. A scratch with the nails.

منګر *mangar*, c. But, etc. See مګر. s.m. Name of the eighth Hindu month, October-November. s. (*aghan*).

منګري *mangarai*, s.m. A viper, a small venomous snake.

منګز *mangaz*, s.f. A hair comb, a comb.

منګنړ *mangaṇr*, s.m. A bug.

منګور *mangor*, s.m. A viper. See منګري.

منګول *mangūl*, s.f. The hand, claw, paw.

منګه *munga*, pr. One of the plural oblique forms of the first personal pronoun زه; us.

منګي *mangai*, s.m. An earthenware pitcher for water. *mangoṭai*, s.m. A small pitcher.

منل *manal*, v.a. To obey, submit, yield, comply, attend; accept, believe, agree, confess. s. (*mānnā*).

منه *manah*, s.m. An arbour, shed (of boughs and leaves).

مني *manai*, s.m. Autumn, autumn harvest. *manī*, s.f. Semen, sperma genitale. A. Egoism, egotism. P. *munai*, s.m. A sage; a devout, pious, or holy man. s. (*munī*)

منړه *maṇra*, s.f. An apple.

مو *mo*, pr. A form of the genitive and instrumental cases plural of the second personal pronoun تۀ. *mū*, pr. A form of the genitive and instrumental cases plural of the first personal pronoun زه. *mū*, s.m. Fat, grease, tallow, suet. The hair (in comp.). P.

مواجب *muwājib*, s.m. Pension, salary. A.

موړه *muwaṛa*, s.f. An instrument for cleaning cotton.

مواس *muwās*, s.m. Backbiter, tell-tale; rebel, mischief maker. *mawās*, s.m. Asylum, protection, refuge. H.

موافق *muwāfiq*, a. Apt, agreeing, conformable, like, consonant, suitable. A.

موافقت *muwāfiqat*, s.m. Analogy, conformity, etc.

موت *maut*, s.m. Death. A.

موټ *moṭ*, s.m. Name of a pulse (*Phaseolus aconitifolius*). H. (*moṭh*). *mūṭ*, s.m. The hand closed, fist; a handful; handle, hilt. s. (*muṭh*).

موج *mauj*, s.m. A wave, billow. A.

موجب *mūjib*, s.m. Cause, motive, reason. A.

موجود *maujūd*, Present; existing. A.

موچنړه *mochaṇra*, s.m. A cobbler's wife; a shoe.

موچي *mochī*, s.m. A cobbler, leather worker. H.

موده *mūda*, s.f. Appointed time, season.

موذن *muwazzin*, s.m. Public crier to prayers. A.

موذي *mūẕī*, a. Pernicious, hurtful, noxious. A.

مور *mor*, s.m. A mother. (pl. *mainde*). P. (*mādar*). *mor*, s.m. A peacock. s. *mor*, s.m. An ant. P.

مورانۍ *morāna-ī*, s.f. Ferule of a knife handle.

مورچنګ *morchang*, s.m. A Jew's harp. P.

مورچه *morcha*, s.f. A battery, redoubt; rust. P.

مورگني *mor·ganai*, s.m. A relative by the mother's side.

مورگه *morga*, s.f. Brim, edge, rim, margin, border, etc.

مورني *moranai*, a. Of the same mother by different fathers.

موروث *maurūs*, a. Hereditary. A.

موري *mora-ī*, s.f. A drain, gutter, waterpipe. H. (*morī*).

موړ *moṛ*, a. Sated, satisfied, surfeited; comfortable, well off, in easy circumstances.

موړه *moṛa*, s.f. A pad, cushion for the back of a baggage animal. A stool. H. (*moṛhā*).

موز *mauz*, s.m. A plantain, A.

موزه *moza*, s.f. A boot; a stocking. P.

موږ *mūg*, pr. A plural form of the first personal pronoun زه. Also written منګ.

موږي *mogai*, s.m. A peg, stake, tent peg.

موسم *mosim*, or *mausim*, s.m. Season, time. A.

موسئ *mosa-ī*, s.f. A stone used in a game like pitch and toss.

موش *mūsh*, s.m. A rat; a mouse. P.

موصوف *mauṣūf*, a. Described; celebrated. praised. A.

موضع *mauẓ'a*, s.f. District, place, village. A.

موقع *mauq'a*, s.f. Contingency, occurrence; proper, fit, suitable. A.

موقوف *mauqūf*, a. Deferred, postponed; relinquished, stopped; dependent. A.

موک *mok*, s.m. A bribe.

مولا *maulā*, s.m. God; judge, lord, master. A.

مولي *molai*, s.m. A wooden pestle; stump of a tree. *mūla-ī*, s.f. A radish. S. (*mūlī*).

موم *mom*, or *mūm*, s.m. Wax. P.

مومن *momin*, a. Believing, orthodox, faithful. A.

موميائي *momyā-ī*, s.f. Name of a waxy substance found in caves, and used as a remedy for fractures, bruises, and sprains; mummy wax. P.

موندره *mūndra*, s.f. A ring, ear-ring, finger ring. S. (*mūndrī*).

موندل *mūndal*, v.a. To find, get, obtain, procure, gain, acquire, etc.

موندي *mūndai*, s.m. A goat or ram with short ears or horns, or without horns.

مونډ *mūnḍ*, s.m. Root of a tree, germ of a plant; source, origin, cause; germ, nucleus, radix.

مونز *mūnz*, s.m. Prayer. See نمونځ.

مونګ *mūng*, pr. See منګ or موږ.

مونړي *mūṇrai*, s,m. A plug of rags, etc. used to stop the hole of a cistern or tank.

مويښې *mawekkhe*, s.f. (pl.). Hemorrhoids, piles; *pruritus ani.*

مه *ma*, ad. of prohibition used with the imperative mood; no, don't.

مهار *muhār*, s.m. A bridle, reins; the nose peg and string by which a camel is led. P.

مهال *mahāl*, s.m. Delay, respite, pause. A.

مهتابئ *mahtāba-ī*, s.f. A kind of firework. P.

مهتر *mihtar*, s.m. A chief, prince; a groom. P.

مهتمم *muhtammim*, s.m. A superintendent, factor. a. Thoughtful, anxious. A.

مهجور *mahjūr*, a. Forsaken, left; separated, cut off. A.

مهر *mahr*, s.m. Marriage portion, settlement. A. *muhr*, s.m. A seal; gold coin equal to sixteen rupees. P. *mihr*, s.m. Affection, kindness. P.

مهرباش *mihrbāsh*, } a. Indulgent, friendly,
مهربان *mihrbān*, } kind, favouring. P.

مهربانګي *mihrbāngī*, } s.f. Favour, friendliness,
مهرباني *mihrbānī*, } kindness. P.

مهرکن *muhr·kan*, s.m. A seal engraver. P.

مهره *muhra*, s.f. A shell; a rubber for smoothing paper, etc. P.

مهري *muhrī*, a. Sealed, stamped. s.f. A gutter, drain, water-pipe. P.

مهلت *muhlat*, a. Deferring, retarding; laziness, indolence; leisure, time. A.

مهلك *muhlik*, a. Deadly, killing, mortal. A.

مهم *muhimm*, a. Important, momentous. s.m. Risk, hazard, danger. A.

مهمان *mihmān*, s.m. A guest, stranger. P.

مهماني *mihmānī*, s.f. Hospitality, entertainment.

مهمند *mahmand*, s.m. Name of an Afghan tribe.

مهميزه *mahmeza*, s.f. A spur. P. (*mahmez*).

مهنړه *mahanṛah*, s.m. A boatman, sailor.

مهي *mahai*, s.m. A fish. P. (*mahī*). *mahe*, s.f. (pl.). A kind of pulse (*Phaseolus max*).

مهيرګه *maherga*, s.f. Epilepsy. See ميرګي.

مهين *mahīn*, a. Fine, subtle, thin. P.

مهينه *mahīnah*, a. Foregoing, preceding, prior; elder, first-born; early sown crops. ad. Before, ere now, previously.

مي *me*, pr. A form of the genitive and instrumental cases singular of the first personal pronoun زه. See م. *mai*, s.m. Wine, spirits. P.

ميا *miyā*, s.m. Title of a religious class; a friar; master, sir. H. (*miyān*).

مياشت *myāsht*, s.f. A month; new moon.

ميان *miyān*, s.m. The loins, middle, waist; sheath, scabbard. p. Between, betwixt. P.

ميانه *miyāna*, s.f. Name of the eleventh Afghan month, between the festivals of Ramazān and Qurbān. P. *miyānah*, a. Middling, medium, medial. P.

ميتل *mītal*, v.a. To piss, make water.

ميچ *mech*, s.m. Measure, scale; measurement, reckoning. P. *mech-kawul*, v.a. To measure.

ميچن *mechan*, s.f. A handmill. A. (*mījan*).

ميخ *mekh*, s.m. A bolt, peg, tent peg. P.

ميخچو *mekhcha*, s.m. A nail, pin, spigot.

ميدان *maidān*, s.m. Area, field, plain; field of battle; parade ground; race course. P.

ميده *maidah*, s.m. Meal, flour, fine meal. P.

مير *mīr*, s.m. Chief, leader; a title given to Sayads. P.

ميرات *mīrāt*, } s.m. Heritage, patrimony. A.
ميراث *mīrāṣ*, }

ميراثي *mīrāṣī*, a. Inherited, hereditary. s.m. Name applied to a class of bards, improvisatores, or singers.

ميرڅمن *mīrtsaman*, a. Deceitful, false, lying; hateful, vile, odious.

ميرڅي *mīrtsī*, s.f. Woe, distress, trouble; malice, spite, enmity; pique, umbrage.

ميرخاني *mīrkhāna-ī*, s.f. A kind of turban; a kind of fine cloth. P.

ميرزا *mīrzā*, s.m. Grandee, noble, prince; title given to a secretary or scribe. P.

ميرسنګ *mīr-sang*, s.m. A conch, a large shell used as a trumpet by hammām keepers, to announce the opening of the baths. S. (*sankh*).

ميرګنج *mīr-ganj*, s.m. A kind of vulture; the royal vulture. P.

ميرګي *mergai*, s.m. Epilepsy. H. (*mirgī*).

ميرمن *merman*, s.f. Lady, matron, madam, mistress, hostess.

ميره *maira*, s.f. Mother-in-law, stepmother. S. (*maibhā*). A desert, open plain.

ميړه *meṛah*, s.m. Husband, lord, master, owner.

ميز *mez*, s.m. A table. P. *mezmān*, s.m. A guest. P.

ميزان *mīzān*, s.m. Balance, pair of scales; metre, measure; addition. P.

ميزر *maizar*, s.m. A veil of fine muslin worn by women.

ميزري *maizarai*, } s.m. The dwarf palm
ميځري *maidzarai*, } (*Chamærops Richiana*).

ميږ *meg*, s.f. An ewe. P. (*mes͟h*).

ميږتون *meg͟atūn*, s.m. An ant's nest.

ميږي *meg͟ai*, s.m. An ant, the black ant.

ميسر *muyassar*, a. Procurable, obtainable. A.

ميشت *mes͟ht*, a. Settled, abiding, residing.

ميشته *mes͟hta*, s.f. Abode, residence, dwelling. A. (*m'aīs͟hat*). *mes͟hta-kawul*, v.a. To inhabit, colonize.

ميښ *mek͟kh*, s.m. A bull buffalo, buffalo. S. (*mahis͟h*).

ميښبه *mek͟khbah*, s.m. A buffalo grazier; owner of buffaloes.

ميښميښ *mīk͟khmīk͟kh*, a. Sick at stomach, nauseated; disappointed, chagrined.

ميعاد *miy'ād*, s.m. Time or place of a promise. A.

ميل *mīl*, s.m. A bodkin, needle, skewer; the barrel of a gun; a horse that stands on its hind legs. P. *mail*, s.m. Dirt, rust, scum. S. *mai-l*, s.m. Partiality, desire, fondness, inclination. A.

ميلان *mai-lān*, a. Inclined, partial, biassed, bent on. A.

ميلمستيا *melmastiyā*, s.f. Hospitality, entertainment.

ميلمه *melmah*, s.m. A guest, visitor. P. (*mezmān*).

ميلو *melū*, s.m. A bear. H. (*mallū*).

ميله *mela*, s.f. A fair; picnic; concourse of people gathered together for religious or commercial purposes. S. (*melā*).

ميمي *meme*, in. The bleating of sheep, kids, etc.; the call of a child for the mother's breast. S.

مين *mayan*, a. Fond of, loving, in love. s.m. A lover. A. (*mail*).

مينا *mainā*, s.f. Name of a bird (*Graculus Indicus*).

مينځ *myan͟dz*, a. Midst. See منځ.

مينځل *mīn͟dzal*, v.a. To wash. P. (*mīsīdan*). See وينځل.

ميانجور *mīnjawar*, s.m. A sweeper at a mosque or shrine. A. (*mujāwir*).

مينده *mīndah*, s.m. A male kept for breeding purposes; bull, ram, etc.

مينه *mīna*, s.f. Affection, love; partiality, regard. *mena*, s.f. Building, habitation, house.

ميو *miyaw*, s.m. The mew of a cat.

ميوه *mewa*, s.f. Fruit in general; raisins. P.

مئي *ma-ī*, s.f. Name of a kind of pulse (*Phaseolus radiatus*).

ن

ن *nūn* is the twenty-fifth letter of the Arabic, and the thirty-sixth of the Puk͟khto alphabet. It is a dental letter, and has the sound of the English *n*. It is added to some nouns to transform them to adjectives, as پم *pam*, mange; پمن *paman*, mangy. Added to the Aorist and Future tenses of verbs it denotes certainty or belief, as کوي *kawī* (he does), کوين *kawīna* (he surely does). It is also used as an adverbial prefix of negation instead of نه *na*, as منل *manal* (to obey), نمنل *namanal* (to disobey).

نا *nā*, No, not; a negative particle prefixed to nouns, participles, and adjectives, has the same meaning as the English prefixes *dis-*, *in-*, *un-*, etc. as ناپاك *nāpāk* (unclean), ناقلار *nāqalār* (discomposed), ناراست *nārāst* (unfair), etc.

ناب *nāb*, a. Pure, genuine. P.

ناړ *nābaṛ*, } a. Clumsy, sturdy, stout; huge,
ناپړ *nāpaṛ*, } gigantic, immense.

ناتار *nātār*, s.m. Plunder, devastation, destruction.

ناتکي *nātka-ī*, s.f. Individuality, oneness, unity.
ناجو *nājū*, s.m. A pine, fir tree. P.
ناڅاپه *nātsāpa*, ad. Suddenly, unawares.
ناچ *nāch*, s.m. A dance. S.
ناخن *nākhun*, s.m. A nail (of finger or toe). P.
ناخنه *nākhuna*, s.f. A disease of the eye, pterygium. P.
نادان *nādān*, a. Ignorant, simple. P. *nādānī*, s.f. Ignorance, stupidity.
نادر *nādir*, a. Exquisite, choice, rare. A.
نار *nār*, s.m. A shoot, sprout. Fire, hell. A. A pomegranate. P.
نارنج *nāranj*, s.m. An orange. P.
نارو *nārū*, s.m. Guinea worm, dracunculus. H.
ناره *nāra*, s.f. A shout, call. See نعره.
نارینه *nārīnah*, a. Male, masculine; manly, bold, brave. P. (*narīnah*).
ناري *hārai*, s.m. Food, refreshment. See نهاري.
ناړ *nāṛ*, s.m. A shoot, sprout; stalk, stem, stubble. H.
ناړه *nāṛa*, s.f. Stalk or stem of a grass or herb.
ناړي *nāṛai*, s.m. Rope made of strips of raw hide.
ناز *nāz*, s.m. Blandishment, coquetry; elegance, gracefulness; fondling, soothing; consequential airs, pride. P.
نازک *nāzak*, a. Delicate, elegant; fragile, tender; light, thin. P.
نازکه *nāzaka*, s.f. A doll; mistress.
نازل *nāzil*, a. Descending, alighting, dismounting; befalling, occurring. A.
نازله *nāzila*, s.f. Calamity, misfortune. A.
نازنین *nāznīn*, a. Delicate, lovely. P.
نازول *nāzawul*, v.a. To fondle, pamper, spoil (as a child).
نازیدل *nāzedal*, v.n. To coquet, assume consequential airs.
ناست *nāst*, a. Seated, sitting.
ناسره *nāsarah*, a. Alloyed, counterfeit, impure; false (as coin), etc. P.
ناسوت *nāsūt*, s.m. Humanity, human nature. A.
ناسور *nāsūr*, s.m. Sinus, fistula. A.
ناسولت *nāsolat*, a. Uncircumcised. A. (*nāsunnat*).
ناشپاتي *nāshpātai*, s.m. A pear. P.
ناشته *nāshta*, s.f. Breakfast, luncheon. P. (*nāshtā*).
ناښنده *nākkhanda*, ناښنه *nākkhana*, s.f. Impropriety, wrong.
ناصح *nāṣiḥ*, s.m. Adviser, counsellor, monitor. A.
ناطق *nāṭiq*, s.m. Speaking, a speaker. A.
ناظر *nāẓir*, s.m. Observing, seeing; inspector, supervisor; an officer in judicial courts, sheriff. A.
ناظم *nāẓim*, s.m. Governor, ruler; arranger, composer. A.
ناغه *nāgha*, s.m. Mulct, fine, poundage; respite, adjournment. *nāghah*, a. Vacant, empty, void; unemployed, out of use. T.
ناف *nāf*, s.m. The navel. P.
نافه *nāfa*, s.f. A musk pod. P.
نافع *nāfi'*, a. Advantageous, profitable, useful. A.
ناقص *nāqiṣ*, a. Deficient, imperfect. A.
ناقل *nāqil*, s.m. A reciter, reporter. A.
ناک *nāk*, s.m. A pear. P. m. A particle added to nouns to denote endowment or possession, and corresponding with the English affix *-ful*, as *gham·nāk* (woeful), *qahr·nāk* (wrathful), *sharm·nāk* (bashful), etc.
ناکار *nākār*, a. Useless. See نکاره.
ناکه *nāka*, s.f. An alligator. S. (*nākā*).
ناګاه *nāgāh*, ad. Suddenly, unawares, unexpectedly, all at once. P.
ناګمان *nāgumān*, ناګهان *nāgahān*, a. Abrupt, sudden, unexpected. ad. Unawares, by surprise. P.
نال *nāl*, s.m. A horse shoe. See نعل.
نالش *nālish*, s.m. Complaint, lament, growl, grumble. P.

نالہ *nāla*, s.f. A canal, stream, rivulet; gutter, drain, watercourse; weeping, lamentation. P.

نالي *nālī*, s.f. A quilt, etc. See نهالي.

نام *nām*, s.m. Name (in comp.). P.

ناموس *nāmūs*, s.m. Renown, fame, reputation; disgrace; female part of a family. A.

نامہ *nāma*, s.f. Book, letter; treatise, writing. P.

نامور *nāmwar*, } a. Celebrated, famous, renowned. P.
نامير *nāmer*, }

نان *nān*, s.m. Baked or leavened bread. P.

نانگه *nānga*, s.f. A blackberry.

نانوائي *nānwā-ī*, s.m. A baker. P.

ناور *nāwar*, s.m. A reservoir, pond, tank, cistern.

ناوك *nāwak*, s.m. An arrow; tube, pipe; bee's sting. P.

ناوكي *nāwaka-ī*, s.f. A doll, plaything. *nāwakai*, s.m. An arrow; name of a plant (*Jasminum revolutum*).

ناوہ *nāwa*, s.f. A canal, gutter; a tube, pipe; a long barrelled gun.

ناوي *nāwe*, s.f. A bride.

ناويات *nāwiyāt*, a. Rare, choice, matchless, peerless.

ناويت *nāwiyat*, s.m. Honeymoon, bridal state.

نائي *nā-ī*, s.m. A barber. S. *nāe*, s.m. A reed, pipe; flute. P.

نائب *nā-ib*, s.m. Deputy, lieutenant. A.

نايك *nāyak*, s.m. Chief, leader, master, patron. S.

نايڼره *nāyanra*, s.f. A barber's wife.

نبات *nabāt*, s.m. Sugar. P. A herb, grass. A.

نبض *nabẓ*, s.m. The pulse (at the wrist). A.

نبي *nabī*, s.m. A prophet. A. *nabūwat*, s.m. Prophecy, prophetship. A.

نتكي *natka-ī*, s.f. A small ring worn in the nose by women. H.

نتل *natal*, v.a. To despoil, plunder, sack, ravage, etc.

نته *nata*, s.f. A ring worn in the nose by women; the peg of wood in a camel's nose. S. (*nath*).

نتيجه *natīja*, s.f. Consequence, result, issue; reward, retribution. A.

نټ *naṭ*, s.m. Name of a caste of Indians who are jugglers, tumblers, ropedancers, etc. A cheat, rogue, knave. S.

نثار *niṣār*, a. Scattering, strewing. A.

نجات *najāt*, s.m. Escape, flight; salvation. A.

نجار *najjār*, s.m. A carpenter. A.

نجاست *najāsat*, s.m. Filth, impurity, dirt, offal. A.

نجتل *njatal*, v.a. To implant, imbed, stick into, thrust. Irr. Pres. *njanī*; Past, *njātah*.

نجس *najis*, a. Nasty, dirty; filthy, foul. A. *najas*, s.m. Dirt, dung, filth, ordure. A.

نجوم *najūm*, s.m. Astrology, astronomy. A. *najūmī*, s.m. Astrologer, fortune-teller. A.

نجيب *najīb*, s.m. A kind of soldier, guardsman. a. Noble, excellent. A. *najīb·zādah*, s.m. A nobleman.

نڅا *natsā*, s.f. Waving, shaking; bounding, dancing. S. (*nachā*).

نڅي *natsa-ī*, s.f. Cord, twine. See انڅي.

نچور *nichor*, s.m. A squeeze, wring. H.

نچورول *nichorawul*, v.a. To squeeze, wring, rinse.

نچه *nicha*, s.f. A weaver's reel; tube of a smoking apparatus or huqqa. P. (*necha*).

نخالص *nakhālas*, a. Genuine, pure, unmixed. A. (*nikhālaṣ*).

نخره *nakhra*, s.f. Coquetry, pretence, artifice; trick, sham; joke, pleasantry. P. A hole, fissure, crevice. See رخنه.

نخره باز *nakhra·bāz*, s.m. An affected person. *nakhra·bāza*, s.f. A coquette. P.

نخبس *nukhakkh*, s.m. A flesh-hook, an iron hook used to draw meat out of a pot.

نخښه *nakhkkha*, s.f. A plan, chart. See نښه.

نخل *nakhl*, s.f. A date tree, palm tree. A. *nakhlistān*, s.m. A palm or date grove.

نخوت *nakhwat*, s.m. Pomp, pride. A.

نخود *nukhūd*, s.m. A kind of pulse (*Cicer arietinum*). P.

ندا *nidā*, s.f. Voice, sound; call, shout. A.

نداپ *naddāp*, } s.m. A cotton carder, cotton
نداف *naddāf*, } dresser. A.

ندامت *nadāmat*, s.m. Contrition, regret. A.

ندرور *ndror*, s.f. pl. *ndrende*, Sister-in-law, husband's sister. S. (*nand*).

نديم *nadīm*, s.m. A courtier; intimate friend. A.

نذر *nazr*, s.m. A gift, present, offering. A.

نذرانه *nazrāna*, s.f. A present offered or received when people of rank meet, or pay their respects to a prince; tribute; fees paid to Government for grants of land, office, etc. A.

نر *nar*, a. Male, masculine; manly, bold. P.

نرخ *nirkh*, s.m. Tariff, price current, rate. P.

نرسوي *narsawai*, s.m. A kind of wild pomegranate. a. Sun-burnt, scorched by the sun.

نرکښ *narkakkh*, s.m. A mountain ram; leader of a herd.

نرکوښ *narkokkh*, s.m. A fish-hook; a hook used to gather fruit from the tree. See نخښ.

نرگس *nargis*, s.m. The narcissus. P.

نرلوخ *narlūkh*, s.m. The bulrush. See لوخه.

نرم *narm*, a. Soft, tender; easy, gentle, silly. P.

نرمي *narma-ī*, s.f. The lobe of the ear. *narmī*, s.f. Softness; mildness; silliness. P.

نرناحق *nar-nāhaqq*, ad. Entirely unjust, altogether wrongfully, without cause, illegally. P. (*bar-nāhaqq*).

نري *narai*, a. Fine, narrow, thin, slender.

نړا *naṛā*, s.f. A bellow, bray, roar, low, shout. A. (*n'ara*).

نړل *naṛal*, v.a. To bray, roar, bellow; call, shout.

نړول *naṛawul*, v.a. To raze, demolish, knock down, level, overthrow (as walls, etc.).

نړۍ *naṛa-ī*, s.f. World, universe, globe.

نړيدل *naṛedal*, v.n. To crumble, fall down, tumble, fall to ruin, subside (as walls, etc.).

نزاکت *nazākat*, s.m. Delicacy, neatness, elegance. P.

نزله *nazla*, s.f. Defluxion of humours; catarrh. A.

نزدي *nizde*, } ad. Close, near, adjacent, con-
نژدي *nijde*, } tiguous. P. (*nizd*).

نژديکي *nijdekī*, ad. Closeness, nearness, contiguity.

نږي *ngai*, s.m. A sneeze.

نږور *ngor*, s.f., pl. *ngende*, Son's wife, daughter-in-law.

نس *nas*, s.m. Abdomen, belly; concupiscence, lust; a sinew, tendon; nerve, vein. A.

نسب *nasab*, s.m. Genealogy, lineage. A.

نسبت *nisbat*, s.m. Affinity, relation; reference, respecting, regarding. A.

نسخه *nuskha*, s.f. Prescription, recipe; exemplar, copy, model; book, letter, writing. A.

نسرين *nasrīn*, s.m. A wild rose. P.

نسغ *nasagh*, s.m. Boring, piercing (as the nose, ears, etc.). A. Order; execution, torture. P. (*nasaq*).

نسکور *naskor*, a. Inverted, upside down.

نسل *nasal* or *nasl*, s.m. Breed, descent, family, origin, pedigree, race. A.

نسوار *naswār*, s.m. Snuff. S. (*nās*).

نسيم *nasīm*, s.m. A breeze, gentle air, zephyr. A.

نسيه *nasiya*, s.f. Credit, money promised. P.

نشان *nishān*, s.m. A mark, sign; scar; butt; family arms; ensign, standard. P.

نشتر *nashtar*, s.m. A lancet. P.

نشته *nishta*, Negative form of شته, Is not. P. (*nest*).

نشست *nishast*, s.m. Sitting, seated (in comp.). P.

نشم *nashm*, s.m. Deceit, craft, artfulness; lewdness, wantonness, extravagance, luxury.

نشمي *nashmī*, a. Luxurious, extravagant; lewd, wanton; crafty, artful.

نشه *nasha*, s.f. Intoxication. A. (*nashā*).

نشيب *nasheb*, s.m. Declivity; hollow. P.

نښان *nikkhān*, s.m. Mark, sign. See نشان.

نښاني *nikkhānī*, s.f. A keepsake, token, sign.

نښتر *nakkhtar*, s.m. A pine tree, conifer.

نښتل *nkkhatal* or *nkshatal*, v.n. To hitch, catch, stick, be caught, entrapped; to cling, cleave to, etc. P. (*nishākhtan*, *nashlīdan*).

نښتيځل *nakkhtedzal*, v.a. To squeeze, wring, strain.

نښلول *nkkhlawul*, v.a. To obstruct, catch, stop, jam, hitch, entrap.

نښه *nakkha* or *naksha*, s.f. Mark, sign, token; emblem, device; banner, flag, standard; target, butt. A. (*naqsha*).

نصب *naṣb*, s.m. Fixing, establishing, planting. A.

نصف *niṣf*, a. Half. A.

نصيب *naṣīb*, s.m. Destiny, fate, lot. A.

نصيحت *naṣīhat*, s.m. Admonition, counsel, advice. A.

نطفه *nuṭfa*, s.f. Seed, sperm; semen. A.

نظام *niẓām*, s.m. Arrangement, order; custom, habit, constitution: sovereign, ruler. A.

نظر *naẓar*, s.m. Sight, vision; look, glance; regard, observation. A.

نظم *naẓm*, s.m. Poetry, verse. A.

نعره *n'ara*, s.f. Bawl, shout, call; noise, clamour. A.

نعل *n'al*, s.m. A horse shoe; ferrule of a scabbard. A.

نعمت *n'imat*, s.m. Favour, benefit; delight, joy; affluence, ease, wealth. A.

نغاره *naghāra*, s.f. A kettle drum. A. (*naqara*).

نغاړل *nghāṛal*, v.a. To fold, envelop, wrap, roll up.

نغري *ngharai*, s.m. A fire-place.

نغړدل *ngharḍal*, v.a. To swallow, gulp.

نغښتل *nghakkhtal*, v.a. To foll, wrap, roll, etc. Def. in pres. ten. See نغاړل.

نغلاند *naghlānd*, a. Hungry.

نغم *nagham*, s.m. A mine, tunnel. P.

نغمه *naghma*, s.f. Melody, music, song. A.

نغوتل *nghwatal*, v.a. To attend, listen, give ear, etc. Irr. Pres. *nghwagī*. Past, *nghwat*.

نغوښيدل *nghwakkhedal*, v.n. To crawl, creep.

نغي *nughai*, s.m. Brand, scar, cicatrix; cutting off the nose, ears, etc.

نفاق *nifāq*, s.m. Enmity, disagreement; hypocrisy, fallacy. A.

نفر *nafar*, s.m. A person, individual; servant, groom. A.

نفرت *nafrat*, s.m. Abomination, aversion; flight, terror. A.

نفرين *nafrīn*, s.m. Malediction, curse, imprecation. P. Detestation, aversion. A.

نفس *nafas*, s.m. Respiration, breath; moment, minute. A. *nafs*, s.m. Spirit, substance, soul; sensuality, concupiscence; lust, desire; envy, pride; vice; gravity; sperm; penis. A.

نفساني *nafsānī*, a. Carnal, sensual, lustful; luxurious. A.

نفعه *naf'a*, s.f. Profit, advantage, gain. A. (*nafa'*).

نفقه *nafaqa*, s.f. Necessary expenses of living (food, clothing, and lodging). A.

نقاب *niqāb*, s.m. A veil. A.

نقاش *naqqāsh*, s.m. A draftsman, sculptor, painter; carver, engraver. A.

نقب *naqb*, s.m. Tunnel, mine, gallery;

burrow; excavation. A. *naqb-zan*, s.m. A miner, excavator; burglar. *naqb-zanī*, s.f. Funnelling; housebreaking by digging through the walls.

نقد *naqd*, s.m. Cash, ready money. A.

نقره *nuqra*, s.f. Silver. A.

نقش *naqsh*, s.m. Carving, painting, embroidering, etc. A.

نقشه *naqsha*, s.f. Map, pattern, model, plan, etc. A.

نقصان *nuqṣān*, s.m. Blemish, defect; injury, loss, damage, etc. A.

نقطه *nuqṭa*, s.f. A spot, dot, point. A.

نقل *naql*, s.m. Fable, anecdote; history, tale; copying, imitating, transcribing; copy; change of place, migration. A.

نکاح *nikāḥ*, s.m. Marriage, matrimony, wedlock. A.

نکاره *nakārah*, a. Useless, worthless; invalid. P.

نکته *nukta*, s.f. A subtle point, mystical meaning. A.

نکریزه *nakrīza*, s.f. Name of a plant (*Lawsonia inermis*), the henna plant. pl. *nakrīze*, Henna leaves; the dye obtained from them.

نکس *nakas*, a. Abject, mean; friendless, poor. P. (*nākas*).

نکیر *nakīr*, s.m. Name of an angel. *Munkir Nakīr*, The names of two angels who examine the spirits of the dead in the grave. A.

نگار *nigār*, s.m. Effigy, picture, idol. P.

نگاه *nigāh*, s.m. A look, glance, sight; observing, watching; custody, care. P. *nigāh-bān*, s.m. Guard, keeper. P.

نکهي *ngakkhai*, s.m. A plaited lock of hair on the temple or forehead (of women).

نګوبي *ngūbai*, s.m. Pommel of a saddle.

نګولي *ngolai*, s.m. Meat, fish, etc., eaten with bread or rice as a relish, a made dish, entrée.

نګون *nigūn*, a. Inverted; hanging downwards. P.

نل *nal*, s.m. A reed; tube, pipe, spout. S.

نله *nala*, s.f. Urinary passage, urethra. S. (*nalā*).

نم *nam*, a. Damp, moist, wet. P. *nam*, a. The ninth. P. (*naham*).

نماز *namāz*, s.m. Prayer. See نمونځ.

نمازل *nmāzal*, v.a. } To rear, sustain, support,
نمانځل *nmāndzal*, } bring up, cherish, nourish; to pamper, spoil. P. (*nawāzīdan*).

نماښام *nmākkhām*, s.m. Evening. See ماښام.

نمد *namad*, s.m. Felt, unwoven woollen stuff. P.

نمر *nmar*, s.m. The sun, sunshine.

نمري *nmarī*, s.m. (pl.) Clothes, garments, dress.

نمړ *numaṛ*, ad. Before, formerly. a. Prior, first; fixed, determined; betrothed, engaged; promised, pledged; bespoken.

نمړي *numaṛai*, a. Former, preceding, etc. *nmaṛa-ī*, s.f. A morsel. See نوړئ.

نمسي *nmasai*, s.m. A grandson. P. (*nawāsa*). *nmasa-ī*, s.f. A granddaughter. P. (*nawāsī*).

نمک *namak*, s.m. Salt (in comp.) P.

نمله *namla*, s.f. A felt pad for a saddle. P. (*namda*).

نمود *namūd*, s.m. Guide, index; display, show. P.

نمودار *namūdār*, a. Conspicuous, famed, noted. s.m. Specimen, model, sample; proof; index. P.

نمونځ *nmūndz*, s.m. Prayer. P. (*namāz*).

نمونه *namūna*, s.f. Pattern, specimen, sample. P.

نن *nan*, ad. To-day. *nan-wradz*, This day, to-day. *nan-shpa*, This night, to-night. *nan-ṣabā*, To-day or to-morrow, in these days, in a day or two.

ننباسل *nanabāsal*, v.a. To insert, etc. Def. in past ten. See ننيستل.

ننداره *nandāra*, s.f. Sight, spectacle, show; glance, look, inspection. P. (*namūdārī*).

نندرور *nandror*, s.f. Husband's sister. See ندرور.

نترړه *nanzaṛah*, s.m. Tar, pitch.

ننكه *nanaka*, s.f. A vesicle, pustule.

ننكئ *nanaka-ī*, s.f. Small pox.

ننگ *nang*, s.m. Honour, reputation; disgrace. P. *nang-o-nāmūs*, Honour, disgrace. P.

ننگو *nangū*, s.m. A span; the space between the thumb and forefinger.

ننگيالي *nang-yālai*, a. Honourable, reputable.

نننى *nananai*, a. Hodiernal, of to-day.

ننواته *nanawātah*, s.m. Entrance, admission; refuge, shelter, asylum.

ننوتل *nanawatal*, v.n. To enter, go in, intrude; to take refuge, seek protection from another.

ننه *nana*, ad. Inside, within.

ننيستل *nanayastal*, v.a. To insert, introduce, draw in, retract, conduct, or lead in, etc. Def. in pres. ten. See ننباسل.

نو *naw*, s.m. Moisture, dampness. P. (*nam*). *nau*, a. Fresh, new, young. P. *nū*, s.m. The navel.

نواب *nawāb*, s.m. A chief, governor of a province. A.

نواحي *nawāḥī*, s.f. Environs; territories. A.

نواره *nawāra*, s.f. Cultivation, habitation, population.

نوار *niwāṛ*, s.m. Broad tape. H.

نواړي *niwāṛai*, s.m. The tape or lacing of a pair of trousers; the hem in which the tape passes.

نواز *nawāz* (in comp.), Cherishing. P.

نوازش *nawāzish*, s.m. Favour, patronage. P.

نوبت *nobat*, or *naubat*, s.m. Period, time, turn; opportunity, occasion; accident; occurrence; degree, pitch; keeping watch; relieving guard; musical instruments sounded at the gate of a great man's house, or at the market place, etc., at fixed intervals. A.

نوبهار *nau-bahār*, s.m. Spring, early spring. P.

نوڅئ *nūtsa-ī*, s.f. Pliers, forceps, pincers. H. (*nochī*).

نور *nor*, a. Other, another, different, more. ad. Besides, moreover, also, likewise. H. (*aur*). *nūr*, s.m. Light, splendour. P. *nwar*, s.m. The sun. See نمر.

نوراني *nūrānī*, a. Bright, light, clear. P.

نوروز *nau-roz*, s.m. New year's day of the Persian calendar. P.

نوري *nwarī*, s.m. Old clothes. See نمري.

نوړز *nwaṛaz*, s.f. A quail.

نوړئ *nwaṛa-ī*, s.f. A mouthful, morsel; food. P. (*nihārī*).

نوړيدل *nwaṛedal*, v.n. To peel, excoriate, strip off.

نوږد *nogd*, } s.m. Genus, kind, source, origin.
نوږي *nogai*, } A. (*nau'*).

نوس *naus* or *naws*, s.m. Spirit, soul; self; lust, sensuality. A. (*nafs*).

نوسي *nwasai*, s.m. Grandson. See نمسي.

نوعه *nau'a*, s.f. Species, kind; manner, mode. A.

نوک *nūk*, s.m. A nail (toe or finger); claw (of an animal or bird). S. (*nakh*).

نوکاره *nūkāra*, s.f. A scratch, claw, scrape; clawing, scratching.

نوکر *nokar*, s.m. A servant. P. *nokarī*, s.f. Service.

نول *nūl*, s.m. Grief, sorrow, affliction. P. (*nāla*).

نولس *nolas*, a. Nineteen. *nolasam*, a. Nineteenth.

نولي *nolai*, s.m. A weasel, mongoose. S. (*newlā*).

نوليدل *nūledal*, v.n. To fret, pine, grieve, sorrow.

نوم *nūm*, s.m. Name; reputation, fame;

honour, character. s. (*nām*). *nūm*, s.m. The navel.

نوماندي *nūmāndai*, a. Named, called, yclept.

نومد *nūmd*, a. Damp, wet. See لوند.

نومړي *nūmaṛai*, a. Named, called; famed, celebrated; eminent, great.

نوميد *naumed*, a. Hopeless, without hope. P.

نوند *nūnd*, a. Damp, wet. See نومد.

نونکي *nūnaka-ī*, s.f. A furuncle, boil, pustule. See ننکي.

نوي *nawai*, a. New, fresh; unused; young, late, modern. P. (*nau*). *nawai*, s.m. The inside one of a drove of oxen treading corn. *nawe*, a. Ninety. *nūe*, s.f. Mother's brother, maternal uncle.

نه *nuh*, a. Nine. *na*, ad. Nay, no. Negative particle. Neither, nor, not.

نهاد *nihād*, s.m. Habit, nature, quality. P.

نهار *nahār*, a Fasting. P.

نهاري *nahārai*, s.m. Breakfast, luncheon, forenoon meal, refreshment. P.

نهال *nihāl*, s.m. A sapling, shoot, sprout, seedling. P.

نهالي *nihālī*, s.f. A cushion, mattress; quilt, coverlet; sapling, seedling, sucker.

نهان *nihān*, a. Concealed, hidden. P.

نهايت *nihāyat*, a. Extreme, excessive. ad. Extremely. s.m. Extremity, limit; excess. A.

نهر *nahr*, s.m. A canal, stream, rivulet. A. *nahar*, a. Fasting, unfed. P.

نهنګ *nahang*, s.m. A whale, leviathan, crocodile. P.

نهوه *nahwa*, s.f. Refusing food, fasting.

نهه *naha*, s.f. Tuesday.

نهيه *nahiya*, s.f. Prohibition; interdict. A. (*nahī*).

ني *nai*, s.m. A reed, tube; flute, pipe. P.

نيا *niyā*, s.f. A grandmother.

نياز *niyāz*, s.m. Petition, supplication; indigence, poverty; a thing dedicated. P. *niyāz-man*, a. Indigent, suppliant. *niyāzī*, s.m. Lover, friend. Name of a Pathan tribe.

نياګانه *niyāgāna*, s.f. A mother's family or relations.

نيام *niyām*, s.m. Sheath, scabbard; bandage for a broken limb; plough tail or handle. P. (*miyān*).

نياو *niyāw*, s.m. Right, equity, justice. S.

نيايه *niyāyah*, s.m. Maternal uncle.

نيبو *nībū*, s.m. A lemon, citron. S.

نيت *niyat*, s.m. Purpose, intention, design; will, desire, wish. A.

نيټه *neṭa*, s.f. Bargain, contract; promise, engagement; appointed time; season.

نيرنګ *nairang*, s.m. Deceit, evasion, fraud; magic, sorcery; miracle, novelty. P.

نيره *nīra*, s.f. A cobbler's awl.

نيز *nīz*, s.m. Deluge, inundation, flood; drift wood, rubbish, etc. carried by floods. ad. Also, again, likewise. P.

نيزه *neza*, s.f. A spear, lance. P.

نيستي *nestī*, s.f. Non-existence. P.

نيشتر *neshtar*, s.m. A lancet, fleam. See نشتر.

نيښ *nekkh*, s.m. A prickle; sting of an insect; puncture, prick; tusk of a camel, dog, etc. P. (*nesh*).

نيغ *negh*, a. Straight, stiff, upright, erect.

نيک *nek*, a. Moral, honest; good; lucky. P. *nayak*, s.m. See نايک.

نيکوکار *nekokār*, a. Righteous, honest, moral. P.

نيکه *nīkah*, s.m. Paternal grandfather, ancestor.

نيکي *nekī*, s.f. Piety, virtue, goodness, morality. P.

نيل *nīl*, s.m. Indigo; blue. S.

نيلاب *nīlāb*, s.m. The river Indus. Name of a town on the Indus below Attak.

نيلم *nīlam*, s.m. A sapphire. S.

نيلي *nīlai*, s.m. A grey horse. P.

نيم *nīm*, a. Half. P. *nīma-khwā*, a. Immature, crude, unripe; changeable, fluctuating; bootless, unavailing.

نيمايه *nīmāyah*, s.m. A half, one half.

نيمبولي *nīmbola-ī*, s.f. A necklace of gold and glass beads (worn by women). H.

نيمتني *nīmtanai*, s.m. A vest, waistcoat, jacket.

نيمګړي *nīmgaṛai*, a. Unfinished, incomplete.

نيمچه *nīmcha*, s.f. A short sleeved fur coat. *nīmchah*, a. Hybrid, mongrel. s.m. Name applied to certain tribes of Kafiristanis who have become converts to Islām.

نيمي *nīmai*, s.m. A half, moiety.

نينزكه *nenzaka*, s.f. See نازكه.

نينكه *nenaka*, s.f. Name of a bird, the tomtit.

نيني *nīne*, s.f. (pl.) Parched grain.

نيوز *niyūz*, s.m. Flood, torrent, inundation. *niyūz-wṛai*, a. Drift wood, rubbish carried by floods.

نيول *nīwul*, v.a. To catch, lay hold of, take, capture, seize. Irr. Pres. *nisī*. Past, *nīwah*.

ڼ

ڼ or نړ *ṛūn*, This compound letter is peculiar to the Pukkhto alphabet, of which it is the thirty-seventh in number. It has a peculiar sound formed by a combined pronunciation of the component letters; the sound of the *n* is nasal, and that of the *r* full and rolling as pronounced by a Frenchman. By some tribes this letter is pronounced as *n* doubled or emphatic, as *rannā* for *raṉṟā*, *gann* for *gaṉṟ*, etc. This letter does not occur at the commencement of any word in the Pukkhto language.

و

و *wāw*, is the twenty-sixth letter of the Arabic and the thirty-eighth of the Pukkhto alphabet. As a consonant it has the sound of *w*, and is sometimes interchanged with ب. As a vowel it has the sound of *o-*, *ū-*, and *au*, as is explained in the Grammar.

وَ *wa*, c. A copulative conjunction used to connect words and sentences; and, also. P. A particle used as the sign of the vocative case. A particle used with signs of the dative case.

وُ *wu*, A particle prefixed to the aorist, future, and perfect tenses, and imperative mood of verbs; it corresponds to the ب similarly used in the Persian, and like that letter is also sometimes rejected as redundant.

وِ *wi*, An abbreviated form of the third person singular, perfect tense of the verb ويل *wayal*, To speak.

وابسته *wābastah*, a. Related, connected, bound. s.m. An adherent, dependent. P.

واپس *wāpas*, ad. Again, back, return. P.

واته *wātah*, s.m. Exit, issue, coming out.

واټ *wāt*, s.f. A road, path. S. (*bāṭ*).

واټن *wātan*, s.m. Distance, interval, space.

واج *wāj*, s.m. Barter, exchange, trading in kind.

واجب *wājib*, a. Expedient, fit, necessary, proper; worthy, just, reasonable. A.

واحد *wāḥid*, a. One, single, sole. A.

واخ *wākh*, in. Alas! sorrow! woe!

واده *wādah*, s.m. Marriage, wedding; marriage festival. *wāda*, s.f. Agreement, promise, vow. A. (*w'ada*).

وار *wār*, s.m. Turn, time, period. P. A blow, stroke; attack, assault. H. Leisure, rest. S. *wār*, A particle added to nouns to denote similitude or endowment. P.

وارث *wāris̤*, s.m. Heir, owner, lord. A.

واريزه *wārīza*, s.f. Intermittent fever.

وارړه *wāṛah*, a. All, the whole. ad. Wholly.

واز *wāz*, a. Open, ajar, gaping. P. Fat, blubber.

وازده *wāzda*, } s.f. Fat, blubber.
وازگه *wāzga*, }

وازه *wāza*, s.f. A fathom, stretch of both arms extended; stride of a horse.

واژگون *wāẓgūn*, a. Inverted, upside-down. P.

واسطه *wāsta*, s.f. Account, cause, sake, reason. A. *wāsiṭa*, s.f. Agency, medium, means. A

واسيکه *wāsīka*, ad. Immediately, now, at once.

واښه *wākkh*, s.m. } Rope or cordage made of
واښکي *wākkhkai*, } goat's or camel's hair.

واښه *wākkhah*, s.m. Fodder, grass, hay; herbage, pasture.

واصل *wāṣil*, a. Arrived, met; coupled, joined. A.

واعظ *wā'iẓ*, s.m. Preacher, lecturer. A.

واف *wāf*, s.m. Nightingale; songster. P.

واقع *wāq'i*, s.m. Befalling, happening, occurring; appearing. A.

واقعه *wāq'ia*, s.f. Event, occurrence, incident.

واقعي *wāq'ī*, a. Proper, right, true. ad. Truly, actually, really. A.

واقف *wāqif*, a. Acquainted, conversant. A.

واك *wāk*, s.m. Authority, command; choice, will; power, force. P.

واگه *wāga*, s.f. A bridle, rein. H. (*bāg*).

وال *wāl*, } A particle added to nouns to denote
والا *wālā*, } resident, inhabitant; agent, owner, keeper, etc. H. Ex. *buner-wāl*, A resident of Buner. *hoti-wālā*, A townsman of Hoti.

والا *wālā*, a. Dignified, sublime, high. A. s.f. A kind of silk, sarcenet. P.

والد *wālid*, s.m. A father. A.

والده *wālida*, s.f. A mother. A.

والدين *wālidain*, s.m. Both parents. A.

واله *wāla*, s.f. Rivulet, canal, stream.

والي *wālī*, s.m. A chief, ruler, prince. A. *wālai*, s.m. An earring. S. (*bālī*). *wālai*, m. A particle affixed to nouns and adjectives to denote endowment or possession, as, *plan* (wide), *plan-wālai* (wideness). H. (*wālā*).

وام *wām*, s.m. Debt, credit, loan; borrowing, lending. P.

وانړه *wānṛa*, s.f. A pile of grain mixed with the husk and chaff as trodden out on the threshing floor, a pile of grain, husk and chaff before winnowing.

واورا *wāwrā*, s.f. A kind of vulture.

واوره *wāwra*, s.f. A flake of snow. pl. *wāwre*, Snow. P. (*barf*).

واويلا *wāwailā*, s.f. Wail, lament, bewailing. A.

واه *wāh*, in. Bravo! well done! excellent. P.

واهمه *wāhima*, s.f. Fancy, imagination. A.

واي *wāe*, in. Alas! woe! woe to you! A.

وبا *wabā*, s.f. Plague, pestilence, epidemic, disease. A.

وبال *wabāl*, s.m. Sin, crime, fault. A.

وبلته *wabulta*, } ad. Together, one with
وبله *wabla*, } another.

وبله باندې *wabla-bānde*, ad. One above another, before and behind, in layers, in folds, together, etc.

وپار *wapār*, s.m. Trade, traffic, commerce. S. (*baipār*).

وپاري *wapārī*, s.m. A merchant, trader.

وت *wat*, s.m. Interval, gap; gorge, defile; pass. *wit*, a. See ويت.

وتر *watar*, a. Watered, saturated, irrigated (field). *witar*, s.m. A voluntary prayer not enjoined by the *farẓ* nor the *sunnat*.

وتراوي *watrāwī*, a. Unaccented, without harmony (as poetry).

وتل *watal*, v.n. To issue, emerge, come out, go forth; to exude, ooze.

وټه *waṭa*, s.f. Discount, exchange; defect, deficiency; injury, blemish. H. (*baṭṭā*).

وجاړ *wujāṛ*, a. Desolate, ruined, waste. H. (*ujāṛ*).

وجاړي *wujāṛai*, s.m. Wilderness, desert, wild.

وجلل *wajlal*, v.a. To kill, slay, put to death. Irr. Pres. *wajnī*; Past. *wājah*.

وجود *wujūd*, s.m. Body, being, substance; penis. A.

وجه *waja*, s.f. Nape, occiput, depression at the back of the neck. *wuja*, s.f. A nerve, vein, tendon, sinew.

وجهه *wajha*, s.f. Cause, reason; manner, way; appearance, visage. A.

وڅکه *wutska*, s.f. A raisin; a kind of raisin without pips.

وچ *wuch*, a. Arid, dry; parched, withered; sapless; without milk, etc.

وچکول *wuchkūl*, } A castrated ram, wether.
وچکولي *wuchkūlai*, }

وچکۍ *wuchaka-ī*, s.f. A burning fever.

وچولي *wuchwulai*, s.m. The forehead, brow.

وحش *waḥsh*, s.m. A wild beast. A.

وحشت *waḥshat*, s.m. Fear, fright; solitude, desert, wild, waste. A.

وحشي *waḥshī*, a. Fierce, savage, ferocious, wild. A.

وخ *wakh*, in. Ugh! Oh! Heigh ho!

وخت *wakht*, s.m. Time, season. A. (*waqt*).

وداع *widā'*, s.m. Adieu, farewell. A.

ودان *wadān*, a. Cultivated, inhabited; peopled, prosperous. *wadānī*, s.f. Prosperity, plenty; cultivation, population. P. (*ābādān*).

ودانول *wadānawul*, v.a. To cultivate, populate, people, colonize.

ودانيدل *wadānedal*, v.n. To flourish, prosper.

ودرول *wudrawul*, v.a. To erect, set up. pitch (as a tent, etc.); prop, support; to stop, stay, halt.

ودريدل *wudredal*, v.n. To stand, stand up, stand still; arise, get up; stay, abide, halt, stop.

ودول *wadawul*, v.a. To marry, give in marriage, take in marriage.

وديدل *wadedal*, v.n. To be married, taken or given in marriage.

وډ *waḍ*, a. Fallow land, land from which the crop has been gathered.

ور *war*, s.m. A door, gate. P. (*dar*). *war*, m. A particle added to nouns to denote possession or endowment, as *dzān* (life), *dzānwar* (an animal). P. *war*, The pronominal dative affix, singular, of the third personal pronoun, as *war-dza*, go to him.

ورا *wrā*, s.f. A marriage procession; party of women who conduct the bride to the house of the bridegroom. S. (*barāt*). *warā*, ad. Afar, far off, yonder; beyond, besides. A.

ورابانړي *wrā-bāṉrai*, s.m. A male member of the *wrā*, or marriage procession; guest at a wedding feast.

وراثت *wirās̤at*, s.m. Heritage, heirship. A.

وراڅه *wrādza*, s.f. A species of louse which infests camels, sheep, dogs, etc.

وراره *wrārah*, s.m. Brother's son, nephew. *wrāra*, s.f. A woman whose brother is dead.

وراشه *wrāsha*, s.f. Language, dialect. H. (*bhāshā*).

وران *wrān*, a. Destroyed, ruined, spoiled; desolate, deserted, waste. P. (*wairān*). *wrānī*, s.f. Desolation, ruin; spoiling, ruining.

ورايه *warāya*, ad. Far, far away; beyond, yonder. *la-warāya*, From afar.

وربوز *wurbūz*, s.m. The snout, muzzle.

ورتګ *wartag*, s.m. Outset, departure, exit.

ورتول *wratawul*, v.a. To fry, grill, roast, broil.

ورتيدل *wratedal*, v.n. To fret; be broiled, fried.
ورټ *wraṭ*, s.m. A gush or flood of tears.
ورځ *wradz*, s.f. A day; daytime. P. (*roz*).
ورځني *wardzane*, } ad. Outside, without (the
ورڇني *warchane*, } house).
ورځه *wrudza*, s.f. The eyebrow.
ورخ *warkh*, s.m. } A small hole or passage in
ورخه *warkha*, s.f. } the side of a watercourse to let out the water for irrigation of fields, etc.
ورخاړي *warkhāṛai*, s.m. Name of a potherb purslain (*Portulaca oleracea*). A disease of goats and sheep, murrain.
ورخته *warkhata*, ad. Firstly, in the first place.
ورخړه *warkhaṛa*, s.f. Rubbish, litter, sweepings.
ورد *wird*, s.m. Reading the Qurān at certain fixed times; daily use, practice, task. A.
وررول *wrarawul*, v.a. To tear, rend, lacerate.
ورريدل *wraredal*, v.n. To tear, be torn, rent, etc.
ورزيدل *warzedal*, v.n. To fly (as a bird).
ورژل *warĵal*, v.a. To chop, mince. Pres. *warĵanī*. Past. *wārĵah*.
ورژي *wriĵe*, s.f. (pl.) Rice (the grain). A. (*aruz*).
ورږ *wrag*, s.m. Mane of a horse, etc.
ورږه *wraga*, s.f. A flea. *wargah*, s.m. Biestings, the first milk after calving or kidding.
ورستو *wrusto*, ad. After, behind, astern.
ورستول *warastawul*, v.a. To send. See آستول.
ورسته *wrustah*, s.m. The rear, stern.
ورستي *wrustai*, } a. Hinder, posterior, rear,
ورستني *wrustanai*, } hindmost, rearmost, backmost.
ورستيدل *wrastedal*, v.n. To decay, rot, putrefy, stink.
ورسركول *warsarkawul*, v.a. To give freely or liberally.
ورشو *warsho*, s.f. A grass plot, lawn, meadow.
ورطه *warṭa*, s.f. A labyrinth, maze; whirlpool, vortex. A.

ورغاڼري *warghāṇrai*, s.m. A paste of butter and flour used to anoint newborn babes and puerperal women with.
ورغلل *waraghlal*, v.n. To arrive at, go to, set out to, depart. Irr. Pres. *wardzam*. Past, *warāghlam*. See راغلل.
ورغومي *warghūmai*, s.m. A young kid.
ورغوي *warghawai*, s.m. The palm, sole.
ورق *warq*, s.m. A card, leaf of a book. A.
ورک *wruk*, a. Lost, mislaid; wasted.
ورکړل *warkṛal*, } v.a. To give, present, be-
ورکول *warkawul*, } stow, grant (to another).
ورکول *wrukawul*, v.a. To lose, mislay; squander, waste. H. (*lukānā*).
ورکه *wruka*, s.f. Deprivation, loss; wasting.
ورکيدل *wrukedal*, v.n. To be lost, to wander, stray; to be mislaid, forgotten.
ورګ *warg*, s.m. The fleece of a sheep. *wrag*, s.m. The mane of a horse, etc.
ورله *warla*, a. Big with young, pregnant.
ورم *waram*, s.m. Swelling, tumour. a. Swelled, tumefied, inflated. A.
ورمارګه *warmārgah*, } s.m. An eruption of boils
ورماګه *warmāgah*, } on the face (of children).
ورمېږ *warmeg*, s.m. The nape, the neck.
وندار *wrandār*, s.f. Brother's wife, sister-in-law.
ؤرنيکه *wa-arnīkah*, s.m. A great grandfather on the father's side; an ancestor.
ورو *wro*, ad. Gently, slowly.
ورو ځه *wrūdza*, s.f. The eyebrow. See ورځه.
ورور *wror*, s.m. A brother. P. (*barādar*). *wrorī*, s.f. Fraternity, brotherhood.
وروست *wrost*, a. Rotten putrid, decayed.
ورون *wrūn*, s.m. The thigh. P. (*rān*).
ورهول *warhawul*, v.a. To liberate, release, set free, save. P. (*rahānīdan*).
ورهيدل *warhedal*, v.n. To escape, become free. P. (*rahīdan*).

وري *wrai*, s.m. A lamb. P. (*barra*). *warai*, s.m. A bundle or load for the head; one of the packs of a camel's or bullock's load.

وريت *wrīt*, a. Broiled, grilled, roasted, fried.

وريځ *waryadz*, } s.f. A cloud.
وريځه *waryadza*, }

وريدل *wuredal*, v.n. To rain, drizzle, shower.

وريره *wrera*, s.f. Brother's daughter, niece.

وريشل *wreshal*, v.a. To spin, twist.

وريښم *wrekkham*, s.m. Silk. P. (*resham*).

ورئيزه *wra-eza*, s.f. Bridesmaid, female guest at a wedding.

وړ *wa-aṛ*, a. Successful, victorious, winning. P. (*burd*): H. (*war*). *waṛ*, s.m. Scab, crust of a sore; miscellany, mass, bits of gold and silver mixed together. *wuṛ*, a. Small. P. (*khurd*). See ووړ.

وړانډِ *wṛāndi*, } ad. Ahead, in front, before,
وړاندې *wṛānde*, } foremost.

وړاندي *wṛāndai*, a. Prior, preceding, foremost. s.m. The front, bow, prow, advance, van.

وړانديني *wṛāndīnai*, a. Foremost, prior, first.

وړانه *wa-aṛāna*, Success, winning, gaining. *wa-aṛāna-pa-aṛāna*, Winning and losing.

وړل *wṛal*, v.a. To bear, support, carry, convey, remove, take away; endure, put up with, etc. (only used with reference to inanimate objects). Def. in past ten. See يوسل. P. (*burdan*).

وړم *waṛam*, ad. Last but one (applied only to times and seasons). *waṛam-kāl*, The year before last. *waṛama-shpa*, The night before last. *la-waṛama-wradz*, Three days ago.

وړمبې *wṛumbe*, ad. Firstly, in the first place.

وړمبي *wṛumbai*, } a. First, principal, fore-
وړمبني *wṛumbanai*, } most, chief.

وړوکي *wṛūkai*, a. Tiny, small, wee.

وړول *wuṛawul*, v.a. To powder, pulverize, grind, triturate.

وړونبې *wṛūnbe*, ad. See وړمبې.

وړه *wuṛah*, s.m. Flour, meal, powder.

وړي *wuṛai*, s.m. Summer. *wṛai*, ad. Removed, carried away; borne, endured. *waṛa-ī*, s.f. Wool, fleece. *ūṛai*, m. A particle affixed to nouns to denote smallness, as *chirg* (a cock), *chirgūṛai* (a cock chicken).

وز *wuz*, s.m. A he-goat; mountain goat. P. (*buz*).

وزر *wazr* or *wazar*, s.m. The wing of a bird or insect; fin of a fish. P. (*bāzū*).

وزګار *wuzgār*, a. Unemployed, unused, unoccupied; idle, inactive, at leisure.

وزګري *wuzgarai*, s.m. A young goat.

وزمه *wazma*, s.f. The charge of a gun.

وزن *wazn*, s.m. Measure, weight; metre (of verse); esteem, reputation. A.

وزير *wazīr*, s.m. A minister of state, prime minister. A.

وزيري *wazīrī*, s.f. The office of Wazīr. s.m. Name of a Pathan tribe, the Wazīrīs.

وزيمه *wazema*, s.f. An ewe or goat seeking the male, in heat.

وژل *wajal*, } v.a. To kill, slay. See وجلل.
وژلل *wajlal*, }

وژه *wuja*, s.f. A nerve, vein, sinew.

وږم *wagm*, s.m. } Breath, vapour, exhalation,
وږمه *wagma*, s.f. } steam.

وږمکۍ *wagmaka-ī*, } s.f. The moon.
وږمۍ *wagma-ī*, }

وږي *wugai*, a. Hungry, famished. *wagai*, s.m. An ear of corn, grasses, etc.

وس *was*, s.m. Endeavour, attempt, trial; ability, power, force; advantage; opportunity; authority. s. (*bas*).

وسته *wasta*, s.f. A pond, pool.

وسک *waska*, } ad. As, as if, as it were.
وسکه *waska*, } Finally, then, therefore.

وسله *wasla*, s.f. Arms, accoutrements, weapons; tools, implements. A. (*silāḥ*).

وسمه *wasma*, s.f. Leaves of the Indigo plant, used as a dye for the hair. A.

وسواس *wiswās*, s.m. Apprehension, suspense, doubt, hesitation; distraction of mind; temptation of the devil. A. *wiswāsī*, a. Apprehensive, distracted; perplexing, causing doubt or suspense.

وسوسه *waswasa*, s.f. Temptation; suspense. A.

وسه *wasa*, s.f. A summer shower, summer rain.

وسيله *wasīla*, s.f. Affinity, conjuncture, cause, medium, means; prop, support, patronage. A. *wasīla-dār*, s.m. Client, defendant.

وشته *washta*, s.f. A joke, jest; joking.

وښتي *wakkhte*, s.f. (pl.). An inferior kind of rice.

وښخور *wakkhkhor*, s.m. An herbivorous animal, grass eater.

وښکل *wukkhkal*, v.a. To pull. See وکښل.

وښي *wakkhai*, s.m. A bracelet.

وصال *wiṣāl*, s.m. Meeting, interview; death. A.

وصف *waṣf*, s.m. Encomium, praise. A.

وصول *wuṣūl*, s.m. Arrival, acquisition; juncture. A.

وصيت *waṣiyat*, s.m. A will, making a will; precept, mandate. A.

وضو *wuẓū*, s.m. A form of purification by ablution before prayer. A.

وطن *waṭan*, s.m. Birthplace, home, native country. A.

وطواط *waṭwāṭ*, s.m. A kind of swallow; a bat; a languid man, timid man. A.

وطي *waṭī*, s.f. Copulation, coition. A.

وظيفه *waẓīfa*, s.f. Pension, stipend, salary; religious duty, task. A.

وعظ *w'aẓ*, s.m. Sermon, lecture; admonition. A.

وغه *wagha*, s.f. A long red worm; a kind of intestinal worm.

وغيره *waghaira*, ad. And so forth, and the rest, et cetera, etc.

وفا *wafā*, s.f. Fidelity, sincerity. A.

وقار *wiqār*, s.m. Dignity, estimation; constancy, steadiness; mildness, modesty; honour, reputation. A.

وقت *waqt*, s.m. Time, season. A.

وقف *waqf*, s.m. Endowment, foundation, legacy for pious purposes. A.

وقوف *wuqūf*, s.m. Sense, understanding; experience, information. A.

وکښل *wukkshal*, v.a. To draw. See کښل.

وکيل *wakīl*, s.m. Attorney, agent; delegate. A. *wakālat*, s.m. Commission, embassy, agency. A.

وګړي *wagaṛai*, s.m. A creature, man, human being.

ول *wal*, s.m. A coil, curl, twist, etc. H. (*bal*). *wul*, A particle added to nouns and adjectives to form the infinitive mood of active verbs. *wal*, s.m. Cheapness. See ويل *wel*.

ولاړ *wulāṛ*, a. Erect, upright, standing.

ولاړ *wulāṛi*, ولاړې *wulāṛe*, ad. A short time, brief interval, somewhat, slightly.

ولايت *wilāyat*, s.m. Abroad, foreign country. A. *wilāyatī*, s.m. A foreigner. a. Foreign.

ولل *wlal*, v.a. To wash.

وله *wala*, s.f. A canal, watercourse, stream; a cane, reed; willow tree. *wula*, s.f. Root of a plant. *wlah*, s.m. Washing. *wala*, p. To, unto; sign of the dative case.

ولې *wali*, ولي *wale*, ad. But, besides, yet, however. A. (*walek*). Why? wherefore?

ولي *walī*, s.m. Lord, prince, master. A. *wilī*, a. Melted. See ويلي.

وليشت *wlesht*, s.m. A span. See لويشت.

وند *wand*, s.m. A bank, dyke, embankment. P. (*band*).

وندر *wandar*, s.m. A tethering rope with

several loops for the feet of goats, sheep, etc.

وندني *wandanai*, s.m. A bandage, binder, wisp of straw used to tie up a sheaf of corn, etc.

وندیار *wandyār*, s.f. Brother's wife. See ورندار.

وند *wanḍ*, s.m. A field, estate, farm, parcel of land.

وندہ *wanḍa*, s.f. Division, portion, quota, share.

ونگرہ *wangara*, s.f. Pond, pool, lake.

ونه *wana*, s.f. A tree, shrub.

وو *wo*, s.m. Air, wind; rheumatism. P. (*bād*).

وودل *wūdal*, v.a. To weave, plait, braid.

وودہ *wūdah*, a. Asleep, sleeping.

وور *wor*, a. Diminutive, minute, small, wee.

ووړکي *woṛkai*, or *woṛukai*, s.m. A little one, child.

ووړوکي *woṛūkai*, a. Minute, tiny, very small.

ووںه *wūna*, s.f. A kind of Damascened sword.

وهل *wahal*, v.a. To beat, hit, strike, wallop, baste.

وهلندي *wahlandai*, a. Wavy, tortuous, meandering, serpentine, winding.

وهم *wahm*, s.m. Idea, fancy, conjecture; anxiety, dread. A. *wahmī*, a. Fanciful, flighty, etc.

وهوہ *wahwah*, in. Bravo! well done!

وهویله *wahwaila*, s.f. Lament. See واویلا.

وهیر *waher*, a. Forgotten.

ویاړ *wiyāṛ*, s.m. Vanity, conceit; envy, jealousy.

ویاړل *wiyāṛal*, v.a. To boast, exult, chuckle.

ویت *wīt*, a. Ajar, open, gaping; pert, saucy; mischievous, wanton.

ویتکي *wītakai*, s.m. A mischievous, pert, precocious, forward, etc. child.

ویته *wīta*, s.f. Impudence, precocity, pertness, etc.

ویخ *wekh*, s.m. Root of a tree; foundation, root; origin, source. P. (*bekh*).

ویر *wīr* or *vīr*, s.m. Mourning, lamentation; beating the breast. P. *wīr-jalai* or *wīra-jalai*, s.m. A mourner, lamenter.

ویران *wairān*, a. Desolate, ruined, waste. P. *wairāna*, s.f. A desert, wilderness, solitude. *wairānī*, s.f. Desolation, ruin. P.

ویرہ *wera*, s.f. Fear, fright, alarm. *werawul*, v.a. To frighten, terrify, alarm.

ویریدل *weredal*, v.n. To fear, be afraid.

ویړ *wīṛ*, a. Open, distended, spread out, expanded.

ویړول *wīṛawul*, v.a. To strew, spread out, scatter, etc.

ویړیدل *wīṛedal*, v.n. To expand, open out, blossom, etc.

ویړیا *weṛiyā*, ad. Free, gratis, for nothing.

ویزار *wīzār*, a. Angry, displeased, chagrined, vexed. P. (*bezār*). *wīzārī*, s.f. Anger, displeasure.

ویسا *wīsā*, s.f. Faith, belief; trust, reliance.

ویساک *wīsāk* or *waisāk*, s.m. Name of the first Hindu month, April-May. S. (*baisākh*).

ویش *wesh*, s.m. Division, distribution; lot, share.

ویشتل *wīshtal*, v.a. To cast, hurl, throw; discharge, propel, shoot. Pres. *wuli*. Past, *wīsht*.

ویشل *weshal*, v.a. To distribute, divide, allot; sift, separate.

ویشله *weshala*, s.f. A kind of unleavened bread, a pancake.

ویښ *wīkkh*, a. Awake, waking, vigilant.

ویښته *wekkhtah*, s.m. Hair, a hair.

ویل *wayal*, v.a. To say, speak, talk, tell. *wel*, s.m. Cheapness, low price. H. (*wārā*).

ویلني *welanai*, s.m. Herb mint, peppermint. P. (*pedīna*).

ویله *wela*, s.f. A brook, small stream, rivulet.

ويلي *wili*, a. Fused, melted; liquefied, thawed. H. (*pighlā*).

وينا *wainā*, s.f. A lament, wail; dirge, funeral song; conversation, speech, talk.

وينځل *windzal*, v.a. To wash, cleanse, purify.

وينځه *windza*, s.f. A bondmaid, slave girl.

وينه *wainah*, s.m. The white ant.

ويني *wine*, s.f. (pl.). Blood.

ويي *wayai*, s.m. A word, saying; talk, speech.

ه *hā* or *he* is the twenty-seventh letter of the Arabic and the thirty-ninth of the Pukkhto alphabet. It is sometimes substituted for ح, and by some hill tribes is used instead of خ and ښ. At the end of a word it is either "perceptible" or aspirated (*hāe-ẓāhir*), or it is "imperceptible" or unsounded (*hāe-khafī*). Words ending in the former are of the masculine gender, and those ending in the latter are of the feminine. *Hāe-khafī* is added to nouns, adjectives, etc. ending in a consonant for the formation of their feminines. Adjectives ending in *hāe-ẓāhir* form their feminines by changing it to *hāe-khafī*, and this letter itself is often dropped and replaced by the short vowel ـَ (*zabar*), especially in poetry. At the end of Arabic words it is generally written with a couple of dots over it (ة) and pronounced as ت.

ها *hā*, s.f. An egg (of bird, insect, reptile, etc.); the testicle. *hā*, ad. Aye, yes. See هو. *hā*, in. Lo! Behold!

هاتنړه *hātanṛa*, s.f. An elephant. S. (*hāthnī*).

هاتي *hātī*, s.m. An elephant. S. (*hāthī*).

هادي *hādī*, s.m. Director, leader, guide. A.

هار *hār*, s.m. Necklace, garland, wreath; herd, flock, drove (of cattle). S. *hār*, A particle affixed to nouns, denoting sound, to form their plurals, as *shṛang* (a jingle). *shṛangahār*.

هاړ *hāṛ*, s.m. Name of the third Hindu month, June-July. S. (*asāṛh*).

هاړه هوړه *hāṛa-hūṛa*, s.f. Clamour, noise, tumult.

هاړي *hāṛe*, s.f. (pl.) Entreating, coaxing, wheedling.

هاله *hāla*, s.f. A halo or circle round the moon. P. *hāla*, ad. Then, at that time.

هامون *hāmūn*, s.m. A desert, plain. P.

هانډئ *hānḍa-ī*, s.f. A cooking pot, stewpan. S. (*hānḍī*). *hānḍa-i-wāl*, s.m. A messmate, pot companion. H.

هاها *hāhā*, s.f. Laughter, laughing loudly. A.

هاهو *hāhū*, s.m. Noise, din, tumult; fame, report, rumour. H. (*hāhā*).

هاي *hāe*, in. Alas! Woe! S. *hāe-hāe*, Alas, alas! Dear, oh dear! *hāe-hūe*, Ah me! Woe, woe! *hā-ī*, pr. See following word.

هايه *hāyah*, pr. An emphatic form of the proximate demonstrative pronoun; this, this very.

هبته *habatah*, a. Worthless, useless, spoiled. A. (*ḥabaṭah*).

هبه *hiba*, s.f. A bequest, gift. A.

هبډبه *hāba-ḍaba*, s.f. Name of a disease, croup.

هپ‌دپ *hap-dap*, a. Hasty, quick, rash. ad. Suddenly, all of a heap, quickly. H. (*hap-jhap*).

هپه *hapa*, s.f. Help, succour, rescue; reprisal, foray, raid, incursion.

هته *hata*, s.f. Beam of a weaver's loom; the cubit, forearm.

هتيات *hatiyāt*, s.m. Foresight, caution, care. A. (*iḥtiyāṭ*).

هتيار *hatiyār*, s.m. Apparatus, arms; implement, tool. S. (*hathyār*).

هټ *haṭ*, s.m. Obstinacy, perversity, stubbornness. s. a. Erect, standing; stationary, stock-still.

هټال *haṭāl*, a. Prevented, stopped, driven back, repelled, hindered. H.

هټالول *haṭālawul*, v.a. To hinder, prevent, repel, push back, etc. H. (*haṭānā*).

هټکي *haṭkai*, s.m. Hiccough. H. (*hichkī*).

هټه *haṭah*, a. Active, stout, vigorous. H. (*haṭā*).

هټۍ *haṭa-ī*, s.f. A chandler's shop, market. s.

هجر *hijr*, s.m. Absence, separation. A.

هجران *hijrān*, s.m. Separation (from friends, etc.).

هجرت *hijrat*, s.m. Flight; the flight of Muhammad from Mecca to Medina; the date or era of that event. *hijrī*, s.f. The Muhammadan era. A.

هجره *hujra*, s.f. A kind of inn or hostelry for the reception of travellers and visitors, free of expense; there is always one of these buildings in each quarter of a village amongst the Yusufzais and Eastern Afghans generally. The *hujra* is also used as a town-hall and vestry-room; also as a club or place of common resort for the men of the quarter in which it is situated.

هجړي *hijṛai*, s.m. An eunuch, hermaphrodite. H. (*hijṛā*).

هجګي *hijgī*, s.f. Spelling. A. (*hajī*).

هڅ *huts*, a. Infatuated, mad. H. (*huch*).

هڅه *hatsa*, s.f. Labour, trouble, toil; desire, inclination, wish.

هچ *hich*, ad. Nothing. See هیچ.

هدایت *hidāyat*, s.m. Guidance, direction. A.

هدف *hadaf*, s.m. A butt, target, mark. A.

هدهد *hudhud*, s.m. The hoopoe. A.

هدیره *hadera*, s.f. Area, enclosure; graveyard.

هدیه *hadiya*, s.f. A present to a teacher, schooling fee. A.

هډ *haḍ*, s.m. A bone; centre or hard part of fruit, etc. s. (*haḍḍī*). Ancestry, lineage; greatness, nobility.

هدو *hado*, ad. Never, not at all, no such thing. in. I say! a term of familiarity or affection.

هډور *haḍawar*, a. Bony, strong.

هډوکي *haḍūkai*, s.m. A bone, stone of fruit.

هډي *haḍai*, s.m. Bone spavin; a node; tongue bone; tonsil. s. (*haḍḍā*)

هر *har*, s.m. A rogue, wag. s. *har*, s.m. Bray of an ass. *har*, a. Every, each, any (in comp.). P. *har-wakht*, Each time. *hara-wradz*, Every day.

هراس *hirās*, s.m. Fear, terror. P.

هراول *harāwul*, s.m. Advanced guard of an army. T.

هراند *harānd*, a. Fearful, timid.

هرتال *hartāl*, s.m. Orpiment. s.

هرټ *haraṭ*, s.m. A Persian wheel for drawing water from a well. H.

هرځاي *hardzā-ī*, s.m. Vagabond, wanderer, rascal.

هرج *harj*, s.m. Interruption, delay; tumult, sedition. A.

هرزه *harzah*, a. Nonsensical, frivolous. *harza*, s.f. A trifle, bagatelle, absurdity. P.

هرکاره *harkārah*, s.m. A courier, messenger; emissary, spy; man of all work. P. *harkāra*, s.f. An iron spoon, a large ladle.

هرګاه *hargāh*, ad. Whenever, wherever. P.

هرګز *hargiz*, ad. Ever, never. P.

هرګوره *hargora*, ad. At least, at all events, by all means; wholly, altogether, entirely.

هرۍ *hira-ī*, s.f. Excuse, pretence, shift, plea. A. (*ḥīla*).

هریړه *hareṛa*, s.f. Name of a nut used in medicine, and as a dye, myrobalan (*Terminalia chebula*).

هرپۍ *harpa-ī*, s.f. A casket, small box.

هزاره *hazārah*, s.m. Name of a Tartar tribe

who possess the hill country between Kabul and Herat.

هزم **hazm**, s.m. Digestion. A. (*hazm*)

هژدات **hajdāt**, s.m. Bell metal, bronze, brass. S. (*ajdhāt*).

هسار **hisār**, s.m. A castle, fort. A. (*hiṣār*). Difficulty, embarrassment. a. Enclosed, surrounded, besieged.

هسارول **hisārawul**, v.a. To enclose, surround, besiege; stop, prevent, keep.

هساريدل **hisāredal**, v.n. To be besieged, en-enclosed, etc., to stick, stop, be stuck, clogged, etc.

هسپه **haspa**, s.f. Erysipelas; quinsy; purpura. *haspa·buṭai*, s.m. Name of a plant used as a remedy for *haspa* (*Indigofera sp.*).

هستي **hastī**, s.f. Being, existence. P.

هسک **hask**, a. High, lofty, tall. p. Above, aloft. *hisk*, s.m. Lottery, hazard, chance; drawing lots, lot.

هسې **hasi**, } ad. As, thus, in like manner,
هسي **hase**, } likewise, therefore.

هښمه **hakkhma**, s.f. An April shower, a spring shower soon passing away (of rain).

هغومبره **haghombra**, ad. So much, that much.

هغه **haghah**, pr. The third personal pronoun; he, she, it. The remote demonstrative pronoun; that. A. (*hazā*).

هفته **hafta**, s.f. A week. P.

هکپک **hak·pak**, a. Aghast, confounded, confused. H. (*hakkā·bakkā*).

هګۍ **haga-ī**, s.f. An egg. See ها.

هل **hal**, s.m. Handle of a plough; a plough. S.

هلاک **halāk**, s.m. Perdition, ruin, death. a. Dead, killed; annihilated, lost, ruined. A.

هلاکت **halākat**, s.m. Perdition, death.

هلاکي **halākī**, s.f. Ruination, destruction A.

هلال **hilāl**, s.m. The new moon; the first and last two or three days of the moon. A. *halāl*, a. Lawful, etc. See حلال.

هلاهل **halāhal**, s.m. Deadly poison. S.

هلته **halta**, ad. } There, yonder, thither, in
هلته‌کي **halta·ke**, } that place, over there.

هلک **halak**, s.m. A boy, lad, youth. a. Small, little; slight, mean; debased, cheap; easy, soft; silly, useless. H. (*halkā*).

هلکت **halakat**, s.m. } Boyhood, youth.
هلکوالي **halak·wālai** }

هلکینه **halkīna**, s.f. Infancy, childhood.

هلم **halam**, s.m. Cress, water cress (*Lepidum sativum*). H. (*hālim*).

هلواک **halwāk**, a. Fast, swift, quick, fleet, rapid.

هله **halla**, s.f. Charge, attack, onset, assault; riot, uproar, tumult. A. *hala*, ad. Then, at that time.

هلي **hale**, ad. Here, hither, in this place.

هم **hum**, c. Also, even, likewise. P. (*ham*) (in comp.). Together, with, same, equal, etc. as *hum·kār*, s.m. A fellow workman. *hum·wazn*, Of equal weight. *hamm*, s.m. Solicitude, anxiety, care. A.

هماي **humāe**, s.m. Phœnix, bird of happy omen. P. (*humā*).

همّت **himmat**, s.m. Bravery, courage; resolution, spirit. A.

همّتناک **himmat·nāk**, } Resolute, daring, bold,
همّتي **himmatī**, a. } courageous.

همراه **hamrāh**, s.m. Companion, fellow-traveller. p. Along with, together. P.

همسا **hamsā**, s.f. A mace, stick. See امسا.

همګي **hamagī**, } a. All, the whole. P.
همه **hamah**, }

هميانې **hamiyānī**, s.f. A purse. P.

هميشه **hamesha**, a. Perpetually, always. P.

هنج **hanj**, s.m. } Assafœtida. S. (*heng*).
هنجه **hanja**, s.f. }

هند **hind**, s.m. India, Hindustan.

هنداره **hindāra**, s.f. A mirror, looking glass.

هندكو *hindko*, s.f. The language of the Indians.

هندكي *hindkī*, s.m. The Indians; name of an Indian tribe (converts to Islam), settled in parts of the Peshawar valley and surrounding hills. *hindkai*, s.m. An Indian (Mussulman). *hindka-ī*, s.f. An Indian woman.

هندو *hindū*, s.m. A Hindu; a pagan, idolater.

هندوبار *hindūbār*, s.m. A place where Hindus dwell or meet; dealings with a Hindu.

هندوستان *hindūstān*, s.m. India, Upper India, the country of the Hindus.

هندوگي *hindūgai*, s.m. A term of abuse. A Hindu grocer, grain dealer.

هندوانه *hindwāna*, s.f. A water melon. P.

هندوانړي *hindwānṛa-ī*, } s.f. A Hindu woman.
هندوه *hindawa*, }

هنډه *hunḍah*, s.m. A wolf. H. *hanḍa*, s.f. Ambition, desire, wish; fancy; want. *hinḍah*, s.m. A stallion, bull, male kept for breeding purposes.

هنډي *hunḍa-ī*, s.f. Bill of exchange, money order. S. (*hunḍī*).

هنر *hunar*, s.m. Art, skill; virtue, quality. P. *hunar-man*, a. Clever, ingenious. P.

هنس *hans*, s.m. A goose, swan. S. (*hāns*).

هنگام *hangām*, s.m. Period, time, season. P.

هنگامه *hangāma*, s.f. Mob, crowd, assembly; uproar, riot, tumult; assault, onset. P.

هنوز *hanoz*, ad, Yet, hitherto, still. P.

هنړ *hanṛ*, s.m. Neigh of a horse, bray of an ass.

هنړهنړيدل *hanṛ-hanṛedal*, v.n. To neigh, bray. H. (*hinhinhānā*).

هو *ho*, ad. Aye, yea, yes. S. (*hān*). in. Halloa! ho! S. Hurrah! An exclamation used when rushing on an enemy in battle.

هوا *hawā*, s.f. Wind, atmosphere, air; lust, desire; affection, love; pride, conceit. A. *hawā*, in. Dear me! Ah! Alas! See هاي.

هوار *hawār*, a. Even, smooth; level, flat; fit, proper; gentle, docile. P. (*hamwār*).

هوباره *hūbārah*, s.m. A kind of bustard. A.

هوبهو *hūbahū*, ad. Exactly, perfectly, quite. A.

هوده *hūda*, s.f. Charming, exorcising, mesmerising (by breathing). Appointment, office, post, business. A. (*'uhda*). *ḥauda*, s.f. A litter or sedan used by women when they travel; a seat or stage placed on the back of an elephant. A.

هوډ *hoḍ*, s.m. The contrary, opposite.

هوډه *hoḍa*, s.f. Perversity, obstinacy.

هوډي *hoḍai*, a, Stubborn, perverse, wayward; opposed, opposite. s.m. Name of a hill opposite Attak (on the Indus), on the top of which are some Buddhist ruins.

هور *hor*, s.m. Time, season. Fire. A deer.

هور *hūri*, } ad. There, thither, over there.
هوري *hūre*, }

هوږه *hūga*, s.f. Garlic.

هوس *hawas*, s.m. Lust, concupiscence; ambition, desire; curiosity. A. *hawas-nāk*, a. Sensual, ambitious, etc.

هوسا *hosā*, a. Refreshed, recruited; untired, unwearied; idle, lazy. P. (*hoshā*). *hosā-kawul*, v.a. To recruit, rest, refresh, repair, refit, etc.

هوسي *hosai*, s.m. A deer, gazelle. P. (*āhū*).

هوښ *hokkh*, s.m. Sense, understanding; mind, soul; judgment. P. (*hosh*).

هوښيار *hokkhyār*, a. Intelligent, sensible, wise; cautious, discreet, prudent.

هوښيارتيا *hokkhyār-tiyā*, } Intelligence, discre-
هوښياري *hokkhyārī*, s.f. } tion, prudence.

هوک *hūk*, a. Flooded, inundated, sunk.

هوكلۍ *hokla-ī*, s.f A large wooden pestle.

هوكه *haukah*, a. Fatigued, tired, weary

هوكي *hokai*, s.m. Assent, consent, saying "yes"; consent of parents to marriage of a daughter.

هول *hūl*, s.m. Bolt or bar of a door. *haul*,

s.m. Horror, fear, terror. A. *haul·nāk*, a. Terrible, awful, dismal, fearful.

هومره *homra*, | ad. So much, that much,
هونبره *honbra*, | this much.

هونړا *honṛā*, s.f. A kind of trap for catching birds; the perch placed over the trap.

هوي *hūe*, in. Alas! See هاي.

هويدا *hawīdā*, a. Evident, manifest, clear. P.

هويه *hoya*, s.f. An egg.

هه *hah*, in. Indeed! Really! Oh ho! Halloa!

هي *hai*, in. Alas! Dear me! *hai·hai*, in. What a pity! Dear me! Wonderful! Strange!

هيات *hayāt*, s.m. Form, aspect, visage, face. A.

هيبت *haibat*, s.m. Panic, terror, awe. A. *haibat·nāk*, a. Terrific, awe-inspiring, fearful.

هيڅ *hets*, ad. Nothing, nought, none. P. (*hech*). *hets·tsok*, Nobody. *hets·shai*, Nothing.

هيڅر *hechari*, | ad. Never, at no time.
هيڅري *hechare*, |

هيڅرته *hecharta*, ad. Nowhere.

هير *her*, a. Forgotten, omitted, lost to memory.

هيرړي *herṛai*, s.m. A sheep of the long-tailed breed. H. (*bheṛā*).

هيرقطار *hīr·qaṭār*, s.m. Indian file, one behind the other, filing along.

هيړ *heṛ*, s.m. Time, season, period. H. (*pher*).

هيړه *heṛa*, s.f. Turn, time. ad. Once, one time. *yawa·heṛa*, Once. *dwa·heṛa*, Twice, etc.

هيړي *heṛai*, s.m. A sheep. See هيرړي.

هيز *hīz*, s.m. Hermaphrodite. P.

هيزگي *hezgī*, s.f. Spelling. See هجگي.

هيسته *hīsta*, ad. Here, hither. *rāhīsta*, Near me. *darhīsta*, Near thee, *warhista*, Near him, her, it, etc.

هيښ *hekkh*, a. Amazed, confounded, perplexed.

هيضه *haiẓa*, s.f. Cholera morbus. A.

هيغ *hegh*, a. Stiff, straight. See فيغ.

هيكل *haikal*, s.m. An ornament for the neck; face, figure, form, person; palace, temple. A.

هيل *hel*, s.m. Cardamoms. A. (*elā*).

هيله *hīla*, s.f. Subterfuge, trick. See حيله.

هيلئ *hīla-ī*, s.m. A duck, water fowl.

هينگ *heng*, s.m. A groan, moan, sigh.

هيواد *hewād*, s.m. Country, region, clime.

هيون *hayūn*, s.m. A horse; camel. P.

هيهات *haihāt*, a. Lamenting, wailing. A. in. Alas! Begone!

ي

ي *yā* or *ye* is the twenty-eighth letter of the Arabic and the fortieth and last of the Pukkhto alphabet. When used as a consonant it has the sound of *y*, if moved by a vowel (*mutaḥarrik*), and of the French *e* or English *ey* (as in *they*), if quiescent or unmoved (*sākin*). When used as a vowel it has the sound of ī (*yāe·m'arūf*), or *e* (*yāe·majhūl*) if preceded by the short vowel *kasra* ـِ, and of the diphthong *ai*, if preceded by the short vowel *fatha* ـَ (*yāe·sākin·māqabl·i·maftūḥ*), as is explained in the Grammar. *Yāe·m'arūf*, preceded by *hamza* ـٔ has the sound of *a-ī*. (*yāe·m'arūf māqabl·i·hamza·i·khafī·i·maksūr*), and is the termination of a number of feminine nouns, both in the singular and plural. In Pukkhto the vowel sounds *yāe·m'arūf* (ī), *yāe·majhūl* (*e*), and *yāe·m'arūf māqabl·i·hamza* (*a-ī*) are often dropped and replaced by the short vowel *kasra* ـِ.

يا *yā*, c. Either, or, whether. P. in. Oh! Vocative particle. Oh! Halloa! A.

ياب *yāb* (in comp.). Finding, obtaining. P. *kam·yāb*, a. Scarce. P.

یابو *yābū*, s.m. A pony. H.

یاد *yād*, s.m. Recollection, memory. P. *yādawul*, v.a. To remind, mention, call to mind. *yādedal*, v.n. To recollect, remember, recur.

یار *yār*, s.m. Paramour, lover, friend; comrade, companion, assistant. P. *yārī*, s.f. Friendship.

یاستي *yāsta-ī*, You are; a form of the second person plural present tense of the defective verb *yam*, I am.

یاسمین *yāsmīn*, s.m. Jasmine. P.

یاغي *yāghī*, a. Mutinous, rebellious. s.m. A rebel, mutineer. A. (*bāghī*).

یاغیگر *yāghī-gar*, s.m. A mutineer, rebel. *yāghī-garī*, s.f. Mutiny, rebellion; sedition, revolt.

یافت *yāft*, s.m. Earnings, perquisites. P.

یاقوت *yāqūt*, s.m. A ruby. A.

یال *yāl*, s.m. The mane of a horse, etc. P.

یاور *yāwar*, a. Aiding, helping, friendly. s.m. Coadjutor, assistant; companion, friend. P. *yāwarī*, s.f. Help, succour, aid.

یاوره *yāwara*, s.f. A bigbellied mare, ass, etc.

یاوه *yāwah*, a. Vain, absurd, futile; ruined, lost. P. *yāwa-goe*, s.m. A talker of nonsense.

یاهو *yāhū*, s.m. Jehovah. A.

یبل *yabl*, a. Barefooted. See ابل.

یتیم *yatīm*, s.m. An orphan. A.

یخ *yakh*, a. Cold, frigid; cooled, damped; satiated; slaked, subsided. s.m. Cold; ice. P.

یخني *yakhnī*, s.f. Coldness, frigidity, chilliness; cold, chill; gravy, jelly. P.

یراق *yarāq*, s.m. Arms, accoutrements, weapons. T.

یرړي *yarṛai*, s.m. A sheep. See هیرړي.

یرز *yarz*, s.m. Ability, skill, fitness, capacity; merit, worth; propriety, expediency; consistency, congruity.

یرزن *yarzan*, a. Expedient, fit, worthy, suitable.

یرغمال *yarghamāl*, s.m. A hostage. P.

یرغه *yarghah*, a. Ambling. s.m. An ambler, an ambling horse or mule; a horse or mule with the ears slit. P.

یرمن *yar-man*, a. Timid, timorous, nervous, fearing, shy.

یره *yara*, s.f. Fear, fright. ad. Really, truly, yes, indeed, verily. P. (*āre*).

یزد *yazd*, }
یزدان *yazdān*, } s.m. God. P.

یږ *yag*, s.m. A bear.

یږه *yaga*, s.f. A she bear. A kind of ulcer.

یساول *yasāwul*, s.m. A mace bearer; equerry, mounted attendant on a man of rank. P.

یستل *yastal*, v.a. To eject, expel, pick out, extract, produce, etc. Def. in pres. ten. See باسل.

یشم *yashm*, s.m. Jasper, jade, agate. P.

یشند *yashand*, a. Boiling, effervescing.

یشنا *yashnā*, s.f. Ebullition, effervescence.

یشول *yashawul*, v.a. To boil, cook, stew.

یشېدل *yashedal*, v.n. To boil, bubble, ferment, effervesce. P. (*joshīdan*). See ایشیدل.

ېښل *yakkhal*, v.a. To put, place, set, deposit, etc. P. (*shāndan*). Applied to inanimate objects. Def. in pres. ten. See ږدل.

ېښودل *yakkhodal*, } v.a. To place, put, set.
ېښول *yakkhawul*, } See ایښودل.

ېښي *yakkhai*, a. Placed, put, set.

یعني *y'ane*, ad. Namely, that is to say, viz., i.e. A.

یغما *yaghma*, s.f. Plunder, booty, spoil. P.

یقین *yaqīn*, a. Certain, sure, true, real. ad. Certainly, surely, truly. A. *yaqīnī*, s.f. Reality, certainty. a. Certain, sure, real.

یقیناً *yaqīnan*, ad. Assuredly, certainly, A.

یک *yak*, a. One (in comp. only). P. *yak-dil*, a. Of one mind, unanimous. *yak-lakhta*, ad. All at once, suddenly.

یکلنگه *yak-linga*, s.f. A lever used to draw water from a well. P. See دنګلي.

يكشمبه *yak-shamba*, s.f. Sunday. P.

يكلائي *yaklā-ī*, s.f. A mantle of a single layer of cloth. P.

يكه *yakah*, a. Unique, single, alone, sole; a one-horse chaise. P.

يكي *yakī*, s.f. Name of a small copper coin.

يگان *yagān*, a. Single, unique. P.

يگانگي *yagānagī*, s.f. Singleness, uniqueness; unanimity, concord, unity. P.

يگانه *yagānah*, a. Single, sole; unanimous, agreed. P.

يگه *yaga*, s.f. A kind of corroding ulcer; a disease affecting the tail of a horse, melanosis; cancer; a she bear. See يږه.

يل *yal*, s m. Hero, champion. P.

يلغر *yalghar*, s.m. Foray, raid, incursion. B.

يله *yalah*, a. Free, liberated; wandering, vagabond. *yala*, s.f. A bog, marsh, morass.

يم *yam*, s.m. The ocean, sea. A. *yam*, I am, the first person singular present tense of the defective verb "to be" (inf. wanting).

ينگ *yang*, s.m. Conduct, behaviour; manner, mode, way.

يو *yo*, a. One; a, an. P. (*yak*).

يواځي *yawādzai*, a. Alone, single, solitary. ad. Separately, alone, apart.

يواڼ *yawād*, s.m. Country, region. See هيواد.

يور *yor*, s.f. Husband's brother's wife. pl. *yūnre*.

يورش *yūrish*, s.m. Assault, charge; invasion. P.

يوز *yūz*, s.m. A lynx; panther. P.

يوسپزي *yūsupzī*, s.m. Name of a powerful clan of Afghans, the Yūsufzais.

يوستوي *yawastawai*, a. Single, without fold or lining (as a garment).

يوسفزي *yūsufzī*, s.m. See يوسپزي.

يوسل *yosal*, v.a. To bear, carry, support, put up with, endure (applied only to inanimate objects). Irr. Pres. *yosī*. Past. *yowaṛ*. See وړل.

يوم *yūm*, s.m. A shovel, spade (with a bar of wood fixed above the blade as a rest for the foot in shoving it into the ground). *yaum*, s.m. A day. A.

يون *yūn*, s.m. Pace, step; gait, carriage; custom, habit; moving, passing.

يوه *yawa*, s.f. A plough. *yawe* or *yiwe*, pl. يويه *yoya*, Ploughing, tilling.

ييښل *yekkhal*, v.a. To put, set: See ښل.

ييم *yīm*, s.m. A shovel. See يوم *yūm*.

يه *ya*, ad. No, not. P.

ئې *e*, A form of the Genitive and Instrumental cases, singular and plural of the third personal pronoun هغه, His, her's, it's, their's, etc. He, she, it, they.

Printed in the United Kingdom by
Lightning Source UK Ltd., Milton Keynes
138025UK00001B/39/P

A Companion to Spanish Cinema

Edited by

Jo Labanyi and Tatjana Pavlović

WILEY Blackwell

This paperback edition first published 2016

Edition History: Blackwell Publishing Ltd. (hardback, 2013)

Registered Office
John Wiley & Sons Ltd, The Atrium, Southern Gate, Chichester, West Sussex, PO19 8SQ, UK

Editorial Offices
350 Main Street, Malden, MA 02148-5020, USA
9600 Garsington Road, Oxford, OX4 2DQ, UK
The Atrium, Southern Gate, Chichester, West Sussex, PO19 8SQ, UK

For details of our global editorial offices, for customer services, and for information about how to apply for permission to reuse the copyright material in this book please see our website at www.wiley.com/wiley-blackwell.

Library of Congress Cataloging-in-Publication Data

A companion to Spanish cinema / edited by Jo Labanyi and Tatjana Pavlović. – 1 p. cm. –
(Wiley-Blackwell companions to national cinemas)
Includes bibliographical references and index.
ISBN 978-1-4051-9438-9 (hardback) ISBN 978-1-119-17013-6 (paperback)
1. Motion pictures–Spain. I. Labanyi, Jo. II. Pavlović, Tatjana.
PN1993.5.S7C6595 2012
791.430946–dc23

2012023050

A catalogue record for this book is available from the British Library.

Cover image: El Sur, 1983, directed by Victor Erice.

Set in 11/13pt Dante by SPi Global, Pondicherry, India
Printed and bound in Malaysia by Vivar Printing Sdn Bhd

1 2016

Contents

Acknowledgments

Our special thanks to Margarita Lobo, Alicia Potes, and Miguel Soria at Filmoteca Española in Madrid for their help with locating and providing graphic material, and with identifying copyright holders. We also thank Elena Baranda of Video Mercury for granting permission to reproduce a significant number of images, including the still from Víctor Erice's *El sur* used on the cover. We are also hugely grateful to Curry O'Day, tech support specialist at Tulane University, for his invaluable technical help with the illustrations. We owe a particular debt to Jayne Fargnoli of Wiley-Blackwell for her faith in our ability to produce an innovative volume, and to Galen Young and Allison Kostka for their efficiency throughout the production process.

List of Figures

List of Contributors

Ferran Alberich is one of Spain's top specialists in film preservation and restoration. The film restorations he has undertaken for several Spanish archives include Sáenz de Heredia's *Raza* (original 1941 version), Llobet Gràcia's *Vida en sombras*, Armand Guerra's *Carne de fieras* (on which he authored the 1993 monograph *Carne de fieras*), and, recently, Luis Buñuel's *Un chien andalou*. He has also directed several film shorts and documentaries, and has worked as a film and television screenwriter.

Josetxo Cerdán is Associate Professor in the Media and Communications Department of the Universitat Rovira i Virgili, Tarragona. He has coauthored *Ricardo Urgoiti: Los trabajos y los días* (2007) and *Del sainete al esperpento* (2011). His coedited volumes include *Mirada, memoria y fascinación: Notas sobre el documental español* (2001), *Documental y vanguardia* (2005), *Suevia Films-Cesáreo González: Treinta años de cine español* (2005), and *Al otro lado de la ficción* (2007). His main current interests are documentary and non-fiction film, and the transnational distribution of Spanish cinema. He is also Artistic Director of the international documentary film festival of Navarre, Punto de Vista, and is guest curator of the 2012 Flaherty Film Seminar.

José Colmeiro holds the Prince of Asturias Chair in Spanish Studies at the University of Auckland, New Zealand. He has published widely on Hispanic cultural studies, contemporary literature, cinema, and popular culture. His major monographs include *La novela policíaca española: Teoría e historia crítica* (1994), *Crónica del desencanto: La narrativa de Manuel Vázquez Montalbán* ("Letras de Oro" prize, 1996), and *Memoria histórica e identidad cultural: De la postguerra a la postmodernidad* (2005). He edited the volume *Manuel Vázquez Montalbán: El compromiso con la memoria* (2007), as well as Francisco García Pavón's *Las hermanas coloradas* (1999) and Silvia Mistral's *Éxodo: Diario de una refugiada española* (2009), and coedited *Spain Today: Essays in Literature, Culture, Society* (1995). His forthcoming book project *Galeg@s sen fronteiras* will explore the effects of globalization on local cultures.

Gerard Dapena is a scholar of Hispanic cinemas and visual culture. He has published and lectured on various aspects of Spanish and Latin American film and art history. He has taught courses in art history and film studies at New York University, Bard College, Macalester College, The New School, and The School of Visual Arts, among other institutions, and currently is Visiting Assistant Professor of Art History in the Liberal Arts Department of Ringling College of Art and Design. Presently, he is working on a monograph on early Francoist cinema.

Marvin D'Lugo is Professor of Spanish and Screen Studies at Clark University, Massachusetts, where he teaches courses on Spanish and Latin American cinemas. Principal editor of *Studies in Hispanic Cinemas* since 2008, he is also the author of *The Films of Carlos Saura: The Practice of Seeing* (1991), *Guide to the Cinema of Spain* (1997), and *Pedro Almodóvar* (2006), and coeditor of *A Companion to Pedro Almodóvar* (forthcoming 2012). He writes frequently on the auteur tradition and transnational aesthetics in Spanish and Latin American film. He is currently completing a book on auditory culture and Hispanic transnational cinemas.

Alberto Elena is Professor of Media Studies at the Universidad Carlos III, Madrid. A member of the editorial boards of *Archivos de la Filmoteca*, *New Cinemas*, and *Secuencias*, he has organized several film retrospectives and has been on the jury of a number of international festivals. His publications include *El cine del Tercer Mundo: Diccionario de realizadores* (1993), *Satyajit Ray* (1998), *Los cines periféricos (África, Oriente Medio, India)* (1999), *The Cinema of Latin America* (2003, coauthored), *The Cinema of Abbas Kiarostami* (2005), and *La llamada de África: Estudios sobre el cine colonial español* (2010), as well as numerous contributions to specialist journals.

Brad Epps is Professor of Romance Languages and Literatures and Studies of Women, Gender, and Sexuality at Harvard University. He has published widely on modern literature, film, art, urban studies, queer theory, and immigration in Catalonia, Spain, Latin America, and the United States. He is the author of *Significant Violence: Oppression and Resistance in the Narratives of Juan Goytisolo* (1996); editor of a special issue of *Catalan Review* on Barcelona and modernity (2004); and coeditor of *Passing Lines: Immigration and Sexuality* (2005), *Spain Beyond Spain: Modernity, Literary History, and National Identity* (2005), a special issue of *GLQ* on Monique Wittig (2007), and *All About Almodóvar: A Passion for Cinema* (2009). He has taught in Spain, Germany, France, Chile, Cuba, the Netherlands, Sweden, and China and is preparing two books: the monograph *Barcelona and Cinema* and the coauthored *El cine como historia: la historia como cine*.

Sally Faulkner is Senior Lecturer in Hispanic Studies at the University of Exeter. Her research and teaching interests include Spanish cinema, modern Spanish literature, cultural studies, film studies, and adaptation studies. She is author of the monographs *Literary Adaptations in Spanish Cinema* (2004) and *A Cinema of Contradiction: Spanish Film in the 1960s* (2006) and coeditor of the special issue *Memory and Exile in Twentieth- and Twenty-First Century Spanish Culture* (2011) for the *Journal of Iberian and Latin American Research*. She currently holds a UK Arts and Humanities Research Council Fellowship for a project entitled "A New History of Spanish Cinema: Middlebrow Films and Mainstream Audiences" and is writing *A History of Spanish Cinema* for Continuum's European Cinema series.

Joseba Gabilondo is Associate Professor in the Department of Romance and Classical Studies at Michigan State University. He has published the essay collection *Nazioaren hondarrak: Euskal literatura garaikidearen historia postnazional baterako hastapenak* (*Remnants of the Nation: Prolegomena to a Postnational History of Basque Literature*, 2006), plus numerous articles on Basque and Spanish nationalism, intellectual discourse, postnationalism, masculinity, queer theory, globalization, and Hollywood cinema. He has also edited the special issue *The Hispanic Atlantic* (2001) for the *Arizona Journal of Hispanic Cultural Studies* and coedited *Empire and Terror: Nationalism / Postnationalism in the New Millennium* (2004). He is currently completing two monographs entitled *Before Babel: A Cultural History of Basque Literatures* (a cultural and postnational history of Basque literatures from the Middle Ages to the twenty-first century) and *Atlantic Spain: Nationalism and the Postcolonial Ghost*.

Román Gubern has been a guest researcher at MIT and Professor of Film History at Cal Tech, the University of Southern California, Venice International University, and the Universidad Autónoma of Barcelona. He has additionally been director of the Instituto Cervantes in Rome and president of the Asociación Española de Historiadores del Cine, and is a member of the Association Française pour la Recherche sur l'Histoire du Cinéma, the Academia de Artes y Ciencias Cinematográficas de España, and the Honorary Committee of the International Association for Visual Semiotics. He has published more than forty books on cinema, mass communications, comics, and popular culture, among them *Godard polémico* (1969), *Cine español en el exilio* (1976), *Benito Perojo: Pionerismo y supervivencia* (1994), *Val del Omar, cinemista* (2004), and most recently *Luis Buñuel: The Red Years* (2011).

Julián Daniel Gutiérrez-Albilla is Assistant Professor of Spanish and Comparative Literature at the University of Southern California. He is author of the monograph *Queering Buñuel: Sexual Dissidence and Psychoanalysis in his Mexican and Spanish Cinema* (2008) and coeditor of *Hispanic and Lusophone Women Filmmakers: Theory, Practice and Difference* (forthcoming 2012). His essays on Spanish and Latin American cinema have appeared in a wide range of academic journals in the United States and United Kingdom, and in the edited volumes *Gender and Spanish Cinema* (2004), *Visual Synergies in Fiction and Documentary Film from Latin America* (2009), and *Spain on Screen: Developments in Contemporary Spanish Cinema* (2011). He is currently preparing a monograph *Ethics, Memory, and Subjectivity in Contemporary Spanish Cinema*.

Jo Labanyi is Professor of Spanish at New York University, where she directs the King Juan Carlos I of Spain Center. A founding editor of the *Journal of Spanish Cultural Studies*, she edits the series *Remapping Cultural History* for Berghahn Books. Her most recent books are *Spanish Literature: A Very Short Introduction* (2010) and the coedited volume *Europe and Love in Cinema* (2012). She is currently coauthoring *A Cultural History of Modern Spanish Literature, Cinema and Everyday Life in 1940s and 1950s Spain: An Oral History* (based on an AHRC-funded collaborative project), and *Film Magazines, Photography, and Fashion in 1940s and 1950s Spain* (based on a British Academy-funded collaborative project). She is a participant in the research project *Los medios audiovisuales en la transición española (1975–1985): Las imágenes del cambio democrático*, directed by Manuel Palacio at the Universidad Carlos III, Madrid. Her research interests include modern Spanish literature, film, photography, popular culture, gender, and memory studies. She was elected Fellow of the British Academy in 2005.

Antonio Lázaro-Reboll is Senior Lecturer in Hispanic Studies at the University of Kent. He is the author of *Spanish Horror Film* (forthcoming 2012) and coeditor of *Spanish Popular Cinema* (2004, with Andrew Willis). His research interests are in Spanish cultural studies and film studies, especially Spanish popular film, the development of film cultures in Spain (reception, consumption, and fandom), and cross-cultural dialogue between Spain and other world cinemas (international traditions of the horror genre, global psychotronic culture). He is currently working on the emergence of subcultural modes of production, reception, and consumption in Spain in the 1970s across different media (film, comics, magazines) and their relation to late Francoism and the transition.

Steven Marsh teaches Spanish film and cultural studies in the Hispanic and Italian Studies Department at the University of Illinois at Chicago, where he is Director of Graduate Studies. He is the author of *Popular Spanish Film under Franco: Comedy and the Weakening of the State* (2006), coeditor of *Gender and Spanish Cinema* (2004), and one of the authors of the forthcoming international collaborative project *Cinema and Everyday Life in 1940s and 1950s Spain: An Oral History*. He has published articles and book chapters in the United States, Britain, Spain, France, and Chile. Currently he is finalizing a counterhistory of Spanish sound cinema from the 1930s to the present day, which proposes a spectral theorization of Spanish independent, underground, and experimental film. He lives in Chicago and Madrid.

Annabel Martín is Associate Professor of Spanish and Comparative Literature and Director of the Women's and Gender Studies Program at Dartmouth College, New Hampshire. Working within the field of cultural studies, she has a particular interest in nationalism and in narratives of cultural and gender identity in contemporary Spain. She is author of the monograph *La gramática de la felicidad: Relecturas franquistas y posmodernas del melodrama* (2005) and is currently preparing a collaborative project with several Basque artists and writers, *Rest in Peace: The Basque Political Contours of the Arts*, which explores the cultural context surrounding the end of ETA terrorism in Spain and the role played by the arts in processes of reconciliation. She is also a member of a research team at the Universitat de València studying tourism and national identity, and is Reviews Editor of the *Journal of Spanish Cultural Studies*.

Susan Martin-Márquez is Professor in the Department of Spanish and Portuguese and in the Program in Comparative Literature at Rutgers University, where she directs the Cinema Studies Program. Her research centers on Spanish-language cinemas and modern Spanish Peninsular literary and cultural studies, and engages with critical race and postcolonial theory and gender and sexuality studies; she is also interested in formal analysis. She is the author of *Feminist Discourse and Spanish Cinema: Sight Unseen* (1999) and *Disorientations: Spanish Colonialism in Africa and the Performance of Identity* (2008; Spanish translation 2011), and a coauthor of the forthcoming *Cinema and Everyday Life in 1940s and 1950s Spain: An Oral History*. She is currently working on two books, one that explores the reconfiguration of imperial space and forced labor regimes in Spain's nineteenth-century penal colonies and another on militant filmmaking and transatlantic encounters and dis-encounters in the long 1960s.

Manuel Palacio is Professor at the Universidad Carlos III, Madrid, where he is currently Dean of the Faculty of Humanities, Communications, and Documentation. His monograph *Historia de la televisión en España* (2001) was joint winner of the Spanish Film Historians Association Book Prize, and he has also coauthored *Práctica fílmica y vanguardia artística en España* (1983). He is the editor of volumes five (1997), six (1995), and twelve (1995) of Cátedra's *Historia General del Cine*, and of *Las cosas que hemos visto: 50 años y más de TVE* (2006). His articles have appeared in academic journals in Spain, Belgium, France, the United Kingdom, and the United States, and in edited volumes published in Spain, France, Italy, and the United Kingdom such as *Cinema d'avanguardia in Europa* (1996), *Antología crítica del cine español* (1997), *L'Oeil critique: Le journaliste critique de télévision* (2002), *The Cinema of Latin America* (2003), *De Goya à Saura: Échos et résonances* (2005), and *La nueva memoria: Historia(s) del cine español* (2005). He currently directs the Spanish state-funded research project *Los medios audiovisuales en la transición española (1975–1985): Las imágenes del cambio democrático*.

Tatjana Pavlović is Associate Professor of Spanish at Tulane University in New Orleans. Her research and teaching interests center on twentieth-century Spanish intellectual history, literature, cultural studies, and film theory. She is author of the monograph *Despotic Bodies and Transgressive Bodies: Spanish Culture from Francisco Franco to Jesús Franco* (2003) and coauthor of the comprehensive survey *100 Years of Spanish Cinema* (2009). Her recent monograph *The Mobile Nation (1954–1964): España cambia de piel* (2011) focuses on a crucial period of transition in the history of Spanish mass culture, examining the publishing industry, the expansion of the television network, popular cinema, the development of mass tourism, and the national automobile manufacturing industry.

Chris Perriam is Professor of Hispanic Studies at the University of Manchester, where he has directed the Film and Languages Program. He has published widely on Spanish star studies, queer writing in Spain, and modern Spanish and Latin American poetry. Recent publications include the coauthored *Carmen on Film: A Cultural History* (2007) and the coedited special issue *The Transnational in Iberian and Latin American Cinemas* (2007) for *Hispanic Research Journal*. His work on Spanish stars has appeared in his monograph *Stars and Masculinities in Spanish Cinema: From Banderas to Bardem* (2003), the edited volume *Spain on Screen: Developments in Contemporary Spanish Cinema* (2011), and his coedited book *Theorizing World Cinema* (forthcoming 2012), as well as in academic journals in the United Kingdom and Spain. He is currently researching a monograph entitled *Film and Spanish Queer Cultures*.

Vicente Rodríguez Ortega is Assistant Professor at the Universidad Carlos III, Madrid and a member of the research group TECMERIN, having graduated in Cinema Studies at New York University. His research interests are new media, issues of globalization, and contemporary cinema. He is the author of *La ciudad global en el cine contemporàneo* (2012) and coeditor of *Contemporary Spanish Cinema and Genre* (2009). He has published essays on transnational cinemas, digital technology, and Spanish cinema and globalization in journals such as *Transnational Cinemas*, *Senses of Cinema*, *Studies in European Cinemas*, and *Film International*. He is a regular contributor to *Reverse Shot* and is cofounder of the website The Water Tapes. He has also made several shorts and a feature-length documentary entitled *Freddy's*.

Vicente Sánchez-Biosca is Professor of Audiovisual Communications at the Universitat de València, editor of the academic journal *Archivos de la Filmoteca*, and a member of the artistic advisory board of the Casa de Velázquez. A Fulbright Scholar in 1991, he has held visiting positions at the universities of Paris III (Sorbonne Nouvelle), Montreal, São Paulo, Buenos Aires, Havana, Princeton, and Paris-Est (Marne-la-Vallée). His most recent books are *Cine y vanguardias artísticas* (2004), *Cine de historia/cine de memoria* (2006), *Cine y guerra civil española* (2006), and the coauthored *NO-DO: El tiempo y la memoria* (2000) and *El pasado es el* *destino: Propaganda y cine del bando nacional en la Guerra Civil* (2011). He has also edited two monographic issues for *Archivos de la Filmoteca*, entitled *Materiales para una iconografía de Francisco Franco* (2002–3) and *Migración de imágenes: Íconos de la guerra civil* (2009). He currently directs a Spanish state-funded research project on visual representation in the memory of the Spanish Civil War.

Paul Julian Smith is Distinguished Professor in the PhD Program in Hispanic and Luso-Brazilian Languages and Literatures at The Graduate Center, CUNY and was previously Professor of Spanish at the University of Cambridge for nineteen years. He has been Visiting Professor at ten universities in the United States and Spain, and has been invited to give more than one hundred guest lectures or conference papers in many countries. He is the author of sixteen books and some seventy articles on Spanish and Spanish American cinema, literature, and culture. His books include *Desire Unlimited: The Cinema of Pedro Almodóvar* (1994, 2nd rev. edn. 2000), *Amores Perros: Modern Classic* (2008), and *Spanish Screen Fiction: Between Cinema and Television* (2009). He is also a pioneer of television studies in Spanish. He is a regular contributor to *Sight and Sound*, the magazine of the British Film Institute; a columnist for *Film Quarterly*, published by University of California Press; and a member of the jury of the Morelia International Film Festival, Mexico. He was elected Fellow of the British Academy in 2008.

Nuria Triana Toribio is Senior Lecturer in Spanish Cinema at the University of Manchester. She is the author of *Spanish National Cinema* (2003) and coauthor of *The Cinema of Álex de la Iglesia* (2007). She is coeditor of the series *Spanish and Latin American Filmmakers* for Manchester University Press. She has published on film festivals, contemporary Spanish film cultures, and new strategies of auteurism, particularly in relation to transnational financing, production, and dissemination. Her most recent work has appeared in *Screen*, *Secuencias*, and *Studies in Hispanic Cinemas*.

Kathleen M. Vernon is Associate Professor of Hispanic Studies at the State University of New York at Stony Brook. She has published and taught on various aspects of Spanish and Latin American cinema from the 1930s to the present, with special focus on historical and musical films, comedy, documentary, and women's cinema. She is coeditor of the first English-language journal devoted to Spanish and Latin American film, *Studies in Hispanic Cinemas*. Her books include the edited volume *The Spanish Civil War and the Visual Arts* (1991), and the coedited *Post-Franco, Postmodern: The Films of Pedro Almodóvar* (1995) and *A Companion to Pedro Almodóvar* (forthcoming 2012). She is currently completing a monograph, *The Rhythms of History: Cinema, Music, and Cultural Memory in Contemporary Spain*, and is a coauthor of the forthcoming multi-authored books, *Cinema and Everyday Life in 1940s and 1950s Spain: An Oral History* and *Film Magazines, Fashion, and Photography in 1940s and 1950s Spain*.

Eva Woods Peiró is Associate Professor in Hispanic Studies at Vassar College, where she also directs the Media Studies Program. Her books include the monograph *White Gypsies: Race and Stardom in Spanish Musicals* (2012) and the coedited volume *Visualizing Spanish Modernity* (2005). She is a coauthor for the forthcoming collaborative book projects *Cinema and Everyday Life in 1940s and 1950s Spain: An Oral History* and its sequel, *Film Magazines, Fashion, and Photography in 1940s and 1950s Spain*. Her published journal and book articles focus on Spanish popular cinema and its projection of race, class, and gender.

Santos Zunzunegui is Professor of Audiovisual Communications and Publicity at the Universidad del País Vasco, Bilbao. His research interests are semiology, textual critique, and film history. He had held visiting positions at the universities of Girona, Paris III (Sorbonne Nouvelle), École Normale Supérieure (Paris), Buenos Aires, Louis Lumière-Lyon II, Geneva, and Idaho. He is a member of the editorial board of the journal *Cahiers du Cinéma España* and of the Honorary Committee of the *Diccionario del Cine Español* published by the Sociedad General de Autores y Editores (SGAE). His many monographs include *El cine en el País Vasco* (1985), *Pensar la imagen* (1989), *Robert Bresson* (2001), *Historias de España: De qué hablamos cuando hablamos de cine español* (2002), *Orson Welles* (2005), and *La mirada plural* (2008, winner of the Francisco Ayala International Audiovisual Communications Prize). He is also coeditor of *La nueva memoria: Historia(s) del cine español* (2005).

1

Introduction

Jo Labanyi and Tatjana Pavlović

The aim of this volume is not only to provide detailed information about cinema made in Spain from its beginnings to the present day but also, above all, to question existing paradigms. A key issue that emerges in its chapters is the transnational nature of Spanish cinema throughout its history – even under the highly nationalistic Franco dictatorship. To talk of Spanish cinema is to talk of its relations with other cinemas, through coproductions, through the sharing of actors and technical personnel, and particularly through its drawing on a common fund of formal, generic, and thematic concerns. Several chapters argue against the notion of Spanish cinema's exceptionalism while also insisting on the importance of considering its historical and geographical specificities. The volume also makes a point of decentering the study of Spanish cinema by stressing the importance of Barcelona as the center of the film industry in its early decades (to our knowledge, the volume offers the first history of cinematic production in Catalonia from its origins to the present available in any book on Spanish cinema) and by giving detailed attention to cinematic production in Spain's major autonomous communities: not just those that have their own language (Catalonia, the Basque Country, and Galicia) but also Andalusia, which has marketed "Andalusian cinema" as a brand – one that is transnational rather than strictly local, since the aim has been to attract filmmakers from outside the area to film there. The transnational and the local are thus seen as intertwined throughout the history of cinematic production in Spain.

The volume also works against the common concentration on art cinema in much discussion of Spanish film. We have given equal attention to production aimed at a discerning elite and that aimed at the popular audiences to which the film industry – for it is an industry – has always catered, examining the often

A Companion to Spanish Cinema, First Edition. Edited by Jo Labanyi and Tatjana Pavlović.

political processes that assign certain directors to the canon or exclude them from it. In this respect, cinema is seen as part of a continuum of cultural production involving other media – such as amusement parks, bullfighting and football, popular theater and the musical revue, literature, and television – and as bound up with other forms of cultural practice such as fashion and political activism. Considerable attention is given to the ways in which audiences have engaged with Spanish films, through their active participation in the star system (one of the industry's major marketing devices, but one gladly embraced by spectators) and fandom (particularly for genres perceived as marginal to hegemonic values, such as horror). The volume consequently considers cinema – especially in the case of cult movies and box-office hits – to be a valuable indicator of how cultural tastes have evolved in Spain over the course of the twentieth and early twenty-first centuries.

While most individual chapters adopt a chronological approach, the volume as a whole has been conceived on a thematic basis – something that again distinguishes it from existing histories of Spanish cinema. This allows consideration not just of individual films (though these are considered too, since many chapters focus on particular case studies) but of how these films form part of a cinematic apparatus comprising production companies, film studios, a broad range of film workers (cameramen, screenwriters, editors, as well as directors and actors), film clubs, festivals, archives, and film magazines directed at both specialist and popular audiences. In addition to the making and exhibition of films, the volume also considers questions of state regulation (censorship and subsidies), including the cinema policies of the major film-producing autonomous communities, and of preservation and restoration. We have made a point of including discussion of non-fiction film, often left out of studies of "national" cinemas since newsreels, documentaries, shorts, and animation have their own conventions and – with the exception of the mid-twentieth-century newsreels screened in cinema theaters, such as the Francoist NO-DO – have different exhibition circuits from the feature film. Experimental film is considered together with other forms of non-fiction film, to avoid subjecting it to the same analytical criteria that govern the fiction film. It is noted that some Spanish practitioners of non-fiction film have obtained a level of international recognition rarely achieved by Spanish feature-film directors.

We have also aimed to avoid the analysis of films primarily in terms of their subject matter, which characterizes much existing work on Spanish cinema. We thus have no chapters devoted to films "about" a particular topic (the city, women, or immigrants, to cite some of the favorites with critics), though of course such issues come up in the process of discussing films grouped together under other headings. One section focuses exclusively on cinematic techniques, visual and acoustic: we believe the discussion in this section of the historical evolution of camerawork, production design, editing, and soundtrack (including dubbing and film music) to be unique as well as enormously productive. Our main category for organizing the discussion of film texts has been not subject matter but genre. Given that genre is a classification system aimed at audiences, through its twin function as a marketing device and as a set of conventions that enable spectators to "read" films associated with a particular generic label, the focus on genre has the advantage of allowing consideration of how films connect with their public. The substantial discussion of genre also provides a historical overview of changing cultural tastes. Our desire to go beyond the discussion of Spanish cinema in terms of subject matter is also the impulse behind our inclusion of a section of theoretically informed analyses of specific film texts.

Despite the fact that Spanish cinema's patterns of production and consumption have from its inception been linked with global film industries, the ingrained critical paradigm of "national" production still dominates the field of Spanish film studies. Part I, "Reframing the National," thus seeks to deterritorialize the concept of national cinema by placing it in dialogue with other film industries both inside and outside Spain. Transnational modes of production are above all economic models, conditioned by the Spanish film industry's limited domestic audience. Expansion has been into two principal areas: (1) the transnational Hispanic market, facilitated by affective affinities of language and culture (yet not without its neo-colonial dimension), and (2) the European market created more recently through political union. Both markets provide the Spanish industry with a means of maintaining autonomy in the face of US hegemony and the growing encroachment of leviathan media corporations. However, Hollywood distributors' mergers and alliances with Spanish companies and the arrival of new technologies (such as cable and satellite provision, digital platforms, and multimedia formats) have threatened the very notion of a uniquely Spanish national film industry. Spain's incorporation into the European Union, with its protectionist laws, subsidies, and cross-European production standards, has created new tensions between, on the one hand, maintaining styles of film production that are understood and marketed as culturally European and, on the other, the pressures of a more standardized audiovisual industry dominated by the large Hollywood corporate media monopolies.

Within these emerging contexts, the cinema production of Spain's autonomous communities has made innovative connections between the local and the transnational, bypassing the national by aligning with world markets. Such ventures show that promotion of area-specific culture can benefit from the "branding" that global capitalism makes possible. Nonetheless, the challenge of reaching sufficiently broad audiences to guarantee box-office success remains. To speak of "Spanish cinema" is thus to speak of a tension between the assertion of local cinemas and homogenizing structural or marketing trends. The essays in Part I also show that transnationalism can correspond to political rather than economic factors – as with the "export" and "import" of film professionals thanks to political exile and the use of international film festivals to consecrate the careers of antiregime directors. In practice, the transnational strategies of cinema production in Spain's contemporary autonomous communities have obeyed ends that are as much nationalist as economic – the two usually but not necessarily working together. We are also reminded that cinema production in Catalonia and Galicia (the former particularly) goes back way before political devolution, and that, although the politics of language is an important factor, Catalan, Galician, and Basque cinemas cannot be limited to films made in the local vernacular. In order to reinforce this last point, we have included Andalusia in this discussion.

Part II, "The Construction of the Auteur," discusses the contentious concept that originated with *Cahiers du Cinéma*'s *politique des auteurs* in the 1960s. Despite focusing on canonical figures who have been perceived as forming the pantheon of Spanish cinema (such as Buñuel, Saura, and Almodóvar), the first of the two chapters questions common assumptions – and their ideological underpinnings – about the canon, including its equation with arthouse cinema and the conception of filmmaking as the artistic product of the director's personal vision. This critique is taken further in the second chapter, which sees auteurism not in terms of the film's qualities but as a strategic practice that can be carried out by directors, critics, and fans alike – as it was by the producers discussed in Part I, who consolidated the reputation of antiregime directors by playing the international film festival circuit. In so doing, this chapter recuperates the less-known, often discordant voices of Spanish cinema obscured by the discourse of auteurist cinema and its dismissive attitude toward the collaborative processes essential to filmmaking. Consequently, the chapter highlights the work of secondary actors, screenwriters, and editors and exposes the explicit androcentrism of the *politique des auteurs*. The chapter also traces a definitive shift away from 1960s auteurist film culture (which had in fact foreshadowed the later critical interest in popular cinema by constructing Hollywood classics as the creation of auteurs) by considering wider "authorial signatures" of understudied popular directors and avant-garde and pulp filmmakers.

Just as critics, academics, and fans strategically construct certain film directors as cult figures, auteurs too – be they avant-garde, popular, pulp, or women – embrace their authorial aura, succumb to self-mythologizing narratives, and invest in self-authorizing strategies. The successful construction of auteurist status in Spanish cinema involves both official recognition at home and the prestige bestowed upon national cinema abroad. Auteurism still predominates because the "director brand" continues to be a key commercial strategy for marketing films and priming audience reception. The synergies and tensions between the two chapters of Part II show how malleable labels associated with auteurism can be, and how fragile – even if deep-seated – are current notions of national cinema, art cinema, cultural prestige, and commercial value.

The three chapters in Part III, "Genre," each discuss two or three cognate film genres: respectively, comedy and musicals; melodrama and historical film; and *noir*, the thriller, and horror. In all cases, genre is considered as a flexible category that groups together a number of features, frequently in combination with features of other genres. Despite this definitional fuzziness, analysis of the historical evolution of films loosely pertaining to a particular genre can be instructive, particularly in revealing continuities as well as change. As is noted, such continuities, while they can be taken to indicate a specifically Spanish tradition (often going beyond cinema to encompass other cultural forms), are in most cases linked to similar trends in other national cinemas and cultures.

We start with a discussion of comedy and the musical in order to rescue them from the subordinate status to which they are often relegated because of their appeal to popular audiences: both genres have had a rich history in Spanish cinema, reinforcing but also challenging received ideas. Melodrama, too, is considered as a popular genre whose emotionalism can encourage acceptance of suffering (especially female suffering, given melodrama's conventional classification as the "woman's film") but that can also trigger emotions that work against the plot resolution, and particularly against conventional gender roles. Frequently overlapping with melodrama, the historical film is shown to be a particularly sensitive barometer for measuring changes in social attitudes, given that its representation of the past necessarily illustrates concerns appropriate to the time of the film's making. The anachronism that is built into the historical film can, despite the genre's ostensible escapism, allow a working through of issues that remain unresolved in the present.

The thriller, too, is shown to obey an evolution that parallels political and social change, with certain periods – the late 1940s with their intense use of *noir* techniques; the transition to democracy when the future remained uncertain – proving particularly conducive to the use of the investigative and/or suspense format. The thriller's focus on deviance has made it an especially important genre for the construction of social norms through the very process of showing how they are flouted; in this sense, the thriller has served to push the boundaries of what, in any given period, has been regarded as permissible in cinema. The horror film – which often merges with the thriller – has played a similar role in testing the limits of the permissible, in this case through the intense participation of fans in the construction of cult movies valued precisely for their positioning on the margins of mainstream culture.

In the case of all the genres discussed in Part III, a common thread emerges in their reliance on haptic forms of visuality that trigger a bodily, material response in the spectator: through farce and the carnivalesque in comedy; through dance and song in the musical; through tears in melodrama; through the emphasis on mise-en-scène in *noir* and on period costume and décor in the historical film; and through the viscerality of horror.

Part IV, "Stars as Cultural Icons," considers how the star system has worked, since the 1920s, to generate audience loyalty through an intense affective engagement with particular actors. The haptic plays a significant role here too, through the erotic charge generated by stars, perhaps particularly in times of sexual prudery, when the taboo on the display of naked flesh makes its limited exhibition on the cinema screen all the more riveting. The construction of a desiring machine built around film stars involved the creation of a whole material infrastructure from publicity photos to fashion tie-ins, disseminated particularly through the film magazines that proliferated from the 1920s on – an infrastructure that measured the appeal of Spanish stars in terms of the same criteria applied to their foreign (especially Hollywood) equivalents. Indeed, as the chapter on the early star system shows, stardom was frequently linked to triumph overseas, in Europe or the Americas, and this theme forms the plotline of innumerable films, as well as being illustrated by the careers of a considerable number of Spanish actors. If glamour had a compensatory function in the largely underdeveloped Spain of the 1920s and 1930s, and for those experiencing the hardships and repression of the early Franco dictatorship, from the 1960s onward stars came to incarnate the contradictions of a belatedly modernizing society – exemplified starkly in the vogue for child stars, precariously poised between infancy and adulthood, that coincided with late-Francoist fast-track capitalist development, and in the career in the same period of Sara Montiel on her return from Mexico and Hollywood as the star of nostalgia films that set new standards of permissiveness for female behavior. Since the transition to democracy, stars have increasingly become sucked into transnational celebrity culture and maligned as much as they are revered – particularly in the case of the considerable number who have engaged in left-wing political activism. From the cosmopolitanism of the stars of the 1920s to the transnationalism of the stars of the early twenty-first century, there is a long historical trajectory that constructs stars as national idols through their ability to transcend national borders.

Part V, "Image and Sound," takes readers through the history of visual and acoustic techniques deployed in Spanish cinema. The discussion of photography, production design, and editing insists on the technical continuum between cinema made in Spain and elsewhere, in some cases through its incorporation of foreign film professionals and in all cases through familiarity with (and sometimes direct experience of working in) other cinemas. At the same time, it is noted that Spanish cinema clung to studio production longer than was the case in most other countries, with the result that the use of location shooting and the concomitant editing and lighting techniques, production design, and use of direct sound were slow to take hold as standard practice. Curiously, the prevalence today of the action film, influenced by the rapid editing of television and the video clip, can be seen as an unacknowledged return to the early "cinema of attractions" designed to subject the spectator to a series of shocks. The transition to sound, which on the one hand severely curtailed the cosmopolitanism of silent cinema, paradoxically meant the internationalization of many Spanish film professionals recruited to work on Hollywood's multilingual and Spanish-language films in the early 1930s. Another phenomenon related simultaneously to internationalism (the viewing of foreign films) and nationalism (their exhibition in Spanish) was dubbing: a significant aspect of the Spanish film industry – particularly with the compulsory dubbing of all foreign films instituted by the Franco dictatorship in 1941 (creating habits that continue today) – and yet one that has mostly been ignored. The discussion of film sound questions assumptions about linear progress by recovering the artistry of Spanish dubbing professionals of the 1940s and 1950s, which was also the great period of the symphonic musical score in Spain as elsewhere. Indeed, it is noted that Spanish film composers of the 1940 and 1950s would have been shocked by the downgrading of the film composer's status in later Spanish cinema, though today the release of musical soundtracks on CD has brought a renewed attention to the film composer as artist, as well as a return to the symphonic score. The questioning of linear progress is also illustrated through discussion of the achievements of postproduction sound in Spanish cinema of the 1950s and 1960s, challenging the assumption that direct sound is always best.

Part VI, "The Film Apparatus: Production, Infrastructure, and Audiences," examines the collaborative medium of motion pictures as a mixture of interconnected industrial, artistic, and political practices, all of which were marked by censorship. Paradoxically, the mechanisms of censorship generated not only strategies of resistance on the part of producers and directors but also an audience of active, savvy spectators. The production apparatus in Spain has been further complicated by tensions between the private sector, state financing, and transnational interests. The latter were a major feature of Spain's early industrial history, with the first studios relying on foreign collaboration in the form of investment, technical expertise, and coproductions but still plagued by bankruptcies. This early economic instability of Spain's cinema infrastructure helps us to understand why, of the two economic models adopted by Spanish production companies from the 1930s to the early 1950s, only one would thrive in the long term. Filmófono and CIFESA imitated the Hollywood studio system by hiring a regular production crew and roster of in-house stars, albeit on a much reduced scale – even CIFESA, the company most often compared to Hollywood, never had its own studios. Other companies – the vast majority – sought greater financial and production flexibility by issuing short-term contracts to directors, film crews, actors, and studios: this was the model that survived. Contrary to received opinion, no production company bore the exclusive ideological stamp of its proprietors. Tellingly, it was the global expansion model pioneered by Cesáreo González's Suevia Films – the marketing of stars popular on both sides of the Atlantic, a worldwide movie-house network, and appeal to a broad transnational base – that anticipated today's independent producers and model of international collaboration. In the early twenty-first century, the picture is complicated by the industry's uneasy relationship with television, exacerbated by the requirement that television companies put five percent of their profits into subsidizing cinema production, which has led them to create their own film companies.

The second chapter in Part VI turns to issues of promotion, by examining the interlinked networks of film clubs, festivals, and magazines, as well as archives, preservation and restoration, and audiences. Film clubs and magazines were, from their inception and during Francoism, key to the promotion of an alternative film culture, the formation of political dissidents, and the recuperation of cinema history. After 1975, film magazines would cease to fulfil their earlier political function and would become absorbed into an increasingly commercial mass culture, as well as contributing to the growth of film studies as an academic discipline in Spain. A similar political function can be seen in film festivals that initially seemed to legitimize the dictatorship but subsequently served the political opposition – paralleling the lionization of dissident filmmakers at international film festivals discussed in Chapter 2. Today, film festival massification illustrates the cultural shift to micropolitics (with increasing specialization tied to genre, gender, autonomous communities, and specific demographics) and an overriding concern with commercial niche marketing. National and regional film archives, and film preservation and restoration, are two other closely connected features of the Spanish cinematic landscape since the former, in addition to functioning as art cinemas, take responsibility for the latter. The study of conservation history reveals the chronic underfunding of Spain's film industry and film patrimony, despite which some excellent restoration work has been carried out in recent years.

Part VI ends by introducing readers to the state of audience studies research in Spain, as well as analyzing audience response in two different periods, in each case adopting a different approach to give an idea of the possibilities available to the researcher. The discussion of spectatorship during cinema's heyday in the 1940s and 1950s, prior to the establishment of television, takes a qualitative approach, based on the analysis of audiences within particular film texts and on ethnographic research, in both cases focusing on the ways in which cinema-going practices enmeshed with everyday life concerns. By contrast, the discussion of audiences from the mid-1960s to the present takes quantitative analysis as its starting point, in order to show how an examination of the top-grossing films in particular periods can serve as the basis for a cultural analysis of changing public tastes. Both approaches assume that audiences are not dupes of the culture industries but that their viewing practices are based on informed choice.

Part VII, "Relations with Other Media," argues that film can only be understood by viewing it in the context of the culture industries as a whole, since viewers mix cinema-going with the consumption of other forms of entertainment. Prior to the consolidation of television in Spain in the 1960s, this meant that cinema coexisted with a range of forms of live entertainment, from the popular theater and music hall to various forms of sport, with stage actors, bullfighters, and even footballers moving between their home terrain and the silver screen. The relation between stage and screen has also taken the form, since cinema's beginnings, of adaptations of theatrical works – particularly popular operettas (*zarzuelas*) and farces (*sainetes*) – as well as of novels, both popular and canonical. Just as historical films tell us more about the period when the film was made than about the past depicted, so too literary adaptations tell us more about the concerns of the historical moment when the adaptation was filmed than about the concerns of the source text, as exemplified by the vogue for adaptations of Spanish literary classics during the period of the transition to democracy. Today, the medium with which cinema has the greatest synergy is undoubtedly television, through the screening of films on the small screen and the sharing of actors and sometimes directors, not to mention television companies' financing of films. It is argued that contemporary Spanish cinema cannot be understood without reference to television, particularly the production of television drama, which – it is suggested – is often more progressive and innovative than cinema in its treatment of social issues.

Part VIII, "Beyond the Fiction Film," focuses on marginalized practices of Spanish cinema: the documentary, experimental film, shorts, and animation. Its single chapter starts by discussing documentary film – newsreels and propaganda – during the Spanish Civil War, challenging the prevailing notion of the creative superiority of Republican production. Stress is placed on the internationalism of wartime film reportage, as foreign film crews flocked to document the war's progress. By contrast, the postwar Francoist newsreel NO-DO was of a piece with the regime's cultural and economic isolationism. Given its monopoly over newsreel production, NO-DO is commonly understood as a propaganda tool yet, paradoxically, it was defined by the exclusion of politics. Instead, it was saturated by the rhetoric of Spain's divine mission and the endless repetition of military and quotidian rituals, producing an atemporality aggravated by distribution problems that meant that cinemas outside urban centers frequently screened old editions. NO-DO's eternal repetition of the same would continue to fit well with the 1960s technocrats' vision of a postideological society, the repetition now being of charts and statistics. Nonetheless, NO-DO remained one of the few outlets for the consumption of non-fictional images, functioning as an audiovisual instrument of socialization.

In contrast to NO-DO's impermeability, experimental film, shorts, and animation have been characterized by a long tradition of mutual borrowings and hybridization with other arts. The chapter's last three sections are conceptually organized around the centrality of the marginal, around hybridization, and around reflexivity, respectively – practices traced from the 1920s to the present day. Oddly enough, experimental film, shorts, and animation have benefited from the backwardness of Spain's film industry, since lack of financing has fostered the development of alternative cinematic practices. This marginal condition has contributed to Spanish cinema's self-consciousness, particularly in non-fiction production, which stands on the margins of the margin. Today, alternative filmic practices exist within a much broader and more complex audiovisual universe, affected – like other phenomena analyzed in this volume – by changing patterns of production, exhibition, and consumption, especially the rise of digital formats and dissemination over the Internet. Specific to non-fiction film is the crossover with the art world, with films exhibited in museums and galleries. Economic pressure also encourages filmmakers to diversify, moving between fictional and non-fictional work. However, documentary, experimental film, shorts, and animation are not just a "bridge" to the commercial feature-film industry but fields in their own right, in which the struggle for visibility frequently leads filmmakers to occupy a broad range of roles, ranging from director to producer to critic.

Part IX, "Reading Films through Theory," functions as a kind of coda, complementing the broad historical sweep of the preceding discussions by providing detailed, theoretically informed analysis of specific film texts. Its three chapters in no way offer comprehensive coverage of the range of theoretical approaches available to film scholars but are offered as case studies that we hope will stimulate readers to undertake their own theoretically informed close readings of Spanish films. It is not coincidence that two of the three essays in this last part are grounded in gender theory, which has been vital to the development of film studies – indeed, it was largely through film studies that gender theory established itself in the academy. Nonetheless, these two essays use gender theory very differently. The essay on the work of Isabel Coixet takes readers through the history of feminist film criticism, establishing a dialogue between its successive stages and two films from different moments in Coixet's career. The following essay, on Pedro Almodóvar's *Todo sobre mi madre*, draws on a range of queer theory to show how the film not only destabilizes gender positions but also functions as a theoretical text in its own right, by making the spectator occupy multiple subject positions that unsettle preconceived conceptions: this is theory expounded through a series of embodied positionalities. The final essay analyzes the work of Iván Zulueta, particularly his feature film *Arrebato*, through an eclectic range of theoretical writing on the mechanisms through which cinema acts on the spectator's sensorial apparatus, highlighting the paradox of predigital film's materiality as celluloid and yet immateriality given its projection of shadows. Indeed, as is noted, cinema produces its effects through the film strip's projection at a speed such that the eye fails to see the gaps between the frames, making it as much about not seeing as about seeing. *Arrebato*, too, could be seen as a film that does not so much illustrate theory as embody it through its own material/immaterial practice. The concept of the haptic features in all three chapters in this last section, which, despite drawing on different theoretical corpuses, coincide in their view of film's capacity to embody philosophical propositions – theory as *corpus* in the most literal sense.

With regard to the conventions adopted throughout the volume, all dates given for films are, to the best of our knowledge, those of their release (rather than of shooting). Full names of directors and dates of films are given on their first mention in each chapter, as are English translations of all film titles: the English release title (taken from www.IMDb.com) has been used where it exists; where there is no English release title or where it is an incorrect or poor translation, the editors have provided their own English version. The many illustrations have been selected on the principle that they should add to the critical discussion; the majority are screengrabs of scenes analyzed in the text. We have acknowledged in the List of Illustrations the many individuals and organizations who supplied images and permission to reproduce them.

In keeping with the aim of showcasing different models of analysis, the essays in the volume bring together outstanding scholars – established and young – from Spain, the United Kingdom, and the United States. Just as the volume stresses the transnationalism of Spanish cinema, we have wanted to offer readers a sample of the best scholarship in all three national critical traditions. In presenting a wide range of critical approaches, we aim not only to give a rounded picture of Spanish cinema but also to offer readers a sense of the possibilities open to them in their own future critical work. We have deliberately not tried to iron out the differences of approach between our twenty-six contributors, since we regard these differences as one of the volume's strengths. To capitalize on this critical diversity, most chapters have been commissioned from two or more authors, often from different countries. For each of these coauthored chapters, one contributor was put in charge of collating the chapter and, where appropriate, adding an introduction, transitions, and conclusion: we are hugely indebted to those contributors who agreed to take this role on. We hope that the result of this working method is a productive mix of coherence and diversity. Our thanks go to all of our many contributors for their patience with our interminable queries during the gestation of this book; their work has been an inspiration to us as fellow scholars, and we hope that it will also inspire our readers to think about Spanish cinema in new ways.

Part I
Reframing the National

2

Transnational Frameworks

Gerard Dapena, Marvin D'Lugo, and Alberto Elena

Introduction (Marvin D'Lugo and Gerard Dapena)

The term "transnational cinema" has been applied broadly in the Spanish context to Spanish films that have involved production with one or more international partners or have included the presence of non-Spanish actors. Although transnationalism has commonly been associated with coproduction strategies (Ezra and Rowden 2006: 1–12; Pardo 2007: 89–127), what is involved is a cultural dynamic that goes well beyond typologies of transnational collaboration based on percentage formulas, such as those proposed by Alejandro Pardo (2007), for example. In speaking of his engagement in coproductions between his own production company, El Deseo, and filmmakers in Chile and Argentina, Agustín Almodóvar has remarked that what drove his efforts was "un encuentro maravilloso de sensibilidades distantes pero muy cercanas" (a marvelous encounter of geographically distant but culturally close sensitivities) (Merayo 2001: 83). These close sensibilities – what Mette Hjort has termed "affinitive coproductions" (2010: 17–18) – have underlain the evolving aesthetics of Spanish transnational cinema since its beginnings in the late silent period (García Fernández 1998: 251–3).

The production and distribution of motion pictures generally has been underpinned by the tacit assumption of their ability to reach audiences beyond geopolitical borders (Ezra and Rowden 2006: 3). The Spanish film industry's awareness of its limited domestic audience, operating in what Hjort has called "small nation contexts and minor cinemas" (2010: 18), is counterbalanced by the colonial dispersion of Spanish-speaking peoples and resulting exchange of cultural

A Companion to Spanish Cinema, First Edition. Edited by Jo Labanyi and Tatjana Pavlović.

products: what amounts to a transnational Hispanic market. This potential audience can be termed a Hispanic "transnation": a deterritorialized population formed through migration and built on the recognition of common linguistic, cultural, and social bonds. While predating cinema, this transnation has been reinforced in the twentieth century through sound technologies (phonograph and radio before motion pictures) that have largely not respected national borders. The "transnational" thus might be said to affirm a desire for identification with an expansive imagined community of shared cultural remembrances and other interests not structured by the narrow logic of the state. The creation of international funding bodies – such as Eurimages, MEDIA, and Ibermedia – to foster the circulation of films beyond national frontiers is a recent historical phenomenon that has made more conspicuous the mechanisms that have allowed Spanish-language cultural exchange across the Hispanic transnational community.

Despite the fact that the film industry has been transnational since its beginnings, standard histories of film have tended to foreground the idea of national cinema, a strategy that has enabled their authors to bestow a certain coherence and common identity on a heterogeneous array of movies. However, in recent years the concept of the transnational has gained ascendancy among film historians as a means to interrogate and problematize this very process of homogenization. If the category of the national has been routinely deployed to describe a series of industrial and artistic practices that are seen as confined to a particular territory (closed to outside influences and immutable to change), in contrast, a transnational film history is structured around the notion of flows, calling attention to movements across borders of film professionals and filmic styles and genres. It seeks to illuminate processes of exchange and interpenetration that are given short shrift and often obscured under the national paradigm, and to remind us that films are far more hybrid, protean texts than this paradigm, with its emphasis on authenticity and purity, is willing to entertain. Ultimately, it is not a matter of jettisoning the national; scholars of transnational cinema are aware that it is a concept that still resonates for many individuals and continues to function as a powerful tool for identity formation and community building. Rather, a transnational approach to the study of cinema seeks to deterritorialize its object of inquiry – rethinking the concept of borders – by placing it in a dialogical relationship with other film industries. In this sense, a transnational perspective on Spain's cinema would ideally go beyond merely noting, for example, the presence of Orson Welles' name on the directorial credits of two films with Spanish financing, assessing the brief Spanish career of Italian filmmaker Marco Ferreri, or recording the international careers of Spanish actors such as Fernando Rey or Francisco Rabal. It would also take into account the flow of foreign and national capital across Spain's borders, the appropriation and adaptation by Spanish filmmakers of cinematic styles, film scores, and genres associated with other national cinemas, and the identity of the intended audiences (national and/or international) for which these films were originally conceived.

As Nuria Triana Toribio has noted (2003: 6–8), the understanding of Spain's film production as a national cinema has been a vexed enterprise, continuously disputed and redefined over decades, under pressure from political, economic, and ideological imperatives. In this sense, films that have met the criteria of Spanishness have included audiovisual narratives that drew their imagery and sounds from other autochthonous cultural manifestations (literature, music, theater) deeply ingrained in popular taste and tradition. Alternatively, the national has been located in audiovisual narratives that looked to contemporary cultural forms that more often than not embodied modern ideals and cosmopolitan structures of feeling. Another point of contention, as Triana Toribio indicates (2003: 10–11), arises over whether one tries to define a national cinematic identity in terms of generic forms with broad mass appeal but low critical esteem or their opposite, an artistically ambitious and socially relevant art cinema for small, elitist audiences. Against this backdrop of contradictory interpretative models, Triana Toribio has argued that one cannot properly speak of a national cinema in the Spanish context until the 1940s; what precedes it is, at best, a proto-national cinema (2003: 17–18). This chapter starts with an examination of early Spanish cinema, seeking to expand and nuance our understanding of the national/transnational binary – and, indeed, to ask whether the two terms might not sometimes work together – by spotlighting some of the various transnational practices and agents involved in the formation or contestation of this national model in the 1920s and 1930s.

Transnational Beginnings (Gerard Dapena)

Spain's early cinema is indebted to the many foreigners who crisscrossed the peninsula at the end of the nineteenth century, peddling competing moving-image technologies or setting the foundation for the local film industry. Among them was José Sellier Loup, a French photographer who had set up his practice in A Coruña. After acquiring the Lumières' camera/projection system soon after its presentation in Madrid in 1896, he filmed General Sánchez Bregua's burial procession in June 1897, a pioneering moment in the history of Spain's early cinema, and later opened one of Spain's first projection spaces. As the silent era unfolded, first in Barcelona, home to the bulk of early film production (see Chapter 3), and later in Madrid and other regional centers, foreign film personnel played an important role. For instance, the first two feature-length films made in and about Galicia were directed by foreigners: Frenchman Henry Vorins cast his wife, French actress Paulette Landais, as the protagonist of *Maruxa* (1923), an adaptation of a famous *zarzuela* (popular operetta), while Cesare Rino Lupo, an Italian filmmaker with a long career in Portugal's film industry, directed *Carmiña, flor de Galicia / Carmiña, the Flower of Galicia* (1926). The contribution of Italian film professionals to Spain's fledging film industry was especially significant. Mario Caserini,

Giovanni Doria, Godofredo Mateldi, and Augusto Turchi were under contract to Catalan production companies, while Mario Roncoroni and his cameraman Giovanni Sessia worked for Valencia's Levantina Films, making movies steeped in Mediterranean scenery. In these works, where the local and the transnational overlap, foreign filmmakers were instrumental in creating the first cinematic signs of regional identity.

Eager to profit from the popularity of the cinema among Spaniards, foreign film producers provided capital for projects with appeal inside and outside Spain. Targeting the middle-class audiences who generally shunned the cinema, Films Cinématographiques of Paris partnered with the Catalan production company Argos Films for a lavish coproduction on the life of Christopher Columbus, *Vida de Cristóbal Colón y su descubrimiento de América / The Life of Christopher Columbus and His Discovery of America* (1916), directed by Gérard Bourgeois with a cast of mostly French actors. Very few Spanish film production companies were financially capable of hiring international talent or embarking on international coproductions. In this regard, Atlántida SACE, based in Madrid, proved to be the exception, engaging the renowned French filmmaker Marcel L'Herbier to supervise the work of his compatriot Jaque Catelain in *La Galerie des monstres / La barraca de los monstruos / Gallery of Monsters* (1924). With its fusion of earthy Spanish imagery and avant-garde visual style, the film proved a box-office hit in France, but in Spain was banned by General Primo de Rivera's censorship, hastening Atlántida's decline.

While many Spanish silent filmmakers turned to Andalusian folklore, bull-fighting, literary classics, and *zarzuelas* as source material for the creation of a cinema endowed with signs of local specificity – which might resonate with domestic audiences and thus deserve to be called national – others looked to Hollywood and European popular film genres in order to fashion a cosmopolitan product with appeal for both Spanish and international audiences. Set in an imaginary kingdom in the Balkans, the spy thriller *Ana Kadowa* (1914), codirected by the Catalan Fructuoso Gelabert and the German Otto Mulhauser with a Spanish cast and financing by an American firm based in Barcelona, exemplified this transnational outlook; the film was released successfully in other European countries and the United States.

The first decades of Spain's cinema witnessed a notable flow of Spanish film professionals beyond the borders of their native land. In 1920s Hollywood, Helena d'Algy appeared in leading roles alongside Rodolfo Valentino and John Barrymore and later starred in the Spanish–German coproduction *Raza de hidalgos / A Race of Noblemen* (1927), directed by her brother, Tony d'Algy, in the Berlin studios of UFA (Universum Film Aktiengesellschaft). Antonio Moreno achieved even greater fame and wealth in Hollywood, mainly in Latin lover roles. During a rare visit to his native Spain, Moreno was persuaded by the journalist Ramón Martínez de la Riva to star in his fictional documentary *En la tierra del sol / In the Land of the Sun* (1927), an appropriately transnational story about a Spanish Hollywood celebrity traveling through Andalusia; basically playing himself, this was Moreno's only appearance in a Spanish film. Among the pioneers of Spain's early cinema, none had as influential a career as Segundo de Chomón (1871–1929). Inventor of a special hand-coloring technique and creator of many special effects and camera tricks, Chomón befriended George Méliès while living in France and worked for the prestigious company Pathé in Paris and later as its representative in Barcelona, furnishing his employer with newsreels on colorful Spanish topics; after 1910, he directed his own short films with Ibérico Films, once again with European markets in mind. In 1913, Chomón moved to Italy on an invitation from Giovanni Pastrone to provide special effects for his large-scale epics – for example, *Cabiria* (1914); a decade later, we find him in France, collaborating on Abel Gance's super-production *Napoléon* (1926). Chomón's special-effects work for a dream sequence in Benito Perojo's *El negro que tenía el alma blanca / The Black with a White Soul* (1927) constituted his final contribution to Spain's cinema.

Like Chomón, Perojo fashioned a professional trajectory with a distinctive international presence. Lured to France by the technical superiority of its facilities, he directed almost all his silent filmography from 1924 onward in French studios (outdoor locations were shot in Spain). Since these Spanish–French coproductions generally featured Spanish actors in leading roles and their narratives were usually set in Spain, Perojo's filmography has been more easily assumed by historians of Spanish national cinema than that of Chomón. Yet throughout his career Perojo confronted accusations that his work was not Spanish enough, on account of his predilection for contemporary Hollywood and European cinematic styles, even when films such as *La bodega / Wine Cellars* (1930) and *El embrujo de Sevilla / The Charm of Seville* (1930, shot in Berlin) evoked the tropes of the *españolada* (a pejorative term used for cultural products that depict stereotypical "Spanishness," usually via Andalusian cultural clichés). Florián Rey's rural melodrama *La aldea maldita / The Cursed Village* (1930) – which he sonorized in Paris, only the original silent version being extant – met with a similarly cool response from certain Spanish critics, who disliked the film's blend of Weimar cinema traits and Soviet-school realism. Finally, the national identity of Luis Buñuel's two collaborations with Salvador Dalí, *Un chien andalou* (1929) and *L'Âge d'or* (1930), is equally fluid; while they are often cited in histories of Spanish cinema, they can be incorporated as easily into the history of French avant-garde cinema.

Breaking the Sound Barrier (Gerard Dapena)

The introduction of sound unleashed a major crisis worldwide. Faced with the exorbitant costs of purchasing and installing the new technology, many undercapitalized film industries, including Spain's, ceased production. Between 1929 and 1932, the majority of sound films in Spanish were made or completed beyond Spain's borders, a fact that upends conceptualizations of the national as contained within the nation-state (see also Chapter 13). From 1930 to 1935, the most active production of Spanish-language films ironically took place under the auspices of Hollywood studios. In order to regain world markets that might be lost to American cinema as local audiences turned to films shot in their native languages, Hollywood executives proceeded to make versions of certain films in various languages. Since the vast numbers of Spanish-language moviegoers promised lucrative box-office returns, Paramount set up a facility in the outskirts of Paris (Joinville) that employed a number of Spanish actors working under mainly American directors. Even more significant was the production that took place in California, which transitioned from adaptations of English originals – shot on the same sets but at a fraction of the budget – such as George Melford's *Dracula* (1931) to original projects such as Enrique Jardiel Poncela's adaptation of his own play, *Angelina o el honor de un brigadier / Angelina or the Honor of a Brigadier* (1935), one of the few Hollywood Spanish-language films to meet with commercial success. Professional ambitions and enticing pay compelled numerous Spanish actors and writers, and the occasional established director such as Perojo, to undertake the trip to Hollywood. Stars with important careers in film, such as Fortunio Bonanova, or on the stage, such as Catalina Bárcena and María Fernanda Ladrón de Guevara, joined rising stars such as Roberto Rey, José Nieto, and María Alba, and newcomers such as Julio Peña and Rosita Díaz Gimeno.

The nationality of the first sound production completed entirely in Spain, *Pax* (1932), is no less debatable. The project originated with Francisco Elías, who obtained financing from the French producer Camille Lemoine to make a film at the newly created Orphea Film studios in Barcelona (see Chapter 14), but only the French version, now lost, was shot. The Swiss-born Artur Porchet and his two sons became Orphea's main cinematographers throughout the 1930s. Although the film production of the short-lived Second Spanish Republic is often referred to as a Golden Age, the country's film industry was still feeble, lacking government support and vying with more polished foreign movies. The most popular Spanish films of this era by and large still resorted to regional folklore, *zarzuelas*, or *sainetes* (low-life farces, often with music) to pull audiences in. Even foreign filmmakers who gravitated toward Spain, as its film industry gradually adjusted to the technological and aesthetic challenges demanded by the transition to sound, worked in this vein. In 1934, Harry D'Abbadie D'Arrast arrived from Hollywood to direct an adaptation of Pedro Antonio de Alarcón's novella *El sombrero de tres picos / The Three-Cornered Hat* entitled *La traviesa molinera / It Happened in Spain* (now lost), starring his wife, American actress Eleanor Boardman; renowned French cinematographer Jules Kruger shot the film, which was the first of several works he lensed in Spain. That same year, Jean Grémillon traveled from France to make a filmed version of the *zarzuela La Dolorosa*. In the meantime, the turmoil unleashed in Germany's film industry by the Nazis' takeover in 1933 provoked an exodus of filmmakers and technical personnel, several of whom found work in Spain, lending their expertise to the development of Spain's cinema and injecting a cosmopolitan look into set design and cinematography. Among those who entered Spain's film industry prior to 1936 were cameramen Heinrich Gaertner (later Enrique Guerner), Fred Mandel, Wilhelm Goldberger and his brother Isidore, Henry Bayerre, and Adolf Schlossy; art directors Herbert Lipschutz and Erwin Scharf; and composer Max Winterfeld (aka Jean Gilbert) (for a discussion of Guerner, see Chapter 12).

War, Isolation, and New Transnational Openings (Gerard Dapena)

General Franco's uprising in 1936 and the ensuing Civil War threw Spain's film industry into disarray, yet opened the door to new transnational ventures. As the majority of the country's studios remained under Republican control, arrangements were made for pro-Nationalist filmmakers to film in Berlin's UFA studios, under the aegis of the Spanish–German production company Hispano-Film-Produktion created for that purpose with Goebbels' blessing as Nazi Minister of Propaganda. There is disagreement about the extent to which the Spanish production company CIFESA (see Chapter 14) was involved in the creation of this joint Spanish–German venture, but CIFESA personnel, directors, and actors were certainly hired to work on its productions. Between 1937 and 1939, Hispano-Film-Produktion produced five films: two were directed by Benito Perojo, starring the *folklórica* (folkloric female singing star) Estrellita Castro, and three by Florián Rey, centered around his wife Imperio Argentina, who had a strong admirer in Hitler himself. These films were released in both German and Spanish versions; both Franco's government and the critical establishment at the time expressed reservations over their Spanish identity. On the Republican side, scarcity of film stock and decreasing funds curtailed film production. Under these dire circumstances, Italian art director Fernando Mignoni, whose striking sets had appeared in Perojo's *La verbena de la Paloma / Festival of the Virgin of the Dove* (1935), made his directorial debut with *Nuestro culpable / Our Culprit* (1938), a comedy financed, oddly enough given the film's formal debt to Hollywood musicals, by the anarchist trade union CNT; its cosmopolitan sensibility stood in contrast to the *españoladas* coming out of Berlin. Moreover, key propaganda films – Republican and Nationalist – had significant transnational components (see Chapter 18). Financed by the Republican government to solicit support from the international community, *Sierra de Teruel / Days of Hope* (1939–45), the foremost Spanish-language fiction film about the Civil War, was directed by French writer André Malraux, on whose novel *L'Espoir* it was based; unfinished by the time Franco's troops vanquished the Republic's army, it was completed by Malraux in France. Defending the Nationalist vision of Spain, Hispano-Film-Produktion funded the compilation film *España heroica / Helden in Spanien / Heroic Spain* (Joaquín Reig, 1938), premiered in Berlin.

The ensuing diplomatic and economic blockade imposed by the Western democracies after the Civil War's end isolated Franco's dictatorship, impacting on Spain's cinema during the 1940s. Although the government favored films that dealt with Spanish history, culture, and folklore, always from a conservative and nationalistic point of view, the debate over what direction Spain's cinema should take was never settled or closed to transnational influences. In fact, despite the nationalistic tone of several early Francoist films, some filmmakers persisted in making movies according to American and European generic and stylistic models: Hollywood screwball comedies (Ignacio F. Iquino's *Boda accidentada / An Eventful Wedding*, 1942), Italian white-telephone romantic comedies (Juan de Orduña's *Ella, él y sus millones / She, He and their Millions*, 1944), *noir*-ish crime thrillers (José Antonio Nieves Conde's *Angustia / Anguish*, 1947), and French poetic realism (Rafael Gil's *La calle sin sol / The Sunless Street*, 1948). The influence of Orson Welles' baroque camerawork pervaded Carlos Serrano de Osma's *La sirena negra / Black Siren* (1947), while Alfred Hitchcock's *Rebecca* (1940) functioned as a key intertext in Lorenzo Llobet Gràcia's *Vida en sombras / Life in Shadows* (1948). It was not only a matter of images: the sounds of American popular music often suffused the soundtracks of the most cosmopolitan of these films.

Despite Franco's autarkic cultural policies, a measure of cinematic collaboration continued with countries sympathetic to his regime: Mussolini's Italy and Salazar's Portugal. Perojo made two films in Rome's Cinecittà's studios in 1939, while Italian filmmaker Augusto Genina directed the coproduction *Sin novedad en el Alcázar / L'assedio del'Alcazar / The Siege of the Alcazar* (1940), which extolled the sacrifices of Nationalist combatants besieged by Republican troops. Spain and Portugal's common history was the subject of the historical melodrama *Inés de Castro* (1944), directed in Spanish and Portuguese versions by José Leitão de Barros. Its Portuguese protagonist, Antonio Vilar, built an important career in Spain, as later did his fellow countryman Virgilio Texeira, who would star in the hyper-nationalistic *Agustina de Aragón* (Juan de Orduña, 1950). The Nazi occupation of France in 1940 provoked another influx of foreign creative talent to Spain's film industry, as a number of film professionals, some of whom had previously fled Germany for Paris, now fled further south to Spain (non-belligerent in World War II), following in the footsteps of the earlier wave of refugees from Nazism. During the 1940s, cinematographers Michel Kelber and Ted Pahle (born in the United States) worked in Spain, as did art directors Hans Scheib (who came to Spain after working in Berlin for Hispano-Film-Produktion) and Pierre Schild (who had worked in Paris on Buñuel and Dalí's *Un chien andalou* (1929) and *L'Âge d'or* (1930)). The German Sigfrido Burmann (originally Sigfried Bürmann), who had worked in Spain as a successful avant-garde stage designer in the 1920s and 1930s, would in the 1940s become one of Spain's top film set designers. Of all European-born directors based in Spain, Hungarian Ladislao Vajda (originally László Vajda Weisz) had the longest and most substantial career. Following his first Spanish film in 1943,

Vadja worked until his death in 1965 in a variety of genres, authoring one of the biggest international hits of early Francoist cinema: *Marcelino, pan y vino / The Miracle of Marcelino* (1955).

The overseas success of Vajda's film, which dovetailed with the end of Spain's political isolation and the resumption of trade relations with Western powers, spurred new transnational developments. Following the signing of agreements with Italy and France in 1953 that regulated filmic coproductions, these operations would grow steadily over the next twenty years. Because labor costs were lower than in other European countries and its film personnel were competent enough, Spain proved immensely attractive to foreign film investors. In addition, it offered varied landscapes of breathtaking, unspoiled beauty and a plethora of artistic and scenic sights. For their part, Spanish producers benefited from access to new markets, while Spanish actors and crews saw opportunities for professional advancement and higher salaries.

Although the bulk of Francoist coproductions belong to the category of popular cinema (and thus have been ignored by historians, who have tended to construct the identity of Spain's national cinema around its arthouse films), Spanish dissident auteurs, laboring under strict censorship laws, availed themselves of the opportunities afforded not only by the presentation of their films at international festivals (discussed later in this chapter) but also by foreign financing. Almost all of Juan Antonio Bardem's major films from the 1950s and 1960s, beginning with *Muerte de un cyclista / Death of a Cyclist* (1955), were coproduced with financing from Italy and/or France, enabling him to thwart the Spanish government's attempts to suppress his movies or alter their meaning; as their protagonists, he cast actresses from Italy (Lucia Bosé), the United States (Betsy Blair), Greece (Melina Mercouri), and France (Corinne Marchand) (see Figure 2.1). Luis García Berlanga also resorted to international casts and financing in *Calabuch / The Rocket from Calabuch* (1956) and *El verdugo / The Executioner* (1963). Likewise, the two films that Buñuel shot in Spain in the 1960s – *Viridiana* (1961) and *Tristana* (1969) – involved international financing and featured foreign actresses in the leading roles. Thus, key works by the main figures of Spain's auteur cinema were essentially transnational projects, problematizing their status as iconic manifestations of an oppositional national cinema. The political implications of this link between auteurism and transnationalism will be developed later in this chapter. The generation of filmmakers that followed in Bardem's and Berlanga's footsteps, the authors of the Nuevo Cine Español (NCE; New Spanish Cinema; see Chapter 5), found themselves in the crossfire of critics and audiences who deemed their formal experimentation and thematic concerns with alienation too derivative of the 1960s European New Waves to be considered properly Spanish. Basilio Martín Patino's *Nueve cartas a Berta / Nine Letters to Bertha* (1996), with its storyline about foreign travel, exile, and interior displacement, exemplifies the use of border crossings as an entry point for a political and moral critique of Francoist society, which found greater echo among foreign spectators than among the majority of Spanish moviegoers.

Figure 2.1 Alberto Closas and Lucía Bosé in *Muerte de un ciclista* (Juan Antonio Bardem, 1955; prod. Suevia Films). Courtesy of Criterion Collection.

Cesáreo González, who distributed many of Bardem's films, became a leading force in the transnationalization of Spain's cinema (see Chapter 14). Although his original field of operations was Latin America, he also participated in European coproductions, often building a bridge between the continents. After signing up Mexican actress María Félix and casting her alongside Italian actors Vittorio Gassman and Rossano Brazzi in *La corona negra / Black Crown* (1950), a *noir*-ish melodrama – allegedly based on an idea by Jean Cocteau – directed by the Argentine Luis Saslavsky, González financed Félix's European career (see Figure 2.2). Despite this, Félix star vehicles such as Carmine Gallone's peplum (the term applied to epics, mostly Italian-made, set in the classical world) *Messalina* (1952) and Richard Pottier's musical *La belle Otero / The Beautiful Otero* (1954) are not generally included in histories of Spanish cinema. González's company, Suevia Films, was also instrumental in raising the international visibility of Spanish movie stars Lola Flores, Sara Montiel, Carmen Sevilla, and Marisol. Having returned to Spain in 1957 after a brief Hollywood interlude that yielded three films, Montiel relaunched a wildly successful career in sultry melodramas and musicals such as Suevia's coproductions *La violetera / The Violet-Seller* (1958) and *Pecado de amor / A Sin of Love* (1961), both directed by Luis Cèsar Amadori. At its height, Montiel's fame reached as far as the Soviet Union and Japan (see Chapter 10 and Chapter 11). Sevilla was second only to

Figure 2.2 Handbill publicizing María Félix and Rossano Brazzi in *La corona negra* (Luis Saslavsky, 1950; prod. Suevia Films). Private collection.

Montiel in international exposure. She was well-known in France for her appearance alongside the popular singer Luis Mariano (a Spanish exile who had made his career in France) in period films such as *Violetas imperiales / Imperial Violets* (Richard Pottier, 1952); appeared in Italian–Spanish films such as *Pan, amor y Andalucía / Bread, Love and Andalusia* (Javier Setó 1959), alongside Vittorio De Sica; and played Mary Magdalene in Nicholas Ray's *King of Kings* (1961).

Ray's biblical epic was one of five English-language super-productions made in Spain under the banner of Hollywood producer Samuel Bronston, who built a short-lived movie empire near Madrid with the support of Franco's government, employing Spanish film personnel under American supervision, in addition to Spanish actors and hundreds of extras (see Chapter 8). Although there is little in the appearance of these films that would identify them as Spanish, their inclusion in a history of Spanish cinema is plausible when we take a transnational perspective. Such a perspective allows us to understand why Anthony Mann's *El Cid* (1961) was declared of National Interest by Spain's film classification board, a privilege rarely bestowed on an English-language movie. Bronston's presence constituted the most visible manifestation of Spain's opening to international capital and tourism.

As the nation's political image became less unpalatable, parts of Spain (the Costa Brava and Almería) quickly became favored locations for Hollywood productions, indirectly participating in Hollywood's dream machine.

The Golden Age of Popular Coproductions (Gerard Dapena)

In 1964, Spain's government freed up the flow of foreign capital into and out of Spain and extended special status to coproductions, which now qualified for generous subsidies. Their number skyrocketed accordingly, reaching a zenith in 1965, when sixty percent of all Spanish films were officially designated as coproductions, a statistic that serves to bracket once again the notion of Spain's cinema as a purely national enterprise. Even more than in the 1950s, the bulk of these coproductions belonged to the popular film genres that until recently were rarely included in histories of European national cinemas: westerns, action/adventure films, peplums, and horror. A number of these transnational productions could be reinscribed into the domain of the national through some connection to Spanish history or culture, even if they starred, or were directed by, foreigners, as was the case with Vincent Sherman's *Cervantes, el manco de Lepanto / Young Rebel* (1966), with German actor Horst Bucholz playing the Spanish novelist, or Vittorio Cottafavi's depiction of the wars between Christians and Muslims in medieval Spain in *Los cien caballeros / 100 Horsemen* (1964). Other pictures in this vein, such as the ultra-modern action movies of Spanish director Antonio Isasi-Isasmendi, undoubtedly pushed the conceptual boundaries of what had previously been considered a Spanish film. Working in English with European and American actors, Isasi-Isasmendi achieved worldwide success with the spy thriller *Estambul 65 / That Man in Istanbul* (1966) and the heist film *Las Vegas, 500 millones / They Came to Rob Las Vegas* (1967).

Although Italian cinema is usually regarded as the cradle of the peplum and the Euro-western, Spanish producers, sometimes nominally and sometimes with substantial financial commitment, played an important role in the consolidation of these genres (see Chapter 8). The Spanish connection to the 1960s revival of the western is particularly noteworthy, as not only was Sergio Leone's seminal *Dollars* trilogy (1964–6) shot in southeastern Andalusia and cofinanced with Spanish money but so were numerous other spaghetti westerns, which additionally featured a gallery of Spanish actors such as Eduardo Fajardo, José Nieto, Julio Peña, Conrado San Martín, and especially Fernando Sancho in supporting roles. The Catalan production company PC Balcázar financed its own line of so-called *paella* westerns (alternatively called *chorizo* westerns), building a Western town in their studios in Esplugas de Llobregat, outside Barcelona, where filming continued until 1974. Shooting in another Wild West set built at Torrejón near Madrid, Joaquín Romero Marchent turned out a string of remarkable westerns such as *El sabor de la venganza* / *Gunfight at High Noon* (1963) and *Antes llega la muerte* / *Hour of Death* (1964). Despite the admiration these films elicit today, in the 1960s neither film critics nor the administration were prone to accept these westerns as unequivocally Spanish, since signs of their Iberian origin were purposefully minimized so that foreign audiences, their primary consumers, could retain the illusion of watching an American movie.

If Spanish horror films and their directors – Jesús Franco, Paul Naschy, Amando de Ossorio, and Carlos Aured – equally lacked the support of the Spanish state and critical establishment, they nonetheless appealed to many Spanish spectators and proved immensely popular abroad (see Chapter 9). As with westerns, all traces of Spanishness were removed from the plots of films such as *La noche de Walpurgis* / *The Werewolf versus the Vampire Woman* (León Klimovsky, 1971) and the coproduction *Non si deve profanare il sonno dei morti* / *No profanar el sueño de los muertos* / *Don't Open the Window* (Jorge Grau, 1974), which generally unfolded in some vague European location. Just as oppositional directors of the 1950s and 1960s had used foreign cofinancing to circumvent censorship, so too, in the case of these popular films of the 1970s, did the frequent participation of international financing and foreign actors allow for the existence of dual versions; the export copy, most often dubbed into English, upped the bloodletting, nudity, and eroticism that Spanish censors excised. Yet, as the dictatorship entered its terminal phase, a timid liberalization allowed for the increased depiction of nudity. The erotic films that comprised the so-called *cine de destape* (nudity films), a mainstay of the film scene in 1970s Spain, frequently had a transnational dimension. The first naked breast in Spanish postwar cinema appeared in a Spanish–German coproduction of a Spanish literary classic, César Fernández Ardavín's *La Celestina* (1969). Several foreign actresses endowed with voluptuous physiques (Helga Liné, Nadiuska, Ornella Muti, Ira de Fürstenberg) found ample work in Spain in these erotic comedies, topical exploitation films, and softcore horror. Conversely, Spanish actresses Soledad Miranda and Lina Romay achieved worldwide iconic status as sex goddesses, partially through their work in Jess Franco's coproductions. If Franco the dictator had wanted to cast Spain's cinema in the mold of an obsolete nationalist ideology, Franco the international master of monster movies and sado-masochistic erotic fantasies can fittingly stand as the embodiment of an entirely different conception of what we might understand as Spanish cinema, one thoroughly steeped in transnational practices and identities (see Pavlović 2003).

The Politics of the Transnational Auteur (Marvin D'Lugo)

The following sections trace the development of Spanish transnational cinema in its contemporary form, dating back to the decline of Spain's studio system, with particular emphasis on the role played in this process by the politics of the auteur or author (I use both terms indistinctly). This development resulted from a shrinking market for films made in Spain, combined with increasing emphasis on lower-cost location shooting thanks to the impact of Italian neo-realism (Gorostiza 1997: 73). It was the recognition by producers, directors, and government bureaucrats of the aesthetic as well as production discrepancies between Spanish films and their international competition that precipitated changes in both style and production. New Spanish Cinema, the Franco government's effort to shore up the industry (see Chapter 5), was, in a real sense, the starting point of concerted efforts to develop what would subsequently be recognized as a high-quality Spanish transnational cinema – by contrast with the popular coproductions that have been emphasized in this chapter so far. In earlier decades, the frequency of coproductions or use of foreign stars had not substantially altered the emphasis on producing a "national cinema." Now, however, this shift of focus would begin to affect Spanish cinema as a corpus and the very concept of national cinema would be called into question through its conflation with the transnational.

The government's promotion of New Spanish Cinema had particular appeal to filmmakers such as Carlos Saura, Víctor Erice, and Basilio Martín Patino, who, voicing internal dissidence in the wake of the spectacular *Viridiana* scandal of 1961 (see Chapter 5), consciously cultivated aesthetic strategies to circumvent the otherwise implacable Francoist censorship apparatus (Salvador Marañón 2006: 454). One of the principal lessons that *Viridiana* taught these filmmakers was the strategic importance of engaging audiences beyond the community defined by political borders. *Viridiana* was a model to emulate less because of its social content – the anachronistic religious credo so closely aligned to the Francoist ideological project – than because it suggested ways of developing a representational aesthetics that could accommodate the censors yet obliquely attack the regime's ideology, and do so by appealing to international audiences.

In part, that transnational perspective was a consequence of the film's nominal status as a Mexican–Spanish coproduction, an effort by novice Mexican producer Gustavo Alatriste to bankroll a film for his wife, Mexican actress Silvia Pinal (see Figure 2.3). The film had originally been planned simply as a Mexican production but Alatriste, needing additional funds, proposed collaboration with the long-standing Spanish directors' collective, UNINCI, whose most famous participants were the key opposition directors of the 1950s, Berlanga and Bardem. The business arrangement was further expanded to include Films 59, the production company of Catalan filmmaker Pere Portabella, though it seems that its involvement was minimal (Salvador López 2004: 13). The original script had been written with a Mexican setting in mind and had to be adjusted when Alatriste proposed more economical shooting arrangements in Spain (Salvador Marañón 2006: 453–4). As with Buñuel's earlier *Nazarín* (1958), the eradication of the script's references to local Mexican place names created a metaphorical textuality that, while overtly referring to the film's specific characters, events, and themes, also operated as a system of allusions to extratextual, largely social and political themes

Figure 2.3 Silvia Pinal in the title role of Luis Buñuel's scandalous transnational hit *Viridiana* (1961; prod. UNINCI / Alatriste).

that resonated with the Francoist obsession with Catholicism. It was the film's aesthetics of allusion, its essential textual dialogism, that made possible wider readings by audiences outside Spain.

At the same time, it was clearly Buñuel's name as auteur (see Chapter 5) that helped to catapult the film into the international arena, connecting it to US, Latin American, and European critical and distribution networks to which Spanish productions seldom gained access. The lesson was well taken. The result was that auteurism came to be viewed less as a label signifying aesthetic quality than as a useful marketing tool in the film-festival circuit. *Viridiana*'s triumph at Cannes made explicit the broad arenas within which Spanish transnational cinema needed to operate. In a transnational system increasingly skewed by the hegemony of Hollywood, the international film-festival network, inaugurated by the Venice Biennale in 1932, had by the 1960s become central to the multiple mechanisms allowing national cinemas to achieve critical recognition and commercial viability. Beyond their publicly stated objectives of recognizing high-quality cinema at an international level, film festivals – then as now – were governed by "hidden agendas" (Valck 2006: 59–61); European festivals have regularly rewarded or castigated certain political positions. Beyond such ideological questions, however, these annual competitions offered a strong commercial incentive: a festival prize translated into marketability at home. This was the case certainly with Carlos Saura's *La caza* / *The Hunt* (1965), which, four years after the *Viridiana* scandal, won the Silver Bear at Berlin, giving its director more visibility in Spain. Here we may speak of a literal "politics of the author" that conflated political dissidence at home with the international image of defiant romantic auteur. What was viewed as art cinema outside Spain was mostly seen by domestic audiences as popular fare, for this was cinema constructed dialogically to allow plural readings at home and overseas.

The Producer-Author as Transnational Entrepreneur (Marvin D'Lugo)

Against this historical backdrop, the producer has to be seen as a pivotal figure in the development of Spanish transnational cinema. This section anticipates the discussion in Chapter 6 of the need to consider as auteurs a range of film workers, and not only directors. Most histories of Spanish film do not adequately take into account the centrality of producers and production companies to an understanding of the development of Spanish cinema. Yet, with the major studios' demise, the producer took on an increased role in the transnational negotiations generated by the marketing and distribution networks that emerged around film festivals during the dictatorship's final decade and the transition period. Small independent production companies had sprung up in the early 1960s, partly in response to Manuel Fraga Iribarne's (Franco's Minister of Information and Tourism) strategy of providing generous subsidies to young filmmakers. Many of these small companies were primarily devoted to promoting a particular director, some being owned or co-owned by the director in question; thus, Elías Querejeta PC promoted Saura, Antxon Eceiza, Víctor Erice, and Montxo Armendáriz, while José Luis Borau's production company El Imán supported Iván Zulueta, Jaime de Armiñán, and Manuel Gutiérrez Aragón, as well as producing Borau's own films. Such arrangements collapsed the conventional distinction between filmmaker and producer, inverting Walter Benjamin's famous aphorism of the "author as producer." This conflation of the two roles had precedents, of course, in 1920s and 1930s Hollywood (Chaplin, Thalberg, Selznick). Although Benjamin's discussion of the author as producer largely ignores questions of the national specificity of artistic production in favor of a consideration of the more general dynamics of industrial mass society, his discussion is appropriately recalled here because it brings into focus important issues of class (1978: 225, 232) that transcend the national. Such a critical perspective implicitly calls into question the validity of nation-based conceptualizations of the arts and commerce. For Benjamin, the producer is a figurative concept: a producer of knowledge or ideology rather than of commodities. Throughout his key essay "The Author as Producer," Benjamin alludes to the producer's disruption of conventional bourgeois modes of cultural consumption, securing a "functional transformation" (1978: 228) of the mass media. "The exemplary character of production," Benjamin writes, "is able first to induce other producers to produce and second to put an improved apparatus at their disposal" (1978: 233).

Benjamin's metaphorical play on the twinned concepts of authorship and production, with both the author and producer regarded as figures whose intervention alters the consciousness of spectators (1978: 225, 230), affords us an understanding of the peculiar dynamics of the small but notable group of filmmaker-producers who emerged from the Francoist state's attempts to alter its international image. Tied to their efforts to challenge the ideological project of Francoism was their seemingly unrelated commitment to a transnational cinematic project. These two projects were, however, logically linked, since opposition to Francoist traditionalism entailed rejection of the pristine sense of nation, of the presumed racial and cultural purity of *la España profunda* (deep Spain) that was intrinsic to it. It is essential to appreciate how a certain genealogy that interweaves producers and filmmakers has been crucial to shaping transnational cinematic aesthetics in Spain since the mid-1960s. Indeed, post-Franco transnational cinema can be reconceptualized as the end product of a series of crucial interventions by producers engaged in radical forms of entrepreneurial authorship.

The most striking producer-author of the late Franco dictatorship, Elías Querejeta, unquestionably provided a model for the producer-authors who would appear during the transition to democracy: anticipating transnational coproduction trends, he was the first truly oppositional producer to strategically engage the Franco regime in an effort to develop films that might be viable both in Spain and overseas. Querejeta is usually credited with definitively shaping the careers and authorial style of the directors Saura, Eceiza, Erice, and Armendáriz (Borau 1998: 722). His earliest engagement in film was with UNINCI in the mid-1950s. A soccer-player turned filmmaker, he had found himself in open confrontation with the Spanish censorship board over his first two films: the documentaries *A través de San Sebastián / By Way of San Sebastián* (1960) and *A través del fútbol / By Way of Football* (1961). In 1963 he set up his own production company to take advantage of Fraga Iribarne's liberalization of film subsidies. Here Querejeta's strategies were clearly distinct from those of other producers. Above all, he was driven by an understanding of how emulation of the aesthetics of quality filmmaking in Europe would allow Spanish films to be integrated into European networks (Gómez 2001: 29). To achieve that goal, he put together a small but highly talented production team able to create and consolidate a particular politically oriented aesthetic. What came to be known as the Querejeta house style was the result of collaboration between Pablo G. del Amo (editing), Primitivo Álvaro (production manager), Luis Cuadrado and later Teo Escamilla (cinematography), and Luis de Pablo (musical score). As Querejeta later insisted, the team produced films whose production values were on a par with those of European producers. This house style often emphasized elliptical editing that, while mirroring chic New Wave stylistics, was also a convenient way to circumvent the censors at home. Equally important was Querejeta's mentoring of select filmmakers in developing small film projects – limited locales, small casts – whose modest budget minimized financial risk.

These films consistently contained implicit and explicit critical commentary on the political regime. Having learned from his head-on clash with the censors over his early attempts at documentary filmmaking, Querejeta now adopted the approach of engaging with the censors by accommodating cinematic style to some of their explicit objections. This would lead his directors – notably Saura and Erice – to develop increasingly metaphorical films whose underlying meaning could be read in and outside Spain while still securing Spanish government support, albeit grudging. Querejeta put his notion of auteur cinema as a team collaboration (Angúlo et al. 1996: 44) in the service of a single, steadfast goal: to appeal to Spanish cinema's "other" – that is, international – audience. In some cases, this involved moving from rural plotlines to narratives set in the modern city or with a directly transnational dimension. This shift is seen in the first three films – *Tasio* (1984), *27 horas / 27 Hours* (1986), *Las cartas de Alou / Letters from Alou* (1990) – of the young Armendáriz, whom Querejeta championed in the 1980s, after terminating his production collaboration with Saura. The denunciation of the abuse of immigrants in Armendáriz's seminal *Las cartas de Alou*, the first Spanish film to deal with illegal immigration, revealed the complexity of the national/transnational interface, in the process mirroring the tendency in contemporary European cinema toward a break with localist, isolationist tendencies. This film was produced shortly after Spain's 1986 entry into the European Community, which provided Spanish producers with access to European subsidies, enhancing Querejeta's efforts to connect with the rest of Europe. Significantly, Querejeta had planned a trilogy of films following Alou from Senegal to Spain, France, and Germany (the last two films were never realized).

Borau, a contemporary of Querejeta, represents a further expansion of the politics of cinematic transnationalism. Like Querejeta, he came to the role of film producer after two failed experiences as a commercial filmmaker. He established his own production company, El Imán, in 1969; as well as enabling him to produce his own films, it provided a financial base through which to produce the work of friends and his former students at the Escuela Oficial de Cine (EOC) – most famously Zulueta's *Un, dos, tres, al escondite inglés / Hide and Seek* (1969) and Armiñán's *Mi querida señorita / My Dear Señorita* (1971) – while engaging in the development of film projects for which he was nominally producer but for which he assumed what amounted to coauthorship (Heredero 1993: 157–79). Underlying nearly all of El Imán's productions was a conception of cinema that challenged the constraining ideology of the national as a mindset concretized in film practice. Commentators have read Borau's work as an assault on the concept of confining borders, at the level of narrative and casting and also in their production mode (Marías 1985: 107; Heredero 1990: 250; Kinder 1993: 347–50). The films Borau produced – including those he directed – may be seen as generally problematizing their Spanishness by self-referentially making Hispanic identity part of the narrative conflict and seeking to relocate that cinematic identity in ways that erase notions of Spain's cultural inferiority. This aim was powerfully expressed in Borau's 1983 essay "Without Weapons," in which he pursued the problematic relation between film and "national" culture. Focusing on Buñuel's assertion that nobody would read American writers such as Dos Passos or Hemingway if they had been born in Paraguay (Borau 1983: 84), he argued that, in part, the presumed cultural superiority of the United States had to do with its status as a military power (1983: 85). Consequently, a country like Spain was "without weapons" in a double sense: it lacked military importance, and the time when it had briefly been able to hold world attention, during its bloody Civil War (1936–9), had long since been forgotten. Picking up on claims put forth by European filmmakers and critics, Borau rejected the ghettoizing mindset that advocates a cinema built around cultural specificity – what he saw as "the ultimate pacifier, devised to calm the creative urge of disinherited authors (you know, the ones from countries without weapons)" (1983: 89). Filmmakers, according to Borau's argument, should not be restricted in their vision or subject matter by national borders or passports.

Borau's career, marked by erratic commercial success overseas, followed a specific border-crossing trajectory, marked – as Marsha Kinder has observed (1993: 345) – by an initial admiration for Hollywood, especially the European émigré directors John Ford, Fritz Lang, and Alfred Hitchcock; then his embrace of the seamless rhetoric of Hollywood-style narrative; and finally the American dream of making a film in Hollywood. Perhaps most indicative of Borau's admiration for Hollywood auteur cinema is his intensive weaving of specific Hollywood texts into the dynamics of his plots and visual regimes. This would, in time, become one of the transnational hallmarks of Spanish cinema.

Hay que matar a B / B Must Die (1973), Borau's first engagement in filmmaking under the aegis of his own production company, was a Swiss–Spanish coproduction made in English. It is one of the earliest examples of the use of English in a Spanish film so as to accommodate an international cast and as a lingua franca for transnational negotiation. Starring American actors Daren McGavin, Burgess Meredith, and Patricia Neal and French actress Stéphane Audran, this political thriller pays homage to Hollywood genre films – notably Welles' *The Lady from Shanghai* (1947). Shot in a clever mix of Madrid streets and the northern port city of Vigo, *Hay que matar a B* is set in a fictitious Latin American dictatorship, inviting symbolic readings that can apply to a generic Latin American country or to the political specificity of Spain (Kinder 1993: 353) (see Figure 2.4). Though it did not do well commercially, due partly to Borau's limited experience as a producer in marketing an unconventional Spanish film abroad, the film remains important for its break with the largely arthouse approach that defined New Spanish Cinema. Instead, it espoused an independent popular cinematic mode, in the style of Orson Welles, that appeared to operate within the Hollywood genre system while working against its commercial features.

Figure 2.4 Stéphane Audran in José Luis Borau's *Hay que matar a B* (1973; prod. El Imán): a cross between one of Hitchcock's icy blondes and a Latin version of Rita Hayworth in Welles's *The Lady from Shanghai* (1947).

After his box-office success, *Furtivos / Poachers* (1975), a not-so-veiled allegory of Spain as what Franco called his "peaceable forest," Borau's next two films further probed the interface between national and transnational cinematic praxis. In *La Sabina* (1979), the use of foreign characters, played by established international actors, engages foreign viewers not so much by bridging Spanish and European culture as by casting a critical, comparative glance at Spain's backwardness. The self-referentiality of the film's scopic regime is explicit in its focus on the tourist gaze at that most highly mythified Spanish mise-en-scène: Andalusia. The film highlights the contrast between the sensuousness of the natural setting, mirrored in the seductive female body (Ángela Molina), and the cerebral response of the foreign intellectual. The result is a cerebral text, as Borau has acknowledged (Martínez de Mingo 1997: 87) that nonetheless plays with the transparency of Hollywood narrative construction.

The defining point of the Borau transnational "adventure," as critics and film historians have called it, was the largely unsuccessful *On the Line / Río abajo* (1983), whose English original title foregrounds the question of borders. A Spanish–US coproduction shot in English in Texas, the film builds on the affective landscape of encounter at the heart of *La Sabina*, lacing it with Hollywood generic inscriptions that blur the sense of the local. Set in a US–Mexican border town, the plotline depicts the love affair between a US border patrolman (David Carradine) and a Mexican prostitute (Victoria Abril), in a striking homage to another great Welles genre film,

Touch of Evil (1958). The film's hybridity – Spanish-made, Mexican-looking, and, in its English-language version, ostensibly American – proved problematic, failing to appeal as a Mexican film but not being identifiably Spanish either. The shortcomings of the film festival system's classification of entries according to nationality was made evident when *On the Line* was denied entry to the Berlin Film Festival because it did not "look" or "sound" Spanish. In many ways, Borau's ambitious, complex vision of the transnational outpaced his financial resources and ability to tap into overseas distribution networks. It would take a subsequent generation of producers to learn how to successfully negotiate the multiple marketing and artistic interests that define the Spanish transnational filmic experience.

By far the principal and most prolific producer of the transition period (stretching back to the early 1970s and continuing into the 1990s and beyond) was Andrés Vicente Gómez, who had worked as an international distribution agent for Querejeta's productions. His first task had been to secure international distribution for Saura's *La madriguera / Honeycomb* (1969), Querejeta's first production with an international cast (Geraldine Chaplin, Per Oscarsson). Having set up his own production company, Eguiluz Films, in 1967, Gómez would in 1972 produce a version of *Treasure Island* directed by John Hough and Andrea Bianchi and starring Orson Welles – the first of a series of collaborations with the legendary Hollywood renegade, including Welles' *F for Fake* (1973) and the never completed *The Other Side of the Wind*. Gómez went on to establish two of the most enterprising and ambitious Spanish production/distribution companies: Iberoamericana Films in Madrid in 1983 and Lola Films in Barcelona in 1992. These companies, intimately involved in coproductions, constituted a major effort to radically internationalize Spanish cinema in accordance with the Socialist government's promotional tagline "Cine español para el mundo" (Spanish Cinema for the World).

Gómez's role as producer-distributor was noteworthy for the intense, complex texture of the transnational machinery underpinning his activities. These encompassed multiple avenues of production and distribution, forging important connections that helped to normalize the international circulation of Spanish films. During the 1980s and 1990s, in addition to promoting a number of novice Spanish filmmakers, he secured overseas distribution for the work of young auteurs coming into their prime (Fernando Trueba, Almodóvar) and for established auteurs (Saura, Mario Camus, Pilar Miró, Vicente Aranda, Jaime Chávarri, Gutiérrez Aragón, José Luis García Sánchez, and Bigas Luna (whose professional name omits his given names)). Gómez was additionally responsible for expanding coproductions with Latin America – for example, Álex de la Iglesia's *Perdita Durango* (1997), and adaptations of stories by Jorge Luis Borges for Televisión Española (TVE; Spanish state television), such as Chávarri's *La intrusa / The Intruder* (1986), Gerardo Vera's *La otra historia de Rosendo Juárez / The Other Story of Rosendo Juárez* (1990), Saura's *El sur / The South* (1991), and Argentine Héctor Olivera's *El evangelio según Marcos / The Gospel according to Mark* (1991). During this same period, Gómez produced films by prominent Latin American filmmakers (Argentine Lautaro

Murúa and Olivera; Peruvian Francisco Lombardi; Mexican Gabriel Retes). He also produced John Malkovich's Spanish–US coproduction *The Dancer Upstairs* (2002), starring Javier Bardem in a genre film of political intrigue set in an unnamed Andean country. Though this last project was an apparent break from his collaboration with Latin American directors, the film, spoken in English but rooted in a Latin American political reality, should be seen as part of Gómez's continuing efforts to develop a prestigious Hispanic-based cinema with a broad transnational appeal.

Gómez's objectives when selecting films for production were threefold. First, as he has stated (Gómez 2001: 70), to make Spanish films that could be exported to a number of overseas constituencies, to compensate for the acknowledged smallness of the Spanish market. Second, to acquire prestige by nurturing auteurs. And third, to prioritize projects that could bridge the gap between the presumed narrowness of Spanish tastes and those of international audiences. This included supporting films that showed historical linkages between Spain and other countries, such as Saura's *El Dorado* (1988) or *Goya en Burdeos / Goya in Bordeaux* (1999), Bigas Luna's *Huevos de oro / Golden Balls* (1993), and Trueba's *Two Much* (1995) – the last two treating contemporary Spanish links to US Latino culture. These films reinforce a sense of borderless cultural spaces while promoting a group of recognizable Spanish stars who, over the coming decades, would become the faces and voices of that Hispanic transnation – Antonio Banderas, Javier Bardem, and Penélope Cruz being the most prominent. Gómez's productions have garnered major international prizes: an Oscar (Trueba's *Belle Époque / The Age of Beauty*, 1993); prestigious awards at Berlin, Cannes, and Venice; and, at home, more Goyas – the Spanish equivalent of the Oscars, given by the Academia de las Artes y las Ciencias Cinematográficas de España (Spanish Film Academy) – than any other Spanish producer in the Film Academy's quarter-century history.

Gómez has argued (2001: 71) that the producer is an essential figure since he has the overall vision required to channel the director's creative energies and talents. Yet, by contrast with Querejeta and Borau, the scale of Gómez's activities is so immense that it does not allow for intimate intervention by the producer in the direction of individual films. What Gómez has provided is, as he says, that necessary broader vision that is capable of translating transnational aesthetics into markets. In his case, the producer's authorial vision has meant emulating Hollywood's polished production values and star system, and a flexible approach to questions of cultural specificity. With his activities in both Europe and the United States, Gómez has succeeded in developing films that normalize the cultural hybridity that critics and scholars regard as the hallmark of transnational cinema (Fornet 1997: xiii–xviii), through the sheer volume of his productions as well as their nuanced border-crossing aesthetic. This is much in evidence in key Gómez productions of the late 1980s and early 1990s: for example, Almodóvar's *Matador* (1986) and Bigas Luna's Iberian myths trilogy – *Jamón jamón* (1992), *Huevos de oro / Golden Balls*, and *La teta y la luna / Tete and the Moon* (1994) – are films that self-referentially act out their Spanishness (in the last case, Catalanness) for international as well as national audiences.

A contemporary of Gómez, Gerardo Herrero, has carved out a distinctive place for himself by expanding still further the volume and complexity of the Gómez network, particularly in building bridges between Spain and Latin America. Starting out as a filmmaker, with only mild commercial success, he became an independent producer with his founding of Tornasol Films in 1987, which produced his own films and several early works by promising young Spanish filmmakers. Over the years, his vision expanded beyond Spanish borders with productions of films by Portuguese director Manoel de Oliveira, Britain's Ken Loach (*Tierra y Libertad / Land and Freedom*, 1995), and a significant number of films by noted Latin American directors. These include the Peruvian Lombardi's *La boca del lobo / The Mouth of the Wolf* (1988), *Caídos del cielo / Fallen from Heaven* (1990), and *Tinta roja / Red Ink* (2000); the Cuban Tomás Gutiérrez Alea's *Guantanamera* (1995), as well as Gutiérrez Aragón's Cuban–Spanish film *Una rosa de Francia / A French Rose* (2006); the Mexican Arturo Ripstein's *El coronel no tiene quien le escriba / No One Writes to the Colonel* (1999) and María Novaro's *Sin dejar huellas / Without a Trace* (2000); and a notable series of Argentine films: Eliseo Subiela's *El lado oscuro del corazón / The Dark Side of the Heart* (1992), Adolfo Aristarain's *Martín Hache / Martin (H)* (1997), Marcelo Pinyero's *Plata quemada / Burnt Money* (2000), plus three important films by Juan José Campanella: *El hijo de la novia / Son of the Bride* (2001), *Luna de Avellaneda / Avellaneda's Moon* (2004), and the Oscar-winning *El secreto de sus ojos / The Secret in Their Eyes* (2009).

For Herrero in the 1980s and 1990s, as for Gómez in the 1970s and 1980s, the effort to expand the geographic imaginary of Spanish cinema relied heavily on a series of institutional supports: subsidies from the Spanish government in the 1980s, subsequently from the European Community (Eurimages and MEDIA), and, beginning in 1997, from Ibermedia, which made possible Gómez's Latin American coproductions. Underpinning this financial support was a conceptualization of the transnational affective bonds that define Spain in Europe while at the same time defining the Spanish-language transnational community. A lynchpin of Herrero's work as producer-author has been his connection to Argentine cinema generally and to Argentine auteur in exile, Adolfo Aristarain, in particular. In the years following Argentina's return to democracy in 1983, Aristarain's films consistently involved international coproductions, primarily with Spain, earning him the dubious accolade of being an invention of Spanish producers. His much-praised 1992 film *Un lugar en el mundo / A Place in the World*, nominally an Argentine–Uruguayan coproduction, was built around a strong cast that reflected its theme of historical and cultural continuities between Spain and Argentina: Argentine actor Federico Luppi, Spaniard José Sacristán, and Cecilia Roth, born in Argentina but with important screen credits in Spanish cinema of the 1980s – most prominently Zulueta's *Arrebato / Rapture* (1980) (see Chapter 21) and early works by Pedro Almodóvar (see Chapter 5). *Un lugar en el mundo* became a major hit in Latin America and Spain, establishing Aristarain's status as a transnational filmmaker.

That status was put to the test by *Martín Hache*, coproduced by Herrero. The film, viewed as Aristarain's masterpiece, picks up conceptually where *Un lugar* left off. In the story of Martín Etchenique (Federico Luppi) – a self-exiled screenwriter living in Madrid who is forced to take in his nineteen-year-old son, also named Martín and nicknamed "Hache" ("H," the first letter of the Spanish for son, *hijo*) – Aristarain has his protagonist ruminate about the nature of father–son relations, bonds to a homeland, and filmmaking. The protagonist's rejection of national affiliations is contested by other characters, setting up a self-referential debate on the relation of identity politics to nation. Though shot almost entirely in Madrid, with one brief early scene in Buenos Aires, the dialogue and musical background continually reinforce the sense of a fluid mise-en-scène that undercuts the usual cinematic affirmation of local space. At the film's end, when Hache returns to Buenos Aires, he leaves his father a video explaining his motives, forcing Martín to acknowledge his nostalgia not for people but places. The film's final position is thus unusually complex: rejecting the "borderless" global position that has defined the protagonist, *Matín Hache* opens up a "slip zone" in which the dynamics of local rootedness and the global are placed under interrogation by characters and audience.

Though operating on a much more modest scale than Gómez or Herrera, Agustín Almodóvar should also be considered here as the producer-author responsible for the strong international profile of El Deseo, the production company he and his director brother Pedro Almodóvar founded in 1986 (see Chapter 14). The aim was to control the production costs of Pedro's films and to ensure appropriate distribution beyond Spain. This family collaboration freed Pedro to devote himself more fully to filmmaking while his younger brother developed the strategies and alliances that would give the Almodóvar imprimatur a presence surpassing the company's limited resources.

The transnational stylistics of Almodóvar's films has long been recognized by film scholars. The integration of Latin American cultural sounds (particularly songs) and images into his work is balanced by the conscious imitation of Hollywood (Sirk, Hitchcock, Cukor). He has also integrated Latin American actors into his films, from Argentine Cecilia Roth in his first film to the star turn of Gael García Bernal in *La mala educación* / *Bad Education* (2004). As Triana Toribio (2007: 159) notes, some of Almodóvar's early films, such as *¿Qué he hecho yo para merecer esto?* / *What Have I Done to Deserve This?* (1985), which includes a German plotline and filming outside Spain, might also qualify as transnational cinema. International coproduction did not begin in earnest for El Deseo until collaboration in the early 1990s with French-based Ciby 2000, however; this initiated a stage in the company's development in which Latin American connections also became part of its growth strategy. One of the earliest of these definition-bending coproductions was

Guillermo del Toro's *El espinazo del diablo / The Devil's Backbone* (2001), shot in Spain by a Mexican director with an Argentine, Mexican, and Spanish cast. As with Buñuel's transposition of *Viridiana* from Mexico to Spain, the script was reworked, changing the setting from the Mexican Revolution to the Spanish Civil War.

More conventional approaches to Latin American coproductions since the turn of the millennium have included modest El Deseo joint-venture funding for Chilean Andrés Wood's *La fiebre del loco / Loco Fever* (2001), Mexican Paul Leduc's *Cobrador / In God We Trust* (2006), and Argentine Lucrecia Martel's *La niña santa / The Holy Girl* (2004) and *La mujer sin cabeza / The Headless Woman* (2008). Esther García, El Deseo's production manager, has emphasized that the main criterion for any coproduction is that "they find quality in the project but that this quality [is] attained without the need for an inflated budget" (Triana Toribio 2007: 158) – "quality" meaning a preference for arthouse films or those willing to experiment with generic conventions (Triana Toribio 2007: 158). In effect, coproductions taken on by El Deseo must be aligned with the broad contours that have defined Almodóvar's own cinema over the decades. The El Deseo imprimatur has worked effectively to secure broad transnational audiences for some of these coproductions by Latin American directors, especially in Spain as the Almodóvar brand becomes increasingly associated with a pan-Hispanic cinematic culture. It is perhaps no coincidence that El Deseo should also have coproduced Isabel Coixet's *My Life Without Me* (2003) and *The Secret Life of Words* (2005), which develop aesthetic forms disengaged from Spanish markers of place and language (see Chapter 14 and Chapter 19). Shot in English in Canada and the Gulf of Mexico respectively, the actors in these films are well-known American independent actors, Tim Robbins and Lili Taylor, which reaffirms Borau's assertion of a Spanish cinema without borders.

The foregrounding of the producer-author disrupts simplistic views of cinematic transnationalism as a series of formulaic categories related narrowly to marketing. As Ezra and Rowden (2006), Palacio (1999), Triana Toribio (2007), and others have noted, the notion of transnational cinema is today increasingly based on audience factors, expanding views of what constitutes Spanish filmmaking and challenging our understanding of who the principal public is. An instance is the career path of Alejandro Amenábar (see Chapter 5), discovered by José Luis Cuerda and developed through Cuerda's production company, Las Producciones del Escorpión. Amenábar's two most recent films – *The Others* (2001), a super-coproduction involving Las Producciones del Escorpión, Sogecine, and Cruise/Wagner and distributed internationally by Miramax, and the equally ambitious *Agora* (2009), with a fifty-million-euro budget, coproduced by Spanish companies (Fernando Bovaira's Mod Productions, Telecinco Cinema, and Canal + España) – are spoken in English and boast international stars Nicole Kidman and Rachel Weisz respectively. The lack of Spanish specificity in the story, setting, and cast of these films suggests the inevitable dissolution of the nation as an operative category for classifying film productions. This is especially notable in *Agora*, a historical drama set in Roman Egypt concerning the female philosopher Hypatia, brutally killed by a Christian mob. There is little beyond the director's renown to suggest that this is a "Spanish" film. The persistence and growth of the transnational dimension of Spanish cinema, while a response to shrinking local markets, is also a recognition of the common ground, given artistic expression by the producer, that links communities of spectators around the acknowledgment of shared experiences, imparted through a medium that has become increasingly globalized. In this system, the role of the producer is to reconcile aesthetic and commercial factors and to author strategies of communication appropriate to a borderless mediasphere.

The Latin American Connection (Alberto Elena)

While the transnational dimension of Spanish cinema has been complex and variegated, it can be plausibly argued that the Spanish film industry has, from a very early stage, enjoyed a privileged relationship with Latin America – equal, if not greater, in quantity and intensity to its many other transnational connections. This section will focus on this particular geographical relationship. The many, not always rigorous, ways in which the term "transnational" has been applied to cinematic practice are hard to pin down, but in the Latin American case a broad repertory of modes of cooperation needs to be considered. Ranging from commercial transactions (film stock, equipment, and films) to the exchange of film professionals (due to contractual arrangements, migration, or exile), from common distribution strategies to frequent coproductions or the creation of funding bodies, the cinematic relationship between Spain and Latin America undoubtedly constitutes an example of what Mette Hjort has called "strong forms of transnational filmmaking" (2010: 14).

As noted at the start of this chapter, and while accepting the validity of other definitions of the transnational, the wide range of models of cooperation between Spain and the Spanish-speaking countries of Latin America can be seen as a prime example of the "affinitive transnationalism" that characterizes world cinema. By this term is meant "a concept of ethnic, linguistic, and cultural affinity that was believed to make cross-border collaboration particularly smooth and therefore cost-efficient, pleasurable, and effective" (Hjort 2010: 17). Although not all periods and relevant cases have been sufficiently studied to date (Elena 2005a; De la Vega Alfaro and Elena 2009), and indeed the origins of this cooperation are still somewhat obscure, it can be asserted that it was the advent of sound that marked a milestone in this process, not least because it was underpinned by the Congreso Hispanoamericano de Cinematografía (Spanish American Film Congress) held in Madrid in October 1931, fed by the nascent but highly influential ideology of *Hispanidad* (Hispanicity) that had been formulated during the Primo de Rivera dictatorship of 1923–30 and would continue to be an important factor, in its successive reworkings, until at least the end of the Franco dictatorship (Pike 1971; Pérez Montfort 1992; Sepúlveda 2005).

This foundational congress (it would have two successors in 1948 and 1966) can be seen as an urgent attempt to establish a pan-Hispanic front, under Spanish leadership, to counteract the devastating effects of Hollywood's foreseeable hegemony in the sound era: language, together with music, was to be the essential weapon of resistance and the key instrument for forging the transnational basis of cinemas in Spanish (D'Lugo 2010). The dream of a vast Spanish-speaking market for film – over 130 million viewers, according to statistics of the time – fitted with the agenda of Hispanic revivalism and its "regenerationist" political inflection within the metropolis: Spain, it was felt, needed to recover a central role on the international stage and the best way of doing that was to capitalize on its influence in Latin America. This notion was so deeply ingrained that the 1948 Certamen Cinematográfico Hispanoamericano (Spanish American Film Competition), promoted by the Franco regime at a time when it was increasingly formalizing diplomatic relations with the countries of Latin America, did little more than repeat the assumptions and aspirations of the 1931 congress, though this time with more tangible results, direct and indirect (Tuñón 2001).

Between 1931 and 1948, however, the dynamic of relations between the Spanish and Spanish American film industries had been altered by a major factor: the exile of many Spanish film workers in the wake of Republican defeat in the Civil War. Professional exchanges were not new: just as the Spaniards Antonio Moreno and Manuel Noriega had made a strong contribution to the development of Mexican cinema, and Manuel Trullen had played a key role in getting the Peruvian film industry off the ground, so too the Mexicans Miguel Contreras Torres and Raphael J. Sevilla, the Peruvian Richard Harlan, and the Chilean Adelqui Millar, among others, had filmed in Spain from the late 1920s to the outbreak of war in 1936. But this bore no comparison to the substantial flow of Spanish film professionals to different parts of Latin America as political refugees. Mexico and Argentina may have played a special role in this process, but the Spanish film industry left its traces in practically every part of Latin America. In addition to celebrated figures such as the directors Luis Buñuel, Carlos Velo, and Luis Alcoriza, a significant number of musicians, set designers, critics, and even poster artists made a major contribution in this respect (Gubern 1976; Gorla 1996). Films such as *Bodas de sangre / Blood Wedding* (Edmundo Guibourg, 1938), building on the successful performance of Lorca's play in Argentina by Margarita Xirgu's theater company in 1933, and *La barraca / The Cabin* (Roberto Gavaldón, 1944), the Mexican adaptation of Vicente Blasco Ibáñez's novel made with the cream of the Spanish exile community in Mexico, are emblematic projects but in no way untypical of the deep artistic symbiosis resulting from this migratory influx.

The legacy of Spanish exiles to Latin American cinema would be long-lasting as they acclimatized fruitfully to local film cultures and practices.

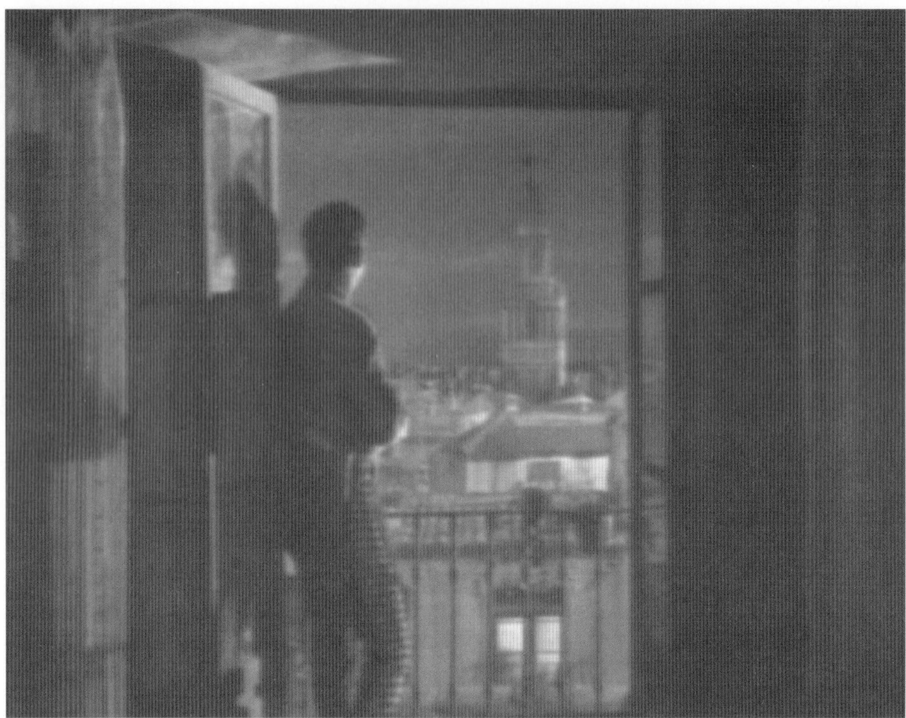

Figure 2.5 Mexican heart throb Jorge Negrete surveys Seville, represented by the iconic image of the Giralda, in the first Spanish–Latin American coproduction, *Jalisco canta en Sevilla* (Fernando de Fuentes, 1948; prod. Chamartín).

Conversely, the 1948 Certamen Cinematográfico Hispanoamericano would provide an incentive and productive framework for many Latin American actors and directors to film in Spain in the 1950s. *Jalisco canta en Sevilla / Jalisco sings in Seville* (Fernando de Fuentes, 1948), a folkloric comedy starring superstar Jorge Negrete and a young Carmen Sevilla (Díaz López 1999), would initiate the wave of Spanish–Latin American coproductions, a substantial corpus that by now amounts to over seven hundred titles and historically has constituted a large proportion of the overall number of Spanish coproductions with other countries (see Figure 2.5). Led by the indefatigable producer Cesáreo González (Dapena 2004; Castro de Paz and Cerdán 2005; see Chapter 14), with CIFESA, Unión Films, and several smaller producers playing a supporting role, Mexican stars such as María Félix and Arturo de Córdova, and Argentine stars such as Libertad Lamarque, Luis Sandrini, and José Iglesias "El Zorro" would become regular fixtures on Spanish screens, immediately recognizable to viewers. Less popular but no less proficient, directors such as Luis César Amadori, Tulio Demicheli, and Luis Saslavsky (from Argentina) and Rafael Baledón, Miguel Zacarías, and even the great Emilio Fernández (from Mexico) would author many of these productions, which were not always successful but were overall deserving of the Spanish public's favor and perfectly compatible with local Latin American markets.

Although it is impossible to analyze this fruitful period of transnational cooperation in detail here, it is crucial to stress how it set up a bridge that, over the years and in different circumstances, would be crossed with different kinds of cultural baggage – for example, in the 1970s and 1980s when it was political exiles from Latin America (the director Patricio Guzmán, the producer Walter Achúgar, and the actors Federico Luppi and Héctor Alterio, among others) who would become productively integrated into the Spanish film industry. Until the late 1980s, coproductions with Latin America were invariably private initiatives since at the time there was no state support specifically for such projects. These transnational collaborations with Latin America were undertaken not only by producers who – like Cesáreo González – reaped the economic benefits of good relations with the Francoist state apparatus but also by UNINCI, the famous production company linked to key figures in the left-wing opposition, which launched ambitious projects with Mexico and Argentina (Salvador Marañon 2006). Similar private collaborations continued throughout the years of the transition to democracy. In this sense, there is a clear continuity in coproduction policies between Spain and Latin America that transcends specific political scenarios while evidently being shaped by them.

The commemorative frenzy accompanying the 1992 celebration of the fifth centenary of the "discovery" of America, under the Socialist Government, marked the start of a new stage in this process. Under the aegis of Spanish state television and the Sociedad Estatal Quinto Centenario (the state body for the fifth-centenary commemorations), an ambitious policy of coproductions with Latin America was launched during the period 1987–92, with an investment – according to some sources (Hoefert de Turégano 2004) – of over twenty million dollars, providing support for over fifty feature films and the occasional television series. The novelty lay in the kind of productions supported: basically arthouse cinema by the top Latin American directors of the day, including some of the big names of the now ailing New Latin American Cinema. Tomás Gutiérrez Alea, Jorge Sanjinés, Miguel Littin, and Ruy Guerra were thus able to make new films, together with younger filmmakers such as María Novaro, Eliseo Subiela, Orlando Rojas, and others. The experiment met with mixed results, not so much because many of the films did not live up to expectations as because their dissemination was sometimes minimal and generally modest. Spanish state television's brusque withdrawal marked the start of a difficult period until the happy coincidence of several big hits – *Como agua para chocolate / Like Water for Chocolate* (Alfonso Arau, 1992), *Un lugar en el mundo* (Aristarain, 1992) and *Fresa y chocolate / Strawberry and Chocolate* (Tomás Gutiérrez Alea and Juan Carlos Tabio, 1993) – allowed a new wave of private investment from the mid-1990s.

The most recent major stage has been marked by the establishment of the funding body Ibermedia, as a result of a major political agreement at the seventh

Ibero-American Summit, bringing together Latin American heads of state and government and held in Venezuela in 1997 (Falicov 2007; Moreno Domínguez 2008). Financed proportionately by the various participating countries but with a formula allowing an equal voice and vote to all members, the program has since its creation envisaged multiple lines of action; over time, however, the promotion of coproductions has emerged as its central strategy. Although it has received occasional criticism as a tool of neo-colonial domination and, more often and plausibly, as a creaky machine suffering from inherent flaws (Villazana 2010), Ibermedia has, for the first time in the region, created a genuine program for transnational coproduction backed by Spain, Portugal, and the Latin American states and, at least tentatively, a common Spanish-speaking (and, to a lesser extent, Portuguese-speaking) audiovisual space. It is true that – as many critics have claimed – Ibermedia follows a purely industrial model that emphasizes a project's financial prospects over any other factor; but it is equally true that its existence is what has allowed certain countries in the region to develop film production (García Canclini 2008; Ripstein 2008). Regardless of this, it has to date done little or nothing to develop and stimulate common Spanish-speaking and Portuguese-speaking exhibition markets, proving itself incapable of guaranteeing adequate circulation of the products it produces and supports and thereby reproducing the major structural flaws of the earlier model of support offered by Spanish state television. Far from learning from that earlier experience, the lack of interest in tackling the problem of the dissemination of Latin American films in the region remains a historical failure.

Cinematic Relations with the Arab World (Alberto Elena)

Spain's privileged relationship with the various countries of Latin America – embodied, as we have seen, in a long and rich history of cinematic collaboration – has tended to eclipse other initiatives that, while undoubtedly slighter, are of political and cultural interest. A parallel rhetoric of brotherhood – based, of course, on very different assumptions – was after the end of the Civil War directed at the Arab world, in an overt attempt to seek international support to relieve the Franco dictatorship's enforced isolation; indeed, it was the mass vote of the Arab nations, together with that of a significant number of Latin American countries, that allowed Spain's admission to the United Nations in 1955. However, this political courting of the Arab countries led only to a number of incidental collaborations (the shooting of films in North African locations). It was only in the late 1960s that joint initiatives started to materialize. The Spanish–Lebanese coproduction *Como un ídolo de arena / Rimal min dhahab / Golden Sands* (Youssef Chahine, 1967) – a stock melodrama with folkloric touches – offered little potential for future development and was barely screened in Spain. The trailblazer was perhaps the small series of Spanish–Tunisian coproductions sponsored by José María Elorrieta for Lacy Films. Of these, *Gallos de pelea / Fighting Cocks* (Rafael Moreno Alba, 1969) and *Las joyas del diablo / The Devil's Jewels* (José María Elorrieta, 1969) were modest action pictures exploiting the North African landscape's attractions. A more substantial contribution was made in the same year by *Une si simple histoire / A Simple Story* (Abdelatif Ben Ammar, 1969), which explored the difficult topic of mixed marriages between Arabs and Europeans.

This kind of "opportunistic transnationalism" (Hjort 2010) characterizes other collaborative ventures with the Arab world. Although in the late 1980s Spanish state television promoted an ambitious project, *Badis* (Mohamed Abderrahmane Tazi, 1988), it was not widely disseminated or followed up, while the conventional historical blockbuster *La batalla de los tres reyes / Tubul al-nar / Tambuori di fuoco / Bitva tryokh koroley / Drums of Fire* (Suheil Ben Barka and Uchkun Nazarov, 1990) – a failed multinational coproduction also involving Italy and the Soviet Union – was hardly a model to imitate. Llorenç Soler's *Said* (1990), a modest but effective look at immigration coproduced by two small independent companies in Spain and Morocco, raised hopes of increased collaboration, but this did not materialize even after the much-vaunted 1998 Acuerdo de Coproducción y de Intercambio Cinematográfico (Film Coproduction and Exchange Agreement) with Morocco. *La vida perra de Juanita Narboni / Juanita de Tanger / Juanita of Tangier* (Farid Benlyazid, 2005), based on Ángel Vázquez's memorable novel, seemed set to usher in a new era but, yet again, the mediocre result and lack of any follow-up frustrated expectations, leaving modest but inspired projects such as Irene Cardona's comedy *Un novio para Yasmina / A Boyfriend for Yasmina* (2008) as the pointers to an ever-postponed increase in cinematic collaboration with the Arab world, specifically Morocco in this instance.

Spanish Cinema by Immigrant Directors (Alberto Elena)

While we can only speculate about the future of collaborative ventures with the Arab world, the emergence within Spanish cinema of a talented cohort of filmmakers of immigrant origin constitutes an undeniable reality (Elena 2005b, 2005c). The first chapter in this story probably corresponds to the Egyptian Basel Ramsis' *El otro lado: Un acercamiento a Lavapiés / The Other Side: A Portrait of Lavapiés* (2003), a full-length documentary that gives a lucid account of the country's new multicultural reality (see Figure 2.6). This was followed up in the same year by two films by Latin Americans resident in Spain: Ana Torres, with *Si nos dejan / If They Let Us*, and Rolando Pardo, with *Cantando bajo la tierra / Singing on the Underground*, which give a fresh look at immigration in an independent, quasi-artisanal mode. In recent years, film projects linked to this emergent cohort of immigrant origin have increased dramatically, particularly in the field of shorts. Sub-Saharan Africa made

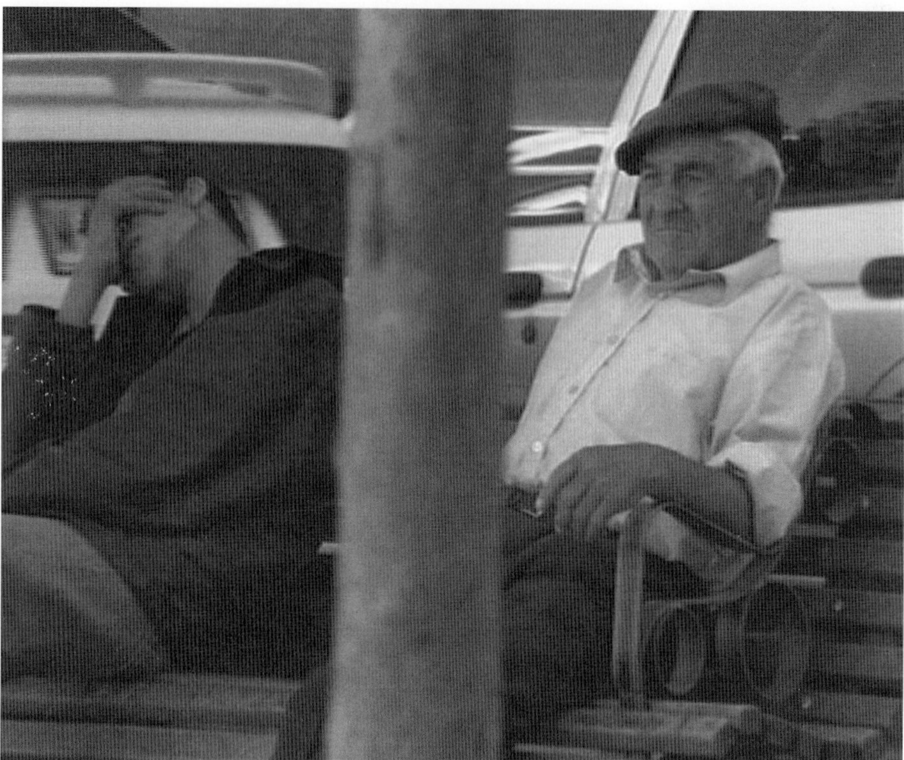

Figure 2.6 A first attempt to depict a broad canvas of immigration in Spain by the Egyptian-born Basel Ramsis: *El otro lado: Un acercamiento a Lavapiés* (2003; prod. Dayra Arts S.L. / Basel Ramsis). Courtesy of Basel Ramsis.

a novel entry into the Spanish film scene with *Querida Bamako / Dear Bamako* (2007), a docudrama on clandestine immigration by the Benin-born and Basque-resident director Omer Oke, codirected by Txarli Llorente. Perhaps the most significant title of all to date is *El truco del manco / The One-Handed Trick* (Santiago A. Zannou, 2008), by a young filmmaker born in Madrid to a father from Benin and a Spanish mother, which won three Goya awards, giving recognition for this promising new form of transnational Spanish cinema. Zannou's most recent film, *La puerta de no retorno / The Gate of No Return* (2011) – a documentary on his father's return to his native country after many years of absence – adds a new, crucial perspective: that of the return in search of roots. This brings the treatment of immigration full-circle, enriching the depiction of transnational flows by considering their multi-directionality.

If the transnational does indeed express "a desire for identification with an expansive imagined community of shared cultural remembrances and other interests not structured by the narrow logic of the state," as argued at the start of this chapter, then this new cinema has an important role to play in today's Spain, affirming a concept of the nation that goes beyond the national, thereby showing that the national and the transnational can indeed work together. Cinema's role in constructing a concept of the nation that goes beyond the national is an issue that will be explored in Chapter 3 and Chapter 4, in relation to the cultural diversity of Spain's historical nationalities and regional cultures.

References

Ángulo, J., Heredero, C. F., and Rebordinos, J. L. (1996) *Elías Querejeta: La producción como discurso*. Donostia-San Sebastián: Filmoteca Vasca.

Benjamin, W. (1978) The Author as Producer. In: Demetz, P. (ed.) *Reflections: Essays, Aphorisms, Autobiographical Writings*. New York: Schocken Books, pp. 220–38.

Borau, J. L. (1983) Without Weapons. *Quarterly Review of Film Studies* 8 (2): 85–90.

Borau, J. L. (ed.) (1998) *Diccionario del cine español*. Madrid: Alianza Editorial.

Castro de Paz, J. L. and Cerdán, J. (eds.) (2005) *Suevia Films-Cesáreo González: Treinta años de cine español*. A Coruña: Xunta de Galicia.

Dapena, G. (2004) *La corona negra*: The International Face of Francoist Cinema. *Studies in Hispanic Cinemas* 1 (2): 119–34.

De la Vega Alfaro, E. and Elena, A. (eds.) (2009) *Abismos de pasión: Una historia de las relaciones cinematográficas hispano-mexicanas*. Madrid: Filmoteca Española.

Díaz López, M. (1999) Las vías de la Hispanidad en una coproducción hispanoamericana de 1948: *Jalisco canta en Sevilla*. In: Díaz López, M. and Fernández Colorado, L. (eds.) *Los límites de la frontera: La coproducción en el cine español (VII Congreso de la AEHC)*. Madrid: Academia de las Artes y las Ciencias Cinematográficas de España, pp. 141–65.

D'Lugo, M. (2010) Aural Identity, Genealogies of Sound Technologies, and Hispanic Transnationality on Screen. In: Durovicova, N. and Newman, K. (eds.) *World Cinemas, Transnational Perspectives*. New York: Routledge, pp. 160–85.

Elena, A. (2005a) Cruce de destinos: Intercambios cinematográficos entre España y América Latina. In: Castro de Paz, J. L., Pérez Perucha, J., and Zunzunegui. S. (eds.) *La nueva memoria: Historia(s) del cine español (1939–2000)*. A Coruña: Vía Láctea Editorial, pp. 332–76.

Elena, A. (2005b) Representaciones de la inmigración en el cine español: La producción comercial y sus márgenes. *Archivos de la Filmoteca* 49: 54–65.

Elena, A. (2005c) Latinoamericanos en el cine español: Los nuevos flujos migratorios, 1975–2005. In: *Cine y migraciones: La experiencia hispanoamericana*. Special issue of *Secuencias: Revista de Historia del Cine* 22: 107–33.

Ezra, E. and Rowden, T. (2006) General Introduction. In: *Transnational Cinemas: The Reader*. New York: Routledge, pp. 1–12.

Falicov, T. (2007) Programa Ibermedia: Co-Production and the Cultural Politics of Constructing an Ibero-American Audiovisual Space. In: Lee, H.-S. (ed.) *Hybrid Media, Ambivalent Feelings,* Dossier in *Spectator* 27 (2): 21–30.

Fornet, A. (1997) Foreword. In: Stock, A. M. (ed.) *Framing Latin American Cinema: Contemporary Critical Perspectives*. Minneapolis: University of Minnesota Press, pp. xi–xviii.

García Canclini, N. (2008) Ibermedia y la coproducción cinematográfica transnacional. *La Jornada de Oriente* (September 8). Online at: www.lajornadadeoriente.com.mx/2008/09/08/puebla/cancli16.php (accessed May 12, 2009).

García Fernández, E. (1998) Coproducción. In: Borau, J. L. (ed.) *Diccionario del cine español*. Madrid: Alianza Editorial, pp. 251–3.

Gómez, A. V. (2001) *El sueño de Andrés Vicente Gómez*. Málaga: Festival de Cine Español de Málaga.

Gorla, P. L. (1996) El exilio del cine español en Hispanoamérica. In: De Llera Esteban, L. (ed.) *El último exilio español en América*. Madrid: Editorial Mapfre, pp. 705–40.

Gorostiza, J. (1997) *Directores artísticos del cine español*. Madrid: Cátedra / Filmoteca Española.

Gubern, R. (1976) *Cine español en el exilio, 1936–1939*. Barcelona: Editorial Lumen.

Heredero, C. F. (1993) *Las huellas del tiempo: Cine español 1951–1961*. Valencia: Filmoteca Generalitat Valenciana.

Hjort, M. (2010) On the Plurality of Cinematic Transnationalism. In: Durovicova, N. and Newman, K. (eds.) *World Cinemas, Transnational Perspectives*. London: Routledge, pp. 12–33.

Hoefert de Turégano, T. (2004) The International Politics of Cinematic Coproduction: Spanish Policy in Latin America. *Film and History* 34 (2): 15–24.

Kinder, M. (1993) *Blood Cinema: The Reconstruction of National Identity in Spain*. Berkeley: University of California Press.

Marías, M. (1985) Borau en la frontera. In: *Cine español 1975–1984*. Murcia: Aula de Cine, pp. 103–9.

Martínez de Mingo, L. (1997) *José Luis Borau*. Madrid: Fundamentos.

Merayo, P. (2001) Agustín Almodóvar: Productor de cine. *La Voz de Avilés* (November 28), 83–4.

Moreno Domínguez, J. M. (2008) Diversidad audiovisual e integración cultural: Analizando el Programa Ibermedia. *Comunicación y Sociedad* (nueva época): 95–118.

Palacio, M. (1999) Elogio posmoderno de las coproducciones. In: *Los límites de la frontera: La coproducción en el cine español*. Special issue of *Cuadernos de la Academia* 5: 221–35.

Pardo, A. (2007) Spanish Co-Productions: Commercial Needs or Common Culture? An Analysis of International Co-Productions in Spain from 2000 to 2004. In: Barriales-Bouche, M. and Attignol Salbodon, M. (eds.) *Zoom In, Zoom Out: Crossing Borders in Contemporary European Cinema*. Newcastle: Cambridge Scholars Publishing, pp. 89–127.

Pavlović, T. (2003) *Despotic Bodies and Transgressive Bodies: Spanish Culture from Francisco Franco to Jesús Franco*. Albany: State University of New York Press.

Pérez Montfort, R. (1992) *Hispanismo y Falange: Los sueños imperiales de la derecha española en México*. México: Fondo de Cultura Económica.

Pike, F. B. (1971) *Hispanismo, 1898–1936: Spanish Liberals and Conservatives and their Relations with Spanish America*. Notre Dame: University of Notre Dame Press.

Ripstein, A. (2008) Por un cine peligroso. Address to I Congreso de la Cultura Iberoamericana (Mexico, October 1–5), reprinted in *Cahiers du Cinéma España* 17 (November): 48–9.

Salvador López, A. (2004) El "caso" *Viridiana*. *Archivos de la Filmoteca* 47: 10–47.

Salvador Marañón, A. (2006) *De "¡Bienvenido, Mr. Marshall!" a "Viridiana." Historia de UNINCI: Una productora cinematográfica bajo el franquismo*. Madrid: EGEDA.

Sepúlveda, I. (2005) *El sueño de la Madre Patria: Hispanoamericanismo y nacionalismo*. Madrid: Fundación Carolina / Marcial Pons Historia.

Triana Toribio, N. (2003) *Spanish National Cinema*. London: Routledge.
Triana Toribio, N. (2007) Journeys of El Deseo between Nation and the Transnational in Spanish Cinema. *Studies in Hispanic Cinemas* 4 (3): 151–63.
Tuñón, J. (2001) Relaciones de celuloide: El Primer Certamen Cinematográfico Hispanoamericano. Madrid, 1948. In: Lida, C. E. (ed.) *México y España en el primer franquismo, 1939–1950: Rupturas formales, relaciones oficiosas*. México: El Colegio de México, pp. 121–61.
Valck, M. de (2006) *Film Festivals: History and Theory of a European Phenomenon that Became a Global Network*. Amsterdam: University of Amsterdam.
Villazana, L. (2010) *Transnational Financial Structures in the Cinema of Latin America: Programa Intermedia in Study*. Saarbrücken: VDM Verlag Dr. Müller.

Further Reading

Aguilar, C. (ed.) (1999) *Cine fantástico y de terror español 1990–1983*. Donostia-San Sebastián: Donostia Kultura.
De España, R. (2002) *Breve historia del Western Mediterráneo*. Barcelona: Glénat.
De la Madrid, J. C. (ed.) (1996) *Primeros tiempos del cinematógrafo en España*. Gijón: Universidad de Oviedo.
Fernández-Armero, A. (1995) *Una aventura americana. Españoles en Hollywood*. Madrid: Compañía Literaria.
Franco, J. (2004) *Memorias del tío Jess*. Madrid: Santillana.
García de Dueñas, J. (1993) *¡Nos vamos a Hollywood!* Madrid: Nickel Odeon.
Gubern, R. (1994) *Benito Perojo: Pionerismo y supervivencia*. Madrid: Filmoteca Española.
Gubern, R., Heinink, J. B., Berriatúa, L., et al. (1993) *El paso del mudo al sonoro en el cine español (Actas del IV Congreso de la AEHC)*. Madrid: Editorial de la Universidad Complutense.
Isasi-Isasmendi, A. (2004) *Memorias tras la cámara. Cincuenta años de UN cine español*. Madrid: Ocho y Medio.
Llinás, F. (1989) *Directores de fotografía del cine español*. Madrid: Filmoteca Española.
Maroney, R. (2004) *Swords, Sandals, and Similar Scope Epics*. Morristown: Lulu Books.
Márquez Úbeda, J. (1999) *Almería, plató de cine*. Almería: Instituto de Estudios Almerienses.
Pérez Perucha, J. (1990) *Mestizajes: Realizadores extranjeros en el cine español (1913–1973)*, vol. I. Valencia: Mostra de València.
Ponce, J. M. (2004) *El destape nacional: Crónica del desnudo en la transición*. Barcelona: Glénat.
Ruiz Álvarez, L. E. (2004) *El cine mudo español en sus películas*. Bilbao: Ed. Mensajero.

3

Echoes and Traces

Catalan Cinema, or Cinema in Catalonia

Brad Epps

Other Voices, Other Scripts: Language, Imagery, and Censorship

Early on in Ignacio F. Iquino's *El tambor del Bruch / The Drummer of Bruch* (1948), a historical epic based on the legend of a young drummer who helps his countrymen repel the Napoleonic invasion of Spain in 1808, an impassioned chorus of patriotic combatants, about to be executed in a manner reminiscent of Goya's famous painting, calls for independence.[1] Amid the repeated cries of "viva la independencia," a lone phrase in Catalan – "visca la independència" – rings out, seemingly echoing, and quickly fading into, the more multitudinous call in Castilian (see Figure 3.1). Fairly early on in Iquino's *El Judas / Judas* (1952), based on the annual production of the Passion play in the town of Esparraguera, a lone word in Catalan – "Passió" – flashes across the screen, inscribed on a public wall as the protagonist's car rushes by (see Figure 3.2).[2] Although in both cases the Catalan language is reduced to little more than a sonorous or scripted blip, that other mainstay of national identity, land, proves more obdurate in its insistence. For, in both films (by one of the most prolific, ambitious, and wily directors and producers in the history of cinema in Spain), the mythically charged mountain of Montserrat, a signal emblem of Catalan culture, appears: in the religiously inspired *El Judas*, as the proximate site of dramatic action (Esparraguera is not far from Montserrat) as well as the backdrop for the credits, and in the militarily inflected *El tambor del Bruch*, as the site of dramatic action as well as the heroine's name. The appearance of Montserrat, together with the echo-like effect of a single spoken phrase and the trace-like effect of a single written word, might serve, however, as an emblem of

A Companion to Spanish Cinema, First Edition. Edited by Jo Labanyi and Tatjana Pavlović.

Figure 3.1 The invisible echo (*El tambor del Bruch*, Ignacio F. Iquino, 1948; prod. Emisora Films).

another sort: that of the troubled state of Catalan film, and by extension of Catalan national culture, under Francoism, a state that, as we shall see, is also troubled – before, during, and after Francoism – by the vicissitudes of multinational market forces and the persistence of a mononational understanding of the Spanish state.

For nearly forty years, and despite a clearer articulation and relative loosening of censorship during José María García Escudero's second stint as Director General de Cinematografía y Teatro (Director General of Film and Theater) from 1962 to 1968, the Francoist dogma of National-Catholic unity and territorial indissolubility zealously reserved a space of privilege for the "language of the Empire," Castilian, inflated and naturalized as Spanish *tout court* at the expense of all other potentially "Spanish" tongues, Catalan most definitely included.[3] Arguably nowhere – other than the political, juridical, and military system, of course – was such monolingual imposition more doggedly in evidence than in the area of cinematic production, where only a handful of films, and almost always with great difficulty, were allowed to express themselves in Catalan. When they were allowed – as with the Argentine Tulio Demicheli's *La herida luminosa* / *La ferida lluminosa* / *The Wound of Light* (1956), Rafael Gil's *Siega verde* / *Verd madur* / *Green Harvest* (1960, but not appearing in Catalan until 1967), Armando Moreno's *Maria Rosa* (1964), Josep Maria Font's *En Baldiri de la costa* / *Baldiri from the Coast* (1968), Francisco Rovira Beleta's *La llarga*

Figure 3.2 The visible trace in *El Judas* (Ignacio F. Iquino, 1952; prod. IFI).

agonia dels peixos fora de l'aigua / *La larga agonía de los peces fuera del agua* / *The Long Agony of Fish out of Water* (1970), and Vicente Lluch's *Laia* (1971) – it was usually in highly controlled dubbed or double versions, with screenings delayed or limited to smaller towns.

A Catalan-language version of *El Judas* itself, *El Judes*, possibly financed by Catalan exiles in Chile (Comas 2003: 232), was scheduled to be screened in Barcelona but at the last moment did not meet with the approval of the authorities, despite the fact that Iquino took pains to make the film as normatively Catholic as possible (citing the approval of an ecclesiastical advisor specially designated by the Bishop of Barcelona) and despite the fact that the majority of the secondary actors were non-professional, Catalan-speaking inhabitants of Esparraguera who reportedly struggled to speak in as standard a Castilian as possible or who in some cases were simply dubbed. Iquino's attempt to render *El Judas* more realistic by shooting it in the very places where the action takes place, a practice he had already performed in *El tambor del Bruch*, in which the battle scenes were shot on location with the collaboration of the army and the *guardia urbana* (Comas 2003: 118), clearly had its linguistic and cultural limits: the supposedly ecumenical story of Christ's passion, *recounted in Catalan* and, to boot, in a medium noted for its mechanical reproducibility and popular appeal, did not sit well with the monolingual account of national reality that the Francoist authorities sought to advance.

As for the patriotic story of the drummer, it would not be until 2010, with Daniel Benmayor's *Bruc, la llegenda / Bruc, the Manhunt*, that an original version in Catalan, Spanish, and French would appear, a double version aimed at a young audience having appeared in the interim, some seven years after Franco's death: Jorge Grau's *La leyenda del tambor / The Legend of the Drummer Boy* (1981). For some forty years, if not in fact much longer, Catalans could be articulated as good patriots and good Catholics only in Castilian Spanish and only, of course, within the parameters of the Spanish state. As Jordi Feliu aptly put it in *Alícia a l'Espanya de les Meravelles / Alice in Spanish Wonderland* (1978; in Catalan, 1986): "el règim parlava en castellà" (the regime spoke in Castilian).

And yet, echoes and traces of that *other* tongue, Catalan, are nonetheless present in both of the aforementioned films by Iquino, complicating any smoothly monologic discourse on God and country – and cinema in Spain. Interestingly, while the one Catalan word that appears in *El Judas* can be read as the trace of a massive censorial erasure by the guardians of the central Spanish state, the one phrase in Catalan that appears in *El tambor del Bruch* can be heard as the echo of a battered if insistent Catalan national alternative. The echo effect is overdetermined, and mightily so, for, as the film makes clear, legend has it that the sound of the drummer boy's drum, amplified by the mountains of Montserrat, led the French invaders to believe, mistakenly, that they were facing a vast, well-organized army when, in reality, their opponents were largely a ragbag group of Catalan civilians. *El tambor del Bruch*, in other ways quite conventional in its triumphant replay of the "War of Independence," is thus shot through with something ambiguous, for the very call for independence, when uttered in Catalan, necessarily troubles, by pluralizing, the referential force of the "fatherland," putting into play a suppressed Catalan "pàtria" alongside the more powerfully expressed Spanish "patria." After all, different understandings of the struggle against Napoleon are at play in the very fact that the war of resistance and liberation that is commonly known in Spanish as the "Guerra de la Independencia" (War of Independence) is commonly known in Catalan as the "Guerra del Francès" (Frenchman's War). Furthermore, although in 1948 France continued to be perceived by the regime in Madrid as unfriendly, and although the film could thus be taken as a cautionary tale about an increasingly unlikely Allied intervention against the regime as well as about Catalans' presumed willingness to risk their lives in defense of Spain (De España 1993: 49), for many in Catalonia and elsewhere in Spain, France continued to be an ambivalent place of refuge and exile (ambivalent because France, with its appalling concentration camps, hardly welcomed Republican exiles with open arms), and the fast-receding possibility of foreign intervention continued to be the stuff of longing, not fear.

Even though it might be a bit too much to designate *El tambor de Bruch* as "pro-Catalan," as Rafael de España (1993: 40) does, it would be difficult to deny that more than one Catalan spectator, recalling the ephemeral life of the Catalan Republic proclaimed by Francesc Macià in 1931 and again by Lluís Companys in 1934, might have heard in the popular cry for "independència" against well-organized military invaders a different story and an alternative history, beyond the control of the censors or the intentions of the director. As confusingly subjective as the censors often were in their determinations, Iquino's intentions were by no means clear either (intentions, even when clearly expressed as such, rarely are), in no small measure because he had to contend with the dual forces of Spanish state censorship *and* multinational capitalist competition. As De España (1993: 52) has perceptively noted, *El tambor del Bruch*, with its sympathetic portrayal of Catalans as *Spanish* patriots, not only stands in stark contrast to Juan de Orduña's *Agustina de Aragón* (1950), which offers what he calls a "rabiosamente propagandística" (rabidly propagandistic) rendition of the war and whose heroes are members of the army, the church, and the aristocracy, but also suggests, in its reliance on an initially depoliticized civilian protagonist, an affinity to the individualistic antiheroes embodied by Humphrey Bogart and Robert Mitchum in US cinema. The reference to the foreign cinematic tradition whose predominance has repeatedly been characterized as an imperialist invasion and occupation in its own right is not incidental, for Iquino has been both celebrated and denigrated for promoting an industrial and financially viable cinematic practice whose most lucrative model was that of Hollywood. As if ironically replaying the *Senyor Esteve* stereotype of the Catalan as more given to commerce than to art, he has been depicted as calculating, even opportunistic, in his negotiations with the Francoist administration.

Neither a devout Catholic nor a fervent nationalist, whether of Spain or of Catalonia, Iquino nonetheless managed to garner state support for *El tambor del Bruch* and *El Judas* in the form of the much-coveted designations of *Interés Nacional* (National Interest) and *Interés Especial* (Special Interest) and, more generally, to instill a business-like attitude in an otherwise beleaguered Spanish film industry, producing, among scores of other films, three early ventures by Josep Maria Forn: *¿Pena de muerte? / Death Penalty?* (1961), *La ruta de los narcóticos / The Drug Route* (1962), and *José María* (1963). Much more politically daring than Iquino, Forn would later go on to make, in Catalan, two unquestionably "pro-Catalan" films that grappled explicitly with the failed Catalan Republic: *Companys, procés a Catalunya / Companys, Catalonia on Trial* (1979) and *El coronel Macià / Colonel Macià* (2006) (De España 1993: 40; Comas 2003: 231; on Forn, see Quintana 2007). But, before Forn and others – such as Antoni Ribas, with *La ciutat cremada / The Burned City* (1976), Eugeni Anglada, with *La ràbia / Rage* (1972–7; 1978), or Jordi Feliu, with the aforementioned *Alícia a l'Espanya de les Meravelles* – could engage in a more defiantly pro-Catalan filmic practice, and before Jaime Camino could delve more deeply into the trauma of historical memory begun with *España, otra vez / Spain Again* (1968) and continued with *Las largas vacaciones del 36 / Long Vacations of 36* (1976), *La vieja memoria / The Old Memory* (1977), *Dragón Rapide* (1986), and *Los niños de Rusia / The Children of Russia* (2001), Iquino, in the terminal phase of the regime and the first heady days of the democratic transition (which is also, in truth, a restoration), would become one of the pioneers in double versions not of a linguistic but rather of a sexual sort, exporting to foreign markets uncensored copies of films awash with erotic scenes in which the naked female body was offered up to masculine delectation.[4]

Along with a barrage of sex comedies and erotically charged crime capers that came to the fore in the final years of the regime and that virtually exploded in the early years of democracy in what has come to be known as the *destape* or "uncovering," Iquino's double versions capitalized on the prurience of the audience but also on the desire for freedom. Although the desire for freedom was repeatedly fused with the desire for sex, or for showing and seeing sex, and to the point that many otherwise anodyne productions enjoyed a dubiously progressive luster, post-Francoist films such as *L'orgia / The Orgy* (1978), *Salut i força al canut / Catalan Cuckold* (1979), *La quinta del porro / The Pot Generation* (1980), and *Pa d'àngel / Pan de ángel / Angel Bread* (1983), all by Francesc Bellmunt and all of which premiered in Catalan with double versions in Castilian, explicitly linked sexual repression and expression to questions of community, marriage, military service, and religious faith. A number of Castilian-language films, some of which also appeared in double versions in Catalan, offered a much more disturbing vision of sexuality – and of life – in Spain: notably, *Bilbao* (1978) and *Caniche / Poodle* (1979), both by Bigas Luna[5]; *Morbo / Morbidness*, by Gonzalo Suárez (1972); *La oscura historia de la prima Montse / The Dark Story of Cousin Monste*, by Jordi Cadena (1977); *Cambio de sexo / Change of Sex* (1977) and, later, *Amantes / Lovers* (1991), *El amante bilingüe / The Bilingual Lover* (1993), and *Intruso / Intruder* (1993), all by Vicente Aranda; and *Tras el cristal / In a Glass Cage* (1986) and *El mar / The Sea* (2000), two of the most artfully perverse films ever made in the country, both by Agustí Villaronga, whose more recent *Pa negre / Black Bread* (2010), filmed in Catalan and set in the post-Civil War Catalan countryside, won an impressive nine Goyas (Spain's equivalent of the Oscars).

Bilbao is particularly remarkable in its darkly gritty presentation of Barcelona's lower depths, reminiscent of contemporaneous deployments of the urban blight of New York City as the backdrop, if not motivation, for similarly disturbing stories (see Figure 3.3). As if to reinforce the interplay of different locales, the title is a red herring: although it invokes the capital of the Basque Country, whose aspirations to national recognition in many respects resemble those of Catalonia, in the film, "Bilbao" is both the name of a prostitute with whom the protagonist, a fetishistic and voyeuristic photographer, is obsessed and the title of a German song performed by Lotte Lenya. As Ángel S. Harguindey noted in a review published shortly after the film's screening in Cannes, *Bilbao* "va mucho más allá de los problemas y condicionantes del franquismo" (goes well beyond the problems and conditions of Francoism) and "ratifica el concepto de que las películas no son *españolas* o *australianas*, sino básicamente personales" (ratifies the concept that films are not *Spanish* or *Australian*, but personal). In Harguindey's reading, Bigas Luna occupies a world apart and unto himself, an auteur whose personal touch stands in contrast to the collective, political pretensions of Chilean Miguel Littín's *El recurso del*

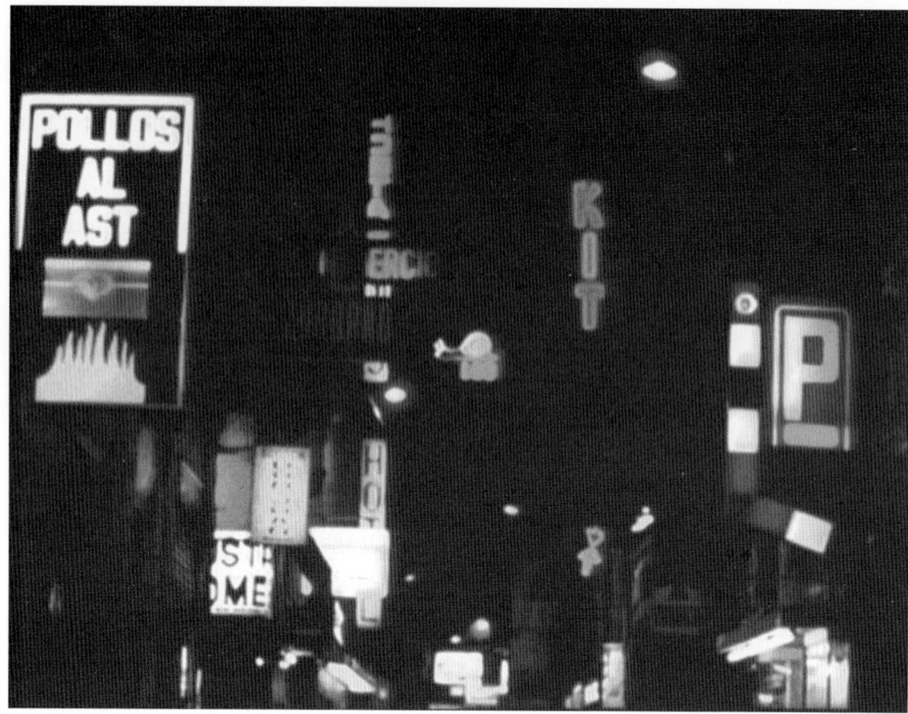

Figure 3.3 Barcelona-cum-New York in *Bilbao* (Bigas Luna, 1978; prod. Figaro-Ona Films).

método / The Recourse to the Method (1978), based on the novel by Alejo Carpentier and screened in Cannes the same year as *Bilbao*. Although it is entirely possible to see *Bilbao* as a devastating portrait of alienation under consumer capitalism, and hence as a *mise en question* of the very auteurist individualism that Harguindey extols, it is by no means simply the politically engaged work of a director like Littín that serves as a counterpoint. Indeed, in Spain, the most immediate and profuse counterpoint is not the often-prohibited work of Littín and other foreigners – nor for that matter the constrained neo-realist work of directors such as Juan Antonio Bardem and Basilio Martín Patino, taken to task, as we shall see, by the antirealist experimenters associated with the Escola de Barcelona (Barcelona School) – but rather the commercial and "industrial" products of someone such as Iquino.

Spectacular (Dis)locations: Art, Business, and Morality

Although Iquino's films are tame in comparison with those of Aranda, Bigas Luna, and Villaronga, they nonetheless point to the appeal of risqué cinematic ventures and to the complex interplay of censorship and freedom, morality and profit, the global and the local. With respect to Iquino, the local refers not just to Catalonia or even Barcelona but also, more specifically still, to a particular neighborhood in the Catalan capital. In the words of Román Gubern (2003c: 12), Iquino "pertenece con toda propiedad a la cultura populista y colorista del Paralelo barcelonés, en donde incardinó precisamente sus estudios de producción" (rightly belongs to the populist and colorful culture of Barcelona's Paral·lel district, where he established his film studios). With its cabarets, music halls, and close proximity to Barcelona's red-light district (variously known as Barri Xino, Districte Cinquè, or Raval), the Paral·lel was indeed a far remove from the National-Catholic pieties of Church, State, and family that undergirded Francoism. The site of dramatic action in films as diverse as *Tuset Street* (begun by Jorge Grau and finished by Luis Marquina, 1968), in which an aging showgirl played by Sara Montiel is calamitously brought into the pretentiously mod sphere of Barcelona's version of Carnaby Street, and *Las alegres chicas de "El Molino" / The Happy Girls of "El Molino"* (José Antonio de la Loma, 1976), in which a variety of sexual dalliances are entertainingly on display, the Paral·lel was one of the earliest locations of cinematic activity in Catalonia (and, hence, in all of Spain). It was preceded only by the Ramblas, where, toward the end of November 1896, a representative of the Lumière brothers, Jean-Claude Villemagne, set up office in the business that two other brothers, the photographers Antonio and Emilio Fernández, popularly known as "Napoleon," had on la Rambla de Santa Mònica (Letamendi and Seguin 2004: 565). In its inception, under the Lumière brothers, Edison, Méliès, Pathé, Gaumont, and others, cinema was indeed geared less to art than to business, and of a rather shady sort at that, with movies screened, often as not, in ramshackle fairs and fly-by-night venues that soon incurred the wrathful opposition of moralists, intellectuals, and politicians who saw in it not only a danger to public safety – fires were not infrequent – but also, and more damningly, an offense to public decency.

As Palmira González (1987), Miquel Porter i Moix (1992), Esteve Riambau (1994), Joan M. Minguet Batllori (2000), and others have demonstrated, cinema, which by the second decade of the twentieth century had spread throughout the Iberian peninsula, was the object of a mixture of intellectual scorn and moral outrage, particularly in its formative years. Eugeni d'Ors, who championed a conservative, institutionally directed concept of Catalan culture known as *noucentisme*, was adamant in his opposition to the new medium, which he characterized in an article from 1906 as a mechanically induced "convulsió gris" (grey convulsion) made of "blancor brutal, entre tenebres" (brutal whiteness amid shadows) in contrast to the natural blue luminosity of the Mediterranean that he extolled as *proper* to Catalonia (D'Ors 1996: 100; see González 1985: 59). D'Ors was not alone in his condemnation. Such major cultural figures as Joan Maragall, Santiago Rusiñol, Josep Carner, Antoni Rovira i Virgili, and Jaume Bofill i Mates also impugned the cinema, though Maragall and Rusiñol, the two foremost figures of *modernisme* that the *noucentistes* likewise rejected, opposed any concerted censorial action. The leading voice for censorship, in conjunction with the much more influential D'Ors, was that of a minor *noucentista*, Ramon Rucabado i Comerna, who launched a campaign against the "cinematographe" from the pages of the review *Cataluña* in 1911 (Minguet Batllori 2000–1: 293). With quasi-apocalyptic fervor, Rucabado railed against the cinema as an affront to public morality and called for governmental intervention in order to stem its putatively nefarious influence on children, the working class, and, indeed, the entirety of society. Linking cinematic spectacle to prostitution, pornography, and degeneracy, Rucabado's moralistic campaign, which brought him into league with the largely anti-Catalanist Comité de Defensa Social (Committee of Social Defense), was consistent with more widespread regenerationist concerns rampant in Spain before and, especially, after its military defeat at the hands of the United States in 1898.

Cinematic spectacle, with its connotations of public and collective vision, was indeed one of the bugbears of the more aesthetically minded D'Ors, who distinguished between the literary endeavors of, for some, such morally questionable writers as Flaubert and Baudelaire and the more readily consumable products on display in cinematic show houses. As Minguet Batllori (2000–1: 299) has noted, screening venues, even as they shifted from itinerant fairs to fixed quasi-theatrical sites in which class divisions were perceptible in the very ordering of space, were nonetheless marked by an "inter-classism" that was at odds with the *noucentistes'* insistence on the hegemony of a cultivated bourgeoisie safely removed from the masses. It is also important to remember, as Julio Pérez Perucha (1995: 22–3) does in an informative account of pre-Republican cinema, that approximately half of the population in Spain was illiterate at the turn of the century, and, as such, sought entertainment, or respite from work, in such visually and musically oriented spectacles as *zarzuelas* (lightweight operettas), bullfights, and comic theater. The first films shot in Spain, by Alexandre Promio, an envoy of the Lumière brothers, confirmed the connection between the newest form of popular spectacle and earlier ones: bullfights and military parades, along with scenes of street life (it is not by accident that Rucabado sees cinema in explicit relation to morality in the street), not only perpetuated deeply rooted stereotypes of Spain but also reinforced a sense of the new medium as eminently populist – and hence as eminently susceptible to politically propagandistic uses. Given the turbulence of the times in which the cinema made it appearance in Spain (the Spanish–American War, the Moroccan conflict, anarchist direct action, anticlericalism, reactionary Catholicism, increasing friction between the working class and the bourgeoisie, burgeoning separatist movements in Catalonia and the Basque Country), it is not surprising that the self-designated arbiters of civic order soon enacted the governmental censorship that D'Ors, Rucabado, and others demanded.

Accordingly, toward the end of 1912, a Royal Decree officially established the censorship of cinematic projects, a measure that was reinforced in 1913 by the Civil Governor in Barcelona – for it was there that cinematic production was then most active – under the title of "Reglamento de Espectáculos" (Regulation of Spectacles) (Martínez Bretón 1993: 112; see Chapter 14). Thus began what

González (1987: 180) has movingly described as "una ombra o fantasma que acompanyarà el nostre cinema en gairebé totes les etapes del seu atzarós camí" (a shadow or phantom that will accompany our cinema in virtually all of the phases of its hazardous trajectory), which flecks, I might add, even the deliberately patriotic and Catholic films of the otherwise salacious and savvy Iquino. Although the moral and political dimensions of censorship were primary, aesthetic and economic considerations also obtained. Charges of artistic turpitude, central to D'Ors' repudiation of the medium, were countered over the next two decades by a diverse array of cultural figures including Víctor Català (Caterina Albert), Carles Soldevila, Josep Maria de Sagarra, Josep Maria Planes, Àngel Ferran, and Josep Palau; Alexandre Plana, arguably the first systematic commentator and theoretician of cinema in Catalonia; Sebastià Gasch and Lluís Montanyà, cosigners, along with Salvador Dalí, of the defiantly "antiartistic" avant-garde *Manifest groc* (Yellow Manifesto); and Adrià Gual, celebrated modernist playwright, founder of the Teatre Íntim, director of the Escola Catalana d'Art Dramàtic (Catalan School of Dramatic Art), and artistic director of the production company Barcinógrafo.[6] Far from bemoaning the cinema as the death of the theater as so many others did, Gual strove to create a cinema of quality, directing films based on Spanish-language classics such as *El alcalde de Zalamea* / *The Mayor of Zalamea* (1914) and on modern works of his own, such as *Misterio de dolor* / *Mystery of Pain* (1914).

Critical as he was to the vindication of cinema as art, Gual built on – and at times contributed to – the work by the pioneers of cinema in Catalonia and, in fact, the Iberian Peninsula as a whole. One pioneeer was Fructuós Gelabert, whose *Salida de los trabajadores de "La España Industrial"* / *Workers Leaving "La España Industrial"* (1897) and *Riña en un café* / *Fight in a Café* (1897, lost but reshot by Gelabert in 1952 in collaboration with Ramon de Baños) are considered to be the first documentary and the first fiction film, respectively, in all of Spain (De Lasa 1988). Another was Segundo de Chomón, born in Teruel but first active in Barcelona, whose dexterity with the fantastic genre has earned him the moniker of "the Spanish Méliès" (Fernández Cuenca 1972; Sánchez Vidal 1992). Others who strove to lesser or greater degrees for an aesthetically viable cinema were Joan Maria Codina, who in collaboration with Gelabert first brought famed Catalanist playwright Àngel Guimerà's *Maria Rosa* to the screen in 1908 (Gelabert had preceded him by adapting Guimerà's most famous play, *Terra baixa* / *Tierra baja* / *Lowlands* in 1907); Josep de Togores, who directed a film based on yet another play by Guimerà, *La festa del blat* / *Fiesta del trigo* / *The Wheat Festival*, in 1914; and Ramon and Ricard de Baños, two brothers who covered a gamut of genres from documentaries and newsreels to historical fictions, melodramas, action-adventure features, and, as if to confirm Rucabado's worst fears, what may well be the first explicit pornographic shorts in the Peninsula, among which was the recently restored *El confesor* / *The Confessor* (1920), possibly commissioned, according to Román Gubern (2003b), by the Count of Romanones for none other than King Alfonso XIII (De Lasa 1996). Needless to say, such early pornographic ventures, far more explicit than Iquino's double versions nearly fifty years later, did not figure in the country's first serious cinematic journal, *Arte y Cinematografía*, published in Barcelona between 1910 and 1936, or in the country's first academic course on cinematic aesthetics, organized by Guillem Díaz-Plaja at the University of Barcelona in 1932.

By the 1920s, and certainly later in the decade when avant-gardists such as Luis Buñuel and Salvador Dalí engaged in it, there could be little doubt as to the aesthetic possibilities of the cinema – though the aesthetic quality of the films actually made was, of course, another matter. Still, the very existence of an innovative journal like *Mirador*, which organized film screenings (including the first showing in all of Spain of the 1929 surrealist masterpiece *Un chien andalou*) and which paid attention to almost everything from the promises and pitfalls of national cinematic production to the growing phenomenon of amateur cinema, stands as testimony to the cultural and aesthetic significance of the new medium.[7] The economic implications, however, were – and continue to be – altogether more vexed. It was not only that artistically, morally, and politically "suspect" films could be profitable, or that profit could prove to be both a powerful disincentive to censorship and a more wily form of censorship in its own right (casting more aesthetically oriented films into a commercially non-viable never-never-land), but also that profit had, both in principle and in practice, a multinational character that outstripped the particularities of established nation-states like Spain, let alone stateless nations like Catalonia. For all the symbolically laden interplays of language and territory, cinema throughout the Spanish state was from the outset an international endeavor, with technological materials and expertise from France, Italy, Denmark, the United States, and other industrialized countries dominating the sector. During World War I, what Riambau (1994: 31) calls the internationalization of Catalan cinema is further fueled by European professionals in exile, a phenomenon that also marks, though on a much grander scale, production in Hollywood, where companies such as Paramount and MGM worked to establish themselves in a Spanish-speaking market that extended to Latin America and the Philippines.

In many respects, the technical nature of cinematic production and distribution is so internationally mixed as to render the very notion of national cinema dubious, if not downright misleading – just as misleading as it is to privilege the name of the director, as I have been doing here, in what is almost always a complex, collaborative endeavor. Be that as it may, nationalism, it seems, will have its way, and not just for nations in dispute, like Catalonia. Accordingly, as early as the second decade of the twentieth century – or perhaps even earlier, in the "patent wars" that marked the highly competitive international debut of cinematic apparatuses themselves – calls for protectionist measures in defense of cinema as a nationally significant industry were increasingly of the order of the day. Notable here is the Mutua de Defensa Cinematográfica Española, a commercial association founded in 1915 that aimed to bring some coherence to a rather chaotic system of cinematic distribution (production in Spain lagging behind that of other countries). Yet it was one thing for companies to come together of their own accord in the name of national unity in order to protect their financial interests and another thing for the government to oversee the industry in the name of national unity in its two-pronged form of political security and civic morality. As Juan Antonio Martínez Bretón (1993: 114) notes, during the 1920s, and especially under the dictatorship of General Miguel Primo de Rivera, "los valores morales de la sociedad van a ser controlados por los poderes públicos, que ven en el cinematógrafo un arma de fácil propagación" (the moral values of society come to be controlled by public forces, which see in the cinematograph an easy arm of propaganda). Though initially supported by sectors of the Catalan bourgeoisie, Primo's regime was bent on centralization and proceeded to dissolve the Mancomunitat de Catalunya in 1925, prohibiting as well all public symbols of Catalanism and persecuting anarchists (the National Confederation of Labor, or CNT, was declared illegal), communists, and others. Although removed from power by early 1930, Primo's campaign of Spanish nationalist centralization, an undeniable precursor of Franco's, marched on.

On April 12, 1930, yet another Royal Decree established a unified censorial apparatus based in Madrid, which met with the ineffective opposition of the Mutua de Defensa Cinematográfica Española, based in Barcelona and accused of unpatriotic leniency by cinematic competitors and centralist politicians in Madrid (Martínez Bretón 1993: 117–18). Thus, even as a system of national protectionism was erected to stem the tide of foreign competitors, whose most assertive representatives hailed from the United States, a system of national centralism was also erected, or better yet reinforced, that made it increasingly clear that Spain was not, at least on a juridical level, a plurinational state. Censorship, which for D'Ors had a largely aesthetic valence and for Rucabado a largely moral one, was also, in short, a matter of internationally inflected mononational politics and finances. Along with the centralizing pull of the mononational state, the homogenizing forces of the international market were such than some national traditions, and languages, were more likely to be promoted, or dismissed, than others. It is in this complex censorial and capitalist context, by no means limited to the first decades of the twentieth century, that any notion of Catalan cinema – or for that matter Spanish cinema – must be located.

Troubled Transitions: The "Talkies," the Republic, the Civil War, the Dictatorship, and Beyond

The advent of the Second Republic in 1931 sparked hopes of change, with regard both to censorship and capitalist competition. Importantly, the late 1920s and early 1930s were also the years in which the cinema underwent one of its most profound transformations: from silence to sound (see Chapter 13). Joaquim Romaguera i

Ramió, in a detailed monograph on the origins of cinema in Catalan (as distinct from cinema in Catalonia), rightly notes that the transformation, at least if understood in terms of a radical cut, is something of a misnomer, for even "silent" films had long been musically and verbally supplemented (1992; see also Cánovas Belchi 2007). While the simplicity of the first "animated views" was such that no supplement was necessary, the upswing in narrative and more complex documentary works soon led entrepreneurs to introduce intertitles and, before the availability of gramophone recordings, to hire musicians and narrators to endow the silent images with atmosphere and voice (Romaguera i Ramió 1992: 26). This practice is beautifully on display in Llorenç Llobet Gràcia's *Vida en sombras / Life in Shadows* (1948, not released until 1953), quite possibly the most astonishingly metacinematic account of the history of cinema in Catalonia produced under Francoism, replete with a short reference in Catalan to a speech by President Companys and a broken statue of the Virgin of Montserrat, both of which function as signs of a violently truncated Catalan national project. Although by no means only because of political turmoil (economic and technologically material factors were also massively at play), a large percentage of silent and early sound films has indeed been lost, including the commercially successful romantic comedy *Mercedes* (Josep Maria Castellví, 1933), which was spoken and sung in Spanish with scenes directly recorded in Catalan (Romaguera i Ramió 1992: 42) and which featured an antagonistic relationship between two fathers, one from Catalonia and the other from Madrid. While it is thus impossible to make any definitive assessment, it seems, as Romaguera has argued, that the overwhelming majority of written intertitles and credits in silent and partially sonorized films were in Castilian, not Catalan, a politically conditioned and market-driven fact that as early as 1923 led at least one journalist to complain that the illiterate Catalan movie-going public was exposed to Castilian, not Catalan, as the language not so much of film as of *writing* itself (Romaguera i Ramió 1992: 43).

The emergence of recorded sound clearly constituted a major event in the history of cinema and, in Spain, reconfirmed and extended the ascendancy of Castilian, leading a number of Catalan critics to lament the passing of the much-touted universality of the image, already compromised, graphically, by intertitles, credits, and publicity. Before that fateful moment, Plana, from his short-lived but ground-breaking column in the evening edition of *La Publicidad* in 1920, had gone so far as to declare (silent) cinema to be "el verdadero y único 'esperanto'" (the true and only Esperanto), the veritable summa of all previous art forms, at once popular and philosophical, accessible to all, and uniquely suited to the perpetually thought-provoking capture of the motility and brevity of life. Sound, with its phenomenal reinstatement, if not indeed renaturalization, of linguistic difference, would lay waste to such an artificial utopia, flickering dumbly across the screen. As a result, a number of writers, especially from the pages of *Mirador*, came to grapple ever more intensely with the question of "national cinema" in both its Spanish and Catalan variants. Sebastià Gasch (1933: 4), for instance, referred to Spain's relation to the United States as that of "una Arcàdia feliç," "un país conquistat," and "una colònia" (a happy Arcadia, a conquered country, and a colony) and placed his hopes in the advancement of locally based companies such as Orphea Film, founded by French producer Camille Lemoine and Andalusian-born director Francisco Elías. Located in one of the buildings of the recently closed International Exposition of 1929 and supported by the Generalitat, it was the first sound studio in the country, opening in 1932 (see Chapter 14). Tellingly, its first project, which became the first "talkie" *produced* in Spain, underscored the international dimension of locally based companies: Elías' *Pax*, filmed in 1932, premiered in Barcelona in mid-1934 not in Catalan, or even in Spanish, but in French with Spanish subtitles (Romaguera i Ramió 1992: 34–5).[8]

Although the Generalitat would later, shortly after the outbreak of Civil War, launch an effort under the guise of Laya Films to promote a cinematic practice in Catalan, Gasch and others writing before the war and during the Republic deemed such a project to be impractical, if not downright utopian: the important thing, they stressed, was not so much cinema in Catalan as cinema made in Catalonia.[9] Describing "national production" in Spanish as the lesser of two evils, Gasch (1933: 4) declared that, "la temptativa sentimental de [Domènec] Pruna, una versió catalana i una altra de castellana, és massa costosa per ésser imitada" (the sentimental attempt by [Domènec] Pruna, one version in Catalan and another in Castilian, is too costly to be imitated). The "sentimental attempt" in question was *El cafè de la Marina* (1933–4), based on a work by Josep Maria de Sagarra, produced by Orphea, and generally considered to be the first feature film in Catalan (Caparrós Lera 1993: 26). The first "talkie" was preceded, nonetheless, by partially sonorized films (usually in the form of accompanying phonographic recordings), now lost, such as *Caramellas* (Josep Amich i Bert, aka "Amichatis," 1928–9), *L'auca del senyor Esteve / Hymn to Senyor Esteve* (Lucas Argilés y Ruiz del Valle, 1928), and a series of musical clips performed by Raquel Meller, among which was the popular Catalan song "El noi de la mare" / "The Mother's Child" or "The Son of Mary." As Joaquim Romaguera i Ramió (1992: 55) makes clear, the first appearance of the Catalan language in sound cinema was through music, some four years before dialogue. Endowed with a lure of universality similar to that of the image, music, when in the form of song, is also shot through with the particularities of language; as such, it signals a tension between the international and the national whose ethical and political charge varies according to context.

Although the days when the mere utterance of Catalan, especially in song, enjoyed a restive, resistant political prestige are long gone, the somewhat muted but unmistakable presence of songs in Catalan in films from the early 1950s to shortly after the death of Franco signals a persistent paradox: song as both a sign of Catalan national identity, pointing to something beyond the current configuration of the Spanish state, and as a note of local or regional color, pointing to something within it.[10] Whatever the case, the one pop-inflected *yé-yé* ditty that Guillermina Motta sings in Catalan in the lone feature film venture by celebrated photographer Ramon Masats, *Topical Spanish* (1972), rings as atypical, or a-topical, and acquires a curious, if indeterminate, political charge, reinforced by the postapocalyptic coda to a narrative of Beatles-like musical success. For, after a series of youthful hijinks in a modish Barcelona, *Topical Spanish* closes in a desolate rural landscape in which an old man, recalling the return to the country by people who had sought fortune in the city, waxes sentimental about a song from the past: "Fantastic Girl," sung, as the title indicates, in English by a group called Los Iberos.

In a diametrically different fashion, though likewise resorting to a postapocalyptic framework, Daniel Mangrané and Carlos Serrano de Osma's *Parsifal* (1951) engages the cult of Wagnerian opera that, centered in Barcelona's Liceu, once characterized the Catalan bourgeoisie, even though the cult certainly counted among its followers less wealthy people as well. Of all of Wagner's works, none enjoyed quite the cachet of *Parsifal* among the so-called "good families" of Catalonia, whose class-specific dreams of grandeur were inflamed by the notion that the site of the Holy Grail was none other than the "sacred mountain" of Montserrat. Portentous in its religiosity and ambiguous in its national implications, *Parsifal* constitutes, as Fèlix Fanés (1986: 348) has so elegantly put it, a work in which "les llegendes del passat resulten el bàlsam per a les ferides del present" (the legends of the past serve as a balm for the wounds of the present). From an international perspective, however, neither of the preceding films – one pop and the other operatic – garnered the attention that accompanied Francesc Rovira Beleta's *Los Tarantos / The Tarantos* (1963), a musically driven story of star-crossed lovers set in a poor neighborhood on the outskirts of Barcelona that was nominated for an Oscar for best foreign film. Starring a vibrant Carmen Amaya, the film resembles a Spanish version of *West Side Story*, which had appeared in movie form some two years earlier, and offers tourist-drenched images of gypsies, flamenco, and amorous passion – so dear to the promotion of Spain as "different" – along with quasi-neo-realist images of social exclusion, racism, and economic marginalization (see Figure 3.4). Not surprisingly, the Catalan language, whether spoken or sung, is absent from *Los Tarantos*, arguably the price for international success, with its profit-driven penchant for stereotypes, but no less arguably a condition of realistic critique.

After all, even Josep Maria Forn, whose Catalanist credentials leave no room for doubt, appreciated the plight of the poor and the marginalized as more than a question of linguistic culture. Forn's most enduring and socially sensitive film, *La piel quemada / Burnt Skin* (Josep Maria Forn, 1967), depicts the travels and travails of various members of a family of impoverished Andalusian immigrants as they interact with generally hardworking (but also at times hardhearted) local Catalans and, in the case of the male protagonist, pleasure-seeking foreign tourists (see Figure 3.5). While there can be no doubt that Francoist censorship typically silenced or pushed the non-Castilian languages of the Spanish state into the background, thus rendering them, in film after film, as sporadic and "exotic" as the French, German, and English of the tourists, there can also be no doubt that the plight of Spanish-speaking immigrants is most accurately conveyed, as

Figure 3.4 Spain is different – but Catalonia is the same: *Los Tarantos* (Francisco Rovira Beleta, 1963; prod. Tecisa / Films Rovira Beleta).

Figure 3.5 Immigrant laborers and foreign tourists in *La piel quemada* (Josep Maria Forn, 1967; prod. Teide PC).

Forn well knows, in the language they actually spoke; at the very least, as Miquel Porter i Moix (1992: 285) notes, the Spanish spoken by the Andalusian immigrants in *La piel quemada* is not the standardized version forcibly showcased in so many other films.

Then again, it is not as if all native-born Catalans spoke – or speak – Catalan as their first language or, more still, that they preferred – or prefer – to speak Catalan. Criticisms, by Catalanist critics, of the Catalan bourgeoisie's putative preference for Castilian as the language of power and prosperity abound, even in many of the studies here cited. Whatever the relation between language and ideological processes and positions, it remains the case that the overwhelming majority of films produced in Catalonia, both before, during, and indeed after the Francoist period, are in Castilian, and to such a degree that it would be foolhardy, historically speaking, to take the Catalan language as an "essential" sign of identity – just as foolhardy as it would be to discount it as "inessential." Language, though undeniably *significant* as a marker of nationality and of a certain cinematic practice, is not so in any stable or univocal way. Thus, while José Luis Sáenz de Heredia, director of the quintessentially Francoist film *Raza / Race* (1942), presented his adaptation of Ignacio Agustí's novel *Mariona Rebull* (1947), whose climax is the anarchist bombing of the Liceu in late 1893, as a veritable hymn to Catalan order, progress, industry, and bourgeois morality in close alliance with the regime (De España 1993: 43), others, such as Josep Lluís Font with *Vida de familia / Family Life* (1964) and Jaime Camino with *Los felices sesenta / The Happy Sixties* (1964) (both of which are filmed in Spanish), offered devastating critiques of the hypocrisy and vacuity of the bourgeoisie that were more devastating, in their subtle use of irony, than Iquino's *La familia Vila / The Vila Family* (1949) or, later on, such melodramatic sagas in Catalan as Antoni Verdaguer's *La teranyina / The Spider's Web* (1990) and *Havanera 1820* (1993), which focused on the colonially inflected rise of commerce and industry.

The critique of the bourgeoisie, which inflects more recent films such as Mar Coll's *Tres dies amb la família / Three Days with the Family* (2009), in which a death in the family exposes the emptiness and alienation of its members (Catalan is the vehicular language, though the protagonist's mother, from France, speaks in Spanish), and *En construcción / Under Construction* (José Luis Guerín, 2001), in which the renovation of the Barri Xino, or Raval, entails the displacement of the poor and marginalized (Catalan is spoken only briefly, most significantly by potential buyers who visit the property and criticize the "ugly" visibility of continuing signs of poverty), has, however, an earlier, more radically concerted formulation, in both Castilian and Catalan, in the anarcho-syndicalist films of the CNT and, more specifically still, the Sindicat de la Indústria de l'Espectacle (SIE; Entertainment Industry Union). Operating in the midst of war, with the cinematic industry effectively collectivized, the SIE produced both documentaries such as *Reportaje del movimiento revolucionario en Barcelona / Report on the Revolutionary Movement in Barcelona* (Mateo Santos, 1936) and *El entierro de Durruti / The Funeral of Durruti* (1936) and, more surprisingly, fiction films that exposed social problems such as drug addiction, alcoholism, prostitution, unemployment, and exploitation. Notable among the fictional ventures are *Aurora de esperanza / Dawn of Hope* (Antonio Sau Olite, 1937), with its idealistic portrayal of consciousness-raising and solidarity (see Figure 3.6), and *Barrios bajos / Poor Neighborhoods* (Pedro Puche, 1937), a tale of crime, passion, and redemption set in the Barri Xino.

Figure 3.6 The new dawn of political consciousness: *Aurora de esperanza* (Antonio Sau Olite, 1937; prod. SIE).

Later on, after the defeat of the anarchists and the Republic as a whole, the Barri Xino returned as the setting of preference for a number of relatively hard-edged crime capers, among them Julio Coll's claustrophobically effective *Distrito quinto / Fifth District* (1957); but, for a short, vertiginously intense time, it served as a stage from which to denounce the injustice of an inequitable order. Although the morality play that is *Barrios bajos* is more melodramatically humanistic than militantly anarchistic, it nonetheless points to extensive concerns about the cinema's propagandistic and pedagogical potential, articulated, for instance, in anarchist leader José Peirats' *Para una nueva concepción del arte: Lo que podría ser un cinema social* (*For a New Conception of Art: What a Social Cinema Could Be*). For Peirats (circa 1935: 5), cinematography is an industry like any other and, as such, is "una nueva modalidad [...] de la explotación del hombre por el hombre" (a new modality [...] of man's exploitation of man). Lambasting the double forces of state censorship and capitalist commodification as hampering a truly socially engaged cinema, Peirats (circa 1935: 12) also upbraids the cinema for promoting homosexuality and sexual inversion in its cult of the star as sex symbol and its use of the screen as narcissistic mirror. For all of the libertarian advances in sexual equality, it would not be until Bilbao-born Pedro Olea's *Un hombre llamado "Flor de otoño" / A Man Called "Autumn Flower"* (1978), released in the year of a new democratic Constitution, that a film would offer a sympathetic portrayal of a gay anarchist, one who performs, moreover, in a burlesque show in Barcelona's red light district and who gives his life in a frustrated attempt to assassinate General Miguel Primo de Rivera and to obtain, as he puts it, the freedom to be "yo mismo las 24 horas del día" (myself twenty-four hours a day).

The melding of sex and violence with marginalization and militancy marks both bourgeois and antibourgeois as well as both revolutionary and antirevolutionary cinema in Catalonia. Not surprisingly, it is a cinema that tends to be set in and around the city of Barcelona and, within it, in the darker, dirtier, more cramped spaces of the Barri Xino and the Paral·lel. These places are far removed from Montserrat, that reservoir of Catalan spiritual culture, and the coast (especially the Costa Brava), that expanse of Catalan material culture increasingly coveted by tourists seeking sun, surf, and sex and which serves as the backdrop for a dizzying array of films, from the aforementioned *La piel quemada*, *Los felices sesenta*, and *Palabras de amor / Words of Love* (Antoni Ribas, 1969) to the decidedly more lighthearted, feminist-inspired *Vámonos, Bárbara / Let's Go, Barbara* (Cecilia Bartolomé, 1978; centering on the relationship between a newly independent mother and her young daughter) and *Costa Brava* (Marta Balletbò-Coll, 1995; a transnational lesbian love story). This is not to say that the coast has not also served as a reservoir of a supposedly purer, if often no less violent and inequitable, Catalan culture, as in *Laia*, *Maria Rosa*, and *La hija del mar / Daughter of the Sea* (Antoni Momplet, 1953), but rather that the city of Barcelona is the preferred site for more impure representations. Starting with *Apartado de correos 1001 / P. O. Box 1001* (Julio Salvador, 1950), which opens with a series of external shots of the city and the shooting of a young man on the busy Via Laietana, and continuing through such films as *El Presidio / The Prison* (Antonio Santillán, 1954), set in Barcelona's Model Prison, and *Los atracadores / The Robbers* (Rovira Beleta, 1961), which ends with a gripping depiction of execution by *garrote vil* (the Spanish mode of execution for common criminals), the Catalan capital serves as the backdrop, and often as not as a coprotagonist, of *noir*-inflected stories centered on criminals, delinquents, detectives, and the police.[11] In a more tendentiously, pseudo-testimonial vein, José Antonio de la Loma, who worked for Iquino in the 1950s, exploited fears of urban insecurity along with the titillation of using real-life delinquents as actors in films such as *Perros callejeros / Street Warriors* (1977) and *Yo, "el Vaquilla" / I, "el Vaquilla"* (1985) that came to be known, along with works by Eloy de la Iglesia and others, as *cine quinqui*.[12]

In none of the aforementioned Francoist-era crime films, however, is the bourgeoisie, let alone the regime, subjected to the sly but biting critique that appears in a scattering of films such as *Vida de familia*, the Gatsby-like *Brillante porvenir / Brilliant Future* (Aranda and Román Gubern, 1964), and, in a markedly different register, Vicent Lluch's absurdist comedy *El certificado / The Certificate* (1969). The closest thing to a more concerted or collective critique of the regime and the Catalan bourgeoisie's complicity in it comes, interestingly enough, largely from within the Catalan bourgeoisie itself: the so-called Escola de Barcelona, with which Aranda and Gubern were also, at least for a time, associated. More a loose collection of shared interests and concerns than a *bona fide* school, the Escola de Barcelona, whose heyday ran from the mid-1960s to the early 1970s, arose as a response to the critical, neo-realist-driven Nuevo Cine Español (NCE; New Spanish Cinema) associated with Carlos Saura, Basilio Martín Patino, Mario Camus, Manuel Summers, and others. The name, or brand, "Escola de Barcelona" appears to have been the brainchild of Ricardo Muñoz Suay, but the Escola promptly came under suspicion and even criticism, not just by more traditional leftists who winced at its ironic reliance on consumer culture and its refusal of narrative "witnessing" but also by proponents of Situationist and anarchist approaches committed to denouncing the bourgeois reformism on display in the Conversaciones Cinematográficas (Cinematic Conversations) associated with the New Spanish Cinema and held in 1955 in Salamanca, a city that many Catalans came to identify with Spanish centralism almost as much as Madrid.

Although Rosalind Galt and others take the so-called "Sitges Manifesto" of October 1967 (spearheaded by Joaquim Jordà) as the closest thing to a programmatic enunciation of the cinematic and political principles of the Escola de Barcelona, Román Gubern, who was vice president of the symposium in Sitges, insists that it was not related to it (personal communication from Gubern; see also Chapter 15). Whatever its relation to the Escola, the "Sitges Manifesto" clearly pitted itself against the efforts on the part of directors such as Saura and Luis García Berlanga to work within the Francoist system of rewards and restrictions. In contrast to the critical collaborationism of the New Spanish Cinema, Jordà and company advocated a calculated indifference to the Francoist system and its officially sanctioned Film Schools and called for – in perhaps good bourgeois fashion – self-financing and alternative lines of distribution (Galt 2006: 2). In a television documentary entitled *La passió possible: l'Escola de Barcelona / The Possible Passion: The Barcelona School* (Jordi Cadena, 2000), Román Gubern, who was himself an important player in cutting-edge cinematic ventures, declares that the Escola de Barcelona constituted an elitist, bourgeois, cosmopolitan, and Parisian response to the Madrid-based and often rurally focused narrative films of the New Spanish Cinema. A Mediterranean variant of the *Gauche Divine*, in which, again in the words of Gubern in *La passió possible*, "Godard era San Godard" (Godard was Saint Godard), the Escola de Barcelona brought together, to often vastly varying degrees, such Catalans as Aranda, Jordà, Camino, Pere Portabella, Jacinto Esteva, Joan Brossa, and Ricardo Bofill, as well as Muñoz Suay (Valencia), José María Nunes (Portugal), and Gonzalo Suárez (Asturias) – Suárez being the creator of an idiosyncratic detective who is at the center of such films as *Ditirambo vela por nosotros / Ditirambo Watches Over Us* (1967), *Ditirambo* (1969), and *Epílogo / Epilogue* (1984) and of a welter of self-consciously bizarre undertakings including *El horrible ser nunca visto / The Horrible Never Seen Being* (1966), *El extraño caso del Doctor*

Fausto / The Strange Case of Doctor Faust (1969), *Aoom* (1970), and reworkings of British gothic classics such as *Remando al viento / Rowing with the Wind* (1988), which depicts the inception of the Frankenstein story, and *Mi nombre es sombra / My Name is Shadow* (1996), which draws on the tale of Dr. Jekyll and Mr. Hyde.

Although the Catalan language continued to be at the mercy of state censors, the "members" of the Escola de Barcelona tended to eschew the established practice of both international leftists and traditional Catalanists. Deliberately enigmatic, elliptical, and fragmentary, their works drew liberally on the trappings of late capitalism, particularly advertising, fashion, and graphic design, and often resorted to only partly intelligible phrasing, as at the beginning of *Dante no es únicamente severo / Dante is Not Only Severe* (Esteva and Jordà, 1967); patently artificial to pop-cultural sound bites, as in *Cada vez que… / Each Time…* (Carles Duran, 1968); to self-consciously lyrical expression, as in the gorgeous *Noche de vino tinto / Night of Red Wine* (José María Nunes, 1967); or, most daringly, to non-verbal sounds and silence, as in Pere Portabella's *Nocturn 29 / Nocturne 29* (1968), *Vampir-Cuadecuc* (1970), and *Umbracle* (1972), the first two in collaboration with poet and artist Joan Brossa. Esteva and Jordà, whose relationship would become increasingly fraught, are two of the most interesting participants in the Escola, with documentary-like films such as Esteva's *Lejos de los árboles / Far from the Trees* (1972, though filming began in 1963) deploying a play of light and darkness and contrasting scenes of traditional and modern life, and deeply self-implicating documentary films such as Jordà's *Monos como Becky / Monkeys like Becky* (1999, with Núria Villazán) and *Más allá del espejo / Beyond the Mirror* (2006) exploring everything from cerebral lesions and personality modification to visual agnosia and neuroimagery, phenomena that are profoundly relevant to the very conditions of possibility of cinematic perception and comprehension.[13] Jordà's passion for the vagaries of vision informs his homage to Buñuel in the excruciating dissection of an eye in *Dante no es únicamente severo*, which also serves as a commentary on the violence done to visual representation under Franco, but it is likewise at play, long after the dictator's death, in Jordà's lengthy meditation on forensic evidence and public perception in the documentary *De nens / About Children* (2003), centered on a scandal involving a ring of pederasts, police manipulations, and real-estate speculation in the rapidly changing Raval.

No incursion into the embattled, if steadfast, field of Catalan cinema and, more widely, the visual arts would be complete without a reflection on the work of Pere Portabella (see also Chapter 6), whose unflinching experimentalism is intricately bound up in his no less unflinching commitment to Catalonia. If Josep Maria Forn can be considered the master of Catalanist historico-political cinema, Iquino the master of a diffusely Catalan commercial cinema under Franco, Ventura Pons (who burst on the scene with the brilliant documentary *Ocaña, retrat intermitent / Ocaña, an Intermittent Portrait* (1978)) the master of a narrative-driven cinema in Catalan after the death of the dictator, and Isabel Coixet the master of a shrewd Catalan internationalism in which English, not Spanish, is the language of preference, Portabella is unquestionably the most internationally recognized master of an experimental

Catalan filmic practice. His impact on Catalan – and Spanish – culture in an international frame far exceeds his financial success and popular appeal. As a producer, he had a hand in three of the most celebrated films in the history of Spanish cinema: Italian Marco Ferreri's *El cochecito* / *The Motorized Wheelchair* (1960), Carlos Saura's *Los golfos* / *The Delinquents* (1961), and Luis Buñuel's *Viridiana* (1961), though with respect to the latter it appears that the financial involvement of Portabella's production company, Films 59, was all but nonexistent. As a political activist, he was a mover and shaker in the Assemblea de Catalunya (Assembly of Catalonia), a senator for Girona in the Entesa dels Catalans (Agreement of the Catalans), an independent deputy affiliated with the Unified Socialist Party of Catalonia (PSUC) in the Parlament de Catalunya, and a veritable master of ceremonies for the triumphant return, in 1977, of Josep Tarradellas, president of the Generalitat in exile.

As a filmmaker, Portabella's commitment to a political and aesthetic exploration of the medium's possibilities and limitations, evident in his filmic tributes to Joan Miró (*Aidez l'Espagne* / *Miró 1937*, 1969; *Miró-la forja* / *Miró-The Forge* and *Miró-tapís* / *Miró-Tapestry*, both from 1973), has left a mark on the work of José Luis Guerín, especially his evocative, metacinematic *Tren de sombras* / *Train of Shadows* (1997), a veritable play of light and shadow. While the work of Jordà is surely of more direct import for younger directors such as Marc Recha and Albert Serra, certain formal similarities – especially in the case of Serra – are nonetheless at play between their work and that of Portabella. Although Portabella's progressive political views are clearer in *El sopar* / *The Supper* (1974) – in which five former political prisoners have a conversation on the night of the execution of the anarchist Salvador Puig Antich (the subject, in 2006, of a gripping film by Manuel Huerga entitled *Salvador*) – and *Informe general sobre unas cuestiones de interés para una proyección pública* / *General Report on Some Questions of Interest for a Public Screening* (1976), the very opacity of such allegorically charged ventures as *Nocturn 29*, *Umbracle*, and *Vampir-Cuadecuc* (the titles refer to twenty-nine years of Francoist darkness and to its shadowy, vampiric system) constitutes perhaps the most eloquent commentary on filmmaking under a repressive regime (see Figure 3.7). With expression anything but free, with entire languages demonized, monitored, and censored, with any alternative national history ridiculed, dismissed, and truncated, and with a public long trained to see what the regime, and Hollywood, had given it to see, it is little wonder that resistance assumed a more tortuous track. In the words of Fèlix Fanés (2008: 31), Portabella's films, "malgrat explicar històries, no són narratives; tenen continuitat, però estan fetes de fragments, escenes isolades" (even though they tell stories, are not narrative; they have continuity, but they are made of fragments, isolated scenes).

Something similar might be said of the fractured entirety of Catalan cinema, dismissed by any number of critics writing, typically, from outside Catalonia (and never in Catalan) and consigned, over and again, to a marginal position in larger projects on "Spanish cinema." And yet, cinema in Spain, and hence "Spanish cinema," is inconceivable without Catalonia and, more specifically, without the

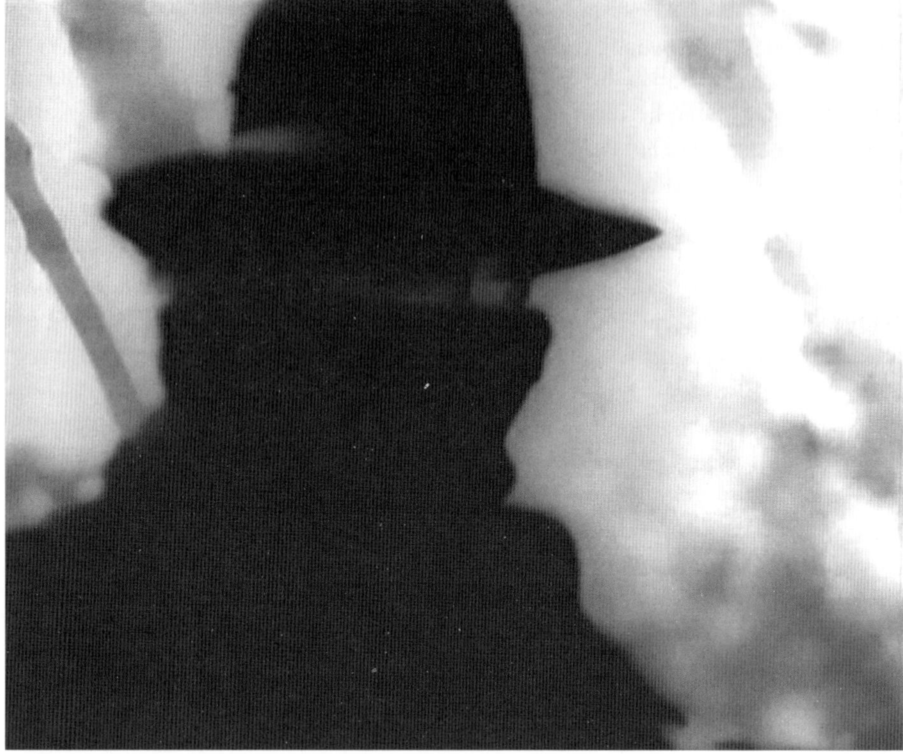

Figure 3.7 The dark face of Francoism: *Vampir-Cuadecuc* (Pere Portabella, 1970; prod. Films 59).

industrial infrastructure that in the early twentieth century made Barcelona a veritable motor of cinematic production; placed it at the forefront of the transition from silence to sound; informed it, now and again, as a site of aesthetic experimentation, academic inquiry, and political contestation; and rendered it, in short, the *other* capital of cinematic production in Spain – and all of this long before the "political devolution" that partly marked the passage from dictatorship to democracy. The relative dearth of attention paid thus far in the present chapter to more recent cinematic practice in Catalonia, and in Catalan, is itself a response to the continued marginalization of Catalan culture in presumably more comprehensive studies and of the mistaken notion that it is only with the death of Franco and the re-establishment of the Generalitat and other institutions that a Catalan cinematic practice begins fitfully to flourish, free from state censorship but still subject to mononational attitudes in Spain and international market forces that continue to leave little room for so-called "minor" languages and cultures, consigning them, often as not, to a realm of echoes, traces, and fragments. Here too there is a play of margins and centers, of major and minor formations, though not necessarily the ones that have come to be expected.

Interestingly, the very year that Jordà and others advanced an experimental project in Sitges (whose most resilient proponent would be Portabella), Ramon (Terenci) Moix published an article that explicitly adduced the bilingual status of Barcelona – though Castilian, he claimed, had never been fully assimilated there – and that at once recognized and criticized the city's centralizing pull. The margin within the margin was, for Moix, the rest of Catalonia, especially the countryside where the Catalan language was more prevalent, but also the Balearic Islands and Valencia, where the very designation of the language – Catalan, Valencian, Mallorcan, and so on – remains a source of contention. Referring explicitly to the commercial cinema of Iquino and, more generally, to both the realist and experimental modalities then cultivated in Barcelona, Moix (1967: 14) complained that the only cinema in which Catalan was given voice was book-bound and mired in the past: "obras de Guimerá y Sagarra, melodrama aprovechadizo de exteriores pirenaicos, Passión [sic] de Esparraguera" (works by Guimerà and by Sagarra, an opportunistic melodrama with shots of the Pyrenees, the Passion play of Esparraguera). The allusions are to *Maria Rosa*, *La herida luminosa*, *Siega verde*, and *El Judas*, respectively, but the upshot is clear: the Catalan language, a critical aspect of Catalan culture (imagine having to say that Castilian is a critical aspect of Spanish culture!), has been confined to the past, to the home, and to the anecdotal (Moix 1967: 10). So confined, the language becomes uncannily exotic (Moix 1967: 15), out of place in the very place where it is spoken – at home, in the streets, but rarely on the screen. It appears, that is, as so much local color and background music – a sort of white noise that disturbs, from time to time, the smooth articulation of what some would still consider, simply yet ever so slyly, Spanish cinema pure and simple.

Alternatively, the Catalan language appears in its disappearance, in the amplification of non-verbal sounds and the recursive nods to the silent era that punctuate Portabella's work up to the present. A recent venture, *Die Stille vor Bach / The Silence before Bach* (2007), celebrated as eminently "European," eschews in its very title the languages of Spain, the languages of the Spanish state, even as it opens with a pianola, that former supplement of silent cinema. Here, however, the pianola is motorized and, far from remaining stationary, moves across a series of white-walled rooms devoid of any human presence, let alone of the patriotic heroes or religious icons of *El tambor del Bruch* or *El Judas*. In so doing, it gestures, ever so ambiguously, to the past, in which some languages, some cultures, were deemed more appropriate than others, and to the future, where the frame of national reference is – or at least could be, perhaps even should be – wider, more complex, more populated by a diversity of non-hegemonic tongues, non-hegemonic traditions. The words of Moix (1967: 14), for whom "las posibilidades concretas de un cine catalán futuro se enfrentan con las contradicciones del pasado" (the concrete possibilities of a future Catalan cinema confront the contradictions of the past), still resonate today, in a new constitutional if not a new (pluri)national order: "el espectador catalán espera de su lengua, en cine, bastante más que palabras" (the Catalan spectator expects from his or her language, in cinema, quite a bit more than words).

And yet, many politicians and administrators in Catalonia, often in tension with centralizing forces in Madrid, appear to have had a very different take on things, seeing in cinema little *but* words, making subsidies contingent on the numbers of tickets sold rather than artistic promise, promoting dubbing – often of US blockbusters – over subtitling, paying little heed to differences in accent and lexicon within Catalan, and generally placing linguistic policy above cinematic art. Such, at least, is the opinion of a wide array of filmmakers, critics, actors, historians, editors, screenwriters, and more than one moviegoer: from Bigas Luna to Eduard Fernández, from Román Gubern to Àngel Comas, whose *Vint anys d'història del cinema a Catalunya (1990–2009)* (2010) offers a comprehensive overview of the vicissitudes of cultural politics, comparable to those of an increasingly globalized market. From the reinvigoration of the Generalitat de Catalunya and the creation of the Servei de Cinematografia in 1981 and, more broadly, the reforms instituted by the Directora General de Cinematografía (Director General of Film), Pilar Miró, in 1983 and others afterwards to the present, cinema in Catalonia as in Spain as a whole has been subject to a vertiginous series of politically and ideologically motivated interventions, protections, stimuli, cuts, quotas, norms, and normalizing, normativizing projects. The picture is further complicated – at times enriched, at times impoverished – by a variety of other factors, ranging from the progressive eclipse of celluloid-based products (though Guerín, Serra, and others hang fire) to the rise and consolidation of film schools, from television coproductions to new interactive modalities such as the Internet and cellular phones, from the longstanding challenges of promotion, distribution, and exhibition to double or dubbed versions that waver not between the prudish and the salacious (as in the days of Iquino) but between Spanish and Catalan (to cite only one among many, Sílvia Munt's *Pretextos / Pretexts*, 2008).

Sometimes, from some perspectives, it would appear that the future of Catalan cinema, or cinema in Catalonia, is as dystopian as what was portrayed, years ago, for the country as a whole in such films as Vicente Aranda's *Fata Morgana / Left-Handed Fate* (1965) and Carles Duran's *Liberxina 90* (1970), in which Barcelona and its industrial surroundings are all but emptied of life and, buffeted by repressive forces, threatened with extinction. For, as Barcelona goes, so, it seems, goes Catalonia, such is the city's centrality in cinematic production still today, a centrality that has led Comas (2010: 24) to claim, in a manner reminiscent of Moix, that "acostumem a parlar de cinema català, quan seria més rigorós dir que parlem de cinema barceloní" (we are in the habit of speaking of Catalan cinema, when it would be more accurate to say that we speak of Barcelonan cinema). Foreign directors would seem to confirm this centrality, for the list of internationally oriented films in which Barcelona looms large is as impressive as it is varied. From Michelangelo Antonioni's starkly stylistic *Professione: reporter / The Passenger* (1976) to Woody Allen's slickly superficial *Vicky Cristina Barcelona* (2008) to Alejandro González Iñárritu's wrenchingly bleak *Biutiful* (2010), together with Whit Stillman's *Barcelona* (1994), Cédric Klapisch's *L'Auberge espagnole / The Spanish Apartment* (2002), Susan Seidelman's *Gaudí Afternoon* (2001), and Pedro Almódovar's *Todo sobre mi madre / All about My Mother* (1999), Barcelona clearly captivates – and sells. Often as not, it captivates – and sells – in English, or French, and certainly Spanish, but at times it does so overwhelmingly in Catalan, as in Ventura Pons' *Barcelona (un mapa) / Barcelona (a Map)* (2007), in which immigrants speak an accented but fluid version of it, and at other times intermittently so, as in Cesc Gay's *V. O. S. / Original Version Subtitled* (2009), in which characters code-switch in a manner that throws the very notion of an "original version" into question (the film even includes a few phrases in Basque). Both situations are, of course, plausible – that is to say, real: many immigrants *do* speak Catalan and many native-born locals *do* code-switch, usually, but by no means only, between Catalan and Castilian. For instance, in Marc Recha's melancholy and meditative *L'arbre de les cireres / The Cherry Tree* (1998), *Pau i el seu germà / Pau and His Brother* (2001), and *Les mans buides / Empty Hands* (2003), the characters express themselves, as many do along the northern border, in Catalan, French, and/or Castilian.

While it may be true, as Comas (2010: 24) contends, that the "decentralization" of Catalan cinema, beyond Barcelona, has yet to be fully realized in favor of "un mosaic idiosincràtic més ampli i més representatiu" (a more ample and representative idiosyncratic mosaic), other Catalan cities and, especially, the countryside are far from absent. Whether it be Joaquim Jordà's *Un cos al bosc / A Body in the Woods* (1996), in which a transplanted Rossy de Palma, best known for her supporting roles in a number of films by Almodóvar, finds herself being commended by a rural resident for speaking Catalan as she investigates what appears to be a murder, or Marc Recha's *Dies d'agost / August Days* (2006), in which two brothers exchange stories amid the sounds, and silences, of nature, the center of attention and attraction is certainly not the capital city. But it is also not necessarily language either: in both of the aforementioned films, and more pointedly in Recha's, the inarticulate image fills the screen, emptying it, in the process, of some of the more mundane chatter that would gainsay Moix's projected expectations – and hopes – for the Catalan spectator. Quite a bit more than words is indeed what the spectator encounters in such diversely located films as Barcelona-based Mercedes Álvarez's *El cielo gira / The Sky Turns* (2004), set in the director's home town in rural Castile; her former collaborator and mentor Guerín's *En la ciudad de Sylvia / In the City of Sylvia* (2007), set in Strasbourg; and, in a more reticently yet insistently Catalan register, Albert Serra's *Honor de cavalleria / Knight's Honor* (2006) and *El cant dels ocells / Birdsong* (2008), which offer an innovatively tedious take on the adventures of Don Quixote and the journey of the Magi, respectively. Quite a bit more than words may also be what the spectator expects, hopes for, and encounters in the films of other young, or relatively young, Catalan directors such as Sílvia Quer, Judith Colell, Maria Ripoll, Pau Freixas, or Albert Espinosa – if not, in fact, in *any* film, not just those that self-consciously court the limits of sense and that set the mind on fire. After all, even in the films of someone as conventional as Iquino, films whose future is partly our past and partly our future, something more – and less – than words, with their frittering echoes and flickering traces, can, just possibly, still impress itself on us in the perpetually passing present.

Notes

1 All translations from works not designated as having been previously translated are mine. I would like to thank Josetxo Cerdán, Jean-Claude Seguin, and Santiago Juan-Navarro for helping me to acquire copies of the less available films; Rosa Saz Alpuente for assisting me so effectively at the Filmoteca de Catalunya; Àngel Quintana for offering a detailed reading of the manuscript; and, most especially, Román Gubern for helping me to refine my understanding of the history of cinema.

2 The word "Passió" first appears in the film's opening credits alongside the acknowledgment of the largely non-professional ensemble cast.

3 For more on censorship, see Gubern (1983, 2003a), Ferrer i Gironès (1985), and Riambau (1994); for more on cinematic production under Franco, see Fernández (1995); for an enlightening interview with García Escudero, see Riambau (2003).

4 The multiple dates of Anglada's and Feliu's films are the effects of censorship.

5 Bigas Luna is his professional name. His given names, when used, appear variously as José Juan (on his own website) and Juan José.

6 For more on Plana's foundational role in the accreditation of cinema, see Donadeu (2011). See also Plana (1920), De Torre (1921), Palau (1929, 1932), Díaz-Plaja (1930a, 1930b), Ferran (1930), Samper (1930), Planes (1931), Gasch (1932, 1933), and D'Ors (1996, 2001). Minguet Batllori (2000) is here of critical importance.

7 Amateur cinema was initially linked to the "excursionista" or hiking movement in which city dwellers rediscovered nature and later to antidictatorial resistance efforts. For more on the relationship between amateur cinema and "excursionisme," see Romaguera i Ramió (1992: 49).

8 There is some debate as to the date of the first "talkie" in Spain. In 1931, Rosario Pi commissioned Edgar Neville to make *Yo quiero que me lleven a Hollywood / Take Me to Hollywood*, which was filmed in Madrid but sonorized in Paris. At least one Catalan did make the jump to Hollywood, and quite spectacularly so: the musician Xavier Cugat.

9 For a full account of the Generalitat's involvement in cinematic production, see Caparrós Lera and Biadiu Cuadrench (1978); for more on anarcho-syndicalist film, see Juan-Navarro (2011).

10 Sung Catalan appears in films as diverse as *La hija del mar* (produced by Iquino), *Laia*, *La llarga agonia dels peixos fora de l'aigua*, and *La piel quemada*. The presence of songs in Catalan is even more pronounced in a number of films that feature such standard-bearers of the politically engaged *Nova Cançó* as Raimon, Lluís Llach, and Joan Manuel Serrat: *Raimon '65* (Carles Duran, 1965), *Palabras de amor*, *Los felices sesenta*, and, shortly after Franco's death, *La nova cançó / New Song* and *Canet Rock* (both Francesc Bellmunt, 1976).

11 For more on the crime genre in cinema, see Espelt (1998). In the 1980s, crime capers situated in Barcelona experienced a revival in such films as Jordi Cadena's *Barcelona sud / Barcelona South* (1981), Aranda's *Fanny "Pelopaja" / Fanny Straw-Top* (1984), Bigas Luna's *Lola* (1986), and Antonio Chavarrías' *Una ombra al jardí / A Shadow in the Garden* (1989).

12 Despite the phonetic resemblance to the English "kinky," the word *quinqui* is derived from *quincallería*, or "scrap metal," and refers to the argot of itinerant vendors or *quincalleros*, also known as *mercheros*, with certain similarities to the *caló* spoken by gypsies. Today, the word is taken more generally to designate a delinquent or drifter, and in the *Dictionary of the Real Academia Española* designates a "persona que pertenece a cierto grupo social marginado de la sociedad por su forma de vida" (person who belongs to a social group marginalized from society for its way of life).

13 For more on the Escola, see especially Riambau and Torreiro (1993) and also Torreiro (1998), Font (2003), Martínez Bretón (2003), and Galt (2006).

References

Cánovas Belchí, J. (2007) Cultura popular e identidad nacional en el cine español mudo de los años veinte. In: Berthier, N. and Seguin, J.-C. (eds.) *Cine, nación y nacionalidades en España*. Madrid: Casa de Velázquez, pp. 25–36.

Caparrós Lera, J. M. (1993) El cine catalán durante la Renaixença. In: Alegre, S., Caparrós Lera, J. M., Crusells, M., et al. *El cine en Cataluña: Una aproximación histórica*. Barcelona: Promociones y Publicaciones Universitarias, pp. 11–38.

Caparrós Lera, J. M. and Biadiu Cuadrench, R. (1978) *Petita història del cinema de la Generalitat (1932–1939)*. Mataró: Edicions Robrenyo.

Comas, A. (2003) *Ignacio F. Iquino, hombre de cine*. Barcelona: Laertes.

Comas, A. (2010) *Vint anys d'història del cinema a Catalunya (1990–2009)*. Barcelona: Laertes.

De España, R. (1993) Cataluña y los catalanes vistos por el cine del franquismo. In: Alegre, S., Caparrós Lera, J. M., Crusells, M., et al. *El cine en Cataluña: Una aproximación histórica*. Barcelona: Promociones y Publicaciones Universitarias, pp. 39–64.

De Lasa, J. F. (1988) *El món de Fructuós Gelabert*. Barcelona: Generalitat de Catalunya, Departament de Cultura.

De Lasa, J. F. (1996) *Aquell primer cinema català: Els germans Baños*. Barcelona: Generalitat de Catalunya, Departament de Cultura.

De Torre, G. (1921) Cinegrafía: El cinema y la novísima literatura: Sus conexiones. *Cosmópolis* 33: 97–107.

Díaz-Plaja, G. (1930a) La nosa de les paraules. *Mirador* 77 (July 17): 6.

Díaz-Plaja, G. (1930b) Els assassinats del sonor. *Mirador* 91(October 23): 6.

D'Ors, E. (1996) El "cimatòfago." In: *Glosari 1906–1907*. Barcelona: Quaderns Crema, pp. 100–1.

D'Ors, E. (2001) Del cinematògraf. In: *Glosari 1908–1909*. Barcelona: Quaderns Crema, pp. 77–9.

Espelt, R. (1998) *Ficció criminal a Barcelona (1950–1963)*. Barcelona: Laertes.

Fanés, F. (1986) El wagnerianisme a la Barcelona dels anys cinquanta: *Parsifal* de Daniel Mangrané i el seu entorn. *Cinematògraf* 3. Barcelona: Federació Catalana de Cine-Club, pp. 333–75.

Fanés, F. (2008) *Pere Portabella: Avantguarda, cinema, política*. Barcelona: Institut Català de les Indústries Culturals / Raval Edicions.

Fernández, A. (1995) El cinema històric espanyol durant el franquisme (1940–1975): La negació de les histories perifèriques. *D'Art* 21: 93–102.

Fernández Cuenca, C. (1972) *Segundo de Chomón: Maestro de la fantasía y de la técnica (1871–1929)*. Madrid: Editora Nacional.

Ferran, A. (1930) La solució ens ve de fora. *La publicitat* (July 19): n.p.

Ferrer i Gironès, F. (1985) *La persecució política de la llengua catalana*. Barcelona: Edicions 62.

Font, D. (2003) D'un temps, d'un país y de un cine anfibio: Sobre la Escuela de Barcelona. In: Heredero, C. F. and Monterde, J. E. (eds.) *Los "Nuevos Cines" en España: Ilusiones y desencantos de los años sesenta*. Valencia: Institut Valencià de Cinematografia Ricardo Muñoz Suay, pp. 175–94.

Galt, R. (2006) Mapping Catalonia in 1967: The Barcelona School in Global Context. *Senses of Cinema*. Online at: http://archive.sensesofcinema.com/contents/06/41/barcelona-school.html (accessed October 11, 2009).

Gasch, S. (1932) El cinema ha tornat a néixer. *Mirador* 182 (July 28): 4.

Gasch, S. (1933) Producció nacional? *Mirador* 241 (September 14): 4.

González (López), P. (1985) Els intel·lectuals catalans i el cinema (1896–1923). *L'Avenç* 79: 42–68.

González (López), P. (1987) *Els anys daurats del cinema clàssic a Barcelona (1906–1923)*. Barcelona: Publicacions de l'Institut del Teatre de la Diputació de Barcelona / Edicions 62.

Gubern, R. (1983) La censura cinematogràfica i la "Qüestió lingüística" sota el franquisme. *L'Avenç* 59: 38–40.

Gubern, R. (2003a) El forcejeo entre censura y reformismo: ¿La primera apertura? In: Heredero, C. F. and Monterde, J. E. (eds.) *Los "Nuevos Cines" en España: Ilusiones y desencantos de los años sesenta*. Valencia: Institut Valencià de Cinematografia Ricardo Muñoz Suay, pp. 69–78.

Gubern, R. (2003b) Los goces secretos del rey pornógrafo. *Clarín* (June 14). Online at: www.sensesofcinema.com/2006/41/barcelona-school (accessed July 12, 2011).

Gubern, R. (2003c) Presentación. In: Comas, A. *Ignacio F. Iquino, hombre de cine*. Barcelona: Laertes, pp. 11–12.

Harguindey, A. S. (1978) XXXI Festival de Cine de Cannes: Lo individual y lo colectivo. *El País* (May 26). Online at: www.elpais.com/diario/1978/05/26/cultura/264981610_850215.html (accessed July 12, 2011).

Iribarren i Donadeu, T. (2011) El primer discurs català d'acreditació artística del cinema: Alexandre Plana i la campanya cinematogràfica de *La Publicidad* (1920). *Els Marges* 95: 20–49.

Juan-Navarro, S. (2011) Un pequeño Hollywood proletario: El cine anarcosindicalista durante la revolución española (Barcelona, 1936–1937). *Bulletin of Spanish Studies* 88 (4): 523–40.

Letamendi, J. and Seguin, J.-C. (2004) *Los orígenes del cine en Cataluña*. Barcelona: Generalitat de Catalunya / Institut Català de les Indústries Culturals.

Martínez Bretón, J. A. (1993) El control cinematográfico en la evolución del mudo al sonoro. Biblioteca Virtual Miguel de Cervantes. In: Gubern, R., Heinink, J. B., Berriatúa, L., et al. *El paso del mudo al sonoro en el cine español (Actas del IV Congreso de la AEHC)*. Madrid: Editorial Complutense, pp. 109–27.

Martínez Bretón, J. A. (2003) La Escuela de Barcelona: De su contexto histórico. In: Heredero, C. F. and Monterde, J. E. (eds.) *Los "Nuevos Cines" en España: Ilusiones y desencantos de los años sesenta*. Valencia: Institut Valencià de Cinematografia Ricardo Muñoz Suay, pp. 163–73.

Minguet Batllori, J. M. (2000) *Cinema, modernitat i avantguarda (1920–1936)*. Barcelona: Edicions 3i4 / Eliseu Climent.

Minguet Batllori, J. M. (2000–1) Classicisme i cinema: Eugeni d'Ors, el noucentisme i les arts industrials. *Locus Amœnus* 5: 291–304.

Moix, R. (1967) Entre un cine de Barcelona y un cine catalán: Introducción a una problemática. *Nuestro Cine* 61: 9–15.

Palau, J. (1929) Orientacions del cinema sonor. *Mirador* 44 (November 28): 6.

Palau, J. (1932) El cinema a la universitat: Un curs de cinema. *Mirador* 167 (April 14): n.p.

Peirats, J. (circa 1935) *Para una nueva concepción del arte: Lo que podría ser un cinema social*. Barcelona: Ediciones de la *Revista Blanca*.

Pérez Perucha, J. (1995) Narración de un aciago destino (1896–1930). In: Gubern, R. (ed.) *Historia del cine español*. Madrid: Cátedra, pp. 19–121.

Plana, A. (1920) *Declaración de propósitos y algunas consideraciones iniciales sobre el cinema*. *La Publicidad* (February 24, evening edition): n.p.

Planes, J. M. (1931) La política i el cinema. *Mirador* 118 (May 7): n.p.

Porter i Moix, M. (1992) *Història del cinema a Catalunya (1895–1990)*. Barcelona: Generalitat de Catalunya, Departament de Cultura.

Quintana, A. (2007) *Josep Maria Forn: Indústria i identitat*. Barcelona: Editorial Pòrtic / Institut Català de les Indústries Culturals / Generalitat de Catalunya.

Riambau, E. (1994) *Paisatge abans de la batalla: El cinema a Catalunya (1896–1939)*. Barcelona: Quaderns de Comunicació.

Riambau, E. (2003) La legislación que hizo posible el NCE: Entrevista con José María García Escudero. In: Heredero, C. F. and Monterde, J. E. (eds.) *Los "Nuevos Cines" en España: Ilusiones y desencantos de los años sesenta*. Valencia: Institut Valencià de Cinematografia Ricardo Muñoz Suay, pp. 53–68.

Riambau, E. and Torreiro, C. (1993) *Temps era temps: El cinema de l'Escola de Barcelona i el seu entorn*. Barcelona: Generalitat de Catalunya, Departament de Cultura.

Romaguera i Ramió, J. (1992) *Quan el cinema començà a parlar en català (1927–1934)*. Barcelona: Fundació Institut del Cinema Català.

Samper, B. (1930) La música: Cinema sonor. *Revista de Catalunya* 63: 257–60.

Sánchez Vidal, A. (1992) *El cine de Chomón*. Zaragoza: Caja de Ahorros de la Inmaculada Aragón.

Torreiro, C. (1998) Aimez-vous la Representation [sic]? Notes on the Cinema of Pere Portabella and on *Informe General*. In: Talens, J. and Zunzunegui, S. (eds.) *Modes of Representation in Spanish Cinema*. Minneapolis: University of Minnesota Press, pp. 303–18.

Further Reading

Gubern, R. (2010) Del cine erótico al cine porno. In: Méndez Baiges, M. and Ruiz Garrido, B. (eds.) *Eros es más: Ensayos sobre arte y erotismo*. Málaga: Fundación Picasso, pp. 193–208.

Nieto, J. (2008) *La memoria cinematográfica de la Guerra Civil española (1939–1982)*. Valencia: Publicacions de la Universitat de València.

Oltra i Costa, R. (1990) *Seixanta anys de cinema català: 1930–1990*. Barcelona: Institut del Cinema Català.

Pedraza, P. (2007) *Agustí Villaronga*. Madrid: Ediciones Akal.

Riambau, E. (2007) *Jaime Camino: La guerra civil i altres històries*. Barcelona: Editorial Pòrtic / Institut Català de les Indústries Culturals / Generalitat de Catalunya.

Romaguera i Ramió, J. (2005) *Diccionari del cinema a Catalunya*. Barcelona: Enciclopèdia Catalana.

Sanabria, C. (2010) *Bigas Luna: El ojo voraz*. Barcelona: Laertes.

4

Negotiating the Local and the Global

Andalusia, the Basque Country, and Galicia

José Colmeiro and Joseba Gabilondo

Introduction: Fragmentation, Invisibility, and Political Devolution (José Colmeiro)

In several vital respects, cinema has since its inception been marked by absence and loss and by a persistent tension between fragmentation and suture, visibility and invisibility, and repression and representation. This tension is perhaps all the more acute in relatively peripheral and invisible cinemas such as that of Spain, and even more so in the various other cinemas that operate on the fringes of the nation-state's official apparatus, such as that of Catalonia (discussed in Chapter 3), and those of Galicia, the Basque Country, and Andalusia (discussed here).

On a general technical level, cinema provides a fragmented virtual take on reality, as a result of both the mechanical reproduction apparatus that magically tricks the human eye (the twenty-four frames per second produce a sutured ghostly illusion of an absent reality) and the particular narrative grammar of cinema based on continuity editing, which sutures a fragmented mosaic of images: the composition frame, the shot, the sequence. On a historical plane, cinema is also indelibly marked by fragmentation: because of the extreme fragility of the medium, the ephemeral nature of cinema, particularly in its first decades, is complicated by belated or insufficient efforts at preservation. Any history of cinema will always be marked by a high degree of loss and fragmented remnants; cinema scholars and institutions aiming to reconstruct a meaningful whole are aware that this is an impossible enterprise. A history of cinema will always be an archeological attempt at suturing the fissures and reconstructing the missing

A Companion to Spanish Cinema, First Edition. Edited by Jo Labanyi and Tatjana Pavlović.

pieces in its narrative. This is especially so in cinemas that, in order to exist at all, have had to contend with major political, structural, and financial obstacles.

The historical mapping of cinema in Spain reveals a complex, fragmented picture composed of several singular cinemas marked by particular political and economic developments as well as by cultural and, in some cases, linguistic diversity. As a mass cultural form, cinema has been used as a vehicle for Spanish nationalism at least since the Second Republic of 1931–6. It has also been crucial to the attempts at nation building in the stateless nations within Spain: not only Catalonia, where an established local film industry operated since cinema's early years, but also in areas such as the Basque Country and Galicia, which have historical claims to political and cultural autonomy, particularly since the transition to democracy and the process of administrative decentralization and political devolution initiated in the late 1970s. This is also true to a lesser extent in Andalusia, for, even though Andalusian cultural identity has generally not been conceptualized in national terms, Andalusian cinema has also been linked to the construction of a differentiated Andalusian cultural and political identity. The historical narrative of Basque and Galician cinemas in particular is necessarily full of discontinuities, silences, and interruptions, marked as they have been by repression, migration, and / or exile during the years of the Franco dictatorship. The emergence of Basque, Galician, and Andalusian cinemas in recent decades has been closely related to the establishment, since the 1978 Constitution, of regional autonomous governments and new audiovisual media, particularly regional public television channels that have hugely boosted the local audiovisual and film sectors. Another key factor is the new global dynamics that have encouraged local film producers to explore transnational initiatives.

Yet these various cinemas have not always developed in tandem; their history is one of uneven and often divergent development. Their response to globalization has also varied, not only in terms of transnational coproduction schemes, film distribution, and marketing for targeted international audiences but also in terms of attracting foreign film production to their territories. This last point raises the question of whether we can really distinguish between "Andalusian cinema" and "cinema made in Andalusia," for example. Any attempt at a unified account that smoothes over the differences and discontinuities, or resorts to a single conceptual model to examine an essentially asymmetrical situation, is inadequate. We need to approach this complex map with a set of lenses that give us both depth of field and sharp focus, and that allow us to examine the interactions of the local and the global, beyond the confines of the national. Marsha Kinder's proposal that we think in terms of "microregional cinemas" and "macroregional cinemas" (1993) can be useful here, since it allows a double focus on the operation of local / regional cinemas both within the nation-state and beyond its borders.

This map is not only fragmented and in flux but also complicated by a number of "invisibility factors." It can be argued that Spanish cinema is literally invisible in that, apart from a handful of exceptional films each year, it fails to reach a broad public. This reality points to the structural problem of Hollywood subsidiaries' monopoly control of distribution, with most new Spanish releases failing to make it commercially, compounded, tellingly, by the rejection of Spanish cinema by Spanish filmgoers, indicating a widespread disconnect between domestic film production and its prime target audience. The distribution problem is acute for films made in, and associated with, "peripheral" autonomous communities. The openness to global currents has transformed the operations of film production but has not resolved its contradictions. A major problem is the general invisibility in Spain's viewing circuits of films made in the autonomous communities, reflecting Spanish nationalist culture's characteristic imperviousness to the multicultural, multilingual reality existing within the nation-state. But this invisibility is evident even within the autonomous communities themselves. It may be easier to see a Galician film in Buenos Aires than Seville, or an Andalusian film in Havana rather than Madrid. We must ask, then, to what extent there is a certain structural and institutional blindness that perpetuates the invisibility of these cinemas for Spanish audiences as well as for audiences in other autonomous communities.

Another potentially problematic issue regarding these cinemas is the use of terms such as "regional" or "peripheral." While it is impossible to avoid these terms altogether, they can appear to reinforce the centrality of the center and the marginality of the margins. We should remember, however, that all Western cinemas are regional and peripheral, as well as partly invisible, in relation to Hollywood – including Spanish cinema. At the same time, the concept of the "national" seems too reductive and exclusionary. Many critics find the notion of national cinema increasingly problematic (Crofts 2002; Higson 2002). It has always been a convenient label that needs to be continually re-examined, and today it seems particularly insufficient to reflect the complexities of a globalized world. However, so long as the concept of Spanish cinema has some critical currency, there are good pragmatic reasons for also talking of Basque, Galician, Andalusian – and Catalan – cinemas, out of parity.

The erosion of the "national cinema" conceptual model has run parallel to the crisis of the nation-state and against the backdrop of re-emerging peripheral nationalisms and the new forces of globalization, all of which has created a new "postnational" paradigm (Bermúdez et al. 2001; Gabilondo 2002a). At a time when the hegemony of the national model is being challenged by regional and national forces from inside the nation-state as well as by supranational and global pressures from outside, it would be a mistake to assume any preconstructed, essentialized notion of what the cinemas of Spain's various autonomous communities should be. The postnational focus of the essays contained in this section aims to rethink the conceptual models used to approach Spain's "peripheral" cinemas. Key questions inflecting the discussion of Basque, Galician, and Andalusian cinemas in the sections that follow include: the difficulty, theoretically and historically, of defining these cinemas marked by fragmentation and invisibility; the role played in shaping them by political and cultural institutions (the autonomous governments,

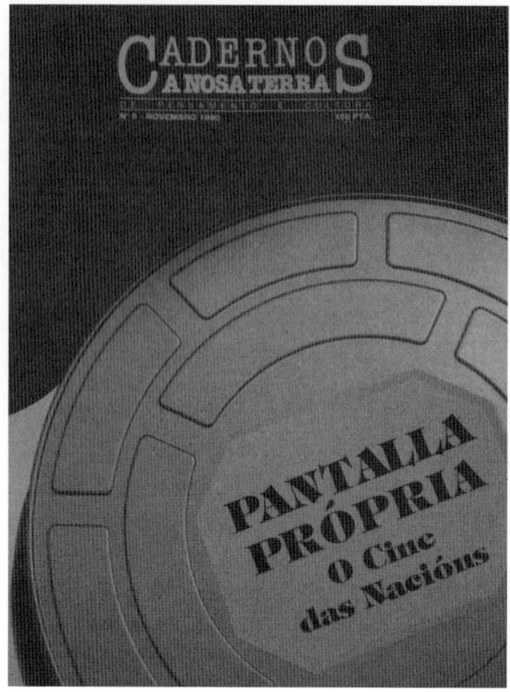

Figure 4.1 *Pantalla Propia: O Cine das Nacións (A Screen of One's Own: The Cinema of Nations).* Special issue of the cultural magazine *Cadernos da Nosa Terra de Pensamento e Cultura* on the cinema of Spain's autonomous communities (November 1990). Courtesy of *Cadernos da Nosa Terra.*

television stations and other media, film schools, professional associations, and film commissions); the persistence of the auteur model; the particular language map involved (monolingualism, bilingualism, diglossia, multilingualism, dialectalism); the intersections of nation, class, race, and gender; and cinema production and commercial branding efforts that exceed the limits of the nation (see Figure 4.1).

With the process of political devolution that took place after the 1978 Constitution – the Basque Country was granted autonomy in 1979, Andalusia and Galicia in 1981 – the administrative control of cinema and audiovisual production passed from the central state to the autonomous governments. The result has been the emergence of a significant corpus of cinematic production in autonomous communities with a strong sense of national identity, such as the Basque Country and Galicia, with their vernacular languages and history of non-state nationalism going back to the mid-nineteenth century, and Andalusia, which, although Castilian-speaking (albeit dialectally inflected), saw the beginnings of a regionalist movement in the 1920s and 1930s. There had, of course, been some film production in the Basque Country, Galicia, and Andalusia before political devolution; what was new now was official recognition and sponsorship – that is, the emergence of the concepts of "Basque cinema," "Galician cinema," and "Andalusian cinema." Basque cinema emerged during the transition period, with a new wave of Basque directors appearing in the early 1990s and significant production in the last decade. Galician cinema officially came into existence in the late 1980s, expanding and diversifying in the late 1990s, while Andalusian cinema was officially born only in the first decade of the twenty-first century. It is not the intention of this chapter to simply present a historical overview of these cinemas but to underscore the historical connections and explore new conceptual models that can offer a fuller picture and better understanding of their development. The visual imagery of the primal scene is a powerful metaphor for cinema, in its tension between visibility and invisibility. The concept of a national primal scene is particularly relevant in the case of these "other cinemas" that have a conflictive relation with Spanish nationalism and authoritarianism and have struggled for visibility since their origins. The following sections on Andalusian, Basque, and Galician cinemas (taken in that order) – or in a broader sense cinemas made in Andalusia, the Basque Country, and Galicia – explore their convergences and divergences in often unexpected ways. What is clear is that, in spite of their obvious differences, these cinemas all share the goal of winning visibility beyond the periphery and making a transnational impact. In this new cartography where the global joins hands with the local, bypassing the nation-state, Spanish cinema may itself become decentered, if not peripheral.

On the Global Formation of Andalusian and Basque Cinemas (Joseba Gabilondo)

The Spanish National Primal Scene

The narrative of Spanish nationalism was founded on the discourse of the War of Independence (1808–14): a postcolonial narrative appropriated from Latin American discourses of independence, according to which a supposedly "colonized" Spain liberated itself from an imperialist France (Álvarez Junco 2001). This appropriation represented the end of the discourse of occidentalism deployed by Spain since the sixteenth century, whereby the Roman Empire found its culmination in Spanish imperial expansion in the Americas and beyond. Moreover, from the late eighteenth century, romantic Europe began to orientalize Spain. In the nineteenth century, Spanish nationalist discourse internalized this orientalization in its manifold celebrations of Spanish difference and exceptionalism. Thus, Spanish nationalist discourse emerged from the intersection or clash between occidentalism and orientalism.

This historical clash has a primal scene: Prosper Mérimée's *Carmen* (1845). The Freudian term "primal scene" is used here in the sense given to it by the art critic

Hal Foster: a "scenario that we invoke to tease out the riddles of our own origins" (2004: x). In this primal scene, these orientalist and occidentalist discourses come together to produce *jouissance*. Although Merimée resorts to the trope of the Gypsy as synecdoche for the Andalusian and sets his story in Seville, the character who serves as focalizer, with the story being told through his eyes, is the Basque Don José Lizarrabengoa. As an Old Christian – of "pure race" and universal nobility – Don José is aligned with the French spectators of the drama: Merimée, the narrator, and readers. When Don José kills Carmen, he stands for the old occidentalist discourse of Spanish conquest, whereas Carmen stands for the orientalist discourse of an othered Spain.

Yet, if Mérimée's novella *Carmen* gave rise to the *españolada* (the stereotypical representation of Spain, largely in terms of Andalusian cultural clichés), there is nothing Spanish about his character Carmen: she and Don José are Spain's "others" who make possible the invisible, phantasmatic Spain that emerges from their deadly clash. They point to a Spanish primal scene founded on the *jouissance* experienced by Spain in seeing itself reflected back at itself in the gaze of its others: the Basque Don José, representing an outdated imperialist occidentalism, and the Gypsy / Andalusian Carmen, representing a fatally seductive orientalism. The deadly encounter between a Basque and an Andalusian can be read as an allegory of a Spanish nation that can only contemplate itself by invoking and annihilating the gaze directed at it by its others.

Today, when the central state's devolution of power to the autonomous communities is "advanced" and Spain has "normalized" its position within a globalized Europe, the political goal of any analysis must be to break out of this othering process by opening up a non-Spanish history inside and outside of Spanish history.

Andalusian Cinema

Although Andalusia has been the site of negotiaton of Spain's orientalization from the "golden age" of Spanish cinema in the 1930s to the present (Delgado 1992: 77–100; Labanyi 2003; Utrera 2005: 135–87), most contemporary histories, although they study films from Andalusia, do not consider there to be such a thing as "Andalusian cinema." The concept first started to be mooted in Andalusia in the 1980s (Utrera and Delgado 1980; Fernández Sánchez 1985; Delgado 1992) but, apart from the Certamen de Cine Andaluz (Andalusian Film Competition) promoted by the Festival Internacional de Cine de Sevilla (Seville International Film Festival) in 1980–2, it was not underpinned by a sustained discourse. In 1996, when the initial debate on "Andalusian cinema" had subsided, Rafael Utrera insisted that the term was still being invoked as a desired or utopian reality (Caparrós Lera 1996: 27). When summarizing Andalusian cinema's twenty-year production record from 1975 to 1996, Utrera named only three directors who had shot more than one film: Gonzalo García Pelayo, Pancho Bautista, and Juan Sebastián Bollaín (Caparrós Lera 1996: 27).

Before attempting to identify a start date for Andalusian cinema, it is important to note that non-Andalusian film production in Andalusia was promoted by local institutions and media before they started to promote Andalusian cinema. Since its creation in 1998, the mission of the Andalucía Film Commission (AFC) has been to promote, not Andalusian cinema as such, but (global) film production in Andalusia. When consulted in June 2010, the AFC's home page (www.andalucia-film.com/index.php/inicio) featured an invitation to the global film industry to film in Andalusia from "Andalusia's most universal film personality," Antonio Banderas. It was within this wider context of film production, and with a clear commercial aim, that in 2004 the AFC joined several Andalusian producers to promote "Andalusian cinema" not in Spain but in the USA, taking advantage of the initial success of films such as *Solas / Alone* (Benito Zambrano, 1999) and *Nadie conoce a nadie / Nobody Knows Anybody* (Mateo Gil, 1999) in Spain, where they were hailed as the beginning of a new realism (Triana Toribio 2003: 155–7). Indeed, "Andalusian cinema" was first promoted as a de facto entity in 2004 at the Instituto Cervantes in New York. This was followed up at Latino film festivals in Chicago, Los Angeles, and Miami with sponsorship from a large number of Andalusian institutions, under the banner "Primera Semana de Cine Andaluz" (First Andalusian Film Week) (Arranca 2004). The same year saw the creation of the "Muestra de Cine Andaluz y del Mediterráneo" (Andalusian and Mediterranean Film Festival), held in Archidona. When this initiative was repeated in 2005, AFC director Carlos Rosado described the AFC as an "ejemplo de desarrollo de la industria en toda Europa" (model of the film industry's development in the whole of Europe) (El IX Festival 2005). Thus, 2004 was the year when "Andalusian cinema" was "born," through its promotion.

From this mapping, it can be inferred that Andalusian cinema is defined by a manifold excess, in the sense that it exceeds the "purely" Andalusian – and, indeed, the purely cinematic. This excess takes several forms. First, geographic excess. From its inception, it has been promoted in international and global settings, linking Seville, Chicago, Los Angeles, Miami, and New York. It thus exceeds the confines of the Andalusian Autonomous Community and of the Spanish state. Second, economic excess. Andalusian cinema is not generally promoted as a body of films made by Andalusian directors (the approach taken by other autonomous communities). The stress is rather on the broad phenomenon of filmmaking in Andalusia, conceived as a strategy for attracting Spanish and foreign investment to the area. Third, visual excess. Andalusian cinema has an inextricable extracinematic function – that of tourist promotion, which has played a major role in defining Andalusia as Europe's internal Orient from the early nineteenth century to today.

The following paragraphs will limit themselves to a brief discussion of Andalusian cinema in the restricted sense of films made by Andalusian directors, taking two examples: Chus Gutiérrez (born in Granada) and Benito Zambrano (born in Lebrija). The focus will be on how Andalusian cinema appropriates the discourses of orientalism and occidentalism, giving rise to a new transnational politics that exceeds the merely Andalusian.

After directing *Sublet* (1991, shot in English in the USA) and *Sexo oral / Oral Sex* (1994), Gutiérrez received wide acclaim with *Alma gitana / Gypsy Soul* (1996), followed by *Insomnio / Insomnia* (1998), *Poniente / Wind from the West* (2002), *El Calentito* (2005), and *Retorno a Hansala / Return to Hansala* (2008), plus several television shorts. In 2009, she received the Premio Archidona Cinema of the Muestra de Cine Andaluz y del Mediterráneo (Andalusian and Mediterranean Film Festival) for her artistic career. Although nominated for a Goya (Spain's equivalent of the Oscars) as Best New Director of 1991, she received no more Goya nominations until 2009, when *Retorno a Hansala* was nominated for Best Original Script, Best Original Song, and Best New Actress; the same film won the 2008 Jury Special Prize at Seminci (Valladolid International Film Festival) and the 2008 Golden Pyramid at the Cairo International Film Festival. Gutiérrez only began to seek coproduction with Andalusian companies in 2008 with *Return to Hansala* (coproduced by the Andalusian Maestranza Films with Madrid-based Muac Films). Prior films were coproduced by companies in Madrid mainly with national television channels, as in the case of *Alma gitana* (Samarkanda with Canal + and Televisión Española), *Insomnio* (Bocaboca with Sogetel), *Poniente* (Amboto and Olmo Films with Antena 3 and Vía Digital), and *El Calentito* (Estudios Picasso and Telespan 2000 with Canal+).

Gutiérrez's films typically employ integrated, multiple narrative structures, ranging from comedy to melodrama. Her goal is to bring together several characters rather than to focus on a single protagonist, in order to explore interpersonal relations (Heredero 1998: 30). Their locations move between Andalusia and Madrid. With the exception of *Insomnio*, her films explore political issues inflected by race and gender, mixing humor and drama with happy endings, within an overarching melodramatic structure and style. According to Thomas Elsaesser (1976), melodrama allows for the representation of complex moments of historical crisis and transition through the excessive, masochistic apparatus of personal feeling and suffering. Melodrama allows the viewer to feel and suffer history in its complex unrepresentability. In this sense, Gutiérrez's filmmaking comprises a very personal and geopolitically situated appropriation and refashioning of the Spanish melodrama tradition of the *españolada*. Between Florián Rey's 1936 box-office hit *Morena Clara / Dark and Bright*, whose female "Gypsy" or Roma protagonist wins the hand of a lawyer, and Gutiérrez's *Alma gitana* (1996), a love story between a Roma girl and a *payo* or non-Roma boy, there is more continuity than break.

Gutiérrez was hired to direct *Alma gitana* when the project was already developed (Camí-Vela 2001: 78–9). The film can be seen as a deconstruction of the Don Juan myth through that of Carmen: the protagonist, a serial seducer, is finally redeemed by the love of an "exotic" Roma girl who remains elusive to his seduction. Yet, the melodramatic celebration of an impossible union allows for a happy, if open, end. In *Poniente*, the sons of Andalusian laborers who migrated to northern Europe in the 1950s and 1960s, now back in Spain, are contrasted with contemporary Maghrebi immigrants to Andalusia, raising questions about both migrations. The film thus gives the viewer a double perspective on the history and geopolitics of migration, which contrasts starkly with the immobility of the traditional Andalusian patriarchal landowning system.

Gutiérrez exploits the dramatic potential of her politicized plots by using shot / reverse-shot sequences with eyeline matches in close-up, establishing a high degree of intimacy between the main characters. The centrality of an interpersonal filmic structure of intimacy, present in most of her films, is supplemented by characteristically diverse and unpredictable camerawork, which reinforces the personal tensions. Such techniques are used to accentuate gender, race, and class divides in a reworking of melodrama's exploitation of binary structures for the purposes of uncompromising social critique.

Gutiérrez's cinematic trajectory moves from the Andalusian myths of Don Juan and Carmen (*Alma gitana*) to the transnational theme of migration binding northern Europe, Africa, and Andalusia (*Poniente, Retorno a Hansala*). In the process, her Andalusian characters move between the positions of orientalized subject and embodiment of the new globalized European Spain, highlighting the orientalist / occidentalist divide that continues to define the historical contradictions of contemporary Andalusia.

Zambrano has made two films so far: *Solas* (1999) and *Habana Blues / Havana Blues* (2005). *Solas* was nominated for eleven Goyas and won five: Best New Actor, Best New Actress, Best New Director, Best Screenplay, and Best Supporting Actress. Utrera and other critics consider *Solas* a watershed in Andalusian cinema produced since 1975 (Utrera 2005: 182). Produced by Maestranza Films in conjunction with Canal Sur (the television channel funded by the Andalusian Autonomous Government), the film is set in Andalusia. It tells the story of an estranged daughter, María, who leaves her family's village for the city of Seville but reconciles with her mother (nameless in the film), who comes to stay when María's abusive father Paco needs hospital treatment in the city. The daughter is an alcoholic involved with an abusive truck driver by whom she becomes pregnant. While the mother is staying with her daughter, she meets a neighbor: an older widower (also nameless) from Asturias, with whom she has an unspoken romance. At the end of the film, the mother dies and the daughter raises her newborn daughter with the elderly Asturian widower.

The final arrangement between the elderly widower and the single mother María points to a rewriting of history, whereby a "good" father figure replaces the previous abusive father. This allows the woman, now a mother, to become the utopian reproductive subject of a new Andalusia that is, nonetheless, haunted by abusive patriarchal figures. Few critics have commented on the fact that the only non-Andalusian character is precisely the elderly Asturian widower. His non-Andalusian accent, biblical white beard, height, and cultivated dialogue (a sign of social distinction) are contrasted with the female protagonist's brutal Andalusian father. Thus, violence, situated within Andalusia, is enacted on the Andalusian female body, but the subject of the Law, the empty signifier that allows the film's ideological suture, is from the north. This resolution reworks the relation between an occidentalized north and orientalized south. As in *Carmen*, the desirable, feminized south is pitted against an enlightened, masculine north, pointing in this case to a utopian refashioning of the northern subject, insofar as the latter's symbolic castration by old age no longer codes it as sexual.

Habana Blues, nominated for four Goyas, of which it won two for editing and original score, was again coproduced by Maestranza Films, with funding from the Andalusian Autonomous Government, but this time with the collaboration and support of two nationwide Spanish television companies (TVE and Canal +) and the Instituto de la Cinematografía y de las Artes Audiovisuales (ICAA) (Spanish Ministry of Culture's Institute of Film and Audiovisual Media), plus Cuba's Instituto Cubano de Arte e Industria Cinematográficos (ICAIC) and the European film-funding body Eurimages. In this film, Zambrano moves the occidental / oriental divide to Cuba, cast in a new form, the stress being on how the country is currently being affected by the economic and cultural imperialism of Spanish and US multinationals. In fact, Zambrano completed his film studies in Cuba, where he wrote the original script for *Solas. Habana Blues* can therefore be read as a metafilmic return to the director's film origins.

In the film, a group of Spanish music producers working for a US company based in Miami and headed by a woman executive, Marta, visits Cuba and becomes interested in the music of two up-and-coming young musicians who lead a band: Ruy and Tito. At the end, the two Cuban musicians face a life-changing dilemma. They are offered a contract that allows them to leave Cuba and record in Spain but, at the same time, requires them, as a promotional strategy, to denounce the Cuban regime and thus abandon any hope of ever returning to a Castrist Cuba. In the end, Ruy stays and Tito leaves for Spain with the producers. The film is structured as a musical melodrama of homosocial bonding. The two women in Ruy's life – his wife, Caridad, who is about to divorce him, and the Spanish producer Marta – leave Cuba for Miami and Spain respectively at the end of the film; the central melodramatic tension is built around the two male protagonists, who quarrel over whether or not to leave for Spain (see Figure 4.2).

The film is structured around its musical numbers, with several songs played by Ruy and Tito's all-male band. To avoid interrupting the film's fast-paced, action-packed rhythm, with its montage of short takes, Zambrano justifies the longer music sequences diegetically by presenting them as rehearsals or concerts, but – and this is the film's structural originality – he intercuts these musical scenes with future events. This intercutting of flash-forward shots with musical sequences advances the action without freezing time, as happens with musical numbers in so many musicals. The film does not so much represent music as perform music cinematically: a performance of music and film-as-music at the same time.

Figure 4.2 *Habana Blues* trio (*Habana Blues*, Benito Zambrano, 2005; prod. Maestranza Films). Courtesy of Maestranza Films.

In centering its non-musical sequences on the band's attempts to secure funding and land a contract for international promotion with the Spanish producers, the film lends itself to metafilmic interpretation, whereby Zambrano allegorizes through Cuban music his own attempts to secure funding for his filmmaking. In a sense, the film can be read as a projection onto Cuba, in the global context of late capitalism, of Andalusia's complex positioning as both Western and other (oriental). The conflictive relationship between the Cuban performers and the Spanish producers is played out between the film's buddy protagonists – one white, one mulatto. The fact that the film ends with the mulatto character alone in Cuba, having made the ethical choice to stay in his country instead of sacrificing his music to late-capitalist corporate interests, speaks to Zambrano's own decision to opt for a situated filmmaking – one that is based in Andalusia and at the same time remains loyal to his professional origins: his filmmaker's apprenticeship in Cuba. Zambrano's Andalusian location – defined by the clash between occidentalism and orientalism – subtends his representation of a Cuba that is othered by globalization as African and Hispanic and yet remains linked to Spain by former colonial ties that place it within Spain's own occidentalist project. The fact that the Spanish producers work for a US multinational in Miami illustrates the new Atlantic redeployment of Spain as a global player in circumstances that are very different from those of its early modern imperial past.

Ever since Tomás Gutiérrez Alea's *Memorias del subdesarrollo / Memories of Underdevelopment* (1968), the gaze at a decaying Havana has been used to underline the alienated positionality of the Western-identified bourgeois and / or tourist. In *Habana Blues*, Zambrano's own Andalusian positionality, predetermined – even overdetermined – by a similar tourist gaze, creates an Atlantic Andalusian–Cuban geography that, although not devoid of contradictions, offers an opportune reflection on globalization, tourism, and film.

Basque Cinema

In his *20 nuevos directores del cine español* (1999), Carlos F. Heredero helps us to situate contemporary debates on "Basque cinema" in the wider Spanish context. He singles out four Basque directors as the core of a new generation of filmmakers that renovated Spanish cinema in the 1990s: Enrique Urbizu, Juanma Bajo Ulloa, Julio Medem, and Álex de la Iglesia. Yet these directors are also seen as bringing about "the end of Basque cinema." Unlike the previous generation of Basque filmmakers (e.g., Pedro Olea, Imanol Uribe, and Montxo Armendáriz), these new directors felt incapable of making films within the constraints established by the Basque Autonomous Government; consequently, they moved to Madrid to work with commercial production companies (for Basque directors not discussed in this chapter, see Zunzunegui 1985; de Pablo 1996, 1998; Roldán-Larreta 1999; Gabilondo 2002b; Martí-Olivella 2003). As a result, most Basque directors started to be considered as Spanish, and their Basque positionality was marginalized or considered secondary. In these circumstances, the debate on Basque cinema became a discussion about its nonexistence. The most telling example of this "end of Basque cinema" narrative is the case of Julio Medem. He has created what can be seen as an auteuristic oeuvre, with his high-quality craftsmanship and singular formalism placing him at the pinnacle of Spanish cinema (see Chapter 5). According to Heredero, Medem's Basque positionality has become subsumed under a broader positionality encompassing Spain and Europe (1999: 250). Isabel Santaolalla observes that Medem's "choice of settings for the films seems to distance him progressively from his homeland: from the Basque–Navarran forests of *Vacas / Cows*, 1992, down to the Riojan countryside for *La ardilla roja / The Red Squirrel*, 1993, to the Aragonese parched vineyards in *Tierra / Earth*, 1996, and, in *Los amantes del círculo polar / Lovers of the Arctic Circle*, 1998, to the edge of the globe" (1999: 312). Santaolalla attempts to read into Medem's move to ever broader geographical canvases an affirmation of his "strong emotional and metaphorical bond" with his homeland; yet, even in her perceptive analysis, she can only hint at "hidden forces raging with turmoil and dissidence, ready to unsettle complacent notions of individual and national identity" (1999: 312) and "heavily symbolic elements and characters" that translate into "universally relevant conflicts, fears and desires" (1998: 336).

The "normalization" or mainstreaming of Medem's cinema as simply Spanish came to an abrupt end when he directed and produced *La pelota vasca: la piel contra la piedra / The Basque Ball Game: Skin against Stone* (2003), a documentary about the Basque political situation. Although *La pelota vasca* received a Goya for Best Documentary in 2004, it became the center of an international political scandal and the target of right-wing parties and Victims of Terrorism groups (Stone 2007: 205). On a political level, the film managed to bring together through editing, despite the absence of representatives of both political extremes (Partido Popular, ETA), a wide range of people who would never agree to meet in the same place, let alone engage in dialogue.

Regardless of the film's "political content," its approach to the Basque situation is radically different from that taken by most previous Basque directors and films. Medem's film thereby marks an important shift in Basque and Spanish cinema – one that speaks to the core of Basque cinema's history. Most critics who have addressed the issue of whether or not "Basque cinema" exists come down on the side of its "nonexistence." Those who address the issue from an empirical or sociological point of view (Zunzunegui 1985; de Pablo 1998; Roldán Larreta 1999) conclude that its existence cannot be denied but that it cannot be defined either, because of its complexity. From a more psychoanalytically imbued perspective, Jaume Martí-Olivella analyzes this negativity or indefinability as precisely the mark of a history that cannot be explained in positivist or empirical terms (2003: 18). Rather, the contradictory negativity of Basque cinema – nonexistent but existent – needs to be analyzed historically as a form of simultaneous repression and representation. Martí-Olivella's groundbreaking definition informs my analysis here.

In *La pelota vasca*, Medem attempts to go beyond this negative logic. For the first time, instead of representing an uncanny history, he set out to represent Basque reality as politically and historically present. He does this by filming a wide spectrum of people speaking about the Basque situation. Importantly, the film continues to use the cinematic techniques and style that had given Medem his reputation as a high-quality, auteuristic Spanish and European director. The long-take format, common in "talking-head" documentaries, is complicated by Medem in a very original way: individuals filmed in medium shot are frequently set against a mise-en-scène of distant landscapes, creating an extreme depth of field. The fact that the talking heads are filmed without establishing shots to ground them in the landscape creates an eerie feeling of disconnection between figure and setting. The landscape acquires such depth that it becomes another historical subject in the film.

Yet, despite Medem's continued use of cinematic techniques that had brought him acclaim, *La pelota vasca*, from its premiere, triggered an irrational, violent response in many sectors of the Spanish state and some sectors of the Basque Country, particularly from the conservative Partido Popular (PP) both within and outside the Basque Country. This reasserted once again what I have elsewhere called the "uncanny" nature of Basque cinema (Gabilondo 2002b), in the sense that its existence is admitted only through its negation and repression. This time the negative logic was not represented through an uncanny, absent violence within the film – as, for example, in *Vacas* (Gabilondo 2002b). The violence was outside: in the movie theater and in the public sphere. The film did not perform Basque violence; a new form of Spanish violence was performed through and upon the film. *La pelota vasca* broke with the logic of the Spanish nationalist primal scene that requires that its othered Basque subject be violently eliminated at the end – a tendency that can be observed from *La Muerte de Mikel / The Death of Mikel* (Imanol Uribe, 1984) to *Yoyes* (Helena Taberna, 2000).

This new way of representing Basque history and politics has in the last few years elicited another kind of filmmaking: Basque cinema in *euskara* (the Basque language). This new cinema has had complex effects on Basque culture, creating new imaginary formations, a new star system, and new debates in the public sphere. Their effects are mostly overlooked by critics because these films have a certain visual opacity that allows them to be dismissed as uneventful, formally unchallenging, parochial, or even *costumbrista* (nostalgically depicting local customs). These films do not elicit any Spanish fantasies about a primal scene in which a Basque subject is supposed to be violent. Although Arantxa Lazkano's *Urte ilunak / Dark Years* (1992) was an important precedent, this new Basque cinema dates from 2005, when the film *Aupa Etxebeste! / Hurray Etxebeste!* (Asier Altuna and Telmo Esnal) was released, ushering in an uninterrupted production of films in Basque, of which the most successful have been *Kutsidazu bidea, Ixabel / Show me the Way, Isabel* (Fernando Bernués and Mireia Gabilondo, 2006) and *Eutsi! / Hold On!* (Alberto Gorritiberea, 2007), while those displaying the highest filmic qualities are probably *Ander* (Roberto Castón, 2009) and *Zorion perfektua / Perfect Happiness* (Jabi Elortegi, 2009). Most of these films were exhibited in film theaters with significant public attendance; for example, on the weekend of its release, *Eutsi!* had the second-highest box-office return in the Basque Autonomous Community and Navarre (Eutsi! 2007).

When analyzing this Basque cinema in *euskara* that emerged in the first decade of the twenty-first century, almost simultaneously with Andalusian cinema, new historical problems and challenges arise. The issue of language is not simply or primarily linguistic: it is geopolitical. Basque cinema in *euskara*, with very rare exceptions, is a cinema made locally in the Basque Country that, by capturing its bilingualism if not trilingualism (Basque, Spanish, French), posits the Basque-speaking public as its target audience while also aiming to reach a broader audience through exhibition with subtitles at international film festivals. *Kutsidazu bidea, Ixabel* was presented at the San Sebastián International Film Festival and won the Special Jury Award at the Festival Internacional de Cinema de Comedia (Peñíscola Comedy Film Festival). *Ander* won the CICAE award at the Berlin International Film Festival and the Violette d'Or at the Tolouse Cinespaña festival.

As Bakhtin's theories of dialogism and heteroglossia explain (1981), the issue of language is also historical. The Basque language raises historical issues of subalternity and repression that are fully articulated only in the language itself – hence the important role that has been played by Basque literature, particularly oral literature and popular theater, since it is the medium that has most represented the conflicts of Basque culture. Discourses and representational strategies developed by literature (oral and written) shape the way in which Basque cinema in *euskara* approaches its Basque subject matter, shifting its discourse from the violence that marks so much earlier Basque cinema to class, gender, and sexual struggles.

With the process of subalternization that the Basque language and culture have undergone since at least the Counter-Reformation – and later, in the seventeenth and eighteenth centuries as an oligarchic elite, backed by the Church, developed the ideology of *foralismo* (legal and economic exceptionalism and particularity) – the Basque rural subaltern classes developed a very rich popular culture of comedy and contestation, even when it took the form of religious performance. Although in the nineteenth century Carlism and Basque nationalism appropriated this popular culture in order to found a political imaginary, it persisted throughout the twentieth century. However, because of its rural origins and religious influence, this popular culture marked by humor, contestation, and excess conflicted with modernizing cultural forms expressed in Spanish and French. The historical contradiction between a rural culture of comedy and contestation and its appropriation by a modernizing nationalism would become the central and enduring axis underpinning Basque visual as well as literary culture. After the Franco dictatorship, as the Basque Autonomous Community – legally instituted in 1979 – developed its own public sphere in *euskara*, media such as television and film took up this popular tradition and its nationalist appropriation, now coding both in *euskara*.

From its beginnings, the oligarchic discourse of *foralismo*, which later took on a nationalist slant, resorted to *euskara* as the cornerstone of the Basque Country's historical uniqueness. Consequently, an occidentalist discourse on the Basque Country was developed that attempted to prove its historical originality by claiming that the Basques were the original founders of the West as well as its sole remaining "indigenous people." Thus, Basques became occidentalism's internal others: the only simultaneously indigenous and Western people left in the West. Basque popular culture was mobilized both in an occidentalist way (as the West's origin and internal other) and in an antioccidentalist fashion (as a subaltern resistance to the local oligarchies' modernizing advances). In short, the modern deployment of popular Basque culture illustrates a founding split within occidentalism: Basques are the "indigenous" others of occidentalism and yet they resort to occidentalism as the ultimate discourse to frame Basque politics (Gabilondo 2008). This split – mainly class-based – at the center of rural popular culture in *euskara* is taken up and refashioned by contemporary Basque film.

I will illustrate this through two case studies: the previously mentioned *Kutsidazu bidea, Ixabel!* (2006) and *Ander* (2009). *Kutsidazu*, a comedy, is the film that is the most aware of and most ironizes the Basque Country's contradictory relationship to occidentalism (see Figure 4.3). The film tells the story of a Basque city boy who, in order to become "truly" Basque by improving his knowledge of *euskara* among

Figure 4.3 Poster for *Kutsidazu bidea, Ixabel* (Fernando Bernués and Mireia Gabilondo, 2006; prod. Tantazioa Produkzioak). Courtesy of Tentazioa Produkzioak.

"authentic speakers," leaves the city of San Sebastián and moves to a rural mountain village to study in a *barnetegi* (a hybrid schooling model whereby the student takes classes in *euskara* during the day and lives with a rural *euskara*-speaking family, helping with the farm work in the evenings and at weekends). The film sends up the Conradian trope of "going native" in a Basque "Heart of Darkness." The main character, Juan Martin, falls in love with the rural family's daughter, Ixabel. In the course of many episodes and adventures in which the city boy is mocked as the most "native" and innocent, the film explores the love triangle between Ixabel, Juan Martin, and Luis-Koldo, a tall, handsome villager who outdoes Juan Martin at every rural activity. At the end, Juan Martin manages to outdo his rival by singing a *bertso* (improvised oral poem) at the village festivities and, in this way, wins Ixabel's heart. Significantly, Ixabel is represented as "less rural" than Juan Martin. In one of the last two sequences, the camera pulls back and reveals the crew and the other cameras filming the village festivities. The film thus becomes a meta-comedy, making the audience aware of its comedic nature and including it in the comedy: the film theater becomes a comedic extension of the village festivities. The film makes the audience part of the contradictions involved in the Basque

Country's contradictory positioning within occidentalism: the audience participates simultaneously in the "native" festivities and in the film's technological spectacle. The audience "goes native" while being reminded, through comedy, that such an experience is mediated through modern film.

Ander is a film that alternates between comedy and melodrama. Unlike the previous film, in which the camerawork and editing create a fast pace attuned to the rhythms of comedy and reveal the movie's metacinematic nature at the end, *Ander* adopts the auteuristic strategy of the long take where the camera barely moves; even when it pans or zooms, it does so to make small adjustments to point of view. The use of silence is perhaps the film's most notable feature, in addition to the use of two-shots with one of the characters positioned with his / her back to the camera, so as to create an inner space of dialogue between the characters that escapes the camera and the spectator.

The film tells the story of a Basque farmstead where the elder sibling, Ander, lives with his mother and sister; the latter is about to get married and move out. Ander has an accident, breaks his leg, and hires a Peruvian immigrant, José, to help him with the farm work until he recovers. Through subtle dialogue, the film makes it clear that neither Ander nor José like city life. As they get to know each other, Ander falls in love with José. When Ander's mother dies and he is close to full recovery, faced with the prospect of loneliness, he asks José to stay with him.

Rather than attempting an ideological suture of the split within occidentalist discourse between the exaltation of primitive origins and the narrative of Western progress, the film hints at the return of a new ruralism across continents – an Atlantic ruralism. The film inserts the occidentalist split into the rural world by incorporating postcolonial difference: the story of immigration shaped by the history of Spanish imperialism. Another (postcolonial) form of ruralism becomes internal to Basque ruralism, inserting the discourse of modernization into the rural world, thereby attempting a new rural suture that counters the split within occidentalism. The desire that emerges from this new ruralism is a gay masculine desire. The fact that José is the subject who stands as the nurturing other that allows the Basque subject to refashion itself at the end does not solve the split – even though the resolution offered is original and full of political potential.

The Deconstruction of the Spanish Primal Scene

The above analysis frames the discussion of Andalusian and Basque cinemas in ways that go beyond homogeneous nationalist formations by placing them in the broader context of occidentalism and orientalism. It also explains such nationalist ideological foreclosures as effects, rather than causes, of Spain's contradictory positioning between occidentalism and orientalism. In this respect, Andalusian and Basque cinemas exceed Spanish cinema. They are thus able to break the circle of othering produced by the Spanish national primal scene and contribute to a political devolution of the power of state devolution; that is, to an autonomy that challenges the central state that regards itself as having granted it. As a result, other issues such as fantasy, desire, gaze, gender, and sexuality are freed from their nationalist overdetermination and can be discussed and analyzed in new ways that situate them in a global context without bypassing their local historicity.

Galician Cinema: Making the Invisible Visible (José Colmeiro)

Another Spanish National Primal Scene

If, as is argued above, *Carmen* can be read as the primal scene of nineteenth-century Spanish nationalism (constructed from outside and later internalized), the film *Raza / Race* (José Luis Sáenz de Heredia, 1942) can be considered the primal scene of twentieth-century Spanish nationalism (constructed from within and imposed from above). A family saga-cum-historical epic, *Raza* traces the national past from Spain's military defeat by the United States in 1898, leading to the definitive loss of its American and Asian possessions, to Franco's victory parade at end of the Spanish Civil War. The film thus rewrites the historical script into a triumphant nationalist epic in accordance with Francoist mythology (as is well-known, the film's original storyline was written by Franco himself under a pseudonym). The Churruca family, which holds the narrative together, is a symbolic stand-in for the Spanish nation – a pedagogical device inviting identification with the film's lament for the end of the global empire where the sun never set, through a post-imperial narrative of loss and fragmentation that seeks historical transcendence. The film effectively announces a new spiritual and cultural empire in the form of *Hispanidad* (Hispanicity), where the traditional values of the lost empire – patriarchalism, militarism, and Catholicism – are resuscitated in a montage of historical images, sutured through dissolves. The anxiety of loss and fragmentation brought by modernity is neutralized through this closing imaginary apotheosis, restoring Spain to its central position in the occidentalist discourse of empire that has defined Europe since the sixteenth century.

The narrative begins in Galicia – specifically Ferrol, Franco's birthplace and one of Spain's oldest naval bases. The film's idealized Spanish patriotic family embodies the fragments of the nation that need to be reconstituted. The lesson taught by this cinematic primal family is the historical continuity and undivided territorial integrity of the motherland and the unity of the "Spanish race." To that effect, the film conveniently erases recent history – in particular the birth of Catalan, Basque, and Galician nationalisms in the nineteenth century, their acquisition of political power and influence in elections and referendums during the Second Spanish Republic, and ultimately their defeat in the Civil War and subsistence in exile.

The Churruca family can be seen as the expression of a national primal scene inasmuch as their family saga rewrites national history so as to produce a mythical narrative of origins. Cultural and political difference is disavowed and integrated into the fabric of the nation. The mise-en-scène depicts the Churruca family mansion as visibly Galician, through its use of traditional Galician imagery and musical soundtrack. Yet no reference is made to specific features of Galician history or language. Galicia is literally a backdrop for Spanish nationalist discourse. The Churruca family may be Galician, but all that matters is that they are Spanish patriots willing to give their lives for the motherland. The navy officer patriarch instructs his children in the patriotic obligations deriving from their lineage. Interestingly, he reveals that one of their ancestors was Cosme Damián de Churruca, a Basque-born admiral of the Spanish fleet who died heroically at the Battle of Trafalgar against the British in 1805. The third example of Spanish patriotism cited by him is that of the Almogavars, a Catalan–Aragonese army during the Middle Ages that was instrumental in the Christian *Reconquista* (wars against the Moors) and in the consolidation of Aragón's Mediterranean empire under the leadership of Roger de Flor, the hero who inspired the Catalan language epic *Tirant le Blanc* (1490). The patriarch's early patriotic lessons are later recited from memory by his grown-up daughter in the film's final montage sequence, subtly suturing the three discordant peripheral nationalisms (Basque, Catalan, and Galician) into the now triumphant narrative of Spanish fascist neo-imperialism.

This rendering invisible of difference through a superficial act of suture, converting representation into a form of repression, has been a historical determinant of Galician cinema production throughout its existence. The history of Galician cinema, like that of modern Galicia itself, is one of migration and dispersion, precariously balanced between the poles of subjugation and emancipation.

The Cinema of Migration and the *Gallegada*

One of the earliest and most distinctive forms of Galician cinema, somewhat neglected by critics, was an autochthonous "cinema of migration." This cinema, sometimes called "epistolary cinema," had the novel format of a two-way exchange of documentary images between Galician migrant societies in Latin America, particularly in the Southern Cone and Cuba, and Galician communities in the homeland. These films were often commissioned by Galician migrant communities, and sometimes by groups of returning migrants, as a form of filmic cultural connection. This cinematic genre produced hundreds of films documenting communal celebrations, cultural activities, traditional Galician scenery, and the migration experience itself, on both sides of the Atlantic.

The "cinema of migration" lasted for several generations, from the early days of the silent era in the 1910s, with pioneer filmmaker José Gil, and continuing well into the 1960s, with directors such as the Argentina-based Manuel Arís

Torres, Elixio González, and Amando Hermida Luaces. These works included documentaries and docudramas, frequently shot in amateur or semi-professional formats but shown in commercial movie theaters. While many of these works remain anonymous and the vast majority have not survived, a few have been recently recovered and restored by the Centro Galego das Artes da Imaxe (CGAI) (González 2000).

This unique phenomenon has no known parallel among other European cultural diasporas in the Americas. What is most noteworthy is that the transatlantic constitution of this "cinema of migration" completely sidesteps the constrictions of Spanish cinema. All the basic elements of this cinema – means of production, technical and artistic crew, cultural themes explored, target audience, and distribution circuits – were Galician. This cinema cannot be called peripheral to Spanish cinema since it was completely independent of Spanish cinema. It exceeded the parameters of Spanish national cinema, just as migration itself represented an excess that could not be successfully integrated into the Spanish nation-state. The "cinema of migration" is thus the first film form that can unequivocally be called "Galician" in the broad sense of transcending national borders; it is also remarkable because of its longevity.

The experience of Galician film directors already active during the Second Republic was also marked by dispersion. Of the three main established prewar Galician directors – José Suárez, Carlos Velo, and Antonio Román – two chose exile: Suárez in Argentina and Velo in Mexico, from where they continued their association with Galicia; Román chose to continue filming in Franco's Spain. During the dictatorship, with Galician film professionals forced to relocate to Madrid or overseas, Galician cinema was subsumed within Spanish cinema.

This absorption of Galician film professionals into Spanish cinema during the dictatorship had its most emblematic figure in producer Cesáreo González. His company Suevia Films (see Chapter 14) became the most important Spanish production company from the 1940s to the 1970s, notable for its well-established transatlantic international distribution circuit and exclusive contracts with some of the megastars of export-oriented popular Spanish cinema of the period – Lola Flores, Sara Montiel, Carmen Sevilla, and the child prodigies Joselito and Marisol – not to mention the Mexican diva María Félix. A returnee Galician migrant who had amassed a fortune in Cuba, González was also responsible for inventing the *gallegada* (films of Galician topicality, customs, landscape, music, and stories of migration) popular in the 1940s and 1950s, including films such as *El famoso Carballeira / The Famous Carballeira* (Fernando Mignoni, 1940) and *¡¡Polizón a bordo!! / Stowaway on Board!* (Ramón Torrado, 1943), and rural caricatures featuring the comic actor Xan das Bolas, which film historian Castro de Paz has called "cine de gaita e pandeireta" (bagpipe-and-tambourine cinema) (quoted in "O cine na Dictadura" n.d.). González was the first film producer to see the commercial potential of deploying the Galician landscape and rural types for a wide Spanish-language audience (Galán 1997), which included the large migrant communities in Latin

America (Suevia Films' remake of the Galician comedy classic *La casa de la Troya / College Boarding House* (Carlos Orellana, 1948) was filmed in Churubusco Studios in Mexico). Thus was born the genre of Galician exploitation cinema, providing a stereotypical or nostalgic tourist-postcard image of Galician life and customs, which proved economically successful in other films such as Ramón Torrado's *Mar abierto / Open Sea* (1946), *Botón de ancla / Naval Cadets* (1948), and *Sabela de Cambados / Sabela from Cambados* (1949). Clearly, the prototype was the *andaluzada* (stereotypical representation of a folkloric Andalusia), which subsumed Andalusian topicality under the Spanish national banner, as González himself acknowledged: "Cada ano fago a miña película e os meus documentais de Galicia, pero Andalucía, para o cine español e para o espectáculo, é unica" (Every year I make a film and documentaries about Galicia but, for Spanish cinema and the entertainment world in general, there is nothing like Andalusia) (cited in Galán 1997: 86).

The Rebirth of a Nation in Cinema: Debates, Consolidation, and Diversification

The 1970s saw the development of highly politicized, sustained debate on the conditions of possibility of Galician cinema, in the context of the rebirth of Galician cultural nationalism. New conceptualizations of Galician cinema were aired through a series of encounters, film festivals, and publications. Particularly important was the Semán do Cine en Ourense (Ourense Film Week), created in 1973, which in the mid-1970s became the epicenter of debates about "national cinemas" in Spain. The first Ourense Film Week's conclusions were somewhat bleak but constituted a real starting point: while confirming the nonexistence of Galician cinema except as an as yet unrealized utopian project, they demonstrated a collective desire for a distinctive self-image and the need to create a sustainable local film industry capable of taking forward its own projects. In 1976 the Ourense Film Week was redefined to include "cine de las nacionalidades y regiones" (cinema from the regions and historic nationalities), bringing together filmmakers from Galicia, Catalonia, the Basque Country, Valencia and the Canary Islands, who published a joint manifesto in the four languages of the Spanish state: "Declaración sobre los cines nacionales" (Declaration on National Cinemas) (Williams 2002: 103; Trenzado Romero 2008: 190–1).

In the same period, various underground film collectives formed across Galicia, and groups of militant filmmakers with extremely low budgets started to produce shorts in amateur formats. Manuel Rivas (1989) has referred to this generation of Galician filmmaking pioneers as believers in the "utopía de un cine autóctono en el *far-west* galaico" (utopia of an autochthonous cinema in the Galician far-west). These early initiatives laid the foundation for the birth of Galician cinema in the 1980s. Chano Piñeiro and Xavier Villaverde, who participated in these early debates on Galician cinema, started their film careers as amateur cinematographers in the

1970s, and would be among the first filmmakers to make the leap into professional cinema in the following decade.

The post-1978 process of political devolution had a direct impact on this process, with the Xunta de Galicia constituted as an autonomous government in 1981 and the public television channel Televisión de Galicia (TVG) established in 1985. Two top-down institutional initiatives instigated by the Xunta were particularly effective: a new policy of official subsidies for Galician film production, and significant support and demand from TVG for autochthonous video and film productions, which generated a large number of audiovisual production companies. In the same period, the exuberant cultural climate and multifaceted activities of the Galician *movida* (the counter-cultural movement in music, video, fashion, and the visual arts that paralleled the better-known Madrid *movida* of the late 1970s and early 1980s) were also decisive factors in the emergence of a new Galician cinema. Key figures here were Antón Reixa and Xavier Villaverde, who in the late 1980s and 1990s moved from highly successful music performance and video work to filmmaking and film production.

The first four major films subsidized by the Xunta were released in the late 1980s. The range of production models, genres, subject matter, and degrees of success of these four films is indicative of the trends as well as the limitations and possibilities of Galician cinema. The first was *Gallego / Galician* (1988), a Galician–Cuban coproduction based on Miguel Barnet's testimonial novel of the same title (1981), which follows the life of two Galician migrants in Cuba. Directed by the Cuban Manuel Octavio Gómez (director of the revolutionary classic *La primera carga al machete / The First Machete Charge*, 1969), the film was shot on location in Galicia and Cuba, with an assortment of Galician (Sancho Gracia, Rosalía Dans), Spanish (Francisco Rabal, Jorge Sanz), and Cuban (Omar Valdés, Caridad Ravelo) actors. It is symptomatic that this first institutionally subsidized project should have been a story of deterritorialization and a transnational initiative that exceeded the geopolitical parameters of both Galicia and Spain, with capital from TVG, Sancho Gracia's production company, and Cuba's ICAIC. In this way, *Gallego* challenged preconceived notions of Galician cinema as being defined by the language spoken or the nationality of the directors, crew, or certificate of origin.

The other three films were premiered together in Vigo in 1989, at the three-day gala event Cinegalicia mounted to inaugurate the new Galician cinema – technically the first ever Galician Film Festival. Considered a pivotal moment in Galician cinema by film critics, *Cinegalicia*'s recent official twenty-year commemoration received wide media coverage from Galician cultural critics, writers, and politicians. The three films launched were *Sempre Xonxa / Always Xonxa* (Chano Piñeiro), *Urxa* (Carlos López Piñeiro and Alfredo G. Pinal), and *Continental* (Xavier Villaverde). *Sempre Xonxa* and *Xurxa* are stories of rural Galicia, shot on location in Galician, with Galician actors and crew and with Galician funding. By contrast, *Continental* is a modern retro *film noir*, with a majority of Spanish actors, shot in Spanish and dubbed into Galician, and filmed entirely in a studio in Madrid, where

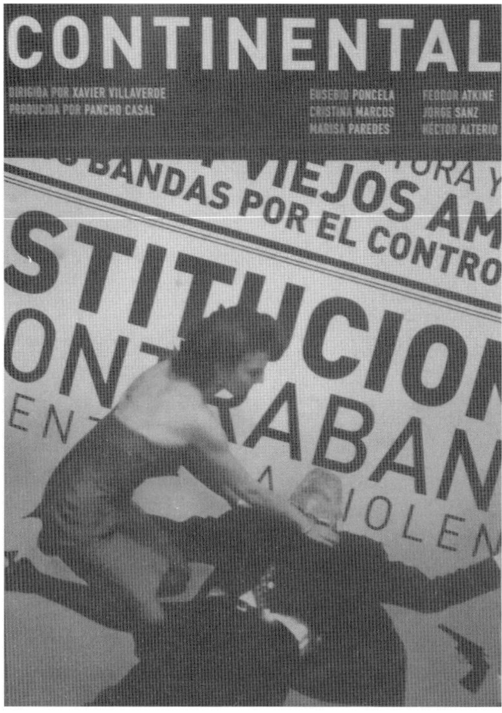

Figure 4.4 Poster for Xavier Villaverde's *Continental* (1989; prod. Contintental Producciones). Courtesy of Continental Producciones.

Villaverde lives and codirects his own multimedia production company, Continental (see Figure 4.4). While *Sempre Xonxa* and *Urxa* are recognizably Galician and possess a visual, linguistic, and cultural aura of "authenticity," mobilizing traditional tropes of Galicianness, *Continental* draws on an international film style, cosmopolitan mise-en-scène, and modern recycling of genres associated with Hollywood. The Galicianness of the first two films is highlighted in their titles, which take a Galician female first name as an untranslatable emblem of the nation; the cosmopolitanism of *Continental*, also figured in its title, does not need translating (at least, not for most European languages, including Spanish).

The first two films opt for a Galician poetic form of "magical realism" that has been common in Galician literature, in various forms, since the mid-nineteenth-century Rexurdimento (literary revival), including, more recently, Álvaro Cunqueiro and Manuel Rivas. Both capitalize on the visual power and spectacularity of the Galician landscape, already present in *Gallego* and a hallmark of much subsequent Galician film production. As in much Galician literature, the land is present not so much as a backdrop but as a constituent element of Galician identity. The shooting of both films in the Galician language was an innovation without precedent in Galician professional cinema, adding a further aura of "authenticity."

The rural Galician setting reinforced this linguistic authenticity since Galician is the prime language spoken in the rural areas, the urban areas being characterized by diglossia or Spanish monolingualism. Both films, set in the postwar years, focus on traditional Galician rural life, giving a somewhat essentialist view of Galician identity at a time in the 1980s when Galicia was rapidly being transformed into an urban-suburban – even "rurban" – community, with traditional farming increasingly abandoned. These films nostalgically recapture the sense of collective loss as well as the experience of migration (*Sempre Xonxa*) but avoid addressing Galicia's modernization. While modern Galician literature was adjusting to social and cultural transformation (Rivas, Suso de Toro), Galician cinema seemed to lag behind, fixated on filling the visual void of a past that had been for the most part cinematically invisible.

By contrast, *Continental* rejects traditional Galician themes associated with rural settings, natural scenery, and magical-realist tropes. Instead, it opts for a neutral urban setting and cosmopolitan look. Indeed, the film is notable for its aesthetic experimentation and postmodern recycling and mixing of genres (*film noir's* sordidness, melodrama's theatricality, the western's archetypal characterization), and for being an ambitious commercial project, with a stellar Spanish and international cast including Eusebio Poncela, Jorge Sanz, Marisa Paredes, Fernando Guillén, Héctor Alterio, and Féodor Atkine. While *Continental* is visually and musically exciting, it ends up falling victim to its overtly ambitious style, which at times disorients the spectator. The marks of its Galicianness are intentionally not obviously inscribed on the film's surface. Critics commented that the film "could well be set in Hamburg, Istanbul, or Brest" (Williams 2002: 105). Its Galicianness is more subtle, embedded in its numerous intertextual allusions to Galician literature (to Ramón Otero Pedrayo and Eduardo Pondal, for example) that would not register with most spectators, especially outside Galicia. Its director has referred to the film's often-misunderstood metaphorical Galician dimension:

> Unha metáfora de Galicia como labirinto de rúas sempre molladas que se entrecruzan, onde ten lugar a traxedia duns personaxes sós, abandonados e de volta de case todo, perdidos na noite interminable de "ese lugar húmido e pequeno" onde transcorre o filme. (Villaverde 2009: 1)
>
> A metaphor of Galicia as a labyrinth of criss-crossing wet streets, where the tragic story unfolds of a lonely, abandoned, and disillusioned set of characters, lost in the endless night of that "small, wet place" where the film's action takes place.

Villaverde's film thus represents a key paradox of Galician cinema. In its effort to create and market a Galician film without obvious surface marks of Galicianness that can travel beyond Galicia, *Continental* could be said to symbolize the general invisibility of Galician cinema; but it also symbolizes a desire to expand the horizons of Galician cinema beyond Galicia itself, and beyond Spain, to the world at large. While *Sempre Xonxa* and *Urxa* were unquestionably Galician, they shared with *Continental* the relative invisibility of Galician cinema, for all three films failed to reach large audiences outside Galicia.

During the 1990s, Galician cinema became consolidated in several key areas: the creation of a functional infrastructure; the establishment of professional film associations; the passing of legislation for the audiovisual sector, giving it official status as a strategic growth area in Galicia thanks to the regularization of film subsidies; the creation of the Galician Film Archives, with a mission to recover and disseminate Galician cinema; and the creation of public and private film schools (Colmeiro 2011). The proliferation of film shorts and short festivals can be attributed to a new generation of film school graduates as well as to the availability of new digital technologies. These various factors have contributed to increased levels of Galician film production since the 1990s. This steady growth of Galician cinema in the last twenty years has been accompanied by a growing diversification, with a large range of genres aimed at different audiences, from children's animation and youth comedies to documentaries, literary adaptations, popular genre films (urban thrillers, horror), and alternative films. Juan Pinzás' *Dogme 95* trilogy – *Era outra vez / Once Upon Another Time* (2000), *Días de voda / Wedding Days* (2002), and *El desenlace / The Outcome* (2005), dealing with issues of cultural identity related to gender, social class, and language use – stand out as the only films made in Spain that have been officially included in Dogme 95, the avant-garde movement initiated by Lars Von Trier, characterized by an anti-studio and bare-bones aesthetic. The movement's rejection of artifice and minimalist aesthetics seem plausible choices for Pinzás' exploration of the difficulties of coming out as both gay and Galician-speaking in a homophobic and diglossic yuppie cultural environment. However, as Ryan Prout has shown (2010), in spite of its promising premises and potential international appeal, the trilogy has enjoyed only marginal success, flawed by its excessive histrionics and lack of linguistic and narrative verisimilitude. By contrast, *Pradolongo* (Ignacio Vilar, 2008), closer to reality and more traditional in narrative style, proved unusually successful with both urban and rural Galician youth audiences. The film depicts rural living as modern and appealing, with an up-to-date, realistic use of the Galician language as spoken dialectally in the Valdeorras area. Given that the Galician language has traditionally been linked with the rural lower classes, and for many young Galicians is associated with an aging population and with the past, the fact that *Pradolongo* was able to connect with young urban, middle-class audiences suggests that this kind of visibly and audibly Galician cinema has potential.

Global Visibility and Technical Innovation

In recent years Galician cinema has become increasingly concerned with internationalizing its operations, both in terms of Galician film productions seeking outside funding and audiences and in terms of attracting film production to Galicia from other parts of Spain and abroad. Official policies were put in place throughout the 1990s to encourage film production in Galicia by non-local film professionals, facilitating coproduction schemes, thus prioritizing the idea of "cinema in Galicia." With that end in mind, in 1999 the official Galician Audiovisual Report was published in English, and a Galicia Film Commission plus a Santiago de Compostela Film Commission were set up in 2002. These initiatives have, in the last decade, coincided with an increase in Galician films screened at international film festivals, and a number of Mostras de Cine Galego (Galician Film Festivals) in various overseas locations, some repeated in successive years – for example, in Portugal (2000), Argentina (2003), Paris (2004), Berlin (2005), Cuba, Brazil, and Chile (2007), and Brussels and New York (2008). Additionally, since 2008 the Galician–Portuguese film festival Filmminho has been held annually in the border towns of Vilanova de Cerveira and Tomiño, on both sides of the River Miño.

In a 2004 article for the North American cinema magazine *Variety*, John Hopewell acknowledges a paradigmatic change in the contemporary Galician audiovisual panorama. The title says it all: "Hit and Myth in the Deep North. Forward-looking Rural Area Transforming into TV and Film Heavyweight." The increase in film and television production in Galicia has undoubtedly been dramatic. Since 2003, Galicia has occupied third place among the various autonomous communities in the statistics for cinema production, ranked after Madrid and Catalonia, with some twenty films produced annually. Yet, while Galician films are being made with increasing regularity, they still remain relatively invisible since most do not reach large audiences. And, while many have received recognition at major film festivals, such as the 2010 award of the Director's Fortnight Prize at Cannes to Oliver Laxe's *Todos vos sodes capitáns* / *You are All Captains* (2010), only occasionally do they break even at the box office. The most successful Galician films of the last two decades have either been coproductions made in Galicia – *La lengua de las mariposas* / *Butterfly Tongues* (José Luis Cuerda, 1999), *Los lunes al sol* / *Mondays in the Sun* (Fernando León de Aranoa, 2002), *Mar adentro* / *The Sea Inside* (Alejandro Amenábar, 2004) – or films made by Galicians or Galician companies outside Galicia, such as *Celda 211* / *Cell 211* (Daniel Monzón, 2009).

The one area of Galician-based and Galician-made cinema production that has been consistently successful at the box office outside Galicia in recent years has been that of digital film animation (see Chapter 18); Galicia holds a leading position in Europe as the top producer of 3D animation films. Some of the highest-grossing Galician films have been in the animation genre, aimed at the local, national, and international family market – for example, *El bosque animado* / *The Living Forest* (Ángel de la Cruz and Manolo Gómez, 2001) and *Pérez, el ratoncito de tus sueños* / *Pérez, the Mouse of your Dreams* (Juan Pablo Buscarini, 2006), both of which had sequels. Fernando Cortizo's *O apóstolo* / *The Apostle* (2010) was the first stereoscopic stop-motion animation film made in Europe, with an estimated budget of nine million euros. This film was also innovative in its mode of financing, with the budget partly covered by selling shares in the film online. While Galician in its theme and

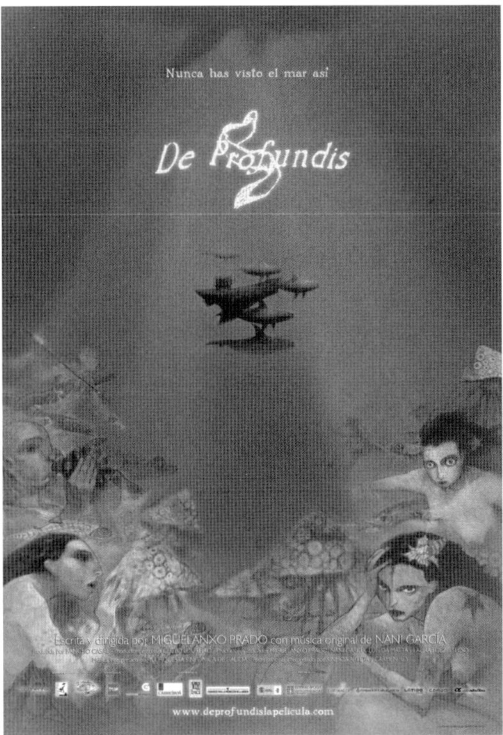

Figure 4.5 Poster for Miguelanxo Prado's *De Profundis* (2006; prod. Continental Producciones). Courtesy of Continental Producciones.

production, the film was clearly transnational in terms of its target audience and the film professionals involved, with the music soundtrack composed by Philip Glass and an international technical team whose members have worked on *The Matrix* (1999), *The Lord of the Rings* (2001–3), and *Coraline* (2009), to cite just some examples.

Indeed, some of the most interesting work in Galician cinema has been in the area of digital technology innovation. A case in point is Miguelanxo Prado's *De profundis* (2006), much more modest in terms of budget and scope than *O Apóstolo* but another fascinating example of how to bridge the two poles between which Galician cinema has swung since the 1980s: Galicianness and cosmopolitanism, the local and the global (see Figure 4.5). Like the pioneering Galician films of the 1980s, *De profundis* shares the visual intensity of a utopian project that has overcome huge structural, technical, and financial obstacles. It almost inevitably invites a symbolic reading in its avoidance of the transparency of mimetic representation. The self-reflexive nature of this fantastic story of longing and loss between a male painter and a female musician further suggests a symbolic dimension. Prado, a Galician graphic novel artist and animator with a brilliant international resumé, responsible for the art design of the *Men in Black* television series, embarked on the herculean task of creating a film single-handedly by digitizing and animating several thousand original oil, acrylic, and watercolor paintings made by him for this purpose, a project completed over an intense four-year period together with Galician musician Nani García. *De profundis* deals with a Galician topic – life and death at sea, inspired by the 2002 Prestige oil spill – and its visual style, cultural referents, music soundtrack, and means of production are recognizably Galician. But the film also creates a new stylized language of images and sounds, without the use of words, that does not require translation, and the result is an exciting audiovisual product that communicates powerfully and effortlessly beyond the confines of Galicia. It does so by combining features traditionally associated with representations of Galician identity – natural settings, the sea-faring world, a poetic magical-realist mode – with universal motifs such as shipwreck, feelings of loss and isolation, the Atlantis myth, exploration of the unknown, imagination and fantasy, and rebirth, in a New-Age-style tapestry of color and sound.

Thoroughly Galician but open in its horizons, *De profundis* takes us to the deep waters of the ocean, and the deep levels of the fantastic imagination, making the impossible seem possible and the invisible visible. More than an example of how Galician cinema can become an autonomous entity, *De profundis* constitutes a symbol of its possibilities. Its sunken ship does not invoke the heroic nationalist naval saga of *Raza*, with its eternal return of the imperial past and Fascist dream of a patriarchal united family that erases all differences. Prado's sunken ship, its fantastic transformation into a living sea creature, and its re-emergence on the face of the ocean stand as powerful metaphors of the death and rebirth of Galician culture, the revitalization of its artistic creativity, and its cinema's increased visibility.

References

Álvarez Junco, J. (2001) *Mater Dolorosa: La idea de España en el siglo XIX*. Madrid: Taurus.

Arranca la I Muestra de Cine Andaluz en Estados Unidos, que se desarrollará en Nueva York y Chicago (2004) Online at: www.porlared.com/noticia.php?not_id=11488 (accessed April 9, 2012).

Bakhtin, M. (1981) *The Dialogic Imagination: Four Essays*. Austin: University of Texas Press.

Bermúdez, S., Cortijo Ocaña, A., and McGovern, T. (eds.) (2001) *From Stateless Nations to Postnational Spain / De naciones sin fronteras a la España postnacional*. Boulder: Society of Spanish and Spanish-American Studies, University of Colorado at Boulder.

Camí-Vela, M. (2001) *Mujeres detrás de la cámara: Entrevistas con cineastas españolas de la década de los 90*. Madrid: Ocho y Medio.

Caparrós Lera, J. M. (1996) *Cine español: Una historia por autonomías*. Barcelona: PPU.

Colmeiro, J. (2011) Contemporary Galician Cinema: Utopian Visions? In: Hooper, K. and Puga, M. (eds.) *Contemporary Galician Studies: Between the Local and the Global*. New York: Modern Language Association of America, pp. 202–20.

Crofts, S. (2002) Reconceptualizing National Cinema/s. In: Williams. A. (ed.) *Film and Nationalism*. New Brunswick: Rutgers University Press, pp. 25–51.

Delgado, J.-F. (1992) *Andalucía y el cine, del 75 al 92*. Seville: El Carro de la Nieve.

De Pablo, S. (ed.) (1996) *Cien años de cine en el País Vasco: 1986–1995*. Gasteiz-Vitoria: Diputación Foral de Álava.

De Pablo, S. (ed.) (1998) *Los cineastas: Historia del cine en Euskal Herria: 1896–1998*. Gasteiz-Vitoria: Fundación Sancho el Sabio.

El IX Festival de Cine Latino de Miami acoge desde hoy la proyección de seis largometrajes sevillanos (2005) Online at: www.lukor.com/cine/noticias/0504/15160631.htm (accessed October 30, 2010).

Elsaesser, T. (1976) Tales of Sound and Fury: Observations on the Family Melodrama. In: Nichols, B. (ed.) *Movies and Methods: An Anthology*, vol. 2. Berkeley: University of California Press, pp. 165–89.

Eutsi! filmak joan den asteburuko bigarren diru-bilketarik handiena lortu zuen Hego Euskal Herrian (2007) Online at: www.kaixo.com/eu/berriak/20070313133033 (accessed July 17, 2011).

Fernández, M. A. (2005) *Rodado en Galicia*. Santiago de Compostela: Consorcio Audiovisual de Galicia.

Fernández Sánchez, M. C. (1985) *Hacia un cine andaluz*. Algeciras: Bahía.

Foster, H. (2004) *Prosthetic Gods*. Cambridge, MA: MIT Press.

Gabilondo, J. (2002a) Postnationalism, Fundamentalism and the Global Real: Historicizing Terror/ism and the New North American/Global Ideology. *Journal of Spanish Cultural Studies* 3 (1): 57–86.

Gabilondo, J. (2002b) Uncanny Identity: Violence, Gaze, and Desire in Contemporary Basque Cinema. In: Labanyi, J. (ed.) *Constructing Identity in Contemporary Spain: Theoretical Debates and Cultural Practice*. Oxford: Oxford University Press, pp. 262–79.

Gabilondo, J. (2008) Imagining the Basques: Dual Otherness from European Imperialism to American Globalization. In: MacClancy, J. and Leoné, S. (eds.) *Imagining the Basques: Foreign Views of the Basque Country. Revista Internacional de Estudios Vascos, Cuadernos 2*. Donostia-San Sebastián: Eusko Ikaskuntza, pp.145–73.

Galán, E. (1997) *O bosque inanimado: Cen anos de cine en Galicia*. A Coruña: Centro Galego de Artes da Imaxe.

González, M. (2000) *Cine restaurado: Nuestras fiestas de allá (1928) Galicia y Buenos Aires (1931)*. A Coruña: CGAI – Consello da Cultura Galeg.

Heredero, C. F. (ed.) (1998) *La mitad del cielo. Directoras españolas de los años 90*. Málaga: Ayuntamiento de Málaga.

Heredero, C. F. (1999) *20 nuevos directores del cine español*. Madrid: Alianza Editorial.

Higson, A. (2002) The Concept of National Cinema. In: Williams, A. (ed.) *Film and Nationalism*. New Brunswick: Rutgers University Press, pp. 52–67.

Hopewell, J. (2004) Hit and Myth in the Deep North. Forward-looking Rural Area Transforming into TV and Film Heavyweight. *Variety* (September 19). Online at: www.variety.com/article/VR1117910645.html?categoryid=&cs=1 (accessed February 15, 2011).

Kinder, M. (1993) *Blood Cinema: The Reconstruction of National Identity in Spain*. Berkeley: University of California Press.

Labanyi, J. (2003) *Lo andaluz en el cine del franquismo. Los estereotipos como estrategia para manejar la contradicción*. Seville: Fundación Centro de Estudios Andaluces.

Martí-Olivella, J. (2003) *Basque Cinema: An Introduction*. Reno: Center for Basque Studies.

O cine na Dictadura (1937–1970) (n.d.) In: *Historia do cine galego (1896–1979)*. Online at: www.culturagalega.org/avg/historia6.php (accessed February 15, 2011).

Prout, R. 2010. Speaking Up / Coming Out: Regions of Authenticity in Juan Pinzás' Gay Galician Dogma Trilogy. *Galicia 21: Journal of Contemporary Galician Studies* B: 68–91. Online at: www.galicia21journal.org/B/pdf/galicia21_4_Prout.pdf (accessed February 15, 2011).

Rivas, M. (1989) Tres películas gallegas. *El País* (December 2). Online at: www.elpais.com/articulo/cultura/peliculas/gallegas/elpepicul/19891202elpepicul_10/Tes (accessed February 15, 2011).

Roldán Larreta, C. (1999) *El cine del País Vasco: De Ama Lur (1968) a Airbag (1997)*. Donostia-San Sebastián: Eusko Ikaskuntza.

Santaolalla, I. C. (1998) Far from Home, Close to Desire: Julio Medem's Landscapes. *Bulletin of Hispanic Studies* 75 (3): 331–8.

Santaolalla, I. C. (1999) Julio Medem's Vacas (1991): Historicizing the Forest. In: Evans, W. P. (ed.) *Spanish Cinema: The Auteurist Tradition*. Oxford: Oxford University Press, pp. 310–24.

Stone, R. (2007) *Julio Medem*. Manchester: Manchester University Press.

Trenzado Romero, M. (2007) La construcción de la identidad andaluza y la cultura de masas: El caso del cine andaluz. *Revista de Estudios Regionales* 58: 185–207.

Triana Toribio, N. (2003) *Spanish National Cinema*. London: Routledge.

Utrera, R. (2005) *Las rutas del cine en Andalucía*. Seville: Fundación José Manuel Lara.

Utrera, R. and Delgado, J. F. (1980) *Cine en Andalucía*. Seville: Argantonio.

Villaverde, X. (2009) 20 anos de Cinegalicia. Online at: www.academiagalegadoaudiovisual.com/attachments/Xavier%20Villaverde.pdf (accessed February 15, 2011).

Williams, B. (2002) Frysky Business: Micro-regionalism in the Era of Post-nationalism. *Film History* 14: 100–12.

Zunzunegui, S. (1985) *El cine en el País Vasco*. Bilbao: Bizkaiko Foru Aldundia/Diputación Foral de Vizcaya.

Further Reading

Acuña, X. (1999) *Chano Piñeiro: Unha historia do cinema galego*. Vigo: Edicións do Cumio.

Berthier, N. and Seguin, J.-C. (2007) *Cine, nación y nacionalidades en España*. Madrid: Casa de Velázquez.

Castro de Paz, J. L. (1996) *Historia do cine en Galicia*. Oleiros: Vía Láctea.

Colmeiro, J. (2009) Nationalising Carmen: Spanish Cinema and the Specter of Francoism. *Journal of Iberian and Latin American Research* 15 (1): 1–26.

D'Lugo, M. (2002) Recent Spanish Cinema in National and Global Contexts. *Post Script* 21 (2): 3–7.

Gómez Pérez, F. J. and Perales Bazo, F. (2001) *Andalucía, una civilización para el cine*. Seville: Padilla.

Nogueira, X. (1997) *O cine en Galicia*. Vigo: Edicións A Nosa Terra.

Rodríguez, M. P. (2002) *Mundos en conflicto: Aproximaciones al cine vasco de los noventa*. Donostia-San Sebastián: Universidad de Deusto.

Part II

The Construction of the Auteur

5

Auteurism and the Construction of the Canon

Marvin D'Lugo and Paul Julian Smith

Auteurism and Spain (Marvin D'Lugo)

This chapter will discuss the history of how auteurism has been received and used in Spain to construct certain perceptions of Spanish cinema and to encourage certain kinds of cinematic production. This is, of course, a process of canon formation. After giving a historical overview, we consider the work of six directors who stand out for the ways in which they have been constructed as auteurs. First, Luis Buñuel, Carlos Saura, and Pedro Almodóvar – arguably the best-known Spanish filmmakers of all time. Following these most visible and perhaps most legible auteurs, we consider two directors whose status as auteurs is linked not only with a measure of international renown, as cult figures with minority audiences, but also and especially with their use of certain idiosyncratic techniques and modes of address: Víctor Erice and Julio Medem. We end by discussing a different kind of auteur, Alejandro Amenábar, for whom authorship is inseparable from the cultivation of transnational commercial genres. A key thread throughout the chapter will be how auteurism moves between the national and the transnational.

Spanish auteurism, which emerged as a recognizable movement of filmmakers and critics in the 1960s, began as an effort to embrace an international model through which to counter the stifling containment of Francoist culture. What we call auteurism today is less a "theory" than a series of interpretative practices, what David Bordwell calls "exegetical film criticism" (1989: 48) – a strategy of reading movies built around the figure of the director as the author of the film. Following the pattern of the French auteurists, the development of auteurism in Spain was

A Companion to Spanish Cinema, First Edition. Edited by Jo Labanyi and Tatjana Pavlović.

connected in its early phases to film journals such as *Objetivo*, *Film Ideal*, and *Nuestro Cine* (Heredero 1993: 347–8; see Chapter 15). Auteurism had a special appeal to the generation of young Spanish filmmakers who read these journals and the critics who wrote in them; coming from different political and cultural positions, they nonetheless saw in the figure of the auteur a broad strategy of artistic freedom but also a politically charged artistic posture.

In his ground-breaking anthology of essays documenting the evolution of movie authorship in French, British, and US contexts, John Caughie (1980: 1–6) inserts a critical preface in which he enumerates problematic aspects of the cultural and intellectual project of auteurism during the three decades of its emergence and stabilization as a critical discourse in Europe and the United States. These included a dearth of critical commentary "on the place of the author within institutions (industrial, cultural, academic) or the way in which the author is constructed by and for commerce" (1980: 2); "a lack of attention to the way in which the author's place within a particular social history is written into the text" (1980: 2–3); and an underlying repositioning of auteur cinema around and even against the model of Hollywood film production practices (1980: 3). Caughie's discussion never involves Spanish cinema, yet it suggests illuminating parallels between French and other international developments and the Spanish situation that help us to better understand the appeal and limits of the auteurist imagination in Spain.

If André Bazin argued that "a film's worth stems from its auteurs" (cited in Bordwell 1989: 45), Alexandre Astruc's influential 1948 article "Birth of a New Avant-garde: La Caméra-Stylo" (1991) established the seminal concept of the auteur as an expansion of the concept of the literary author, with the film seen as an analogue to the literary text. The camera is thus viewed as a pen and the filmmaker as the author. Astruc's article, presented as a manifesto, aimed to dislodge film from the French "Tradition of Quality," subservient to literary adaptations and theatrical codes of acting (Greene 2007: 8), by espousing the notion of cinema as an independent art form built around the figure of the cinematic artist-director-auteur. Astruc insisted on differentiating between the *metteur-en-scène*, the director as craftsman, and the auteur, the filmmaker as complete creative author. This distinction would lead François Truffaut, in his fiery polemical essay of 1954, "A Certain Tendency in French Cinema," published in *Cahiers du Cinéma*, to propose an implicit canon of auteurs to the exclusion of merely artisanal directors (2008). Bordwell claims that it was not authorship as such that *Cahier du Cinéma*'s "Young Turks" introduced in the early 1950s but rather a *politique des auteurs*, a policy of favoring particular directors (1989: 46–7). Among the directors favored by Truffaut, Eric Rohmer, and other members of the *Cahiers* group were Hitchcock, Rossellini, and Welles. More moderate than his disciples, the journal's founding editor, André Bazin, proposed a pantheon of auteurs that included Chaplin, Buñuel, and Renoir (Andrew 2010: 122).

From a geopolitical perspective, what is perhaps most notable about the early identification of particular auteurs is that the emerging canon valorized filmmakers who represented France, Italy, and the United States – precisely the film industries that were filling Parisian movie screens in the post-World War II years. The canon would expand over time to include German, Japanese, and even Indian directors, but that essential Euro-American core of canonical auteurs would remain. In early critical commentary, the national seemed to have little to do with the auteurist bent. Auteurism did not so much ignore the logic of the state as an ordering principle of aesthetic quality as affirm a borderless community of spectators taking shape around the universality of the medium and the shared assumptions of a seemingly timeless canon of values, a sustained aesthetic vision, and a praxis through which to embody that aesthetic.

By contrast, the Spanish appropriation of auteurism could never fully obviate the national context, unavoidably acknowledging the legacy of Spain's uneven intellectual and cultural development and its authoritarian legacy. The Spanish auteur tradition would implicitly be synonymous with anti-Francoism. Well after the dictator's demise, the peculiar anchoring of the auteur in Spanish cultural contexts remains a curious feature that to some degree sets the Spanish canonical auteurs apart from their European counterparts.

Within its effort to establish a high art canon for cinema, intuitively following the pattern of the literary establishment, the *Cahiers* group was drawn to popular directors who were closely linked to the Hollywood studio system (John Ford, Howard Hawks, Orson Welles). In a sense to justify this seeming paradox, it was stressed that the auteur text required "an operation of decipherment" (Peter Wollen cited in Bordwell 1989: 44). Like avant-garde cinema and art cinema more generally, auteurist films required exegesis to illuminate their aesthetic and conceptual coherence.

As this French rethinking of film as art in the 1960s spread to the United Kingdom and the United States, it began to appeal to a generation of academics, first at Oxford University around the student journal *The Oxford Opinion* (Ian Cameron, V. F. Perkins, Mark Shivas) and later in the British Film Institute's magazine *Sight and Sound* and the journal *Movie*. In the United States, Andrew Sarris would codify the terms of what was meant by the film auteur in his famous "Notes on the Auteur Theory in 1962" (1980). The timely "migration" of auteur theory beyond its original French contexts reflects a broader social scenario that, as Caughie observes, is not accompanied by any attention to the way in which "the author's place with a particular social history is written into the text" (1980: 2–3). Scholarly publishing, as Bordwell notes (1989: 53), was the precondition for the expansion of auteurism into academic contexts. This was the period in which Tantivy Press in the United Kingdom and MIT Press, Indiana University Press, and University of California Press in the United States began to publish extensive series of film books, with a marked emphasis on auteurist approaches.

By the end of the 1960s, and again following the model of literary canonical coherence, film courses began to be offered in North American and British universities by scholars who themselves had "migrated" from traditional literary studies, usually in English departments. For them, auteurism had an obvious advantage in offering a pattern of critical approach that seemed the natural extension of literary study, especially in its reliance on close textual analysis of films to decipher authorial signatures, replacing the interrogation of production history with an exclusive focus on aesthetic consistency.

Just as there had been other directors in the prior history of international cinema, in addition to those proposed by Bazin and the *Cahiers* group, whose bodies of work could have been considered auteurist (Fritz Lang, René Clair, and Jean Renoir, for example), there had been Spanish filmmakers whose corpus could well have merited serious auteurist consideration. Among these certainly were two key figures of the early sound period, Benito Perojo and Florián Rey. What was perhaps lacking in appreciation of their work was a key ingredient: evidence of the director's creativity as a unifying vision that could be seen as aesthetically guiding a series of productions over time – the logic that would lift individual effort above the level of mere commercial fare to what auteurists would deem an art form.

If we accept Sarris' description of the auteur as an independent filmmaker whose vision is at odds with the system, then institutionalized censorship in Spain, which necessarily affected all film production, would surely preclude the possibility of a truly critical scholarly discourse around a directorial vision. Certainly, outside Spain at this time, the appeal of those filmmakers identified as auteurs combined this notion of resistance with the sense of the independent personal vision, especially appealing to a student population engaged in the cultural politics that would produce the crucible of 1968 in France, the United States, and beyond. In effect, by the late 1960s, auteurism had become a generational cause. Most tellingly in this regard, the interests of the *Cahiers* writers who had given birth to the first wave of auteurist writings now evolved from a formalistic aesthetics of the text to larger questions of ideology, as noted, for instance, in the editorial board's 1970 collective reading of the ideology of John Ford's *Young Mister Lincoln* (*Cahiers du Cinéma* 1972).

Understandably, much of the intellectual upheaval of the period bypassed Francoist Spain. Some of the process of political and cultural ferment that would give rise to the Spanish cult of the auteur derived from the Cine-Club movement of the mid-1950s (Heredero 1993: 346–9; see Chapter 15). It was, of course, the University of Salamanca film club, run by Basilio Martín Patino, that had been one of the principal organizers of the historic 1955 Salamanca Conversations. Up until the founding the National Film School (Instituto de Investigaciones y Experiencias Cinematográficas (IIEC)) in 1947, movie culture had been viewed in Spain as little more than entertainment, or else as an ideological arm of the state. Being constrained by the censorship system, like other forms of cultural expression, films that did not adhere to the state line were marginalized, even if they could get produced in the first place. When a modest grassroots auteur movement did arise in the 1950s through the works of Juan Antonio Bardem and Luis García Berlanga, and later those of Carlos Saura, it was, because of the censorship, posed as an effort to revitalize the artistic qualities of Spanish cinema and not as head-on social critique.

On the surface, these filmmakers were romanticized figures who, with the exception of Bardem, who was always the most politically outspoken of the group, limited their early work to opposition to the aesthetic norms that dominated national cinema. That they had learned from foreign movements was clear in their cultivation of a recognizable visual mastery of the medium that enabled critics in *Film Ideal* and *Nuestro Cine* to speak of the signature styles of these young filmmakers. At the same time, however, Bardem and Martín Patino were members of the clandestine Communist Party, further underscoring the ideological investment in auteurism as an oppositional strategy. The film collective UNINCI, which produced Berlanga's *¡Bienvenido Mister Marshall! / Welcome Mr. Marshall!* (1953) and would be the Spanish production partner for Buñuel's *Viridiana* (1961), also had strong ties to the Communist Party (Sánchez-Biosca 1999: 21).

The modern Spanish version of auteurist cinema, as Peter Evans writes (1999: 3), reflects a "shift in the sociology of spectatorship for auteurist films" from 1960s New Spanish Cinema (Nuevo Cine Español) to the rise of popular auteurs in the 1980s and 1990s. Coinciding with the Spanish critical embrace of the director as auteur, the auteurist packaging of films had emerged in the early 1960s under the impetus of the liberalizing moves of Franco's Minister of Information and Tourism, Manuel Fraga Iribarne, who designed a promotion of what was labelled "New Spanish Cinema," which, it was hoped, would shore up the industry and update Francoism's authoritarian image. Thus, paradoxically, the Spanish state became one of the players in the construction of the Spanish canon – or, at least, as it sought to gain propagandistic leverage during the Cold War, it attempted to use auteurism, through its support for New Spanish Cinema, to its own political advantage. In doing so it followed a strategy that Thomas Elsaesser describes in relation to New German Cinema of this period as "a cultural mode of production" – that is, a formulation of state-subsidized film production around the packaging of the works of directors whose artistic vision, though clearly idiosyncratic and personal, is used to represent a national culture in its projection to international markets (1988: 40–4). Given foreign perceptions of the repressive Francoist state, foreign critics and festival juries, among others, recognized the ploy for what it was; it became apparent that it was the regime that was being exploited by Spanish producers who used the government's efforts for their own ends.

The publicity for this New Spanish Cinema played freely with the label of auteur in an effort to align these political efforts with allusions to artistically valid film-making and a presumed freedom of artistic expression. During the first decade of the government's promotion of New Spanish Cinema, as many as ninety aspiring commercial filmmakers had made their debut films with government subsidies, seeking the accolade of auteur (Torres 1973: 13). Given what amounted to a wholesale production of auteurs, the effect of this promotion of New Spanish Cinema was in many respects to trivialize the notion of the auteur, since it came to be seen as merely a state-orchestrated publicity strategy.

One of the key avenues for aligning the auteur with the nation has conventionally been through international film festivals. Indeed, in 1955, mindful of the growing international recognition of film as a form of cultural capital, the Spanish government had taken over the locally established San Sebastián Film Festival, transforming it into a national showcase to rival the three principal European festivals of Venice, Cannes, and Berlin (see Chapter 15). Spain's entries to international film festivals took on a political dimension since at such competitions – according to the guidelines of the three aforementioned festivals – specific film entries implicitly represented their respective national film industry. While functioning as a synecdoche for an exotic Romantic trope, Spain – as evoked in festival screenings of the 1950s, 1960s, and 1970s – shifted from being a site of picturesque backwardness to being the arena for an ideological battle against Francoist officialdom, in which antiestablishment views were aired.

This shift was irrevocably clinched by the award of the Palme d'Or to Buñuel's *Viridiana* at the 1961 Cannes Film Festival, where, in Buñuel's absence, the award was accepted by José Muñoz-Fontán, the director of the Spanish government film office. The film was immediately denounced by the Vatican newspaper, *L'Osservatore Romano*, and the Franco regime was made to play the dupe in Buñuel's master plan. The ensuing "*Viridiana* scandal" crystallized the tensions between the Spanish state and receptive foreign audiences, who saw the auteur as a resistance fighter. In this regard, the biographical auteur – in Buñuel's case, an exiled dissident – gained additional extratextual weight.

With the dictatorship's demise and the dismantling of its censorial apparatus in the late 1970s, what remained of stable film production in Spain was a combination of popular genres that were throwbacks to Francoist cinema (Vicente Escrivá, Pedro Lazaga, etc.) and a notable group of auteurs, principal among them Saura, Erice, Jaime de Armiñán, and Manuel Gutiérrez Aragón. The 1982 election victory of the Socialist Party (PSOE) brought Pilar Miró to the directorship of the Ministry of Culture's Film Division in 1983. The film legislation of that year, which became known as the Miró Law (*Ley Miró*), singled out auteurs for subsidy. Ironically, this produced a return to the very "Tradition of Quality" against which young artists and intellectuals in 1950s France had reacted.

The decade of the transition (1978–88) in Spain coincided with further critique of auteurism in European critical discourse. As Caughie notes, the shift away from a formalistic auteurism toward what he terms "auteur-structuralism" brought a series of conceptual approaches that questioned the authority of the author and the primacy of the text (1980: 128). In rejecting the "empiricist epistemology" of earlier approaches to auteurist texts (Caughie 1980: 128), these approaches opened the door to a broader range of critical inquiry into the nature of language and textuality in the cinematic text, thereby diminishing the aura of the creative genius that had so often surrounded the auteur. This conceptual realignment of cinematic critical discourse coincided with the beginnings of an intensified interest in Spanish cinema by a new generation of Hispanic film scholars in Spain, France, the United Kingdom, and the United States, some of whom appeared to take little note of these radical conceptual changes in the dynamics of auteurist criticism, often reinventing the earlier phase of Anglo-European auteurist criticism in relation to Spanish auteurs. At the same time, an increasing number of auteur studies broke new ground by challenging the premises of the first auteurist wave by questioning what Susan Martin-Márquez, in Chapter 6, calls the "androcentrism" of the original *Cahiers* group. Indeed, questions of gender, class, and region have become progressively central to discussion of the malleable Spanish canon.

Part of the thinking at the root of the Miró Law had been to exploit the cultural capital deriving from the alignment of the recognized auteur with national cultural production for the purposes of international marketing. A logo and tagline were invented to market the strategy: "Cine español para el mundo" (Spanish Film for the World). Though anachronistic as a policy of state intervention in the film industry, this slogan anticipated to some degree what Mette Hjort understands as "auteuristic transnationalism" (2010: 22–4), which rallies the particular aura of the individual director in the service of a commercial circulation of conceptual and artistic tropes. Not surprisingly, given the biographical vicissitudes and career evolution of Spain's major canonical auteurs (Buñuel, Saura, Almodóvar), the notion of Spanish rootedness emerges as a key marker, at once defining a form of cultural identity in relation to the auteurist signature and transposing those marks of identity onto international contexts through the mediatization of the "name of the author." Critical commentary on these three auteurs has only in recent years begun to take note of the problematics of the national/transnational interface of Spanish auteurism as Spain itself becomes geopolitically repositioned.

Luis Buñuel (Marvin D'Lugo)

Luis Buñuel's body of films, imbued with a highly personal vision of film as a social practice, enabled him to maintain a distinctive authorial signature that was remarkably consistent throughout much of his fifty-year career. Commentators refer to certain stylistic features, usually related to violent eroticism, fetishism, and dream sequences, as "Buñuelian." It is worth noting that these same stylistic traits, so prominent in his early surrealist films, recur as well in many of the Mexican popular genre films that constitute the bulk of Buñuel's subsequent filmography. In general, these elements function less as expressions of narrative detail or character motivation than as ways of disturbing conventional viewing habits.

Of his early surrealist films, perhaps the most consistently cited to exemplify these features is his first short, made in collaboration with Salvador Dalí, *Un chien andalou* (1929). Inspired by the surrealists' appreciation of dream discourse, Buñuel would later formalize his view of the cinematic medium as a dream mode in a 1958 presentation, "El cine, instrumento de poesía" (Cinema as an Instrument of Poetry) (2000). His basic premise, as he summarized it in his memoirs, was that the operation of the cinematic apparatus – the projection of hypnotic images seen by the spectator in a darkened room – loosens the viewer's inhibitions and approximates to the dream state (Buñuel 1982: 34–6). To reinforce their notion of film as the spectator's dream, Buñuel and Dalí incorporated a number of striking editing features into *Un chien andalou*, aligning what they understood as rhetorical elements in the dream process (condensation, displacement, word play) with key components of conventional narrative film practice, used in new, startling ways (framing and cross-cuts that characteristically focus on body parts, often as if the camera frame were vivisecting the human body; montage that enables the filmmakers to construct visual "gags" that disrupt the illusion of cinematic realism). The most famous of these cinematic gags is the opening image, in which we see Buñuel appear to slash open the eye of a woman seated on a chair at his side. An additional feature is disjunctive editing that disrupts the conventional illusion of a continuous space of action, thereby transforming the movie screen into an oneiric mise-en-scène. Operating in tandem, these techniques were aimed at disrupting the spectator's general passivity toward screen representations.

Un chien andalou introduces one of the dominant narrative tropes that remained fairly constant in Buñuel's subsequent work: a plot built around the male character's desiring gaze, which triggers his aggressive pursuit of the female. From that narrative trope come the visual erotics of the female body, treated in the surrealist short through segmented images of eyes, legs, breasts, and naked buttocks in close-up at various points. These images – which recur in the imagery of women's legs in *Ensayo de un crimen / The Criminal Life of Archibaldo de la Cruz* (1955), *Viridiana* (1961), and, most prominently, in the heroine's amputated leg in *Tristana* (1970) – are striking in that they transpose a surrealist aesthetic practice onto an apparently realistic narrative milieu (see Figure 5.1).

This obsessive treatment of the female by the camera contributes to the sense of the fetishized female body as the object of male desire. The narrative pursuit of the woman by the obsessed male – the central plotline of *Un chien andalou* – will in time become a way to channel spectatorial desire, turning the film's viewer into an involuntary voyeur whose scopic desire is thwarted by a series of physical obstacles within the diegetic space. Variations on this trope are found in later films as diverse as *Los olvidados / The Young and the Damned* (1950), in which Jaibo and the blind man Don Carmelo each attempt to violently subdue the young girl Meche, and *Cet obscur objet du désir / That Obscure Object of Desire* (1978), whose entire plot centers around the old rake Mateo's attempts to have sex with the elusive Conchita. In all of these films, sexual desire is transposed onto a visual narrative of the male's scopic urge to see and thereby possess the female. Not surprisingly, the Buñuelian visual motif of the male spying on the female through a peephole abounds in these films.

In his first sound film, *L'Âge d'or* (1930), these same elements are repeated, now with the added focus of a striking use of sound to enhance the erotics. We note this in the early scene in which a pompous dignitary is interrupted as he is about to

Figure 5.1 The leg fetishism in Buñuel's *Ensayo de un crimen* (1955) would inspire Almodóvar's *Carne trémula* (1997; prod. El Deseo), as illustrated in this shot.

give a speech by the off-screen sounds of sexual panting. The on-screen crowd's and the spectator's view of the erotic source is blocked by the edge of screen. We are allowed to see the protagonists (played by Lya Lys and Gaston Modot) embracing in the mud only after the cinematic interdiction has engaged our voyeuristic curiosity. Sound is thus used to channel the characters' and the spectator's scopic drive toward the sight of the scandalous sexual encounter.

Marsha Kinder finds Buñuel's use of sound to be a persistent feature of his cinematic production, running counter to the dominant use of soundtrack to naturalize narrative (1993: 294). In *L'Âge d'or*, for example, the sound of cowbells, identified with Lys, is mysteriously heard by Modot in another part of the city as he is being dragged away by the police. As Lys sits before the mirror in her bedroom, she hears a dog barking, a sound that is diegetically located in the spaces through which Modot passes. *Belle de jour* (1967) begins with the sound of sleigh bells jingling from horses that carry the film's heroine Séverine and her husband Pierre in a landau along the road of a country estate. The ensuing sequence is retrospectively recognized as the heroine's sexual fantasy. In this way, sound is aligned for both character and spectator with the dream mode and the expression of repressed individual desire. A similar structure of non-linear sequencing involving dreams serves to undercut the presumed linear narrative of *Tristana*. As in *Belle de jour*, the dream – this time of a creaking church bell – is only acknowledged retrospectively and thereby thwarts the spectator's efforts to read the film as a linear narrative.

Sound is explicitly linked to the dream mode in what is arguably Buñuel's most accomplished dream sequence: Pedro's dream in *Los olvidados*. What is notable about this sequence is that the mise-en-scène of the dream is the same space inhabited by the dreamer in his waking state. In this way, the dream appears to disrupt the presumed realism of the characters' waking actions by inserting an oneiric dimension into the mise-en-scène. The sequence begins as we hear the sound of a cock crowing and the strange chords of Gustavo Pittaluga's musical film score. It is at once a disruption of the seemingly neo-realist style of the rest of the film and an expression of the protagonist's desires embodied in his pleading to be fed by his mother. Pedro arises from his bed in slow motion in the darkened room in which his brothers, sisters, and mother sleep. He speaks to his mother but his words are out of sync with the movement of his lips. The ensuing action, all in slow motion, presents in condensed form the elements of the film's plot involving the rivalry with Jaibo and the murder of Julián. What sets this sequence apart from the rest of the film is precisely the antirealist deployment of sound devices that challenge the spectator's perception of what constitutes social reality.

The most notable Buñuelian signature sound is that of the ritual drums of Calanda, part of the Holy Week ritual in the filmmaker's native Aragonese village. Their sound first accompanies Modot's delirious rage as he rips pillows apart in *L'Âge d'or* and reappears over the final images of the traumatized protagonist of *Nazarín* (1959). Such use of sound reinforces the seemingly irrational, dreamlike qualities of the film medium that are central to the larger project of Buñuel's auteurist vision, destabilizing the spectator's passive acceptance of conventional cinematic narrative.

L'Âge d'or added a visual element that also became a staple of the Buñuelian signature: the erotics of feet, first introduced with the suggestive image of Lya Lys sucking the big toe of a statue as a surrogate for her absent lover. This sense of the scandalous, linked to specific cinematic techniques, has come to be identified as Buñuel's key auteurist signature. However, throughout the twenty-two films that comprise Buñuel's Mexican period, the scandalous disruption of the cinematic frame by on- and off-screen voyeurism is largely absent, except in two masterpieces: *Los olvidados* and *Él / This Strange Passion* (1952). It was not until *Viridiana* that this disruption was foregrounded in what is perhaps his most scandalous work – a disruption that is particularly striking since the film's construction is congruent with the most standard modes of classical cinematic narrative. This film occupies a crucial place in Buñuel's filmography for bringing together various formal aspects of his authorial signature, especially its use of anti-Catholic imagery and its anticipation of the characteristically disruptive narrative style of his later films. It combines elements traceable back to his surrealist period, such as the sexualized body, the male character as voyeur, and the visual fetish in the form of the naked legs that are the object of the character's and spectator's gaze.

The male protagonist Don Jaime, the would-be good Christian, is the perfect cinematic embodiment of sexual fetishism and voyeurism (Sánchez-Biosca 1999: 38–40). An exemplar of the sexually repressed bourgeois males who populate Buñuel's earlier films, he is also, importantly, the on-screen agency through whose eyes the spectator's own scopic desires are mediated. Don Jaime has, in fact,

Figure 5.2 The Buñuelian specular ritual aligns the gaze of characters on screen with the extradiegetic gaze of the camera and spectators: *Belle de jour* (Buñuel, 1967; prod. Robert and Raymond Hakim / Paris Film Production).

transformed his life into a mise-en-scène populated by fetish objects, principally foot fetishes, displayed for his visual delectation (the young Rita's legs and knees as she skips with her skipping rope; the bare feet of his niece Viridiana). The fetish is triggered by the power of a gaze that, thanks to Buñuel's camerawork, makes the spectator share the voyeur's diegetic point of view. In this way, Buñuel incorporates essential tropes of Hollywood classical cinema – the eyeline-match and glance-object shots – into a mechanism within which the fetish is specularized and the film spectator is implicated in the fetishism.

Specular rituals are an essential part of the Buñuelian staging of *Viridiana*, anticipating later films. In one key scene, Don Jaime plays a religious dirge on the organ as his housekeeper Ramona, who has been sent to spy on Viridiana, looks through the keyhole at her performing a religious ritual that has its own fetish objects (a crown of thorns and a cross), and reports back to Jaime on what she has seen. In this way the gaze is transformed into a protean voyeurism, becoming a perverse expression of sacred love turned into profane desire. The device is a simple one: the camera follows a character viewing a scene in which another character or characters are also shown to be voyeurs. We see this again, for instance, in *Belle de jour*, where the rooms in the brothel have peep-holes through which the characters can view sexual acts. At a key moment, an Asian gentleman presents Séverine with a box that she peeps into. Her visual curiosity, like that of the spectator and other characters, is part of a specular ritual play that aligns the diegetic gaze of the character with the extradiegetic gaze of camera and spectator (see Figure 5.2).

In basic ways, *Viridiana* embodies the paradoxes of Buñuelian auteurism. The film is built on a personal vision of the contradictions of societal norms that thwart and thereby reinforce instinctual desires. It is at once part of a recognizable cinematic narrative identified with the "name of the author" and discursively posed in ways that disrupt and destabilize the spectator's passive reception of the story. Yet, its universal appeal is often linked to the contingency of its localism: the specificity of Francoist Spain and repressive Catholic dogma; the social marginality and industrial limitations of Mexican cinema. This same paradoxical tension between local constraints and the universal features of the auteurist project would in time, as we shall see, help to define the direction of Saura's and Almodóvar's authorial cinemas as they learned to balance the peculiarities of the Spanish circumstance with the larger contours of universal auteurist aspirations.

Carlos Saura (Marvin D'Lugo)

By contrast with Buñuel's engagement with popular as well as avant-garde cinematic forms, Carlos Saura's filmography emphasizes film as art, with a persistent focus on protagonists who are painters, writers, choreographers, or filmmakers and their struggle to create in repressive political and cultural environments. These thinly disguised stand-ins for the director abound in films as diverse as *Antonieta* (1982), *Carmen* (1983), *La noche oscura / The Dark Night*

(1988), *Tango* (1998), *Goya en Burdeos / Goya in Bordeaux* (1999), and *Salomé* (2005); they derive from the narrative formula of the spectator-in-the-text, the dominant trope of Saura's earlier films (D'Lugo 1990: 29–66), reminding us of the persistent sense of allegory through which Saura inscribes local and transnational meanings into his films. In that narrative-visual formulation, he frequently aligned his on-screen characters' efforts to decipher the meaning of the world around them with the spectator's line of sight. Expanding the classical cinematic narrative formula of masking editing cuts between images and new camera set-ups by recourse to the rhetoric of eye-line matches or glance-object shots, Saura often positioned his protagonists standing back from action in order to observe and question their immediate surroundings. The story of these characters' self-conscious visual interrogation of their social milieu thus operated as social and often political allegory, illustrating the ideologically confining positions of sight and understanding imposed on individuals in Spanish or any other repressive society.

Commentators generally divide Saura's career into two periods. The first period, mostly under the Franco dictatorship but continuing through 1979, is seen as focusing on characters who, having been traumatized by the Civil War, are now victims of involuntary memories of the war, their stories often serving as allegories of the Spanish nation. The second period, from the early 1980s to the present, is seen as built around dance performances, frequently of a folkloric nature (flamenco above all but also Argentine tango). The first three of these films comprise his celebrated flamenco trilogy made with dancer Antonio Gades and producer Emiliano Piedra. The first and third films in the trilogy – *Bodas de sangre / Blood Wedding* (1981) and *El amor brujo / Love the Magician* (1986) – were based on canonical Spanish stage works (Federico García Lorca's 1933 play and Manuel de Falla's 1915 ballet respectively), while the second – *Carmen* (1983) – was based on what is probably the most famous literary text ever written about Spain: Prosper Mérimée's 1845 novella of that title, dramatized in Bizet's opera of 1875. In Chapter 2, I discussed how Saura was projected as an auteur through international film festivals by his producer for the period 1965–82, Elías Querejeta. That a director firmly associated with arthouse cinema should make eight films based on flamenco between 1981 and 2010 indicates that we have here a reworking of Spanish cinema's love affair with Andalusian song and dance that on the one hand caters to foreign visions of a stereotypically exotic Spain while on the other it breaks resolutely with the earlier (despised) popular film genre of the folkloric musical. This division of Saura's work into two periods, while roughly accurate, ignores those films that, in both periods, do not fit this overall scheme. Further, chronology goes only so far in illuminating Saura's artistic development since various stylistic features from his earlier films are expanded in the later dance-based works. Additionally, films of both periods reflect a sustained effort to appeal to arthouse audiences abroad through internationally recognized tropes aligned with Spanishness (the Civil War, atavistic violence, Andalusian culture). Here I will focus substantially on the later work, less discussed by scholars, in order to show how Saura draws on, and in some cases takes further, techniques that his earlier films had established as his authorial signature. If, as I have argued elsewhere (D'Lugo 1990), Saura's earlier work provides a reflection on the act of looking, often associated with memory, much of the later work constitutes a reflection on performance and artistic creativity in which looking and remembering play a crucial part.

Those of Saura's later films that explore literary or artistic creation (*La noche oscura* – titled after the most famous poem of St. John of the Cross – and *Goya en Burdeos*) highlight the writer or artist's act of remembering his past life. These works rely heavily on camera movement and editing patterns in which the distinction between the present moment and the remembered past collapses. The present-day action may be interrupted by a cut to, or a slow lateral tracking across, what appears to be a contiguous space, only to reveal that we are relocated in a moment from the past. The trick continuity editing used here to bridge the past and present reprises the use of the same device in so many earlier films (*El jardín de las delicias / Garden of Delights*, 1970; *La prima Angélica / Cousin Angelica*, 1974; *Cría cuervos*, 1975) in which characters do not merely recall the past; they relive it.

This narrative strategy is succinctly deployed in *Elisa, vida mía / Elisa, My Life* (1977), which involves the merging of creative outlooks and values of an aging father (Fernando Rey) and his daughter (Geraldine Chaplin). In one scene, we see Elisa seated at her father's desk in his country cottage, reading a passage her father has underlined in a copy of the seventeenth-century Spanish writer Gracián's *El criticón*. We hear Elisa's voiceover reading Gracián's words to the background strains of an Eric Satie *Gnosienne*. On the desk there is a framed photograph of Elisa and her sister as small children. The camera frames the reflection of Elisa's adult face reflected on the surface of her photographic portrait as a child. Breaking away to the window, the camera reveals the bright Castilian landscape framed by the dark interior of the room. The photographs and the text she is reading lead Elisa to imagine that she sees her estranged husband in the field outside the cottage, but it is only a subjective recollection; then the camera picks up Elisa's father cycling toward the house. Camera movement works in this scene to break the boundaries between lived and imagined spaces, between present and past. Words cede to images, with off-screen music, as one critic notes, "choreographing" Elisa's search for her father (Sánchez Vidal 1988: 116).

The dance films, which also often involve the interplay of looks to construct complex and self-referential narratives, are generally built around the narrative trope that details the rote exercise sessions by dancers in a rehearsal hall as they practice standard dance movements in preparation for an assumed public performance that we never actually see. Through such collective rote exercise, individual dancers begin to form a dance troupe; then, through progressive rehearsals of specific narrative sequences, they immerse themselves in the characters of the story that will be narrated through their dance. Besides the fictional story told in this manner, each film also constitutes its own self-referential "story," a documentary that traces the inner journey of the performers and choreographer, the protagonists of this backstage documentary, from rehearsal to performance. Adding to that documentary style, in *Bodas de sangre* and *Salomé*, for instance, Saura includes voiceovers by the performers offering brief biographical commentary.

As part of that complex story-telling process, Saura often employs mobile cameras that circle the dancers and provide close-ups of their faces and bodies. In *Tango*, the rehearsal space includes panels that work like movie screens, projecting videocam images of the same character from different vantage points within the performance space. This provides a prismatic view of the dancers in a vertiginous display of planes. In general, the ubiquitous mirrors used in all of the dance films function for the dancer as a stand-in for the viewpoint of the audience, which is internalized as the performer's own, thus fusing the perspectives of performer and public. In this way, the dancers' metanarrative about rehearsal and performance represents the ritual of their submission to the audience's gaze (Chijona 1983: 40–1). This use of mirrors reflecting the dancer's image allows Saura to probe the doubling of identity, making the performer-characters part of a wider community as they view themselves in the mirror through the imagined view of others. Saura thereby refines the use of mirrors as a narrative device in his Franco-era films, whose protagonists take a detached look at themselves by contemplating their image in an actual or figurative mirror, creatively viewing their lives as performance. In *Cría cuervos*, for example, the film's narrative structure – with the child Ana imagining herself as an adult in the future looking back to her present circumstance as the past – established this mirror effect as a creative strategy for understanding experience.

Such narrative strategies connect to one of the constants of Saura's broader artistic design: the effort to capture the intersection of the pictorial, the photographic, and the cinematic as they construct a complex intertextual weave that shapes the representation of human experience and offers the individual self-understanding in historical, cultural, and personal terms. We see this in *Tango* (1998), Saura's effort to capitalize on the previous international success of his Spain-themed film *Carmen*, by transposing the scenario to an Argentine locale. The plot details the efforts of a choreographer to stage a dance version of the history of ethnic culture in Buenos Aires; in the course of the rehearsal process, he becomes sentimentally involved with his lead dancer. In the interior spaces of the rehearsal hall, the filming of the dancers as they go through their collective routines is paired with photographic panels of Argentine social history, thereby inviting the spectator to connect the two and linking the social scenario to the artist's emotional biography.

For Saura, a former photographer, the emotional impact of photographs is exploited as a way to historicize personal and collective memories. For instance, a daguerreotype-style group photograph of the Antonio Gades Company in costumes for their dance production of Lorca's *Bodas de sangre* accompanies the opening and closing credits of Saura's film version. The sequences enclosed by the two projections of this photograph document the drama of the dancers' transformation from individuals into members of a dance company, then into the characters they perform in the restaging of Lorca's tragedy, and finally into a static tableau that suggests that they have become objects of contemplation and nostalgia for audiences. The photograph thus prompts the viewing subject to engage with the dance film as an ongoing interplay between lived and remembered experiences. A similar use of photographs of early twentieth-century migrants arriving in Buenos Aires, accompanied by the strains of a milonga, introduces us to the world of Borges' story "El sur" in Saura's television adaptation of 1993: a narrative in which the lines between lived, remembered, and imagined experiences are again blurred. We are reminded of the strategic use of the photograph as a harsh reminder of the past in Saura's earlier films *El jardín de las delicias* and *La prima Angélica*. In some of these earlier films – *La prima Angélica*; *Elisa, vida mía*; *Dulces horas / Sweet Hours* (1982) – characters view a photograph and question their own faulty memory.

Growing out of this emphasis on the photograph, Saura often uses the self-referential device of freeze-frames, in the style of the ending of Truffaut's *Les quatre cents coups / The Four-Hundred Blows* (1959), to sum up a narrative situation. The spectator responds to the freeze-frame in much the same way that the characters – or spectator – "relive" past events by looking at an old photo. Key examples are the final images of *La caza / The Hunt* (1965), *El jardín de las delicias, Ana y los lobos / Ana and the Wolves* (1972), and *Dulces horas* (see Figure 5.3). The freeze-framed image is closely connected to Saura's use of *tableaux vivants* in a number of his films, as enactments of painterly scenes. In the early *Llanto por un bandido / Lament for a Bandit* (1963), for instance, a notable scene of Andalusian folkloric customs related to violence takes the form of a "battle with cudgels" that brings to life the famous Goya painting of that title. Variations on this interplay between familiar painterly images and social experience recur in later Saura films; for example, in the *tableaux vivants* of Goya images in *Los zancos / Stilts* (1984) and perhaps most elaborately in the recreation of Goya's *Disasters of War* in *Goya en Burdeos*.

At the center of the visual tropes that comprise Saura's authorial signature is the concept of performance. Saura's later performance-based films can be seen as the final stage in the elaboration of a concept that underlies his whole cinematic trajectory, which teaches us to understand performance as the process through which the individual either learns social conformity or rebels against established authority. The images of schoolchildren in *La prima Angélica*, *Cría cuervos*, and *Elisa, vida mía*, for instance, emphasize the mise-en-scènes of childhood (home, school, church) that function as spaces for disciplining the child's free spirit. In *Dulces horas*, by contrast, the protagonist is repressed precisely by recollections of the Civil War, which he recalls as the happiest time of his life. Seeking to relive his past, he hires actors to perform his scripted memories. Performance for him means

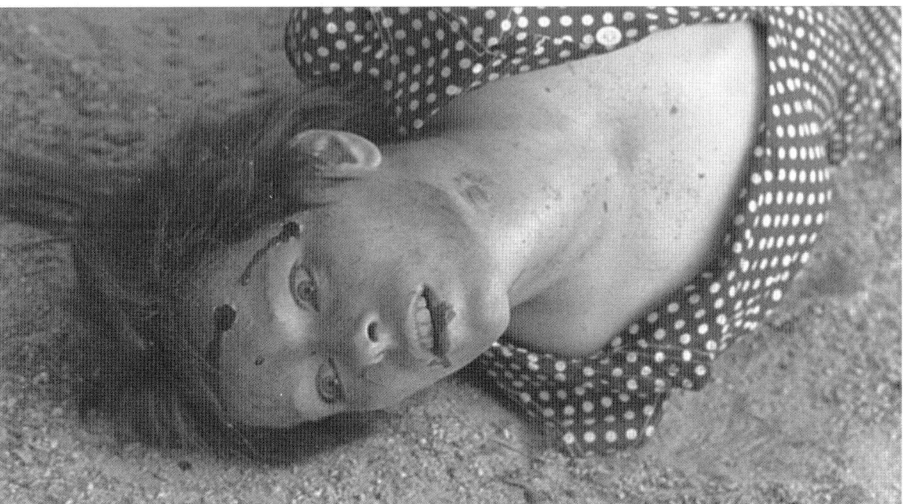

Figure 5.3 Saura's use of freeze-frames at the end of *La caza* (1965) and *Ana y los lobos* (1973; both prod. Elías Querejeta PC) gives them a photographic quality that encourages spectators to "relive" the characters' fictional past.

pleasurable submission to the order of the past, which, as the film suggests, is a dangerous form of self-imposed containment. The impulse to lose oneself in the past is countered visually by the film's parodic mock happy ending, with the characters lip-synching a popular song from the 1930s.

The same theme of performance as the crucible of conformity or rebellion is given further historical and political specificity in *¡Ay, Carmela!* (1990), the third film in Saura's long career to be set during the Civil War period. In this instance, the stage itself becomes a mirror reflecting the shifting social allegiances of the divided nation during the Civil War. Carmela (Carmen Maura), the personification of the Second Republic (Pillado-Miller 1997: 131), is forced to comply with the Nationalist forces who have taken her traveling vaudeville troupe prisoner and ordered them to perform a parody of their variety show. The new show is a Francoist reworking of the skits that the traveling troupe performed earlier in the Republican zone. When Carmela shows her defiance of the Nationalists by acknowledging the heroism of the incarcerated members of the International Brigade, present at the performance, she is shot dead by a Nationalist officer. Through Carmela's dangerous act of disobedience, Saura underscores the need to rebel against the imposition of political conformity by reaffirming individual creativity within the performance of social life. Performance – whether on or off stage – is shown to be intensely political.

¡Ay, Carmela! ends with the surviving members of the traveling troupe honoring Carmela's grave. Memory is closely interwoven with performance in Saura's work, whether in the earlier films where characters "stage" and work through a repressive past or in the later dance-based films that rework creative traditions, dramatizing through the insistence on rehearsals the ways in which repetition is a way of moving forward: a literal "working through" based on collective labor – that of the performance ensemble. While some of these dance films come close to being tributes to the star performers lovingly depicted, they retain a strong sense, through their choreography, of performance as what constructs community. The near-abstraction of the performance spaces allows these works to speak to wider international audiences at the same time as they celebrate a living national artistic heritage. If most Spanish cinema of the democratic period abandoned the allegorical bent of work produced under censorship during the dictatorship (exemplified by Saura's own Franco-era production), Saura is an unusual case of a director who opted, after the return to democracy, for increasingly non-representational forms of expression: that is, for a concept of art as performative. In this respect, his later *oeuvre* takes forward many of the concerns of the earlier, more explicitly political work – and it does so by refining the cinematic techniques that established his auteurist status as the Franco dictatorship's leading dissident filmmaker.

Pedro Almodóvar (Paul Julian Smith)

After thirty years of successful filmmaking in a country whose cinema industry seems always to be in crisis and after (at the time of writing) eighteen feature films that have won immense critical and audience approval, Pedro Almodóvar would seem to be in a class of his own. On the UK release of *La piel que habito / The Skin I Live In* (2011), the reverent interviewer of one national daily could write: "no major nation in the world has one director who enjoys such dominance over his native industry" (Gritten 2011). Some Spaniards would beg to differ. Indeed, the same film was attacked by the lead critic of *El País* (a long-term sparring partner of the director) as "hollow," an attempted "tragedy" that inadvertently provokes only "laughter" (Boyero 2011).

Almodóvar's auteurist prestige and hence his canonicity within an assumed Spanish film tradition thus remain unstable. And this is in spite of the fact that, as Nuria Triana Toribio argues, in the 1990s (the decade when Almodóvar received his definitive consecration abroad) "Spanishness" was conceived under a broad "generic umbrella" of a "discourse on diversity" that would have appeared to have benefited a filmmaker known for his protean nature (2003: 146). Rather, it remains the case that although "widely seen as the main representative of Spanish cinema outside Spain and the recipient of numerous international accolades [...] Almodóvar is still the source of some embarrassment in his own country" (Triana Toribio 2003: 158).

This tension between the national and transnational (the subject of Chapter 2) is one of the three themes I will treat in this section. The others will be the breach in the barrier between art and commerce effected by Almodóvar's reconciliation of critical and popular success, cited earlier, and the vexed question of postmodernism, which I argue should be taken back to its philosophical roots. These themes will be illustrated with reference to three representative features from Almodóvar's now lengthy career: *¿Qué he hecho yo para merecer esto? / What Have I Done to Deserve This?* (1984), widely thought to mark the end his early experimental period; *Todo sobre mi madre / All about My Mother* (1999), heralded as evidence of a newly mature style; and *La piel que habito*, yet darker and more self-referential than any of its predecessors in the creator's late period. Arguing that technique is central to Almodóvar's artistic signature or commercial trademark, sequences from each film will also be briefly examined.

To begin with the last theme, "posmoderno" has been an adjective loosely and often pejoratively ascribed to Almodóvar from the start of his career. Indeed, in Chapter 12 Vicente Sánchez-Biosca reads the opening sequence of *Mujeres al borde de un ataque de nervios / Women on the Verge of a Nervous Breakdown* (1988), with its credits collaged from vintage magazines and its allusions to Hollywood genres of earlier eras, as representing forms of pastiche and kitsch that he calls "postmodern." If this latter phenomenon is identified, as Sánchez-Biosca does, with the recycling of pre-existing fragments, then "postmodern auteurism" is something of a contradiction in terms, for the cinematic auteur would seem to stake his (more rarely her) claim to distinction on artistic innovation and a break with the past. If we return to the scholarly origins of the term in the 1980s, however, we find a more precise definition, one that is not without interest for Almodóvar's practice of cinema.

As should be better known, philosopher Jean François Lyotard defined the postmodern condition as one of "incredulity towards metanarratives," especially those that were once sought to explain the totality of political or psychic structures (1986: xxiv). For Lyotard, the formal trope of this condition is "incommensurability" – a kind of diversity so radical that the diverse elements it juxtaposes cannot even be compared or contrasted.

We can apply this paradigm to Almodóvar's *¿Qué he hecho … ?*. This film, initially at least, seems to come closest to being both a sociopolitical critique (a denunciation of the living conditions of the urban poor on the fringes of Madrid) and a case study in psychoanalysis (an investigation of the near breakdown of depressed housewife Gloria, so movingly played by Carmen Maura). Exiled to a monstrous housing project on the edge of the M30 beltway and brutalized by her sexually and financially selfish taxi-driver husband, Gloria would appear to embody the perfect victim of class and gender exploitation. But Almodóvar juxtaposes this metanarrative dimension of political and psychic critique with radically heterogeneous ("incommensurable") elements that resist totalization or assimilation. We see this in the three sequences treated by Tatjana Pavlović and her coauthors in their account of the film (Pavlović et al. 2009). Thus, when Gloria cleans or shops (a transparent opportunity for neo-realist documentation and denunciation), Almodóvar favors a jarring and unusual technique: shooting his character from inside ovens, washing machines, and shop windows. Subjects are thus shown "from the point of view of objects" (Pavlović et al. 2009: 174), an anomalous and disconcerting perspective (see Figure 5.4). Likewise, when Gloria and her husband make brief and unsatisfactory love (as she pleads for money for the dentist), the sequence is set to a popular song about a prostitute, ironically comparing the positions of housewife and streetwalker. But this potentially political commentary is undercut by the implausible performance of that song as shown on the family's television set: lip-synched by Almodóvar himself to his musical collaborator Fanny McNamara, who is dressed in drag as Scarlett O'Hara (Pavlović et al. 2009: 175). Finally, grandmother and son Toni watch an unlikely film in a movie theatre: Elia Kazan's *Splendor in the Grass* (1961). Here the example of the Warren Beatty character's desire to stay in Kansas and not relocate to the East Coast will inspire Almodóvar's urban misfits to move back from the city to their village, a reverse migration that contradicts some forty years of historical Spanish population movement. Pavlović writes: "Through the intertextual use of a Hollywood film, Almodóvar touches on important themes such as failed rural integration" (Pavlović et al. 2009: 177). It remains the case, however, that the use of such cinematic references both transcends facile pastiche ("postmodernism" as it is commonly understood) and configures a radical hybridity of constitutive elements that resist integration into a whole (the incommensurability of philosophical postmodernism).

Some fifteen years later, Almodóvar's hard-won mastery of cinematic technique would seem to make such formal and ideological ruptures less self-evident. And the cultural distinction claimed by and for *Todo sobre mi madre* was underwritten by its receipt of the most prestigious awards at home and abroad (the Goya for Best Spanish Feature and the Oscar for Best Foreign Film). A new austerity of theme

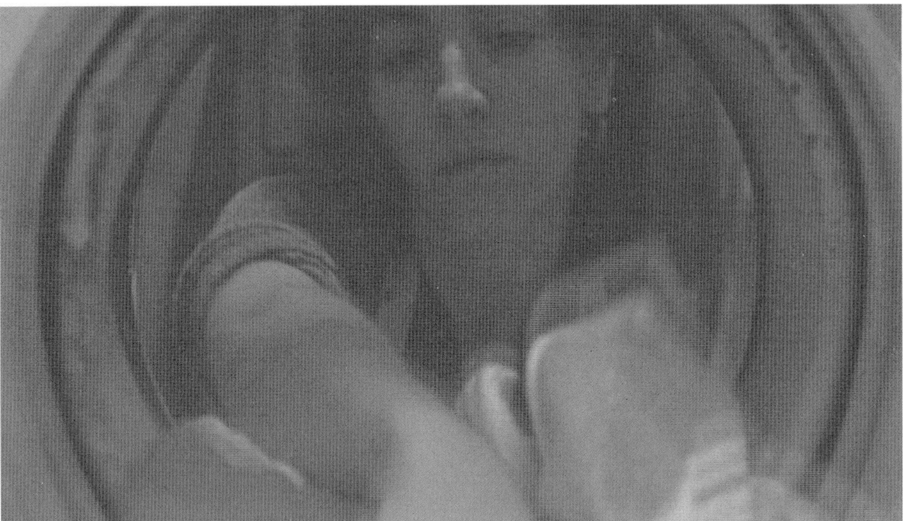

Figure 5.4 Almodóvar's *¿Qué he hecho yo para merecer esto?* (1984; prod. Kaktus PC/ Tesauro SA): domestic objects look back at housewife Gloria.

barely troubled by comic elements (a mother's mourning on the death of her son, with Cecilia Roth as affecting as Maura before her) was confirmed by a certain austerity of technique.

Thus, in an early sequence the car accident in which the son dies is not directly shown. Almodóvar cuts from a suddenly shattered windshield to a blurry pan of a rainy street at night. The camera comes to rest at a canted angle and Roth's Manuela comes wailing into frame. The shot, blurred and distorted, fades to black, as we realize that this is the perspective of the dying youth. While the unusual point-of-view shot perhaps echoes the viewpoints from objects we saw in *¿Qué he hecho ... ?*, it is far less showy and more subtle. Later, Manuela's arrival in Barcelona (an astonishing first for the Madrid-centric Almodóvar oeuvre) is also filmed with economy and precision. A panoramic aerial view of the city at night gives way to a travelling shot of Manuela in a taxi, the Sagrada Familia glittering gold in its window. Point-of-view shots once more show the prostitutes working a desolate area outside the city, before Almodóvar cuts to another high angle: the cars of punters circle the girls as in some Dantesque inferno. In traditional style we are here "sutured" into the protagonist's point of view, seeing the elements of the urban spectacle, diverse and even "incommensurable" as they are, within a certain unifying subjectivity. A third vital sequence is the late monologue performed in a theatre by Agrado, the transsexual prostitute turned PA who provides (limited and qualified) comic relief here. While Agrado's text confirms the stress on performativity that is the greatest academic cliché in criticism on Almodóvar's cinema (she claims that "authenticity" is simply the result of a self-fashioning achieved through plastic surgery), the sequence's shooting style is defiantly plain: Almodóvar simply sets up the camera in the stalls to observe an impeccably theatrical routine.

Unlike in the case of *¿Qué he hecho ... ?*, *Todo* subtly orchestrates tones and registers that remain, nonetheless, radically diverse. But this newly modulated artistic technique is inseparable from the industrial conditions of its production. As the eighth feature made by and for El Deseo, the independent production company headed by Pedro's brother Agustín, *Todo* benefited from a creative freedom earlier features did not enjoy. And, as Nuria Triana Toribio writes in Chapter 14, ties of family and friendship are vital here, protecting the auteur from the pressures of unsympathetic corporate management. Yet, as Triana Toribio writes once more – and as I myself have documented elsewhere (Smith 2009b: 18–20) – artistic "quality" is as much a part of the business model of El Deseo as such strictly financial precepts as the determination to keep budgets within reasonable levels or the preselling of features to foreign distributors before production begins. The new "maturity" of Almodóvar's style, much trumpeted by critics, is thus also a commercial strategy, intended to create a profitable and sustainable position for Almodóvar in a turbulent audiovisual sector.

With the passing of another decade, Almodóvar perhaps found the continuing pressures of celebrity more demanding. The dark-hued *La piel que habito*, like *Los abrazos rotos / Broken Embraces* (2009) immediately before it, marked his densest assemblage of self-citations, approaching an anthology of the director's back catalogue. The unlikely story of a plastic surgeon (Antonio Banderas) who takes revenge on the attempted rapist of his daughter by transforming him into a beautiful female captive (Elena Anaya), *La piel*'s kidnap/bondage premise evokes *Átame / Tie Me Up! Tie Me Down!* (1990), also made with Banderas some twenty years earlier. A lengthy and troubling rape sequence echoes *Kika* (1993) shot for shot. The hosing down of a scantily clad soon-to-be transsexual replays a famous sequence starring Carmen Maura's transsexual character in *La ley del deseo / The Law of Desire* (1987), while the obsessive focus on medical paraphernalia has been unnervingly prominent in each of Almodóvar's films since *La flor de mi secreto / The Flower of My Secret* (1995). This collaging of film fragments is confirmed by at least two *mise-en-abymes* within the film itself: the surgeon pieces together samples of skin to remake his victim and s/he in turn spends her captivity making doll-like mannequins covered by swatches of cloth, reassembled to make a whole surface.

Like the cinematic references in *¿Qué he hecho ... ?*, such emphatic quotation, even to Almodóvar himself, remains ambivalent here. Is the director (like the surgeon) a Frankenstein, feeding parasitically on past body parts? Or is he, like Prometheus (also referenced in the film), a hero who transforms human creativity through his theft? While such self-citation clearly serves the purposes of auteurship (making the strongest claim for thematic and stylistic continuity in an expanding oeuvre), in this case it also raises the problem of the disjunction between national and transnational reception. Thus we saw at the start of this piece that critical response (mixed at home, ecstatic abroad) was widely varying. Within the film itself it is striking how distant Almodóvar's fictional universe had grown from the social concerns of contemporary Spain, which he once addressed, however obliquely and ambivalently, in films such as *¿Qué he hecho ... ?*. Nominally set in Toledo, much of *La piel* was shot in a rainy Galicia and the local newspaper shown in the film is Barcelona's *La Vanguardia*. *La piel*'s moneyed milieu (surgeons and socialites secluded in country houses) remains unperturbed by the financial crisis and social unrest so prominent in Spanish life during the film's lengthy production process.

Clearly such contradictions, which confirm the hermetic claustrophobia of the film's premise, prove untroubling to foreign viewers more willing than some locals to suspend disbelief. And they could be read perhaps as continuations of that "incommensurability" that we saw so nakedly in *¿Qué he hecho ... ?* and more masked by consistent artistic "quality" in *Todo*. Perhaps the answer to this conundrum lies in the most durable and original of Almodóvar's repertoire of auteurist motifs. The avenging transsexual, pivotal in *La piel*, can be traced back through *La mala educación / Bad Education* (2008) and *La ley del deseo* to an unpublished short story of the 1970s (Smith 2009a). The familiar loosely postmodern trope of performance can here be qualified in a way presciently suggested by Isolina Ballesteros before *La piel*'s release: "performativity [has] become [in Almodóvar's later films] a curse and punishment, a painful burden to others, a tragic irony" (2009: 96). If, then, Almodóvar is indeed in a cinematic class of his own (perilously poised between art and commerce, home and abroad), his is an institutional position that embodies unique strains and tensions, which have become increasingly visible in the text of his films.

Víctor Erice (Paul Julian Smith)

The creator of just three feature films in over thirty years, Erice has no rival for the role of quintessential auteur in Spanish cinema. Here auteurism is to be understood in its most traditional sense as denoting filmmakers with a uniquely personal style and thematics that are sustained over a lengthy period of time and whose practice is identified with the most prestigious forms of art cinema. Although, as we shall see, Erice has benefited from collaboration with skilled practitioners in, say, screenwriting, acting, and cinematography, he is widely acknowledged as the only begetter of his small but highly rated oeuvre.

Emilio G. García Fernández claims, in words often echoed by Spanish critics, that Erice's first feature was "inexplicable and unexplained," "timeless [and] unrepeatable" (1985: 270). This film, *El espíritu de la colmena / The Spirit of the Beehive* (1973), in which a child is fascinated by the figure of Frankenstein shortly after the Civil War, remains one of the most celebrated of all works in Spanish cinema. *El sur / The South* (1983), in which a girl explores her father's tragic past, is a notorious case of a mutilated masterpiece, abandoned when producer Andrés Vicente Gómez, alarmed by escalating costs, pulled the plug on the project. *El sol del membrillo / The Quince Tree Sun* (1992), about Madrid hyper-realist painter Antonio López, is an austere and elegant documentary about the artistic process, a transparent allegory for Erice's own painstaking struggle to capture reality through his chosen medium. As Nuria Triana Toribio writes with some skepticism, Erice and a select number of directors identified with the short-lived movement called New Spanish Cinema have thus become "synonymous not just with Spanish art cinema but with national cinema as a whole" (2003: 83).

Although his features were shot in Spain and are held to be essential landmarks in Spanish filmmaking, Erice is one of the very few Spanish directors who have attained the highest levels of international prestige. It was symptomatic that in 2006 he was invited to undertake a cinematic "correspondence" with gnomic Iranian auteur Abbas Kiarostami, which served as the basis for an art exhibition. In the catalogue the two directors, in spite of their very different backgrounds, are held to exhibit the same characteristics, practicing as they do a "twofold cinema of childhood" (i.e., both focusing on children as protagonists and making the audience see film as if for the first time); further, having come of age under repressive regimes, they are said to exhibit "an intransigent morality of creation" and an "ethics of form" that transcend their immediate social and political context (Kiarostami and Erice 2006: 10). The catalogue reminds us that Erice's work goes beyond feature film, as its filmography lists four shorts made by the director when he attended the Francoist Official Film School (Escuela Oficial de Cine; EOC) from1961 to 1963); a mid-length episode in the portmanteau movie, *Los desafíos / The Challenges* (1969); and five shorts shot mainly on video (1996–2006) after the release of *El sol del membrillo*.

While Erice's corpus remains severely restricted, it clearly fulfills the criteria for authorship enumerated by Foucault (1986: 108–12) in a famous essay: its value is held to be consistent, with all three films highly prized by critics; its concepts are thought to be coherent, including as they do mortality and the passing of time, the primacy of the imagination, and the mystery of human identity; and its style is considered to be unified, exemplifying as the corpus does the tenets of art-movie storytelling identified by David Bordwell in *Narration in the Fiction Film* (1990). To be more precise: while classical, or canonic, Hollywood narration relies on "character-centered causality and the definition of the action as the attempt to achieve a goal" (Bordwell 1990: 157), transnational art-cinema narration "loosen[s] causal relations," leaving gaps or lacunae, silencing motivations, and employing a "subjective" or "expressive" notion of realism, based more on contradictory characters than on clearcut actions (Bordwell 1990: 207).

In *El espíritu*, this leaving of gaps was clearly conscious and came to the director late in the production process. While the finished film is resolutely (and resonantly) ambiguous, the original script included a voiceover narration spoken by the now adult Ana (Ana Torrent), the child protagonist, that explained the troubling ellipses of the narrative. Likewise, in the original script of *El sur*, main character Estrella (Icíar Bollaín) resolves the mysteries of her father's past by visiting her family in Andalusia, where she encounters the son he secretly had with an actress lover. As the film in its final, truncated form breaks off before this resolution, the characters remain contradictory and their actions incomplete. *El sol del membrillo* at first seems less formally complex than its predecessors, consisting as it does of a linear diary of Antonio López's heroic, but frustrated, attempt to capture the tree of the title on canvas. But this third feature also ends with subjective or expressive elements that are difficult to resolve: López recounts a disturbing dream, and Erice gives us an extended shot of his own camera and arc light abandoned beneath the tree. Rotting fruit litters the ground underfoot, in an apparent reminder of the death that can be delayed, but not defeated, by the artistic process.

But, if Erice's works conform so closely to the criteria of the international art movie, it does not follow that his corpus (valued not in spite but because of its scarcity) is aesthetically autonomous. Rather it takes up its position, like all artistic products, within a specific cultural field. Manuel Palacio (2005) has shown how the myth of *El espíritu* was actively constructed by its author and sympathetic critics soon after its release. For example, Palacio cites a surprising interview with Erice published on the day of *El espíritu*'s premiere at the San Sebastián Festival (September 19, 1973) in which he expresses a desire to "channel" or "direct" the promotion for his film and to make sure that its audience is properly "alerted" in advance as to what they will be seeing (2005: 197). Palacio further suggests that Erice's current position in the "Olympus" of Spanish film has erased memories of the contingencies of the film's initial reception: critics were bitterly divided as to its merit, and the audience received the news that it had been awarded the grand prize with the noisiest boos ever heard at the festival (2005: 198). Palacio also shows that two comments by a journalist published on the day of the premiere became "central" to readings of the film for the next thirty years: namely, that the poetic and emotional character of Erice's text is radically opposed to conventional cinematic narration and that *El espíritu* is a "homage" to the viewer's first experience of cinema.

I myself have documented elsewhere (Smith 2000) how the legend of the solitary auteur is subverted by Erice's collaboration with artistic comrades: his expert cinematographer, young star, and co-screenwriter. Thus, the "magical" effect of *El espíritu* was produced to a large extent by specific techniques of Luis Cuadrado's shooting style, of which Erice had no specialist knowledge (Smith 2000: 33). While Erice himself stressed the innocence of the young Ana Torrent (who, like her character, saw Frankenstein on film for the first time during the shoot), some press coverage of the period stresses her precocious ambition and professionalism (Smith 2000: 35–7). Finally, Ángel Fernández Santos' childhood experiences were as vital as those of Erice himself to the screenplay they wrote together. Yet the creative claims of the subsequent critic of *El País* tended to fade out of the narrative of the film's authorship (Smith 2000: 37–8).

Moreover, the reverence shown toward even such slight works as Erice's more recent short *Lifeline* (2002) reveals that his auteurist signature now serves, like that of a fashion designer, almost magically to distinguish even minor creations. It could be argued, then, that the fact that Erice has been unable to mount a feature project for almost twenty years – he published a script, *La promesa de Shanghai / The Shanghai Promise* (Erice 2001), for his adaptation of Juan Marsé's novella *El embrujo de Shanghai / The Shanghai Spell*, but it was brought to the screen by another director – speaks more to the particularity of his own temperament than to the general state of Spanish cinema as a whole. After all, Julio Medem, a director whose work is as personal, even eccentric, as that of Erice, has managed to make no fewer than seven theatrically released features over a much shorter time period.

In Spain, however, Erice's reputation remains unassailable. Thus, when a textbook seeks to demonstrate the "fundamental components of cinema narration" (spatial and temporal structure, montage, and soundtrack), it is through the analysis of just one film: *El sur* (Villafañe and Mínguez 2006: 314–23). Erice's use of "ellipses" and flashback (which problematize the relation between story and plot) prove especially well-matched for formalist academic analysis, which is displayed here in the form of a diagram (2006: 323). In his essay on *El sol del membrillo*, the respected Spanish academic Santos Zunzunegui focuses rather on Erice's use of dissolves, which, he claims, serve to fuse the two moments of the "concrete" time of shooting and the "abstract" time of montage (the terms are taken from Erice himself) (2002: 72). Citing in rapid succession Paul Cézanne, André Bazin, and Jean-Luc Godard, Zunzunegui claims that Erice returns us to an "age of innocence" in which cinema and the world itself are "reinvented" (2002: 76). As we have seen, this argument has been echoed by critics with remarkable consistency for some thirty years.

There are signs, however, that after almost two decades without a new feature Erice's prestige is waning outside Spain. Already in their *Contemporary Spanish Cinema*,

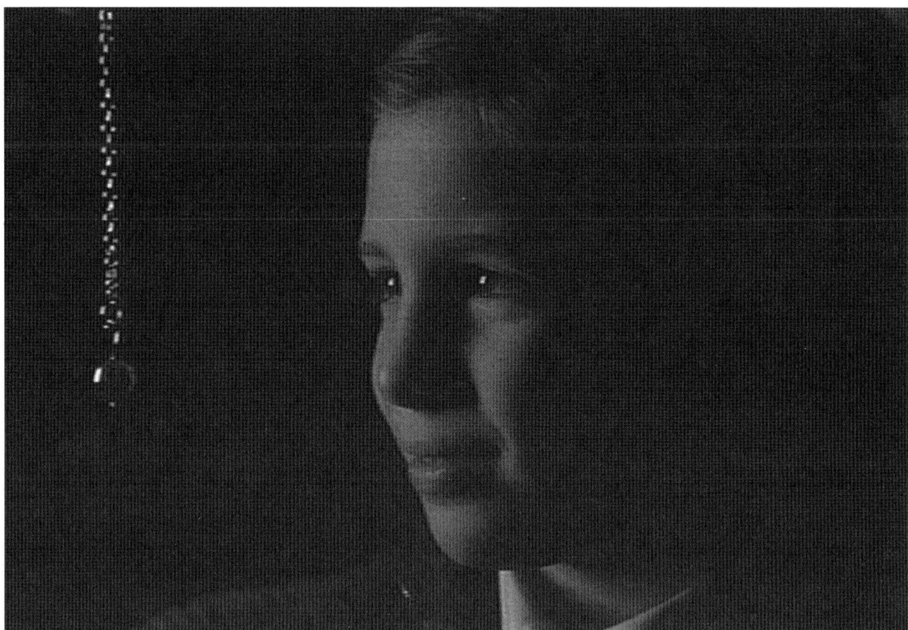

Figure 5.5 The magic pendulum in Víctor Erice's *El sur* (1983; prod. Elías Querejeta PC): Sonsoles Aranguren as the young Estrella (1983).

Barry Jordan and Ricky Morgan-Tamosunas acknowledge that *El espíritu* and *El sur* are "fascinating, evocative, richly textured studies of family life on the losing side under Francoism in the 1940s and 1950s, as seen through the confused eyes of children" (1998: 200) but go on to note, more skeptically, that, appealing as he did to international audiences enamored of Bergman and Godard, Erice "became a prism through which arthouse audiences and academic specialists abroad tended to approach Spanish cinema and through whom they constructed their views of what a quality Spanish cinema ought to look like" (1998: 200). In 2003 Erice was barely mentioned in Nuria Triana Toribio's *Spanish National Cinema*. Likewise, Tatjana Pavlović and her team, who in 2009 published *100 Years of Spanish Cinema* as a guide to "the most important movements, films, and directors of twentieth-century Spain" (jacket), did not see fit to include a film by Erice among their twenty-two case studies.

But to say that Erice's Olympian auteur status should be historicized is not to diminish his achievement. There is little doubt that each of Erice's films contains a "magical" moment in which an object bathed in light seems to stand outside time, inexplicable and unexplained. Thus, Ana's rapt face gleams white out of the darkness in the improvised cinema where she sees Frankenstein for the first time; Estrella's precious pendulum, a gift from her beloved father, shines and spins golden in the shadowy space of her bedroom; and the little tree displays its fragile fruit for the contemplation of the painter and filmmaker who seek to memorialize its beauty (see Figure 5.5).

But these three films also offer a historical critique of the processes they document, however hidden or ambivalent that critique may be. Ana's silent and shadowy household is resolutely mysterious (Erice himself confessed that he did not know to whom the mother was writing her letters). Yet, although the family does not seem to suffer the cruel deprivations of many Spaniards in the 1940s, their melancholia is clearly an allegory for the mood of the nation in the most repressive period of the regime. Likewise, *El sur* is mainly concerned with the (frustrated) personal journey of young Estrella and her family romance with her depressed father. But the latter (unlike the father in *El espíritu*) is openly identified as one of the losers in the Civil War. The characters' exile in the chilly north is thus emblematic once more of the alienation of those estranged from the regime. *El sol del membrillo* takes place in the most secluded of spaces: a tiny walled garden where an artist struggles with his craft. Yet Antonio López's lone quest, that of painters through the centuries, is precisely located and contextualized: the painter receives visits from Spanish friends or admirers from China; he chats with the Polish workmen who are renovating his house; and he listens to the radio that gives repeated reports on the distant Gulf War. The final moral of Erice's art cinema, however abstract it may be, is thus that aesthetics and politics, those eternal enemies, are by no means hermetically sealed off from one another.

Julio Medem (Paul Julian Smith)

The Basque-born Julio Medem is positively prolific compared to his predecessor Víctor Erice, a director with similar artistic ambitions. Yet Medem is problematic as a "Spanish" auteur. While *Vacas / Cows* (1992) was an eccentric historical epic staged in a lush Basque valley and *La ardilla roja / The Red Squirrel* (1993) an amnesiac love story set mainly on a campsite in Euskadi's neighboring region of La Rioja, the enigmatic *Tierra / Earth* (1996) played out in a red-earthed no man's land, devoid of geographic markers, and the tragic romance *Los amantes del círculo polar / Lovers of the Arctic Circle* (1998) strayed as far as Lapland. Medem's biggest popular success, *Lucía y el sexo / Sex and Lucía* (2001), shuttled between Madrid and the Balearics, while his critical failure *Caótica Ana / Chaotic Ana* (2007) tracked its time-traveling heroine from the ancient Sahara to contemporary Manhattan.

In her *Spanish National Cinema*, Nuria Triana Toribio has argued that it was precisely this cosmopolitan or transnational quality that enabled Medem to serve as the consecrated auteur of the 1990s. His conceptual difficulty and stylistic modernism were felt by the local critics who championed him to redeem the "misdemeanors" of a Spanish cinema otherwise characterized by coarse comedies with a markedly localist flavour. She writes: "Julio Medem's cinema can be understood as an instrument by which the discourse that locates the Spanishness of Spanish cinema in high art and the intellectual traditions of the country is maintained" (2003: 149). Triana Toribio's is of course a functionalist reading of auteurism, stressing such external factors as criticism and curriculum, as opposed to the traditional conception of the term, which focuses on personal expressivity. Yet there is no doubt about the consistency and continuity of Medem's corpus, whose formal and narrative techniques extend into his controversial feature-length documentary *La pelota vasca / The Basque Ball Game* (2003) (see Chapter 4).

In his excellent book on the director, Rob Stone lists the elements of Medem's signature style: "colorful eroticism, subjective camerawork, elaborate plotting, structural equations, straight-faced absurdity, and obsessions with symmetry, duality, and chance" (2007: 1). In spite of the self-consciousness of this concern with film form (which would seem to preclude direct personal expression), critics inevitably stress the particularity of his biographical situation. In his study and interview (1997, 1999), major Spanish critic Carlos F. Heredero (cited with various degrees of skepticism by Triana Toribio, Stone, and Jo Evans, who also authored a book (2007) on Medem) sought to establish Medem as the vital figure in Spanish cinema of the 1990s. Heredero invokes genealogy to explain the auteur's complexities, as the son of a politically liberal mother of mixed French / Basque origins and a reactionary father of mixed German / Valencian origins (1999: 248). Disappointed in a youthful love affair, the shy Medem gave up the chance to train as an Olympic athlete to study medicine, specializing in surgery and, then, psychiatry (1999: 250), training clearly appropriate for a director who would come to focus on stories of psychic disturbance. For Heredero, Medem has staged a "journey to maturity" through his feature films, held to constitute a "renewed personal exorcism" (1999: 251). Dedicating each of his features to a different member of his family, Medem himself has encouraged this personalized understanding of his cinema, even as he came to fame as an exponent of the collective movement baptized "New Basque Cinema." It is a label that, as Evans suggests, is highly problematic (2007: 11), given continuing and violent conflicts over what it means to be Basque in Euskadi and beyond.

If Erice, the earlier critics' darling, exemplified the tenets of the art movie narration as specified by Bordwell (1990), then Medem coincides closely with the conception of style that distances international art film from the classical or Hollywood standard. Borrowing from his collaborator Kristin Thompson, Bordwell notes that, while in the canonic mode stylistic elements (whether visual or auditory) are subordinated to the communication of plot, in non-classical film "lines, colours, expressions, and textures" can constitute an "excess" that transcends both denotation and connotation (1990: 53). Medem's dazzlingly complex signature style exploits such "unjustified" elements to suggest a "strangeness" that "escapes unifying impulses," appealing to critics and select audiences alike.

The openings of Medem's films are especially virtuoso. According to Evans, the director calls them "zero sequences," intended to "seduce and hypnotize the viewer" (2007: 26). Thus, *Vacas* begins with a man in traditional Basque dress chopping wood as he stands on a log. With dynamic editing and in extreme close-up, we see multiple shots of chips flying and the axe falling perilously close to his bare feet. *La ardilla roja*, on the other hand, starts with a slow and eerie underwater shot of a flooded forest, which will prove to be the reservoir where the main characters, a failed musician and a young woman who is feigning amnesia, will take an uneasy vacation. *Tierra* stages perhaps the most complex "zero sequence." Beginning with shots of outer space and set to the portentous voiceover of main character Ángel (who may be extraterrestrial or simply mad), the camera, in a sequence of masked cuts, falls through the clouds to earth, flying over barren red fields before coming to rest on a tiny woodlouse, one of a host who are plaguing the anonymous village that is the film's main location.

The key color throughout *Tierra* is the warm brownish red of the landscape, which Medem found only in the region of Aragón, where he shot his film. *Los amantes del círculo polar*, however, stresses from the very start (in which star-crossed lovers Ana and Otto meet as children) a chilly palette of blue and white. The startling use of color in these two films is clearly excessive or unjustified, producing a sense of strangeness in the viewer even as it reminds us of the unifying vision of the auteur. Some critics have reacted negatively to such recurring visual techniques. *Vacas* was praised for its shots from the viewpoints of cows, mute and ironic observers of the tragic Basque conflict. But *La ardilla roja* was attacked for subjective shooting from the perspective of the scurrying rodent, a technique that by now seemed more of a formalist tic than an expressive necessity.

There is perhaps a tension here between the all-too-evident brilliance of Medem's images and the insufficiencies of his narrative. Certainly, Medem's plots stress not classic narrative dynamism but rather the circular symmetries implied in the palindromic names he favors for his characters, and which are of course influenced by his own (exceptionally rare) surname. Thus, in *Vacas* the names of the characters and the actors who play them return compulsively as one generation succeeds another. In *Los amantes*, Otto and Ana repeatedly fail to coincide, even as they search desperately for one another; and Medem provides us with two alternative endings in which the couple may live or die but, typically, see themselves reflected in each other eyes. *Lucía y el sexo*, in which the titular character has a passionate affair with a writer in Madrid before fleeing to the Balearic islands, ends with the couple inexplicably back in the capital once more, apparently some time earlier. Like palindromes, it would seem, Medem's stories can be read indifferently backwards and forwards in time.

Perhaps it would be fairer to suggest that, at his best, Medem can fuse image and narrative in a common dream-like expressivity. This is what Heredero, citing his interview with the director, calls the "narrative image" that "vibrates on the screen" because it comes from "the territory of passion, desire [and] instinct" (1999: 251). While this is perhaps a curious description of the technique of a director who can be clinically cerebral in his own accounts of his films, it seems likely that the "narrative image" that most resonantly recurs in Medem's films is the gap or hole (see Figure 5.6). *Vacas* boasts an enigmatic empty tree trunk from which

Figure 5.6 Looking into the void in Medem's *Vacas* (1992; prod. Sogetel): Emma Suárez (Cristina) and Txema Blasco (Manuel).

strange messages emerge, and *La ardilla roja* features the empty forest, drowned by the reservoir. Lucía, a new Alice in Wonderland, falls down a hole in the island where she has fled, only to emerge at another point in her story. When we first meet the chaotic Ana, she is living in a cave.

But, if Medem focuses in art cinema style on narrative gaps or ellipses, he also stages journeys for his characters. While the villagers of *Vacas* remain in their verdant valley, retreating only into madness or incest, the lovers of the subsequent films travel restlessly, even if their motives and goals remain studiously obscure. And, in spite of his solitary, even narcissistic, auteurism (most of the male characters are clearly stand-ins for the director himself), Medem's own cinematic journey has been in the company of others who have decisively affected its trajectory. In the first place, Medem's career would have been impossible without continuing financial support from the production company Sogecine, a division of Prisa, Spain's largest media conglomerate. Stone also cites challenges to the director's authority during the fraught shoot of *Tierra*, coming both from the disoriented star, experienced actor Carmelo Gómez, and the strong-willed veteran cinematographer, Javier Aguirresarobe (Stone 2007: 113). Skilled composer Alberto Iglesias (who was later to provide the soundtracks for Almodóvar's recent films) is also a "crucial" collaborator (Stone 2007: 164) in establishing the complex mood of Medem's films. Emma Suárez, expert female lead in the first two features, became estranged from the director only when next cast in *Tierra* in the thankless role of a submissive wife and mother.

This brings us to the sticking point of gender. While *La ardilla roja* was explicitly presented by Medem as a parody of machismo (the male who imposes an identity on the female amnesiac is in fact hoodwinked by her), *Tierra* was based on the most conventional of oppositions, with the male protagonist choosing a sex-crazed teenager over a mature mother. (The fact that in his personal life Medem himself was making a similar decision reinforced the auteurist credentials of the film without making its plot more palatable.) In *Lucía y el sexo* as well, the more graphic sexual scenes are clearly directed to a heterosexual male viewer: as part of their lovemaking, Lucía (Paz Vega) stages an erotic striptease for her partner Lorenzo (Tristán Ulloa); he reciprocates with a comically unsexy version, his pants getting caught around his ankles as he struggles to remove them. However, even this most crowd-pleasing of Medem's techniques, the increasing appeal to sexual content, can be read within a European art movie context. It is no secret that a potent attraction of otherwise austere old-school auteurs was their freedom to include such graphic images at a time when sex was subject to strict censorship in Hollywood movies.

Medem's claim to seriousness (to what Triana Toribio calls high art and intellectual tradition) was, however, bolstered by his documentary *La pelota vasca*, an unexpected incursion into politics (see Chapter 4). While the film's reception in Spain was hugely polarized, with Medem receiving both standing ovations and death threats (Evans 2007: 9), most striking is the way in which the director carried his fictional techniques, such as fissiparous editing, into the more tricky terrain of actuality. Crosscutting between a bewildering variety of talking heads and leaving jump cuts that testified to his editing of their testimony, Medem reproduced the dueling and unresolved subjectivities that are so characteristic of his fictions.

Medem's next feature, *Caótica Ana* (whose heroine was named for his recently deceased sister), seemed to suggest to the contrary a retreat from the real, featuring as it did the director's most implausible premise yet: a young girl who, on undergoing regressive therapy, relives several centuries of reincarnated selves (Smith 2007–8). Presented as an open attack on patriarchy and war, the film was criticized for the naivety of its politics and, a sad first for Medem, failed to obtain distribution abroad. In spite of this setback (and *Ana* clearly connected in Spain with its youthful target audience), it remains the case that Medem has produced a substantial body of work that constitutes a uniquely distinctive contribution to Basque, Spanish, and world cinema.

Alejandro Amenábar (Paul Julian Smith)

Alejandro Amenábar is a unique case among Spanish auteurs. While directors such as the cerebral Erice and Medem have inscribed themselves in their different ways in a prestigious European tradition, Amenábar followed the riskier path of naturalizing or acculturating Hollywood genres and shooting styles within Spain. Thus, *Tesis / Thesis* (1996) was a serial-killer and snuff-movie-themed thriller that expertly reproduced US techniques (albeit with ironic echoes of Erice's 1973 *El espíritu de la colmena*, signaled by the presence of the now adult Ana Torrent) and *Abre los ojos / Open Your Eyes* (1997) was an enigmatic mystery focusing on virtual reality *avant la lettre*, a premise that was so easily translatable to other cultural contexts that it became one of the very few Spanish features to be remade in Hollywood (as the Tom Cruise vehicle *Vanilla Sky*, 2001).

Amenábar has thus been able to create a new and widely accepted form of auteurism that unites Spain and the United States, and art cinema and commercial moviemaking to the satisfaction of both critics and audiences alike. Given the persistent hostility of the Spanish critical establishment to Hollywood and to popular genres and the equally engrained skepticism of Spanish audiences toward their own local cinema and its pretensions to quality, this radical revision of the notion of auteurism is no small feat.

Yet, in spite of this high-profile hybridity, even the English-language ghost story *The Others* (2001), which starred Nicole Kidman and boasted a plot twist highly reminiscent of the Hollywood hit *The Sixth Sense* (M. Night Shyamalan, 1999), was shot in Spain, with a Spanish crew, and with an impressively gloomy art design and palette borrowed from Spanish Old Master painting. And Amenábar followed this transnational project (faithfully acclaimed by the local press as the most successful "Spanish" film of all time) with *Mar adentro / The Sea Inside* (2004), a highly localist feature. This real-life story of euthanasia activist Ramón Sampedro, a figure unfamiliar to international audiences, was shot mainly on location in Galicia and scripted in no fewer than three of the Spanish state's official languages: Castilian, Catalan, and Galician. Amenábar's most recent project, the English-language historical epic *Agora* (2009), which chronicles the conflict between paganism and Christianity in late Antiquity, confirms the idiosyncrasy of his thematic choices, which refuse to be pigeonholed within either the Hollywood or the European canon. An unlikely popular hit in Spain, with over three and a half million admissions, *Agora* (like Medem's *Caótica Ana*) has, nonetheless, yet to secure distribution abroad at the time of writing.

Carlos Heredero, the key commentator on Spanish directors of the 1990s, derives Amenábar's artistic imagination from his conflicted early life: born in Allende's Chile, as a child Amenábar went with his parents into Spanish exile, where, as a timid introvert, he rarely left the family home (1999: 31–2). In his introduction to a book-length interview by Oti Rodríguez Marchante, Amenábar's early mentor and producer José Luis Cuerda writes of Amenábar's subsequent career that "never in the history of cinema" has there been a case like that of Amenábar, whose first feature was sold in markets around the world, whose second was remade in Hollywood, and whose third was the biggest grossing European film ever in the United States (Rodríguez Marchante 2002: 9). Yet, beyond this strictly commercial criterion, Cuerda also claims that his protégé places "ethical questions" at the top of his "scale of values," comparing him to an architect or mason who builds something he believes in and values highly (Rodríguez Marchante

2002: 9). Rodríguez Marchante himself writes that in the field of Spanish cinema Amenábar combines two current trends, which Rodríguez Marchante baptizes "muscle" and "feeling" (2002: 14). This makes the young cineaste as skilled in action sequences as, say, Álex de la Iglesia and as intensely attuned to emotion as Julio Medem.

As these quotes suggest, Amenábar's affection for commercial genres and Hollywood technique has not diminished the regard in which he is generally held by Spanish critics. Indeed, while Almodóvar was attacked for citing Hollywood melodramas such as those of Douglas Sirk, Amenábar was praised for his reworking of Hitchcock's thrillers. And there is no doubt that, in traditional auteurist style, Amenábar's small but diverse oeuvre exhibits clear thematic continuities. Rodríguez Marchante rehearses what he calls the director's "obsessions" – the act of looking; the treatment of violence; the thin line between fiction and reality, beauty and terror, death and deformity; and an "exalted romanticism" (2002: 14–15).

The first monograph on the director (Sempere 2000), written when he had released only two features, gives a rather different list of "keys" to Amenábar's work, stressing not his subject matter but rather his practice as a filmmaker: Amenábar rejects the "orthopedic" cinema whose shooting style feels fake or constrained (2000: 35); he consciously recycles existing elements in his attempt to produce something new (2000: 36); he is conscious of the "pressure" of public expectations, even as he aims for a "personal" cinema (2000: 37); he attempts a "balance" between European and North American styles (2000: 40); he chooses protagonists close to his own (then tender) age (2000: 43); and, finally, he conceives his work as "operatic" – the self-composed soundtrack is inextricable from the images (Sempere 2000: 51).

Sociologist Pierre Bourdieu (1996) traced the emergence in nineteenth-century Paris of two "economies" based, respectively, on art and money: the avant-garde artist rejected the immediate success of the commercial painter for the more lasting, but less lucrative, reward of cultural prestige. Amenábar, whose features have both made more money and won more prizes than any other Spanish director, is thus indeed in a unique position, having successfully combined these two economies of art and money, held to be mutually exclusive by Bourdieu. Moreover, he has done so without overexploiting his own rather modest figure in the press. It is an achievement that should not be underestimated and that, as we shall now see, is also visible at the textual level of his films.

When *Tesis* achieved a clean sweep of the Goya awards (the Spanish equivalent of the Oscars) for 1996, it was the least likely of successes. It boasted a first-time director who had failed to complete the filmmaking course at Madrid's Complutense University; a cast of relative unknowns (including male lead Eduardo Noriega, later to be a major star); and a premise, that of snuff movies, almost unknown to Spanish audiences. In the "making of" included on the UK DVD, Amenábar explains in some detail his chosen shooting style, which surprised his crew with its novelty. For a sequence where, say, a character goes to a drawer and removes a gun, a Spanish director would generally use a single take. Amenábar chose rather to break down the scene in the Hollywood manner into a series of separate shots: a wide shot of the actor walking, a medium shot from his point of view of the drawer, and a close-up of the gun itself. This shooting style, which clearly takes longer to film than more leisurely European sequence shots, not only quickens the pace of *Tesis* but also subtly cues the spectator to respond to an international genre film.

Yet there are still national, even localist, elements to *Tesis* that were essential to its success. The presence of the dark-eyed Ana Torrent as a student obsessed with video horror inevitably recalls the same actress' encounter with Frankenstein so many years before in Erice's *El espíritu de la colmena*. Cheekily shooting in the highly recognizable concrete bunker of his own university's faculty building, Amenábar even lends his fictional professor (who tells his students to "give the audience what they want") the name of the real-life academic who failed him on the directing course. And, if the plot is packed with twists and full of Hitchcockian suspense, it also engages the ethical dimension that José Luis Cuerda identified in his protégé: Torrent's prim Angela, outwardly academic in her interest in the media, is secretly fascinated by cinematic violence, just as she is fatally drawn to Noriega's seductive Bosco, a fellow student whom she suspects of being a serial killer. The poster for *Tesis* was brutally simple. Over an image of Torrent's face the tagline read: "My name is Angela. They're going to kill me." But the film's final moral was more complex. In the last sequence, shot in a hospital, Amenábar lingers on anonymous patients, mesmerized by the everyday horrors they are watching on the television news bulletin.

Abre los ojos boasted a more baroque plot. César (Noriega, once more) is a young and wealthy man suddenly disfigured in a car crash. Miraculously cured, or so it seems, he resumes his affair with Sofía (a young Penélope Cruz) but is troubled by strange events: a crowded bar suddenly falls silent and he is followed everywhere by a mysterious Frenchman. This time the plot twist is that César's life since his accident is a kind of living fantasy, a virtual reality created as he lies in cryogenic suspension awaiting resuscitation. Leaping from a tall building at the film's close he hopes to "open his eyes" to (future) life in the real world.

While this second film was remade by Cameron Crowe as *Vanilla Sky* in New York, the original featured prominent references to a Madrid location that remained unnamed in its script. Thus, in the opening dream sequence, César runs down an eerily empty avenue: it is the Gran Vía, leading down to the Plaza de España, a location that could hardly be better known to Spanish audiences (in the unusually faithful remake Times Square stands in for it) (see Figure 5.7). Likewise, the final rooftop confrontation takes place on what was then Madrid's tallest building, the Picasso Tower, and is framed so that clearly visible behind Cruz are the distinctive leaning twin towers known as the Gate to Europe. Amenábar's transnational shooting style is thus firmly anchored in settings as distinctively Castilian as the spoken accents of his young stars. Beyond this, he was himself concerned with a specific technical problem: how could he shoot consistently in

Figure 5.7 The Gran Vía emptied for the opening sequence of Amenábar's *Abre los ojos* (1997; prod. Las Producciones del Escorpión).

the first person, reproducing the viewpoint of the fantasizing César, without giving away the game too soon to his audience?

The Others was, once more, a very different project in both scale and substance and a new test case for what counts as "Spanish cinema." As Nuria Triana Toribio writes: "it is a film that Spanish audiences must watch dubbed into Spanish from the original English … [for which] Nicole Kidman was nominated for both an Oscar […] and a Goya […] [and which] was funded partly by [Spanish producer] Sogecine but mainly by [US independent] Miramax International" (2003: 162). Interestingly, Amenábar himself stressed not US but British influences on this expert haunted house movie, citing as a precedent the "English air" of Jack Clayton's *The Innocents* (1961), itself based on Henry James' *The Turn of the Screw* (Rodríguez Marchante 2002: 121). And *The Others'* dizzying final revelation, namely that it is Kidman and her children who are ghosts, was scripted before the release of *The Sixth Sense*, which played a very similar trick on audiences.

Mar adentro appeared to be an unexpected project for a director famed for the mobility of his camera. Star Javier Bardem, heavily made up to play the paralyzed Sampedro, was confined to his bed for almost the duration of the film. Moreover, as a hardcore drama, this project put to rest the continuing concern that Amenábar was only a genre director. But, if Amenábar's transnational thrillers were scattered with localist references, here his national drama (the struggle for euthanasia in a Spain where it remains illegal) was somewhat sweetened by prodigiously realized virtuoso scenes: for example, the fantasy sequence where Sampedro abandons his bed and (in a single seamless shot) flies over the green Galician hills to rendezvous on an Atlantic beach with the blonde lawyer played by television star Belén Rueda. In spite of its very specific Spanish content, then, *Mar adentro* was close enough to US generic conventions (such as the "disease of the week" television movie) to connect with international audiences and secure an Oscar for Best Foreign Language Film (Smith 2009c: 108).

Amenábar's features are thus strikingly diverse in thematics and genre. But their significance lies not so much in the way in which they adopt and adapt Hollywood norms as in their continuing exploration of the ethical stance identified so early on by José Luis Cuerda. There seems little doubt that the critique of media violence suggested in *Tesis* continues through the attack on fatal self-delusion in both *Abre los ojos* and *The Others* and into the overtly political argument for the right to die made by *Mar adentro*. If Amenábar is that oxymoron, a commercial auteur, he is also that equally rare creature: a crowd-pleasing moralist.

Indeed, paradox lies at the heart of auteurism, which, as we have seen in the case studies discussed in this chapter, constructs national "authors" in large measure through the status they attain abroad. While this is not new – we have only to remember the extreme case of the cosmopolitan exile Buñuel – auteurism and transnationalism are today inseparable. The spectacular careers of Almodóvar and of the youngest filmmaker discussed here, Amenábar, are paradigmatic examples.

References

Andrew, D. (2010) *What Cinema Is*. Chichester: Wiley-Blackwell.

Astruc, A. (1991) Birth of a New Avant-garde: La Caméra-Stylo. In: Corrigan, T. (ed.) *Film and Literature: An Introduction and Reader*. Upper Saddle River: Prentice Hall, pp. 158–62.

Ballesteros, I. (2009) Performing Identities in the Cinema of Pedro Almodóvar. In: Epps, B. and Kakoudaki, D. (eds.) *All About Almodóvar*. Minneapolis: University of Minnesota Press, pp. 71–100.

Bordwell, D. (1989) *Making Meaning: Inference and Rhetoric in the Interpretation of Cinema*. Cambridge, MA: Harvard University Press.

Bordwell, D. (1990) *Narration in the Fiction Film*. London: Routledge.

Bourdieu, P. (1996) *The Rules of Art*. Cambridge: Polity.

Boyero, C. (2011) Retrato de un horror aún más hueco que frío. *El País* (May 20). Online at: www.elpais.com/articulo/cultura/Retrato/horror/hueco/frio/elpepicul/20110520elpepicul_1/Tes (accessed March 24, 2012).

Buñuel, L. (1982) *Mi último suspiro (memorias)*. Barcelona: Plaza & Janés.

Buñuel, L. (2000) Cinema as an Instrument of Poetry. In: *An Unspeakable Betrayal: Selected Writings of Luis Buñuel*. Berkeley: University of California Press, pp. 136–41.

Cahiers du Cinéma (1972) John Ford's Young Mr. Lincoln. A Collective Text by the Editors of *Cahiers du Cinéma*. *Screen* 13 (3): 5–44. Translation of original published in *Cahiers du Cinéma* 223 (August 1970).

Caughie, J. (ed.) (1980) *Theories of Authorship: A Reader*. London: Routledge & Kegan Paul.

Chijona, G. (1983) La cámara detrás del espejo: Entrevista con Carlos Saura sobre *Bodas de sangre*. *Cine Cubano* 104: 37–42.

D'Lugo, M. (1990) *The Films of Carlos Saura: The Practice of Seeing*. Princeton: Princeton University Press.

Elsaesser, T. (1988) *The New German Cinema*. New Brunswick: Rutgers University Press.

Erice, V. (2001) *La promesa de Shanghai*. Barcelona: Plaza & Janés.

Evans, J. (2007) *Julio Medem*. London: Grant & Cutler.

Evans, P. W. (1999). "Introduction." In: *Spanish Cinema: The Auteurist Tradition*. Oxford: Oxford University Press, pp. 1–7.

Foucault, M. (1986) What is an Author? In: Rabinow, P. (ed.) *The Foucault Reader*. Harmondsworth: Penguin, pp. 101–20.

García Fernández, E. G. (1985) *Historia ilustrada del cine español*. Barcelona: Planeta.

Greene, N. (2007) *The French New Wave: A New Look*. London: Wallflower Press.

Gritten, D. (2011) Pedro Almodóvar: Interview for *The Skin I Live In*. *The Daily Telegraph* (August 13). Online at: www.telegraph.co.uk/culture/film/filmmakersonfilm/8695522/Pedro-Almodovar-interview-for-The-Skin-I-Live-In.html (accessed March 24, 2012).

Heredero, C. F. (1993) *Las huellas del tiempo: Cine español 1951–1961*. Valencia/Madrid: Filmoteca de la Generalitat Valenciana/Filmoteca Española.

Heredero, C. F. (1997) *Espejo de miradas: Entrevistas con nuevos directores del cine español de los años noventa*. Alcalá de Henares: Ayuntamiento.

Heredero, C. F. (1999) *20 nuevos directores del cine español*. Madrid: Alianza.

Hjort, M. (2010) On the Plurality of Cinematic Transnationalism. In: Durovicova, N. and Newman, K. (eds.) *World Cinemas: Transnational Perspectives*. New York: Routledge, pp. 12–33.

Jordan, B. and Morgan-Tamosunas, R. (1998) *Contemporary Spanish Cinema*. Manchester: Manchester University Press.

Kiarostami, A. and Erice, V. (2006) *Correspondences*. Barcelona: Diputació.

Kinder, M. (1993) *Blood Cinema: The Reconstruction of National Identity in Spain*. Berkeley: University of California Press.

Lyotard, J.-F. (1986) *The Postmodern Condition*. Manchester: Manchester University Press.

Palacio, M. (2005) Lluvia fina: Contingencias preliminares de la recepción. El caso del Festival de Cine de San Sebastián. In: Pérez Perucha, J. (ed.) *El espíritu de la colmena: 31 años después*. Valencia: Filmoteca de la Generalitat Valenciana, pp. 193–215.

Pavlović, T. et al. (2009) *100 Years of Spanish Cinema*. Oxford: Blackwell.

Pillado-Miller, M. (1997) La República va al doctor: Síntomas de la Guerra Civil en tres películas de Carlos Saura. *Arizona Journal of Hispanic Cultural Studies* 1 (1): 129–40.

Rodríguez Marchante, O. (2002) *Amenábar: Vocación de intriga*. Madrid: Espuma.

Sánchez-Biosca, V.(1999) *Estudio crítico: Luis Buñuel, "Viridiana."* Barcelona: Paidós.

Sánchez Vidal, A. (1988) *El cine de Carlos Saura*. Zaragoza: Caja de Ahorros de La Inmaculada.

Sarris, A. (1980) Notes on the Auteur Theory in 1962. In: Caughie, J. (ed.) *Theories of Authorship: A Reader*. London: Routledge & Kegan Paul, pp. 62–5.

Sempere, A. (2000) *Alejandro Amenábar: Cine en las venas*. Madrid: Nuer.

Smith, P. J. (2000) Between Metaphysics and Scientism: Rehistoricizing Víctor Erice. In: *The Moderns: Time, Space, and Subjectivity in Contemporary Spanish Culture*. Oxford: University Press, pp. 23–41.

Smith, P. J. (2007–8) Chaotic Ana. *Film Quarterly* 61–2: 30–4.

Smith, P. J. (2009a) Almodóvar's Unpublished Short Stories and the Question of Queer Auteurism. *Screen* 50 (4): 439–49.
Smith, P. J. (2009b) *Spanish Screen Fiction: Between Cinema and Television*. Liverpool: Liverpool University Press.
Smith, P. J. (2009c) Two Suicides and a Funeral: The Euthanasia Debate on Film and Television. In: *Spanish Screen Fiction: Between Cinema and Television*. Liverpool: Liverpool University Press, pp. 105–21.
Stone, R. (2007) *Julio Medem*. Manchester: Manchester University Press.
Torres, A. M. (1973) *Cine español, años sesenta*. Barcelona: Anagrama.
Triana Toribio, N. (2003) *Spanish National Cinema*. London: Routledge.
Truffaut, F. (2008 [1954]) A Certain Tendency in French Cinema. In: Grant, B. K. (ed.) *Auteurs and Authorship: A Film Reader*. Oxford: Wiley-Blackwell, pp. 9–18.
Villafañe, J. and Mínguez, N. (2006) *Principios de teoría general de la imagen*. Madrid: Pirámide.
Zunzunegui, S. (2002) La edad de la inocencia (*El sol del membrillo*, Víctor Erice, 1993). In: *Historias de España: De qué hablamos cuando hablamos de cine español*. Valencia, Filmoteca de la Generalitat Valenciana, pp. 67–76.

Further Reading

Allinson, M. (2001) *A Spanish Labyrinth: The Films of Pedro Almodóvar*. London: I. B. Tauris.
Aranda, J. Francisco (1970) *Luis Buñuel: Biografía crítica*. Barcelona: Editorial Lumen.
Corrigan, T. (1991) *A Cinema without Walls: Movies and Culture after Vietnam*. New Brunswick: Rutgers University Press.
D'Lugo, M. (1998) Buñuel in the Cathedral of Culture: Reterritorializing the Film Auteur. In: Kinder, M. (ed.) *Luis Buñuel's "The Discreet Charm of the Bourgeoisie."* Cambridge: Cambridge University Press, pp. 101–10.
D'Lugo, M. (2006). *Pedro Almodóvar*. Chicago: University of Illinois Press.
Ehrlich, L. C. (ed.) (2000) *An Open Window: The Cinema of Víctor Erice*. Lanham: Scarecrow.
Epps, B. and Kakoudaki, D. (eds.) (2009) *All About Almodóvar*. Minneapolis: University of Minnesota Press.
Jordan, B. (forthcoming) *Alejandro Amenábar*. Manchester: Manchester University Press.
Kinder, M. (1983) The Children of Franco in the New Spanish Cinema. *Quarterly Review of Film Studies* 8 (2): 57–76.
Sánchez Vidal, A. (1994). *Luis Buñuel: Obra cinematográfica*. Madrid: Ediciones JC.
Smith, P. J (1994) *Desire Unlimited: The Cinema of Pedro Almodóvar*. London: Verso. 2nd rev. edn. 2000.
Subirats, E. (ed.) (2002) *Intransiciones: Crítica de la cultura española*. Madrid: Biblioteca Nueva.
Vernon, K. M. and Morris, B. (eds.) (1995) *Post-Franco, Postmodern: The Films of Pedro Almodóvar*. Westport: Greenwood Press.
Wood, G. (2010) *"La caza" de Carlos Saura*. Zaragoza: Prensa Universitaria de Zaragoza.

6

Strategic Auteurism

Antonio Lázaro-Reboll, Steven Marsh,
Susan Martin-Márquez, and Santos Zunzunegui

Introduction (Susan Martin-Márquez)

While Chapter 5 treated a variety of "canonical" directors such as Luis Buñuel, Carlos Saura, and Pedro Almodóvar who are frequently labeled "auteurs," this chapter instead explores a range of directors and others essential to the filmmaking process, such as screenwriters and editors, who are not generally characterized as such. Throughout our discussion we will make reference to a variety of different formulations of auteur "policy" or "theory." In general terms, it can be said that auteurism, which as we have seen originated in France in the 1950s, quickly rose to dominance in Western film criticism and sought to establish the director as the central creative force behind the cinematic text. In the pages that follow, we will analyze why many important contributors to Spanish cinema have not been welcomed into the auteurist fold, and we will also examine the case of a number of figures who might strategically be constructed (or who have sought strategically to present themselves) as auteurs.

We will begin this chapter by elucidating the disruptive nature of the auteurist "signatures" of three directors – Edgar Neville, Luis García Berlanga, and Eloy de la Iglesia – who produced cinematic texts that were at once popular, drawing upon national traditions and often appealing to a broad audience, and marginal, exploring the contradictions of dominant discourses. The collaborative relationship Berlanga established with Rafael Azcona then prompts a consideration of the "authorship" of screenwriters within a Spanish context in which the art of the script has not traditionally been lauded; we juxtapose Azcona's relative fame with the critical neglect of his fellow scriptwriter Pedro Beltrán, who ironically might better

A Companion to Spanish Cinema, First Edition. Edited by Jo Labanyi and Tatjana Pavlović.

fit the definition of auteur. We then consider the fascinating case of Jesús Franco, a "pulp" director who has recently been recuperated by critics and who himself has sought strategically to adopt the auteurist mantle. From here we move to the "rarified" realm inhabited by the director Pere Portabella, who is often considered a major artistic figure, yet he too has failed to be incorporated into the "canon" of Spanish cinema; we explore the possibility that Portabella's collaborative work with prestigious artists and his self-construction as a unique creator have perhaps set him apart too radically from other filmmakers in Spain. And, finally, we discuss an entire sector of filmmakers who, like Franco, may also decide strategically to declare themselves auteurs, despite the fact that auteurism has systematically sought to exclude them: women. Here, alongside the historical emergence of female directors in Spain, we also consider how the "auteur policy" managed to subalternize film editing, a profession that has often been dominated by women such as Margarita Ochoa, the subject of a brief case study.

Neville, Berlanga, and de la Iglesia: A Strategically Disruptive Auteurism (Steven Marsh)

Auteurism is often defined (and correspondingly repudiated) in conservative terms as the artistic product of a personal vision, of an individual genius. In fact its entrance into film theory – via François Truffaut's celebrated *Cahiers du Cinéma* article, "A Certain Tendency in French Cinema" (2008 [1954]) – posited auteurism precisely in strategic terms. Truffaut decried the literary pretensions of the French film industry in favor of popular US cinema (John Ford, Howard Hawks, Nicholas Ray, and, above all, Alfred Hitchcock). Later, in 1962, Andrew Sarris, as mentioned in Chapter 5, drew up a pantheon of auteurs in the vein of F. R. Leavis' literary great tradition. Sarris, the most influential North American theorist of auteurism, outlined three characteristics in his definition: the particular "technical competence" of a director that identifies him as a good filmmaker; signature, the "recurrent characteristics of style"; and finally the "tension between a director's personality and his material" (1962: 562). (The association of auteurism with exclusively masculine pronouns will be interrogated at the end of this chapter.) In this section I will consider three directors (Edgar Neville, Luis García Berlanga, and Eloy de la Iglesia) in two ways. First, as distinctive and discordant voices working within and against the dominant discourses of their times; and, second, in an appropriation of Sarris' term, as cineastes whose signatures as auteurs produce a *mise-en-abyme*; that is, they open doorways to corresponding counter-signatures, thereby contradicting Sarris' claims.

European auteurism has long been associated with national canons, in part as resistance to the encroachment of Hollywood, as a reaction to the perceived threat of US cultural imperialism. While the work of Neville, Berlanga, and de la Iglesia functions with (and within) what has been construed as a Spanish "native tradition" – *sainete, esperpento, costumbrismo* (popular farce, grotesque distortion, local color) – they have all proved disruptive of the very discourse that associates generic taxonomy with the Spanish nation (Marsh 2006). Indeed, the individual style of the auteur is measured against a larger system (generally conditioned by commercial interests), whether a studio, a nation, an ideology, or a global network. In this sense too, auteurism might be considered strategic. Further, auteurism tends to refer to the director's corpus as a whole rather than to individual films. The three films I discuss here are case studies; that is, they seek to highlight key elements in the overall production of their filmmakers and to exemplify the critical stance adopted by these cineastes: their nonconformism with respect to the different political regimes of the historical periods in which they lived.

Edgar Neville was unquestionably one of Spain's most personal filmmakers. Although his career began in the late 1920s (in Los Angeles) and would continue through the early 1960s, his finest work, by general consensus, was produced in the 1940s. His output in this period can be seen as an extension of the urban, cosmopolitan direction he had in some ways pioneered during the Second Republic, such as his screen adaptation of Carlos Arniches' play *La señorita de Trevélez / The Lady from Trevélez* (1935) and his work as scriptwriter on Harry d'Abbadie d'Arrast's *La traviesa molinera / It Happened in Spain* (1934) and Benito Perojo's *Rumbo al Cairo / Bound for Cairo* (1935). He was, moreover, a significant influence on future generations of Spanish cineastes, first for those younger contemporary filmmakers – such as Berlanga and Juan Antonio Bardem – who emerged with the first graduating class of the Official Film School (Escuela Oficial de Cine; EOC): Neville was a screenwriter on Berlanga's second feature, *Novio a la vista / Boyfriend in Sight* (1954), and Bardem would follow Neville's example by also adapting the play *La señorita de Trevélez* for his 1956 masterpiece *Calle Mayor / Main Street.* Neville's importance for future Spanish filmmaking, though, extends beyond Berlanga's generation to the 1980s comedies set in Madrid, the work of Pedro Almodóvar, and the films of the "La Cuadrilla" partnership of the 1990s.

In spite of this influence, Neville (partly because of the critical neglect of his work until recently) is often regarded as a "cult" director (López n.d.). The epithet, while relegating him to a cineaste of interest to a reduced and select coterie of specialists or to an eccentric fan base, also suggests a filmmaker with a distinctive style. *La torre de los siete jorobados / Tower of the Seven Hunchbacks* (1944) is typical of this "cult"-like status (see Figure 6.1). The film is rarely screened and was unobtainable commercially until the 2011 collectors' edition. It is, in these senses, enshrouded in the mystique of auteurism and yet its diegesis revolves paradoxically around a potboiling content. Like Emilio Carrère's pulp novel, on which it was based, the film is a mélange of popular genres: detective story, comic romance, and ghost tale wrapped together with the demotic culture and customs of central Madrid. Its cinematography, conversely, owes a great deal to German expressionism and particularly to Robert Wiene's *The Cabinet of Doctor Caligari* (1920) and (in terms of

Figure 6.1 The ghost of Robinson de Mantua (Félix de Pomés) emerges from a mirror in *La torre de los siete jorobados* (Edgar Neville, 1944; prod. España Films).

symbolic urban palimpsest) to Fritz Lang's *Metropolis* (1927). Typically of Neville's work, *La torre de los siete jorobados* is a film whose register and subject matter combine the avant-garde and the popular. One central aspect to its distinctive tone is its location. Neville's association with Madrid is perhaps the most distinctive feature of his oeuvre: the majority of his films were shot there and they evidence his familiarity with the rhythms and motifs of the city's popular culture. Street names, specific buildings, and historical and literary figures from the city's past combine to make the Madrid of *La torre de los siete jorobados* a distorting prism tense with hermeneutic implications. However, it is precisely the film's enigmatic quality – the product of its generic mixture of fantasy and realism – that disturbs and disrupts the national tradition of *costumbrismo*, associated particularly with central Madrid. It is fitting, then, that the film should end with the implosion of the city as the void beneath its foundations gives way in a quite literal collapse.

Neville's friend and collaborator Luis García Berlanga, the most outstanding heir to the filmic tradition that commenced during the Second Republic, is possibly the only Spanish director other than Luis Buñuel and Pedro Almodóvar to warrant an adjective applied to his style. The term *berlangiano* conjures up a cacophonic, crowded, and seemingly chaotic scenario – the site of multiple activities conducted simultaneously – and the eschewing of montage in favor of the prolonged sequence shot. Like the other two filmmakers discussed here, on one level Berlanga, as a cineaste of "the popular," resists classification as an auteur. On another, though, as we have just seen, he is indeed a distinct and recognizable auteur. He also has the kind of "signature" that signals his work as *berlangiano*, similar to the cameo appearances that Hitchcock made his hallmark (and that Almodóvar has also adopted by inserting his brother Agustín into his films). In Berlanga's case, his signature is so coy as to be almost imperceptible: in each and every one of his films, somebody mentions the Austro-Hungarian Empire. Dudley Andrew reflects upon the signature:

> Always a problematic and very special sign, the signature of the author is a mark on the surface of the text signaling its source. The signature embeds within it – as in hypertext – a genuine fourth dimension, the temporal process that brought the text into being in the first place." (2000: 25)

The observation is interesting for, contrary to the positing of the auteur as originator (the "genius" as genus), it points to antecedents and to the auteur's legacy, the traces that he leaves in his wake.

La escopeta nacional / The National Shotgun (1978) has not attracted as much interest from commentators outside Spain as some of Berlanga's other films. It is, though, representative of Berlanga's individual style in terms of technique, cast, and its oblique intervention, beyond the confines of the screen, in social and political discourse. Just as *¡Bienvenido Mister Marshall! / Welcome Mr. Marshall!* (1952), the first film Berlanga directed alone, offered a parodic view of relations between the United States and Spain in the context of the latter's exclusion from the Marshall Plan, *La escopeta nacional* provides a wry view of politics as conducted under new "democratic" conditions. As always with Berlanga, the film is choral and populated by verbose repertory actors. This cast (Agustín González, José Luis López Vázquez, José Zazatornil, Amparo Soler Leal, Luis Ciges), by and large, worked with him from the late 1950s and early 1960s until his retirement in 1999 (see Figure 6.2). On this occasion, moreover, the actress Conchita Montes appears, as if Berlanga were indirectly alluding to his filmic predecessor: Montes, of course, was the muse and common-law wife of Edgar Neville. While all of Berlanga's work is densely verbal, it is also visually fluid owing to his frequent use of the long take. This formal particularity, together with an obsessive but consistent interest in scatology, marks out Berlanga's style. His cinematic world view, founded on comic incongruity, is compounded by the scripts of Rafael Azcona, his screenwriting collaborator from the early 1960s to the 1980s (see the next section of this chapter). Furthermore, since the action of the film takes place in the course of a weekend hunt, the film contributes to an important tradition in Spanish cinema, where the hunt functions as allegory for political discourse, as in Carlos Saura's *La caza / The Hunt* (1965) and José Luis Borau's *Furtivos / Poachers* (1975). In *La escopeta nacional*, Berlanga lampoons the tendency of politicians and businessmen (and their cheerleaders in the Catholic clergy) to use hunting as a scenario in which to contract mutual favors. Just as he is sensitive to the political and historical conjuncture

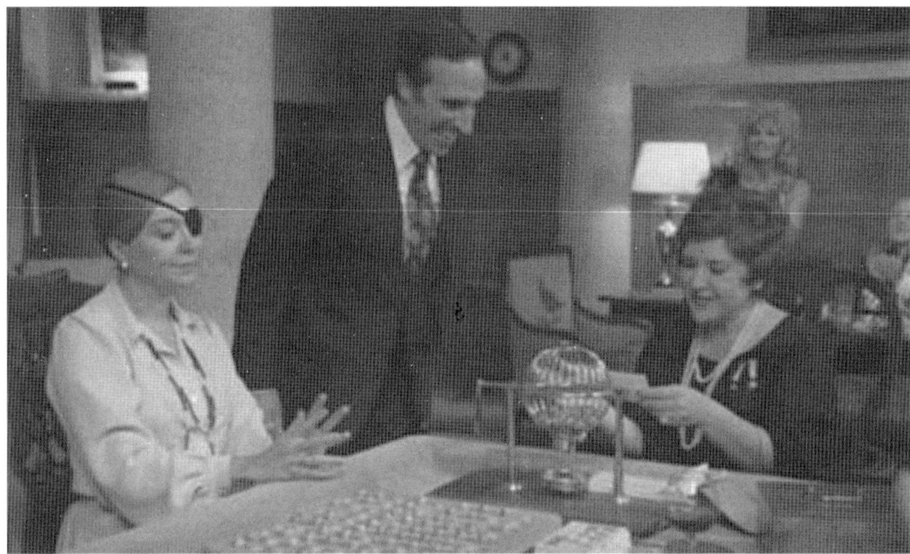

Figure 6.2 Jaume Canivell (José Zazatornil) attempts small talk in the company of Chus (Amparo Soler Leal) and Laura (Laly Soldevila) in *La escopeta nacional* (Luis García Berlanga, 1978; prod. Impala).

in his mockery, Berlanga also parodies the cinematic trends of the time (something he does frequently in many of his films but particularly in *¡Bienvenido Mister Marshall!*). In its use of the starlet Bárbara Rey, for example, *La escopeta nacional* comments on *destape* (literally "uncovering"), the soft porn fashion that seized Spanish filmmaking of the early to mid-1970s, a commentary that in Berlanga's hands slyly correlates *destape* with unmasking the scandals of broader society.

At first sight Eloy de la Iglesia might seem a long way from the arthouse criteria associated with the *Cahiers du Cinéma* of the early 1960s, and even further from Andrew Sarris' list of great filmmakers. However, de la Iglesia did attract the attention of the writers of *Contracampo*, the short-lived Spanish theoretical journal of the late 1970s, some of whose contributors today write for the Spanish version of *Cahiers du Cinéma*. De la Iglesia's raw style has been labeled *tremendista*: sensationalist, populist, and lurid. His most celebrated films, those of the late 1970s and early 1980s, deal principally with teenage delinquency and are set against political and historical backdrops (the transition, the Basque conflict). Homosexual, Basque, Communist, and a heroin addict, de la Iglesia – unique among the filmmakers discussed here – would foreground these autobiographical elements in his films. His "signature" – like that of Pier Paolo Pasolini before him – lies in his fascination with the disturbance produced by the meeting of the marginal and the mainstream. Indeed, his entire work might be described as a search for a cinematic form that adequately converges with this very subject matter.

Part of this Pasolini-like dialectic can be seen in de la Iglesia's combination of well-known popular actors (José Sacristán, Carmen Sevilla, Agustín González, Rafaela Aparicio, Maruchi Fresno, and Amparo Muñoz) with non-professionals whom he "discovered" in the slums on the outskirts of Madrid. This use of actors helps to emphasize de la Iglesia's interest in the contradictions in political and social discourse. Paradox and contradiction – more than hypocrisy – are unveiled by fringe elements who, by their very presence, destabilize discourse. Whether it be the Catholic Church in *El sacerdote / The Priest* (1978), the Communist Party in *El diputado / Confessions of a Congressman* (1979), Basque nationalism and the Guardia Civil in *El pico / Overdose* (1983) and *El pico 2 / Overdose 2* (1984), or, as we will see, the gay-friendly, tolerant world of Madrid's Chueca in *Los novios búlgaros / Bulgarian Lovers* (2003), de la Iglesia remains resolute in his fascination with the potential of the excluded. Like Neville half a century before him, de la Iglesia's concern with the marginal – expressed through sexual practice, drugs, poverty, or immigration – intersects with genre (science fiction, melodrama, the thriller) in ways in which the discourse of "the popular" takes on a particular and personal register while its premises are disrupted.

After a sixteen-year hiatus, owing to his own addiction to heroin, de la Iglesia returned to cinema to make one final film, *Los novios búlgaros* (2003). As engaged as in his previous work with the issues of the day, this film deals with recent immigration into Spain. However, if in the earlier films space played an important role, it was one that was limited to city or national space. In the films of the 1970s and 1980s, the marginalized characters were located either on the edges of Madrid or in an ambiguous zone with respect to national space, as in the case of the Basque Country. In *Los novios búlgaros*, a new marginal space – paralleling the prosperity of a democratic Spain in the era of globalization – has emerged from the East, from the former satellites of the Soviet Union, once the imagined utopias of de la Iglesia's erstwhile Communist Party affiliation. Ostensibly in tune with another generic group of films that first emerged in the 1990s and that reflected the new-found "tolerance" toward homosexuality – Chris Perriam (2004) terms this "heterosociality" – evident in Spanish civil society (and to which the state responded in legislative form in the 2005 same-sex marriage law), *Los novios búlgaros* significantly departs from the genre. As in the films of the transition, there is a marked class element here that cuts across discursive lines defined by sexuality. Much of the film's action is shot in Madrid's wealthy gay neighborhood of Chueca and revolves around a set of economically buoyant, successful professionals and the displaced lumpen foreigners upon whom they bestow favors in exchange for sex (see Figure 6.3). If the earlier films are in some way pre-gay – that is, prior to a discourse of gayness – in *Los novios búlgaros* gayness has arrived and become commodified. Just as de la Iglesia's film disturbs the subgenre of "heterosocial" film, he has also made a film about immigration that, unlike very many films of the same ilk, actually grants agency to immigrants. By outwitting their wealthy clientele with surreptitious ingenuity and a keen sense of tactics born of necessity,

Figure 6.3 Kyril (Dritan Biba) bids a final farewell to Daniel (Fernando Guillén Cuervo) in a Chueca café in *Los novios búlgaros* (Eloy de la Iglesia, 2003; prod. Altube Filmeak SL).

the immigrants of *Los novios búlgaros* put paid to their habitual condition as objects of liberal pity.

None of the three filmmakers discussed in this section conforms to the dominant discourses of their age. Neville, who originally supported the Francoist uprising, was committed to a cosmopolitan and secular filmmaking that sat ill with the National-Catholic regime of the 1940s. Berlanga was a constant thorn in the side of the Francoist regime, yet was equally mocking of the democratic pretensions of its successors. De la Iglesia is as harsh a critic of the democratic acceptance of homosexuality – the ideology of tolerance – as he was of the Communist Party's prejudice. Key to the work of all three cineastes, moreover, is its common engagement with the popular, in terms of genre, film language, and register. In this confluence of elements and interests, these three directors lay bare the links in a chain of what habitually we term a tradition. It is a tradition nonetheless characterized precisely by strategy, or more specifically by a counterstrategy, rather than by national affiliation. The three cineastes introduce discordant voices into the national discourse; all three play upon the topical and the typical and yet in doing so – in this popular variant of auteurism – they carve out alternatives to the dominant paradigms and open up different, often non-linear or "unauthorized" routes. Their distinctive voices and styles – signatures that are "not reducible to the name of an 'author' or to signing a proper name" (Caputo 1997: 189) – vibrate with implications that exceed and expand the conditions of their making and their textual materiality. That is to say, they both cinematically respond to and elicit critical and popular reaction – countersignatures – from within and beyond the filmic text. Neville, Berlanga, and de la Iglesia are auteurs in the sense suggested by Andrew when he glosses Peter Wollen's view of auteurism: "Isolating the auteur's signal within the noise of the text carried for Wollen a strategic function, initiating further analyses to disentangle other signals – other codes – that contribute to the textual (dis)organization" (2000: 21–2).

Authorizing Screenwriting: Rafael Azcona and Pedro Beltrán (Santos Zunzunegui)

While the previous section characterized Rafael Azcona as a "collaborator" of the (strategically defined) auteur Berlanga, it is important to note that within the Spanish context screenwriters have generally failed to enjoy any status whatsoever, let alone the imprimatur of auteur. Furthermore, in locating film authorship in the director, the mid-twentieth-century originators of the *politique des auteurs* – the "Young Turks" grouped around André Bazin in the fledgling *Cahiers du Cinéma* – had studiously sought to shift attention away from the fact that films depend on teamwork. The result was to give the figure of the director a supremacy that would never be lost in the cinephile imagination. Overlooking the other roles involved in filmmaking was a price deemed worth paying to ensure that cinema was appreciated as an art freed from all traces of the literary; this rejection of the literary made it especially important to play down the screenwriter's role. Still today, in order to claim authorial status for a screenwriter, it is necessary to make a special case – except when the writer has prior literary credentials, in which case the status is awarded on non-cinematic grounds.

It is true that in Hollywood cinema (in the golden years of the studio system, at least) the screenwriter was considered an essential cog in a machine organized around a strict division of labor that assigned functions and tasks according to the principle of maximum specialization. Thus, although the screenwriter's role was, in Brecht's famous phrase of 1942, that of "selling lies" (Brecht 1968: 133), it was seen as having a specific function in a sophisticated, complex apparatus. An industrialized vision of this kind did not exist in Spanish cinema, making it even more difficult to claim auteur status for screenwriters. Added to the industrial weakness of Spanish cinema was the proverbially ill-defined nature of the screenwriter's creative input as writer of a text that is superseded by the film itself, further complicated by the distinction between the literary screenplay and the shooting script plus a lack of regard for screenwriting as a profession that characterizes the whole of Spanish film history. Indeed, in Spain, screenwriting has hardly ever been a profession; rather, it has been a way in which journalists, novelists, or playwrights (canonical or popular) could supplement an inadequate income. For many years, being a screenwriter in Spanish cinema meant trying to survive in a world of making do and double-dipping (Riambau and Torreiro 1988). Also militating against recognition of the screenwriter's essential function is the fact that Spanish film workers have often played multiple roles, as producer-screenwriter (Ignacio F. Iquino, José Luis Dibildos,

Luis Megino), director-screenwriter (Antonio Román, Pedro Lazaga, Luis García Berlanga, Carlos Saura, Mario Camus), and even producer-director-screenwriter (José Luis Borau is the classic example). Pedro Beltrán summed the situation up when he said:

> Para ser guionista en España hace falta tener la humildad de Francisco de Asís, la capacidad de soportar el hambre de Gandhi, el sentido del honor de un hidalgo y una familia con dinero que te mantenga en este *hobby*. (cited in Riambau and Torreiro 1988: 9)
>
> To be a screenwriter in Spain you need St. Francis of Assisi's humility, Ghandhi's ability to cope with hunger, a feudal nobleman's sense of honor, and a wealthy family to support you while you indulge in this *hobby*.

In such a context, the figures of Rafael Azcona and Pedro Beltrán himself stand out. Born in 1926 and 1927 respectively, they belong to the same generation and their work has several points of contact – perhaps even a similar authorial "signature" – though it differs in quantity and level of success. While today it is accepted that Azcona has made a signal contribution to Spanish cinema (despite which in-depth analysis of his work is still lacking), Beltrán has received only occasional recognition. Azcona's greater fame stems not only from the fact that he has scripted nearly a hundred films and television series but also from his additional literary profile as a poet and novelist. By contrast, Beltrán has few publications to his name: one short story, a poetic anthology released in record-book form, one play, a dictionary of bullfighting terms, plus, most importantly for this discussion, six feature-length scripts written over the course of an irregular career. But, if we shift our focus from the quantitative to the qualitative, we will be better able to judge the relative merits of their work as well as the paradoxes of their inclusion or not in the auteurist pantheon.

What makes both these writers special is the fact that their work opens up a creative vein previously untapped in Spanish cinema, with the exception of parts of Neville's postwar production and certain films made under the 1931–6 Republic. Azcona's first collaboration with Marco Ferreri (*El pisito / The Little Apartment*, 1959), like that shortly after with Berlanga (*Plácido*, 1961), gave birth to a creative output that has been described as a "sainete absurdo que busca soluciones macabras a la miseria en la que están inmersos los personajes" (absurd *sainete* that seeks macabre solutions to the misfortunes overwhelming the characters) (Pedraza Jiménez and Rodríguez Cáceres 2000: 408). As the same authors note, this "tétrico ambiente costumbrista" (bleak local color) is combined with "un humor agrio y esperpéntico" (bitter, grotesque humor) that lampoons the down-trodden characters' "manías y obsesiones, gritos y pataletas" (manias and obsessions, tantrums and fits) (2000: 408).

In an interview (Angulo 2000), the film director José Luis García Sánchez eloquently summed up Azcona's strengths; the features he identifies apply also to Beltrán. First, the ability to tap into a vibrant current in Spanish literature and art

(Pío Baroja, Ramón del Valle-Inclán, Francisco de Goya, or Juan de Valdés Leal), which Azcona integrates into Spanish cinema through his particular brand of black humor. Second, the ability to present himself as the "poeta de la narración, de la tristeza, del suburbio" (poet of narration, of sadness, of the suburb), together with his obsession with capturing the real. Here García Sánchez hints at the documentary dimension that always underpins Azcona's grotesque vision. It is impossible not to see the teeming world of *El pisito* in the shocking description (no political correctness here) that Azcona gave, in an interview, of the boarding-house where he lodged in Madrid on first arriving in the capital from his native Logroño:

> Esa pensión estaba especializada en opositores a Correos. La criada era una enana, la cocinera una señora octogenaria, totalmente calva, y el dueño un homosexual vergonzante y encantador, Paquito se llamaba. A la criada enana la llevaban constantemente al hospital con desgarros de vagina, porque los opositores, excitados por la visión de unas modistas que los provocaban desde el piso de abajo, en cuanto se descuidaba la atacaban. (Harguindey 1998: 93–4)

> The boarding house specialized in students preparing for the qualifying exam to work in the state postal service. The maid was a dwarf, the cook in her eighties, completely bald, and the owner a charming, shameless homosexual who everyone called Paquito. The dwarf maid was always being taken to hospital with a torn vagina since the students, aroused by some seamstresses who teased them from the floor below, attacked her whenever they caught her off-guard.

The initial idea for Azcona's novel *El pisito*, on which the film was based, had in fact come from a real event of the time in Barcelona. *El cochecito / The Motorized Wheelchair* (Ferreri, 1960) too was based on a real incident, which Azcona frequently recounted:

> Una tarde de los primeros años cincuenta esperaba yo para cruzar la Castellana cuando, entre una riada de automóviles que bajaban hacia Cibeles, apareció un enjambre de cochecitos tripulados por vociferantes inválidos; el semáforo se les puso en rojo, y mientras cruzaba tuve ocasión de escuchar por encima del petardeo de sus motores fragmentos del apasionado debate, que los traía enzarzados desde el estadio Bernabeu: -"¡Si no pueden ni con las botas, hombre!." –"¡Un equipo de baldados, te lo digo yo!" (cited in Harguindey 1998: 24–5)

> One afternoon in the early 1950s I was waiting to cross the Paseo de la Castellana when, among the flood of cars going south towards Cibeles, there appeared a flotilla of motorized wheelchairs manned by a boisterous crew of invalids; the lights went red on them, and as I crossed the road I happened to hear, over them revving up their engines, scraps of the passionate argument engrossing them on their drive back from the Bernabeu Stadium [home of Real Madrid football club]: "They don't know what to do with their boots, for Christ's sake!" "A team of cripples, that's what I say!"

A situation typical of the false charity encouraged in National-Catholic Spain was the basis for *Plácido* (1961), as expressed in the original title rejected by the censors: *Siente un pobre a su mesa / Seat a Poor Person at Your Table. El verdugo / The Executioner* (Berlanga, 1963) updates a *sainete* by Pedro Muñoz Seca and Enrique García Álvarez – *El verdugo de Sevilla / The Executioner of Seville* (1916) – whose protagonist is inveigled into unwittingly signing his appointment as executioner to pay off a debt, with clear reminiscences of the character in Camilo José Cela's 1949 story "Un verdugo" (An Executioner) who became an executioner hoping he would never have to kill anyone (Cela 1994). The Azcona–Berlanga team subjects the heroes of these two films to singular twists of fate. The plotline of *Plácido* moves from a public urinal to a barracks (the site of Franco's headquarters in the Civil War, as a plaque makes clear); *El verdugo* turns a funeral parlor employee into an executioner, moving from prettifying corpses to producing them. And *Las cuatro verdades / Four Truths* (Berlanga, 1962) draws on a source removed from Franco's Spain, La Fontaine's fable "Death and the Woodcutter," only to turn it into a priceless portrait of Spain in the early years of fast-track capitalist development (*desarrollismo*), with funeral carriages being used to transport little girls to compete in radio song contests.

A similar black humor is found in the work of Beltrán, who considered the *esperpento* (the term coined by the early-twentieth-century dramatist Ramón del Valle-Inclán to refer to his technique of systematic distortion) to be what he saw around him every day, in the street and in private life, in the press and on television. As in Azcona's case, we have here a critical, nihilistic gaze in which a tragicomic, grotesque humor serves to denounce the sordidness of a prudish, self-engrossed society. But, if Azcona's world has no glimmer of human solidarity, one has only to look at Beltrán's gaze at the helpless Paquita (Rafaela Aparicio) and Venancio Vidal (Jesús Franco) in *El extraño viaje / Strange Voyage* (Fernando Fernán Gómez, 1964) to appreciate that it is shot through with the tender complicity of someone who knows and shares much of their frustrations.

In practice, the best of both screenwriters' work – in Azcona's case in collaboration with Ferreri and Berlanga, in Beltrán's with Fernán Gómez – ends up producing (to borrow Valle-Inclán's phrase) an "imán de conjunciones grotescas" (force field of grotesque collisions) in which, as in Valle-Inclán's amalgam of tragedy and comedy, the horrific is contaminated by the preposterous, the bizarre, and the extravagant, with paradox ruling the day. This use of paradox means in *El cochecito* that "to be like everyone else" is to join a marginal group; in *El pisito* that "to marry one person you have to marry another"; in *El verdugo* that you have to "kill to live" (all three scripted by Azcona); and in the Beltrán-scripted *El extraño viaje*, as Carlos F. Heredero has noted (2008: 146), that the characters who are ostensibly oppressors are presented as victims: "una patética galería de niños humillados digna de la España de Quevedo y Valle-Inclán" (a pathetic gallery of humiliated children worthy of the Spain of Quevedo or Valle-Inclán). All these paradoxes are inflected by an aesthetics at once tragic and grotesque, in a series of works that circle around the idea of death. This is taken to the point of paroxysm in *¡Vivan los novios! / Long Live the Bride and Groom!* (Berlanga with Azcona, 1970), with the old woman's corpse decomposing in the bathtub as the ice stacked up to conserve it melts – "¡la muerta se está mojando!" (the corpse is getting wet!). The film occupies a paradoxical space in which marriage and burial converge.

How did progressive critics of the 1960s receive these works in which populist local color was displaced by a new satirical "realism," and that supposed the transposition to cinema of the grotesque vein of black humor so strong in past Spanish literature and art? With considerable suspicion, it must be said (Zunzunegui 2005: 161–72). This is patent in two key discussions of Berlanga's *Plácido* published in the magazine *Nuestro Cine* (Erice et al. 1961; San Miguel and Erice 1962). After noting Azcona's evolution as a writer from the playful wit of the satirical magazine *La Cordoniz* to the black humor of his recent fiction and early screenplays, Santiago San Miguel and Víctor Erice (1962) – anticipating later critics – recognized Azcona's continuation of a particular Spanish tradition of realism exemplified in the picaresque and the *esperpento*: what they called "el humor español" (Spanish humor). However, when they compared him with his illustrious precursors (Goya, Quevedo, etc.) – a comparison that, we may note, implicitly grants Azcona authorial status – they found lacking in Azcona the call to moral awareness that characterized earlier Spanish artists' and writers' use of techniques of distortion. While recognizing that *El pisito* (which had dealt with housing shortages) responded to a social reality, they felt that Azcona's next two films – *El cochecito* and *Plácido* – had abandoned traditional Spanish realism for a new abstract concept of humanity, figured by a freaks' gallery whose problems were metaphysical rather than social. In the earlier collective review of *Plácido* in *Nuestro Cine* (Erice et al. 1961), Jesús García de Dueñas had similarly suggested that the film disarmed social testimony through its particular kind of black humor that "nos da como insólito y exótico algo que es concreto y real" (presents as extraordinary and exotic something that is concrete and real). San Miguel and Erice (1962) concluded their article with an appeal to "volver al realismo casi de urgencia" (return to realism with some urgency) – a notion of realism as limited as the model they were attacking. This blinkered view placed a prohibition on the exploration in 1960s Spanish cinema of this mode of gruesome distortion that converts persons into personae, exploding any narrow notion of photographic realism.

So far we have explored how Azcona and Beltrán draw on a common cultural fund. When we move to consider the differences between them, the most obvious is that Azcona started to work in cinema after a respectable, more or less conventional literary career. He had published assorted poems – "yo no era un poeta, era una caja de resonancias" (I wasn't a poet, I was a sounding board) (cited in Riambau and Torreiro 2000: 17) – plus several short stories; some novellas under the penname Jack O'Relly, "translated by Rafael Azcona," for the popular Biblioteca Chicas (specializing in love stories for adolescent girls); regular contributions to the satirical magazine *La Cordorniz*; and a list of comic novels including *La vida del repelente niño Vicente / The Life of the Disgusting Child Vicente* (1955), *Los muertos no se tocan, nene / Don't Touch the Dead, Child* (1956), and most particularly *El pisito: Novela de amor e inquilinato / The Little Apartment: A Novel of Love and Leasehold* (1957), in which he had given free rein to his idiosyncratic vision. It was this vision that caught Ferreri's eye when in 1958, after several fruitless attempts at collaboration, he directed *El pisito* with Azcona as the screenwriter. This film, based on the central story in Azcona's 1960 collection *Pobre, paralítico y muerto / Poor, Paralyzed, and Dead*, together with his other collaboration with the "Spanish Ferreri," *El cochecito*, plus his three collaborations with Berlanga in the early 1960s, form the "hard core" of Azcona's *oeuvre* (to which we could add the vitriolic, scatological *¡Vivan los novios!* of 1970, also made with Berlanga), making his irruption into Spanish cinema in the late 1950s and early 1960s a key moment. My point here is that Azcona the author is best represented not in his literary works but in his screenplays. A curious detail suggests that Azcona himself recognized this: when in 1999 he published revised versions of some of his literary works – ostensibly to make up for the previous impact of censorship – he produced a reworking of *El cochecito* that is effectively a prose adaptation of his screenplay, while his rewrite of *El pisito* bends over backwards to be faithful to Ferreri's film.

If we take Azcona's work overall – we should not forget that it spans half a century – it falls into a series of clusters marked by the personalities of the filmmakers with whom he collaborated: possibly an argument for considering the directors he worked with as having a greater authorial presence than the screenwriter, but certainly an argument for regarding Azcona's authorial trajectory as being marked by cinema rather than literature. One cluster is his work for the "Italian Ferreri," covering several major films from *La donna scimmia / The Ape Woman* (1964) to *Ciao maschio / Bye Bye Monkey* (1978) and including such suggestive titles as *La Grande bouffe / The Big Feast* (1973). Another cluster is formed by his five collaborations with Carlos Saura in Francoism's later years; their temporal games and accumulation of symbols dilute the previous material precision of Azcona's characters. Paradoxically, it was when the grotesque vein in his work became softened in screenplays of the utmost professionalism (I would include here his work for Fernando Trueba and José Luis Cuerda) that Azcona's recognition as an author peaked – as if the weakening of his critical vision were the entry ticket to social acceptance in a cinema that had jettisoned its bitter side. In this respect, we need only consider his late collaborations with Berlanga, from *La escopeta nacional / The National Shotgun* (1979) to *Moros y cristianos / Moors and Christians* (1987), in which – as Heredero notes (1997) – black humor and distortion give way to an "astracanada fallera" (burlesque farce), his early work's corrosive force being replaced by a gentler focus on the unseemly. In the last years of his career, Azcona would strike up a more productive relationship with a filmmaker in whom he seemed to have found a new kindred spirit. Working with José Luis García Sánchez allowed him to return to his earlier predilection for the grotesque (albeit slightly mannered), in a collaboration that lasted from the splendid *La corte de Faraón / The Court of the Pharaoh* (1985) to the television adaptation of Valle-Inclán's *Martes de carnaval / Military Charades* (2007).

A very different path was followed by Pedro Beltrán, whose critical recognition never went much beyond specialist circles. His multiple activities speak to his unfocused career: student, tap dancer, medical assistant, occasional actor, singer, fireman, impersonator, flamencologist, bullfighting specialist, advertiser, playwright, tavern poet, indefatigable conversationalist, professional idler, inveterate bohemian, and, of course, screenwriter. Manuel Vicent (1981) described him as a walking *esperpento* of the Madrid bar scene. If we leave aside his variegated acting appearances – starting with *Ronda española / Spanish Tour* (Ladislao Vajda, 1951), and most notably in the films of friends such as Berlanga, Juan Estelrich, and, of course, Fernando Fernán Gómez (including *Yo la vi primero / I Saw Her First* (1974); *Bruja más que bruja / Witch* (1977, also screenwriter); *Mambrú se fue a la guerra / Mambru Went to War* (1986, also screenwriter); *El viaje a ninguna parte / Voyage to Nowhere* (1986); and *Siete mil días juntos / Long Life Together* (1994)) – Beltrán's film output consists of his three screenplays for feature films by Fernando Fernán Gómez, as well as for two documentary shorts and two very different bullfighting films (*Il momento della verità / The Moment of Truth* (Francesco Rosi, 1965) and *El monosabio / The Wise Monkey* (Ray Rivas, 1977)) plus the comedy he wrote for Ramón Fernández (*¿Quién soy yo? / Who Am I?* (1970)).

The answer to why Beltrán's screenwriting output is so meager when he worked in cinema for over forty years lies in the previously mentioned conditions of the profession (or, rather, non-profession) in Spain. But Beltrán also indicated that "no puedo trabajar *al estilo de* porque, además entiendo que para tal empeño, siempre habrá otro que posea ese estilo de manera natural y que podrá hacerlo mejor" (I can't work *in the style of* because I'm always aware there will be someone else who intuitively has that style and could do it better) (cited in Heredero 2008: 90). While Azcona opted for a supremely professional career, Beltrán chose a much more anarchic path – one that, one might argue, was considerably more "auteurist" than that of Azcona, since Beltrán affirmed the unique "imprint" of personality on the artistic text (the definition of auteurism given by *Cahiers du Cinéma*'s "Young Turks"). If Azcona steered his early assault on society toward a highly codified, socially accepted auteurist practice, Beltrán stayed on the margins of any kind of institutionalization of his work. The results in terms of critical and social recognition are self-evident: the fanfares that accompanied Azcona's last years – Premio Nacional de Cinematografía (National Film Award) in 1982, Medalla de Oro de las Bellas Artes (Gold Medal for Fine Arts) in 1994, and the dozens of Goyas awarded to his screenplays between 1988 and 2008 (the year of his death) – are matched in Beltrán's case by a hush in which his merits have received scant mention.

Indeed, several of Beltrán's screenplays remain unpublished, including the suggestive projects *El desguace / The Scrapyard* and *Música de viento / Wind Music* that he embarked on for Berlanga, in the latter case in collaboration with Azcona. The first of these, written around 1976, told the story of a marchioness' family united around her deathbed; the second (date of writing unknown) related the vicissitudes of an actor-bullfighter troupe that earned its living during the Civil War by passing back and forth between the enemy zones, changing their repertoire accordingly. The traces of these on Berlanga's *La escopeta nacional* and

La vaquilla / The Heifer (1984), both in the end scripted by Azcona, are immediately evident. It is equally lamentable that no one has published Beltrán's screenplay *Las aventuras de Don Juan* (date of writing again unknown), which continued his personal assault on Spanish machismo and the exploration of transvestism initiated in the last scenes of *El extraño viaje* (Heredero 2008: 144). *El desguace* also pointed in that direction with the character of the marchioness' husband, who, transformed into an "*esperpento* femenino" (female freak) (Beltrán cited in Heredero 2008: 144), earns a living in a sleazy Hamburg cabaret.

Sadly, the career of Pedro Beltrán, a writer doomed to failure (much to his chagrin) who used Madrid's bars and cafés as his personal sitting room and the elevators of not a few buildings as his occasional bedroom, came to an end in 2007 in the dismal loneliness of a boarding house, where his body was found one morning by his friend, the actor Gabino Diego.

Jesús Franco: From Pulp Auteur to Cult Auteur (Antonio Lázaro-Reboll)

Jesús ("Jess") Franco has produced almost two hundred films that trade in pulp and pop, crime and horror, and softcore and hardcore porn. A retrospective organized by the Cinématheque Française in 2008 aptly described his work as "Fragments d'une filmographie impossible" (Fragments of an impossible filmography). A blog dedicated to "the archaeology of Jess Franco's films" since 2006 and entitled "I'm in a Jess Franco State of Mind" is indicative of the consuming passion of a fan, and, by extension, the affective dimensions of fandom.[1] These are two recent examples of how Franco is seen as an auteur by players in the development of auteurist film cultures: the former a traditional film institution strongly associated with cinephilia and the artistic validation of film authors; the latter a new form of subcultural expression made possible by digital culture and connected to cult movie fandom. Franco himself has actively cultivated his (pulp) auteur status, trafficked in cinephile and popular culture connoisseurship, and prepared the ground for the making of his cult auteur reputation. Franco has made so many films and directed under so many different male and female pseudonyms that "an entire subculture was required to keep track of his activities" as well as the "multilingual variants and alternative titles and repackagings" of his films (O'Brien 1993: 183, 184).

Any archaeology of Jesús Franco's cult credentials must therefore be seen as part of specific historical and cultural junctures that go beyond histories of Spanish cinema. Such an archaeology would plunge us into the messy histories of international production, distribution, exhibition, reception, and consumption of horror, exploitation, and sexploitation. While this might be a painstakingly challenging task, it would shed light on how constructions of particular cult auteurs such as Franco go hand in hand with changing patterns of film consumption, the role of specific producers and international distribution strategies, the impact of changing technologies, the shifting terrains of reception and taste, and/or different types of cult film fandom. His films have been enjoyed by perverse audiences in New York's downtown grindhouses such as the Cinerama and the Liberty in the late 1960s and early 1970s[2] and celebrated by American (*European Trash Cinema, Psychotronic, Video Watchdog*, and *Sleazoid Express*) and European (*Mad Movies* in France, *Eyeball* and *Flesh and Blood* in the United Kingdom, and *2000maníacos* in Spain) paracinematic publications linked to the home video generation of the 1980s and 1990s, and are persistently discussed by devoted online communities such as "The Franco Lounge" across the globe at the turn of the twenty-first century (see, for example "The Latarnia Forums," www.thelatarniaforums.yuku.com). The international and transcultural dimension of Franco's cult auteur status has also shaped the celebration and revival of his work for new generations of fans in Spain. With the exception of the journalistic and cinéphile interventions – and fan enthusiasms – of Carlos Aguilar, Joan Bassa, and Ramón Freixas in the early 1990s,[3] and the official recognition attached to the recently awarded Goya de Honor (2009) for his lifetime achievement in Spanish cinema, the reception and consumption of Franco in Spain have always been mediated and constructed through fandom culture (see Figure 6.4). Fan consumption, connoisseurship, and reading strategies of Franco's films have come via foreign psychotronic film distributors (Something Weird, Sinister Cinema, Image Entertainment, Mondo Macabro) and lately via cyberspace, namely through Internet file sharing and YouTube, now part of a common everyday practice of consumption and distribution among fans.

From very early on, the director forged a biographical template that is told and retold in interviews, recollected in his autobiography *Memorias del tío Jess* (Franco 2004; "tío Jess" is his nickname), and, in turn, reproduced by journalistic film criticism, fans, and – lately – academics. I will zoom in on two of these biographical moments that have been regularly and strategically invoked by Franco to frame his entry into film culture and his self-mythologizing narrative: his fictional pulp past and his cinephilia.

References to a pulp past are frequently mobilized by the director. Franco has long claimed that under the pseudonym David Khune he wrote pulp novels (detective fiction, westerns, and horror) in the 1950s. Such claims have been readily accepted by interviewers, fans, and critics. Thus, Tombs and Tohill state that the young Franco "supported himself by writing pulp novels [...]. These youthful pulps were crazed, fantastic creations. Many of their plots and strange scenarios were later to provide inspiration for his films. He wrote over a hundred crime thrillers and horror stories and was paid around $20 per title" (1995: 80; see also Pavlović 2003: 108). Franco's claims, however, fly in the face of the evidence. Research into the pulp production of David Khune yields no traces, sending the Franco aficionado on a wild goose chase that leaves him wondering whether these novels actually existed in the first place. But why would Franco invent this writer of nonexistent novels? What would be the purpose of such an autobiographical

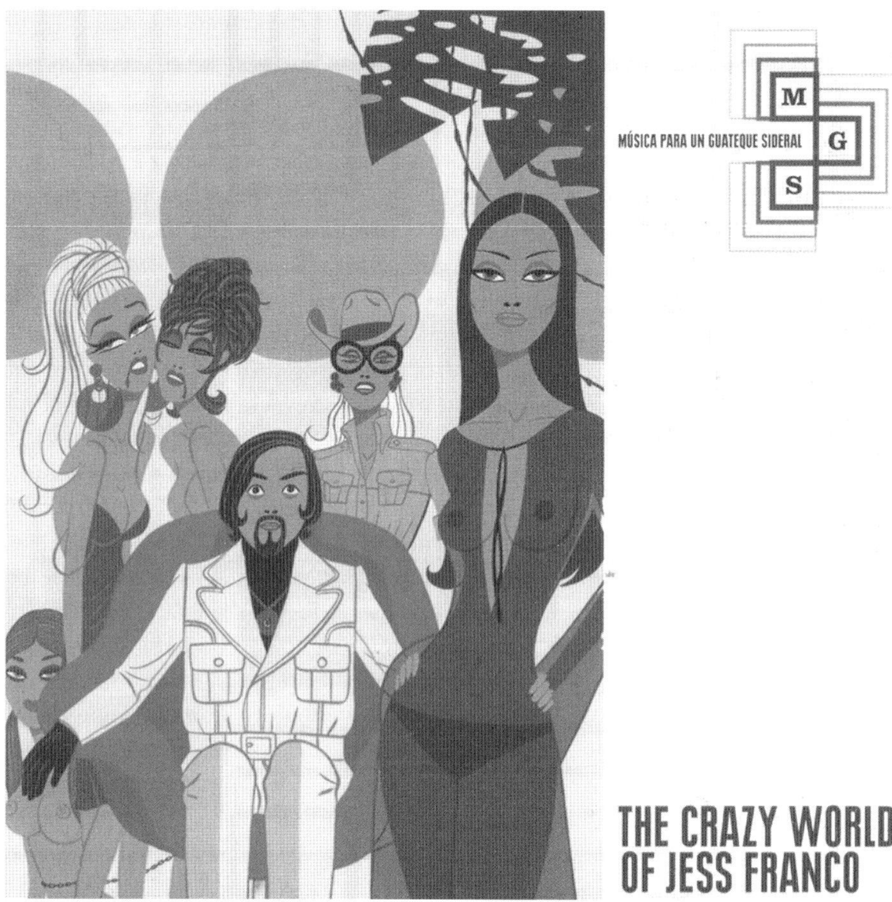

Figure 6.4 Cover of the December 2008 issue of *Academia*, the magazine of the Spanish Film Academy, commemorating the Goya Lifetime Achievement Award to Jesús Franco. The artwork by Jordi Labanda was originally created for the 1997 CD of soundtracks of Franco's films, *The Crazy World of Jess Franco* (Subterfuge Records). Courtesy of Jordi Labanda.

move? And how does this fictional pulp past affect the reading of, for example, his Dr. Orloff cycle in the early 1960s (according to the credit titles, *Gritos en la noche / The Awful Dr. Orloff* (1961), *El secreto del Dr. Orlof / The Secret of Dr. Orloff* (1964) and *Miss Muerte / The Diabolical Dr. Z* (1965) are all adaptations for the screen from "novels" by Franco's pulp fiction alter ego David Khune)? An obvious answer is that the foreign name of David Khune lent these films a certain degree of authenticity and commercial viability. More importantly, however, Franco inserts himself into a popular film tradition harking back to the Fantômas series of Louis Feuillade in the early 1910s, the Dr. Mabuse saga adapted to cinema by German Fritz Lang in the 1920s and 1930s, and the Fu Manchu films made in the United

States during the 1930s and 1940s; these adapted for the screen the pulp fiction works of Pierre Souvestre and Marcel Allain, Norbert Jacques, and Sax Rohmer, respectively. At the same time, Franco is acknowledging the reciprocal influence of these mass culture forms, pulp movies and pulp novels, on his filmmaking.[4] What is at stake here is Franco's own construction of a pulp auteur past that lends the director and his films a pulp sensibility, thereby granting his filmic production a (sub)cultural value that aligns him with American and European pulp fiction and pulp movie traditions. Furthermore, it underlies his desire to be linked to a set of US and European cultural histories far removed from the Spain of the 1950s.[5]

Another iterated moment in Franco's personal narrative is his stay in Paris in the early 1950s. Franco has frequently talked about his experience as a regular filmgoer at the Cinémathèque Française and that momentous episode when Henri Langlois, then Director of the Cinémathèque, arranged special screenings for him on his last day in Paris. His conscious rehearsal of this episode about his entry into film culture and his film education can be interpreted as an act of strategic auteurism. Cult fans have subsequently lapped up and repeated endlessly these and other stories, such as his work for Orson Welles in *Chimes at Midnight* in 1965, a well-known episode of Franco's biographical template. One story has it as follows: "the Spanish producers for *Chimes at Midnight*, horrified by Welles' choice of the second-unit director of photography, dug out *Rififí en la ciudad / Rififi in the City* (1963) to show Welles just how bad Franco's camerawork could be. Unfortunately for the producers, Welles was charmed by *Rififí*'s obvious homage to *The Lady from Shanghai* (Welles, 1948)" and hired him (Hawkins 2000: 243). Franco's constant references to maverick filmmakers such as Orson Welles contribute to his self-mythologizing. There are a number of auteurist investments in the Henri Langlois and the Cinémathèque Française narrative as well as in the referencing of filmmakers: apart from establishing Franco as a cineaste, it places the director geographically and historically as part of a cinephile audience that was about to have a major influence on the development of film culture, constructions of modern *auteur* cinema, and re-evaluations of American "pop" culture, and it also links him to a generation of kindred spirits formed by Langlois, some of whom, like Franco, went on to make films that broke away from dominant models of officially approved cinema film production. In this respect, Franco's films have always been associated with an illegitimate strand of Spanish cinema, making him a marginal and anomalous figure in Spanish film history. And illegitimacy, marginality, and anomaly are the stuff of which cult reputations are made. Whether or not Franco was aware of an emerging critical discourse about film authorship, his own strategic auteurism has certainly served him well. Both the retrospective and the blog to which I referred above attest to Franco's recognized auteur status and to the ongoing construction, promotion, and perpetuation of his cult reputation. Indeed, Franco's Cinémathèque Française narrative has come full circle: sixty-nine of his films were screened in the Henri Langlois and Georges Franju cinemas as part of the activities of its "Space Cinéphile." But the way to cult in the case of Franco is to be traced not only in the role played by retrospectives programmed by established film institutions but also in the subcultural ideologies of blogs and online forums, genre magazines and fanzines, mail-order video, and DVD and Blu-ray catalogues across the globe. The making of his cult reputation is the result both of localized cult responses in the United States, Europe, and Spain since the 1960s and the more recent emergence of the "cult movie" and "cult director" as niche markets for global consumption.

Pere Portabella: The Politics and Aesthetics of Auteurism (Santos Zunzunegui)

Jess Franco and Pere Portabella are two directors who could not be more different, and yet there is a connection between them in that Portabella's *Vampir-Cuadecuc* (1970) is built around the shooting that year of Franco's film *Count Dracula* (see Figure 6.5). They are similar also in that both have strategically constructed an authorial status for themselves through criteria – very different in each case – unusual in a film industry like that of Spain. Any consideration of Portabella's position in Spanish cinema has to start from two basic premises. First, his work has to be considered in dialogue with other artistic practices outside the field of cinema. Second, while those of his films that initially seem the most "political" are always marked by the endeavor to achieve the status of "art object" (e.g., *Informe general / General Report*, 1976), conversely those that are most obviously art films (e.g., *Umbracle*, 1972) have important political dimensions. This section explores the ways in which Portabella's cinema strategically articulates a complex notion of "authorship" through this double relationship: between film and other artistic practices, and between film and politics. (For the Catalan dimensions of his work, see Chapter 3.) That his work has found a home in the museum in itself demonstrates that it has implications that transcend the cinematic. Likewise, all his films propose singular ways of broadening any narrowly defined notion of political activism in order to claim the broader terrain of "the political," always linked to the exploration of avant-garde expressive forms conducive to such a conception. The hallmark of Portabella's cinema – his principal authorial "signature" – is thus its dialogism, its will to heterogeneity.

Portabella's trajectory was from the start eccentric in relation to the cinema of his time. His early work as a producer, through his company Films 59, illustrates the point made by Marvin D'Lugo in Chapter 2 about the importance of seeing producers as *auteurs*. *Los golfos / The Delinquents* (Carlos Saura, 1959) – the first film Portabella produced – was novel in offering itself as an exercise in "realist cinema" that at the same time took an interest in the New Waves then starting to make an impact throughout Europe. Films 59's second production, *El cochecito* (Ferreri, 1960; see "Authorizing Screenwriting" above), can again be seen as the exploration of an "alternative realism" – in this case based on the Spanish *esperpento* tradition

Figure 6.5 *Vampir-Cuadecuc* (1970; prod. Films 59): Portabella's avant-garde film constructed its metaphorical universe around the shooting of Jesús Franco's horror film *Count Dracula*. Courtesy of Films 59.

of grotesque distortion as a formula for achieving what Portabella, talking later of his own work as a director, would call a "realismo de resultados" (intervention in the real) (Torres and Molina Foix 1969: 30). The next film produced – albeit with minimal financial investment – by Films 59, taking stylistic density and radicalization further, was none other than Luis Buñuel's *Viridiana* (1961). The rumpus surrounding the film's prize at Cannes, with its consequent banning in Spain (see Chapter 5), forced Films 59 to suspend operations temporarily, obliging Portabella to rethink his future in cinema. It is logical that his next step should have taken him to avant-garde film (see Chapter 18). If we jump ahead a few years, we find Portabella producing Antonio Maenza's sadly unfinished *Hortensia / Béance* (1969) and the more recent *Tren de sombras / Train of Shadows* of José Luis Guerín (1997).

Portabella's immediate engagement with avant-garde film was, however, realized by moving into film direction. Given that Portabella's conception of cinema did not divorce it from other artistic practices, his work (as well as his self-representation) harmonizes perfectly with the auteurists' emphasis on the uniquely creative role of the director. On the home page of his website, Portabella metaphorically relates the gestational process of his work to that of writers and painters:

> In order to conceive a film I simply need to situate myself in front of a blank page. That's the shortest path to arrive, under the best of conditions, at the blank, white screen. In a certain sense, it's like working directly on the screen. It's only necessary to allow a situation, a chance occurrence, a starting point, to fall onto the page, black on white [...] a splotch. (www.pereportabella.com/home)

Portabella's biography confirms this interest in other artistic processes that appear to be separate from cinema only if one forgets that they are grounded in, and given meaning by, a common impulse. Relevant here is his participation in the Grup de Treball (Working Group), a collective engaged in conceptual, artistic, and political interventions in Barcelona between 1973 and 1976 (Museu d'Art Contemporani de Barcelona 1999), and particularly his collaboration with several figures in the Barcelona literary and artistic world such as Joan Brossa and Joan Miró, whose "high art" credibility enhanced the cachet of Portabella's films.

Portabella's first artistic partner, Brossa, was a poet, playwright, painter, lover of crosswords, and untiring experimenter with language (Brossa 1997; Guerrero 2001), whose heterogeneous interests and crossing of artistic boundaries would make a strong impact on Portabella's future career as a film director. The fruits of this collaboration, a testament to the creative synergy between a filmmaker and a poet, were a short (*No compteu amb els dits / No contéis con los dedos / Don't Count with Your Fingers*, 1967) and three feature films (*Nocturn 29 / Nocturno 29 / Nocturne 29*, 1968; *Vampir-Cuadecuc*; and *Umbracle*). In tandem with his work with Brossa (at its most intense in *Nocturn 29*, tailing off progressively in the next two feature films), Portabella found a new partner in the avant-garde musician Carles Santos, who would himself develop a separate career as an experimental filmmaker. After appearing in *No compteu amb els dits* and *Nocturn 29* (where his piano performances are stunning), Santos would be responsible for the soundtracks of all Portabella's subsequent films, creating a unique sonic environment that plays an essential role in the generation of meaning.

A similar process of hybridization is found in the series of films Portabella made around the figure of the painter Joan Miró between 1969 and 1973. The three shorts that comprise the first cluster were linked to Miró's 1969 retrospective at Barcelona's Col·legi d'Arquitectes (Architects' Association). The first of these, *Aidez l'Espagne / Miró 37* (1969), attempted to encapsulate the tragedy engulfing Spain in 1936–9 by actualizing the call for aid depicted in the postage stamp Miró designed for the French postal services in 1937, while the second, *Miró l'altre / The Other Miró* (1969), documented Miró's painting of a mural on the glass façade of the Architects' Association building, only to bear testimony in its second part to its erasure by the painter and, finally, to the façade's return to its original state as a window thanks to an army of cleaning ladies, such that "nada había tenido lugar salvo el lugar" (nothing had taken place other than the place). This is the record of a performance, but also a meditation on the banality of art and its claim to timelessness, here explored through the indexical nature of the cinematic image, manipulated in full awareness that it is the trace of an absence. The third film in this triptych, *Premios nacionales / National Prizes* (1969), takes us to the basement of Spain's National Library, to the rhythms of the late-nineteenth-century *zarzuelas* (popular operettas) *La revoltosa / The Troublemaker* and *El tambor de granaderos / The Grenadiers' Drum*, where we see piled up on the floor the works awarded official prizes by successive Francoist juries in a show of intellectual vacuity and artistic myopia. Although this last film was made to be screened in a section devoted to kitsch art, providing a counterpoint to the avant-gardism of the work by Miró in the exhibition, it stands on its own as an ironic testimony to the inanity of the official art of the Franco dictatorship.

The next cluster of Miró films appeared in 1974, in connection with the Miró exhibition held that year at the Grand Palais in Paris. This time Portabella chose to focus on the artisanal nature of the manufacturing processes involved in some of Miró's work. Both *Miró-la forja / Miró-The Forge* (which documents the casting of three huge gates designed by Miró but crafted by expert foundry workers) and *Miró-tapís / Miró-Tapestry* (showing the production by craftsmen of a vast tapestry measuring sixty square meters and weighing almost 3500 kilos, based on a small cartoon by Miró) invite the spectator to reflect on key aspects of art in the age of technological reproduction. In these films, Portebella affirms his status as an auteur reflecting on the creative process while at the same time affirming a concept of art as collective labor. It is entirely appropriate that his first works as experimental documentarist should have been collaborative projects with other artists.

As Portabella's collaboration with Brossa came to an end, his filmmaking underwent a decisive change. Both *Vampir-Cuadecuc* and *Umbracle* were made in 16 mm, were not submitted to the censors for prior approval before shooting, and consequently circulated via alternative platforms linked to clandestine political opposition circles. This consciously assumed marginalization has to be seen as a search for new spaces of freedom, political and artistic. A film like *Umbracle* is exemplary in both respects: in its challenge to Aristotelian narrative conventions through its avoidance of plot in order to "ir directamente a la temática" (go straight to the point) (Portabella cited in Torres and Molina-Foix 1969: 30) but also in its reconstruction of the Francoist uncanny. Accordingly, from this point on, Portabella's work would explore ways of navigating the system's margins – *Advocats laboralistes / Labor Lawyers* (1973) and *El sopar / The Supper* (1974) – culminating in the programmatically titled *Informe general sobre algunas cuestiones de interés para una proyección pública / General Report on Some Questions of Interest for a Public Screening* (1976), in which he traced the public emergence in Spain of a will to democracy and the persistence at its core of the black hole of the former dictatorship and its monarchist future. This was achieved by breaking with the dictatorship of the reality effect, which tends to contaminate documentary production, by using a rhetorical structure punctuated by returns to a series of emblematic spaces associated with Francoism's real or imaginary demise. In this case, the film is not presented as an art object in its own right but as a pretext for subsequent debate.

What we have here is the idea of film as performance (doing things with images). This places a new spin on the concept of the author: not the creator of a text but the stager of an event – or, rather, of a series of events whose montage produces the intervention in reality that is the film.

Informe general was followed by a thirteen-year gap in Portabella's film career, in which he was engaged in intense political activity, extending into democracy his prolonged anti-Francoist commitment – elected a member of the Spanish Senate in 1977 in the first elections after the return to democracy, he was a member of the commission that drafted the 1978 democratic constitution; from 1980 to 1988 he served as a deputy to the Generalitat (Catalan autonomous government). His return to filmmaking was marked by *Pont de Varsovi / Warsaw Bridge* (1989). This time Portabella did not shun plot ("no se da la espalda al argumento," as he put it) (Monterde and Riambau 1990: 29), but the filmic structure remained healthily provocative: taking as its starting point an unlikely news story – later used by Paul Thomas Anderson in *Magnolia* (1999) – it offers a flashback that is barely perceptible as such, adopts a rhizomatic form that makes many of its sequences narrative dead ends, and stresses the purely plastic dimension of the cinematic image.

Recent years have seen an explosion of international interest in Portabella's films: the 2001 retrospective at MACBA (Museu d'Art Contemporani de Barcelona), the films' screening at the 2002 Kassel Documenta, and the film cycles at the Centre Georges Pompidou in 2003, at New York's MoMA in 2007, and at London's Tate Modern in 2011 – all art museums – have confirmed his films' strategic dialogue with other arts. This dialogue – returning to his interest in music – has been continued by his last feature film, *Die Stille vor Bach / The Silence before Bach* (2007), whose "pre-text" is the figure of Johann Sebastian Bach, going beyond biography to explore the persistence of Bach's work by literally transporting his music to our day (see Figure 6.6). Portabella thereby creates a new cinematic genre of the variation, which has no center and is built on the black hole in Europe's catastrophic history – a dimension made explicit through the focus on Dresden and presence of the near-unrepresentable event that was the Holocaust. As in his earlier cinema, the different sequences straddle the boundary between fiction and documentary. We move constantly between the different moments of a narration that unravels what it weaves together, blurring genres in the process; not so much a structured narration as a notebook. The hybridization that is such a striking feature of Portabella's work is found again in his 2008 short, *Mudanza / Removal*. Conceived as a museum piece for the Patronato García Lorca in Fuentevaqueros, it occupies a conceptual space close to minimalism, offering an allegorical representation, based on the idea of absence ("disappearance" in the political sense), of the tragedy of Lorca's death.

Portabella's privileged terrain, then, is structured by the renunciation of classical narration and an uncompromising dialogue between cinema and other arts – a no-man's-land that is unique in Spanish cinema. His resolutely non-commercial approach to film has given him political and artistic freedom – a freedom enhanced

Figure 6.6 *Die Stille vor Bach*, Portabella's exploration of the relationship between image and music (2007; prod. Films 59). Courtesy of Films 59.

by the fact that his own production company, Films 59, has produced all his work. The absence of his films from mainstream distribution circuits has made them into museum pieces appreciated by connoisseurs, granting him authorial status despite his concept of the film as process rather than text, and despite the stress in much of his cinema on collaborative labor.

Editing in the Woman Auteur (Susan Martin-Márquez)

The explicit androcentrism of the *politique des auteurs* as defined by contributors to *Cahiers du Cinéma* from the mid-1950s to the 1960s certainly facilitated the exclusion of women filmmakers from the global canon of great directors. Later in this section I will explore the ways in which a number of Spanish women directors from different periods have negotiated that phenomenon by strategically adopting or rejecting the "auteur" mantle. First, however, I will examine another less recognized manner in which the internationally influential *politique* functioned to consign women's contributions to filmmaking to obscurity, and I will engage in a recuperative practice of auteurism by undertaking a brief case study of the Franco-era film editor Margarita Ochoa.

As mentioned at the start of this chapter, in his 1954 *Cahiers* essay "A Certain Tendency in French Cinema," François Truffaut railed against the French "Tradition of Quality" style of filmmaking. France's studio system, modeled on Hollywood, turned out some hundred films a year, and the best of those works were routinely praised at home and abroad, garnering top prizes at Cannes and other prestigious festivals. Many were based on literary works, adapted for the screen by a small number of screenwriters who were not, in Truffaut's estimation, true "men of cinema." To counter the resulting impoverishment of the film medium, Truffaut and his colleagues at *Cahiers* called for a shift in valorization away from (supposedly second-rate) screenwriter-centered films and toward a "cinéma d'auteurs," created by directors who succeeded in gaining control of all the formal properties of the medium in order to achieve personal expression. While Hollywood directors such as Alfred Hitchcock and John Ford were some of the first auteurs identified in *Cahiers*, lauded for the genius required to imprint their unique personalities on works produced within the studio system, when it came to films created outside Hollywood the *politique des auteurs* tended to exalt directors working independently of established national industries, if not outside national canons – a practice that Truffaut and his French New Wave colleagues themselves adopted.

Both the rejection of studio-based forms of production and the emphasis on the director as the true originator of the film text prompted critics to shift their attention away from the collaborative processes that are essential to most forms of filmmaking. In this way, the *politique* effected a double erasure of women's contributions, by figuring the director-auteur as necessarily male (as we shall see later) and by characterizing the other participants in the filmmaking process – any number of whom might be women – as subordinate to the will of the auteur.[6] The case of screenwriting was discussed earlier in this chapter, but perhaps the most glaring instance of erasure involves editing, an essential aspect of cinematic creation that throughout the first half of the twentieth century was frequently dominated by women. Yet the achievements of women editors are typically left on the cutting room floor. For French film scholar Colin Crisp,

> it is undeniable that a contributing factor to this invisibility is the gender differentiation which early on marked the editing task as appropriate for females rather than males [...] it was early assimilated to the role of the seamstress, with the little woman snipping busily away in her backroom, tidying up after the men. (1987: 62)

In Spain and during the Franco regime in particular, dozens of women served as editors-in-chief as well as assistant editors, as documented in industry directories of the era.[7] However, women editors are almost completely absent from the history and criticism of Spanish cinema. If they appear at all in the literature, it is often because of their relationship to men who were also involved in the film industry, sometimes in less significant roles. This is the case, for example, of Sara Ontañón, whose professional accomplishments over three decades (cutting films for directors such as José Luis Sáenz de Heredia, Edgar Neville, and Rafael Gil) are only highlighted after her status as sister to the supporting actor and set designer Santiago Ontañón is affirmed (compare the entries in Borau 1998: 642–4)

Figure 6.7 From the 1940s to the 1960s dozens of women worked in film editing, as did this unidentified friend of Sara Ontañón, in a photograph from the latter's personal collection. Courtesy of Alfonso Orueta, with kind assistance from Esther López Sobrado.

(see Figure 6.7). Margarita Ochoa, who edited over fifty films, including some of the most significant works produced under the Franco regime, has fared even worse: she is not listed at all in the presumably authoritative *Diccionario del cine español* (Borau 1998) or in other major encyclopedias or handbooks (e.g., Torres 1999). As with Ontañón, in the few sources where Ochoa's name does appear, it is usually in relation to her husband Arcadio Ochoa, a hair and makeup artist, or their son, the assistant director José María ("Joe") Ochoa, who worked on several Hollywood super-productions shot in Spain (Roldán Larreta 2003: 262–5).

A close examination of Ochoa's editing practices suggests that she in fact left an indelible imprint on a number of Spanish films, akin to the "authorial signature" emphasized by the *politique des auteurs*. Ochoa edited a wide range of commercial films beginning in the 1940s, but by the 1950s she had also begun to work with two of Spain's highest-profile directors, both of whom would become associated with the creation of an oppositional cinema under Franco, albeit from different ideological positions: José Antonio Nieves Conde and Juan Antonio Bardem. Nieves Conde called upon Ochoa to edit seven of the eleven films he produced in the first half of his career. For his part, after his first film and until Ochoa's death in the mid-1960s, Bardem would entrust the editing of his films to no one else. Interestingly, both filmmakers are associated with a unique visual style, based in part on a superb deployment of editing.

Nieves Conde's inaugural films were edited exclusively by Ochoa. The director's first extant film, the 1947 *Angustia / Anguish*, is a taut *noir*-inspired murder mystery that exemplifies the way in which the dissident Falangist Nieves Conde's films often expose the seamier aspects of life in Franco's Spain. The film employs a number of visual techniques to reflect the tortured psychology of its characters, including an unusual and emphatic pattern of editing that underlines the exchange of paranoid gazes through multiple eyeline matches, and foregrounds the guilty gestures that might otherwise remain hidden from view through a quick and insistent montage of close-ups. Although they make no mention of Ochoa, critics have characterized the film's editing as "brilliant" (Company 2003: 23; see also Zunzunegui 1997: 228). Nieves Conde's most famous film is *Surcos / Furrows* (1951), which is considered one of the first films directly to critique the conditions of urban working-class life under Franco. The editing in this work again functions to transmit the characters' psychological and physical suffering to the audience. In one celebrated scene, for example, an older farmer named Manuel who has migrated to the city with his family struggles to keep up with mechanized factory work; the accelerating rhythm of the montage, which alternates shots of the pounding metalworking machine with canted frames of the exhausted Manuel, imbues the image track with the character's subjective experience and prompts viewers to feel sympathy for him. The increasingly rapid crosscutting between shots of Manuel and the phallic machine functions as a classic example of Soviet-style dialectical montage; the symbolism underlines the destruction of the patriarch's traditional masculine identity and his enforced submission to a more powerful socioeconomic regime (Zumalde Arregi 1997: 296). Although Ochoa's name is nowhere mentioned in the critical literature on *Surcos*, this editing was singled out at the time of the work's release and continues to be praised by film scholars (e.g., *Surcos* 1960; Kinder 1993: 46; Zumalde Arregi 1997: 296).

Nieves Conde did not prepare detailed technical scripts indicating his editing vision. In interviews, the director tends to assign credit for most of the positive aspects of his films to himself and, though he never mentions his partnership with Ochoa, he is particularly dismissive of the work of editors (e.g., Llinás 1995: 61–8). For that reason, it is difficult to determine to what extent Ochoa was involved in creative invention and crucial decision-making with respect to the editing of Nieves Conde's cinematic texts – though it seems likely that her input was significant. At a minimum, her skill in producing the final cut contributed to the notable effectiveness of these films.

We have substantially more information concerning the creative relationship between Ochoa and Bardem, an oppositional filmmaker who was an active member of the clandestine Communist Party. Bardem indicates in his memoirs that he learned to edit film himself very early on, and that he was inspired by V. I. Pudovkin's mandate that montage be considered the foundation of cinematic art; he also claims that his filming techniques left few options to the editor (2002: 62–3, 200). Yet his reliance on Ochoa was absolute: he planned to vacation while

Ochoa edited one of his films (Bardem 2002: 324), and after her death he was exasperated when he was required to take a more hands-on approach while working with other editors. After shooting his 1982 Eastern Block superproduction *La advertencia / The Warning*, he was assigned a Bulgarian editor who "se negó a cortar el más mímimo trozo de las tomas elegidas por mí sin que yo estuviera presente. Así que durante meses estuve yo montando la película junto a ella, que solo cortaba y empalmaba lo que yo le decía" (refused to cut the smallest piece from the shots I selected unless I was present. Thus for months I was editing the film alongside her; she only cut and spliced what I told her to) (Bardem 2002: 228). Bardem is generally known as a director who disliked sharing the limelight, yet his memoirs include numerous references to his "beloved" and "venerable" Madame Ochoa, "mi colaboradora más constante y fiel" (my most constant and faithful collaborator) (Bardem 2002: 206, 234, 248, 287, 340).

Ochoa's influence on Bardem's filmmaking might be gauged by comparing the director's first solo film, *Cómicos / Actors* (1954), which was edited by others, with his third, the highly acclaimed *Muerte de un ciclista / Death of a Cyclist* (1955), edited by Ochoa. In *Cómicos* we clearly see the emergence of Bardem's "signature style" of framing – characterized by tight close-ups, dramatically lit profiles, and unusual camera angles – which early in his career tended to carry over from one film to the next, regardless of the cinematographer he worked with. Yet the cutting in the film is far more pedestrian. In fact, the editing on *Cómicos* was rushed, since Bardem had already begun shooting his next film; Bardem was also unhappy with his editor, Antonio Gimeno, and he called on another filmmaker, León Klimovsky, to help with the final cut (Egido 1958: 18; Bardem 2002: 200). One critic has asserted of *Cómicos* that "la película debía salvarse en la mesa de montaje, pero no ocurrió así" (the film should have been saved on the editing table, but that didn't happen), underlining that *Muerte de un ciclista* is far more successful in terms of its overall "calligraphic" qualities (Minguet 2004: 68).

Indeed, *Muerte de un ciclista*, produced just a year after *Cómicos* (in 1954), is characterized by a significantly more dramatic editing style, similar to the showier passages of editing that we find in earlier films cut by Ochoa. Critics have generally ascribed the editing style of this film to Bardem's admiration for Pudovkin and early Soviet montage theory (Cerón Gómez 1998: 47, 129; Evans 2007). Yet it is curious that it was not until he began working with Ochoa that Bardem utilized more dynamic editing passages that energize the narrative and heighten the psychological complexity as well as the ideological valence of his characters. *Muerte de un ciclista* centers on an adulterous couple, María José and Juan, who accidentally run over a cyclist on the way home from a tryst and leave the man to die so that their affair will not be discovered. In one of the most critically acclaimed scenes of the film, María José and Juan attend a flamenco show together with María José's husband Miguel, as well as with Rafa, a would-be blackmailer who threatens to reveal all during the performance. The script includes no technical details, but does call for an anguished play of gazes against an increasingly grating backdrop of clapping, stomping, strumming, and singing (Bardem 1962: 76–80). It is Ochoa's editing that brings this charged atmosphere into being, through a rapid succession of two- and three-second shots with tight chains of eyeline matches between increasingly closer views of the protagonists alternating with cutaways to the flamenco artists, which both relieve and enhance the level of tension in the scene. As always, Ochoa's name is never mentioned by the critics who have singled out the impact of this film's editing (e.g., Kinder 1993: 77–84; Evans 2007) – a consequence, it might be argued, of the gendered auteurist legacy within film studies.

The emergence of the *politique des auteurs* was in fact accompanied by anxiety over the abundance of women editors. In a 1956 series of articles devoted to montage in *Cahiers du Cinéma*, one critic justifies his use of the masculine form of the noun when referring to film editors by noting that, while women have customarily been associated with the profession, the intense effort involved in editing in reality demands a certain "virility," further claiming that the number of male editors was on the rise for that reason (Colpi 1956: 28 n. 3). Indeed, *Cahiers*' champions of auteurism labored to define the essence of film creation, and particularly the essence of film direction, as exclusively masculine. This is of course evident from the fact that all of the auteurs they identified were men, but it also emerges from their pointed rhetorical choices. Jacques Rivette, for example, praised the violence and "virile anger" of a number of auteurs, who "impose themselves" on the audience; here his discourse is evocative of a rape scenario (Caughie 1981: 41).

This was the challenging critical context within which the range of women's participation in filmmaking broadened and within which women directors began to emerge in significant numbers in a variety of nations, including Spain. By the 1950s, two Spanish women had moved into film direction: Ana Mariscal and Margarita Aleixandre.[8] Both had begun their film careers as actresses within the Spanish industry of the 1940s; while Aleixandre's acting profile was more modest, Mariscal had become a major star whose image was significantly more complex than has traditionally been acknowledged by those who underline her support for the Franco regime (Martin-Márquez 1999: 85–112; Triana Toribio 2000). As they gravitated toward directing, both women clearly understood that they would only be able to take on that role outside the studio system, and as a result their practices might be characterized as "authorial." They established independent production companies in conjunction with their creative collaborators and future husbands: Mariscal set up Bosco Films with her cinematographer Valentín Javier, while Aleixandre created Nervión Films together with her codirector Rafael Torrecilla. They also chose their own projects – producing a total of ten and three films, respectively – and in many cases wrote their own scripts. Most significantly, despite the strict censorship norms that often limited their freedom of expression, both women produced "personal" works that departed from hegemonic forms of filmmaking. In *Segundo López, aventurero urbano / Segundo López, Urban Adventurer* (1952), for example, Mariscal was one of the first directors in Spain to draw upon the techniques of Italian neo-realism as well as melodrama to underline the pathos of ongoing economic stratification in Spain (the film was also edited, importantly, by Margarita Ochoa). In *La gata / The She-Cat* (1956), Spain's first film shot in Cinemascope, Aleixandre countered the dominant "folkloric" images of Andalusia and foregrounded her female protagonist's sexual assertiveness (Martin-Márquez 1999: 113–19, 249–64; Martín 2002). Notwithstanding their accomplishments, however, Mariscal and Aleixandre did not contribute to the burgeoning auteurist discourse that began to be articulated by other independent (or would-be independent) filmmakers in Spain, many of whom were the first graduates of the state-run Official Film School. The case of Mariscal in particular makes clear that the gender politics of the era often required women directors strategically to minimize their own ambitions and achievements, though heavy doses of irony or the deployment of a double-voiced discourse might temper the gestures of self-effacement (Martin-Márquez 1999: 121–5).

Not surprisingly, no women spoke at the famous Salamanca Conversations of 1955, where cineastes such as Bardem criticized the poverty of the Spanish film industry and the repressive constraints of censorship, even as they sought to solidify their efforts to establish alternative and/or oppositional modes of production. By the following decade, however, auteurism had been coopted and converted into a governmental policy designed to improve Spain's image abroad and, as Kathleen Vernon and Nuria Triana Toribio have explained, three women were implicitly invited to become "autores de cine" upon their acceptance into the Official Film School: Josefina Molina (the School's first woman graduate), Pilar Miró, and Cecilia Bartolomé.

In contrast to their predecessors, this cohort of women directors did explicitly view and present themselves as auteurs, though they each adopted a different perspective on the intersection of film authorship with gender issues, with Miró most vehemently seeking to distance herself from any association with feminism or a "cine de mujer" (women's cinema) (Triana Toribio 2002; Vernon 2002: 97). Yet all three faced similar challenges. Though ostensibly trained to become auteurs, their first films were all commissioned works, and they sometimes sidestepped original stories by opting for "quality" literary adaptations (Vernon 2002: 98) – a practice at odds with Truffaut's original conceptualization of a "cinéma d'auteur" but that Miró would later promote when she became Director General of Film in 1982. Their work in television and their early association with B-genre films were subject to a disparagement not experienced by male colleagues who had taken similar professional paths, and reviewers frequently employed essentialist clichés to belittle these women directors' projects (Triana Toribio 2002: 87–8). However, many of the films the three created from the 1970s to the 1990s present an incisive engagement with the complex political challenges the nation faced in the aftermath of Franco's death, including the ongoing problem of gender discrimination; some of their works are formally inventive as well. In her treatment of the breakdown of a marriage between two well-known Spanish actors in *Función de noche / Night*

Performance (1981), for instance, Molina cannily melds melodrama and cinéma vérité in order to dissect the institutional repression of Francoism, even as she exposes gendered behaviors as essentially performative (Martin-Márquez 1999: 202–17; Vernon 2002: 103–4). Bartolomé's *Vámonos, Bárbara / Let's Go, Barbara* (1977) hijacks the male-dominated road movie genre by literally and figuratively placing female characters in the driver's seat, foregrounding Spanish women's desires for multifaceted forms of liberation while condemning the sexism and homophobia that continued to be reinforced by law even after the end of the dictatorship (Vernon 2002: 101; Pérez 2008). While Miró addresses the nation's legacy of violence in *El crimen de Cuenca / The Cuenca Crime* (1981), subversively exposing abject male bodies, in *Gary Cooper, que estás en los cielos / Gary Cooper, Who Art in Heaven* (1980) it is constraints upon the female body that are foregrounded, as film production is conflated with ill-fated reproduction (a uterine cancer suffered by the film director-protagonist) in order to allegorize resistance to women's authorship (Martin-Márquez 1999: 141–82; Vernon 2002:107–10).

While all three directors were compelled to negotiate the gendered valences of the predominantly auteurist paradigms of the time, Cecilia Bartolomé's transition-era documentary *Después de … / Afterwards …* (1981–3) also calls forth the legacy of alternative modes of filmmaking that depart from auteurism.[9] Directed in collaboration with her brother, José Bartolomé, who assisted Patricio Guzmán on *La Batalla de Chile / The Battle of Chile* (1974–9), the documentary is an heir to the more militant and sometimes clandestine forms of film production that emerged in a number of contexts in the 1960s and 1970s and that (in theory at least) eschewed the ethos of individualism so essential to the *politique des auteurs*. One of the most significant representatives of this tendency in Spain is Helena Lumbreras, who (co)directed eleven films from 1968 to 1983 and who, as María Camí-Vela observes, "se posiciona en contra del concepto de cine de autor para realizar un cine colectivo cuyos objetivos (informar, educar, y movilizar) se conciben desde y para la clase trabajadora, incluyendo a la mujer" (positions herself in opposition to the concept of author cinema in order to produce a collective cinema whose objectives (to inform, educate, and mobilize) are conceived from and for the working class, including women) (2009: 208). It is important to note, however, that Lumbreras' works do not prioritize gender over class-based analysis. Her career perhaps reflects the acute tensions of "double militancy" experienced by Spanish women on the left (Vernon 2002: 102), which may explain the fact that feminist filmmaking collectives never prospered in Spain. Lumbreras' collaborators were men, and it has taken their efforts, in conjunction with a number of pointedly "auteurist" endeavors initiated over the last five years – film series, symposia, homages, and academic publications – to rescue Lumbreras (who passed away in 1995) from almost complete critical oblivion.

Since the 1990s, the number of women directors working in Spain has increased dramatically relative to earlier periods, and the *cine de autor* model has again tended to dominate (Camí-Vela 2005: 33).[10] Rosanna Maule has argued that, in an era (problematically) characterized as "postfeminist," women filmmakers have often found it more strategic to represent themselves as "gender neutral" film authors, exercising "a type of agency premised on pragmatic and localized tactics of personal and professional affirmation that purposefully ignore sexual difference and gendered identity as binding and limiting concepts" (2008: 192–3). This attitude is perhaps best represented by Isabel Coixet, the most visible Spanish woman director beyond the nation's borders, and the first, for example, to be invited to screen a film at the Cannes Film Festival (see Chapter 19). Coixet has insisted that, if she were a man, her first feature film, shot in Barcelona in 1989, would not have been cruelly derided by Spanish critics, nor would her filmmaking career have been so difficult (Febrés 2008: 30). Coixet's second feature was filmed outside Spain (in the United States) and was not undertaken until 1996, after she had already established a successful career in advertising, a move that eventually enabled her to deploy one of the tactics of her earlier predecessors Mariscal and Aleixandre: founding her own production company, Miss Wasabi Films (see Chapter 14). Nuria Triana Toribio, Valeria Camporesi, and Belén Vidal all contend that Coixet carefully marshals her marketing expertise in order to construct her image as auteur. Like Pedro Almodóvar, Coixet keeps fans apprised of her activities through an eye-catching website (http://misswasabi.com); she also makes frequent appearances on television and in a wide variety of public cultural fora (Triana Toribio 2006: 50–1). The global range of Coixet's "authorial signature" is becoming increasingly evident as she continues to shoot many of her films abroad, and as she has expanded into high-profile forms of international installation art (such as her enormous animatronic (male) infant – "Miguelín" – in the Spanish Pavillion at the 2010 World Expo in Shanghai). As Vidal has asserted, "through such carefully staged interventions, the director inserts herself into a preferred lineage of cinephile filmmakers, bypassing other more contested categories such as 'Spanish director' or even 'Spanish woman director'" (2008: 222).

Coixet's status as international auteur, however, is exceptional among contemporary Spanish women directors, who continue to experience significant marginalization. Just eight percent of Spanish films are directed by women, while only twenty percent have women in significant production roles – statistics that are now available on the website of CIMA (Asociación de Mujeres Cineastas y de Medios Audiovisuales (Association of Women in Cinema and Audiovisual Media); www.cimamujerescineastas.es). CIMA, which currently boasts two hundred members, was formed in 2006 to elevate the numbers and position of women working in the nation's film industry and to foster the creation of less distorted images of women in the media. But, as Susan Larson has underlined, the effort has been controversial: when the subject of CIMA was raised in a joint interview, "sparks flew" between Icíar Bollaín, one of the organization's founding members, and Gracia Querejeta, who belongs instead to ARPA (Asociación de Realizadores y Productores Audiovisuales/Association of Filmmakers and Audiovisual

Producers). Querejeta characterized CIMA as an "error," an initiative that would only reify the segregation of women filmmakers (Sardá 2007).[11]

CIMA's impact on the Spanish film industry remains to be seen. Until strategic forms of collaboration and activism among women filmmakers are proven effective, then, it seems likely that many of Spain's female directors will continue to prefer to engage in a more "gender neutral" practice of strategic auteurism.

Notes

1 See Robert Monell's blog: http://robertmonell.blogspot.com. See also http://franconomicon.wordpress.com, a blog in Spanish written by Álex Mendíbil.

2 For Landis and Clifford (2002: 177), "The king of the Deuce Eurosex movie was and is Jess Franco." The same authors note that Franco's *99 mujeres / Island of Despair* (1968) and *Necronomicón* (aka *Succubus*, 1969) were among the first films to be awarded X tags once the MPPA ratings were created, and were shown alongside "violent thrillers known as giallos, cannibal vomitoriums and zombie rip-offs" (2002: 177).

3 In the same year (1991), Aguilar organized a Franco retrospective at Filmoteca Española; Freixas and Bassa interviewed him for *Archivos de la Filmoteca* (Freixas and Bassa 1990–1); and Aguilar and Freixas (1990–1) produced a Franco filmography in *Dezine*. Aguilar, Freixas, and Bassa were the main contributors to the 1990–1 *Dezine* special issue on Franco's work (*Dezine* 1990–1: 4–11, 12–23).

4 Franco's relationship with pulp writing and pulp movies is undeniable when most of his filmic output is considered: the well-known intensity of his cultural production and the time constraints of demanding production schedules, the repetition of limited story plots and the interchangeable use of stock characters and devices, and the rhetorical excess and inclusion of shock elements.

5 A similar argument could be made of his jazz obsession or his love for comics, genre cinema, and pop culture in general.

6 While the long-dominant critical focus on the independent auteur has been supplemented in recent years by the turn to exploration of non-elite and studio-based filmmaking, ironically that "corrective" gesture has often itself adopted an auteurist stance, establishing an alternative pantheon of revered popular (male) directors that continues to marginalize the majority of other participants in filmmaking.

7 Together with more than fifty women working as assistant editors, the directories for 1956 and 1962 list the following female editors-in-chief: Teresa Alcocer López, Mercedes Alonso Ciller, María Rosa Ester Güera, Rosa G. Salgado, Mercedes Gimeno García, Ángela Grau Ralla, Margarita Ochoa, Sara Ontañón Fernández, Josefa Orduña López, María Paredes Martín, Gaby Peñalva Elzo, Magdalena Pulido Martín, Petra Rodríguez García, and Pilar Serrano García (Cuevas 1956: 469–70; Valle Fernández 1962: 569–73).

8 They had been preceded by Helena Cortesina and Rosario Pi, who directed films in the pre-Civil War (and preauteurist) period (Martin-Márquez 1999: 6–7, 49–84).

9 Margarita Aleixandre also became involved in alternative forms of filmmaking after she and Rafael Torrecilla left Spain (out of frustration over Aleixandre's inability to dissolve her first marriage) and ended up in revolutionary Cuba. Aleixandre was

quickly recruited by ICAIC, the state-run Cuban film production company, where she served as executive producer on seven films, including some of Tomás Gutiérrez Alea's early work, such as *La muerte de un burócrata / Death of a Bureaucrat* (1966). But Aleixandre eventually lost patience with ICAIC's internal politics. For more on the director's experiences, see Camí-Vela's published interview (2007).

10 In their published conversations, Isabel Coixet and Cesc Gay argue that all Spanish filmmakers in Spain are forced to function as auteurs, since Spanish producers no longer pursue commissioned works; both acknowledge, however, that in the contemporary context auteurism is not necessarily divorced from more commercial forms of filmmaking (Febrés 2008: 53–4).

11 I am indebted to Susan Larson's unpublished paper (Larson 2009) for this information.

References

Aguilar, C. (1999) *Jess Franco. El sexo del horror*. Florence: Glittering Images.

Aguilar, C. and Freixas, R. (1990–1) Filmografía. *Dezine* 4: 61–3.

Andrew, D. (2000) The Unauthorized Auteur Today. In: Stam R. and Miller T. (eds.) *Film and Theory: An Anthology*. Oxford: Blackwell, pp. 20–9.

Ángulo, J. (2000) Un caudaloso río subterráneo. Entrevista con José Luis García Sánchez. *Nosferatu* 3 (April): 61–5. Online at: http://bib.cervantesvirtual.com/bib_autor/Azcona/estentre.shtml (accessed July 29, 2011).

Bardem, J. A. (1962) *Muerte de un ciclista* (film script). Xalapa: Universidad Veracruzana.

Bardem, J. A. (2002) *Y todavía sigue: Memorias de un hombre de cine*. Barcelona: Ediciones B.

Borau, J. L. (1998) *Diccionario del cine español*. Madrid: Alianza.

Brecht, B. (1968 [1942]) Hollywood. In: *Poemas y canciones*. Alianza Editorial: Madrid, p. 133.

Brossa, J. (1997) *Poesía visual*. Valencia: IVAM Centre Julio González.

Camí-Vela, M. (2005) *Mujeres detrás de la cámara: Entrevistas con cineastas españolas 1990–2004*. Madrid: Ocho y Medio.

Camí-Vela, M. (2009) Entre la esperanza y el desencanto: El cine militante de Helena Lumbreras. In: Aranda, D., Esquirol, M., and Sánchez-Navarro, J. (eds.) *Puntos de vista: Una mirada poliédrica a la historia del cine*. Barcelona: UOC, pp. 207–23.

Caputo, J. D. (ed.) (1997) *Deconstruction in a Nutshell: A Conversation with Jacques Derrida*. New York: Fordham University Press.

Caughie, J. (1981) *Theories of Authorship*. London: Routledge.

Cela, C. J. (1994 [1949]) Un verdugo. In: *El gallego y su cuadrilla y otros apuntes carpetovetónicos*. Barcelona: RBA, pp. 258–68.

Cerón Gómez, J. F. (1998) *El cine de Juan Antonio Bardem*. Murcia: Universidad de Murcia.

Colpi, H. (1956) Dégradation d'un art: Le montage. *Cahiers du Cinéma* 11 (65): 26–9.

Company, J. M. (2003) Torturas del espíritu: A propósito de *Angustia* (1947) y *Balarrasa* (1950). In: Castro de Paz, J. L. and Pérez Perucha, J. (eds.) *Tragedia e ironía: El cine de Nieves Conde*. Ourense: Festival Internacional de Cine, pp. 19–27.

Crisp, C. (1987) The Rediscovery of Editing in French Cinema, 1930–1945. In: O'Regan, T. and Shoesmith, B. (eds.) *History on/and/in Film*. Perth: History and Film Association of Australia, pp. 57–67.

Cuevas, A. (1956) *Anuario del cine español 1955–56*. Madrid: Sindicato Nacional del Espectáculo.

Dezine (1990–1) *Jesús Franco: Francotirador del cine español*. Special issue of *Dezine* 4.

Egido, L. G. (1958) *Bardem*. Madrid: Visor.

Erice, V., García de Dueñas, J., San Miguel, S., et al. (1961) *Plácido* de Luis Berlanga. *Nuestro Cine* 5: 47–51.

Evans, J. (2007) Pudovkin and the Censors: Juan Antonio Bardem's *Muerte de un ciclista*. *Hispanic Research Journal* 8 (3): 253–65.

Febrés, X. (ed.) (2008) *Isabel Coixet i Cesc Gay: Converses trascrites per Xavier Febrés*. Barcelona: La Magrana.

Franco, J. (2004) *Memorias del tío Jess*. Madrid: Aguilar.

Freixas, R. and Bassa, J. (1990–1) El increíble hombre mutante (Entrevista con el heterónimo Jesús Franco). *Archivos de la Filmoteca* 8 (December–February): 39–51.

Guerrero, M. (ed.) (2001) *Joan Brossa o la revuelta poética*. Barcelona: Generalitat de Catalunya / Fundació Joan Brossa / Fundación Joan Miró.

Harguindey, Á. S. (1998) *Conversaciones con Rafael Azcona y Manuel Vicent*. Madrid: Alfaguara.

Hawkins, J. (2000) The Anxiety of Influence: Georges Franju and the Medical Horrorshows of Jess Franco. In: *Cutting Edge, Art-Horror and the Horrific Avant-garde*. Minneapolis: University of Minnesota Press, pp. 87–113.

Heredero, C. F. (1997) Azcona frente a Berlanga. Del esperpento negro a la astracanada fallera. In: Cabezón, L. A. (ed.) *Rafael Azcona, con perdón*. Logroño: Ayuntamiento de Logroño / Instituto de Estudios Riojanos, pp. 307–28.

Heredero, C. F. (2008) *Pedro Beltrán, la humanidad del esperpento*. Murcia: Filmoteca Regional Francisco Rabal.

Kinder, M. (1993) *Blood Cinema: The Reconstruction of National Identity in Spain*. Berkeley: University of California Press.

Landis, B. and Clifford, M. (2002) The Liberty and the Cinerama: Showcases for Eurosleaze. In: *Sleazoid Express*. New York: Fireside, pp. 177–213.

Larson, S. (2009) Gender Difference: Social Realism and the Films of Icíar Bollaín. Women on the Other Side of the Lens. Unpublished conference paper (University of Washington, April 24).

Llinás, F. (1995) *José Antonio Nieves Conde: El oficio del cineasta*. Valladolid: Semana Internacional de Cine.

López, J. A (n.d.) Edgar Neville el primer director español de culto. Online at: www.grancanariaweb.com / cine / edgar / lopez.htm (accessed September 18, 2010).

Marsh, S. (2006) *Popular Spanish Film Under Franco: Comedy and the Weakening of the State*. Basingstoke: Palgrave.

Martín, A. (2002) Fictions of Equality: Rethinking Melodrama and Neorealism in Ana Mariscal's *Segundo López, aventurero urbano*. In: Ferrán, O. and Glenn, K. M. (eds.) *Women's Narrative and Film in Twentieth-Century Spain*. New York: Routledge, pp. 59–74.

Martin-Márquez, S. (1999) *Feminist Discourse and Spanish Cinema: Sight Unseen*. Oxford: Oxford University Press.

Maule, R. (2008) *Beyond Auteurism: New Directions in Authorial Film Practices in France, Italy, and Spain since the 1980s*. Bristol: Intellect.

Minguet, J. M. (2004) Las vacilaciones iniciales de Bardem (a propósito de *Cómicos* y *Felices Pascuas*). In: Castro de Paz, J. L. and Pérez Perucha, J. (eds.) *El cine a codazos: Juan Antonio Bardem*. Ourense: Festival Internacional de Cine, pp. 63–70.

Monterde, J. E. and Riambau, E. (1990) Volver para perseverar (entrevista con Pere Portabella). *Archivos de la Filmoteca* 7: 27–33.

Museu d'Art Contemporani de Barcelona (1999) *Grup de Treball (exhibition catalog).* Barcelona: MACBA.

O'Brien, G. (1993) *A Ticket to Hell. In: The Phantom Empire. Movies in Mind of the 20th Century.* New York: W. W. Norton and Company, pp. 173–96.

Pavlović, T. (2003) Transgressive Bodies of the Other Franco. In: *Despotic Bodies and Transgressive Bodies: Spanish Culture from Francisco Franco to Jesús Franco.* Albany: SUNY Press, pp. 107–22.

Pedraza Jiménez, F. B. and Rodríguez Cáceres, M. (2000) *Manual de literatura española.* Vol. XIII: *Posguerra: Narradores.* Pamplona: Cénlit Ediciones.

Pérez, J. (2008) Spanish Women behind the Wheel: Gendering the Transition to Democracy in *Vámonos, Bárbara. Revista de Estudios Hispánicos* 42: 215–36.

Perriam, C. (2004) Heterosociality in *Segunda piel* (Gerardo Vera, 2000) and *Sobreviviré* (Alfonso Albacete and David Menkes, 1999): Strong Women, or the Same Old Story? In: Marsh, S. and Nair, P. (eds.) *Gender and Spanish Cinema.* Oxford: Berg, pp. 151–63.

Riambau, E. (2000) Una manera de ver el mundo. Entrevista con Rafael Azcona. In: *Rafael Azcona.* Special issue of *Nosferatu*: 4–28.

Riambau, E. and Torreiro, C. (1998) *Guionistas en el cine español. Quimeras, picarescas y pluriempleo.* Madrid: Cátedra.

Roldán Larreta, C. (2003) *Los vascos y el séptimo arte: Diccionario enciclopédico de cineastas vascos.* Donostia-San Sebastián: Filmoteca Vasca.

San Miguel, S. and Erice, V. (1962) Rafael Azcona, iniciador de una nueva corriente cinematográfica. *Nuestro Cine* 15: 2–7.

Sardá, J. (2007) Icíar Bollaín y Gracia Querejeta: *Mataharis* y *Siete mesas* a competición. *El Cultural* (September 20). Online at: www.elcultural.es/articulo_imp.aspx?id=21259 (accessed August 30, 2010).

Surcos (1960) *Esquemas Film-Ideal* 45.

Tombs, P. and Tohill C. (1995) The Labyrinth of Sex. The Films of Jesús Franco. In: *Immoral Tales. Sex and Horror Cinema in Europe 1956–1984.* London: Titan Books, pp. 77–133.

Torres, A. M. (1999) *Diccionario Espasa del cine español.* Madrid: Espasa-Calpe.

Torres, A. M. and Molina Foix, V. (1969) Nocturno año 30. Introducción a Pedro Portabella. *Nuestro Cine* 91: 26–33.

Triana Toribio, N. (2000) Ana Mariscal: Franco's Disavowed Star. In: Sieglohr, U. (ed.) *Heroines without Heroes: Reconstructing Female and National Identities.* London and New York: Cassel, pp. 184–95.

Triana Toribio, N. (2002) Transitions that Count: Josefina Molina. *International Journal of Iberian Studies* 15 (2): 84–90.

Triana Toribio, N. (2006) Anyplace North American: On the Transnational Road with Isabel Coixet. *Studies in Hispanic Cinemas* 3 (1): 47–64.

Truffaut, F. (2008 [1954]) A Certain Tendency in French Cinema. In: Grant, B. K. (ed.) *Auteurs and Authorship: A Film Reader.* Oxford: Blackwell, pp. 9–18.

Valle Fernández, R. del. (1962) *Anuario español de cinematografía.* Madrid: Sindicato Nacional del Espectáculo.

Vernon, K. (2002) Screening Room: Spanish Women Filmmakers View the Transition. In: Ferrán, O. and Glenn, K. M. (eds.) *Women's Narrative and Film in Twentieth-Century Spain.* London: Routledge, pp. 95–113.

Vicent, M. (1981) *Retratos de la transición*. Madrid: Ed. Penthalon.

Vidal, B. (2008) Love, Loneliness and Laundromats: Affect and Artifice in the Melodramas of Isabel Coixet. In: Beck, J. and Rodríguez Ortega, V. (eds.) *Contemporary Spanish Cinema and Genre*. Manchester: Manchester University Press, pp. 219–38.

Zumalde Arregi, I. (1997) Surcos. In: Pérez Perucha, J. (ed.) *Antología crítica del cine español, 1906–1995: Flor en la sombra*. Madrid: Cátedra, pp. 294–6.

Zunzunegui, S. (1997) Angustia. In: Pérez Perucha, J. (ed.) *Antología crítica del cine español, 1906–1995: Flor en la sombra*. Madrid: Cátedra, pp. 227–9.

Zunzunegui, S. (2005) *Los felices sesenta. Aventuras y desventuras del cine español (1959–1971)*. Barcelona: Paidós.

Further Reading

Azcona, R. (1999) *Estrafalario*, vol. I (includes *Los muertos no se tocan, nene*; *El pisito*; *El cochecito*). Madrid: Alfaguara.

Balbo. L. (ed.) (1993) *Obsession: The Films of Jess Franco*. Berlin: Graf Haufen and Frank Trebbin.

Camí-Vela, M. (2007) Una cineasta española en la Revolución cubana. *El Viejo Topo* 231 (April): 100–7.

Expósito, M. (ed.) (2001) *Historias sin argumento: El cine de Pere Portabella*. Barcelona: Ediciones de la Mirada/MACBA.

Fanés, F. (2008) *Pere Portabella: Avantguarda, cinema, politica*. Barcelona: Filmoteca de Catalunya.

García Ferrer, J. M. and Martí Rom (1975) *Pere Portabella*. Barcelona: Cine Club de Ingenieros.

Lucas, T. (1990) How to Read a Franco Film. *Video Watchdog* 1: 18–34.

Lucas, T. (2010) Jess Franco's Declaration of Principles: How to Read the Early Films 1959–67. *Video Watchdog* 157: 16–49.

Marsh, S. (2010) The Legacies of Pere Portabella: Between Heritage and Inheritance. *Hispanic Review* 78 (4): 551–67.

Rubio, R. (ed.) (1986) *La comedia en el cine español*. Madrid: Imagfic 86/Dicrefilm.

Part III

Genre

7

Comedy and Musicals

Steven Marsh, Chris Perriam, Eva Woods Peiró, and Santos Zunzunegui

Comedy in Spanish Cinema: An Overview (Steven Marsh)

In 1962 the future writers Manuel Vázquez Montalbán and Salvador Clotas were arrested and jailed for publically singing "Asturias, patria querida" (Asturias, beloved fatherland) in solidarity with striking Asturian miners suffering repression unleashed by the Francoist state in northern Spain. Three years earlier, Tony Leblanc and Antonio Ozores had led a rousing chorus of gulled foreign tourists in a drunken rendition of the same song in the 1959 comedy *Los tramposos / The Swindlers* (Pedro Lazaga). While the coincidence is just that, coincidence, it is nonetheless a telling one. Comedy has an uncanny knack of emerging in the most unlikely and unexpected of circumstances; the politics of comedy often depends on the coincidental and the arbitary. Indeed, it is precisely this kind of incongruous juxtaposition that constitutes the comic.

Often based on misunderstandings, things out of place, confusion, impotence, the thwarting of desire, and deviations from convention, comedy is so broad and contradictory a field that it is practically impossible to reach a critical consensus on its substance. Is it conservative in generating a sense of wellbeing designed to innure the spectator against harsh reality? Theodor Adorno and Max Horkheimer (2002: 112) famously wrote that "Fun is a medicinal bath. The pleasure industry never fails to prescribe it." Is it reactionary, as the abundance of racist, sexist, and homophobic jokes might suggest? Or is it subversive and transgressive; does it hold up a critical mirror to corrupt, self-satisfied, and hypocritical power? These are the broad fields within which comedy is frequently located. Meanwhile, although there is little consensus as to the "essence" of comedy, there is general agreement

A Companion to Spanish Cinema, First Edition. Edited by Jo Labanyi and Tatjana Pavlović.

that it has a complex relation to cultural identities as produced by the connections between comedy and national or ethnic discourse. We often talk of a distinctive British sense of humor (one whose articulation marks a differential from other predominantly English-speaking countries). Likewise, it is a commonplace to refer to Jewish humor and point to a long tradition of Jewish comedians. In the case of Spain, there are theatrical and musical traditions stretching back to the medieval period that resonate in cinema and often have an ironic relevance to the contradictory impulses of the historical conjuncture (in Luis García Berlanga's 1963 *El verdugo / The Executioner*, for example, the popular traditional scatological figure, the *caganer* – who defecates in a corner of the Catalan nativity scene – is in one sequence ironically juxtaposed to images of the nation's modernization process). But, as Bakhtin (1984) has demonstrated in his work on medieval popular culture, such comic traditions are not exclusive to Spain. Salaün (1990), one of the most respected authorities on the *género chico* (the amalgam of short popular theatrical and musical forms from which, together with the longer *zarzuela* (operetta), much of today's Spanish film comedy derives), has criticized the critical tendency within Spain to adopt a specific taxonomy so as to create a false sense of difference.

However, to insist that popular culture exceeds national frontiers is not to deny the importance of local specificity and topicality, upon which comedy thrives. Indeed, while making claims to universality, comedy is often – and most effectively – locally specific in its frame of reference. In this Spain is indeed – albeit paradoxically – emblematic. Comedy is considered by many as the distinctively national "form" – from the picaresque novel to Pedro Almodóvar or the work of contemporary filmmakers such as Santiago Segura and Álex de la Iglesia. Yet invariably what is comic conflicts with what is national. Berlanga's apparent lack of success abroad, for example, has often been attributed to a kind of "untranslatable" national sense of humor, while Almodóvar has been criticized at home precisely for being overly accessible to a public beyond national frontiers. Indeed, Berlanga provides us with one of the most graphic examples of the double-edged reception to which film comedy is susceptible, in the famous controversy that greeted the screening of *El verdugo* at the 1963 Venice film festival. Berlanga's film was attacked first by Italian anarchists who misread it as an apology for Francoism, and then by the Spanish Ambassador to Italy at the time, Alfredo Sánchez Bella, who was outraged by what he saw as a "slander" of Spain.

Film comedy has from its beginnings been marked by a particular physicality; by exacerbated, hyperbolic gesture; by the grotesque; by deformation; and by corporeal evacuation (as will be discussed later in this chapter). While comedy often plays upon physical deformation (the fatness or shortness of its protagonists, large noses, baldness, crossed eyes), it is itself a mutant form, bifurcating, unfolding, and unfinalized; unfinalized in the sense of Bakhtin's carnival, in which the consuming, defecating body – and its corresponding social corpus – dies and is renewed. The mutant nature of comedy corresponds to a notion of being as a process of constantly becoming, a metaphysical struggle at the center of comic disorder (Marsh 2006). One of the enduring life-inspiring elements of comedy is precisely the use of laughter in the face of mortality: laughing at death and death by laughter constitute key elements in a folk tradition that dates from antiquity to the contemporary period. In Spanish film, one need only look to Álex de la Iglesia's 1999 *Muertos de risa / Dying of Laughter*. Popular comedy is here closely related to – and occasionally overlaps with – horror. In filmic terms, traditional critical theory has tended to label both collectively as genre cinema to distinguish them from arthouse productions, thus establishing another hierarchy – which is ironic, since the erosion of hierarchy is what comedy is about.

Comedy is largely, though not exclusively, an urban phenomenon; indeed, it is often a product of the clash of rural and urban cultures, of traditional and modern outlooks, and, as such, a sign of uneven development and its contradictions. This motif is evident in the prevalence of different kinds of city comedies, whether socially oriented and realist, as in Marco Ferreri's *El pisito / The Little Apartment* (1958), or escapist, of which Fernando Palacios' *La gran familia / The Big Family* (1962, discussed below) and its sequels are representative. In this escapist vein, one thinks of the plethora of productions featuring one of the more ignominious stars of this kind of comedy in the 1960s, Paco Martínez Soria. Whether realist or diversionary, comedy is unquestionably a social force. It is the preserve of life's losers; the marginalized, the displaced, the downtrodden. It is often dependent on local forms of speech (such as the distinctive accents of Madrid nightwatchmen, almost exclusively from Galicia and Asturias) and recognizable stock-in-trade types (from rogues to mothers-in-law). A pioneer of the early period, Benito Perojo (who reappears later in this chapter) had made use of a Chaplinesque character, Peladilla, and his work combines liberal sophistication and cosmopolitanism – as in *Rumbo al Cairo / Bound for Cairo* (1935) – with filmic sketches (*sainetes*) full of the local color and customs of central Madrid, as in *Es mi hombre / He's My Man* (1934) and *La verbena de la paloma / Festival of the Virgin of the Dove* (1935). A contemporary of Perojo, Edgar Neville – a precursor of and mentor to Berlanga's generation, trained, like several Spanish directors of his time, in the Hollywood studios of the late 1920s and early 1930s – had commenced his career in Spain as a screenwriter on the legendary comedy *La traviesa molinera / It Happened in Spain* (Harry d'Abbadie d'Arrast, 1934), now lost. In the 1930s, Neville would make such tragicomedies as *El malvado Carabel / Carabel the Wicked* (1935) and *La señorita de Trevélez / The Spinster from Trevélez* (1936) before becoming one of the most interesting directors of the 1940s. On the left of the political spectrum, Luis Buñuel, in his role as executive producer of the Second Republic's attempt to create a secular popular cinema, Filmófono, recognized the potential of comedy in that company's four productions (see Chapter 14). The enterprise also kickstarted the career of the man who, in time, would become Franco's favorite filmmaker, José Luis Saénz de Heredia. Further to the left, Fernando Mignoni's *Nuestro culpable / Our Culprit* (1937) – a comedy that, by combining the spirit of comic reversal and anarchism, exalted the values of theft – was produced by the anarcho-syndicalist federation, the CNT (Confederación Nacional de Trabajadores).

This multifaceted tradition of comedy survived the Civil War with satirical magazines such as *La Ametralladora*, edited by Miguel Mihura while serving on the front with the Nationalists, and later (most famously) *La Codorniz*, with figures such as Mihura, Neville, Antonio de Lara (Tono), and the man destined to become the doyen of Spanish screenwriters, Rafael Azcona (see Chapter 6). Miguel Mihura and his brother Jerónimo would prove key figures in the evolution of modern film comedy in Spain, with Miguel helping to script Berlanga's landmark comedy *¡Bienvenido Mister Marshall! / Welcome Mr. Marshall!* (1953). In the 1940s, Jerónimo – heavily dependent on Miguel's screenwriting skills – would direct such madcap films as *Castillo de naipes / House of Cards* (1943), *Camino de Babel / The Road to Babel* (1945), and *Mi adorado Juan / My Beloved Juan* (1949), with their overtones of screwball comedy and the Marx brothers. Miguel Mihura and Neville had learned their trade working in Los Angeles on Hollywood Spanish-language productions in the late 1920s and early 1930s.

The ambivalence of comedy and its consequent enduring capacity to elude classificatory discourse (critical, national, ethnic) extends to political affiliation. Interviewed live on television in May 2010 at the entrance to one of Madrid's funeral parlors following the death the previous day of Antonio Ozores, whose brother Mariano directed a number of right-wing comedies, actor José Sacristán (politically linked to the Communist Party) recognized a personal debt. "The Ozores," he said, "are like family to me" (Sacristán 2010). The figure of Sacristán and his association with the Ozores family hark back to the mildly ribald comedies of innuendo of the 1960s in which Sacristán often starred; these are reminiscent of the contemporaneous British *Carry On…* series of film comedies, and with origins once again in music hall and burlesque. These hugely popular (and reactionary) films came to be known by the sobriquet *Landismo*, owing to the frequent presence in them of actor Alfredo Landa, playing the caricatured "Latin lover" who preys upon foreign female tourists with an improbable degree of success. These films are still shown regularly on Spanish state television in the Saturday afternoon slot *Cine de Barrio / Neighborhood Movie Theater*. Indeed, it is a measure of the enduring populism of successive political administrations (and of the nuances of nostalgia) that the presenters of *Cine de Barrio* should have switched in 2011 from the seemingly innocent conservativism of Carmen Sevilla to Concha Velasco, an actress well known for her closeness to the ruling Socialist Party (PSOE). Both actresses, in turn, established their reputations in comedies of the 1950s and 1960s.

The death of Franco in 1975 and the easing of film censorship had many consequences for Spanish cinema in general and, while film comedy was undoubtedly marked by certain ruptures associated with the new freedoms, it was also distinguished by formal continuities. The so-called Nueva Comedia Madrileña (New Madrid Comedy) of the late 1970s and early 1980s illustrates this reluctance to make a complete break with the past or with traditional culture. Future

Oscar-winning filmmakers such as Pedro Almodóvar (with his first three full-length films made between 1980 and 1983) and Fernando Trueba (with his 1980 debut feature *Opera prima*) first won critical and commercial acclaim as part of this "movement," but it is their contemporary Fernando Colomo who stands out as the model exponent of film comedy of this period. His first two features, *Tigres de papel / Paper Tigers* (1977) and *¿Qué hace una chica como tú en un sitio como éste? / What's a Girl Like You Doing in a Place Like This?* (1978), are emblematic films of the transition. Both exploit the new-found freedoms of sex, drugs, and rock music within the framework of the urban *sainete* (popular farce). While sex and drugs (as well as political discourse, often lampooned) figure in these films in ways that would have been previously unthinkable, their musical interludes have a similar choral function to the traditionally Madrilenian *chotis* of Neville's 1940s films and the flamenco of those produced by Filmófono in the 1930s. Indeed, the title song of *¿Qué hace una chica como tú en un sitio como éste?*, performed by the Madrid rock band Burning, became one of the anthems of the Madrid counter-cultural movement of the late 1970s and early 1980s, the *movida madrileña*. This film also features – in a typically quirky minor role – Luis Ciges, who has been a constant presence in Spanish cinema (comic and otherwise) from *Plácido* (Berlanga, 1961) to *El milagro de P. Tinto / The Miracle of P. Tinto* (Javier Fesser, 1998).

Ciges appeared again in José Luis Cuerda's *Amanece, que no es poco / Dawn is Breaking, and That is Something* (1988), together with many of the country's leading and most recognizable comic actors of several generations. Of the roster of actors in this film, Manuel Alexandre, Agustín González, Chus Lampreave, and Alfredo Landa – like Ciges – belong to a group that first emerged in the 1950s and 1960s; Antonio Resines and Guillermo Montesinos were stalwarts of the 1980s *comedia madrileña*; while the film's younger actors, notably Gabino Diego and Fernando Valverde, were figures who only came to prominence in the 1990s. Cuerda's comedies of the late 1980s and early 1990s draw on a rich vein of absurdist humour that is suggestive of surrealism. Offbeat and bizarre, *Amanece, que no es poco* has become a comic cult film since its release. Unlike many of the other films discussed here, it is located in the countryside. Cuerda himself has labelled it – and the other two films with which it forms an informal triptych: *Total* (1983) and *Así en el Cielo como en la Tierra / In Heaven as On Earth* (1995) – wryly as "surruralism," but it also feeds on a tradition of rural film comedy indebted to the *sainete* (Berlanga's *¡Bienvenido Mister Marshall!* being an obvious example) and the *zarzuela* (e.g., Fernando Fernán Gómez's *El extraño viaje / Strange Voyage*, 1964). The key features of *Amanece, que no es poco* – reinforced by its rural setting – are its atemporality and its spatial ambiguity. While in an utterly recognizable location – the utopian and originary *pueblo* (village) of the Spanish imaginary – the spectator's expectations are repeatedly displaced by the extraordinary turn of everyday events in this particular rural community. Ever since adapting (with Rafael Azcona) Wenceslao Fernández Flórez's novel *El bosque animado / The Living Forest* (1987), Cuerda – who often makes dramatic, non-comic films – has had a keen sense of the comically magical possibilities of the countryside. Moreover, Cuerda's work of the 1980s and early 1990s, in its exploitation of the comic possibilities of the conjunction of surrealism and the everyday, helps to break down the traditional critical dichotomy between arthouse cinema and popular film.

The persistence of the tradition of Spanish film comedy extends to the present day, most significantly in the figures of Álex de la Iglesia and Santiago Segura. De la Iglesia's 1995 *El día de la bestia / Day of the Beast* combines multiple references to the comedic style of Berlanga and Azcona with the mise-en-scène of the postmodern city. Its hyperbole is expressed through the characteristically deformed bodies of its protagonists in the context of a bustling and violent urban setting in which televisual reproduction serves as both an enticing narcotic and sinister state surveilance. De la Iglesia is seemingly fully conscious of the Bakhtinian comic tradition in which he operates and its potential in the localized circumstances of Spain and its recent history. His 2010 *Balada triste de trompeta / The Last Circus* details the rivalry between two professional clowns (one bold and vicious, the other melancholic) and brings that universal age-old tradition into the sharp focus of historical specificity by means of reference to 1960s pop star Raphael and in the film's precipitous finale at the cross above Franco's tomb at the Valle de los Caídos.

Knowingness, too, is what informs Santiago Segura's continuing *Torrente* series (see Chapter 12). Segura's parody combines the local with the global from its eponymous racist, misogynist antihero (an ex-policeman nostalgic for the Francoist period) to the send up of Sylvester Stallone's Cobra character. Segura plumbs the musical archives of 1960s and 1970s Spanish popular culture in its use of the long-out-of-fashion crooner El Fary. In the same way the *Torrente* series has rescuscitated, after a thiry-year lull, the career of Tony Leblanc, mentioned at the start of this chapter and one of the great stars of film comedy of the 1950s and 1960s.

Bakhtin has termed carnival a "second life" of the people "organized on the basis of laughter" (1984: 17). The term is interesting for reasons to which I will refer later in my discussion of Berlanga's French-produced *Tamaño natural / Grandeur nature / Life Size* (1974). What interests me here is how it suggests both a platonic utopia and a parody, a simulacrum of sorts; something whose relation with an original is intimate while – simultaneously and paradoxically – serving to expose claims to originality. Comedy is thus a process of both masking and unmasking claims to origin. The notion of a "second life" is key to understanding the contradictions of comedy – its tendency to combine and complicate apparent oppositions. In the two case studies that follow, I appropriate Geoff King's observation that comedy is "best understood as a mode rather than as a genre" (2002: 2) in order to avoid the schematic critical division between genre cinema and auteur or arthouse cinema. The following discussion focuses on two films that are not only representative of their respective decades (the 1960s and the 1970s) but also serve to highlight the central elements, outlined above, of a lengthy tradition of film comedy that endures to the present day.

La gran familia (Fernando Palacios, 1962)

La gran familia is not, by any standards, a progressive film, but its ambivalent aspects reveal that even in the most retrograde of comedies certain carnivalesque features emerge. The film is a paean to Francoist notions of happiness; that is, to the joys of procreation irrespective of economic hardship and social realities. Starring Alberto Closas as Carlos, the paternal head of a family of fifteen children (with another on the way) and Amparo Soler Leal as Mercedes, his dutiful and doe-eyed wife, *La gran familia* (the first of what would become a trilogy extending into the democratic period) presents us with an idealized metaphor of the Francoist state in miniature. As has been well documented, the family formed the foundational unit of Francoist ideology, and this film both reflects and dramatizes that fact. From the beginning we can appreciate a relation between the thing (Francoism) and its representation (the family). While this is not to suggest that the latter is a parody of the former, it does point to the potential tension – the contradiction inherent in comedy – between the thing and its representation.

From the outset there is that central element of comedy: excess. In an early establishing sequence, the various members of the family awake early one morning and form an impromptu and cacophonic line of complaint outside the occupied bathroom. The immediate effect is one of cheerful discord amid corporeal function. One by one, the members of the immense brood are thus introduced by means of the Bakhtinian site of the bathroom, the scene of bodily discharge, the unruly preserve of "the material bodily lower stratum" (Bakhtin 1984: 368).

This domestic space suggests the more general importance of constructed space in the film. Carlos is an architectural engineer, "both building the modernizing new Spain and populating it" (Faulkner 2006: 35), and the film is played out against a backdrop of early 1960s commodity culture vying with traditional values – a conflict reflected in the urbanization boom. Carlos' precarious, discontinuous career is representative of the times, with all its connotations of economic modernization. Two central set pieces involve space in different ways and both take place in a festive atmosphere. The first is the holiday that the family take to Tarragona, a collective bonding of the family as unit, complete with the idealized love story of one of the adolescent offspring. The collective displacement to the national margins (it is noteworthy that the family travels to the disruptive confines of Catalonia) constitutes a celebratory interlude before the film's (and the family's) crisis, which concerns the loss of the family's smallest child, Chencho, in the public square, Madrid's Plaza Mayor with its Yuletide market stalls, the day before Christmas.

If this family represents the folksy, benignly dictatorial values of Francoism's image of itself, the Plaza Mayor – Bakhtin's marketplace, "the place for working out a new mode of interrelationship between individuals" where "impenetrable hierarchical barriers" are dissolved (Bakhtin 1984: 123) – poses a potential threat.

Figure 7.1 *La gran familia* (Fernando Palacios, 1962; prod. Pedro Masó Producciones): the godfather, Juan (José Luis López Vázquez), soaks up the sun during the family's holiday in Tarragona.

"The marketplace," writes Bakhtin, "was the center of all that is unofficial; it enjoyed a certain extraterritoriality in a world of official order and official ideology, it always remained 'with the people'" (1984: 153–4). The comic juxtaposition of *La gran familia* lies in the unfolding of the idealized private space of the family within the potentially sinister, dangerous (and morally corrupt) public arena. And, indeed, it transpires that Chencho has been kidnapped – though the word is never used – by a childless (and thus suspect) couple desperate to form a family. The uncontrollable dangers posed by public space cut across other spaces and combine in contradictory mode the traditional and the modern. The space of the public square is medieval – topologically linked to the origin of the urban nucleus – while the intervention of the public in the domestic sphere is produced via television in its public service modality (television in 1962 was controlled exclusively by the state): television proves key to finding the lost Chencho.

Although the childless couple who have adopted/kidnapped Chencho are depicted as sad and misguided figures, morally and physically defective, another childless character in the film, the godfather to the entire family (played by one of the great comic actors of his generation, José Luis López Vázquez) is a figure of pure pleasure (see Figure 7.1). Comically irascible, with moods that swing from irritation to clownishness, and the butt of the family's mirth, he is also, as the owner of a bakery, the source of a seemingly unlimited supply of pastries and cakes. Despite his unreliability, he bankrolls the family, innoculating it against "the virus that threatens its existence," financial instability (Evans 2000: 84). As an ancillary member of the family, he is both inside it and outside it, and his appearance at the family party on Christmas Eve is symptomatic: leaping through the doorway (he is, after all, a threshold figure, not fully a member of the family) as a bouncing jester in full costume, his jocularity is abruptly curtailed – signalled as inappropriate – by the sombre atmosphere he confronts.

Together with the godfather, the family grandfather, played by veteran actor José Isbert (the year previous to his extraordinary role in Berlanga's *El verdugo*), is another marginal and thus potentially disruptive character. These two characters – precisely by virtue of their comic status – provide unwitting alternatives to Carlos' function as father; they both, in different ways, constitute a parody of the patriarch in that they suggest second-hand, *ersatz* versions that either refute blood ties or disturb generational order. Throughout the film the grandfather is allied with the children (he accompanies them on the fateful excursion to the Plaza Mayor). In a comic spatial twist, the grandfather shares a bedroom with Chencho, the youngest child. As Bakhtin observes, the carnivalesque thrives on the "threshold of the grave and the crib" (1984: 21).

Tamaño natural (Luis García Berlanga, 1974)

The choice of a film as bleak and cruel as *Tamaño natural*, whose subject matter is masculine solitude and which ends in suicide, is perhaps an odd one for comedy. And yet, while far removed from the insouciant sunniness of *La gran familia*, it is nonetheless representative of the work of the most emblematic and lacerating exponent of Spanish film comedy: Luis García Berlanga. In spite of the tragic aura that enshrouds it, *Tamaño natural* also contains all the comic elements of Berlanga's corpus: a group of actors that functions as a choral (and cacophonic) foil to a protagonist in plight, a fixation with what Bakhtin terms "bodily topography" (1984: 102–15), and a lampooning of the national. It is also a film that counts on the screenwriting collaboration (habitual in Berlanga since *Plácido*, 1961) of Rafael Azcona, whose humor consistently hinges upon the haplessness of the perennial loser (see Chapter 6).

Tamaño natural is a tragicomic love story of sorts between a Parisian dentist and a life-sized doll that he has imported from Japan (see Figure 7.2). In an early sequence of the film, Michel (Michel Piccoli), at work in his dental surgery, adjusts the braces of a young girl. In a jump cut that switches from the lips of the patient to those of Michel's doll, we see an example of the kind of ironic visual gag in which Berlanga specializes. The jump in continuity and the matching images of the respective mechanical artifices grafted onto the human are symptomatic of the film as a whole. Here we see two Bakhtinian moments: the carnivalesque "second life" of prosthetic virtuality and the importance of the mouth itself. Michel is, after all, a dentist. For Bakhtin, "The encounter of man with the world, which takes place inside the open, biting, rending, chewing mouth, is one of the most ancient, and most important objects of human thought and imagery" (1984: 281).

Figure 7.2 Michel (Michel Piccoli) kisses his new life-size doll in *Tamaño natural* (Luis García Berlanga, 1974; prod. Uranus Productions France).

The other key image of the film is that of the polystyrene mold in which the doll has been delivered. The mold functions as a kind of mnemonic, a polystyrene imprint, a distant plastic echo. Its resonance extends to the parodic familial relation that Michel maintains with the doll (unlike his wife – who in a later sequence will herself imitate the doll – she neither ages nor answers back) as well as operating filmically. Recalling the plastercast images of the Pompeii corpses in Rosselini's 1953 *Viaggio a Italia / Journey to Italy* (another film about matrimonial decay), the mold functions as a comic trace that marks the absence of the thing (the doll) itself. In this respect, it is an ineludible supplement to the doll, just as the doll is a supplementary reminder of the deficiencies (yet more absences) in Michel's life.

*Tamaño natu*ral is one of two films that Berlanga shot outside Spain, and its non-Spanish locations are emphasized from the start. As Michel collects the doll at Orly Airport, we hear the distant notes of "The Marsellaise" drifting within the diegesis. Moments later, as Michel's taxi parks outside his apartment building, the view is of the Eiffel Tower. The final sequence, as Michel's car careers into the Seine, returns us once more, amid comic tragedy (the immortal doll bursting to the surface of the river as Michel plunges deeper to his death in the water), to picture-postcard Paris and another view of the Eiffel Tower. False representation, whether in the form of picturesque tourist imagery or prosthetic artifice, forms *Tamaño natural*'s ironic structure. There is, moreover, an added dimension to the comic processes of simulacra in this film. Michel makes use of a Super 8 camera first to document his life with the doll and then as a surveillance device to determine the apparent faithlessness of his plastic lover. However, unlike *La gran familia*, the (at times delirious) virtuality at the heart of the comic aesthetic of *Tamaño natural* engages directly with social reality. Indeed, it is through its playful interrogation of forms of representation and its surrogates that the film proves to be most effective.

Michel abandons his wife to go and live in a large, old apartment owned by his mother, where he and his plastic doll simulate first a wedding and then its consummation, complete with fake blood stain to demonstrate – performatively – the purity of his new compliant partner. Yet this is not the film's only instance of virtual virginity. In what will become a wholesale parody of the nation, Michel is introduced to a community of expatriate Spaniards through his maid, a ham Andalusian ("You should learn to speak Spanish," she bawls at her employer. "I do. You're the one who doesn't," responds Frenchman Michel Piccoli). In a performance of Spanishness – complete with *paella*, guitar, and *anís* – the group invades Michel's home while he languishes in bed stricken with influenza, and steal the doll. Later the kidnapped doll – an effigy dressed up as the Virgin of the Macarena – is made the centerpiece of a grotesque parody of the Seville Holy Week procession, in another, national example of virtual virginity. On one level representation in surrogate form, the performance of national identity helps to identify the comicity of the film, its comic achievement. "Laughter," writes Butler on the politics of parody, "emerges in the realization that all along the original was derived" (2004: 113). On another level, meanwhile, the radical contrast between Michel's bourgeois surroundings and the very real living conditions of the Spanish emigrant workforce stresses the film's social relevance. Remarkably, in a film whose comedy depends on the incongruity of the verisimilar, on the confusion between reality and falsehood, simulacra and parody do not obscure the real, they reinforce it.

Queridos cómicos: Actors and Entertainment[1] (Santos Zunzunegui)

There have not been many attempts to evaluate the contribution to Spanish cinema made by particular actors in the course of its history, nor their role in embedding in the medium some of Spain's most enduring artistic traditions and developing their cinematic potential. There have been even fewer attempts to map Spanish film actors' various acting styles, and to situate these in the complex, heterogeneous configuration of Spanish cinema as a specific entity. In particular, it has been common, and easy, to underplay the contribution to Spanish cinema by actors as entertainers, in comic or light-hearted roles, as character actors or supporting cast.

Even if, relatively speaking, Spanish cinema's star system is small scale (see Part IV of this volume), it can safely be claimed that it has fashioned a whole gallery of singular types with few equivalents in the national cinemas of neighboring countries, and that their high level of popular acceptance is often attributable to the very concrete way in which specific actors – and the characters played by them – have staged for the camera's benefit a whole repertoire of firmly established popular artistic modes. While, as noted in this chapter's first section, there is in Spanish film comedy a rich vein of exploitation of indigenous popular theatrical and musical forms (*sainete*, *género chico*, *zarzuela*, the *copla* (traditional popular song), and the revue; see also Zunzunegui 2002), it should not be forgotten that this could not have happened without the creative contribution of actors, whose role goes far beyond that of dutifully reciting a written script. For we are not dealing here with high-cultural forms that obey strict rules but with a terrain in which a key role is played, not only by the actor's capacity for improvisation or greater or lesser ability to engage audiences but also by factors such as singularity of performance style, manner of occupying and negotiating space, and bodily presence.

In a pioneering text devoted to the role of actors in Spanish cinema, Juan Miguel Company suggested that:

> Una lectura crítica y germinativa de la Historia del Cine Español, pasaría, entre otras cosas, por la fijación del estatuto teórico en el que se ha basado su star-system y, más concretamente, el del actor secundario. La tradición en la que éste se inserta y sus múltiples perversiones de film en film, nos darían algunas de las claves metodológicas necesarias para acercarnos a un cine al que tanto las aproximaciones sociologistas como las exclusivamente ideológicas han sepultado en un lugar donde es muy posible que sí habite el olvido. (1984: 54)
>
> A critical, productive reading of the history of Spanish cinema would, among other things, explore the conformation of its star system's theoretical underpinnings, particularly with regard to secondary actors. The tradition on which the latter draw and its multiple perversions across different films would give us essential methodological tools for understanding a cinema that sociological or excessively ideological approaches have relegated to what runs the risk of being a place of oblivion.

How, then, can we theorize the cinematic practice of the film actor without falling into a purely technical evaluation of acting styles or into regarding such styles as a mere reflection of social mores? The former approach to the "actor's work" limits itself to describing the various acting methods and techniques (e.g., Actors Studio) available as professional tools; that is, the production of a more or less complete inventory of the different "technologies" that generate what we call "acting." The latter approach considers that actors and their roles can and should be studied, not just on their own terms but as projections for a series of social configurations that themselves become the principal object of study, interposing themselves between the scholar and the actor's on-screen presence. This makes the film actor anything but the physical person who uses his or her body, image, and voice to create a character through a repertoire of technical maneuvers that stage feelings and passions that are not his or her own. For actors project themselves beyond their persons through the characters they take on, fashioning a mask that invites the spectator's complicity. The actor, then, works from the inside out, as the support for a succession of ephemeral, shifting personae: one body, an infinite number of masks. Among these is the mask of comedy, the guise of the entertainer.

If we look at the history of cinema, we can see that there have been various moments when it has been felt that fiction film needed to go beyond codified norms in order to achieve a higher degree of "realism." I will focus on two such moments that have had a major impact on film criticism. When André Bazin (1967–71), in a series of memorable texts originally published between 1946 and 1949, discussed the key characteristics of Italian neo-realism, he stressed that its regime of verisimilitude stemmed in good part from what he called its "neo-realist mix." What was that "mix"? Simply, the careful combination of professional and non-professional actors achieved by Italian filmmakers' casting practices. What specifically interests me here is what this use of "non-actors" was aiming to achieve. As Bazin makes clear, the major aim was to produce a naturalness that would erase any sense of acting. But equally important was the need to use the non-actors' lack of experience and ingenuousness in such a way that they would give the impression of being suited to their part, for which the only thing required was their "physical or biographical likeness" to the characters they were playing. In this respect, what neo-realist filmmakers were intuitively doing was an elementary version of what, in the context of Soviet silent film, Sergei M. Eisenstein had theorized in his 1933–4 film-directing classes at the VGIK (Soviet State Film School) as *tipazh* ("typage") – a technique used in his earlier silent films. Comparing "typage" to the use of masks in the Commedia dell'arte, Eisenstein suggested that the two practices were two sides of the same coin (1949). If the aim of the mask was to make the character's nature clear to the audience, like a kind of ID card, "typage" – while similarly seeking to express a cluster of expressive possibilities in concentrated form – aimed at something radically different: instead of the seven or eight masks used by the Commedia dell'arte, cinema would use an unlimited range of faces. As Eisenstein noted, a face on screen narrates a whole biography. He went on to note that, while the masks of the Commedia dell'arte serve to reinforce and stylize pre-established character roles, the function of "typage" was to offer the audience a face (a figure) able to say it all in terms of social and biological experience. In reality, Eisenstein's ideas put into practice the "phantasmagoria of the *flâneur*" as described by Walter Benjamin (1999: 429): "to read from faces the profession, the ancestry, the character."

These considerations provide the basis for a new form of critical practice, which I propose to term "refiguration," using the expression coined by Mikhail Bakhtin (1989) – an appropriate term in the case of actors who express everything through their figure. An alternative term, closer to home, might be "restylization" – the term used by the literary critic Amado Alonso (1928) to describe the techniques used by the early-twentieth-century Spanish writer Ramón del Valle-Inclán to rework the concept of the real. When talking of the realist orientation of "low" genres, Bakhtin talked of a kind of laughter, produced by sudden close contact, that could subvert respect for certain social objects in such a way that familiarity might lead to unbiased analysis. This ability to make us look anew, though a material contact with the real that produces laughter, is, roughly speaking, what Bakhtin understands by "refiguration." Bakhtin reminded us (1974: 12) that carnivalesque forms (whose popular status is evident) are closely related to animated artistic images – for example, in theater – while stressing the importance in the Middle Ages and Renaissance of buffoons and actors who, as he put it, remained clowns all their lives.

Refiguration is, I suggest, a useful term to describe the cinematic practice of a whole series of actors in whom everything is figurative – that is, on show, visible to the spectator – and whose onscreen presence is that of bodies endowed with autonomy. This autonomy allows them to move from one film to another, one theme to another, one story to another, one narrative situation to another, while remaining always themselves. This is a perverse kind of sameness, evoking the "multiple perversions" noted in the earlier quote by Company as a trait of the secondary actor, and suggesting a model of refiguration as perverse repetition. They are that group of actors who the director Luis García Berlanga described as "cómicos de tripa" (gut actors), who replace "showing" (what actors do) with minimalist performance and psychology achieved through the unique "gestus" (Brecht's term) of the particular. Actors with singular bodies in the extreme; bodies that in some cases tend to the grotesque (the gherkin-shaped head of José Isbert, to take an obvious example), giving material expression to the "models of plastic abjection" that Pedro Salinas (1970) perceived in the characters of Valle-Inclán's *esperpentos* (the term coined by Valle-Inclán to refer to his literary technique of systematic distortion) (see Figure 7.3). Bodies that can sustain certain forms of behavior even in the absence of coherent characterization, through their mere presence on screen. Residual bodies with *gravitas*, that are not afraid to show the signs of age, and the wear and tear of individual experience and of Spain's calamitous history. Bodies inhabited by grainy voices, whose speech is phatic, colorful, metonymic, and hyperbolic, moving between the stutter and onomatopoeia. A signal example is the memorable performance of José Isbert in the police station scene in *La vida por delante* / *Life Ahead* (Fernando Fernán Gómez, 1958), which is not just a Spanish version of *Rashomon* (Akira Kurosawa, 1950) but a singular display of gestuality that seeks to subvert the serious nature of the situation, basing the scene's metafilmic dimension on an attribute of one of those implicated. That attribute is the stutter of Isbert – "el señor bajito" (the short gentleman) – when it is his turn to tell the police officer the details of the traffic accident in which he has been involved; this stutter will end up contaminating the very flow of images, with an element of the diegesis driving the mode of cinematic enunciation.

Let us focus for a moment on a significant but less well known figure, Luis Heredia. Discovered for cinema by Buñuel (his stage training was in the revue), he acted in three of the four films that Buñuel produced for Filmófono (see Chapter 14)

Figure 7.3 The gherkhin-shaped head of José "Pepe" Isbert in *El cochecito* (Marco Ferreri, 1960; prod. Films 59).

in the last years of the Second Republic, re-emerging in 1961 in the role of El Poca, the "gracioso desesperado" (desperate fool) in Buñuel's *Viridiana* (see Figure 7.4). Thin as a stick and utterly shameless, he had under the Republic incarnated the Madrid low-life braggart Angelito (*Don Quintín el amargao / Don Quintin the Bitter* (Luis Marquina, 1935)); Supito, the pickpocket-turned-nanny with his unending pursuit of any bit of skirt (*¿Quién me quiere a mí? / Who Loves Me?* (José Luis Sáenz de Heredia, 1936)); and Tiburcio Canales, the soldier-cum-bootblack who ends up as a cheapsgate Sherlock Holmes (*¡¡Centinela alerta!! / Guard! Alert!* (Jean Grémillon, 1936)), allowing him to develop a notorious gestural repertory and irremediable verbosity. When Buñuel recovered him for *Viridiana*, it would be as a toothless, scheming beggar who uses his verbosity to stir up the other beggars, rubbing salt in every wound. Here, then, is one of those bodies that end up becoming a particular way of giving shape to a world that, without them, would be mired in a uniform greyness, from which they escape though the subtle exaggeration of a tiny detail, the calculated exaggeration of a gesture. These bodies encapsulate a series of performances almost always on the margins, if not against the grain, of the narrative they are supposedly driving forward, displacing it, deferring it, at times making it opaque, finally finding themselves back at its center after multiple to-ings and fro-ings. These are performances that delineate a second text that ends up cancelling (or perhaps giving solidity to) the main narrative in which we more or less believe, creating what Vicente Ponce (1984) has called "surplus narrative value."

It should be stressed that this is possible because of the existence of what has been called the "typically Spanish school" of acting, which, as Vicente Molina Foix

Figure 7.4 Luis Heredia as El Poca, one of the beggars in Buñuel's *Viridiana* (1961; prod. UNINCI / Alatriste).

has noted (1984), survived thanks to the fact that Spanish theater did not undergo the methodological renewals that revolutionalized the European stage in the early decades of the twentieth century. Spanish audiences have remained attuned not so much to the vertiginous replacement of one acting model with another as to the repeated re-encounter with these actors, able through their mere physical presence, to justify the daily renewal of a cinematic or theatrical ritual. This is a skill (and a response) rooted in the popular forms discussed throughout this chapter. What is key is acceptance of the tacit compact of trust between audience and actor, which, by virtue of its continuity and the ever-renewed fascination with the same, turns over time into a familiarity that, in the last instance, allows the transmutation of a body into an index of something other than what it originally seemed to be. Talking of the late-eigthteenth-century *sainetes* of Ramón de la Cruz, José Ortega y Gasset stressed that

> todo su propósito y su valor radicaban en ser algo parecido a lo que hoy son los guiones de las películas: un cañamazo donde las actrices y actores podían lucir sus donaires. De aquí que acabase por hacer de los histriones las figuras mismas de sus argumentos. (1983: 528)
>
> their *raison d'être* and value lay in being the rough equivalent of today's filmscripts: a canvas where actresses and actors could showcase their talents. As a result, their plots came to be figured in the actors themselves.

That substratum would persist to our day, fed by various forms of popular theater, giving birth to the constellation of "cuerpos gloriosos" (glorious bodies)[2] – in most cases relegated time and time again to secondary roles – that have fed Spanish cinema for much of its history, from José Isbert to Javier Gurruchaga, from Guadalupe Muñoz Sampedro to Chus Lampreave. One has only to look at Filmófono's productions of the 1930s, Edgar Neville's films of the 1940s, singular works such as *Historias de la radio / Radio Stories* (Sáenz de Heredia, 1955) and Berlanga's *Plácido* in the 1960s, or *La colmena / The Hive* (Mario Camus, 1983) and *La corte de Faraón / The Pharaoh's Court* (José Luis García Sánchez, 1985) in the 1980s to appreciate the persistence of this particular acting tradition.

We need, then, to define the conceptual space in which these actors move. It is a terrain by definition unstable, a terrain of transit between two opposing poles (that of the "actor proper" and that of the "non-actor") that might appear to be in conflict but that can be negotiated by those with sufficient talent. This is the art of so many Spanish secondary film actors (the Spanish term "cómicos" is really the only appropriate one), and it has a lot to do with caricature as a privileged medium for revealing the man beneath the mask – a mask that displays his fundamental vanity and deformed condition (Gombrich 1968). Precisely for that reason, while the "actor" expresses the singular and the "type" lends his body to habitation by the general, these "queridos cómicos," who navigate the space of the in-between, have the special mission of actualizing the very idea of the particular and the irreducible. This is what guarantees them a permanent place in the memory of Spanish cinema. So too do these entertainers – embodying not only the disruptive comic moment but a plot of their own, an ironic standing-aside from the conventional stories of national cinematic entertainment – become cultural icons, such as those that will be discussed in Part IV of this volume.

The Heyday of the Musical Film (Eva Woods Peiró)

The Spanish musical film had its beginnings in several different performance and literary practices: music theater, comic opera (*zarzuela*), popular plays, circus and vaudeville acts, bullfights, popular novels, and, later, radio shows. During its first three decades, cinema was an unabashed forum for mainly comic spectacles that nevertheless served as vehicles for society's most acute concerns about race, sex, and social mobility. It was precisely such anxieties, folded into the comedy and entertainment of musical films, that contributed to the lasting, even mythic appeal of this genre throughout the twentieth century, peaking from the 1930s to the 1950s. While the musical films discussed in this section are largely musical comedies, some have a strong melodramatic element – and even in the latter case there are usually comic moments since these are, above all, entertainment films.

The resilience of vaudeville during cinema's emergence had a major impact on the direction and shape of later musical film. The cross-fertilization between the two makes it possible to claim – paradoxically – that the musical film's heyday (not just in Spain) stretches back to the period of silent cinema. Live dance and song, on a film set or as a filmed stage performance, were integral to film practice as early as 1905, when Ricardo de Baños filmed *zarzuelas* with the Gaumont Chronophone (Gubern 1993: 5). This dual focus of cinema continued throughout the 1910s, with Segundo de Chomón filming dozens of *zarzuelas* (Fernández Cuenca 1948). It climaxed in the mid-1920s in feature-length films such as *Currito de la Cruz / Currito of the Cross* (Alejandro Pérez Lugín, 1925), *Nobleza baturra / Aragonese Virtue* (Juan Vilà i Vilamala, 1925), and *Gigantes y cabezudos / Carnival Figures* (Florián Rey, 1925). This thematic and structural dependence upon theater would be inscribed in several full-length film adaptations in the 1920s through "silent" song and dance performances that would later be amplified in sound musical remakes; for example, *La verbena de la paloma / Festival of the Virgin of the Dove* (José Buchs, 1921; Perojo, 1935; Sáenz de Heredia, 1963) and *La revoltosa / The Troublemaker* (Rey, 1924; José Díaz Morales 1949, 1963; Orduña, 1969).

Until the end of the 1920s, with the closing of Teatro Apolo, Madrid's premier musical theater, cinema and live entertainment shared the same venues. Films of song, dance, or circus acts were projected in the theaters and cafés where *zarzuelas*, *espectáculos de variedades* (vaudeville variety shows), *revistas* (revues, including the erotic *género ínfimo*), and the *cuplé* (a short narrative song derived from the French *couplet*) were also performed (Salaün 1990: 142–3). Conversely, whole stage sequences found a place within feature films, as did masters of ceremonies. Cabaret, circus, and theater scenes abound in *El negro que tenía el alma blanca / The Black with a White Soul* (Perojo, 1926) and the French-produced *La malchanceuse / La sin ventura / Hapless Woman* (E. B. Donatien and Perojo, 1925–6). *Frivolinas / Bagatelle* (Arturo Carballo, 1926) – a filmed revue of skits that included comedy routines, striptease, orientalist opium homages, and parodies of prostitution – encouraged spectators to imagine a comically irreverent world of drug dens, harems, and raunchy theaters. In *La venenosa / Venemous Woman* (Roger Lion, 1928) the Parisian Cirque d'Hiver was the stage for *cuplé* performer Raquel Meller as Liana, an orientalized trapeze artist. The *cuplé* "La violetera," written by José Padilla for Meller and performed during the circus scenes, became absurdly popular and inspired the score for Chaplin's *City Lights* (1930). According to one anecdote, Meller's nightly performances – while singing she languidly tossed bouquets of violets to the audience – were mimicked by an elephant (*The Living Age* 1928).

Cinema made particular use of the *cuplé*. The performer was usually a singer-showgirl working the cafés, lyric theaters, and low-brow clubs, and the *cuplé*'s themes of lost loves, sexual escapades, poverty, politics, or patriotic feelings developed in close relationship with the nascent star system (Salaün 1990). The opening scene – functioning much like a trailer – of *La gitana blanca / The White Gypsy* (De Baños, 1923; revised version of *Los arlequines de seda y oro / Silk and Gold Harlequins*, 1919) underscores the reciprocal relationship between cinematic spectacle and stage entertainment. The camera opens on a striking woman in an ornate black dress with the traditional Andalusian *mantilla*; she walks away from the camera to the base of a staircase to examine a publicity poster mounted on the wall. As she slowly turns toward the camera, we realize it is Meller herself. Glancing to her left, she beckons coquettishly to a spectator out of the frame, then proceeds up the stairs. In this residual remnant of the peekshow, Meller is a *femme fatale*, emphatically not the picture of innocence or victimhood she will play during the rest of the film. This segment, seemingly irrelevant to the film's plot, orients spectators to the star's extrafilmic status, fusing her erotic appeal with the film's message about racial identity (she is herself a white Gypsy). This kind of proto-trailer prefaced the incorporation of musical numbers by female dancers such as Pastora Imperio in *La danza fatal / Danse Fatale / Dance of Fate* (José de Togores, 1915), La Fornarina (biographed in *La sin ventura*), and Concha Piquer in Lee DeForest's synchronized sound film shorts shot in New York in 1923.

Film adaptations of popular musical theater and variety shows vacillated between semi-respectable light entertainment and sexually explicit comedy. These combinations of cinema and musical shows were seen as a threat by moral and civil authorities who were increasingly alarmed by the encroachment of women and the lower classes into the public sphere. What had been considered a "healthy" genre – the *género chico* (light one-acter) – had declined into the ultimately more profitable *género ínfimo* (naughty act), notorious for its shameless ingénues and sexually suggestive "piernografía" ("leggy" porn) (Retana 1964: 17).[3] Given the financial gains for producers, exploitation of women became more widespread; the theaters and cafés of the *género ínfimo* had become an escape from poverty and mediocrity, and singing *cuplés* was also a way to rise above routine work as an entertainer. When cinema (and later radio) offered similar opportunities, the rise and escape to stardom became a common and enduring theme – as illustrated in the retrospective look back at this period in *El último cuplé / The Last Torch Song* (Orduña, 1957), evoking Meller, and *La violetera / The Violet-Seller* (Luis César Amadori, 1958).

Another lucrative element of the *género ínfimo* and film up to and during the twenties was the raciness perceived in mixing white performers and performers of color, offering what Gubern (2005) describes as a "cosquilleo interracista" (interracial *frisson*). The genres that provided this thrill – blackface, *teatro bufo*, and jazz – were considered the anarchic progeny of African Americans and Cubans. Racialized entertainment with domestic or foreign performers appeared in Madrid as early as the 1880 s (García Martínez 1996). It proliferated during the 1920s in films such as *El negro que tenía el alma blanca*, which was advertised by blackface on the labels of commodity tie-ins and was built around the unself-conscious blackface performance of Raymond de Sarka, the Egyptian actor who played the Afro-Cuban male dancing lead, Peter Wald (see Figure 7.5). Concha Piquer, the famous *cupletista* (singer of *cuplés*) who played the female dancing lead, symbolized white stardom yet put on blackface for a "sambo" scene and later performed the Charleston with Peter. What remains of the sexually irreverent *Frivolinas* confirms that Spanish

Figure 7.5 Peter Wald (Raymond de Sarka), a bellboy and aspiring dancer in *El negro que tenía el alma blanca* (Benito Perojo, 1926; prod. Goya Producciones Cinematográficas). Courtesy of Filmoteca Española.

silent cinema spectacularized and racialized female sexuality by recounting the same lurid social ills that had deliciously scandalized European and American audiences. If *Frivolinas'* songs celebrated opium, its oriental sets and costumes made it clear that the East was the true site of hedonism. Racialized entertainment was also available in the parallel tradition of the Gypsy entertainer. The obsession with Andalusian topics and Gypsy characters spanned the new century, manifesting itself in early silents such as *Amor gitano / Gypsy Love* (Segundo de Chomón, 1910) and surfacing in every decade. Racial visibility and anxiety had coded cultural production from Cervantes to Romantic and turn-of-the-century novels and plays, through to the popular theater of the Álvarez Quintero brothers, which fed the folkloric musical comedy genre. Race remained a salient element in these early films because the stories upon which they were based were themselves obsessed with questions of racial identity. In *La chavala / The Young Lass* (Rey, 1924), a Gypsy girl sings *cante jondo* ("deep song," a particularly guttural form of flamenco) in a *café cantante* (cabaret), as also occurs in *Los claveles de la Virgen / The Virgin's Carnations* (Rey, 1928).

Malvaloca (Perojo, 1926), based on a 1912 play by the Álvarez Quintero brothers, contained the basic ingredients of later folkloric musical films and was readily remade as a film musical in 1942 (Marquina) and again in 1954 (Ramón Torrado).

Its protagonist, Rosita, is a fallen woman from Málaga with a heart of gold whose abusive upbringing had compelled her to seek refuge in the arms of the local playboy (similar plotlines were used in other Andalusian musicals such as *Mariquilla Terremoto / Mariquilla the Fireball* (Perojo, 1939) and *Filigrana* (Marquina, 1949)). Now known as Malvaloca, Rosita emerges from her backstory with a child out of wedlock and better financial prospects owing to – it is assumed – intimate relationships with men. In one scene – a set piece of several *folklórica* narratives (the term *folklórica* applies both to the folkloric film musical and to its female singing star) – we see a blurred double image of Rosita dancing on a table from the perspective of a drunken army officer. Such film musicals, and others such as the twice-remade *La hermana San Sulpicio / Sister San Sulpicio* (Rey, 1927, 1934; Luis Lucia, 1952; an early example of the singing nun cinematic subgenre), displayed a fascination with female singing stars, often associated with Gypsy culture if not ethnicity.

Frequently underlying these treatments of sexualized racial identities is the dry irony of Spanish comedy. *El misterio de la Puerta del Sol / The Mystery of the Puerta del Sol* (Francisco Elías, 1930), arguably the first full-length sound film in Spain (Fernández Cuenca 1948: 276), is, among other things, a witty commentary on the conflict between folkloric and cosmopolitan filmmakers in their attempts to recreate their own entertainment styles on screen. *El misterio*'s organizing motif is a tour de force display of cinematic reflexivity (prevalent in the film musical) in which the cinephile's dream merges with the filmic material. The wannabe movie stars Pompello Pimpollo (the youthful Juan de Orduña, who would later direct several musical films) and Rodolfo Bambolino audition with the foreign director, Edward Carawa – a reference to the North American director Edwin Carewe, who sought to establish sound film in Spain (Sánchez Oliveira 2003: 65). Waiting for their screen test, they flirt with a *cupletista*, Lia de Golfi (a reference to Lya di Putti) and meet two parodic figures, El niño del Mausoleo and La Terele, the latter "more Madrilenian than the Cibeles fountain," having become a Gypsy "out of mere enthusiasm for cinema." The director tells these flamenco fakes to perform "flamenco made in the USA." Watching this pitiful show in the making, spectator Rodolfo falls asleep and dreams a cosmopolitan adventure, macabre and sensationalist, that comprises the bulk of the film. The transition to sound was thus wryly understood by many to be a battle over what kind of entertainment – including musical entertainment – would prevail.

Film musicals ran the gamut of regional folklore – from Aragonese *La Dolores* (Fructuoso Gelabert, 1898, 1908; José Gaspar, 1923; Rey, 1940) and *Nobleza baturra / Aragonese Virtue* (Rey, 1935; Orduña, 1965) to the Arab-orientalist *La canción de Aixa / Aixa's Song* (Rey, 1939). Yet musical films largely preferred female folkloric stars and other white actors playing the role of Andalusian Gypsies. The casting of non-Gypsy actors as screen Gypsies made racial hybridity a key element of these films, in addition to their interracial romance plots. After 1936, musical *españoladas* (the pejorative term used of stereoptypical representations of Spanishness, usually via Andalusian tropes) proliferated with formulaic stories of (usually Gypsy) flamenco dancers/singers and bullfighters, who either entertained or broke the law. It was, as Terenci Moix termed it (1993: 19), the "dictadura del andalucismo escénico" (dictatorship of stage Andalusianism), and race – particularly interracial romance – was a key ingredient. *La gitana blanca*, *Morena Clara / Dark and Bright* (literally "light-skinned brown girl"; Rey, 1936), *Torbellino / Whirlwind* (Marquina, 1941), *Canelita en rama / Cinnamon Flower* (Eduardo García Maroto, 1942), *La cigarra / Cricket* (Rey, 1948), and *La venenosa* (Miguel Morayta's 1949 remake) trumpeted racial hybridity with their Gypsy or Gypsy-associated heroines, covering the color spectrum from white to dark brown. The most paradigmatic of these musicals makes the point through its hit song, "Soy Morena Clara" (I'm the light-skinned brown girl). *Morena Clara* starred Imperio Argentina, the famous half-Gibraltarian, half-Malaguenian singer and dancer, born in Argentina and not the least bit brown.

Despite the demand for Andalusianism, both left- and right-wing camps of the Spanish filmmaking community lamented the lack of true Spanishness in what they considered a vulgar misrepresentation of the nation (Triana Toribio 2003: 14–31). Alternative non-folkloric and cosmopolitan musicals – such as *El bailarín y el trabajador / The Dancer and the Worker* (Marquina, 1936) – challenged Hollywood's economic and ideological domination but were equally criticized, in this case for being degenerate and foreign-inspired. An exception was perhaps Perojo's *La verbena de la paloma* (1935), which brilliantly blended a slick cosmopolitan visuality and fast-paced editing with the Spanish *zarzuela* musical tradition.

In the 1940s and 1950s, the folkloric film musical would predominate, with scores of musical films featuring a Gypsy-*folklórica* in an interracial romance plot that projected a resolution to class (and racial) conflict but also staged the negotiation of different musical styles, with the Andalusian folkloric style inevitably "winning" over bourgeois or foreign musical forms (Labanyi 2002). These films do not so much return to premodern rural scenarios as use rural (and sometimes urban) settings as a stage for the battle between tradition and modernity. Such is the case with *Torbellino*, *Canelita en rama*, *El sueño de Andalucía / The Dream of Andalusia* (Lucia, 1950), *La niña de la venta / The Girl at the Inn* (Torrado, 1951), *Estrella de Sierra Morena* (Torrado, 1952), and *Gloria Mairena* (Lucia, 1952). But it was also in the 1950s that the folkloric genre reached its last breath, exhausting even its most brilliant, self-reflexive parodies. In the course of the 1950s the folklorical musical underwent a dual process of whitening and masculinization (with non-Gypsy male protagonists). Miguel de Molina, who as a highly successful Andalusian singing star had represented a queer masculinity during the Republic, had been driven into exile in 1942. In the mid-1950s, Antonio Molina became a major singing star of the previously female-dominated folkloric musical genre, with an often camp look but playing clearly heterosexual roles, as in *El pescador de coplas / The Fisher of Songs* (Antonio del Amo, 1954), *Esta voz es una mina / This Voice is a Mine* (Lucia, 1956), and *El Cristo de los faroles / Christ of the Lanterns*

Figure 7.6 Camp and masculinity converge in this publicity still of Antonio Molina in miner's overalls in *Esa voz es una mina* (Luis Lucia, 1956; prod. Producciones Cinematográficas Ariel). Courtesy of Video Mercury and Filmoteca Española.

(Gonzalo Delgrás, 1958) (see Figure 7.6). Other leading males such as Jorge Mistral – with Carmen Sevilla in *El caballero andaluz / The Andalusian Gentleman* (Lucia, 1954) – and Luis Aguilar – with Lola Flores in *Pena, penita pena / Oh Sadness, Oh Grief* (Morayta, 1953) – lent the genre a recognizable machismo that nurtured a series of Spanish–Mexican coproductions.

The other notable development of the 1950s was a return, toward the decade's end, to the urban *cuplé* culture that had flourished prior to Francoism. *El último cuplé* (1957), starring Sara Montiel, was arguably postwar Spain's "first authentic 'blockbuster'" (Vernon 2004: 183), dwelling nostalgically on *cuplé* culture but avoiding race – so tied up with early twentieth-century musical entertainment in Spain – entirely. Another nostalgic return to prewar musical culture was *Vampiresas 1930 / Female Vamps 1930* (Jesús Franco, 1962), which – at the same time that a new generation of child singing stars such as Joselito and Marisol was definitively taking over the musical film (see Chapter 11) – replayed the rise of the talkies, this time reintroducing race into the picture. Presenting itself as a tribute to *Singing in the Rain* (Stanley Donen and Gene Kelly, 1952), *Vampiresas* witnesses the demise of silent film through the story of four down-and-out silent film actors and musicians. Dora (Mikaela Wood), a singer and silent film actress pigeonholed as a vamp and "savage Indian," longs to be herself, a wholesome girl from the

Figure 7.7 Spanish entertainers in blackface in *Vampiresas 1930* (Jesús Franco, 1962; prod. Hispamer Films).

Canaries; Trini (Lina Morgan) and two male musicians want to be appreciated by Spanish audiences. With the triumph of sound film, newspapers announce mass suicides of silent film actors and directors, and the job ads only want (Black) jazz musicians. The Spanish artists are thus pitted against foreign performers of color (a nod to *El negro que tenía el alma blanca* (1926; remade by Perojo in 1934 and Hugo del Carril in 1951) and *Some Like it Hot* (Billy Wilder, 1959)), specifically a female jazz ensemble – an apparently random mix of African and African American women. Wearing blackface and (cross-)dressing like the jazz singers, Dora, Lina and friends regain footing in the entertainment world by tricking the women of color into taking the train to Siberia (see Figure 7.7). If *Vampiresas* brought race back into the film musical, as well as introducing transvestism into it, Luis María Delgado's *Diferente / Different* (1962) would dramatically destabilize gender roles with its gay dance fantasy sequences, as well as modernizing the Spanish musical through its nods to *West Side Story* (Jerome Robbins and Robert Wise, 1961) (see Chapter 12).

The nostalgic recycling of folkloric fare continued after 1975 with musical films such as *La corte de Faraón / The Pharaoh's Court* (José Luis García Sánchez, 1985), *Las cosas del querer / The Things of Love* (Jaime Chávarri, 1989, 1995), *Yo soy ésa / I Am the One* (Luis Sanz, 1990), *El día que nací yo / The Day I Was Born* (Pedro Olea, 1991), *La Lola se va a los puertos / Lola Goes off to Sea* (Josefina Molina, 1993), and *La niña de tus ojos / The Girl of Your Dreams* (Fernando Trueba, 1998). In many of these films, the simultaneous hyper-visualization and denial of race would remain an integral feature.

Contemporary Musical Comedy, Sex, and Gender (Chris Perriam)

As we have seen, the Spanish musical lends itself well to the revival mode. Harking back to such already nostalgic show films as *Teatro Apolo / The Apollo Theater* (Rafael Gil, 1950), *Dos chicas de revista / The Two Showgirls* (Mariano Ozores, 1972) starring Lina Morgan, and TVE's variety show *La revista* (1995–6, directed by José Luis Moreno), Spanish revivals reinforce the move away from the idea of the "musical" as defined by its Anglo-American origins (e.g., by the *Diccionario de la Real Academia Española*) by localizing the glamour. Sketches and musical numbers do this in their allusions, musical range, and format; casting is emphatically Spanish, and stereotyping plays its part. A favorite tactic of the show films and programs of the 1970s carries forward into the 1980s and 1990s, harnessing comedy to complicity: sensual Spanish femininity as spectacle is pitted, light-heartedly, against (usually) virile and capable Spanish men. *La corte de Faraón* (1985), for example, is an elaborate and eroticized take on the original biblical operetta,[4] which exploits the sex appeal and frequently scantily clad bodies of both Ana Belén and Antonio Banderas, positioning the latter in the characteristic naif, dim, and weak younger man role of his early career. The humor, in keeping with the vein of comedy outlined in the introduction to this chapter, is corporeal, the music enlivening, and the glamour highlights issues of gender. Similarly localized and sensitized to the gendered body – their lyrics mainly deep in a Southern Spanish and more or less folk-historical stratum of culture and their melodrama linked to erotic distress and the politics of sexuality – are the intense music- and show-based dramas that flourished in the 1990s, such as those listed at the end of the previous section.

Of more contemporary, cosmopolitan resonance, though just as interesting for the tensions between the song work and the gender work embedded in them (Biddle and Fouz Hernández 2012), are two romantic comedies of urban coupledom, part of a mini-boom in battle-of-the-sexes films in Spain (Bentley 2008: 295): *El otro lado de la cama / The Other Side of the Bed* and *Los dos lados de la cama / The 2 Sides of the Bed* (Emilio Martínez Lázaro, 2002 and 2005), plus a Televisión Española spin-off, *Paco y Veva / Paco and Veva* (2004). Pertinently enough, in the light of this chapter's earlier discussion of the undecidability of political affiliation in relation to comedy performance, they feature a group of young actors from the Animalario company (Guillermo Toledo, Alberto San Juan, Ernesto Alterio), whose vociferously leftist members still dominate much contemporary cinema, comic and otherwise.

Heather Gilmour observes of the romantic comedy of remarriage in particular that its success lies in the way "the films are constructed so that several discourses may be kept running at once [and] what is more important [to the characters] than taking firm ideological stands is the fun that's had along the way" (1998: 38). In these two Spanish films, these several discourses stagger along separately as much as they keep running in tandem. The musical references in both are a mix of World Popular and Spanish Youth. *El otro lado de la cama* starts right in with the music, though in banal sentimental mode, as Sonia (Paz Vega) and Paula (Natalia Verbeke) sing to their men in bed at dawn in semi-speech mode. The second number comes several episodes and more than ten minutes later and is also low-key; Javier (Ernesto Alterio) sing-speaks his way through the far-from-comical dilemma caused by his having an affair with the partner (Paula) of his best friend Pedro (Guillermo Toledo) and his cheating on Sonia. It is not until the sixth number, "Salta" (Jump), that musical comedy proper sets in, with a mildly lively dance routine back in a condo patio subsequent to Sonia awarding Pedro 7.5 out of 10 for his lovemaking now that they too are cheating on their partners. A similar attempt to lighten the gender complications and make the characters quirky comes in an acrobatic dance number epilogue, set, with redundant reflexivity, in a large rehearsal-cum-dance aerobics space. But music and comedy both lead directly back into misogyny: Javier's view that an ex is better than a stable girlfriend, since you can screw the ex whenever you want, and "Las chicas son guerreras" (The Girls Are Fighters) (the third musical number, with pseudo-rock electric guitar riffs) are two examples, even if machismo is challenged directly by the women's dialogue, indirectly by the plot (setting the men up for a fall), and satirically (the superficiality of the views of all the men in the film is encapsulated in the macho taxi-driving Rafa, played by Alberto San Juan, whose clichés fill the last scene of the narrative proper with painfully self-deflating humor).

The lesbian affair in the second film between Marta (Verónica Sánchez) and Raquel (Lucía Jiménez), which prevents the wedding of Marta and Javier, is used as a light foil to point up some obvious redundancies of heterosexual coupledom and to provoke some amusing gender reversals. For example, Javier and Pedro exchange tittle-tattle about marriage while their fiancées make out in the women's toilets on the stag/hen night. When Pedro and Javier's own homosociality is amplified into frank erotic closeness by way of a threesome with Carlota (Pilar Castro) and they finally kiss, there is a gentle oscillation between the old cliché that "todos somos bisexuales, o sea" (everyone's a bit bi, you know) and a simple affirmation of close friendship.

While the eight musical numbers (two of them perfunctory) and corny choreography of *Los dos lados* are, in the main, lessons in how not to punctuate a musical comedy with vitality, the music in the more off-beat *¿Por qué se frotan las patitas? / Scandalous* (Álvaro Begines, 2006), conversely, is dynamically disruptive and well sutured in. Central to the plot is character actor Antonio Dechent's role (reprising a long career that has included several generic roles as authority figures, as well as comedy) as the oblivious, insensitive, and lazy husband, Luis. His daughter Laura (Julia García) also has to contend with a commitment-shy lover "El Utrera" (Raúl Arévalo), whose wild, nomadic life as an *okupa* (squatter) refusenik is referenced by the film's title (which alludes to the way in which flies continually rub their front limbs to stop them sticking to any one place for too long). Men who cannot comprehend or respond to the pain of an older woman are the issue for María

(Lola Herrera), whose singing career has faded away, who fears she is dying, and who has wasted much of her emotional life (and her earnings) on a negligent, alcoholic husband, now dead. These gender-based dramatic situations have their corresponding musical numbers – a mélange of traditional flamenco-*copla* (María was once the *copla* singer La Niña María) and new numbers, set in Seville (coded as traditional) and Sitges (more modern). The participation of the flamenco-rock-pop star Tomasito in the opening and closing numbers epitomizes the fusion of styles. Dance routines and location-set action (on the streets and the beach of Sitges) resituate the traditional numbers and give variety and dynamism to the new pieces. "Loco" (Crazy), with a large plaster-dust-white, spooky-but-lively ensemble, is performed in a fantasy dimension on the other side of a wall that the troupe have jumped through in super-hero style, and the teaser and the trailer both emphasize the element of refreshing zaniness. The iconic number "Nadie se lleva nada" (We Take Nothing With Us When We Go; written by veteran Cuban performer Jorge Zamora and sung here by Carmen Linares) performed on the temporary stage on the sands by María is bitter-sweet and as ambivalent in its message as any cultural item in the *carpe diem* subtradition. Tomasito and Los Atlánticos follow it up with "De momento" (Just For Now; by Queco), which is scarcely less double-edged, for all its quick pulse and patter.

El Calentito (Chus Gutiérrez, 2005, also using Dechent) deploys the music performed in the eponymous underground club-bar as the catalyst for a standard narrative of intergenerational and national-political conflicts between tradition/control and progress/anarchy. The wit of the film is helped by the variable length and relative volume of the musical numbers and fragments: from full-number performance through brief interruptions of dramatic diegesis to more-or-less meaningful background for dialogue and action. Although this is more musical (a fictionalized rock biopic) than comical, the linkage of a personality-based, fun storyline and national history – via the coming-of-age story of Ana and the 1981 setting with its key narrative event of the attempted military coup of February 23 (known as the "23-F" or "Tejerazo") – make this a classic of feel-good comedy with a political and cultural edge, framed in the already polysemic narrative of the Madrid *movida* (Stapell 2009). A parody of the coup itself, with the club-bar substituting for the parliament and far-rightist reactionary, noise-hating neighbor José for Tejero, the film allows sexual and democratic freedoms to come together in an amusing but pointed allegory.

20 centímetros / Twenty Centimeters (Ramón Salazar, 2005) uses a similar ludic mix of historical memory and commentary on sexuality, but with a much more emphatic closeness to the musical proper, and making its history almost exclusively musical too (see Figure 7.8). There is plenty that is structurally counter-hegemonic here (Biddle and Fouz-Hernández 2012). The 1982 "Quiero ser santa" (I Want to Be a Saint) – also used in *El Calentito* – allows the reclaiming of sex-work and "nightlife" as spaces of liberation and catharsis for the transitioning protagonist Marieta (Mónica Cervera). The aesthetic mix and match here is with

Figure 7.8 Marieta (Mónica Cervera) and chorus dancing on the Gran Vía in *20 centímetros* (Ramón Salazar, 2005; prod. Estudios Picasso).

Michael Jackson's pop video *Thriller* (as Biddle and Fouz-Hernández remind us). The 1960s are visually and musically cited in "Tómbola" (from the Marisol film of the same title; Luis Lucia, 1962) and in a queer/S&M/leather performance of "La máscara'" (The Mask; written by Augusto Algueró and Antonio Guijarro, 1964). The mix also includes Madonna, Alaska, and Dalida, visual echoes of nineteenth-century *zarzuela* (especially the still much reperformed *La Gran Vía* by Chueca and Valverde), and early Almodóvar (the iconic Rossy de Palma's role as the redoubtable trans hooker Ice Box emphasizes this echo). Marieta's twenty-centimetre-long obstacle to sexual happiness constitutes a challenge to standard feminist and queer positions on the representation of sexual politics, and it becomes an effective and often very funny destabilizing technique, akin to that deployed in *Hedwig and the Angry Inch* (John Cameron Mitchell, 2001). Carnivalesque overturnings of established gender and sex roles abound: Marieta comments, to the straight-acting hunk of a barrow boy (Pablo Puyol) who falls for her, "muy activo no te veo" (you don't look much like a top to me) as they attempt anal sex, with the lottery – that token of straight, state-sanctioned domesticity – playing on the television in the family sitting room just next door; at the film's happy end Marieta is told "no llores […] que llorar es cosa de hombres" (don't cry, only men cry). The film revels in its overall representation of masculinity as a state of near idiocy, and uses the camp appeal and resetting of many of its musical numbers to champion its flamboyant approach to transsexuality and glamour in the face of adversity.

Conclusion (Chris Perriam)

This chapter began with two comedies dealing in different ways with families, which had at their center Bakhtin's notion of carnival as a "second life." It has ended with a musical comedy that ludically stresses the alternative through disruptive attention to the body and through musical hybridity. While carnival as a "second life" may well be a utopian concept, it does posit – as does comedy in general – the notion of an "alternative" that helps us to understand the simulacrum as something other than pure vacuity, as something potentially subversive. Richard Dyer has stressed the utopian impulse of the musical as an entertainment form (2002: 19–35): escapist but offering a glimpse of other possible worlds. The films discussed in this chapter have shown how film comedies and musicals can, despite – or because of – their apparent frivolity, or alternatively through the use of a very Spanish tradition of black humor, serve to work through conflicts in the areas of gender, race, or class, and between what is perceived as traditional and what is perceived as modern. Not all the comedies discussed in this chapter (musical or otherwise) end with closure but, even when they do (as in the standard romance plot), the final closure cannot cancel out the trouble had along the way. For comedy, no matter how much it may strive toward a happy end, is generated by things going wrong, by mismatches and misunderstandings, by things refusing to be in their "proper" place. Comedy allows us to enjoy the experience of dislocation; for that reason, as suggested at the start of this chapter and notwithstanding the existence of national styles of humor and comic genres that feed off national stereotypes, comedy and the nation are uncomfortable bedfellows.

Notes

1 The heading "Queridos cómicos" (Actors We Love) pays tribute to Diego Galán's splendid twenty-three-episode television series of that title, broadcast on Televisión Española over the 1992–3 season.

2 The term "cuerpos gloriosos" is borrowed from Francisco Umbral's 1992 book title *Memorias eróticas (cuerpos gloriosos)*; I am, of course, applying the term to very different kinds of bodies.

3 The origin of the *género ínfimo* is generally accepted to be the 1901 musical play *El género ínfimo / The Naughty Act* by the Álvarez Quintero brothers, but the work that became its emblem was *La corte de Faraón* (Guillermo Perrín and Miguel de Palacios, with music by Vicent Lleó, 1910), adapted to film in 1985 by José Luis García Sánchez (discussed in this chapter).

4 See note 3.

References

Adorno, T. and Horkenheimer, M. (2002) *Dialectic of Enlightenment: Philosophical Fragments*. Stanford: Stanford University Press.

Alonso, A. (1928) Estructuras de las *Sonatas* de Valle-Inclán. *Verbum* 21: 7–42. Repr. in: Alonso, A. (1955) *Materia y forma en poesía*. Madrid: Gredos, pp. 222–57.

Bajtín [Bakhtin], M. (1974) *La cultura popular en la Edad Media y en el Renacimiento. El contexto de François Rabelais*. Barcelona: Barral Editores.

Bakhtin, M. (1984) *Rabelais and His World*. Bloomington: Indiana University Press.

Bajtín [Bakhtin], M. (1989) *Teoría y estética de la novela* (1924–1973). Taurus: Madrid.

Bazin, A. (1967–71) *What is Cinema?*, 2 vols. Berkeley: University of California Press.

Benjamin, W. (1999) *The Arcades Project*. Cambridge, MA: Harvard University Press.

Bentley, B. (2008) *A Companion to Spanish Cinema*. London: Tamesis.

Biddle, I. and Fouz-Hernández, S. (2012) Voicing Gender: Transgender Performance and the National Imaginary in the Spanish Cinema of the Democratic Era. In: Shaw, L. and Stone, R. (eds.) *Screening Songs in Hispanic and Lusophone Cinema*. Manchester: Manchester University Press, pp. 30–50.

Butler, J. (2004) Bodily Inscriptions: Performative Subversions. In: Salih, S. and Butler, J. (eds.) *The Judith Butler Reader*. Oxford: Blackwell, pp. 90–118.

Company, J. M. (1984) El grano de una voz secundaria. In: Pérez Perucha, J. (ed.) *El cine de José Isbert*. Valencia: Excmo. Ayuntamiento de Valencia, pp. 53–4.

Dyer, R. (2002) *Only Entertainment*. London: Routledge.

Eisenstein, S. M. (1949) Through Theater to Cinema. In: *Film Form: Essays in Film Theory*. New York: Harcourt, Brace, pp. 3–17.

Evans, P. (2000) Cheaper by the Dozen: *La gran familia*, Francoism and Spanish Family Comedy. In: Holmes, D. and Smith, A. (eds.) *100 years of European Cinema: Entertainment or Ideology?* Manchester: Manchester University Press, pp. 77–88.

Faulkner, S. (2006) *A Cinema of Contradiction: Spanish Film in the 1960s*. Edinburgh: Edinburgh University Press.

Fernández Cuenca, J. C. (1948) *Historia del cine*. Madrid: A. Aguado.

García Martínez, J. M. (1996) *Del fox-trot al jazz flamenco: El jazz en España. 1919–1996*. Madrid: Alianza.

Gombrich, E. H. (1968) El arsenal del caricaturista. In: *Meditaciones sobre un caballo de juguete*. Barcelona: Seix Barral, pp. 163–81.

Gilmour, H. (1998) Different, Except in a Different Way: Marriage, Divorce, and Gender in the Hollywood Comedy of Remarriage. *Journal of Film and Video* 50 (2): 26–39.

Gubern, R. (1993) La traumática transición del cine español del mudo al sonoro. In: Gubern, R., Heinink, J. B., Berriatúa, L., et al. *El paso del mudo al sonoro en el cine español (Actas del IV Congreso de la AEHC)*. Madrid: Editorial Complutense, pp. 3–24.

Gubern, R. (2005) Ruido, furia y négritude: Nuevos ritmos y nuevos sones para la vanguardia. In: Mechthild, A. (ed.) *Vanguardia española e intermedialidad: Artes escénicas, cine y radio*. Madrid: Iberoamericana, pp. 273–302.

King, G. (2002) *Film Comedy*. Brighton: Wallflower Press.

Labanyi, J. (2002) Musical Battles: Populism and Hegemony in the Early Francoist Folkloric Film. In: Labanyi, J. (ed.) *Constructing Identity in Contemporary Spain: Theoretical Debates and Cultural Practice*. Oxford: Oxford University Press, pp. 206–21.

Marsh, S. (2006) *Popular Spanish Film under Franco: Comedy and the Weakening of the State*. Basingstoke: Palgrave Macmillan.
Moix, T. (1993) *Suspiros de España: La copla y el cine de nuestro recuerdo*. Barcelona: Plaza & Janés.
Molina Foix, V. (1984) José Isbert y los recuerdos. In: Pérez Perucha, J. (ed.) *El cine de José Isbert*. Valencia: Excmo. Ayuntamiento de Valencia, pp. 59–60.
Ortega y Gasset, J. (1983) Preludio a un Goya. In: *Obras completas, vol. VII*. Madrid: Revista de Occidente / Alianza Editorial, pp. 505–73.
Ponce, V. (1984) Don José o la plusvalía en la narración. In: Pérez Perucha, J. (ed.) *El cine de José Isbert*. Valencia: Excmo. Ayuntamiento de Valencia, pp. 15–18.
Retana, Á. (1964) *Historia del arte frívolo*. Madrid: Tesoro.
Sacristán, J. (2010) Con Ozores aprendí y dí de comer a los míos. Serie Grandes Cómicos. *La Razón*. Online at: www.larazon.es/noticia/4184-jose-sacristan-con-ozores-aprendi-y-di-de-comer-a-los-mios (accessed January 3, 2011).
Salaün, S. (1990) *El cuplé*. Madrid: Espasa Calpe.
Salinas, P. (1970) Significación del esperpento o Valle-Inclán, hijo pródigo del 98. In: *Literatura española siglo XX*. Madrid: Alianza Editorial, pp. 86–114.
Sánchez Oliveira, E. (2003) *Aproximación histórica al cineasta Francisco Elías Riquelme (1890–1977)*. Seville: Universidad de Sevilla.
Stapell, H. M. (2009) Just a Teardrop in the Rain? The *movida madrileña* and Democratic Identity Formation in the Capital, 1979–1986. *Bulletin of Spanish Studies* 86 (3): 345–69.
The Living Age (1928) Metropolitana. *The Living Age* 334 (July): 987.
Triana Toribio, N. (2003) *Spanish National Cinema*. London: Routledge.
Umbral, F. (1992) *Memorias eróticas: Los cuerpos gloriosos*. Madrid: Ediciones Temas de Hoy.
Vernon, K. M. (2004) Theatricality, Melodrama and Stardom. In: Marsh, S. and Nair, P. (eds.) *Gender and Spanish Cinema*. Oxford: Berg, pp. 183–201.
Zunzunegui, S. (2002) *Historias de España: De qué hablamos cuando hablamos de cine español*. Valencia: IVAC.

Further Reading

Dyer, R. (1997) *White*. London: Routledge.
Labanyi, J. (1997) Race, Gender and Disavowal in Spanish Cinema of the Early Franco Period: The Missionary Film and the Folkloric Musical. *Screen* 38 (3): 215–31.
Medhurst, A. (2007) *The National Joke: Popular Comedy and English Cultural Identities*. London: Routledge.
Woods Peiró, E. (2012) *White Gypsies: Race and Stardom in Spanish Musicals*. Minneapolis: University of Minnesota Press.

8

Melodrama and Historical Film

Jo Labanyi, Annabel Martín,
and Vicente Rodríguez Ortega

Melodrama: Modernity's Rebellious Genre (Annabel Martín)

There is no straightforward way to address feeling and its cultural representations. We tend to get stuck when it comes to emotion, embarrassed to acknowledge what moves us, still wedded to the old and unproductive dichotomies, to the artificial splintering of thought and feeling. In *A Lover's Discourse*, Roland Barthes underscores that we live in a time where the sentimental (and not the sexual) has become obscene (Barthes 1978: 177; Pérez Firmat 2007: 38); in other words, a time that prohibits the undressing of the soul instead of the body. Culturally, emotion has many embodiments and manifestations, one of them being filmic melodrama. Many qualifications come to mind in reference to this genre: its binary language, Manichaean universe, hyperbolic affect, and expressionistic aesthetic and epistemology, to name a few. The "melodramatic" has usually carried very little cultural weight for it is too histrionic, too fixed in the popular, too vulgar and low-brow, too entangled with the domestic, too explicit and "obscene" in its exhibition of tears. But melodrama is also a cultural imagination, one that scholars (Brooks 1976; Herlinghaus 2002) locate in the backroom of the house of modernity – an uncomfortable reminder of modernity's abuses, rationalist excesses, and hierarchies, and, of course, of its push toward the universality of capitalist logic, exploitation, and ill-treatment of the individual and family. Melodrama hides in the attic, with all the other misfits, and demands (because modernity does not) a rethinking of the categories underlying reason and emotion, a readjustment of the notion of the subject (and its gender), an affirmation of the weak and wronged, a pulse toward justice, reparation, and the good. Melodrama moves us; pathos

A Companion to Spanish Cinema, First Edition. Edited by Jo Labanyi and Tatjana Pavlović.

"feminizes" us (it genders and transgenders us), making us stronger and better – or so the tears in the "happy end" hope.

Mass culture has been targeted as the natural camp for melodrama, given how its aesthetic preferences find an easy translation into elements of popular appeal. Mass culture has been critiqued for its complicity with structures of power, for promoting structures of feeling complicit with hegemonic forces of society, for being gentle with the ideological status quo. Beginning in the 1930s with Antonio Gramsci's (1985) rethinking of the "reactionary" corseting of the popular, the revitalization of melodrama in literature, theater, and film has a solid history (e.g., Heilman 1968; Elsaesser 1972; Gubern 1974; Brooks 1976; Kleinhans 1976; Neale 1986; Gledhill 1987; Sobejano 1996; Ríos-Font 1997; Linda Williams 1998, 2005; Herlinghaus 2002; Rodríguez 2004; Epps 2005; Gabilondo 2005; Martín 2005). These studies all share the insight that literary, theatrical, or filmic genres are not closed systems of signification but rather complex languages whose meanings and values are as dependent on their internal generic features as they are on what they "do" in cultural/ideological terms as they elicit responses from readers and spectators. In the case of melodrama, the "doing" is about understanding affect as a cultural hermeneutics that derives its meaning from its generic packaging but also from what Deleuze calls a "thing's longitude and latitude" (Thrift 2008: 179) or its place on a broader grid of cultural productions. The high/low split does not adequately address these more nuanced locations of texts because binary classifications like these simplify the actual epistemological operations of culture and its contestation (or not) of power.

In his study of melodrama, Hermann Herlinghaus (2002) explains that there is a long tradition in Western philosophical thought that has relentlessly tried to iron out the inconsistencies generated by the notion of a rational, speculative subject who administers the world of culture. He lucidly affirms that

> los imaginarios que acompañan el actuar humano no se subordinan a la norma que un sujeto autorreflexivo establece. La modernidad, en su proyecto más ambicioso, se encaminó a superar o reprimir esa aporía sin dejar de producir, a su vez, imaginarios heterogéneos. (Herlinghaus 2002: 22)
>
> the imaginaries that accompany human activity are not subordinate to the norm that the self-reflexive subject establishes. Modernity, in its most ambitious terms, tried to overcome or repress that aporia without ever ceasing to produce heterogeneous imaginaries.

The latter are, naturally, set aside and barred from the dominant cultural matrix. One of these heterogeneous imaginaries is the melodramatic in all of its ideological ambiguity. Melodrama is a meaning-making system shared by many cultural languages, high and low, visual and narrative alike; it is a particularly powerful enterprise because it deals with affect as a *moral imagination* that demands justice. In melodrama, affect (sometimes love) transcends the interpersonal and becomes an issue of societal relevance, an ethics, a politics, begging for engagement through tears. An underlying moral legibility is at stake (Linda Williams 1998: 52), one that can be extrapolated to society at large and bids action.

Most intellectual historians agree that melodrama became tragedy's counterpart in the eighteenth century, melodrama being a hermeneutic response to the rapid secularization of society, one where divine cause or intervention can no longer explain the tragic destiny that afflicts the hero. It is this "orphaning" of the subject that melodrama tries to appease, in all of its modern secular garb, usually by cross-dressing conflict and turning it into a language of femininity and desire. This is a theater of good versus evil, a dramaturgy where order is restored by magic with deep anarchic threads running throughout, a genre that rebels against the atomization of society while simultaneously restoring equilibrium in the most absolute, black-and-white, and desperate of terms. It is melodrama's forced endings that have gotten it into trouble, resolutions that control the unleashing of emotions that fall prey to the powers at hand. These are simplistic answers, those suspicious of mass culture have argued, to what are otherwise complex social questions, answers that insufficiently address and satisfy a desire for a more realistic and nuanced understanding of our time and its dysfunctions and operations of power. The re-evaluation of melodrama that has steadily taken place since the 1970s has, conversely, rethought this Manichean universe on different terms and underscored how this binary simplicity allows for a magnificent exhibition of melodrama's "plus" (Sarlo 1985: 226) or excessiveness, a "surplus" that, once reigned in, either restores and secures the status quo or is deemed so brutally undeserved and violent that it makes a plea for a radical alternative – what I have termed, respectively, the avenues of compensatory and crisis melodrama in film (Martín 2005).

In the contemporary Spanish context, the revaluation of melodrama's language and modus operandi took place in the early years of the transition to democracy, most predominantly in the world of literary creation. Writers and cultural analysts such as Manuel Vázquez Montalbán (1970, 1974a, 1974b, 2000), Carmen Martín Gaite (1978, 1987, 2002), and Juan Marsé (1971) exhibited a special sensitivity toward understanding the "grammar of happiness" embedded both in the design of Francoism and in its survival. Starting with Vázquez Montalbán's work in the early 1970s, Spanish mass culture became a direct window onto understanding the ways in which consent and hegemony turn into a kind of overarching cultural paradigm or language in and of themselves (Williams 1977). In the case at hand, mapping a generation's complicity, frustration, and reaction against the regime required revisiting the archive of official discourses and understanding how Francoism's social policy and models of national and sexual identity were embedded in those articulations. Drawn to melodrama's bilingual nature, to that peculiar epistemology that can simultaneously reaffirm, neutralize, or critique cultural displays, writers such as Martín Gaite, Marsé, and Vázquez Montalbán were quick to revisit the mass culture texts of their youth to pinpoint just how Francoism embodied the language of feeling that became the backdrop (and soundtrack) to its peculiar and anachronistic models of citizenry. In Martín Gaite's words, these texts lend us "sus propios ojos [...], proporcionan patrones con arreglo a los cuales mirar lo que pasa, escuchar lo que nos dicen, adornar nuestros sueños e interpretar las noches de la propia novela" (2002: 460) (their eyes [...], modeling ways for us to see what surrounds us, hear what we are told, embellish our dreams, and interpret the nights of our own novel). Their work avoids the tempting, yet facile, rejection of the regime's cultural production as ideologically perverse – which it undoubtedly was – and instead teaches us that "resistance" or countercultural critique is located more in what culture can "do" as a praxis and not so much in what it "is" in ontological terms.

Within this framework, film, song, radio, popular novels, and comics are as much cultural documents of a period illustrating a given ideological focus as they are pockets of affect that intertwine the historical and ideological with lived cultural and personal experiences capable of turning this semiotic system against itself, one of the most successful examples in film being Basilio Martín Patino's magnificent *Canciones para después de una guerra* / *Song for after a War* (1971, banned until 1976). However, in the late 1970s, National Catholicism's excesses were not only about the manipulation of desire, limitation of freedom, and constriction of identity; they also constituted a language that was turning the everyday of their coming of age into a foreign terrain, a space occupied by a piece of themselves that democracy was quickly turning into an unrecognizable other. Much like a family photo album full of "strangers," writers like the three mentioned here were aiming to rescue that ineffable part of history that escapes the archive of the real, that epistemology of feeling that fractures the simplicity of every model of cultural and political identity. Melodrama (in film, popular song, or the romance genre) became a historiographical strategy that rescued a less visible version of history, one that flowed at times parallel or counter to official discourses and at others was inextricably linked to the Francoist master narrative.

In the remainder of this section, I will provide examples of melodrama's incarnations during the Franco period and address several recent samples of its success in Spanish filmmaking. Filmmakers as diverse as Jose Luis Sáenz de Heredia, Luis Lucia, Manuel Mur Oti, Luis García Berlanga, Mariano Ozores, Pedro Lazaga, Basilio Martín Patino, Pedro Almodóvar, and Isabel Coixet have turned to this peculiar epistemology because of the moral pulse that beats within its walls, a pulse that has been known and critiqued for serving very different ideological agendas. No group could come to filmmaking from more ideologically diverse camps, but these filmmakers do share a special interest and attraction toward a semiotic code that, in Linda Williams' terms: (1) begins and wants to end in a space of innocence (1998: 65); (2) focuses on victim-heroes/heroines and the recognition of their virtue (1998: 66); (3) employs an aesthetics of astonishment or contraction between the "happy end" and what this entails (1998: 67); (4) involves a dialectic of pathos and action: a give and take of "too late" and "in the nick of time" (1998: 69); and (5) presents characters who embody primary psychic roles organized in Manichean conflicts between good and evil, or what is also known as melodrama's monopathy (1998: 77). In Gonzalo Sobejano's formulation, this means that the psychic structure of the melodramatic hero is disjunctive while that of the tragic hero is conjunctive (1996: 18), a formulation that had already been suggested in Robert Heilman's foundational *Tragedy and Melodrama* (1968).

When studying melodrama in the Spanish context, its service to the Francoist cause inevitably takes center stage. One needs only to recall how strictly Spanish screens were controlled through the Board of Censors to understand that all films, domestic and international productions alike, were in one way or another in dialogue with the regime (Gubern 1981; see Chapter 14). In the eyes of the Francoist centers of propaganda, mass culture in general, but filmmaking in particular, had the nationalist mission of promoting shamelessly tranquilizing identitarian, historical, or consumerist narratives in which a collective, unified body of citizens would feel at home in the postwar reconstruction efforts. Francoism understood the power of mass culture and therefore gave it a privileged role in its identity-building efforts, an undertaking that needed a repressive legal system as much as it required an effective and fruitful manipulation of tears.

The birth of this "new" National Catholic society demanded painful instances of sacrifice and renunciation as it attempted to instill in Spaniards, who unquestionably needed to overcome the disasters of civil war, an "honorable mission" in history, an uncomfortable yet longed-for place of reconciliation. No matter how unsuccessful the regime might have been in its anachronistic nationalist efforts, its instruments of propaganda were conceived, nevertheless, as homogenizing venues. In the case of film, the manipulation of the language of melodrama throughout the genres of folkloric, historical, or Hollywood-like productions became key for this message of coerced "happiness" embedded in regime-friendly films. Spectators witnessed plot resolutions in which the integration of the unruly character into this reimagined Spain – at times achieved with a brutal iron fist – provided a restoration of order, a sense of purpose, and psychological peace – what Ben Singer terms melodrama's ability to grant "an ethical simplicity and legibility that makes the world more secure, if not socially or economically then at least psychologically" (2001: 137). In the Spanish context, this is what I have termed "compensatory melodrama" (Martín 2005) or a theory of the integration of the marginal, of the social misfit, into the center of ideological hegemony. It is a theory that explains how excess is "corrected" and turns normative. Francoism and melodrama share the same Manichean simplicity that runs throughout the former's nationalist fundamentalism, as well as an attraction to hyperbolic situations that result in crisis and demand easy solutions, simplistic teleological narratives, and outrageously reductionist embodiments of cultural and sexual identity. And yet, tears can potentially destabilize Francoist propaganda. How is this accomplished?

When theorizing the politics of the state as a process of textual entanglements with happiness in Latin American mass culture, Beatriz Sarlo explained the disruptive power of melodrama in these terms:

> La felicidad establece, en la trama de estas narraciones, una relación subterránea con lo prohibido, mientras que los desenlaces tienden a reprimirlo según un modelo de realización que armonice los órdenes individual y social. Todo el interés narrativo está en la oscilación entre dos polos básicos: un ideal de plenitud física que se contrapone al orden moral y un estado de beatitud moral fundado en la represión de la plenitud física. Muchas veces las narraciones parecen tentadas a postular un horizonte de felicidad que integre la transgresión y la aceptación de la norma, proponiendo una *solución imaginaria*, que los desenlaces generalmente no confirman. (1985: 164)

> In the plot of these narratives, happiness establishes a subterranean relation with the prohibited, while the endings tend to repress it as they instead follow a model that harmonizes the personal and social orders. Narrative interest is based on the oscillation between two primary extremes: an ideal of physical plenitude that is in opposition to the moral order and an ideal of moral sanctity founded on the repression of physical plenitude. Oftentimes the narratives seem tempted to propose a space of happiness that combines transgression and acceptance of the norm, hence offering an *imaginary solution* that the endings seldom confirm.

Melodrama generates a semiotic and emotional surplus that needs to find a home. It is this epistemological contradiction, this capability of simultaneously affirming order and its upheaval, this plea for "what could have been," this impossibility of total closure, that turns melodrama into a heterotopic paradigm in the Foucauldian sense (Foucault 1986). Under this formulation, melodrama becomes a text in crisis, a symptomatic and anxious text that converts tears (feeling) into an epistemological filter that, when read against the grain, begs reparation and justice. As we will see shortly in several filmic examples, what on one level performs as an example of Francoist propaganda, a mimetic underpinning of ideology and text, a simplistic rendering of how the politics of the state get inscribed in family, national, or cultural narratives, on another becomes a much more unsettled, troubled, and resistant space. The ambiguity embedded in these texts and the roles of the spectator in the act of interpretation facilitate this shift.

Domestic melodrama plays a significant role in Francoism's call for a new Spain. This special subgenre of melodrama places the family at its center and stages the assaults that the excesses of capitalism perform on its security and stability, attacks that more often than not center on women and range from the effects of poverty on morality to the dangers of modernity and consumerism for family (reproductive) stability. As has been well documented by many cultural critics focusing on the postwar years, in their roles of saintly mother, devoted daughter, or loyal and obedient wife to the paternal spouse, women not only represent the pure and uncontaminated private sphere of the family but also its *Spanish* rendition, given how women are asked to link the ethos of the family with the values of the nation (Ballesteros 1999; Labanyi 2004, 2007). This version of compensatory melodrama is key for the ideologues of the regime for they understand the value of this language (its Manichaeanism and restorative impulse) in the quest to legitimize the regime's cultural and moral matrix. The family, therefore, is depicted as always being at risk from either exterior "contamination" or internally from an unruly member (usually female) in need of punishment or "domestication." The films invite us to believe that *internal* diegetic order translates into its *external* equivalent in postwar Spanish society, a disposition only attainable if we disregard most of the diegetic violence (literal and/or symbolic) needed to tame the unruly. The tears spectators shed in movie theaters help to invoke this loss or subjugation of spirit, a clash between opposites that the story tells us has been resolved by reducing the tension between desire and reality (Moretti 1983: 157–81). If heightened pathos triggers action in these films, its decrease provides the crevice from which tears can flow, because "when we let go of this desire, the sadness that results is also a kind of relief. Tears can thus be interpreted as both a homage to the desire for happiness and the recognition that it is lost" (Williams 1998: 69–70). When the layer of cultural propaganda is added to the narrative, tears shared in a movie theater can turn individual emotion into a call for collective awareness; they might just untie the knot that Francoism so desperately attempts to tie.

Luis Lucia's *De mujer a mujer / From Woman to Woman* (1950) is a prime example of this melodramatic paradigm. This is a film about female sterility, female insanity, redesigned motherhood, marital infidelity, female friendship, and suicide displaced onto the Spanish fin de siècle and written onto the mise-en-scène in all of its melodramatic glory: from hyperbolic rooms that simultaneously materialize wealth, tragedy, and pathos to life-size children's toys, oversized furniture, and excessive décor that highlight the irreparable loss of a child (see Figure 8.1). Consistent with Francoist ideology (and other repressive sociopolitical contexts), *De mujer a mujer* assumes reproductive sexuality to be the core of the family and the child to be the ultimate bond between husband and wife. The accidental death of this family's daughter pulverizes their stability. They face a dead end in terms of family lineage given the wife's (Isabel) sterility after childbirth but new bonds will be made after Isabel suffers a severe mental breakdown and is hospitalized. As melodramatic destiny would have it, husband Luis falls in love with Emilia, Isabel's nurse and confidant. After numerous medical examinations and a patient, hopeful wait for recovery, it becomes painfully obvious that Isabel will never be cured. Hence, despite his family's disapproval and solidarity with the sick Isabel, Luis begins an extramarital love affair with Emilia and from this relationship a baby girl is born. This is, of course, an illicit family unit for the ideological times but Lucia makes it a forgivable one for part of the film because we are made to sympathize with the lot of the new couple, understanding their predicament and frustration, allowing us to imagine how things could be very

Figure 8.1 Bourgeois opulence and psychic disorder: the life-size doll that will become a child substitute in *De mujer a mujer* (Luis Lucia, 1950; prod. CIFESA). Courtesy of Video Mercury and Filmoteca Española.

different if the legal system were otherwise. However, in line with National Catholicism, Emilia (not Luis) will be punished for having crossed society's moral expectations and fallen prey to her desire: as the "fallen woman" that she is, Emilia will die at the end of the film and order will be restored when the miraculously cured Isabel accepts the baby as her daughter, rejoins the marriage, and assumes her place as mother and wife.

This film would be a poor example of melodramatic excess and its contestatory epistemology if Lucia had not triangulated the desire between husband, wife, and lover. Isabel's mental illness stems from her vehement rejection of the world of masculine power her husband represents. Unconsciously blaming him for her daughter's death due to his carelessness when pushing the child on a swing, Isabel suffers from a paranoid mindset and violently rejects all things masculine. It is at the psychiatric hospital that she befriends Emilia and turns her into her confidant, a situation, the film makes clear, that benefits Isabel's recovery and mental stability for, in psychoanalytic terms, the heterotopic space of the hospital makes evident the kind of cultural violence Isabel fears and from which Emilia protects her. Isabel longs for a precultural limbo of sorts that the hospital can provide; she does not yearn for a marriage lost to illness but rather for the irreplaceable primary bond between mother and daughter, a bond that, in the film, is replaced by the friendship between the two women. It is this wish for and impossibility of restoration and justice – death always makes it too late – that evokes the pathos in viewers. I find this to be the most convincing way to explain both women's mutual sacrifice when the truth is revealed once Isabel is cured and released from the hospital, an interpretation that extends to Isabel's sacrificial wish to return to this prison house of sorts so that Emilia can enjoy a life of happiness with Isabel's husband and their baby. How else can we explain Emilia's attempted suicide and deathbed wish that Isabel take her daughter and care for her as her own? In the words of Jo Labanyi,

> The conventional narrative of a woman's self-sacrifice to redeem the hero is here twisted to become her self-sacrifice for the sake of another woman, as the title implies. Although the wife is thereby safely restored to the role of bourgeois mother, the film effectively writes the husband [...] out of the script, reduced to the instrumental role of fathering daughters by both women. (2007: 178)

Order is not restored because the unruly has been tamed or because a normative family unit is stitched back together – or not only. Order is attained because an alternative model of love is expelled from societal legitimacy. This is what dies on Emilia's deathbed as little men give way to a model of heroic female sacrifice that spectators feel to be unnecessary and that runs counter to the possibilities of desire. This is compensatory melodrama turned upside down and melodrama's destabilizing effect at work.

Manuel Mur Oti's *Orgullo* / *Pride* (1955) is a prime example of another modality of the social reconfiguration of the feminine through melodrama, but this time, instead of a reimagined triangular family unit that unsettles the status quo, we follow woman's heroic and sacrificial upholding and consolidation of the nation in what film critics call Spain's first western. A visually complex and sophisticated film, *Orgullo* is the story of how the transmission of power and wealth from mother to daughter demands a moral stature and a degree of family loyalty that will only be complete when it finds a mutual home in the domestic arena and not only in the world of state-like politics.

Orgullo is epic melodrama at its best. The cinematography is heavily inspired by the awesome landscapes that filmmakers such as John Ford and Howard Hawks underscored and made representative of the nation in their own films: long shots of the natural beauty of mountains, lakes, and rivers; large numbers of cattle always on the move, symptomatic of the flow of fortune and power at stake (see Figure 8.2); a carefully composed musical score of intense, iterative rhythm that underlines the effort, the labor, and moral value of working the land; and an emphasis on the cyclical nature of life, a cycle where land and its fruits have their own implacable demands, as, in this case, the fight for water rights illustrates. Nevertheless, although the aesthetic inspiration comes from Hollywood's melodramas of the west, *Orgullo* takes its cues from National

Figure 8.2 Melodrama linked to nation and power through landscape and the movement of cattle (*Orgullo*, Manuel Mur Oti, 1955; prod. Celta Films SA). Courtesy of Video Mercury and Filmoteca Española.

Catholicism, for here the nation is not one inscribed in capitalism's linkage of successful economic power with change, progress, and individualism but rather in an atavistic, premodern conceptualization of political and economic merit, values that emanate from and are imbued in the land itself and that extend to those who govern.

The economic machine is alive in Dos Cumbres and it rests in the hands of two aristocratic families responsible for the land, the animals, and the farmers and families who steward this wealth: Teresa and Laura Mendoza (mother and daughter) and Luis and Enrique Alzaga (father and son). Operating more like monarchs than private landowners, both families operate under a psychological logic that Bataille described as peculiar to fascism: a pseudo-democratic apparatus of equal responsibility and commitment to the general wellbeing held in place by the moral legitimacy this "equality" in purpose inspires and by an underlying immobile social structure of extreme hierarchy. The romantic interests in the film intersect with Oti's conceptualization of power and wealth. In their youth, Teresa and Luis were engaged to be married; however, a dispute concerning water rights broke out on their wedding day between their respective farm hands, unable to deal in peaceful terms with the shortage of water that affects the women's ranch when a dry season takes hold. Anarchy breaks loose, frustrating their future together since Luis chooses responsibility (land preservation) over love, therefore spurning Teresa and fatally wounding her sense of pride (the title of the film). Today, their children face the same dilemma on their wedding day for the cycle of chaos and anarchy among their workers has returned, their survival instincts taking hold of their actions, their natural "inferiority" explaining their disregard of the common good and of the future happiness of their superiors. Given how, in fascism, "the immediate needs of men must be renounced, under constraint, in favor of a transcendent principle that cannot be the object of an exact explanation" (Bataille 1985: 144), the young couple will also postpone their wedding because social order trumps their individual bliss.

However, what is most fascinating about *Orgullo* is how the justification of power, its transmission in the psychosocial context, is developed through the eyes of the women, from mother to daughter and not father to son. This adds a nuanced subtext to the version of power described above, for the usual renunciation of the sphere of the maternal, of affect, in order to enter the realm of the public sphere is no longer necessary nor warranted. The mother's authority stems not only from her deep knowledge of the atavistic laws that govern people and land – issues the daughter will be brutally confronted with in all their materiality, as, for example, in the senseless slaughtering of animals. Her power is also legitimized because she sentimentalizes the public sphere with actions that pertain to her personal circumstances. This complicates that "transcendent principle" that guides her rule for, in this film, Francoism seems to be legitimizing authority in the public sphere only when it touches the realm of affect. In other words, the film posits that authority can only be fully understood and followed when social actors incorporate their personal narratives into their decision-making, into the foundation of the national project. This makes the working of ideology quite modern but it reverses the usual players and importance of spheres.

Following Nancy Armstrong's lead on desire and domestic fiction in the British nineteenth-century context and the separation of the private and public in that literature (1987), Doris Sommer (1991) points out that the opposition of polis and Eros in the Latin American context of the same period offers a very interesting complication, for in this literature feeling and power were inextricably linked through the figures of sentimentalized men entering the public sphere. When we look closely at the structuring of *Orgullo*, we find that this film adds another refinement to the paradigm, given how affect is reintroduced into the public sphere, not by sentimentalized men but rather by deeply politicized women. In the case at hand, the finest melodramatic moment of the film comes when mother and daughter meet on common ground the day Laura's ultimate defiance – her decision to marry – is to be announced to her mother. Teresa, the great strategist, is in her bedroom where she is expecting Laura; she has laid out on the bed the wedding dress that she had been wearing on the day in the past when Luis had

Figure 8.3 Melodrama's domestic family drama at play: confrontation between mother and daughter in *Orgullo* (Manuel Mur Oti, 1955; prod. Celta Films SA). Courtesy of Video Mercury and Filmoteca Española.

spurned her love. As Teresa tells her story to Laura, we witness the moving effects of these words on the daughter's face. In response to her mother's final question asking whether she has decided to leave their home and join the Mendozas, Laura's affirmative reply surprises us at first but then brings us to tears (or so the language suggests) when she conditions her independence on reparation of the slight to her mother (see Figure 8.3). The "Queen" is now comforted to know that the generational transmission of power lies on a solid moral and ethical footing. The rest of the film pays close attention to the lessons in governance that the daughter must learn in order to safely transition between the public and the domestic. What *Orgullo* does brilliantly through melodrama's quest for justice, metonymic language, and intermingling of spheres is prove the case that modernity entails, in Doris Sommer's terms, "the erotic or sentimental investment in the state" (1991: 32).

The list of Spanish melodramas is quite long, as many films, despite their more historical, war-related, musical, or even comedic narratives, contain many of the structural and epistemological threads of melodrama. Examples range from *La malquerida / Loveless* (José López Rubio, 1940) to *Raza / Race* (José Luis Sáenz de Heredia, 1942), *Un marido a precio fijo / The Hired Husband* (Gonzalo Delgrás, 1942),

Rosas de otoño / *Autumn Roses* (Juan de Orduña, 1943), *El escándalo* / *The Scandal* (Sáenz de Heredia, 1943), *La vida en un hilo* / *Hanging on a Thread* (Edgar Neville, 1945), *Los últimos de Filipinas* / *Last Stand in the Philippines* (Antonio Román, 1945), *Audiencia pública* / *Public Trial* (Florián Rey, 1946), portions of *¡Bienvenido Mister Marshall!* / *Welcome Mr. Marshall!* (Luis García Berlanga, 1953), *El último cuplé* / *The Last Torch Song* (Orduña, 1957), *Faustina* (Sáenz de Heredia, 1957), *Una chica de Chicago* / *A Girl from Chicago* (Mur Oti, 1958), *El camino* / *The Road* (Ana Mariscal, 1963), *El verdugo* / *The Executioner* (Berlanga, 1963), *Nueve cartas a Berta* / *Nine Letters to Berta* (Basilio Martín Patino, 1966), *El próximo otoño* / *Next Autumn* (Antxon Eceiza, 1967), and *Pero ¿en qué país vivimos?* / *What Country Are We Living In?* (Sáenz de Heredia, 1967). Films such as these offer an insightful complication of the gender-related biases and upheavals taking place during these three decades, presented to audiences through the language of melodrama. More recent revitalization of filmic melodrama in the Spanish context lies in the hands of two of its contemporary masters, Pedro Almodóvar (see Chapter 5 and Chapter 20) and Isabel Coixet (see Chapter 6 and Chapter 19).

Interested in how the semiotic codes of the high and the low intersect and mesmerized by the pulse toward emotional truth that he sees embedded in the Hollywood models of 1950s melodrama, Almodóvar adopts the structural elements of the genre (its sexual roles, pathos and action dichotomy, crumbling internal psychological world, and metonymic epistemology, depicted through his brilliant use of color, sound, and mise-en-scène) if only to empty these elements of their socially conditioned meaning. It is the "shell" that interests him, for Almodóvar is involved in a metacinematic dialogue with melodrama that, as Mark Allinson notes, is full of "anti-illusionistic gestures, self-reference, and parody, all of which undermine the 'naturalizing' logic of cinema" (2001: 123). Films such as *¿Qué he hecho yo para merecer ésto?* / *What Have I Done to Deserve This?* (1984), *La flor de mi secreto* / *The Flower of My Secret* (1995), and *Volver* / *To Return* (2006) are melodramas of crisis that emphasize the metonymic display of meaning – articulated from within the psychology of a wounded self – and the embodied and material translation of affect into creative structure. They are melodramas that underscore compassion and solidarity over reproductive sexuality; films that link affect and ethics (a sense of personal and social justice) to the realm of the "feminine" – a world inhabited by displaced men, shattered women, and healing mothers (sisters, friends, and neighbors), lost souls that seek the reverberation and peace that love instills in us. In the Almodóvarian universe, love and family are inextricably linked to the melodramatic "echo" the loved one seeks in the other, whether it be at the hands of the lover or in the multiple incarnations of the caregiver.

In this respect I remind readers of the magnificent play with sound, love, and memory that Almodóvar achieves in scenes like that in *The Flower of My Secret* where a frustrated and abandoned Leo throws a picture of her beloved Paco to the floor, a picture whose frame falls apart into dozens of beautiful glass marbles that bounce and slide on the floor, reverberating into a hollow echo of no return

Figure 8.4 Almodóvar translates melodrama's intensity of emotion into sight and sound in *La flor de mi secreto* (1995; prod. El Deseo).

(see Figure 8.4). Sound takes center stage again in this film when Leo "returns from the dead" when she hears her mother's desperate voice on the phone, and, yet again, in a third scene when mother and daughter finally recognize each other and hear each other's pain and helplessness – the famous "vacas sin cencerro" (cows without cowbells) scene – as we witness a profoundly intimate mother–daughter conversation on loneliness filmed through the delicate lace curtains of the needlepoint of their female neighbors. *Volver* also pays special attention to the non-verbal in mother–daughter recognition and communication, as is the case between Raimunda (Penélope Cruz) and Irene (Carmen Maura), as exemplified through body odor or song; the same is true between Rebeca (Victoria Abril) and Becky (Marisa Paredes) in *Tacones lejanos / High Heels* (1991). In Almodóvar's work, filmic resolution – his "happy endings" – is never regressive, as it is in compensatory melodrama; the transgression never has to be discerned by reading "against the grain." The surplus in his melodramas always lies with the character embodying unrequited love, a social "misfit" of sorts that takes many forms (gay men, desperate mothers, wounded daughters, transsexual fathers) and who achieves a "happy end" when she or he consolidates an alternative space of care.

If Almodóvar defamiliarizes Hollywood's excesses and uses its heightened sensibility to reclaim the healing power of care and family under patriarchy, Isabel Coixet develops a model of melodrama that, while also based on the "medicinal" values of the domestic, is governed less by the pull of its more recognizable language (the hyperbole of gesture, color, or sound that has become Almodóvar's signature) and more by its less explored features, those of silence and confinement. It is the "muteness" of the melodramatic text, the traumatic unspoken, that interests her. Coixet's work offers a portrait of the extremities of the human experience, its unfathomable cruelty and unthinkable kindness, in situations that range from a young mother's preparation for her untimely death to the suicide of a best friend, the trauma of torture, the experience of war, and the labor of recovery. For this Catalan filmmaker, melodrama is the language that best expresses the randomness and unfairness of these struggles and extreme predicaments. Working with the categories of excess and surplus (tears and silence), the marginal, and space as heterotopia (e.g., the interior of a trailer home or an oil rig in the North Sea), Coixet uses the language of silence and trauma to equip melodrama with a broader social agenda and even with a political underbelly.

In the case of *My Life without Me* (2003), viewers are invited to give up that piece of themselves that focuses on the "smallness" of the self in order to learn how to become a custodian for the "other," a theme that Coixet also develops in detail in *The Secret Life of Words* (2005). In *My Life without Me*, she uses the hermeneutics of melodrama (the individual's fight against injustice – in this case, a terminal illness) to bring us closer to the banality that surrounds us in our daily lives, to the distracting lies of consumerism, to the false narratives of happiness that belie our frustrations. This is a melodrama that undermines simplistic mass culture, a melodrama that places the protagonist in the most extreme of situations and peels away, with razor-sharp precision, the layers of distraction from the "real" fabricated by mass culture's histrionic call to anesthetize. It is by understanding the magnitude of Ann's plight and the beauty of her last two months of life that we stop, if only briefly, the kind of vision machine with which consumer society tempts and distracts us. The empathy and pathos her predicament elicits instigates viewers into confronting their own unpreparedness for death, as we watch this wise, twenty-three-year-old woman confront her illness, make plans for a short future, and turn this personal tragedy into a story about memory, mothering after death, profound individual growth, and generosity. We are the witnesses to a young woman's last secrets, precious knowledge about her life choices, frustrated dreams, sadness and regrets, taped birthday stories for her daughters, and last love affair. We cry and we feel; we are moved and a shift takes place.

The Secret Life of Words additionally links this special epistemology with a social agenda concerned with the ravages of war and female victimhood. Here, the muteness of the wounded text (the life of the nurse, Hannah), the scars on Hannah's beautiful body, and the torture of her mind and soul transform the loquacity of her injured, enamored, and temporarily blinded patient (Josef) into silence and awe. In times of war, evil comes in melodramatic dressings because of its extreme senselessness, its inexplicable absurdity, its random and unpredictable targets. Yet, if it is hyperbole that drives evil in these moments, Coixet uses silence (muteness) as a call to cure. Touch, tears, and silence are all that are needed for these two enamored social orphans to find themselves in each other, and to repair what is so unimaginably painful. Secluded on an oilrig in the North Sea where twenty-five million waves beat against its foundation, nurse Hannah and patient Josef find refuge from the weight of the past and

Figure 8.5 The scarred body that cures the wounded I–You in its powerful muteness (*The Secret Life of Words*, Isabel Coixet, 2005; prod. El Deseo).

learn how the enamored "I–you" can cure. Unaware of her secret, Josef asks one day, revealing his own, "How do you live with the dead, Hannah?" and she looks into his "mute" eyes and responds from a place of darkness in her own soul, "Some go on living. Others don't."

The day she bares her scars to Josef, we too become witnesses to her tragedy and victimhood. Coixet moves us deeply not through the histrionic but through touch, words, and tears, tears that bond Hannah and Josef forever and that scar us as well (see Figure 8.5). The ugliness of what is revealed, as we finally hear and see Hannah's story on her body, directs us to a "you" located in the irreducible experience of evil. The witnessing of this revelation, the unraveling of Hannah's unthinkable life story, turns us into custodians for the "other," once again. She uses the romantic story, the place where "you are tender," as Barthes would have it, as the site where you "speak your plural" (Barthes 1978: 225) and pushes us in the best of melodrama's ways from love to solidarity, to justice. The "wrinkles of the face," the "epidermal" writing of history appeal to a "remainder" (Finkielkraut 1999), to a piece of ourselves and of history, that begs an ethical stance. In this case, it is Coixet's striving for memory, for honoring the experiences of female war and torture victims like Hannah and of those who have committed their lives to safeguarding that story, to keeping the dead alive, and to rescuing those victims from their own private hells that instigates Coixet to take the story off the oilrig and into the offices of the International Rehabilitation Council for Torture Victims, a repository of those memories. Here lies the social dimension of Coixet's melodrama, in its call to bear witness. In *The Secret Life of Words*, Coixet puts a very high price on happiness for she links it to a system of values that are "respuestas a situaciones que duelen" (answers to situations that hurt) (Mate 2005: 52). Coixet's film is a fine example of melodrama's desire for *what could be*, for bringing back into our lives a sense of the "sacred" – what John Berger terms, in his discussion of the film, "the unsayable or the indescribable" (2005: 8) – through silence, the traumatic: the secret life of words.

Melodrama has a long and fruitful history in the Spanish context. Its Manichaeanism, hyperbole, facile sentimentalism, kitschiness, and low and feminized features are the usual qualifications for those who have not revisited the complexity of the genre. Its "natural" alliances with Francoist ideology made it suspect for most critics of the regime, but, as we have seen above, the tears elicited, the push for order, are most often painful and rebellious. In more recent years, tears have become hermeneutic instruments for documenting the Francoist past: writers interested in this function of mass culture turned into chroniclers of the contradictory alliances of postwar society, into compilers of the imaginaries contained in generational offerings of music, sports, or beauty ideals, into students of the postwar uses of love for men and women, into documentarians of an "old-fashioned" language. Today, melodramatic tears slow down time, making us more cognizant of the dream-like fantasy into which consumerism traps us. "Good" feeling brings us closer to the realities of life, to more compassionate models of citizenry, to dialoguing with the "other." This hermeneutics needs a piece of the heart in its claim for justice.

In the following sections we turn to the historical film – which often overlaps with melodrama – and its particular coding and dialogue with reality both present and past. Special attention will be given to this genre's hermeneutic strategies; its own reading against the grain, especially during Francoism; and its excess in the performativity of gender, time, and the nation. While it is highly relevant for understanding how Spanish filmmakers reworked Francoist historiography during the transition to democracy, this filmic genre today is also pertinent for understanding the ways in which globalized film markets affect our entanglement with the past.

The Historical Film: Genre and Legibility (Vicente Rodríguez Ortega)

The label "historical film" embraces a diverse range of film genres, an understanding of whose conventions – for example, those of the horror film or musical – is necessary in order to identify the particular past recreated. In certain genres, such as the western, the setting itself is crucial to generic categorization. It is through genre that historical films train their viewers to identify their "history-building" function: to appreciate a biblical epic or a nineteenth-century costume drama, for example, one needs to have watched a number of such films in order to master the skills required to decode their narrative and formal strategies. In addition, it must be remembered that the modes of enunciation that give historical films a specific identifiable historicity invariably conform to ideological and aesthetic codes contemporaneous not with the period represented but with their date of production (Sánchez Noriega 2004: 111–22). Historical films necessarily engage with the present, through a set of audiovisual discourses that strive to create a degree of verisimilitude for the contemporary spectator (Monterde 1999: 10). Genres also rely on "specific systems of expectations and hypothesis which spectators bring with them to the cinema and which interact with films themselves during the course of the viewing process" (Neale 2000: 31). These extracinematic systems facilitate recognition. In short, historical films are perceived as such because spectators have learned to codify them in a specific way, even if they overlap with other genres such as melodrama, the action film, or the thriller.

The historical film is thus most usefully understood as a multi-generic template that, while thematically and aesthetically recognizable (especially in terms of production design and often camerawork; for example, extensive use of the panoramic format), mobilizes a variety of generic registers in order to typically offer an understandable, linear, and ideologically skewed rereading of the past. Historical rigor almost inevitably succumbs to the pleasures of cinematic spectacle. If there is one thing that binds historical films together it is perhaps their spectacularity: that is, their mobilization of the audiovisual (especially visual) resources of cinema for the purposes of transporting the spectator to another time. The historical film has to be able to make the spectator want to inhabit that "other time" while also using it to comment on the present.

The Ambivalent Attractions of the Past: Historical Film of the Early Franco Period (Jo Labanyi)

The 1940s and early 1950s are the period most associated in Spain with historical cinema. However, films set in the past were made from cinema's beginnings. These were often literary adaptations – for example, Ricardo de Baños' *Don Juan Tenorio* (1906) and *Los amantes de Teruel / The Lovers of Teruel* (1912) – but recreations of national history became popular from the late 1920s, as in José Buch's *El dos de mayo / The May 2nd Revolt* (1927) and *El guerrillero / The Guerrilla Fighter* (1928), both set during the early-nineteenth-century War of Independence against Napoleonic invasion, and *Isabel de Solís, reina de Granada / Isabel de Solís, Queen of Granada* (1931), set in Muslim al-Andalus. Florián Rey's silent *Agustina de Aragón* (1929, also set in the War of Independence) preceded Juan de Orduña's famous 1950 remake by twenty-three years. Indeed, the repertoire of episodes from national history that appeared on Spanish screens, in the silent and sound periods, was fixed in the second half of the nineteenth century by the historical painting genre promoted for nation-building purposes by liberal and conservative governments (Labanyi 2005). Pradilla's 1877 painting of Juana la Loca, staged in Orduña's 1948 *Locura de amor / The Mad Queen*, disturbs national destiny with its focus on madness, while Gisbert's 1860 painting *Ejecución de los Comuneros de Castilla / Execution of the Comuneros*, staged in Orduña's *La leona de Castilla / The Lioness of Castile* (1951) and dramatizing the sixteenth-century burghers' revolt against Habsburg centralizing power, was bought by Congress at the instigation of liberal politicians.

If representations of the past were popular from cinema's start, it is because they play on the moving image's magic promise to animate the dead (Moore 2000) – an "animation" that caters to popular audiences' love of spectacle. Since the 1920s, historical film has been despised as "vulgar" because of its spectacularity, but spectacle – often producing a tableau effect – can disrupt linearity and continuity, "exposing the artifice of histories" (Hughes-Warrington 2007: 45, 74–5). Early Francoist historical film has been criticized for its lack of realism – what has been called "Francoist kitsch" (González González 2009). This misses the point, which is the conversion of history into masquerade: spectator pleasure comes from awareness of the constructed nature of the past enacted on screen. As Cook notes (1996), lavish costumes were central to this enjoyment of history as masquerade, generating a concept of identity as performance that anticipated Judith Butler's insights (1990). Fanés attributes the mistaken identity trope in so many 1940s CIFESA films to war-derived traumas (1989: 216–20); a more basic explanation is that audiences loved the equivocations produced by the reduction of identity to costume – masquerade has always been a feature of popular culture. Reflexivity is likewise produced by the excessive décor – like the costumes, researched from paintings and producing a similar tableau effect (Castro de Paz 2002: 145). Criticism of early Francoist historical films – especially its patriotic epics – has tended to focus on plot and dialogue, which invariably conform to Francoist ideology since scripts had to be approved by the censor prior to filming. But the meanings of these films, given their spectacularity and use of pictorial sources, are constructed much more by their visual language, which can work with and against the script.

A distinction can be made between films that focus on historical figures in order to dramatize events from national history and films set in the past whose protagonists may be historical or fictional but where historical events merely form a backdrop or are absent; the latter will be referred to here as costume dramas. The two categories can blur, as in Orduña's *Lola la piconera* (1951): a costume drama with fictional characters whose War of Independence setting is nonetheless prominent. Hughes-Warrington notes that not all historical films are concerned with instilling a concept of national identity (2007: 10). In many costume dramas there is no patriotic intent – for example, Edgar Neville's comedies *Domingo de carnaval / Carnival Sunday* (1945) and *El crimen de la calle de Bordadores / The Crime on Calle Bordadores* (1946), which pastiche stereotypical images of nineteenth-century popular Madrid as well as the thriller genre, born in the nineteenth century.

Despite the common misperception that the patriotic epic (usually equated with the production company CIFESA) was the main early Francoist cinematic genre, in fact CIFESA made only four such films, all directed by Orduña: *Locura de amor, Agustina de Aragón, Alba de América / Dawn of America* (1951), *La leona de Castilla* (on CIFESA, see Chapter 14). If we include other production companies, the number of historical epics grows; and the number of historical films made by CIFESA increases considerably if we include costume dramas as well as epics. Nonetheless, the historical films of the 1940s and 1950s discsussed here were made by a total of fourteen production companies. The epics of CIFESA were preceded by *El abanderado / The Flag Bearer* (Eusebio Fernández Ardavín, 1943), the Spanish–Portuguese coproduction *Inés de Castro* (J. M. Leitão de Barros, 1944), *Reina santa / The Holy Queen* (Rafael Gil, 1946), and *Doña María la Brava* (Luis Marquina, 1947), establishing as preferred settings the Middle Ages and War of Independence (see Figure 8.6). The medieval period is embodied by female heroines: *Reina Santa* and *Doña María la Brava* create a paradigm for representing the Middle Ages as a period of effeminate (poet and/or philandering) kings, with strong women restoring order to the realm. *Inés de Castro* and *Reina santa* depict the impact of Spanish queens on Portuguese history. Arturo Ruiz-Castillo's *Catalina de Inglaterra / Catherine of England* (1951) portrays Catherine of Aragon as a positive force in English history, wining battles, and conducting her own legal defense when Henry VIII divorces her.

The Habsburg period (sixteenth and seventeenth centuries) was absent prior to CIFESA's first incursion into the patriotic epic genre with the spectacularly successful *Locura de amor*, which constructs Habsburg rule as a foreign occupation, the Flemish Felipe el Hermoso (Philip the Beautiful) being another philandering king. Audience identification is clearly with Juana la Loca (daughter of Isabel la Católica) as Philip's victim. Unlike Vicente Aranda's 2001 remake *Juana la Loca, Locura de amor* is not just a melodrama but a political film dramatizing the usurpation of Juana's rights as queen. CIFESA repeated this period setting in *La leona de Castilla*, which similarly constructs Habsburg rule (of the Holy Roman Emperor, Charles V) as a foreign usurpation. It is not true that early Francoist patriotic epics promote the Habsburg period as an age of empire. The only epic to celebrate empire – the ill-fated *Alba de América* (see Chapter 14) – associates it explicitly with Isabel la Católica (played in a disastrous miscasting by the period melodrama star Amparo Rivelles). The film ends with Columbus landing in America (staging another nineteenth-century painting, Puebla's 1862 *Primer desembarco de Colón en América / Columbus' First Landing in America*), stopping as empire starts. Its last scene shows the presentation to the Catholic Kings in Burgos Cathedral of the natives brought back by Columbus. The rear-view tracking shot undermines the solemnity by foregrounding their buttocks in skimpy loincloths – here the term "Francoist kitsch" is entirely appropriate. The only other early Francoist film to dramatize empire in the Americas is the missionary film *La manigua sin Dios / The Godless*

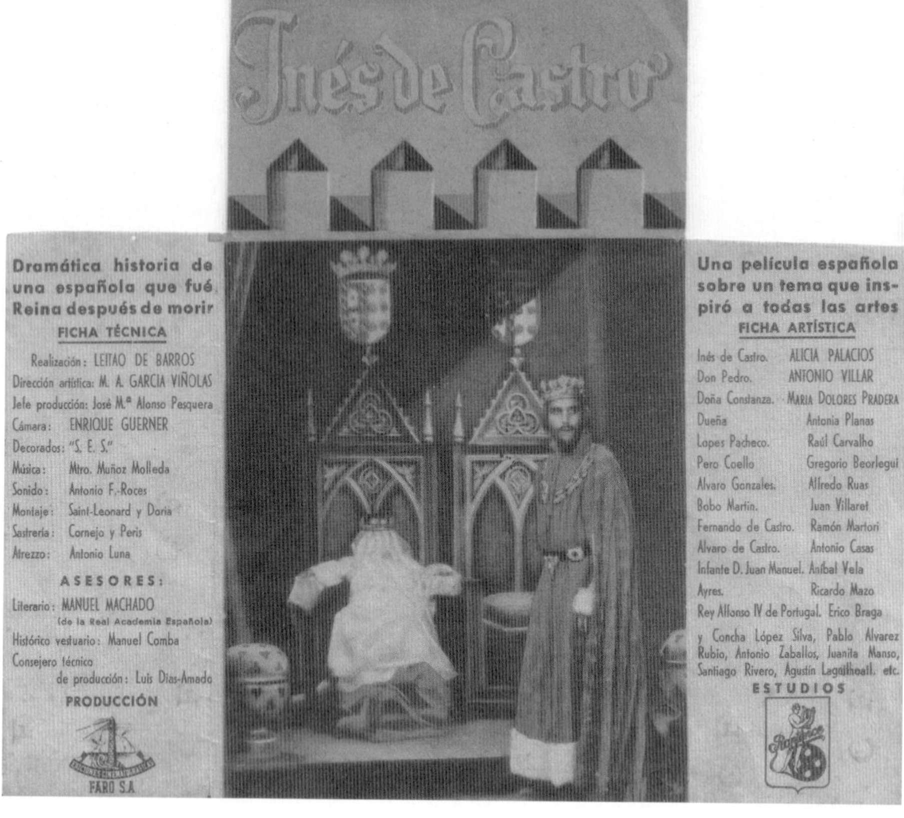

Figure 8.6 Handbill for the historical epic *Inés de Castro* (1944), made four years before CIFESA's first incursion into the genre, in the form of a medieval castle whose gates open to reveal the details (J. M. Leitão de Barros; prod. Faro Producciones Cinematográficas). Private collection.

Swamp (Arturo Ruiz-Castillo, 1947), set in Paraguay at the time of the Jesuits' expulsion by the Enlightenment monarch Charles III. The message is that Spain's imperial mission was realized by the Church against Crown opposition. The film's main attraction is not the missionaries but the semi-naked body of Jorge Mistral as the native male hero.

If *Agustina de Aragón* is CIFESA's most successful patriotic epic, it is partly because it taps into the "siege mentality" (Triana Toribio 2003: 48) of a Spain under United Nations boycott but also because it appropriates for representation of the War of Independence the "strong heroine saves the nation from effeminate men" formula developed in earlier films set in the Middle Ages. As in *Locura de amor*, Aurora Bautista's hyperbolic acting style turns national history into pure

Figure 8.7 Agustina firing the phallic cannon in *Agustina de Aragón* (Juan de Orduña, 1950; prod. CIFESA).

performance. In both films, it also provides female spectators (the majority audience) with the pleasurable spectacle of female agency, at a time when the dictatorship had rescinded all women's rights (see Figure 8.7).

Theorization of the "heritage movie" – a concept rarely applied to Spanish cinema – has stressed its nostalgic depiction of the national past (Higson 2003). It is commonly assumed that early Francoist patriotic epics encouraged a view of the past as embodying superior values so as to legitimize those values' restoration by the Franco dictatorship at the time. While this is true in terms of the portrayal of patriotic sacrifice, the past depicted is one in which, in the majority of movies, women have agency and dominate the screen – as in international cinema of the time, thanks to the studio system's high-earning female stars. The flashback format of many of these patriotic epics, framed by a character telling the story in retrospect (especially pronounced in *Locura de amor* and *Agustina de Aragón*), encourages a nostalgic vision of a past now lost. But what has been lost is, in most cases, a female agency that is far from the patriarchal society the Franco dictatorship sought to restore. In effect, the flashback structure encourages spectators to accept that a better past has to be left behind – nostalgia in the sense of attraction to a past that one knows is gone forever. A similar structure operates in *Los últimos de Filipinas / Last Stand in the Philippines* (Antonio Román, 1945), depicting loss of empire. Its military protagonists have to accept at the end that their heroic resistance has been futile, since Spain had surrendered to the United States six months before.

Several costume dramas perform a similar trope in encouraging spectator identification with a beautiful past that has at the end to be relinquished (Labanyi 2007). In this sense, one could argue that early Francoist historical films encourage identification with regime ideology insofar as Francoism was, like other European fascisms, a form of conservative modernity predicated on the violent break with a democratic past. Regardless of whether such films set out to instill a notion of the historical necessity of loss, they are likely to have helped audiences grappling with loss in the Civil War's aftermath to come to terms with the need to put the past behind them. The huge majority of the many costume dramas produced in the period opted for the nineteenth and occasionally eighteenth centuries, negatively associated in Francoist rhetoric with liberalism and Enlightenment respectively. This time frame allowed them to include the War of Independence period favored by epics.

The 1940s was the great decade of costume dramas in Western cinema generally, with many set in the nineteenth century. Harper (1994) and Cook (1996) have explored how Gainsborough's British costume dramas offered female spectators the spectacle of wayward women skilled in the arts of disguise and escapology. Early Francoist cinema, which remained in private hands and therefore had to be commercially viable, had to satisfy not only the censors but also audiences who flocked to see English-language movies. The historical film tradition in fascist Germany and Italy, also influential in Spain, likewise mostly comprised entertainment cinema (Gubern et al. 1995: 361). The emphasis in costume drama on nineteenth-century settings allowed the depiction of a sexual license whose pleasures are likely to have been enjoyed, regardless of the moralizing end whose conventionality robbed it of impact. A classic case was *El escándalo / The Scandal* (José Luis Sáenz de Heredia, 1943). Hyped by the state-run film magazine *Primer Plano* as a model of quality national cinema, the film's depiction of cynical amorality provoked an outcry from the Church. Many costume dramas were adaptations of conservative or inoffensive nineteenth-century writers, whose status helped to get wayward sexual behavior past the censors. Rafael Gil's 1944 *El clavo / The Nail* (see Chapter 12) and 1947 *La fe / The Faith* were adapted from Alarcón and Palacio Valdés respectively – the latter, whose heroine tries to seduce a priest, produced another Church outcry. A much-adapted novelist was the Jesuit Padre Coloma. Orduña's 1950 *Pequeñeces / Trifles*, based on Coloma's 1890 novel, depicts a truly shocking serial adulteress, played with such gusto by Aurora Bautista that her final repentance fails to convince. Luis Lucia's 1953 *Jeromín* adapted Coloma's novel about the young Don Juan de Austria simply to secure Jesuit investment (*CIFESA* 1990: 132).

Another reason for the preference for nineteenth- (or eighteenth-)century settings was that they allowed low necklines (*escotes*); these did appear in early Francoist cinema but only in costume dramas. Sumptuous examples are Lucia's

Figure 8.8 Cross-class romance between Amparo Rivelles as duchess and Jorge Mistral as bandit leader. Low necklines were allowed by the censors in costume dramas (*La duquesa de Benamejí*, Luis Lucia, 1949; prod. CIFESA). Courtesy of Video Mercury and Filmoteca Española.

1947 *La princesa de los Ursinos* / *The Princesse des Ursins*, a swashbuckling musical romp set during the early-eighteenth-century War of Succession, starring Ana Mariscal at her witty best, and his 1949 *La duquesa de Benamejí* / *The Duchess of Benamejí*, based on the Machado brothers' verse drama – another musical, starring Amparo Rivelles in ravishing costumes as both the duchess and her Gypsy look-alike (see Figure 8.8). Set in the mid-nineteenth century, the film is surprising for its cross-class romance (with Jorge Mistral as a bandit leader) and for its positive treatment of the bandits (in 1949 the Francoist military were hunting down the rural resistance fighters, officially called *bandoleros*) (Fernández Colorado in Pérez Perucha 1997: 254). Cross-class romance and (male) cross-class and (female) cross-gender transvestism provide the pleasure in another musical romp set at the nineteenth century's start: Benito Perojo's 1942 *Goyescas*, in which Imperio Argentina plays both a duchess and a music-hall singer. The film's look is as much Hollywood as Goya.

The folkloric substratum to the last two films reminds us that many folkloric musicals (see Chapter 7) were set in the early to mid-nineteenth century, literally turning the past into a performance. As in Gainsborough's costume dramas (Cook 1996: 74), female Gypsy characters represent a freedom of movement that would end for women with the implantation of modern concepts of sexual difference in the mid-nineteenth century. The choice of this period in so many costume films, including *folklóricas*, allows them to dramatize a freedom – illustrated by bandits and gypsies as non-settled elements of the population – prior to the imposition of state control (Labanyi 2004). Many period *folklóricas* end with the Gypsy heroine marrying a landowner, "settling" her nomadic impulses; the ostensibly happy end "tames" the heroine, again signalling the need to leave a beautiful past behind. Curiously, the first fiction films made in Berlin in 1938 by the Nazi–Spanish coproduction company Hispano-Film-Produktion were folkloric musicals set in the nineteenth century: Rey's *Carmen, la de Triana / Carmen from Triana* and (anachronistically) Perojo's *El barbero de Sevilla / The Barber of Seville*, catering to north European stereotypes of an exotic premodern Spain.

Finally, we should consider films set in the recent past of the Civil War. These ranged from direct propaganda – the infamous but well-crafted *Raza / Race* (Sáenz de Heredia, 1941), scripted under a pseudonym by General Franco – to melodramas such as *Porque te vi llorar / Because I Saw You Cry* (Orduña, 1941), whose bizarre plot sanctions cross-class marriage while implying that the ideal husband is a castrated Nationalist. The latter film's idealization of the caring, feminine man fits ill with the exaltation of the virile warrior (typically played by Alfredo Mayo) found in most of the *cine de cruzada* (Civil War films exalting the Nationalist "crusade"), which filled Spanish screens from 1939 to 1942. Equally anomalous in gender terms is *Rojo y negro / Red and Black* (Carlos Arévalo, 1942), whose explicit fascist values are incarnated by its female protagonist. The Civil War returned as a subject in 1949 with Ruiz-Castillo's *¡El santuario no se rinde! / The Sanctuary Will Not Surrender!*, whose love story between a Republican (played by Alfredo Mayo, going against his fascist star image) and a Nationalist proposes reconciliation in another example of the historical film's use to encourage leaving the past behind. Narrated in flashback form, the film is a possibly unique case of a war film relayed through female voiceover. Equally surprising is Carlos Serrano de Osma's 1951 *Rostro al mar / Face to the Sea*, which reunites its Republican hero and heroine after his odyssey through exile and internment in a German concentration camp. Both Ruiz-Castillo and Serrano de Osma had made pro-Republican documentaries during the war. While these pleas for national reconciliation tapped into Francoist rhetoric of the time (coexisting with extermination of the rural resistance fighters), in the late 1950s they were taken up, following the Spanish Communist Party's 1956 adoption of a policy of national reconciliation, in a further spate of Civil War films. Pedro Lazaga's *La fiel infantería / The Proud Infantry* (1959) is dedicated to "todos los españoles que hicieron esta Guerra, estén donde estén, vivos o muertos" (all Spaniards who fought in this war, wherever they are dead or alive). Antonio Isasi-Isasmendi's *Tierra de todos / All Men's Land* (1962) ends with a baby being born in the crater where the Republican and Nationalist military protagonists, jointly undertaking a mercy mission, have been blown up (Heredero 1993: 207–8). Only in the mid-1970s would it start to become possible to depict what Nationalist victory really meant for the losers.

Between the National and the Global: The Historical Film from the 1960s to the Present (Vicente Rodríguez Ortega)

This section will address how Spanish filmmakers codified the past during, and from the vantage point of, a period of massive change: the fast-track economic development of the 1960s, the transition to democracy, and the country's definitive modernization starting in the mid-1980s, resulting in full integration into global capitalism's economic and cultural circuits.

In fact, the globalization of Spanish historical cinema started in the late 1950s, through the adoption of a set of transnational modes of representation and production. The European western and peplum (the term used for films of this period, usually Italian, set in the ancient world; also called "sword-and-sandal" films) – two international genres that brought together film workers and producers from across Europe and the United States – were extensively produced on Spanish soil. Peplum films started to be made in Spain late in the genre's peak period, with Robert Rossen's *Alexander the Great* (1956). Films such as *La rivolta de gli schiavi / Revolt of the Slaves* (Nunzio Malasomma, 1960), starring Rhonda Flemming; *Goliath contro i giganti / Goliath against the Giants* (Guido Malatesta, 1961); and *I sette gladiatori / Gladiators 7* (Pedro Lazaga, 1962), which included a well-known star of the genre, Richard Harrison, epitomize early-1960s international coproductions made in Spain, the last with a Spanish director. These were period pieces codified through a popular generic format, capitalizing on the use of renowned English-speaking stars and favored by Spanish-government tax breaks. The aim of the 1959 Stabilization Plan and subsequent Development Plans of the 1960s was to open Spain's doors to the global economy, and international production companies specializing in popular European genre films grasped the opportunity. Having established his production company in Spain, in the early 1960s Samuel Bronston produced high-profile blockbusters such as *El Cid* (Anthony Mann, 1961), *55 Days in Peking* (Nicholas Ray, 1963), and *Circus World* (Henry Hathaway, 1964). Attempting to compete globally from his European outpost, after a few years Bronston was dropped by his financial backers (García de Dueñas 1999).

Spanish European westerns – sometimes called *chorizo* or *paella* westerns; sometimes subsumed within the broader category of spaghetti westerns – are a particularly interesting case. Not bound by the historical resonances of westerns produced in the United States, European filmmakers could take the genre's mise-en-scène, empty it of its American ideological referents, and create abstract narratives that dealt metaphorically with the dangers of late capitalism, at the time being embraced enthusiastically by the Spanish state. Santos Zunzunegui has observed that the western's mythical features served in these films as a pretext to deliver an anticapitalist parable, escaping the censors' attention (2005: 96). From 1963 to 1969, over 160 westerns were shot in Almería, Esplugas de Llobregat, and Torrejón (Bentley 2008: 173). These films were often produced, scripted, and directed by established

Spanish directors under a pseudonym: for example, Ignacio F. Iquino made *Oeste Nevada Joe / Guns of Nevada* (1965) and *Cinco pistolas de Texas / Five Dollars for Ringo* (1966) under the alias John Dexter. These coproductions included canonical spaghetti westerns such as Sergio Leone's *A Fistful of Dollars* (1964) and *For a Few Dollars More* (1965), as well as lesser known efforts by Spanish directors such as Joaquín Luis Romero Marchent's *Antes llega la muerte / Hour of Death* (1964) and Eugenio Martín's *El precio de un hombre / The Ugly Ones* (1967).

Not all 1960s historical films were transnational products. Some continued the nationalist slant of the earlier historical epics based on national history. The fact that General Director of Cinema José María García Escudero's attempt in 1950 to grant the "National Interest" rating to the neo-realist *Surcos / Furrows* (José Antonio Nieves Conde, 1951), instead of *Alba de América* (Orduña, 1951), cost him his job makes clear the resistance to abandoning patriotic rhetoric for social critique. However, the "historical kitsch" that continued through the early 1970s was updated with a new, modern look. Films such as *Los guerilleros / The Guerrilla Fighters* (Pedro Luis Ramírez, 1963) and *La guerrilla / The Guerrilla War* (Rafael Gil, 1972) returned to the War of Independence, depicting, like their early Francoist predecessors, a Manichean world of "them" (foreigners) and "us" (Spaniards). *Los guerrilleros* is remarkable for starring folk icons Manolo Escobar and Rocío Jurado as members of the "bandit" resistance to the French occupation, in a winning formula: Spanishness conveyed through popular music and easily decipherable melodramatic conventions.

In the 1970s the historical genre came to be seen as a vehicle of political critique, with a consequent switch of focus to Spain's recent history. The few historical productions from the early 1970s to the inception of democracy recreated the past to offer a diagnosis of a country on the brink of political change (Pérez 1999: 69). Pedro Olea's *Pim pam pum, ¡fuego! / Ready, Aim, Fire!* (1975) paved the way – along with other period pieces more typically labelled as art films: *El espíritu de la colmena / The Spirit of the Beehive* (Víctor Erice, 1973), *La prima Angélica / Cousin Angelica* (Carlos Saura, 1974), and *Las largas vacaciones del 36 / Long Vacations of 36* (Jaime Camino, 1976) – for a critical revaluation of the forty-year Franco dictatorship, initiating what would become a major vein in Spanish cinema in subsequent decades. Olea's film, released a month before Franco died, revisits the Civil War's aftermath with a realist lens that foregrounds the corruption and sexual exploitation of the winners and a cinematically unprecedented solidarity among the losers (Pérez 1999: 71). In addition, the film reinvents Concha Velasco as a star: previously an icon of the dictatorship's "smiling face" as in *Las chicas de la Cruz Roja / Red Cross Girls* (Rafael J. Salvia, 1958), Olea's film recycles her as a powerful sexual onscreen presence identified with the political left. *Pim pam pum, ¡fuego!* opens the door to a revaluation of the demonized figure of the *maquis* (anti-Franco resistance fighters), in a kind of updating of the heroic treatment of the resistance fighters of the War of Independence in earlier cinema, at a time before Spanish cinema could openly treat the Civil War without incurring censorship (Heredero

1999: 215–32). Saura's trilogy *El jardín de las delicias / The Garden of Delights* (1970), *Ana y los lobos / Ana and the Wolves* (1973), and the above-mentioned *La prima Angélica* explore the residues of the Civil War in Spanish collective memory (see Chapter 5). The trilogy chronicles the regime's decomposition, indicting the military and the Church for instilling self-punishing urges in Spaniards. While helping to counter decades of Francoist ideological indoctrination, these films also contribute to the consensus that marked the transition to democracy, suggesting a need to forget the past, close the transgenerational wounds that had split the country in two, and move forward toward full-blown modernization and integration into Europe.

More politically radical than Saura's trilogy, Imanol Uribe's trilogy on Basque nationalism – *El proceso de Burgos / The Burgos Trial* (1979), *Fuga de Segovia / Escape from Segovia* (1981), and *La muerte de Mikel / The Death of Mikel* (1984) – openly treats the history of the Basque pro-independence group ETA, in a classic case of historical film's retroactive readjustment of the past to fit a specific political juncture (Zunzunegui 2005: 160). In the second film especially, Uribe takes a historical event as a point of departure in order to play with the conventions of the documentary and the thriller, creating a hybrid aesthetic that calls attention to the mechanisms through which historical fictions are constructed. The historical genre has also been important in Catalan cinema. Antoni Ribas' *La ciutat cremada / The Burned City* (1976), spanning the decade between loss of empire in 1898 and the 1909 "Tragic Week," constructs the democratic impulse and the Catalan nationalist agenda as largely convergent. Another milestone was Francesc Beltriu's *La plaça del Diamant / The Time of the Doves* (1982), based on Mercè Rodoreda's classic novel set in Barcelona before, during, and after the Civil War.

The year after gaining power in 1982, the Spanish Socialist Party (PSOE) appointed Pilar Miró Director General of Film. The Miró Law (1983) marked a shift in the state's handling of film subsidies. Miró's desire to foster "quality cinema" went together with a desire to disseminate liberal ideology through the medium of film. The policy of promoting Spanish cinema in international festival and arthouse circuits, competing with other European cinemas in increasingly globalized markets and favoring films with a high degree of exportability, was also conceived as a way of curtailing production of the popular genres that were a staple of Spanish cinema (Gubern et al. 1995: 421). This triggered the production of films that attempted to rewrite Spanish history from a left-wing perspective. A key example is Mario Camus' *Los santos inocentes / The Holy Innocents* (1984), an adaptation of Miguel Delibes' novel that revisits Spain's feudal past with polished camerawork and an unambiguous mode of narration in keeping with the PSOE's goal of using the audiovisual media to promote social awareness. Camus performs a political operation in which the ideological is deemed ethical; modernity is a goal to reach but violence invariably leaves its indelible stains (Moreiras-Menor 2007). The film's stars, Alfredo Landa and Paco Rabal, jointly won the Best Actor award at the Cannes Film Festival. In the late 1980s the Miró decree also facilitated the making of potential historical blockbusters such as Saura's self-indulgent "Euro-pudding" (with French, Italian, and Spanish funding), *El Dorado* (1988), about the Spanish conquest of America, and Gonzalo Suárez's English-language reimagining of Lord Byron and Mary Shelley's lives in *Rowing in the Wind / Remando al viento* (1988). The failure of these films at home and abroad forced a rethinking of state policy, bringing in box-office performance as a funding criterion (see Chapter 16).

The early to mid-1990s saw a cycle of films that refigured the Spanish Civil War by framing it from the losers' point of view. These included transnational coproductions such as Camino's *El largo invierno / The Long Winter* (1992), starring Vittorio Gassman, Elizabeth Hurley, and Jean Rochefort alongside Spanish star José Luis López Vázquez. Equally praised and attacked, films such as *Land and Freedom* (Ken Loach, 1995; filmed in Spain with a wide range of European funding) and *Libertarias / Freedomfighters* (Vicente Aranda, 1996) gave voice to previously silenced stories while displaying high production values, enabling them to compete in international markets. Although Loach's coproduction was criticized by some for depicting the war through foreign eyes and for its "unbalanced" focus on Trotskyists and anarchists, it successfully utilized a realist aesthetic to show the growing disillusionment of international volunteers and their Spanish comrades in the Republican militias with their side's progressive self-destruction. Filmed multilingually in English, Spanish, and Catalan, it was one of the few films about the Civil War to make it internationally as well as in Spain. Made on a low budget, the film engaged with a tradition of realist cinema by shooting on location, using non-professional actors, and utilizing a non-intrusive, non-declarative camera aesthetic that leaves room for the spectator to think through the traumatic events it depicts (Crusells 2000: 292). Loach refuses to aestheticize the left through ornate mise-en-scène and self-indulgent camerawork, as has been the case in so many films that treat the Civil War. By contrast, *Libertarias* is in thrall to its saturated reds and the beautified costumes and make-up of its supposedly rugged female anarchist protagonists. As Sánchez-Biosca notes, the film's obsessively pristine mise-en-scène sinks any attempt at a realist mode of representation, with the image trapped in a series of visual anachronisms. At the end, under the alibi of realism, violence takes over the narrative to provide the dose of voyeuristic excitement craved by contemporary spectators (Sánchez-Biosca 2006: 295). Another Civil War film, *La lengua de las mariposas / Butterfly Tongues* (José Luis Cuerda, 1999), while adopting different strategies (sentimentalism, the use of ochre tones), similarly resorts to cliché, stock characters, and a standard repertoire of melodramatic formulae. We should not forget here a tradition of Spanish Civil War comedies encompassing films such as *La vaquilla / The Heifer* (Berlanga, 1985), *¡Ay, Carmela!* (Saura, 1990), and the 1992 Academy Award winner for Best Foreign Picture, Fernando Trueba's *Belle Époque / The Age of Beauty* (set before the war's start but overshadowed by spectators' knowledge of its imminence).

In the first decade of the twenty-first century, we can observe two strands of historical film: one that continues this critical exploration of the Civil War and its legacy, and another that opts for a transnational aesthetic and subject matter. The latter is exemplified by films such as *Alatriste* (Agustín Díaz Yanes, 2006), based on Arturo Pérez-Reverte's bestselling fiction series set in seventeenth-century Flanders and Spain, and by Alejandro Amenábar's *Agora* (2009; see Chapter 5), set in fourth-century Alexandria and made in English. Both were attempts to make international blockbusters within a national film industry that has historically failed to produce international hits. Respectively starring Viggo Mortensen and Rachel Weisz, *Alatriste* and *Agora* are epics for mass consumption that guarantee transnational readability by deploying the look of popular generic modes and displaying production values comparable to their Hollywood equivalents. By contrast, David Trueba's *Soldados de Salamina / Soldiers of Salamis* (2003), based on Javier Cercas' bestselling novel, centers on the importance of researching difficult aspects of the Civil War: in this case, controversially, the real-life story of a prominent Spanish fascist's survival of a Republican firing squad. Incorporating generic features of the detective movie, this docudrama explores multiple layers of (contradictory) evidence in the form of oral testimonies, audiovisual and written documents, and home movies. The polarized political debates around the 2004–7 passage through parliament of the Socialist government's Law of Historical Memory intensified cinematic production on the Civil War and its repressive aftermath, the result being some outstanding documentaries but, in the field of fiction film, a succession of feel-good nostalgia movies that all too often romanticize their subject matter (something that *Soldados de Salamina* is not entirely free of). An unforgiveable example is *Las 13 rosas / 13 Roses* (Emilio Martínez Lázaro, 2007), whose concern with achieving a period look aestheticizes and glamourizes the young Communist women shot for a crime they did not commit.

Ironically, the director who has perhaps provided the best model of how to engage with Spain's historical past and succeed in both domestic and international circuits is the Mexican Guillermo del Toro, with *El espinazo del diablo / The Devil's Backbone* (2001) and *El laberinto del fauno / Pan's Labyrinth* (2006), both filmed in Spain. Both are Spanish–Mexican–US coproductions with impeccable production design and cinematography, notable for rethinking the representation of the Civil War and its aftermath by playing with generic boundaries – those of the thriller, horror, and fantasy (see Figure 8.9). Working within these globally operative modes of address, Del Toro's films are nonetheless not afraid to point fingers at perpetrators. At the same time, their mixing of cinematic genres poses disturbing questions about history and how we relate to it. The international success of these films suggests that the way forward for historical cinema may be to conceive of it as a deconstruction rather than reconstruction of the past, achieved by producing a meticulous reconstruction that is disrupted by dissonant elements, provoking questions rather than providing answers. Del Toro's lesson seems to have been learned in Agustí Villaronga's recent film in Catalan on the Civil War's repressive aftermath, *Pa negre / Black Bread* (2010), which swept up nine Goya awards and in September 2011 was honored with the Premio Nacional de Cinematografía (National Cinema

Figure 8.9 The threatening monster opens its eyes for the first time in *El laberinto del fauno* (Guillermo del Toro, 2006; prod. Estudios Picasso / Tequila Gang).

Figure 8.10 The boy protagonist of *Pa negre* contemplates the photograph that will trigger a series of imaginative projections relating to homoerotic desire in the aftermath of the Civil War (Agustí Villaronga, 2010; prod. Massa d'Or Produccions).

Prize). The film's stunning cinematography is deployed in the service of a story that mixes grim realism with imaginative projection, in a world where everyone (whether oppressor or victim) is lying to cover up some unpalatable truth – imagination thus being the only way of negotiating the real (see Figure 8.10). Disconcertingly, what comes over as the hyper-realistic revelation of the horrific homophobic crime at the film's center, acknowledged in distorted form through local legend, is, we discover, a nightmare – what could be more appropriate when dealing with a historical reality whose monstrosity defies understanding?

References

Allinson, M. (2001) *A Spanish Labyrinth: The Films of Pedro Almodóvar*. London: I. B. Tauris.

Armstrong, N. (1987) *Desire and Domestic Fiction: A Political History of the Novel*. New York: Oxford University Press.

Ballesteros, I. (1999) Mujer y nación en el cine español de posguerra: Los años 40. *Arizona Journal of Hispanic Cultural Studies* 3: 51–70.

Barthes, R. (1978) *A Lover's Discourse: Fragments*. New York: Farrar, Straus, and Giroux.

Bataille, G. (1985) *Visions of Excess: Selected Writings (1927–1939)*. Ed. Allan Stoekl. Minneapolis: University of Minnesota Press.

Bentley, B. P. (2008) *A Companion to Spanish Cinema*. Woodbridge: Tamesis Books.

Berger, J. (2005) Cuatro notas sobre *La vida secreta de las palabras* (escrita y dirigida por Isabel Coixet). In: *Isabel Coixet, La vida secreta de las palabras: El guión*. Barcelona: Ediciones B, pp. 7–10.

Brooks, P. (1976) *The Melodramatic Imagination: Balzac, Henry James, Melodrama, and the Mode of Excess*. New Haven: Yale University Press.

Butler, J. (1990) *Gender Trouble: Feminism and the Subversion of Identity*. New York: Routledge.

Castro de Paz, J. L. (2002) *Un cinema herido: Los turbios años cuarenta en el cine español (1939–1956)*. Barcelona: Paidós.

CIFESA, de la antorcha de los éxitos a las cenizas del fracaso (1990) Special issue of *Archivos de la Filmoteca* 1 (4).

Cook, P. (1996) *Fashioning the Nation: Costume and Identity in British Cinema*. London: BFI.

Crusells, M. (2000) *La Guerra Civil española: Cine y propaganda*. Barcelona: Ariel.

Elsaesser, T. (1972) Tales of Sound and Fury. In: Gledhill, C. (ed.) *Home is where the Heart is: Studies in Melodrama and the Women's Film*. London: BFI, pp. 43–69.

Epps, B. (2005) Entre la efusividad multicolor y la desesperación monocromática: Melodrama, pornografía y abstracción en *Hable con ella*. In: Zurian, F. and Vázquez Varela, C. (eds.) *Almodóvar: El cine como pasión*. Cuenca: Ediciones de la Universidad Castilla-La Mancha, pp. 269–86.

Fanés, F. (1989) *El cas CIFESA: Vint anys de cine espanyol (1932–1951)*. Valencia: Filmoteca Generalitat Valenciana.

Finkielkraut, A. (1999) *La sabiduría del amor: Generosidad y posesión*. Barcelona: Editorial Gedisa.

Foucault, M. (1986) Of Other Spaces. *Diacritics* 16: 22–7.

Gabilondo, J. (2005) Melodrama atlántico y migrancia materna. Apuntes sobre *Todo sobre mi madre*. In: Zurian, F. and Vázquez Varela, C. (eds.) *Almodóvar: El cine como pasión*. Cuenca: Ediciones de la Universidad Castilla-La Mancha, pp. 287–306.

García de Dueñas, J. (1999) Samuel Bronston, una quimera española. In: Monterde, J. E. (ed.) *Ficciones históricas: El cine histórico español*. Special issue of *Cuadernos de la Academia* 6: 233–50.

Gledhill, C. (1987) The Melodramatic Field: An Investigation. In: Gledhill, C. (ed.) *Home is where the Heart is: Studies in Melodrama and the Woman's Film*. London: BFI, pp. 5–39.

González González, L. M. (2009) *Fascismo, "kitsch" y cine histórico español (1939–1953)*. Cuenca: Universidad de Castilla-La Mancha.

Gramsci, A. (1985) *Selections from Cultural Writings*. Ed. Forgacs, D. and Nowell-Smith, G. Cambridge, MA: Harvard University Press.

Gubern, R. (1974) *Mensajes icónicos en la cultura de masas*. Barcelona: Lumen.

Gubern, R. (1981) *La censura: Función política y reordenamiento jurídico bajo el franquismo (1936–1975)*. Barcelona: Península.

Gubern, R. (1994) *Benito Perojo: Pionerismo y superviviencia*. Madrid: Filmoteca Española.

Gubern, R., Monterde, J. E., Pérez Perucha, J., et al. (1995) *Historia del cine español*, 2nd edn. Madrid: Cátedra.

Harper, S. (1994) *Picturing the Past: The Rise and Fall of the British Costume Film*. London: BFI.

Heilman, R. (1968) *Tragedy and Melodrama: Versions of Experience*. Seattle: University of Washington Press.

Heredero, C. F. (1993) *Las huellas del tiempo: Cine español 1951–1961*. Valencia: Filmoteca Generalitat Valenciana.

Heredero, C. F. (1999) Historias del maquis en el cine español: Entre el arrepentimiento y la reivindicación. In: Monterde, J. E. (ed.) *Ficciones históricas: El cine histórico español*. Special issue of *Cuadernos de la Academia* 6: 215–32.

Herlinghaus, H. (2002) La imaginación melodramatica: Rasgos intermediales y heterogéneos de una categoría precaria. In: Herlinghaus, H. (ed.) *Narraciones anacrónicas de la modernidad: Melodrama e intermedialidad en América Latina*. Santiago de Chile: Editorial Cuarto Propio, pp. 21–59.

Higson, A. (2003) *English Heritage, English Cinema: Costume Drama since 1980*. Oxford: Oxford University Press.

Hughes-Warrington, M. (2007) *History Goes to the Movies: Studying History on Film*. London: Routledge.

Kleinhans, C. (1976) Notes on Melodrama and the Family under Capitalism. *Film Reader* 3: 40–7.

Labanyi, J. (2004) Costume, Identity and Spectator Pleasure in Historical Films of the Early Franco Period. In: Marsh, S. and Nair, P. (eds.) *Gender and Spanish Cinema*. Oxford: Berg, pp. 33–51.

Labanyi, J. (2005) Horror, Spectacle and Nation-Formation: Historical Painting in Late Nineteenth-Century Spain. In: Larson, S. and Woods, E. (eds.) *Visualizing Spanish Modernity*. Oxford: Berg, pp. 64–80.

Labanyi, J. (2007) Negotiating Modernity through the Past: Costume Films of the Early Franco Period. *Journal of Iberian and Latin American Studies* 13: 241–58.

Marsé, J. (1971) *Años de penitencia (1939–1950)*. Barcelona: Difusora Internacional.

Martín, A. (2005) *La gramática de la felicidad: Relecturas franquistas y posmodernas del melodrama*. Madrid: Libertarias/Prodhufi.

Martín Gaite, C. (1978) *El cuarto de atrás*. Madrid: Destino.

Martín Gaite, C. (1987) *Usos amorosos de la postguerra española*. Barcelona: Anagrama.

Martín Gaite, C. (2002) *Cuadernos de todo*. Barcelona: Random House-Mondadori.

Mate, R. (2005) *A contraluz de las ideas políticamente correctas*. Barcelona: Anthropos.

Monterde, J. E. (ed.) (1999) *Ficciones históricas: El cine histórico español*. Special issue of *Cuadernos de la Academia* 6.

Moore, Rachel O. (2000) *Savage Theory: Cinema as Modern Magic*. Durham: Duke University Press.

Moreiras-Menor, C. (2007) De lo natural a lo histórico, de lo ético a lo político: Temporalidades violentas en Delibes y Camus. *Dissidences: Hispanic Journal of Theory and Criticism* 3 (1): 1–19.

Moretti, F. (1983) *Kindergarten. Signs Taken for Wonders: On the Sociology of Literary Forms*. London: Verso, pp. 157–81.

Neale, S. (1986) Melodrama and Tears. *Screen* 27 (6): 6–22.

Neale, S. (2000) *Genre and Hollywood*. London: Routledge.

Pérez, P. (1999) Entre la apertura, el bunker y la disidencia (Presencias de la historia en el cine español, 1970–1976). In: Monterde, J. E. (ed.) *Ficciones históricas: El cine histórico español*. Special issue of *Cuadernos de la Academia* 6: 67–78.

Pérez Firmat, G. (2007) Reading for Feeling: Pablo Neruda's "Poema 20." *Hispania* 90 (1): 32–41.

Pérez Perucha, J. (ed.) (1997) *Antología crítica del cine español 1906–1995*. Madrid: Cátedra / Filmoteca Española.

Ríos Font, W. (1997) *Rewriting Melodrama: The Hidden Paradigm in Modern Spanish Theater*. Lewisburg: Bucknell University Press.

Rodríguez, J. (2004) *Almodóvar y el melodrama de Hollywood: Historia de una pasión*. Valladolid: Maxtor.

Sánchez-Biosca, V. (2006) *Cine y guerra civil española: Del mito a la memoria*. Madrid: Alianza.

Sánchez Noriega, J. L. (2004) *Apuntes sobre las relaciones entre el cine y la historia (el caso español)*. Salamanca: Junta de Castilla y León.

Sarlo, B. (1985) *El imperio de los sentimientos: Narraciones de circulación periódica en la Argentina. 1917–1927*. Buenos Aires: Grupo Editorial Norma.

Singer, B. (2001) *Melodrama and Modernity: Early Sensational Cinema and its Context*. New York: Columbia University Press.

Sobejano, G. (1996) Política y melodrama en el teatro de Galdós. *Boletín de la Fundación Federico García Lorca* 19–20: 13–26.

Sommer, D. (1991) *Foundational Fictions: The National Romances of Latin America*. Berkeley: University of California Press.

Thrift, N. (2008) *Non-Representational Theory: Space, Politics, Affect*. London: Routledge.

Triana Toribio, N. (2003) *Spanish National Cinema*. London: Routledge.

Vázquez Montalbán, M. (1970) *Manifiesto subnormal: Escritos subnormales*. Barcelona: Grijalbo.

Vázquez Montalbán, M. (1974a) *Happy End: Escritos subnormales*. Barcelona: Grijalbo.

Vázquez Montalbán, M. (1974b) *La penetración americana en España*. Madrid: Cuadernos para el Diálogo.

Vázquez Montalbán, M. (2000) *Cancionero general del franquismo (1939–1975)*. Barcelona: Editorial Crítica.

Williams, L. (1998) Melodrama Revised. In: Browne, N. (ed.) *Refiguring American Film Genres: History and Theory*. Berkeley: University of California Press, pp. 42–88.

Williams, L. (2005) El melodrama melancólico: El dolor y las relaciones homosexuales perdidas en el cine de Almodóvar. In: Zurian, F. and Vázquez Varela, C. (eds.) *Almodóvar: El cine como pasión*. Cuenca: Ediciones de la Universidad Castilla-La Mancha, pp. 307–16.

Williams, R. (1977). *Marxism and Literature*. Oxford: Oxford University Press.

Zunzunegui, S. (2005) *Los felices sesenta: Aventuras y desventuras del cine español (1959–1971)*. Madrid: Paidós.

Further Reading

Altman, R. (1999) *Film / Genre*. London: BFI.

Labanyi, J. (2000) Feminizing the Nation: Women, Subordination, and Subversion in Post-Civil War Spanish Cinema. In: Sieglohr, U. (ed.) *Heroines without Heroes: Reconstructing Female and National Identities in European Cinema 1945–51*. London: Cassell, pp. 163–82.

Pérez Rojas, J. and Alcaide, J. L. (1992) Apropiaciones y recreaciones de la pintura de historia. In: Díez, J. L. (ed.) *La pintura de historia en España en el siglo XIX*. Madrid: Museo del Prado, pp. 103–18.

Vázquez Montalbán, M. (1998) *Crónica sentimental de España*. Barcelona: Grijalbo.

Zunzunegui, S. (2002) *Historias de España. ¿De qué hablamos cuando hablamos de cine español?* Valencia: Filmoteca Generalitat Valenciana.

9

Film Noir, the Thriller, and Horror

Jo Labanyi, Antonio Lázaro-Reboll, and Vicente Rodríguez Ortega

Introduction (Antonio Lázaro-Reboll)

Genres "depend directly and heavily on the identity and purpose of those using and evaluating them" (Altman 1999: 98); that is, on the discursive activities of "genre users" or "user groups" that function as "discursive claims made by real speakers for particular purposes in specific situations" (Altman 1999: 101). The industry, critical commentators, audiences, and fans participate in the classification of genres, understood as a social process. Rather than stable, consistent bodies of work, genre theorists such as Rick Altman have argued that genres are unstable, ambiguous, and resistant to easy categorization and definition (1999: 123–4).

This chapter insists on genre as a process. Definitions of genres change over time – from the term *film noir* coined by French critics after World War II to describe 1940s and 1950s American films that shared an aesthetic sensibility, to the reinterpretation of the crime film in different cultures, to the ways in which the horror genre is constructed by different social groups. Rather than idealized objects that conform to the paradigms produced by critics and theorists, genre films are hybrid entities. The overlap of *film noir*, the thriller, and horror with other genres works on two levels: on the one hand, films relate to one another and evoke other genres to appeal to different audiences; on the other, as Joan Hawkins puts it, "not only there is slippage between genres, there is also slippage between evaluative classifications" (2000: 27). For example, Ladislao Vajda's film *El cebo / It Happened in Broad Daylight* (1958) features in the discussion here of both *noir* and horror, while Eloy de la Iglesia's *La semana del asesino / Cannibal Man* (1971) is discussed as both thriller and horror film. While Rodríguez Ortega considers *El cebo*

A Companion to Spanish Cinema, First Edition. Edited by Jo Labanyi and Tatjana Pavlović.

to be part of the internationalization of 1950s Spanish *noir* and *La semana del asesino* as a distinctive thriller of the late Francoist period, Lázaro-Reboll notes that Vajda's film has become a canonical text in some histories of Spanish horror film and that de la Iglesia's became a classic of European exploitation cinema once it was included in the inventory of horror titles known as "video nasties."

Traditional histories of Spanish cinema have dismissed *film noir*, the thriller, and horror as "mimetic," "imitative," or "derivative" of American models; this has contributed to the marginalization of these genres. As Jay Beck and Vicente Rodríguez Ortega observe in *Contemporary Spanish Cinema and Genre*, "the view of genre [in the case of Spanish film scholarship] has almost exclusively been constructed negatively" (2008: 5). However, as this chapter argues, the transnational sensibility associated with these two genres is key to their understanding, cutting across not only their mode of production and aesthetics but also their modes of reception and consumption. Indeed, this type of Spanish genre production establishes a fruitful dialogue with wider Hollywood and European cinematic traditions in a variety of ways: for instance, the numerous transnational coproductions of *film noir* in the 1950s and of horror in the 1960s and 1970s, and the transnational modes of reception of Spanish *noir* and Spanish horror whereby they are marketed and consumed as "Euronoir" and "Eurohorror," respectively.

The chapter starts with chronological overviews of Spanish *noir* and the thriller, relating local production to Hollywood trends and cycles as well as to the wider Spanish social, political, and ideological contexts. It then goes on to focus on the horror genre, examining the discursive activities of "genre users" in constructions of the field of Spanish horror film.

Film Noir (Jo Labanyi and Vicente Rodríguez Ortega)

Film noir has typically been theorized as a confluence of four factors: the adaptation of hardboiled fiction for the silver screen; an evolving paradigm of representation deriving from the 1930s gangster film; the importation into Hollywood of German Expressionism's low-key lighting and skewed angles; and the attempt to capture the bleak underworlds of the 1940s US cityscape. However, it is imperative to remember that, in its very beginnings, *film noir* was fundamentally a critical rather than industrial category. That is, *film noir* became a genre as a result of a series of French critical essays, written shortly after the end of World War II, that attempted to define the contours of a cycle of Hollywood films with specific characteristics that had begun a few years before. The term did not become standard in film scholarship and criticism to refer to a specific body of films of the 1940s and 1950s until several decades later. As Martin Rubin states in relation to the *noir* genre, "neither the term nor the concept behind it received wide circulation in English-language film criticism until ca. 1970" (1999: 90).

Noir, thus, did not spring from a conscious effort on the part of studios and filmmakers to create a genre. As James Naremore states, *film noir* is "a baggy concept, elaborated largely after the fact of the films themselves" (1998: 5). When discussing *film noir*, we have to remember that those films now labeled *noir* that date from before 1946 were made before the term existed, and those made in the late 1940s or 1950s were mostly made without knowledge of the term. All the same, there is a certain aesthetic and thematic consistency to a cycle of films made in Hollywood from the early 1940s through the mid-1950s, peaking between 1946 and 1950 and expanding transnationally to other film industries, including those of France, Japan, and Spain. The retrospective application to this cycle of films of the label *film noir* functions industrially and aesthetically as a roughly recognizable generic register that has the practical function of allowing filmmakers and spectators to identify a particular cinematic corpus. Although the term *noir* is applied to contemporary cinema – in the broad sense of the thriller (*serie negra* in Spanish), as in the term *Euronoir* mentioned at the end of this chapter – this section will use the term in the restricted sense of that body of films from the 1940s and 1950s recognized as sharing certain cinematic and thematic features.

Early Spanish *noir* is clearly derivative, which should not be interpreted as a failure of creative imagination but rather as an attempt to situate Spanish cinema within the contours of a transnational cinematic mode of address that was swiftly expanding from the United States to Europe and East Asia. Being made during the dictatorship, Spanish *noir* – like the thriller, as we shall see – walked a thin line since it focused on the dark underbelly of society, revealing the moral rot of postwar Spanish society, contradicting the illusion of wellbeing that Francoism attempted to instill into its citizens. Predictably, censors were quick to pounce on any explicit condemnation of the regime. To make a *film noir* in Spain was, consequently, a continuous process of ideological and aesthetic negotiation between the demands of the internationally operative mode of address and the idiosyncrasies of Spain's political environment.

What most clearly distinguishes *noir* from the thriller is its focus on the dark side of human subjectivity, trapped in a downward spiral, without the relief of a morally satisfying ending. The Central European exiles from Nazism who arrived in Hollywood from the mid-1930s brought with them not only familiarity with German expressionist cinematography but also a knowledge of Freud's exploration of pathology, which the expressionist aesthetic of distortion and shadows was perfectly suited to express. Spanish *noir* of the late 1940s is mostly concerned not with a detective's investigation of a crime but with a character-investigator probing a case of pathological disturbance; as in Hollywoood *noir*, the murky world under observation frequently theatens to suck the character-investigator in. Like Hollywood, 1930s Spain saw a significant influx of Central European filmmakers fleeing Nazism – in this case, cameramen and art directors who were welcomed into the Spanish film industry because of their technical expertise (Llinás 1989: 45–50) – with more arriving after Hitler's occupation of France in 1940, several of them staying in Spain after the end of World War II. Curiously, the examples of Spanish *noir* made in the late 1940s were not their work but that of indigenous cameramen and art directors – though the German Sigfrido Burmann, who had arrived in Spain in 1914, did the sets for the films by Neville discussed here.

Three directors stand out for the production of *noir* films in late 1940s Spain: Carlos Serrano de Osma, Edgar Neville, and Llorenç Llobet Gràcia (the last coming out of the Catalan amateur cinema movement). The first two were professionally imbued with US film culture: Serrano de Osma as a film critic from 1933–47 and Neville via his work in Hollywood and at Paramount's Joinville (Paris) studios in the late 1920s and early 1930s. Serrano de Osma's film criticism of 1945–7 discusses in detail the features of the contemporary Hollywood cinema we now call *noir*, noting that Orson Welles was an antecedent. In 1945 Serrano de Osma (cited in Labanyi 1995: 10) remarked that Hollywood was delivering a "diariamente, con profusión exhaustiva" (daily, overwhelming) dose of distorted images constructing "visiones de pesadilla, obsesión o neurastenia" (nightmarish, obssessive, or neurasthenic visions). Serrano de Osma's four films between 1946 and 1948 represent an attempt to create a Spanish *noir* tradition (the term is never used by him) that picks up on the gender anxieties that feminist film critics have seen as intrinsic to the genre, which classically depicts the anxious masculinity of an investigator probing the riddle of femininity and torn between a dark *femme fatale* and a blonde nurturing woman (Thomas 1992: 59–67; Cowie 1993). Serrano de Osma's first film, *Abel Sánchez* (1946), intelligently adapts Miguel de Unamuno's novel of disturbed masculinity through a *noir* lens, with profuse use of visual distortions (including a dramatic hallucination sequence), shadows, and low- and high-angle shots to create a sense of unbearable claustrophia – that of the protagonist's mind as he probes his own sexual obsessions. *Embrujo / Bewitched* (1947) was an extraordinary attempt to create an arthouse movie out of the folkloric musical genre, with Lola Flores' dancing viewed through the drunken hallucinations of her male dancing partner (and real-life performing and romantic partner), Manolo Caracol. *La sirena negra / The Black Siren* (1947) adapted Emilia Pardo Bazán's 1908 modernist novel as a drama of erotic obsession (acted by Fernando Fernán Gómez) with a dying woman. The protagonist of *La sombra iluminada / The Illuminated Shadow* (1948) – whose title evokes *noir* cinematography – is an escaped mental patient who investigates the crime for which he was locked up. Serrano de Osma helped to finance Llobet Gràcia's rediscovered masterpiece *Vida en sombras / Life in Shadows* (made in 1948, released in 1953), which brilliantly uses *noir* cinematography to dramatize its protagonist's (Fernando Fernán Gómez) obsessive sense of guilt at his wife's accidental death in the Civil War.

Neville's films from 1944 to 1947 draw regularly on expressionist techniques in plots that mostly feature the investigation of a crime (or of a literal underworld in *La torre de los siete jorobados / The Tower of the Seven Hunchbacks*, 1944; see Chapter 6), but in a comic vein. However, the brilliantly disturbing *Nada / Nothing* (1947),

Figure 9.1 The *noir* stairwell in *Nada*: the predatory Román watches Andrea from above (Edgar Neville, 1947; prod. CIFESA).

based on Carmen Laforet's contemporary novel of the same name, remains the most accomplished example of *noir* in the history of Spanish cinema. As Vicente Sánchez-Biosca explains in Chapter 12, the production company CIFESA cut thirty minutes from the film in a vain attempt to alleviate its unrelieved atmosphere of claustrophia and suppressed hysteria, only to concentrate it even more. For the film's striking use of camerawork and production design, readers are referred to Chapter 12; what deserves mention here is the gender twist that Neville gives to the *noir* format. Instead of the usual insecure male investigating the riddle of femininity, we have a cool-headed young woman, Andrea (played by Neville's common-law wife, Conchita Montes), investigating the pathological psychology of her two uncles, Román and Juan. While the extensive use of shadows (particularly the classic *noir* stairwell) and oppressive low ceilings threaten to engulf Andrea in the claustrophobic family drama (see Figure 9.1), she remains intact. In a brilliant touch, it is the camera itself that falls victim to the murky world it is investigating as, at the film's end, no sooner has Andrea escaped into the daylight than the camera is sucked back into the *noir* hell of the stairwell, filmed – with the help of the nightmarish musical soundtrack – as an inescapable vortex. There is a political twist too, thanks to the casting of Fosco Giachetti – known for playing the role of virile warrior hero in Italian fascist epics, in which he typically appears in sun-drenched exteriors – as the predatory blackmarketeer Román, filmed here in shadowy, distorted interiors.

The intensive production of films with a *noir* aesthetic and thematics between 1946 and 1948 was not continued. However, the 1950s saw a number of films that productively drew on *noir* cinematography and, as in Hollywood *noir*, refused a morally comforting ending. Set in North Africa, *La corona negra / Black Crown* (Luis Saslavsky, 1950), a Suevia Films production written by Miguel Mihura, whose cast included the Mexican María Félix and the Italian Vittorio Gassman (see Chapter 2), displayed a "by-the-book" *noir* aesthetic through the extensive use of low-key lighting, skewed camera angles, and a narrative structure designed around a series of flashbacks. The film shares the sense of impending doom that characterizes classic *films noirs* such as *Double Indemnity* (Billy Wilder, 1943) and *Out of the Past* (Jacques Tourneur, 1947). Juan Antonio Nieves Conde's *Los peces rojos / Red Fish* (1952) – a box-office hit set in the northern town of Gijón – uses the phantasmagoric presence of a nonexistent son and a claustrophobic, storm-buffeted hotel to capture the psychological disturbance of a failed writer hiding from himself as well as from the authorities. The use of *noir* cinematography and production design had, in fact, accounted for much of the success of Nieves Conde's famous *Surcos / Furrows* of 1951, whose non-*noir* topic of migration from city to country was expressed through the representation of the city as a form of entrapment. *Los peces rojos* capitalized on the use of depth of field and high- and low-angle shots, blatantly appropriating the aesthetic of *Citizen Kane* as its immediate visual referent (see Figure 9.2). The poster for the film – dominated by oblique lines, slanted angles, and multiplane composition – highlighted the film's reliance on the internationally operative aesthetic of *noir* as an organizing framework to catch the audience's attention. In their marketing of these 1950s Spanish *noir* films, producers and studios stressed the *noir* thematics of criminality and violence in partnership with romance.

Also deserving of mention is *Los ojos dejan huellas / Eyes Leave Traces* (José Luis Sáenz de Heredia, 1952), starring Raf Vallone, Elena Varzi, and Fernando Fernán Gómez, which creates a claustrophobic mise-en-scène to graphically represent the protagonist's progressive psychological deterioration. Like *La corona negra*, this film illustrates the progressive internationalization of the genre and the corresponding practice of transnational coproduction (see Chapter 2) – also exemplified by *El cebo*, Vajda's German–Spanish film based on a story by Friedrich Dürrenmatt. *El cebo* is thematically and aesthetically reminiscent of Fritz Lang's *M* (1931) in chronicling the search for a serial child killer in the Swiss cantons. Also in 1958, Julio Coll made *Un vaso de whisky/A Glass of Whiskey*, a tale of false friendship and revenge involving two former university colleagues separated by class difference. The film uses the metaphor of night and a series of sleazy spaces (a cabaret among others) to depict the domino effect – materialized literally in the film's opening credits – of a series of unethical decisions that end up condemning the protagonist. As Antonio José Navarro aptly comments, the urban atmosphere of films such as *Un vaso de whisky* reveals the greyness of characters whose evil has more to do with

Figure 9.2 The tormented writer in *Los peces rojos* (Antonio Nieves Conde, 1952; prod. Yago Films / Estela Films).

the drastic cultural and economic deprivations of Spain at the time than with their inner personae (2006: 341). If early Francoism proved a propitious period for *noir* techniques to flourish in Spanish cinema, it was because the political and economic conditions translated easily into the murky world of *noir* that in Hollywood had been used to express inner-city decay and, some have argued (Maltby 1992: 39–48), the paranoia of persecuting political right and persecuted political left in the McCarthyite era of anticommunist witch hunts – a paranoia that was even more keenly felt in the politically repressive climate of 1940s and 1950s Spain.

The Thriller (Vicente Rodríguez Ortega)

The thriller is one of those genres that is easier to identify than to define with precision, since its contours are typically liminal: it exists in a criss-cross of generic categories ranging across the adventure film, romance, melodrama, horror, the gangster film, and the detective film. As we shall see, its overlap with *noir* is substantial. As Martin Rubin has written, "the thriller can be conceptualized as a 'metagenre' that gathers several other genres under its umbrella, and as a band in the spectrum that colors each of those particular genres" (1999: 4). In short, it is a fundamentally hybrid mode of representation. In addition, the term "thriller" nominally refers to the ability to *thrill*: to physically and psychologically engage the spectator through the deployment of a variety of cinematic techniques, which constitute its generic codes. Alternatively, the thriller may be understood as an ideological canvas through which behavioral practices and social formations are evaluated morally in the context of the crime film. Thus, the plot typically pits unscrupulous criminals against the law and, intertwined with the problematics of heterosexual romance, in most cases enables society to suppress the menace of deviance and re-establish the parameters of the accepted social order. In the context of Spanish cinema during the Franco dictatorship, the vast majority of crime films served to condemn those forms of behavior that bent the rules of social conduct as dictated by the regime's ideological fabric. If the thriller remained a marginal genre during the dictatorship's first decades, this was evidently because of the strict censorship policies imposed by the state, with the Church members of the Board of Censors having a veto (Llorens 1988; Heredero 1993; Cueto 2002; see Chapter 14). Organized crime, poverty, social marginalization, and psychological or sexual deviance could not be recognized as part of Spanish society.

The history of the thriller in Spanish cinema starts in the 1950s with the birth of the so-called *género policíaco*. As Antonio José Navarro (2006) explains, the characteristics that allow a film to be identified as belonging to the *género policíaco* are the presence of crime in its multiple variants, a psychological structure in which the notion of crime disrupts the peaceful coexistence of a particular community, and a visual style that fosters claustrophobia, nihilism, the unbearable force of fate, and a tragic sense of despair. In addition, such films utilize a dense, obtrusive soundscape that reverberates powerfully throughout the narrative, functioning as an aural counterpart to its protagonists' psychological imbalance.

To make a thriller under the dictatorship meant entering the slippery terrain of a genre that by definition focused on morally, sexually, or politically deviant behavior. A higher "ethical" authority, embodied by the law, had to remain intact to avoid the censors' red pen. Thus, in these early Spanish thrillers, criminals and wrongdoers are invariably punished. The law and its "heroic agents" solve all crimes, emphasizing their higher authority as agents of the regime; we do not find in Spanish thrillers of this period the "private eye" who in many Hollywood thrillers replaces a police force viewed as corrupt. However, as Elena Medina de la Viña (2000) argues, many of these early Spanish thrillers had a critical, realist dimension despite the sanitization required by censorship. Medina de la Viña suggests that this realist slant had two sources: first, the Italian neo-realist aesthetic concurrently having an impact on Spanish filmmakers; second, the fact that Ignacio F. Iquino's Barcelona-based studio, IFI, had the distribution rights to 20th Century Fox productions at a time when Fox had started to shoot on location with non-professional actors. There is, indeed, a realist vein in the thrillers produced by Iquino's production company, Emisora Films, such as *Apartado de correos 1001 / P. O. Box 1001* (Julio Salvador, 1950) and *Brigada criminal / Crime Squad* (Ignacio

F. Iquino, 1950). Yet these films – even if pointing to a realist tradition derived from the thriller's and *noir*'s attention to society's underside, as well as to some extent Italian neo-realism – also offer a stock repertoire of *noir* stylistic commonplaces, such as the constant emphasis on slatted blinds to create a claustrophobic effect, and extensive use of high-contrast shots and oblique camera angles. This skewed, expressionist visuality can undermine the moral tone that directors were obliged to add to appease the regime, suggesting a world that is less black and white (Navarro 2006: 349). Other remarkable titles that follow the police versus criminal formula with similar morally upright endings are *Persecución en Madrid / Persecution in Madrid* (Enrique Gómez Bascuas, 1952), *Contraband Spain / Contrabando* (Julio Salvador, 1955; filmed in English and Spanish), *El cerco / The Cordon* (Miguel Iglesias, 1955), and *A sangre fría / In Cold Blood* (Juan Bosch, 1959), as well as the adaptation of Emilio Hernández Pino's play *Duda / Doubt* (Julio Salvador, 1951), which mixes the suspense thriller and melodrama (Cueto 2002: 359).

Stepping into the 1960s, the Spanish thriller evolved in three directions: progressive hybridization with other generic categories and cinematic movements, such as black comedy or the French New Wave; increasing use of non-studio locations; and explicit depiction of violence, which went together with a new privileging of the criminals' point of view over that of the agents of the law. It is imperative to highlight the importance of José María Forqué's *Atraco a las tres / Robbery at 3 O'clock* (1962) and Francisco Pérez-Dolz's *A tiro limpio / Shoot-out* (1963). The former combines acerbic black humor, *noir* visuality, and realist drama to depict the failed attempt of a group of well-intentioned but pathetic bank employees to pull off a heist at their workplace. The latter mixes a realist impulse, manifest in the use of real locations, with a highly stylized mise-en-scène. *Las manos sucias / Dirty Hands* (Juan Antonio de la Loma, 1963) is a reimagining of Luchino Visconti's *Ossessione / Obsession* (1943) that plays with the figure of a hard-working gas station owner and his unhealthy obsession with a small-town beauty / *femme fatale*. *Los atracadores / The Robbers* (Francisco Rovira Beleta, 1961), based on a novel by a former secret police agent, is narrated from the point of view of one of the three robbers, a delinquent who seems to be motivated purely by existential angst. *No dispares contra mí / Don't Fire at Me* (José María Nunes, 1961) is a mix of B-movie and arthouse film that unabashedly imitates Truffaut's self-referential *noir Tirez sur le pianiste / Shoot the Piano Player* (1960) (Cueto 2002: 464–5).

With Franco's death in 1975, although censorship was not formally replaced by a ratings system until November 1977, both state censorship and the Church lost their moral grip on Spanish cinema. Critics and fans were able to acknowledge the thriller's critical and cultural importance openly; the genre no longer had to "apologize" for its existence (Cueto 2002: 366). The genre's newly acquired intellectual pedigree was facilitated by the emergence of a new cohort of filmmakers who consciously set out to redefine its contours. The transition period saw the birth of a social cinema that crossed the thriller with the action film so as to account for unspoken social realities such as teenage delinquency or drug addiction. Perhaps the pivotal film was *Deprisa, deprisa / Fast, Fast* (Carlos Saura, 1980), which updated what has been seen as Saura's "neo-realist" masterpiece *Los golfos / The Delinquents* (1960). With *Los golfos'* focus on delinquency as his starting point, Saura attempted in *Deprisa, deprisa* to create a fresh kind of popular cinema that engaged with the new democratic historical reality. The film opens to the rhythms of the rumba band Los Chunguitos as two teenagers steal a car. In what follows, Saura plunges us into the protagonists' downtrodden, economically blighted neighborhood on Madrid's outskirts. The film focuses on a gang of young males plus the local bartender Ángela, who soon turns into a key player in their increasingly dangerous robberies. Saura confronts the spectator with one of those forgotten pockets of deprivation that the euphoric accounts of democratic change seldom took into account. The characters' accented slang anchors the narrative in their cultural idiosyncrasies. The extensive use of wide panoramic shots foregrounds the ugliness of the world depicted, unequivocally situating the film in a tradition of social cinema, filtered through the thriller's generic lens, for *Deprisa, deprisa* is both a denunciation of socioeconomic conditions during the democratic period's early stages and a reinvention of the thriller as a legitimate format for the expression of social content. As the teenagers leave and re-enter their neighborhood before and after their robberies, Saura repeatedly foregrounds a handwritten sign that reads "Los vecinos de la colonia no pedimos por piedad sino por justicia" (The neighborhood's demands seek justice, not pity). In addition, the constant presence of buildings under construction signals the pervasive urban alienation that the overdevelopment of outer Madrid was generating at the start of the 1980s.

After a bank hold-up goes wrong and death catches up with most of the teenage gang, the film concludes with Ángela, the gang's only female member and the only one who survives, walking away from her neighborhood and dying boyfriend over derelict land framed on both sides by anonymous high-rise apartment blocks. She has the stolen money; perhaps that is her passport to a different life elsewhere. Saura's pre-1975 films were well known for their focus on female characters and examination of oppressive gender roles under Francoism, and his focus on gender continued into the transition period. On the one hand, Ángela may be seen as the embryonic model of a type of woman who is no longer subordinated to male authority or to her marginalized place of origin, pointing to newly formed modes of agency in Spanish society. On the other hand, the film's attempt to depict its marginal subjects faithfully sometimes tips into social determinism, replicating their oppression.

Saura's focus on delinquency and social marginality via the thriller/action combo has much in common with the so-called *quinqui* (street thug) cinema, of which *Perros callejeros / Street Warriors* (José Antonio de la Loma, 1977) is the outstanding example; De la Loma would exploit this new subgenre by making a series of sequels and spin-offs with female protagonists. As Rubén Lardín states (2006), this was the Spanish version of blaxploitation cinema: a set of films that used violence, sex, and drugs as springboards for a series of action sequences that attempted to capture an undesirable, unrepresented part of society. In a similar vein, but bringing to the fore the previously forbidden depiction of homosexuality, Eloy de la Iglesia's *El pico / Overdose* (1983) and *El pico 2 / Overdose 2* (1984) depicted the doomed world of youth drug culture, with graphic representations of nudity and the physical processes of drug addiction (for Eloy de la Iglesia's cinema, see Chapter 6).

The thriller of the transition period was marked by the constant tension between a growing attempt to create cinematic products that could function in international markets and a commitment to the specifics of Spanish social reality. This tension is reflected in critical disagreement over these films. Carmen Herrero notes that critics have tended to see the Spanish thriller as increasingly imitative of its Hollywood counterpart, in an attempt to achieve a certain internationalization of the "product" (2007). Ann Davies rejects this critical view, insisting that the Spanish thriller is marked by the particular social, economic, and political changes that took place in Spain from the end of the dictatorship through the 1990s (2007). Peter Evans suggests that Spanish thrillers of the 1980s follow two different directions, "one focus[ing] on private or public investigative figures, big-city crime and underworld *ambientes* [and] another, avoiding the complexities of the detective narrative, concentrat[ing] on transgressive, fatal desires" (1999: 93).

Pivotal thrillers of the transition era that set new levels of permissiveness with regard to the representation of sex and violence in Spanish cinema were *Bilbao* (Bigas Luna, 1978), *Matador* (Pedro Almodóvar, 1986), and Vicente Aranda's two films *Fanny Pelopaja / Fanny Straw-top* (1984) and *Amantes/Lovers: A True Story* (1991). These films conform to a haptic conceptualization of the thriller genre, which relies for its effects on engaging the spectator at a bodily level. Wandering between a variety of generic registers, they foreground the spectacle of the body caught in the grip of intense sensation, demanding from the spectator what Linda Williams – in her seminal essay on melodrama, pornography, and horror, "Film Bodies: Gender, Genre, and Excess" – has called "a lack of aesthetic distance, a sense of overinvolvement in sensation and emotion" (2003: 145). As previously noted, the thriller ultimately aims to thrill, often subordinating the dictates of narrative progression to the production of an excessive discourse that functions as an end in its own right. Spanish filmmakers of the 1980s and 1990s used the thriller genre to push back the limits of representation.

In this respect, the thrillers of the transition period were anticipated by Eloy de la Iglesia's *La semana del asesino* (1971), which focused on a factory worker, Marcos (Vicente Parra), living with his brother Esteban in a shack on Madrid's outskirts. One night, on the way home with his girlfriend Paula (Emma Cohen), he has a row with a taxi driver, who subsequently attacks him and to whom he delivers a fatal blow with a rock. He then embarks on a number of progressively brutal killings – his brother Esteban's fiancée, Paula's father, and the waitress in the local bar – to cover up his previous crimes and avoid arrest. Marcos accumulates the bodies in his bedroom and disposes of them in the meat factory where he works. Néstor (Eusebio Poncela), a resident in a new apartment block overlooking the

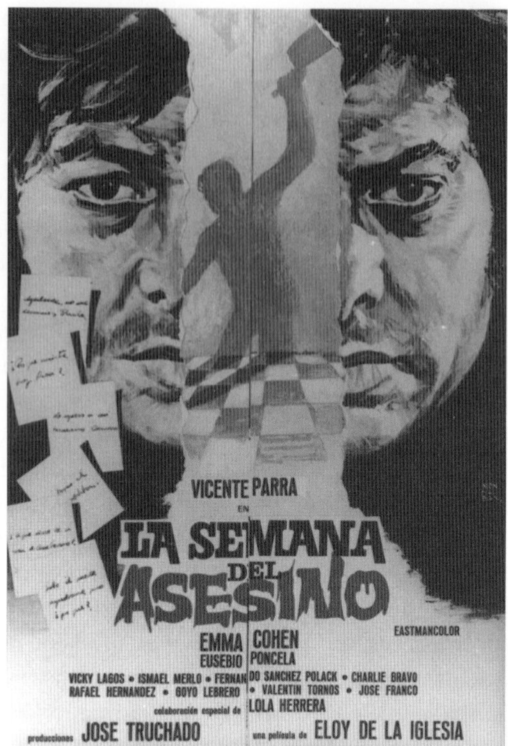

Figure 9.3 Poster for *La semana del asesino* portraying the protagonist Marcos as a divided man, his face split in two (Eloy de la Iglesia, 1971; prod. Atlas International Film). Courtesy of Video Mercury.

shack, witnesses Marcos' crimes from his balcony but does not denounce him. Finally, in an ending imposed by the censors, Marcos turns himself in to the police.

From its opening scene, the film juxtaposes two scopic regimes. Marcos sits in his *chabola* (shack) staring at photos of naked women, while Néstor's voyeuristic gaze observes him from his apartment block. Highlighting these two gazes, divergent in their object of desire but equally unsatisfied, the film depicts a universe of sexual mismatches that will eventually turn violent. While acknowledging the unequivocal presence of a homoerotic sensibility within the Spanish social fabric, de la Iglesia explores the connection between sexuality and murder: the narrative tracks the protagonist's daily life as he becomes immersed in a cycle of serial killings that ends up dominating his psyche and social existence (see Figure 9.3). The murders bring nothing but the putrid stink of corpses that decompose in the protagonist's bedroom. Becoming more and more graphic, the film established an unprecedented permissiveness that made possible the films that followed in the next two decades.

Of these, Bigas Luna's *Bilbao* is a tale of sexual perversion that depicts a man's growing obsession with a prostitute. Visually anchored in extreme close-ups of sexual organs, female garments, and dead animals, the film's depiction of the monetary exchange between client and prostitute moves into the terrain of the exploitation film, figuring the dark consequences of the progressive liberalization of the Spanish market as it opted for full-blown late capitalism. As Marvin D'Lugo affirms, *Bilbao*

> might appear to be only one more of the chain of pornographic films released in Spain during the early post-Franco years. [...] A closer inspection, however, reveals a precise and highly controlled visual and narrational structure charged with a series of other, "oppositional" messages. At the very least, the depiction of Leo's sexual obsessions forces the audience to question the illusion of post-Franco social freedom. (1997: 37)

Focusing on the marginalized underbelly of Barcelona's nightlife, *Bilbao* depicts a perverse middle-class exchange economy that culminates in psychotic violence. It capitalizes on the transition period's new permissiveness with regard to the representation of sex and violence to provoke horror (another example of how the thriller and horror frequently blur), demanding a physical response from the spectator to its thrilling yet repellent mode of address. The combination of perverse sexual obsession and violence would be continued by Aranda's French–Spanish coproduction *Fanny Pelopaja* and his later *Amantes*.

Almodóvar's contribution to the reinvention of the thriller genre – first in *Matador*, coinciding with the films of the transition discussed here, but also in the later movies *Tacones lejanos / High Heels* (1991), *Carne trémula / Live Flesh* (1997), and *La mala educación / Bad Education* (2004) – takes it in very different directions. Extensively documented elsewhere (Acevedo-Muñoz 2008; D'Lugo 2008; Epps and Kakoudaki 2009; Marcantonio 2009), one of Almodóvar's main merits is his reworking of icons and commonplaces of Spanish culture by re-viewing them through the lens of a transnational sensibility based on the mixing of genres and appropriation of a variety of cinematic traditions ranging from 1950s Hollywood melodrama to exploitation film, screwball comedy, and soap opera, among others. To this list we can add the thriller. *Matador* remains perhaps his most iconoclastic appropriation of a symbol of Spanishness – bullfighting – that had been harnessed to a nationalistic agenda by the Franco regime, as a pretext for immersing the spectator in a twisted universe of sex, murder, and perversion (see Figure 9.4). *Tacones lejanos*, for its part, maps out a hybrid terrain where melodramatic excess – what we could call the "diva imagination" – and the thriller meet. Based on crime-fiction writer Ruth Rendell's novel *Live Flesh*, *Carne trémula* is an erotically charged pyschological thriller with plenty of plot twists that traverses a variety of generic codes as diverse as soap opera, *noir*, and the comedic / melodramatic. *La mala educación* subjects the investigative mode to an increasing reflexivity, to the point of becoming "meta-Almodovarian." In all these films, Almodóvar mixes the thriller format with the melodramatic imagination and the strategic deployment of comedic

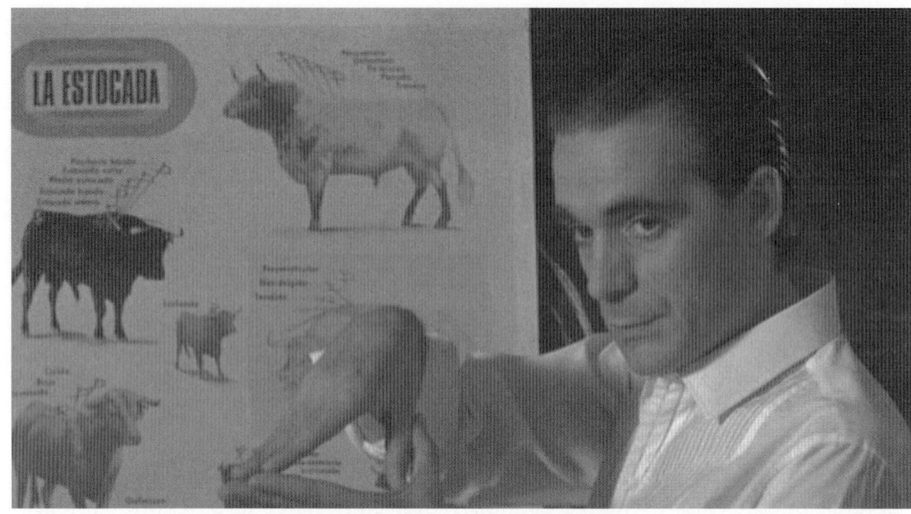

Figure 9.4 Ángel (Antonio Banderas) mesmerized by the lecture on the art of killing (*Matador*, Pedro Almodóvar, 1986; prod. Compañía Iberoamericana de TV).

excess in order to reinvent commonplaces of the thriller genre – such as the *femme fatale* or the private investigator.

While recognized as a hallmark of Almodóvar's *oeuvre*, this process of hybridization via the appropriation and resemanticization of other filmic texts is, in fact, a major feature of Spanish cinema of the last few decades. Rick Altman argues that the rise of mass media and consumerism "along with the proliferation of narrative entertainment [...] have tilted the typical generic mix of life experience / textual experience radically toward the experience of previous texts" (1999: 190).

In keeping with this premise, Carlos F. Heredero and Antonio Santamarina (1998) see Spanish filmmaking from the 1990s onward as marked by a postmodern combination of the generic commonplaces of a variety of Hollywood film registers (the thriller, sci-fi, sophisticated comedy) with traditional Spanish representational templates such as the *esperpento* (aesthetic of grotesque distortion), *costumbrismo* (gently humorous depiction of popular customs), and social drama. As they argue, this type of filmmaking strategically appropriates American representational models to reject the auteurist stamp of the previous generation of Spanish filmmakers, and to reclaim an understanding of film as an industrial practice that engages with its audiences. Thrillers that adopt this kind of industrially oriented *modus operandi* include *Los lobos de Washington / Washington Wolves* (Mariano Barroso, 1999), *Nadie conoce a nadie / Nobody Knows Anybody* (Mateo Gil, 1999), *Yoyes* (Helena Taberna, 2000), *El viaje de Arián / Arian's Journey* (Eduard Bosch, 2000), and *Juego de Luna / Luna's Game* (Mónica Laguna, 2001).

In the 1990s, Imanol Uribe and Daniel Calparsoro renewed the political thriller subgenre by interrogating the specificities of the Basque conflict while simultaneously mobilizing stylistic and narrative techniques operative in transnational markets. As mentioned in Chapter 8, in the late 1970s and early 1980s Uribe had made a trilogy of films dealing with the history of the Basque separatist group ETA – *El proceso de Burgos / The Burgos Trial* (1979), *La fuga de Segovia / Escape from Segovia* (1981), and *La muerte de Mikel / The Death of Mikel* (1984). In 1994 he took this subject matter up again with the thriller *Días contados / Running out of Time*. Based on the novel by crime-fiction writer Juan Madrid, *Días contados* dwells on the existential angst of the modern subject in contemporary Madrid, with an ETA commando thrown into the equation. As Ibon Izurieta points out (2008), rather than explore the political complexities of Basque separatism, the film concentrates on a sordid, postmodern Madrid in the wake of the *movida*, opting for a melodramatic mode in which social denunciation and political critique give way to a love story between an ETA operative and a local prostitute. While Uribe's commitment to political cinema in the late 1970s and early 1980s is unquestionable, films such as *Días contados* use social and political issues as a backdrop to sensational entertainment rides that capitalize on explicit nudity and action set pieces supposedly legitimated ideologically by the foregrounding of the terrorist's sentimental and existential dilemmas. In practice, the film barely scratches the surface of the fundamentally political conflict it purports to depict.

Calparsoro also touched on the issue of ETA with *A ciegas / Blindness* (1997), but perhaps his most remarkable thriller is his urban tale *Salto al vacío / Leap into the Void* (1995). The film relies on claustrophobic cinematography, the ubiquity of explicit violence, and a punk-rock soundtrack to depict the criminal, lower-class world of Sestao, a small industrial Basque town near Bilbao. On the one hand, the film clearly belongs to the Tarantinesque mode of 1990s action filming in terms of editing and narrative tempo. On the other, it points out the inescapability of violence and its devastating effects on the social fabric by resorting to the explicit depiction of bloodletting, representing Sestao as an asphyxiating postindustrial urban landscape that entraps its inhabitants. Calparsoro anchors his film firmly in the social effects on the Basque country of the so-called "industrial reconversion" that had devastated the area, traditionally dependent on heavy industry, creating rampant unemployment. At the same time, in stylistic terms, *Salto al vacío* marks an embrace of the representational templates of an action cinema dominant transnationally in the 1990s, redefining the contours of the Spanish political thriller through its visual and acoustic regimes.

Other than Almodóvar, Alejandro Amenábar is perhaps the key figure in Spanish cinema from the mid-1990s to the present, as far as the thriller genre is concened (on Amenábar's *oeuvre*, see Chapter 5). He has steadily built a strong national and international market base, alternating between English- and Spanish-language productions that touch upon a variety of generic categories, the thriller being a key part of the mix. Films such as *Tesis / Thesis* (1996) and *Abre los ojos / Open Your Eyes* (1997) are characterized by an undeniable transnational stamp – that is, the utilization of generic codes deeply in tune with the international-popular that Hollywood propagates as a globally operative aesthetic and narrative mode.

Tesis is a first-time director's low-budget tale that effectively appropriates generic commonplaces of the thriller to perform a political critique of the violence-saturated Spanish film panorama of the 1990s. Although hardly original in its aesthetic modes and narrative structure, its importance lies in the fact that it signalled unambiguously the need to appropriate internationally operative generic categories so as to engage with both domestic and foreign audiences, in order to rescue Spanish cinema from self-ghettoization within its own geopolitical borders. *Tesis* effectively intertwines a number of key features: sensorial engagement with the spectator at a physical level, producing a string of carefully timed thrills; the use of melodramatic formulas to produce specific spectator identifications; and the strategic deployment of a visibility/invisibility dynamic with regard to the "real" images of the snuff movie format that lies at the film's center (see Figure 9.5). *Abre los ojos* – at the time of its relase, the highest-grossing Spanish film of all time – not only confirmed Amenábar's generic craftmanship in persuasively combining the codes of the thriller and melodrama but also enabled him to reinvent the sci-fi thriller in a Spanish context while securing substantial international distribution. In addition, *Abre los ojos* was remade as *Vanilla Sky* (Cameron Crowe, 2001), starring Tom Cruise, Penélope Cruz, and Cameron Diaz, demonstrating that the "Amenabarian" thriller formula had proven commercially viable abroad. Not accidentally, Amenábar found his way into English-language markets with *The Others* (2001), a film that mixes the visual fabric of gothic horror with the editing patterns and musical cues of the thriller genre, creating a generic hybrid that signals the dominance of genre-mixing in the contemporary transnational film panorama.

Negotiating the contours of an increasingly fragmented and saturated media-scape, in which spectators watch movies not only in the cinema, on television, or

Figure 9.5 The materiality of the video image comes to the fore as the serial killer gets ready to slaughter Ángela in Amenábar's *Tesis* (1995; prod. Las Producciones del Escorpión / Sogepaq).

on DVD but also – increasingly – by streaming and downloading them from the Internet, Spanish thrillers continue to move in the direction of an increasing transnationalism, adopting generic codes and aesthetics that are globally operative, which in turn entails the hybridization of generic discourses. This does not prevent them from engaging sporadically with the evolving patterns of Spain's social and political reality. In the past, criticism of the Spanish thriller has tended to focus on its role as a vehicle of social and political critique. The thrillers being made in Spain today make it clear that it is necessary also to engage critically with the genre's transnational dimensions – indeed, as should be clear from this chapter so far, this has always been the case.

The Horror Genre (Antonio Lázaro-Reboll)

Recent developments in genre theory (Altman 1999; Neale 2000) are particularly productive in the case of the horror film, since they open discussion of the genre up to broader questions of production, reception, mediation, and consumption. Jancovich's recent theorizations of the horror genre have established that it is not just defined differently by different user groups but that "genres are bound up with struggles for distinction in which different social groups compete for authority over one another" (2002: 18). In other words, "rather than horror having a single meaning, different social groups construct it in different, competing ways as they seek to identify with or distance themselves from the term, and associate different texts with these constructions of horror" (2002: 159). Constructions of the field of Spanish horror film and questions of cultural analysis are the focus of this section. Initially I consider two competing accounts of Spanish horror film history to discuss not only how different cultural commentators think and write about the genre and its history but also how these accounts serve as cultural platforms for the construction of Spanish horror film history and its canon. I then examine how these differing accounts are bound up with cultural assumptions and distinctions in the field of Spanish horror film. Both of these narrative histories of the genre focus on production, with their main protagonists being the auteur and his work, neglecting the circulation, critical reception, and consumption of this popular genre in and beyond Spain. Consequently, the second half of the section argues that discussion of issues such as cultural and technological mediation, genre fandom, and media consumption may provide more productive ways of thinking about (re)configurations of the genre. As Peter Hutchings has argued in relation to the horror genre, changing experiences of watching and consuming film genres "are mediated by institutions and technologies that have their own historical specificity" (2008: 220). My argument will be illustrated through two brief case studies that examine the impact of specific technologies and institutions in the field of Spanish horror. First, I trace the changing generic status and historical circulation of a particular film, *La semana del asesino* (Eloy de la Iglesia, 1972; discussed as a thriller in the preceding section), to emphasize that any history of Spanish horror cinema must consider its relation to transnational cultural flows and international traditions of horror cinema. Second, I argue for a more inclusive cultural geography of horror that would take into account the function of horror film festivals as specific sites of cultural formation, with particular attention to the San Sebastián Semana de Cine Fantástico y de Terror (Horror and Fantasy Film Festival), which has been running since 1990.

Two accounts of Spanish horror cinema published in the national newspaper *El Mundo*'s cultural supplement "El Cultural" in 2001 frame my opening section. Under the title "El cine español mete miedo" (Spanish Cinema Scares), academic Román Gubern and autochthonous horror star Jacinto Molina (aka Paul Naschy) map the evolution of the genre in Spain, tracing its artistic roots and identifying precursors, key directors, and films (some of which are not readily associated with the genre), and offer their own narrative histories (Gubern and Naschy 2001). Notwithstanding the context in which these accounts were written (mainstream journalism, requiring brevity and targeting a particular readership), both show how legitimations of Spanish horror cinema are framed and underpinned by specific cultural assumptions, tastes, and values.

Gubern's and Molina's articles were prefaced by an accurate résumé of the history of Spanish horror cinema: "ha sido durante décadas el género apestado de la cinematografía española, denostado por la crítica y arrinconado a producciones de serie B" (for decades it has been the disreputable genre of Spanish cinema, reviled by critics and sidelined to B-movie productions), but the last few years of the twentieth century and the first few of the twenty-first witnessed the genre's commercial and critical renaissance thanks to filmmakers who revitalized the form by "aportando dosis autorales a producciones de indudable calidad que han seducido al público" (injecting a dose of auteurism into products of evident quality that have attracted audiences). To this historical résumé I would add the fact that box-office and critical success throughout the first decade of the twenty-first century has made the academic study of contemporary Spanish horror critically acceptable. This brief summary encapsulates the key critical issues involved in the horror genre's positioning in dominant histories of Spanish cinema: on the one hand, dismissed and ghettoized by critics and scholars, it has been pushed to the margins of the industry, the cultural field, and the academy; on the other hand, auteurism and artistic adequacy (or quality) have become the prevailing critical frameworks for discussion of the genre.

Gubern's opening statement lamented what he saw as the Spanish horror film's lack of grounding in a genuinely Spanish cultural tradition, whether literary or artistic: neither the "filón tremendista" (literary seam of exaggerated violence) nor the "inquietantes mundos de Goya o de Gutiérrez Solana" (disturbing worlds of Goya or Gutiérrez Solana) had been translated to the screen. Furthermore, "la cosecha del género no ha sido muy grande" (the crop has not been that large) and "ha mimetizado con frecuencia los modelos canónicos internacionales" (has repeatedly imitated international canonical models), making it therefore "apátrida" (non-Spanish). Gubern did concede, however, that the genre had become a vehicle for the powerful metaphorical cinema of specific auteurs through the inscription of "fantasmas que han poblado el imaginario social español a lo largo de casi un siglo" (ghosts that have haunted the Spanish social imaginary for almost a century) – exemplified most notably, perhaps, in Víctor Erice's *El espíritu de la colmena / The Spirit of the Beehive* (1973). While Gubern mentioned the output of Jesús Franco, Paul Naschy, and Narciso Ibáñez Serrador in relation to the genre's commercial resurgence in international markets during the 1960s, his overall narrative focused on films that were either not conceived as horror when they were originally released in the 1930s, 1940s, and 1950s – therefore raising questions about genre classification – or that belong to the post-1960s auteurist tradition, associated with the New Spanish Cinema modelled on the young European cinema movements of the 1960s. In the former group he included some Spanish titles: *Una de miedo / Scary Movie* (Eduardo García Maroto, 1935), *Una mujer en peligro / Woman in Danger* (José Santugini, 1935), *Viaje sin destino / Journey to Nowhere* (Rafael Gil, 1942). But he also included a film by a cosmopolitan director who had worked in Hollywood – Edgar Neville's *La torre de los siete jorobados / Tower of the Seven Hunchbacks* (1944; discussed in Chapter 6), which he praised as "la obra maestra del cine terrorífico bajo el franquismo" (the masterpiece of the horror genre under Francoism) for its "original mezcla de costumbrismo finisecular y ritualismo hermético" (original mix of fin de siècle local color and esoteric ritualism) – and another by the Hungarian-born Ladislao Vajda – *El cebo* (1958; discussed in the previous section), which he described as having modernized the genre with its narrative of a psychopathic murderer, which intelligently echoed Fritz Lang's *M*. Post-1960s cinema was represented in Gubern's article by what he saw as the exceptional creative handling of the genre by emergent auteurs such as Vicente Aranda, who "dignificó el género" (dignified the genre) with *Fata Morgana / Left-Handed Fate* (1965); José María Vallés, Emilio Martínez Lázaro, Francesc Bellmunt, and Jaime Chávarri, who delivered an ironic take on the genre in their composite *Pastel de sangre / Blood Pie* (1971); Bigas Luna's reflexive originality in *Angustia / Anguish* (1987); and Gonzalo Suárez's "inteligente recreación" (intelligent recreation) of Mary Shelley's *Frankenstein* in *Remando al viento / Rowing with the Wind* (1988). More recent productions referenced by Gubern included the forays into the horror genre of debutant filmmakers Juanma Bajo Ulloa (*Alas de mariposa / Butterfly Wings*, 1991; *La madre muerta / The Dead Mother*, 1993); Alejandro Amenábar (*Tesis*, 1995; *Abre los ojos*, 1997); and Álex de la Iglesia (*El día de la bestia / The Day of the Beast*, 1995). Arguably, these three directors used the horror genre in their shorts and first feature films as a way of breaking into mainstream filmmaking.

In his contribution, Molina declared that genre and authorship can coexist: "el cine de género [...] es también de autor" (genre cinema [...] is also auteur cinema). To back this claim, he noted the rich international tradition of fantasy and horror stretching from the 1920s to the late 1950s (German expressionism, Universal, and British Hammer), which had generated "autores geniales y [...] obras maestras" (brilliantly original authors and [...] masterpieces). Regrettably, Molina observed, both the Spanish film industry and its critical establishment had for decades ignored local and international horror traditions. He then provided an account of the proto-history of the horror genre in Spain – rooted in a cinema of fantasy (the French term *fantastique*, used by him, includes fantasy, adventure, and the visionary) and associated with pioneers such as Segundo de Chomón, Alberto Marro, Magín Muriá, Ramón Caralt, and Nemesio Sobrevila in the 1910s and 1920s, as well as the singular achievements of Neville's *La torre de los siete jorobados* and Jesús Franco's *Gritos en la noche / The Awful Dr. Orlof* (1961) – before moving on to the central protagonist of his narrative: Jacinto Molina himself. The success of *La marca del hombre lobo / Frankenstein's Bloody Terror* (Enrique L. Eguíluz, 1968), scripted by Molina, established his screen alter ego Paul Naschy in the serial role of the werewolf Waldemar Daninsky, ushering in the "Golden Age of Spanish horror cinema." What followed was a list of eleven Molina/Naschy films produced between 1968 (*La marca del hombre lobo*) and 1984 (sic; actually 1983) (*La bestia y la espada mágica / The Beast and the Magic Sword*). Other authors who had genuinely cultivated the genre, Molina conceded, were Narciso Ibáñez Serrador (*La residencia / The House that Screamed*, 1969; *¿Quién puede matar a un niño? / Island of the Damned*, 1975); Eugenio Martín (*Pánico en el Transiberiano / Horror Express*, 1976 (sic; actually 1972)); and Jorge Grau (*Non si deve profanare il sonno dei morti / No profanar el sueño de los muertos / Don't Open the Window*, 1974), while Amando de

Ossorio and Juan Piquer were, in his view, "cineastas de menor impronta" (minor filmmakers). The contemporary outputs of Alejandro Amenábar, Álex de la Iglesia, Jaume Balagueró, and Álvaro Fernández Armero were, according to a blatantly self-serving Molina, a far cry from the achievements of the genre's heyday; correspondingly, Molina placed his hopes for a genuine revival of Spanish horror at the turn of the twenty-first century in his latest acting role as protagonist of Carlos Gil's *School Killer / El vigilante* (2001).

Although Gubern's and Molina's contributions to "El cine español mete miedo" did not seek to complement each other, their juxtaposition makes interesting reading, for they share similar methods of constructing the history of Spanish horror film while, at the same time, highlighting different classificatory frameworks, tastes, and aesthetic values. Both narratives are auteurist-led, giving the individual author the central role in the development of Spanish horror film. Likewise, both recall their individual interventions in the Spanish horror field over the preceding thirty years, beginning with their respective contributions to the first critical study devoted to Spanish genre cinema, *Cine español, cine de subgéneros* (*Spanish Cinema, a Cinema of Sub-Genres*) (1974)[1] – specifically, the foreword written by Gubern, and Juan Manuel Company's chapter on horror, "El rito y la sangre (aproximaciones al sub-terror hispano)" (Ritual and Blood: Approaches to the Hispanic Sub-genre of Horror), which included an interview with Molina. There Molina had bemoaned critics' dismissal of the genre and the "falta de especialización en el género" (lack of specialist genre criticism) (Company 1974: 35), arguing for the elevation of a (sometimes) banal horror film production to the artistic refinement of other (his own) horror output. Twenty-seven years later, in "El cine español mete miedo," Molina expressed similar views, contructing a familiar narrative with himelf in the starring role as the most significant contributor to the development of Spanish horror films.[2] With this mythologizing self-construction as auteur, Molina was seeking to generate credibility and vindicate his place in the history of Spanish horror cinema.

Likewise, Gubern's words in 2001 echoed his introductory remarks in *Cine español, cine de subgéneros*, where he had already established that Spanish horror films of the late 1960s and early 1970s were "sucedáneos miméticos y repetitivos de otros modelos previos, también repetitivos, pero de carácter cultural genuino o arquetípico" (mimetic, repetitive products in their imitation of previous models [German expressionism, Universal Pictures, and Hammer films], which are also repetitive but at least are culturally genuine or archetypal) (1974: 13). Spanish horror was thus not rooted in an autochthonous tradition, whether literary or cinematic. And not being associated with a literary tradition meant that the genre could not be legitimated artistically or aesthetically, thereby attaining respectability. Horror for Gubern was therefore not peculiarly Spanish. Gubern's 1974 prophecy on the back cover of *Cine español, cine de subgéneros* – "esta deleznable producción hispana no pasará jamás a las historias del cine, como no sea en una escueta nota a pie de página" (this paltry Spanish cinematic production will never make it into histories of Spanish cinema, except as a brief footnote) – has held sway until very recently.[3]

Analysis of these differing positions within the field of Spanish horror shows how different historical accounts of the genre are bound up with an economy of taste and auteurist models of canon formation. What was, and still seems to be, at stake in Gubern's writing about Spanish horror cinema are specific critical and ideological operations deeply entrenched in narratives of Spanish film history: the exclusion of genre and subgenre film production from accounts of Spanish cinema, thereby privileging the political (and cultural) economy that sustains "legitimate" (i.e., auteurist) cinema; the deployment of an aesthetic order based on cultural hierarchies of aesthetic value; and the guardianship of taste, ignoring other ways in which audiences use, and construct meanings from, the commodities they consume. Recent academic studies of Spanish popular cinema and genre have taken issue with the partisan implications of such critical operations and as a consequence have questioned accepted histories of Spanish cinema, shifting the focus away from histories of production and of canonical auteurs and films toward a consideration of popular genres and their circulation, critical reception, and consumption, with the aim of recovering marginalized film practices and filmmakers, and, by extension, re-examining the role specific cultural agents play in the constructions of the canon and of Spanish film history (Triana Toribio 2003; Lázaro-Reboll and Willis 2004; Marsh 2006; Beck and Rodríguez Ortega 2008). As far as the academic study of Spanish horror film is concerned, the work of Lázaro-Reboll (2008, 2012) and Willis (2004, 2008) illustrates this critical shift. *Spanish Horror Film* (Lázaro-Reboll 2012), for example, considers Spanish horror, past and present, to be bound up with transnational patterns of production and consumption, examining how specific films and cycles respond to industrial practices of standardization and differentiation of the horror product in the marketplace, whether in the 1970s or in the first decade of the twenty-first century, as well as the ways in which institutions and technologies, genre users, and consumers shape and participate in the process of genre classification and reconfiguration.

My first case study is the previously discussed *La semana del asesino*, which provides an example not only of slippage between genres and evaluative classifications but also of the impact of VCR technology on the cultural afterlife of a specific film. I will look at the promotional material and critical reception of this film in Spain in the early 1970s, before moving on to its circulation and reception abroad in relation to different sites of reception and various technologies, in particular the "video nasties" debate in the United Kingdom in the 1980s.[4] As we shall see, in the context of the emerging home-video market in the 1980s and then in the 1990s and the following decade with DVD and Blue-ray, *La semana del asesino* has acquired the status of a cult classic of European exploitation.

Although both the title and plot summary of *La semana del asesino* alike frame Marcos as a serial killer, the promotional campaign cued a range of alternative generic features to attract different audiences. The film was billed as offering "romance," "suspense," and "shocks." Some posters sold the film on the basis of the star image of the actor playing Marcos, Vicente Parra, whose previous career had been as romantic lead in melodramas, musicals, and plays. The fluid legibility of genre was also mobilized by the director in promotional interviews in which he defined his production as "una película comercial y popular. Y, en primer lugar, es una película de humor. Luego también es una película de sangre, y, en definitiva, es una historia de amor" (a commercial and popular film. First of all, it's a film with humour. It's also a bloody film, and, above all, a love story) (de la Iglesia 1972). One of the main marketing strategies used in the press-book and publicity material was the generation of suspense, imitating Hitchcock's policy in *Psycho* of allowing no one into the cinema theater once the film had begun: "Se suplica a los espectadores la máxima puntualidad. La violencia empieza desde el principio" (Spectators are expected to arrive punctually. The violence starts at the very beginning). The stress on suspense linked the film to the thriller genre, but the emphasis on violence went beyond this. The film's violence was a feature explicitly highlighted by trade journals such as *Pantallas y escenarios*, with warnings that effectively encouraged distributors and exhibitors to market it on this basis: "Quizás una de las películas más violentas que se hayan filmado en España" (Perhaps one the most violent films ever made in Spain). Enmeshed in controversy for two years, *La semana del asesino* could not be released until 1974; the Francoist censorship mutilated the film with sixty-two cuts (up to a hundred, according to some sources), imposed a narrative closure whereby the murderer turns himself in to the police (as previously mentioned), and classified it as "gravemente peligrosa" (seriously dangerous).

Contemporary reviewers read the film through differing generic and aesthetic lenses. While the mainstream daily press read it in relation to realist frameworks associated with Spanish literary traditions and works such as Camilo José Cela's 1942 novel *La familia de Pascual Duarte* – "recuerda en su tremendismo y en la desolación del personaje protagonista [...] a cierta literatura española enraizada en nuestra tradición" (its exagerated violence and the desolation of the main protagonist are reminiscent of [...] certain Spanish literary works rooted in our tradition) (Rubio 1974) – film publications such as *Nuevo Fotogramas* and specialist film magazine *Terror Fantastic* read it through the lens of horror. *Nuevo Fotogramas* described the film as a "Grand Guignol" (sensational, often macabre entertainment) that graphically reflected "la impotencia y la soledad del proletario" (the impotence and isolation of the proletariat) (*La semana del asesino* 1972: 70), linking the film to contemporary social issues. *Terror Fantastic* criticized the director's use of the horror genre because it fell between two stools, on the one hand offering a "terror intelectualizado (posibles implicaciones a la desbocada conducta homicida de Marcos)" (intellectualized horror (the possible implications of Marcos' uncontrollable murderous behavior)), and, on the other hand, mere gore (Montaner 1972: 55). The range of responses to Eloy de la Iglesias' work was noted by Paul Julian Smith in his seminal analysis of de la Iglesias' cinema (1992: 129–62), which focused on his post-1975 films: "the central paradox of the director's work" is "the curious combination of mass technique (sex and violence) and personal, indeed idiosyncratic, obsessions" (1992: 136). While Eloy de la Iglesias' films of the mid-1970s and early 1980s have been the object of analysis in several studies (Hopewell 1986; Smith 1992; Troppiano 1997; Mira 2004) – in particular his representation of homosexuality and use of the codes and conventions of popular genres, especially melodrama, in films such as *Los placeres ocultos* / *Hidden Pleasures* (1976), *El diputado* / *Confessions of a Congressman* (1978), and *El pico* / *Overdose* (1983) – *La semana del asesino* has been overlooked, as have his other early 1970s productions, and no attempts have been made to establish links between his pre- and post-1975 output. As Smith rightly observed in relation to Eloy de la Iglesia's cinema of the transition, "critical abuse of de la Iglesia has been [...] motivated by an inability to 'read' his use of genre" (1992: 130).

In the early 1980s, British censors also slaughtered the film, this time for completely different reasons. When *La semana del asesino* was released uncut on video by Intervision in November 1981 for the US and European market, under the title *Cannibal Man*, it was included in the inventory of horror titles known as "video nasties" and banned in the United Kingdom in July 1983. Under the 1984 British Video Recordings Act, all videotapes for the home-video market had to be approved and classified by the BBFC (British Board of Film Classification) in order to circulate legally. Despite its retitling, there are no scenes of cannibalism in *La semana del asesino*. The reputation acquired by the "video nasties" has made Eloy de la Iglesia's film a must-have cult movie among horror fans and collectors over the last twenty-five years. According to one of several websites devoted to the "video nasties" phenomenon, the film "stayed on the list throughout the panic and became one of the collectable DPP39s, that is to say, the 39 films, of a total of 74, withdrawn from the shops and successfully prosecuted by the Director of Public Prosecutions."[5] *La semana del asesino* highlights the relevance of cultural mediation and media consumption in constructions of the field of Spanish horror. The reception and consumption of films like *La semana del asesino*, as well as that of many other Spanish (and international) horror films from the second half of the 1980s onward, came to be mediated through fandom culture once video stores and mail-order catalogs began to make previously unobtainable films available for Spanish viewers and fans. As Kendrick has argued in relation to the British market, though the point holds for Spain too, US distributors flooded the video market with low-budget films on VHS, heralding "a new form of transnationalism emerging from the introduction of a new media technology: the VCR" (2004: 156).

While Eloy de la Iglesia's *La semana del asesino* was carving out a cult reputation among Spanish and international horror fans from the mid-1980s onward, his critical recuperation in mainstream Spanish reception contexts did not come until 1996 when the Festival Internacional de Cine de San Sebastián organized a retrospective of the director's work and published the multi-authored volume *Conocer a Eloy de la Iglesia*. The Filmoteca Vasca (Basque Film Archive), Donostia Kultura (San Sebastián Cultural Office), and the festival were the institutional

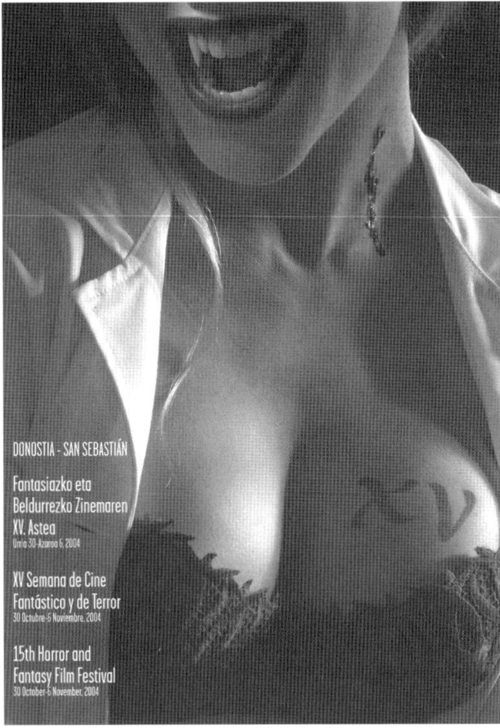

Figure 9.6 Poster for the 2004 San Sebastián Horror and Fantasy Film Festival. Courtesy of Donostia Kultura.

agents championing de la Iglesia's auteur status. It is to the role of another festival, the Semana de Cine Fantástico y de Terror (Horror and Fantasy Film Festival), which also takes place in San Sebastián (Donostia in *euskara*) and is organized under the auspices of Donostia Kultura, that I now turn to conclude this section.

The Semana de Cine Fantástico y de Terror is a horror-themed festival, whose programming, activities, and publications in the last decade of the twentieth century and first of the twenty-first contributed significantly to the field of popular cultural production (see Figure 9.6).[6] The festival has established a firm reputation in the international specialized film festival circuit – it is a subscribing member of the European Fantastic Film Festivals Federation (EFFFF) – bringing together commercial interests, specialized horror film knowledge, and boisterous horror aficionados. In fact, one of the distinctive features of the festival is the active participation of the festival-goers; as the EFFFF web-site puts it, "this is not your standard film festival, it's also an enormous horror and fantasy knees up" (European Fantastic Film Festivals Federation n.d.). A panoply of artistic, cultural, and educational activities (exhibitions, comic-book encounters, fanzine conventions, workshops) adds a rich cultural and subcultural dimension to the festival's programming.

While the festival is international in its scope, its origins are firmly grounded in local film culture, in particular the drive of cinema enthusiast José Luis Rebordinos[7] and the cultural activities promoted by Donostia Kultura. At the request of the Cultural Office, in October 1990 Rebordinos organized a film season aimed at attracting young audiences. The youth emphasis of the first two horror-themed seasons, "Terroríficamente modernos" (Terrifyingly Modern) and "De la B a la Z" (From B to Z), organized the following year, was a success. The film seasons were soon upgraded to festival status in 1992 with Rebordinos at the helm, under its current name, Semana de Cine Fantástico y de Terror. "Terroríficamente modernos" and "De la B a la Z" announced the programmers' genre credentials and their broad understanding of fantasy and horror: the former screened the films of contemporary US horror auteurs such as Larry Cohen, David Cronenberg, and Brian Yuzna; the latter cut across Japanese animation *Akira* (Katsuhiro Otomo, 1988), European arthouse *Delicatessen* (Marc Caro and Jean Pierre Jeunet, 1991) and US low-fare exploitation *The Toxic Avenger* (Lloyd Kaufman, 1985). Since the 1990s, the festival has contributed to the dissemination of local and international horror traditions by giving screen space to amateur film production; championing obscure, underground strands of horror; programming retrospectives of horror auteurs and key moments in the development of the horror film; and showcasing the latest world horror production. Official competitions have been instituted as the festival has evolved: the short film competition in 1994, the feature film competition in 2001, and the inter-festival Golden Méliès Award for Best European Fantastic Short Film in 2004, which links the festival to other EFFF members. Audience participation has remained at the heart of the festival experience with audience awards for both short and feature films since 1992.[8] The festival's publishing ventures, supported by Donostia Kultura, range from monographs and edited collections on individual filmmakers and international horror traditions to the periodical *Dezine*, which for six volumes acted as an unofficial publication for the festival, to regular collaborations with fanzines *2000maniacos* and *ojalatemueras* from the mid-1990s onward.[9] The festival has thus provided different generations of horror fans with venues to indulge in horror pleasures as well as with networks where "fans from different walks of life gather together to share their fandom" (Hills 2002: 61) and invest their (sub)cultural capital as consumers and/or producers.

As material sites for the formation of cultural tastes, horror-themed film festivals play an important role as industrial and cultural platforms for the distribution, exhibition, and consumption of the genre, in its variegated international and cross-generic aspects. Specialist festivals also provide a key site for the social process of classification of the horror and fantasy genres through the discursive activities of "genre users," which range from the discourses of the industry circulated through the trade press to the discourses generated by the press, specialist magazines, and horror aficionados in alternative publications, as well as the innovative takes inscribed in the films themselves. In this respect, the San Sebastián Horror and Fantasy Film Festival has become a training ground for emergent Spanish directors – in particular the figure of the horror auteur, as in the cases of Jaume Balagueró and Nacho Cerdà – and also for film critics, whose professional development can be traced from fanzines to specialist film publications to the mainstream press. Balagueró, whose use of and engagement with the genre emerged out of a horror fan subculture linked to alternative publications, has been a festival regular both as author of the fanzine *Zineshock (Revista de cine oscuro y brutal)* (*Zineshock (Journal of Brutal, Dark Cinema)*) in the early 1990s and as amateur and professional filmmaker: first through his shorts in the mid-1990s – *Alicia* (1994) and *Días sin luz / Dark Days* (1995) – and later with his first feature film, *Los sin nombre / The Nameless* (1999). Likewise, film critics Rubén Lardín and Borja Crespo, who came out of the late 1990s fanzine scene (the former as coeditor with Hernán Migoya of the fanzine *ojalatemueras*, the latter as a coauthor of the horror, fantasy, and science-fiction magazine *Quatermass*) have also been regular festival-goers who have contributed to the festival's publications.

Genre festivals and fanzines are invaluable resources for the study of the field of Spanish horror, facilitating re-examination of accepted accounts of the genre, such as those given by Gubern and Molina. Critics such as Lardín, Antonio José Navarro, and Jesús Palacios belong to a new generation of Spanish film critics whose work not only has re-evaluated and reclaimed Spanish cinematic traditions such as the *género policíaco* and the *cine fantástico y de terror* but also considers them in relation to wider US and European literary and cinematic traditions of representation (pulp fiction, crime, and horror films) in fanzines, specialist genre publications, and multi-authored volumes in the course of the 1990s and the first decade of the twenty-first century. The volume *Euronoir: Serie negra con sabor europeo* (Palacios 2006), in which the three participate, is a case in point. Here, for example, Spanish early thrillers and crime films feature next to chapters on the French *polar* or *film policier*, the Italian *poliziesco*, the Brit *noir*, and the German *krimi* film. Equally, to acknowledge the true scope of contemporary Spanish thrillers and horror cinema today demands an acknowledgment of the critical intersections and interactions between various fields of cultural production, critical reception, and consumption, and of the transnational dimension of these popular genres. Any adequately formulated history of popular cinema and genre cinema needs to address the role of institutional, technological, and cultural mediation in shaping Spanish film culture.

Notes

1 Gubern and Molina also appeared side by side in 1981 in the film journal *Contracampo* (see Gubern 1981 and the interview with Molina in García Santamaría 1981).

2 This accrual to Molina of symbolic capital in the field of Spanish horror is traceable in interviews and articles in the daily press, popular film publications, and specialist film

magazines of the 1970s and 1980s, and, more recently, in his own autobiography, *Memorias de un hombre lobo / Memoirs of a Werewolf* (1997), fanzines, and DVD special features on his films.

3 See Beck and Rodríguez Ortega (2008: 5–14) for the lasting imprint of Gubern's views on discussions of Spanish cinema and genre.

4 As *Video Watchdog* has noted, the film was distributed in the United States in 1973, before it was released in Spain in 1974, as *The Apartment on the 13th Floor*, and later teamed in a double bill with a Spanish–Italian horror film made in Italian, *Non si deve profanare il sonno dei morti / No profanar el sueño de los muertos / Don't Open the Window* (US title) (Jorge Grau, 1972) for the drive-in circuit, but it was "never licensed for the home video market in the United States until Anchor Bay Entertainment released it on DVD and VHS in the late 1990s" (Smith 2000: 46).

5 See www.melonfarmers.co.uk/nasties.htm: "The cover was a flimsy slip case that didn't last long so adding to the rarity of a mint condition cover. [The film] was re-released after 3 BBFC cuts in 1993 (Redemption). Current UK status: Passed 18 with 3 cuts." While most films came from the United States and Italy, there were also four other Spanish films that made it into the list: *Non si deve profanare il sonno dei morti / No profanar el sueño de los muertos / Don't Open the Window* (UK title: *Let Sleeping Corpses Lie*) (Jorge Grau, 1974), a Spanish–Italian coproduction; *La maldición de la bestia / The Werewolf and the Yeti* (Miguel Iglesias, 1975); *El caníbal / The Devil Hunter* (Jesús Franco, 1980), a Italian–Spanish–German coproduction; and *Die Säge des Todes / Colegialas violadas / Bloody Moon* (Jesús Franco, 1981), a Spanish–German coproduction made in German.

6 Festivals devoted to horror and fantasy cinema in Spain represent a sizeable percentage of the festival industry – more than twenty percent. The oldest horror film festival in the Spanish state is the Festival Internacional de Cinema de Catalunya (International Film Festival of Catalonia) – Semana Internacional de Cine Fantástico y de Terror (International Fantasy and Horror Film Festival) in its original denomination – which has been running since 1968. The 1990s and the first decade of the twenty-first century witnessed a boom of specialized genre festivals in this field, among them Semana Internacional de Cine Fantástico de Málaga (Málaga International Fantasy Film Festival, 1991), Semana de Cine Fantástico de Sevilla (Seville Fantasy Film Festival, 1995), Muestra de Cine de Terror de A Coruña (La Coruña Horror Film Festival, 1996), Semana de Cine Fantástico y de Terror de Cáceres (Cáceres Fantasy and Horror Film Festival, 1998), Festival Fantastosfreak de Cortometrajes de Cerdanyola del Vallés (Cerdanyola de Vallés Fantastosfreak Short Festival, 2000), Semana Internacional de Cine Fantástico y de Terror de Estepona (Estepona International Fantasy and Horror Film Festival, 2000), and Festival de Cortometrajes Fantásticos y de Terror de Molins del Rei (Molins del Rei Fantasy and Horror Shorts Festival, 2001). For film festivals in Spain generally, see Chapter 15.

7 Rebordinos had been running a film club since the late 1970s. In 1989 he founded the specialist film magazine *Nosferatu*, also funded by Donostia Kultura, whose Film Department he heads as of 2012.

8 For quantitative data on the numbers of films screened, spectators attending, and revenue see www.donostiakultura.com. Throughout the first decade of the twenty-first century, the festival has shown seventy-plus films per year and welcomed an average of fifty

thousand spectators. For a full list of awards see www.donostiakultura.com/terror/2010/es/doc/palmares.pdf.

9 Since 1997 the festival has published several volumes on international horror film traditions: for example, *Del giallo al gore: Cine fantástico y de terror italiano* (1997), *Cine fantástico y de terror español, 1900–1983* (1999), *El cine fantástico y de terror de la Universal* (2000), *Cine fantástico y de terror alemán, 1913–1927* (2002), *Cine fantástico y de terror español, 1984–2004* (2005), *David Cronenberg: Los misterios del organismo* (2006), and *American Gothic: Cine de terror USA, 1968–1980* (2007).

References

Acevedo-Muñoz, E. (2008) *Pedro Almodóvar*. London: BFI.

Altman, R. (1999) *Film/Genre*. London: BFI.

Beck, J. and Rodríguez Ortega, V. (eds.) (2008) *Contemporary Spanish Cinema and Genre*. Manchester: Manchester University Press.

Company, J. M. (1974). El rito y la sangre (aproximaciones al subterror hispano). In: Equipo Cartelera Turia (eds.) *Cine español: Cine de subgéneros*. Valencia: Fernando Torres.

Cowie, E. (1993) *Film Noir* and Women. In: Copjec, J. (ed.) *Shades of Noir*. London: Verso, pp. 121–65.

Cueto, R. (2002). Entre el desprecio y el olvido: La novela criminal en el cine español. In: Heredero, C. F. (ed.) *La imprenta dinámica: Literatura española en el cine español*. Madrid: Cuadernos de la Academia de las Artes y Ciencias Cinematográficas de España, pp. 255–378.

Davies, A. (2007) Spanish neo-noir. In: Spicer, A. (ed.) *European Film Noir*. Manchester: Manchester University Press, pp. 210–35.

D'Lugo, M. (1997). *Guide to the Cinema of Spain*. Wesport: Greenwood Press.

D'Lugo, M. (2008). *Pedro Almodóvar*. Chicago: University of Illinois Press.

De la Iglesia, E. (1972) Bebo en las fuentes del pueblo. *Nuevo Fotogramas* 1221: 12–13.

Epps, B. S. and Kakoudaki, V. (eds.) (2009) *All about Almodóvar: A Passion for Cinema*. Minneapolis: University of Minnesota Press.

European Fantastic Film Festivals Federation (n.d.) San Sebastián Horror and Fantasy Film Festival. Online at: www.melies.org/festival.asp?ID=19 (accessed May 27, 2010).

Evans, P. W. (1999) The Dame in the Kimono: *Amantes*, Spanish *Noir* and the *Femme Fatale*. *Bulletin of Hispanic Studies* 76: 93–100.

García Santamaría, J. V. (1981). Entrevista con PAUL (Jacinto) NASCHY (Molina). *Contracampo* 24: 51–6.

Gubern, R. (1974). Prólogo. In: Equipo Cartelera Turia (eds.) *Cine español: Cine de subgéneros*. Valencia: Fernando Torres, pp. 9–16.

Gubern, R. (1981) La nueva edad del terror. *Contracampo* 24: 35–46.

Gubern, R. and Naschy, P. [Jacinto Molina] (2001) El cine español mete miedo. *El Cultural* (June 27). Online at: www.elcultural.es/version_papel/CINE/751/El_cine_espanol_mete_miedo (originally accessed May 27, 2005; when accessed on April 21, 2012, only Gubern's contribution to this feature remained online).

Hawkins, J. (2000) *Cutting Edge: Art-Horror and the Horrific Avant-garde*. Minneapolis: University of Minnesota Press.

Heredero, C. F. (1993) *Las huellas del tiempo: Cine español 1951–1961*. Valencia: Filmoteca Generalitat Valenciana.

Heredero, C. F. and Santamarina, A. (1998) *El cine negro: Maduración y crisis de la escritura clásica*. Barcelona: Ediciones Paidós Ibérica.

Herrero, H. (2007) Paisajes urbanos y "no lugares" en el thriller español contemporáneo: *Fausto 5.0* y *La Caja 507*. *Romance Studies* 25 (2): 137–49.

Hills, M. (2002) *Fan Cultures*. London: Routledge.

Hopewell, J. (1986) *Out of the Past: Spanish Cinema after Franco*. London: BFI.

Hutchings, P. (2008) Monster Legacies: Memory, Technology and Horror History. In: Geraghty, L. and Jancovich, M. (eds.) *The Shifting Definitions of Genre*. Jefferson: McFarland Press, pp. 216–28.

Izurieta, I. (2008) Performative Identities and the Representation of E. T. A. in Basque Film and Novel. *Romance Studies* 26 (1): 87–98.

Jancovich, M. (ed.) (2002) *The Horror Film Reader*. London: Routledge.

Kendrick, J. (2004) A Nasty Situation: Social Panics, Transnationalism and the Video Nasty. In: Hantke, S. (ed.) *Horror Film: Creating and Marketing Fear*. Jackson: University Press of Mississippi, pp. 153–72.

Labanyi, J. (1995) Masculinity and the Family in Crisis: Reading Unamuno through *Film Noir* (Serrano de Osma's 1945 adaptation of *Abel Sánchez*). *Romance Studies* 26: 7–21.

Lardín, R. (2006) Menos que nada: Una aproximación al último cine negro español (1980–2005). In: Palacios, J. (ed.) *Euronoir: Serie negra con sabor europeo*. Madrid: T&B, pp. 389–401.

Lázaro-Reboll, A. (2008) Now Playing Everywhere: Spanish Horror Film in the Marketplace. In: Beck, J. and Rodríguez Ortega, V. (eds.) *Contemporary Spanish Cinema and Genre*. Manchester: Manchester University Press, pp. 65–83.

Lázaro-Reboll, A. (2012) *Spanish Horror Film*. Edinburgh: Edinburgh University Press.

Lázaro-Reboll, A. and Willis, A. (eds.) (2004) *Spanish Popular Cinema*. Manchester: Manchester University Press.

Llinás, F. (1989) *Directores de fotografía del cine español*. Madrid: Filmoteca Española.

Llorens, A. (1988) *El cine negro español*. Valladolid: Ed. 33 Semana Internacional de Cine de Valladolid.

Maltby, R. (1992) The Politics of the Maladjusted Text. In: Cameron, I. (ed.) *The Movie Book of Film Noir*. London: Studio Vista, pp. 39–48.

Marcantonio, M. (2009) The Transvestite Figure and *Film Noir*: Pedro Almodóvar's Transnational Imaginary. In: Beck, J. and Rodríguez Ortega, V. (eds.) *Contemporary Spanish Cinema and Genre*. Manchester: Manchester University Press, pp. 157–78.

Marsh, S. (2006) *Popular Spanish Film under Franco: Comedy and the Weakening of the State*. Basingstoke: Palgrave Macmillan.

Medina de la Viña, E. (2000) *Cine negro y policiaco español de los años cincuenta*. Madrid: Laertes.

Mira, A. (2004) *De Sodoma a Chueca: Historia cultural de la homosexualidad en España, 1914–1990*. Madrid: Egales.

Montaner, A. (1972) La semana del asesino. *Terror Fantastic* 11: 55.

Naremore, J. (1998) *More than Night: Film Noir in its Contexts*. Berkeley: University of California Press.

Navarro, A. J. (2006). El cine negro y el thriller español (1950–1975): Historia de un desencuentro. In: Palacios, J. (ed.) *Euronoir: Serie negra con sabor europeo*. Madrid: T&B, pp. 335–55.

Neale, S. (2000) *Genre and Hollywood*. London: Routledge.

Palacios, J. (ed.) (2006) *Euronoir: Serie negra con sabor europeo*. Madrid: T&B Editores.

Rubio, M. (1974) La semana del asesino. *Nuevo Diario* 27: n.p.

Rubin, M. (1999) *Thrillers (Genres in American Cinema)*. Cambridge: Cambridge University Press.

Smith, P. J. (1992) *Laws of Desire: Questions of Homosexuality in Spanish Writing and Film, 1960–1990*. Oxford: Clarendon Press.

Smith, R. H. (2000) Cannibal Man. *Video Watchdog* 66: 46–8.

Thomas, D. (1992) How Hollywood Deals with the Deviant Male. In: Cameron, I. (ed.) *The Movie Book of Film Noir*. London: Studio Vista, pp. 59–70.

Triana Toribio, N. (2003) *Spanish National Cinema*. London: Routledge.

Troppiano, S. (1997) Out of the Cinematic Closet: Homosexuality in the Films of Eloy de la Iglesia. In: Kinder, M. (ed.) *Reconfiguring Spain: Cinema/Media/Representation*. Durham: Duke University Press, pp. 157–77.

Williams, L. (2003) Film Bodies: Gender, Genre, and Excess. In: Grant, B. K. (ed.) *Film Genre Reader III*. Austin: University of Texas Press, pp. 141–59.

Willis, A. (2004) From the Margins to the Mainstream: Trends in Recent Spanish Horror Cinema. In: Lázaro-Reboll, A. and Willis, A. (eds.) *Spanish Popular Cinema*. Manchester: Manchester University Press, pp. 237–49.

Willis, A. (2008) The Fantastic Factory: The Horror Genre and Contemporary Spanish Cinema. In: Beck, J. and Rodríguez Ortega, V. (eds.) *Contemporary Spanish Cinema and Genre*. Manchester: Manchester University Press, pp. 27–43.

Further Reading

Aguilar, C. (ed.) (2005) *Cine fantástico y de terror español: 1984–2004*. San Sebastián: Donostia Kultura.

Conrich, I. (2010) (ed.) *Horror Zone: The Cultural Experience of Contemporary Horror Cinema*. London: I. B. Tauris.

De Abajo de Pablos, J. J. (2001–2003) *Los thrillers españoles: El cine español policíaco desde los años 40 hasta los años 90*. Fancy: Valladolid.

Dopazo Jover, A. (1972) La semana del asesino. *Pantallas y escenarios* 117: n.p.

Hantke, S. (ed.) (2004) *Horror Film: Creating and Marketing Fear*. Jackson: University Press of Mississippi.

Hills, M. (2005) *The Pleasures of Horror*. London: Continuum.

Hutchings, P. (2004) *The Horror Film*. London: Pearson Longman.

Jancovich, M. (2002) Cult Fictions: Cult Movies, Subcultural Capital and the Production of Cultural Distinctions. *Cultural Studies* 16 (2): 306–22.

La semana del asesino (1972) *Nuevo Fotogramas* 1235: 70.

Morales, G. (2010) España criminal. El cine negro español. *Mondo Brutto* 41: 14–54.

Naschy, P. (1997). *Paul Naschy: Memorias de un hombre lobo*. Madrid: Alberto Santos.

Rodríguez Ortega, V. (2005) "Snuffing Hollywood": Transmedia Horror in *Tesis*. *Senses of Cinema: An Online Film Journal*. Online at: www.sensesofcinema.com/contents/05/36/tesis.html (accessed May 4, 2012).

Schneider, S. J. and Williams, T. (2005) *Horror International*. Detroit: Wayne State University Press

Serrano Cueto, J. M. (2007) *Horrormanía: Enciclopedia del cine de terror*. Madrid: Alberto Santos.

Williams, L. R. (2005).*The Erotic Thriller in Contemporary Cinema*. Edinburgh: Edinburgh University Press.

Part IV

Stars as Cultural Icons

10

The Construction of the Star System

Kathleen M. Vernon and Eva Woods Peiró

The 1920s and 1930s

While no one can dispute the mammoth impact that Hollywood has had on cinema and star cultures across the globe, the understudied Spanish cinema of the 1920s and 1930s offers a wealth of fascinating case studies. This neglect has been due in part to the long-held view that stardom was not as fully developed in Spain as it was in Hollywood or even neighboring countries such as France or Italy. Scholars have noted the lack of investment in Spain's cinema, the haphazard nature of the private commercial and state sectors, and the general poverty of the industry before the appearance of full-length sound films and the establishment of companies such as CIFESA in 1932 (Fanés 1982; Pozo Arenas 1984; Pérez Perucha 2000; Vallés Copeiro del Villar 2000; see also Chapter 14). Although large amounts of capital were not available to film producers and directors from either the private or state sectors, a cultural awareness about stardom nevertheless emerged in Spain and mimicked, to the extent of its ability, the capital-intensive industries of Hollywood and other European countries. At the same time, and to no less a degree, the development of a star system in Spain was related to more general trends in popular visual culture in which theater and popular music audiences became spectators of film as these performance traditions increasingly overlapped and merged with cinema (see Chapter 15).

Understanding the evolution and expansion of the Spanish star system thus involves shifting focus from the number of films produced in Spain versus Hollywood and instead considering the role of private production and distribution companies and individual entrepreneurial directors that accompanied the state's

A Companion to Spanish Cinema, First Edition. Edited by Jo Labanyi and Tatjana Pavlović.

equally modest financial, legislative, and censorship apparatus. If we include the shared mass-media networks – magazines, newspapers, fashion media, advertisements, posters, *programas de mano* (handbills), *cromos* (trading cards), pulp fiction, and radio – that informed and fed off the nascent cinema industry, and the dynamic discourse concerning the national aesthetic they generated, then we greatly amplify the picture of the incipient star system over these two decades.

Commercialization: Stars as Capital Value

While the Hollywood imaginary was in large part responsible for mobilizing a cinema-going public, the Spanish government soon recognized the cinema and its stars as a profit-making machine. As early as 1911 it sought to benefit from sales by mandating tax collection on cinema ticket income (Vallés Copeiro del Villar 2000). The state also intervened in proto-star culture when it came to dictating public morality regarding the control of female sexuality. A 1909 Royal Decree aimed at mitigating the prostitution of female performers who worked in public theaters prohibited such employment for women aged under sixteen, stipulating that contracts with minors under age twenty-three had to be signed by their parents or legal guardians (Scanlon 1986: 115). In 1923, as the Spanish public clamored to see more Hollywood stars, the state stepped in with customs tariffs on foreign cinema imports (Vallés Copeiro del Villar 2000: 37). Another Royal Decree of 1929 stipulated specifically that only twenty-five percent of artists in Spanish films could be foreign (Vallés Copeiro del Villar 2000: 39) – a requirement intended to increase Spanish cinema's marketability. Yet, despite these attempts by the state to assert control, the press and fashion would have far more influence on the direction of Spanish stardom.

Diversification

Combining images of stars and textual commentary was one way in which mass print media intersected with and bolstered star consciousness. By fusing images and text, stars and other objects of cinema could be packaged in a way that guided the reader-spectator. Posters – like *programas de mano* and *cromos*, the most important publicity elements of any production – were part of the commercial network that buttressed cinema. In the 1910s, Spanish actors did not have the symbolic capital or fame to be able to compete with foreign stars, so Spanish posters initially featured a significant scene of the film, as for *Los intereses creados / The Bonds of Interest* (Jacinto Benavente and Ricardo Puga, 1919), or a photographic tribute to the writer of the original literary work, such as the bust of Jacinto Benavente that advertises the film *Más allá de la muerte / Beyond Death* (Benito Perojo, 1924) (Gubern 1994: 76, 90). With the arrival of full-length feature films, however, posters increasingly placed star protagonists at the visual center of gravity (Baena Palma 1998: 14), displacing the film's content and aesthetic as the primary commercial draw.

The press that specialized in reporting on entertainment – for example, *Arte y Cinematografía* (first published 1910), *El Cine: Semanario Popular de Espectáculos* (first published 1912), and *Cinema Variedades* (first published 1918), all of which continued publication through to the mid-1930s – became increasingly attuned to cinema. Articles and photos featuring *zarzuela* actors, comedians, or especially popular female singers (Raquel Meller, La Goya, or La Serós) were juxtaposed with news about the latest films, thus associating the protagonists of these various spectacles with notions of individual fame and an inchoate stardom. The resulting synergy was evident in the case of singers who crossed over to silent film: Pastora Imperio starred in *La danza fatal / The Fatal Dance* (José de Togores, 1915) and *Gitana cañí / Authentic Gypsy* (Armando Pou, 1917); Raquel Meller debuted in 1919 in *Los arlequines de seda y oro / Silk and Gold Harlequins* (Ricardo de Baños); and Concha Piquer would star in one of the first sound-on-film movies to be released commercially, a short of her song performances recorded and premiered in New York in 1923 with Lee De Forest's synchronized Phonofilm system. Radio continued to reinforce this bridge with cinema by broadcasting stars' songs and advertisements for their records and films.

Weekly novelized versions of films, such as the *Novela Semanal Cinematográfica*, contributed to the mechanism of star-building by publishing photos of star actors on their covers. When this weekly series published a novelized version of *Boy* (Perojo, 1925), its front cover featured the young Juan de Orduña, who starred in other important early films – *La casa de la Troya / College Boarding House* (Manuel Noriega and Alejandro Pérez Lugín, 1925) and *El misterio de la Puerta del Sol / The Mystery of the Puerta del Sol* (Francisco Elías, 1930) – and would later gain renown as a "woman's director" celebrated for his work with female stars. From this point onward, stars would be the central icon in the image–text complex.

In the mid-1920s, magazines went from summarizing movie plots to including film analysis and opinion and more elaborate photomontages and articles on stars. *Popular Film* (Barcelona 1926–38) included articles on fashion, beauty product advertisements, competitions, doctored interviews with stars and directors, and film commentary and review, in addition to articles on the state of the domestic and international film industry. In several issues of *Popular Film* during 1928 (e.g., May 3, 1928), the Concurso de Semblanzas Literarias (Literary Portrait Competition) invited fans to write a winning panegyric on their favorite star, to be published in an upcoming issue (*Popular Film* 1928). Fans were thus collectively courted and their involvement bound them to star texts in ways both personal and public.

The creation of star consciousness through the linkage of stars to fashion was instrumental in closing the distance between fans and their stars. In Madrid's *La Pantalla* (December 2, 1927), debate about female pyjamas was enhanced by photos of Joan Crawford and Leandrice Joy modeling this ultra-modern trend

Figure 10.1 Raquel Meller on the cover of *Nuevo Mundo* (June 17, 1932). The caption informs readers that she has been made a Chevalier de la Légion d'Honneur by the French government. Private collection.

(De Diego 1986: 156).[1] Marantz Cohen notes that "the development of personal information about stars was a gradual movement to narrative form" and that, conversely, as film narratives became more complex with the rise of the feature-length film, constructed star personas were better able to convey the intimacy of private life (2001: 141).

The incipient star system was best exemplified by Raquel Meller, a *cupletista* (cabaret or music-hall singer and performer) and later star of radio and the silver screen. She was the first Spanish star to have an identity thoroughly buttressed and defined by film magazines and product advertising, merging her star text, her films, and her private life. The second issue of *Popular Film* (December 8, 1926) featured a piece entitled "La fama de Raquel Meller es mundial" (Raquel Meller's Fame is Worldwide) in its editorial section (see Figure 10.1). In the 1910s and 1920s, the brand name "Meller" proliferated on objects such as hats, perfumes, ties, fans, and cigarette papers (Salaün 1990: 95). Knowledge of Meller as a champion of consumerism reinforced spectators' buying habits. That Meller was the first Spanish actress to appear on stage smoking a cigarette surely had an impact on both male and female audiences, perhaps foreshadowing the publicity myth that equates cigarette smoking with the acquisition or consumption of the sexualized female body (Gómez Santos 1959: 41). Ads in the *New York Times* for Lord & Taylor department stores advertised dresses that could "bring on a Raquel Meller feeling," while fashion columns talked about the latest fabrics that, when worked into "swishing ruffles on a sinuous train" were "as worldly as Raquel Meller" (*New York Times* 1933: 4). Meller was a model for consumers and a fashion leader; her jewels and gowns were spectacularized and fetishized in almost all of her films, which dealt self-reflexively with narratives of stardom, and this amplified the awe and excitement that energized her performance sequences. The credit sequence of *La Venenosa / Venemous Woman* (Roger Lion, 1928), for instance, announces that Meller will be modeling dresses by the Parisian designer Jeanne Lanvin.

Meller's cosmopolitanism, displayed through her minglings with the international star crowd of the 1920s (Charlie Chaplin, Rudolph Valentino), royalty (Alfonso XIII and several famous aristocrats), and intellectuals (her husband Enrique Gómez Carillo and Manuel Machado), added sophistication to her star persona. With Meller, consumerist stardom intersected with the older notion of fame that was reserved for the nobility, intellectuals, and politicians. In the film *La malcasada / The Unhappy Wife* (Francisco Gómez Hidalgo, 1926), we see the merging of new and old kinds of fame through the mingling of *cupletistas* with the dozens of distinguished personalities who appear in cameo in the film's party and dinner sequences. *Folklóricas* (female stars who performed in folkloric, usually Andalusian, style on stage or screen) after Meller would continue this love affair with the aristocracy.

Despite residues of older discourses, female stars were being sold as "new women" – individuals in the process of becoming, emblems of modernity, and the embodiment of social mobility. The press contributed to the mythification of stars such as Meller in articles and interviews that dwelled on anecdotes about her vast wealth, revealing details such as her 1926 contract with the company Empire in New York that earned her fifty thousand dollars (Díaz de Quijano 1960: 129). Inventories of her stock of luxury items were minutely documented in the press: Rodin sculptures, drawings by Matisse, and a piano that had supposedly belonged to Mozart (Gómez Santos 1959: 41). Gossip about entertainers' salaries was a constant in pulp fiction as well as journalistic coverage of the popular stage. The director Perojo, for instance, affirmed in an interview that another singer-turned-actress, the previously mentioned Concha Piquer, made twelve thousand pesetas for three months' work in his 1926 film *El negro que tenía el alma blanca / The Black with the White Soul*, more than any other Spanish actress was earning at the time (Gubern 1994: 121) (see Figure 10.2).

Figure 10.2 Promotional still showcasing Emma (Concha Piquer) as a stylish showgirl on the beach with Afro-Cuban star Peter Wald (Raymond de Sarka) in *El negro que tenía el alma blanca* (Benito Perojo, 1926; prod. Goya Producciones Cinematográficas SA). Courtesy of Filmoteca Española.

Star Exchange

As commodities, stars were consumed but also exchanged between competing national cinema industries and between warring intranational political factions. Exchange created competition and sparked nationalist debates about the direction and mission of Spanish cinema, thereby influencing expectations about who was an appropriate star. While exchange was not always equally weighted, it included consumption of both foreign and Hollywood stars by Spanish spectators.

Despite claims that the French film industry was the first to promote an early form of star branding in its comedy and *films d'art* around 1908 (Hayward 2000: 349), a vibrant, witty consciousness of stardom had already emerged in Spain by the mid-1910s. Spanish audiences had become so familiar with Hollywood actors and other international artists that Spanish films and posters knowingly teased their audiences with references to the figure of Charlie Chaplin, even though he did not appear in the films in question, such as *Charlot, torero español / Chaplin, Spanish Bullfighter* (José Calvache "Walken," 1928; poster by F. Martínez) and *Ya t'oyí / I heard'ja* (Vicente Suárez Arango, 1928; poster by Germán Oracio). Prior to those examples, Perojo founded Patria Films (1915), making several shorts in a comic cycle about Peladilla, a figure based on Charlie Chaplin and played by Perojo himself, imitating Chaplin's gestures and costume. Although this kind of managerial improvization was considered by critics to be an indicator of Spain's insufficiently diversified industry (Pérez Perucha 2000: 98–9; Fanés 1982: 55), it also attests to the gumption of individuals like Perojo, who not only starred in his own films but also personally carried out the casting and contracting of stars for them.

Toward the end of the 1920s, several big Hollywood studios installed distribution offices in Spain (Los Artistas Asociados, Hispano Fox Film, and JUFA), which published their own posters and magazines out of their local branches: *Revista Paramount* (1928), *Paramount Gráfico* (1929), Fox's *El Faro* (1929), Metro-Goldwyn-Mayer's *El Rugido del León* (1935), Columbia's *La Antorcha*, Radio Films' *Titán Radio*, and Universal's *Universal* (1936). This turf war spawned a range of Spanish studio magazines such as CIFESA's *Noticiario CIFESA* (1935).

The film musicals and comedies produced between 1932 and 1936 constitute for historians a golden age of Spanish cinema and it was also during this time that the star system was consolidated by star-makers such as Perojo and production companies such as CIFESA, Filmófono, and the future director Rosario Pi's Star Film. Star Film not only produced and provided actresses for films such as Edgar Neville's *Yo quiero que me lleven a Hollywood / Take Me to Hollywood* (1931), *El hombre que se reía del amor / The Man who Laughed at Love* (Perojo, 1932), and Pi's own *El gato montés / The Wild Cat* (1935); it also offered opportunities for wanna-be female stars (Martin-Márquez 1999: 55–62). During this golden age, agents such as Pi were responsible for the creation of star duos such as Imperio Argentina and Miguel Ligero, and Rosita Díaz Gimeno and Ricardo Núñez, and individual stars (female and male) such as Antoñita Colomé, Angelillo, Ana María Custodio, Roberto Rey, Manuel Luna, Raquel Rodrigo, and Charito Leonís.

Spain's most influential production company, CIFESA (see Chapter 14), founded and run by the Valencian Manuel Casanova, produced three of the biggest box-office hits in Republican Spain – *La verbena de la paloma / Festival of the Virgin of the Dove* (Perojo, 1935), *Nobleza baturra / Aragonese Virtue* (Florián Rey, 1935), and *Morena Clara / Dark and Bright* (Rey, 1936). With its novel, aggressive publicity campaigns, CIFESA was the Spanish production company whose operational mode most resembled that of Hollywood. Modeling itself explicitly on the Hollywood majors, Casanova's company fused a capitalist mentality with conservative national values, striving both for ultra-Spanishness and a conservative regionalism (Fanés 1982: 27–9). CIFESA implemented basic elements of capitalist logic: programmatic production, the creation of infrastructure, and a solid distribution network (Fanés 1982: 51, 52) that provided carefully chosen, profitable films. Often compared to Adolph Zukor, Casanova competitively monopolized talent around a star system reinforced by granting exclusive year-long contracts to primary stars and the best secondary actors, directors, set designers, cameramen, and musicians (Fanés 1982: 56). The ambition of CIFESA to conquer new markets, a practice compatible and contemporaneous with Spain's expansionist discourse of Hispanidad (Fanés 1982: 57), materialized in 1935 in the creation of branches in Latin America (Mexico, Cuba, Argentina, Chile) and even in Paris and Berlin, leading to further exchange of capital and stars. During the period 1935–6, CIFESA enjoyed the highest ticket sales in Spanish history with *La hermana San Sulpicio / Sister San Sulpicio* (Florián Rey, 1934), *Nobleza baturra*, and *Morena Clara*, all starring Imperio Argentina.

Imperio Argentina would embody the shape of things to come. Born in Argentina (hence her stage name) to an Andalusian mother and a father from Gibraltar, her star image had already begun to circulate internationally in the 1920s when the silent version of *La hermana San Sulpicio* (Rey, 1927) had debuted in Germany. When Perojo set about making *Corazones sin rumbo / Restless Hearts* in 1928, he chose her as the winner of a star contest that had been run by the weekly magazine *El Cine*, the German producer Phoebus, and the German studio Emelka (Gubern 1994: 154). Yet *Corazones sin rumbo* was attacked by Spanish critics who thought Spanish actors had been relegated to the second tier, which was regarded as an affront considering Spanish investment in this coproduction (Gubern 1994: 161).

The introduction of sound film in the early 1930s had huge consequences for cinema production and star-making. As sound technology became a stressful reality for Spain's inadequate sound equipment infrastructure, debates raged in cinema magazines about how to launch a film industry that was not a "colonia de Francia" (French colony) (Santos 1932: n.p.). Sound film would allow cinema to capture nationalist sentiment through language (more rooted in local speech patterns than silent film intertitles) and songs sung by nationally celebrated performers such as Argentina, Piquer, Colomé, and Estrellita Castro, who increasingly responded to the demand for folkloric repertoires. As in the United States with *The Jazz Singer*, Spanish blackface died with its most celebrated incarnation, *El negro que tenía el alma blanca*. But on its coat-tails rode the Andalusian musical comedy film starring white actresses who in effect performed "Gypsyface," albeit without "browning up" (see Chapter 7). Replacing the international cosmopolitan ambience of the silent film with an "authentic" (in practice, stereotypical) Andalusian backdrop, directors and producers retained the formulas that had proved so successful in silent films about the world of entertainment and stardom while avoiding the criticisms launched at Perojo for making what looked like a "foreign film." In Piquer's limited but significant cinematic career, she would play non-folkloric performers in *El negro que tenía el alma blanca*; *Yo canto para ti / I Sing for You* (Fernando Roldán, 1934), based on the life of the *cupletista* La Fornarina; and *Me casé con una estrella / I Married a Star* (Luis César Amadori, 1951), based on the Argentine stage scene. Her folklore films included *La Dolores* (Rey, 1940) and *Filigrana* (Luis Marquina, 1949).

Rosita Díaz Giméno would counter the image that Imperio Argentina personified: the nationalist symbol of the cute, rural, chaste girl next door. Díaz Giméno, in contrast, was the female archetype of the Republican "gal" – urban, emancipated (in real life she had begun a degree in medicine), and star of several of Perojo's cosmopolitan comedies: *El hombre que se reía del amor / The Man Who Laughed at Love* (1932), *Susana tiene un secreto / Susana Has a Secret* (1933), and *Se ha fugado un preso / A Prisoner has Escaped* (1933) (Gubern unpublished). While she was filming *El genio alegre / The Cheerful Temper* (Fernando Delgado, 1939) at the end of the Civil War, she was arrested in Córdoba and condemned to death by the Nationalists, but finally exchanged for a Francoist prisoner. Managing to escape to exile in Mexico, she made three more films: *Pepita Jiménez* (Emilio "El Indio" Fernández, 1946), *El último amor de Goya / Goya's Last Love* (Jaime Salvador, 1946), and *El canto de la sirena / Siren Song* (Norman Foster, 1948).

Another notable Spanish star who would go into exile was Angelillo. A popular male idol of Andalusian song styles, his first screen role was in Perojo's 1934 musical film remake of *El negro que tenía el alma blanca*. He would star in two more films, *La hija de Juan Simón / Juan Simón's Daughter* (José Luis Sáenz de Heredia, 1935) and *¡¡Centinela, alerta!! / Guard! Alert!* (Jean Grémillon, 1937), a box-office smash of the Civil War period in which he copied the Hollywood and German technique of looking directly at the camera when singing. Like other stars who did not conform to the Nationalist model, his Republican ideas led him into exile in Mexico and Argentina while his failed marriage fed rumors about his purported homosexuality.

While few male performers achieved the impact or celebrity of female stars such as Argentina, Díaz Gimeno, or Castro (the last a *folklórica* who specialized in cheeky, lower-class roles, usually in a modern urban setting), a handful stand out. Both Miguel Ligero and Manuel Luna accompanied Argentina in her greatest successes of the 1930s. Ligero specialized in broadly comic roles, such as the Argentina character's rascal brother in *Morena Clara*, capitalizing on his rubbery features and physique. In contrast, Luna, with his impassive countenance and somewhat stolid acting style, played the villain in *Nobleza baturra* and the straight-arrow lawyer won over by the Gypsy heroine in *Morena Clara*. Roberto Rey, characterized by Antonio Comás (2004: 122) as the Spanish equivalent of Maurice Chevalier, was highly effective as the romantic singing lead in films such as *La verbena de la paloma* (Benito Perojo, 1935), *El bailarín y el trabajador / The Dancer and the Worker* (Luis Marquina, 1936), and *Suspiros de España / Sighs of Spain* (Perojo, 1939).

The outbreak of the Civil War in 1936 signaled exile for certain stars as well as an invigorated push by the Nationalist insurgents to mold Spanish cinema. In 1936 the Nazi German film industry, under the concerted efforts of Goebbels as Minister of Propaganda, sought to sponsor the production of Spanish-language films in German studios that could serve as a commercial locomotive for German productions in the Latin American market. The resulting Spanish–German coproduction company Hispano-Film-Produktion (see Chapter 2) invited Spanish directors Rey and Perojo to make films in the UFA studios starring Imperio Argentina (of whom Hitler had reputedly become enamored after seeing her in

Nobleza baturra) and Estrellita Castro. Of the feature films produced under this arrangement, three were directed by Perojo – *El barbero de Sevilla / The Barber of Seville* (1938), *Mariquilla Terremoto / Mariquilla the Fireball* (1938), and *Suspiros de España*, all starring Castro, with Ligero co-starring in the first two – and two by Rey – *Carmen, la de Triana / Carmen, from Triana* (1938) and *La canción de Aixa / The Song of Aixa* (1939), both starring Argentina. This was a fundamentally star-driven venture.

Genres and Techniques

Stars and stardom were the core of the "cinephile" film, a genre emerging in the 1920s that played with the critical awareness of stardom through a conspicuous reflexivity about making and viewing cinema (Gubern 1994: 156): for example, *Una aventura de cine / A Cinema Adventure* (Orduña, 1928); *El misterio de la Puerta del Sol* (Elías, 1930); *Cinópolis / Elle veut faire du cinema / She Wants to be in a Movie* (José María Castellví, 1931); *Yo quiero que me lleven a Hollywood* (Neville, 1931); *Falso noticiario / Fake Newsreel* (Neville, 1933); *Patricio miró a una estrella / Patricio Looked at a Star* (Sáenz de Heredia, 1934); *El veneno del cine / The Poison of Cinema* (Mauro Azcona, 1935); *No me mates* aka *Los misterios del Barrio Chino / Don't Kill Me* aka *The Mysteries of the Red Light District* (Pedro Puche, 1935); and *Sesenta horas en el cielo / Sixty Hours in Heaven* (Raymond Chevalier, 1935).

A subcategory of the cinephile genre focused on the making or furthering of a star's career. Typical were *El bailarín y el trabajador* (Marquina, 1936); *Currito de la Cruz / Currito of the Cross* (Alejandro Pérez Lugín, 1926; remade three times: Delgado, 1936; Luis Lucia, 1949, 1965); *Mariquilla Terremoto* (Perojo, 1938); and *Suspiros de España* (Perojo, 1939). Films portraying the negative side of stardom (whether on screen or on stage, or in allusions to nightlife-as-performance), such as *La terrible lección / The Terrible Lesson* (Delgado, 1927), enjoyed particular appeal and several were remade (sometimes more than once), such as *Malvaloca* (Perojo, 1926; Marquina, 1942; Ramón Torrado, 1954) and *María de la O* (Elías, 1936; Torrado, 1959). Some film directors, such as Perojo and Rey, dedicated much of their careers to making films about stars, whether singers, dancers, bullfighters, or football players (Gubern 1994: 45).

Camera techniques were central to the development of the star. The close-up or title cards using dialogue (*rótulos de diálogo*) were at first infrequently employed, inhibiting character individualization, but by the mid-1920s they were common fare in Spanish cinema (Sánchez Salas 2007: 420). Another technique that nurtured the star gaze among spectators was parallel editing between intradiegetic spectators and stars, which was used most frequently in performance sequences of musical comedies. Musicals about travelling *folklóricas* (*Mariquilla Terremoto* and *Suspiros de España*) made use of conventional visual shortcuts to show the star's itinerary through the Americas via montages of trains, planes, and cars, or newspapers stacked one atop the other, displaying front page news of the star's arrival in a major foreign city. Monuments of cultural capitals such as New York, Paris, or Buenos Aires were often used metonymically in these travel sequences to denote the star's ascent to fame, in the form of postcard-like shots of the Eiffel Tower or of the star posing against similar cosmopolitan icons.

Star Typology and Performance

Stars sold films, but their exchange value surpassed their filmic image. The multimedia and intertextual nature of star texts was evident in posters that recalled Catholic images of saints or the Virgin Mary, a readily recognizable feature of Spanish visual culture. Thus, stars might appear outlined by a glittering halo that verged on the sublime (Baena Palma 1998: 17). A cinematic type that developed in accord with this iconography was that of the "saintly" girlfriend or wife.

Another type cultivated in literature and song before making its way into Spanish films was the *peliculera*, a blonde who imitated Hollywood stars, divorced her husband, kissed "for real" (*besos de verdad*), and most often left her boyfriend for a man in the movie industry. Avant-garde novels such as Ramón Gómez de la Serna's *Cinelandia* (1923), and the weekly subscription series *Novela Cómica*, paid homage to this prototype (De Diego 1986: 155). Various cinema magazines educated readers in the science of kissing practiced by stars, in articles such as "Los besos cinematográficos" (Movie Kisses), "Cómo besan los ases de la pantalla: Clases e importancia de los besos" (How the Stars Kiss: Categories and Importance of Kisses), and "¿Sabría usted besar para el celuloide?" (Would You Know How to Kiss in the Movies?) (Morris 1980: 168 n. 25).

Cinema was early on integrated with variety shows, which began to incorporate film showings, either in alternating sessions or projecting them simultaneously with live performances, in order to boost ticket sales. And, when performers of popular spectacles, such as singers (*cupletistas*), dancers (*bailaoras*), saucy performers (*cocottes*), or aspiring stars (*vedettes*), appeared in films, it meant that the star system had become a fusion of these two entertainment traditions. The Spanish vamp was a product of this merger, a blend of the morally dubious Spanish female performer and the melodramatic Italian diva made famous in the 1910s (Sánchez Salas: 2007).

Raquel Meller's star text shows the broadening of the spectrum of female subjectivity and, at the same time, the effects of a national effort to maintain proper (white) womanhood. Meller's brand of femininity was a powerful version of the vamp, a charged mode of alterity that signified the liminality of being caught between the old and the new Spain. This uncontainable sexuality, haunted as it was through Meller's star roles by the ghosts of racial and social tensions (see Chapter 7), was brought into disturbing proximity with other roles that Meller could enter almost too easily – those of perfect wife and mother, both of them necessary models of womanhood for keeping order in the home and on the streets. The creation of a modern Spanish woman who could entice while retaining a veneer of wholesomeness would be the fundamental balancing act underlying the star image of Imperio Argentina, allowing her star career to extend into the postwar period when Francoism imposed female decorum. This balancing act would be pronounced for the *folklórica* stars of the early Franco period. A similar sign of changing times is found in the uncomfortable contrast between the ambiguous sexuality of the prewar male idol Angelillo and masculine stars of the 1940s and 1950s such as Alfredo Mayo and Rafael Durán.

The 1940s and 1950s

Rather than rejecting the Hollywood-inspired model of stardom, the Franco dictatorship sought to adapt it to its own needs and purposes. Following the lead of fascist Germany and Italy, the regime recognized cinema as an important vehicle for the transmission of national myths and values, with performers playing an obvious and indispensable role – at least potentially – in embodying Spanish virtues. By the early 1940s, a full range of measures intended to support and regulate cinema production and exhibition were in place. On the production side, financing for the Spanish industry, such as it was, was cobbled together from a range of direct and indirect public subsidies and credits (Pozo Arenas 1984: 43–127). The Nationalists created a unified censorship apparatus in Salamanca in 1937, two years before the Civil War's end, and during the 1940s and 1950s the Francoist government continued to police film content through prior scrutiny of film scripts plus subsidy policies designed to promote films in the "national interest" (see Chapter 14). On the consumption side, cinema was recognized as an item of "primera necesidad" (basic necessity) and ticket prices were subject to price controls to ensure that attendance remained in reach for even the most modest household budgets (Comás 2004: 29).

Although originally designed to safeguard Spanish audiences against ideas and indeed actors deemed inimical to the principles espoused by the new regime,[2] these regulations had the effect of delivering a nearly fatal blow to a domestic film industry ravaged by the war and the ensuing exile of Republican talent. The Ministerial Order of April 1941, which imposed the obligatory dubbing of all foreign-language films, effectively opened the floodgates to what would become an irresistible onslaught of technologically superior and artistically more appealing Hollywood products that could now compete with Spanish films on a linguistically equal footing. Even the policy of awarding subsidies for the production of Spanish films was linked to the financial reward of import licenses for the dubbing and distribution of foreign (largely Hollywood) films. The consequences were predictable. As Ángel Comás (2004: 36) observed, if Gary Cooper, Marlene

Dietrich, or James Stewart spoke in Spanish, why would audiences go to see minor Spanish stars in insignificant Spanish films? Setting the stage for cultural habits and practices that continue to the present day, Spanish actors would coexist and compete with foreign performers across a range of film-related outlets and offerings, in movies themselves but also in film magazines and the media at large.

Star-Makers: CIFESA and Suevia Films

Faced with the need to rebuild Spanish film production quickly following the war, CIFESA, now under the control of Vicente Casanova, son of the founder, soon cemented its role as the preeminent studio (see Chapter 14). With import restrictions initially limiting the competition with foreign films, CIFESA took advantage of its position to supply the national market with a series of quickly and inexpensively made escapist comedies. Continuing to pattern itself on the Hollywood studio model, the company sought to maintain and renew its stable of domestic stars, with names that included prewar stars such as Piquer, Castro, Luna, Conchita Montenegro, Luis Peña, and Josita Hernán; actors whose film careers had just started before the Civil War, such as Alfredo Mayo, Rafael Durán, and Luchy Soto; and new names such as Amparito Rivelles, Antonio Casal, Marta Santaolalla, Isabel de Pomés, and Mary Delgado. In the late 1940s it also incorporated seasoned actors who had made their names with other production companies such as Fernando Rey and Jorge Mistral, as well as the new discoveries Sara Montiel and Aurora Bautista (Comás 2004: 38). In the midst of early postwar depravations, CIFESA sought to inject a note of Hollywood-ish glamour into its operations, sponsoring lavish public premieres for selected films. Nevertheless, as Fèlix Fanés reports, the results were not always up to expectations:

> En vez de los espléndidos sueños de mármol, que eran las *stars* americanas, la gente tenía que conformarse con el exiguo esplendor de las artistas locales, a menudo demasiado gorditas y, sobre todo, siempre excesivamente bien peinadas. (1982: 108)

> Instead of the splendid sculptural dreams that were American stars, people had to be satisfied with the paltry splendor of local artists, often a little too plump, and always excessively well coiffed.

Where CIFESA could and did compete with Hollywood was in contracts for top performers. Following her success in the films *Alma de Dios / The Simple Soul* (Ignacio F. Iquino, 1941), *Los ladrones somos gente honrada / We Thieves are Honest Folks* (Iquino, 1942), and *Malvaloca* (Marquina, 1942), Amparo (then known as Amparito) Rivelles was signed up by CIFESA to a three-year contract renewable annually. She was paid ten thousand pesetas a week, whether she worked or not, and had the right to choose the director and co-star for films she worked in (Fanés 1982: 111). Her partner in *Malvaloca*, *Un caballero famoso / A Famous*

Gentleman (José Buchs, 1942), and *Deliciosamente tontos / Delightfully Foolish* (Orduña, 1943), and in a much-talked-about off-screen romance, Alfredo Mayo, was reportedly earning a hundred thousand pesetas per film in the early 1940s, a sum that rose to two hundred thousand for *Arribada forzosa / Emergency Call* (Esteban Montaño, 1944) (Comás 2004: 111–12). In his quest to monopolize the best talent, Fanés observes, Casanova was prepared to go to any lengths, spending lavishly to achieve his ends (1982: 111).

If the goal of the star system as an industrial strategy was, as Fanés argues (1982: 189), to achieve "el buen entendimiento con el público" (a strong connection with the public) as a means of consolidating the domestic market while attempting to conquer new external markets, then Casanova more than met his match in the person of Cesáreo González, owner of Suevia Films (see Chapter 14). González had spent his youth in Cuba and Mexico working in a variety of jobs. Returning to Galicia in the early 1930s, he established an advertising agency and automobile dealerships, adding Suevia Films to his list of business ventures in 1940. By the mid-1940s, Suevia Films had become CIFESA's chief competitor and in 1951 it took over CIFESA's position as the dominant studio in Spain. Rather than seeking to corner the star market with exclusive and expensive contracts, González took advantage of existing arrangements and audience preferences in the countries where he wished to do business (Fanés 1982: 189–90). He traded on the value of stars in a kind of broad-ranging cinematic diplomacy, promoting Spanish cinema in Mexico, South America, and the United States in ways that sought to accomplish what official foreign policy could not.[3] In the face of the continuing absence of official diplomatic relations between Mexico and Franco's Spain, he offered his services: "A falta de otra embajada, yo mismo pienso ser un embajador cinematográfico de España en México en todo momento" (Given the lack of an embassy, I plan to act myself on every occasion as a cinematic ambassador for Spain in Mexico) (Durán 2003: 147). González most famously brought to Spain a host of Mexican stars – María Félix, Jorge Negrete, Cantinflas, the songwriter/actor Augustín Lara – while promoting the careers of Spanish counterparts such as Lola Flores abroad. In the 1950s, González was the prime mover behind a second wave of folkloric films and perfomers, including Flores, with whom he would make twelve films, as well as Carmen Sevilla and Paquita Rico. These star vehicles sold well in the Latin American market.

Film Magazines and Star Discourse

None of the film magazines of the 1920s and 1930s – such as *Popular Film*, *Nuestro Cinema*, *Cinegramas*, and *Cinelandia Films* – survived the Civil War, but new publications soon emerged to take their place.[4] The first, *Radio y Cinema* (promptly renamed *Radiocinema*), was created in 1938 in La Coruña by the Falangist writer Joaquín Romero Marchent. The cover image for its debut issue, a photomontage highlighting the fragmentary close-up of a glamorous young woman framed by the title headlines "Por España y por Franco ¡Todo! Gran Revista Ilustrada de Radio y Cine: La única en su género en la España Nacional" (For Spain and for Franco, Our All! Illustrated Review of Radio and Film: The Only One of its Kind in Nationalist Spain) spoke to its schizophrenic mission of pro-Francoist propaganda on the one hand and the coverage and promotion of the film industry in Spain and abroad on the other. Both *Radiocinema* and *Primer Plano*, which began publication in October 1940 as the official organ of the Falangist-controlled cinema sub-ministry, struggled openly with the resulting tensions and contradictions between ideological orthodoxy, commercial priorities, and popular tastes. During the early 1940s, as Spain flirted with entering World War II on the Axis side, both magazines promoted German cinema and film stars as an antidote to Hollywood. While seeking to combat the widespread perception that audiences preferred foreign – and especially Hollywood – films over national productions, as in a 1940 article by Francisco Casares that directly posed the question "¿por qué no le gusta el cine español?" (why don't you like Spanish cinema?), critics and editorialists were also keen to define what a suitable Spanish cinema should or should not be. Despite a handful of dissenting voices (Camporesi 1993: 29–39), multiple writers denounced the persistence of folkloric themes and character types as offering unworthy subject matter for representations of the "New Spain." For some critics the overemphasis on stars was itself a source of the problem. Romero Marchent put the blame, perhaps only partly in jest, on actress Imperio Argentina:

> Se diría que nuestros proyectos de cine son una consecuencia de Imperio Argentina, en vez de Imperio Argentina ser una resultante del Cinema español. [...] Aquí en España, no preguntamos, "¿Has visto "Carmen'?" Aquí decimos que hemos visto a Imperio Argentina en "Carmen" porque ni "Morena Clara" ni Nobleza baturra" ni "Carmen" tienen fuerza nacional, ni artística, ni cinematográfica bastantes para sobreponerse a la personalidad del intérprete. La fuerza expresiva de Imperio, su gracia, su "personalidad," su "belleza," su modo han creado escuela, hasta el punto de que todos los filmes españoles donde aparece una gitana, aquella gitana, sea quien sea, quiere parecerse a Imperio Argentina. (1939: n.p.)

> It could be said that our films are a consequence of Imperio Argentina, instead of Imperio Argentina being a result of Spanish Cinema. [...] Here in Spain we don't ask, "Have you seen *Carmen*?" Here we say we've seen Imperio Argentina in *Carmen* because neither *Morena clara* nor *Nobleza baturra* nor *Carmen* possess the national, artistic, or cinematic power sufficient to outweigh the personality of the actress. The expressive force of Imperio, her charm, her "personality," her "beauty," her style have created a school, to the degree that in any Spanish film where a female Gypsy character appears, that Gypsy wants to be like Imperio Argentina.[5]

Six issues later, filmmaker Antonio Román would return to the attack on the institution of stardom but from another flank. In an article entitled "Valor real del actor en el Cinema" (The True Value of the Actor in Cinema), he warned against the "admiración fetichista que el actor ejerce en cierto sector del público" (the fetishistic attraction that the actor exercises on a certain sector of the public). Claiming that this fetishism had reached alarming levels, he noted that theater actors had never been the object of such vehement devotion despite the technical and artistic superiority of their craft compared to film performers. In films, he argued, citing the case of Marlene Dietrich in the films of Josef von Sternberg, actors were often mere marionettes in the director's hands. Román declared the need to rebalance our understanding and appreciation of cinema by directing greater attention to the role of the director, "verdadero deus ex machina de cada película" (the real deus ex machina of every film). Fetishism was

> siempre peligroso, máxime cuando, como aquí, tiene determinadas raíces psicopatológicas encarnadas en lo que los americanos, en su afán de quitar importancia a ciertas cuestiones, han dado en llamar "sex appeal," adjetivo que nosotros preferimos dejar sin traducir. (Román 1939: n.p.)

> always dangerous, especially when, as here, it stems from particular psychopathological sources rooted in what the Americans, in their insistence on trivializing certain matters, call "sex appeal," an adjective [sic] we prefer to leave untranslated.

Ultimately, these objections seemed to hold little sway and both *Radiocinema* and *Primer Plano* settled for a kind of devil's bargain. Stars' faces and lives would be used to sell the magazine to readers and advertisers but editorial content could and did denounce and disdain their influence.

Two other important film magazines of the period – *Cámara*, founded in October 1941 by writer, humorist, and sketch artist Antonio de Lara (Tono), and the Barcelona-based *Fotogramas*, created in November 1946 by radio and newspaper critic Antonio Nadal Rodó – mostly side-stepped such ideological concerns and embraced the cause of star-making in all its facets. While all the magazines studied published full-page photos of well-known actors and actresses, sometimes as tear-out sheets or centerfolds suitable for tacking to a wall or pasting into a scrapbook, *Cámara* specialized in glamour shots of both Spanish and international stars by well-known photographers of the day such as Gyenes, Campúa, Ortiz, Nicolás, and Cervera.

With this acceptance if not endorsement of star-centered content, the pages of film magazines were transformed into cultural "cease-fire" zones where Spanish and foreign stars (and lifestyles) cohabited but also competed, sometimes overtly. While a host of moralizing articles denounced Hollywood stars for their supposed lack of traditional values, evidenced in fervent reporting on their multiple marriages and divorces ("Desde Hollywood, 'Tío Vivo Matrimonial'" (From Hollywood, "Matrimonial Merry-Go-Round") (*Radiocinema* 1955a)), an October 1948 feature in *Cámara* offered "Dos fórmulas para ser feliz en el matrimonio" (Two formulas for marital happiness) with pictures of Spanish actors José María Rodero and Elvira Quintillá at home with their baby (*Cámara* 1948: 46). Other contemporary articles seemed to search out counterexamples of reassuring family behavior among foreign actors. Thus, *Cámara* (1946: 4–5, 13) would report in an article acompanied by photos of Maria Montez and Hedy Lamar that "Las vampiresas de hoy son excelentes madres de familia" (Today's *femmes fatales* are excellent mothers), and a two-page photo spread in *Fotogramas*, "Cara y Cruz ... de Hollywood" (Heads and Tails ... of Hollywood) sought to correct the impression that Hollywood was "sin city." Citing statistics, the article noted that seventy-three percent of film professionals were married and seventy-five percent of those "tienen hijos y viven felices y contentos en la tranquila y risueña paz del hogar" (have children and live happy and content in the tranquil bliss of a harmonious home) (*Fotogramas* 1947). An August 1948 article in *Cámara* offered a paean to "Las actrices con delantal" (Actresses in aprons), noting that:

> Las estrellas de cine no son solamente diosas paganas sujetas a la propaganda de los estudios y la devoción y adoración de sus admiradores; también son mujercitas hacendosas, plenas de femineidad, que en sus hogares cumplen su papel a la perfección, sin focos, cámaras, micrófonos ni maquillaje, como cualquier mujer de las muchas que estamos diseminadas por el mundo. (Laguna 1948: 16–17)
>
> Cinema actresses are not just pagan goddesses beholden to studio publicity and the devotion and adoration of their admirers; they are also diligent wives, brimming with femininity, who in their homes fulfill their role to perfection, without spotlights, cameras, microphones or makeup, just like us and the many other women all over the world.

In addition to attesting to actresses' domestic virtues, such coverage tapped into a key characteristic of star discourse: the contradictory insistence that stars are different (i.e., superior and worthy of adulation) but also, deep down, in their intimate moments, just like us.

The comparison of Spanish stars with their foreign equivalents, while often serving, as Carmen Martín Gaite observed in her thoroughly documented study of social behavior and customs in postwar Spain (2004: 34), as a transparent bid to promote the nation's antimodern "moral superiority," could also function in reverse, to claim for Spain and Spanish performers the attributes of the "modern girl" or guy. Such was the case of an article touting Spanish actress Ana Mariscal's off-screen style as representative of her "true" nature:

> La personalidad de Ana, a pesar de los trajes de época con la que la "decoran" algunas veces en el cine, responde a la de una chica moderna. Una chica con pantalones de pescador y un pañuelo anudado al cuello a lo pirata. Una chica de pelo corto y flequillo, que tome "gin-fizz" y se pasee en "Vespa" por Serrano. Una chica que, con sus 10 o 12 trajes de noche [...] y su estola de renards blancos, no nos dejará quedar mal al lado de una Elizabeth Taylor o cualquier Silvana Pampanini. (*Radiocinema* 1954a: n.p.)
>
> Ana's personality, despite the period costumes with which she is sometimes "decorated" in films, is that of a modern girl. A girl in capri pants with a scarf tied

> around her neck, pirate style. A girl with short hair and bangs, who drinks gin-fizzes and rides her Vespa around Serrano [a fashionable street of Madrid]. A girl who, with her 10 or 12 evening gowns […] and white fox-fur stole, would not take a backseat to an Elizabeth Taylor or any Silvana Pampanini.

In fact, such contradictory attitudes toward international stars were rampant in film magazines. The increasing presence in the country throughout the 1950s of stars from Hollywood, Italy, and Mexico as tourists and working professionals (see Chapter 2), avidly reported in the national media, put Spain back on the international map and validated the country's status as an important nation. Both film magazines and the NO-DO (see Chapter 18) documented their arrival at Madrid's airport – "El aeropuerto de Barajas, etapa obligada de las estrellas de cine" (Barajas airport, an obligatory stop for film stars) (*Cámara* 1951) – to the extent that such scenes became a cliché. A 1958 article in *Radiocinema* would go so far as to claim that "Madrid es el Hollywood europeo" (Madrid is the Hollywood of Europe) thanks to the constant stream of famous visitors:

> Hace apenas un par de lustros, querer ver personalmente a alguna celebridad de Hollywood era una quimera. Hoy, en cambio, no es muy difícil ver de cerca a cualquier figura famosa del séptimo arte en una cafetería, como se se tratara de un "night club" hollywoodense cualquiera. (Romo 1958: n.p.)

> A scant ten years ago, the thought of seeing a Hollywood celebrity in person was a pipe dream. Today, in contrast, it is not difficult to catch a close-up view of almost any famous representative of the seventh art in a café, as if it were some Hollywood night club.

The arrival of foreign stars on Spanish soil was read to mean that Spain, too, had arrived.

Star Texts

Ultimately neither governments nor would-be cultural leaders had much success in exercising control over the accumulated meanings adhering to and communicated by what Richard Dyer (1979) has termed the "star text," an "intertextual construct" that combines the star's acting ability and style in individual films and across a career with other discursive projections of his or her off-screen lifestyle, personality, and behavior, and exists to be read by audiences and critics as a text in its own right. Spanish stars of the 1940s and 1950s, whose images were forged in a crucible of complex and contradictory national and international forces, offer a revealing set of case studies for analyzing these processes in their social, political, economic, geocultural, and historical contexts.

Perhaps the only Spanish actor of the 1940s to approach the Hollywood standard of glamour and erotic allure was Alfredo Mayo. Coming off his service in the Civil War as a lieutenant in the Nationalist airforce, Mayo projected a masculine ideal of physical aplomb and matinee idol looks in the role of military hero that he played in early films such as *¡Harka!* (Carlos Arévalo, 1941), *Escuadrilla / Squadron* (Antonio Román, 1941), *¡A mí la legion! / Follow the Legion!* (Orduña, 1942) and *Raza / Race* (Sáenz de Heredia, 1942). His identification as Francoist leading man *par excellence* was cemented in his role as José Churruca, the fictionalized alter ego of the dictator himself in *Raza*, the Franco-scripted retelling of the Civil War as a melodramatic family saga. Nevertheless it is his performances in the African-themed *¡Harka!* and *¡A mí la legión!* that have garnered more contemporary critical attention for their homoerotic subtexts (Evans 1995; Pavlović 2003; Mira 2004; Martin-Márquez 2008). Amid these films' almost exclusively male casts, the Mayo characters stand out for their costume choices and personal style. In *¡Harka!*, alone among the Spanish officers, as Susan Martin-Márquez points out, Mayo wears a *djellaba* (Arab robe) over his uniform and a Moroccan fez instead of the standard brimmed cap (2008: 209). At other times he tops his uniform with a dashing cape. A recurring fashion statement in his films, whether in military or civilian roles, such as the comedy *Deliciosamente tontos*, was the tightly rolled shirt-sleeve that revealed the curve of his biceps. Years later, when interviewed for the documentary *Raza, el espíritu de Franco / Race, the spirit of Franco* (Gonzalo Herralde, 1977), the actor showed a certain ironic self-awareness of his impact on audiences. Because of his background and physical appearance, he recalls, he was a natural for heroic roles: "A mí me sentaba bien el uniforme militar. [...] Por lo visto, yo, cuando me arremangaba las mangas de la camisa, era como el striptease aquél que hizo Rita Hayworth, en fin, cuando se quitaba el guante" (I looked good in military uniform. When I rolled up my shirt sleeves it was like that striptease of Rita Hayworth when she took off her glove [in *Gilda*]).

Among the most popular and, as we have seen, best-compensated actresses of the 1940s and early 1950s, Amparo Rivelles struck a decidedly modern note in the shape and conduct of her career. Building on an initial image as the girl next door, she developed her comedic gifts in such films as *Eloísa está debajo de un almendro / Eloisa Under an Almond Tree* (Rafael Gil, 1943) and *Deliciosamente tontos*. Paired in contemporary roles with the two principal romantic leads of the period, Mayo and Rafael Durán, she was also cast in (melo)dramatic period pieces of distinguished literary pedigree such as *El clavo / The Nail* (Gil, 1944; see Chapter 12) and *La fe / The Faith* (Gil, 1947) (see Figure 10.3). Riding the subsequent wave of historical costume dramas, she appeared in the title roles of *Eugenia de Montijo* (José López Rubio, 1944) and *La Leona de Castilla / The Lioness of Castille* (Orduña, 1951) and as Queen Isabella in the Columbus epic *Alba de América / Dawn of America* (Orduña, 1951). She also followed in the footsteps of such disparate screen divas as Bette Davis and Imperio Argentina, playing the dual role of the duchess and her Gypsy rival in *La Duquesa de Benameji / The Duchess of Benameji* (Lucia, 1949). With the exception of films such as Gil's effective exercise in poetic realism, *La calle sin sol / The Sunless Street* (1948), Rivelles was nearly always better

Figure 10.3 Handbill for *El clavo* (Rafael Gil, 1944; prod. CIFESA). Private collection.

than her roles. If she had been born in Italy, notes Comás, she would have been more than the "número uno del cine de teléfonos blancos, por su físico, por su clase y por su ya apreciable sentido de humor" (number one in white telephone films, thanks to her physical beauty, her distinction, and her considerable sense of humor) (2004: 124). Her wit was perhaps more clearly expressed in the advice column she wrote for *Primer Plano* in the mid-to-late 1940s.[6] Dubbed by the same magazine "la cara más bonita del cine español" (the prettiest face in Spanish cinema) (Navarro and Rodríguez Martínez 1988: 9–10), she was more than a pretty face, showing great savvy in managing her career. Unlike Hollywood stars, for whom a studio contract often meant a form of slavery, while still with CIFESA Rivelles parried offers from Suevia Films, which she accepted, later returning to CIFESA. In the late 1950s she left for a six-week theater run in Mexico but ended up staying twenty-four years, working in film, theater, and a number of highly successful television soap operas (Navarro and Rodríguez Martínez 1988: 66).

Figure 10.4 Jorge Mistral as bandit leader, with open shirt displaying his physical attractions (*La duquesa de Benamejí*, Luis Lucia, 1949; prod. CIFESA). Courtesy of Video Mercury and Filmoteca Española

Signed to an exclusive contract with CIFESA in 1945, Jorge Mistral (born Modesto Llosas Rosell) rose to fame in a series of high-impact roles in *Currito de la Cruz* (Lucia, 1949), *La duquesa de Benamejí* (where he was paired with Rivelles), *Locura de amor / The Mad Queen* (Orduña, 1950), and *Pequeñeces / Trifles* (Orduña, 1950) (see Figure 10.4). Darkly handsome, Mistral was seemingly appreciated for his well-toned physique as much as for his acting skills. Typical of his portrayal on and off screen is a 1955 interview piece on the set of the film *La gata / The She-Cat* (Margarita Alexandre and Rafael María Torreccila, 1956), featuring a photo of the actor bare-chested before a dressing room mirror. The caption declares: "Jorge no necesita maquillaje. Únicamente un poco de loción y dos o tres pasadas del peine" (Jorge doesn't need makeup. Only a bit of lotion and a few flicks of the comb) (*Radiocinema* 1955b: n.p.). Throughout the 1940s and 1950s, evidence points to the fact that there was much greater leeway for male physical display than for that of female performers, visible in the contrast between Mayo's bared biceps and Mistral's naked torso and the covered necklines and modest hems of their female co-stars. Still, his roles as the native other in two earlier missionary films – *Misión blanca / White Mission* (Juan de Orduña, 1946), filmed on location in Equatorial Guinea, in which he plays, in blackface and body, one of the two main African characters, and *La manigua sin Dios / The Godless Swamp* (Arturo Ruiz Castillo, 1949), in which he appears as a rather

Figure 10.5 A double dose of the transgressive Montiel on the cover of a 1958 serialized photo-novel version of *El último cuplé* (Juan de Orduña, 1957; prod. Producciones Orduña Films). Private collection.

Hollywood-looking Guaraní "Indian" chief – suggest that a narrative alibi had to be found to justify such corporal display. Another reading of the films suggests the inescapable effects of the camera's objectifying gaze, in which the fetishized male body is doubly marked as a feminized, native other (Labanyi 1997: 217–19).

Although the young Maria Antonieta Abad was first "discovered" in the course of a CIFESA-sponsored contest in Madrid's Retiro Park during the summer of 1942 (Fanés 1982: 109), the actress known as Sara (or Sarita) Montiel would achieve her definitive consecration as Spain's first home-grown female sex symbol thanks to her role in *El último cuplé / The Last Torch Song* (Orduña, 1957), a melodramatic anthology of popular cabaret-style songs from the 1910s and 1920s that catapulted her to fame and fortune throughout and beyond the Spanish-speaking world and spawned a series of sequels (see Figure 10.5 and Figure 10.6). After appearing

Figure 10.6 Sara Montiel strikes an inviting pose in *La violetera* (Luis César Amadori, 1958; prod. Producciones Benito Perojo), one of the sequels that capitalized on the success of *El último cuplé*.

in a handful of films in her native country, Montiel had abandoned the Spanish film industry in 1950 for greater acting opportunities in Mexico and Hollywood. The performer who returned to Spain had honed her acting skills along with her technical knowledge of the medium, consequently harnessing a greater control over her own screen image. In *El último cuplé*, the actress projects an anachronistic 1950s sensibility and sensuality as well as a highly developed concept of star power schooled in North America's two most potent film industries, qualities that she grafts onto the historical persona of the 1920s *cupletista*. Dyer (1991) links the development of intense star–audience relations, projected through the star's "charisma," to performers' embodiment of ideological contradiction, suggesting that the rise of particular stars can be traced to their condensation of values felt to be under threat or in flux at a particular moment in time. To that extent, Montiel was perhaps the quintessential female icon of her day, personifying the ambivalences of a society caught between moralizing and modernizing impulses, and reflecting back at spectators the face of Spain as shaped by their own beliefs and desires. In this sense, the figure of Montiel provides an appropriate link between this chapter, on the earlier history of star making, and Chapter 11, which will consider subsequent decades.

Notes

1 Other fashion magazines of the time that constantly referenced cinema were *Siluetas* (Madrid, 1930–) and *Moda y Elegancia* (Madrid, 1932–).

2 In addition to controlling film content, a 1940 order from the National Press Department outlawed the mention in film credits and publicity materials of the names of twenty-nine American actors who had supported the Republic. These included Charlie Chaplin, Joan Crawford, and James Cagney. See Coma (2002) and the film *Hollywood contra Franco* (Oriol Porta, 2008).

3 A May 1954 issue of *Radiocinema* brought news on González's recent trip to "America," including the comment that he found that "El general Perón es un gobernante maravilloso y un hombre simpático como pocos" (General Perón is a marvelous leader and remarkably likeable man) (*Radiocinema* 1954b).

4 This section draws on research supported by grants from the British Arts and Humanities Research Council and the British Academy to an international research team directed by Jo Labanyi. Our thanks to Jo Labanyi and Susan Martin-Márquez for generously sharing materials and insights.

5 Ideological agendas aside, Romero Marchent's analysis is remarkably consistent with De Cordova's classic account of the role of "personality" in the development of star images: "Personality existed as an effect of [...] the representation of character across a number of films" (1990: 86).

6 Responding to a Mr. José Fernández Marcelo's request to know "dónde está Greer Garson?" (where is Greer Garson?), Rivelles playfully replied: "¿Le ha hecho algo Greer Garson? Me lo pregunta de un modo tan así, que me hace el efecto, poco más o menos, de que la quiere matar" (What did Greer Garson do to you? You ask me the question in such a way that it makes me kind of think you want to kill her) (Rivelles 1948: n.p.).

References

Baena Palma, P. (1998) *El cartel de cine en España 1910–1965*. New York: Samuel French.

Cámara (1946) Las vampiresas de hoy son excelentes madres de familia. (May 1): 13.

Cámara (1948) Dos fórmulas para ser feliz en el matrimonio. (October 15): 46.

Cámara (1951) El aeropuerto de Barajas, etapa obligada de las estrellas de cine. (March 1): n.p.

Camporesi, V. (1993) *Para grandes y chicos: Un cine para los españoles 1940–1990*. Madrid: Ediciones Turfan.

Casares, F. (1940) A Usted, ¿por qué no le gusta el cine español? *Radiocinema* 49 (March 30), n.p.

Coma, J. (2002) *La brigada Hollywood: Guerra española y cine americano*. Barcelona: Flor de Viento Ediciones.

Comás, A. (2004) *El star system del cine español de postguerra (1939–1945)*. Madrid: T&B Editores.

De Cordova, R. (1990) *Picture Personalities: The Emergence of the Star System in America*. Urbana: University of Illinois Press.

De Diego, E. (1986) Buscando a Hollywood desesperadamente: Una aproximación a las revistas de cine madrileño. In: Barranco Gallardo, J. A. (ed.) *El cinematógrafo en Madrid 1896–1960*. Madrid: Museo Municipal / Concejalía de Cultura, pp. 155–9.

Díaz de Quijano, M. (1960) *Tonadilleras y cupletistas: Historia del cuplé*. Madrid: Cultura Clásica y Moderna.

Durán, J. A. (2003) *Cesáreo González: El empresario-espectáculo*. Madrid: Taller de Ediciones J. A. Durán.

Dyer, R. (1979) *Stars*. London: BFI.

Dyer, R. (1991) Charisma. In: Gledhill, C. (ed.) *Stardom: Industry of Desire*. London: Routledge, pp. 57–9.

Evans, P. (1995) Cifesa, Cinema and Authoritarian Aesthetics. In: Graham, H. and Labanyi, J. (eds.) *Spanish Cultural Studies: An Introduction*. Oxford: Oxford University Press, pp. 215–22.

Fanés, F. (1982) *Cifesa, la antorcha de los éxitos*. Valencia: Institución Alfonso el Magnánimo.

Fotogramas (1947) Cara y Cruz ... de Hollywood. 4 (January 1): n.p.

Gómez Santos, M. (1959) *Mujeres solas*. Barcelona: Pareja y Borrás.

Gubern, R. (1994) *Benito Perojo: Pionerismo y supervivencia*. Madrid: Filmoteca Española.

Gubern, R. (unpublished) *Lo mejor es reír (1929–1939)*. Typescript.

Hayward, S. (2000) *Cinema Studies: The Key Concepts*. New York: Routledge.

Labanyi, J. (1997) Race, Gender and Disavowal in Spanish Cinema of the Early Franco Period: The Missionary Films and the Folkloric Musical. *Screen* 38 (3): 215–31.

Laguna, R. (1948) Las actrices con delantal. *Cámara* (August 1): 16–17.

La Pantalla (1927) Joan Crawford and Leandrice Joy. (December 2): n.p.

Marantz Cohen, P. (2001) *Silent Film and the Triumph of the American Myth*. New York: Oxford University Press.

Martín Gaite, C. (2004) *Courtship Customs in Postwar Spain*. Lewisburg: Bucknell University Press.

Martin-Márquez, S. (1999) *Feminist Discourse and Spanish Cinema: Sight Unseen*. Oxford: Oxford University Press.

Martin-Márquez, S. (2008) *Disorientations: Spanish Colonialism in Africa and the Performance of Identity*. New Haven: Yale University Press.

Mira, A. (2004) *De Sodoma a Chueca: Una historia cultural de la homosexualidad en España en el siglo XX*. Barcelona: Egales.

Morris, C. B. (1980) *This Loving Darkness*. Oxford: Oxford University Press.

Navarro, J. de P. and Rodríguez Martínez, J. (1988) *Amparo Rivelles, pasión de actriz*. Murcia: Filmoteca Regional de Murcia.

New York Times (1933) Lord & Taylor Advertisment. (April 4): 4.

Pavlović, T. (2003) *Despotic Bodies and Transgressive Bodies: Spanish Culture from Francisco Franco to Jesús Franco*. Albany: State University of New York Press.

Pérez Perucha, J. (2000) Narración de un aciago destino (1896–1930). In: Gubern, R., Monterde, J. E., Pérez Perucha, J., et al. (eds.) *Historia del cine español*. Madrid: Cátedra, pp. 19–121.

Popular Film (1926) La fama de Raquel Meller es mundial. (December 8): n.p.

Popular Film (1928) Concurso de semblanzas literarias. (May 3): 11.

Pozo Arenas, S. (1984) *La industria del cine en España: Legislación y aspectos económicos (1896–1970)*. Barcelona: Edicions Universitat de Barcelona.

Radiocinema (1954a) Ana Mariscal. 188 (February 27): n.p.

Radiocinema (1954b) Cesáreo González nos habla de su viaje por América. 199 (May 15): n.p.

Radiocinema (1955a) Desde Hollywood, "Tío Vivo Matrimonial." 244 (March 26): n.p.

Radiocinema (1955b) Se rueda: *La gata*. 267 (September 3): n.p.

Rivelles, A. (1948) Consultorio sentimental. *Primer Plano* 391 (April 11).

Román, A. (1939) Valor real del actor en el cinema. *Radiocinema* 27: n.p.

Romero Marchent, J. (1939) Cinema nacional: Comentarios al margen. Imperio Argentina y el cinema español. *Radiocinema* 21 (January 30): n.p.

Romo, A. (1958) Madrid es el Hollywood europeo. *Radiocinema* 401 (March 29): n.p.

Salaün, S. (1990) *El cuplé*. Madrid: Espasa Calpe.

Sánchez Salas, D. (2007) *Historias de luz y papel: El cine español de los años veinte, a través de su adaptación de narrativa literaria española*. Murcia: Filmoteca Regional Francisco Rabal.

Santos, M. (1932) Raquel en España. *Popular Film* 313 (August 11): n.p.

Scanlon, G. M. (1986) *La polémica feminista en la España contemporánea 1868–1974*. Madrid: Akal.

Vallés Copeiro del Villar, A. (2000) *Historia de la política de fomento del cine español*. Valencia: Ediciones de la Filmoteca.

Further Reading

De la Madrid, J. C. (1996) *Cinematógrafo y "Varietés" en Asturias (1896–1915)*. Asturias: Asturgraf.

Dyer, R. (1986) *Heavenly Bodies: Film Stars and Society*. London: Routledge.

Moix, T. (1993) *Suspiros de España: La copla y el cine de nuestro recuerdo*. Barcelona: Plaza & Janés.

Retana, Á. (1967) *Historia de la canción española*. Madrid: Tesoro.

Román, M. (1993) *Memoria de la copla: La canción española. De Conchita Piquer a Isabel Pantoja*. Madrid: Alianza Editorial.

Sánchez Vidal, A. (1991) *El cine de Florián Rey*. Zaragoza: Caja de Ahorros de la Inmaculada de Aragón.

Vázquez Montalbán, M. (1998 [1971]) *Crónica sentimental de España*. Barcelona: Grijalbo.

Woods Peiró, E. (2012) *White Gypsies: Race and Stardom in Spanish Musicals*. Minneapolis: University of Minnesota Press.

11

Stars, Modernity, and Celebrity Culture

Tatjana Pavlović, Chris Perriam, and Nuria Triana Toribio

Introduction (Chris Perriam)

Contributors to this volume have found themselves alighting on key names in screen performance, analyzing aspects of actors' roles and images that, to adapt Paul McDonald in his supplementation of Richard Dyer's classic study of stars (1998), "influence the ways in which we think about ourselves [and Spain] and others" (McDonald 1998: 176). Spanish cinema has a rich history of finding, creating, nurturing, and marketing the distinctive, special, charismatic, or somehow representative *estrella* (Aguilar and Genover 1996; Dyer 1998: 1–59; Triana Toribio 2003: 7–8). Sometimes, as in the cases of Imperio Argentina, Amparo Rivelles, and Jorge Mistral, studied in the previous chapter, or of Sara Montiel and Antonio Banderas, studied here, substantial structures and patterns of film commissioning and distribution arise around the already ideologically and socially coded phenomenon of high-profile screen performance (Dyer 1998). They become the core of a trend or microsystem in Spanish and transnationally Hispanic cinema. Classically speaking, the star is not a star without a system; and that system requires a massive industrial base, such as that of Hollywood in the years of the "studio system" or of Bollywood. As Santos Zunzunegui observes in Chapter 7, Spain's star system is small (see also Perriam 2003: 1–4); for some it is not a star system at all but an intermittent and decentered phenomenon, such as might be thought of as represented by sets of films starring Penélope Cruz or Javier Bardem (or both), occasionally lifting Spanish filmmakers into global prominence against a historical background of critical neglect (Bentley 2008: xiv, 251) (see Figure 11.1).

In this chapter, which covers the period from the mid-1950s to the present day, we focus on individual filmmakers – in this case, actors – whose aesthetically and

A Companion to Spanish Cinema, First Edition. Edited by Jo Labanyi and Tatjana Pavlović.

Figure 11.1 Penélope Cruz as Raimunda in *Volver* (Pedro Almodóvar, 2006; prod. El Deseo).

commercially mediated imbrication with the cultural movements and social dynamics of their time makes them intensely indicative of the experience of late modernity, cinema's temporal home, for the viewers and audiences beholding and enjoying them. The child "stars" of the 1950s and 1960s are read as closely bound to national preoccupations while radically resituating the presuppositions that might underlie these. With regard to the period after the transition to democracy, the chapter suggests that an illuminating perspective on the fame and effects of Spanish screen actors might come from viewing their fortunes in the frame of an increasingly explicit alignment of acting and activism, of stardom and – paradoxically enough – opprobium. Finally, the necessary question – the twin to the basic question "what is a star?" – is asked: "what, in the transnationalized world, is a 'Spanish' star?"

Child Stars: Pablito Calvo, Joselito, Marisol, Pili and Mili, Rocío Dúrcal (Tatjana Pavlović)

A consensus has emerged among critics that Ladislao Vajda's 1955 film *Marcelino, pan y vino / The Miracle of Marcelino*, debuting seven-year-old Pablito Calvo, marks the onset of a true child-star system in Spain, in the sense of a celebrity-focused, organized, and highly resonant production of screen voice and image giving meaning and energy to crucial debates and private musings on identities national, regional, and personal. The melodrama of an orphan adopted by friars captivated the audience, and *Marcelino, pan y vino* created a formula for success that would be exploited in subsequent films. The tale was an adaptation of a religious fairytale by the devout Catholic and Falangist writer José María Sánchez Silva. Pablito Calvo, a charismatic child actor, impeccably embodied an abandoned infant, conveying

Figure 11.2 Joselito in his film début *El pequeño ruiseñor* (Antonio del Amo, 1957; prod. Argos SLPC). Courtesy of Video Mercury and Filmoteca Española.

problematics of origin and issues of filiation, paternity, and community. Ladislao Vajda, a well-known Hungarian film director who had lived in Spain since 1942, was of Jewish origin, having arrived in Spain fleeing anti-Semitic persecution in Hungary and then fascist Italy (Camporesi 2007). Yet he found the story's religious overtones, melodramatic plot, and mysticism an ideal setting for his artistic explorations: German expressionism, fascination with light, and directing children.

The massive success of *Marcelino, pan y vino* prepared Spanish audiences for yet another screen orphan, and two years later *El pequeño ruiseñor / The Little Nightingale* (Antonio del Amo, 1957), starring fourteen-year-old Joselito (José Jiménez Fernández), opened in Madrid's Cine Rex and Cine Muñoz Seca. Joselito would become known as the "little nightingale" from that moment on, his real-life person becoming inextricably blurred with his screen persona (see Figure 11.2). Three years after the release of *El pequeño ruiseñor*, Marisol (Josefa Flores; her adult career as Pepa Flores is considered later in this chapter) became the second early adolescent to achieve child stardom. Her debut on the silver screen at the age of twelve in *Un rayo de luz / A Ray of Sunshine* (Luis Lucia, 1960) was also as an orphan. Joselito's and Marisol's early films spanned the period 1957–62; that is, from the technocrats' entry into the cabinet, marking the end of the Falangist grip on power, to the economic Stabilization Plan and the first of the Development Plans that followed. The institutionalization of a "child stardom machine" thus coincided with Spain's tumultuous passage to consumer capitalism in the early 1960s, with all the political and economic complexities that this entailed.

What distinguishes the early adolescent Joselito and Marisol from their much younger predecessor Pablito Calvo is that they were subjected to the star-making system. Modernized forms of production, distribution, and exhibition were tied to exclusive contracts, the morphing of the actors' personal lives with their star personae, and the myriad marketing ploys aimed at promoting their image, such as fan clubs, franchises, and merchandize endorsements, in an industrial and ideological process that rendered these child stars a cultural commodity. Their story is inseparable from that of their creators: Cesáreo González, who issued an exclusive contract to Joselito; the producer Manuel Goyanes, who considered Marisol his discovery; and Benito Perojo (Goyanes' father-in-law), who reaped the profits of Marisol's stardom by coproducing her films – three of the most influential producers of Francoist Spain. Child stardom was a product of economic interests feeding on cultural practices. Both Joselito and Marisol came from desperately poor homes. Their discovery attests to a historical moment when "la ascención hasta la fama y el reconocimiento artístico desde los estratos más humildes de la sociedad" (the rise from the bottom of society to fame and artistic recognition) appealed to an audience that was emerging from years of deprivation (Heredero 1993: 232). The tale of childhood poverty that was an intrinsic part of their "star text" struck a chord with the public and was crucial in cementing their success.

El pequeño ruiseñor, Saeta del ruiseñor / The Nightingale's Holy Week Song (1957) and *El ruiseñor de las cumbres / The Nightingale of the Peaks* (1958) – all directed by Antonio del Amo – loosely form a trilogy, cleverly synthesizing and refashioning formulas that had proved successful. Besides lifting elements from *Marcelino, pan y vino*, Joselito's opus dissolves generic boundaries, skillfully blending the plotlines of nineteenth-century popular fiction with the formulas of religious cinema and folkloric melodramas (Heredero 1993: 231). Antonio del Amo, to whom the beginning of Joselito's career was linked, was a filmmaker with a past of leftist political views, who directed Joselito in order to finance his future films, which were more socially engaged. Joselito was considered a parenthesis in del Amo's career, and yet the latter's trajectory became inseparable from that of "el niño de la voz de oro" (the boy with the golden voice). The first three films set the tone for most of Joselito's work. There is an obsessive replaying of certain themes: (1) real or apocryphal orphanhood, family discord, and the restoration of broken family ties; (2) maternal and paternal oedipal dramas; (3) profound religious sentiment; (4) disinterest in the material and elevation of the spiritual realm; (5) lack of social conflict; and (6) the social immobility of traditional rural Spain.

Of all the recurring traits of child-exploitative cinema, the choice of orphaned protagonists was the most prominent and persistent. As writer and film critic Terenci Moix observed (1993: 268), Joselito seemed to be a professional orphan

("Joselito, de profesión huerfanito"). His films' elemental affective charge stems from this real or apocryphal orphanhood. Regardless of whether one reads orphanhood as a traumatic replaying of postwar devastation or as a cleverly manipulated formula with charged melodramatic potential, what is impressive is its insistent repetition – replayed and exploited for over a decade and persisting throughout Joselito's entire career, including his Latin American odyssey and later "urban" films. The visual claustrophobia of Joselito's films mirrors the matrix of rural immobility and static social relationships idealized by Francoism. Joselito's cinema did not appeal because it faithfully depicted reality but because audiences, confronted with the challenges of modernization (emigration to the city, urban life), responded nostalgically to the way in which Joselito's unsettling, distinctive voice seemed to conjure up ghosts of an innocent, lost (and nonexistent) past. They also responded to the emotional excess of his singing, for from the body of this idealized child of early Francoism sprang adult songs, mostly of passion and transgression, directly opposing the ideals incarnated in his screen persona.

Marisol's films, too, left a powerful imprint on the popular imagination and similarly bear witness to drastically changing times. While some of her film scenarios closely resemble those of Joselito, others perfected and modernized his successful formulas. Marisol's striking appearance helped to make her an icon of modernity:

> Rubia y de ojos azules en un país latino en que predominan las morenas, pero preservando su identidad y gracejo andaluz, ofrecía un look muy personalizado en nuestro star-system [...] resultaba exótica y próxima a la vez, reuniendo el atractivo y las ventajas de ambas condiciones. (Gubern 2001: 13)

> Blonde and blue eyes in a Latin country where most girls are dark, but conserving an Andalusian character and wit, she offered a very personal look in our star system [...] she was exotic and accessible at the same time, fusing the attractions and advantages of both.

The start of Marisol's career was tied to Luis Lucia, an extraordinarily able filmmaker associated with popular entertainment cinema who established a formula that became the core of the Marisol myth. Some recurrent themes of Marisol's early cinema are: (1) real or apocryphal orphanhood, family discord, and the restoration of broken family ties; (2) class mobility; (3) focus on Marisol as the epitome of modernity; (4) secularization of religious values; (5) displacement of erotic and sexual elements onto the child; (6) lack of social conflict; and (7) an emphasis on fantasy and pleasure. As should be clear, this list has similarities to but also significant differences from that given above for Joselito's films. *Tómbola* (Luis Lucia, 1962) was one of Marisol's most popular films and its song of the same name was one of her biggest musical hits (as Chapter 7 notes, it would be referenced in Ramón Salazar's 2005 musical comedy *20 centímetros / 20 Centimeters*) and is illustrative of the spirit of both her films and the times (see Figure 11.3). The song is

Figure 11.3 Marisol in *Tómbola* (Luis Lucia, 1962; prod. Guión Producciones Cinemátográficas).

reminiscent of other light ditties that swept Europe in the early 1960s, the time of pop hits and Eurovision song contests, when "los gustos del público estaban evolucionando hacia la modernidad, personificada en la música ligera con sus victorias sobre la copla, antes dominante" (public tastes were evolving toward modernity, personified in light music's triumph over the previously dominant *copla* [traditional popular song, with highly melodramatic, tragic, lyrics]) (Moix 1993: 275).

As Joselito and Marisol matured, a conflict arose between the established image of the child star and the reality of adolescence. They were not allowed to grow up, forced to linger in the arrested space of childhood so dear to their audiences and so profitable to their producers. By 1963 and 1964 respectively, both had finally abandoned their infantile roles, discarding their stage names, the trademarks of their commodity status, and reclaiming their original names. In 1963, age twenty and with nine films behind him, Joselito left the "Joselito role" behind and became successively Tony, Tomy, Johnny, and Marcos. His last film, *Prisionero en la ciudad / Captive in the City* (Antonio de Jaén, 1969) can be read as a denunciation of the entertainment world. In the film, Marcos Villena (Joselito) feels stranded in his chic urban environment and returns to his village and his origins. Thus, in his very last film, Joselito returns to origins that were, from the start, invented – a quest for origins, as in the earlier works, but now the origins are further displaced inasmuch as they function as a citation of earlier postwar films promoting an idyllic, rural Spain contrasting with the urban decay and corruption of a troubled modernity. As we shall see later in this chapter, Marisol's transition (back) into Pepa Flores brought with it similar concerns.

Besides Joselito and Marisol, there were other child stars who had an impact on Spanish screens and the popular imagination of the time. The sixteen-year-old twin actors Pili and Mili (Pilar and Emilia Bayona Sarriá) were launched by Benito Perojo with *Como dos gotas de agua / Like Two Peas in a Pod* (Luis César Amadori, 1964), an unsuccessful attempt to replicate Marisol's hit *Marisol rumbo a Río / Marisol Bound for Rio* (Fernando Palacios, 1963), which exploited the doppelgänger theme taken from the successful American film *The Parent Trap* (David Swift, 1961; known in Spanish as *Tú a Boston y yo a California*). With Pili and Mili, Perojo also produced *Whisky y vodka / Whisky and Vodka* (Fernando Palacios, 1965), in which the twins played Russian and American girls, respectively. Though the twins never achieved Marisol's charisma nor accumulated a substantial oeuvre in terms of quantity, revivals of their films nevertheless provoke postmodern nostalgia in latterday critics and spectators of their work.

More important was the career of María de los Ángeles de las Heras Ortiz, better known by her artistic name Rocío Dúrcal. Like her predescessors, she came from a modest background and large family, and at the time of her discovery was working as an apprentice hairdresser. Luis Lucia, "Marisol's director," directed several of Dúrcal's films, including her first two hits, *Canción de juventud / Song of Youth* (1962) and *Rocío de la Mancha / Rocío of La Mancha* (1963). She was seen as an imitation of Marisol – or at least as a continuation of cinema à la Marisol and of the "cine con niño" (films with child protagonists) – and her work was considered second-rate commercial cinema, dismissed as "sub-musical" or "cine de subgénero" (sub-generic) or even "subnormal" (Gubern 1974: 11). Such critical disdain does not match her films' box-office success nor her popularity as an actress. She would become one of the most important figures in the Spanish star system of the late 1960s.

Terenci Moix has emphasized that the explotation of Rocío Dúrcal resembled the Diana Durbin model more than the Marisol/Shirley Temple model (1993: 292); indeed, Dúrcal's adolescent cinema does not quite fit the child prodigy niche. As noted by Lucia, "Rocío es la clase de actriz que no existía en España. Un término medio entre la niña prodigio y la damita joven" (Rocío is a type of actor that didn't exist in Spain before: halfway between child prodigy and young lady) (quoted in Moix 1993: 292). When she filmed *Canción de juventud* she was already eighteen. Her films form a hybrid genre, drawing on sentimental comedy, musical comedy, the "cine con niño," and the "comedia del desarrollismo" (comedies based on the modernization phenomenon). Rocío Dúrcal exemplified social mobility, women's entrance into the working world, rapidly changing women's roles, and the new opportunities of the fast-developing "España del desarrollo." A model of adolescent femininity, she was the epitome of modernity. Nevertheless, her modern look contained a mixture of traditional and modern values, exemplifying the ambivalence of 1960s femininity and social mobility. Rocío Dúrcal illustrates well Sally Faulkner's claim that "the contradictions inherent in trying to reconcile tradition and modernity characterized 1960s Spain" (2006: 3).

The films of Joselito and Marisol, and of other child stars of the period, are generally not regarded as directly representative of the Francoist cultural and ideological agenda. Far from being tools of indoctrination, these films reveal tensions between tradition and modernity and between immobility and movement. These child stars, each in their own way, participated in a symbolic settling of accounts. Their voices emerged at the critical, conflictive moment when autarky gave way to incipient capitalist development. At times, they resonated with progress as they illuminated the problematic course of modernity. However, the most charismatic of these child actors – Joselito and Marisol – would ultimately turn into the wounded voices of the transition: when his voice broke, Joselito fell out of favor and his film career ended at the age of twenty-six. Marisol would publicly denounce the exploitative marketing of her child persona and went on to work with the politically engaged directors Juan Antonio Bardem, Mario Camus, and Carlos Saura (for her adult career, see the following section). From their very first appearance on screen, all these child stars were tied to the construction of a national image. Their voices and careers were a by-product of the dictatorship. However, they were also the nation's recalcitrant remainder, resistant to whatever the state might officially wish to communicate. Paradoxically, the very same voices that were supposed to epitomize what is national would point out what lingered buried beneath the national narrative.

The Politics of Stardom and Celebrity (Chris Perriam and Nuria Triana Toribio)

The Struggle to be a Star

The introduction to this chapter has already noted the cultural-contextual and economic restrictions that affect stardom in Spain. Indeed, it could be said that being an actor in Spain is no entertainment at all. This professional group has come under so much criticism in the course of its history that it is astonishing that anyone would still want to join it – so much so that Carlos Aguilar and Jaume Genover, authors of one of Spain's main resources on actors, justify the need for their work by declaring that actors in Spain "siempre ha[n] padecido una infravaloración excesiva, tanto por parte de los medios de comunicación como entre la prensa especializada, el público en general y hasta la propia industria" (have always suffered from being excessively undervalued, in the media in general and the specialized press in particular, by the public, and even by the film industry itself) (Aguilar and Genover 1996: 12). Attacks on Spanish actors have come from many sources. In recent years, the conservative radio station La Cope[1] in its program *La mañana* (particularly when the programme was presented by Federico Jiménez Losantos) has routinely called Spanish actors *titiriteros* (puppeteers), while newspapers such as *La Razón* and *El Mundo*, in much smaller measure, often level charges against some of Spain's most important performers of moral turpitude and of engaging in excessive left-wing political involvement, particularly since 2003 and the demonstrations by the "No a la Guerra" campaigners against Spain's involvement in the Iraq War. Ángeles González-Sinde, Spain's Minister of Culture at the time of writing, looked back over more than five years of repeated attacks against Spanish cinema by the Partido Popular, declaring "No conozco ningún partido politico en Europa que tenga tan malas relaciones con su cine" (I know of no European political party with such bad relations with its country's film industry) (reported in García 2009: 1).

Why are actors censured like this in Spain? As already indicated, the matter is, in part, partisan. José Luis Zapatero himself, in 2004, reinforced the political link by attending the première of a Spanish film shortly after his election to office: *Mar adentro / The Sea Inside* (Alejandro Amenábar), starring Javier Bardem, whose role in linking acting with activism is explored in the last section of this chapter. That term *titiriteros* continued to be used of the pro-Zapatero alliance PAZ (Plataforma de Apoyo a Zapatero), whose supporters – producers and directors, as well as actors – were customarily deemed to be champagne socialists about to grow fat on the new 2007 Ley del Cine (Film Law). The reasons are also to be found perhaps in the roles and meanings that actors fulfil for a society (Dyer 1998: 7–32; McDonald 1998); their typicality (Dyer 1998: 47–59); their glamorous prominence (Dyer 1998: 35–46), which provokes attention and envy in equal measure; and their function as scapegoat, victim, source of *schadenfreude*, or symbol of decline (Shickel 1985).

For instance, in the early 1960s Sara Montiel had the dubious honor of being hailed and condemned at the same time. She was undoubtedly CIFESA's most prominent star, someone who had managed to become a Spanish presence within Hollywood (as an actor and as the wife of Hollywood director Anthony Mann) at a time when this was a near impossible feat: "her appearance in mainstream Hollywood films served to establish her as the one Spanish film actress of the decade with an important international presence" (D'Lugo 1997: 248). As noted in Chapter 10, the most commercially successful film in 1950s Spain – *El último cuplé / The Last Torch Song* (Juan de Orduña, 1957) – was a vehicle for her. She should also be celebrated for the challenge she constituted to the rigid morality with which the regime and the Catholic Church were straight-jacketing Spanish cinema in particular and society in general: as D'Lugo points out, "in the midst of the prudish Franco dictatorship, her eroticism seemed to defy the usual constraints of the Spanish film censors" (1997: 248). However, for the filmmakers who held the famed Salamanca Conversations of 1955 (see Chapter 15) to discuss their preferred model of national cinema, and for that sector of the regime (with José María García Escudero at its head) who wanted a controlled reform of Spanish filmmaking, Montiel was a symbol of all that was wrong with the cinema of their time. In fact, for García Escudero, writing at the start of his second period in office as

Director General of Film and Theater, she was the lowest of the low, even worse than "bobaditas en tecnicolor" (technicolor fripperies), among other forms of cinema he despised: "lo mejor es que el público se entretenga con [aquellas] a que lo haga llorando con Sara Montiel" (better that the public amuse themselves watching [these technicolor films] than sobbing along to Montiel) (1962: 25).

Montiel came under attack not for being fetishized by audiences, nor for lending herself to the objectification afforded to female screen stars, but because this scopophilia and reification occurred in the wrong context and genres (Triana Toribio 2003: 67–8). Her very centrality to melodrama within 1960s popular cinema was what required that she be expurgated from Spanish cinema altogether, in order to make it a cinema worthy of domestic audiences and consumption abroad. García Escudero thus proposed that this most international of stars had to go, alongside "el nefasto imperio del cuplé" (the baleful predominance of the cabaret form) (1962: 24).

Luckily, and perhaps justifiably, subsequent generations have been willing to recuperate Montiel as a major figure in the history of national cinema and have restored this now undisputed icon of Spanish popular culture to a place where her work and cultural role in the 1950s and 1960s can be appreciated without the blinkers of fear of the popular. From very different theoretical positions to those of 1960s critics, later writers have focused on how disruptive her presence can be when read for its challenge to the regime's strictures in denying desire and pleasure (Moix 1993: 222–47; Perriam 2005: 89–96). As part of this rereading, her legacy has been celebrated in contemporary films such as *La mala educación / Bad Education* (Pedro Almodóvar, 2004) and in Alaska and Nacho Canut's electro pop band Fangoria's release of *Absolutamente* (DRO Atlantic, 2009), which includes a collaboration with Montiel, confirming her continued relevance as popular culture icon (see Figure 11.4).

Montiel's case is hardly isolated. Another female star who paid a high price for challenging with her presence and star persona the very narrow space allocated to women by the regime was Marisol – as we have seen earlier in this chapter, a child actor whose films generated the greatest of expectations and the longest of queues in the 1960s, and whose career is crucial to understanding concepts embedded in the category of Spanish national cinema in the 1960s and 1970s (Triana Toribio 2003: 84). As the 2008 television coverage of her sixtieth birthday put it (restating a fond cliché), "[ella] creció ante nuestros ojos" (we watched her grow up) (*Corazón, Corazón* 2008). It must be emphasized that the physical aspects of this star persona, as she grew, and of the associated, constructed, and contested Spanishness around it and underlying it, were carefully prefabricated (Evans 2004: 131). Marisol, embodying unthreatening femininity with some modernizing (and surgical) touches, continued retrospectively in the 1970s to be a construct of heteronormative Spanishness – and, arguably, also through to the present day, with her continuing presence in magazines such as *¡Hola!* and the image she conveys in television interviews, as witnessed by the wide selection of clips currently on YouTube.

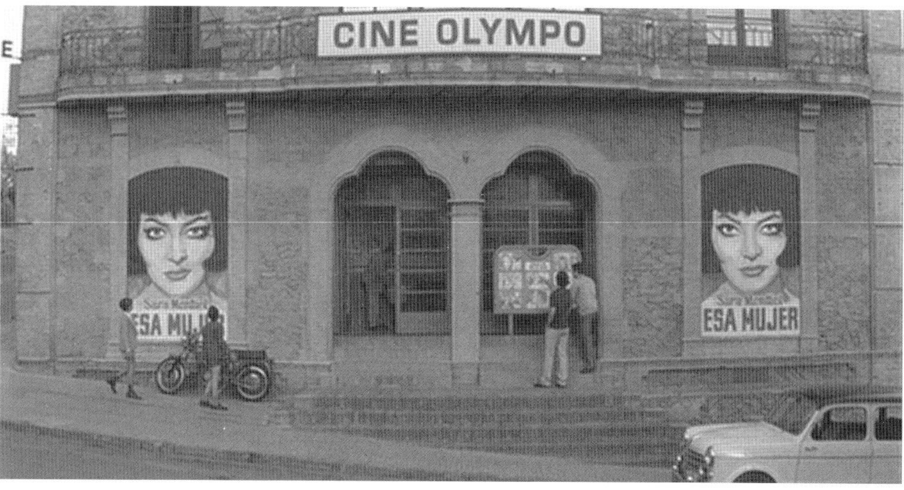

Figure 11.4 The protagonists of *La mala educación* (Pedro Almodóvar, 2004; prod. El Deseo) walk into a screening of Sara Montiel's *Esa mujer* (1969). Almodóvar's homage illustrates Montiel's continued popularity as a cultural icon, particularly for gay spectators.

Moving her career forward under the shortened version of her real name, Pepa Flores, her personal and political commitment to socialism became as high-profile as her celebrity image generally (Martín 2003: 155–60; Evans 2004: 133). But the authentic political elements to her persona and actions were greedily appropriated and sabotaged by the unreconstructed liberal left, at least in its mediatic manifestations – for instance, the magazine *Interviú* in September 1976 used the cynically exploitative strapline "El bello camino de la democracia" (The Road to Democracy's Looking Good) to link politics and sexual exploitation by publishing (out-of-date) unauthorized nude pictures of her (Martín 2003: 156; Evans 2004: 132–3). Furthermore, her separation after only three years from Carlos Goyanes, son of Marisol's producer Manuel, shocked (some of) her public for its deviation from convention and from the moral practices of the outgoing regime (Martín 2003: 156); her decision to cohabit with the communist dancer-choreographer Antonio Gades provoked "considerable animosity towards her, which led to her being insulted in the streets and graffiti being painted on her house in Altea" (Martín 2003: 156). While one study talks in terms of her retiring early out of choice (Monterde 1998: 546), it seems clear that this is another classic tale of the celebrity's fall from grace (Dyer 1998: 21–3, 44). What was to become the theme song of her adult career – "Soy una muchacha igual que todas" (I'm a girl like any other), from the film *Carola de día, Carola de noche / Carola by Day, Carola by Night* (Jaime de Armiñán, 1968) – sounds like a "lament for her kidnapped childhood" (Evans 2004: 140). Public opinion and the industry itself would go on to kidnap Flores' adult career, making her a scapegoat for public anxieties over political change and female agency. Flores' awareness of this was evident, for example, in her interview in 2000 on TVE-1's *Cine de Barrio / Neighborhood Movie Theater*; when the (male) reporter asked her to comment on this song (the end of whose title he tellingly mis-remembered as "muchacha normal" (normal girl)), she responded straight to camera: "pues eso, yo quiero ser una mujer como todas" (well, quite; I want to be a woman like any other) (*Cine de Barrio* 2000).

Like Marisol, many stars whose careers straddled the dictatorship and the transition to democracy have suffered from fluctuations in their fame and fortune, partly by dint of that very historical positioning. The cases of Alfredo Landa and José Luis López Vázquez, to name just two representatives of a generation, are highly illustrative in this respect. López Vázquez was awarded a Goya for lifetime achievement in 2005, and the presentation was preceded and followed by ten-minute standing ovations (Granado 2006: 286–7). His obituary in *El País* in November 2009 was entitled "López Vázquez, patrimonio nacional" (López Vázquez, a National Treasure) (Fernández-Santos and Torres 2009: 38), recalling the iconic satirical film *Patrimonio nacional* (Luis García Berlanga, 1981) in which he featured; but we must not forget that this epithet conflates and glosses over a number of stages in his career. The beginnings of his career featured many of those comedies that often are included only with reluctance and a certain disdain in traditional histories of Spanish cinema: *La gran familia / The Big Family* (Fernando Palacios, 1967) and *Sor Citroën / Sister Citroen* (Pedro Lazaga, 1967) are set alongside other comedy roles in films that proved to be more to the taste of academic film historians; for instance, *El pisito / The Little Apartment* (Marco Ferreri, 1959) and *El verdugo / The Executioner* (García Berlanga, 1963) (Boyero 2009: 39). In the early 1970s, Lopez Vazquez's association with, and roles in, Carlos Saura's films (particularly *La prima Angélica / Cousin Angelica*, 1974) positioned him as one of the visible cultural icons for audiences abroad (the film won a Grand Prix du Jury at Cannes), among other reasons because it was a film taken as representing the political opposition within Spain (see Figure 11.5). This seam in his career meant that López Vázquez's performances became more to the taste of traditional cinephiles but in equal measure also the target of right-wing violence: when cinemas showing *La prima Angélica* were attacked by paramilitary right-wing groups (on one occasion, coinciding with the Cannes festival, involving the theft of reels of the film and thus of López Vázquez's image), the film was banned (Galán 1974: 127–43).

Actors such as López Vázquez have had to bear the violent appropriation, or disappearance, of their image and the burden of their career choice within a relatively small national cinema whose sociopolitical contexts have had a highly restrictive effect on the free choice or agency that actors might exercise. Positioned between the thuggish and the snobbish, the critical establishment, as Carlos Boyero suggests, only gave López Vázquez his "certificado de artista como dios manda" (certificate as a "proper" actor) once he had been obliged to "despojarse del tonillo al hablar, contener el gesto o hacerlo atormentado, expresar tinieblas interiores [...] y demás sensaciones prestigiosas" (get rid of his characteristic pitch

Figure 11.5 José Luis López Vázquez in *La prima Angélica* (Carlos Saura, 1974; prod. Elías Querejeta PC).

when speaking, show restraint, or at least show inner turmoil and express dark feelings and other similar signs of a superior sensitivity) in a purging of associations with popular genres perceived as reactionary (Boyero 2009: 39). Boyero does not entirely disapprove of this process of stellar decontamination, even if he is quick to see the process for what it is; and he is not alone. Critics of the generation of cinephiles who cut their teeth on the French New Wave, and for whom only auteurist cinema had the prerequisites for quality, saw the transition to becoming part of the national heritage, and a star, as necessarily taking the actor into the new realms of prestige. Connections with the auteurs who mattered – Carlos Saura, Mario Camus, Jaime Camino – and with films that would be lauded abroad at festivals such as Cannes or Berlin were what was needed, from this point of view – although López Vázquez had consistently woven into the fabric of his career star and cameo performances in high comedy, with Berlanga, as mentioned above, in *Disparate nacional / National Folly* (Mariano Ozores, 1990) and, more recently, *Torrente 2: Misión en Marbella / Torrente 2: Mission in Marbella* (Santiago Segura, 2001).

It was through his own association with Mario Camus and particularly the success at Berlin in 1984 of *Los santos inocentes / The Holy Innocents* that Alfredo Landa, the second of these representative actors, purged and altered his career. It is perhaps illustrative to use the annual Goya awards celebrated by the Spanish Film Academy (Academia de las Artes y Ciencias Cinematográficas de España) as an entry point into the narrative of Landa's change in cultural value, since these awards "can tell us a great deal about how the guardians of the national cinema want the national cinema to be perceived both internally and externally" (Triana Toribio 2003: 158). In 2008, Landa received a Goya de Honor for his career. The preliminaries to the presentation of the award can be read as a visual re-enactment of the first part of the purgation process under discussion here. The gala ceremony's presenter was the actor and director José Corbacho, whose own career has transitioned from the comic to the serious – from acting in *El amor perjudica seriamente la salud / Love Can Seriously Damage Your Health* (Manuel Gómez Pereira, 1996) to codirecting *Tapas* (2005) and *Cobardes / Cowards* (2008) (both with Juan Cruz). Corbacho appeared on stage surrounded by scantily clad blonde women representing the so-called foreign tourists who featured in the films with which Landa is mainly associated – the films that created the 1970s cultural phenomenon called *landismo*. Only once these women were invited to leave the stage was a montage of Landa's more prestigious roles, particularly *Los santos inocentes*, screened at the back of the stage. Many of Landa's iconic roles, such as Antón in *No desearás al vecino del quinto / Thou Shalt Not Covet Thy Fifth Floor Neighbor* (Ramón Fernández, 1970) and Pepe in *Vente a Alemania, Pepe / Come to Germany, Pepe* (Pedro Lazaga, 1971), are thus often presented as a preamble, as a condition of possibility for a perceived respectability that is only acquired once national cinema itself has been purged of the *sub-productos* (sub-products) that are the popular genres – the reforms brought in by Pilar Miró during her time as Director General of Film (1983–6) were one well-known manifestation of this process (Bentley 2008: 256–7).

Professional respectability – celebrity rather than stardom – is also recognized, however, as a direct by-product of regular appearances in popular genres, even – as one obituarist (of the character actor Antonio Ozores) put it – "en un entorno de cine rastrero y ridícula exaltación patriótica" (in a context of base, reactionary cinema and ridiculous jingoism) (Análisis: El acento 2010). Ozores represents, for this *El País* writer, "una casta de actores [...] capaces de construir miniaturas impagables" (a breed of actor capable of constructing a series of priceless cameos). The cumulative effect of such cameos constitutes these actors' popular fame; how they negotiate these roles and manage this part of their career represents the fine-tuning of the machinery devoted to the production of potential minor stardom. Fernándo Fernán Gómez, Lola Gaos, Gracita Morales, Francisco Rabal, Fernando Rey, and Concha Velasco could all be said to have negotiated highly restrictive career paths through the second half of Francoism, neutering the "base, reactionary" elements in Spanish cinema with microstrategies of resistance.

Several actors of this generation have died since the turn of the millennium, and commemorating their contribution to Spanish cinema has meant that important re-evaluations of the conditions in which they worked have taken place. Among these actors was Fernando Fernán Gómez, whose death in November 2007 was marked by a special program in state-owned TVE-2's prestigious series *Versión española* (November 14) and by the naming of an iconic performance space situated underneath the Plaza Colón, Madrid, as the Teatro y Centro de Arte Fernán Gómez. Fernán Gómez had made a career of playing and directing quietly dissident, off-beat, and antiestablishment figures (Brasó 2002: 14, 144–8, 213–18; see also Freixas 1993), gradually building a position as a substantial and intellectually committed celebrity and creative artist. Upon his death, his name was, to use a favorite term of Spanish cultural journalism, consecrated. He has become a star of the whole delicate and heroic enterprise of screening the memories of Spain's mid-twentieth century (Bentley 2008: 262–3).

Transmedia Stardom

We have been seeing how different and changing historical and cultural environments configure actors' careers, shifting them between celebrity and stardom, adulation and reproach. Focusing now on film, television (on which Smith (2000b: 4) considers the "incipient Spanish star system" to be "parasitic"), and the celebrity press, this section will consider the careers of Imanol Arias and Carmen Maura. Imanol Arias' entry in the canonical *Diccionario del cine español* (Weinrichter 1998: 82–3) gives a detailed account of his roles in iconic films of the transition such as *Demonios en el jardín / Demons in the Garden* (Manuel Gutiérrez Aragón, 1982) and *Laberinto de pasiones / Labyrinth of Passion* (Pedro Almodóvar, 1982), but does not seem to see it as relevant to list or comment very much on any of his numerous and equally iconic roles for television. Moreover, the *Diccionario* avoids any indication that this actor's public persona has been largely transmitted and constructed as a celebrity via the *prensa del corazón* (gossip magazines). Arias is in fact an actor who has worked extensively for all the main broadcasting channels, and the press coverage that he has commanded across three decades now has been extensive (Internet coverage is growing to be just as extensive: his divorce from Pastora Vega toward the end of 2009, for example, yielded some one hundred relevant hits when Googled in July 2010).

Nowadays, the image of Imanol Arias is indeed indelibly associated with television and particularly with the audience-record-breaking series *Cuéntame cómo pasó / Tell me How it Happened* (TVE-1, 2001–), in which he plays the role of the father of the Alcántara family. Arguably, his televisual family in the age of multi-channel digital provision has become as close to Spanish audiences as the families of the series that were broadcast when there was little choice of channel or objects of identification. As Paul Julian Smith argues, the secret of the series' success is that it has inherited that brand of authority of the "era when a monopoly public service addressed the whole nation" (2006a: 18); it is by way of the series' characters that viewers are invited to "work through" the national differences and conflicts over the transition that remain unresolved in its wake (2006a: 23). Arias, as the patriarch of the Alcántaras, can be seen, then, as one crucial player in this process of "working through" and in the pursuit of a desirable outcome to the Spanish nation's move beyond the transition's violent legacy (Smith 2006b: 23–5) (see Figure 11.6). His performance as the *pater familias* whose authority is

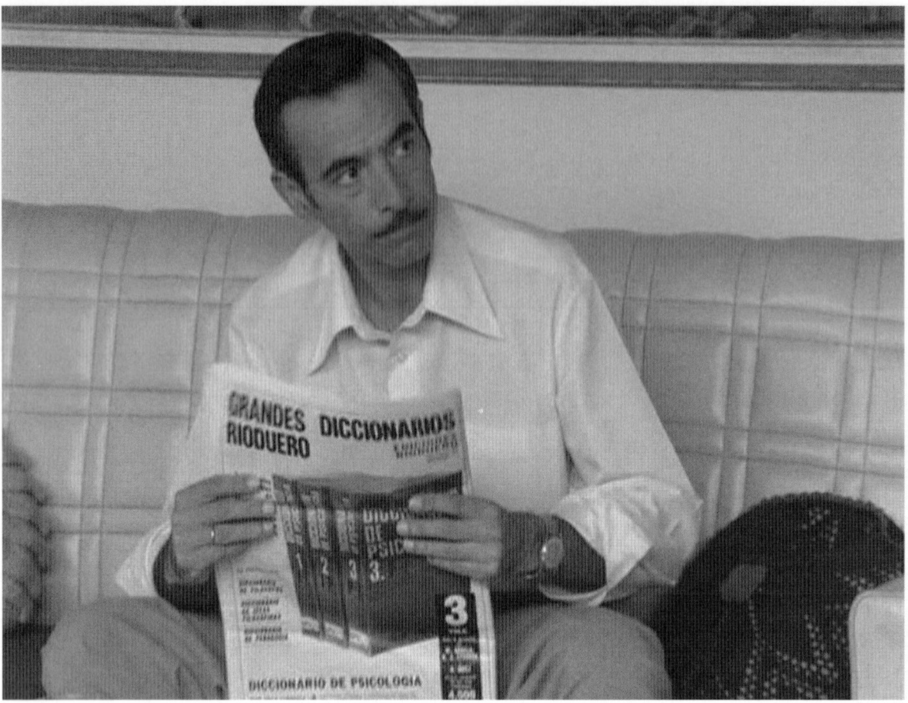

Figure 11.6 The patriarch Antonio Alcántara (Imanol Arias) in the first episode of the television series *Cuéntame cómo pasó* (TVE-1, 2001–).

questioned, and who is often seen as ambivalent and fearful of what the future after Franco would bring, offers a recognizable mirror image for the generations who lived through the transition years. His presence on screen facilitates a fictional confrontation with that crucial recent past, in a present time when it is increasingly clear that such a confrontation – so long evaded – is vital. If Spain felt that it had watched Marisol grow up into Pepa Flores and mapped a semi-politicized sentimental education onto that reception process, in this case audiences have accompanied Arias on a trajectory through some intensely coded narratives of Spanish history of the past fifty years. He is "most memorable for his representations of masculinity's relationships with crime, civil strife, war, and domestic and psychological abuse, and for how these are articulated about moments in the national drama" (Perriam 2003: 22). This facet of his career ranges from *Demonios en el jardín* (1982) and *La muerte de Mikel / The Death of Mikel* (Imanol Uribe, 1984), on national identities, religion, family, and sexuality, through *La colmena / The Hive* (Mario Camus, 1982) and *Tiempo de silencio / Time of Silence* (Vicente Aranda, 1986), in literary, retrospective mode, to *Territorio comanche / Comanche Territory* (Gerardo Herrero, 1996) and *Salvajes / Savages* (Carlos Molinero, 2001), on war, ethnic and racial hatred, immigration, and social disintegration.

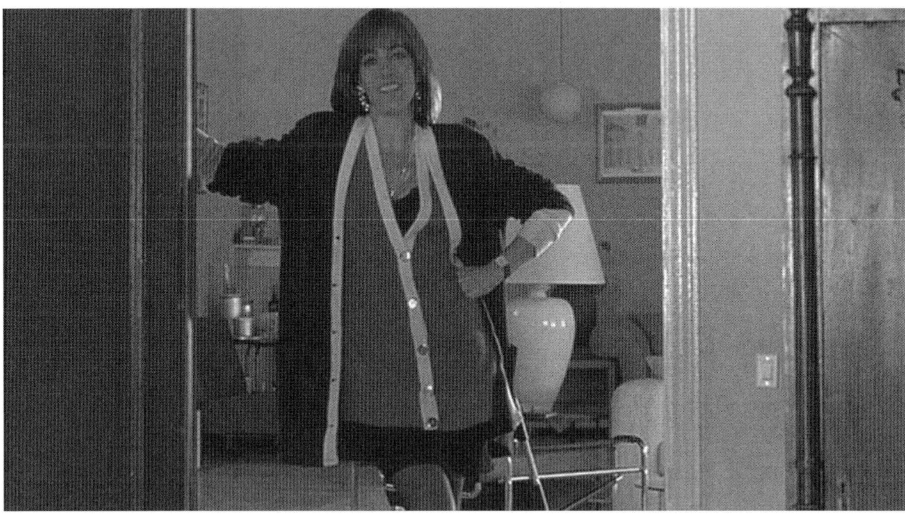

Figure 11.7 Carmen Maura in *Mujeres al borde de un ataque de nervios* (Pedro Almodóvar, 1988; prod. El Deseo).

Dubbed Spain's sweetheart (Perriam 2003: 22), and with a substantial side in comedy (Perriam 2003: 37–9), Arias is also Spain's amenable, if sometimes severe and always serious-minded, guide to the stories of its recent collective heritage.

Like Arias, Carmen Maura is a star and a celebrity of substance who challenges the validity of studies of actors that concentrate solely on cinema (Vincendeau 1998: 445). Widely known nowadays as one of Spain's most international stars, Maura has to be celebrated also for a crucial celebrity role in TVE-1's *Esta noche / Tonight*, a programme that lasted only a year (from April 1981 to April 1982) but that launched her career and made her familiar to millions of Spaniards (Ponga 1993: 69). It has been easily assumed that Maura's career was defined by her intervention in Pedro Almodóvar's films of the 1980s, up to *Mujeres al borde de un ataque de nervios / Women on the Verge of a Nervous Breakdown* (1988), and that she was somehow launched by the (in fact paralyzing) condition of becoming known as the director's *musa* (muse), and indeed subsequently *ex-musa*, and a "chica Almodóvar" – the terms were and are ubiqitous in press coverage, particularly around the time of the filming and release of *Volver / To Return* (2006), as an Internet search on them and on Maura's name will readily demonstrate (see Figure 11.7). It is, however, necessary also to analyze the function of *Esta noche*, and of Maura as its charismatic presenter, in order to ascertain how much the director's career was also benefiting from his use of her. The expression "Nena, tú vales mucho" (Girl! You're worth your weight in gold), which Maura used from the first program as part of a monologue in which her televisual persona related fictional episodes of her career as a star, became a set phrase overnight in a Spain still reeling from the effects of the failed *coup d'état* of February 23, 1981; she suddenly came to "formar parte de la cotidianeidad de millones de españoles, a personificar el aperturismo televisivo de la transición y la efervescencia de la llamada postmodernidad" (form part of the daily life of millions of Spaniards and to personify the openness of television in this period of transition as well as the glitz and sparkle of what was then being called the postmodern) (Ponga 1993: 69). These hard-won values were transferable signifiers that Maura endowed on Almodóvar's films, reinforcing his engagement with those themes of connection and representativity, making them instantly legible through her voice and image throughout the 1980s. Changing times would bring different sets of roles and the star persona of Maura accrued new signification when performing, for instance, the central role in Saura's 1990 *¡Ay, Carmela!*, which, among other prizes, earned her the European Film Award for Best Female Actor that year; *Sombras en una batalla / Shadows in a Battle* (Mario Camus, 1993); and *La comunidad / The Community* (Álex de la Iglesia, 2000), which won her the Goya for Best Female Actor. *La Comunidad* was a film in which the acting, Maura's included, was particularly praised by the critics (Buse et al. 2007: 120–2), and was an instance of Spanish cinema in which one generation (Maura's) was clearly endorsing and reinforcing the importance of another, as noted by the director: "actors like these, the traditional kind, authentic classics of Spanish cinema, television and theatre [...] give a different dimension to the dialogue, they triple its strength; they improve it" (De la Iglesia quoted in Buse et al. 2007: 122).

Acting and Activism

Links between screen actors and political action arise out of the historically specific social phenomenon of celebrity activism and humanitarianism and the unionization and associationism of actors – most famously in the North American Actors' Guild but also in the Unión de Actores, as recent calls to protest show (Europa Press 2009). Strongly naturalized connections between performance and politics in theater contribute to the strength of these links (Goodman and De Gay 2000). Many prominent film stars have "new-found global agendas" (Drezner 2007: 23) – new-found because of the comparative autonomy of present-day actors: "Stars may have always cared about politics, but they have not always been able to act on these impulses" (Drezner 2007: 23). The list is long and is dominated by Bollywood and Hollywood figures: most famously Shabana Azmi (world poverty), George Clooney (UN Messenger of Peace), Leonardo DiCaprio (environmental issues), Richard Gere (Survival International), Celina Jaitley (gay rights), Angelina Jolie (UN Goodwill Ambassador), Aamir Khan (human rights), Brad Pitt (environment, world poverty, HIV/AIDS in the developing world), and Natalie Portman (world poverty).

In Spain, globally significant issues have also mobilized screen actors, and the filmmaking community more widely. Javier Bardem's acceptance speech for his 2008 Oscar for Best Supporting Actor in the Coen Brothers' *No Country for Old Men* (2007) evoked pride in a multiple heritage (professional, familial, linguistic, political, and ethical) whose outline details were already familiar to Spanish audiences and to those studying recent Spanish film culture (Green 2006; Wood 2008); specifically a heritage of resistance to the values of Francoism – a heritage that he associated with his mother Pilar Bardem and a whole family tradition, through his grandparents Rafael Bardem and Matilde Muñoz Sampedro and his uncle Juan Antonio Bardem. Bardem's mass-broadcast reference to the Spanish generation of actors involved in resistance to Francoism can also be understood to signify, more generally, cultural agendas of rebellion against illiberalism in various forms, engaging with issues common across Europe from the 1960s onward. These agendas, or the sentiments underlying them, have most frequently been manifested only within actors' film roles, within performance, and not in their public lives. It has only been since around the turn of the millennium and perhaps the previous decade – in line with the increased autonomy of actors noted by Drezner – that Spanish screen actors and larger social and political issues have become aligned at the biographical as well as histrionic level. Objections to Spain's involvement in the war against Iraq (under the Partido Popular government) coalesced in 2002–4 around the Plataforma de la Cultura contra la Guerra (Anti-War Cultural Platform), with Pilar Bardem being one of the most prominent spokespersons.[2] The "No a la Guerra" (No to War) campaign, for example, led the press reporting on the seventeenth Goya Gala Awards ceremony to focus on "la militancia antibelicista" through which "el cine español cumplió su papel reivindicativo a la perfección" (antiwar militancy through which Spanish cinema played its role as an agent of protest perfectly) (Aparicio et al. 2003).

The Plataforma highlighted the many tensions and pitfalls that the activist-humanitarian screen actor must negotiate. As well as prompting adverse reactions to semi-politicized filmmaking practices and cultural policies, it developed, for example, a conflicted relationship with the Asociación de Víctimas del Terrorismo (Victims of [Basque] Terrorism Association). Tensions between support for freedom of cultural expression (notably around Julio Medem's *La pelota vasca / The Basque Ball Game*, 2003; see Chapter 4) and opposition to the use of violence for the achievement of political ends became very publicly noticeable (Quíles 2004). Thus, Pilar Bardem was joined by Juan Diego Botto and Aitana Sánchez Gijón, among others, in the protest march against ETA's truce-breaking bombing at Barajas airport on December 31, 2006 (Europa Press 2007) as part of an ostensibly non-partisan political intervention.

The presence of these latter two mid-generation actors in this march was one of numerous moments and positionings in which a news-aware public and a cinephile fanbase could see, in Spain since the year 2000, significant alignments of performed roles (acting) and social roles (agency) across a range of sometimes overlapping issues. Botto's playing of a young, politically revolutionary actor in *Los abajo firmantes / With George Bush on My Mind* (Joaquín Oristrell, 2005) – with an antiwar soliloquy improvised on stage as a key ingredient – and in a plot with an oblique connection to the politics of ETA in *Plenilunio / Plenilune* (Imanol Uribe, 1999) had already connected his on- and off-screen personalities with key sociopolitical issues. As Justo, in *La mujer del anarquista / La Femme de l'anarchiste / The Anarchist's Wife* (Marie Noelle and Peter Sehr, 2008), he was later able to link up with the cultural politics of re-remembering the Civil War. Similarly, Sánchez Gijón's role as Vera, uncovering the Spanish past in an Argentine context equally resonant of repression and exile, in *La puta y la ballena / The Whore and the Whale* (Luis Puenzo, 2004) had locked screen presence into a certain persistence of historical memory. Elsewhere, José Coronado – whose filmography includes *Frontera Sur / Southern Frontier* (Gerardo Herrero, 1998), on Spanish emigration to Buenos Aires; *Poniente / Wind from the West* (Chus Gutiérrez, 2002), on immigrant labor and racism in southern Spain; and *Lobo / Wolf* (Miguel Courtois, 2004), on ETA activism and the dilemmas and challenges it presents for society – can be seen in full-page color ads and in television slots endorsing, with his son, the activities of Ayuda en Acción (Aid in Action).[3] Likewise, Rosa Maria Sardà, along with Javier Bardem and Juan Diego Botto, protested against Israel's offensive against Palestine in 2009[4] and Carmelo Gómez made connections in an interview between large-scale environmental and human rights issues and local green activism, specifically the Asociación de Vecinos Urbe (Urbe Neighborhood Association) (Sevillano 2009).

Activism around the issue of the Saharawi people of the western Sahara and refugee camps around Tinduf (Algeria) has involved a large numbers of actors.[5] Guillermo (Willy) Toledo shared Saharawi activist Aminetu Haidar's November 2009 hunger strike at Arrecife airport on Lanzarote after her expulsion from Morocco and the withholding of her passport by Spanish authorities, adding to the social pointedness of many of his comedy roles a further level of relevance. But the most famous name is that of Javier Bardem: to the arguably nation-specific iconicity outlined in the previous section, his roles in *Los lunes al sol / Mondays in the Sun* (Fernando León de Aranoa, 2002) and *Mar adentro* offered serious engagement with postindustrial long-term unemployment and alienation and with the plight of the quadriplegic and euthanasia, respectively. As producer of the compendium documentary for Médecins Sans Frontières *Invisibles / Invisible* (2007), Bardem made a clear, practical connection between filmmaking – acting, then hands-on producing – and ethical agency. His own close involvement in the cause of the Saharawi Arab Democratic Republic, his backing of the Sahara International Film Festival (Fisahara), and the creation of the Plataforma Todos con el Sahara (All with the Sahara Platform), whose website his voice introduced,[6] all contribute a moral weight to his stardom within Spain and beyond.

Transnational Spanish Stars

The definition of the "Spanish star" has never, of course, been contained by the borders of the national nor by the space in front of the camera, and it has to accommodate the effects of transnational commercial and cultural exchange. Sara Montiel's Mexican and American period (1950–5) is a case in point, making her the exotic from within (Powrie et al. 2007: 215–16); the same can be said of Victoria Abril, between Spain and France, and of Sergi López, between France and Catalonia. The political awareness of Javier Bardem, and the activism of his family, as much as the image of Penélope Cruz, have made of them, in the same way as Antonio Banderas before them, multi-mediatic and pluri-territorial celebrity phenomena. They flare up from time to time as Spanish-born stars of world cinema status, rather than just Spanish stars, Banderas most of all for his readiness from the late 1990s onward to stay close to film as colorful entertainment aimed at cross-generational audiences: *Once Upon a Time in Mexico* (Robert Rodriguez, 2003), *The Legend of Zorro* (Martin Campbell, 2005), the *Spy Kids* and *Shrek* films, and video-games series.

The construction of the star personas of actors accepted and celebrated as national icons – such as Imperio Argentina, discussed in Chapter 10 – cannot be understood without taking into account the transnational dynamics that contribute to the definition of the nation by reference to otherness or through the heightening effects of expert mimicry (Triana Toribio 2003: 30–1). What Marina Díaz López neatly terms "la configuración de unas identidades en tránsito" (the configuration of identities in transit) (2005: 111) continues to enrich Spanish cinema through its actors, whatever their provenance. This configuration is, precisely, a process that can, as it were, create Spanish actors out of non-Spanish ones with subtle but surprising immediacy. For example, years after Imperio Argentina, as Díaz López observes (2005: 116), the combination of the box-office successes of the Argentine–Spanish coproduction *El hijo de la novia / Son of the Bride* (Juan José Campanella, 2001) and the Spanish *El otro lado de la cama / The Other Side of the Bed* (Emilio Martínez Lázaro, 2002; discussed in Chapter 7) gave the Argentine but Madrid-based Natalia Verbeke a prominent place in the new Spanish generation of film actors, as well as making of her "una peculiar sex-symbol" (a very particular kind of sex symbol) for Spain. A simultaneous Argentine-turned-Spanish case is that of Leonardo Sbaraglia, who in his ten-year Spanish phase (ending with a return to Buenos Aires in 2010) entered rapidly into the national circulation of celebrity images and made a series of films bonding his growing star persona to Spanish preoccupations. In *En la ciudad sin límites / The City of No Limits* (Antonio Hernández, 2002), this process received a considerable boost through Sbaraglia's alignment with two iconic actors of the Spanish screen since the 1970s, Geraldine Chaplin and Fernán Gómez, in the frame of an intense plot focusing on memories of resistance to Franco and to conservative ideologies; in *Carmen* (Vicente Aranda, 2003), no less, Sbaraglia was placed at the core of a potent mythic construct of Spanishness and its others (Powrie et al. 2007: 182–9).

Notes

1 La COPE (Cadena de Ondas Populares de España) is a privately owned radio station whose main shareholders are associations linked to the Catholic Church. See www.cope.es. Our thanks to Carlos Álvarez for the information and contextualization provided.

2 The 2003 website archive is available at www.culturacontralaguerra.org/plataforma.html.

3 See related coverage at www.youtube.com/watch?v=NjCnwy24Q-0.

4 See www.radical.es/informacion.php?iinfo=9817.

5 See www.publico.es/espana/276029/actores/activistas/protestan/madrid; www.lavanguardia.es/gente-y-tv/noticias/20080920/53542887329/acaudalados-y-dadivosos-naciones-unidas-america-latina-susan-sarandon-unicef-iraq-leonardo-dicaprio-.html; and www.saharalibre.es/modules.php?name=News&file=article&sid=3200.

6 See www.youtube.com/watch?v=iM-9DHjIt5w.

References

Aguilar, C. and Genover, J. (1996) *Las estrellas de nuestro cine: El cine español en sus intérpretes*. Madrid: Alianza Editorial.

Análisis: El acento (2010) Secundarios olvidados. *El País* (May 17). Online at: www.elpais.com/articulo/opinion/Secundarios/olvidados/elpepiopi/20100517elpepiopi_3/Tes (accessed June 1, 2010).

Aparicio, S., Arroyo, M., Cabezas, R., et al. (2003) Especial Goya 2003. *El Mundo* (February 2). Online at: www.elmundo.es/especiales/2003/02/cultura/goya/index.html (accessed January 4, 2010).

Bentley, B. P. E. (2008) *A Companion to Spanish Cinema*.Woodbridge: Tamesis.

Boyero, C. (2009) Risa sin mancha, gravedad forzada. *El País* (November 3). Online at: www.elpais.com/articulo/cultura/Risa/mancha/gravedad/forzada/elpepicul/20091103elpepicul_4/Tes (accessed July 28, 2010).

Brasó, E. (2002) *Conversaciones con Fernando Fernán Gómez*. Madrid: Espasa Calpe.

Buse, P., Triana Toribio, N., and Willis, A. (2007) *The Cinema of Álex de la Iglesia*. Manchester: Manchester University Press.

Camporesi, V. (2007) Para una historia de lo no nacional en el cine español: Ladislao Vajda y el caso de los huidos de las persecuciones antisemitas en España. In: Berthier, N. and Seguin, J.-C. (eds.) *Cine, nación y nacionalidades en España*. Madrid: Casa de Velázquez, pp. 61–74.

Cine de barrio (2000). Televisión Española, TVE-1 (November). Online at: www.youtube.com/watch?v=Nj70XIdzvq8&feature=related (accessed July 28, 2010).

Corazón, Corazón (2008). Marisol (Pepa Flores) en su 60 cumpleaños. Televisión Española, TVE-1 (February 3). Online at: www.youtube.com/watch?v=FO_GZoZvwsg&feature=related (accessed July 15, 2010).

Díaz López, M. (2005) Maletas que viajan: Natalia Verbeke y Gael García Bernal, presencias y sentidos en un cine transnacional latino. *Archivos de la Filmoteca* 49: 109–23.

D'Lugo, M. (1997) *Guide to the Cinema of Spain*. Westport: Greenwood Press.

Drezner, D. (2007) Foreign Policy Goes Glam. *The National Interest* (November–December): 22–8.

Dyer, R. (1998) *Stars*, 2nd edn. London: BFI.

Europa Press (2007) Los actores reclaman participar en la manifestación "sin colores politicos" porque la justificación es "grave." Online at: http://noticias.cine.hispavista.com/n1274-eta-los-actores-reclaman-participar-en-la-manifestacion-sin-colores-politicos-porque-la-justificacion-es-grave (accessed April 20, 2010).

Europa Press (2009) "Por apoyar causas sociales, a los del cine nos han recordado que estamos subvencionados," afirma Fernando Colomo. *El Economista* (December 11). Online at: http://ecodiario.eleconomista.es/cultura/noticias/1764533/12/09/Por-apoyar-causas-sociales-a-los-del-cine-nos-han-recordado-que-estamos-subvencionados-afirma-Fernando-Colomo.html (accessed January 5, 2010).

Evans, P. W. (2004) Marisol: The Spanish Cinderella. In: Lázaro Reboll, A. and Willis, A. (eds.) *Spanish Popular Cinema*. Manchester: Manchester University Press, pp. 129–51.

Fernández-Santos, E. and Torres, R. (2009) López Vázquez, Patrimonio Nacional. *El País* (November 3): 38.

Freixas, R. (1993) Entre la convención y la sumisión. In: Ángulo, J. and Llinás, F. (eds.) *Fernando Fernán Gómez: El hombre que quiso ser Jackie Cooper*. Donosti-San Sebastián: Patronato Municipal de Cultura, pp. 59–76.

Galán, D. (1974) *Venturas y desventuras de "La prima Angélica."* Valencia: Fernando Torres.

García, R. (2009) Ángeles González-Sinde al PP: "No hagan listas negras con el cine español." Online at: http://cultura.elpais.com/cultura/2009/12/01/actualidad/1259622023_850215.html (accessed December 2, 2009).

García Escudero, J. L. (1962) *Cine español*. Madrid: Rialp.

Goodman, L. and De Gay, J. (eds.) (2000) *The Routledge Reader in Politics and Performance*. London: Routledge.

Granado, V. P. (2006) *20 años de Goyas al cine español*. Madrid: Aguilar.

Green, J. (2006) El cine español: Imagen e industria. In: Rodríguez, H. J. (ed.) *Miradas para un nuevo milenio: Fragmentos para una historia futura del cine español*. Alcalá de Henares: Festival de Cine de Alcalá de Henares, pp. 235–40.

Gubern, R. (1974) Prólogo. In: Equipo Cartelera Turia (eds.) *Cine español: Cine de subgéneros*. Valencia: Fernando Torres, pp. 9–16.

Gubern, R. (2001) Teoría y práctica del star-system infantil. *Archivos de la Filmoteca* 38: 9–15.

Heredero, C. F. (1993) *Las huellas del tiempo: Cine español 1951–61*. Madrid: Filmoteca Española.

Martín, C. (2003) Defying Common Sense: Casting Pepa Flores/Marisol as Mariana Pineda. *Journal of Iberian and Latin American Studies* 9 (2): 149–61.

McDonald, P. (1998) Reconceptualising Stardom. In: Dyer, R. *Stars*, 2nd edn. London: BFI, pp. 177–200.

Moix, T. (1993) *Suspiros de España: La copla y el cine de nuestro recuerdo*. Barcelona: Plaza & Janés.

Monterde, J. E. (1998) Marisol. In: Borau, J. L. (ed.) *Diccionario del cine español*. Madrid: Academia de las Artes y las Ciencias Cinematográficas / Fundación Autor / Alianza Editorial, pp. 545–6.

Perriam, C. (2003) *Stars and Masculinities in Spanish Cinema*. Oxford: Oxford University Press.
Perriam, C. (2005) *El último cuplé / The Last Torch Song*, Juan de Orduña Spain 1957. In: Mira, A. (ed.) *The Cinema of Spain and Portugal*. London: Wallflower, pp. 89–96.
Ponga, P. (1993) *Carmen Maura*. Barcelona: Icaria Editorial.
Powrie, P., Babington, B., Davies, A., and Perriam, C. (2007) *Carmen on Film: A Cultural History*. Bloomington: Indiana University Press.
Quílez, R. (2004) El cine español convierte la gala de los Goya en una firme defensa de la libertad de expresión. *El Mundo* (February 1). Online at: www.elmundo.es/elmundo/2004/01/31/cultura/1075573076.html (accessed April 15, 2010).
Sevillano, E. (2009). Carmelo Gómez: "Soy un paleto, no me adapto a la ciudad." *El País, Sección Tierra (September 19)*: 10.
Schickel, R. (1985) *Intimate Strangers: The Culture of Celebrity in America*. Chicago: Ivan R. Dee.
Smith, P. J. (2006a) *Television in Spain: From Franco to Almodóvar*. Woodbridge: Tamesis.
Smith, P. J. (2006b) *Spanish Visual Culture: Cinema, Television, Internet*. Manchester: Manchester University Press.
Triana Toribio, N. (2003) *Spanish National Cinema*. London: Routledge.
Vincendeau, G. (1998) Issues in European Cinema. In: Hill, J. and Church Gibson, P. (eds.) *The Oxford Guide to Film Studies*. Oxford: Oxford University Press, pp. 440–8.
Weinrichter, A. (1998) Imanol Arias. In: Borau, J.-L. (ed.) *Diccionario del cine español*. Madrid: Academia de las Artes y las Ciencias Cinematográficas / Fundación Autor / Alianza Editorial, pp. 82–3.
Wood, D. (2008) Javier Bardem Finds that Spain is No Country for Stupid Remarks. *The Independent* (September 11). Online at: www.independent.co.uk/arts-entertainment/films/news/javier-bardem-finds-that-spain-is-no-country-for-stupid-remarks-925562.html (accessed July 15, 2009).

Further Reading

Cook, P. (1980) Star Signs. *Screen* 20 (3–4): 80–8.
Elena, A. (2001) El cantor del cine Rex: Una revisión del cine de Joselito. *Archivos de la Filmoteca* 38: 49–61.
Faulkner S. (2006) *A Cinema of Contradictions: Spanish Film in the 1960s*. Edinburgh: Edinburgh University Press.
Gledhill, C. (1991) *Stardom: Industry of Desire*. London: Routledge.
McDonald, P. (2000) *The Star System: Hollywood's Production of Popular Identities*. London: Wallflower Press.
Sánchez-Biosca, V. (ed.) (2001) *Infancia y juventud en el cine franquista*. Special issue of *Archivos de la Filmoteca* 38: 5–84.
Stone, R. (2002) Seeing Stars: Banderas, Abril, Bardem, Cruz. In: *Spanish Cinema*. Harlow: Pearson Education, pp. 183–205.

Part V

Image and Sound

12

Photography, Production Design, and Editing

Vicente Sánchez-Biosca

An Anomalous Cinema?

Film historians frequently lament what they insist on seeing as the "exceptionalism" of Spanish cinema. But a comparative study of photography, production design, and editing reveals a substantial measure of normality with respect to styles, techniques, and fashions existing in other national cinema traditions. The specificity of Spanish cinema has to be sought in its periodization and the ways in which such styles, techniques, and fashions were adapted. To discuss all this in detail would mean writing a history of film form in Spain covering more than a century – obviously impossible here. My aim will rather be to highlight some specific modes of stylistic expression through brief analysis of relevant case studies.

It is crucial here to remember that photography, production design, and editing are inseparably linked. While they are different in technical, artistic, and professional terms, analysis of their intersection can offer useful insights into the study of film form. For example, the arcane practice of reconstructing historical paintings in the sets of CIFESA's historical films involved meticulous attention to props and costumes, and also affected the dynamics of editing, since each cut broke the frame's compositional coherence. Additionally, the interiors crammed with detail determined the kind of lighting equipment to be used. By contrast, the exteriors preferred in modern film go together with a preference for more balanced natural light, as well as lightweight cameras and direct cinema.

Nonetheless, recognition of this interconnectedness should not make us forget the relatively autonomous historical trajectory of each of these three processes.

A Companion to Spanish Cinema, First Edition. Edited by Jo Labanyi and Tatjana Pavlović.

The importance of art direction dates back to the 1920s, and increased in the 1930s with the construction of film studios – CEA (1932), Orphea Film (1932), Ballesteros (1933), ECESA (1933), Iberia Films (1933) – that would continue to operate over a longer period than in other countries (Gorostiza 1997; see also Chapter 14). As far as editing techniques are concerned, these have been influenced by many factors, from the creativity of the avant-garde to the international style in genre cinema, and also the way of photographing exteriors that dominated the two first decades of studio photography (inspired by painting) until the impact of neo-realism and the New Waves brought about a radical change of sensibility.

The case studies chosen for discussion in this chapter all involve photography, production design, and editing in varying combinations and to different extents. In each case, the analysis seeks to illustrate a moment of stasis or change, highlighting features that permit comparative study: iconography, realism, experimentalism, the sound/image dialectic, the autonomization of design, and the adoption of techniques borrowed from television and the video clip, among other things.

A Cinema of Attractions

In 1906, a short film entitled *El ciego de la aldea* / *The Village Blind Man* was shot in the Valencian village of Godella. Made by the production company Cuesta, its author was the photographer and, from this point on, filmmaker Ángel García Cardona. His figure encapsulated the efforts to endow cinema with an industrial and leisure infrastructure (dedicated cinema theaters, regular production, films with a plotline, etc.) – something that had only existed since the previous year – in a city that was taking a decisive leap into modernity: Valencia's Regional Exhibition of 1909 would be crucial in that respect (see Lahoz 2010). This exhibition would embrace cinema, making it one of the exhibition's biggest popular draws but, symptomatically, situating it within a complex system of attractions in which the fairground, with its mechanical attractions, and the circus would be its closest neighbors (Sánchez-Biosca 2010; see "A Strange Attraction" in Chapter 17). *El ciego de la aldea* tells a simple story culminating in what Hollywood cinema would call "the last-minute rescue." A blind man and a little girl begging in the streets are given alms by a bourgeois couple, watched keenly by a band of robbers. The action commences with the pursuit and kidnap of the wealthy couple, and their rescue by the police thanks to the quick-wittedness of the blind man and little girl. The structure was a familiar one in American cinema but a novelty in relation to the literary adaptations being made at the time in Barcelona's film studios, and the film shows considerable technical accomplishment, exploiting the potential of depth of field in open spaces. By contrast, the moments of high drama are highly theatricalized, as was the case in American cinema. This occurs at the moment when the three groups of characters converge in the frame, unaware of each other's presence, thereby setting up the plot. When the conflict is resolved in the interior of the cave where the robbers are holding their kidnap victims, the sets are exaggerated. It is in this interior that the police, tipped off by the little girl and with the blind man's help, set a trap for the villains. The drama of the scene when the latter are caught *in flagranti* is conveyed by freezing the actors in a tableau – a convention that the cinema borrowed from late-nineteenth-century popular stage melodrama (Fell 1974).

El ciego de la aldea is thus a precocious model of what early Spanish narrative cinema is likely to have been like (the vast majority is lost). This cinema, in Tom Gunning's felicitous formulation (1986), stood halfway between the fairground attraction and narrative integration: popular in inspiration, with a gulf separating the visual regimes governing the exteriors (which make brilliant use of photography and landscape) and the interiors (whose sets are claustrophobic and rigid).

Dialectics of the Avant-Garde

One of the most radical metaphors produced on screen by the surrealist imaginary was authored in Paris by two Spaniards, Luis Buñuel and Salvador Dalí: a beautiful full moon intersected by a cloud triggered the violent irrational association of a woman's eye being slit by a razor blade (see Figure 12.1). This famous start of *Un chien andalou* (1929) is, however, inconceivable without the French avant-garde cultural influence propagated by Madrid's Residencia de Estudiantes (elite student hall of residence), where Buñuel, Dalí, and Lorca were formed intellectually, as well as the Paris cinema scene in which Buñuel had worked under Jean Epstein.

Despite this cultural influence, the Spanish avant-garde, although fascinated by the attempt to produce cinematic effects in words, contributed little to cinema as such, and examples of editing based on Soviet-style shock effects or intellectual montage, surrealist free association, Dadaist chance or play, futurist automation, or constructivist engineering are rare. *El sexto sentido / The Sixth Sense* (Nemesio Sobrevila, 1929) illustrates the ambiguous use of montage in avant-garde-influenced Spanish cinema, which remains grounded in a melodramatic imaginary. The film features a kind of drunken artist and philosopher, Kamus, who postulates the existence of a sixth sense revealed in the cinematograph. His cabinet, plunged into shadow and furnished with a camera and projector, is a stage on which the events of real life are transfigured in unexpected ways. The images projected in his cabinet are a compendium of avant-garde allusions and experiment with different forms of montage.

The first allusion is to Dziga Vertov's futurist conception of film technology as a mechanical eye, to which the protagonist attributes special powers that make

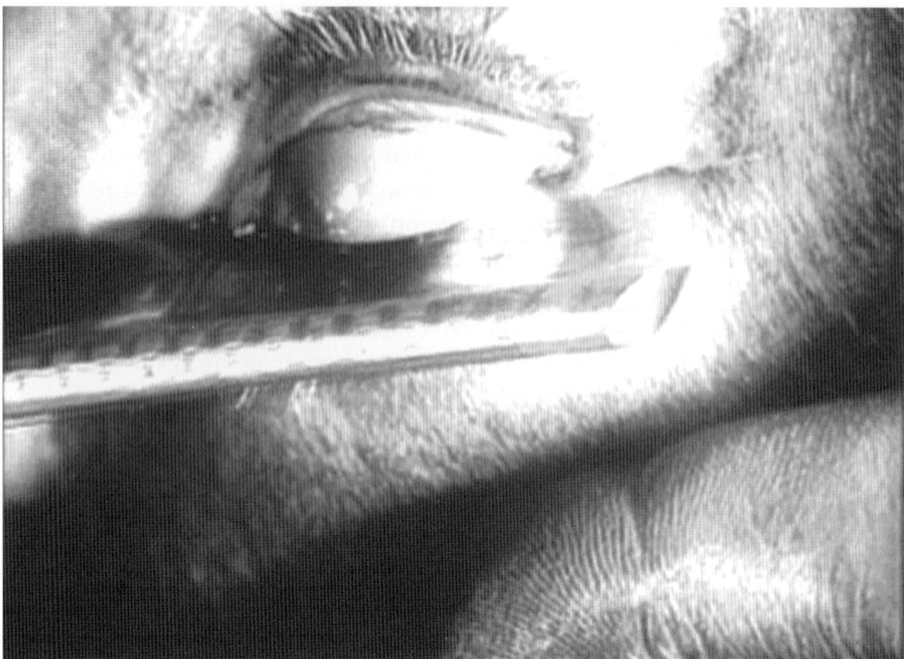

Figure 12.1 Woman's eye slit by a razor blade: the shocking prologue to Luis Buñuel's *Un chien andalou* (1929; prod. Pierre Schilzneck / María Portolés [Buñuel's mother]).

it a hybrid mix of Vertov's concepts of *kino-pravda* (film-truth) and *kino-glaz* (film-eye). Kamus' divinatory postulates are transcribed on intertitles:

> Este ojo extrahumano nos traerá la verdad. Ve más profundamente que nosotros … más grande, más pequeño, más deprisa, más despacio […] pero yo le dejo solo … libre y él me trae lo que ve con precisión matemática. Verá usted los casos de una manera distinta. Con nuestro sexto sentido.
>
> This extrahuman eye will bring us the truth. It's more penetrating than the human eye … bigger, smaller, faster, slower […] but I let it operate on its own … freely and it gives me what it sees with mathematical precision. You'll see things differently. With our sixth sense.

Despite all this, there is no automatism, no worship of technology, no homage to speed in the flow of images. The film's model of montage is reminiscent of the poetic trends that in the immediately preceding years had been the rage in France (Jean Epstein, Germaine Dulac, Marcel L'Herbier, etc.). The camera-voyeur penetrates hidden places, like a journalist's roving eye, subjected through editing to a succession of special effects: superimpositions, out-of-focus shots, sudden pans, reflections, and so on – in short, a whole catalog of techniques taken from the cinematic trend that would become known as *absolute Film*: the abstract films made by European artists such as Vikking Eggeling, Hans Richter, and Walter Ruttman, which were combined with figurative forms in Ruttman's *Berlin: Die Symphonie einer Grosstadt / Berlin: Symphony of a Great City* (1927). *El sexto sentido* thus shows itself to be familiar with editing techniques then in vogue among the French, German, and Soviet avant-gardes, but it assimilates them not programmatically but with an ironic, even burlesque, distance. Classical editing, a melodramatic structure, and a comic tone are the basic ingredients, which have grafted onto them French poetic associations, abstractions reminiscent of German experimentalism, and futurist echoes of a Vertov positioned midway between the impressionism of his newsreels and his later constructivism. A veritable cocktail.

However, the influence of 1920s avant-garde film could also lead in more conservative directions, as in *La aldea maldita / The Cursed Village* (Florián Rey, 1930). A rural honor drama depicting the plight of Castilian villages dependent on the land and thus on the whims of nature, it has an emotional intensity, tragic dimension, and sense of Spanishness conveyed through highly compact, confined scenarios in which the characters effectively become abstractions – that is, types or archetypes. In these earthy interiors with only interior light sources, allowing the gaze no possibility of escape, we can spot the legacy of the German *Kammerspielfilm* (intimate, intense psychological drama with a minimalist, almost abstract set), which, derived from theater, produced its best results in the early 1920s, gradually losing its abstract quality and veering toward the social melodrama of the decade's end. *La aldea maldita* still has that abstract quality. After years of drought and hailstorms, the starving peasants can see no future ahead. Acacia, a young mother, rocks the cradle of her newborn son with a mechanical gesture, her head bowed in an expression of apathy, bathed in a diffuse light. Her husband Juan approaches, bows his head in a similar gesture, and halts, not knowing what to do. That frozen, claustrophobic tableau, which the lighting turns into a space closed in on itself, evokes a host of scenes in *Scherben / Shattered* (Lupu Pick, 1921), *Sylvester / New Year's Eve* (Lupu Pick, 1924), and other metaphysical dramas scripted by Carl Mayer that were shown on German screens between 1921 and 1924.

Shortly after, the peasants, having decided to emigrate, set off in a caravan and Magda, a frivolous friend of Acacia, persuades her to leave the village, her husband (who is in jail), and their child for a better future in the city. Magda's tale mutates on screen into a collage of Madrid street scenes, materializing the fascination her words hold for the peasant woman. This sequence inevitably evokes the scene in *Sunrise* (F. W. Murnau, 1927) when the vamp conjures up an image of the teeming city to the male peasant Ansass, whom she has seduced. In Murnau's film, the character played by Margaret Livingston, the archetypical wicked urban vamp, gyrates wildly in front of Ansass, a peasant who has never before set eyes on the sexual license of the big city. *La aldea maldita* lacks the eroticism exuded by the female body in *Sunrise*. Nevertheless, the shared topic of the conflict between city and country, the success of Murnau's first film made in Hollywood, and Rey's knowledge of postexpressionist German cinema make clear the debt of his film not only to *Sunrise* but to 1920s German cinema in general. *La aldea maldita* retains the abstraction of the best of this tradition, dramatizing the tragedy of confinement.

Two Iconographies of the Popular

One of the perennial conflicts in Spanish cinema has been that between the defenders of "Spanish" forms, traditions, and iconography and those who have rejected these for more international, cosmopolitan modes. The debate, at whose heart is the so-called *españolada* ("typical," usually folkloric, representation of Spain; see Chapter 7), goes beyond cinema and back to at least the nineteenth century. Film was a privileged scenario for this polemic. "Typical Spanishness" could take the form of the folkloric musical, regional costumes, bullfighting scenes, rural customs, regional or ethnic stereotypes (Andalusian, Madrilenian, Aragonese, Gypsy, etc.), inflected by popular theatrical forms (*zarzuela* (popular operetta) or *sainete* (one-act farce, often with songs)), in all these cases habitually depicting the lower classes. Films drawing on this repertoire came with a ready-made stock of plastic forms (set design, costume design, props) and musical numbers (popular songs, folkloric singing stars), requiring editing techniques that showcased choreography, set design, and the centrality of performance, as in Hollywood musicals.

The 1930s were especially important in this respect. With the consolidation of sound and the construction of film studios, an array of sets were constructed and cameramen devised ways of filming them that generated a highly standardized grammar of montage (shot/reverse shot, elementary continuity editing, lack of depth of field, etc.). CEA Studios at Ciudad Lineal in Madrid were a practice ground for this codification. Two films were shot there in 1935 that encapsulate two different ways of understanding typecasting, in both cases subordinating form to choreography and musical numbers: *Nobleza baturra / Aragonese Virtue* (Florián Rey), by the Valencian production company CIFESA, and *Don Quintín el amargao / Don Quintin the Bitter* (Luis Marquina), Filmófono's first production. The shooting of the latter – an adaptation of the musical *sainete* by Carlos Arniches and Antonio Estremera – started on May 20, 1935, directed by Marquina under Buñuel's supervision. The film was shot in eight weeks, with a modest business plan and a technical crew hired on a fixed-term contract, including the set decorator, José María Torres, and the director of photography, José María Beltrán.

Conceived as a mix of melodrama (illegitimate children, abandonment, orphanhood, deception and revelation, expiation of guilt) and comedy (steeped in popular repartee), its lighting and editing tend to be classical and self-effacing, with the set recreating a single Madrid street – austere in comparison with the reconstruction of popular Madrid in Benito Perojo's *La verbena de la Paloma /*

Festival of the Virgin of the Dove, shot the same year in the same studios (with sets by Fernando Mignoni). But one special feature stands out in this grotesque tragicomedy: the staging of the musical numbers. Filmófono's director, Ricardo Urgoiti, had been the head of Unión Radio, the founder of the record label Rékord, and had launched a system of synchronized film sound based on the Vitaphone sound-on-disk system. The soundtrack of *Don Quintín* is notable in two respects: the *costumbrista* ("typical" lower-class) language, colloquialisms, and popular intonation of most of the characters; and the way it handles the songs.

Let us take an example. Don Quintín's bitterness has become a talking point throughout the city, and a song about it is sung in bars and public places, and has even been issued as a gramophone record. At the customers' request, a waiter gets out a copy of the record, which he keeps carefully stored, and plays it to everyone's delight. As if by magic, the regulars engaged in conversation, the lovers petting, and the beggars eking out their daily ration join in and sing along. Out of the blue, Don Quintín comes into the bar and, although the waiter takes the record off the gramophone and turns on the radio, it happens that the radio announces to its listeners the famous song… "Don Quintín el amargao." Furious, Don Quintín insists that the record be handed over to him; he puts it on and then smashes it. We thus see how, in no time at all, the song's success has spread to every corner of Madrid. As well as being sung and played on the gramophone and radio within the diegesis, the song of Don Quintín was also the film's extradiegetic theme tune. Urgoiti thus inscribed his multiple professional activities onto the film at a structural level.

Turning to *Nobleza baturra*, the film opens with a striking sequence. In a sea of wheat extending as far as the eye can see, men and women are busy harvesting. Brilliant light and meticulously orchestrated crosscutting between the men and women alternate with lavish travelling shots following the protagonist, María del Pilar (Imperio Argentina), as she drives a pair of oxen. The camera movements together with the editing and sunlit exteriors are a technical tour de force that additionally testifies to CIFESA's economic capacity, combining Enrique Guerner's skills as a cameraman with Rey's directorial preciosity. The spectacularity achieved by the camerawork is not undermined by the constant crosscutting, thanks to the continuity provided by the song "La Magallonera" sung by the protagonist. This use of a striking opening travelling shot would be repeated in at least two later CIFESA films involving Rey and Guerner. The first is the travelling shot that opens *Morena Clara / Dark and Bright* (1936), in which the camera enters the Venta de los Platillos as if representing the gaze of a character, fades into the arrival of a waiter whom the camera then tracks, moves to frame a scene taking place the other side of a doorway, and returns to the waiter. All this meant complicated acrobatics for a heavy camera in 1936, and coordination between direction of the actors, narrative point of view, and adjustment of the camera lens to film at variable distances, exploiting depth of field and movement. In the second example, from 1940, with a plot similar to that of *Nobleza baturra*, the super-production *La Dolores* would start with a sophisticated travelling shot that takes us through the varied activities of rural life, from agriculture to cattle-raising. The travelling shot ends with the camera coming to rest on the protagonist, Concha Piquer, who starts to sing as she milks a cow. All the resources of mise-en-scène are mobilized here to showcase the star.

Also worth mentioning is the way in which *Nobleza baturra* adapts camerawork to set design in its depiction of the Aragonese village in the scene of the procession of the Virgin of the Rosary, when María del Pilar is slandered. Guerner sought out his camera positions with care, framing his shots through archways with a background of black silhouettes illumined by the lanterns carried by the men. This constant virtuoso camerawork became Guerner's authorial signature. The same virtuosity is found in the spectacular dance in the Andalusian patio of *Morena Clara*, celebrating the fiesta of the Cruces de Mayo, for which Guerner both positioned a camera behind a window grille and used a bird's eye view shot to highlight the fountain and female costumes. This use of depth of field and the positioning of the camera behind an object in the foreground are also found in the dancing and singing numbers in *La Dolores*, in which Guerner filmed through both a cartwheel and a window grille. In sum, the camera's arabesques are placed in the service of a lavish, recognizable typecasting, whose principal ingredients are directorial style, set design, lighting, and the centrality of the female star.

From Propaganda Documentary to Plush Interiors

Just when the number of films shot in film studios was taking off, civil war broke out as a result of the military uprising of July 1936. Spain was overrun by news cameramen, and those who had developed expertise in filming pictorially conceived studio sets were thrust into the unpredictability of the battlefield. Newsreels and documentaries of the Civil War are discussed in Chapter 18; here I limit myself to noting the technical upheaval that the war entailed: anarchist documentary filmmakers rushed to the front; Guerner and other exquisite cameramen had to turn to making propaganda films; Nazi models of montage (counterpropaganda, recycling of enemy footage) reached Spain; and Buñuel helped to edit *España 1936 / Spain 1936* (Jean-Paul Le Chanois, 1937), in which he accentuated the film's capacity to shock. Nothing illustrates the change so graphically as this last film, together with, on the Nationalist side, *España heroica / Heroic Spain* (1938), in which Joaquín Reig forged a model of intellectual montage without shooting a single take (see Chapter 18). However, Franco's victory in 1939 would soon take Spanish cinema back to the studios, and to the production of genre films and a new kind of standardization. How should this postwar production be defined?

El clavo / The Nail (Rafael Gil, 1944) offers a model. Adapted from a novel by the canonical late-nineteenth-century novelist Pedro Antonio de Alarcón and drawing on the genre of the fantastic, the film, produced by CIFESA in the early postwar period with sets by Enrique Alarcón and photography by Alfredo Fraile, is a significant example of the return to films characterized by a self-contained environment, making reality opaque. This effect was created by meticulous attention to mise-en-scène, with sets modeled on a stereotypical vision of the nineteenth century, camerawork that showcased the actors (Rafael Durán and Amparo Rivelles) and added a sinister note to the action, and a self-effacing editing style in keeping with the models of classical narration developed by Hollywood after the move to sound. Certain aspects of this film speak eloquently to the hermetic quality that cinema strove to achieve in the great age of the studio system, with its roster of stars, recourse to genre cinema, and unassertive editing. Neutral to the point of excess, *El clavo* represents a style within Spanish cinema that would be slow to decline, keeping the protective environment of the film studio in operation until very late.

Claustrophic Lighting

Nada / Nothing (Edgar Neville, 1947) opens and closes with the voiceover of Andrea narrating her arrival in Barcelona from the countryside in order to study at university, full of illusions about her future prospects. A few months later, having lived through a devastating drama, that same voice picks up the story as she leaves, taking away with her "absolutamente nada" (absolutely nothing). This voiceover reproduces the first-person narration used by Carmen Laforet in her novel of the same title. In the film, the opening first-person voiceover economically announces the personal focus that will impregnate the whole narrative. On a rainy night, a taxi pulls up outside an apartment block, and the camera accompanies the female protagonist as she enters a dark world where there is no electric light. Lit by the flame of a match, she goes up the stairs, the camera following her from behind, and waits outside the apartment door, viewed from behind the banisters. The camera slowly zooms in on the young woman, highlighting her entry into the hermetically sealed, sinister world where her relatives tear each other apart and where she will be greeted like a ghost from the past. After the brief return of her voiceover at the end, the camera turns 180 degrees to go back inside the building, from which it frames a brightly lit street. As Andrea leaves, the camera, now in the doorway, goes indoors, pans the darkness, moves through the archway leading to the inner courtyard, and turns so as to aim up the empty stairwell down which Román had flung himself shortly before in a strange "accidental" suicide. Dissonant music adds to the sinister quality of this closing travelling shot.

This narrative framework illustrates the oppressive atmosphere that camerawork and set design will, throughout the film, imprint on a succession of events structured by the sordid relationships of Andrea's relatives, creating a sense of entrapment that echoes her feelings as a newly arrived observer. The unhinged plot probably benefited from the cuts that CIFESA imposed to alleviate the film's depressing atmosphere (Pérez Perucha 1982). The grandmother and her children – Angustias (who has an obscure past relating to the war and is her boss' lover), Román (imprisoned during the war and now a musician, black-marketeer, and above all sadistic seducer who ruined the life of the mother of Andrea's friend Ena, who takes her revenge during the course of the film), and Juan (mentally unstable and married to Gloria, who has an equally sordid background and maintains the family by gambling in the red-light district) – configure a narrative web of which only loose strands emerge. Two things are responsible for the film's mood: camerawork and sets. It is a world of cramped interiors, with the ceilings weighing on the characters and a pronounced depth of field, reinforced by an acting style of barely suppressed hysteria. The set recalls the low ceilings designed by Perry Ferguson for *Citizen Kane* (Orson Wells, 1941), filmed by Gregg Toland with extreme low-angle shots. Since Welles' first film was not released in Spain until 1967, it is likely that the similar but less obviously distorted camerawork of Stanley Cortez for *The Magnificent Ambersons* (Welles, 1942) was the inspiration for *Nada*'s director of photography, Manuel Berenguer. Sigfrido Burmann's set designs for Román's attic show the express aim of creating a tortured look (Gorostiza 1997: 59). Indeed, the combination of plot, subjective point of view, cramped sets, and the photography's strong black/white contrasts and sense of unreality produce one of the most asphyxiating environments in Spanish cinema, giving plastic form to the sense of derangement. This is so much the case that even Juan and Andrea's night-time expedition to Barcelona's red-light district, with its maze of narrow streets, takes on a claustrophobic quality, if one compares it to the incipient realism of a film of the following year, *La calle sin sol / The Sunless Street* (Rafael Gil, 1948).

Sets for a Cardboard Version of History

The highly successful *Locura de amor / The Mad Queen* (Juan de Orduña, 1948) was part of the cycle of historical epics that scholars have so despised, condemning these films as retrograde and as unquestioningly propounding official dogma. It has become standard for histories of Spanish cinema to say that, at the end of 1950, *Alba de América / Dawn of America* (Orduña, released 1951) represented the historical trappings of a outdated cinema, while *Surcos / Furrows* (José Antonio Nieves Conde, released 1951) represented the realist future for which the short-lived Director General of Film and Theater, José María García Escudero, fought and was defeated (see the sections in Chapter 14 on censorship and CIFESA). *Locura de amor*'s start hints at its mode of composition: the image over which the opening credits appear is a rendering of Francisco Pradilla's painting *Doña Juana la Loca* (1877). Over it appears the title of Manuel Tamayo y Baus' historical drama *Locura de amor* (1855), on which the screenplay (written by none other than

Figure 12.2 An example of the statuesque, theatrical mise-en-scène favored by CIFESA's historical epics: Aurora Batista as Juana la Loca in *Locura de amor* (Juan de Orduña, 1948). Courtesy of Video Mercury and Filmoteca Española.

the dramatist's grandson Manuel Tamayo together with Alfredo Echegaray) was based. The painterly reference attests to the authority of an iconography generated by the historical painting genre that shaped nineteenth-century cultural tastes, instituting a visual imaginary and repertoire of legends surrounding national history, which was co-opted by the nation-formation process. In drawing on this source, the film reinforced pictorialism and frozen tableau effects at the expense of dynamic editing and narrative pace. Tamayo y Baus' play added a dose of post-Romantic emotionalism, played up by Aurora Bautista's exaggerated diction in the role of Juana. The film's opening image thus evoked a recognizable universe.

The static pictorial-theatrical quality of the sets, props, and camerawork (see Figure 12.2) is offset by certain traumatic editing effects, such as that triggered in the now aged, confined queen by the sight of the insignia of the Golden Fleece, which cuts to her hallucination of the villain Filiberto de Vere. As occurs frequently in CIFESA's historical epic cycle, the story from the past is framed by a narrator recounting it at a later point of time – in this case Alvar de Estúñiga, who relates it to none other than the Holy Roman Emperor Charles V (King Charles I of Spain). The narrator's voice gives way to a heavily furnished interior in which Juana's mother, Queen Isabella, lies dying. The composition of this frame, which serves as a portico to the drama, is modeled on another nineteenth-century canvas,

Eduardo Rosales' *El testamento de Isabel la Católica / The Testament of Isabella the Catholic* (1864), though this time the stasis is broken by a gentle travelling shot.

These two paintings represent the two poles between which the film moves: Pradilla's canvas highlights the truculent element, with its ghoulish coffin, the Habsburg coat of arms, and the pregnant widow in the midst of a windswept landscape, whereas that of Rosales transmits a maternal serenity to a scene that presages future disintegration. Just before the film's end, Juana caresses her husband Philip I – known as Felipe el Hermoso (Philip the Handsome) – on his sick bed, not realizing he is dead. To her courtiers' stupefaction, she stands up and requests silence since "el rey se ha dormido" (the king is asleep). With this Orduña inscribes another classic pictorial reference, to Lorenzo Vallés' painting *Demencia de doña Juana / Madness of Doña Juana* of 1866.

The film's self-conscious staginess (diction, entrances and exits, costumes, and sets and props) is reinforced by the omnipresent pictorial references: Albert Bouts, Van Eyck, Roger van der Weyden, among others (Seguin 1997). The historical research and costumes were entrusted to Manuel Comba (son of the court painter of Alfonso XII and Alfonso XIII, Juan Comba), who was married to the great-granddaughter of the historical painter Eduardo Rosales. To produce this painterly effect, no less than thirty set designs by Sigfrido Burmann were constructed by Enrique Bronchalo. The film's end is highly indicative of this desire to create historical tableaux derived from nineteenth-century historical painting: the dark scene of the coffin that opened the film reappears, this time painstakingly recreated by the actors, bearing witness to the morbid, death-obsessed legend. The rigidity of the sets and the overacting were such between 1947 and 1951 (Fanés 1982: 164–81) that when Juan Antonio Bardem and Luis García Berlanga made their first film – *Esa pareja feliz / That Happy Couple* (filmed 1951, released 1953) – they opened it with the shooting of a historical film; the sequence ends with the destruction of the set and all the lighting equipment.

Openings to Modernity: Realism and Editing

In the history of film form, perhaps the most significant break occurred at the end of the 1950s. Even if we allow for a certain amount of temporal slippage, a series of factors – industrial, technical, aesthetic, and relating to social sensibility – determined the end of an era centered on the great Hollywood studios, genre cinema, and mass production. These multiple factors ranged from the jolt produced by television to a new perception of the real heralded by neo-realism but that only became standard with the generalized use of direct sound and high-sensitivity film. The fondness for exteriors, use of lighter cameras, and influence of news reporting went together with a preference for using lighting to create atmosphere rather than to showcase the stars. Spain was not a pioneer in these changes; the daring innovations came from New York, the *Nouvelle Vague*, Free Cinema in Britain, and even New German Cinema. Symptomatic of this conservatism was the fact that film studios survived in Spain until the late 1970s. However, the main lines of modern cinema can be squarely identified in Spanish film. Four areas of aesthetic renewal deserve mention.

First, the perceptible efforts from the early 1950s to accommodate techniques of fragmentation and location shooting show the influence of news reporting, especially in a genre little studied from a formal point of view: the thriller (Medina 2000). Getting out of the studios, lighting real-life interiors, segmenting narrative and space in keeping with the techniques of modern mass culture – all these are reactions against the grammar of continuity editing and theatrical illumination that went with the studio system. *Brigada criminal / Crime Squad* (Ignacio F. Iquino, 1950) is a curious example of the stylistic crossings that took place in the early 1950s: on the one hand, the traces of the American thriller and courtroom drama (Palacio 1997) are evident in the strong black/white contrasts, iconography of the gangster, and phantasmagoric interiors with almost abstract lighting; on the other, the documentation of urban life (Madrid and Barcelona) gives an impression of randomness and improvisation. Added to this is the use of journalistic techniques of condensation through the voiceover narration of a police chief, modeled on Fritz Lang's *M* (1931).

Second, there was an attempt in this same period to create the impression that the reality being filmed exists independently from what is captured by the camera. A sophisticated use of camerawork goes together with meticulous directing of the actors, crosscutting, the layering of sound, and the overlapping of storylines. Nothing illustrates this better than Berlanga's long takes of choral actions that are not subjected to the restrictions of controlled dramatic composition, as if the camera had been "invited in." In an interview given in 1964, Francisco Sempere, the director of photography for Berlanga's *Plácido* (1961), described Berlanga's shooting method as follows:

> Para rodar estos planos-secuencia, en donde luego no se puede cortar ni intercalar nada, hay que saber [...] marcar ya en el rodaje el ritmo de la interpretación y del movimiento de los actores. En una palabra, hay que poseer un completo dominio de todos los factores que entran en juego y tener una intención. En cuanto al método de trabajo, empezábamos por ensayar mucho, con la grúa, actores, luces. A las dos de la tarde estábamos en el plató y se iniciaban los ensayos. Unas cuatro horas después, hacia las seis, empezábamos a rodar. (López Clemente 1989: 349)

> To shoot these sequence shots, where you can't make cuts or add anything later, you have to know, at the time of shooting, how to [...] maintain the rhythm of the actors' performance and movements. That is, you need to have complete control of all the factors involved and know where you are going. As for our working method, first we'd rehearse intensively, with the crane, the actors, the lighting. We'd be on the set at 2 p.m. and the rehearsals would begin. Four hours later, around 6 p.m., we'd start to shoot.

It is worth comparing this strategy with that of Guerner-Florián Rey, discussed above. In that example, the camera drew attention to itself in a composition where the light was trained on the actors and the director organized what appears on screen according to a hierarchy of dramatic intensity. In Berlanga's case, by contrast, the camera loses that aloofness and tends toward self-effacement. The movements are made by the characters, with their mobility conveyed through a layering of sounds (with several characters talking at once) and images (with several groups of characters passing each other in different directions, or the action splitting into two or being interrupted by another action). Sempere's camera tries to capture something going on just out of reach, though it is of course his manipulation of the camera that creates that impression. These are not so much sequence shots as a multiplicity of characters, images, and sounds held together by unity of time and place. *Plácido* is a good example since it has several overlaid plotlines, none of which takes priority over the others. Plácido (Cassen) tries to pay the next instalment on the three-wheeler he has bought on credit; Gabino Quintinilla (José Luis López Vázquez) takes charge of organizing the festivities; the chairman of Cocinex Cookware oversees the publicity for his product. These actions overlap with the misadventures of the beggars and artists seated at the tables of their wealthy hosts. On top of this, other actions and characters intrude sporadically, only to vanish. The direction of the actors has to be perfectly synchronized with the manipulation of the camera, so that the camera can mingle with the actors without attracting attention or prioritizing any particular aspect.

A more radical sign of this modernity – the third feature discussed here – is found in *Los chicos / The Young Ones* (Marco Ferreri, 1960), for which Sempere was also director of photography. At the edge of the frame, leaning against a tree, one of the young protagonists, El Negro, is waiting for something. In the background is a busy street. El Negro's gaze is trained on a bar whose exterior he watched keenly in a previous scene. A couple comes out of the bar and walks to an alleyway on the right. At that point, El Negro moves toward the couple, who disappear into the alleyway. The next shot picks up the action from the alleyway, filmed in deep focus but with no visual distortion. The couple – El Negro's mother and her lover – pass in front of the camera and continue on their way; the camera waits for their pursuer and then follows him in a pan after which we see him disappear into the distance. The sense of real time is crucial to this shot, as is the neutrality of the camera's gaze, filming everything in its view without emphasizing anything in particular. The couple disappears at the entrance to a boarding house; El Negro's face, now filmed in medium shot, stiffens; behind him, a group of passersby comment on how such "boarding houses" are great money-makers, "happening" to express what the boy's face registers as a stab of pain. This sequence is symptomatic of Sempere's use of the camera/gaze in *Los chicos*: the depiction of the four boy protagonists in their different habitats by means of deep-focus compositions,with objects in the foreground, fills in the moral and psychological context of family and work. But, as with Berlanga, there is a complete absence of dramatization. Filming in the street, refusing to prioritize, opting for multiple protagonists – all of these factors signal the modernity that would put an end to the studios' mystique. Subject matter and expression, editing and composition, exterior locations, and the large cast of characters combine to announce new times. Of course the radical aesthetics of John Cassavetes' *Shadows* (1960) is on a different scale from the innovations of *Los chicos*: Ferreri's film has no jump cuts, documentary-style grainy 16 mm images, or actors improvising. The script, photography, composition, directing of the actors, and editing follow more classical guidelines.

The fourth feature that deserves to be singled out does take experimentation further: namely, the combination of realism and allegory, of the apparently real and the hallucinatory, achieved by the photography of Luis Cuadrado in *La caza / The Hunt* (Carlos Saura, 1965), where the use of a mobile camera (borrowed from television reporting) and long takes are combined with overexposures, black/white contrasts taken to the extreme, and near-experimental editing of narrative and sound. *La caza* is untypical of 1960s Spanish cinema: it picks up on the decade's fondness for exteriors and its agile camera roves around the bleakness of the barren hills; but it also experiments with the characters' interior monologues, and with the dissonance and atonalism of Luis de Pablo's musical score. Converting the landscape into a tragic scenario, exploring the effects on faces and bodies of the sweltering heat, Luis Cuadrado produced a strange blend of realism and experimentalism, shooting through a filter to accentuate the contrasts and overexposing the film to produce an almost burned look (see Figure 12.3). Nor is editing neglected, with its unexpected jumps that alternate establishing shots of the landscape with extreme close-ups of the characters that probe their states of mind, its shifts of focus, and its zooms. In short, the film combines the resources of editing with those of a mobile camera. The paradoxical result is a film that shades into allegory precisely because of its extreme realism.

Choreography and Musical Design: Something *Different*

Diferente / Different (Luis María Delgado, 1962) is an anomalous film within Spanish cinema. A bizarre narrative built around a homosexual imaginary (by the dancer and choreographer Alfredo Alaria) whose (unspoken) theme is just that, it was a unique example at that time of a film musical that had nothing to do with the *españolada*, with its folkloric or popular female singing star. The film is structured around a series of set designs with a pre-cinematic function: that of showcasing choreography and dance. If in the *españolada* the sets, costumes, and props serve to highlight an exotic Spain, in *Diferente* the dancer's personal imaginary invades the whole production design: the sets are those of the successive dance numbers that make up the film, and the latter, in turn, are not narrative performances by the actor (as in the backstage musical) but dream

Figure 12.3 Sunburned landscape and faces as harbingers of tragedy in Carlos Saura's *La caza* (1965; prod. Elías Querejeta PC).

sequences, ideas, divertimentos. In other words, the whole film depends on the sets inasmuch as they are a metaphorical, narrative, and psychological projection of the demiurge that gives birth to it.

The film's production design involves the integration of several features: first, the set designs for the locations depicted (associated with jazz, native dance, etc.); second, the choreography or movement of the dancers on stage, starting with the protagonist; and third, the imaginative condensation of these spaces, liberated from the tyranny of the real and giving way to abstraction (saturation of color, allegory, etc.). The film's self-referentiality also derives from its citations: *West*

Side Story (Jerome Robbins and Robert Wise, 1961), in the scene of a rough fight in a night club; the use of recurring motifs in Kenneth Anger's *Fireworks* (1947), in the deflationary toppling of the Christmas tree.

Holding the Image: The Aesthetics of the Static Shot

The credits of *El espíritu de la colmena / The Spirit of the Beehive* (Víctor Erice, 1973) plunge the spectator into a child's world of make-believe: drawings by the two child protagonists (Isabel and Ana); a banner with the fairy-tale invocation "Érase una vez" (Once upon a time); a vaguely specified time and place (start of the 1940s, a village in Castile). The whole film retains this dimension of make-believe: songs and jingles, leafing through a family album, viewing a film, a sense of the mysteries of death hovering in every corner. This recreation of childhood experience takes on a particular tone thanks to the use of color, the composition of the frame, the length of the takes, and the takes' relation to the soundtrack.

Luis Cuadrado (the cinematographer for Saura's *La caza*, as we have seen) gave the camerawork an ochre color that seems to emanate from the bees buzzing around the hive tended by the father of the family, Fernando (Fernando Fernán Gomez). This honey color bathes the interior spaces, and Fernando's room looks out onto the garden through a window made of ochre-colored glass panes shaped like the cells of a honeycomb. This yellow hue is one of the features that give the film its melancholy atmosphere, reinforced by the scale of many of the shots. Erice chose to film the Castilian plain through long shots of the open horizon, which forms an unattainable or infinite vanishing point, literalized in the shot of the railway tracks whose lines stretching into the distance will never meet. Within this vastness, the figure of a little girl, her back turned to us, scrutinizes the barren landscape, fixing her gaze on the ruined hut with a well where the ghost of the past (for Ana, an emanation of the monster in the film *Frankenstein*; for us as spectators, the past of the Civil War) will appear. The takes are long and silent, or at least wordless, the only sound being the relentless howling of the wind.

This minimalist composition and the predilection for persistent, static long takes (each space is represented by a take that is repeated each time it reappears) have their correlation in the film's muteness. The lack of sound makes the film's effects audible. The characters gaze and meditate, write letters to an addressee they will not reach (the children's mother, Teresa), get bogged down in literary descriptions of the buzzing of the bees (Fernando), whisper in the quiet of the night (the little girls), and contemplate the traces of an unknown past via a family photo album (Ana). The sense of absence is echoed in the shots of the open plain, which stress how tiny Ana and Isabel are in comparison with the imposing landscape. In these long shots, the figures of the little girls, especially Ana, act as a prop against which the vastness of the open horizon makes itself felt; on occasion they lose themselves in it as they run into the distance. At such moments the empty countryside becomes an actor, indicating a temporal ellipsis, as in the sequence in which Ana goes back to the recently discovered spot that she intuits is the haunt of the spirit her sister has told her about – the passage of time is subtly suggested by the change of color of her socks.

This scenario of solitude and reverie, where the gaze confronts an empty landscape, has a counterpart in the sequence in which Ana's fascinated gaze acts as the reverse shot to the screen on which the film *Frankenstein* (James Whale, 1931) is being shown – the only part of the film we see is the encounter between the little girl and the monster. In the darkness of the improvised cinema, the shot/reverse shot alternation between the screen image's interpellation of Ana and her intense look back forms a self-contained loop that will culminate in the materialization of the ghost in the wounded resistance fighter whom the little girl will tend and feed. After this shot/reverse shot exchange between the screen and Ana's passionate gaze back at it, Ana is overwhelmed by the specter of absence and, on the night she runs away, imagines her encounter with the monster in the film. The compositional minimalism, the extreme economy in the selection of shots, and the capacity of the camerawork to recreate states of mind are perhaps the reasons why this film has so influenced later Spanish cinema. One can even talk of a "Querejeta look," given the recognizable style that characterizes the films he produced – whether directed by Saura or Erice, Jaime Chávarri or Manuel Gutiérrez Aragón, Francisco Regueiro or Montxo Armendáriz – and which impregnates the photography of cameramen as different as José Luis Alcaine, Teo Escamilla, and Cuadrado (see the section "The Producer-Author as Transational Entrepreneur" in Chapter 2). Numerous films of the 1980s would inherit this style in their lingering recreation of places and times marking the sentimental education of Spanish children – a sentimental education soured by the Civil War or Francoism. Most of these would lack the equilibrium that *El espíritu de la colmena* achieved between emotional tone, camerawork, sobriety, silence, length of take, and the sense of time lived as reverie.

A New Experimental Avant-Garde

Arrebato / Rapture (Iván Zulueta, 1980; see Chapter 21) is imbued with US underground culture, making use of collage, fragmentation, and recycling. Its visual regime draws on comics and horror films, and has little to do with the literary-based cinema dominant in Spain at the time. Having previously authored several experimentally inspired shorts, in *Arrebato* Zulueta gives narrative form – visually attractive and delirious in its treatment of drugs – to a series of topics that had been recurrent in experimental cinema since the 1950s: home movies, found footage, conceptualism, and minimalism, including the "rediscovery" of cinema in Warhol's early films, such as *Sleep* (1963). The central theme of *Arrebato* is the pause, the suspension of movement, a concern of those filmmakers who had set out to rethink the mechanisms for capturing and projecting images: Michael Snow, Hollis Frampton, and Ernie Gehr in North America, but also Kurt Kren and Peter Kubelka in Europe. Indeed, the red frame to which Pedro (Will More) attributes the camera's devouring of his life is a reference to *Schwechater*, a film made by Kubelka in 1957–8 with 1440 different units in black and white. Kubelka had in his montage used a structure based on blocks of red, each lasting for thirty frames and recurring at decreasing intervals, comprising what he called "metric cinema." Pedro, however – like the protagonist José (Eusebio Poncela) on his behalf – responds to this meditation on red in a passionate, compulsive manner.

At the same time, Zulueta's two main characters probe their everyday surroundings with their camera pretty much as if they were making a home movie, except that they have no memorializing impulse (as in the work of Jonas Mekas) and are not driven by an interrogating inner eye that transfigures the real (as in Stan Brakhage) nor by an urge to exhibit the private in public (as in Carolee Schneeman). Much of the footage projected within the film comes from a Super 8 mm travelogue shot by Pedro, speeded up so as to become something unrecognizable, if not sinister. This mix of sources, textures, and formats – including the recycling of material previously filmed by Zulueta himself – evokes the indiscriminate hybridization that contemporary documentary calls "found footage."

That this atypical film, with its complex intertextual references, should have become a cult movie for much of the general public is quite extraordinary. The reasons were partly to do with the author's reputation as a *maldito* (doomed artist) but also with the film's treatment of the topic of heroin at a key moment in Spanish culture (the transition to democracy) – a topic that the film assimilates to the metaphor of vampirism. If Almodóvar introduced pastiche into Spanish cinema of the same period – in the sense of a masquerade or detached ironic allusion, the definition of the term given by Fredric Jameson in his study of postmodernism (1992) – Zulueta played up the passion and drama of the modern subject, its inner lacerations and eventual destruction. This and the many cinephile textual references in the film obscured for the general public the film's recourse to the subject matter, style, genres, and problematics of experimental cinema.

From Eccentricity to Designer Look

The screen is taken over by cuttings from fashion magazines; the colors are bright, the contours clear. Lingerie, gloves, evening gowns, high-heeled shoes – all highly sophisticated. Painted fingernails drying after a manicure, red lipstick, dressmakers' scissors, an eye painted with eye-shadow repeated in a strip of pristine shots from a photo booth. Over these images, the beat of a *bolero* with its inevitable lyrics of betrayal in love. The culminating image of these credits: a camera on a film set. Immediately, a female voice transports us to what appears to be a farmyard but turns out to be an improvised chicken coop on a city terrace. A single shot condenses the core of the melodrama: the back of an old LP, on which a red felt-tip pen has turned the title of a song into a declaration of eternal love; to its left, an ashtray filled with sweet wrappers and a cigarette end; behind it, a coaster with a forgotten drink against a red background. A man's voice repeats the promise of love. Next, an alarm clock; the camera pans to the photograph of a couple, inscribed with a handwritten message signed by someone called "Iván"; then an empty pack of pills; then another alarm clock, its hands indicating the same time as the last one: eight o'clock.

This is the start of *Mujeres al borde de un ataque de nervios / Women on the Verge of a Nervous Breakdown* (Pedro Almodóvar, 1988). The essence of melodrama is condensed in these shots: the *bolero*, the woman's story, the kitsch picture, redundancy. Even before we are made aware of the standard plot of love betrayed, the credits indicate an aesthetic: the fragment, the magazine cuttings, fashion, fetishization of the female body and women's clothes, in frames saturated with bright colors and littered with scraps of dress material (see Figure 12.4). We could be in the workshop of a dressmaker or fashion designer. All the same, the tone is uniform; José Luis Alcaine's camerawork homogenizes the fragments in a postmodern design that is impeccably kitsch and camp.

This start is remarkably similar to that of Almodóvar's first film, *Pepi, Luci, Bom y otras chicas del montón / Pepi, Luci, Bom and Other Girls on the Heap* (1980): grotesque drawings, references to comics, accompanied by rock music of the day, and again ending with the image of a camera on a film set, cutting to the same actress, Carmen Maura, this time collapsed on a bed. And yet, even before the narrative has started, we can see a host of revealing differences with regard to *Mujeres*: the coarse quality of the sound and image, the provocatively grungy textures, the glaring references to Warhol. Separating these two films – nearly a decade apart – is the conquest of a designer look, an elegant style that, no matter how outrageous the storylines, enhances its flawless composition by citing hallowed sources: Douglas Sirk and his mannerist use of color, framing a universe of postmodern female fetishes where retro and design-consciousness rule. This formal slickness, which encompasses editing, camerawork, and production design, would become a constant of Almodóvar's subsequent work. Collage but without disorder, pastiche but with its nods to the underground subtly designed.

What is involved here is the harmonization of a style to which all formal elements are subordinated, artificially provoking the desired effect, as in Umberto Eco's definition of kitsch (1968: 82). Nothing illustrates this so well as *Todo sobre mi madre / All about My Mother* (1999), released just over a decade after *Mujeres*. The references are to an array of gay icons that time and tradition have codified as ingredients of over-the-top melodrama: *All about Eve* (Joseph L. Mankiewicz,

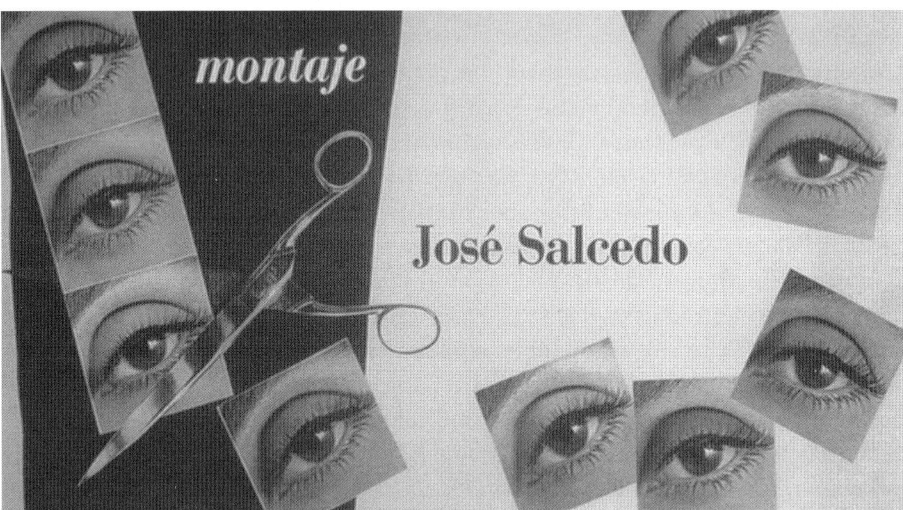

Figure 12.4 *Mujeres al borde de un ataque de nervios* (Pedro Almodóvar, 1988; prod. El Deseo): fetishization, collage, and postmodern design.

1950), the theater world as a scenario of exaggerated performance and fakery, and the explicit quotation of *Opening Night* (John Cassavetes, 1977).

Stylistic Diversification

The highly fragmented panorama of the last few decades invites analysis from a political, cultural, or gender perspective more obviously than from a formal point of view. Nonetheless, I will end by sketching out a few formal trends, with no pretensions to comprehensive coverage. One identifiable avenue is that opened up by *El espíritu de la colmena*, exploring the dimensions of time and silence in an everyday life ever more lacking in dramatic potential. Erice's *El sol del membrillo / The Quince Tree Sun* (1992) follows this line in its focus on the supremely cinematic phenomenon of light transformed into time and time transformed into light; that is, the ungraspable ephemerality that Antonio López attempts to capture in his painting. Symptomatic in this respect is the interest in recent years in the documentary format. *En construcción / Under Construction* (José Luis Guerín, 2001) starts with the banner "Cosas vistas y oídas durante la construcción de un nuevo inmueble en 'el Chino,' un barrio popular de Barcelona que nace y muere con el siglo" (Things seen and heard during the construction of a new apartment block in the "Barrio Chino," a Barcelona working-class neighborhood born and dying with the century's end). This can be read as a manifesto of the film's working methods: its approach to observation and filming, editing and length of takes, acoustic match and mismatch. By patiently and persistently observing a historical enclave in the Catalan capital over three years, with the help of a team of students from the Universitat Pompeu Fabra's masters program in creative documentary, Guerín was able to offer a gaze that is the opposite of that of the news reporter: no sensationalist out-of-focus shots, no pans or rapid camera movements, no quick cutting or sense of urgency. On the contrary, carefully-thought-out long takes are employed, highlighting subtle contrasts (depth of field connecting the local inhabitants' everyday lives to the labor of the builders constructing the apartment block; passersby coinciding in the streets; posters, graffiti, or advertisements in the background). Sound follows the same rhythmic interactions: the voices are sometimes synchronous, sometimes out of sync; in some cases they are off-screen comments by passersby whose faces we do not see, but in other cases they appear on screen later. Image and sound are woven together freely. Nothing illustrates this so clearly as the sequence in which the drilling unearths some skeletons, which become the center of attention of the locals, the media, and experts alike – a veritable X-ray of the neighborhood. In this respect, Erice, Guerín, and Mercedes Álvarez (the editor of *En construcción* and director of *El cielo gira / The Sky Turns* (2004)) share a similar imaginative trajectory, an approach to reality grounded in documentary and fiction in equal doses.

A second – diametrically opposed – trend is that which packages together a series of attractions, as if returning to early cinema's origins in the fairground, albeit in blockbuster format. In this respect, the techniques of the video clip – hyper-fragmentation and glossy design – play a major role. Juanma Bajo Ulloa's *Airbag* (1997) was presented as a provocative *comedia gamberra*; that is, a crazy comedy characterized by a rapid succession of events that mix the absurd, the iconoclastic, and the spectacular. This was followed two years later by Javier Fesser's *El milagro de P. Tinto / The Miracle of P. Tinto* (1998), a hilarious comedy with a somewhat more controlled visual imagination thanks to the meticulous photography of Javier Aguirresarobe. The editing created all manner of perceptual anomalies (extreme close-ups followed by establishing shots; high-speed hyper-fragmentation; special effects, for which it won a Goya award). The fast-paced rhythm of such films suggests a resuscitation of the attractions that were cinema's principal selling point in its early days, with the entertainment sources that provide equivalent thrills today – the shopping mall, the slot machine, the computer game – reproducing their sensory regimes within the film as a succession of electric discharges. *Torrente, el brazo tonto de la ley / Torrente, the Dumb Arm of the Law* (Santiago Segura, 1998) and its sequels are eloquent examples of this modality.

In a context in which the editing and compositional conventions of the television series (shot/reverse shot, transitions via a theme tune, use of three-dimensional models for sets) and its styles of production design (glossy, impersonal, lacking signs of everyday wear and tear) are becoming standard, it is not surprising that a series of genre formulas, modeled on American cinema, are becoming codified, grounded in classical continuity editing but enriched with new sound technologies and the possibilities opened up by digital photography and digital editing. The potential of this kind of filmmaking is illustrated by Alejandro Amenábar, whose first film *Tesis / Thesis* (1996) drew on Hitchcockian suspense and the topic of snuff movies, and who skillfully exploited special effects in *Abre los ojos / Open your Eyes* (1997), which uses digital technology to enhance narrative artifice, and in *The Others* (2001), which at the same time draws on a US/British classic, *The Innocents* (Jack Clayton, 1961). Daniel Monzón's *Celda 211 / Cell 211* (2009) also draws on classical Hollywood cinema, productively exploring the genre of the prison movie, undeveloped in Spain. The return to the transparent conventions associated with genre cinema goes together with modest auteurist pretensions, through the development of a recognizable brand. If Aménabar incarnates this trend (see Chapter 5), films such as *Barrio / The Neighborhood* (Fernando León de Aranoa, 1998) illustrate a curious mix of realist observation with stylized auteurist traits. The credits draw our attention to the precariousness of the zoom lens, the limits of reportage, and the scope for technical imprecision with out-of-focus shots; nonetheless, the film is meticulous in its composition and editing, creating a kind of storyboard realism. This auteurist cinema has nothing to do with the grunge and lack of polish that gave the films of José Antonio de la Loma – such as *Perros callejeros / Street Warriors* (1977) – their vitality, as was also the case with the films of Eloy de la Iglesia from *El pico / Overdose* (1983) onward (see Chapter 6). The author's imprint imposes itself on reality, filters it, and aestheticizes it, turning it into an object of beauty.

Conclusion

The formal features that have made Spanish cinema what it is and the technical processes behind them (camerawork, production design, editing) have passed through the same stages of trial and error, hurdles, crises, and conflicts as has been the case with other national cinemas. The notion of the exceptionalism of Spanish cinema is not supported by evidence, unless by "anomaly" we just mean "cultural specificity." Cultural specificities there have been, as there are today: the highly idiosyncratic set designs of popular adaptations (of *zarzuelas*, of literary texts) in the 1920s; the enforced experimentation of the Civil War; the claustrophobic atmosphere of the postwar years; the prolongation of the studio age perhaps longer than in any other country; and the modest impact of lightweight cameras and direct sound in the modernizing phase that began in the late 1950s. But are these cultural specificities any greater than those represented by 1920s German expressionism and Soviet montage, 1930s French poetic realism, the New York underground, or the cyclical recurrence of genres in Japan? A good case can be made for giving Spanish cinema back its normality; that is, its unsurprising singularity.

References

Eco, U. (1968) *Apocalípticos e integrados*. Barcelona: Lumen.

Fanés, F. (1982) *Cifesa, la antorcha de los éxitos*. Valencia: Institución Alfonso el Magnánimo.

Fell, J. (1974) *Film and the Narrative Tradition*. Norman: University of Oklahoma Press.

Gorostiza, J. (1997) *Directores artísticos del cine español*. Madrid: Cátedra / Filmoteca Española.

Gunning, T. (1986) The Cinema of Attraction: Early Film, its Spectator, and the Avant-Garde. *Wide Angle* **8** (3–4): 63–70.

Jameson, F. (1992) *Postmodernism; or, the Cultural Logic of Late Capitalism*. Durham: Duke University Press.

Lahoz, J. I. (ed.) (2010) *A propósito de Cuesta. Escritos sobre cine español. 1896–1920*. Valencia: Institut Valencià de l'Audiovisual i de la Cinematografia (IVAC).

López Clemente, J. (1989) Entrevista con Francisco Sempere. In: Llinás, F. (ed.) *Directores de fotografía del cine español*. Madrid: Filmoteca Española, pp. 347–53.

Medina, E. (2000). *Cine negro y policiaco español de los años cincuenta*. Barcelona: Laertes.

Palacio, M. (1997). Brigada criminal. In: Pérez Perucha, J. (ed.) *Antología crítica del cine español 1906–1995*. Madrid: Cátedra / Filmoteca Española, pp. 279–81.

Pérez Perucha, J. (ed.) (1982) *El cinema de Edgar Neville*. Valladolid: 27 Seminci.

Seguin, J.-C. (1997) *Locura de amor*. In: Pérez Perucha, J. (ed.) *Antología crítica del cine español 1906–1995*. Madrid: Cátedra / Filmoteca Española, pp. 230–2.

Sánchez-Biosca, V. (2010) El cine en la época de la Exposición Regional Valenciana. In: De la Calle, R. (ed.) *El contexto artístico-cultural valenciano en torno a la Exposición Regional de 1909*. Valencia: Real Academia de Bellas Artes de San Carlos, pp. 179–99.

Further Reading

Alarcón, E. (1984) *El decorador en el cine*. Torrejón de Ardoz: Festival de Cine de Alcalá de Henares.

Fernández Colorado, L. and Cerdán, J. (2007). *Ricardo Urgoiti: Los trabajos y los días*. Madrid: Filmoteca Española.

García de Dueñas, J. and Gorostiza, J. (2001) *Los estudios cinematográficos españoles*. Special issue of *Cuadernos de la Academia* 10 (December).

Gorostiza, J. (2001) *La arquitectura de los sueños: Entrevistas con directores artísticos del cine español*. Alcalá de Henares: 31 Festival de Cine.

Heredero, C. F. (1993) *Las huellas del tiempo: Cine español 1951–1961*. Valencia: Filmoteca de la Generalitat Valenciana / Filmoteca Española.

Heredero, C. F. and Monterde, J. E. (2003) *Los "nuevos cines" en España: Ilusiones y desencantos de los años sesenta*. Valencia: Institut Valencià de l'Audiovisual i de la Cinematografia (IVAC).

Llinás, F. (ed.) (1989) *Directores de fotografía del cine español*. Madrid: Filmoteca Española.

Sánchez Vidal, A. (1991) *El cine de Florián Rey*. Zaragoza: Caja de Ahorros de la Inmaculada.

13

Soundtrack

Román Gubern and Kathleen M. Vernon

Introduction (Kathleen M. Vernon)

The story of film sound in Spain crosses multiple geographic and disciplinary boundaries, embracing elements of economic, industrial, political, and artistic histories. It has become commonplace to lament the lack of critical attention to sound as opposed to visual techniques and expression, although this situation has changed dramatically since the 1990s. During that time the work of Mary Ann Doane, Rick Altman, and Michel Chion, among others, has taught us to consider the complex and often contradictory role of sound in anchoring the illusionary power of cinema, while new research on the development and deployment of sound technologies in national cinemas (Sider et al. 2003; Harper 2009) has opened our ears to the critical role of sound in soliciting and confirming collective identities. (For the importance of the musical film in Spain, see Chapter 7.) Beginning with a detailed account of the introduction of sound film in Spain, this chapter will go on to examine the role of dubbing, sound design, and musical score in the construction of a national soundscape within the larger context of a global film industry.

The Transition from Silent to Sound Cinema (Román Gubern)

The advent of sound cinema produced a major upheaval in the film industry, both for producers, who had to work through several years of costly and frustrating experimentation with assorted new forms of recording equipment, and for

A Companion to Spanish Cinema, First Edition. Edited by Jo Labanyi and Tatjana Pavlović.

exhibitors, who had to re-equip their cinema theaters. Beyond the economic impact, the move to sound meant a complete rethinking of the geopolitical organization and conceptualization of cinema. By comparison, the later transition from black and white to color, though it involved another costly updating of equipment, would have relatively minor, largely aesthetic repercussions. Spain's technological and economic underdevelopment at the time of the transition to sound made inevitable the dependence on foreign technical innovation. The resulting intensified transnational collaboration (see Chapter 2) had a positive flip side for Spanish directors and actors, as producers – accustomed in the silent era to targeting international audiences – experimented with ways of continuing to allow their films to reach audiences who spoke different languages, with their eye particularly on the vast Spanish-speaking market in Latin America. The resulting multilinguals and Hollywood Spanish-language productions provided first-class training for the numerous Spanish film professionals recruited to make them, as well as a cosmopolitan attitude that would carry over into the new era of "national cinemas" that would develop worldwide in the course of the 1930s and become consolidated in the 1940s – partly for political reasons but also because, as dubbing became the standard way of making films accessible to audiences who spoke another language, film producers settled down to a pattern of making films only in the language of the country where they were located.

As we shall see, the transitional period of experimentation with new sound recording technologies was marked by many dead ends and hybrid solutions. The story in Spain starts in 1926, when, on May 2, Valencia's Teatro Lírico projected a monologue by the filmmaker Armand Guerra, recorded in Berlin with the Danish sound system invented by Peterson and Poulsen. It was one of various trial runs leading up to the introduction of sound cinema in Spain, at a time when silent film versions of *zarzuelas* (popular Spanish operettas) were screened with live orchestral accompaniment and with the audience, familiar with the words, singing along – even, on occasions, with professional choirs appearing on stage to perform the most popular numbers. Also in 1926, in New York's Fox Case Movietone Corp. studios, equipped with Western Electric's Movietone system, Raquel Meller – directed by Marcel Silver – recorded various short musical numbers sung in Castilian and Catalan, some of them screened at the start of the New York premiere of Raoul Walsh's *What Price Glory?* on January 21, 1927, and later in Spain. In February 1927, the American engineer Lee DeForest arrived in Madrid, after a fruitless visit to England, to promote his Phonofilm sound-on-film system, recorded on a separate film from the image – a system in which Hollywood studios had shown no interest, since they were at the time committed to sound-on-disk systems. DeForest had previously used his system to film Conchita Piquer singing several songs in New York, screening the recording in 1923 at New York's Cine Rivoli and in London. 1923 thus marked the start of Spain's involvement in the transition to sound beyond Spanish shores (this recording of Piquer, recently rediscovered in the Library of Congress, is now held to be among the earliest sound films ever made).

On arrival in Madrid, DeForest filmed a speech by the military dictator Miguel Primo de Rivera, and in March travelled to Barcelona, where the film distribution business was based. There he sold his equipment to the Cuban Enrique Uranzadi and the itinerant film projectionist Feliciano Vitores, who from June 13, 1927 exhibited their recordings to the public at Barcelona's Cine Kursaal. In September, again in Barcelona, Uranzadi and Vitores founded Hispano DeForest Phonofilm, in partnership with the entrepreneur Agustín Bellapart, while DeForest travelled on to Italy in the hope of filming Mussolini. Phonofilm projections were held in Madrid in October 1927, with the Phonofilm system used to film short performances of popular figures, such as the clown Ramper and a parodic monologue by the writer Ramón Gómez de la Serna. The only feature film shot with Phonofilm was Francisco Elías' *El misterio de la Puerta del Sol / The Mystery of the Puerta del Sol*, in October and November 1929 – a rudimentary comedy made in Madrid with a budget of eighteen thousand pesetas and whose plot hinges self-reflexively on the casting of actors in a sound film studio (see Chapter 7). It was premiered in February 1930 in Burgos, Uranzadi's city of origin, but flopped thanks to Phonofilm's technical incompatibility with the available equipment. A symptomatic film, it reflects the fascination with the new sound cinema, with virtuoso acoustic displays such as the gong struck by the director on giving orders. But it also illustrates cinema's false promise of access to the star system, equating cinematic representation with the dream world – as Buster Keaton had done earlier in *Sherlock Jr.* (1924).

Before shooting for *El misterio de la Puerta del Sol* started, in March 1929 the cameraman J. E. Delgado had arrived in Spain with a Movietone sound truck to make a number of short films for Fox: musical numbers by the Argentine trio Irusta, Fugazot, and Demare; interviews with the painters Ignacio Zuloaga and Julio Romero de Torres and the sculptor Mariano Benlliure, among others; and a speech by King Alfonso XIII.

In January 1929, Alan Crosland's *The Jazz Singer* (1927) was premiered at Madrid's Cineclub Español, run by Luis Buñuel. It was introduced by Gómez de la Serna, who gave a peroration on jazz in blackface. It was shown not with the original soundtrack but with live musical accompaniment, prompting protests from the audience. In June 1929, Crosland's film was screened again at Madrid's Cine Callao with the Melodión sound-on-disk system, invented by Antonio Graciani of the distribution company Exclusivas Diana. Again it provoked protests, being shown with the original soundtrack for the first time only in 1931, with the title *El ídolo de Broadway / The Idol of Broadway*. Also in 1929, the impresario Ricardo Urgoiti introduced the Filmófono sound system, using two synchronized disks with independent volume controls. It was first tried out on the public at the Cineclub Español's screening of Erich von Stroheim's *Greed* in May 1929, and subsequently used by Florián Rey in *Fútbol, amor y toros / Football, Love, and Bullfighting* (1929). In Barcelona, the writer of stage comedies Amichatis (Josep Amich i Bert) introduced the Parlophone sound-on-disk system, which was used in Sabino Micón's *La alegría que pasa / Passing Happiness* (1930). All these systems would prove flawed and short-lived.

The last silent Spanish film was *Los hijos mandan / The Children are in Charge* (1930), shot by Antonio Martínez Ferry in 1929. In that same year, on September 19, the Paramount production *Innocents of Paris* (1928), directed by Richard Wallace and starring Maurice Chevalier, was premiered in Barcelona – the first Hollywood sound film exhibited under relatively normal conditions: Western Electric's American engineer responsible for the projection played the sound only for the song routines, to avoid protests at the untranslated English-language dialogue, as had happened in other European cities. October 4, 1929 saw the release at Barcelona's Cine Tívoli of a feature-length sound film promoting the World Exposition inaugurated in the city that May. Made in Hollywood with the title *Barcelona Trailer*, it showed the journalist Marcel Ventura presenting a parade of Hollywood stars, including Harold Lloyd, Clara Bow, Maurice Chevalier, Dolores del Río, Norma Talmadge, Bebe Daniels, Norma Shearer, Lupe Vélez, Louise Fazenda, and Raquel Torres.

The first Spanish attempts to produce technically viable sound cinema relied on the use of foreign studios (the first complete French sound film had also been shot abroad, in England). The two key examples – illustrating the two options: multilingual or Spanish-only production respectively – are George B. Samuelson's *La canción del día / Spanish Eyes* (1930), filmed in British studios, and Benito Perojo's *La bodega / Wine Cellars* (1930), shot in French studios. *La canción del día* was a venture of the producer Ricardo Urgoiti, in collaboration with the Anglo-German consortium BIP (British International Pictures)/UFA (Universum Film Aktiengesellschaft), created to make multilingual productions. The script was written by Pedro Muñoz Seca and Pedro Pérez Fernández, with musical score by Jacinto Guerrero; the sound system was General Electric's RCA Photophone. The exteriors of this *costumbrista* melodrama, reminiscent of Chaplin's *City Lights* (1930), were filmed in Madrid and its interiors in England, in Spanish and English versions. It was premiered in Madrid on April 19, 1930. *La bodega*, based on Vicente Blasco Ibáñez's novel, was a coproduction of the Spanish company Julio César and the French Compagnie Générale de Productions. Perojo started to shoot it in July 1929 at the Nathan studios in Paris, travelling to Seville the next month to film the exteriors. In September it was announced that the film would be sonorized and its protagonist Conchita Piquer provided recordings of two song performances, rerecorded on disk at the Billancourt studios together with background music taken from recordings of Albéniz, Granados, and Turina. *La bodega* was shown in silent and sound versions (the former slightly longer), depending on the market; in 1931 it was edited in sound-on-film form. The film was premiered in Madrid on March 10, 1930, still in sound-on-disk format, and the next month in Barcelona with the French sound system Cronophone Gaumont. Perojo's next sound coproduction, *El embrujo de Sevilla / L'ensorcellement de Séville / The Spell of Seville* (1930), was filmed with the German Tobis sound system in UFA's Berlin studios and at the Éclair studios at Épinay-sur-Seine.

Two more multilinguals deserve mention to illustrate this phase of transnational collaboration. One is Robert Florey's *L'Amour chante / El amor solfeando* aka *El profesor de mi mujer / Love in Song* aka *My Wife's Teacher* (1930), a vaudeville comedy shot in UFA's Berlin studios as a coproduction of Harmonic Films (Berlin) and Pierre Braunberger (Paris), with the Spanish distributors Renacimiento Films (Madrid) and Cinaes (Barcelona) acting as coproducers for the Spanish version, shot with a different cast headed by Imperio Argentina. Argentina also starred in *Cinópolis / Elle veut faire du cinema / She Wants to Be in a Movie* (1931), filmed for Gaumont in Paris by José María Castellví, whose Spanish version, later extended by Francisco Elías, can be considered a Spanish production, having been commissioned by the Barcelona distributor Enrique Huet. Premiered in September 1931, it describes the frustrations of a would-be movie star.

Another survival strategy in the new market was the sonorization in French studios of silent films made in Spain. This was the case with Florián Rey's *La aldea maldita / The Cursed Village* (1930), sonorized at the suggestion of its Cuban importer at the Épinay-sur-Seine studios with the Tobis sound system, adding music and dialogue and refilming some scenes in new sets. Rey also sonorized in Paris his comedy *Tiene su corazoncito / He Has a Heart* (1930). A similar procedure was used for José Buch's historical films *Prim* (1931) and *Isabel de Solís* (1931); Leopoldo Alonso's documentary *Salamanca* (1930); Fernando Roldán's homage to the recently executed republican soldier *Fermín Galán* (1931); and Edgar Neville's musical *Yo quiero que me lleven a Hollywood / Take Me to Hollywood* (1931), which was sonorized with the Seletone system at the Baroncelli studios.

It was at this moment of crisis, when Spanish cinema was dependent on foreign sound technology and when the practice of making multilingual versions meant that foreign production companies were making films in Spanish, that the Congreso Hispanoamericano de Cinematografía (Spanish American Film Congress) was held in Madrid on October 2–12, 1931, with the aim of taking advantage of the new sound cinema to create a Spanish-language front, bringing together the Spanish-speaking countries of Latin America under the leadership of Spain to counter the expansion of Hollywood cinema made in Spanish. The Congress yielded few tangible results. Ever since their start in 1929 with *Sombras habaneras / Havana Shadows*, produced by Hispania Talking Film Corp. and directed by Cliff Wheeler, Hollywood's Spanish-language films had been seen as a commercial threat, as well as offering an annoying mix of vernacular colloquialisms and accents that was a constant source of complaint on the part of audiences and reviewers. Hollywood's production of films made exclusively in Spanish would end up outstripping its production of multilinguals, thanks to the size of the Spanish-speaking market, and would involve many Spanish film professionals, including (as writers) Edgar Neville, Eduardo Ugarte, José López Rubio, Tono (Antonio de Lara), Gregorio Martínez Sierra, and Enrique Jardiel Poncela, and (as actors) Xavier Cugat, María Alba, Rosita Moreno, José Crespo, and Conchita Montenegro, some of whom would also act in English-language films. The first

Figure 13.1 Poster for *El presidio* (Edgar Neville and Ward Wing, 1931), MGM's Spanish version of its English-language production *The Big House* (George W. Hill, 1931). Private collection.

Spanish-language productions were multilinguals – that is, Spanish versions of English-language productions – but Fox started the practice of filming original scripts in Spanish with Perojo's *Mamá* (1931), based on a play by Martínez Sierra. It continued this practice until 1935, making a total of forty-five films in Spanish, compared to thirteen by MGM and Universal Pictures, six by Warner Bros.–First National Pictures, and five by Columbia Pictures. They were generally second-rate productions, though US film historians have regarded George Melford's *Drácula* (1931), made in Spanish, as superior to Tod Browning's *Dracula* made the same year. Multilingual production continued, however (see Figure 13.1). In 1930, Paramount had set up its multilingual film factory at Joinville-le-Pont, outside Paris, its first Spanish-language production being Perojo's *Un hombre de suerte / A Lucky Man* (1930), also made in French and Swedish versions. Only three Spanish directors were hired at Joinville: Perojo; Luis Fernández Ardavín, as adapter and writer of dialogues; and Florián Rey, as dialogue supervisor. While at Joinville, Rey directed the musical short *Buenos días / Good Morning* (1932). Joinville's Spanish section produced seventeen feature films and two shorts until ending Spanish-language production in December 1932. After that, it devoted itself to dubbing films into Spanish, with Buñuel hired to head the section from September 1932 to the end of 1933.

In 1932 the director Francisco Elías shot the French-language film *Pax* for the French producer Orphea Film in the latter's newly equipped studio in Barcelona (see Chapter 14). The next film made at Orphea's Barcelona studio would be José Buchs' *Carceleras / Prison Songs* (1932), based on the *zarzuela* by Vicente Peydró and Ricardo Flores, with exteriors filmed in Cordoba: the first Spanish sound film shot with direct sound to be exhibited in Spain. The country's technical backwardness restricted the exploitation of films recorded with sound-on-disk systems, and, when sound systems were belatedly installed in Spanish cinemas in the course of the 1932–3 season, sound-on-film was the only option. This put an end to ambiguous formulas such as "just with music" or "semi-sonorized." It also signaled an end to the hybrid solutions of filmed theater or filmed musical performance that in 1931 had threatened to become a veritable epidemic. From now on, sound film would be just that: film.

Listening to Spanish Cinema (Kathleen M. Vernon)

The Role of Dubbing

With the apocalyptic-sounding title "El cine español se asoma al absimo" (Spanish Cinema Nears the Abyss), a February 2011 newspaper article reported a loss of market share during the previous year to the point that nearly ninety percent of the films screened in domestic movie houses were non-Spanish (Belinchón 2011). Although the implications were many, one consequence was that audiences were clearly hearing a lot more of non-Spanish actors such as Johnny Depp, Leonardo DiCaprio, and Colin Firth than they were of Spanish actors such as Luis Tósar, Javier Cámara, and Carmen Machi; or, more accurately, that they were hearing a lot more of the actors and actresses providing the dubbed Spanish voices for the mostly English-speaking performers appearing in the year's top-grossing films. Far from being an anomaly, this statistic reflects the continuing dominance of Spanish markets by foreign-language films, a fact of life since the introduction of sound and one only exacerbated by the development and growth of a highly professional dubbing industry in Spain. The reality is that dubbing is a central factor, the elephant in the sound studio, in any discussion of the sounds and voices of Spanish cinema, or cinema in Spain, and one that should be addressed in any account of film sound in the peninsula. Accordingly, in her prologue to Alejandro Ávila's *La historia del doblaje cinematográfico* (*History of Film Dubbing*), film historian Palmira González calls for the expansion of the field of "nuestro cine" – that is, Spanish cinema history – to include

> No sólo el cine realizado por cineastas autóctonos sino también el cine de origen foráneo que se exhibe en nuestras pantallas y que es visto – y oído – por nuestro

> público y que constituye en buena parte el "clima" cinematográfico que se respira en el país en una época determinada. (Ávila 1997b: 14–15)
>
> Not only the films directed by domestic directors but also the foreign cinema exhibited on our screens that is seen – and heard – by our audiences and that constitutes to a large extent the cinematic "climate" that informs the country during a given era.

The role of dubbing has been a controversial topic since the beginnings of sound cinema in Spain. Although conventionally held to be a politically driven imposition that dates from the first years of the Franco dictatorship, the practice of dubbing initially took hold during the Republic, with the first Spanish dubbing studios established in Barcelona from 1932 onward (Ávila 1997b: 74). The pros and cons of dubbing versus the use of subtitles were amply debated in the press of the period, with arguments distributed in unexpected ways across political lines. Certainly nationalism had its place. As an alternative to the Spanish versions of Hollywood films produced by Paramount and Fox with their pan-Hispanic jumble of accents, films dubbed in Spain had the advantage of preserving the "integrity" of standard Castilian Spanish. Film critics on the left such as Juan Piqueras, while arguing for the need to devote more resources to the production of Spanish films that might better express the national character and explore national problems, also set forth a series of populist and economic arguments in favor of dubbing as a means to ensure access to popular foreign films for a mass audience uncomfortable with or unable to read subtitles, while providing a source of steady employment for actors and technicians in the cinema industry (Ballester Casado 2000: 64, 104–10).

Following the Civil War, the Franco regime made dubbing obligatory, although the April 23, 1941 Ministerial Order proclaming that fact was never published (Gubern 1997: 12–14), as required, in the *Boletín Oficial del Estado*; in fact it initially appeared in print in the Falangist film magazine *Primer Plano*, which also became the subsequent venue for bitter denunciations of the dubbing law on the part of critics, directors, and producers who regarded it as a dagger to the heart of the national film industry.[1] The prohibition of films in languages other than Castilian stayed in effect until 1967, when the establishment of small urban art cinemas (*salas de arte y ensayo*) opened the door to the showing of films in their original languages. Much of the research and writing on the history of dubbing in Spain has dealt with its industrial and ideological consequences, especially the opportunity it presented to Franco-era censors who effectively rewrote dialogue in the passage from the original language to Spanish in the attempt to cleanse films of their transgressive political or sexual charge. But beyond the much-cited anecdotes about films such as *Mogambo* (John Ford, 1953) – where in their zeal to erase evidence of adultery the censors created a case of incest – or *Casablanca* (Michael Curtiz, 1942) – where references to Rick Blaine's (Humphrey Bogart) past as a volunteer for the Republic during the Civil War were wiped from the voice track – there is much more to be learned about the broader cultural and material effects of dubbing.

Figure 13.2 Handbill for the 1950 Spanish release of *Gone with the Wind / Lo que el viento se llevó* (Victor Fleming, 1939; prod. Warner Bros): the effort involved in dubbing the film into Spanish was massive. Private collection.

Scholars such as Ávila, the author of three books on various aspects of dubbing in Spain, have done important work in reconstructing the industrial and political history of the practice, in the process promoting recognition of the professionalism and talent of the actresses and actors working in the sector. Ávila devotes a subchapter of *La historia del doblaje* to the Spanish version of *Gone with the Wind* (Victor Fleming, 1939), which he terms "el gran doblaje de todas las décadas" (the greatest dubbing operation ever) (1997b: 172) (see Figure 13.2). When the film finally arrived for dubbing in Spain in 1947 – due to censorship problems it would not open until 1950 – the prestigious project was assigned to the historic Metro studios in Barcelona. Ávila includes a list of the full Spanish vocal cast with their Hollywood counterparts, led by Elsa Fábregas and Rafael Luis Calvo in the roles of Scarlett O'Hara (played by Vivien Leigh) and Rhett Butler (Clark Gable) respectively. Among the supporting players, he singles out the work of Carmen Robles who, with what he terms her characteristic "pseudo-Cuban" accent, dubbed the role of Mammy (Hattie McDaniel), Scarlett O'Hara's servant. Ávila reports, "La juventud española de los años cincuenta solía gastar bromas en fiestas y reuniones, imitando a la gorda sirvienta negra con su peculiar acento diciendo aquello de [...] 'Zeñorita Ecal·lata'" (Spanish young people of the 1950s used to joke around during parties and get-togethers, imitating the fat black servant with her peculiar accent, repeating the frequently heard phrase ... "Miss Scarlett" [Ávila's phonetic transcription highlights the dubber's exaggerated Caribbean dialect with its use of the *ceceo* and aspirated "s"]) (Ávila 1997b: 175). Among its other potential meanings and impact, *Lo que el viento se llevó* (the Spanish title of *Gone with the Wind*) showcased the impressive level of achievement of the Spanish dubbing industry when drawing upon the best voices and technical resources.

Recently, this line of academic research has been supplemented by a number of websites devoted to recuperating the names and actual voices of these invisible protagonists of Spanish film sound history. One of these, the Internet-based archive and searchable database eldoblaje.com – part online employment office, part nostalgia, and part recuperation of another piece in the mosaic of cultural and historical memory – provides a wealth of resources and suggestions for future study. Its search function allows one to follow the careers of and listen to sample dialogue by the better-known voice actors and actresses of the "golden age" of dubbing: Félix Acaso as the voice of Henry Fonda, Robert Mitchum, David Niven, and Joseph Cotten; Rafael Luis Calvo, hailed for his work as the voice of Clark Gable as well as Stewart Granger, Gregory Peck, and John Wayne; Matilde Conesa, the "voz habitual" (usual voice) for Bette Davis, Lauren Bacall, Jane Wyman, and Jean Arthur; and the great Elsa Fábregas, who, in addition to the voice of Vivien Leigh, regularly dubbed the voices of Katherine Hepburn, Doris Day, and Gena Rowlands, as well as Rita Hayworth in *Gilda* (Charles Vidor, 1946) and Betsy Blair in *Calle Mayor / Main Street* (Juan Antonio Bardem, 1956).[2]

Greater access to these matters allows us to formulate, if not yet answer, a series of questions: How much of a performance and of an actor or actress' star image and relation to spectators is attributable to the voice? What are the consequences for Spanish audiences of never hearing the real voice of a given actor or actress? What is lost and what is gained in the revoicing of foreign stories for domestic consumption? Looking beyond the virtuoso performances of films such as *Lo que el viento se llevó*, it is important to consider an often overlooked consequence of the pervasive practice of dubbing – one arguably more troubling than the loss of the original actorial voices – that has to do with its role in promoting a standardization and typification of voices in Spanish original-language films. In Ávila's book *El doblaje*, which includes a section directed at readers interested in exploring a career in dubbing, he includes a table enumerating a series of theatrical character types (male lead, male villain, female lead, female villain, child, etc.) and their vocal equivalents (1997a: 67). This prescriptive codification in which the male lead is characterized by a deep (*grave*) voice and the female lead by her soft, feminine voice (*dulce y femenina*) alludes to a series of unwritten expectations and rules that continue to shape and restrict the kinds of voices Spanish audiences hear on screen. For, while non-standard voices may be permitted and are even cultivated for comic and character actor parts – one thinks of José Isbert, Rafaela Aparicio, Gracita Morales, and Lola Gaos – leading roles continue to demand the "phonogenic" expression of the unproblematically feminine *dama buena* (virtuous heroine) or appropriately masculine *galán bueno* (virtuous hero).

In practice, this vocal orthodoxy has even led to the dubbing of well-known Spanish actors and (more often) actresses. Particularly striking is the case of the late Emma Penella. Nancy Berthier notes, in a study of *El verdugo / The Executioner* (Luis García Berlanga, 1963), that Penella's voice was considered "tellement inhabituelle" (so unusual) that she was regularly dubbed until director Juan Antonio Bardem "restored" her original voice to her in his 1953 film *Cómicos / Actors* (1998: 86). In consulting eldoblaje.com, we find a list of at least six films in which Penella was dubbed by the likes of Elsa Fábregas and Mireya Mercedes. Given the roiling debates over the topic of dubbing, it is perhaps not suprising to find an article in the film magazine *Radiocinema* devoted to the subject of "La voz de Emma Penella" (The Voice of Emma Penella) (Gil de la Serna 1958). Remarking that Penella was the Spanish star who had created the most work for dubbing studios, the author confesses his incomprehension at the "manía" (mania) afflicting directors who claimed that her voice was not "microfónica" (phonogenic). How is it possible, he asks, that

> Hasta ahora, si exceptuamos a Bardem, directores de la talla de Mur Oti, Sáenz de Heredia, Ruiz Castillo, Ladislao Vadja, etc., de probada solvencia artística, hicieron que la voz de Emma Penella fuese doblada, con la que se nos robaba [...] su voz inconfundible. [...] Es indudable que con esto se hace un mal al espectador y a la misma actriz, pues ni aquél llega a comprender todo el arte de ella, ni ésta llega al espectador con la fuerza y la personalidad que indudablemente tendría si su verdadera voz fuese la oída desde la butaca del cine. (Gil de la Serna 1958: n.p.)

> Until now, with the exception of Bardem, distinguished directors of proven accomplishment, such as Mur Oti, Sáenz de Heredia, Ruiz Castillo, and Ladislao Vajda, have had Emma Penella's voice dubbed, thus robbing us [...] of her unmistakable voice. [...] There is no doubt that this is as damaging for the spectator as for the actress herself, since the former is unable to comprehend the full measure of her art and her performance is prevented from reaching the spectator with the force and personality it would unquestionably possess were her real voice heard in the cinema stalls.

What was it about Penella's voice that led to its silencing? The author of the *Radiocinema* article provides an answer in his defense of the actress: "Emma Penella, entre otras virtudes, tiene la de poseer una voz pastosa, hasta si se quiere demasiado ronca para ser de mujer pero de una atraccíon poderosa" (Emma Penella, among her other virtues, has a rich and mellow voice, perhaps too husky to be thought a woman's voice, but powerfully attractive) (Gil de la Serna 1958: n.p.). In considering the distinctive quality of Penella's voice, we find an example of what Roland Barthes has famously called "the grain of the voice" – a discernable texture or roughness that carries, in Barthes' words "the materiality of the body

Figure 13.3 The embodiment of an aural-corporal eroticism still new to Spanish cinema: Emma Penella *en deshabillé* with Nino Manfredi in *El verdugo* (Luis García Berlanga, 1964; prod. Inter Lagar SA / Zebra Film).

speaking its mother tongue" (1978: 181). In watching and listening to Penella in *Cómicos*, or later as the sensual everywoman Carmen in *El verdugo*, we witness the actress, through the fusion of voice and corporal presence, as the literal embodiment of an eroticism then unwelcome on Spanish screens (see Figure 13.3). What former collaborators Bardem and Berlanga sought in aesthetic and ethical terms through their break with the cinematic *ancien régime* was also communicated in their insistence on using atypical and presumably more authentic voices.

With Franco's censorship long gone, both dubbing and the restrictions on voices in Spanish cinema continue, as does the controversy. In an August 2010 article published in *El País* entitled "El problema más grave del cine español" (Spanish Cinema's Big Problem), John J. Healey offered a drastic diagnosis of the causes of the ongoing crisis in Spanish cinema, stating baldly that "la lengua española tal y como está expresada en España no casa bien con el cine" (the Spanish language, as spoken and expressed in Spain, is incompatible with cinema). The problem, he noted, is that all characters sound alike and speak the same way, with the same gestures and tones of voice across classes, regions, and even languages. The practice of dubbing, in his estimation, bears much responsibility. The most knowledgeable filmgoers, fans, and cinema professsionals, he writes, came to know the films of their favorite foreign directors through the voices of a handful of dubbing actors. With the films' naturalness, authenticity, and spontaneity surpressed, "se impuso el filtro de un castellano duro y revestido de los mismos clichés de tono que se oyen hoy en los teatros de la Gran Vía" (dialogues were heard through the filter of a hard-sounding Castilian Spanish, characterized by the same clichéd intonation patterns heard today in the theaters of Madrid's Gran Vía) (Healey 2010: n.p.). As a consequence, he argues, future directors learned not to value the importance of the voice in acting.

Sound Recording and Design

Interviewed by Patricia Hart in 2006, film editor Leopoldo González Aledo confirmed the opinion of many that in Spanish cinema "el sonido ha sido siempre el niño feo" (sound has always been the ugly stepchild) (Hart 2007: 143). This supposed neglect or tone-deafness when it comes to sound recording and design is generally attributed to the fact that, until relatively recently, Spanish film production relied on postproduction or postsynchronized sound (studio-recorded sound) rather than embracing, as had its more "modern" and "authentic" counterparts in other countries, the use of direct or location sound (sound – at least for dialogue and ambient sound and sound effects – recorded on location). In fact, Spain followed Italy in this practice, as in so many others, well into the 1960s, 1970s, and even 1980s. The original advantages of postproduction sound were primarily practical and economic. Achieving high-quality synchronized sound in either studio or exterior shooting required more advanced equipment and above all strict control over unpredictable surroundings and conditions. During the 1950s and 1960s, when coproductions were common in both countries, postproduction recording of dialogue could easily accommodate the presence of foreign actors. In films such as *Calle Mayor / Main Street* (Bardem, 1956) spectators with passable lip-reading skills can discern the fact that the lead actress, the American Betsy Blair, and the sympathetic Madrid "outsider," played by Yves Massard, are mouthing their lines in French.

The situation began to change, albeit slowly, in 1970 with Carlos Saura's *El jardín de las delicias / The Garden of Delights* (1970) (D'Lugo 1991: 104). As Hart documents in her fascinating 2007 study, it was the arrival in the late 1970s and early 1980s of sound specialists from France (Gilles and Bernard Ortion, Pierre Gamet) and the United Kingdom (James Willis) that initiated a sea change in sound production in Spain. Working with influential directors Fernando Trueba and Pedro Almodóvar on most of their early films, this group was important in the training of many of the current generation of sound specialists.[3]

In many respects, however, too much has been made of the distinction between direct sound and postproduction sound. In practice, most films use a mixture of both, despite the denunciations of the latter by proponents of pure cinema such as Lars von Trier and Jean Marie Straub – for whom postproduction and dialogue replacement produce a "cinema of lies, mental laziness and violence" (Straub and Huillet 1985: 150). The Spanish case provides reasons to question the doctrine of direct sound and the assumption that technology always moves forward if we turn back to consider the irrefutable achievements in the creation of complex and expressive sound worlds by films and filmmakers from the postproduction sound "generation," such as Berlanga and Bardem in *Esa pareja feliz / That Happy Couple* (1951) and Marco Ferreri with *El cochecito / The Motorized Wheelchair* (1960). In their directorial debut, Berlanga and Bardem introduced scenes of overlapping dialogue that would have delighted the English-language master of the technique, Robert Altman, to convey the oppressively chaotic existence of the title couple living in a crowded sublet. In the darkly comic *El cochecito*, whose striking sonic texture has also been studied by Hart (2007: 139–40), the lack of communication that bedevils the three-generation household at the center of the story and leads to the grandfather's murder by poison of his entire family is expressed by the layering of muttered comments, asides, and angry scolding – set against the dissonant sounds of apartment life in mid-century Madrid, including squawking chickens and insistent violin playing – of characters who hardly ever address, and virtually never listen to, each other.

Film Music

Writing in the CD booklet that accompanies José Nieto's contemporary orchestral recording of Juan Quintero's scores for four classic films of the 1940s and early 1950s, Julio Arce laments the near total silence regarding film music and musicians in the 1995 *Historia del cine español* published by Cátedra. In his view, any approach to national cinema history that overlooks the achievements of composers of the stature of Juan Quintero, Manuel Parada, Jesús García Leoz, Antón García Abril, Carmelo Bernaola, or José Nieto can only be considered a "sorda e incompleta historia del cine español" (a deaf and incomplete history of Spanish cinema) (Arce 1998: 5). While recent research by film historians and critics has begun to remedy the situation (Padrol 1986, 2006; Pachón Ramírez 1992, 2007; Álvares 1996; Colón Perales et al. 1997; Cueto 2003; Vernon and Eisen 2006; Fraile Prieto 2010), the artistic and industrial history of film music in Spain remains poorly known to students and scholars of Spanish cinema. Nieto – himself a prolific and influential composer and current director of the sound department at the Madrid Autonomous Community Film and Media School (Escuela de Cinematografía y del Audiovisual de la Comunidad de Madrid (ECAM)) – and Arce have played a central role in filling the critical and musical void with respect to Spain's neglected "golden age" of symphonic film composing and composers in the 1940s and 1950s through their three-volume set of film scores by Quintero (1998), García Leoz (1999), and Parada (2000) issued by the Fundación Autor.

Contrary to the common view of the early post-Civil War film industry as a chronically underfunded operation devoted to the production of pro-Franco propaganda, recent studies have come to reveal a more complex picture of a relatively successful, if minor, national industry modeled on the Hollywood studio system that included a role for symphonic film scores and provided a basic infrastructure designed to support their production. In Arce's estimation, music constitutes what is best about Spanish cinema of the 1940s, and, despite the pervasive censorship and structural deficiencies that left their mark on film content, "la maestría de nuestros compositores [...] manifiesta un nivel equiparable al de Francia, Italia o Estados Unidos" (the mastery of our composers [...] is on the same level as those from France, Italy, or the United States) (1998: 6). In style and scoring practices, Spanish film music and musicians were fully congruent with the international language of post-Romantic symphonism that dominated European and Hollywood film composition. There was no room for avant-garde experimentation here. As Arce notes,

> El cine, a pesar de ser una nueva forma de comunciación artística, era también una industria y la música formaba parte del último engranaje de la producción fílmica; se buscaron aquellos códigos musicales comprensibles a partir de la tradición sínfónica y operística para que la banda sonora fuese efectiva, por encima de su calidad artística en el contexto de la creación musical contemporánea. (Arce 1998: 6–7)

> Cinema, despite being a new form of artistic communication, was also an industry and music formed part of the last stage in the assembly line of film production; for the score to do its work, composers sought out musical codes comprehensible to audiences through their reliance on existing symphonic and operatic traditions, over and above the work's artistic quality in the light of contemporary standards of musical creation.

The 1940s marked the emergence of the first generation of professional film composers in Spain. Earlier scores were the work of musicians such as Joaquín Turina or Ernesto Halffter, whose main focus was the concert hall, with only sporadic incursions into film work (Arce 1999: 6). Roberto Cueto's research on the period testifies to the standing of the film composer, customarily the fourth-highest-paid professional for a film, following the director, scriptwriter, and producer (although presumably certain highly coveted stars earned higher salaries; see Chapter 10). Significantly, from the 1930s onward, film composers were guaranteed separate authorship rights to their music for film by the Spanish Authors and Publishers Collecting Society (Sociedad General de Autores y Editores (SGAE)) (Cueto 2003: 27). Nevertheless, the resemblance to the Hollywood model only went so far. Arce reports that instead of working with independent departments responsible for the different functions or stages in the elaboration of a film score (composition, orchestration, direction, and recording), as was the practice in Hollywood studios, composers such as Quintero and García Leoz were responsible for the whole process, from composition and orchestration to hiring the musicians, directing rehearsals, conducting the performance, and even participating in the mixing of the soundtrack (Arce 1998: 12, 1999: 5).

In the decades that followed, despite the country's ongoing political marginalization, developments in Spanish film music largely paralleled tendencies in the rest of Europe. The 1950s brought about a change in subject matter and modes of production away from the genre cinema and studio shooting that dominated the previous period and toward location filming and "critical realism" (Cueto 2003: 30). With the dismantling of many of the studios, film production could no longer sustain the needs of symphonic scores. Spanish critical realism, Álvares tells us, required "un tipo diferente de música" (a different type of music) (1996: 194). Cueto compares the scores for Berlanga's films to the intellectualized populist ("un tono populista deliberadamente intelectualizado") compositions of Nino Rota for Fellini's first films (2003: 31). The subsequent Spanish "New Wave" directors, grouped under the banner of the Nuevo Cine Español (New Spanish Cinema) of the 1960s, shared common ground with their counterparts in the world of Spanish concert music. A group of young composers – members of the so-called Generation of '51 including Luis de Pablo, Carmelo Bernaola, Antón García Abril, Cristóbal Halffter, and Antonio Pérez Olea who banded together under the rubric of Nueva Música (New Music) – sought nothing less than to bring Spanish classical music into the (mid-)twentieth century and out of the isolation imposed by the Civil War and Francoist cultural values and policies. The majority combined their work as "serious" composers (in that sense returning to the pre-"golden age" model) with collaborations with directors such as Carlos Saura, Basilio Martín Patino, Miguel Picazo, Antxon Eceiza, Mario Camus, and later Víctor Erice and Manuel Gutiérrez Aragón. The exception to the dominant strain of cinematic and musical modernism among this group was the extraordinarily versatile García Abril, who early in his career became an assiduous collaborator of director Pedro Lazaga, responsible for the scores of films such as *La ciudad no es para mí / City Life is Not for Me* (1965) and *Vente a Alemania, Pepe / Come to Germany, Pepe* (1971) (Hernández Ruíz and Pérez Rubio 2002). By the late 1970s, however, this second burst of film musical creativity had run its course, as most of the New Music composers retired from film work and the art cinema paradigm lost its dominance. During the 1980s, the majority of films had recourse to prerecorded music and popular songs. Tight budgets resulted in ever-poorer working conditions for recording and synchronization, a situation that would have shocked the filmmakers and composers of the 1940s.

Such was the immediate context for the emergence of a group of widely celebrated film composers in the 1990s, including Alberto Iglesias, Roque Baños, Carles Cases, Ángel Illarramendi, Bingen Mendizábal, and Eva Gancedo. If the work of Luis de Pablo and others of his generation often evinced a modernist discomfort with the conventions of the classic film score, composers such as Iglesias and Baños in their collaborations with Julio Medem and Pedro Almodóvar or Álex de la Iglesia and Santiago Segura, respectively, proposed a new normativity for film music. Indeed, since 1990 Spanish cinema has seen a rebirth of the large-scale and symphonic film score, favored by higher film production budgets, technological advances in digital recording and Dolby sound, and a new recognition of film music as recorded music evident in regular releases of Spanish film scores

(Cueto 2003; Kennedy 2001). Michel Chion identifies a parallel phenomenon in European and Hollywood cinema over the same period – an era he cinematically dubs "back to the future" – consisting not of a simple return to traditional musical practices but of an opportunity for innovation based both on technical advances in film sound recording and projection and on dialogue with earlier symphonic traditions (1995: 152–4). Thanks to their training and experience in classical as well as contemporary idioms, including jazz, rock, folk, and electronic music, the creative identity of these Spanish composers is tied to an ability to integrate a range of musical styles and discourses (Saenz de Tejada 1994). Iglesias is perhaps the most recognizable and certainly the most successful representative of this group. The winner of nine Goya awards for Best Film Score; an Oscar nominee for *The Constant Gardener* (Fernando Meirelles, 2005), *The Kite Runner* (Marc Forster, 2007), and *Tinker, Tailor, Spy* (Thomas Alfredson, 2011); and celebrated for his work with Steven Soderbergh and the "guest appearance" of an excerpt from his score for Medem's *Lucía y el sexo / Lucía and Sex* (2001) in an episode of the US television series *Mad Men*, Iglesias has achieved a level of visibility and renown rare for any film composer and unheard of among Spanish practitioners of the form.

Notes

1 The text of the law reads as follows: "Queda prohibida la proyección cinematográfica en otro idioma que no sea el español, salvo autorización especial, que concederá el Sindicato Nacional del Espectáculo, de acuerdo con el Ministerio de Industria y Comercio y siempre que las películas en cuestión hayan sido previamente dobladas. El doblaje debe realizarse en estudios españoles que radiquen en territorio nacional y por personal español" (The projection of cinema in any language other than Spanish is prohibited, except through special authorization by the National Entertainment Syndicate in accordance with the Ministry of Industry and Commerce, and only following the prior dubbing of the films in question. Dubbing must be carried out in Spanish studios on Spanish territory by Spanish personnel) (cited in Ávila 1997b: 158).

2 A clip of the Elsa Fábregas-dubbed version of Scarlett O'Hara's "As God is my witness" scene is available on YouTube: www.youtube.com/watch?v=IwFgmZDfKtI.

3 It is notable that the Goya awards have included a Best Sound category from their first iteration in 1987 (see the Wikipedia entry "Anexo: Premio Goya al mejor sonido") although the prize designation apparently does not distinguish between work in sound recording, mixing, editing, and Foley (sound) effects.

References

Álvares, R. (1996) *La harmonía que rompe el silencio: Conversaciones con José Nieto*. Valladolid: Semana Internacional de Cine.

"Anexo: Premio Goya al mejor sonido" (n.d.) Online at: http://es.wikipedia.org/wiki/Anexo:Premio_Goya_al_mejor_sonido (accessed September 25, 2011).

Arce, J. (1998) *José Nieto dirige la música de Juan Quintero (CD booklet)*. Madrid: Fundación Autor / Polygram Ibérica, S. A.

Arce, J. (1999) *José Nieto dirige la música de Jesús García Leoz (CD booklet)*. Madrid: Fundación Autor / Karonte.

Arce, J. (2000) *José Nieto dirige la música de Manuel Parada (CD booklet)*. Madrid: Fundación Autor / Iberautor Promocciones Culturales, S. R. L.

Ávila, A. (1997a) *El doblaje*. Madrid: Cátedra.

Ávila, A. (1997b) *La historia del doblaje*. Barcelona: CIMS.

Ballester Casado, A. (2000) *Traducción y nacionalismo: La recepción del cine americano en España a través del doblaje*. Granada: Editorial Comares.

Barthes, R. (1978) The Grain of the Voice. In: *Image, Music, Text*. New York: Hill and Wang, pp. 179–89.

Belinchón, G. (2011) El cine español se asoma al abismo. *El País* (February 7). Online at: www.elpais.com/articulo/cultura/cine/espanol/asoma/abismo/elpepicul/20110207elpepicul_4/Tes?print=1 (accessed September 24, 2011).

Berthier, N. (1998) Prénom Carmen (Images de la femme dans *El verdugo*). In: Larraz, E. (ed.) *El verdugo*. Dijon: Hispanistica XX, pp. 83–105.

Chion, M. (1995) *La Musique au cinéma*. Paris: Fayard.

Colón Perales, C., Infante del Rosal, F., and Lombardo Ortega, M. (eds.) (1997) *Historia y teoría de la música en el cine: Presencias afectivas*. Seville: Alfar.

Cueto, R. (2003) *El lenguaje invisible: Entrevistas con compositores del cine español*. Alcalá de Henares: Festival de Cine de Alcalá de Henares.

D'Lugo, M. (1991). *The Films of Carlos Saura*. Princeton: Princeton University Press.

"Elsa Fabregas doblaje *Lo que el viento se llevo*." Online at: www.youtube.com/watch?v=IwFgmZDfKtI (accessed February 1, 2011).

Fraile Prieto, T. (2010) *Música de cine en España*. Badajoz: Festival Ibérico de Cine.

Gil de la Serna, A. (1958) La voz de Emma Penella. *Radiocinema* 407 (May 10): n.p.

Gubern, R. (1997) Prólogo. In: Ávila, A. *La censura del doblaje en España*. Barcelona: CIMS, pp. 11–17.

Harper, G. (2009) *Sound and Music in Film and Visual Media*. New York: Continuum.

Hart, P. (2007) Sound Ideas or Unsound Practices? Listening for "Spanishness" in Peninsular Film. In: Sánchez-Conejero, C. (ed.) *Spanishness in the Spanish Novel and Cinema of the 20th–21st Century*. Newcastle upon Tyne: Cambridge Scholars, pp. 133–46.

Healey, J. J. (2010) El problema más grave del cine español. *El País* (August 2). Online at: www.elpais.com/articulo/opinion/problema/grave/cine/espanol/elpepiopi/20100802elpepiopi_10/Tes (accessed February 1, 2011).

Hernández Ruíz, J. and Pérez Rubio, P. (2002) *Antón García Abril: El cine y la televisión*. Zaragoza: Diputación Provincial de Zaragoza.

Kennedy, S. A. (2001) Film Scores from Spain. *Film Score Monthly* (May 28). Online at: www.filmscoremonthly.com/articles/2001/28_May---Film_Scores_from_Spain.asp (accessed September 1, 2011).

Pachón Ramírez, A. (1992) *La música contemporánea en el cine*. Badajoz: Diputación Provincial de Badajoz.

Pachón Ramírez, A. (2007) *Música y cine: Géneros para una generación*. Badajoz: Festival Ibérico de Cine.

Padrol, J. (ed.) (1986) *Evolución de la banda sonora en España: Carmelo Bernaola*. Alcalá de Henares: 16 Festival de Cine de Alcalá de Henares.

Padrol, J. (2006) *Conversaciones con músicos de cine*. Badajoz: Festival Ibérico de Cine.

Sáenz de Tejada, I. (1994) El ojo que escucha. *El País* (May 30): n.p. Online at: http://elpais.com/diario/1994/05/30/cultura/770248803_850215.html (accessed April 25, 2012).

Sider, L., Freeman, D., and Sider, J. (2003) *Soundscape: The School of Sound Lectures 1998–2001*. London: Wallflower.

Straub, J.-M. and Huillet, D. (1985) Direct Sound: An Interview with Jean-Marie Straub and Danièle Huillet. In: Weiss, E. and Belton, J. (eds.) *Theory and Practice of Film Sound*. New York: Columbia University Press, pp. 150–3.

Vernon, K. M. and Eisen, C. (2006) Contemporary Spanish Film Music: Carlos Saura and Pedro Almodóvar. In: Mera, M. and Burnand, D. (eds.) *European Film Music*. London: Ashgate, pp. 41–59.

Further Reading

Altman, R. (ed.) (1992) *Sound Theory, Sound Practice*. London: Routledge.

Ávila, A. (1997) *La censura del doblaje en España*. Barcelona: CIMS.

Belaygue, C. (ed.) (1988) *Le Passage du muet au parlant*. Toulouse: Cinémathèque de Toulouse / Éditions Milan.

Cerdán, J. (1998) Técnica y estética: Apuntes para una aproximación a algunos aspectos del primer cine sonoro español. *Vértigo* 13–14 (November): 37–43.

Chion, M. (2003) *Film, a Sound Art*. New York: Columbia University Press.

De la Escalera, M. (1971) *Cuando el cine rompió a hablar*. Madrid: Taurus.

Doane, M. A. (1985) Ideology and the Practice of Sound Editing and Mixing. In: Weiss, E. and Belton, J. (eds.) *Theory and Practice of Film Sound*. New York: Columbia University Press, pp. 54–62.

Fernández Colorado, L. and Cerdán, J. (2007) *Ricardo Urgoiti: Los trabajos y los días*. Madrid: Filmoteca Española.

García de Dueñas, J. (1993) *¡Nos vamos a Hollywood!* Madrid: Nickelodeón.

Gubern, R., Heinink, J. B., Berriatúa, L., et al. (1993) *El paso del mudo al sonoro en el cine español (Actas del IV Congreso de la AEHC)*. Madrid: Editorial Complutense.

Gubern, R. (1994) *Benito Perojo: Pionerismo y supervivencia*. Madrid: Filmoteca Española.

Heinink, J. B. and Dickson, R. G. (1990) *Cita en Hollywood*. Bilbao: Mensajero.

Hernández Girbal, F. (1992) *Los que pasaron por Hollywood*. Madrid: Verdoux.

Sánchez Vidal, A. (1991) *El cine de Florián Rey*. Zaragoza: Caja de Ahorros de la Inmaculada de Aragón.

Part VI

The Film Apparatus

Production, Infrastructure, and Audiences

14

Censorship, Film Studios, and Production Companies

Josetxo Cerdán, Román Gubern, Jo Labanyi, Steven Marsh, Tatjana Pavlović, and Nuria Triana Toribio

Film Censorship (Román Gubern)

This section provides a brief survey of the organization of state censorship of cinema in Spain from its beginnings to its abolition in 1977. Although the Spanish film industry has always remained in private hands, even during the Franco dictatorship (unlike in Nazi Germany and fascist Italy), the existence of some form of state censorship for much of its history has been a major factor affecting what could or could not be produced – other factors being the availability of finance (tied up with censorship, as we shall see) and questions of audience taste. Chapter 2 shows how producers found ways of getting round the censors; directors too became adept at strategies of evasion, while a major consequence of censorship was the creation of active spectators ever ready to read between the lines – sometimes imagining things that were not the case, as with the widespread popular supposition that the censors had prevented Spanish audiences from seeing Rita Hayworth strip completely in *Gilda* (Charles Vidor, 1946), and not just remove that famous glove. Nonetheless, contestation had its limits and the restrictive effects of censorship on the film industry were all too real.

Film censorship was first instituted in Spain by the November 27, 1912 Royal Decree of the Ministerio de Gobernación (Interior Ministry), ratified the following year at the request of the Governor of Barcelona, the city that acted as the national distribution center. The censorship office was consequently established in Barcelona, with a further office in Madrid set up in 1914, creating a two-pronged control mechanism operating independently in both cities. This system allowed Barcelona, from 1912, to authorize the exhibition of hardcore pornographic

A Companion to Spanish Cinema, First Edition. Edited by Jo Labanyi and Tatjana Pavlović.

movies in certain theaters, after the last evening session. The Catholic Church in Spain, as the official religion of state, followed a notably conservative line, and many mayors, under pressure from local priests, practised additional forms of censorship, provoking protests from film professionals.

In 1921 the Ministerio de Estado (Foreign Ministry) established the Oficina de Relaciones Culturales (Office of Cultural Relations) to defend Spain's public image and culture, including cinema, abroad. Following its instructions, Spanish embassies protested against foreign films that treated sensitive issues, such as Spain's defeat in the Spanish–American colonial war of 1898 in Cuba and the Philippines, and the government threatened to ban the films of certain foreign production companies. Films attacked included *Les Opprimés / Flanders under Philip II* (Henri Roussell, 1922), starring Raquel Meller, accused of offering a brutal image of Spanish rule in Flanders; *Rosita* (Ernst Lubitsch, 1923), for its depraved depiction of an eighteenth-century Bourbon monarch; and *Don Q. Son of Zorro* (Donald Crisp, 1925), set in Madrid, whose hero flirted with the queen (it was approved after revising the intertitles so as to set the action in Mexico). Also found offensive was *Carmen* (Jacques Feyder, 1926), again starring Raquel Meller, though it was eventually authorized. In 1926, the government threatened to ban all MGM films if the studio did not withdraw from distribution *Valencia* (Dimitri Buchowetzki, 1926) and, later, *The Road to Romance* (John S. Robertson, 1927), which in the end was released with major cuts. Other offending films were *The Two Lovers* (Fred Niblo, 1928), set under Spain's occupation of Flanders, and *In Gay Madrid* (Robert Z. Leonard, 1930), based on Alejandro Pérez Lugín's 1915 novel and 1925 film *La casa de la Troya / College Boarding House*. From 1929, a tiny number of Soviet films were authorized for exhibition to minority audiences at Madrid and Barcelona film clubs, with special permits, such as Sergei Eisenstein's *Battleship Potemkin* (1925) and *Old and New* (1929), and Pudovkin's *Storm over Asia* (1929).

Spanish silent films also underwent censorship, which was particularly strict under the Primo de Rivera dictatorship of 1923–30. Banned films included *Venganza isleña / Island Revenge* (Manuel Noriega, 1924), the remarkable 1924 French–Spanish coproduction *La Galerie des monsters / La barraca de los monstruos / Gallery of Monsters* (Jaque Catelain, 1924), and *El héroe de Cascorro / The Hero of Cascorro* (Emilio Bautista, 1929), set in the Cuban War of Independence, which was not released until 1932 under the Second Republic.

The two-pronged system, with censors' offices in Barcelona and Madrid, ended with the April 14, 1930 Royal Decree, which centralized censorship in the Dirección General de Seguridad (General Directorate of Security) in Madrid but gave the Governor of Barcelona control of film comedies and newsreels. Neither office had clear guidelines on what was considered tolerable, though both took a highly conservative stance.

With the monarchy's replacement by a Republican regime on April 14, 1931, censorship was again decentralized and put under the control of the governors of Madrid and Barcelona, under the Order of June 18, 1931. In October 1931, the first

Congreso Hispanoamericano de Cinematografía (Spanish American Film Congress), held in Madrid, stressed the importance of ensuring that foreign films gave a "correct" image of those Spanish-speaking countries in which they were set, threatening with sanctions any offending production company. Censorship hardened notably under the conservative government from November 1933 to February 1936. In December 1933, Luis Buñuel screened his documentary *Las Hurdes / Land without Bread*, without sound and with the director improvising a commentary, but the government banned the film, advising its embassies to look out for any overseas screenings. The film was not shown again in Madrid until April 1936, after the Popular Front's February election victory. In April 1935, the Governor of Barcelona prohibited nudist and gangster films, while in May 1935 Buñuel's *L'Âge d'or* (1930) was banned at the Surrealist Exhibition in Tenerife. In October 1935, the government ordered Paramount to destroy the negative of Josef von Sternberg's *The Devil Is a Woman*, considered offensive to the Civil Guard, threatening to ban all Paramount productions. It seems that, under pressure from the US State Department, at the time negotiating a trade deal with Spain, Paramount burned a supposed negative of the film in the presence of an official from the Spanish Embassy. This incident led to an Interior Ministry Order of October 25, 1935 banning all films "que traten de desnaturalizar hechos históricos o tiendan a menoscabar el prestigio debido a instituciones o personalidades de nuestra patria" (that attempt to misrepresent historical events or undermine the prestige of our fatherland's institutions or public figures). Soviet cinema was treated harshly by the censors during this period of conservative rule, to the point that the magazine *Nuestro Cinema* ran a survey in August 1935 in which the writers Francisco Ayala, Antonio Espina, Federico García Lorca, and Ramón J. Sender protested at its banning.

With the fascist uprising against the Republic in July 1936, triggering Civil War, both the Nationalist and Republican authorities paid considerable attention to censorship, especially of films with political or military content. On the rebel side, from September 1936 the military command of the Army of the South obliged reporters and laboratories to submit their footage to their control, while the Army, as it advanced, confiscated films deemed subversive or immoral. A Junta de Censura (Censorship Board) was set up in Seville on December 8, 1936; given the geographic split between the northern and southern territories under rebel control, another Censorship Board was set up in La Coruña on March 27, 1937. Both Boards included representatives of the army, the Spanish Fascist Party (Falange Española), the Catholic Church, and industry – there were frequent disagreements when the industrialists saw their commercial interests threatened by the Boards' intolerance. On May 29, 1937, prior censorship of scripts was instituted, and on October 19 both Boards were put under the new Delegación del Estado para Prensa y Propaganda (State Delegation for Press and Propaganda). On November 18, 1937, the Junta Superior de Censura Cinematográfica (Higher Film Censorship Board) was set up in Salamanca (later transferred to Burgos) and for a while coexisted with the board in Seville. In January 1938, Franco formed his first government, putting the new Departamento Nacional de Cinematografía (National Cinema Department) under the Dirección General de Propaganda (General Directorate of Propaganda), within the Interior Ministry. In June 1938, this new department asked the Foreign Ministry to inform it of foreign films about the Civil War. The ensuing surveillance threatened to ban the films of companies producing or distributing "offensive" films – such as *Blockade* (William Dieterle, 1938), distributed by United Artists. On November 2, 1938, the Interior Ministry created the Comisión de Censura Cinematográfica (Film Censorship Commission), under a newly defined Higher Film Censorship Board, responsible for documentaries and newsreels as well as for reviewing decisions and appeals. Upon the Nationalist occupation of Barcelona and Madrid in 1939, Comisiones Provisionales de Censura (Provisional Censorship Commissions) were set up, under military control, to inspect the vast amount of film stock in the two cities and to reorganize the operation of movie theaters.

After Nationalist victory, on July 15, 1939 obligatory prior censorship of scripts was instituted for all forms of entertainment, and in September cinema attendance was banned for minors under the age of fourteen. A casualty of the new climate was Edgar Neville's *Frente de Madrid / Madrid Front* (1939), a Spanish–Italian coproduction: despite the fact that Neville had made wartime documentaries for the rebels, the film's end, showing the fraternization in a shell crater of two seriously wounded enemy soldiers, was mutilated. And the propaganda film *El crucero Baleares / Warship Baleares* (Enrique del Campo, 1941), produced by RKO to help the United States compete against Germany and Italy in the Spanish film market, was banned for its poor quality and its naval officers' frivolous intrigues. In the same period, the German Embassy complained about excessively strict censorship of German films, which had already undergone censorship in Germany. From April 2, 1940, it was forbidden to mention in film credits and publicity the names of Hollywood film professionals who had supported the Republic, such as Charlie Chaplin, Joan Crawford, Bette Davis, Bing Crosby, James Cagney, Lewis Milestone, or Clifford Odets. Further, the institution of obligatory dubbing into Spanish in April 1941 (calqued on Mussolini's similar decree of October 1930) facilitated manipulation of the dialogue (for dubbing in Spain, see Chapter 13).

May 20, 1941 saw the creation of the Vicesecretaría de Educación Popular (Sub-Secretariat of Popular Education), which in October assumed overall control of the media (its name evoked Mussolini's Ministry of Popular Culture). The Dirección General de Cine y Teatro (General Directorate of Film and Theater) and its censorship offices were placed under this Sub-Secretariat. The cycle of propaganda films aimed at legitimizing the 1936 uprising – whose high point was *Raza / Race* (1942), based on a script by Franco – came to an end in 1942 when World War II swung in the Allies' favor. This motivated the creation in December 1942 of the state-controlled newsreel NO-DO (Noticiarios y Documentales / Newreels and Documentaries; see Chapter 18); it was given a monopoly over newsreel production and its screening was made mandatory in movie theaters, thus eliminating Movietone Fox, the German UFA, and the Italian Luce from the market. The control of film content was enhanced from 1943 through a system of state subsidies to production companies, the amount corresponding to the state rating of each film's content. From June 1944 the top rating was given the name "Interés Nacional" (National Interest), granted to those films "que contengan muestras inequívocas de exaltación de valores raciales y de enseñanzas de nuestros principios morales y políticos" (that unequivocally exalt racial values and transmit our moral and political principles) (Gubern 1981: 79). As Allied victory loomed, financial incentives were given to escapist literary adaptations set in the nineteenth century, while foreign films referring to the Civil War were banned and Falangist groups boycotted English-language Allied propaganda films. Sam Wood's 1943 Hemmingway adaptation *For Whom the Bell Tolls* led to the government's blocking of Paramount imports for several years. The censors also altered the dialogues referring to the Civil War in Michael Curtiz's *Casablanca* (1942), Orson Welles' *The Lady from Shanghai* (1948), and Lewis Milestone's *Arch of Triumph* (1948). When Spanish cinema resumed treatment of the Civil War from a politically distanced perspective, with Lorenzo Llobet Gràcia's *Vida en sombras / Life in Shadows* (1948), bureaucratic problems prevented its release until 1953.

In June 1946 the Censorship Board was given the sanitized name of Junta Superior de Orientación Cinematográfica (Higher Film Guidance Board), with the Church censor granted a veto. In 1947 there were two scandals: Rafael Gil's *La Fe / The Faith*, whose heroine falls in love with a priest, and the release in Spain of Vidor's *Gilda* (1946), starring Rita Hayworth, which prompted protests from bishops and from Catholic posses in film theaters. Reacting against what it saw as the excessive permissiveness of state censorship, in March 1950 the Comisión Episcopal de Ortodoxia y Moralidad (Episcopal Commission for Orthodoxy and Morality) created the Oficina Nacional Clasificadora de Espectáculos (National Entertainment Classification Office), to guide Catholic viewers; it succeeded in getting Catholic newspapers to ban advertising for blacklisted films.

July 18, 1951 saw the establishment of the Ministerio de Información y Turismo (Ministry of Information and Tourism), under Gabriel Arias Salgado, whose Catholic fundamentalism was reinforced by the 1953 Concordat with the Vatican. Responsibility for entertainment passed to this new ministry. Until March 1952, José María García Escudero was in charge of the ministry's cinema policy, but he resigned over his "excessively liberal" support of José Antonio Nieves Conde's 1951 film *Surcos / Furrows*, which dealt with the problems of rural emigration to the cities, and his attempt to refuse the award of "National Interest" to Juan de Orduña's glorification of the discovery of America, *Alba de America / Dawn of America* (1951), made with state support to counter David MacDonald's British film *Christopher Columbus* (1949), considered insulting to Spain. García Escudero's successor, Joaquín Argamasilla, was sacked in 1955 over the two different versions of the historical coproduction *La princesa de Éboli / That Lady*, made in Spain by Terence Young, whose British version was deemed offensive to Spain. The practice of making double versions had started shortly before with the producer-director Ignacio F. Iquino, who added erotic shots to his films for export. This commercial ploy provoked a scandal when his 1960 film *Juventud a la intemperie / The Unsatisfied* was released in Brussels with the title *La Reine du strip-tease / The Queen of Strip-tease* just before the royal wedding of Bauduoin of Belgium to the Spanish Fabiola Mora; Spanish officials rushed to see the film, discovering to their surprise that it was Spanish. Foreign films, often with the distributors' complicity, had their plotlines and dialogues changed to satisfy the censors. In John Ford's *Mogambo* (1953), Donald Sinden and Grace Kelly (a married couple) were made into brother and sister so her relationship with Clark Gable would not appear adulterous; the result was barely disguised incest. The censors' rigor did not stop Church protests nor the withdrawal of authorized films. The Bishop of the Canaries threatened to excommunicate anyone who went to see the Italian film *Riso amaro / Bitter Rice* (Giuseppe de Santis, 1948).

Cuts were made to Spanish films of the calibre of *¡Bienvenido Mister Marshall! / Welcome Mr. Marshall!* (1953) and *Los jueves, milagro / Miracles of Thursday* (1957), both by Luis García Berlanga, who tried to list the censors as co-screenwriters for the latter. Other cases were Juan Antonio Bardem's *Muerte de un ciclista / Death of a Cyclist* (1955), *Calle Mayor / Main Street* (1956), and *La venganza / Vengeance* (1957); Antonio del Amo's *Sierra maldita / Cursed Mountain* (1954); and Nieves Conde's *El inquilino / The Tenant* (1957), which, after being authorized, was withdrawn and forced to undergo further editing. The Italian director Marco Ferreri saw his film *El pisito / The Little Apartment* (1958) banned for six months and the end of *El cochecito / The Motorized Wheelchair* (1960) altered. Spanish filmmakers' indignation at state film policy was aired at the Salamanca Conversations of May 1955 (see "Film Clubs" in Chapter 15), which demanded a censorship code to counter the censors' arbitrariness and film clubs' exemption from censorship.

The censors' arbitrariness gave rise to paradoxical situations (see Figure 14.1 and Figure 14.2). They failed to pick up the homosexual choreographic fantasies of Luis María Delgado's 1961 *Diferente / Different*, starring the dancer Alfredo Alaria (see Chapter 12), and in the same year authorized *Viridiana*, Buñuel's first film made in Spain since his Mexican exile, only to subsequently ban it after the angry comments of the Vatican newspaper *L'Osservatore Romano* on the film's submission as Spain's entry to the Cannes Film Festival, where it won the top prize. José Muñoz Fontán, in charge of film policy, was sacked and *Viridiana* would not be shown in Spain until 1977. Its production company, UNINCI, formed by various Communist professionals under Bardem's chairmanship, suffered sanctions and Bardem had to make his next film, *Los inocentes / The Innocents* (1962), in Buenos Aires.

The evolution of Spanish society thanks to economic development produced a cabinet reshuffle in July 1962, with Manuel Fraga Iribarne appointed Minister of Information and Tourism. Fraga Iribarne introduced a more flexible, modernizing

Figure 14.1 Publicity for the Barcelona premiere of *Gilda* (Charles Vidor, 1946; prod. Columbia Pictures) in the magazine *Fotogramas* (January 1, 1948). Rita Hayworth's dress has been touched up by the censors to cover her bare shoulders. Sony Pictures © 1946, renewed 1973 Columbia Pictures Industries, Inc. All Rights Reserved. Courtesy of Columbia Pictures.

Figure 14.2 A similar image of Rita Hayworth in *Gilda* (see Figure 14.1) appeared shortly before in *¡Hola!* magazine (December 20, 1947), announcing the film's Madrid premiere. This time the censors let Rita Hayworth's bare shoulders through; censorship was arbitrary. Sony Pictures © 1946, renewed 1973 Columbia Pictures Industries, Inc. All Rights Reserved. Courtesy of Columbia Pictures.

cultural policy, naming the reformist García Escudero – who had participated in the Salamanca Conversations – as Director General of Film and Theater. García Escudero instituted a Censorship Code in February 1963: its criteria included the banning of apologies for suicide, euthanasia, revenge crimes and duels, divorce, adultery, illicit sexual relations, prostitution, abortion, or contraception; the representation of sexual perversions, drug addiction, alcoholism, or overly explicit crimes; scenes of brutality and cruelty or that were in bad taste; antireligious sentiment, historical misrepresentations, incitement to racial or class hatred, or questioning the duty to defend the fatherland; and slurs against the Catholic Church, the fundamental principles of the regime, national dignity, or the person of the head of state. This "liberalizing" measure had its hiccups. After sounding out the ministry, in 1963 CIFESA imported Fellini's *La dolce vita* (1959), which the minister had expressed willingness to authorize with minor cuts, to show off the new liberal attitude. But his good intentions were frustrated by the veto of the Church representatives on the censorship board.

Despite its many restrictions, the Censorship Code raised Spanish film directors' hopes somewhat, particularly with the August 1964 Orden para el Desarrollo de la Cinematografía Nacional (Order for National Cinema Development), which introduced new subsidies as an incentive to the new directors emerging from the Escuela Oficial de Cine (EOC; Official Film School) to stimulate an auteurist cinema with higher artistic standards – an equivalent of the French New Wave, able to compete at international festivals. Although the censorship criteria applied to both Spanish and imported films, Spanish films had to undergo prior censorship of their scripts. The new system initiated a "controlled dissent," since the new, young directors were invited to present innovative projects to win subsidies but with censorship acting as a brake on what they could get away with – this tense situation explains the nervous quality of much of the Nuevo Cine Español (NCE; New Spanish Cinema) of the time. Saura's *La Caza / The Hunt* (1965) was forced to drop its original title *La caza del conejo / The Rabbit Hunt* because of its sexual connotations (*conejo* being slang for "cunt") and to cut its mentions of the Civil War. In fact, censorship restrictions helped to shape the very personal elliptical style of Saura's powerful allegorical and symbolic films about the dictatorship, such as *El jardín de las delicias / The Garden of Delights* (1970), banned for six months, and *Ana y los lobos / Anna and the Wolves* (1972), which underwent several cuts. Some notable titles of the New Spanish Cinema suffered mutilation, such as Mario Camus' *Los farsantes / The Actors* (1964/8), Miguel Picazo's *La tía Tula / Aunt Tula* (1964, five minutes cut), Manuel Summers' *La niña de luto / The Girl in Mourning* (1964) and *Juguetes rotos / Broken Toys* (1966), and Francisco Regueiro's *Amador* (1965), among others. And, when Jaime Camino's *España, otra vez / Spain Again* (1968) chose as its protagonist an American who had served as a surgeon in the International Brigades – the first anti-Franco militant to appear as a positive character in the cinema of the dictatorship – the censors insisted on massive cuts to the script, with warnings such as:

> En la realización de la película se deberá evitar cuidadosamente todo aquello que, de una manera implícita o explícita, pueda suponer una referencia o interpretación de nuestra guerra que no tenga un carácter absolutamente integrador, así como la presentación de aspectos negativos de la vida española actual a los que pudiera darse, dentro del contexto de la obra, un significado inconveniente. (anonymous censor's report)

> In making the film, care must be taken to avoid anything that could, implicitly or explicitly, be taken as a mention or interpretation of our war that is not clearly in a reconciliatory spirit, as well as any depiction of negative aspects of Spanish life that, in the film's context, could take on an inappropriate meaning.

The script of Camino's next film, *Un invierno en Mallorca / A Winter in Majorca* (1969), based on Georges Sand's autobiographical text, was initially banned, judged by the censors to offer an image of "la España negra" (Black Spain), and underwent numerous amputations.

On January 12, 1967, *salas especiales* (special exhibition venues) – including *salas de arte y ensayo* (art cinemas) – were authorized in cities with populations of over fifty thousand and with a maximum capacity of five hundred spectators; these were licensed to show films in their original uncut versions. The contrast between their programming (films by Polanski, Losey, Pasolini, Glauber Rocha) and Spanish film production made clear the discriminatory effects of censorship. On occasions, the state threatened producers with sanctions for "anti-Spanish" projects, such as Fred Zinnemann's *Behold a Pale Horse* (1964), which led to a ban on imports of Columbia Pictures productions and closure of its Spanish office.

The frustration of young Spanish filmmakers exploded at the Primeras Jornadas Internacionales de Escuelas de Cinematografía (First International Symposium of Film Schools) held at Sitges from 1–6 October 1967, whose conclusions – drafted by Joaquín Jordá, Antonio Artero, Julián Marcos, and Manuel Revuelta – included criticism of the Salamanca Conversations' "reformism," demanding an end to censorship and to all official control of the industry (see the section on film festivals in Chapter 15). In November 1967, for economic reasons, the General Directorate of Cinema and Theater was axed, replaced by a Dirección General de Cultura Popular y Espectáculos (General Directorate of Popular Culture and Entertainment), under Carlos Robles Piquer. This coincided with the emergence of the Escuela de Barcelona (Barcelona School), with its experimental and avant-garde tendencies, which Jordá justified with the statement "como no podemos hacer Victor Hugo, hacemos Mallarmé" (since we can't do Victor Hugo, we do Mallarmé) (Riambau and Torreiro 1999: 122). The Barcelona School came to a close with Carlos Durán's 1970 *Liberxina 90*, a political fiction film that, despite being invited to participate at the Venice Biennale, was first banned and then mutilated. José María Nunes also saw his *Sexperiencias / Sexperiences* banned in 1969, despite its script having been approved. The *apertura* (liberalization) of 1963 came to a definitive end in 1969 with the appointment of the hard-line Alfredo Sánchez Bella as Minister of Information and Tourism.

In March 1970, ASDREC (Agrupación Sindical de Directores-Realizadores Españoles de Cinematografía / Union of Spanish Filmmakers) demanded the abolition of censorship, the arbitrariness of which was illustrated once more with the authorization and subsequent banning of Basilio Martín Patino's *Canciones para después de una guerra / Songs for After a War* (1971). In January 1974, Pío Cabanillas was appointed Minister of Information and Tourism, and tried to resume the previous liberalization. But the scandal over Saura's *La prima Angélica / Cousin Angélica*, which ridicules a Falangist during the Civil War, awarded the Jury Prize at Cannes in 1974, provoked official protests and attacks on some cinemas. Franco sacked Cabanillas in October, replacing him with León Herrera Esteban, who embarked on reform of the Censorship Code. Its revised version, approved in February 1975, authorized on-screen nudity for the first time "siempre que esté exigido por la unidad total del film, rechazándose cuando se presente con intención de despertar pasiones en el espectador normal o incida en la pornografía" (provided it is required by the film as a whole, and inadmissible when it has the aim of arousing passions in the normal spectator or lapses into pornography) (Gubern 1981: 279). But in May 1975 an assembly of producers rejected the reform, demanding that there be no restrictions on freedom of expression other than those covered by the Penal Code. Franco died on November 20, 1975 and the Censorship Code was rescinded by the Royal Decree of November 11, 1977.

This decree set up a Ministerial Commision to issue exhibition licenses indicating the age range of the audience authorized to view each film. The S rating for viewers over eighteen indicated that the film "puede herir la sensibilidad del público" (may offend audience sensibilities) (Gubern 1987: 8) and allowed screening only in special venues (Salas S). But, in the course of a complex political transition, a district attorney secured the judicial confiscation of Pasolini's *Salò, o le 120 giornate di Sodoma* (1975) when it was about to be shown at the Barcelona Semana Internacional de Cine (International Cinema Week), applying the "public scandal" clause of the Francoist Penal Code. Article 20 of the 1978 Constitution confirmed the abolition of all forms of censorship. Nonetheless, irregularities continued well into the 1980s. Imanol Uribe's 1980 *El proceso de Burgos / The Burgos Trial*, depicting the trial of ETA members, was refused a statutory subsidy on the grounds that most of its footage was documentary. In 1981 a Seville court confiscated Fernando Ruiz Vergara's documentary *Rocío* (1980), alleging "burla a la religión católica" (mockery of the Catholic religion) and "insulto a persona difunta" (offence to a deceased person), though it was subsequently screened with cuts (Gubern 1987: 10). Oshima's *The Empire of the Senses* (1977) was given an X rating before *salas X* (venues authorized to show X films) existed, but finally was allowed to be shown in a *sala S* (*salas X* were authorized in April 1983 by the Socialist government). The most serious case was that of Pilar Miró's 1979 *El crimen de Cuenca / The Cuenca Crime*, which dramatized a real-life event of 1910 in which two men confessed under torture to being guilty of a murder they had not committed. In December 1979, the film was refused an exhibition licence; in 1980 it was shown at the Berlin Film Festival but was confiscated and its director tried by a military court in April for "injurias a la guardia civil" (slurs against the Civil Guard) (Gubern 1987: 9–10). The case was resolved in March 1981 thanks to a reform of the Francoist Military Justice Code. In this same year, the climate created by the attempted military coup of February 23, 1981 prevented Stanley Kubrick's *Paths of Glory* (1957) from being shown in Spain until October 1986.

Film Studios (Román Gubern)

Little has been written on the material infrastructure of Spanish cinema. This section aims to fill a gap. As should emerge from what follows, the history of Spanish film studios, while making possible a Spanish national cinema, is interlaced with transnational connections (investment, ownership, equipment, and their use to shoot foreign films). This is a chequered history plagued by fires and bankruptcies: we should remember the material and financial precariousness of the film industry in its early days – not to mention the elementary material environment in which early Spanish cinema was filmed. It should also be noted that the history of film studios is linked to the history of dubbing (see Chapter 13).

The film industry's beginnings in Spain date back to 1905, when a modest production output in Barcelona generated the necessary infrastructures. In 1908, Fructuoso Gelabert converted an old glass greenhouse in a private garden into a studio measuring six by nine meters. In 1910, Segundo de Chomón, back from Paris, built another glass studio in Barcelona, this time measuring twelve by twenty meters. In Madrid in 1915, Patria Films inaugurated a glass studio of eight by four meters – so small that establishing shots had to be filmed from outside its door. The first important Madrid production company was Atlántida SACE, set up in 1919 with Alfonso XIII as patron, with studio space of 224 square meters, equipped with electric light. In 1923, some of Atlántida's film professionals left to set up their own production company, Film Española, backed by the Banco Urquijo, with warehouses and a laboratory as well as studios measuring twenty by twenty-five meters and with ceilings eighteen meters high.

The advent of sound required production infrastructures that were more sophisticated technically. In 1932, at the suggestion of the director Francisco Elías, the French production company Orphea Film, owned by Camille Lemoine, rented from Barcelona City Council the Palacio de la Química (Palace of Chemistry) built for the 1929 Universal Exposition, and in May started to shoot *Pax*, in French, with French sound recording equipment housed in a truck outside the building and a French sound engineer, René Renault. As the only Spanish studio equipped with sound recording facilities, Orphea Studios was used for all Spanish productions of 1932, starting with the *zarzuela* (popular operetta) *Carceleras / Prison Songs* (José Buchs, 1932; see Chapter 13 on the transition to sound) and allowing Benito

Perojo to give up his film career in Paris, returning to shoot *El hombre que se reía del amor* / *The Man who Laughed at Love* (1932). In 1933, by when Orphea had two sets, it embarked on distribution alongside producing five films. Fourteen of the seventeen films made in Spain in 1933 were filmed at Orphea, but by 1934 this had gone down to a third of the total national output, due partly to financial and legal problems but mainly to the opening of other studios. In 1934, Orphea set up a subsidiary, Publi-Orphea, specializing in shorts and documentaries, but internal issues and competition from Madrid eroded Orphea's former hegemony. Thus, in 1934 Perojo filmed *Se ha fugado un preso* / *A Prisoner Has Escaped* at Orphea but sonorized it at the ECESA studios in Aranjuez (see later in this section), while in the same year he filmed the exteriors for his sound remake of *El negro que tenía el alma blanca* / *The Black with a White Soul* in Nice and Barcelona, and its interiors at ECESA. In February 1936, Orphea's roof was damaged by a fire.

During the Civil War, the anarchist trade union CNT (Confederación Nacional del Trabajo (National Labor Confederation)) took over Orphea and shot several of its propaganda films there, including the interiors of André Malraux's *Sierra de Teruel* / *Espoir* / *Days of Hope* (1938–9). Upon the war's end in 1939, Orphea Studios passed to Laboratorios Cinefoto, becoming the base of producer Saturnino Ulargui. Its output declined progressively but low costs attracted some foreign projects, such as Michael Todd's *Scent of Mystery* (1959), shot in Odorama/ Aromarama/Smell-O-Vision. In April 1962 it was destroyed by a fire in obscure circumstances.

March 1932 saw the creation in Madrid of CEA (Cinematografía Española Americana (Spanish American Film)), with the dramatist Jacinto Benavente as honorary director and managed by a group of writers and musicians (including the Álvarez Quintero brothers, Carlos Arniches, Eduardo Marquina, and Pedro Muñoz Seca), who ceded their next three years' royalties to the company. The managing director was Rafael Salgado. Building work for CEA's studios, which housed three sets equipped with Tobis sound, was completed in October 1933. Eusebio Fernández Ardavín, CEA's technical director, inaugurated the new studios with his short *Saeta* (1933), followed by *El agua en el suelo* / *Water in the Ground* (1934), with a screenplay by Serafín Álvarez Quintero. It was at CEA, which in 1934 stopped producing its own films, that Luis Buñuel embarked on his dubbing work for Warner Bros. The CEA studios were also used for significant films such as Jean Grémillon's *La Dolorosa* (1934), Perojo's *Crisis mundial* / *World Crisis* (1934) and *La verbena de la Paloma* / *The Festival of the Virgin of the Dove* (1935), and Luis Marquina's *Don Quintín el amargao* / *Don Quintín the Bitter* (1935) and *El bailarín y el trabajador* / *The Dancer and the Worker* (1936). After the Civil War – during which CEA's management had supported the Nationalist rebels but its studios had nonetheless been used for the anarchist film *Nuestro culpable* / *Our Culprit* (1938) by the Italian-Argentine director Fernando Mignoni – CEA's studios were revamped, and it was there that José Luis Sáenz de Heredia would in 1941 shoot the Franco-scripted *Raza*. In 1946, fifteen of the thirty-eight films filmed in Spain were shot at

CEA, which continued to operate until November 1966, its production facilities having been used the previous year for David Lean's *Doctor Zhivago* (1965).

In October 1931, with the nationalist fervor generated by the Congreso Hispanoamericano de Cinematografía (see Chapter 2), Aranjuez City Council offered land to build a film school. The offer transmuted into the construction of film studios, designed by the architect Casto Fernández Shaw to be "the Spanish-speaking world's Hollywood" (Sánchez Salas 2001: 81). This was the origin of ECESA (Estudios Cinema Español SA), formally created in January 1932 but without supporting capital. Some writers provided backing (Pío Baroja, Alberto Insúa, Armando Palacio Valdés), and a truck toured Spain seeking investors in this "patriotic" project. Technically equipped by the Dutch company Philips, the shooting of its first production – *Invasión / Invasion*, directed by the above-mentioned Mignoni, its chief set designer – started in November 1933, but the film was never released. ECESA's official inauguration took place in January 1934. The sound of its first film, Florián Rey's *El novio de mamá / My Mother's Boyfriend* (1934), was so poor that the soundtrack had to be redone at postproduction stage. CIFESA made its first film there – Rey's *La hermana San Sulpicio / Sister San Sulpicio* (1934) – but in September 1934 ECESA suspended payments and its assets were seized by Philips Ibérica. In April 1935 it was reconstituted as Estudios Aranjuez SA, but a month later it was damaged by fire. In 1936 it was equipped with RCA Photophone sound, used for Benito Perojo's production that year of *Nuestra Natacha / Our Natacha* (never released because of the outbreak of the Civil War). After the war, ECESA was used by CIFESA for some of its productions, and for a number of Spanish–Italian coproductions. It closed after the shooting of Raffaello Matarazzo's *Empezó en boda / It Started with the Wedding* (1944).

In 1933–4 the young Falangist Serafín Ballesteros built facilities to house technical services for cinema and a warehouse, which in October 1935 moved to the new Estudios Ballesteros, whose first production was the comedy *Patricio miró a una estrella / Patricio Looked at a Star* (1934), directed initially by Fernando Delgado and concluded by Sáenz de Heredia. Estudios Ballesteros also included dubbing studios and a laboratory. During the Civil War the company was run by a workers' committee, and it resumed activities in 1939 with José Buchs' *zarzuela El rey que rabió / The Rabid King* (1940). Sáenz de Heredia's major films – *El escándalo / The Scandal* (1943), *El destino se disculpa / With Apologies from Fate* (1944), and *Mariona Rebull* (1947) – were shot there, but in 1949 it was seriously damaged by a fire. In the 1950s, Estudios Ballesteros embarked on the production and export to Spanish America, through 20th Century Fox, of musicals in color and wide-screen format, but this venture failed and the studios closed temporarily in 1958, going bankrupt finally in 1974. Dating from the same period was the more successful Estudios Cinearte, which opened in Madrid in January 1933 and is still active today after several remodellings.

In Barcelona, Estudios Trilla – conceived in 1931 and inaugurated as dubbing studios in 1932 by the jeweler Aberlardo Trilla together with the radio pioneers the

De la Riva brothers – was used for its productions by CIFESA (1941–4) and Emisora Films (1948–51), despite its modest facilities. It ceased operations in 1956. Estudios Lepanto was also set up in Barcelona in 1935, by the distributor and producer Enrique Huet, with one set – extended to thirty-six by fifteen meters in 1936 – equipped with Marconi Vistatone sound; it closed in 1943.

Madrid's Estudios Roptence grew out of a 1932 patent on portable sound projection equipment taken out by Miguel Lapuente Irigoyen and Antonio Fernández-Roces Heredia. In 1935, thanks to an injection of capital, the premises used by them to manufacture and sell this equipment became Estudios Roptence, with one set that could be subdivided, allowing two films to be made simultaneously. It started operations in June with the filming of Perojo's CIFESA production *Es mi hombre / He's My Man* (1934), followed by Filmófono's *La hija de Juan Simón / Juan Simón's Daughter* (Sáenz de Heredia, 1935) and *¡¡Centinela alerta!! / Guard! Alert!* (Jean Grémillon, 1937). Roptence started its activity as a production company with León Artola's *Rinconcito madrileño / Corner of Madrid* (1936). Its installations survived the Civil War intact, and in 1940 it was used for ten productions and was consequently expanded in 1941–2. In 1941, Roptence joined forces with the production company Ediciones Cinematográficas Faro, which specialized in coproductions with Portugal, but from 1946 it declined. Roptence closed in 1956.

Estudios Chamartín, at Las Rozas outside Madrid, grew out of a 1935 project of the Bilbao financier Tomás de Bordegaray, postponed because of the Civil War. Inaugurated in April 1941, it comprised 32 000 square meters, with five sets, two of which could be joined together to make one space measuring twenty by seventy meters. José Val del Omar was hired to manage special effects. Several ambitious projects were filmed there, including *La aldea maldita / The Cursed Village* (Rey, 1942), *Goyescas* (Perojo, 1942), and *El abanderado / The Standard Bearer* (Fernández Ardavín, 1942), and it became the preferred studio for Cesáreo González's Suevia Films (see "Cesáreo González and Suevia Films" later in this chapter), which shot some thirty productions there, including Juan Antonio Bardem's *Muerte de un ciclista*, *Calle Mayor*, and *La venganza / Vengeance*. After 1945, Estudios Chamartín also operated as a production company, its biggest hit being Ladislao Vajda's *Marcelino, pan y vino / The Miracle of Marcelino* (1955; see Chapter 11). In 1962, the US producer Samuel Bronston, then based in Spain in order to make blockbuster spectacles (see Chapter 2 and Chapter 8), bought the studios, changing their name to Estudios Bronston. In May 1984, the Ministry of Culture purchased the premises, unused since 1965 and impounded for the previous twelve years, and they were acquired by Televisión Española (Spanish state television) and renamed Estudios Buñuel.

In July 1938, in the middle of the Civil War, a monarchist group linked to the Marqués de Luca de Tena, with technical assistance from the previously mentioned French producer Camille Lemoine, founded the production company Estudios Sevilla in Seville, in the Nationalist zone. It planned to start by filming the Italian–Spanish coproduction *A Madrid: 682 / To Madrid: 682*, a glorification of the military uprising scripted by Luca de Tena. After the war, its first production was Juan Parellada's *Gloria de Moncayo / Glory of Moncayo*, shot in April 1940 in Barcelona's modest Estudios Kinefón (1940–53), owned by Juan Homedes. In 1943, Estudios Sevilla Films was inaugurated on the edge of Madrid, built in the style of an Andalusian *cortijo* (ranch), with six sets and 250 employees. It signed an agreement with CIFESA, the first fruit of which was Rafael Gil's *Eloísa está debajo de un almendro / Eloisa under an Almond Tree* (1943). The films made there included such significant titles as José Antonio Nieves Conde's *Surcos*, Orson Welles' *Mr. Arkadin* aka *Confidential Report* (1954), Robert Rossen's *Alexander the Great* (1956), King Vidor's *Solomon and Sheba* (1958), Carlos Saura's *Los golfos / The Delinquents* (1959), Marco Ferreri's *Los chicos / The Young Ones* (1960; see Chapter 12), and the Bronston productions *John Paul Jones* (John Farrow, 1959), *King of Kings* (Nicholas Ray, 1961), and *El Cid* (Anthony Mann, 1961). Estudios Sevilla Films was later rented by Televisión Española, until in 1973 the company was dissolved.

In Barcelona, the producer-director Ignacio F. Iquino, after a period of collaboration with Emisora Films (1943–8), in 1950 kitted out his own studios, IFI, in the Avenida Paralelo (Barcelona's equivalent of Broadway) with three sets and hired José María Nunes to lead a team of screenwriters. Iquino later added to this enterprise the dubbing studio Parlo Films, headed by Antonio Santillán. Iquino, a skilled producer of B movies, especially thrillers, produced seventy-two feature films in his studios between 1950 and 1970, including Mario Camus' *Los farsantes / The Actors* and *Young Sánchez* (both released in Barcelona in 1964 and in Madrid in 1968). IFI's studios closed in May 1970.

In 1964, at Esplugas de Llobregat on Barcelona's outskirts, Producciones Cinematográficas Balcázar, founded in 1951 by Alfonso Balcázar, built a Western outpost of some sixteen thousand square meters, with five sets, where sixty-five films were shot between 1964 and 1974 – chiefly spaghetti westerns, many coproduced with Italy (see Chapter 2 and Chapter 8). However, between 1965 and 1973, after the success of Sergio Leone's *La muerte tenía un precio / Per qualche dollari in più / For a Few Dollars More* (1965), the genre relocated to Almería, where some 150 such films were made.

By the 1980s, on the threshhold of the digital age, the studio era was over, though, with the rapid expansion of television channels on the return to democracy, at national and at regional levels, new infrastructures were created (as with Televisión Española's development of Estudios Buñuel) to produce their programs and fiction series, as well as producing films for distribution in cinema theaters. Going against the current of the times, in 2005 the Valencian Autonomous Government built the Ciudad de la Luz (City of Light) near Alicante – a vast audiovisual production complex of eleven thousand square meters with studios and an adjoining film school headed for some years by Luis García Berlanga – a polemical political venture that has been criticized by some as megalomaniac and by others for subsidizing production companies to lure them to film in its facilities, going against the logic of the market.

Filmófono (Steven Marsh)

The chapter now moves on to production companies, which will be discussed in chronological order, starting with the 1930s. The first production company singled out for discussion, Filmófono, was a singular (albeit short-lived) attempt to create a secular popular cinema that sought to bring together nationally specific cultural traditions with Hollywood-style studio practices. It might also be seen as loosely aligned with the Second Republic's efforts to secure a progressive hegemony through culture by means of Lorca's traveling theater company La Barraca, the Museo Circulante (Traveling Art Museum), and the Misiones Pedagógicas (Pedagogical Missions), by which the public (in a largely rural country with widespread illiteracy and intellectually dominated by the Catholic Church) was introduced to hitherto elitist culture.

Created by the radio empresario Ricardo Urgoiti – son of the liberal publisher Nicolás María Urgoiti – Filmófono became a fully fledged production company in 1935 after having first pioneered sound technology for film in the late 1920s. Urgoiti was also responsible for the importation and distribution of foreign films within the Spanish market. Further, owing to his friendship with Luis Buñuel, Urgoiti would establish Filmófono's Cineclub on Madrid's central thoroughfare, the Gran Vía, for screenings of both foreign and domestic avant-garde films (Gubern 1977: 84–5). Upon expanding into filmmaking, Urgoiti teamed up with Buñuel, who was named Filmófono's executive producer and charged with organizing and supervising the company's productions (Buñuel already had some experience in this kind of work, having supervised the dubbing of Warner Bros. productions the previous year). According to Luis Fernández Colorado and Josetxo Cerdán, Urgoiti, following the precedent of Hollywood studios, insisted on the convergence of what he saw as three essential factors: a permanent production crew, established stars for whom the films would serve as vehicles, and scripts that would appeal to a popular audience without sacrificing the film's artistic quality (2007: 98).

These three criteria and the significant presence of Buñuel suggest a convergence between what has traditionally been a dichotomy in writing on film: popular or genre cinema and the avant-garde. Indeed, Filmófono's very philosophy – its identification with the cultural initiatives of the state, in which progressive intellectuals sought to bind the popular classes (both industrial workers and peasantry) to their project – is suggestive of the national-popular that the Italian Communist Party leader Antonio Gramsci (languishing in prison at the time that Filmófono's productions were underway) saw as a preliminary and provisional educational necessity for social transformation. Gramsci was equally conscious, however, of the ideological ambiguity of the national-popular. Indeed, the Filmófono model – in the hands of its 1930s rivals, the Catholic-minded CIFESA – would serve Francoism in the years immediately following the Spanish Civil War. As Gramsci commented:

> In my opinion, the most reasonable and concrete thing that can be said about the ethical State, the cultural State, is this: every State is ethical inasmuch as one of its most important functions is to raise the great mass of the population to a particular cultural and moral level [...]. The school as a positive educative function, and the courts as a repressive and negative educative function, are the most important State activities in this sense: but, in reality, a multitude of other so-called private initiatives and activities tend to the same end – initiatives and activities which form the apparatus of the political and cultural hegemony of the ruling classes. (1971: 258)

Under Buñuel's supervision, Filmófono released four films before the onset of the Civil War brought production to an untimely end. Fernández Colorado and Cerdán have documented Urgoiti's efforts to resuscitate the company while in exile in Argentina (1937–42), but the atomization of the crew (dispersed in exile or dead), the lack of infrastructure, and (perhaps above all else) the absence of the ideological conditions that had prevailed in Spain's Second Republic were to frustrate his endeavors.

The four films – *Don Quintín el amargao* (Luis Marquina, 1935), *La hija de Juan Simón* (Nemesio Sobrevila and José Luis Sáenz de Heredia, 1935), *¿Quién me quiere a mí? / Who Loves Me?* (Sáenz de Heredia, 1936), and *¡¡Centinela alerta!!* (Grémillon, 1937) – all bear signs of Buñuel's influence. It is noteworthy that Buñuel himself, while disavowing the Filmófono productions as execrable in his autobiography, would go on to direct his own version of *Don Quintín el amargao* – entitled *La hija del engaño / Daughter of Deceit* – in Mexico in 1951. Likewise, it is clear from individual testimonies by Buñuel and others and from the textual evidence of the films themselves that Buñuel actively participated on set and that his involvement was not limited to mere supervision. Further, in a telling irony, Buñuel was responsible for consolidating the incipient career of José Luis Sáenz de Heredia. The latter – who had made only one other film prior to directing *La hija de Juan Simón* and *¿Quién me quiere a mí?* – was a cousin of the Falangist leader José Antonio Primo de Rivera and supported the 1936 military uprising. Arrested and sentenced to death in Republican Madrid during the war, he was spared only after Buñuel intervened on his behalf. Sáenz de Heredia would go on to an illustrious filmmaking career (and his friendship with Buñuel survived their political differences), although he is best known for directing the notorious Franco-scripted *Raza*. Given the model pioneered by Urgoiti and appropriated by the right-wing CIFESA, it is perhaps not so surprising that the progressive Filmófono should also have produced one of the most celebrated directors of the Francoist period.

In accordance with Urgoiti's stipulations, the four films adopt popular modes. The first – *Don Quintín el amargao* – was based on one of Carlos Arniches' celebrated *sainetes* (low-life farces). Arniches' work was adapted for the screen on numerous occasions before and after *Don Quintín*, and the playwright's son-in-law, the screenwriter Eduardo Ugarte, formed part of Filmófono's regular team of collaborators. Directed by Luis Marquina, its publicity slogan – typical of Urgoiti's philosophy – proclaimed it "Una comedia madrileña con el ritmo de una película americana" (A Madrid comedy with the rhythm of an American film) (Gubern 1977: 87). *¿Quién me quiere a mí?* was an attempt to cash in on the popularity in Hollywood of child stars in the vein of Shirley Temple, who two years before had achieved fame at the age of six in 20th Century Fox's production of *Bright Eyes* (David Butler, 1934). Accordingly, Filmófono organized a competition to select its star, Mari-Tere Pacheco. Unlike Filmófono's other productions, it proved a box-office failure in spite of its opportunistic use of a child star and the topical nature of its subject matter (it deals with custody issues in the wake of Spain's divorce law of 1932). The final Filmófono film, *¡¡Centinela alerta!!*, conversely, was the company's most successful production in spite (or perhaps because) of its release during the Civil War. This final film was originally directed by the well-known French filmmaker Jean Grémillon, who had previously worked in Spain as director of the filmed *zarzuela La Dolorosa* (1934). Owing to illness, Grémillon was unable to continue working during the shoot and his functions were taken over (anonymously) by Buñuel himself.

I will conclude this section by offering a brief analysis of *La hija de Juan Simón* as a representative case study of Filmófono's productions. Román Gubern cites the publicity for the film: "lo que la música de Falla o los romances gitanos de García Lorca: la superación de la raíz popular del arte" (the equivalent of Falla's music or García Lorca's Gypsy ballads: a reworking of the popular roots of art) (1977: 90). Customarily referred to as an *españolada* (representation of stereotypical tropes of Spanishness) (George et al. 2007: 76), the film is – in accordance once again with Urgoiti's Filmófono thesis – a curious mixture of the popular and the avant-garde within a national discourse. This combination is evidenced by the film's two directors. Nemesio M. Sobrevila, an architect by training, was a major figure in 1920s experimental filmmaking, known particularly for his 1929 *El sexto sentido / The Sixth Sense* (see Chapter 12). Sobrevila was fired by Buñuel after the first week's shoot for his erratic behavior and failure to follow the schedule marked out by its tight budget. Buñuel replaced Sobrevila with the more reliable Sáenz de Heredia. One of the film's most interesting features is its formal adventurousness: the linking devices, match cuts, and superimpositions, together with the play on space and spacing in its editing. In a Spain whose filmic infrastructure was at best rudimentary, this is a film shot through with modernist innovation. It is worth considering the film's introductory sequences as exemplary of its elliptical narrative technique, its specifically filmic economy. Gravedigger Juan Simón – the eponymous character (albeit a secondary one) of the film's title – is shot from an appropriately mid-to-low angle against the shadow of a bare tree trunk and looming clouds at twilight, made stark by the diaphanous illumination as he shovels earth. In this way he outlines – by means of simile – the melodramatic familial crisis at the heart of the film's action. Shortly thereafter, Carmen (Pilar Muñoz), the film's female protagonist, reminisces via a photograph spiralling into mise-en-abyme. The stylistic cinematic flourish employed here – the flashback – not only functions

Figure 14.3 Angelillo, the popular singing star for whom *La hija de Juan Simón* (Nemesio M. Sobrevila / José Luis Sáenz de Heredia, 1935; prod. Filmófono) was a star vehicle.

as a narrative technique locating the antecedents of Carmen and Ángel's (Ángel Sampedro Montero "Angelillo") courtship but also offers up a critique of circus-style illusionary representation. Indeed, the fairground sequences recall the importance of spectacle in early film. The fairground is both a site of "the popular" and a favorite of the filmic avant-garde – exemplary of this, within Spain, are Ernesto Giménez Caballero's film *Esencia de verbena / Essence of Carnival* (1930) and Luis García Berlanga's student short *El circo / The Circus* (1949). The photo that triggers Carmen's flashback, moreover, re-emerges as a narrative touchstone later in the film, in her dressing room at the cabaret shortly before her attempted suicide, as a key moment in her re-encounter with Ángel.

The film's self-conscious editing emphasizes the importance of spacing; editing is largely a question of the distribution of celluloid space, while filming is a matter of capturing space within the frame. In the architecture of the film's mise-en-scène, there is a marked contrast between the sinister, claustrophobic interiors (the prison, the flamenco *tablao*) on the one hand and the wide, open optimistic spaces with "natural" lighting, imbued with a sense of liberty – part western, part ethnographic film – on the other. This use of space is marked by the melodramatic genre of the film's narrative (for some, a sign of contamination by mass culture) but also by the film's self-referential quality as film.

While it is a tongue-in-cheek rags to riches story, *La hija de Juan Simón* is principally a film designed for the promotion of Angelillo, not only the film's star but also the leading flamenco singer of his day and a member of the Communist Party who was forced into exile after the war (see Figure 14.3). To this end, *La hija de Juan Simón*'s key sequence takes place when Ángel, imprisoned unjustly for a crime of which he is innocent, sings "Soy un pobre presidiario" (I'm a poor convict) to the rousing choral accompaniment of jailors and fellow prisoners. In scenes such as this, the film – via the aura surrounding its star, reinforced in this central song – proves emblematic of Filmófono's progressive politics in its affinity with the national-popular project of the state.

CIFESA (Jo Labanyi)

The production company CIFESA (Compañía Industrial Film Español SA) is often discussed as if its cinematic output were a mere extension of early Francoist ideology. The reality is more complex. The Valencian company was founded in 1932 under the Second Republic. Having bought majority shares in the new firm, Manuel Casanova became its president in 1933, with his two eldest sons, Vicente and Luis, members of its board. In his superb monograph, on which this section draws heavily, Fèlix Fanés outlines Manuel Casanova's Valencian bourgeois background as a self-made man who made his fortune through olive oil manufacture, land speculation, importation of foreign automobiles, and purchase of majority shares in the Banco de Valencia (1989: 45–56). His motive in buying up CIFESA was to give his sons – particularly Vicente, interested in cinema – gainful employment. The Casanovas' political links were with the Derecha Regional Valenciana (Valencian Regional Right), a Catholic, anti-Marxist, anti-Centralist party – a key element in the conservative political alliance CEDA (Confederación Española de Derechas Autónomas) that from 1934 to 1936 held major positions in Lerroux's coalition government. CIFESA's theme tune quotes the Valencian anthem's opening chords. The exaltation of regional culture (not Valencian, curiously) typifies several CIFESA movies, especially of the Republican period.

The Casanovas' background confirms Fanés' point that early Spanish cinema was championed by the political right: the Franco dictatorship, following fascist Germany and Italy, was the first Spanish government to enact legislation to protect the medium (Fanés 1989: 15–43, 135–6). As Fanés notes (1989: 33, 37), CIFESA was founded at a moment when the shift to sound cinema generated hopes that Castilian's world-language status would give Spanish cinema a global influence; demands for a "racially Hispanic" cinema appear in early 1930s rhetoric of the political right and left. CIFESA's mix of regionalism and nationalism – anticipating the Franco dictatorship's promotion of regional culture for nationalist ends – coexisted harmoniously with global capitalism: Vicente Casanova's first coup in 1933 was to sign a contract with Columbia Pictures for exclusive distribution rights in Spain.

Like other 1930s Spanish film companies, CIFESA started as a distributor, moving into production in 1934. After terminating production in 1952, it continued as a distributor until its demise in 1964. When its contract with Columbia Pictures ended in 1935, it switched to importing largely European films (French, German, and British). As a major distributor of foreign films, CIFESA benefited hugely from the Francoist state's protectionist measures, introduced in 1941, which rewarded films given top state ratings with profitable import licenses. Throughout its thirty-one years, CIFESA was also a substantial distributor of films made by other Spanish production companies (for titles, see *CIFESA* 1990: 136–8); its last financial break came in 1957 from distributing Juan de Orduña's smash-hit musical *El último cuplé / The Last Torch Song*, starring Sara Montiel (see Chapter 10 and Chapter 11). Indeed, many CIFESA films were coproductions with other Spanish companies, and there were attempts at coproductions with Italy in 1940–1 and 1952 (Fanés 1989: 278; *CIFESA* 1990: 134). Some of the Spanish films distributed after 1951 – including Jess Franco's 1962 *Vampiresas 1930 / Female Vamps 1930* – were de facto coproductions made with CIFESA's investment. CIFESA's distribution network was transnational: by 1936 it had branches in Buenos Aires, Santiago de Chile, Havana, Mexico City, Paris, Berlin, and Oran (Fanés 1989: 96). However, Vicente Casanova never realized his dream of securing widespread exhibition in Spanish America, despite repeated trips there from 1947 onward (Fanés 1989: 260).

During the Civil War, CIFESA operated from Valencia and Madrid (in the Republican zone) and Seville (under Nationalist control), with filming taking place almost entirely in Seville. CIFESA's Seville office made a number of pro-Nationalist documentary shorts. CIFESA's substantial production of shorts (on political, military, regional, artistic, agricultural, and medical topics) from 1934 through 1959 should not be forgotten (for titles, see *CIFESA* 1990: 134–6). CIFESA's relationship to the Nazi–Spanish coproduction company of 1937–9, Hispano-Film-Produktion, is unclear. Gubern (1994: 291–3) concludes tentatively that it was tenuous, with the company created in Berlin, with Goebbels' approval, by CIFESA's representative in Havana, Norberto Soliño, without CIFESA's direct involvement. Nonetheless, Hispano-Film-Produktion hired CIFESA directors (Florián Rey, Benito Perojo) and stars (Imperio Argentina, Miguel Ligero), and CIFESA distributed its brilliantly edited propaganda film *España heroica / Heroic Spain* (Joaquín Reig, 1938).

Although the Francoist state did not nationalize the film industry, CIFESA made its allegiance clear by donating a film projector to Franco in June 1939. In 1943–4, Vicente Casanova established close friendships with General Rada (two of whose sons held top positions at CIFESA) and Franco's right-hand man, Admiral Carrero Blanco (Fanés 1989: 196). The company's prewar belief in the need for a national cinema based on (premodern) Spanish values fitted perfectly with Francoist ideology. Nevertheless – and this must be stressed – the majority of CIFESA's early 1940s productions are cosmopolitan film comedies, expressing the values of urban modernity. Indeed, CIFESA's postwar comedies are more modern and urban than its largely rural prewar comedies.

Effectively, the productions of CIFESA both before and after the war are heterogeneous, regardless of the Casanovas' political connections. CIFESA's two main prewar directors, Florián Rey and Benito Perojo, were strikingly different, the former favoring premodern rural dramas and the latter – having worked in the French and German film industries, for MGM and Fox in Hollywood, and at Paramount's Joinville (Paris) studios – slick, cosmopolitan comedies. Of the six films made in CIFESA's second year of production (1935), three were comedies directed by Perojo: the cosmopolitan romp *Rumbo al Cairo / Bound for Cairo* and the low-life urban farces *Es mi hombre / He's My Man* and *La verbena de la Paloma / Festival of the Virgin of the Dove* (which turns a popular *zarzuela* into a Hollywood-style musical). The remaining three comprise two rural dramas exalting traditional morality – including Rey's musical *Nobleza baturra / Aragonese Virtue* – plus Eduardo García Maroto's *La hija del penal / The Penitentiary's Daughter*: a zany social comedy scripted by Miguel Mihura (founder of the postwar satirical magazine *La Codorniz*) in which the workers at a prison threatened with closure engineer the marriage of the last remaining prisoner to the prison director's daughter, securing the prison's survival. This plotline is worthy of the social comedies produced by Buñuel for Filmófono during the Republic (see the previous section of this chapter). Two major CIFESA films of 1936 also illustrate its productions' political complexity. Rey's musical comedy *Morena Clara / Dark and Bright*, Spain's biggest box-office hit up to that date, caters to conservative audiences through the precapitalist values of its folkloric Gypsy protagonists (Imperio Argentina, Miguel Ligero), but their picaresque humor subverts the bourgeois order into which the heroine succeeds in marrying. The film's social justice message is entirely compatible with the newly elected Popular Front government's program of social inclusion. Indeed, the film was hugely popular in both Republican and Nationalist zones during the Civil War, until the Republic banned it because of Rey's and Argentina's pro-Nationalist stance (Fanés 1989: 112 n. 57). Perojo's *Nuestra Natacha / Our Natacha*, never screened and now lost, was a progressive, feminist social drama based on a play by Alejandro Casona, director of the theater group of the Republican government's Misiones Pedagógicas (Pedagogical Missions). Perojo, who despite his progressive cinema supported the Nationalists, withheld the film during the war; upon Nationalist victory it was banned.

A repeated plotline in CIFESA's prewar comedies is social ascent through marriage. Surprisingly, the same is true of CIFESA's postwar comedies, which also frequently celebrate cross-class romance (Fanés 1989: 181–2) – for example, *Torbellino / Whirlwind* (Luis Marquina, 1941) and *Huella de luz / A Sight of Light* (Rafael Gil, 1943). Fanés notes (1989: 217–20) the recurrent concern in CIFESA's postwar films with mistaken identity – a trope found in other 1940s national cinemas, undermining Fanés' suggestion that this betrays anxieties resulting from the Civil War.

Figure 14.4 The crazy modern dance "El Tipolino" in *Un marido a precio fijo* (Gonzalo Delgrás, 1942) – one of CIFESA's cosmopolitan modern comedies of the early 1940s. Courtesy of Video Mercury and Filmoteca Española.

Of the forty-one films produced or coproduced by CIFESA in 1940–4, the overwhelming majority were comedies. Curiously, given that these were the early years of the Franco Dictatorship, almost all of these were modern urban comedies of the "white telephones" variety (the name given to the contemporary brand of Italian comedies set in luxury mansions or hotels). Typical examples are *Un marido a precio fijo / The Hired Husband* (Gonzalo Delgrás, 1942), *La chica del gato / The Girl with the Cat* (Ramón Quadreny, 1943), and *La vida empieza a medianoche / Life Starts at Midnight* (Juan de Orduña, 1944) (see Figure 14.4). The two films exalting military values – *¡Harka!* (Carlos Arévalo, 1941), *¡A mí la Legión! / Follow the Legion!* (Orduña, 1942) – could equally be classified as homoerotic romances. The most memorable productions are melodramas, a surprisingly infrequent genre in CIFESA's productions prior to 1948: *Malvaloca* (Marquina, 1942) and *El clavo / The Nail* (Gil, 1944; see Chapter 12), which between them established Amparo Rivelles as a CIFESA star.

In 1945 CIFESA hit financial trouble, attributed by Vicente Casanova to the Motion Picture Association of America's blacklisting of pro-Axis film companies. Fanés (1989: 229–33) dismisses this explanation as a cover-up for bad management, and is scathing about Casanova's remedy of opting for fewer, big-budget films in the Hollywood blockbuster tradition. This decision gave rise to the historical epics based on a patriotic interpretation of national history with which CIFESA has become almost exclusively associated. Strictly they number only four: *Locura de amor / The Mad Queen* (1948), *Agustina de Aragón* (1950), *La leona de Castilla / The Lioness of Castile* (1951), and *Alba de América / Dawn of America* (1951), all directed by Orduña – and *Locura de amor* is more melodrama than epic. As argued in Chapter 8, CIFESA's five other 1947–51 historical films are better seen as costume dramas (of which CIFESA made several before the 1945 crisis), given that national history is absent or marginal. It is, however, significant that CIFESA's early 1940s productions have almost entirely modern settings, while the large majority of its 1947–51 productions are set in the past: a change consonant with the shift of hegemony within the regime from the Falange (bent on creating a fascist modernity) to the Church (bent on extirpating all modern values) upon fascism's defeat in World War II.

If CIFESA has become identified with its historical epics, it is not only because its productions are often seen as coterminous with regime ideology but also because these films most clearly embody CIFESA's trademark: the "look" it cultivated through the hiring, on fixed-term contracts, of particular directors, stars, and technicians. In this respect, CIFESA achieved its aim of creating a "quality brand" that boosted distribution and attendance for its products. This quality brand was enhanced by the stress on literary adaptations: a good example is *Pequeñeces / Trifles* (Orduña, 1950), adapted from the 1890 novel by the Jesuit Padre Coloma (thus legitimizing the depiction of scandalous behavior), whose publicity stressed Aurora Bautista's nineteen luxury costumes made from authentic fabrics of the period and commissioned, down to the underwear, from top designer Pedro Rodríguez (Labanyi 2007: 244) (see Figure 14.5). CIFESA's first film in 1934, Rey's *La hermana San Sulpicio / Sister San Sulpicio*, dramatized a popular Alarcón novel (previously adapted as a silent film by Rey in 1927), and a high proportion of its movies were based on popular novels or plays. Its remakes of silent movies – others are *Malvalovca* (1942; original version Perojo, 1926), *La condesa María / Countess María* (Delgrás, 1942; original version Perojo, 1924), *Currito de la Cruz / Currito of the Cross* (Luis Lucia, 1948; original version Alejandro Pérez Lugín, 1926; first remake Fernando Delgado, 1936), *Agustina de Aragón* (1951; original version Florián Rey, 1929) – also conferred prestige through the creation of a cinematic genealogy.

It was, however, CIFESA's imitation of the Hollywood studio system that most contributed to its brand. This dates back to the prewar period with exclusive contracts for Rey and Perojo as directors, Imperio Argentina and Miguel Ligero as stars, and the German-trained Jewish refugees from Nazism Fred Mandel and Enrique Gaertner (originally Heinrich Gärtner, subsequently Enrique Guerner) as cameramen (for discussion of Guerner, see Chapter 12). This buying of directors', actors', and technicians' loyalty was mirrored by CIFESA's treatment of its employees, who were given a share of profits and welfare benefits (Fanés 1989: 170). After the war, CIFESA focused on the creation of new in-house directors – Juan de

Figure 14.5 The CIFESA "look" illustrated by costume drama *Pequeñeces* (Juan de Orduña, 1950), adapted from the 1890 novel by the Jesuit Padre Coloma, starring Aurora Bautista (center) as a serial adulteress, with Sara Montiel (right) as a French courtesan. An example of CIFESA's use of literary adaptations to promote a "quality brand." Courtesy of Video Mercury and Filmoteca Española.

Orduña (a prewar CIFESA actor), Rafael Gil, and Luis Lucia – and new in-house stars such as Alfredo Mayo, Amparo Rivelles, Fernando Rey, Jorge Mistral, and Aurora Bautista (Sara Montiel was "discovered" through a CIFESA talent-spotting competition). The contracts offered to Bautista and Mistral were record-breaking – and also bank-breaking since they did not make all the films contracted.

Fanés accuses Vicente Casanova of megalomania in imitating the Hollywood studios' promotion of their stars through gala events (including attendance at Valencia's Fallas). But the resulting glamour gave Spanish audiences, at a time of hardship, what they wanted and they mostly responded as loyal viewers. What eventually broke CIFESA was the regime's lack of loyalty to a company that had cultivated good relations with it. In 1951, the regime banned CIFESA's planned biopic of Saint Teresa, for which Aurora Bautista had been paid. In the same year, the new Director General of Film, José María García Escudero, awarded the top National Interest rating to José Antonio Nieves Conde's social drama *Surcos* instead of CIFESA's *Alba de América* – the only feature film that CIFESA made in direct collaboration with the regime. Incensed by the 1949 British film *Christopher Columbus*, the Instituto de Cultura Hispánica commissioned CIFESA to produce a riposte, with the Institute's director Alfredo Sánchez Bella – and some say Admiral

Carrero Blanco (Mira 2004: 73; González González 2009: 114) – intervening in the (dreadful) script. Vicente Casanova's protests gained *Alba de América* the National Interest category in 1952, on García Escudero's resignation, but CIFESA's other three films of 1951 were given second- and third-class ratings. Vicente Casanova declared that he would cease production as a point of honor; in reality, the regime had broken CIFESA financially.

There was, however, an additional factor that ultimately broke CIFESA: the emergence of Cesáreo González (see the following section of this chapter), whose hard-nosed entrepreneurship won out over the Casanovas' bourgeois model. A former card-sharper who had emigrated to Cuba to escape poverty in his youth and had made his fortune there and in Mexico (Zunzunegui in Castro de Paz and Cerdán 2005: 159), González opted for a canny business model based on quantity and diversification, and engaged in a bidding war to steal CIFESA's top stars. Having lived in Cuba and Mexico, he succeeded where Vicente Casanova failed in establishing good relations with Spanish American distributors – crucial to economic success (Fanés 1989: 261). CIFESA is credited with being the first Spanish production company to run itself on capitalist lines, but its bourgeois capitalist model was outdated. Ironically for a company that professed allegiance to the Franco regime, the death blow was triggered by CIFESA's 1963 attempt to import Fellini's *La dolce vita* (1960); when – as mentioned in the first section of this chapter – the censors banned the film after CIFESA had paid a large advance for the rights, bankruptcy was inevitable.

Cesáreo González and Suevia Films (Josetxo Cerdán)

The case of Cesáreo González is a paradoxical one: he is as the same time the individual most responsible for what can be seen as Francoist cinema and a unique, isolated case in the Spanish film industry (Castro and Cerdán 2005). The cinema he produced under the brand name Suevia Films (later also a trading company) most clearly represents the contours of Francoist cinema from the late 1940s to the late 1960s. Suevia Films was responsible for a good share of popular commercial cinema of the period, opting from the start for topics and approaches that might attract a mass public but also paying attention to production values. The first title Cesáreo González produced, *¡¡Polizón a bordo!! / Stowaway on Board!* (1941), was directed by one of the most prestigious filmmakers of the day, Florián Rey, while the second, *¡Campeones! / Champions!* (Ramón Torrado, 1943), was one of the first Spanish films to approach what was already at the time a mass sport, football. To attract the public, *Campeones* included in its cast some of the top footballers of the day. By contrast, González was responsible for titles such as *Duende y misterio del flamenco / Flamenco* (Edgar Neville, 1952), *La laguna negra / The Black Lagoon* (Arturo Ruiz-Castillo, 1952), and *Muerte de un ciclista / Death of a Cyclist* (Juan Antonio Bardem, 1955), to

Figure 14.6 Publicity still for *Faustina* (José Luis Sáenz de Heredia, 1957; prod. Suevia Films / Chapalo Films) showcasing the Mexican diva María Félix with Spanish co-star Fernando Fernán Gómez. Suevia pioneered cinematic collaboration between Spain and Latin America in the late 1940s and 1950s. Courtesy of Video Mercury and Filmoteca Española.

give just three examples, which distanced themselves from popular commercial models. It is the range of Suevia's productions that makes the company illustrative of Spanish cinema of the 1940s and 1950s. Indeed, its films correspond to a series of formulas that are indissolubly linked with the period. González would be a pioneer in the field of coproductions (with Latin America and Europe; see Chapter 2) and would consolidate a transatlantic Spanish-speaking star system through the exploitation on various fronts (film, stage tours, records) of charismatic figures such as Lola Flores, María Félix (see Figure 14.6), and Marisol (see Chapter 11). At the same time, González's productions had a clear advantage over much of Spanish cinema: from the 1950s, Suevia Films had a broad distribution network, with offices not just in Spain but also in Latin America and other parts of the world, ensuring that its productions would reach cinema theaters.

Cesáreo González registered Suevia Films as a production company in the summer of 1941. A former emigrant, he was at the time a hotel proprietor and owner of a transport company, as well as a board member of the football club of his native Vigo (Galicia). His first involvement with the film industry had been just a few months before, when he participated as a one-off financial partner in *El famoso Carballeira / The Famous Carballeira* (Fernando Mignoni, 1940). Despite the country's evident economic devastation at the time (one year after the end of the Civil War), González sensed that the film industry could be a money-spinner and hired a fellow Galician, the writer of stage comedies Adolfo Torrado, to write a script that would become Suevia Films' first production. Suevia Films' central office opened in Madrid in 1941, and González set about attracting the necessary capital. He cut a highly advantageous deal with Tomás de Bordegaray, president of Chamartín Producciones y Distribuciones Cinematográficas SA, allowing him to use the Chamartín studios, with his films being distributed by Chamartín on preferential terms. To embark on this project, González used the first dubbing permits he obtained to import Republic Pictures' serial *Drums of Fu Manchu* (John English and William Witney, 1940), clearly indicating his commitment to popular cinema and his aim of reaching the biggest possible audience. This package of pictures was part of his deal with Chamartín, which undertook to distribute them; it was by ceding to Chamartín a large cut of the profits that González was able to negotiate hugely favorable terms to film in its facilities.

Despite declaring repeatedly throughout his long career that he was considering opening his own film studios, González never had any serious intention of doing so; his announcements to that effect were publicity stunts. The business formula he put into practice from the start, and to which he remained faithful all his life, was to manage a small number of loyal collaborators (many of them trained at Suevia) while issuing a series of exclusive contracts to a handful of transnational stars. His technical and artistic crews were hired on one-off contracts for individual films. This meant that they were not a financial drain on the company when inactive. Nothing could have been further from the production model of the studio conceived as film factory – a mistake made by González's major competitor of the 1940s, CIFESA, that lead to its bankruptcy in the early 1950s (see the previous section). While CIFESA clearly ascribed to the system of the great Hollywood studios (a model also followed in France and Germany), Suevia Films anticipated the concept of the independent producer that would become standard, at least in Europe, from the 1950s. This business configuration would allow Suevia great flexibility and, importantly, the ability to adapt to the changing circumstances of the Spanish film industry.

A quick look at the first pictures made by Suevia Films shows how González set out to explore the various popular film genres cultivated in Spain at the time: urban melodrama, as in *Unos pasos de mujer / A Woman's Steps* (Fernández Ardavín, 1942); romantic comedy with box-office hit potential, such as *El rey de las finanzas / The King of Finance* (Ramón Torrado, 1944); a gesture toward the folkloric film, as in *Castañuela / Castanet* (Torrado, 1945); and the historical epic, which he first attempted, several years before CIFESA's cultivation of the genre, with *El abanderado / The Standard Bearer* (Fernández Ardavín, 1943) – a relatively low-key but nonetheless ambitious project aimed at attracting the attention of those responsible for awarding state film subsidies. And there is no doubt that Cesáreo González knew how to cultivate key figures in the Francoist state apparatus. That is clear if one looks at the ratings and prizes awarded to his films from the start.

Despite this cultivation of national connections, González had also from the start shown a clear transnational vocation: he appreciated that his films needed to travel beyond national borders to reach other markets. And that would be his goal once he had got his company established at home. As a former emigrant, he would not hesitate to exploit the topic of emigration, both in his first production, *¡¡Polizón a bordo!!*, and in *El emigrado / The Emigrant* (Torrado, 1946). But he would also target transnational audiences through plots with a regional setting (preferably Galician, given the huge Galician communities in Latin America, especially Cuba and Argentina) – for example, *Mar abierto / Open Sea* (Torrado, 1946). However, his first big transnational bid was the contract he signed with the British-born Hollywood actress Madeleine Carroll to star in his historical epic *Reina santa / The Holy Queen* (Rafael Gil, 1947). Later disagreements led to Carroll dropping out of the project (she was replaced by the Spanish actress Maruchi Fresno), but the attempt made clear the direction González was heading in. His major center of business operations was Latin America – the "twenty Spanish-speaking nations" that González constantly talked of "conquering" with his films and to which he travelled incessantly. To that end, he set up an efficient grid of offices and partner distributors (eventually also producers), mainly in Mexico and Argentina but also in other countries in the region. But, for this operation to work, González first had to control the circulation of his films, which is why in 1947 he registered the trading company Suevia Films – Distribuciones Cinematográficas (Suevia Films – Film Distributors), with majority control of the shares.

The 1950s would see Suevia Films blossom definitively, becoming Spain's principal production company. To achieve this, it resorted to all kinds of formulas (productions on its own, national or international coproductions, associations, purchase of film rights, participation in production or in subsequent exploitation, diverse financing models, the cession of rights for particular or worldwide markets, and financial support with a role in production), thus multiplying its presence at home but above all abroad. Latin American stars had started to appear in González's films in the late 1940s: the Argentine Luis Sandrini starred in *¡Olé, torero! / Olé, Matador!* (Benito Perojo, 1948) and the Mexican Jorge Negrete in *Teatro Apolo / The Apollo Theater* (Rafael Gil, 1950). In 1951, the Argentine director Hugo del Carril filmed for Suevia the remake of Perojo's 1926–7 *El negro que tenía el alma blanca*, and that same year González formalized his contract with Lola Flores for five films over two years, with the star receiving five million pesetas and daily subsistence of two thousand more. She would be followed by the Mexican María Félix, and later the Spanish actresses Carmen Sevilla, Paquita Rico, and Sara Montiel and child stars Joselito and Marisol (see Chapter 11). The bulk of the films in which these stars acted – all of them showing a clear transnational vocation, through their narrative model of Spanish and Latin American co-stars, or a Spanish star who goes to Latin America, as, for example, in *Marisol rumbo a Rio / Marisol bound for Rio* (Fernando Palacios, 1963) – have over the years become the principal, lasting image of Suevia Films. Not for nothing were they the company's chief source of revenue as well as accounting for a large number of its productions.

However, even in the 1950s Suevia Films did not limit itself to this kind of popular cinematic register. Seeking to achieve a balance between the different emergent tendencies in Spanish cinema and wishing out of vanity to silence certain critics who accused him of producing formulaic movies with no artistic value, Cesáreo González participated in the production of Juan Antonio Bardem's famous films *Muerte de un ciclista* and *Calle Mayor*, as well as Manuel Mur Oti's singular *Fedra / Phaedra* (1956). The take-off of international coproductions in the 1950s would offer fertile terrain for Suevia's production model, and its films – whether produced solo or jointly with other partners, such as Guión PC (the production company of Manuel Goyanes, Suevia's former general production manager) or Producciones Benito Perojo – would be exported widely, at least partly thanks to the appeal of its stars.

In 1962 González turned his company into a corporation: Suevia Films – Cesáreo González PCSA This change was an attempt to put his personal estate in order. González continued to run Suevia Films until his death in March 1968. The company maintained its rhythm of production during this final period but it seems that, after Marisol, its capacity to launch new stars that connected with popular audiences had exhausted itself.

Telecinco Cinema and El Deseo (Nuria Triana Toribio)

The Hated Five Percent Ruling

In early 2011, the future of film production in Spain was uncertain: the financing model of the previous decade was under attack and in danger of collapse. At stake was the participation of television companies in the funding of cinema. In 1999, the Partido Popular (Conservative) Government modified the 1994 Cinema Law by obliging television companies, private and public, to put five percent of their annual profits (six percent in the case of public television) into financing Spanish cinema. This was a far from negligible figure. It meant that between 1999 and 2009 television companies invested around a billion euros in Spanish cinema. As Rocío García and R. G. Gómez (2009: n.p.) state, "sólo en 2007 [...] las cadenas invirtieron un total de 153 millones de euros en obra audiovisual europea, de los que 124 fueron destinados a películas en lengua original española" (in 2007 alone [...] television channels invested 153 million euros in European audiovisual content, 124 million euros of which was devoted to films with Spanish as their original language). This model was a compromise, part of an attempt from the mid-1990s to free Spanish film from the heavy state subsidies introduced by the *Ley Miró* (Miró Law) in 1983. The Miró Law had attempted to stimulate the production of "quality" films, and was widely considered a failure in that respect, as well as proving financially debilitating (Besas 1997; Ansola González 2004). As part of the process of Spain's integration into the European Union, the subsequent Cinema Law of 1994 had tried to push cinema production toward a free-market model, with audiences the ultimate arbiter. That Spanish cinema was not ready for direct exposure to the market was recognized by the 1999 law; instead, it prompted a move to a mixed public/private funding system, with public funding coming from the state indirectly via public television.

This kind of funding model is not unheard of – both Italy and France operate comparable strategies (García 2009). As Esther Bintliff explains, in France "commercial television broadcasters [...] must invest a certain amount of their revenue in film production [...] and must also help out with distribution" (2011: n.p.). Like much Spanish legislation, the 1999 Cinema Law was modeled on French measures, but in the case of Spain the measure was controversial and unpopular from the start, especially with private television companies (Green 2007: 13). These companies awaited their opportunity to contest the legislation – an opportunity that arose in December 2009 when the Ley General del Audiovisual (General Audiovisual Media Law) was debated in parliament. At this point, the Unión de Televisiones Comerciales Asociadas (UTECA; Associated Commercial Television Channels Union) appealed to the Supreme Court and Constitutional Court against the mandatory five percent ruling, arguing that the requirement that one industrial sector subsidize another was unconstitutional (García and Gómez 2009).

The protest by UTECA threw the Spanish cinema world into disarray, provoking apocalyptic headlines such as "El cine español no sobrevivirá" (Spanish Cinema Will Not Survive) (García and Gómez 2009). Meanwhile, UTECA's president, Alejandro Echevarría (also chairman of Gestevisión Telecinco's board of directors), argued that, rather than being funded by imposition, the Spanish film industry should rethink its output so that national audiences would no longer reject Spanish films, as is currently the case (*El País* 2009). As of April 2012, the debate is ongoing and the courts have yet to deliver a verdict. Regardless of whether the five percent ruling is repealed or not, one thing is likely to remain a sensitive issue, provoking heated debate and anguished headlines: the fact that Spain is a country whose cinema is viable only if it can recoup its investment through international distribution and exhibition (Triana Toribio 2007: 154), and, it seems, a country hostile to its own cinema. Echevarría has a point.

These circumstances notwithstanding, the Partido Popular's 1999 five percent ruling created one of the two planks supporting Spanish cinema production today. As Jara Yáñez argues:

> A partir del inicio del siglo XXI el modelo de financiación de la mayor parte de las películas españolas no se concibe sin la participación de alguna cadena y su influencia

> acaba extendiéndose incluso al tipo de film que se empieza a producir a través de ellas o a los nuevos métodos de promoción y marketing que ponen en marcha. (2009: 39)
>
> Since the start of the twenty-first century, the financial model for most Spanish films has necessarily involved the participation of a television company and this additionally ends up affecting the kinds of films that start to be produced or the new promotion and marketing methods brought into play.

Television companies sustain all types of production, whether small films (with budgets of about two million euros) – which tend to seek state finance and have limited chances of reaching an international audience beyond film festivals, thus making coproduction with a television company essential – or big-budget films (over twelve million euros), which can be undertaken only by large transnational production companies and by television channel subsidiaries (see Triana Toribio 2007: 155).

The other plank had been created much earlier, in 1983, when the PSOE (Socialist) Government, through the Miró Law, had encouraged directors to act as independent producers for their own films. Currently, the independent producer is expected to apply for government grants and, where possible, join forces with a television company as a reluctant big partner. This paradigm is enshrined in the 2007 Cinema Law (Ley del Cine 55/2007), which, despite numerous challenges and hiccups, regulates Spanish cinema today. An independent producer is defined precisely as one who has no links to a television company:

> Aquella persona física o jurídica que no sea objeto de influencia dominante por parte de un prestador de servicio de comunicación-difusión audiovisual ni de un titular de canal televisivo privado, ni, por su parte, ejerza una influencia dominante, ya sea, en cualesquiera de los supuestos, por razones de propiedad, participación financiera o por tener la facultad de condicionar, de algún modo, la toma de decisiones de los órganos de administración o gestión respectivos. (Garanto 2009: 399)
>
> The physical or legal person who is not subject to dominant influence by an audiovisual communication/broadcasting service provider or by the owner of a private television channel and who does not exercise a dominant influence due to reasons of ownership, financial participation, or through being likely to affect in any way the decision-making processes of the administration or management of any such body.

If we look at recent figures, a Spanish film costs on average three million euros (ICAA 2007, 2008, 2009). Once the money has been secured, how is it spent? Regardless of the funding sources, the answer is the same in all cases. According to the Ministry of Culture's Instituto de la Cinematografía y de las Artes Audiovisuales (ICAA; Institute of Film and Audiovisual Media), most of the budget of a Spanish film goes toward paying the cast and crew, while the percentage dedicated to screenwriting and postproduction is lower than in other cinema industries.

Finally, as I have outlined elsewhere (Triana Toribio 2008: 259–60), the area that is most consistently neglected is promotion and marketing (ICAA 2008, 2009).

The following subsections will focus on two very different production companies: Telecinco Cinema, a subsidiary of the private television channel Telecinco, and the independent producer El Deseo. These have been chosen as two particularly successful as well as contrasting instances. It must be remembered that Telecinco Cinema is just one of several television-owned production companies, and that El Deseo cannot be seen as representative of all independent producers. Nevertheless, these two case studies should give some idea of the contemporary Spanish industry's diversity and versatility.

Telecinco Cinema SAU

2008 was an excellent year for Telecinco Cinema, the film production subsidiary of the television channel Telecinco (full name: Gestevisión Telecinco SA). It topped the list of biggest grossing producers in Spain with eighteen feature films, which attracted an audience of 3 810 847 and made 22 041 815 euros. The following year, 2009, was no less successful: *Celda 211 / Cell 211* (Daniel Monzón, 2009) and *Agora* (Alejandro Amenábar, 2009) were not only the undisputed box-office successes of the year but were also nominated for thirty-two Goya awards between them, with *Celda 211* winning eight (Juste 2010). *Agora*, as proudly announced at the time on Telecino Cinema's webpages (www.telecinco.es/t5cinema), secured a deal with Newmarket Films for distribution in the United States in January 2010. Given the paramount importance that international distribution has for Spanish cinema, this is a key indication of the company's strengths.

Telecinco Cinema's director Álvaro Augustín, who became a cinema producer as a consequence of the obligation to contribute five percent to film production, declared to Yáñez that his loyalties are to television's managerial mode of production, although he wants to be perceived as a television executive who is sympathetic to cinema. His priorities determine which projects are considered viable as well as the company's conception of cinema (Yáñez 2009: 81–111). However, his choices have to meet with the approval of key corporate members of the parent company Gestevisión Telecinco, such as its co-chief executive producer, Paolo Vasile, who is also chairman of Telecinco Cinema and has an extensive cinema background, having worked in the Italian film industry for over ten years before joining Gestevisión Telecinco (Reuters 2011) – Telecinco Gestevisión is, of course, part of the Italian media conglomerate Mediaset, controlled by media mogul Silvio Berlusconi.

In Augustín's view, the industry can accommodate only a very small number of experimental or arthouse films, but

> La mayoría de las personas que estamos dentro del sector queremos que las películas que producimos se vean – ya no sólo por ganar dinero, pues nos gustaría recuperar

> la inversión – , pero que también nuestros títulos [...] perduren en la memoria del espectador. Eso se consigue a través de la conexión con el público. Y muchas veces en este país [...] eso se olvida. (cited in Yáñez 2009: 91)
>
> Most of us in the sector want the films we produce to be seen – not just to make a profit, since we do want to recoup our investment – but we also want our films [...] to remain in audiences' memories. This can only be achieved by connecting with viewers. And in this country [...] that connection has been often neglected.

Telecinco's desire to find audiences for its films does not, however, extend to screening them on its own television channel, where commercial Hollywood fare dominates. This absence of Telecinco films from Telecinco's programming is yet further evidence of how precarious the five percent ruling is, and of how television companies regard it as an imposition.

Pre-empting accusations that this managerial strategy could make television-owned film companies favor repetition and sameness, since all decisions are taken by a committee with audience statistics being a prime consideration, Agustín insists that "Nunca hemos buscado una especialización en ningún género concreto" (we do not seek genre specialization) (cited in Yáñez 2009: 96). This declaration is consistent with Telecinco's approach to serial television drama, which aims to create "series that benefit from their own 'popular style,' and are 'intended to satisfy all kinds of audience'" (Smith 2003: 19). Telecinco Cinema's net is cast equally widely and since 2004, with Augustín as its helm, it has produced, as well as the Goya winners mentioned above, such box-office successes as *El otro lado de la cama / The Other Side of the Bed* (Emilio Martínez Lázaro, 2002), *Días de fútbol / Football Days* (David Serrano, 2003), and *El orfanato / The Orphanage* (Juan Antonio Bayona, 2007). Its big hits for 2006 were *Alatriste* (Agustín Díaz Yanes) and *El laberinto del fauno / Pan's Labyrinth* (Guillermo del Toro), the latter not only an international box-office hit but also a success with film critics.

El Deseo SA

Pedro and Agustín Almodóvar registered El Deseo as a limited company (*sociedad anónima*) on June 14, 1985, with both brothers as partners. Smith has emphasized the importance of the company's "fraternal" conception:

> Few visitors could fail to be impressed by the loyalty and industry of Almodóvar's "family" of coworkers (most particularly by his producer-brother Agustín) and by their determination to protect him from the unsympathetic critics [...]. It would be difficult to underestimate the role of such a collaborative enterprise in the success of films identified [...] by the single name "Almodóvar". (1994: 4)

For Brown (2003), too, the secret behind El Deseo's resilience is that, as a production outfit, it is the work of a team of close collaborators: the Almodóvar brothers and their trusted production manager Esther García. This is a business run very much on family company lines. Nothing could be more removed from Telecinco Cinema's committee-led managerial model.

As Esther García has explained in an interview, tight control and modest budgets are the key to the company's survival (Triana Toribio 2006b). El Deseo echoes the production strategy outlined by Telecinco Cinema's director Agustín in that it does not aim for specialization beyond producing "quality films." However, as I have observed elsewhere, "quality means for El Deseo a preference for films that show arthouse characteristics or those which are willing to push the boundaries of genre and experiment with any aesthetic dictated by generic conventions" (Triana Toribio 2007: 158). Whenever El Deseo collaborates with other companies as production partners (as it has done with the Spanish division of Warner Bros., Catalan television, and the film company Mediapro), it has always been on a film-by-film basis, without committing to big-budget projects (Evans 2007), reining in spending in compliance with a strategy that has served it well since the 1980s. Despite its modest aims and tightly controlled strategies, El Deseo has nurtured new talent and helped to launch careers such as those of Álex de la Iglesia and Isabel Coixet. Moreover, international filmmakers such as Lucrecia Martel and Guillermo del Toro first gained entry to the world of Spanish cinema coproduction with El Deseo's support, even if they subsequently worked with other producers – in Del Toro's case, principally large television companies. All of El Deseo's collaborations have been more or less hand-picked by its production team, and have involved working with trusted partners with whom they felt an affinity.

Marketing and the Internet

The 2007 Cinema Law aims, unambiguously, to protect independent national producers against the Hollywood "majors" and to encourage them to work alongside film production companies founded on television money. According to a report in *El País* on the Law's first presentation to the media, tellingly entitled "Espaldarazo al productor independiente" (A Leg-up for Independent Producers), this course of action was intended primarily to benefit Spain's strongest and most established production companies, identified in the article as El Deseo (Agustín y Pedro Almodóvar), Tornasol Films (Gerardo Herrero), Lola Films (Andrés Vicente Gómez), Enrique Cerezo PC (Enrique Cerezo), and Filmax (Julio Fernández) (García 2006). The 2007 legislation indicates evident will on the government's part to protect such independent producers' status and freedom of action, irrespective of their very different production priorities.

A notable effect of the mandatory involvement of television companies in the financing of cinema has been an improvement in marketing and publicity. Since these companies' priority has been "not to lose money making films" (Triana Toribio 2006a: 161), they have indeed lifted the bar of publicity budgets and costly campaigns. One relatively economical way to improve publicity is through the Internet. That El Deseo SA and Telecinco Cinema have very different understandings of the Spanish film industry is very evident in their modes of self-presentation as found on their respective websites.

Telecinco Cinema's webpages (www.telecinco.es/t5cinema) are accessed via the television channel's main website (www.telecinco.es). One has to trawl through innumerable spots on Telecinco's home page – devoted to current serials, gossip and sports programs, and the ongoing reality-TV contest *Gran Hermano / Big Brother* – before finally arriving at the link to Telecinco Cinema almost at the bottom on the left (as of April 17, 2012, when most recently accessed). Telecinco Cinema clearly does not share space with the other sections of Telecinco's home page on an equal footing. The secondary position of cinema production at Telecinco is thus explicitly indicated in graphic form on its website. The main function of www.telecinco.es is undoubtedly to serve as a showcase for its television programs, to offer access to schedules, and to provide web links so that viewers can rewatch the most iconic moments of recent episodes, rather than to serve as a display case for its cinema production. The cinema pages themselves are in no way differentiated from the main television pages in style or mode of presentation, and make a striking contrast to www.eldeseo.es. The sole purpose of El Deseo's webpage is to showcase the films it produces and to provide information about prizes, events, and future projects. Its pages are aesthetically very different from those of Telecinco Cinema. In contrast to the image-rich, wall-to-wall market-stall presentation of Telecinco Cinema, El Deseo displays its content against a white background on which sparse headlines and links are located. The images are smaller and there is consistency in the colors used for banners and links. In other words, as might be expected, aesthetic values come to the fore on El Deseo's site, which was designed by the award-winning David Guaita (see www.davidguaita.com/trabajosdef.htm), while commercial values predominate on the Telecinco site, which does not identify its designer.

Despite the discrepancy between the ethos of Telecinco Cinema and El Deseo as (respectively) television-owned film producer and independent film producer, it must be remembered that both kinds of production company underpin the Spanish film industry. Regardless of the many criticisms leveled against this polarized two-pronged model and its frequently aired shortcomings (it has become a cliché to say that Spanish cinema has no industry or that the industry, such as it is, is in perpetual crisis), Spanish films continue to be made and shown.

Producciones La Iguana, Lamia Producciones, and Miss Wasabi Films (Tatjana Pavlović)

Icíar Bollaín, Helena Taberna, and Isabel Coixet – Spain's foremost contemporary women filmmakers – also run their own production companies, which mainly produce their own films: Producciones La Iguana S. L. (founded 1991, co-owned), Lamia Producciones (founded 2001), and Miss Wasabi Films (founded 2000), respectively. Bollaín's long and successful acting career preceded her directing and producing in the mid-1990s. As Susan Martin-Márquez has argued, Bollaín's socially aware themes manifest the present-day cultural turn wherein "the treatment of notions of home, of displacement, and of cultural difference emerges from contemporary contexts of globalization rather than from the traumas of the post-Civil War period" (2002: 257). Taberna has participated in Spain's film industry since 1994 through shorts and documentaries and in 2000 she directed her first feature, *Yoyes*, the fictionalized biography of a former member of the terrorist group ETA. Taberna focuses on the themes of gender and history and their intersection, as well as the use of cinema as a pedagogical tool. Coixet entered Spain's film scene in the late 1980s with *Demasiado viejo para morir joven / Too Old to Die Young* (1988), a critical and box-office disappointment. Her second feature film, the transnational success *Things that I Never Told You* (1996), appeared nearly a decade later. Initially trained in audiovisual advertising, Coixet became one of the most thriving film directors of her generation, in the age of postmodern global authorship.

All three filmmakers have been categorized as "women directors," given the prominence in their films of themes such as domestic violence, the female body, rape, emotional trauma, and female terrorism. However, of these three, Taberna is the only one who embraces that label: she is the founder of the Asociación de Mujeres Cineastas y de Medios Audiovisuales (CIMA; Association of Women in Cinema and Audiovisual Media). Coixet, conversely, has invented her own cinematic genealogy. As Belén Vidal has pointed out: "the director inserts herself into a preferred lineage of cinephile filmmakers, bypassing other more contested categories such as a 'Spanish director' or even 'Spanish woman director'" (2008: 222). It is worth remembering that Coixet's debut film was aided by the government funding for young directors that the Miró decree (popularly known as the Miró Law) enabled (Triana Toribio 2008: 63). This subvention mechanism also assisted the careers of Bollaín and Taberna, whose beginnings coincided with a moment when the economic and social structures of Spanish cinema were changing. A product of the Socialist ethos of 1980s film production, the Miró Law has often been criticized for its excessive subsidies for "quality cinema." It nevertheless contributed to the 1990s boom of Spanish women directors.

As producers, all three women survived the economic liberalization of the film market in the 1990s and forged successful careers in an extremely volatile industry, marked by domestic and foreign competition for funding and audiences. Each producer has cultivated her own niche sector, a differentiation mechanism that targets a particular class of audience across national boundaries. Bollaín enjoys a mainstream, intellectual following among socially engaged and politically liberal audiences. Her films' critical and popular success is the result of their contemporaneity, exploring problems plaguing Spain's rapidly changing social structures. Well known before venturing into directing, Bollaín had long established herself as a "trusted brand" among her target audience.

While Bollaín operates from Madrid, Taberna created Lamia Producciones in order to develop film projects outside Spain's major film production centers (see www.lamiaproducciones.com). She strategically aligns herself with "women's cinema" and "Basque film," using both labels as leverage to secure promotion and funding. Coixet's work, in contrast, belongs to a new current of international filmmakers who are experimenting with innovative methods of narration. These methods include the separation of films from their national context and the adoption of English as a lingua franca. Her cinema involves trans-European and global cooperative efforts, transnational casts and crews, and often a polyglot sound track. It models itself on the aesthetic and marketing strategies of both European art cinema and American independent cinema (Triana Toribio 2006a; Camporesi 2007; Vidal 2008).

For each director, market and artistic vision are interrelated. This is above all true for Coixet. Triana Toribio describes her as a "directora mediática" (media-savvy director) who illustrates the "increasing importance of the auteur as a *commercial* strategy for organizing audience reception, as a critical concept bound to distribution and marketing aims that identify and address the potential cult status of an auteur" (2008: 261; emphasis in original). The marketing of Coixet's films is partly done via her official website, www.misswasabi.com, a subsidiary of www.clubcultura.com, a portal that supports other Spanish directors such as Almodóvar and Amenábar. ClubCultura.com is in turn hosted by FNAC, a French multinational culture industry company that provides commercial links to products available on the FNAC online shopping site, including videos, books, DVDs, and video games. As Triana Toribio has observed, "in promoting filmmakers as auteurs [these homepages] undermine the usual romantic view of authorship by presenting it as a marketing device, a way of organizing the merchandise" (2008: 268).

Producciones La Iguana, Lamia Producciones, and Miss Wasabi are connected to a variety of outside sources that make possible their success in today's competitive production market: (1) domestic and global coproductions; (2) private and public financing; and (3) new sales platforms that disseminate films through a wide variety of cultural venues. The involvement with globally interlinked production, distribution, and exhibition companies is extensive. Bollaín and La Iguana have collaborated with Fernando Colomo PC, Alta Films, and Sogecine; Taberna and Lamia Producciones have worked with HT Producciones, Enrique Cerezo's CIPI Cinematográfica, Mact Productions, Marvel Movies, Sherlock Films, Golem, Columbia Tristar, and Italian Intrafilms; and Coixet and Miss Wasabi have operated largely in the English-language context, through collaborations with Carbo Films, Eddie Saeta SA, Seventh Art Releasing Production Co., Sony Classics, and Lakeshore Entertainment, as well as El Deseo and the Catalan Mediapro and Versátil Cinema. These creative partnerships point to the new transnational cast of Europe's national cinemas. Given Hollywood distributors' mergers and alliances with local European companies, it is obsolete to speak of Spanish production and distribution models as being in opposition to those of Hollywood (Pardo and Yordan 2005; Triana Toribio 2006a).

The three directors embrace a range of funding models. This is especially visible in the work of Taberna and Coixet. Taberna has generally opted for the local model, relying above all on Basque institutions and funding networks. Coixet has refused to direct and produce within the strict limits of the national context, a decision that has brought economic consequences, particularly in the light of Catalan funding "censorship" and restrictive language policies (Triana Toribio 2006a: 54–6). Despite the tensions between Spanish film funding policy and Coixet's transnational focus, *The Secret Life of Words* (2005) received significant recognition from the Spanish film industry in 2006, winning the Goya awards for Best Director, Best Original Screenplay, Best Production, and Best Picture. Moreover, it was the first time in Spanish film history that an English-language work, filmed and produced abroad, had been awarded the prize for Best Picture. Coixet's case signals a paradox: national subsidies intended for the promotion of local culture at times conflict with filmmakers' transnational artistic ambitions.

Finally, the promotion strategies of these filmmakers mirror their production and funding models. Their films are showcased, promoted, and disseminated through festivals, retrospectives, and cultural institutes. Historically, the Spanish film industry has suffered from poor marketing. During the 1980s, the Miró Law "concentrated resources on heavily subsidizing film production and protecting its exhibition" (Triana Toribio 2008: 261), and in the next decade the promotional budget rarely surpassed twenty percent of a film's total budget, a sum inadequate to compete in the global market. Marketing strategies are crucial, now that theatrical exhibition is no longer the primary forum in which films are consumed. The average commercial run in cinemas is merely four weeks, due to competition from video, television schedules, and issue of soundtracks. La Iguana, Lamia, and Miss Wasabi have responded to the changes in format, production platform, and consumption. Today, revenues come from the repackaging of films by distributors of new technologies: television (selling screening rights to national and international television channels such as Televisión Española, Canal Plus, ETB, and Vía Digital); DVD; screenings outside commercial cinema venues; and dissemination at specialized fora and congresses.

Bollaín's, Taberna's, and Coixet's production companies have responded to social, economic, industrial, and political shifts by using new, dynamic industrial practices, production techniques, and marketing strategies. This cinema brings to the fore questions regarding the relationship between national cinema, Hollywood, and art cinema, as these categories acquire new meaning in today's global context. Each filmmaker's body of work illuminates the ways in which the concepts of nation and national identity align or clash with institutional funding, promotion, and distribution in Spain, Europe, and even globally. Bollaín, Taberna, and Coixet have earned a place in Spain's film industry even while contesting the limits of national cinema: Taberna by operating within a smaller-scale audience and revenue niche; Bollaín by attending to the local as well as the global; and Coixet by reaching new heights in both audience and revenue figures. Through aesthetic innovation, personal authorial vision, and novel commercial practices, Spain's women director-producers have successfully navigated the recent transformations in Spain's film industry. Ownership of their own production companies has helped them to do so.

References

Ansola González, T. (2004) El decreto Miró: Una propuesta ambiciosa pero fallida para impulsar el cine español de los 80. *Archivos de la Filmoteca* 48: 102–21.

Besas, P. (1997) The Financial Structure of Spanish Cinema. In: Kinder, M. (ed.) *Refiguring Spain: Cinema/Media/Representation*. Durham: Duke University Press, pp. 41–59.

Bintliff, E. (2011) What's Holding the U. K. Film Industry Back? Online at: www.slate.com/articles/life/ft/2011/01/whats_holding_the_uk_film_industry_back.html (accessed January 15, 2011).

Brown, C. (2003) Almodóvar Pair Comes into Focus. *Screen International* (February 10). Online at: www.screendaily.com/almodovar-pair-comes-into-focus/4012208.article (accessed February 15, 2006).

Camporesi V. (2007) A ambos lados de todas las fronteras: Isabel Coixet y el cine contemporáneo. In: Peña Ardid, C. and Millán Muñio, M. A. (eds.) *Las mujeres y los espacios fronterizos*. Zaragoza: Prensas Universitarias de Zaragoza, pp. 55–69.

Castro de Paz, J. L. and Cerdán, J. (eds.) (2005) *Suevia Films-Cesáreo González: Treinta años de cine español*. A Coruña: Centro Galego de Artes da Imaxe / IVAC / Filmoteca Española / AEHC.

CIFESA, de la antorcha de los éxitos a las cenizas del fracaso (1990) Special issue of *Archivos de la Filmoteca* 1 (4).

El País (2009) González-Sinde defiende la "constitucionalidad" de las ayudas de las televisiones al cine (December 22, 2009). Online at: http://sociedad.elpais.com/sociedad/2009/12/22/actualidad/1261436403_850215.html (accessed December 22, 2009).

Evans, C. (2007) Warner Bros in Spain to Develop and Co-produce El Deseo Films. Online at: www.screendaily.com/warner-bros-in-spain-to-develop-and-co-produce-el-deseo-films/4035068.article (accessed May 30, 2010).

Fanés, F. (1989) *El cas CIFESA: Vint anys de cine espanyol (1932–1951)*. Valencia: Filmoteca Generalitat Valenciana.

Fernández Colorado, L. and Cerdán, J. (2007) *Ricardo Urgoiti: Los trabajos y los días*. Madrid: Filmoteca Española.

Garanto, A. (2009) Glosario. In: Yáñez, J. *La aritmética de la creación: Entrevistas con productores del cine español contemporáneo*. Alcalá de Henares: Festival de Cine de Alcalá de Henares / Comunidad de Madrid, pp. 389–401.

García, R. (2006) Espaldarazo al productor independiente: Cultura presenta al sector cinematográfico y de televisión las bases de la nueva ley del cine. *El País* (December 29): 39.

García, R. (2009) Entre la tranquilidad y la preocupación. *El País* (December 22). Online at: http://elpais.com/diario/2009/12/22/sociedad/1261436402_850215.html (accessed December 22, 2009).

García, R. and Gómez, R. G. (2009) El cine español no sobrevivirá. *El País* (December 23). Online at: http://elpais.com/diario/2009/12/23/cultura/1261522801_850215.html (accessed December 23, 2009).

George, D., Larson, S., and Mercer, L. (2007) Disintegrating Pictures: Studies in Early Spanish Film. *Studies in Hispanic Cinemas* 4 (2): 73–8.

González González, L. M. (2009) *Fascismo, "kitsch" y cine histórico español (1939–1953)*. Cuenca: Universidad de Castilla-La Mancha.

Gramsci, A. (1971) *Selections from the Prison Notebooks*. London: Lawrence & Wishart.

Green, J. (2007) The Art of Picasso. *Screen International* (Berlin 2007 special issue): 12–13.

Gubern, R. (1977) *El cine sonoro en la II República (1929–1936)*. Barcelona: Lumen.

Gubern, R. (1981) *La censura: Función política y ordenamiento jurídico bajo el franquismo (1936–1975)*. Barcelona: Península.

Gubern, R. (1987) Spagna: Dieci anni senza censura. *Bianco e nero* 1: 7–22.

Gubern, R. (1994) *Benito Perojo: Pionerismo y supervivencia*. Madrid: Filmoteca Española.

ICAA (2007) *Boletín Informativo*. Online at: www.mcu.es/cine/CE/Boletin/Boletin.html (accessed January 14, 2011).

ICAA (2008) *Boletín Informativo*. Online at: www.mcu.es/cine/CE/Boletin/Boletin.html (accessed January 14, 2011).

ICAA (2009) *Boletín Informativo*. Online at: www.mcu.es/cine/CE/Boletin/Boletin.html (accessed January 14, 2011).

Juste, M. (2010) Telecinco triunfa en los premios Goya 2010 (February 15). Online at: www.expansion.com/2010/02/15/empresas/medios/1266249116.html (accessed January 14, 2011).

Labanyi, J. (2007) Negotiating Modernity through the Past: Spanish Costume Film of the Early Franco Period. In: Delgado, L. E., Mendelson. J., and Vázquez, O. (eds.) *Recalcitrant Modernities: Spain, Difference, and the Construction of European Modernism*. Special double issue of *Journal of Iberian and Latin American Studies* 13 (2–3): 241–58.

Martin-Márquez, S. (2002) A World of Difference in Home-making: The Films of Icíar Bollaín. In: Ferrán, O. and Glenn, K. (eds.) *Women's Narrative and Film in Twentieth-Century Spain*. New York: Routledge / Garland, pp. 256–72.

Mira, A. (2004) Spectacular Metaphors: The Rhetoric of Historical Representation in CIFESA Epics. In: Lázaro Reboll, A. and Willis, A. (eds.) *Spanish Popular Cinema*. Manchester: Manchester University Press, pp. 60–75.

Pardo, A. and Yordan, P. (2005) Paradoxes of Survival in the Europe vs. Hollywood Battle: The Case of the Spanish Film Industry. Unpublished paper given at Society for Cinema and Media Studies Conference, London (March 31–April 3).

Reuters (2011) People: Gestevisión Telecinco, SA. (TL5.MC). Online at: www.reuters.com/finance/stocks/companyOfficers?symbol=TL5.MC (accessed January 14, 2011).

Riambau, E. and Torreiro, C. (1999) *La Escuela de Barcelona: El cine de la "gauche divine."* Barcelona: Anagrama.

Sánchez Salas, D. (2001) A diez kilómetros de Hollywood (La historia de E.C.E.S.A./Estudios de Aranjuez). In: J. García de Dueñas, and Gorostiza, J. (eds.) *Los estudios cinematográficos españoles*. Special issue of *Cuadernos de la Academia* 10 (December): 81–117.

Smith, P. J. (1994) *Desire Unlimited: The Cinema de Pedro Almodóvar*. London: Verso.

Smith, P. J. (2003) Quality TV? The *Periodistas* Notebook. In: *Contemporary Spanish Culture: TV, Fashion, Art and Film*. Oxford: Polity Press, pp. 5–33.

Triana Toribio, N. (2006a) Anyplace North America: On the Transnational Road with Isabel Coixet. *Studies in Hispanic Cinemas* 3 (1): 49–66.

Triana Toribio, N. (2006b) Interview with Esther García, *El Deseo*, Madrid (unpublished).

Triana Toribio, N. (2007) Journeys of *El Deseo* between the Nation and the Transnational in Spanish Cinema. *Studies in Hispanic Cinema* 4 (3): 151–63.

Triana Toribio, N. (2008) Auteurism and Commerce in Contemporary Spanish Cinema: Directores mediáticos. *Screen* 49 (3): 259–76.

Vidal, B. (2008) Love, Loneliness and Laundromats: Affect and Artifice in the Melodramas of Isabel Coixet. In: Beck, J. and Rodríguez Ortega, V. (eds.) *Contemporary Spanish Cinema and Genre*. Manchester: Manchester University Press, pp. 219–238.

Yáñez, J. (2009) *La aritmética de la creación: Entrevistas con productores del cine español contemporáneo*. Alcalá de Henares: Festival de Cine de Alcalá de Henares / Comunidad de Madrid.

Further Reading

Ávila, A. (1997) *La censura del guión en España*. Barcelona: CIMS.

Benet, V. J. (2005) Estilo, industria e institución: Reflexiones sobre el canon del cine español actual. *Archivos de la Filmoteca* 49: 67–81.

Buñuel, L. (1982) *Mi último suspiro*. Barcelona: Mondadori.

Cebollada, P. (1963) *La censura de cine en España*. Madrid: Centro Español de Estudios Cinematográficos.

Durán, J. A. (2003) *Cesáreo González: El empresario espectáculo. Viaje al Taller de Cine, Fútbol y Varietés del general Franco*. Pontevedra: Diputación de Pontevedra / Taller de Ediciones J. A. Durán.

Fanés, F. (1982) *CIFESA, la antorcha de los exitos*. Valencia: Institución Alfonso el Magnánimo (Shorter version of the 1989 book in Catalan listed in "References" above, included here for readers without a knowledge of Catalan.).

García de Dueñas, J. (2000) *El imperio Bronston*. Madrid: Ediciones el Imán / Filmoteca Generalitat Valenciana.

García de Dueñas, J. and Gorostiza, J. (eds.) (2001) *Los estudios cinematográficos españoles*. Special issue of *Cuadernos de la Academia* 10 (December).

García Escudero, J. M. (1978) *La primera apertura: Diario de un director general*. Barcelona: Planeta.

García Fernández, E. C. (1990) Aproximación a la obra de Cesáreo González productor cinematográfico. In: Romaguera i Ramio, J., Aldazábal Bardaji, P., and Aldazábal Sergio, M. (eds.) *Hora actual del cine de las autonomías del estado español: II Encuentro de la AEHC*. San Sebastián: Filmoteca Vasca, pp. 287–304.

González Ballesteros, T. (1981) *Aspectos jurídicos de la censura cinematográfica en España: Con especial referencia al período 1936–1977*. Madrid: Universidad Complutense.

Green, J. (2002) Spain's Independents Face Wealth Gap. *Screen International* 1341: 1–2.

Gubern, R. and Font, D. (1975) *Un cine para el cadalso: Cuarenta años de censura cinematográfica en España*. Barcelona: Euros.
Heredero García, R. (2000) *La censura del guión en España*. Valencia: Filmoteca Generalitat Valenciana.
Jäckel, A. (2003) *European Film Industries*. London: BFI.
Labanyi, J. (2004) Buñuel's Cinematic Collaboration with Sáenz de Heredia 1935–36. In: Evans, P. and Santaolalla, I. (eds.) *Buñuel 2000*. Zaragoza: Institución Fernando el Católico / Prensas Universitarias de Zaragoza, pp. 293–301.
Martínez Breton, J. A. (1987) *Influencia de la Iglesia católica en la cinematografía española (1951–1962)*. Madrid: Harofarma.
Neuschäfer, H.-J. (1994) *Adiós a la España eterna: La dialéctica de la censura. Novela, teatro y cine bajo el franquismo*. Barcelona: Anthropos.
Sánchez Vidal, A. (1984) *Luis Buñuel: Obra cinematográfica*. Madrid: Ediciones J. C.
Sánchez Vidal, A. (1991) *El cine de Florián Rey*. Zaragoza: Caja de Ahorros de la Inmaculada de Aragón.
Taibo I, P. I. (2002) *Un cine para un Imperio*. Madrid: Oberón.

15

Film Clubs, Festivals, Archives, and Magazines

Ferran Alberich, Román Gubern, and Vicente Sánchez-Biosca

Film Clubs (Román Gubern)

Film clubs have played a major role in Spain, in introducing the late 1920s Spanish avant-garde to European experimental cinema, and, under the Franco dictatorship, in exposing largely student audiences to a wider range of international cinema than was accessible in commercial venues, as well as encouraging social readings of film texts that helped to shape the consciousness of the anti-Franco opposition. A key feature of these film clubs was a pedagogical concern to produce an intellectual elite that, whether for artistic or political reasons, sought to distinguish itself from the general public for commercial cinema.

Private screenings were organized for film lovers in several cities throughout the 1920s, but the start of *cineclubismo*, as the phenomenon is called in Spain, is usually given as May 1927, when Luis Buñuel started to organize cinema sessions at Madrid's elite university hall of residence, the Residencia de Estudiantes, as part of its extracurricular program (see Gubern 1999: 260–70). Buñuel introduced the sessions personally. The first May 1927 session screened *Rien que les heures / Nothing but Time* (Alberto Cavalcanti, 1930) and *Entr'acte* (René Clair, 1924), together with examples of accelerated and slow motion and a dream sequence from *La Fille de l'eau / Whirlpool of Fate* (Jean Renoir, 1924). The March 1928 session screened *La Coquille et le clergyman / The Seashell and the Clergyman* (Germaine Dulac, 1927) and *La Glace à trois faces / The Three-sided Mirror* (Jean Epstein, 1927). The December 1928 session, held at the Teatro Princesa, screened *La Passion de Jeanne d'Arc / The Passion of Joan of Arc* (Carl Th. Dreyer, 1928), with an introductory lecture by Valentine Victor Hugo. The success of these screenings led to the creation of the

A Companion to Spanish Cinema, First Edition. Edited by Jo Labanyi and Tatjana Pavlović.

Cineclub Español, linked to the cultural magazine *La Gaceta Literaria* (see Gubern 1999: 271–389). Both the film club and the magazine were directed by Ernesto Giménez Caballero; the magazine's film feature was, from the second issue in January 1927, run by Buñuel, who would write ten articles for it through April 1929. Cineclub Español's creation was announced in October 1928, though its first session did not take place until December 23. Its organizing committee combined intellectuals and aristocrats, and Buñuel did the programming from Paris up to its sixth session, devoted to film comedies (May 4, 1929). From then on, Giménez Caballero took over programming with input from César M. Arconada, Juan Piqueras, Luis Gómez Mesa, and Miguel Pérez Ferrero. Its members included avant-garde writers and artists such as Ramón Gómez de la Serna, Rafael Alberti, Federico García Lorca, Rosa Chacel, Maruja Mallo, José Moreno Villa, Vicente Aleixandre, and José Bergamín, and the radio (and later film) empresario Ricardo Urgoiti (for Urgoiti, see the section "Filmófono" in Chapter 15). This cinephile elite was captured on celluloid by Giménez Caballero in his remarkable avant-garde documentary *Noticiario del cineclub / Film Club News* (1930).

Buñuel had wanted to inaugurate the Cineclub Español's sessions with Erich von Stroheim's *Greed* (1923) but MGM refused permission, fearing it would go down badly. Programming for its twenty-one sessions, held between December 1928 and May 1931, was eclectic. It combined work by established directors (*Das Wachsfigurenkabinett / Waxworks* (Paul Leni, 1924), *Tartüff / Tartuffe* (F. W. Murnau 1925), *Feu Mathias Pascal / The Living Dead Man* (Marcel L'Herbier, 1926), *La Chute de la maison Usher / The Fall of the House of Usher* (Jean Epstein, 1928), *Un chapeau de paille d'Italie / The Horse Ate the Hat* (René Clair, 1928), *Sous les toits de Paris / Under the Roofs of Paris* (Clair, 1930)) with experimental films (*Schatten / Warning Shadows* (Artur Robison, 1923), *Le Ballet mécanique* (Dudley Murphy and Fernand Léger, 1924), *La Marche des machines / The March of the Machines* (Eugène Deslaw, 1927), *Lonesome* (Paul Fejos, 1928), *La Perle / The Pearl* (Georges Hugnet, 1929), and Buñuel's own *Un chien andalou* (1929), shown on December 8, 1929). In addition, it screened documentary films (*Moana* (Robert Flaherty, 1926), *Skyscraper Symphony* (Robert Florey, 1929), *Esencia de verbena / Essence of Carnival* (Giménez Caballero, 1930), the zoological documentaries of Jean Painlevé); feminist cinema (*La Souriante madame Beudet / The Smiling Madame Beudet* (Germaine Dulac, 1923)); the new sound cinema (*The Jazz Singer* (Alan Crosland, 1927), which was booed because it was not shown with the original soundtrack, *Deutsche Rundfunk / German Radio Broadcasting* (Walter Ruttmann, 1928)); Soviet cinema (*Battleship Potemkin* (Sergei M. Eisenstein, 1925), which was screened at the final session, *Storm over Asia* (Vsevolod Pudovkin, 1928), *Women of Ryazan* (Olga Preobrazhenskaya, 1928), *The General Line* (Eisenstein, 1929)); Chinese cinema; film comedies; and cartoons. The only Spanish film shown was fragments of Francisco Camacho's 1929 *Zalacaín el aventurero / Zalacaín the Adventurer*, based on Pío Baroja's novel and then at postproduction stage. The presenters included Giménez Caballero, as well as Buñuel, the French director Dulac, Urgoiti, the eminent doctor Gregorio Marañón, and the writers Gómez de la Serna, Alberti, García Lorca, Baroja, Benjamín Jarnés, and Eugenio Montes.

Barcelona's role as the center of the early Spanish film industry should not be forgotten. In April 1929 the Barcelona cultural weekly *Mirador* (1929–37), whose film column was run by Josep Palau, started its Sesiones Mirador, with similar programming including films by Buñuel, Epstein, Clair, Deslaw, Man Ray, Cavalcanti, Henri Chomette, Hugnet, Murnau, Pudovkin, and Howard Hawks, among others. It organized the Spanish première of *Un chien andalou* (October 24, 1929) and the first screening in Spain of Soviet cinema (Pudovkin's *Storm over Asia* on November 28, 1929). In November 1930, after its eleventh session, *Mirador* announced that its screenings would be organized in collaboration with the distributor Cinaes, which had been running its own film club since that January. Their first joint session (November 7, 1930) again scored a first, with the Spanish première of *Battleship Potemkin* (screened by Madrid's Cineclub Español in May 1931). This collaboration was short-lived and Cinestudio Cinaes' private sessions continued independently of Sesiones Mirador, while other film clubs sprang up in the city: Barcelona Film Club, Horitzons, and Cine Amateur.

The declaration of the Second Republic in April 1931, ushering in new public freedoms, stimulated a rapid growth of film clubs. The Madrid distributor Filmófono, headed by Urgoiti with Buñuel as advisor, started private screenings at the Proa-Filmófono film studio on December 20, 1932 with *Kameradeschaft / Comradeship* (G. W. Pabst, 1931). Urgoiti invited Giménez Caballero to its inaugural session, which it regarded as a continuation of his Cineclub Español, but the latter publicly declined, bitterly alleging that he had been sidelined by the new Republican regime. Proa-Filmófono studio's programming favored Soviet cinema, chosen by Juan Piqueras from Paris. Its 1932 sessions included *The General Line* (Eisenstein), *October* (Eisenstein, 1929), *Turksib* (Victor Turin, 1929; a documentary on the building of the Turkestan–Siberia railroad), *Earth* (Aleksandr Dovzhenko, 1930), and *Das Lied von Leben / Song of Life* (Alexis Granowski, 1931). Also screened in 1932 were *The Crowd* (King Vidor, 1928), *The Wind* (Victor Sjöström, 1928), *Melodie der Welt / Melody of the World* (Ruttmann, 1929), *Le Sang d'un poète / Blood of a Poet* (Jean Cocteau, 1930; presented by Rafael Gil), *À nous la liberté* (Clair, 1931), *Berlin Alexanderplatz* (Phil Jutzi, 1931), and *Die Koffer des Herrn O. F. / Mr. O. F.'s Suitcases* (Granowsky, 1931). Included in its 1933 program were *Regen / Rain* (Joris Ivens, 1929), *La Chienne / Isn't Life a Bitch?* (Renoir, 1931), *L'Opéra des quat'sous / The Threepenny Opera* (Pabst, 1931), *Road to Life* (Nikolai Ekk, 1931), *Kuhle Wampe* (Slatan Dudow, 1932), and *Vampyr / Not against the Flesh* (Dreyer, 1932). This mix of artistic and political innovation was the hallmark of film club programming in those years. Filmófono, like Cinaes, was a distributor, which allowed it to promote certain films that it then released commercially in cinema theaters. Thus, between March and May 1931 (spanning the transition to the Republic), Cinaes exhibited in Barcelona *Mother* (Pudovkin, 1926), *Voyage au Congo / Journey to the Congo* (Marc Allégret and André Gide, 1927), *Les Deux timides / Two Timid Souls* (Clair, 1928),

Vormittagspuk / Ghosts before Breakfast (Hans Richter, 1928), *Regen* (1929), *China Express* (Ilya Trauberg, 1930), *The Dawn Patrol* (Howard Hawks, 1930), *Esencia de verbena* (1930), *Liliom* (Frank Borzage, 1930), and *Stürme über dem Montblanc / Avalanche* (Arnold Fanck, 1930). Although Spanish cinema was rarely screened by these film clubs, Cinestudio Cinaes did show Edgar Neville's *Falso noticiario / Fake Newsreel* (1933).

Film clubs fulfilled a useful function by offering private screenings of controversial film that, even with the general permissiveness under the Republic, could be screened only with precautionary measures. Banned in France, Buñuel's *L'Âge d'or* was shown in a private session at Urgoiti's Palacio de la Prensa Cinema in Madrid on November 22, 1931, and was screened again at the same venue, with *Un chien andalou*, on October 29, 1933. Barcelona's Cinestudio Cinaes and Cineclub Mirador screened it in January 1933 and May 1934 respectively, with some cuts ordered by the civil governor, though in June 1934 the Agrupació d'Amics de l'Art Nou (ADLAN; Association of Friends of Modern Art) advertised its exhibition in uncut form. The Grupo de Escritores Cinematográficos Independientes (GECI; Independent Film Writers Group), comprising Antonio Barbero, Rafael Gil, Luis Gómez Mesa, Benjamín Jarnés, and Manuel Villegas López, issued a founding manifesto in Madrid on September 26, 1933 blaming commercial publicity for corrupting film criticism. GECI's film club, inaugurated in November 1933, held thirty sessions through 1936, and published Villegas López's *Cita de ensueños (Appointment with Dreams)* and Gil's *Luz del cinema (Film Light)*. Villegas López was also the driving force behind Madrid's Cinestudio Imagen (not to be confused with the film club Cinestudio 33, also created in 1933). In December 1933, Cinestudio Imagen premiered Buñuel's documentary *Las Hurdes / Land without Bread* in a screening without soundtrack but with live commentary by the filmmaker. As noted in the section on censorship in Chapter 14, this documentary was banned from exhibition under the Radical-CEDA (Confederación Española de Derechas Autónomas) coalition government of November 1933 to January 1936 and not shown again until after Popular Front victory in February 1936, when it was screened at the same film club.

Under the Republic, film clubs also became a proletarian phenomenon. The magazine *Nuestro Cinema*, directed by the communist Juan Piqueras, convened a meeting of film club organizers in Madrid in July 1933, which produced a manifesto entitled "Hacia una Federación de Cineclubs Proletarios" (Towards a Federation of Proletarian Film Clubs), published in the magazine in October 1933, though the federation never materialized. Piqueras' Cinestudio *Nuestro Cinema* launched its first session in December 1934 with *Das blaue Licht / The Blue Light* (Leni Reifenstahl, 1932), introduced by Antonio del Amo; the participation of the Hungarian communist Béla Balázs in its script and shooting presumably made it ideologically acceptable. Cinestudio *Nuestro Cinema*'s programming followed the pattern of "proletarian film clubs," with their predilection for Soviet cinema, attempt to cater to a working-class public, irregular sessions, and ideological

Figure 15.1 *Nuestro Cinema* (June–July 1933) featuring a still from Joris Ivens' *Konsomolsk* (1932). Private collection.

instrumentalization of screenings through discussion sessions (see Figure 15.1). Cine-Teatro Club, linked to the Spanish Communist Party's daily *Mundo Obrero*, screened Soviet films and exhibited Party documentaries (e.g., *Primero de mayo en Madrid / 1st of May in Madrid*). Student and white-collar unions also created their own film clubs. The Federación Universitaria Escolar (FUE; Federation of University Students) ran the Cineclub FUE, directed by biologist Carlos Velo and journalist Fernando G. Mantilla, holding its sessions in Urgoiti's Palacio de la Prensa from 1933. Also active in 1933 was the Cineclub de los Empleados y Banca y Bolsa (Bank and Stock Exchange Workers Film Club), which produced the film *El despertar bancario / The Banks' Awakening*, a history of the Bank and Stock Exchange Workers Union.

In 1934 the film club scene expanded as specific groups set up their own organizations: Cineclub de la Juventud Roja (Red Youth Film Club), Cine-Studio Lyceum Club Femenino (Women's Lyceum Club Film Studio), Centro Cultural Deportivo Obrero Avanti (Avanti Workers Cultural and Sports Center), Cineclub La Lucha (The Fight Film Club), Cineclub Trabajadores de la Distribución y Producción de Material Cinematográfico (Film Distribution and Production Workers Film Club), Cineclub de Trabajadores de Comercio (Shopworkers Film Club), Cineclub del

Socorro Obrero Español (Spanish Workers Aid Film Club), Cineclub Frente Universitario (University Front Film Club), Cineclub del Socorro Obrero en el Cinema (Cinema Workers Aid Film Club), and Cineclub de la Biblioteca Circulante de Chamartín de la Rosa (Chamartín de la Rosa Lending Library Film Club), organized by the ubiquitous *cineclubista* Julio González Vázquez, who was linked to several "proletarian film clubs" and attracted Alberti and his fellow communist intellectual Wenceslao Roces to introduce its sessions.

The 1930s also saw the film club phenomenon spread throughout the country. Film clubs sprang up in Valencia, Seville, Toledo, Santander, Oviedo, and Cartagena. The Cine-Club Valencia held its first session on May 18, 1930, organized by Piqueras, while the Cine-Studio Popular de Valencia was linked to the communist magazine *Nuestra Cultura*, edited by the poster artist Josep Renau. The anarchists also took an interest in cinema, as seen in José Peirats' 1935 leaflet *Lo que podría ser un cine social* (*Blueprint for a Social Cinema*).

Fascism too paid attention to film, a communications medium to which Mussolini, Hitler, and Goebbels attached great importance. In December 1934, the Falangist Carlos Ruiz de la Fuente suggested to the Falange's founder, José Antonio Primo de Rivera, that they should use film as a propaganda tool, since Primo de Rivera was known to admire certain "social" films as conceived in Mussolini's Italy, as well as Henry Hathaway's colonial film *Lives of a Bengal Lancer* (1935). On February 23, 1935, the Film Club of the Sindicato Español Universitario (SUE; fascist Spanish University Students' Union), organized by Ruiz de la Fuente, held its first screening at Madrid's Cine Bilbao, at which it showed *Camicie nera* / *Blackshirts* (Giovacchino Forzano, 1933), described as "the Fascist Potemkin." Two months later, its second session screened the German film *Morgenrot* / *Dawn* (Gustav Ucicky, 1933), which extolled submarine warfare and heroic death.

After the Civil War, Valencia's Cineclub Mediterráneo, linked to Radio Mediterráneo, owned by the Falangist future film director, scriptwriter, and producer Vicente Escrivá, started to operate in late 1940. In Madrid in January 1941, the National Film Department created the government body Círculo Cinematográfico Español (CIRCE; Spanish Film Circle) to bring together film professionals and deal with their concerns; its film club was inaugurated in February with a screening of *Ninotchka* (Ernst Lubitsch, 1939). This state-run film club screened films banned by the censors, but the (also state-run) film magazine *Primer Plano* warned against attending its sessions out of idle curiosity rather than a thirst for knowledge. Again run by the state, the Círculo de Escritores Cinematográficos (CEC; Circle of Film Writers) founded its film club in Madrid in November 1945, holding 105 sessions through June 1951. 1945 also saw the creation of the Cineclub de Zaragoza (Zaragoza Film Club), founded by Eduardo Ducay, Manuel Rotellar, Antonio Serrano, and Orencio Ortega Frisón.

In November 1951, the Italian Cultural Institute in Madrid, which enjoyed diplomatic immunity, held its first Italian Film Week; a second followed in March

1953. These film series would form a landmark in the history of Spanish cinema. Their screenings of Italian neo-realist films previously unknown in Spain made a huge impact on Juan Antonio Bardem, Luis García Berlanga, and other young Spanish filmmakers, sending their careers in new directions. In 1951, the French Institute in Barcelona opened its Cercle Lumière. Foreign cultural institutes, with private film screenings for members, provided a haven for Spanish cinephiles for the almost forty years of the dictatorship.

University film clubs took on a similar dissident political function. The SEU, a Falangist organization, as explained above, was under the Franco dictatorship the mandatory, sole university students' union, run by the state; as such, it had responsibility for cultural activities across the whole Spanish university system. Film clubs started to be organized within its framework from 1940. The Cineclub del SEU in Barcelona, run by José María Castellet, was created in 1949, and organized a lecture cycle in the same year. In the 1950s, the SEU film clubs would grow into a network with government backing but frequently infiltrated by dissident cinephiles who turned its branches into sites of ideological resistance to the regime, as had happened in fascist Italy. Competing with them were the film clubs run by the Catholic Church – such as Madrid's Cineclub Vinces (1952–8) – under the umbrella of Acción Católica, which used cinema as form of proselytizing. When, in April 1952, the Madrid Ateneo held the first Congreso Nacional de Cineclubs (National Congress of Film Clubs), twenty-six organizations attended.

At this time, non-Church film clubs depended on the SEU's Departamento Nacional de Actividades Culturales (National Cultural Activities Department); from 1954 the latter's national leader was the communist activist Manuel Rabanal Taylor. To give an idea of programming: in 1955 the Salamanca SEU film club screened fragments of Eisenstein's *October* and Pudovkin's *Storm over Asia*, while from February to May 1956 its Barcelona equivalent, run by Román Gubern, programmed three Soviet films: Vladimir Petrov's *Thunderstorm* (1934), Aleksandr Ptushko's *The New Gulliver* (1935), and *Battleship Potemkin* – the screening of the last film was banned by the civil governor.

One of the most active SEU film clubs was the one in Salamanca, launched in March 1953 by a group led by Basilio Martín Patino, which from 1955 to 1963 published the magazine *Cinema Universitario*. It was this group that in 1955 would hold the controversial Salamanca Conversations. The first issue of *Cinema Universitario*, dated January–March 1955, defended neo-realism as a model for Spanish cinema, going against Francoist cultural policy. This first issue published the call for the Conversaciones Cinematográficas Nacionales (National Cinema Conversations), as they were officially titled. Its second issue – October–December 1955, after the Conversations had taken place, and edited by Luciano G. Egido, Joaquín de Prada and José María Gutiérrez – defended the meeting against government criticism. In its fourth issue (December 1956), J. F. Aranda reclaimed Buñuel for Spain in his essay "Buñuel nacional" while the eleventh issue (March 1960) was devoted to Joris Ivens. Contributors to the magazine included Bardem, Berlanga, Carlos Saura,

Ricardo Muñoz Suay, Ducay, Joaquín Jordà Gubern, Enrique Tierno Galván, and Mario Vargas Llosa. After its January–May 1963 issue, the magazine was banned. This was because of the hostile letter sent by Carlos Álvarez, a contributor to the magazine, to the censor and director of Filmoteca Nacional, Carlos Fernández Cuenca, commenting on the latter's criticisms of Orson Welles' *Le Procès / The Trial* (1962) and on the trial of the communist activist Julián Grimau, executed in April 1963 – an episode that led to Álvarez's own trial and imprisonment.

The call for the National Film Conversations was drafted jointly by the organizers of the SEU film club at Salamanca and the editorial team of the magazine *Objetivo*, affiliated to the clandestine Communist Party, in consultation with representatives of progressive Catholic sectors (such as José María Pérez Lozano) and of the critical wing of Falangism (such as Marcelo Arroita-Jáuregui). It criticized Spanish cinema for having abdicated its responsibility to be a "testigo de nuestro tiempo" (witness to our times), invoking the realist tradition of Spanish art and literature as a model for film. After obtaining government authorization, the encounter was held at Salamanca University from 14 to 19 May 1955, with the participation of Spanish film professionals and invited foreign speakers (Cesare Zavattini, Guido Aritarco, and Manoel de Oliveira; Georges Sadoul's attendance was not authorized). The papers coincided in their criticisms of Spanish cinema, asking for a more rational system of state production subsidies, distribution guarantees, a censorship code to replace the censors' current ad hoc mode of operating, the creation of a federation of film clubs, and an end to the monopoly of the state newsreel NO-DO. The critique formulated at Salamanca was summed up in Bardem's verdict that Spanish cinema was "políticamente ineficaz, socialmente falso, intelectualmente ínfimo, estéticamente nulo e industrialmente raquítico" (politically inept, socially hollow, intellectually vacuous, aesthetically worthless, and industrially stunted). The direct and indirect attacks on state control of Spanish cinema were accused in official quarters of being "subversive" but were supported by *Objetivo* and *Cinema Universitario*, and their reformist proposals were in large measure adopted by José María Garcìa Escudero (a participant in the Conversations) when in July 1962 he was appointed Director General of Film and Theater. But they were attacked by the radical left at the Primeras Jornadas Internacionales de Escuelas de Cinematografía (First International Film School Festival) at Sitges in 1967 (see the following section).

The Salamanca film club remained active but only in 1960 was it allowed to screen Rossellini's antifascist manifesto *Roma, città aperta / Rome, Open City* (1945). The second half of the 1950s saw a spectacular explosion of film clubs. In 1956, SEU film clubs were created in Seville and Pamplona (the latter an offshoot of the Zaragoza parent club). The magazine *Cine-Club*, the organ of SEU film clubs, started publication in May 1956, with fifteen issues through April 1958. This effervescence led the Ministry of Information and Tourism to issue an order of March 11, 1957 setting up a "Registro Oficial de Cine-Clubs" (State Register of Film Clubs); this was matched by the call for a Conference of Film Clubs in Madrid, to set up a federation to oversee their development and activities. But those film clubs linked to the Church refused to participate after a stormy conference in April of that year. On December 15, 1957, the Federación Española de Cineclubs (Spanish Federation of Film Clubs) was created, with José G. Maesso as president. Awareness of film clubs' social relevance lay behind the activities of the Cine-Club Monterols, housed in an Opus Dei residence in Barcelona, founded in 1951 but from 1957 launching an intensive program of activities, geared to the aesthetic concerns of the magazine *Cahiers du Cinéma*. In May 1960, this film club launched the magazine *Documentos Cinematográficos* with contributions from Jorge Grau, José Luis Guarner, and Javier Coma, paying particular attention to the financial and industrial aspects of cinema. It ceased publication in 1963.

By 1961 the Federation had eighty-six member film clubs. A government order of July 1963 authorized them to import foreign films. Another order of January 12, 1967 authorized "salas de arte y ensayo" (exclusive theaters licensed to screen art-house cinema) in cities with over fifty thousand inhabitants; their specialist programming produced strong competition for the film club network. In 1969 there were 244 federated film clubs. After Franco's death in 1975 and the abolition of censorship in November 1977 (when Buñuel's 1961 film *Viridiana* was finally premiered in Spain), things changed radically. 1977 saw the creation of the Confederación de Cineclubs del Estado Español (Confederation of Film Clubs of the Spanish State), which recognized the new political decentralization. But the dissident political agenda that had been such an important offshoot of film clubs under the dictatorship disappeared, at a time when television, regional *filmotecas*, and soon the appearance of domestic video players took over many of the functions that film clubs had previously fulfilled.

Film Festivals (Román Gubern)

The first film festivals in Spain were inaugurated during the Franco dictatorship, when – like film clubs, as we have seen – they had a significant political function. Initially designed to benefit the regime, they pushed the boundaries of what was or was not officially regarded as permissible, in some cases becoming spaces of more-or-less open dissidence.

After the United Nations announced its diplomatic boycott of the dictatorship on February 9, 1946, the government tried to break its international isolation by reactivating its relations with the countries of Spanish America, with the aim of integrating them into one big Hispanic political and cultural family (see Chapter 2). Already in November 1940 the regime had created the Consejo de la Hispanidad (Council of Hispanicity), one of whose first tasks was to produce the film *Raza / Race* (1942), a patriotic epic based on a screenplay by Franco and directed by the Falangist José Luis Sáenz de Heredia. In accordance with this strategy, the Sindicato

Nacional del Espectáculo (state-run National Entertainment Union) organized the first Certamen Cinematográfico Hispanoamericano (Spanish American Film Competition) in Madrid from June 27 to July 4, 1948, with the participation of Spain, Argentina, Mexico (which did not have diplomatic relations with Spain), Cuba, and a representative from Colombia. Although its aim was to encourage coproductions and commercial exchange in the field of cinema, it also functioned as a film festival, with films being screened from the participating countries; a jury diplomatically awarded the top three prizes to the Spanish film *Locura de amor / The Mad Queen* (Juan de Orduña, 1948), the Argentine *Dios se lo pague / God Reward You* (Luis César Amadori, 1948), and the Mexican *Río escondido / Hidden River* (Emilio Fernández, 1948), respectively. The plans to make this competition an ongoing event did not come to fruition but it did lead to some joint ventures (see "The Latin American Connection" in Chapter 2).

This conception of the film festival as a window onto cultural exchange with the outside world was not taken up again until the 1950s. The Semana Internacional de Cine de San Sebastián (San Sebastián International Film Week) was inaugurated on September 21, 1953 and promoted by local commercial and tourist organizations. Authorization was given to screen the occasional film banned from commercial release, such as Jacques Becker's *Casque d'or / Golden Marie* (1951), but the awards for Best Film, Best Director, and Best Leading Actor went to Rafael Gil's Catholic propaganda film *La guerra de Dios / I Was a Parish Priest* (1953). The following year the festival changed its name to Festival Internacional de Cine de San Sebastián (San Sebastián International Film Festival). The censorship board took a permissive line in authorizing films to be screened at the festival. Thus, in July 1958 the award for Best Film was given to Tadeusz Chmielewski's *Ewa chce spac / Eva quiere dormir / Eva Wants to Sleep*, from communist Poland, at a time when films from Eastern Europe could not be exhibited in Spain. Further, in July 1960 the Best Film award went to the Czech director Jiri Weiss' *Romeo, Julia a tma / Romeo, Julieta y las tinieblas / Romeo, Juliet and Darkness*. It was not until December 1965 that the Ministry of Information and Tourism, responsible for film censorship, would normalize the import of Soviet films and the export of Spanish films to the USSR. The San Sebastián Film Festival participated in the promotion of the New Spanish Cinema encouraged by the "liberalizing" policies of José María García Escudero as General Director of Film and Theater since 1962. Accordingly, it awarded the Concha de Plata (second prize) to Manuel Summers' *Del rosa ... al amarillo / From Pink ... to Yellow* in 1963 and to Basilio Martín Patino's *Nueve cartas a Berta / Nine Letters to Bertha* in 1966, and the Best Director award to Miguel Picazo's *La tía Tula / Aunt Tula* in 1964, as well as awarding the Concha de Oro (top prize) to Víctor Erice's *El espíritu de la colmena / The Spirit of the Beehive* in 1973, and to José Luis Borau's *Furtivos / Poachers* in 1975 (two months before Franco's death).

After the end of the dictatorship, the San Sebastián Film Festival, established as Spain's most influential film competition, continued to operate as a commercial platform for national cinema, thanks to the awards given to Jaime Chávarri's *A un dios desconocido / To an Unknown God* (1977), Jaime Camino's *La vieja memoria / The Old Memory* (1977), Manuel Gutiérrez Aragón's *Sonámbulos / Sleepwalkers* (1978), Gonzalo Herralde's *El asesino de Pedralbes / The Murder of Pedralbes* (1979), Carlos Saura's *Mamá cumple cien años / Mama turns 100* (1979), Imanol Uribe's *El proceso de Burgos / The Burgos Trial* (1980), and Gutiérerez Aragón's *Demonios en el jardín / Demons in the Garden* (1982), among other Spanish films.

In March 1956, the Catholic-inspired Primera Semana de Cine Religioso y de Valores Morales (First Religious and Moral Cinema Week) was held in Valladolid. The censors adopted a tolerant line toward this festival too, with its third edition of March 1958 awarding first prize to Jules Dassin's *Celui qui doit mourir / He Who Must Die* (1957), based on a novel by Nikos Kazantzakis; the film had been banned from general release in Spain. In 1960, this festival – which from that year regularly programmed films by Ingmar Bergman – was subdivided into two separate sections, "Religious Values" and "Human Values," which allowed it to broaden its scope and to give a special award to Manuel Summers' documentary *Juguetes rotos / Broken Toys* (1966). In 1972 it abandoned its initial thematic focus, changing its name to Seminci (Semana Internacional de Cine (International Film Week)). Fernando Lara, its director from 1983 to 2004, built the festival up into a prestige event, thanks to its rigorous selection criteria. Seminci also published monographic studies on Edgar Neville (1982), Luis Marquina (1983), and Carlos Serrano de Osma (1983), all by Julio Pérez Perucha, which helped to revive interest in the work of these neglected directors. When Fernando Lara had to give up directing Seminci, on receiving a government appointment as director of the Instituto de la Cinematografía y de las Artes Audiovisuales (ICAA; Institute of Film and Audiovisual Media), the festival entered into a period of instability.

September 1959 saw the beginning of the Semana Internacional de Cine de Color de Barcelona (Barcelona International Color Film Week), sponsored by the Cineclub Monterols, affiliated to an Opus Dei residence in the city (see the previous section). From 1975 it changed its name to Semana Internacional de Cine de Barcelona (Barcelona International Film Week), under the directorship of film critic José Luis Guarner. The political turbulence of the transition to democracy impacted on this Barcelona film festival, with the legal sequestration in October 1978 of Pier Paolo Pasolini's *Salò o le 120 giornate di Sodoma / Salò, or the 120 Days of Sodom*, thanks to a denunciation lodged with a local police court by a private citizen. In July 1987 it became the Primer Festival de Cine de Barcelona (First Barcelona Film Festival), in that year giving the awards for Best Film, Best Script, and Best Director to Agustí's Villaronga's *Tras el cristal / In a Glass Cage*; it subsequently declined.

In October 1959, the Certamen Internacional de Cine Documental Americano y Filipino (International American and Filipino Documentary Film Competition) opened in Bilbao, later becoming the Certamen Internacional de Cine Documental y Cortometraje de Bilbao (Bilbao International Documentary and Shorts Competition). From 1979 to 1981 it pioneered screenings of films made during the

Civil War, some of which had previously been shown only at the Filmoteca Nacional in Madrid, as well as publishing brochures on the topic.

The Primeras Jornadas Internacionales de Escuelas de Cinematografía (First International Film School Festival) took place in Sitges from 1 to 6 October 1967, screening work by film schools from a range of cities worldwide, including Moscow, Prague, and some Asian countries. During the discussion time, a group of radical Spanish filmmakers – Manuel Revuelta, Antonio Artero, Joaquín Jordà, and Julián Marcos – read out a manifesto, which was approved at the closing assesmbly. This demanded the abolition of the Sindicato Nacional del Espectáculo (state-run National Entertainment Union), censorship, government subsidies, and all control mechanisms, in strident opposition to the cautious "bourgeois reformism" of the May 1955 Salamanca Conversations. The police broke into the closing dinner, making several arrests, and the following year the festival was replaced with the more innocuous Festival Internacional de Cine Fantástico de Sitges (Sitges International Fantastic Cinema Festival), first held in September 1968. This festival has consolidated its reputation as a specialist competition. The revolutionary 1967 Sitges Manifesto became a reference point for critical sectors (mainly Maoist) to the left of the Communist Party, such as the "Marta Hernández" collective and the brothers Carlos and David Pérez Merinero (authors of the 1975 book *Cine y control* (*Cinema and Control*)).

In November 1969, the Primera Semana de Cine de Autor de Benalmádena (Benalmádena First Auteur Cinema Week), directed by Julio Diamante, was held in Málaga province. This competition, whose prizes were awarded by popular vote, offered rigorous programming, screening cinemas previously unknown in Spain (Chinese, Palestinian, Chicano, etc.), but suffered a police raid leading to arrests in 1970; it was held for the last time in April 1989.

Effectively, in the dictatorship's twilight years, certain film festivals and magazines became sites of cultural and political resistance, fighting for an alternative cinema culture to that espoused by the regime. As seen in Chapter 2, international film festivals also provided a haven for certain dissident Spanish filmmakers. Spain participated in the Cannes Film Festival for the first time in April 1953, with Neville's *Duende y misterio del flamenco* / *Flamenco* and Berlanga's *¡Bienvenido Mister Marshall!* / *Welcome Mr. Marshall!* The latter won a prize and generated a polemic (Edward G. Robinson, serving on the jury, demanded that an "anti-American" shot be cut), which led Franco to ask to see the film. In May 1961, Cannes awarded the Palme d'Or to Luis Buñuel's *Viridiana* but, as previously noted, the film was banned in Spain and would not be shown there until April 1977. The Venice Biennale of September 1956 gave the FIPRESCI prize (awarded by the International Critics Federation) to *Calle Mayor* / *Main Street* by Bardem, a communist activist who had been arrested by the Francoist police while shooting the film. And the same festival, in September 1960, awarded the same prize to the Italian director Marco Ferreri's Spanish production *El cochecito* / *The Motorized Wheelchair*, which was mutilated by the Spanish censors, leading to cancellation of the director's Spanish residence permit. This kind of complicity by international festival juries led the Ministry of Information and Tourism to issue an order on January 31, 1964 requiring Spanish producers to seek prior government authorization to submit their films to film festivals.

Chapter 2 has shown how Carlos Saura was one of the dissident directors who most benefitted from this international complicity. Not only did his film *La caza / The Hunt* (1965), whose script had suffered significant cuts at the censors' hands, win the Silver Bear for Best Director at the Berlin Film Festival of July 1966, but in July 1968 the same festival awarded a prize to his 1967 film *Peppermint frappé*. Although his *El jardín de las delicias / The Garden of Delights* (1970) was banned for seven months, it was authorized to enter the New York Film Festival; as a result of its enthusiastic reception there, it was authorized for release with three major cuts. In addition, Saura's *La prima Angélica / Cousin Angelica* (1974) received the Jury Special Award at Cannes in 1974, before its screening produced fascist protests in Spain, leading to the sacking of Pío Cabanillas as Minister of Information for having authorized the film's release.

General Franco's death in November 1975 marked the start of a new permissiveness in cinema, which impacted on festival programming. December 1975 saw the inauguration of the Primera Semana Internacional de Cine Iberoamericano de Huelva (Huelva First International Ibero-American Cinema Week – later renamed the Festival de Cine Iberoamericano de Huelva (Huelva Ibero-American Film Festival) – which the following year paid tribute to Buñuel, who travelled to Huelva for the event.

From 1977, when the first general elections since the 1930s were held, the climate of democratic euphoria produced an explosion in the number of festivals (though many would prove short-lived) at a time when cinema attendance was declining thanks to competition from television. In January 1980, the Primera Muestra de Cine Imaginario y Ciencia Ficción (IMAGFIC; First Festival of Imaginary and Science Fiction Film) opened in Madrid, continuing successfully until 1993. November 1980 saw the Primera Mostra de Valencia: Cinema del Mediterrani (First Valencia Mediterranean Cinema Festival), still active today.

Since the early 1990s, there has been a proliferation in Spain of specialist festivals, even microfestivals, focusing on Spanish cinema (Málaga), Latin American cinema (Lleida), African cinema (Barcelona), European cinema (Seville), comedy (Alfàs del Pi, Valencia), documentary (Barcelona, Pamplona, and Madrid), sports films (Seville), horror films (San Sebastián), youth cinema (Valencia), women filmmakers (Barcelona), gay and lesbian cinema (Barcelona), cinema of the south (Granada), erotic cinema (Barcelona, Madrid, and Seville), and so on. In 2009, a total of 233 film festivals were held in Spain. This illustrates a concern with niche marketing that is partly commercial and partly educative, and also a desire on the part of the various local communities to gain cultural capital and media attention. At a time when there are concerns about the future of cinema-going in Spain, the way forward may be intensive, specialist programming of this kind.

Film Archives (Román Gubern)

What follows is a story of loss, thanks to a late start, offset by a proliferation of activity in Spain's present-day autonomous communities. The result is a conception of national heritage in which the cultural diversity of Spain's regions plays a major role, while costly activities such as recuperation and restoration remain largely centralized in the national archives in Madrid, which are integrated into the central state apparatus.

The first national film archive conceived on modern cultural and technical lines was that of Sweden, founded in 1933, in a country whose film industry had blossomed economically and artistically in the 1920s. In the United States, the MoMA Film Library was created in 1935. At that time, the position of the Spanish film industry was precarious, while its productions enjoyed little cultural capital and attracted little government interest. Consequently, Spain was slow to organize an efficient storehouse to conserve its audiovisual heritage. The Spanish National Film Archives (Filmoteca Nacional) in Madrid were created by decree on February 13, 1953 as a state body within the Ministry of Information and Tourism, with the film historian and critic Carlos Fernández Cuenca serving as director until 1966. A year later, on April 2, 1954, the Cinemateca Educativa Nacional (National Educational Film Archive) was also set up in Madrid, within the Ministry of Education, specializing in pedagogical documentaries. Both initiatives were part of the modernizing cultural agenda that succeeded the prolonged period of political isolationism (autarky) from the Civil War's end in 1939 to the lifting of the United Nations' diplomatic boycott on the Franco regime in November 1950. By the time the Filmoteca Nacional was created, most silent cinema and films of the 1930s had definitively vanished from circulation and could not easily be recovered. The Filmoteca's founding collection came chiefly from the film stock that had been impounded by the Francoist authorities on military victory in 1939 (mainly Republican and Soviet films, plus wartime newsreels and documentaries) and that had survived the fire on August 16, 1945 at Madrid's Laboratorios Cinematiraje Riera, where this confiscated material was stored. The date of this fire, which destroyed the cinematic memory of the Republic and the war, and whose causes were never clarified, is politically suspicious since it coincides with the end of World War II, when it was felt that the Franco regime was likely to suffer reprisals because of its close political relations with the Axis powers (films from the Republican zone were kept in red tins and those from the Nationalist zone in blue tins). This fire plus four others at major laboratories make it likely that little more than ten percent of pre-1936 Spanish cinema has been conserved. A contributing factor to this devastation is the paradoxical "success syndrome," whereby the greater and more immediate a film's success, the more likely it is to suffer damage as a result of overuse of the negative to make copies. Another result of success is the generation of remakes, leading to neglect of the original version. Fernández Cuenca allowed occasional exhibition of films from the Filmoteca's archives (usually private screenings at film clubs), sometimes introduced by himself. These screenings helped to make the material deterioration irreversible, at a time when no professional preservation work was undertaken.

On his appointment as Director General of Film and Theater in July 1962, José María García Escudero encouraged an active program of activities at the Filmoteca. In 1963 it started weekly public screenings in Madrid and Barcelona, sometimes accompanied by the publication of monographs by Carlos Fernández Cuenca. The result, from 1963 on, was a series of studies of the work of Georges Méliès, E. A. Dupont, F. W. Murnau, Erich von Stroheim, Carl Dreyer, Robert Flaherty, Sergei Eisenstein, Jean Renoir, Florián Rey (cowritten with Florentino Soria), and the French New Wave. A decree of February 20, 1964 required all producers and distributors to deposit a copy of their films with Filmoteca Nacional if they had received some kind official credit or subsidy, but in practice the copies sent to the Filmoteca were often incomplete or defective (e.g., black-and-white copies of color films, or copies that included rejected footage).

After García Escudero was sacked in November 1967, the Filmoteca's activities declined until, on November 17, 1970, the Ministry of Information and Tourism reorganized it, naming Florentino Soria as director. After the institution of democracy, an order dated May 20, 1980 transferred to the Filmoteca the archives of the state newsreel NO-DO. In February 1982 the archives' name was changed to Filmoteca Española, constituted as an autonomous institution affiliated with the Ministry of Culture, with Berlanga briefly serving as its director. During the 1980s, which saw the start of a program of recovery and restoration of films, the Filmoteca was directed from April 1983 by Juan Antonio Pérez Millán and from October 1986 by Miguel Marías, who was replaced in October 1989 by the current director, José María Prado. In February 1989, thanks to the Madrid City Council's sponsorship, the Cine Doré – one of Madrid's oldest cinemas – was completely refurbished and inaugurated as the venue for Filmoteca Española's regular screenings. But the Filmoteca did not attain the planned administrative goal of operational autonomy; in the end its legal status was formalized as that of a general subdirectorate of the Institute of Film and Audiovisual Media (created in January 1985), within the Ministry of Culture.

The consolidation of democracy and the creation of autonomous regional governments allowed the gradual emergence of regional film archives, though the extent of their holdings and activities would vary greatly. The Basque Filmoteca (Euskadiko Filmategia) was established in May 1978, in San Sebastián, as a private initiative linked to the Partido Nacionalista Vasco (PNV; Basque Nationalist Party), legally constituted as a cultural association. Peio Aldazabal was appointed its first director. On January 1, 1981, at the Primeros Encuentros de Cine de Autor e de Arte i Ensaio (First Symposium on Auteur and Arthouse Cinema) in Vigo, the Filmoteca do Pobo Galego (Film Archives of the Galician People) was created, housed in Vigo's Municipal Cultural Center, but it proved short-lived. In Barcelona, a city with a major history of activity in the field of cinema, the Filmoteca of the

Generalitat de Catalunya (Catalan Autonomous Government) was instituted on June 1, 1981 under a decree transferring the operation of cultural services from the state to the Generalitat. Its first directors were Ramón Herreros and Ramón Font. Also in June 1981, Zaragoza City Council voted to institute the Filmoteca of Zaragoza, which would be headed by the historian Manuel Rotellar, with public programming starting on February 4, 1982. The Filmoteca Canaria, in Las Palmas de Gran Canaria, was set up on November 3, 1984 by an order of the Cultural Office of the Autonomous Government of the Canaries; this was followed on November 22 by the creation of the Filmoteca de Galicia by the Galician Autonomous Government – with a library, video library, and photo library – based in A Coruña. In February 1985, the Valencian Government established the Filmoteca de la Generalitat Valenciana, under the directorship of Muñoz Suay, which from May 1989 would publish the film journal *Archivos de la Filmoteca* (see the final section of this chapter). March 1987 saw the creation of the Filmoteca Regional de Murcia, effectively operational since January 1986. In December 1987, the Junta de Andalucía instituted the Filmoteca de Andalucía, based in Córdoba. In October 1989 the Centro Galego de Artes da Imaxe (Galician Center for the Visual Arts) was created in Santiago de Compostela; it functioned as a film archive with regular screenings. The Filmoteca de Castilla y León was established in January 1991 in Salamanca and opened in March with Juan Antonio Pérez Millán as director. And, on May 11, 1999 the Archivo del Sonido y de la Imagen de Mallorca (Audiovisual Archive of Majorca) was inaugurated, in Palma de Mallorca, directed by Margalida Alberti under the Consejo de Mallorca's Department of Culture and Heritage; this would become the future Filmoteca de Mallorca.

Not all the film archives listed here have been equally active. Although Filmoteca Española remains the most important because of the size of its holdings – some 34 000 items – and level of activities, the Filmotecas of Valencia and Catalonia (the latter holding an important collection of films by Segundo de Chomón) have also been extremely dynamic, as well as publishing major book series. The regional archives have had to rely on the technical services of Filmoteca Española for the preservation and restoration of their holdings. Filmoteca Española has pioneered the recuperation and restoration of historical material since the 1980s, thanks to the efforts of competent professionals such as Alfonso del Amo, Luciano Berriatúa, and Ferran Alberich (see the next section by Alberich). A major contribution to recuperation has been Filmoteca Española's acquisition of the Archivo Luis Buñuel from the filmmaker's family. Alfonso del Amo was responsible for the fundamental catalog of Spanish Civil War cinema (Del Amo 1996), published by Filmoteca Española as the first of an important collection of reference works, including inventories of Spanish directors of photography (Llinás 1989), art directors (Gorostiza 1997), screenwriters (Riambau and Torreiro 1998), and producers (Riambau and Torreiro 2008). These volumes, like those published jointly with the San Sebastián Film Festival, have made a notable contribution to the bibliography on cinema in Spain.

Film Preservation and Restoration (Ferran Alberich)

The expansion of film archives in the last few decades, discussed in the previous section, has hugely increased the availability to the public of Spanish films, through screenings, video libraries, and viewing facilities. However, it is not enough to build up film holdings; conservation needs to be supplemented by expert preservation and restoration work. The weakness of the Spanish film industry has been a major problem here. In the past, lack of continuity of production companies, with ownership of exhibition rights changing hands, meant that responsibility for the conservation of film stock fell on film laboratories, which became producers' de facto archives. The appearance of new forms of commercialization – first television broadcasting, then analog and digital home video – raised hopes that, given the new business opportunities, the holders of the rights would take an interest in preservation, but that did not happen. In Spain, television broadcast of films did not become regular until well into the 1960s. For these transmissions, as well as for the first video transfers, exhibition copies were used; the standard practice, when the copy to be broadcast showed signs of wear (scratches, tears, etc.), was to cut the whole sequence – the effect of this on the subsequent study of many films has been catastrophic. Since Spanish films were mostly made for domestic consumption rather than export, the number of copies made for exhibition was relatively small; consequently, it was not economically viable for the producer to make intermediary copies, with the result that all copies were made from the original negative. As noted in the previous section, original negatives of successful films have particularly suffered, since more copies were made.

Given this situation, in Spain responsibility for preservation and restoration work has been taken by the public sector: that is, film archives under central state, autonomous government, or municipal control (in practice, mostly the state archives in Madrid). When in the mid-1980s the first studies were made of the state of preservation of films in Spanish archives, a complicated picture emerged. As noted in the previous section, by the time the first public archive, Filmoteca Nacional, was created in 1953, practically the whole of silent cinema had been lost, and fires at the Cinematiraje Riera laboratories in 1945 and the Madrid Film Laboratories in 1951 had had devastating effects. The Cinematiraje Riera laboratories had housed all the films produced during the Civil War in both Republican and Nationalist zones as well as a large proportion of those produced from 1931 to 1936 under the Republic – that is, virtually the whole of early Spanish sound cinema. The Madrid Film laboratories had housed the majority of original negatives for films made in the years immediately following the Civil War. In July 1953, the Ministry of the Interior issued an order banning the transport and handling of inflammable film material. This aggravated production companies' neglect of film negatives, which were literally abandoned to their fate in warehouses. Many Spanish producers destroyed the inflammable negatives and copies of their films without previously copying them to a non-flammable film base. In sum, it is fair to say that original negatives of almost the entirety of Spanish films made before 1953 have been lost. The best that film restorers can expect is to work with duplicate materials, almost always exhibition copies, and often 16 mm copies that do not match the originals (both because of the different aspect ratio and because of the differences in photographic quality).

What can be considered the first state ruling on the conservation of the national cinema heritage came in 1964, as part of José María García Escudero's package of cinema reforms as General Director of Cinema and Theater. García Escudero's ruling requiring producers and distributors to deposit with the Filmoteca Nacional a copy of all films for which they had obtained state support did not solve the problem, however. As we now know, the existence of a positive copy of a color film negative does not in itself guarantee that the film will have survived in good condition, since the quality of duplication masters and conservation prints, positive and negative copies, CRI (color reversal intermediate) prints, camera negatives, and so on is very different from that of exhibition prints, which are not expected to have a working life of more than a few years. The color prints held by the Filmoteca in compliance with the 1964 legal deposit requirements are mostly badly deteriorated since, in addition to the irregularities mentioned in the previous section, a high proportion were used exhibition copies. It was only in the 1990s that the legislation on legal deposit was addressed, requiring producers to deposit conservation prints, production of which is subsidized by the state.

The chief preservation issue today is the transfer of acetate material to polyester, which is much more stable; this process has not yet begun to be addressed, since so far acetate degradation has not become a significant problem at the Madrid Filmoteca, which has by far the largest holdings of Spanish film stock. It is, however, an appreciable problem at the Barcelona and Valencia film archives, which have a much higher humidity level. The new film archives created after the return to democracy in 1975, under autonomous government or municipal control, plus the many other institutions that today bear the name *filmoteca*, in practice do not have a conservation function but serve as exhibition venues for films that would not otherwise be screened. Since no Spanish film archives have their own laboratories, preservation and restoration work that requires the production of a new print – practically all of it – has to be undertaken off-site in private film laboratories. In Spain, since the introduction of sound cinema these have existed only in Madrid and Barcelona; consequently, the Madrid and Barcelona Filmotecas are the most active in the fields of preservation and restoration.

What could be seen as the earliest restoration work in Spain was undertaken at the Filmoteca Nacional in the late 1950s and 1960s. It involved transferring to acetate some surviving copies of silent films, which was done without prior inspection. The results were defective, since the shrinkage of the original materials resulted in an incorrect relationship between the perforations and the image. In keeping with widely accepted practice in film archives of the time, when nitrate was considered a dangerous substance, the originals were destroyed after the transfer to acetate, which means that this restoration work cannot be redone again today, under better conditions. In 1992, Filmoteca Española (as it was renamed in 1982) made a valiant effort to recover one of these films – *Currito de la Cruz / Currito of the Cross* (Alejandro Pérez Lugín, 1926) – which was restored by the director of photography, Juan Mariné, by selecting the stills that had retained the most detail and repeating them in place of those where most of the image had been lost. The result allows the film to be screened with spectators being able to follow the story, but the movement on screen does not flow as smoothly as would have been the case with the original.

After the early attempts of the late 1950s and 1960s, there was a hiatus until restoration work was resumed in the 1980s, again at Filmoteca Española. While studying F. W. Murnau's *Nosferatu* (1922), the filmmaker Luciano Berriatúa found in the copy held in Madrid a shot that was not in the copies in any other archive (he would complete the restoration of *Nosferatu* in 2006). This discovery awoke new interest in Filmoteca Española's holdings, triggering further investigation by Berriatúa and others. The resulting research made it possible to embark on the restoration of Lorenzo Llobet Gràcia's *Vida en sombras / Life in Shadows* (1948) – previously unknown to critics and the public. When the restored copy was screened in 1983, it was hailed as a classic of Spanish cinema. This success marked the start of concerted film restoration work in Spain.

Although there has not been a coordinated plan for restoration work across the various film archives, there have been productive collaborations in the form of the exchange of materials or information. These collaborations have led to the restoration of films such as *Frivolinas / Bagatelle* (Arturo Carballo, 1926), *Un chien andalou* (Buñuel), *La aldea maldita / The Cursed Village* (Florián Rey, 1930), *La verbena de la Paloma / Festival of the Virgin of the Dove* (Benito Perojo, 1935), *Carne de fieras / Food for the Lions* (Armand Guerra, 1936; see Alberich 1993), *Rojo y negro / Red and Black* (Carlos Arévalo, 1942), *Don Juan Tenorio* (Alejandro Perla, 1952, with costumes and sets by Dalí), and *Mañana / Tomorrow* (José María Nunes, 1957). A particularly interesting case was the restoration of the original version of *Raza* (José Luis Sáenz de Heredia), which revealed how political censorship under the early Franco dictatorship affected even films exalting the regime. The film, shot in 1941 and released in early 1942, was produced by the Consejo de la Hispanidad (Council of Hispanicity), a Spanish state body, based on a screenplay written under a pseudonym by General Franco himself. After the defeat of fascism in 1945, it was deemed appropriate to produce a new version, modifying some dialogues (thereby stressing communism as the enemy) and suppressing the fascist salutes, the references to the US military as Spain's enemy in the 1898 Spanish–American War, and the hostile remarks against parliamentary democracy (see Figure 15.2). The remake was released in the summer of 1950, at the height of Spain's political and economic overtures to the United States, with the revised title *Espíritu de una raza / Spirit of a Race*. Copies of the original version were destroyed in an attempt to

Figure 15.2 Children giving the fascist salute in the original version of *Raza* (José Luis Sáenz de Heredia, 1942; prod. Consejo de la Hispanidad), excised in the 1950 bowdlerized version. The original version was recently restored by Ferran Alberich for Filmoteca Española.

airbrush the early Franco regime's pro-fascist stance out of its film propaganda. After the fall of the Berlin Wall in 1989, when East and West German film archives were merged, a positive print of the original 1942 version was found in the former UFA archives in East Berlin. Thanks to collaboration between the Bundesarchiv and Filmoteca Española, the original version could be restored, revealing the exact changes to the original and thus providing an insight into Spain's repositioning of itself in the new Cold War climate after World War II (Alberich 1997).

The restoration work described so far was carried out by public-sector organizations. But there has also been some recent restoration work by the private sector. Most notable is that undertaken by the production company El Deseo of Pedro Almodóvar's early films, and by the producer Elías Querejeta, who restored the original negative of Víctor Erice's *El espíritu de la colmena / Sprit of the Beehive* (1973) – all damaged as a result of the previously mentioned "success syndrome." It should be noted that, with the new policy of state subsidies to make conservation prints, most recent Spanish films have been conserved in an appropriate form. The outstanding problem remains, though, of how to fund the restoration of cinema from earlier periods, whether on a nitrate or acetate film base. But there is also the challenge of how cinema – increasingly in digital format – will be preserved in the future. The only method currently known for ensuring the survival of digital copies deposited in archives is for them to be recopied periodically to new formats, since the durability of digital material is still unclear.

Film Magazines from the 1930s to the 1960s (Román Gubern)

This section covers film magazines in two politically charged periods: the 1930s, under the Second Spanish Republic, and the 1940s to the 1960s, under the Franco dictatorship. In both periods, film magazines staged ideological debates that went well beyond cinema as such, with film conceived not only as an art or as entertainment but also as a site of struggle between conflicting worldviews.

With the proclamation of the Republic in April 1931, there was an explosion of new film magazines, filling the gap left by the disappearance of the notable Madrid weekly *La Pantalla* (November 1927–August 1929). New titles in Madrid were *Supercine* (1932), *Cinema* (1932), *Cinema Sparta* (1932, financed by Ricardo Urgoiti's production company Filmófono), *Cinegramas* (1934), *Crítica Cinematográfica* (1934), *Madrid Cinema* (1934), *Guirigay* (1935), *Gran Film* (1935, directed by Rafael Gil), and *Cine Star* (1935). Barcelona saw the appearance of *Cine y Hogar* (1931), *Cinema Amateur* (1932), *Filmópolis* (1933), *Cine-Art* (1934, founded by Antonio Momplet), *Cine Farsa* (1934), *Proyector* (1935), *Película* (1935), and *Última Hora* (1935). New magazines in Seville were *Altavoz* (1934) and *Andalucía Films* (1935).

The most singular magazine was *Nuestro Cinema*, founded by the Valencian Juan Piqueras, a member of the Communist Party who had settled in Paris in May 1930. From Paris he contributed to Spanish newspapers and magazines such as *La Gaceta Literaria*, *El Sol*, *Mundo Obrero*, and *Popular Film*, and selected films for the distributor Filmófono and its film club Proa-Filmófono (see the section on film clubs earlier in this chapter). *Nuestro Cinema* (Paris and Madrid, June 1932–August 1935) was codirected by Piqueras in Paris and Antonio del Amo in Madrid. It established Soviet cinema as the model of "proletarian cinema" and was the only communist film magazine of the time in Western Europe. Its thirteenth issue (October 1933) marked the end of its first period. It resumed publication in January 1935, when it toned down its revolutionary rhetoric in accordance with the Komintern's new strategy of creating cross-class Popular Fronts. The magazine avoided cover photos promoting the star system, instead showing stills from documentary or Soviet cinema. It featured articles praising these cinematic forms by writers such as Eisenstein, I. Anissimov, Karl Radek, Léon Moussinac, Arconada, and Ramón J. Sender. In October 1933 it published a manifesto of the Association of Friends of *Nuestro Cinema*, with twenty-eight signatures including Arconada, Sender, Alberti, María Teresa León, and Emilio Prados. The February 1935 issue included an interview with Luis Buñuel by José Castellón Díaz and a review of the former's documentary *Las Hurdes / Land without Bread* by Arconada. Its last number featured a survey of Soviet cinema, with strongly favorable responses by Sender, Francisco Ayala,

Figure 15.3 The first issue of *Popular Film* (August 1926). Private collection.

Antonio Espina, Benjamin Jarnés, and Federico García Lorca. (For *Nuestro Cinema*'s attempt to set up a federation of proletarian film clubs and for its own film club Cinestudio *Nuestro Cinema*, see this chapter's earlier section on film clubs.) Piqueras was shot by fascists in Palencia in July 1936 at the start of the Civil War.

The most influential magazines of the 1930s were *Popular Film* and *Cinegramas*. Directed by the anarchist Mateo Santos, the weekly *Popular Film* was published in Barcelona from August 1926 through 1937, when it fell victim to the Civil War (see Figure 15.3). Despite its profile as a frivolous magazine devoted to the promotion of stars, it took a combative stand on several polemical issues; for example, its criticisms of censorship and of the Congreso Hispanoamericano de Cinematografía (Spanish American Film Congress), its defense of Soviet cinema, and its negative views of Hollywood films made in Spanish. This combative stance led it to sack several contributors, such as Gómez Mesa in 1931, while Juan Piqueras was replaced as Paris correspondent by José Luis Salado. From 1935 it was directed by Lope F. Martínez de Ribera. The weekly *Cinegramas* was launched in Madrid in August 1934, with a large format and copious illustrations, directed by A. Valero de Bernabé. It closed in July 1936 on the outbreak of war.

During the Civil War, in March 1938 *Radio y Cinema: Revista ilustrada de la España Nacional*, based in La Coruña in the Nationalist zone, started to publish, moving to Madrid in May 1940, at which point it became a monthly magazine called *Radiocinema* (though it no longer covered radio). Directed by the Falangist writer Joaquín Romero Marchent, it sought to give political definition to the cinema of the "New Spain," with contributions from Antonio Román, Gómez Mesa, Fernández Cuenca, and José María Salaverría. It continued to publish until July 1963. Its ideological mission was taken up from October 1940 by the influential weekly *Primer Plano*, the voice of state cinema policy, directed by Manuel Augusto García Viñolas, head of the Departamento Nacional de Cinematografía (National Cinema Department). Its first issue cited Mussolini's notion of the three stages of civilization, characterized by print, photography, and cinema respectively. In March 1941 an editorial by Luigi Chiarini, director of Italy's Centro Sperimentale di Cinematografía (Experimental Cinema Center), extolled the virtues of the fascist industrial organization of cinema. In the high period of autarky, it was directed by Carlos Fernández Cuenca (from April 1942) and Adriano del Valle (from December 1942 until October 1955). It ceased publication in October 1963.

By contrast, *Cámara*, founded in Madrid in October 1941 by Tono (Antonio de Lara), took a more reader-friendly and eclectic ideological line, its contributors including Miguel Mihura, Wenceslao Fernández Flórez, Ángel Zúñiga, Alfonso Sánchez, and Enrique Llovet. It ceased publication in 1952. An even more striking contrast was provided by *Cine Experimental*, directed by the engineer Victoriano López García, founded in Madrid in December 1944. Aimed at an educated elite, it focused on technical and formal questions. Its contributor Carlos Serrano de Osma became managing editor from the fifth issue, taking over as director from the seventh issue until the magazine's demise in 1946. *Cine Experimental* paved the way for the Instituto de Investigaciones y Experiencias Cinematográficas (Institute for Film Research and Innovation), created in February 1947 within Madrid's Escuela de Ingenieros Industriales (Industrial Engineering School), transformed in 1962 into the Escuela Oficial de Cinematografía (EOC; Official Film School). While filming *Abel Sánchez* in Barcelona in 1946, Serrano de Osma took further his interests in theoretical inquiry by forming the "Telluric" cinephile group (Los Telúricos) with Pedro Lazaga and the set designer José G. Ubieta.

In July 1953, the film magazine *Objetivo* was launched in Madrid, taking a dissident line with regard to Francoist cultural politics through its defense of neo-realism. Its editorial board included the communists Bardem, Muñoz Suay, and Ducay as well as the Orteguian philosopher Paulino Garagorri. It supported the May 1955 Salamanca Conversations (see the earlier section on film clubs), to which it devoted its sixth issue, and was closed down by the regime, its last issue appearing in October 1955. *Objetivo*'s contributors included, in addition to the above, Martín Patino, J. F. Aranda, Julio Caro Baroja, Jorge Semprún (under the alias Federico S. Artigas), Manuel Villegas López (returned from exile in Argentina), and the pro-regime García Escudero and Marcelo Arroita-Jáuregui, plus some foreign filmmakers: Cesare Zavattini, Carlo Lizzani, Georges Sadoul, and John Grierson.

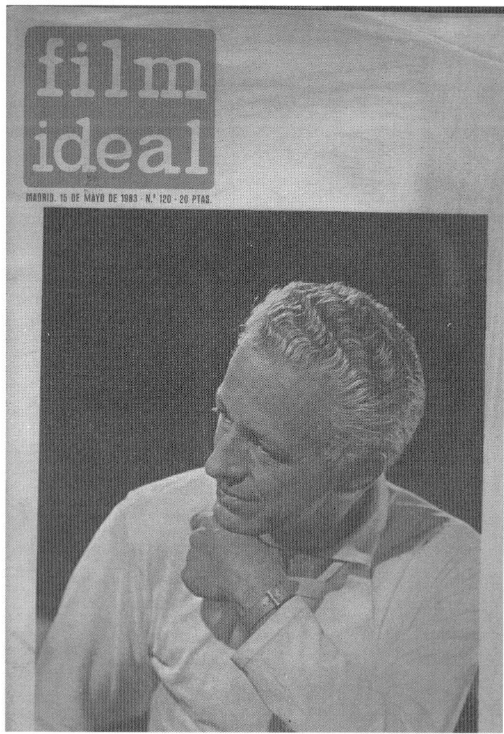

Figure 15.4 Nicholas Ray on the cover of *Film Ideal* (May 1963). Private collection.

October 1956 saw the launch in Madrid of *Film Ideal*, published by Publicaciones Populares Católicas (see Figure 15.4). Its founders were José María Pérez Lozano, Juan Cobos, the military officer Félix Martialay, and the Jesuits José A. Sobrino and Félix de Landaburu. A product of the ideological ferment generated by the Salamanca Conversations, in its first period (1956–61) it tenaciously defended cinema as a vehicle for Catholic doctrine and morality. In 1961 it suffered an editorial break-up, with Pérez Lozano leaving to become director of the new magazine *Cinestudio* (founded in May 1961), which took a more eclectic line. Cobos, Martialay, and Francisco Izquierdo became the new directors of *Film Ideal*, which now aligned itself with *Cahiers du Cinéma*'s defence of auteurism, emphasis on mise-en-scène, and re-evaluation of Hollywood. Its principal new contributors in the 1960s were José Luis Guarner, Pere (then Pedro) Gimferrer, and Miguel Rubio. In this new phase, a clear political rift developed between *Film Ideal* and the Madrid monthly *Nuestro Cine*, which took an orthodox Marxist line. *Film Ideal*'s support for the New Spanish Cinema promoted since 1962 by García Escudero was lukewarm and conflictive. After several more crises and changes of format and frequency, it closed in 1970.

Nuestro Cine had appeared in July 1961 as an offshoot of the theater magazine *Primer Acto*, both directed by José Monleón (see Figure 15.5). Continuing the line of

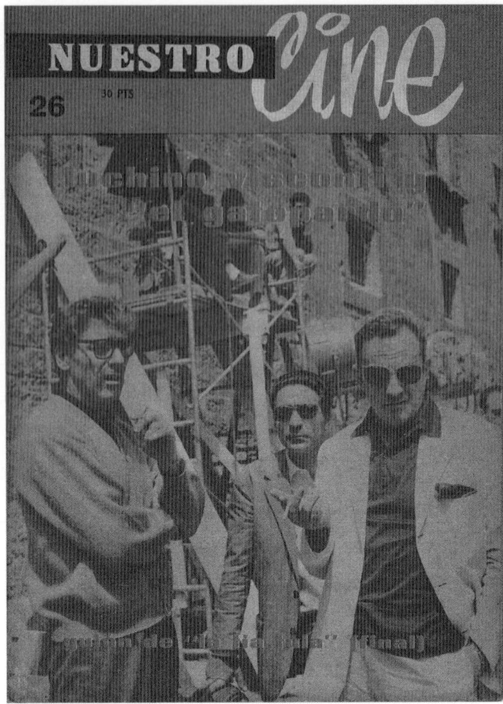

Figure 15.5 Luchino Visconti shooting *Il Gatopardo* (1963), featured on the cover of *Nuestro Cine* (January 1964). Private collection.

Objetivo and complementing *Cinema Universitario* (the magazine of the Salamanca SEU film club, headed by Martín Patino; see the previous section on film clubs), its title paid homage to Piqueras' prewar *Nuestro Cinema*. Some of its contributors – such as Víctor Erice and Antxon (then Antonio) Eceiza – were products of the Official Film School, and its Marxist ideological line was influenced by the Italian magazine *Cinema Nuovo* – faithful to the aesthetic theories of the Hungarian Marxist Georg Lukács – and the French journal *Positif*. Its defense of critical realism manifested itself in admiration for Italian cinema (Luchino Visconti, Michelangelo Antonioni, Francesco Rosi, Valerio Zurlini) and its critical attitude to Hollywood, which contrasted with its praise for New American Cinema, British Free Cinema, and French cinéma vérité. It supported García Escudero's appointment as Director General of Film and Theater in July 1962 and the New Spanish Cinema that he promoted. An ideological opponent of *Film Ideal*, in the latter's period of decline it stole several of its contributors (Vicente Molina Foix, Miguel Marías, Manuel Pérez Estremera), becoming more eclectic as a result. Its last issue appeared in February 1971.

After 1975, film magazines would cease to fulfill the political function that had been so important during the Franco dictatorship (as it had been previously under the Republic), and would increasingly become absorbed into the commercial mainstream. The academic journals that are the exception are discussed in the next section.

Academic Film Journals since the 1980s (Vicente Sánchez-Biosca)

In the late 1970s, Spanish film magazines started to divide into those aimed at the general public and academic journals, but with evident overlap. In the former category, *Fotogramas* (founded in Barcelona in 1946) was in the early 1980s (under the editorship of Elisenda Nadal) offering substantial information about festivals, new releases, and reviews, while *Dirigido Por* (founded in 1972) followed the French *politique des auteurs* (see Chapter 5 and Chapter 6), though less so after Enrique Aragonés took over as editor. A new departure has been *Cahiers du Cinéma España*, created in 2007 under Carlos Heredero's editorship, which has actively championed an auteurist cinema that rarely gets taken up by exhibition circuits.

Academic cinema journals as such are, then, a relatively recent phenomenon in Spain, though they obey the same impulse as in other countries. That is, their appearance is linked to the inclusion of film studies as an academic discipline in Spanish universities, in the field of "comunicación e imagen" (communications and visual media). On the closure in 1976 of the Official Film School, film studies moved into faculties of information science, with Madrid's Universidad Complutense and Barcelona's Universidad Autónoma leading the way. The creation of a university market stimulated new publishing initiatives, such as the book series launched in the 1970s by Fernando Torres in Valencia, and in Barcelona by Gustavo Gili and by Lumen in the communications field. These developments inevitably led to an increase in academic research into cinema. This new space positioned itself at a remove from cinema practitioners on the one hand and from film reviewers and film festivals on the other.

Nonetheless, things are never as simple as they seem and formulas were fairly diversified in the years of the transition to democracy, given that historical and theoretical reflection was at the time tied up with political and social intervention, and given that festivals were (and sometimes still are) arenas that lent themselves to specialization and research. The first journal to attempt to fill the gap left by the disappearance in 1970 of *Film Ideal* and *Nuestro Cine* (see the previous section) was *La Mirada* (1978–9) – a short-lived magazine that only managed four issues but that succeeded in giving voice to a collective need that materialized in a longer-lasting, more substantial publication, *Contracampo* (see Talens and Zunzunegui 2007). Edited by Francisco Llinàs with the involvement of a group of intellectuals in Madrid, Barcelona, and Valencia, from its first issue of April 1979 *Contracampo* juggled the roles of critical review, arguing for a politically daring arthouse cinema; of historical journal devoted to the analysis and promotion of film classics at a level that went beyond cinephilia; and of theoretical journal indebted to French structuralism, especially semiotics (Roland Barthes and Julia Kristeva were major reference points) and psychoanalysis (Freud, Lacan, etc.). It is not hard to discern here the traces of publications such as the *Cahiers du Cinéma* of the late 1960s and early 1970s, which, through analysis of the 1920s Russian avant-garde, the French *nouveau roman*, the May 68 movement and Godard's political militancy, and the New Latin American cinema (among other things), changed the relationship between criticism and politics, engaging in a polemic with *Cinéthique*, for example. Spanish cinema, film history and theory, and the contemporary scene constituted *Contracampo*'s primary lines of inquiry, set out in its first issue's editorial and maintained until the journal's demise in 1987, after a short period when it published from Valencia. Perhaps symptomatic of this focus was the dossier published in its twentieth volume (March 1981) entitled "El golpe como representación" (The Coup as Representation), in which various contributors analyzed, still close to the events, the random filming by television cameras of Tejero's attempted coup of February 23, 1981.

If *Contracampo* was characterized by an aesthetic, historical, and (sometimes) political approach, another project, important less for its results than for its focus, was *Film-Historia*. Created in the early 1990s, around scholars at Barcelona's Universidad Autónoma, it drew on the work of French film historian Marc Ferro in order to analyze cinema's relations with history – a line that its editor José María Caparrós pursued not only through the journal but also through symposia and book publications. *Film-Historia*'s content included less-academic features, such as interviews with directors, and rarely delved into the methodological issues of concern to the French historians that it cited, such as Pierre Sorlin, Michèle Lagny, and, later, J.-P. Bertin-Maghit, Sylvie Lindeperg, Christian Delage, and others.

In the last two decades, the university discipline of film studies has been reconfigured at curricular and research levels, impacting on publications in the field. Cinema is increasingly subsumed in the ambiguous terms "lo audiovisual" (audiovisual media) or "lo comunicativo" (communications), as well as being increasingly included in journals of contemporary history, art, sociology, and even political science. Two Spanish journals stand out as reference points in the systematic study of cinema: *Secuencias: Revista de Historia del Cine* (*Sequences: Journal of Film History*) and, especially, *Archivos de la Filmoteca* (*Archives of the Filmoteca*). With their well-established publication records, institutional connections, international editorial boards, systems of peer review, and range of disciplinary coverage, both play an important role in the dissemination of state-of-the-art film research.

Secuencias, created in 1994 under the editorship of Alberto Elena, grew out of the Film Program of the Universidad Autónoma de Madrid. Its aim was to give film history the respectability and rigor of other areas of historical inquiry. Although its publication frequency has sometimes been erratic, the journal has maintained and expanded its presence in the market, thanks in part to collaboration with the film publisher Ocho y Medio, again showing the close link between journals and book publication. One of *Secuencias*' major features is the large amount of space it gives to reviews of books in any of the major academic languages. In 2009 it published the volume *El espíritu del caos: Representación y recepción de las imágenes durante el franquismo* (*The Spirit of Chaos: The Representation and Reception of Images under Francoism*), edited by Laura Gómez Vaquero and Daniel Sánchez Salas, which brings together a significant number of articles on Spanish cinema published in the journal.

Archivos de la Filmoteca is a special case because of its institutional base, which has guaranteed quality design, abundant illustrations, and an international projection through FIAF (International Federation of Film Archives), not to mention a twenty-year history. Created by Muñoz Suay as part of his founding vision for the Filmoteca de la Generalitat Valenciana (Film Archive of the Valencian Autonomous Government), it first appeared in Spring 1989 and was edited for its first two years by Vicente Ponce. Its line was close to that of *Contracampo* but with a broader base of collaborators, including the more academic wing of *Dirigido Por*. In November 1992, Vicente Sánchez-Biosca became editor, with Vicente J. Benet as managing editor, instituting features that at the time were novel: international exchanges, a range of authors writing on a common theme, lack of attention to new releases and film reviews, listings in US databases, and in 2006 the issue of a DVD of the journal's first fifty issues (*Archivos de la Filmoteca* 2006). The aim of *Archivos* was not just to turn film studies into a historical field but to embed the journal in the debates taking place in film studies, historical studies, and cultural theory in universities, research centers, and progressive *filmotecas* with a research agenda. This led to wide collaboration with overseas authors and monographic issues on (for example) the future of narrative at the turn of the millennium (vol. 21), the Middle East (vol. 44), political charisma (vol. 46), the homosexual gaze (vol. 54), Carmen in Hollywood (vol. 51), and documentary (vols. 57–8). The objective is not analysis of the field by a small group of writers but recognition of the fact that the field has been enriched by an infinite range of bibliographic, filmographic, and historical sources that require discussion by the appropriate specialists.

But, if *Archivos* has contributed to knowledge of cinema as a whole, its main contribution has been its articles on Spanish, and also Latin American, cinema. Encouraging debate between different schools of thought, its studies on Spanish and Latin American cinema have ranged across cultural studies, aesthetic and formal analysis, scholarly historical inquiry, film archaeology as practiced in film archives, auteur theory, and issues of gender and ethnicity, with contributors from many countries. In its nearly sixty-five issues, the journal has been able to offer a range of approaches normally confined to separate book or periodical publications, in keeping with their particular editorial line. The frequent publication of dossiers or monographic issues has favored debate between different views, on occasions including articles on sculpture or stamps when relevant to the iconographic analysis. Among the most innovative volumes are those devoted to television in Spain (vols. 23–4), Latin American mythologies (vol. 31), Brazil between modernism and modernity (vol. 36), the iconography of Franco (vols. 42–3), cinema and the Cuban Revolution (vol. 59), the migration of images of the Spanish Civil War (vols. 60–1), and Guernica (vols. 63–4). The same eclectic approach is illustrated in the 2010 volume in French edited by Benet and Sánchez-Biosca, *Visions du cinéma espagnol* (*Visions of Spanish Cinema*), containing twelve articles previously published in *Archivos*.

In summary, *Secuencias* and *Archivos de la Filmoteca* stand on a par with international research-oriented publications such as *Screen*, which has played a central role in British film studies through its openness to theoretical innovation, while their breadth of focus, methodology, and subject matter differentiate them from the specialization of, for example, the Italian *Griffithiana* (linked to the Giornate del Cinema Muto (Silent Cinema Festival) and limited to cinema's first three decades), the French *1895*, and the English-language *Film History* (which focuses on historical issues). The synergy between all of these magazines is shown by the fact that they share many contributors.

References

Alberich, F. (1993) *Carne de fieras*. Madrid: Filmoteca Española.

Alberich, F. (1997) *Raza*: Cine y propaganda en la inmediata posguerra. *Archivos de la Filmoteca* 27 (October): 50–61.

Archivos de la Filmoteca (2006) *Interactive DVD containing vols. 1–50 of the journal (1989–2005)*. Valencia: Institut Valencià de Cinematografia (IVAC).

Benet, V. and Sánchez-Biosca, V. (2010) *Visions du cinéma espagnol*. Paris: L'Harmattan.

Del Amo, A. with Ibáñez Ferradas, M. L. (1996) *Catálogo general del cine de la Guerra Civil*. Madrid: Cátedra / Filmoteca Española.

Gómez Vaquero, L. and Sánchez Salas, D. (2009) *El espíritu del caos: Representación y recepción de las imágenes durante el franquismo*. Madrid: Ocho y Medio.

Gorostiza, J. (1997) *Directores artísticos del cine español*. Madrid: Cátedra / Filmoteca Española.

Gubern, R. (1999) *Proyector de luna: La Generación del 27 y el cine*. Barcelona: Anagrama.

Llinás, F. (1989) *Directores de fotografía del cine español*. Madrid: Filmoteca Española.

Peirats, J. (1935) *Lo que podría ser un cine social*. Barcelona: La Revista Blanca.

Pérez Merinero, C. and Pérez Merinero D. (1975) *Del cinema como arma de clase: Antología de "Nuestro Cinema" 1932–35*. Valencia: Fernando Torres Editor.

Riambau, E. (2008) *Productores en el cine español*. Madrid: Cátedra / Filmoteca Española.

Riambau, E. and Torreiro, C. (1998) *Guionistas en el cine español*. Madrid: Cátedra / Filmoteca Española.

Talens, J. and Zunzunegui, S. (2007) *Contracampo: Ensayos sobre teoría e historia del cine*. Madrid: Cátedra.

Further Reading

Caparrós Lera, J. M. (2000) *Cine y vanguardismo: "Documentos Cinematográficos" y "Cine-Club Monterols" (1955–1966)*. Barcelona: Flor del Viento.

Hernández Marcos, J. L. and Butrón, E. (1978) *Historia de los cineclubs en España*. Madrid: Ministerio de Cultura.

Nieto Ferrández, J. (2009) *Cine en papel: Cultura y crítica cinematográfica en España (1939–1962)*. Valencia: Filmoteca Generalitat Valenciana.

Tubau, I. (1983) *Crítica cinematográfica española. Bazin contra Aristarco: La gran controversia de los años 60*. Barcelona: Universitat de Barcelona.

Tuñón, J. (2009) *Relaciones de celuloide: El Primer Certamen Cinematográfico Hispanoamericano.* Madrid, 1948. In: Lida, C. E. (ed.) *México y España en el primer franquismo, 1939–1950: Rupturas oficiales, relaciones oficiosas*. Mexico City: El Colegio de México, pp. 121–61.

16

Audiences

Manuel Palacio and Kathleen M. Vernon

Introduction: Audiences and Audience Research (Kathleen M. Vernon)

The relatively recent interest in audiences within the discipline of cinema studies stems from a convergence of influences and concerns both internal and external to the field. In their anthology *The Audience Studies Reader*, editors Will Brooker and Deborah Jermyn speak of the "journey" undertaken in film studies "from the primacy of the 'spectator' as a hypothetical subject position constructed by the filmic text, to an increasingly expansive recognition of 'the audience,' as actual, empirical viewers belonging to distinct sociohistorical contexts" (2003: 127). Pierre Sorlin, a central figure in European cinema studies for his role in bridging the methodologies of sociology, history, and film analysis, locates the origin of audience research in the response to the challenge posed by the arrival of television, which put an end to the "golden age" of cinema attendance in Europe, as ticket sales plummeted across the continent from some four billion in 1952 to half of that in 1962 (2002: 24–5, 2005: 95). Forced to compete for viewers, film producers, distributors, and exhibitors sought to measure and anticipate audience composition and tastes as a way to (re)capture market share. Television studies from the beginning boasted a strong empirical component, as researchers gathered and analyzed data on audience demographics and viewing patterns that proved useful for both academics and advertisers. But research on historical audiences also responds to the impetus from developments in the qualitative social sciences and cultural studies, with their emphasis on the recovery of microhistories and the material details of everyday life in the reconstruction of the cultural and social realities, or mentalities, of a given time and place.

A Companion to Spanish Cinema, First Edition. Edited by Jo Labanyi and Tatjana Pavlović.

In her 2002 study of cinema audiences in 1930s Britain, Annette Kuhn distinguishes four approaches to the study of spectator response: a text-centered focus on the spectator-in-the-text addressed or constructed by the film; contextual analysis of film reception based on information derived from historical sources, primarily contemporary film reviews; quantitative media research designed to identify attitudes, trends, and behaviors among audience groups; and smaller-scale ethnographic studies carried out through in-depth interviews with individual spectators (2002: 4–5). In her study, borrowing from the methods of cultural anthropology, Kuhn both narrows and expands the scope of research to consider not only the direct interaction between spectator and text but also the wider implications of cinema-going as cultural practice and social ritual carried out in a specific socioeconomic and historical context.

The research on Spanish cinema audiences presented in this chapter reflects the range of approaches to the topic, from textual analysis and ethnographic work to study of the patterns of box-office receipts. With a concentrated focus on the period from the end of the Civil War to the present, the two main sections work from methodologically diverse points of departure toward a common goal of providing insight into the cinema-going habits of Spanish audiences and into what those practices have to tell us about the changing shape of Spanish society.

From Patterns to Passion: Cinema-Going Prior to the 1960s (Kathleen M. Vernon)

Writing in his travel diary *The Face of Spain*, British writer and Hispanophile Gerald Brenan remarked on the importance of cinema in postwar life: "In no other country in Europe does one find such a passion for cinema. Madrid, which has very few churches, has over seventy cinemas" (1956: 16). Stressing a similar point, contemporary Spanish researcher Mercedes Montero brings documentary precision to Brenan's observations, citing statistics from the Junta de Protección de Menores to the effect that in 1948 Madrileñans spent a total of 250 million pesetas on film and theater attendance (in comparison, in the same year in Buenos Aires, a population twice the size spent the equivalent of 180 million pesetas on the same pursuits). On average, she reports, in 1948 each inhabitant of the Spanish capital went to the movies forty-five times. Between 1938 and 1945, thirty-eight new cinemas were constructed, as opposed to twenty-five churches during the same period (2002: 180).[1]

The question of how to document and account for not only the fact of cinema attendance during a given period but also the nature of the motivations for and conditions and experiences of cinema-going has increasingly occupied Spanish scholars and reseachers. Sorlin addresses these issues in essays published in two recent anthologies, *Ver cine: Los públicos cinematográficos en el siglo XX* (Pelaz and Rueda 2002) and *Por el precio de una entrada* (Montero and Cabeza 2005).[2] As he notes, it is often through the study and analysis of local contexts and practices that one gains knowledge of audience composition and tastes and of the specific role played by the division of social space, and by different socioeconomic levels and cultural traditions (2005: 101). In the case of Spain, he cites a wealth of studies devoted to reconstructing the history of cinema exhibition and reception in Catalonia, Valencia, Alicante, and Seville among other regions and cities (2005: 102). Exemplary in its breadth and detailed documentation is Agustín Sánchez Vidal's two-volume study, *El siglo de la luz: Aproximaciones a una cartelera* (1996–7), which offers information on cinema distribution, exhibition, promotion, and reception in Zaragoza from the origins of cinema to 1996. Valeria Camporesi's *Para grandes y chicos: Un cine para los españoles 1940–1990* is a pioneering model of the study of cinema reception in Spain that seeks to use empirical and archival evidence to go beyond the "facts" of audiences' preferences to address "los sueños colectivos, las modificaciones de la geografía y de la historia mental del espectador, los cambios en el gusto, las modificaciones de las necesidades y de los deseos" (collective dreams, the evolving mental geography and history of spectators, changes in taste, evolving needs and desires) (1993: 69).

A "Golden Age" of Spectatorship? Cinema and Everyday Life in the 1940s and 1950s

As noted above, Sorlin and others have identified the 1940s and 1950s, prior to the establishment of television as a competing form of mass entertainment, as the high point for cinema attendance across Europe and much of the West. In this respect, Spain was no exception; indeed, it may have exceeded its neighbors in the frecuency and intensity of its devotion to the seventh art, perhaps surprisingly given the dire economic and political conditions resulting from the Civil War and Franco dictatorship. And yet, as César Santos Fontenla observed in a 1966 study, those same constraints were key to creating and shaping the cinema-going culture of mid-century Spain. He cites the relatively low cost of movie tickets compared to other forms of entertainment, and even basic necessities, as well as the peculiar moral codes ("especialísmas reglas morales") that made the darkened movie house the inevitable refuge for courting couples (Santos Fontenla 1966: 49). But how does one get from these explanations of assiduous film attendance to the nature and contents of the "collective dreams" and "needs and desires" expressed in the act of spectatorship? Such questions are related to the way in which the film text and the spectator's experience of it mobilize existing needs and aspirations on the viewer's part and also to the way the spectator is able to use the film-going experience to his or her individual ends, above and beyond the explicit meaning of a particular film.

Bridging the gap between the reconstruction of the spectator-in-the-text and the historical audience, Sorlin solicits the testimonial value of fictional depictions of cinema-going as a first stage in accessing the deeper level of spectator attitudes and behavior (2002: 30). It is surely no coincidence that three of the most critically esteemed Spanish films from the Francoist era – Luis García Berlanga and Juan Antonio Bardem's *Esa pareja feliz* / *That Happy Couple* (made 1951 but not released until 1953), Berlanga's *¡Bienvenido Mister Marshall!* / *Welcome Mr. Marshall!* (1953, with Bardem as co-screenwriter), and Víctor Erice's *El espíritu de la colmena* / *The Spirit of the Beehive* (1973) – include scenes that offer detailed accounts of film-going during the period.

Film dominates the everyday lives of the protagonists of *Esa pareja feliz*: Juan (Fernando Fernán Gómez), an electrician at the CEA film studios in Madrid, and his wife Carmen (Elvira Quintillá), a seamstress whose evenings are spent immersed in the romantic plotlines of Hollywood movies. At just under five minutes, an extended early sequence set in a neighborhood movie house offers invaluable insights into the cinema-going habits of the urban lower-middle-class population. Cutting between shots from the film (an ocean liner, the ensuing romance, obstacles to the same, and the final reunion) and the rows of spectators that fill the theater, the camera singles out a rapt Carmen, her eyes fixed on the screen as she munches on a loosely wrapped sandwich. Juan arrives shortly thereafter, led to her row by the usher. Her husband at her side, she praises the film and hands him a sandwich, which he will consume despite grumbling that he doesn't like to eat supper in the movie theater (see Figure 16.1). As soon becomes clear, Carmen and Juan offer contrasting models of audience response. When she dreams out loud of taking an ocean voyage like the characters onscreen, Juan corrects her: "pero allí no viaja nadie" (nobody is traveling anywhere). All too aware of the technology behind the movie magic, he proceeds to explain the workings of rear projection, to the dismay of at least one of his fellow spectators who actively protests the intervention of "el Juan de Orduña ese" (that guy who thinks he's [the film director] Juan de Orduña). While holding tight to cinema's promised illusions, the audience portrayed in *Esa pareja feliz* is nevertheless firmly anchored in the here and now of its immediate socioeconomic and political circumstances. When the movie couple's concluding kiss is visibly censored, a woman spectator takes note, exclaiming, "Vaya, ya han cortado el beso" (Great, they've cut the kiss again). As the lights come up, the formerly anonymous spectators acknowledge each other's presence. A woman seated in the row behind passes her toddler to Carmen to hold while she steps out. The cries of vendors hawking refreshments are heard and Juan asks another man to buy him a soft drink before the next feature begins. For urban dwellers like Carmen and Juan, living in the cramped quarters of a one-room sublet, the cinema offers a place to socialize in the form of a communal supplement to their own inadequate domestic space.

In all three films, the scenes devoted to cinema-related activity go beyond their role in setting up the plot and character motivation, offering ethnographic detail in

Figure 16.1 Cinema as everyday family entertainment: eating supper in the movie theater in *Esa pareja feliz* (Juan Antonio Bardem and Luis García Berlanga, 1953; prod. Altamira Industria Cinematográfica).

the portrayal of cinema's reach into the texture and habits of daily life. A very different cinema-going experience is reflected in the rural, small-town settings of *¡Bienvenido, Míster Marshall!* and *El espíritu de la colmena*, where the arrival of the weekly film is an event of note in itself. For the citizens of *Bienvenido*'s Villar del Río, film attendance is a social ritual like the dances in the town square or gossip sessions in the barbershop. Westerns are the favored genre and men, women, and children attend the regular Saturday-night showing. In *El espíritu*, a group of children greet the truck transporting the projector and the film cannisters. Their excitement bubbles over as they question the impresario who presides over the unloading about the film's content: is it "de miedo, de pistoleros, hay indios?" (a horror film, a gangster movie, are there Indians?). As the scene demonstrates, even children as young as six or seven have absorbed a thorough knowledge of generic conventions. Publicity for the film is provided by the town crier, who announces the title, time, and price of admission (one peseta for adults, two reales for minors). The children are the first to enter the makeshift theater set up in the town hall, each carrying his or her chair to the front of the room. The women follow, also dragging chairs. As he collects the admission fees, the impresario greets some of the women by name, promising one a better film than last time, cautioning

Figure 16.2 The avid engagement of early 1940s rural cinema audiences recreated in *El espíritu de la colmena* (Víctor Erice, 1973; prod. Elías Querejeta PC).

another not to burn down the building with the charcoal brazier she has brought along to provide some heat. When the space is full, a light bulb hanging from the ceiling is extinguished and the projection begins. The noise from the projector at the back of the room reminds us of the gulf between the urban and rural cinema-going experiences but as the light from the screen illuminates the faces of the spectators, mostly children and older women but also some men and a handful of couples, it is clear that the intensity of their immersion in the onscreen action is undiminished (see Figure 16.2).

A further step toward direct analysis of the responses of real audiences was inspired by Kuhn's work with British cinema-goers. With funding from the British Arts and Humanities Research Council, Jo Labanyi assembled an international team of researchers from the United Kingdom, Spain, and the United States to carry out an oral history of cinema-going in 1940s and 1950s Spain. Conducting and analyzing eighty-five unstructured interviews, from one to three hours in duration, with 112 film-goers from Madrid and Valencia (interviewed individually or in groups of two to three), the team has published articles on cinema-going as urban cartography (Marsh 2005), the role of the cinema house as a site for sexual activity in the context of Francoist repression (Martin-Márquez 2005), identification and melodrama (Woods Peiró 2005), and material culture and the cinema collector (Vernon 2005), with book-length studies in English and Spanish under preparation.[3] As Labanyi notes, rather than documenting cinema-going practices per se, the project is conceived as an exercise in memory work, exploring "how people remember now the affective charge that cinema had" for them at the time (2005: 106).

In the remainder of this section I include two brief case studies drawn from this oral history study. Overall, the testimonies collected confirm Brenan's impressions of Spaniards as mad about cinema. Many if not most of the interviewees reported going to the movies at least twice a week and several, similarly to the protagonists of *Esa pareja feliz*, described taking advantage of double and triple feature programs that lasted four to six hours. While the majority of participants stressed their preference for Hollywood cinema over Spanish productions, in their interviews the two women profiled below devoted most of their comments to the role of Spanish cinema and films in their lives. The other determining factor in my pairing of the two, both of whom were Madrid residents during the two decades studied, is their very different backgrounds and experiences, which inform the ways they perceive and make use of films and film culture generally. The advantage of the oral history approach is the access it provides to individual subjectivities, attitudes, and affects. Focus on individual experience does not allow one to make claims to representativeness, but this loss is more than compensated for by the richness of anecdotal detail and depth.

The interview with Gloria Madrigal Hortelano (GMH), born in 1929, provides an entirely unique account of her experience as a film spectator, with the focus less on particular films or special moments recalled than on the integration of cinema-going into the daily routines of everyday life.[4] GMH's husband was a civil guard assigned to duty at Franco's official residence at El Pardo palace outside Madrid. Her memories revolve around her recollections of the free film showings at the civil guard barracks for the families of the guards stationed there. She explained the scheduling of movies and her "system" for seeing films, taking turns with her husband so that one would see the film while the other took care of their children:

> La misma película la ponían dos veces en dos días. Lo hicieron así y así que cuando yo bajaba mi marido se quedaba con los niños y luego el día siguiente iba él y yo me quedaba con los niños. Las vecinas decían, mañana cine a las cuatro. Bajábamos todas tan contentas al cine. [...] Yo iba al cine y luego él iba pero me decía, cuéntamela, y yo, pero has ido tú. Y él, pero me gusta como tú me la cuentas. A mí me encantaba.

> The same film would be shown two days running. That's how it was, so when I went down to see the film my husband stayed with the kids and then the next day he'd go and I'd stay with the kids. The women on the block would say, tomorrow there's a film at four o'clock. We'd all go down to the movie theater feeling really happy. [...] I'd go to the movie and then he'd go but he'd say to me, tell me the story, and I'd say, but you saw it. And he'd say, but I like the way you tell it. I loved it.

GMH was an enthusiastic spectator of Spanish cinema, which, predictably, dominated the screenings at El Pardo; she expressed her admiration for the official newsreel: "El NO-DO que era muy bonito. Era precioso, no me lo quería perder. No como las noticias ahora en la tele. El ministro tal ha dado credenciales ..."

(The NO-DO was so nice. It was lovely, I never wanted to miss it. Not like the news on television today. Minister so-and-so has presented his credentials …). She also expressed her enthusiasm for "los actores que teníamos" (the actors we had) and their roles: "Imperio Argentina, Malvaloca, Rosario la cortijera"[5] – interestingly, all those mentioned are female.

Movies were central to the life GMH lived as a young wife and mother (which she later contrasted to the more complicated present-day world of her daughters-in-law), the details of which she evoked with some nostalgia:

> Fue tan bonito. No teníamos la ansia o vanidad o el mercado de todo, que queríamos tener más. Con aquello estamos felices. […] Hacer la cena, fregar tus platitos, organizar a tus hijos, hacerles sus pantalones, sus jerseys, nos entreteníamos, salíamos a coser al sol, salían del colegio, hacíamos comentarios de la pelicula que hemos visto, éramos menos exigentes.
>
> It was so nice. We didn't have anxieties or pretensions, or everything available in the stores, making us want more. We were happy with what we had. […] Making supper, washing your dishes, organizing your children, making their trousers, their sweaters, we had fun, we'd go out to sew in the sun, the kids came home from school, we talked about the film we'd seen, we were less demanding.

The crowning point of her description of domestic bliss is the communal discussion of the most recently viewed movie.

Born in 1925, María García Rodríguez (MGR), in contrast, displayed a remarkable memory for the films she saw during the 1940s and 1950s, even as she defended postwar Spanish cinema in general: "La gente parece que está en contra del cine español pero yo soy todo lo contrario. Me gustaban mucho las películas españolas" (People seem to be against Spanish cinema but I'm completely the opposite. I liked Spanish films a lot).[6] Citing a number of films and actors to illustrate her point, she centered on one, *Porque te vi llorar / Because I Saw You Cry* (Juan de Orduña, 1941). Her memories of the film, released a scant year and a half after the end of the Civil War, appear intimately tied to her experiences during the period, as the oldest of seven children from a poor and openly left-wing family. Speaking of why the film made such an impact, she recalled:

> Trabajaron Luis Peña y Pastora Peña. […] La película me impresionó muchísmo porque él era un hombre, era un obrero que estaba trabajando en una iglesia. Recuerdo esa película y me impactó y me impresionó tanto y lloré. Fíjate que el título era *Porque te vi llorar* y yo también lloré.
>
> Luis Peña and Pastora Peña were in it. […] The film impressed me a lot because he was a man, he was a worker who was working in a church. I remember that film and it made such a big impact and impression on me and I cried. And just imagine, the title was *Because I Saw You Cry* and I cried too.

MGR's recollection of *Porque te vi llorar* actively rewrites the film, deactivating its original ideological message, which casts the war as the story of a wealthy family sundered by wanton Republican violence only to be healed by the generosity of its humble Falangist hero. Her account significantly elides a series of inconvenient plot details: the rape of the heroine María Victoria (Pastora Peña) on the night of her engagement party, when she is carried off by a raging band of Republican militiamen who kill her fiancé; her subsequent pregnancy and rejection by her family; the sordid financial bargain proposed by her father, who pays an electrician (Luis Peña) hired to repair a radio to marry his daughter and give a name to his bastard grandson; not to mention the final revelation of the would-be husband's identity – following plot twists that point to him as her possible rapist – as a war-wounded Falangist veteran. In her initial description of the plot, MGR emphasized the electrician's status as a worker, "un obrero." The richest nugget of memory followed in her subsequent reconstruction of a love scene. As she recalled:

> Y él era un electricista que estaba trabjando en una iglesia y ella estaba rezando y estaba llorando y él se aproximó a esa chica y entonces se enamoraron. Y de ese llanto él le preguntó por qué lloraba y le dio unas explicaciones y no me acuerdo precisamente cuáles eran las explicaciones que ella le dio a él que era obrero, electricista. Y entonces de allí salió que se enamoró de ella y salieron novios. Y el fin de esa película fue que se casó con ella.

> And he was an electrician who was working in a church and she was praying and crying and he came up to the girl and then they fell in love. And because of her sobbing he asked her why she was crying and she gave him some explanation and I don't remember exactly what the explanation was that she gave the man who was a worker, an electrician. And that led to him falling in love with her and they became engaged. And at the end of the film he married her.

The church scene is indeed crucial, but not in the way MGR "remembers" it. María Victoria has sought emotional refuge in church, where she is seen weeping before the statue of the Virgin. As the lights suddenly flicker on and off, the camera cuts to a close-up of a pair of hands twisting electrical wires. Only later does the now-properly-identified groom confess his real motivation, born the first time he saw her, for agreeing to the marriage: "porque te vi llorar" (because I saw you crying).

MGR's reading recreates the film narrative as a cross-class romance, seemingly the product of a dual identification with both the proletarian but noble hero, the electrician, and the wealthy but emotionally bereft victim of war violence, the daughter/mother, María Victoria. As MGR's response demonstrates, the active work of negotiating and reaffirming identity and personal history overwrites the surface details of manifest film content. That a film as politically loaded as Juan de Orduña's crusade melodrama – part of the early 1940s cycle of *cine de cruzada* (films that glorify the Nationalist "Crusade") – is susceptible to this kind of reappropriation offers confirmation of the instability of textual meaning in the face of spectator wishes and desires.

Spanish Cinema Audiences from the mid-1960s to the Present (Manuel Palacio)

This section will analyze changing patterns of cinema attendance over the last four and a half decades, something that can be done only for the period since 1966 – the first year for which official statistics on cinema-going in Spain are available. Cinema ticket sales in Spain since then total around five billion. Needless to say, this is a very respectable figure that firmly establishes cinema-goers as the largest audience for any form of public entertainment.

The initial reporting requirements instituted to provide information on numbers of spectators as well as income earned by films were introduced as part of the package of measures to support Spanish cinema designed by José María García Escudero, and are still today considered to have informed all subsequent policies regarding cinema. Appointed in 1962 by Manuel Fraga Iribarne (Franco's Minister of Information and Tourism) to oversee the workings of cinema in Spain, García Escudero drew up a series of protectionist measures to ensure that Spanish films were sufficiently represented in cinema theaters. To that end, he introduced new rulings on exhibition and distribution quotas, and established the obligatory reporting of box-office takings so as to be able to partially link the financing of production to income (García Escudero 1967).

Exhibition and Distribution Quotas

Quotas for exhibition and distribution go back to the first years of the Franco dictatorship. Their aim was to correct the imbalance of a film market disproportionately governed by foreign interests. Exhibition quotas required cinema theaters to project a certain percentage of Spanish films. Distribution quotas ruled that distributors wanting to import foreign films and dub them into Spanish had to reach a certain level of takings on the Spanish films they sold to theaters.

Such quotas obviously necessitated finding some kind of middle ground between conflicting interventionist and free-market policies. For that reason, since their introduction, they have been subject to fluctuation, depending on the stance of successive governments and on the degree of solidity achieved by the Spanish film industry. When first instituted in 1941, exhibition quotas were fixed at six to one (i.e., one Spanish film for every six foreign films); over the 1940s and early 1950s as a whole, quotas averaged at five to one; and from 1955 to the end of the dictatorship they stood at four to one. Today, given Spain's current international commitments, quotas are not limited to protecting Spanish cinema but cover European cinema in general. At present, according to article 18 of Law 55/2007, exhibition venues are obliged to devote at least twenty-five percent of their programming to European films (Ley del Cine 2007). Clause 6 of this same article 18 states that, after five years, the impact of this exhibition quota will be evaluated with a view to phasing it out. A similar approach of setting a future date for implementation of a decision announced in prior legislation had been taken in Law 17/1994, which set a future date for the elimination of distribution quotas, which were finally abolished in 1999 (Ley del Cine 1994).

Exhibition and distribution quotas have always created friction between the exhibition and distribution sectors and the state administration – so much so that they led to strikes by cinema theater owners in 1994 and 2007. There has been recent talk of using specific exhibition quotas not to help the Spanish film industry but to further processes of linguistic normalization: in 2009 the Catalan autonomous government presented to the Catalan Parliament a Catalan Cinema Law with the requirement to dub or subtitle in Catalan at least fifty percent of non-European films exhibited in Catalonia.

Reporting of Box-Office Takings

All countries have methods for gathering statistics about cinema audiences. In the case of Spain, the collection of such data started, as we have seen, in the second half of the 1960s. The rationale for the requirement to report box-office takings is very simple: if legal rulings stipulate that certain state support for production is to be linked to audience satisfaction, it is necessary to have official statistics on box-office takings. The gathering of box-office data has always been the responsibility of the same state organization: that known today as the Instituto de la Cinematografía y de las Artes Audiovisuales (ICAA; Institute of Film and Audiovisual Media), within the Ministry of Culture. Over time the collection of box-office data has taken on a function going beyond their relationship to state support: the figures regarding audiences for Spanish films and for their market share of the total film-going public are prominent in media and parliamentary debates on the financial and even creative health of national cinema production.

For the purposes of undertaking an analysis of film audiences, Table 16.1 below gives statistics for 1966, 1975, 1982, 1990, 2000, and 2009. This allows a general overview of patterns of cinema-going for the late Franco dictatorship (1966–75), the transition to democracy (1975–82), and the subsequent three decades of fully consolidated democracy (1983–2009). In relation to population figures, the overall consumption of cinema in Spain remained at the same level of attendance per spectator as in the countries of Western Europe generally. However, a striking feature of these figures is the reduced market share of Spanish cinema in recent years. A more detailed breakdown of the figures since 1990 than that given in this

Table 16.1 Cinema Audiences in Spain: Changes in the Number of Spectators

	Total cinema audience (millions)	*Audience for Spanish cinema (millions)*	*Market share of Spanish cinema (percent)*
1966	403.0	101.1	25.0
1975	255.7	78.8	30.8
1982	155.9	36.1	23.1
1990	78.5	8.6	10.9
2000	135.3	13.4	9.0
2009	94.4	13.1	13.8

Source: Author's calculations based on box-office receipts reported in ICAA annual bulletins.

table reveals a low point for Spanish cinema's market share of 7.29 percent in 1994 and a high point of 17.87 percent in 2001, while the average for the first decade of the twenty-first century stands at 13.8 percent, which is the figure achieved in 2009 (figures taken from ICAA annual bulletins).

By way of comparison, we can add that the market share for US films in the last two decades has oscillated between roughly sixty percent in 2005 and roughly eighty percent in 2000, averaging a steady seventy percent (ICAA annual bulletins). If we go further back in time, the picture changes. In the period 1970–5, the market share of Spanish cinema was greater than that of US films; in 1977 they balanced each other out; and from then on Spanish cinema would never come close to challenging US cinema's supremacy (José i Solsona 1989). What seems to be Spaniards' limited support for their own cinema has been analyzed from industry and academic points of view. The film industry's explanation stresses the unequal conditions governing the respective positions of Spanish and US films in the market and in exhibition venues, an argument usually backed with reference to the overwhelming monopoly of US companies over the distribution sector and their rental policies (bordering on the illegal), which bludgeon exhibitors into taking US films. This argument had already been used at the time of the transition, as can be seen in the conclusions of the I Congreso Democrático del Cine Español (First Democratic Spanish Cinema Congress), organized in December 1978 by the Socialist Party (PSOE) and supported by the Communist Party (PCE), Manuel Fraga's Alianza Popular (AP), and the two main trade unions, among other organizations (Pérez Perucha 1979). A quarter of a century later, in the last major agreement reached by the Spanish film industry, the representatives of sixteen influential cinema associations – including the Spanish Film Academy (AACCE; Academia de las Artes y las Ciencias Cinematográficas de España), Spanish Film Directors Assembly (ADIRCE; Asamblea de Directores Cinematográficos Españoles), Spanish Film Photographers Association (AEC; Asociación Española de Autores de Obras Fotográficas Cinematográficas), Federation of Spanish Audiovisual Producer Associations (FAPAE; Federación de Asociaciones de Productores Audiovisuales Españoles), Actors Collecting Society (AISGE; Artistas Intérpretes Sociedad de

Gestión), Screenwriters Association (ALMA; Autores Literarios de Medios Audiovisuales), and Spain's two major trade unions – drew up, on February 10, 2003, fourteen proposals to strengthen the Spanish film industry. The agreement's title, "El cine español exige unánimemente igualdad de condiciones para competir en su propio mercado" (Spanish cinema unanimously demands equal conditions allowing it to compete in its own market), its arguments, and the measures outlined reproduce the same arguments about skewed distribution and exhibition putting Spanish cinema at an insuperable disadvantage (*Academia* 2003).

For their part, Spanish scholars, while not denying the skewed nature of the market, have suggested other explanations. For example, in the collective volume *Once miradas sobre la crisis y el cine español* (*Eleven Views of the Crisis and Spanish Cinema*), José Luis Castro de Paz and Josetxo Cerdán argued that Spanish film professionals could benefit from greater knowledge of the history of Spanish cinema and its particular traditions (Alonso García 2003: 23–40), while Txomin Ansola González saw the current situation as the legacy of the policies of heavy state subsidies for arthouse cinema implemented by Pilar Miró in the early 1980s (Alonso García 2003: 41–57), and Emilio García Fernández asked for a measure of self-criticism and acceptance of responsibility on the part of Spanish film professionals (Alonso García 2003: 23–40). In a 2008 article, Román Gubern outlined eight scenarios that might explain why Spaniards do not like Spanish cinema. In addition to giving an lucid account of arguments aired before, he added a new one: that Spanish cinema still suffers from a lack of cultural legitimacy among certain cultural elites that goes back to the days of Francoism (Gubern 2008).

It is true that the image of Spanish cinema has not been good. To be more precise, there has been a gulf between popular attitudes and those of the better-educated social sectors who shape public opinion. One of the earliest surveys of the 1960s on how Spanish cinema was regarded showed that in sectors that represented a numerical minority but that played a major role in the configuration of public space and opinion – such as professionals and academics – Spanish cinema was held in low esteem (Instituto de la Opinión Pública 1968). Things do not seem to have changed substantially in more recent times: a 2000 survey by the Spanish Authors and Publishers Collecting Society (SGAE; Sociedad General de Autores y Editores) that compared opinions on Spanish and US cinemas came up with the result that men, the upper and upper-middle classes, the university educated, and young people have a higher opinion of US cinema than of its Spanish counterpart (SGAE 2000).

This is despite the Film Academy's efforts to change Spanish cinema's image. The Academy's Goya awards (the Spanish equivalent of the Oscars), instituted in 1987, have undeniably succeeded in creating an aura of social prestige around the top-voted Spanish films, which feeds into public attitudes. Recent years have seen a novelty: coinciding with the public alignment of many Spanish film professionals with agendas of the political left, and specifically of the government of José Luis

Rodríguez Zapatero (2004–11), much of the right-wing media has transmitted a highly negative view of the Spanish cinema world today. Thus, at the Madrid premiere on March 22, 2004 of Pedro Almodóvar's *La mala educación / Bad Education*, members of the conservative Partido Popular (PP), incensed by Almodóvar's previous negative comments on the then conservative prime minister José María Aznar, hurled insults, eggs, and coins at the guests attending the gala performance (see the last section of Chapter 11).

What Can Box Office Figures Tell Us?

The success of a film is heavily conditioned by purely economic factors, such as the number of copies available for release, and easy access to distribution and exhibition circuits. Nonetheless, a look at the lists of top-grossing films in particular periods can reveal other factors, such as a film's ability to tap into national collective imaginaries or connect with the social context at the time of the film's release. What follows is a critical survey of some of Spanish cinema's biggest hits, organized chronologically into periods that have a certain economic or symbolic coherence.

During the five-year period 1966–70, at the height of the Franco dictatorship's accelerated capitalist development, the films shown in the first section of Table 16.2 achieved audiences of around four million, according to data compiled in 1977. In these top rankings, apart from one international coproduction (the spaghetti western *La muerte tenía un precio / For a Few Dollars More* (Sergio Leone, 1965), shot in Spain; see Chapter 8), we find one film (*La ciudad no es para mí / City Life Is Not for Me* (Pedro Lazaga, 1966)) that narrates the urban trials and tribulations of the time-honored commonplace of a dying rural Spain (incarnated by Paco Martínez Soria). In three of the five top-grossing films – *Mi canción es para ti / My Song is for You* (Ramón Torrado, 1965), *Pero ¿en qué país vivimos? / What Kind of Country Are We Living In?* (José Luis Sáenz de Heredia, 1967), and *Un beso en el puerto / A Kiss in the Harbor* (Ramón Torrado, 1965) – Manolo Escobar was without doubt the luminary of the 1960s Spanish star system (see Figure 16.3). An Andalusian singer and actor who specialized in acting popular characters bent on social ascent (often involved with tourists, male or female, as in *Un beso en el puerto*), his mere presence on screen would remind moderately aware Spanish viewers that he and his family were, like so many other Spanish families, caught up in the mass migratory flows on which Spain's economic development was built: a life trajectory represented at plot level in several of the films in which he starred. The hits in this list also reflect the new male–female dynamics in this rapidly modernizing Spain – exemplified particularly well by another hit of Sáenz de la Heredia from this period, *Relaciones casi públicas / Almost Public Relations* (1968; 2 860 334 viewers) (see Figure 16.4). Conchita Velasco was the principal female star in these films, playing professional roles that were novel for women under late Francoism, habitually better educated than men but deferring to their hierarchy of values.

Table 16.2 Top-Grossing Spanish Films, 1966–2009

Film	*Viewers*
1966–70	
La ciudad no es para mí / City Life Is Not for Me (Pedro Lazaga, 1966)	4 280 000
La muerte tenía un precio / For a Few Dollars More (Sergio Leone, 1965)	4 245 000
Mi canción es para ti / My Song Is for You (Ramón Torrado, 1965)	3 962 000
Pero ¿en qué país vivimos? / What Kind of Country Are We Living In? (José Luis Sáenz de Heredia, 1967)	3 949 000
Un beso en el puerto / A Kiss in the Harbor (Ramón Torrado, 1965)	3 947 000
1971–5	
No desearás al vecino del quinto / Thou Shalt Not Covet Thy Fifth Floor Neighbor (Ramón Fernández, 1971)	3 941 000
Furtivos / Poachers (José Luis Borau, 1975)	3 418 000
Adiós cigüeña, adiós / Goodbye, Stork, Goodbye (Manuel Summers, 1971)	3 154 000
Las adolescentes / The Adolescents (Pedro Masó, 1975)	2 770 000
Experiencia prematrimonial / Pre-Matrimonial Experience (Masó, 1975)	2 640 000
1976–82	
La guerra de papá / Daddy's War (Antonio Mercero, 1977)	3 493 000
La trastienda / Blood and Passion (Jorge Grau, 1976)	2 635 000
El crimen de Cuenca / The Cuenca Crime (Pilar Miró, 1981)	2 412 000
La lozana andaluza / The Lusty Andalusian Woman (Vicente Escrivá, 1976)	2 370 000
Asignatura pendiente / Unfinished Business (José Luis Garci, 1976)	2 302 000
1983–90	
Mujeres al borde de un ataque de nervios / Women on the Verge of a Nervous Breakdown (Pedro Almodóvar, 1988)	3 314 000
Los santos inocentes / The Holy Innocents (Mario Camus, 1984)	2 033 000
La vaquilla / The Heifer (Luis García Berlanga, 1985)	1 907 000
1991–2000	
Torrente el brazo tonto de la ley / Torrente, the Dumb Arm of the Law (Santiago Segura, 1998)	3 010 000
Todo sobre mi madre / All about My Mother (Almodóvar, 1999)	2 590 000
La niña de tus ojos / The Girl of Your Dreams (Fernando Trueba, 1998)	2 497 000
Airbag (Juanma Bajo Ulloa, 1997)	2 195 000
Two Much (Fernando Trueba, 1995)	2 141 000
Tacones lejanos / High Heels (Almodóvar, 1991)	2 072 000
2001–8	
The Others (Alejandro Amenábar, 2001)	6 410 000
Torrente 2: misión en Marbella / Torrente 2: Mission in Marbella (Segura, 2001)	5 312 000
La gran aventura de Mortadelo y Filemón / Mortadelo and Filemon: The Big Adventure (Javier Fesser, 2003)	4 985 000
El orfanato / The Orphanage (Juan Antonio Bayona, 2007)	4 419 000
Mar adentro / The Sea Inside (Amenábar, 2004)	4 099 000
Torrente 3, el protector / Torrente 3: The Bodyguard (Segura, 2005)	3 575 000
Agora (Amenábar, 2008)	3 400 000*
Alatriste (Agustín Díaz Yanes, 2006)	3 182 000

*Provisional figure.

Source: *Boletín Informativo del Control de Taquilla* (1980, 1983); *Boletín Informativo* (1992, 2001, 2008).

Figure 16.3 Manolo Escobar and Conchita Velasco as co-stars in one of the highest-grossing comedies of the late 1960s, *Pero ¿en qué país vivimos?* (José Luis Sáenz de Heredia, 1967; prod. Arturo González Producciones Cinematográficas).

Figure 16.4 Conchita Velasco in one of her many unconventional female roles with co-star Manolo Escobar in *Relaciones casi públicas* (José Luis Sáenz de Heredia, 1968; prod. Arturo González Producciones Cinematográficas).

The top-grossing Spanish films in the next five-year period (1971–5) are shown in the second section of Table 16.2. Comparison with the hits of the previous five-year period suggests drastic changes. If the tradition versus modernity scenario featured strongly in the tastes of 1960s audiences, it seems that early-1970s film-goers were looking for new images of a sexuality repressed under the dictatorship. Practically all the films in this list have that as their explicit or implicit focus. Today it is commonplace to claim that Spanish cinema went downhill with the transition to democracy and to see that period as characterized by the so-called *cine de destape* (nudity cinema), with its fondness for peppering its narratives with images of naked bodies, mostly female; but the list of top hits of the early 1970s shows that this tendency started earlier, in the dictatorship's closing years. It is also striking that, for the first time in Spanish film history, the top five hits include a movie recognized as an enduring contribution to Spain's cinematic cultural heritage: *Furtivos / Poachers* (José Luis Borau, 1975).

The years of the transition (1976–82) were inevitably marked by the necessary apprenticeship in the exercise of freedom. This period saw the formal abolition of censorship in November 1977, and also the gradual disappearance of age ratings determining the audiences permitted to see particular films. Since the transition, uniquely in the world, entry to Spanish cinema theatres has been open to all age groups, regardless of the (purely advisory) classification given to a film by the state. The films that, during this five-year period, topped more than two million spectators are given in the third section of Table 16.2. It seems clear that all these hits introduced Spaniards to new social and political imaginaries that would become widely accepted under democracy. The plots refer to the Civil War (*La guerra de papá / Daddy's War* (Antonio Mercero, 1977)) or to a real or figurative Francoism (*Asignatura pendiente / Unfinished Business* (José Luis Garci, 1976), *El crimen de Cuenca / The Cuenca Crime* (Pilar Miró, 1981)), but they also evidence the new roles assigned to relations between the sexes, especially in the field of sexuality (a factor in almost all these films, in one way or another).

With the legislation enacted by successive Socialist governments – particularly the 1983 Miró Law (named after Pilar Miró as Director General of Cinema), which privileged arthouse cinema, and the 1989 Semprún Decree (named after Jorge Semprún as Minister of Culture), which modified it – the 1980s saw fundamental changes to the basic model of Spanish cinema: popular cinema genres, often ideologically conservative, progressively disappeared from Spanish screens, replaced by films aligned with the dominant canon of Spanish cinema established by critics. The top-grossing films with around two million spectators according to 1991 figures are given in the fourth section of Table 16.2. These successes show the diversity of Spaniards' tastes at the time: there are films that reflect the new aspirations to modernity (*Mujeres al borde de un ataque de nervios / Women on the Verge of a Nervous Breakdown* (Almodóvar, 1988)), left-wing readings of the dark side of 1960s fast-track economic development (*Los santos inocentes / The Holy Innocents* (Mario Camus, 1984)), and the first revisionist take on the Civil War (*La vaquilla / The Heifer* (Luis García Berlanga, 1985)). From another angle, in this decade it became difficult to talk of a cinematic star system consolidated by public tastes.

The 1990s supposed a shift in Spanish cinema's positioning in the public sphere. The Film Academy – particularly televised broadcast of its Goya awards – would in this decade become a key structural feature of cinema's institutional presence in Spain. The films that, according to 2000 figures, sold more than two million tickets are listed in the fifth section of Table 16.2. What is striking in this period is the concentration of hits around works by a small number of directors; the generic preponderance of comedy; and the emergence of the subgenre of the *comedia gamberra* (gross-out comedy) favored by young directors (*Airbag* (Juanma Bajo Ulloa, 1977), *Torrente el brazo tonto de la ley / Torrente, the Dumb Arm of the Law* (Santiago Segura, 1998)). On a second level, one can detect the appearance of a new star system in the persons of Penélope Cruz and Santiago Segura. Cruz, who appears in two of these hits (*Todo sobre mi madre / All about My Mother* (Almodóvar, 1999), *La niña de tus ojos / The Girl of Your Dreams* (Fernando Trueba, 1998)), is a young, beautiful, ideal woman whose image is diametrically opposed to that of Segura. Appearing in *Torrente* and *La niña de tus ojos*, the latter comes over as engaging and extravert but also crass and horny. It is as if Spanish cinema has decided to leave unfilled the position of traditional male star designed to appeal to female audiences.

The years since the millennium – a quarter of a century after the end of Francoism and the transition to democracy – have seen the Spanish film industry's definitive immersion in the international capitalist system, in terms of both production and consumption. Perhaps for that reason, or maybe thanks to the emergence of a generation of front-line filmmakers who work with very different imaginaries from those of previous generations, box-office figures are up on those of the previous periods. The films that, according to 2008 figures, have sold over three million tickets are given in the sixth section of Table 16.2. This list points to two things: first, that today Alejandro Amenábar is one of the most firmly established figures in Spanish cinema; and, second, that three of the top-grossing films – (*The Others* (Amenábar, 2001), *El orfanato / The Orphanage* (Juan Antonio Bayona, 2007), *Agora* (Amenábar, 2008)) – have either been made in English or are indebted to a highly international conception of filmmaking. This probably accounts for why the list of hits for the contemporary period is the most diversified of all those considered so far, with a striking mix of Spanish comedy traditions (*Torrente 2: misión en Marbella / Torrente 2: Mission in Marbella* and *Torrente 3, el protector / Torrente 3: The Bodyguard* (Segura 2001, 2005), plus the adaptation of the cartoon *Mortadelo y Filemón* in *La gran aventura de Mortadelo y Filemón / Mortadelo y Filemón: The Great Adventure* (Javier Fesser, 2003)) and international style and content – this is a mix that favors sales.

The Future of Film Audiences (Kathleen M. Vernon)

Beyond continuing concerns about the domestic market share for Spanish films lies the broader question of radical changes in the nature of viewing practices. Sorlin (2005) cites a major decline in European cinema attendance between 1952 and 1962; Table 16.1, based on official Spanish figures, attests to a drop in the total cinema audience from just over 400 million in 1966 to some 94 million in 2009. During those years movies have had to contend with competition not only from television but also from home video, video games, and the Internet. Additionally, certainly some of the drop in box-office numbers can be attributed to the availability of video, DVD, and now Internet downloads and streaming as alternative modes of consumption of film content.

These issues were thrust into the spotlight in dramatic fashion in Spain in February 2011 as a result of the so-called *Ley Sinde*. The Sinde Law – named after screenwriter, director, and Minister of Culture Ángeles González Sinde – was designed to combat the growing threat of online piracy by creating judicial panels empowered to close those websites determined to encourage or permit the unauthorized download of copyrighted materials. As discussions pitted well-known artists, performers, and producers against the *internautas* (Internet users), the filmmaker and then president of the Spanish Film Academy Álex de la Iglesia offered to mediate. When de la Iglesia appeared to side with the *internautas* against many of his colleagues, he resigned as the Academy's president. In his last official act as host of the 2011 Goya awards ceremony, he addressed the core concerns of the debate and the relation between the work of film and its public, affirming the latter's fundamental role:

> Una película no es una película hasta que alguien se sienta delante y la ve. La esencia del cine se define por dos conceptos: una pantalla y una gente que la disfruta. Sin público esto no tiene sentido. (De la Iglesia 2011: n.p.)
>
> A film is not a film until someone sits in front of it and watches it. The essence of cinema is defined by two concepts: the screen and people who enjoy what they see there. Without an audience, it is meaningless.

Whatever the future of cinema and cinema spectatorship, it seems apparent that the old model, studied in this chapter, of film-going as a group activity and social ritual, in which different individuals gather in a darkened hall to gaze at the images and stories projected on a large screen, is no longer the dominant option. With the highest rate of Internet piracy in Europe, among the top thirteen countries worldwide, according to a 2011 report of the International Intellectual Property Alliance (*El Público* 2011), Spain is perhaps in the vanguard of these changes.

Notes

1 This phenomenon was not restricted to Madrid. Both Sánchez Vidal (1996–7: vol. 1 29) and Camporesi (1993: 73) report figures for 1945 and 1946 respectively that identify Barcelona as the city with the most movie theaters, followed by Madrid, Seville, Valencia, Zaragoza, and Bilbao. All researchers concur in noting the urban character of most cinema-going activity in Spain (as elsewhere) while signaling the differences between the urban and the small-town film-going experience (Sorlin 2002: 29).

2 Several of the essays in Montero and Cabeza's volume are the product of work conducted under the Spanish Ministerio de Ciencia y Tecnología-sponsored research project "Ir al cine en España (1896–1939): La organizción del entretenimento como factor de la modernización" (Cinema-going in Spain (1896–1939): The Organization of Entertainment as a Factor in Modernization).

3 The research team also includes Vicente Sánchez-Biosca and María José Millán. For an overview of the project, see Labanyi (2007).

4 Interview with Gloria Madrigal Hortelano conducted by Steven Marsh in Madrid on January 22, 2000.

5 The last two names are the protagonists of *Malvaloca* (Luis Marquina, 1942) and *Rosario la cortijera / Rosario, the estate overseer's daughter* (León Artola, 1935). The last film was made before the Civil War; several of those interviewed confused films made before and after the war, understandably since many prewar films were shown in the postwar period.

6 Interview with María García Rodríguez conducted by Steven Marsh in Madrid on April 12, 1999. The outline of this case study draws on Woods Peiró (2005) and the unpublished draft of a book chapter entitled "The Postwar Economy of Affect: Identification as Expenditure, Investment, and Consumption" (Woods Peiró and Vernon).

References

Academia: Noticias del Cine Español (2003) El cine español exige unánimemente igualdad de condiciones para competir en su propio mercado. 88: 8–12.

Alonso García, L. (ed.) (2003) *Once miradas sobre la crisis y el cine español*. Madrid: Ocho y Medio / Asociación Española de Historiadores de Cine (AEHC).

Boletín Informativo del Control de Taquilla: 1977–1978–1979 (1980) Madrid: Dirección General de Promoción del Libro y de la Cinematografía / Ministerio de Cultura.

Boletín Informativo del Control de Taquilla: 1982 (1983) Madrid: Dirección General de Cinematografía / Ministerio de Cultura.

Boletín Informativo: Datos de 1991 (1992) Madrid: Instituto de la Cinematografía y de las Artes Audiovisuales (ICAA) / Ministerio de Cultura.

Boletín Informativo. Datos de 2000 (2001) Madrid: Instituto de la Cinematografía y de las Artes Audiovisuales (ICAA) / Ministerio de Educación, Cultura y Deportes.

Boletin Informativo 2008 (2008). Madrid: Instituto de la Cinematografía y de las Artes Audiovisuales (ICAA) / Ministerio de Cultura. Online at: www.mcu.es/cine/MC/BIC/2008/Portada.html (accessed January 12, 2010).

Brenan, G. (1956) *The Face of Spain*. New York: Grove Press.

Brooker, W. and Jermyn, D. (eds.) (2003) *The Audience Studies Reader*. London: Routledge.

Camporesi, V. (1993) *Para grandes y chicos: Un cine para los españoles 1940–1990*. Madrid: Ediciones Turfan.

De la Iglesia, Á. (2011) Discurso íntegro de Álex de la Iglesia en la entrega de los Goya. *El País* (February 13). Online at: www.elpais.com/articulo/cultura/Discurso/integro/Alex/Iglesia/entrega/Goya/elpepucul/20110213elpepucul_9/Tes (accessed February 14, 2011).

El Público (2011) La industria audiovisual sitúa a España entre los 13 países "más piratas" (March 3). Online at: www.publico.es/culturas/364330/la-industria-audiovisual-situa-a-espana-entre-los-13-paises-mas-piratas (accessed October 16, 2011).

García Escudero, J. M. (1967) *Una política para el cine español*. Madrid: Editora Nacional.

Gubern, R. (2008) ¿Por qué no gusta el cine español? *El País* (February 2): 29.

Instituto de la Opinión Pública (1968) *Estudio sobre la situación del cine en España*. Madrid: Instituto de la Opinión Pública.

José i Solsona, C. (1989) *Cinema europeu i cinema americà a Espanya*. Barcelona: Institut del Cinema Catalá.

Kuhn, A. (2002) *Dreaming of Fred and Ginger: Cinema and Cultural Memory*. New York: New York University Press.

Labanyi, J. (2005) The Mediation of Everyday Life: An Oral History of Cinema-Going in 1940s and 1950s Spain. An Introduction to a Dossier. *Studies in Hispanic Cinemas* 2 (2): 105–8.

Labanyi, J. (2007) Cinema and the Mediation of Everyday Life in 1940s and 1950s Spain. In: Topping, M. and Armstrong, G. (eds.) *Alternative Voices in European Cinemas*. Special issue of *New Readings* 8. Online at: http://ojs.cf.ac.uk/index.php/newreadings/issue/view/6 (accessed April 21, 2012).

Ley del Cine (1994) Ley 17/1994 de 8 de junio de Protección y Fomento de la Cinematografía. *Boletín Oficial del Estado* (June 10).

Ley del Cine (2007) Ley 55/2007 de 28 de diciembre del Cine. *Boletín Oficial de la Cinematografía* (December 29).

Marsh, S. (2005) The Haptic in Hindsight: Neighborhood Cinema-Going in Post-War Spain. *Studies in Hispanic Cinemas* 2 (2): 109–15.

Martin-Márquez, S. (2005) Sex in the Cinema: Film Going Practices and the Construction of Sexuality and Ideology in Franco's Spain. *Studies in Hispanic Cinemas* 2 (2): 117–24.

Montero, M. (2002) Cine para la cohesión social durante el primer franquismo. In: Pelaz, J. V. and Rueda, J. C. (eds.) *Ver cine: Los públicos cinematográficos en el siglo XX*. Madrid: Rialp, pp. 175–89.

Montero, J. and Cabeza, J. (eds.) (2005) *Por el precio de una entrada*. Madrid: Rialp.

Pelaz, J.-V. and Rueda, J. C. (eds.) (2002). *Ver cine: Los públicos cinematográficos en el siglo XX*. Madrid: Rialp.

Pérez Perucha, J. (1979) Primer Congreso Democrático del Cine Español: Conclusiones. *Contracampo* 1: 24–34.

Sánchez Vidal, A. (1996–7) *El siglo de la luz: Aproximaciones a una cartelera*, 2 vols. Zaragoza: Caja de Ahorros de la Inmaculada.

Santos Fontenla, C. (1966) *Cine español en la encrucijada*. Madrid: Editorial Ciencia Nueva.

SGAE (2000) *Informe SGAE sobre hábitos de consumo cultural*. Madrid: Sociedad General de Autores de España (SGAE) / Fundación Autor.

Sorlin, P. (2002) ¿Público o públicos? Cómo plantear la cuestión. In: Pelaz, J. V. and Rueda, J. C. (eds.) *Ver cine: Los públicos cinematográficos en el siglo XX*. Madrid: Rialp, pp. 23–31.
Sorlin, P. (2005) Formas de ir al cine en Europa Occidental en 1950. In: Montero, J. and Cabeza, J. (eds.) *Por el precio de una entrada*. Madrid: Rialp, pp. 95–131.
Vernon, K. M. (2005) Material Culture and the Cinema Collector: A Case Study from Franco-Era Spain. *Studies in Hispanic Cinemas* 2 (2): 137–44.
Woods Peiró, E. (2005) Identification and Disconnect through Melodrama. *Studies in Hispanic Cinemas* 2 (2): 125–35.

Further Reading

Álvarez, J. M. and López Villanueva, J. (2006) *La situación de la industria cinematográfica española: Políticas públicas ante los mercados digitales*. Madrid: Fundación Alternativas.
Ciento volando (2000) Placeres públicos: Balance del consumo del cine español contemporáneo. *El Viejo Topo* 141 (June–July): 44–9.
Fernández Blanco, V., Prieto Rodríguez, J., Muñiz Artime, C., et al. (2002) *Cinéfilos, videoadictos y telespectadores*. Madrid: Sociedad General de Autores de España (SGAE) / Fundación Autor.
Otero, J. M. (2005) *¿Por qué se va al cine?* Huesca: Festival de Cine de Huesca.
Palacio, M. (2005) El público en las salas. In: Castro de Paz, J. L., Pérez Perucha J., and Zunzunegui. S. (eds.) *La nueva memoria: Historia (s) del cine español (1939–2000)*. A Coruña: Vía Láctea, pp. 378–419.
Redondo. I. (2000) *Marketing en el cine*. Madrid: Pirámide / Esic.

Part VII

Relations with Other Media

17

Cinema, Popular Entertainment, Literature, and Television

Sally Faulkner, Vicente Sánchez-Biosca, and Paul Julian Smith

Cinema and Other Forms of Entertainment Prior to the Arrival of Television (Vicente Sánchez-Biosca)

In an excellent methodological essay, Rick Altman (1996) has argued that the notion that cinema has a stable identity across time is, at best, an illusion. Specifically, its identity has become diffuse at moments when it has entered into circuits of transformative exchange and competition with other forms of leisure activity. Altman focused on the age of the nickelodeon (exhibition at fairgrounds or amusement parks, early cinema theaters) and on the sound revolution (producing forms such as "radio with images" and filmed theater), proposing a "crisis model" of historiography in which what we call cinema includes heterogeneous, unstable scenarios that have emerged at crisis points in its history.

Spanish cinema – like cinema elsewhere – has existed within a relational economy of leisure, entertainment, and representation that makes it difficult to consider it as a separate entity. Research is still needed into the relationship of cinema to the broad range of cultural and entertainment practices with which it forms a continuum, and into the ways in which this relationship has changed at certain critical junctures; in Spain such research has not been attempted to date. Such a study would have to consider cinema-going in relation to the full range of leisure activities available in any given period: the forms of entertainment open to different social classes; family circles and their domestic economy, which made certain cultural practices accessible to some of their members rather than others; and the social, sexual, or gender constituencies for particular forms of cultural consumption. Who goes to see what with whom may depend on the day of the week; for example,

A Companion to Spanish Cinema, First Edition. Edited by Jo Labanyi and Tatjana Pavlović.

the whole family might go to the cinema on Sundays, the males to a cabaret on Saturdays (with a female partner or other males), the mother and children to the neighborhood cinema on Thursdays (the maid's day off), the adults maybe to a *corrida* in the bullfighting season, or the males to a football match on Sundays. Sometimes these cultural options might clash; for example, if their days of the week coincided (in the examples above, the family outing to the cinema and the football match), or if they appealed to incompatible social sectors. In other, more complex instances they might overlap, exchanging attributes or imitating each other: actresses who combined theater with music hall, bullfighters recruited to act in bullfighting films, folkloric stage singers discovered by film producers (as Lola Flores was by Cesáreo González), or footballers from the other side of the Iron Curtain who became stars of anticommunist movies (such as the Hungarian Ladislao Kubala in *Los ases buscan la paz / Aces in Search of Peace* (Arturo Ruiz-Castillo, 1955)).

Sport (especially football, which the Franco regime turned into the mass sport *par excellence*); theater (particularly the popular *sainete* (one-act low-life farce), the musical revue, and *zarzuela* (popular operetta)); radio; and bullfighting all shared a leisure economy with cinema prior to the arrival of television. Based in the home – after the early 1960s when Manuel Fraga Iribarne, as Minister of Information and Tourism, encouraged *teleclubes* (television clubs) – television followed a strategy of absorption of other cultural forms, rather than entering into conflict with them. Accordingly, it gradually came to accommodate most forms of entertainment that required a venue, an audience, and specific material conditions; this substantially modified the previous cultural dynamic. Nonetheless, the lateness of the small screen's implantation in Spain (one cannot talk of the medium's social penetration until the mid-1960s) leaves an extended period in the history of cinema to be analyzed in terms of comparative leisure consumption.

This section can only make an initial attempt at exploration of this field; it will do so by focusing on two symptomatic case studies. The first is a concrete but highly revealing event: the Exposición Regional y Nacional (Regional and National Exhibition) held in Valencia in 1909 and 1910. Its organization shows the liminal position of cinema and its uncertain status in a city whose economic and political leaders had opted for modernization. The second will discuss the relationship to cinema of the *cuplé* (a narrative song form popularized by cabaret; see Chapter 7), which in turn is connected with the history of song and of the musical revue – indeed, all of these terms are conceptually and historically polyvalent. The premise will be that these cultural formulas or scenarios exist both inside and outside cinema, and that the case of the *cuplé* is a story of absences, ellipses, come-backs, and areas of overlap. Other phenomena that could fruitfully have been studied are (among others) the bullfighting film genre, which rewrites the silver screen's star system, or football, which gave rise to an idiosyncratic rhetoric – for example, Matías Prats, as football commentator for the NO-DO newsreels (see Chapter 18), shaped a specific language or jargon from which audiovisual sports journalism would not free itself for decades.

A Strange Attraction

In 1909, the city of Valencia was turned upside down by an initiative aimed at plunging it into modernity, in its industrial, urban, touristic, and leisure facets. The Ateneo Mercantil (Chamber of Commerce), headed by Tomás Trénor, mounted a Regional Exhibition that the following year would be renamed "National Exhibition." February 13, 1909 saw the publication of the terms of exploitation of the *Cinematógrafo y Parque de Atracciones* (Cinema and Amusement Park) (Pingarrón-Esaín 2009), showing that the two things were seen as a unit, both in the minds of a committee whose members were educated businessmen and in the social imaginary of the period that made it a success. The physical context for the cinema was, then, the *glissoire roulant* aka *tobogán* (helter skelter), the *globo mariposa* (hot-air balloon, literally "butterfly balloon"), the *tapis volant* (flying carpet), the mechanical staircase, the roller coaster, and other funfair attractions. This regional exhibition supposed access to technological modernity (inventions, stunts, fascination with the latest mechanical devices) but also a new experience of time and spatial vertigo that were constants of the World Fairs of the nineteenth century, especially those of Paris, as lucidly analyzed by Walter Benjamin (1982). Moreover, the cinema was located in the first purpose-built, solid-structure building to be constructed in the city of Valencia expressly for the screening of films. The exhibition coincided, then, with a key moment in the history of cinema in which it was starting to be housed in spaces designed for that purpose and, at the same time, itinerant cinema was starting to become a thing of the past. The success of the film screenings at the exhibition led to their move to another venue in the grounds, the Teatro-Circo (solid-structure circus venue), with additional open-air sessions at the Fuente Luminosa (Illuminated Fountain), taking advantage of the temperate Mediterranean climate.

Thus, cinema was – in terms of how it was perceived socially and as a form of entertainment, both of which have technical and formal consequences – a space of the imagination related to the surrounding attractions, the circus, the outdoor location, and strong perceptual and emotional experiences. In addition to the initial lack of a fixed or even specifically designated space for the film screenings, no one – whether in the press of the time or in the memoirs of those responsible for the venture – mentioned the actual content of the films projected. What made it a success was the spectacle as such. This tells us what cinema represented to the public imaginary in a privileged enclave in Spain in 1909 and 1910: a multifaceted instrument, unrelated to and distanced from art, paradoxically since its creators – for example, the Valencian photographer and cinema pioneer Ángel García Cardona (see Chapter 12) – were cameramen with a gift for composition and a skilled technical eye. But what triumphed was the idea of leisure, of the technical gimmick, internally geared to the production of sensational (rather than artistic) effects, and externally merging with other attractions on a grander scale (Gunning 1986). In its spectacularity and sensationalism, Spanish cinema of 1909 would be incomprehensible if viewed solely as cinema. It should be added that, at the time, Valencia was the home of the Cuesta production company, which would be decisive in giving shape to early cinema in Spain (Lahoz 2010).

Those Times of the *Cuplé*

In 1958, José Luis Merino made *Aquellos tiempos del cuplé / Those Times of the "Cuplé"* – a nostalgic film that recreates, with excessive concessions to public decorum, the period when this particular entertainment form, originating in France (its name derives from the French *couplet*), triumphed in Spain (see "The Heyday of the Musical Film" in Chapter 6 and "The 1920s and 1930s" in Chapter 7). The film's star, Lilian de Celis, came from the same cabaret tradition depicted in the film. This was the time of *El último cuplé / The Last Torch Song* (Juan de Orduña, 1957), starring Sara Montiel, which starts in Barcelona in the 1950s, as a former singing star, who had left the stage for love, makes a come-back. A flashback takes us back three decades to when Barcelona's Paralelo (the city's entertainment district) was at its height, and transports us to Paris, the cradle of the genre and of variety theater and the revue.

The *cuplé* dominated the Spanish stage from the start of the twentieth century, acting as a popular counterpoint to sophisticated operatic performance. Drawing on certain stage traditions and popular song, and replacing the late-nineteenth-century vogue for the *zarzuela* and *género chico* (one-act musical play), it continued the tradition of the revue that had originated in the 1860s. The most striking feature of the *cuplé* is that, during the first decade of the twentieth century, it was characterized by what at the time was called *sicalipsis*, which Serge Salaün (1990) defines as a "perversion del género chico en género ínfimo, mediante el erotismo" (degradation of the *género chico* [light genre] to the *género ínfimo* [lightest genre; a term then used for saucy stage acts], thanks to its eroticism). This "naughty" slant was exemplified in the so-called *canción de doble intención* (song based on *double entendre*), the sexual innuendo of its lyrics, or the mismatch between innocent lyrics and the erotic gestuality of the female performer – as in the famous song "La pulga" (The Flea) – but also in the moderate or heavy sexual license surrounding its venues and stars, and the love lives of the latter. This, however, is not what passed into cinema, if we look at the films of the internationally famous *cupletista* Raquel Meller, whose films included *Los arlequines de seda y oro / Silk and Gold Harlequins* (Ricardo de Baños, 1919) and *Violetas imperiales / Imperial Violets* (Henry Roussell, 1923) and who would immortalize the songs "La violetera" (The Violet Seller) and "El relicario" (The Reliquary). Not surprisingly, the *cuplé* disappeared from cinema altogether during the first decades of the Franco dictatorship because of its associations with a tawdry sexual underworld (though a degree of sexual innuendo was tolerated in select venues). It was Sara Montiel who would, around 1960, be responsible, almost single-handedly, for bringing back this female prototype; despite the sanitization perceptible in these revivals, the relation of the *cuplé* to sexual license was made clear. If *El último cuplé* meant a revival of the genre (Montiel 2000: 236), Montiel's subsequent films – *Pecado de amor / Sin of Love* (Luis César Amadori, 1961), *La bella Lola* (Alfonso Balcázar, 1962), *La reina del Chantecler / Queen of the Chantecler* (Rafael Gil, 1962), *La dama de Beirut / The Woman from Beirut* (Ladislao Vajda, 1965), and *Tuset Street* (Jorge Grau and Luis Marquina, 1968) – would continue in the same vein with great success.

The earlier ellipsis of several decades during which cinema avoided the *cuplé*, although it had continued as live performance under a cloak of discretion if not semi-clandestinity, had been filled with the costumes and narrative plotlines – and explosion on the radio and in the record industry – of another kind of song: that of the chaste folkloric female star, the performer of Andalusian song and the traditional *copla*, morally puritanical and anatomically much more decorous, embodied successfully by Imperio Argentina, Estrellita Castro, Lola Flores, Paquita Rico, Gracia de Triana, and Marifé de Triana, even though their private lives (sometimes aired in public) did not correspond to the moral norms of the day. It is curious to note that a figure like Carmen Sevilla would in the 1960s opt for an extraordinary mix of the folkloric and the permissive, which went down well with French audiences – a kind of *flamenca lite*, as Terenci Moix called her (1993). But that would take us into another period.

Literary Adaptations (Sally Faulkner)

Literary adaptations – just one of many possible connections between film and literature – have been central to the history of cinema, popular with practitioners and audiences from the silent era to the present, and have ranged across genres as varied as costume drama, *film noir*, and youth movies. As Linda Hutcheon notes, most Best Picture awards at the Oscars, which are selected by industry professionals, have gone to films based on literary works (2006: 4). Yet critics remain divided, raising concerns about "purity" or, conversely, stressing originality.

The case of Spain is no exception. If one were to write the history of Spanish cinema referring only to literary adaptations, virtually no period, genre, political orientation, or degree of success would be left out. As in other countries, literary adaptations of classic texts played a key role in the early constitution of film as the seventh art – for instance, via versions of Cervantes' *Don Quijote* (first adapted by Narciso Cuyàs in 1908) and Calderón's plays (as in Adrià Gual's 1914 version of *El alcalde de Zalamea / The Mayor of Zalamea*). Following José Buchs' popular 1921 *La verbena de la Paloma / Festival of the Virgin of the Dove*, adaptations of *zarzuelas* dominated Spanish cinema of the early 1920s, constituting over half of films produced in 1923 (Pérez Perucha 1995: 90). Notwithstanding later successes (Benito Perojo made a sound version of *La verbena* in 1935), 1925 saw the beginning of an alternative vogue for adaptations of novels (Alejandro Pérez Lugín successfully filmed his novels *La casa de la Troya / College Boarding House* and *Currito de la Cruz / Currito of the Cross* that year) that has continued to the present (Sánchez Salas 2007: 408).

Under the Franco dictatorship, literary adaptations became politicized. Critics have questioned the frequent supposition that the cinema of early Francoism uniformly promoted regime ideology, and this holds true for adaptations of the period. For instance, while Antonio Román's version of Lope de Vega's *Fuenteovejuna* (1947) used Spain's literary Golden Age (sixteenth and seventeenth centuries) as a mirror for Francoist values, Peter Evans notes that the star Amparo Rivelles disrupts its promotion of a conservative gender ideology (1997: 5–6). In other cases, adaptations allowed directors to smuggle sexually racy plots past the censors – for example, via Alarcón in *El escándalo / The Scandal* (José Luis Sáenz de Heredia, 1943) and Palacio Valdés in *La fe / The Faith* (Rafael Gil, 1947) (Labanyi 1995: 7–8). Adaptations of antiauthoritarian writers that got past the censors implicitly critized the regime by displaying social injustice (Perojo's 1940 version of Galdós' *Marianela*) or what Jo Labanyi (1995) terms the "family in crisis" (Carlos Serrano de Osma's 1946 adaptation of Unamuno's *Abel Sánchez*).

This potential for creative adaptation to function as a political act of dissent was consolidated in the late dictatorship and transition periods. For example, Miguel Picazo used the early-twentieth-century writer and philosopher Miguel de Unamuno to condemn the stifling patriarchal restrictions of 1960s provincial Spain (aided by the performance of Aurora Bautista) in *La tía Tula / Aunt Tula* (1964) (Faulkner 2006: 101–24). The first case study below examines how Pedro Olea effected a similar critique via the nineteenth-century realist novelist Benito Pérez Galdós in *Tormento / Torment* (1974). In the early post-Franco years, despite the fact that many films were based on nineteenth- and early-to-mid-twentieth-century originals, literary adaptations in Spanish cinema and television alike articulated the values of a new democratic Spain. Thus, in *La colmena / The Beehive* (1982), Mario Camus turned to Camilo José Cela's nihilistic novel of 1951, originally banned by the Francoist censorship, to enunciate antiauthoritarian values in the present (Faulkner 2004: 24–33). This film's combination of a complex work by a major author with popular actors and high production values indicated a successful middlebrow trend. Manuel Palacio (2001: 153) has traced a similar didactic drive to promote democratic values through literary classics in television adaptations of the transition period – for example, via Galdós again in Camus' ten-part *Fortunata y Jacinta / Fortunata and Jacinta* (1980). No longer enjoying the state subsidies available to literary adaptations in the 1980s – under both UCD (centre-right) and PSOE (socialist) governments – directors in the 1990s and beyond have nonetheless continued successfully, if occasionally, to connect with audiences through adaptations, on both large and small screens; for example, Pilar Miró's film version of Lope de Vega's *El perro del hortelano / The Dog in the Manger* (1996), discussed as the second case study below, and Fernando Méndez Leite's three-part television production of Leopoldo Alas' 1885–6 novel *La Regenta* (1995).

Adaptation Theory

Following the first book on the subject, by George Bluestone in 1957, early adaptation studies focused principally on the question of fidelity. This approach had the merit of dealing with the material differences between the written medium of literature and the audiovisual medium of film, asking, for example, how character might be created through descriptive passages in a novel or dialogue and stage directions in a play, versus casting, performance style, screenplay, mise-en-scène, cinematography, editing, and sound in film. However, whether because too many studies judged film "worse" or because the authors were often literary rather than film scholars, "fidelity criticism" – first condemned by Andrew Horton and Joan Magretta in 1981 – became the straw man of adaptation studies. Whatever adaptation theory was, critics protested from the 1980s onward, it was not "fidelity criticism." While it can be argued that subjective judgments about "fidelity" to some elusive "essence" of a literary text have no place in adaptation theory today, much is lost if we dismiss fidelity completely. Linda Hutcheon argues that, whatever an adapter aims to do, it is rarely to be faithful (2006: xiii). Surely this is counterintuitive. If there is no desire to conjure up the literary text, albeit it in an entirely different form, why bother to adapt at all? A key risk in dismissing "fidelity" is that we lose the important work of close textual analysis of the two media. Dismissing "fidelity" also means dismissing audience response, since that tends to be the key issue for spectators familiar with the source text. While the case studies below address audience reception through critics' reviews in the press and box-office statistics, both available to scholars, a fruitful direction for further enquiry might be reintroduction of the issue of fidelity through audience research in cases where access to viewers is feasible.

The avoidance of audience response that resulted from the rejection of "fidelity criticism" was continued by the belated turn to structuralism by adaptation critics in the 1990s (e.g., McFarlane 1996). Structuralist critics dissected films and their sources in terms of narrative codes, permitting what they claimed were "objective" conclusions about the extent to which an adaptation duplicated or departed from its source, as an antidote to what they saw as the reliance on "subjective" opinions in "fidelity criticism." Also lost in this structuralist turn was the crucial question of context: that is, consideration of the commercial, cultural, and political reasons why certain texts are adapted at certain times, and of how adaptations are shaped by changing institutional, social, and political environments.

Since the start of the twenty-first century, adaptation studies has transformed itself by energetically, if belatedly, embracing poststructuralist theory – for example, Derridean deconstruction, the Lacanian questioning of the unified subject, and the Foucauldian rethinking of the author (Stam 2005) – as well as cultural studies. In 1999, Deborah Cartmell and Imelda Whelehan identified the largely cultural issues of "history, nostalgia, ideology" and "audience, pleasure and intertextuality" (1999: 11, 15) as key concerns of the field. In 2000, James Naremore reprinted articles by André Bazin (originally 1948) and Dudley Andrew (originally 1984), which adaptation critics had missed in their embrace of structuralism. By rejecting both the subjective hierarchy of "better/worse" inherent in "fidelity criticism" and the avoidance of context that limits structuralist methodology, these two articles point to a cultural studies approach *avant la lettre* (Naremore 2000: 1). Today adaptation studies is attracting the attention of major film, cultural, and literary scholars (Vincendeau 2001; Hutcheon 2006; Sanders 2006), and 2008 saw the launch of the specialist academic journal *Adaptation*.

Scholarship on literary adaptations within Spanish film studies has followed this same trajectory, with structuralism dominant in the 1990s and with recent critics in the United Kingdom and Spain exploring cultural issues (Sánchez Salas 2002, 2007; Faulkner 2004; Pérez Bowie 2004). By considering two films from different decades – the 1970s and the 1990s – the two case studies offered here stress the importance of taking cultural context into account. The aim is to explore how adaptation can serve political and gender critique. This will be analyzed through attention to casting, performance style, and film form in the genres of melodrama and romantic comedy.

Tormento / Torment (Pedro Olea, 1974)

Spanish cinema of the early 1970s saw a mini-boom of classic literary adaptations. The catalyst was Luis Buñuel's 1970 *Tristana* – also based on a novel by Galdós – which was passed by the censors with only minor objections (Sánchez Salas 2002: 201) and, according to the Ministry of Culture database (www.mcu.es/cine/index.html), attracted nearly two million viewers and made over four hundred thousand euros. Producers, mired in one of Spanish cinema's perennial financial crises, saw the commercial possibilities here; the ensuing copycat adaptations of a wide range of literary texts were producer-led. A new university-educated, relatively wealthy, and predominantly urban audience was the target for this middlebrow fare; the graduates of the Escuela Oficial de Cine (EOC; Official Film School), for whom government subsidies had dried up, were its ideal directors. Thus, the producer José Frade commissioned Olea to direct a film version of Galdós' 1884 novel *Tormento*.

The only kind of audience response available for this film – press reviews – cannot be taken to be indicative of public opinion since the press was censored. The film was released a year before Franco's death; there was a return to hard-line censorship in the last two years of his rule. Reviews sampled at Filmoteca Española show that hostile reviewers used the stock fidelity argument to pass moral judgment on the film. Olea's change to the ending, which explicitly verbalizes both Rosalía's annoyance and Agustín's extramarital arrangement, was a particular source of outrage to critics in the pro-regime press (Arroita Jauregui 1974, writing in *Arriba*; Ramos 1974, writing in *El Alcázar*). In a more progressive review, the fidelity issue was also raised but as a smokescreen to critique the current situation in Spain (López Sancho 1974, writing in the conservative but more open-minded *ABC*). Today, we can make explicit what was implicit here: Galdós' social critique serves as a "scalpel" (the word used by the *ABC* reviewer) for Olea to dissect the dying days of Francoism. The censors fixated on the plot's potential sensationalism – a priest's love affair – requiring the script to be revised three times before filming could proceed (Navarrete 2003: 134). But the film's critique lies not in its anticlericalism (from the 1960s onward, progressive elements of the clergy had opposed the regime) but in its portrayal of the hollow values of the bourgeoisie and the disruptive presence of strong female characters. These two points of critique struck at the ideological core of late Francoism, the economic policies of which, from the 1959 Stabilization Plan onward, had focused on consolidating the middle classes, unleashing social mobility while continuing to protect patriarchy. The film's critique of Francoist values was reinforced by the fact that the author of its source text was the "liberal crusader" Galdós (Berkowitz 1948), whose work had been blacklisted in the ideologically stricter years of early Francoism (Faulkner 2004: 90). The tentative nature of the film's critique is in line with the tentative approach to political change that would follow Franco's death the following year; it is appropriately set in the late-nineteenth-century Restoration period (named after the restoration of the Bourbon monarchy in 1874), anticipating the second restoration of the Bourbon monarchy under Juan Carlos I, who viewers knew was Franco's designated successor.

Turning from context to text, *Tormento* was a critical and commercial success, attracting over two million spectators and winning the Best Spanish-Language Film award at the San Sebastián Film Festival. This was thanks to the casting of the actors (the experienced Concha Velasco alongside the aspiring *progre* (radical) Ana Belén and the known Socialist-sympathizer Paco Rabal), their performances, and the adaptation's harnessing of the source novel's explicit melodramatic qualities to the film genre of melodrama. As Velasco's three awards for her role attest, the film owes much of its success to her performance as Rosalía, the slightly dim, middle-aged, endlessly scheming petite bourgeoise bent on social ascent, known to Galdós enthusiasts from this novel or its sequel of the same year, *La de Bringas* (1884). Drawing on her experience in popular comedy, Velasco perfectly judges her portrayal of this shrewish stereotype, presenting Rosalía's pomposity and hypocrisy as objects of satire rather than caricature. Olea and Velasco take full advantage of the prancing, puffing, and preening indicated by Galdós throughout his text (the actress put on eleven kilos to take on the role). A good example is Velasco's performance of the passage in which Galdós describes a conversation between Rosalía and Agustín. With a self-reflexive nod, Galdós' narrator writes that an "attentive observer" would have noted Rosalía's desire to leave her relative in no doubt over her beauty: done up in carefully chosen clothes and accessories, "cómo enseñaba sus blancos dientes, cómo contorneaba su cuello, cómo se erguía para dar a su bien fajado cuerpo esbeltez momentánea" (how she flashed her white teeth, how she showed off the shape of her neck, how straight she held herself to make her tightly corseted body look momentarily slender) (Pérez Galdós 1977: 175). Olea is the ideal "attentive observer" and Velasco's interpretation of Rosalía was so successful that the director expanded her role in the film compared to the novel (Navarrete 2003: 136).

The final sequence is especially revealing of Olea's intentions as it departs significantly from the novel. In Galdós' original, we learn that Amparo has become Agustín's mistress when Rosalía's husband Bringas alone sees Agustín off at the station (chapter 40); Rosalía's reaction occurs when Bringas relays the information to her in the following chapter. The novelist can only signal Rosalía's disgust through language: questions, exclamations, and – a Galdós favourite – ellipsis, heavy here with pent-up, unarticulated emotion: "¿Y tuviste paciencia para presenciar tal escándalo? … Conque no la puede hacer su mujer porque es una … ¡y la hace su querida …!" (And you had the patience to witness such a scandal? … So he can't make her his wife because she's a … and he makes her his mistress …!) (Pérez Galdós 1977: 194). In the film, both Rosalía and her husband turn up at the station to say goodbye. As Ramón Navarrete points out, this draws the adaptation full circle and conveys the impression of a closed world to the viewer (2003: 135), since Olea also eliminates the novel's opening conversation and begins with Agustín's arrival by train. Rosalía is particularly keen to see off a man she believes she has saved from a dishonorable marriage and whom she hopes may be a future son-in-law, if not a second husband for herself. Velasco's gloating gaze at Agustín in the train clouds over with horror when her former maid Amparo steps forward in the carriage (see Figure 17.1), a point emphasized cinematically through the zoom. "¡Puta, puta, puta!" ("Bitch, bitch, bitch!") we hear her furiously mutter (though the script had promised the censors these words would be masked by the departing noise of the train).

Amparo's triumphant gaze is a mirror image of Rosalía's here. Up to this point, Belén's performance as the angelic Amparo – admittedly a less juicy role – had been insipid compared to Velasco, even though the maid's past shadowy love affair with a priest and present rosy romance drive the film narrative. In terms of the diegesis, the final shot of Belén's Amparo is climactic: through it, the viewer learns that Amparo and Agustín will live in sin. But there is an extradiegetic story here too about the two actresses' performance style. The matching shots of Velasco's and Belén's gloating gazes triggers Belén's performance to shift gear from holier-than-thou servant girl to triumphant mistress, as if she had learned from the more experienced actress in the course of the shoot. This apprenticeship would serve her well when she embodied Galdós' most famous heroine, the working-class Fortunata, in Camus' 1980 television series *Fortunata y Jacinta* – though her performance there is still slightly uneven.

A brilliant Velasco and an improving Bélen aside, another success of Olea's *Tormento* is its attention to secondary roles. The character of the wealthy relative who returns to Madrid after making his fortune abroad, Agustín Caballero, was hardly a challenge for Paco Rabal, whose star trajectory had included portraying the protagonist of Buñuel's Mexican *Nazarín* (1959) and the cocksure Jorge of his

Figure 17.1 Amparo (Ana Belén) gazes triumphantly as Agustín (Paco Rabal) draws her into view in *Tormento* (Pedro Olea, 1974; prod. José Frade PC).

Spanish-made *Viridiana* (1961), subsequently going on to earn his colors with major European and Latin American auteurs such as Michelangelo Antonioni, Claude Chabrol, Leopoldo Torre Nilsson, and Glauber Rocha. Rabal's career, with his extensive experience of filming overseas, felicitously matched his on-screen role in *Tormento* as the self-made Agustín whose career has been forged in the Americas. As Rabal's Agustín draws Belén's Amparo into view for the triumphant final shot described above, it again seems that an older generation of veteran actors is guiding a younger generation forwards.

It has frequently been stated that the nineteenth-century novel provided fiction film with its (realist) narrative codes. Galdós' *Tormento* demonstrates that it provided film with a model for melodrama too (a genre explicitly referenced in the novel's parodic first chapter). Olea reads his source text through the lens of the female-focused narratives, theatrical performance style, and narrativized mise-en-scène of film melodramas made in Hollywood (e.g., Douglas Sirk) and Spain (e.g., Miguel Picazo). The film's mise-en-scène in general and costume in particular illustrate this influence. Setting reinforces characterization, inviting viewers to contrast the tacky pretentiousness of the Bringas' apartment with the austerity of Amparo's home and the grandeur of Agustín's mansion. But the use of costume is multi-layered. In the light, perhaps, of the attention given to dress in the sequel novel, *La de Bringas*, Olea expands on Galdós' mention that Rosalía takes charge of purchasing Amparo's new clothes following the announcement of her engagement to Agustín (Pérez Galdós 1977: 129). Costume is narrativized as Amparo's shift from servant to *Señora* is registered in her dress. But for Rosalía this is about control. Amparo may have won the battle for Agustín, but Rosalía will win the war of clothes: Rosalía accuses Amparo of lacking "taste" and "style" (those ultimate signifiers of class) (Pérez Galdós 1977: 129, 134) and takes more care to dress sexily herself, in the home and out, following the engagement (135). As the example of Amparo's attire in the last scene demonstrates, Rosalía's attempt to pin her down and hem her in through clothes fails. Olea, working in a visual medium and a genre attentive to mise-en-scène, is able throughout the film to capitalize on this power-dressing.

El perro del hortelano / *The Dog in the Manger* (Pilar Miró, 1996)

Olea's *Tormento* and Pilar Miró's *El perro del hortelano* are separated by the explosion in the number and popularity of classic adaptations – known collectively as "heritage film" (Higson 2003) – in the 1980s. These included Merchant Ivory productions and quality British television adaptations. This trend was echoed in 1980s Spanish cinema. However, these "Miró" films – so named since they were financed by the subsidies for quality cinema introduced by Pilar Miró in 1983 when Director General of Film, a post she held from 1982 to 1986 – perform an awkward balancing act that distinguishes them from their foreign counterparts. While adopting the high production values often used to portray the aristocracy in European heritage movies, Spanish classic adaptations of this period take as source texts the gritty, politically oppositional texts of Spain's fraught twentieth century, which tend to focus on the poor (e.g., Francesc Betriu's 1985 adaptation of Sender's *Réquiem por un campesino español* / *Requiem for a Spanish Peasant*). The term "heritage film" can thus be used of Spanish classic adaptations of this period only with qualifications. Despite the awkwardness of some of these films, and the fact that successes such as *Tormento* were forgotten in the desire to dismiss culture produced under the dictatorship once democracy arrived, classic literary adaptations continued to find audiences in the 1990s and after. Miró's 1996 film version of Lope de Vega's 1618 play *El perro del hortelano* is a key example.

Like Olea, Miró was a graduate of the Madrid Film School and a director for whom literature and film went hand in hand. Apart from her support for literary adaptations when Director General of Film and subsequently (1986–9) Director of Spanish State Television (TVE), her own filmography includes five adaptations plus television work in this area. *El perro* – which attracted almost a million viewers in Spain, earned over three million euros in box-office receipts, and received twelve awards including seven Goyas – pulled off what many saw as its audacious retention of almost all of Lope's original verse: only one fifth is cut (Allinson 1999: 35).

Miró's work builds on the 1980s boom in adaptations of literary classics. Press reviewers of the 1990s were writing for a very different readership from those who reviewed Olea's film in 1974 – a readership that was cine-literate, internationally aware, and sensitive to gender issues. With the odd exception (Monterde cited in

Evans 1997: 9), press reviews echoed the enthusiasm indicated by high audience attendance and awards. Critics praised the adaptation for its fidelity (Bermejo 1997; Canning 2005: 82) and its successful deployment of cinematic techniques (Riambau cited in Evans 1997: 9). Following prompts from Miró herself regarding her admiration for international heritage cinema – *Cyrano de Bergerac* (Jean-Paul Rappeneau, 1990), an obvious model also scripted entirely in verse, and *Much Ado about Nothing* (Kenneth Branagh, 1993) were mentioned by her in interviews of 1995 and 1997, before and after the film's premiere, respectively (Paz 2001: 259; Fernández Soto and Checa y Olmos 2010: 86) – critics hailed the film as the first Spanish movie to rival these foreign successes (García-Posada 1997). Miró also guided critics toward an interpretation of the film as a reworking of Lope that is sensitive to gender critique (Torres 1997).

If *Tormento*, made in 1974 on the eve of the transition, appeared when the chief concern was the need to redefine political identities rather than gender issues, a very different feminist politics of identity, appropriate to the changed historical context of the 1990s, emerges as central to *El perro*. As an example of Spain's modest heritage cinema (Perriam 2003: 85), Miró's film is usefully interpreted through theoretical work on this trend. In terms of form, Ginette Vincendeau argues that what differentiates heritage cinema from earlier period films (thus *El perro* from *Tormento*) is, first, an emphasis on setting and, second, a "mannerist and postmodern" self-consciousness about narrative conventions (2001: xviii). In terms of ideology, critics of the prominent British heritage cinema – Charles Barr (1986: 11) coined the term and Higson has subsequently focused specifically on "English heritage" – and of its limited Spanish equivalent concur that "there is a tension between narrative and spectacle," the former "progressive" and the latter "reactionary" (Smith 2006b: 111–12). Weighing Vincendeau's identification of formal characteristics against this ideological tension, the following analysis will argue a case for interpreting Miró's period picture as a feminist text that, in its knowing adoption of heritage form, exhibits the reflexivity that is central to postmodern cultural production.

In accordance with the first characteristic outlined by Vincendeau, mise-en-scène is fundamental to *El perro*. The vibrant costumes worn by Emma Suárez's Diana, and the sumptuous interior and exterior settings of her palace, are a major source of visual pleasure. However, this is not a "museum aesthetic" (Vincendeau 2001: xviii) where narrative depth is displaced by surface spectacle, because this mise-en-scène is made to serve the narrative. We do not just marvel at the frills and bustles of Diana's dresses, which in any case were not authentic – they date from the mid-seventeenth century whereas the play is from 1618 (Canning 2005: 84). Dress is clearly aligned with plot development, as the colors of Diana's costumes encode emotion: blue for coldness; red for passion; gold and orange at the opening and conclusion for social status (Canning 2005: 90). Settings similarly enhance the narrative: palatial interiors reference Diana's social standing; exteriors in the garden express a loosening of restrictions that allows her to flirt with her secretary

(Canning 2005: 84). The director capitalizes too on the liminal spaces that connect these two spheres, such as the steps, and on fluid spaces such as the river (Allinson 1999: 36). If the inauthenticity in costume may have been lost on audiences, newspaper readers would have been aware of the inauthentic locations since Miró explained that the film was shot in Portugal because permits were easier to obtain there (Evans 1997: 9). This geographical displacement has the additional advantage of making it clear that the faithful portrayal of period was not Miró's concern. Thus the film does not fully comply with Vincendeau's view of the heritage movie's attitude to setting, since it avoids the superficial stress on spectacle that scholars have criticized.

If we turn to Vincendeau's second formal definition of heritage film – its reflexivity – an analysis of performance style in *El perro* allows us to appreciate how the film promotes a progressive narrative in gender terms. If Velasco, Belén, and Rabal made *Tormento* a success, so Emma Suárez and Carmelo Gómez account for much of *El perro*'s appeal. But, while Velasco's intelligent performance can be attributed to her previous work in popular film and Rabal's to his experience in auteur cinema, Suárez's and Gómez's success is best appreciated through their recourse to the acting conventions of foreign heritage cinema. Chris Perriam argues that Gómez's costume, long hair, and beard self-consciously echo Gérard Depardieu's look in *Cyrano de Bergerac*, while the delivery of his lines is knowingly "postmodern" (2003: 85). In the case of Suárez, the intelligence that actresses such as Emma Thompson have brought to British heritage cinema is surely a model. Elaine Canning argues that Miró's Diana is "a more coquettish creature than her Lopean counterpart" (2005: 84), and, while we cannot know how a seventeenth-century stage actress would have performed this role, Canning's point regarding Suárez's performance stands. Breathless, wistful, or lusty by turns in her delivery of Lope's lines, Suárez's Diana oozes intelligence and self-awareness. Crucial here for a gendered interpretation is Suárez's "mannerist" performance – playfully peeping through her veil at mass, or suggestively clutching a rose as she muses "Mil veces he advertido en la belleza, / gracia y entendimiento de Teodoro; / que a no ser desigual a mi decoro, / estimara su ingenio y gentileza" (I've noticed a thousand times in Teodoro's beauty, grace and wit that, if it were not inappropriate to my sense of decorum, I might admire their ingenuity and gallantry) (Vega 1991: 68) (see Figure 17.2). This ensures that her coyness merges suggestively with cunning, making her role satisfying to feminist audiences in Spain, who since 1975 have enjoyed increasing numbers of films (by women and otherwise) that "articulat[e] the changing definitions of female subjectivity and the relations between the sexes" (Evans 1997: 12). *El perro*, then, adapts the characteristics of the heritage trend to suit its purpose. By playing down the genre's "museum aesthetic" and playing up its self-consciousness, Miró avoids the seductions of surface and foregrounds a feminist reading of Lope's play.

While the film only partially adopts the formal characteristics of foreign heritage, its success is explained by a more consistent generic affiliation with romantic

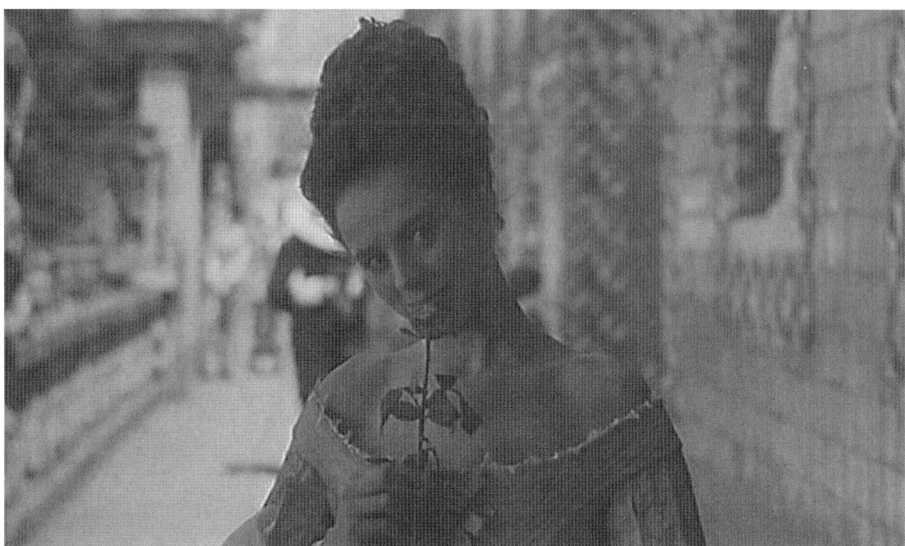

Figure 17.2 Emma Suárez's knowing performance as Diana in Pilar Miró's film version of Lope de Vega's *El perro del hortelano* (1996; prod. Enrique Cerrezo Producciones Cinematograficas).

comedy (Evans 1997: 10–11; Allinson 1999: 34). It is relevant in this context that Branagh's *Much Ado*, one of Miró's models, was also marketed as a romantic comedy. Thus, the Portuguese palaces that provide the setting evoke romantic comedy's recourse to a lovers' "place apart" (Evans 1997: 10), while the cinematography portrays the unfolding of romance through the point-of-view shots, facial close-ups, dissolves, and soft-focus photography that are typical of the genre (see Allinson's (1999: 37) formal analysis of the end of Act II). The opening kiss between Teodoro and Diana's love rival Marcela – a departure from the play (Canning 2005: 83) – also signals the romantic comedy genre. Just as it is helpful to consider *Tormento* as a melodrama, analyzing *El perro* as a romantic comedy highlights its intelligent use of film technique. Mark Allinson goes so far as to suggest that the film does not belong to the heritage category at all (1999: 34). It can be argued that *El perro*'s generic mix of heritage movie and romantic comedy reveals the film's indebtedness to the 1990s contexts of feminism and postmodernism.

Literary Adaptations: Methodological Conclusions

If we take a literary adaptation to be an "extended, deliberate, announced revisitation of a particular work of art" (Hutcheon 2006: 170), comparison is bound to be the business of adaptation studies. Since a literary adaptation is first and foremost a film, that comparison must be shaped by the methodology of film studies rather than of literary studies. This avoids the potential to close down interpretation implied in the approach proposed by Seymour Chatman in 1980 in his essay entitled "What Novels Can Do that Film Can't (and Vice Versa)." The analysis here of *Tormento* and *El perro* has been guided by questions raised by film studies: casting, star image, performance style, generic traits of melodrama and film comedy, and (in so far as is possible) reception. Such an analysis shows Olea, in collaboration with his actors and technical crew, to be an "attentive observer" of his source novel, who capitalizes on the performance and star images of actors such as Velasco, Belén, and Rabal (associated with comedy, lost innocence, and world-weariness, respectively) and draws on conventions of mise-en-scène typical of melodrama (the use of interior spaces and clothes) to infuse Galdós' literary text with a cautious critique of class and gender roles in the twilight of the dictatorship. Miró's collaboration with her actors and technical crew may be likened to that of a theater director – her work in the theater in the early 1990s is relevant here (Fernández Soto and Checa y Olmos 2010: 86). Her familiarity with theater as performance art allows her to elicit Suárez and Gómez's knowing delivery of Lope's lines, and to dress, accessorize, and position them within the frame in playful response to the text. But *El perro* could not be further from filmed theater: the formal characteristics of romantic comedy as a film genre, especially settings and cinematography, enrich performance style and mise-en-scène to offer a reflexive, feminist reworking of the 1618 stage original.

Film and Television (Paul Julian Smith)

Anyone reading the Spanish press in 2009 could be excused for thinking that the audiovisual sector was in a critical condition. Journalists and filmmakers predicted the death of Spanish cinema, which had been identified by the director of the Ministry of Culture's Instituto de la Cinematografía y de las Artes Audiovisuales (ICAA; Institute of Film and Audiovisual Media) as the "image" or "calling card" of Spain to the world (G. B. 2009). While the traditional foe of the film industry was always Hollywood, there was now also an enemy within: television. A Supreme Court judge had ruled that the substantial subsidies paid by the television channels to film producers, legally enforced by the government in its recently renewed Cinema Law, were unconstitutional. How, then, asked press and industry alike, could Spanish national cinema survive this new betrayal by the upstart electronic medium (García 2009)?

El País cited veteran Fernando Bovaira, producer of Alejandro Amenábar's successful feature *Agora* (2009), on the negative prognosis for the film industry in Spain if it was indeed deprived of financial support from the television business. The article noted that television companies had been obliged since 1999 to invest five percent of their income in film, and that in 2007 that sum had risen to as high as 153 million euros (García 2009; see Chapter 14). The television companies replied that the practice had been "arbitrary" – if filmmakers received subsidies from television, why not sportsmen or dentists? Ironically, 2009 had proved to be a record-breaking year for Spanish cinema at the box office, with the historical epic *Agora* joining forces with genre films such as prison drama *Celda 211* / *Cell 211* (Daniel Monzón); teen movies *Mentiras y gordas* / *Sex, Party, and Lies* (Alfonso Albacete and David Menkes) and *Fuga de cerebros* / *Brain Drain* (Fernando González Molina); and Pedro Almodóvar's typically polished melodrama *Los abrazos rotos* / *Broken Embraces*.

Historians of Spanish film have commented that this rhetoric of "crisis" has been constant in a field known throughout its history for "unrelieved industrial decapitalization" (Hopewell 1986: 4). The repeated predictions of the death of Spanish cinema have thus been greatly exaggerated. Moreover, as scholars such as Josep Lluís Fecé and Cristina Pujol (2003) remarked of a now forgotten cinema scare that had taken place as recently as 2001–2, a financial crisis for current industry practitioners should not be conflated with a crisis for all those groups who are stakeholders in Spanish cinema; to put it more plainly, unlike producers, spectators do not benefit from the production of feature films that fail to connect with the audiences for whom they are supposedly intended. Fecé and Pujol wrote rather of an "imaginary" crisis for a "cinema without an audience" (2003: 147–65).

While the polemic between the two media was especially acute in 2009, rivalry between them has been continuous since regular television broadcasting began in Spain at the late date of 1956. And I shall suggest, against received wisdom, that cinema has been for some time dependent on television, not just industrially but also artistically. In their monumental history of producers in Spanish cinema, Esteve Riambau and Casimiro Torreiro argue that the period since 1995, when the Law for the Protection and Promotion of Cinema first came into effect, should be called "the era of the audiovisual"; cross-subsidies combined with the consolidation of "the great [media] conglomerates" meant that it no longer made sense to speak of a separate "film industry" and "TV business" in Spain (2008: 901). Using the evidence of parallel case studies of audiovisual products, I have argued myself in a recent book (Smith 2009a) that the convergence between the two media, both commercially and aesthetically, suggests that they can no longer be considered in isolation from one another.

Before tracing this somewhat fraught history, let us begin with a brief industrial survey of the current conditions of the two media. In all three areas – production, distribution, and exhibition – the first decade of the twenty-first century had been a success story for the Spanish film industry. To take some statistics from the official source of the Ministry of Culture website (Ministerio de Cultura n.d.), feature film production fell to a low of forty-seven in 1990, but by 2006 it had risen to 209; the audience for those Spanish films was 13.9 million in 1997, but by 2005 it was 21.29 million, giving the industry an enviable market share of 20.35 percent; due to the belated multiplexing of Spanish theaters, the number of screens more than doubled in the decade between 1996 and 2005. Although television had been instrumental in the collapse of cinema-going as a mass activity in the late 1960s and the 1970s, it seemed that Spaniards had now been tempted back into the movie theaters in spite of the proliferation of offerings on the small screen.

If this cinematic success has been somewhat obscured by pessimistic journalists or self-interested professionals, then the blossoming of television fiction remained almost unknown outside limited academic circles in Spain, such as the research groups headed by Lorenzo Vilches in Barcelona and Manuel Palacio in Madrid. Since the early 1990s the production of quality local fiction, spearheaded by the autonomous communities of Catalonia and the Basque Country (less innovative in feature film than in television fiction), has pushed once-dominant US series to the margins of the schedule. Milly Buonanno's Euro Fiction Group has noted that the number of hours taken up by local production nearly tripled between 1996 and 2001, far outstripping France and Italy, and that Spain has a higher seriality index than those nations, meaning that it produces more episodes of single titles for faithful fans (Eurofiction 2007). In spite of competition from the Internet, those viewers watched more television than ever in the first decade of the new millennium. In 1993, women viewed on average 223 minutes a day; by 2005 the figure had risen to 246, one of the highest in Europe (Rueda Laffond and Chicharro Merayo 2006: 449). With the exportation of innovative fiction formats such as period drama – for example, *Cuéntame cómo pasó / Tell Me How It Happened* (TVE-1, 2001–) – Spain had produced a mature industry of primetime weekly series whose production values were much higher than Latin American *telenovelas* (soap operas, usually running for a fixed period unlike the British and US variety) and that could be compared only to the fiction factories of Hollywood (see Figure 17.3).

It was Raymond Williams, father of British cultural studies, who first called attention to the paradox of the audience's early preference for television over film in spite of the former's "visual inefficiency" (1990: 28). Viewers were prepared to accept the technical impoverishment of the small screen with its flickering black and white image because the new medium was richer in its "social definition" (1990: 29). While cinema was confined to "discrete and specific works" shown in a "special kind of theater," broadcasting was "general" in its content (music, news, entertainment) and was consumed in the "privatized home" in which citizens of the 1950s were increasingly invested (1990: 29). More recent theorists of television have stressed the medium's continuing flexibility. Milly Buonanno writes that "it is precisely because television allows us to switch between looking and listening, between involvement and detachment, and because it offers us both demanding and relaxing form of cultural entertainment and social participation that it can claim to [be] an open medium" (2008: 41).

On a more formal level (but still stressing "openness"), Kristin Thompson argues for "redundant and dispersed exposition" (2003: 37) in television narratives, which, unlike classic movie plots, are often left without definitive closure. Thompson notes, however, the adaptation of films into television series and vice versa (2003:

Figure 17.3 The Alcántara family watches Massiel win the Eurovision Song Contest for Spain in 1968, in the first episode of *Cuéntame cómo pasó* (TVE-1, 2001–).

83–98). On an industrial level, the convergence of the two media has been dissected by Spanish media academics. Enrique Bustamante distinguishes between "vertical integration" within a single medium (when, say, producers take control of distribution); "horizontal integration" (when broadcasters increase their range of stations); and "multimedia integration" (when producers attempt to produce synergy or mutual reinforcement between their products or sectors) (2004: 88).

In the historical survey that follows, we shall see how each of these questions (of social address, consumption, narrative form, and industrial synergy) has played out in the Spanish audiovisual sector.

After the arrival of broadcast television – rigorously controlled by the state – in 1956, Spanish commentators, more accustomed to film, proved nonetheless open to the artistic possibilities of the new medium. In his introduction to a 1963 book of television scripts by pioneer Jaime de Armiñán – later to direct the remarkable cross-dressing feature *Mi querida señorita / My Dearest Señorita* (1972) – the critic "Viriato" (penname) cited the already classic live television drama made in the United States by creators such as Paddy Chayefsky and set out to define the televisual medium, which he regarded as a new and unexpected dramatic field (Armiñan 1963: 27). According to media historian Mario García de Castro, Spanish television drama (of which there was already twelve hours a week in 1966 and 1967) was thought at the time to constitute a distinctive "third way" between theater and cinema (2002: 25, 35). As Tatjana Pavlović has noted, it is ironic that the few surviving images of such early fiction (which was either live or wiped) are preserved on film, often in the newsreels that reported on the new medium for cinema audiences (2007: 9).

Curious hybrids also appeared in this early period, crossing the boundaries between media. Pavlović, again, has studied *Historias de la television / Television Stories* (1965), a comic feature directed by Francoist film veteran Sáenz de Heredia. This film combined the trends of consumerism and modernity with the changing role of women, as illustrated by its female protagonist, the enthusiastic would-be singing star and hopeless housewife played by Conchita Velasco (Pavlović 2007: 15). A lesser-known later example is *La casa de los Martínez / At Home with the Martínez* (Agustín Navarro, 1971). A curious blend of sitcom and chat show, the television version, which ran from 1967 to 1971, showed a "typical" Spanish family (albeit with two live-in maids) who entertained a celebrity in their home each week, granting them a key to their (televisual) house. The feature film of this show, which was made as the television series came to the end of its run, begins with a curious prologue in which varied households are shown getting ready to watch the show: a butler announces to a posh couple that "the television is served"; a working-class man shouts out of his apartment window to a woman hanging up the washing, alerting her to the start of her favorite program; and a family with eight children solemnly introduce themselves to the camera before settling down to watch.

This imagined community of television viewers is, in the feature film that follows, undercut by the anxieties provoked by the new medium. Old-fashioned Señor Martínez fears, given his wife's new stardom and the close attentions of the series' director, that he is no longer master in his own house. A relaxing trip to the country, away from the bright lights of celebrity-plagued Madrid, is ruined when even the village hicks recognize Spain's most heartwarming family and insist on loudly celebrating the latter's presence among them. There is a constant refrain in the dialogue here that Spain has to modernize and become European. It is a process identified with feminism, modernity, and television itself that seems at once desired and feared. Film audiences of the time (almost half a million saw this feature) were no doubt also disconcerted to see their domesticated friends, hitherto glimpsed in blurry black and white, displayed in full color on the big screen of their local picture palace. The "visual inefficiency" of television noted by Williams was here partially eclipsed by the technical superiority of a film medium that lacked, nonetheless, the "social definition" of its younger rival. Much later, television would return the favor to Francoist cinema: since 1995, TVE-1 has devoted Saturday afternoons to the screening of a feature film of the dictatorship in a slot known significantly as *Cine de barrio / Neighborhood Movie Theater*.

According to Manuel Palacio, the 1960s and the first half of the 1970s marked the "golden age" of Spanish television drama (as the 1950s did for the United States). Commentators even lamented that, with the end of live performance in the studio, the "distinguishing characteristic" of television drama had been lost (Palacio 2001: 86). Palacio gives a list of some thirty distinguished cineastes who worked for television at the time (2001: 87); and, taking advantage of the relative freedom of the minority second channel (TVE-2, which began broadcasting in 1966), future film directors such as Pilar Miró and Josefina Molina produced some of their riskiest works for the small screen, which proved to be a more open medium than cinema even under the dictatorship (Palacio 2001: 132).

While Palacio states that television fiction has always had a logic distinct to that of film and theater (2001: 143), he also recounts radical changes in the medium. For example, at the time of the transition to democracy, the studio-bound drama of the 1970s (one distinguished and long-lasting slot was actually called *Estudio 1*) gave way to the classic prestige serials of the 1980s (often literary adaptations), which were shot on celluloid and used feature film techniques (Palacio 2001: 153; see the previous section of this chapter). Such series not only played a vital pedagogic role, educating Spaniards in the new ideals of democracy; they also offered some explicit space for radical politics, not always present in film of the period. According to director Josefina Molina, *Teresa de Jesús / Teresa of Ávila* (TVE-1, 1984), again starring Concha Velasco, reworked a Counter-Reformation heroine in order to celebrate women's freedom of initiative (Palacio 2006: 102). Faulkner has noted the complex multimedia dialogue between novels of the nineteenth century, their film adaptations in the 1970s, and the television versions of the same works in the 1980s (2004: 81).

Yet television auteurs thrived in very different technical and institutional conditions. Narciso Ibáñez Serrador's gothic series *Historias para no dormir / Stories to Keep You Awake* (TVE, 1966–8) exploited the gloomy claustrophobia of studio sets to scare Francoist audiences, and Antonio Mercero's more expansive and optimistic location-shot serials, some of the best-known titles in Spanish television history, warmed the hearts of viewers in the dictatorship (*Crónicas de un pueblo / Chronicles of a Village* (TVE, 1971–3)) and the new democracy (*Verano azul / Blue Summer* (TVE-1, 1981)). While both directors also worked in feature film, they remain best and most fondly remembered for their innovative work in television (see Smith 2009a: 145–74). Much later, in a cinematic tribute to his low-budget television dramas, five film directors (Álex de la Iglesia, Jaume Balagueró, Mateo Gil, Enrique Urbizu, and Paco Plaza) were to join Narciso Ibáñez Serrador in making feature-length fictions that were released under the umbrella title *Películas para no dormir / Films to Keep You Awake* (2006).

As we have seen, feature film production fell to a record low in Spain at the end of the 1980s, the same decade in which prestige television series took on cinematic production values. But the much-delayed launch of commercial television in Spain at the start of the 1990s led to a perceived decline in quality and a controversy over so-called *telebasura* (junk television). One unique figure in the crossover between film and television here is "popular auteur" Álex de la Iglesia. As Buse, Triana Toribio, and Willis have argued in their excellent monograph on the director (2007: 61), De la Iglesia pays affectionate homage to television, citing horror auteur Ibáñez Serrador in his black comedy *El día de la bestia / The Day of the Beast* (1995). And yet, de la Iglesia's plot, in which a phony television medium joins forces with an eccentric priest, is clearly a savage satire on private television, with the film's fictional "Tele 3" combining the names of the two principal real-life commercial channels Antena 3 and Telecinco (Buse et al. 2007: 73).

As I have documented elsewhere, Almodóvar reveals a similar ambivalence to the small screen (Smith 2006a: 143–56). While his early features of the 1980s gleefully celebrate television genres such as commercials and, indeed, popular culture in general, Almodóvar has made a continuing attack on the medium since his critique in *Kika* (1993) of the new genre of reality shows, the supposed epitome of *telebasura*. The social presence of the medium is such, however, that it has remained ubiquitous in his cinema (see Figure 17.4). It is perhaps no accident that both de la Iglesia and Almodóvar have dabbled (with mixed results) in the production of television series that were screened on TVE-2, the minority public channel: El Deseo made the working-class dramedy *Mujeres / Women* (2006) while de la Iglesia wrote and directed the sci-fi sitcom *Plutón B. R. B. Nero* (2008–9).

In 2000, Richard Maxwell, the Cassandra of Spanish television studies, claimed that a multi-channel environment would lead to "unprecedented demand for imported films and television shows from Hollywood" (2000: 176) and a "decline in the quality and timeliness of domestic productions broadcast free of charge" (2000: 177). Fortunately, this has not proved to be the case. Writing in 2007, Vilches noted that, even after the introduction of two new national channels into a crowded marketplace (Cuatro and la Sexta), local television series still dominated in the schedule over feature films, especially in prime time and on stations with a national reach (2007: 165). Moreover Telecinco, then the frontrunner among all the channels, owed its success mainly to its home-produced quality dramas, a tradition that stretched back to the start of the previous decade. It is perhaps no

Figure 17.4 Pedro Almodóvar's *Volver* (2006; prod. El Deseo): Agustina (Blanca Portillo) appears on television.

surprise, then, that the influence of television should be felt so strongly in the content of feature films of the new millennium.

Let us look more closely at the year 2009, which boasted a number of innovative new titles in television fiction (Smith 2009b). As mentioned earlier, the most popular domestic feature films for that year, far out-grossing even an established auteur such as Almodóvar, include *Mentiras y gordas* (a teen melodrama boasting copious quantities of drugs and sex) and *Fuga de cerebros* (a teen comedy reveling in crude jokes on such topics as blindness and necrophilia). While these commercial hits are often dismissed as mere facsimiles of their US generic equivalents (in this case, youth movies), unlike art films they receive no distribution abroad and are thus precisely targeted to uniquely Spanish audiences. They thus encourage the national "social participation" that is for Buonanno characteristic of television fiction.

Moreover, the principal selling point of such popular cinema is the presence of young actors familiar to audiences only from domestic television. While the Spanish edition of *Cahiers du Cinéma* complained of the "servidumbres televisivas" (servility to television) that it discerned in the more high-minded of the current crop of Spanish film releases (De Pedro and Monterrubio 2009), the more populist *Fotogramas* celebrated multimedia integration with a feature promoting no fewer than thirteen of what they baptized "teletalentos made in Spain" (homegrown television talents) (*Fotogramas* 2009). The mise-en-scène of this glossy photo spread is an unlikely classroom where young actors with "un pie en el cine" (one foot in the cinema) (*Fotogramas* 2009: 104) are being lectured on the technical terms of television: a blackboard boasts such anglicisms as "share," "primetime," and "late night" written in chalk. The brief biographies that follow in the text accompanying the image give the fledgling stars' credits in television first, then in film. Rarely has media convergence been more self-evident.

A special case in this context is Mario Casas, the leading actor in both of the teen feature films mentioned above, whose previously supporting role in Antena 3's quirky ensemble police series *Los hombres de Paco / Paco's Men* (2005–10) was punched up to coincide with his new status as a cinematic leading man. Hoping for synergy in spring 2009, the channel aired frequent cross-promotions of *Fuga de cerebros* in the advertising breaks for this series. Given that most Spanish films fail to appeal to the teenage demographic that comprises the most assiduous group of visitors to cinemas, the success of local youth movies of this kind, which attract audiences in their millions, is no small achievement. Such successes also contradict the "crisis" narrative of Spanish film promoted by more mature producers and journalists, who are, of course, temperamentally hostile to youth movies.

These films no doubt benefited from the disrobing of their young stars' bodies, which are kept somewhat better covered on television. And it is striking that, in these parallel narratives that cast the same actors across two media, it was the television fiction that was more mature in its coverage of social issues. Thus, the premise of the film *Mentiras y gordas* (which could have been unchanged since the 1960s) was that Mario Casas' character was a closeted gay youth, doomed to a tragic death because of his unavowed love for his straight best friend. Yet, in the television high-school drama *Física o química / Physics or Chemistry* (Antena 3, 2008), one of the main training grounds for the casts of these youth pictures, a central gay character was treated with much greater sophistication, well integrated with his peer community, and even rewarded in spring 2009 with a steady boyfriend (most of the heterosexual characters in the series have failed relationships).

To take another pressing social issue, Spanish cinema has produced in the last decade of the twentieth century and the first of the twenty-first a restricted number of feature films on the theme of immigration. These are much studied by Hispanists abroad (e.g., Santaolalla 2005) but are little seen in Spain itself. In the same period, long-running television series such as *El comisario / The Police Chief* (Telecinco, 1999–2009) and *Hospital Central* (Telecinco, 2000–) have produced a corpus of several hundred episodes dealing with the same theme, all of which were seen by audiences in their millions. More sensitive than feature films to changing social circumstances, these series also trace a shift in the representation of immigrant and ethnic-minority characters from criminals and victims to authentic individuals. Increasingly fused with the host society, they now inspire not repulsion but sympathy and empathy (Lacalle 2008: 124–5).

Such series exemplify the concepts of Buonanno, doyenne of European television studies. They embody cultural proximity, engaging a unique closeness to local audiences, and operate a process of "indigenization," whereby US genres, such as the medical drama or police procedural, are radically adapted and adopted by the various national networks. Serving as both cultural entertainment and social participation, they also employ Thompson's technique of "dispersed exposition" (2003) through the mouthpieces of their large ensemble casts and set in motion multiple plot strands that, unlike goal-directed movie plots, resist simple resolution.

Spanish television drama is also known for its attention to the past. The public channel TVE-1's weekly series *Cuéntame cómo pasó* (2001–) and daily serial *Amar en tiempos revueltos / Loving in Troubled Times* (2005–) have both investigated for mass audiences the texture (and sometimes the terror) of everyday life under Francoism. Such shows are at once demanding in their depiction of real trauma and relaxing in the familiarity of the fictional world they recreate for viewers. Critics who complain of historical "amnesia" in contemporary Spain would do well, then, to pay more attention to this very visible national narrative, which is embedded not in cinema or literature but in television.

One unintended effect of the financial transfers from television to cinema has been the recent rise of a television genre that owes much in its form to film: the historical miniseries. Spring 2009 boasted no fewer than three projects that depicted for the first time on screen the figure of King Juan Carlos. The most notable of these, and the most widely watched program of all time on Spanish television, was TVE-1's *23F: El día más difícil del Rey / February 23rd: The King's Most Difficult Day*, which recreated the attempted coup d'état that took place in 1981. As the King, the distinguished theater veteran Lluís Homar combines sympathy for a man betrayed by the generals whom he believes to be his friends with respect for the man who remains Spain's head of state.

By coincidence, Lluís Homar also played the male lead in the highest-profile international release in Spanish cinema that year, Almodóvar's *Los abrazos rotos*, which premiered just days after the miniseries screened. Both texts seek to explore the past in their different ways and media. Indeed, both contain scenes in which the dignified Homar engages in a kind of personal pedagogy with a younger male, who is (or will prove to be) his son. It is an educational process, which, as Manuel Palacio has suggested (2001), is more often undertaken on television than in cinema in Spain. It is no accident that the year 2009 also saw the publication of two excellent books on the representation of history in Spanish television fiction (López et al. 2009; Rueda Laffond and Coronado Ruiz 2009). Another volume, published in the same year, which treats "discourses of the national on global television," also devoted substantial space to content from Spain, including the televisually rich *autonomías* of Catalonia and the Basque Country (Castelló et al. 2009).

The link between film and television is thus industrial (the television companies fund both media), generic (popular movies and television series are mutually reinforcing), and artistic (young television-trained actors venture for the first time on to the big screen, even as established film stars cross over to television, attracted by the steady work in series). The well-known virtues of television (its familiarity, domesticity, and cultural closeness to a local audience) might thus well be imitated in a film medium that has sometimes turned its back on national spectators.

While critics and viewers have reason to fear vertical and horizontal integration in the audiovisual sector (which tends to increase monopolies in and across production and distribution), multimedia corporations have still produced some of the most distinguished work of recent years in Spain. To take just one example,

Telecinco has through its production arm Estudios Picasso created some of the best-quality television drama and some of the most challenging feature films (such as Guillermo del Toro's *El laberinto del fauno / Pan's Labyrinth*, 2006). There seems little doubt that, in spite of persistent rumors of its demise, cinema will continue to be the calling card of Spain to the world. It is likely, however, that television fiction will remain the mirror that reflects back to local viewers the image that they most recognize of themselves.

References

Allinson, M. (1999) Pilar Miró's Last Two Films: History, Adaptation and Genre. In: Rix, R. and Rodríguez-Saona, R. (eds.) *Spanish Cinema: Calling the Shots*. Leeds: Trinity and All Saints, pp. 33–45.

Altman, R. (1996) Otra forma de pensar la Historia (del cine): Un modelo de crisis. *Archivos de la Filmoteca* 22: 6–19.

Armiñán, J. de (1963) *Guiones de TV*. Barcelona: Rialp.

Arroita Jauregui, M. (1974) Galdós como coartada. *Arriba* (September 4): n.p.

Barr, C. (1986) Introduction: Amnesia and Schizophrenia. In: Barr, C. (ed.) *All Our Yesterdays: Ninety Years of British Cinema*. London: BFI, pp. 1–30.

Benjamin, W. (1982) *Das Passgen-Werk*. Frankfurt: Suhrkamp.

Berkowitz, H. (1948) *Pérez Gáldos: Spanish Liberal Crusader*. Madison: Wisconsin University Press.

Bermejo, A. (1997) Fiel, sobria y brillante. *El Mundo* (January 25): 3.

Bluestone, G. (1957) *Novels into Film: The Metamorphosis of Fiction into Cinema*. Berkeley: California University Press.

Buonanno, M. (2008) *The Age of Television: Experiences and Theories*. Bristol: Intellect.

Buse, P., Triana Toribio, N., and Willis, A. (2007) *The Cinema of Álex de la Iglesia*. Manchester: Manchester University Press.

Bustamante, E. (2004) *La televisión económica*. Barcelona: Gedisa.

Canning, E. (2005) "Not I, My Shadow": Pilar Miró's Adaptation of Lope de Vega's *The Dog in the Manger* (1996). *Studies in European Cinema* 2 (2): 81–92.

Cartmell, D. and Whelehan, I. (eds.) (1999) *Adaptations: From Text to Screen, Screen to Text*. London: Routledge.

Castelló, E., Dhoest, A., and O'Donnell, H. (2009) *The Nation on Screen: Discourses of the National on Global Television*. Newcastle: Cambridge Scholars.

Chatman, S. (1980) What Novels Can Do that Film Can't (and Vice Versa). *Critical Inquiry* 7 (1): 121–40.

De Pedro, G. and Monterrubio, L. (2009) Servidumbres televisivas. *Cahiers du Cinéma España* 23 (May): 50.

Eurofiction (M. Buonanno and the European Audiovisual Observatory) (2007) *Television Fiction in Europe* (November 18). Online at: www.obs.coe.int/oea_publ/eurofic (accessed June 6, 2010).

Evans, P. (1997) From Golden Age to Silver Screen: The *comedia* on Film. *Papers in Spanish Theater* 5: 1–13.

Faulkner, S. (2004) *Literary Adaptations in Spanish Cinema*. London: Tamesis.
Faulkner, S. (2006) *A Cinema of Contradiction: Spanish Film in the 1960s*. Edinburgh: Edinburgh University Press.
Fecé, J. L. and Pujol, C. (2003) La crisis imaginada de un cine sin público. In: *Once miradas sobre la crisis y el cine español*. Madrid: Ocho y Medio, pp. 147–65.
Fernández Soto, C. and Checa y Olmos, F. (2010) El cine de Pilar Miró: Homenaje y puente hacia la literatura. *Arbor* 186 (741): 79–88.
Fotogramas (2009) Generación TV 2009. *Fotogramas* 1986 (April): 104–11.
García, R. (2009) El cine español no sobrevivirá. *El País* (December 23). Online at: http://elpais.com/diario/2009/12/23/cultura/1261522801_850215.html (accessed June 6, 2010).
García de Castro, M. (2002) *La ficción televisiva popular*. Barcelona: Gedisa.
García-Posada, M. (1997) Un perro muy particular. *El País* (June 2). Online at: http://elpais.com/diario/1997/02/06/cultura/855183606_850215.html (accessed May 22, 2010).
G. B. (2009) La mejor imagen de España. *El País* (May 29): 50.
Gunning, T. (1986) The Cinema of Attraction: Early Film, Its Spectator and the Avant-Garde. *Wide Angle* 8: 3–4.
Higson, A. (2003) *English Heritage, English Cinema: Costume Drama since 1980*. Oxford: Oxford University Press.
Hopewell, J. (1986) *Out of the Past: Spanish Cinema after Franco*. London: BFI.
Horton, A. and Magretta, J. (eds.) (1981) *Modern European Filmmakers and the Art of Adaptation*. New York: Ungar.
Hutcheon, L. (2006) *A Theory of Adaptation*. London: Routledge.
Labanyi, J. (1995) Masculinity and the Family in Crisis: Reading Unamuno through *Film Noir* (Serrano de Osma's 1946 Adaptation of *Abel Sánchez*). *Romance Studies* 26: 7–21.
Lacalle, C. (2008) *El discurso televisivo sobre la inmigración*. Barcelona: Omega.
Lahoz, I. (ed.) (2010) *A propósito de Cuesta: Estudios sobre los comienzos del cine español 1896–1920*. Valencia: IVAC.
López, F., Cueto Asín, E., and George, D. R. (eds.) (2009) *Historias de la pequeña pantalla: Representaciones históricas en la televisión de la España democrática*. Madrid: Iberoamericana.
López Sancho, L. (1974) *Tormento*, buen espejo galdosiano de situaciones pasadas para realidades de hoy. *ABC* (September 9): 81.
Maxwell, R. (2000) New Media Technologies in Spain: A Healthy Pluralism? In: Jordan, B. and Morgan-Tamosunas, R. (eds.) *Contemporary Spanish Cultural Studies*. London: Arnold, pp. 170–8.
McFarlane, B. (1996) *Novel to Film: An Introduction to the Theory of Adaptation*. Oxford: Clarendon Press.
Ministerio de Cultura (n.d.) Cine y audiovisuales. Online at: www.mcu.es/cine (accessed June 6, 2010).
Moix, T. (1993) *Suspiros de España: La copla y el cine en nuestro recuerdo*. Barcelona: Plaza & Janés.
Montiel, S. (2000) *Memorias: Vivir es un placer*. Barcelona: Plaza & Janés.
Naremore, J. (2000) Introduction: Film and the Reign of Adaptation. In: Naremore, J. (ed.) *Film Adaptation*. London: Athlone Press, pp. 1–16.
Navarrete, R. (2003) *Galdós en el cine español*. Madrid: T&B Editores.
Palacio, M. (2001) *Historia de la televisión en España*. Barcelona: Gedisa.
Palacio, M. (2006) *Las cosas que hemos visto: 50 años y más de TVE*. Madrid: RTVE.

Pavlović, T. (2007) Television (Hi)stories: "Un escaparate en cada hogar." *Journal of Spanish Cultural Studies* 8 (1): 5–22.

Paz, N. de la (2001) Pilar Miró ante el teatro clásico. *Anales de la Literatura Española Contemporánea* 26 (1): 255–76.

Pérez Bowie, J. A. (2004) La adaptación cinematográfica a la luz de algunas aportaciones teóricas recientes. *Signa* 13: 277–300.

Peréz Galdós, B. (1977) *Tormento*. Oxford: Pergamon.

Pérez Perucha, J. (1995) Narración de un aciago destino (1896–1930). In: Gubern, R., Monterde, J. E., Pérez Perucha, J., et al. (eds.) *Historia del cine español*. Madrid: Cátedra, pp. 19–121.

Perriam, C. (2003) *Stars and Masculinites in Spanish Cinema*. Oxford: Oxford University Press.

Pingarrón-Esaín, F. (2009) Preparativos para la Exposición Valenciana de 1909: Acuerdos y concursos para ciertas obras, actividades y acontecimientos. In: *El Ateneo Mercantil y la Exposición Valenciana de 1909. El espectáculo de la modernidad o la modernidad como espectáculo*. Valencia: Ateneo Mercantil, pp. 83–103.

Ramos, P. (1974) *Tormento*, de Pedro Olea. *Alcázar* (September 6): n.p.

Riambau, E. and Torreiro, C. (2008) *Productores en el cine español: Estado, dependencias, y mercado*. Madrid: Cátedra.

Rueda Laffond, J. C. and Chicharro Merayo, M. (2006) *La televisión en España (1956–2006)*. Madrid: Fragua.

Rueda Laffond, J. C. and Coronado Ruiz, C. (2009) *La mirada televisiva: Ficción y representación histórica en España*. Madrid: Fragua.

Salaün, S. (1990) *El cuplé (1900–1936)*. Madrid: Espasa-Calpe.

Sánchez Salas, D. (2002) En otras realidades: La obra de Clarín, Galdós y Valera en el cine español. In: Heredero. C. (ed.) *La imprenta dinámica: Literatura española en el cine español*. Madrid: Academia de las Artes y las Ciencias Cinematográficas de España, pp. 189–209.

Sánchez Salas, D. (2007) *Historias de luz y papel: El cine español de los años veinte, a través de su adaptación de la narrativa española*. Murcia: Murcia Cultural.

Sanders, J. (2006) *Adaptation and Appropriation*. London: Routledge.

Santaolalla, I. (2005) *Los "otros": "Etnicidad y "raza" en el cine español*. Zaragoza: Universidad de Zaragoza.

Smith, P. J. (2006a) *Television in Spain: From Franco to Almodóvar*. Woodbridge: Boydell and Brewer.

Smith, P. J. (2006b) *Spanish Visual Culture: Cinema, Television, Internet*. Manchester: Manchester University Press.

Smith, P. J. (2009a) *Spanish Screen Fiction: Between Cinema and Television*. Liverpool: Liverpool University Press.

Smith, P. J. (2009b) Media Migration and Cultural Proximity: Television Fiction in Spain. *Studies in Hispanic Cinemas* 5 (1–2): 73–84.

Stam, R. (2005) Introduction: The theory and practice of adaptation. In: Stam, R. and Raengo, A. (eds.) *Literature and Film: A Guide to the Theory and Practice of Film Adaptation*. Oxford: Blackwell, pp. 1–52.

Thompson, K. (2003) *Storytelling in Film and Television*. Cambridge, MA: Harvard University Press.

Torres, R. (1997) Pilar Miró: "Lope se adelanta a su tiempo en los personajes femeninos." *El País* (March 5). Online at: http://elpais.com/diario/1997/05/03/cultura/862610407_850215.html (accessed May 22, 2010).
Vega, L. de (1991) *El perro del hortelano*. Madrid: Espasa Calpe.
Vilches, L. (2007) *Culturas y mercados de la ficción televisiva en Iberoamérica*. Barcelona: Gedisa.
Vincendeau, G. (2001) Introduction. In: Vincendeau, G. (ed.) *Film/Literature/Heritage: A Sight and Sound Reader*. London: BFI, pp. xi–xxxi.
Williams, R. (1990) *Television: Technology and Cultural Form*. London: Routledge.

Further Reading

Deveny. T. G. (1999) *Contemporary Spanish Film from Fiction*. Lanham: Scarecrow Press.
Diego, P. (2010) *La ficción de la pequeña pantalla: Cincuenta años de series en España*. Pamplona: Universidad de Navarra.
Martínez-Carazo, C. (2008) Novela española y cine a partir de 1939. Online at: http://descargas.cervantesvirtual.com/servlet/SirveObras/nec/34692843210125086521457/029293.pdf?incr=1 (accessed May 23, 2010).
Martin-Márquez, S. (2009) Spanish Literature and the Language of New Media. In: Gies, D. T. (ed.) *The Cambridge History of Spanish Literature*. Cambridge: Cambridge University Press, pp. 739–55.
Mínguez Arranz, N. (1988) *La novela y el cine: Análisis comparado de los discursos narratives*. Valencia: Ediciones de la mirada.
Román, M. (1994) *Memorias de la copla. La canción española: De Conchita Piquer a Isabel Pantoja*. Madrid: Alianza.
Sánchez Noriega, J. L. (2000) *De la literatura al cine: Teoría y análisis de la adaptación*. Barcelona: Paidós.
Vegas López-Manzanares, F. (2003) *La arquitectura de la Exposición Regional Valenciana de 1909 y de la Exposición Nacional de 1910*. Valencia: Biblioteca TC.

Part VIII

Beyond the Fiction Film

18

Newsreels, Documentary, Experimental Film, Shorts, and Animation

Josetxo Cerdán and Vicente Sánchez-Biosca

Introduction (Josetxo Cerdán)

This chapter focuses on key elements of Spanish cinema that lie outside the limits of the narrative feature film conceived for exhibition in commercial theaters. Its sections are intended as tasters to give an idea of certain features of newsreels, documentary, experimental film, shorts, and animation throughout Spanish cinema's long history. Two issues are singled out for separate treatment, since they are structurally central to the history not just of Spanish cinema but of Spain itself: non-fictional cinematic production during the Spanish Civil War (1936–9) and NO-DO, the state newsreel that the Franco dictatorship created in late 1942 and that continued to operate until 1981. The Civil War and NO-DO occupy the chapter's first two sections. We then pass to a methodological consideration of factors that need to be taken into account when considering alternative cinematic practices. The last part of the chapter proposes three conceptual axes for thinking about these alternative cinematic practices that go beyond genre or chronology while not abandoning either: the relations between center and margins, hybridization, and reflexivity.

Non-Fiction Film during the Civil War (Vicente Sánchez-Biosca)

Newsreels and Documentaries

After the resolutely avant-garde 1920s, the following decade saw the dramatic rise of the documentary format. The Depression, increased social tensions, and the

A Companion to Spanish Cinema, First Edition. Edited by Jo Labanyi and Tatjana Pavlović.

rise of totalitarianisms and their all-out propaganda war were contributing factors. The fracture supposed by the Spanish Civil War was merely an acceleration of this tendency. The documentary field of the time was divided into two different rhetorical systems: the first resulting from the triumph of a new concept of "news" embodied in the newsreel; the second being propaganda and social critique, optimally expressed in documentary, which consequently took on a strong agitprop slant. There was no clear boundary between the two, but they obeyed recognizably different regimes of verisimilitude. In the former case, press correspondents, photographers, photo-journalists, and, of interest to us here, news cameramen mobilized to cover events "live." In the latter, dehumanization of the enemy, social confrontation, and the "brutalization of politics" became hallmarks of the propaganda documentary. Neither of these rhetorical systems was born with the Civil War. But, between 1936 and 1939 both faced a cleavage of international dimensions.

As the eye of the looming international storm, for three years Spain found itself traversed by newsreel crews from France, Germany, Italy, Britain, the USSR, and the United States, among other countries, who disseminated their images throughout the world (Alessandrini et al. 1999). To them we owe the configuration of an iconography of the Civil War that left indelible traces on the imaginary of the world war that followed (Sontag 2003). If the shots of air raids on Madrid or Bilbao – issued between 1936 and 1937 by the Soviet news agency Soiuzkinochronika for the newsreel series *Events in Spain* (Kowalsky 2003) – bear the stamp of the Soviet cameramen Roman Karmen and his assistant Boris Makaseev, the so-called "retreat" of the Republican Army and civilian population after the fall of Barcelona, in late January and early February 1939, was captured chiefly by the cameras of the French news agencies Gaumont Actualités, Pathé Journal, and Éclair Journal (Cadé 2010). While the overall mobilization was spectacular, the biggest single initiative was that of Fox Movietone News, which prided itself on showing only its own images; with up to fifteen film crews shooting throughout Spain, it became a vast visual arsenal (Romeiser 1991).

In practice, a fair proportion of these newsreel images, obeying criteria of verisimilitude appropriate to news journalism, were almost immediately put to propaganda use in documentaries: inflected though intellectual montage and subjected to agitprop voiceover, news became propaganda. A classic case is that of the footage taken in Madrid by Roman Karmen, using the "live report" method of filming. Edited and sonorized in Moscow, with strident voiceover and music, Karmen's images take on a certain heroic tone; borrowed or appropriated by dozens of propaganda documentaries, they express the pathos and anxiety of the civilian victims; when edited by Esther Shub, they generate a compilation film that is a brilliant example of montage: *Ispaniia / Spain* (Shub, 1939).

When we consider the production side of this documentary output, the frontiers between what is Spanish and what is foreign also frequently blur. Nationalist propaganda made more use of Nazi Germany than of Fascist Italy or Portugal.

Berlin became its center of operations, both because of the rhetoric elaborated some years before by Goebbels' Ministry of Propaganda, which now took up the war in Spain as a central motif (Goebbels 1937), and because of the Geyer laboratories' material assistance. Decisive here was the figure of Joaquín Reig, who edited his films for the Falange (Spanish Fascist Party) in the German capital, and, after the creation of the Spanish–German production company Hispano-Film-Produktion in Autumn 1936 (see Chapter 2 and Chapter 14), participated in a series of effective anticommunist films that followed on from the company's first documentary production, *Die Geissel der Welt* / *Scourge of the World* (H. Weidemann, 1937): *España heroica* / *Heroic Spain* (1938) and its two German versions, *Helden in Spanien* / *Heroes in Spain* (1938 and 1939) (Nicolás Meseguer 2008). A more unusual anticommunist message is conveyed by the pro-Nationalist documentary *Romancero marroquí* / *Der Stern von Tetuan* / *Tetuan Sky* (Carlos Velo (uncredited) and Enrique Domínguez Rodiño, 1938–9), produced by the Spanish High Commission in Morocco, which presents Muslims and Christians as united by a common cause (Elena 2004). More complex, but not that different, is the relationship between Spanish and foreign initiatives in the case of pro-Republican documentary. Some of these productions were effectively independent, such as *The Spanish Earth* (Joris Ivens, 1937) undertaken by Contemporary Historians of New York. Others were solidarity initiatives of the political left, directly or indirectly indebted to popular-front agendas, such as Frontier Films' *Heart of Spain* (Herbert Kline and Geza Karpathi, 1937) and the films made by Henri Cartier-Bresson (*With the Abraham Lincoln Brigade*, 1938, recently restored; *L'Espagne vivra* / *Spain will Live*, 1939; and *Victoire de la vie* / *Triumph of Life*, 1939). But the involvement of Spain's Ministry of Propaganda, created in November 1936 by the Socialist Francisco Largo Caballero, was fundamental to the gestation of *Espagne 1936* / *España leal en armas* / *Loyalist Spain at Arms* (1937), conceived for overseas exhibition by Cine-Liberté together with the Spanish Embassy in Paris under Luis Araquistáin, and directed by the French Popular Front filmmaker Jean-Paul Le Chanois (Dreyfus) with the intervention of Luis Buñuel (Gubern and Hammond 2009: 303–17).

Propaganda Models

For many years, historians repeated the accepted notion that cinema produced in the Republican zone was rich, diverse, and vibrant whereas that of Nationalist Spain was the opposite: characterized by paranoid censorship and a glaring lack of imagination. This view is no longer sustainable. It is true that the first initiatives were on the Republican side and that the early months show a marked disproportion, partly due to the fact that the equipment, laboratories, and professionals were mainly in the territory under Republican control (Gubern 1986; Sala 1993). Nonetheless, with the exception of anarchist production, the propaganda models mobilized in Spain's war show the same features found in the Europe-wide propaganda war of the time, in terms of both motifs and formal properties: after all, anticommunism and antifascism were not a national matter (see Sánchez-Biosca 2006).

As mentioned, the surprising anomaly is the anarchist response to the military uprising, especially in Barcelona. The Anarchist trade union CNT (Confederación Nacional de Trabajo (National Labor Confederation)), which since 1930 had controlled the Sindicato Único de Espectáculos Públicos (SUEP; Single Public Entertainment Union) took over the Orphea and Trilla Studios (see Chapter 14) and, under the Office of Information and Propaganda directed by Jacinto Toryho, produced a considerable number of documentaries, among which the pioneering *Reportaje del movimiento revolucionario en Barcelona / Report on the Revolutionary Movement in Barcelona* (Mateo Santos, 1936) stands out. Its object was not the war, which had not yet started, but the social revolution that had taken over the Catalan capital in response to the military insurrection. By means of a "friendly" camera, involved in the events it is narrating, this on-the-spot report, lacking any sense of perspective, captured the libertarian rejoicing at the collectivizations, the taking over of the streets, the barricades, the opening of prisons, the burning of churches, and the departure of the first columns for the Aragonese front. These images would be a gift to the enemy, which almost immediately used them to denounce the chaos and destruction unleashed not by libertarian idealism but by communism (Sánchez-Biosca 2008–9). However, subsequent anarchist documentaries gave a highly novel angle on the war: in their desire to show the revolution, the series *Aguiluchos de la FAI por tierras de Aragón / Eaglets of the FAI in the Fields of Aragón* (1936) assembled images of daily life in the villages taken over by the FAI (Federación Anarquista Ibérica (Iberian Anarchist Federation)), reconstructions of battle scenes, and eulogies of its heroes (especially Durruti). In the same way, *La toma de Siétamo / The Taking of Siétamo* (Adrien Porchet, 1936) and *La silla vacía / The Empty Chair* (Valentín González, 1937) represent the particularities of this atypical war more successfully than the Madrid anarchists of the FRIEP (Federación Regional de la Industria de Espectáculos Públicos (Regional Federation of the Public Entertainment Industry)) were able to do in their series *Estampas guerreras / Images of War* (Armand Guerra, 1936).

Particularly efficient because of its speedy response, and crucial because of its length of operations, was the Commisariat de Propaganda de la Generalitat de Catalunya (Propaganda Commisariat of the Catalan Autonomous Government). In November 1936 it set up a cinema section, Laya Films, under Joan Castanyer. Equipped with two sets of sound-recording equipment, a production manager, an editor, six cameramen, a sound engineer, and assistants, from January 1937 it embarked on production of a weekly news report in Catalan, *Espanya al dia / Spain Today,* which it also issued in Castilian, English, and French. Closely connected to Laya Films was the production and distribution company Film Popular, created in Barcelona in fall 1936 and linked to the PCE-PSUC (Partido

Comunista de España-Partit Socialista Unificat de Catalunya (Communist Party of Spain-Unified Socialist Party of Catalonia)). Indeed, Film Popular would issue the Castilian-language newsreel *España al dia* jointly with Laya Films from March 1937 until the fall of Catalonia to the Nationalists; its content and commentary differed from those of the Catalan version. Also significant among productions linked to Marxist organizations was *Defensa de Madrid / Defense of Madrid* (Ángel Villatoro, 1936), made by the International Red Cross in collaboration with the Alliance of Anti-Fascist Intellectuals.

Nationalist production was faced with a very different situation. With the exception of the Falange, none of the sectors grouped under the Nationalist umbrella had a concept of propaganda. Neither CIFESA (responsible for around twenty documentaries) nor CEA, the two companies responsible for the first Nationalist films, showed themselves to have an adequate grasp of the needs of the moment. Neither did the military authorities feel any desire to entrust propaganda to political hands. It was the documentary production of the Falange's Film Section that would forge an iconography seen simultaneously in the illustrated magazines *Fotos*, *Vertice*, and *Y*, among others. Its films *Alma y nervio de España / Soul and Sinew of Spain* (J. Martínez Arboleya, 1937), *Frente de Vizcaya y el 18 de julio / Vizcaya Front and the 18th July* (1937), and *Los conquistadores del Norte / Conquerors of the North* (1937) display features that would remain constants of Nationalist film propaganda: newsreel-style voiceover, ceremonies commemorating the dead, and a rhetorical mode of locution. *Frente de Vizcaya* includes the first example of counterpropaganda relating to Guernica. If we compare this film to *España heroica*, we can see the innovation introduced by Berlin: the reappropriation and re-editing of enemy material, which would be a basic feature of later Francoist propaganda.

With the establishment of the first Francoist government in late January 1938 and the reorganization of the Press and Propaganda Services within its Interior Ministry (headed by Franco's brother-in-law, the lawyer Ramón Serrano Suñer), the Departamento Nacional de Cinematografía (DNC; National Cinema Department) was created the following April, under the direction of the poet, former member of the Foreign Legion, and journalist Manuel Augusto García Viñolas. The dynamism of the DNC's propaganda effort made an immediate impact. In coordination with the Nationalists' other propaganda instruments (radio, press, magazines) in a project that the first Nationalist Head of Propaganda, Dionisio Ridruejo, would describe as "totalitarian" (1976: 130), the newsreel *Noticiario Español* was issued from June 1938, together with a series of documentaries that illustrate the key components of Nationalist propaganda: the treatment of prisoners (*Prisioneros de guerra / Prisoners of War*, García Viñolas, 1938); denunciation of Communist repression and torture (*Vivan los hombres libres / Long Live Free Men*, Edgar Neville, 1939); the cult of the dead in the person of Falange's founder, José Antonio Primo de Rivera, executed in Alicante prison on November 20, 1936 (*¡Presente!*, 1939); some war reports (disappointing compared to the

Republican material); parades, celebrations, and triumphal tours by the Caudillo (*El gran desfile de la victoria en Madrid / The Great Victory Parade in Madrid*, 1939; *Viaje triunfal del Caudillo por Andalucía / The Caudillo's Triumphal Tour of Andalusia*, 1939); and activities of organizations charged with indoctrinating the population (*Juventudes de España*, Edgard Neville, 1939; *La concentración de la Sección Femenina en Medina del Campo*, 1939) (Tranche and Sánchez-Biosca 2011: 491–6).

In sum, in the light of recent studies we can conclude the following: first, that the international dimension of the Civil War makes it impossible to treat national and foreign production separately; second, that it is necessary to consider the always shifting relationship between the regime of verisimilitude corresponding to news journalism, as in the live coverage of photo-reportage and newsreels, and that corresponding to powerful propaganda machines; and, finally, that it is necessary to examine documentary production on the Nationalist side without prejudice or blinkers, situating it on the same level as anticommunist production of the period elsewhere.

NO-DO: The Francoist Newsreel (Vicente Sánchez-Biosca)

On January 4, 1943, the first Spanish cinemas opened their program with a ten-minute newsreel covering what the Franco regime – locked in the grip of World War II (non-belligerent but explicitly pro-Axis) – regarded as "national news." The newsreel was preceded by a prologue that served as a mission statement (see Figure 18.1). Although it was not conceived as a purely short-term instrument, its duration – until 1981, when cinema newsreels were a distant memory – exceeded all expectations. The machinery had been set in motion some months before. An agreement dated September 29, 1942 of the Vicesecretaría de Educación Popular de FET y de las JONS (Vice-Secretariat for Popular Education of the FET y de las JONS (the official title of the political grouping resulting from Franco's forced merger of the fascist Falange with the traditionalist Carlists in 1937)) had set out the guidelines for the organization and operation of the Noticiarios y Documentales (Newsreels and Documentaries; NO-DO for short). A December 17, 1942 disposition of the same Vice-Secretariat announced its monopoly over newsreel production and the requirement that its news bulletins be screened in all Spanish cinemas. It was, then, a fast, energetic start, and, four months later, with its twentieth bulletin, NO-DO would inaugurate a second edition. This and the privilege of being the only institution allowed to produce newsreels in Spain make it clear that NO-DO's arsenal of images was, especially before television became widely available in the course of the 1960s, the almost exclusive source of documentary footage for public consumption under Francoism and its most efficient audiovisual instrument of socialization (Tranche and Sánchez-Biosca 2000) (see Figure 18.2).

Figure 18.1 NO-DO's camera enters Franco's residence at the Palacio del Pardo: prologue to the first NO-DO (4 January 1943). Courtesy of Filmoteca Española.

Figure 18.2 Behind the scenes at NO-DO: Joaquín Soriano (director) and Alberto Reig (assistant director) on the moviola (NO-DO 105 A, 1945). Courtesy of Filmoteca Española.

Paradoxes

One inevitably has to start by considering NO-DO as a propaganda instrument, as were the other media of the time (press, radio, cinema). All the fundamental values of Francoism appear in its images; the regime's institutions loom large and proud in its news coverage and reports; the enemy is lambasted and refuted acrimoniously in its voiceovers; and the professionals responsible for its making rarely had brushes with their superiors. Nonetheless, the term "propaganda" proves inadequate as a way of understanding the newsreel's logic and, while not untrue, is more confusing than enlightening. Effectively, what needs to be examined is NO-DO's time lag with respect to front-line propaganda of the interwar period – a time lag that chronologically is slight but in stylistic and rhetorical terms is fundamental.

NO-DO's first paradox is that it represented a tenacious effort, unheard-of in a news medium, to avoid "news" and to sideline political information. The historian trawls its images in vain for precise details about national or even international events. The ideological warfare in which it unsurprisingly engaged did not take place on the terrain of current affairs. Considering that it was made in a country that was highly ideologized, close to other European fascisms, and with an iron control over communications, NO-DO is positively laconic. Its omissions, absences, even frivolity leave the researcher perplexed – curiosities, amusements, social functions, fashion, nature, sport, bullfighting, and natural disasters take on an importance not found in other newsreels. In practice, NO-DO would not cease, in its most ideologized sections, to remind viewers of the "crusade" (as the regime termed the Civil War), lingering over ceremonies to honor the "fallen" (on the Nationalist side) or over the regime's sites of memory, and taking viewers round the schools of Sección Femenina (Women's Section of the Falange) or the camps of the Frente de Juventudes (Youth Front), immersing viewers in an unequivocal symbolic repertoire. And yet, its lack of dramatic tension, the primacy given to the secondary, and omission of the political would be its immediately distinctive traits.

This is better understood if we consider the political conjuncture from which NO-DO was born in 1942–3. After a period of Falangist hegemony in documentary film production (1938–41), the team led by Serrano Suñer fell in the cabinet reshuffle of May 1941, with Press and Propaganda Services moving from the Interior Ministry to the recently created Vice-Secretariat of Popular Education. After the Falangist bombings at Begoña (Bilbao) on August 16, 1942, Serrano was definitively relegated, the totalitarian dream collapsing with him. The international context of World War II must also be taken into account. When NO-DO was launched in January 1943, the likelihood of German victory on the Eastern front was already in question, and indeed Marshal von Paulus surrendered at Stalingrad on February 2. That produced a climate of uncertainty that made advisable a more cautious position on Spain's part, which in October 1943 translated into abandonment of the policy of non-belligerence for a return to neutrality.

After unconditional victory in the Civil War and the ensuing repression and extermination of the enemy, as the regime took on an increasingly conservative slant and the most revolutionary sectors of the Falange were disbanded, and with the prospect of Allied victory exposing Spain to reprisals, the propaganda project that ended up imposing itself was one of encouraging acceptance of Francoism rather than one of political agitation. It was a matter not of mobilizing the masses but of demobilizing them, while maintaining the display of religious, political, and charismatic symbols together with a formal, figurative rhetoric that had been supplied by the Falange (and, to a lesser extent, by the Carlists and a baroque-inspired Catholic liturgy). NO-DO was born at a moment when the regime was repositioning itself, backing off (apart from some significant moments) from the confrontational stance of previous years.

Two further factors define the newsreel. Unlike the radio and press, NO-DO had no ideological diversity, no rough edges. While the differences (even of tone) between the monarchist, Falangist, war veterans', and Church press provide the historian with substantial insights into the frictions and dynamics of the *koine* that was Francoism, NO-DO, by contrast, operated as the regime's sole newsreel, with no signs of ideological in-fighting. Thus, NO-DO spoke as the regime's single, standardized voice, free of fissures and conflicts, Francoism's *doxa*. A practical circumstance reinforced its atemporal sameness: the lack of exhibition copies. The more lowly the category of cinema, the older the newsreels shown, producing the comic situation, noted as late as 1952 by NO-DO's deputy director, that at Christmas some cinemas screened the news corresponding to the same time last year. In sum, everything favored the lack of topicality, with preference given to what we might call "news of the period" (the *longue durée*) rather than "the latest news."

Document and Ritual

To appreciate the role played by NO-DO in Francoism's first decades, it is necessary to understand the period's visual climate and expectations about access to information: a single audiovisual news medium; isolation from the outside world; little familiarity with the culture of travel; curiosity about the exotic. With no television and homes equipped only with radio sets that, by definition, were limited to sound commentary, censorship was all-pervasive; enforced silence sealed the lips of those who had avoided exile, prison, or execution; and the institutions of socialization and indoctrination operated at the microlevel of the village or neighborhood, workplace, school, or parish. In this context, NO-DO had a hugely powerful role to play: that of providing Spaniards with knowledge of a previously codified reality in a visually attractive manner.

As one of Francoism's instruments of socialization, NO-DO was responsible for creating what is ambiguously called "sociological Francoism," though its success in this respect is hard to measure. But what does a newsreel document when it avoids "news" but for the most part does not engage in direct propaganda either? This is a key question. NO-DO's inertia reflects the regime's creative apathy. The newsreel's images plunge the spectator into a world that seems not to move: immune to change, always identical to itself, subject to perpetual ceremonial – albeit dotted with exotic and curious trivia. Its succession of ritual commemorations followed an immovable calendar: April 1, with its celebration of Nationalist victory and the military parade at its center; May 1, with the parades of the single state-controlled union; April 18, with its exaltation of work, its inaugurations, and the inevitable reception of the diplomatic corps; October 29, a day of mourning, and even more so November 20, the day of remembrance of the death of José Antonio, buried in the Escorial and in 1959 moved to the Valle de los Caídos (Valley of the Fallen). These date markers combined with others of lesser ideological intensity to conjugate the calendar year: Christmas, imbued with the melancholy, kitsch mood that Francoism bestowed on it; Epiphany, with its stilted infantile chants addressed to the Reyes Magos (the Three Kings, Spain's equivalent of Santa Claus); the "profound Spanishness" of Holy Week, austere in Castile, tragic in Andalusia; plus those local fiestas that merited remembrance in the "national interest." With these ingredients, NO-DO stitched together a hermetically sealed, atemporal circle. Time, in the sense of change and the singular event, disappeared. In its place was ritual, the memory of another time of plenitude and intensity that Francoism yearned for.

Few documents match NO-DO's capacity to represent the Franco regime's ritualistic basis: decisive historical events were replaced by static commemoration, as if the last heroic gesture (the Civil War, the "crusade") had exhausted energies and suspended the country in a dream of plenitude (national, imperial, religious) such that nothing else could ever happen – a historical mirage but also an arrest of history. This spectral dimension of time would be overlaid by the proliferation of symbolically overcharged spaces, the expression in spatial terms of this same ritualism. Three of these stand out – the Valle de los Caídos, the monumental mausoleum dreamed up by Franco as a burial place for the victims (especially on the Nationalist side) in the Civil War; the Toledo Alcázar, where Colonel Moscardó held out against the republican siege in the summer of 1936; and the Escorial, built on Philip II's orders as an embodiment of the spirit of the Counter-Reformation, which would inspire Francoism – though one could add others, such as the Ciudad Universitaria, Paracuellos de Jarama, or Cerro de los Ángeles. This list should suffice to give a clear idea of the Francoist conception of time and space, which NO-DO translated into images.

To conclude, through its representation of time and space, NO-DO became the weekly ritual of a ritualistic, ceremonial state; repetitive ad nauseam, indifferent to change. The more it repeats itself and the more echoes it generates with its unchanging annual liturgy, the more it tells us about the model of society that the regime wished to impose: static, acclamatory, but socially and politically deactivated. This sensation comes over especially strongly to today's historian, attentive to the symbolic significance of décor and place, scenography and verbal rhetoric. NO-DO's message hits the cultural historian in the face.

Change, Finally

Ritualism is necessarily bound up in an intense dialectical relationship with the pressure of change, and NO-DO underwent a major upheaval in the course of the 1960s. The rhetoric of Francoist motifs (its sites of memory and liturgical calendar) did not disappear, but it had to face the emergence of a parallel rhetoric that either tacitly contradicted it or took over its spaces, testifying to their transformation. The language of development was a new rhetorical regime based on the incontestable authority of numbers and calculations, technocratic, often opaque, and apparently deideologized. This discourse coexisted with the previous one in accordance with Francoism's facility for co-opting incompatible linguistic practices, mixing those derived from its military origins with others relating to its more recent legitimization through its achievements (peace, prosperity, work). NO-DO underwent this curious metamorphosis through its relationship to television, for some years in tandem and collaboration (the highpoint was perhaps the 1964 commemoration of the "25 Years of Peace"), but in 1968 it was absorbed into the Dirección General de Radiodifusión y Televisión (Directorate General of Radio and Television). This allowed the news of tourism and economic development to coexist alongside the sites of memory and commemorations of the past, in a syncretism that at some times was masterly and at others bordered on the ludicrous. NO-DO's use of language, defiance of logic, and stubborn persistence in the use of certain symbols speak volumes of Francoism. That is NO-DO's documentary value – as a cultural document.

Shorts, Documentary, Experimental Film, and Animation in Transhistorical Perspective (Josetxo Cerdán)

Historical Change

At the end of 2007, the Academia de las Artes y las Ciencias Cinematográficas de España (Spanish Film Academy), which gives the Goya awards (Spain's equivalent of the Oscars), announced publicly that it was planning to eliminate from the gala ceremony the handing over of its three awards for Best Short (in the categories of animation, documentary, and fiction). Spanish short directors were quick to respond and showed an impressive capacity for mobilization; as a result, the Academy was forced to back down. This incident illustrates the weight that directors of short films have acquired, as a collective, in twenty-first-century Spain.

At no earlier point of time can we talk of an organized collective of short filmmakers able to make a public impact.

This raises a fundamental question: although the term "short" (*cortometraje*) is used generically to refer to a body of films lasting less than thirty minutes, the social, cultural, and indeed formal value attached to such productions has varied hugely at different historical moments. The term "short" can be used to refer to *Una de fieras / Wild Animal Movie* (Eduardo García Maroto, 1934), *Verbena / Carnival* (Edgar Neville, 1942), *Pompurrutas imperiales / Imperial Jingles* (Fernando Colomo, 1976), *Mirindas asesinas / Killer Mirindas* (Álex de la Iglesia, 1991), and *7:35 de la mañana / 7:35 a.m.* (Nacho Vigalondo, 2003), but the different historical circumstances in which these various films originated make them very different cinematic exercises. They do not even all share the common denominator usually attributed to shorts (questioned by some short filmmakers): that of being "trampoline" films helping young directors to establish themselves in the field and to go on to make full-length features. Neville had already directed several feature films when he accepted Saturnino Ulargui's invitation to make *Verbena* in 1942, and, as the above anecdote implies, in the last decade one can talk of short filmmaking as an established field in its own right. Indeed, Vigalondo's aim when he made *7:35 de la mañana* was not to establish himself as a feature filmmaker but to be nominated for an Oscar for Best Fiction Short. Six years later, Javier Recio also got an Oscar nomination, this time for Best Animation Short, with *La dama y la muerte / Death and the Lady* (2009).

Thus, we can call all these films "shorts" but the different historical conditions under which they were shot make them very different cinematic objects. Recio's and Vigalondo's films share the same codes of production, circulation, and consumption, which set them apart from the earlier films listed above. For, since the late 1990s, Spanish shorts have entered a phase marked by the decentralization of production subsidies, with the production and dissemination of shorts becoming a way in which the autonomous communities can promote their image and "brand." The first to do this was the Basque Country, which set up Kimuak to turn the short into the flagship defining a concept of Basque cinema from 1998 onward (see Chapter 4). Other autonomous communities followed suit with similar initiatives. Thus, for the first time in history, there are structures for the production and dissemination of shorts outside the historical centers of production in Madrid, Barcelona, and Valencia. This has two immediate consequences: the production of shorts as a means of self-promotion for new directors has shifted to digital format and dissemination via the Internet (www.notodofilmfest.com/#/Home) and specialist distributors for shorts have sprung up (e.g., Lolita peliculitas). While we are still talking about "shorts," this has nothing to do with shorts as they were conceived in earlier periods.

The same need to distinguish between production in different periods arises when we consider animation, documentary, or experimental cinema. The first full-length animation film made in Spain – *Garbancito de la Mancha* (Arturo Moreno, 1945), scripted by the Falangist Julián Pemartín and made in the middle of the period of autarky (isolation and economic self-sufficiency) after the Civil War – had a clear propaganda message aimed at a public cut off from the outside world. At the other historical extreme, *Planet 51* (Jorge Blanco, Javier Abad, and Marcos Martínez, 2009) was the first Spanish animation film made with a transnational exhibition plan allowing it to be released in over thirty countries, distributed in the United States by TriStar (for theaters) and Sony Pictures Home Entertainment (for home-entertainment formats).

With regard to documentary production (leaving aside newsreels): in the 1920s and 1930s it had a fundamentally propagandistic function, often relating to national identity politics, including from at least the late 1920s that of Spain's historical nationalities. In the course of the Franco dictatorship, in a very small number of productions made outside the framework of NO-DO – for example, *Juguetes rotos / Broken Toys* (Manuel Summers, 1966) – documentary started to take on new forms. Not surprisingly, the flood of documentary production in the 1970s obeyed a strong political impulse, but in many cases these films would be very different formally from the traditional propaganda film. *El desencanto / The Disenchantment* (Jaime Chávarri, 1976), *La vieja memoria / The Old Memory* (Jaime Camino, 1977), *Raza, el espíritu de Franco / Race, the Spirit of Franco* (Gonzalo Herralde, 1977), and *Ocaña, retrat intermitent / Ocaña, an Intermittent Portrait* (Ventura Pons, 1978) are four films that settle accounts with the dictatorship in different ways, but they do so with no intention of indoctrinating the spectator (see Català et al. 2001).

In the case of experimental cinema, the historical discontinuity is total. If we consider its beginnings, critics are still divided over whether films such as *El sexto sentido / The Sixth Sense* (Nemesio M. Sobrevila, 1929) are avant-garde or anti-avant-garde, while Luis Buñuel's first two films – *Un chien andalou* (1929) and *L'Âge d'or* (1930) – are French. It was only in 1930 that two works by the Falangist writer and cultural entrepreneur Ernesto Giménez Caballero – *Noticiario del cineclub / Film Club News* and *Esencia de verbena / Essence of Carnival* – would acclimatize experimental cinema in Spain. These experiments – which Giménez Caballero arranged to have screened abroad (Gubern 1999: 442–3) – have a closer relationship to certain works by Catalan amateur filmmakers of the time (e.g., Delmiro de Caralt or Domènech Giménez) than to the experimental films made by certain Spanish artists from the 1950s on, such as *Aguaespejo granadino / Granada Water Mirror* (José Val del Omar, 1955; see below) or *Operación H / Operation H* (Néstor Bastarretxea, 1963).

It is therefore crucial to consider how the production models and formal properties of shorts, animation, documentary, and experimental film have changed over time, rather than making generalizations about them as a series of discrete cinematic forms. Even more important is the need to consider the different ways in which, at different historical moments, they have been circulated, viewed, and consumed by their various audiences. The following sections will consider these cinematic forms in terms of a series of transhistorical conceptual axes, but in each case will take historical factors into account.

The Centrality of the Marginal

At least two historical factors have to be borne in mind in order to understand the particular relationship in Spanish cinema between mainstream industrial production (centered on narrative feature films) and production taking place on the industry's margins (shorts, documentary, experimental film, animation). First of all, Spain's incorporation into the industrial revolution and modernity was late and achieved at high cost. A backward country in terms of all the criteria used to measure development in the late nineteenth century, this became notoriously evident with the loss in 1898 of Spain's last significant colonies in a war with the technologically more advanced United States. In these conditions of backwardness and general demoralization, the introduction of a modern form of entertainment such as the cinematograph was bound to be difficult. Second, we should remember that the outcomes of the Spanish Civil War and of World War II – conflicts that were in many respects intimately related, with a gap of only a few months between them – were diametrically opposed. While the end of World War II meant the defeat of fascism in Western Europe and the adoption of liberal democratic models, in Spain Franco's victory led to an autarkic dictatorship that imposed a politics of revenge, extermination, and pillage, with many forced into exile. Only with the passage of time, chiefly to ensure the regime's survival, were certain minimum social and economic freedoms permitted, always under police surveillance and subject to suppression at any moment. Almost forty years of Francoism made an indelible mark, not only on the development of the film industry but also on the possibility of developing alternative cinematic practices on its margins.

Given the first of these factors, it is hardly surprising that, as Pérez Perucha has observed (1993), during the whole period of silent cinema in Spain, production companies, economically precarious and with limited possibilities of commercial exploitation in the national market, were forced to channel their efforts into producing panoramas (a distant cinematic antecedent of the documentary film) and newsreels instead of fiction films, since the latter required more resources (lighting in order to shoot interiors, the hire of actors and scriptwriters, etc.). The producers of Spain's fledgling cinema were economically dependent on their ability to sell their newsreels, panoramas, and other pre-documentary material abroad. It is important to note that the great figures of early Spanish cinema also operated in these marginal areas. The first Spanish filmmaker to acquire an international name was Segundo de Chomón, who did so thanks to his mastery of techniques linked to animation, such as superimposition, hand coloring, and frame-by-frame shooting. His skills were recognized when Pathé contracted him in 1906 to work in France, where he would make some of his best-known films, such as *El hotel eléctrico / The Electric Hotel* (1906) (Minguet Batllori 2010). The other outstanding figure of the silent period is Buñuel, who made his name in experimental film with *Un chien andalou* and *L'Âge d'or* – both filmed in France, though the first was financed with money from Spain and the second contains a few scenes shot on the Costa Brava. Both films brought Buñuel recognition in Paris avant-garde circles of the late 1920s. When Buñuel made his first film in Spain, it would be a propaganda documentary: *Las Hurdes / Land without Bread* (1933). While Spanish silent cinema had a prolonged dependence on newsreels, panoramas, and other pre-documentary material, and its most remarkable creators were a precocious pioneer of animation (Chomón) and a central figure in the avant-garde (Buñuel), narrative fiction film produced in Spain barely reached national audiences until virtually the end of the 1920s.

This centrality of the margins is found again at other moments. During the late Franco period, when to make a film one first had to obtain a shooting permit (i.e., get the censor's approval), a significant number of filmmakers decided to work "illegally" on the industry's margins, creating an oppositional cinematic corpus that, although unseen in commercial theaters, took on great importance in alternative exhibition circuits. Perhaps the figure who best exemplifies this move from professional to underground filmmaking is Basilio Martín Patino, who saw his *Canciones para después de una guerra / Songs for After a War* banned (made in 1971, it would not be screened until 1976) and decided to go underground, making two more unauthorized documentaries before the dictator's death in 1975: *Queridísimos verdugos / Dearest Executioners* (1973) and *Caudillo* (1974). These underground filmmakers had varied profiles: from the documentary filmmaker Helena Lumbreras, linked to the Communist Party, who made militant films (*El campo para el hombre / The Land for Men*, 1973) to an iconoclast like Antoni Padrós (*Lock Out*, 1973; *Shirley Temple Story*, 1976). The underground film movement took on such importance that in 1974 a distribution company was created for this kind of work, La Central del Curt, which contined to operate until 1981.

With cinema converted into a digital industry in the twenty-first century, few production companies operating in Spain make only narrative feature films for the big screen: first, because significant holdings in production companies are held by media and pressure groups who oblige them to diversify production; and, second, because cinema is now part of a much broader audiovisual system that includes the production of content for television, the Internet, or institutions of every kind. In this new audiovisual universe, transnational and yet atomized, Spanish cinema continues to occupy certain niches that permit the creation of "anomalous" projects that, on occasion, impact on the industry's center. This is the case with, for example, two animated features films made in the last decade: *Un perro llamado Dolor / A Dog called Pain* (by the singer and painter Luis Eduardo Aute, 2001) and *De profundis* (by the graphic novel artist Miguelanxo Prado, 2006; see Chapter 4) – both formally eccentric in their balancing of industrial and artisanal production. A similar eccentric position is occupied by the experimental films of Albert Serra (*Honor de cavalleria / Quixotic*, 2006) and the documentaries of Óscar Pérez (*El sastre / The Tailor*, 2007): produced on the industry's margins, these films have garnered considerable accolades and won awards at some of the most prestigious

Figure 18.3 *El sastre* (2007) – directed, shot, edited, and produced by Óscar Pérez – won the Best Short Documentary Film award at the Amsterdam International Documentary Film Festival. Courtesy of Óscar Pérez.

international festivals, achieving a global recognition rarely attained by mainstream Spanish cinema (see Figure 18.3).

Hybridization

There is no doubt that, throughout the history of cinema, the border between animation and experimental film, and between the latter and documentary, has been highly porous. Already in the 1920s, visual music and urban symphonies illustrated these two kinds of hybridization. In the case of an underdeveloped film industry such as that of Spain, these mixtures have possibly occurred even more frequently. This is not just because their creators had an interest in innovation but also because, lacking a well-established tradition, they found themselves operating on shifting terrain. In this respect, it is not surprising that many figures have occupied different roles in one or other of these fields. In current times, Begoña Vicario is a clear example of this mobility. She started out directing and producing her experimental animation work in the mid-1990s – her best-known piece is *Pregunta por mí / Ask after Me* (1996). Then she wrote *Breve historia del cine de animación experimental vasco* (*Short History of Basque Experimental Animation*, 1998), which sketches the work of ten key figures, including herself. Later, she appeared as producer for a film by another female experimental animation director, *Hezurbeltzak / A Common Grave* (Izibene Oñederra, 2007). The low level of professionalization encourages a proliferation of hybrid products; conversely, moving around different roles within the creative community can help to achieve professionalization – thus, Vicario can promote the field to which she contributes creatively as director by also operating as critic or producer. This hybridization process should not be seen as a limitation; on the contrary, it pushes boundaries in all three of these marginal fields: experimental film, documentary, and animation. Additionally, the practice of moving between production, direction, and even criticism helps to create a sense of community.

Six decades before Vicario, José Val del Omar had already cultivated the hybridization of documentary and avant-garde in the 1930s (*Vibración de Granada / Granada Vibration*, 1935). Two decades later, opting resolutely for technical experimentation, he would add to that mix elements more usually associated with animation, with his two most important works: *Aguaespejo granadino* (1955) and *Fuego en Castilla / Fire in Castile* (1960). Both fuse technical and formal experimentation with a documentary focus on Andalusia and Castile that oscillates between myth and ethnography. Also during the Republic, Carlos Velo introduced into his documentary film projects some of the innovations of Soviet avant-garde cinema of the previous decade.

In the 1960s, some of the figures associated with the Barcelona School (see Chapter 3) would make a series of interventions in documentary film with a clear experimental vocation. Three very different examples are *Lejos de los árboles / Far from the Trees* (Jacinto Esteva, 1970), *El sopar / The Dinner* (Pere Portabella, 1974), and *Numax presenta … / Numax presents …* (Joaquín Jordà, 1980). Portabella expanded into collaborations that went beyond the cinematic, working with artists in various media: music (*Playback*, 1970) with Carles Santos, painting (*Miró l'altre / The Other Miró*, 1969) with Joan Miró, and poetry (*Lectura Brossa / Brossa Reading*, 2003) with Joan Brossa (see Chapter 3 and Chapter 6). This cross-fertilization between cinema and other arts had been anticipated by the first experiments with visual music on the part of Equipo 57, a collective of Spanish artists founded in Paris in 1957, though perhaps the most remarkable experiment of this kind was *Ere erera baleibu icik subua arauren* (José Antonio Sistiaga, 1970; the title is Basque-sounding nonsense language), a full-length seventy-five-minute film consisting entirely of hand-painted celluloid.

At the opposite end of the spectrum, in the 1960s animation also joined hands with fiction feature film in some interesting hybrid products. What made this possible was animation's professionalization in the field of advertising, especially thanks to television. The chief contribution of animators here was the creation of credit sequences, but in some cases it was more extensive – for example, in José María Forqué's 1968 film featuring the rock group Los Bravos, *Dame un poco de amooor … ! / Bring a Little Loving*, whose pop-inspired animations were created by Francisco Macián.

Iván Zulueta's work must be included in any discussion of animation and experimentalism (see Chapter 21). Zulueta's experimental films made in Super

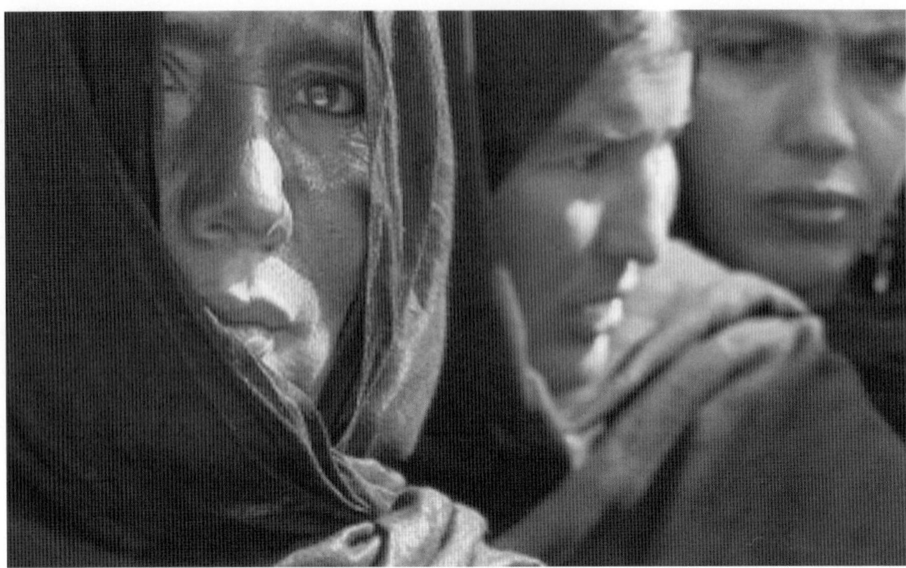

Figure 18.4 Tuareg women protect themselves from the sun in the desert, captured with an intense realism by Lluís Escartín's camera in *Amanar Tamasheq* (2010, prod. Lluis Escartín / Green Valley). Courtesy of Lluis Escartín.

8 and 16 mm, with their extraordinary plasticity, incorporate a whole repertoire of trick photography associated with animation – though perhaps his most outstanding works in this field are those made for television. During the two seasons when he was responsible for the youth program *Último grito / The Latest Craze* (1968–70), he used various animation techniques to make pop songs of the time come alive. Nonetheless, Zulueta's major work is beyond doubt *Arrebato / Rapture* (1980), a fiction film produced within a relatively normal industrial framework, appealing to the generic features of horror film but with a plotline that allowed him to introduce fragments from his earlier experimental shorts, making the film a hybrid mix of genre film and experimental film.

Finally, it should be noted that the irruption of digital systems into cinema in the 1990s has produced a new convergence between cinema and art at an institutional level. In Spain this process is very evident in what is known as experimental documentary. Works such as those of Virginia García del Pino have found funding from art institutions but are released at film festivals. The work of María Cañas is as likely to be shown in an art gallery as in a touring film series. Andrés Duque has been nominated for Goya awards, but his works are shown in exhibition spaces such as La Casa Encendida and MNCARS (Museo Nacional Centro de Arte Reina Sofía). Lluís Escartín won the prize for Best Short with his film *Amanar Tamasheq* (2010) at the international documentary film festival Punto de Vista, but his work is deposited in the video library of the Fundació La Caixa (see Figure 18.4). Isaki Lacuesta alternates between fiction films for exhibition in commercial theaters (e.g., *Los condenados / The Condemned*, 2009) and very different joint projects with the filmmaker Naomi Kawase, the novelist and theater critic Marcos Ordóñez, or the painter Miquel Barceló. All these filmmakers share a common mobility and capacity for hybridization. That perhaps does not make them a "generation," but they comprise the first group of Spanish creators who see their work as occupying a hybrid space somewhere in between cinema and the museum, both formally and in terms of production and exhibition.

Reflexivity

One of the obsessions of Spanish critics writing about Spanish cinema has been the issue of "realism." This dates back to the initial attempts at constructing a national cinema in the late 1920s, which set up an opposition between the *españolada* (stereotypical representation of Spain) and a cinema that would depict Spain as it "really" was; that is, an opposition between the artificial and the genuinely Spanish. This was reactivated after the Civil War by Francoism, which equated realism with its own discourse (initially Falangist, later National-Catholic) on the essence of Spain. The topos took on new life with the impact on Spain of Italian neo-realism and the European New Waves. And it has been revived recently by critics who reject the "postmodernity" of Spanish cinema as a sign of its disconnect from the country's reality. It is striking that there have been few critical texts devoted to the reflexive side of Spanish cinema, when this has been an evident feature throughout its history (Castro de Paz and Cerdán 2007). Reflexivity is understood here in the sense given to the term by Robert Stam (1992) as a "different tradition" from that of realism – one that formally highlights the process of textual construction. Stam's key examples are taken from Spanish culture: Cervantes, Velázquez, Goya.

This reflexivity, as widespread as it is understudied, is even more marked, if such a thing is possible, in those cinematic forms on the industry's margins – for example, it has been claimed as a characteristic of Brazilian cinema (Vieira 1982). There is no need to insist on the reflexivity of Spanish experimental cinema, since experimentalism by definition involves reflexivity. But attention does need to be called to the reflexivity of shorts, since this is where it is most evident, especially in periods when cinematic models have tended, through various strategies of erasure, to hide their enunciative mechanisms. Early works such as the already mentioned *El sexto sentido* or Edgar Neville's *Yo quiero que me lleven a Hollywood / Take Me to Hollywood* (1931), a film that revolves around the mechanics of stardom, are clear examples of this reflexivity. But it is even more striking in the series of three shorts – *Una de fieras / Wild Animal Movie*; *Una de miedo / Scary Movie*; *Y, ahora, una de ladrones / And Now a Gangster Movie* – made by Eduardo García Maroto between 1934 and 1936, which parody successful film genres of the time. The first, *Una de fieras*, starts by showing a three-thousand-peseta check – the money raised to make the film – and continues with images of the film crew together with the actors, a selection of the settings to be used, and so on; in a nutshell, it is a film about its own making. If we consider the contemporary period, some of the most outstanding Spanish shorts of the 1990s and early twenty-first century have a similar reflexive note of parody of Hollywood genres. This is the case, for example, with *Mirindas asesinas* (Álex de la Iglesia), *Perturbado / Disturbed* (Santiago Segura, 1993), and *7:35 a.m.* – the last of these being a reflexive, hypertextual parody of the musical.

The marginal condition of Spanish cinema in the transnational market has from early on been a factor in these parodic retakes on genre cinema. This is evident in short fiction films, which, being made at the far edge of the industry's margins, are especially prone to plotlines that reflect on their own forms and limits. However, conditions of production alone do not explain the existence of shorts such as Vicente Lluch's *Documento secreto / Secret Document*, a parody of the spy film with a female protagonist who travels to the French–Spanish border to realize a dangerous secret mission while her boyfriend stays at home. This sixteen-minute film was made in 1942, when the Franco regime had not yet started to disengage itself from the Axis powers. Reflexivity, then, is about the renewal of cultural forms.

There is, however, a kind of reflexivity that is not concerned with parody. This is the case with the previously mentioned documentary compilation film *Canciones para después de una guerra*, in which Martín Patino takes apart the historical memory of Francoism. A non-parodic mode of reflexivity characterized the whole of documentary production during the transition to democracy, as seen in *El desencanto* (1976), *El asesino de Pedralbes / The Murder of Pedralbes* (Gonzalo Herralde, 1978), *Ocaña, retrat intermitent*, *Rocío* (Fernando Ruiz Vergara, 1980), *Animación en la sala de espera / Animation in the Waiting Room* (Carlos Rodríguez Sanz and Manuel Coronado, 1981), and *Cada ver es / Every Sight Is* (Ángel García del Val, 1981; the title is a pun on the Spanish for "corpses"). A similar non-parodic form of reflexivity is found in Aute's *Un perro llamado Dolor*, which comprises seven reflections in animated form on a series of Spanish and non-Spanish visual artists – particularly Goya and including Velázquez and Buñuel – with the director appearing on screen in person. Several recent reflexive documentaries are similarly anything but parodic. Andrés Duque dedicated his first film *Iván Z* (2003) to the figure of Iván Zulueta. Much more than a survey of Zulueta's life and work, Duque's film takes up the challenge of Zulueta's experimental project, adapting it to his own creative agenda. The result avoids imitation by offering a reflection on the forms of experimental documentary at the time of the film's production. Duque would use one of the phrases spoken by Zulueta in *Iván Z* as the title of his *No es la imagen sino el objeto / It's not the Image but the Object* (2008), a performative film that takes further the circle of meditations woven around Zulueta's figure. Equally striking is Carlos García Alix's *El honor de las injurias / The Honor of the Wronged* (2007), which tells the story of the anarchist Felipe Sandoval by resemanticizing iconic shots in the history of international documentary production together with others from Spanish fiction film, generating a highly productive interaction between both visual traditions (see Figure 18.5).

Figure 18.5 Shot in high-contrast black and white, *El honor de las injurias* (Carlos García Alix, 2007; prod. Andrea Santaolaya / No hay penas SL) undertakes a criminal investigation into the figure of the anarchist Felipe Sandoval. Courtesy of Andrea Santaolaya / No hay penas SL.

Consideration of Spanish documentary, animation, experimental film, and shorts in the light of the three conceptual categories proposed here goes some way toward giving a sense of their complexity, always bearing in mind the importance of chronology, which generic classifications so often ignore.

References

Alessandrini, L., Arbizzani, L., Bertrand de Muñoz, M., et al. (1999) *Immagini nemiche: La Guerra civile spagnola e le sue rappresentazioni*. Bologna: Editrice Compositori.

Cadé, M. (2010) *La Retirada en images mouvantes*. Canet: Trabucaire / Institut Jean Vigo.

Castro de Paz, J. L. and Cerdán, J. (2007) Tra(d)iciones y traslaciones del ensayo fílmico en España. In: Weinrichter, A. (ed.) *La forma que piensa*. Pamplona: Gobierno de Navarra, pp. 110–24.

Català, J. M., Cerdán, J., and Torreiro, C. (2001) *Imagen, memoria y fascinación: Notas sobre el documental en España*. Madrid: Ocho y Medio.

Elena, A. (2004) *Romancero marroquí: El cine africanista durante la Guerra Civil*. Madrid: Filmoteca Española.

Goebbels, J. (1937) "Die Wahrheit über Spanien." Speech given at 1937 *National Party Congress in Nüremberg*. Berlín: Müller und Sohn.

Gubern, R. (1986) *1936–1939. La guerra de España en la pantalla*. Madrid: Filmoteca Española.
Gubern, R. (1999) *Proyector de luna: La generación del 27 y el cine*. Barcelona: Anagrama.
Gubern, R. and Hammond, P. (2009) *Los años rojos de Luis Buñuel*. Madrid: Cátedra.
Kowalsky, D. (2003) *La Unión Soviética y la guerra civil española: Una revisión crítica*. Barcelona. Crítica.
Minguet Batllori, J. (2010) *Segundo de Chomón: The Cinema of Fascination*. Barcelona: Filmoteca de Catalunya.
Nicolás Meseguer, M. (2008) *Las relaciones cinematográficas hispano-alemanas durante la guerra civil española y los inicios del franquismo (1936–1945)*. Unpublished PhD thesis. Universidad de Murcia: Departamento de Historia del Arte.
Pérez Perucha, J. (1993) La larga marcha. In: Llinás, F. (ed.) *Directores de fotografía del cine español*. Madrid: Filmoteca Española, pp. 22–55.
Ridruejo, D. (1976) *Con fuego y con raíces: Casi unas memorias*. Barcelona: Planeta.
Romeiser, J. B. (1991) The Spanish Civil War and Fox Movietonews, 1936–1939. In: Vernon, K. (ed.) *The Spanish Civil War and the Visual Arts*. Ithaca: Cornell University Press, pp. 71–7.
Sala, R. (1993) *El cine en la España republicana durante la guerra civil*. Bilbao: Mensajero.
Sánchez-Biosca, V. (2006) *Cine y guerra civil española: Del mito a la memoria*. Madrid: Alianza.
Sánchez-Biosca, V. (ed.) (2008–9) *Imágenes en migración: Íconos de la guerra civil española*. Special double issue of *Archivos de la Filmoteca* 60–1.
Sontag, S. (2003) *Regarding the Pain of Others*. New York: Farrar, Straus and Giroux.
Stam, R. (1992) *Reflexivity in Film and Literature: From Don Quixote to Jean-Luc Godard*. New York: Columbia University Press.
Tranche, R. and Sánchez-Biosca, V. (2000) *NO-DO: El tiempo y la memoria*. Madrid: Cátedra / Filmoteca Española.
Tranche, R. and Sánchez-Biosca, V. (2011) *El pasado es el destino: Propaganda y cine del bando nacional en la Guerra Civil*. Madrid: Cátedra / Filmoteca Española.
Vicario, B. (1998) *Breve historia del cine de animación experimental vasco*. Madrid: Semana de Cine Experimental.
Vieira, J. L. (1982) From *High Noon* to *Jaws*: Carnival and Parody in Brazilian Cinema. In: Johnson, R. and Stam, R. (eds.) *Brazilian Cinema*. Cranbury: Associated University Presses, pp. 256–69.

Further Reading

Del Amo, A., with Ibáñez Ferradas, M. L. (1996) *Catálogo general del cine de la Guerra Civil*. Madrid: Filmoteca Española / Cátedra.
Fernández Cuenca, C. (1972) *La guerra de España y el cine*. Madrid: Editora Nacional.
Martínez Barrionuevo, M. L. (2003) *El cine de animación en España* (1908–2001). Madrid: Fancy Ediciones.
Medina, P., González, L. M., and Velázquez, J. M. (eds.) (1996) *Historia del cortometraje español*. Madrid: Festival de Cine de Alcalá de Henares.

Part IX

Reading Films through Theory

19

Isabel Coixet's Engagement with Feminist Film Theory

From G (the Gaze) to H (the Haptic)

Susan Martin-Márquez

While Catalan director Isabel Coixet's works eschew the radically experimental nature of films that are more commonly associated with theoretical exploration, they do in fact manifest the director's decades-long engagement with contemporary theory. That engagement is perhaps most evident from her friendship and collaboration with the British essayist, art historian, painter, and literary author John Berger, which culminated in Coixet's dedication of her 2005 film *The Secret Life of Words* to him, and her 2009 museum installation *From I to J*, a tribute to Berger's epistolary novel *From A to X*. Although it would certainly be fruitful to focus on the symbiosis between Coixet's and Berger's work, my project here is somewhat different, for I am more interested in the director's involvement in a theoretical exchange that may have been initiated by the British author but that was subsequently pushed in different directions by other academic and cultural figures. Berger's 1972 book *Ways of Seeing* anticipated a fascinating series of debates concerning the viewing practices that are mobilized and extended through cinema spectatorship – practices that are profoundly tied up with gender constructions. As I shall argue in the following pages, Coixet's films may productively be placed in dialogue with both the psychoanalytically based feminist "gaze theory" that rose to the fore from the late 1970s to the 1990s and also the burgeoning theorization of a "haptic" or embodied cinema, which has emerged out of phenomenological approaches to the medium. I will show how Coixet's work contributes to these theoretical discourses through a close analysis of two films produced at different moments in the director's career: the 1984 short *Mira y verás / Look and You Will See* (Coixet's directorial debut) and the 2003 feature *My Life without Me*.

Coixet has explained that her first "encounter" with John Berger took place years ago in London, when she purchased a well-worn copy of *Ways of Seeing*, a

A Companion to Spanish Cinema, First Edition. Edited by Jo Labanyi and Tatjana Pavlović.

book she characterizes as transformative: "the world was no longer the same; I was no longer the same [...] after reading the book, you can no longer look at anything in the same way" (Berger and Coixet 2009: 12; the book also appears in a character's room in *The Secret Life of Words*). Berger's cowritten volume followed upon his popular BBC television series of the same title, and laid the groundwork for a practice of visual analysis that acknowledged the technical accomplishments and affective impact of Western artworks (or their reproductions) while exposing signs of the economic and gendered power relationships that they exemplified and reaffirmed. Berger explained how the development of the oil painting was caught up in the rise of capitalism, presenting richly tactile representations of objects to viewers who delighted in the affirmation of their own wealth (in the case of the art owners themselves) or enjoyed a vicarious form of possession (in the case of the general public) (1977: 83–112). By means of visual as well as narrative essays, Berger also showed how artistic works, as well as later forms of advertising inspired by the painterly tradition, converted entire groups of people – racialized others and most especially women – into objects to be possessed, through particular compositional strategies and a careful channeling of the viewer's gaze. This dynamic was then internalized by those who were objectified. In Berger's famous formulation,

> *men act* and *women appear*. Men look at women. Women watch themselves being looked at. This determines not only most relations between men and women but also the relation of women to themselves. The surveyor of woman in herself is male: the surveyed female. Thus she turns herself into an object – and most particularly an object of vision: a sight. (1977: 47; emphasis in original)

While the British scholar Laura Mulvey's 1975 essay "Visual Pleasure and Narrative Cinema" (reprinted in Mulvey 1989: 14–26), often characterized as one of the single most influential works of film theory, is grounded in a densely psychoanalytic frame of reference absent from *Ways of Seeing*, her arguments are clearly an extension of Berger's ideas into the cinematic context. Mulvey asserts that the female figure onscreen is objectified in classical Hollywood films, which are organized around a mobilization of two forms of visual pleasure highlighted by psychoanalysis. Spectators enjoy a narcissistic pleasure when they see and identify with the "ego-ideal" represented by the male protagonist, gaining a sense of omnipotence as well as possession of the female protagonist by the narrative's end, as frequently happens in Hollywood film; and they indulge in scopophilic pleasure when they become voyeurs, gazing upon the female bodies that are displayed for them, bodies that connote "to-be-looked-at-ness," in Mulvey's well-known expression. Yet, according to psychoanalytic theory, contemplation of the female figure may provoke castration anxiety. Mulvey claims that this anxiety is resolved when spectators, along with the male protagonist in the narrative, replay the complex by subjecting the female to investigation and then punishing or pardoning her, or are prompted to disavow the complex altogether when the figure of the woman is converted, through fragmentation or other means, into a fetish that covers over the presumed "lack" (1989: 14–26). Mulvey's widely debated theoretical model has been challenged, refined, and extended over the years. For example, in response to early objections that the essay left aside female viewers, the author herself published a second piece in 1981, "Afterthoughts on 'Visual Pleasure and Narrative Cinema'" (reprinted in Mulvey 1989: 29–38), in which she argued that classical cinema in essence "masculinizes" the spectator position (Mulvey 1989: 29), an assertion similar to Berger's claim that "the 'ideal' spectator is always assumed to be male" (Berger 1977: 64). Mulvey again turns to psychoanalysis to posit that female viewers might in fact draw satisfaction from that masculinization, which enables them psychically to return to the "phallic phase" that Freud claims boys and girls alike experience before the imposition of sexual difference (1989: 29–38).

Gaze Theory and *Mira y verás*

Coixet launched her directorial career in Barcelona in 1984 with the short film *Mira y verás*, whose title, narrative, and visual logic reflect her early fascination with the objectifying gaze that had been theorized by Berger and Mulvey.[1] Indeed, the very first image of *Mira y verás* is an extreme close-up of an eye, in black and white and pixelated, as if it were a magnified detail of a newspaper photograph or some other form of low-resolution illustration. The pixelation immediately foregrounds the ways in which still and moving-image technologies are grounded in the special characteristics of the human visual apparatus: our eyes' ability to roam over a moderately pixelated image enables us to perceive it as sharply defined, much as the phenomenon of persistence of vision enables us to "see" a seamless movement in a series of frozen images. This brief invocation of the mechanics of image-making and perception is followed by a reference to viewing practices within a social context, as the title of the film is subsequently superimposed in chartreuse letters over the pixelated eye. While a viewing subject is emphasized by the two verbs of the title – "look" and "see" – a reciprocity of gazes is implied in the image of the black retina, which features a white light reflection that converts the eye into an illuminated object, as well as a "bearer of the look," as Mulvey would term it (1989: 19). Similarly, the direct address of the second-person verb forms of the title also deconstructs the viewer/viewed hierarchy, as audience members are simultaneously invited to gaze upon, and identify with, the image of the eye. The opening of the film thus suggests that the position of the voyeur – seeing yet unseen – is in fact an unstable one, an instability that the film's spectators as well as its protagonists will come to share.

The playfully worded chartreuse-on-black credits that follow anticipate the amusingly iconoclastic tone of the narrative. If classical Hollywood cinema, according to Mulvey, promotes a gendered "division of labor" between masculine viewing subject and feminine object, Coixet's film begins first with a parody, and then with an equally satirical reversal, of that dynamic. Although Mulvey insists that radical filmmakers must destroy pleasure in order to counter the "active/passive mechanisms" of classical cinema (1989: 16, 26), it might be argued that *Mira y verás* encourages viewers critically to distance themselves from those mechanisms by deploying a pointedly politicized yet still pleasurable form of humor. After a brief presentation of the female protagonist – listed in the credits as "La Chica" (The Girl) and played by Ester Rabinad – as she settles into a new apartment, there is a cut to a scene of her disastrous first day at work as a stripper. Before a tacky gold and silver lamé curtain, dressed in a pink sequined bikini, The Girl sways her hips as she peels off one of her black elbow-length gloves and tosses it into the audience. The medium shot is framed so that the audience members remain offscreen, yet the presence of "unseen voyeurs" is suddenly revealed as the glove flies back into the left of the frame, apparently thrown at The Girl by an unsatisfied spectator. As the hackneyed burlesque music continues on the soundtrack, there is a cut to a decidedly untitillating close-up of The Girl as she showers – only her head and neck are shown – and then to shots of her attempting to finish dressing and of a large run in her stockings, as she laments in voiceover that she has already ruined five pairs in one morning. The glove scene in particular might be characterized as a degraded evocation of Rita Hayworth's celebrated "Put the Blame on Mame" performance in *Gilda*, which caused a scandal in Franco-era Spain since it was mistakenly presumed to be a censored version of a full striptease (Gubern and Font 1975: 57).[2] Moreover, Coixet's entire sequence studiously avoids or perverts the classical Hollywood techniques – glamorous costuming, bodily fragmentation through framing, and the fetishistic use of lighting and filters – that Mulvey identifies as promoting a gendered circuit of voyeurism/scopophilia and objectification (1989: 22–3). Instead of a seamless spectacle of "to-be-looked-at-ness," the opening of Coixet's short offers us – comically – the shredded remnants of an illusory "visual pleasure."

In the next scene, The Girl accidentally uncovers a peephole in her living-room wall, and after looking through it she discovers that it opens onto the bedroom of her neighbor in the apartment next door, who happens to be sitting directly in front of her, on the edge of his bed in his black underwear, putting on his socks. While in the earlier striptease scene our gaze is not channeled through onscreen male spectators, here, by contrast, we are invited to adopt the viewing position of The Girl through a point-of-view shot of the neighbor, with an iris mimicking the shape of the peephole. As this schema is repeated in successive scenes, The Girl will eventually come to characterize herself as a "vulgar voyeur"; the neighbor, for his part, lingers over his gestures, as if he were aware of, and even enjoyed, his own objectification. Here, female viewers have no need to adopt the "restless transvestism" that Mulvey claims is their customary lot (1989: 33, 37). Rather, it is male viewers who are perhaps forced to oscillate (uncomfortably, or in secret pleasure?) between identification with an objectified man, who is far from an "ego-ideal," and the "cross-gender" identification with The Girl that they must take up in order to enjoy the pleasure, freedom, and control generally granted to male protagonists and spectators.[3]

The peephole scenes might appear to be precisely the kind of reversal of the voyeurism–objectification relationship that has been problematized by feminist film theorists such as Mary Ann Doane, who notes that the exceptional case of the man on display maintains the binary opposition and thus "simply reinforces the dominant system of aligning sexual difference with a subject/object dichotomy" (1991: 20–1). However, in *Mira y verás* the reversal is effected through the same humorous distancing devices as the initial striptease. At first The Girl hardly seems to garner "visual pleasure" from her gaze: her immediate reaction upon peering through the peephole is to draw back and rub her eye, commenting in voiceover that the neighbor – listed as "Calcetín Man" (Sock Man) in the credits, and played by Manel Barceló – is definitely not her type. Neither the man's sartorial choices – particularly his "horrible" black argyle socks, as The Girl describes them – nor his physique conform to the conventional norms of sexual attractiveness circulated through the media; moreover, the overblown orchestral music that swells when the socks are slowly slid onto the feet only underlines the incongruousness of their structural status as fetish objects. Yet, as The Girl continues to spy upon her neighbor, even after they begin dating and making out at the movies,[4] and even after she insists again that he is not "her type," it becomes less obvious precisely why she feels compelled to return to the peephole. *Mira y verás* might be juxtaposed to Spanish writer Ana Rossetti's widely discussed 1987 poem "Calvin Klein, Underdrawers," in which the poetic voice, inspired by a popular underwear ad of the period, delights in the erotic display of a finely sculpted man clad only in well-filled white briefs. Yet, as Cristina Moreiras-Menor has argued, the ostensibly subversive figure of a female (or, alternatively, gay male) voyeur who actively gazes upon an objectified male body simply masks the image of a passive consumer whose desires are predetermined by the latest advertising campaigns (2002: 106–8). Coixet's film, by contrast, does not claim to "speak" for female desire, nor does it conflate that desire with the commercialized forms of erotic images that John Berger interrogates in *Ways of Seeing*.

Instead, in its deconstruction of the processes of voyeurism and objectification promoted by visual media, *Mira y verás* substitutes hegemonically erotic images with numerous glimpses of daily life. Sock Man's bedroom wall is adorned with a female pin-up who lies provocatively on her stomach, wearing black thigh-high stockings (no runs); Sock Man himself, however, reclines in his underwear (clearly not Calvin Klein) and those unappealing socks, scratching his testicles, as the non-diegetic burlesque music is again heard on the soundtrack. Another spying session reveals Sock Man's pitiful efforts to exercise: he can only touch his toes if he bends his knees, and he collapses to the floor after two push-ups. Meanwhile, The Girl is shown shuffling around her apartment in a plush robe and slippers with her hair wrapped in a towel and cold cream on her face; poking her head into the refrigerator and sniffing at a suspicious item; or cramming food into her mouth in the middle of the night. Interestingly, the only nudity in the film is framed within this quotidian context, when we see a brief medium shot of The Girl with bare breasts as she applies deodorant in her bathroom, which is festooned with her drying lingerie (multicolored, but certainly not sequined). This scene contrasts with the only other view we are offered of The Girl at her stripping job, where she struggles and ultimately fails to remove her sparkling pink bikini top while on stage.

It could be argued that, even though the film's narrative explicitly presents The Girl as far more skilled at voyeuristic gazing than at objectifying herself, the partially nude scene in the bathroom nonetheless represents a capitulation to traditional forms of "visual pleasure." The ending of the film also suggests that, despite her apparent desire to control the terms of, or at least profit from, her own objectification, The Girl will always be "caught unaware," subjected to a hidden male gaze. *Mira y verás* closes on the rooftop of the couple's apartment building as the two hang up their laundry. In the film's first and only dialogue, Sock Man interrupts The Girl after she blurts out that she has something to tell him, confessing that, before they began dating, he created a peephole so that he could spy on her. The Girl, silencing her own appropriation of that peephole, feigns indignation and then rushes into Sock Man's arms as the film closes – almost – with a Hollywood-style "happy ending": a kiss. What I have characterized as the film's destabilization of the viewer/viewed hierarchy, synthesized in the opening graphic of the pixelated eye with the light reflection, as well as in The Girl's final voiceover realization that "por un agujero puedes mirar y ver, pero también puedes ser visto" (you can gaze and see through a peephole, but you can also be seen) is further complicated in the last seconds of the film. After focusing on Sock Man and The Girl, the camera pans left until they are out of frame, and then zooms in to reveal a man standing on a nearby rooftop, observing the couple through binoculars, accompanied by the non-diegetic burlesque music. While The Girl's gaze has been dominant throughout the film, in many cases authorizing the spectators' own access to specific scenes, it is supplanted in the end by the image of an anonymous, omnipotent male gaze, seemingly a cipher for the masculine, or masculinized, film viewer theorized by Mulvey.

Although many scenes of *Mira y verás* clearly ally the gaze with gendered processes of objectification (a central concern of the psychoanalytically based feminist film theory that emerged out of Mulvey's work), much of the short also evokes the broader sensory stimulation of daily life: the enveloping softness of a fuzzy robe; the soothing density of cold cream; the pungent aroma of spoiling food. Indeed, *Mira y verás* suggests that, while the gaze may be associated with a distanced form of visual mastery, it may also draw us in closer to a world of multisensory experiences, engaging in synaesthesic fashion with our perception (for example) of touch and smell – a cinematic phenomenon that has come to be referred to with the term "haptic." By supplementing the "ocularcentric" with an attention to the broader range of everyday sensory experiences, Coixet's inaugural work anticipates a recent development in film theory – the turn to exploration of the haptic qualities of cinema – that I will treat in more detail later in this chapter.

Melodrama, the Woman's Film, and *My Life without Me*

Notwithstanding the occasional moments of levity, Coixet's 2003 feature film *My Life without Me* is in many respects radically different in tone from *Mira y verás*. Yet it shares with the earlier short a critique of the gendered narratives and visual structures of classical Hollywood cinema as well as a (significantly more extensive) mobilization of haptic techniques. The narrative, which was shot in Vancouver, centers on the twenty-three-year-old Ann (Sarah Polley), who is married to Don (Scott Speedman), the teenage sweetheart she met at a Nirvana concert. Ann, who works as a cleaner at the local university, and Don, a construction worker, live with their two young girls in a cramped trailer home in the backyard of the home of Ann's mother (Deborah Harry). When Ann learns that her bouts of nausea and acute abdominal pain are not the result of another pregnancy but rather the symptoms of a late-stage ovarian cancer that has spread to her stomach and liver, leaving her with only a few months left to live, she decides to hide the news from her family, and creates a list of ten things she wishes to do in her final days. The list includes telling her daughters, Patsy and Penny, that she loves them every day and recording audio messages for all their birthdays until they turn eighteen; finding a new wife for Don and by extension a new mother for the girls; and making love with, and inspiring love in, a man other than her husband. The central subject matter – a young woman facing a terminal illness – is of course a staple of classical film melodrama. Even as it draws upon a number of melodramatic techniques, however, Coixet's work, like much of feminist film theory, also interrogates Hollywood's traditional interpellation of female subjects through the genre.

Indeed, the narrative of *My Life without Me* recalls two of the subgenres of the melodramatic "woman's film" analyzed by Mary Ann Doane in her 1987 volume *The Desire to Desire*: the medical discourse film, featuring an ill woman and a male doctor who must function as "reader or interpreter, as the site of knowledge which dominates and controls female subjectivity" (1987: 43), and the maternal melodrama, which foregrounds the all-consuming "sacrifice and suffering" of a mother facing a separation, or threatened separation, from her children (1987: 73). Yet in both cases Coixet's film breaks with generic norms. Ann's doctor, who initially has difficulty looking his patient in the eye, is a radical departure from the male protagonist of the medical discourse film, whose penetrating gaze signals his omnipotence. In fact, *My Life without Me* is now used in bioethics courses to instigate frank discussions of doctors' emotional investment in their patients' wellbeing, and to exemplify an approach that restores agency to patients themselves (Shapiro 2006; Casado da Rocha 2008).[5] Coixet's filming style underlines the profoundly intersubjective nature of the doctor–patient relationship. When the doctor reveals the diagnosis, he and Ann are seated side by side in an empty hospital waiting room; the conversation is presented through a modified shot/reverse-shot structure that maintains both characters in the frame, as the camera is positioned, alternately, next to each of them. While the selective focus of the lateral shots shifts our attention between the doctor's pained communication of the terrible news and Ann's stunned reaction, the blurrier presence of the figure nearest the camera heightens our awareness of the intense emotional resonance of the conversation for both. The camera positioning also amplifies the impact of the moment in which the doctor finally brings himself to look directly into Ann's eyes (see Figure 19.1). The doctor ultimately supports Ann's decision not to share the news with her family or seek further medical tests or treatment – though he does insist on offering her palliative care – and he also agrees to deliver the taped birthday messages to Patsy and Penny after Ann's death.

Ann's devotion to her daughters, represented in the tapes and in her desire to spare them the trauma of witnessing fruitless cancer treatments and a medicalized death, does not, however, entail the "noble" forms of self-denial traditionally demanded of maternal melodrama heroines (Vidal 2008: 227). In the alternative moral universe of Coixet's film, Ann's pursuit of personal happiness in the last few weeks of her life, including her affair with a man named Lee (Mark Ruffalo) whom she meets in a laundromat, does not contravene the interests of her daughters, or even of her husband. This represents a dramatic reworking of the ethos of maternal melodramas such as *Stella Dallas* (King Vidor, 1937) and *Mildred Pierce* (Michael Curtiz, 1945), both of which are discussed by Doane and incorporated into *My Life without Me* through pointed intertextual reference. In *Mildred Pierce*, for example, the title character makes constant sacrifices on behalf of her two daughters, especially after she separates from her husband. Even so, on the one day that Mildred takes a break from her responsibilities to enjoy herself with a suitor, she is in effect "punished" for her "selfishness" as her younger daughter falls ill and dies of pneumonia. *Mildred Pierce* is explicitly referenced in *My Life without Me* when Ann's mother watches, tearfully, another scene from the film on television, the showdown between Mildred (Joan Crawford) and her ungrateful older daughter, Veda (Ann Blyth), who cruelly derides her mother, calling her a "common frump," and vows to escape from her "stinking" surroundings (see Figure 19.2).[6] Ann's mother later narrates a "Joan Crawford" film to her granddaughters, emphasizing that the female protagonist made "a huge sacrifice and she suffered a whole lot," though in fact the snippet of plot description we overhear – a mother hides her identity so as not to spoil her daughter's chances at a favorable marriage – corresponds not to *Mildred Pierce* but to *Stella Dallas* (which stars Barbara Stanwyck). This conflation of the two movies underlines the unchanging message of maternal abnegation imparted by the "woman's film," a message that Ann hastens to condemn, chiding her mother for filling the girls' heads with narratives of "moth-

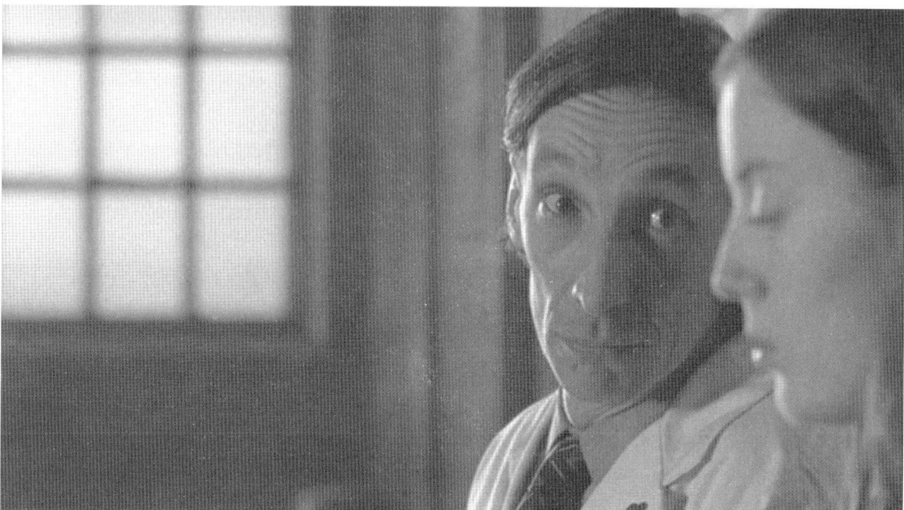

Figure 19.1 As the doctor reveals the diagnosis to Ann, lateral shot/reverse-shots and selective focus highlight the intense emotional impact on both characters (*My Life without Me,* Isabel Coixet, 2003; prod. El Deseo).

ers making dumb-ass sacrifices." Ironically, although the scene can be read as excoriating the ideological thrust of Hollywood melodrama, the argument between Ann and her mother quickly escalates, coming to resemble a more subdued version of the encounter between Mildred and Veda (Ann's mother thinks she is unappreciative of her sacrifices; Ann dislikes the fact that she resembles her mother). Resonating beneath the surface, too, is Ann's own forbearance, as she endures all the references to suffering women while suppressing the devastating secret of her own terminal illness.

Figure 19.2 Ann's mother sobs while watching *Mildred Pierce's* mother–daughter showdown on television (*My Life without Me*, Isabel Coixet, 2003; prod. El Deseo).

From Body Genres to the Haptic

My Life without Me thus censures Hollywood's gendered deployment of melodrama, even as it mobilizes the genre's undeniably powerful address to viewers. The precise nature of that power has intrigued feminist theorists for decades. Scholars working within a psychoanalytic frame of reference such as Doane, Gaylyn Studlar (1988), and Kaja Silverman (1992) have emphasized the masochistic positioning of female as well as male viewers of melodrama; as Doane writes of the woman's film in particular, "spectatorial pleasure is often indissociable from pain" (1987: 16). In her 1991 reconsideration of the genre, Linda Williams also drew on psychoanalysis, shifting the focus from Freudian considerations of perversion to the structures of fantasy that melodrama engages (2000: 216–20). At the same time, she moved the debate in a particularly productive new direction, classifying melodrama as one of a number of "body genres" (including pornography and horror) that foreground the images and sounds of a (characteristically female) body "caught in the grip of intense sensation or emotion" (2000: 209). Williams underlines the fact that watching these low-status genres entails a failure to maintain a presumably "proper aesthetic distance": "the body of the spectator is caught up in an almost involuntary mimicry of the emotion or sensation of the body on screen" (2000: 210). Thus, when Ann's mother wipes away her tears while watching *Mildred Pierce*, she models the type of bodily response that viewers of *My Life without Me* may be prompted to share.

Williams' article is now viewed as an important bridge between the psychoanalytically based feminist film theory that followed upon Mulvey's pioneering essay and the ever-growing corpus of theoretical work on the haptic, which also pays close attention to questions of gender. That work may be traced back to Vivian Sobchack's phenomenological approach to film, as evidenced in her *The Address of the Eye* (1991) as well as the more recent *Carnal Thoughts* (2004). Sobchack counters much of film theory's treatment of sight as purely a "distance sense" (leading to the association of "the gaze" with mastery and control), as well as the more commonplace notion that film may only be experienced through the eyes and ears:

> Even at the movies our vision and hearing are informed and given meaning by our other modes of sensory access to the world: our capacity not only to see and hear but also to proprioceptively feel our weight, dimension, gravity, and movement in the world. In sum, the film experience is meaningful *not to the side of our bodies but because of our bodies*. (2004: 59, 60; emphasis in original)

Sobchack exemplifies this phenomenon by discussing how her own fingers instantly "knew" that the first shot in Jane Campion's 1993 film *The Piano* was an extreme close-up of the female protagonist's fingers as she peered through them, even before the visual information from that and the clarifying second reverse shot had been sent from her eyes to her brain and been consciously decoded (2004: 62–4).

While ongoing scientific research on mirror neurons seems to support some of Sobchack's insights concerning the ways in which spectators' embodied experiences may reflect those of the characters onscreen,[7] within the realm of film theory a number of scholars have also extended the reach of Sobchack's formulations concerning the profound sensory and emotional impact of cinema. Laura Marks, for instance, introduces the concept of a "haptic visuality [...] that functions like the sense of touch" (2000: 22). Haptic visuality may depend in part on spectator predisposition, but Marks argues that some films also include particularly "haptic" images, which may be created, for example, with extreme close-ups and/or out-of-focus, underexposed or overexposed, or grainy shots; haptic images are often not immediately discernible, prompting the eye to move over or "caress" the surface of the visual field, to be "more inclined to graze than to gaze," in the author's felicitous phrase (2000: 170–6, 162). Giuliana Bruno also describes the eye of the film viewer as capable of caressing and being caressed by the moving image (2002: 252), though her conceptualization of the haptic shifts the emphasis from the "surface" to the "habitable space" of cinema (2002: 250). Bruno adopts the distinct graphic form "*e*motion" to encapsulate the way in which film viewers "move into" and undertake a tactile exploration of filmic spaces and are "moved" by the emotional resonance of the sensory stimuli they experience in that process (2002: 247–62). Jennifer Barker, for her part, shares Bruno's interest in the affective valence of the broader range of "haptic" sensations of the cinema – from the tactile to the kinaesthetic to the proprioceptive – exploring viewers' responses to so-called immersive technologies (such as camerawork or computer-generated effects that mimic or magnify our own bodily movement) as well as other materially engaging techniques. Barker insists, however, that the cinema-viewing experience is unique, not because we are simply absorbed by cinematic works, but rather because we are "doubly situated," feeling ourselves to be at once outside the film looking on *and* inside the space of the moving images, inhabiting what she terms the "film's body" (2009: 84). Barker relates this simultaneous being in oneself and in the other to phenomenological treatments of intersubjectivity. Complementing Bruno's reflections on "*emotion*," Barker draws upon Glen Mazis' conceptualization of a fully reversible "e-motion," where subject/object and active/passive distinctions fall away, and affect and meaning circulate within a dynamic of interconnectedness (Barker 2009: 155–6).

The Haptic and *My Life without Me*

In *My Life without Me*, as in *Mira y verás*, there are numerous representations of the characters' sensory experiences, as they savor comfort food, listen to music or Mandarin language tapes, or revel in the warmth of a partner's body in bed. However, even more significant than these "indexical" references – which Marks would characterize as relying more on traditional processes of identification (2000: 171) – are the cinematographic strategies that Coixet deploys to create "haptic images" and by extension to promote embodied viewing practices. *My Life without Me* marked the beginning of Coixet's extended collaboration with cinematographer Jean-Claude Larrieu, who designs the lighting while she operates the camera. Coixet's earlier films were often characterized by steadily framed long takes shot from a tripod or other stabilizing device, but in *My Life without Me*, in response to the challenge of shooting in a trailer home, she began to employ hand-held camerawork, a technique that has subsequently come to characterize her filmmaking (Cerrato 2008: 43–4). Coixet's method, however, must be distinguished from the now-clichéd shaky hand-held shooting style, often characterized by an abundance of whip pans and other abrupt movements, that emerged in foreign and American independent film over the course of the 1990s to represent the disaffection of youth and the increasingly frenetic pace of contemporary life. The Catalan director, by contrast, has developed a more flowing, "organic" form of hand-held camerawork (sometimes aided by an improvised suspension system) in which the image itself almost appears to "breathe" and emote; as Dennis Hopper (who appeared in Coixet's later film *Elegy*, 2008) has described it, "it's like being alive, the cinema is *alive*" (*Charlie Rose* 2008). Other actors who have worked with the director, such as Sarah Polley and Penélope Cruz, have also noted the intense intimacy of shoots in which Coixet, often positioned just a few steps away from them, herself mirrors the emotions of the scene from behind the camera (Cerrato 2008: 10; *Charlie Rose* 2008). While Barker notes that it is important not to confuse the theorization of the "film's body" with the bodies of the actors or even of the cameraperson (2009: 7–9), in the case of Coixet's work the director's specific filmmaking strategies certainly shape viewers' apprehension of her films as perceiving and expressive entities.

In addition to inaugurating her particular style of hand-held camerawork, in *My Life without Me* Coixet shoots on a grainier super 16 mm stock and deploys a number of specific techniques – such as extreme close-ups, selective focus, lens flare, slow and fast motion, and unsynchronized sound – that also increase the haptic quality of the film. Interestingly, these techniques are used most extensively in scenes of Ann when she is alone, intensifying the viewer's embodied connection to the female protagonist. Although a number of different moments in the film exemplify this process, I will focus in detail on the opening sequence.

Like *Mira y verás*, *My Life without Me* begins with a direct address to the viewer as the female protagonist initiates her voiceover in the second person, while a close-up of her as she stands outside in the rain slowly fades in from an all-white screen. However, Ann's opening phrase, "This is you," far more pointedly draws the viewer into the text; in the words of Belén Vidal, it "encloses the spectator in Ann's fantasy" (2008: 224). The film's use of language is, moreover, quite complicated. The phrase "this is you" is in fact repeated twice, with an initial slight questioning tone that later resolves into a statement. Although on a first viewing we are unaware of Ann's situation, in retrospect her ongoing recourse to the second person functions in part to represent her "out-of-body" experience as she struggles to assimilate her diagnosis. That "out-of-body" quality is also suggested as we watch and hear Ann, who otherwise appears silent, breathing heavily in the rain, even as we listen to her voiceover: "You never saw yourself as, I don't know how you describe it, it's like one of those people who like looking up at the moon, or who spend hours gazing at the waves, or at the sunset, or … I guess you know what kind of people I'm talking about. Maybe you don't." Ann's comment "Maybe you don't" also implies a capacious "you" that encompasses her own personal turmoil as well as other subjectivities that may not share her worldview or experiences. Ann is thus represented as "here and there," inhabiting her body while moving into the space of mutual encounter, just as the film's spectators are, as Barker would describe it, "doubly situated."

That "double situation" is effected through concrete visual and aural strategies. Some of the images clearly function to "illustrate" the sensory experiences highlighted in Ann's voiceover: the camera frames her bare feet on the grass as she mentions the feel of the ground softening beneath her, and focuses on her nose and open mouth as she comments on the smell of the rain; an extreme close-up of the raised hairs on her arm, and longer shots that reveal her soaked shirt and erect nipples, accompany her references to the sensation of the cold and of the water seeping into her clothing. The profound tactility of many of the images, however, moves viewers beyond the realm of the illustrative and into the haptic. A studied use of selective focus maintains Ann in sharp view while producing a pronounced layering of textures that draws out the materiality of her body as well as of her immediate surroundings. The blurred image of the rain converts the falling drops into heavy vertical threads of light against a dark background that echo in form

Figure 19.3 Ann in the rain: the sensual textures of haptic images evoke the embodied experiences of characters, and prompt an embodied response in viewers (*My Life without Me*, Isabel Coixet, 2003; prod. El Deseo).

even as they contrast in color with the darkly dripping strands of hair against the smooth pallor of Ann's face (an effect that is rendered abstract in another close-up shot featuring the back of Ann's head to the left of the screen, with the rain to the right). While in several shots the use of slow motion draws our attention to the individual droplets of water that roll down the contours of Ann's features and dangle from her nose, lips, and brow, in the extreme foreground of these images isolated drops of water also slowly descend, so "close" to us that we may catch ourselves blinking in response, much as Ann does (see Figure 19.3). A final extreme close-up of Ann's left eye in profile then fades to a black screen.

While the first half of this opening sequence is eminently carnal, the second is decidedly more ethereal. We hear Ann utter "this is you" again, as well as the tones of an otherworldly music, and then the black screen fades in to an extreme close-up of numerous glass vessels filled with clear and amber-colored liquids. It is initially hard to discern precisely what we are seeing, and the music itself is similarly difficult to "place," until the next shot, which includes an image of fingers rubbing along the rims of the glasses, enables us to realize that we are witnessing the playing of a glass harp, an instrument associated with altered mental and physical states (see Figure 19.4).[8] Isabel Navarro's discussion of Coixet's fascination with water as well as glass, which she characterizes as representing "lo incorpóreo dentro de lo corpóreo" (the incorporeal within the corporeal) is particularly germane here (2007: 33). In contrast to the first scene, in which the hand-held camera hovers around and draws close to Ann in an anthropomorphically embodied manner, here the "film's body" moves (us) through space in a way impossible for any human to achieve. There are four editing dissolves in quick succession that superimpose

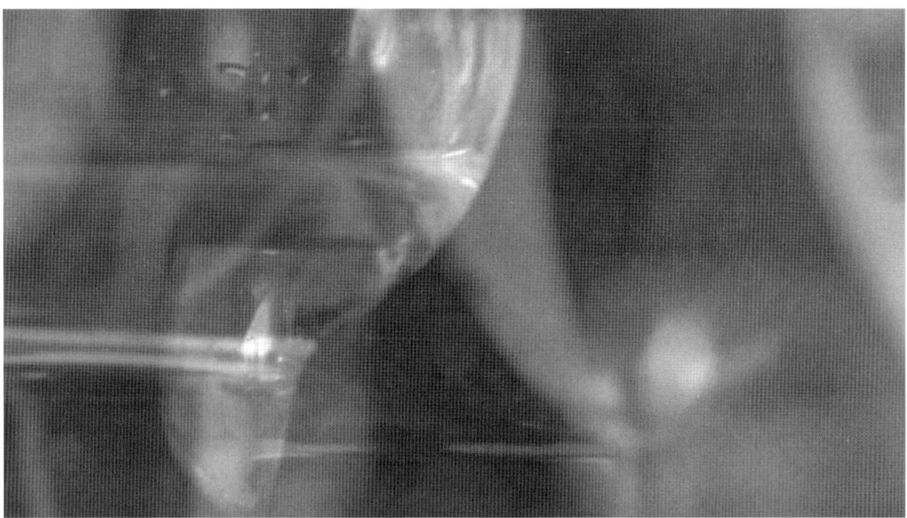

Figure 19.4 The glass harp: haptic images are created in *My Life without Me* through the use of extreme close-ups, superimpositions, selective focus, lighting contrasts, reflections, and lens flare (*My Life without Me*, Isabel Coixet, 2003; prod. El Deseo).

roving extreme close-ups of the glasses, all of which reflect light (and perhaps a fleeting glimpse of the filmmaker herself) but only some of which are in focus; the result is a mobile palimpsest of soft luminosity and transparency, as the music, melded with the faint strains of seagulls and children laughing, washes over the soundtrack. The effect is deeply sensorial yet unearthly, an "inhabitable" figuration of Ann's vibrant yet intangible presence as she appears to narrate the film from a space and time beyond death. The final panning shot of this filmic prologue shifts our eyes away from the glasses to a blurred and foggy landscape, and a racking focus then reveals the city of Vancouver in the distance, scintillating with lens flare; we are thus delivered to the setting for the narrative proper, which begins after another fade to black.

The opening of *My Life without Me*, then, renounces the objectifying relay of gazes associated with the gendered regimes of visual mastery analyzed and condemned by John Berger, Laura Mulvey, and others. Instead, Coixet deploys a panoply of haptic techniques to "incorporate" viewers into the film and enable them to share in the embodied humanity – and mortality – of her film's female protagonist. While Laura Marks is careful not to claim that haptic cinema constitutes a uniquely "feminine" form of filmmaking (what might be termed a filmic *écriture féminine*), she does associate the haptic with "alternative visual practices, including women's and feminist practices" (2000: 169–70). Coixet, too, rejects essentializing characterizations of the films of women (Camí-Vela 2005: 67–8), yet it is clear from a close analysis of her work that she is profoundly committed to interrogating the cinema's traditional modes of gendered interpellation, and to formulating different, more haptic, forms of representation that respect the full dignity of her characters – as well as of her viewers.

Notes

1 After graduating with a university degree in history, Coixet began working at an advertising agency, where she surreptitiously collected remnants of 35 mm film stock left over from publicity shoots in order to produce her first short (Febrés 2008: 37–8). The field of advertising, where Coixet quickly rose to prominence, has quite literally "sustained" the director's filmmaking career, notwithstanding the highly critical view of commercialized media images (and the clear-eyed view of socioeconomic stratification within consumerist societies) present in much of her cinematic work.

2 In Richard Dyer's (1980) revisionist reading of *Gilda*, Rita Hayworth's star image works against the characteristic processes of objectification, facilitating her reading as a figure of resistance. In an essay on the prevalence of domestic violence in Spain, however, Coixet casts the character in the role of victim when she condemns viewers' "reverence" for the scene (immediately after the "Mame" performance) in which Gilda's husband Johnny hits her in the face (Coixet 2004: 71–2). For more on the enduring resonance of *Gilda* in Spain, see Vernon (1997: 47–61).

3 Carol Clover (1992) has explored a similar dynamic in her discussion of teenage boys' identification with the "final girl" figure in slasher films.

4 The Girl and Sock Man emerge from "making out" in a cinema showing both Franco Nero in the Italian antiwar film *Marcia trionfale / Victory March* (Marco Bellocchio, 1976) and the Spanish porn flick *Apocalipsis sexual / Sexual Apocalypse* (Carlos Aured and Sergio Bergonzelli, 1982), featuring transvestite star Ajita Wilson. Space limitations preclude extended analysis of this intriguing scene, as well as alternative readings of the film's complex treatment of the relationship between spectacle, the gaze, gender, and desire.

5 This is not the only one of Coixet's films to have been taken up by bioethicists and the medical community. *The Secret Life of Words* has been discussed in relation to counseling for torture victims (Cook 2008), and the short *Cartas a Nora / Letters to Nora* (2007) has been studied as a contribution to healthcare justice issues (Ródenas Cantero and García Capilla 2009). Articles such as these suggest that Coixet has achieved her stated goal of creating films that have a tangible impact on the world (Coixet 2004: 64, 109), an aspect of her work that has been treated by Camporesi (2008).

6 After her outburst, Veda slaps her mother in the face, and Mildred responds by expressing a desire to kill her daughter. Coixet's film excises this violence, seamlessly editing in a later excerpt from a conversation between Veda and Mildred in its place (this is in fact the only portion of *Mildred Pierce* we actually see, and the camera is positioned behind Ann's mother so that her body blocks part of the television screen and occupies, symbolically, the space of Mildred).

7 As the neuroscientist Marco Iacobini explains (2008), mirror neurons fire when we complete a particular activity ourselves *and also* when we see (or in some cases simply hear) another perform the same activity; above and beyond the notion of "vicarious experience," our bodies register the impact of others' expressions, gestures, and movements. Some researchers now hypothesize that mirror neurons are essential to the development of human empathy. The possible implications of mirror neurons for film spectatorship are now beginning to be addressed by film theorists, and have been mentioned by scientists working in this area. Iacoboni, for example, asks, "Why do we give

ourselves over to emotion in the carefully crafted, heartrending scenes in certain movies? Because mirror neurons in our brains re-create for us the distress we see on the screen. We have empathy for the fictional characters – we know how they're feeling – because we literally experience the same feelings ourselves" (2008: 4). It is important to note that this area of scientific exploration is still quite new. It is also essential to resist the temptation to reduce the embodied film-viewing experience to "hard-wiring." As Laura Marks insists, our sensory perceptions are not mechanical processes isolated from cultural formations; they must be "educated," and for that reason culture itself is, in essence, inscribed in the body (2000: 145).

8 Because of the glass harp's complex production of harmonic tones, the human ear has difficulty "locating" its sounds. In the eighteenth and nineteenth centuries, the instrument was believed to induce trance-like states, and Franz Anton Mesmer came to use it in therapeutic séances (Gallo and Finger 2000).

References

Barker, J. M. (2009) *The Tactile Eye: Touch and the Cinematic Experience*. Berkeley: University of California Press.

Berger, J., with Blomberg, S., Fox, C., Dibb, M., et al. (1977) *Ways of Seeing*. London: Penguin.

Berger, J. and Coixet, I. (2009) *From I to J*. Barcelona: Actar.

Bruno, G. (2002) *Atlas of Emotion: Journeys in Art, Architecture, and Film*. New York: Verso.

Camí-Vela, M. (2005) *Mujeres detrás de la cámara: Entrevistas con cineastas españolas 1990–2004*. Madrid: Ocho y Medio.

Camporesi, V. (2008) Ante el dolor de los demás: *La vida secreta de las palabras* (I. Coixet, 2003) y las nuevas formas del cine de compromiso. In: Cabañas Bravo, M., López-Yarto Elizalde, A., and Rincón García, W. (eds.) *Arte, poder y sociedad en la España de los siglos XV a XX*. Madrid: CSIC, pp. 91–100.

Casado da Rocha, A. (2008) El primado de la autonomía en *Mi vida sin mí* (2002). *Revista de Medicina y Cine* 4 (2): 66–75.

Cerrato, R. (2008) *Isabel Coixet*. Madrid: Ediciones JC.

Charlie Rose (2008) Talk Show. PBS (August 7).

Clover, C. (1992) *Men, Women, and Chain Saws: Gender in the Modern Horror Film*. Princeton: Princeton University Press.

Coixet, I. (2004) *La vida es un guión*. Barcelona: El Aleph.

Cook, K. (2008) The Movie *The Secret Life of Words*: Implications for Counselors. *Journal of Creativity in Mental Health* 3 (3): 330–7.

Doane, M. A. (1987) *The Desire to Desire: The Woman's Film of the 1940s*. Bloomington: Indiana University Press.

Doane, M. A. (1991) *Femmes Fatales: Feminism, Film Theory, Psychoanalysis*. New York: Routledge.

Dyer, R. (1980) Resistance through Charisma: Rita Hayworth and *Gilda*. In: Kaplan, E. A. (ed.) *Women in Film Noir*. London: BFI, pp. 91–9.

Febrés, X. (ed.) (2008) *Isabel Coixet i Cesc Gay: Converses trascrites per Xavier Febrés*. Barcelona: La Magrana.

Gallo, D. A. and Finger, S. (2000) The Power of a Musical Instrument: Franklin, the Mozarts, Mesmer, and the Glass Armonica. *History of Psychology* 3 (4): 326–43.

Gubern, R. and Font, D. (1975) *Un cine para el cadalso: 40 años de censura cinematográfica en España*. Barcelona: Editorial Euros.

Iacoboni, M. (2008) *Mirroring People: The New Science of How We Connect with Others*. New York: Farrar, Straus and Giroux.

Marks, L. (2000) *The Skin of the Film: Intercultural Cinema, Embodiment, and the Senses*. Durham: Duke University Press.

Moreiras-Menor, C. (2002) *Cultura herida: Literatura y cine en la España democrática*. Madrid: Libertarias.

Mulvey, L. (1989) *Visual and Other Pleasures*. Bloomington: Indiana University Press.

Navarro, I. (2007) Los teléfonos dicen lo que los personajes callan: La elocuencia de los objetos en el cine de Isabel Coixet. In: Navarro, I. (ed.) *De los que aman: El cine de Isabel Coixet*. Madrid: Ayuntamiento de Madrid, pp. 26–39.

Ródenas Cantero, G. and García Capilla, D. J. (2009) *Cartas a Nora* from *Invisibles* (2007): Chagas Disease from a Bioethical Point of View. *Journal of Medicine and Movies* 5: 98–105.

Shapiro, J. (2006) The "Bad News Scene" as Clinical Drama Part 2: Viewing Scenes. *Family Medicine* 38 (7): 474–5.

Silverman, K. (1992) *Male Subjectivity at the Margins*. New York: Routledge.

Sobchack, V. (1991) *The Address of the Eye: A Phenomenology of Film Experience*. Princeton: Princeton University Press.

Sobchack, V. (2004) *Carnal Thoughts: Embodiment and Moving Image Culture*. Berkeley: University of California Press.

Studlar, G. (1988) *In the Realm of Pleasure: Von Sternberg, Dietrich, and the Masochistic Aesthetic*. New York: Columbia University Press.

Vernon, K. M. (1997) Reading Hollywood in/and Spanish Cinema: From Trade Wars to Transculturation. In: Kinder, M. (ed.) *Refiguring Spain: Cinema/Media/Representation*. Durham: Duke University Press, pp. 35–64.

Vidal, B. (2008) Love, Loneliness and Laundromats: Affect and Artifice in the Melodramas of Isabel Coixet. In: Beck, J. and Rodríguez Ortega, V. (eds.) *Contemporary Spanish Cinema and Genre*. Manchester: Manchester University Press, pp. 219–38.

Williams, L. (2000) Film Bodies: Gender, Genre, and Excess. In: Stam, R. and Miller, T. (eds.) *Film and Theory: An Anthology*. Oxford: Blackwell, pp. 207–21.

Further Reading

Beugnet, M. (2007) *Cinema and Sensation: French Film and the Art of Transgression*. Edinburgh: Edinburgh University Press.

Elsaesser, T. and Hagener, M. (2010) *Film Theory: An Introduction through the Senses*. New York: Routledge.

Laine, T. (2011) *Feeling Cinema: Emotional Dynamics in Film Studies*. New York: Continuum.

McMahon, L. (2012) *Cinema and Contact: The Withdrawal of Touch in Nancy, Bresson, Duras and Denis*. Oxford: Legenda.

Nessel, S., Paulet, W., Rüffert, C., et al. (eds.) (2008) *Word and Flesh: Cinema Between Text and the Body*. Berlin: Bertz + Fischer.

20

Becoming a Queer (M)Other in/and/through Film

Transsexuality, Trans-subjectivity, and Maternal Relationality in Almodóvar's Todo sobre mi madre

Julián Daniel Gutiérrez-Albilla

Introduction

This chapter explores the ways in which Pedro Almodóvar's 1999 film *Todo sobre mi madre/All about my Mother*, winner of an Academy Award in 2000, lends itself to interpretation through, or intersects with, concepts that are particularly theorized by queer theory and by queer film theory. The specific concepts I will explore are: first, the supposition that sex and gender are performative, multiple, interchangeable, and transmissible embodiments of feminine and masculine identity, subjectivity, and desire beyond patriarchal and heteronormative psychic and ideological frameworks; second, a heterosocial notion of community as an alternative ethical model of relationship based on solidarity between a heterogeneous, transgenerational group of women;[1] and, third and most importantly in the context of my discussion, the idea of becoming a mother beyond biological, heterosexual reproduction and the Oedipal nuclear family.

As will become clear, I am not the first to pursue such issues in relation to this film (see particularly Maddison 2000; Martin-Márquez 2004; Bersani and Dutoit 2009). What I hope to add to the existing discussion is, first, an exploration of the film's representation of sex and gender in the light of Bracha Ettinger's concept of the "matrixial" (2005); and, second, a reflection on the film's relationship to theory. In stressing the intersections and productive tensions between cinema and theory, I aim to move beyond the interpretative and epistemological limitations that are

A Companion to Spanish Cinema, First Edition. Edited by Jo Labanyi and Tatjana Pavlović.

imposed when one simply "applies" theory to cinematic practices. In particular, I want to explore the possibility of thinking of Almodóvar's film itself as a kind of theoretical text (Bal 1999), by opening it up to a reflection on the cognitive and phenomenological effects that the film's aesthetic and ethical possibilities produce in us as spectators. This epistemological and interpretative shift maximizes the content of the film by moving between a focus on the film's textual signification and a focus on how the spectator may experience the film as a more porous space between the viewing subject and the projection screen. I focus primarily on three sequences in order to tease out my theoretical interpretation of Almodóvar's film from a close perceptual and cognitive engagement with their textuality: the death of Esteban, Agrado's monologue, and Manuela's journey by train from Madrid to Barcelona. I argue that these three sequences allegorically encapsulate the spectator's aesthetic and thematic engagement with the entire film. From this perspective, while I seek to conceptualize the ways in which the film may represent "queer motherhood," I propose that it is the working of the film that produces effects in the spectator in relation to the notion of becoming a "queer (m)other."

The chapter thus explores how we may draw on the notion that sex and gender are performative – as theorized by queer theory, particularly in the early work of Judith Butler[2] – as a way of reflecting on how *Todo* proposes a notion of sex and gender identity that is articulated through iterative and imitative practices. This reconceptualization of sex and gender identity here challenges, or even deconstructs, the naturalization of sex and gender, thereby destabilizing heteronormative conceptions of sex and gender identity. In order to move beyond the points of reference of phallocentrism, which regulates and controls people's modes of conduct and codes of identity, I explore how we can redefine gender, sexuality, and subjectivity in *Todo* less by relying on a critical or political resistance to hegemonic paradigms than by drifting away from a dialectical mode of opposition, thereby putting the emphasis on the transformative and expansive potential for thinking and rethinking the processes of being and becoming beyond fixed categories.

Although Butler is not entirely concerned with formulating a theory of the psyche, she is still preoccupied with the way in which the unconscious, the concept on which psychoanalysis is founded, remains an excess or, as she calls it, an opacity that has to be linguistically articulated, even if, according to Butler, the psyche is still socially, historically, and culturally contingent (2005). Concerned as I am here with psychoanalysis, I want to pay attention to the ways in which the film engages with the specificity of the feminine in human subjectivity, which lies beyond and beside patriarchal and heterosexist ideological and psychoanalytic conceptions of subjectivity. Drawing on Ettinger's psychoanalytic notion of the "matrixial," this chapter argues that *Todo* evokes a sub-symbolic psychic sphere in which "the 'I' and 'non I' are crossprinting psychic traces in one another and continuously transform their shareable threads and sphere" (2005: 74). By looking at how the film shifts from subjectivity or intersubjectivity to trans-subjectivity or subjectivity as "encounter at shared border-spaces," I pay attention to the interconnections and productive tensions – the "resonances and disjunctions," to use Sudeep Dasgupta's (2009) terms – between queer theory and matrixial psychoanalysis.

Finally, I explore the ethical implications underpinning *Todo*'s emphasis on motherhood as practiced by the film's feminine characters (whether they are biological women or transgendered subjects). Rethinking Susan Martin-Márquez's sophisticated feminist analysis of maternal subjectivity and the "ethics of care" in the film (2004), I argue that such an ethics of motherhood, beyond patriarchal and heterosexist conceptions of maternity, is based on a compassionate relationality that derives from our "*joining-in-difference* with others in transference relations" (Dasgupta 2009: 2; emphasis in original). While I focus on the film's ethical mode of relationality, my chapter pays attention to the process by which the spectator embraces the ethics of queer motherhood proposed here in the phenomenological and cognitive encounter with the film.

Acting and Re-enacting the Loss of the Child

We begin our discussion of *Todo* with the scene almost at the beginning of the film that shows Esteban II's death. As the camera pulls away from Manuela, the film's female protagonist, a subjective shot from Manuela's point of view shows Esteban running on a wet street behind the taxi that Huma, his favorite diva, has taken, in order to ask her for an autograph. A subjective shot from an unidentified driver cuts to a close-up of Manuela, whose facial expression seems to anticipate the tragedy that is about to occur. A shot from inside the car shows someone getting hit by the car, who we assume is Esteban. A shot of the shattered glass of the windshield produces a disturbing opacity in our field of vision and reflects in cinematic terms the disturbing pain that Esteban's body must be suffering at the moment of encountering death. Such a disturbing opacity, produced by the shattered glass of the windshield, which becomes a trace of looking, also anticipates in cinematic terms the emotional and psychic pain that Manuela suffers at the sight of her son's death. Emma Wilson describes the ensuing sequence as follows: "disconcertingly, the film cuts to Esteban's point of view as we suddenly view the scene tip sideways, upset from its axis [...]. We see Manuela's legs as she runs towards him [...]. The scene closes with her screams" (2003: 71). I shall return later to this rather disorienting shot from Esteban's point of view (see Figure 20.1). At this stage it is interesting to note that Manuela's psychic and emotional pain is reflected in cinematic terms by the lack of synchronization between her image and the sound of her screams. This painful disruption between sound and image, which emphasizes the shattering of Manuela's subjectivity, creates a slippage between voice and speaker. It also produces a painful haptic and corporal resonance in our own body and subjectivity, as if our corporeal engagement must complete the meaning of this death scene – a meaning that resides in the interstices of language.[3]

Figure 20.1 The sobbing Manuela seen from the dying Esteban's point of view (*Todo sobre mi madre*, Pedro Almodóvar, 1999; prod. El Deseo).

This tragic scene reminds us of Manuela's previous simulated enactment, witnessed by her son, in which she played the part of a widow during a seminar on organ donation. Within the diegetic reality of the film, Manuela will enact this "real" situation after her son's death. These repeated, and yet different, actions within the film occur on several occasions. For instance, a television intertext shows the scene in Joseph L. Mankiewicz's *All About Eve* (1950) when Margo (Bette Davis) accuses Eve Harrington (Anne Baxter) of wanting to take her place. Later on in *Todo*, Nina accuses Manuela of wanting to take her place as Estella in Tennessee Williams' play *A Streetcar Named Desire* (1947). Likewise, Manuela's "real" weeping over the death of Esteban is repeated differently when she herself plays the pregnant Estella in Williams' play. The haptic and corporal resonance of the sound of Manuela weeping in labor here reminds us of the previous disruptive sound of her cries at the sight of Esteban's death. Manuela's performative act could thus be interpreted as a compulsive re-enactment of her traumatic experience, associated with the tragic loss of Esteban, "involuntarily and repeatedly reliving her trauma as a belated experience" (Guerin and Hallas 2007: 8). Huma's rehearsal of the scene in Lorca's *Bodas de sangre* (1932), in which a mother mourns the death of her murdered son, can also be read as a repeated, and yet different, re-enactment of that previous catastrophic event, which, like a specter coming in and out of time, is constantly made manifest, repeated, throughout the film. These infinitely repetitive series of echoes and looping returns and reverberations of scenes and actions within the film foreshadow or recall material that will occur later on or that has already occurred in the narrative, thus functioning as déjà vu, constantly haunting and transforming the present by evoking how "different temporalities and memories commingle, inscribe and inflect each other" (Skoller 2005: xv).

In *Todo*, the sequences related to the diegetic reality of the film and those related to the reality of the theatrical pieces, *A Streetcar* and *Bodas*, or the television intertext, *All About Eve*, coexist and interact with each other, thereby emphasizing the passages of fantasies, anxieties, and realities across psychic and physical thresholds that cannot be contained within a single temporality, space, and place. The film registers a mobility of consciousness through what Leo Bersani (1986) defines as "concentric circles" that imply the blurrings, slippings, and/or juxtapositions of visual and textual registers. Almodóvar does not collapse the distinctions between the "fictionalized" space and time, associated with theater, and the "real" space and time, associated with the characters' ordinary lives. Nonetheless, *Todo* consists of reversals, inversions, and conflations of textual references, images, dialogues, characters, scenes, actions, and voices, producing or generating a precarious space of coexistence between multiple, interchangeable, and transmissible textualities and, particularly relevant to this discussion, identities and subjectivities.[4]

Transsexuality

An instance of this coexistence and interaction of the diegetic reality of the film and the reality of the theatrical pieces contained within it is the scene when Agrado, recalling somehow the figure of the *gracioso* (character who provides comic relief) in Spanish Golden Age dramas, steps away from the theater scenario in order to interact with the theater audience, even though she is about to perform a monologue.[5] Unmotivated by plot, a panning shot of the theater's red velvet curtain avoids depth of field, turning the image of the curtain into an almost monochromatic abstract red surface, as if color "became the register of experience" (Fer 2004: 172) (see Figure 20.2). Yet, as Briony Fer suggests in relation to Michelangelo Antonioni's *Red Desert* (1964), "a dialectic between color and monochromy becomes the motor of a poetics of cinema" (2004: 172). This unyielding and mobile surface produced by the panning shot fills the spectator's field of vision and creates an overproximity to the aesthetic object, running the risk of contributing to a dislocation of experience. Yet, the impact that the aesthetic object has on the spectator produces a mobility of consciousness that "cannot be contained, since it remains always already continuous with consciousness of the world" (Dean 2010: 391). Despite this overproximity of the look, which might create a disturbance in the field of vision, the spectator can haptically perceive the texture of the velvet material and the series of tonal differences within the red surface. The dark spaces within the folds of the red curtain become vertical black stripes interrupting the uniformity of the red color that one would strictly associate with a monochromatic red surface.

As the camera moves rightwards, a close-up of Agrado's profile (see Figure 20.3) is followed by a quick subjective shot, from her point of view, of the theater audience. At this point, a beam of light, which we assume comes from a spotlight

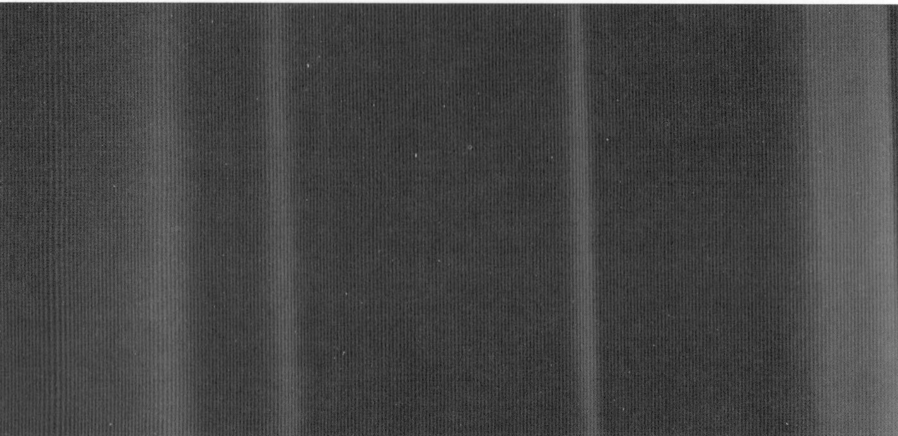

Figure 20.2 Panning shot of the theater's red velvet curtain (*Todo sobre mi madre*, Pedro Almodóvar, 1999; prod. El Deseo).

Figure 20.3 Close-up of Agrado's profile (*Todo sobre mi madre*, Pedro Almodóvar, 1999; prod. El Deseo).

trained on Agrado as she stands on the edge of the stage in front of the curtains, cuts across and fills the cinema screen to such an extent that it blinds us. This blinding light ambivalently inscribes the dialectic between opacity and transparency as a fundamental condition of vision and perception. This is followed by a long shot of Agrado announcing the cancellation of the play and offering, instead, to tell the narrative of her life. As the camera moves toward the stage until Agrado is seen in medium shot, she starts telling her life story. If the very act of describing the theater's red velvet curtain allows us to visualize how a process of metamorphosis – a curtain becoming an abstract red surface – is already inherent in the poetics of the cinematic form, I suggest that such a process of becoming (an)other is the subject of Agrado's monologue. Crosscutting between shots of Agrado and reaction shots of a sympathetic audience, the film focuses on how the narrative of Agrado's life is based on the repetitive series of cosmetic surgical operations to which her material body and face have been submitted to allow her to feel the emancipatory potential that can be found in the process of becoming a transitional/transgendered embodied feminine subject.

Agrado's transformed, artificially manufactured body can be related to Almodóvar's preoccupation with surface and style, and can be read as a parodic signifier that connotes an excessive investment in the performativity of feminine identity. In a similar way, the film's mise-en-scène emphasizes costumes, blond and red-haired wigs worn by Huma, and the interior design of both Catalan bourgeois households (the Gaudiesque apartment of Sister Rosa's mother) and more modest homes (the apartments of Agrado and Manuela), which are so artificial that they seem almost as theatrical as the scenarios of Williams' and Lorca's plays represented within the film. The film's mise-en-scène thus reinforces a kind of hyperbolic engagement with characters and objects, whether biological women, transgendered subjects, clothes, or décor. This loss of the boundary between "artificiality" and "naturalness" is also made manifest by associating a "real" baby – Sister Rosa's child, Esteban III – with the baby doll that Nina and Agrado hold in their arms during the staging of *A Streetcar*. In the same way that Agrado's monologue puts emphasis on becoming (an)other instead of on the final product of the change (Weidner-Maluf 2005: 11), the uncanny confusion between the animate baby, Esteban III, and the inanimate baby doll blurs the distinction between "one" and "another."

Agrado's transgendered embodied feminine subjectivity and the representation of Lola as a transgendered mother and/or father enable us to read *Todo* as advocating subject positions that are excluded from and articulated beyond the dominant social and symbolic order. This is a challenge to the "naturalness" of gender and sexuality and a deconstruction of essentialist notions of identities and subjectivities within heteronormativity. The latter, as Butler suggests, is itself a mimetic repetition of its own idealization (1999: 338). From this perspective, Agrado's and Lola's transgendered embodied feminine subjectivity undoes, through a process of citation, the arbitrary dichotomy between original gender and its imitations within heteronormativity. For Butler, the performativity of sex and gender cannot be interpreted as an intentional act since, she argues, we are already constituted by what is before us and outside us (2004: 3). Thus, the displacement or resignification of hegemonic social and cultural norms through subversive repetition already depends on the norms that constrain, precede, and exceed the subject (Harris: 1999). Although Butler does emphasize the fact that performativity is related to bodily practices as well as to speech acts, her focus on the body's construction within social and cultural discourses seems to overlook the materiality and the expressiveness of the body as formative of the self. In addition, although Butler reflects on the production of new meanings through reiteration or repetition, her emphasis on improvisational possibility within a field of culturally predetermined constraints seems to neglect the "potential process of radical emergence, of becoming, of creative evolution" (Tuhkanen 2009: 21). Agrado's and Lola's transgendered embodied feminine subjectivities are articulated less in the moment of shifting from a fixed notion of masculine identity to another fixed notion of feminine identity than in the moment of the transition,[6] thereby extending the process of being and becoming and opening up a space for nomadic modes of thought that mobilize the transformative and expansive potential of bodies and subjectivities in an endless process of becoming what is still unknown.[7] From this perspective, the film puts an emphasis on "the processes of the constant folding and unfolding of experience associated less with fixed centers than with bits and pieces constantly moving in and out of the folds to become intertwined with other surrounding unfoldings in a spiraling distributive process" (Hequembourg 2007: 158). If Agrado and Lola engage in an endless, incomplete process of "becoming" another being by altering their material bodies, I shall now focus on how the film itself produces in the viewer's own body and psyche the sensation of occupying another space: the body of the film.

Trans-subjectivity

After Esteban's death in Madrid, Manuela decides to go back to Barcelona in search of Esteban's father. As we later learn, Esteban's father is the transgendered Lola (Esteban I), who has had an unprotected sexual relationship with Sister Rosa, resulting in her death from AIDS. In recent formulations in queer theory about the rectum, for example by Leo Bersani and Adam Phillips (2008) or Tim Dean (2009), the sexual practice of barebacking becomes a mode of relationality based on an impersonal intimacy not only between the passive subject and the active subject but also between the passive subject and all those who have previously established an impersonal intimacy with the one penetrating him. Barebacking thus becomes a mode of relationality that is based less on social intelligibility than on the way in which the self plunges himself into non-meaning and self-shattering (Dasgupta 2009: 2). Although Rosa's generous gesture of looking after and receiving Lola in her body leads to her fatal encounter with death, plunging herself into self-shattering, her unprotected intimacy with Lola and with all those who had sex or shared needles with Lola before her, unlike Bersani's and Dean's emphasis on the rectum as the place for conceiving death, leads to her giving birth to a child who will live on after her. The child becomes the generous gift that, without expecting anything in return, Sister Rosa offers to Manuela as a replacement or substitute for her own dead child, transforming Manuela from biological to adoptive mother. Manuela had previously performed the same ethical gesture by taking care of Sister Rosa during her pregnancy until the latter encountered death at the moment of bringing Esteban III to life.

Figure 20.4 Sister Rosa with some transgendered prostitutes, seen via Manuela's point-of-view shot (*Todo sobre mi madre*, Pedro Almodóvar, 1999; prod. El Deseo).

As a nun and social worker (as she is defined by Manuela during Rosa's visit to the gynecologist), Sister Rosa spends her life helping those who are often expelled from or aggressively assimilated into the body of late 1990s Spanish society, such as African immigrants, prostitutes, and transgendered subjects. We are introduced to Sister Rosa when Manuela is in a taxi looking for Lola in Barcelona and the taxi drives around an area outside the city where, as Paul Julian Smith aptly describes it, "cars slowly cruise prostitutes as if in some lower circle of suburban hell" (1999: 29). A subjective shot from Manuela's point of view shows Sister Rosa giving something to a couple of transgendered prostitutes (see Figure 20.4). It is also interesting to note that faceless, nameless, voiceless African immigrants figure constantly in the film – they populate the Raval neighborhood where Agrado lives, or they stand behind Sister Rosa and Manuela during their visit to the Hospital del Mar. Although they merely fulfill the function of *figurants* in the film, the presence of these disenfranchised non-citizens forces the spectator to confront the face of the other, thereby recognizing the other's experiences as real, even if they may be incomprehensible to the spectator, and encouraging a mode of seeing that can support and tolerate difference and alterity rather than repudiating it or assimilating the experience of the other to the self (Bennett 2005: 105).[8]

Instead of a conventional image of a train cutting across the cinematic screen, which could be symbolically associated with phallic penetration (Acevedo-Muñoz 2004: 29), Almodóvar shows us a shot of the inside of a long dark tunnel, which seems to be drained of color, from the camera's, and thus the director's, point of view instead of from the point of view of Manuela, as we listen to the soundtrack playing a Senegalese song, "Tajabone," sung by Ismaël Lô, further emphasizing our above-mentioned encounter with alterity (see Figure 20.5). As previously

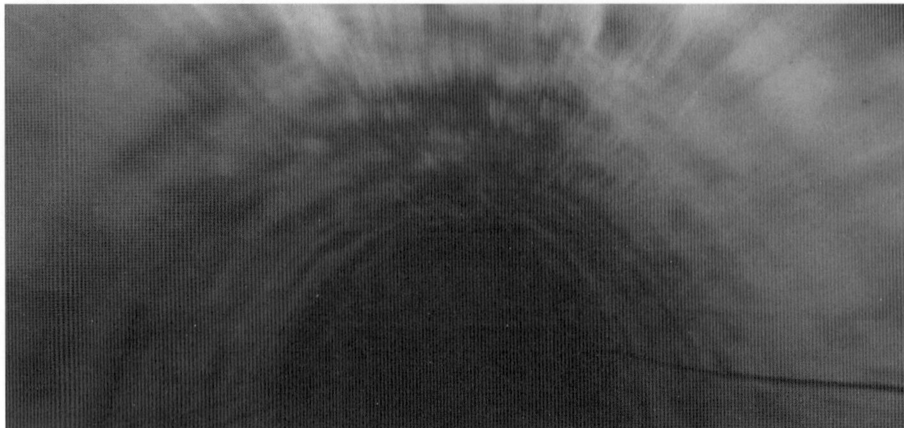

Figure 20.5 The image of the tunnel, indirectly conveying Manuela's journey to Barcelona, involves the spectator in its textured materiality (*Todo sobre mi madre*, Pedro Almodóvar, 1999; prod. El Deseo).

noted, the sequence that shows Esteban's death is seen from his point of view. The spectator's point of view merges with that of the dead Esteban, thus unveiling the principle of suture, the process by which the subject is joined to the signifying chain. Martin-Márquez rightly suggests that this subjective shot from Esteban's point of view could imply that the film's narrative is told from beyond the grave and that, from "this particular frame, the narrative that follows centers on Manuela as ur-mother" (2004: 502). Martin-Márquez raises a crucial issue vis-à-vis spectatorship theory: challenging a unidirectional mode of looking at the screen, she implicitly reflects on the way in which the spectator is "at once receptive and form-giving" (Kuhn 2009: 7), thus thinking of film spectatorship as an embodied experience.

Based on this more interactive and participatory mode of spectatorship, I suggest that the dislocating shot of the long, dark tunnel makes us feel as if our bodies were entering or were located in the space of the film or as if the film itself were coming out of frame, thus entering the spectator's space. As Tanya Leighton puts it in a different context, the film might point to "the illusory dissolution of the boundary between the viewing subject and the projection screen, opening up a new psychological space for a more inclusive sensory environment" (Leighton 2008: 33) and altering the spectator's perceptions without reconciling the contradictions between the failures or excesses of our perceptions and our consciousness of the embodiment required for the knowability of self-presence (O'Bryan 2005: xvi). The first shot of the long, dark tunnel, through which Manuela travels from Madrid to Barcelona (and later will travel back from Barcelona to Madrid), cuts to a ravishing aerial shot of Barcelona at dusk, as if the Mediterranean city were embracing the Argentine Manuela as a daughter, as if she were being reborn into a multicultural, multi-racial Barcelona, or as if she were giving birth to a multi-sexual, multi-class Barcelona. Our own difficulty in forcing language to adequately articulate something that we sense in fully rational discourse, to describe the effects that the working of the film produces in us as spectators, points symptomatically and ambivalently to the fear and/or comfort of expressing a return to and/or a memory of a particular familiar/strange place: the shattering fantasy or anxiety of intrauterine existence in the maternal body. I am not interested in associating the long, dark tunnel with metaphors of the body, such as the maternal uterus or womb.[9] Such a metaphorical association would identify the womb as an object, which is already haunted by the process of being abjected as the phobic object. Instead, I put emphasis on how the shot of the long, dark tunnel enacts some psychic processes that are at work here. The repeated scene of the long, dark tunnel, which could become a signifier of the shared border-space that is associated with our primary source of becoming, emphasizes the porosity of the borders of the subject (Dasgupta 2009: 3).

From this perspective, I want to suggest that *Todo* represents and creates several affective relationships and spaces of coemergence and coaffection within and beyond the diegetic space of the film, thus creating trans-subjective encounters. These trans-subjective encounters point to the traces of what Ettinger has defined as the matrixial process – which spreads across the threshold of culture via art, thereby expanding the symbolic itself – in which the "outside" is beyond any "inside–outside" spatial oppositions. Since Ettinger is concerned with the specificity of feminine difference, it is important to engage deeply with Ettinger's theoretical paradigm in order to understand the way in which *Todo* could point to a rearticulation of feminine subjectivity beyond a patriarchal and heteronormative psychic and ideological framework. Such a framework, which has historically excluded the feminine from Western metaphysics, reduces femininity, as Griselda Pollock rightly suggests, to a physiological, anatomical, or biological essence (2009: 12). I want to establish a connection between the film's emphasis on trans-subjective encounters – such as, for instance, Esteban living after his death in the form of a heart transplanted into the body of a Galician patient, narrating the story and haunting the film's characters beyond the grave, as Martin-Márquez argues, or being resurrected as Esteban III – and Ettinger's groundbreaking theoretical propositions. Such a porous intersection between theory and practice allows us to explore how *Todo* points to the interconnections and productive tensions between queer theory's challenge to phallic Oedipal logic and Ettinger's emphasis on the specificity of feminine difference as that which remains outside the feminine and masculine opposition, in human subjectivity.[10]

Ettinger reflects on the possibility of thinking of the feminine in human subjectivity as remaining outside the dominant economy of symbolic representation that is associated with the phallic signifier, without relegating femininity to the realm of the psychotic. From this perspective, an alternative feminine sub-symbolic sphere continuously affects the symbolic, based less on undifferentiated subjectivity (associated with pre-Oedipality) or on differentiated subjectivity (associated with Oedipality) than on what Ettinger defines as a "matrixial subjectivity." For Ettinger, subjectivity is conceived of as an encounter between the "I" and the "non-I" at shared border-spaces where several partial subjects, composed of the known as well as the not-rejected and not-assimilated unknown, become vulnerable and fragile through "borderlinking" (1996). Moreover, according to Ettinger, in the matrixial border-space "we metabolize mental imprints and traces for one another in each matrixial web whose psychic grains, virtual and affective strings and unconscious threads participate in other matrixial webs and transform them by borderlinking in 'metra-morphosis'" (2005: 705). The matrixial border-space thus creates a redistribution in the shared field and a change in common subjectivity, offering the potential for transformation in these trans-subjective encounters.[11]

In the light of Ettinger's redefinition of subjectivity as encounter, we may think of *Todo* as proposing a notion of feminine subjectivity within the matrixial sub-symbolic psychic sphere that comes neither after the founding cut of castration and splitting nor by means of a regression to the pre-Oedipal, archaic psychic stage, as the latter would still be haunted by its position relative to the dominant phallic signifier. Ettinger's emphasis on the specificity and contribution of the feminine in and to human subjectivity seems to stand in a mutually exclusive relationship to the dominant strand in queer theory, which advocates a politics of identity beyond gender. However, according to Dasgupta, both matrixial psychoanalysis and queer theory "share a re-formulation of subjectivity beyond an enclosed, essentialized subject, and suggest a breaking of the boundaries which have circumscribed theories of the subject based primarily on a focus on the phallus" (2009: 1). From this perspective, if we move beyond the Freudian Oedipal semantic universe and/or Lacanian phallocentrism, we can associate the film with a more complex articulation of the feminine in human subjectivity, within Ettinger's matrixial paradigm – an articulation that can be celebrated by queer subjects.

Maternal Relationality

If the matrixial is inexorably related to the maternal, as we can see from the description of the above sequences, we could argue that *Todo*'s emphasis on feminine difference is inextricably linked to the empathic acts and maternal practices adopted by its feminine characters, which form the core of their relationships. Despite Almodóvar's long association with queer politics, he has been extensively criticized for representing women in an exaggeratedly emotional – to the point of being hysterical or overly sexual – manner, thereby exercising a Pygmalion-like power over women. Is the filmmaker, consciously or unconsciously, reinserting motherhood into a patriarchal and heteronormative ideological framework in which women are articulated within the boundaries and signs of a self-abnegating maternity? Although the film represents different relationships that point to both biological and symbolic maternal relations, does the film's emphasis on maternity perpetuate the patriarchal and heteronormative notions of kinship based on biological reproduction and the Oedipal nuclear family in which the child figures as "a dense site for the transfer and reproduction of culture" (Butler 2002: 22)?

Apart from the lesbian Nina, who ends up in a heterosexual relationship with a biological child and returns to her own village, I contend that in *Todo* the feminine characters' self-conscious choice to embrace an other – whether a natural child (Manuela raising Esteban II by herself or Lola, as Esteban III's biological female father, cradling him); an adoptive child (Manuela becoming the adoptive mother of Esteban III); an adoptive sister (Manuela taking care of Sister Rosa); an actress (Agrado looking after Huma); a dead non-biological child (Huma getting hold of the picture of Esteban II that has been circulating among several of the characters throughout the film); or prostitutes, transgendered subjects, or African immigrants (Sister Rosa helping these marginalized people) – cannot be reduced to a sign of their accepting their "natural" feminine role within a patriarchal and heteronormative framework. Rather, it is a materialization of an ethical gesture that is associated with a capacity to hold the other, beyond normative conceptions of the family, opening up the radical difference of alterity. As Seán Hand notes, in Levinasian ethics, in which the notions of dwelling and of the feminine are explicitly linked, "otherness and ethical care are already present in the structures of 'interiority' and 'habitation,' and already imply a feminine dimension, a dimension which disrupts the virility of the force of Being" (1996: 11). In this context, the film offers a mode of relationality that symbolizes the primordial affective interactions that we experienced during our bodily encounter with the mother. This potentially threatening re-encounter with maternal alterity, instead of perpetuating heteronormative kinship relations, becomes an opportunity to open ourselves to an ethical gesture that becomes associated with our expansive capacity to embrace and welcome alterity without mastering, reducing, capturing, or flattening out the other's specificity (Hand 1996: 13).

Todo thus proposes that, as Pollock (2007) reminds us, maternity can be associated with a structure of thought, or with an openness to an ethical gesture, that is adopted by women, transgendered subjects, and men of all possible sexual orientations, and that has to do with relinquishing or curving away from our individual narcissism so that we can create a social, psychic, and affective space for the other to be able to become – even if, as with Manuela's son or Sister Rosa, there is a risk that the self or the other will not be able to go on living. Martin-Márquez forcefully argues that the film "exemplifies an 'ethics of care' to remind us that compassionate solicitude is a universally human need, demanding a universally human response" (2004: 497). For Martin-Márquez, the apparent self-sacrifice underpinning this "ethics of care," which could perpetuate a "masochistic suffering underlying traditionally-defined practices of maternal benevolence" (2004: 497), can "cycle back to serve self-interests" (2004: 497); she thereby detects an emancipatory potential at the core of this "ethics of care." I would like to add to Martin-Márquez's propositions the claim that this structure of thought, associated with a maternity that can be adopted by any human being regardless of gender and sexual identity, is not based on a narcissistic desire to claim back what we have given away (Pollock 2007). Therefore, such an ethical gesture – associated with a maternity beyond biological, heterosexual reproduction and the Oedipal nuclear family – is a movement without return that allows the other to be able to become beyond and beside us. Openness to such an ethical gesture does not perpetuate a notion of reproduction as the rationale of sexuality and as a means of self-transcendence (Warner 1991: 9). The emancipatory potential of such an ethical gesture resides less in its serving our self-interests than in our active engagement with and acknowledgment of this mode of relationality.

Conclusion

I want to end by proposing that we think of *Todo* in terms of the work it performs in producing a particular kind of spectator. That is, the film invites the spectator to become a "queer (m)other" through the phenomenological and cognitive process of encountering, experimenting with, understanding, and sharing the ethics underpinning the film. As I have attempted to demonstrate in my description of the film's aesthetics and thematics and of the effects that it produces in our bodies and psyches, the film could be interpreted less as a text than as a process that produces the subject (De Zeguer 1996: 23). This turn shifts our engagement with the film from detached textual analysis to a more physical and more intimate exchange with its materiality, thereby enhancing our critical and hermeneutic practices.[12] From this perspective, we could theorize the spectator as becoming a "queer (m) other" beyond patriarchal and heteronormative conceptions of maternity. Such a reconceptualization of maternity within a notion of becoming a "queer (m)other" is based on an asymmetry rather than on a mirroring symmetry between the I and the irreducible alterity that can never be fully comprehended or accessed and that invokes one's hospitality, responsibility, and compassion for the irreducible other in what Pollock defines as all her or his otherness and in one's own alterity (2009: 10). This ethical and aesthetic process of becoming a "queer (m)other" makes us think of cinema less in terms of "reflecting" an external reality or an external referent than as a means of producing theory itself. In this context, Almodóvar's film foregrounds what Mieke Bal identifies as both the theoretical thought and the cinematic articulation of that thought (1999: 104). To sum up, *Todo*'s emphasis on trans-sexuality, trans-subjectivity, and maternal relationality allows for the possibility of thinking of a mode of queer relationality and of our queer being-in-the-world that would reverse Tenessee Williams' famous sentence: "I have always depended on the kindness of strangers" – constantly repeated throughout the film during and after the staging of *A Streetcar*. On several occasions, Agrado admits that her artistic name comes from her ethical gesture of having tried, throughout her entire life, to offer kindness to others by giving them pleasure. Unlike Williams' sentence, Agrado's admission encapsulates the ethics of ontological relatedness underpinning Almodóvar's film. In other words, our conditions of existence depend on our giving pleasure and kindness to a stranger in order to enable her or him to become beyond and beside us.

Notes

1 For a discussion of *Todo sobre mi madre*'s female identification in the context of gay or queer dissidence, see Maddison's fine discussion of the film (2000).

2 While I connect queer theory to Butler's early work (Butler 1990), this chapter does not provide an exhaustive history of queer theory. Instead, I focus on some of the concepts theorized by queer theory and by other epistemological frameworks, such as, for instance, psychoanalytic feminism or phenomenology, to problematize some of the most common notions in queer theory, such as the notion that gender and sexuality are performative.

3 For an excellent theorization of sound in Almodóvar's cinema, see Vernon (2009).

4 See Kinder's fine analysis of the film in terms of a fluid intertextual trans-subjectivity (2005). I have been inspired by Kinder's emphasis on a trans-subjective intertextuality, which she sees as energizing the narrative and extending "the life, meaning and mobility of all discreet parts" (2005: 15).

5 For a discussion of the *gracioso* figure, see Greer-Johnson (2001).

6 Bersani and Dutoit also argue that Agrado and Lola are "gender transitions without normative end points" (2009: 245).

7 See Ballesteros' discussion of the film in terms of the subversive, as well as normative, implications of the representation of transgendered subjects (2009). While I agree with her that some of the transgendered characters in the film, such as Lola, can be rather disturbing, and even sexist, my theoretical analysis goes beyond a focus on positive and negative images of queer characters in film.

8 For a wonderful discussion of *figurants* in film, see Didi-Huberman (2009).

9 Acevedo-Muñoz provides an allegorical reading of the film that associates the human body with the body of the nation (2004).

10 For a discussion of Ettinger's theories in relation to thinking of the filmmaker not so much as a feminist or feminine filmmaker but rather as a filmmaker produced within the feminine, see Gutiérrez-Albilla (forthcoming).

11 Griselda Pollock remains, to my knowledge, one of the most important interpreters of Ettinger's artistic work, aesthetic theory, and psychoanalytic focus on the "matrixial borderspace," on which she has written extensively. Especially fine introductions to Ettinger's complex theories are Pollock's article on feminine aesthetic practices and Ettinger's concepts of "matrix" and "metramorphosis" (Pollock 2004) and Pollock's

introductory essay in Ettinger's first English monograph (Ettinger 2006: 1–37). Connecting the philosophy of art and psychoanalytic theory, Ettinger undoes psychoanalysis from within by shifting from psychoanalysis' focus on subjectivity and intersubjectivity to "subjectivity as encounter" or trans-subjectivity. Ettinger provides us with an alternative language to account for psychic "borderspaces" and transubjective, affective transactions that relate back to prenatal experiences and that are associated with the realm of the feminine. This was previously unthought in the phallocentric psychoanalysis of Freud and Lacan, as well as in the psychoanalysis of Kristeva, Cixous, and Irigaray, which still emphasizes a language of objects that remain haunted by their relationship to the cut of castration and to the Lacanian phallic signifier. See Ettinger (2005).

12 I am indebted to recent theoretical work on gallery films, such as that of Catherine Fowler (2004). For Fowler, although gallery films still borrow from the specific *dispositif* of cinema, one has to take into consideration how the out-of-frame affects our viewing experience. I suggest that, since we are now exposed to a variety of screen media, we bring to the viewing of a film our experience of being exposed to different *dispositifs*, even though the film studied here relies on the specific *dispositif* of cinema. Likewise, cinema itself has expanded into other media, such as digital media. In this respect, Spanish cinema studies need new theoretical tools that can account for these new ways of understanding and expanding our cinematic viewing experience.

References

Acevedo-Muñoz, E. (2004) The Body and Spain: Pedro Almodóvar's *All about My Mother*. *Quarterly Review of Film and Video* 21 (1): 25–38.

Bal, M. (1999) Narrative Inside Out: Louise Bourgeois' Spider as Theoretical Object. *Oxford Art Journal* 22 (2): 101–26.

Ballesteros, I. (2009) Performing Identities in the Cinema of Almodóvar. In: Epps, B. and Kakoudaki, D. (eds.) *All About Almodóvar: A Passion for Cinema*. Minneapolis: University of Minnesota Press, pp. 71–100.

Bennett, J. (2005) *Empathic Vision: Affect, Trauma, and Contemporary Art*. Stanford: Stanford University Press.

Bersani, L. (1986) "The Culture of Redemption": Marcel Proust and Melanie Klein. *Critical Quarterly* 12: 399–421.

Bersani, L. and Dutoit, U. (2009) Almodóvar's Girls. In: Epps, B. and Kakoudaki, D. (eds.) *All About Almodóvar: A Passion for Cinema*. Minneapolis: University of Minnesota Press, pp. 241–66.

Bersani, L. and Phillips, A. (2008) *Intimacies*. Chicago: Chicago University Press.

Butler, J. (1990) *Gender Trouble: Feminism and the Subversion of Identity*. London: Routledge.

Butler, J. (1999) Gender is Burning: Questions of Appropriation and Subversion. In: Thornham, S. (ed.) *Feminist Film Theory: A Reader*. Edinburgh: Edinburgh University Press, pp. 336–49.

Butler, J. (2002) Is Kinship always already Heterosexual? *Differences: A Journal of Feminist Cultural Studies* 13 (1): 14–44.

Butler, J. (2004) *Undoing Gender*. London: Routledge.

Butler, J. (2005) *Giving an Account of Oneself*. New York: Fordham University Press.

Dasgupta, S. (2009) Resonances and Disjunctions: Matrixial Subjectivity and Queer Theory. *Studies in the Maternal* 1 (2): 1–5.

Dean, T. (2009) *Unlimited Intimacy: Reflections on the Subculture of Barebacking*. Chicago: Chicago University Press.

Dean, T. (2010) Sex and the Aesthetics of Existence. *PMLA* 125 (2): 387–92.

De Zeguer, C. (1996) Introduction. In: de Zegher, C. (ed.) *Inside the Visible: An Elliptical Traverse of 20th Century Art in, of, and from the Feminine*. Cambridge, MA: MIT Press, pp. 19–41.

Didi-Huberman, G. (2009) Peuples exposés, peuples figurants. *De(s)générations* 9: 7–17.

Ettinger, B. (1996) Metramorphic Borderlinks and Matrixial Borderspace in Subjectivity as Encounter. In: Welchman, J. (ed.) *Rethinking Borders*. New York: Macmillan, pp. 125–59.

Ettinger, B. (2005) Co-poiesis. *Framework X Ephemera* 5 (10): 703–13.

Ettinger, B. (2006) *The Matrixial Borderspace*. Minneapolis: University of Minnesota Press.

Fer, B. (2004) *The Infinite Line: Remaking Art after Modernism*. New Haven: Yale University Press.

Fowler, C. (2004) Room for Experiment: Gallery Films and the Vertical Time from Maya Deren to Eija Liisa Ahtila. *Screen* 45: 324–41.

Greer-Johnson, J. (2001) Sor Juana Castaño: From *gracioso* to Comic Hero. *South Atlantic Review* 66 (4): 94–108.

Guerin, F. and Hallas, R. (2007) Introduction. In: Guerin, F. and Hallas, R. (eds.) *The Image and the Witness: Trauma, Memory and Visual Culture*. London: Wallflower, pp. 1–20.

Gutiérrez-Albilla, J. D. (forthcoming) Filming in the Feminine: Subjective Realism, Disintegration and Bodily Affection in Lucrecia Martel's *La ciénaga*. In: Nair, P. and Gutiérrez-Albilla, J. D. (eds.) *Hispanic and Lusophone Women Filmmakers: Theory, Practice and Difference*. Manchester: Manchester University Press.

Hand, S. (1996) *Facing the Other: The Ethics of Emmanuel Levinas*. Richmond: Curzon Press.

Harris, G. (1999) *Staging Femininities: Performance and Performativity*. Manchester: Manchester University Press.

Hequembourg, A. (2007) Becoming Lesbian Mothers. *Journal of Homosexuality* 53 (3): 153–80.

Kinder, M. (2005) Reinventing the Motherland: Almodóvar's Brain-dead Trilogy. *Film Quarterly* 5 (2): 9–25.

Kuhn, A. (2009) Screen and Screen Theorizing Today. *Screen* 50 (1): 1–12.

Leighton, T. (2008) Introduction. In: Leighton, T. (ed.) *Art and the Moving Image: A Critical Reader*. London: Tate and Afterall, pp. 7–40.

Maddison, S. (2000) All about Women: Pedro Almodóvar and the Heterosocial Dynamic. *Textual Practice* 14 (2): 265–84.

Martin-Márquez, S. (2004) Pedro Almodóvar's Maternal Transplants: From *Matador* to *All about My Mother*. *Bulletin of Hispanic Studies* 81 (4): 497–509.

O'Bryan, J. (2005) *Carnal Art: Orlan's Refacing*. Minneapolis: University of Minnesota Press.

Pollock, G. (2004) Thinking the Feminine Aesthetic Practice as Introduction to Bracha Ettinger and the Concepts of Matrix and Metramorphosis. *Theory, Culture and Society* 21 (1): 5–65.

Pollock, G. (2007) Notes from a Feminist Front. Unpublished paper given at Feminist Futures: Theory and Practice in the Visual Arts, MoMA, New York (May 26).

Pollock, G. (2009) Mother Trouble: The Maternal-Feminine in Phallic and Feminist Theory in Relation to Bracha Ettinger's Elaboration of Matrixial/Aesthetics. *Studies in the Maternal* 1 (1): 1–31.
Skoller, J. (2005) *Shadows, Specters, Shards: Making History in Avant-garde Film*. Minneapolis: Minnesota University Press.
Smith, P. J. (1999) Silicone and Sentiment. *Sight and Sound* 9 (9): 28–30.
Tuhkanen, M. (2009) Performativity and Becoming. *Cultural Critique* 72: 1–35.
Vernon, K. M. (2009) Queer Sound: Musical Otherness in Three Films by Pedro Almodóvar. In: Epps, B. and Kakoudaki, D. (eds.) *All About Almodóvar: A Passion for Cinema*. Minneapolis: University of Minnesota Press, pp. 51–70.
Warner, M. (1991) Fear of a Queer Planet. *Social Text* 29 (3): 3–17.
Weidner-Maluf, S. (2005) Embodiment and Desire: *All About my Mother* and Gender at the Margins. *Gender Institute New Working Paper Series* 14: 1–17.
Wilson, E. (2003) *Cinema's Missing Children*. London: Wallflower.

Further Reading

Allinson, M. (2001) *A Spanish Labyrinth: The Films of Pedro Almodóvar*. London: I. B. Tauris.
Beugnet, M. and Ezra, E. (2009) A Portrait of the Twenty-First Century. *Screen* 50 (1): 77–85.
Marks, L. (2000) *The Skin of the Film: Intercultural Cinema, Embodiment, and the Senses*. Durham: Duke University Press.
Silverman, K. (1983) *The Subject of Semiotics*. New York: Oxford University Press.
Smith, P. J. (1994) *Desire Unlimited: The Cinema of Pedro Almodóvar*. London: Verso.

21

The Space of the Vampire

Materiality and Disappearance in the Films of Iván Zulueta

Brad Epps

> *The cinema combines, perhaps more perfectly than any other medium, two human fascinations: one with the boundary between life and death and the other with the mechanical animation of the inanimate, particularly human, figure.*
>
> (Laura Mulvey, *Death 24× a Second*, 2006: 11)

> *If the eye were more perceptive it would see the sleight of 24 individual pictures and an equal number of utter blacknesses every second of the show.*
>
> (Stan Brakhage, "The Camera Eye," 2001: 19)

> *What manner of man is this, or what manner of creature is it in the semblance of man?*
>
> (Bram Stoker, *Dracula*, 1998 [1897]: 34)

The eye blinks, often imperceptibly, and in the blink something imperceptible is lost. So too, in a sense, does the camera, where the shutter blots out what then becomes a sliver of the profilmic image, losing it in the interstitial spaces of the frames. So too does the projector, where the shutter blocks light – reflected and condensed – three times per frame, twenty-four frames a second, in order to ensure a smooth and steady sense of apparent motion – the so-called flicker fusion threshold – rather than a blearing of static images. For all their obvious differences, in all three ocular apparatuses, one fleshly and two mechanical, continuity and plenitude are illusory, part and parcel of a powerfully persistent myth of the persistence of vision, with its ghost- or after-images, whose perceived clarity and sharpness – crucial to dominant realist practice – are the effects of an unperceived blinking, blotting, and blocking. In celluloid-based films, the blink, linked to the flicker, is, however, of a visible, even palpable order – *there* for all to see and touch in the form

A Companion to Spanish Cinema, First Edition. Edited by Jo Labanyi and Tatjana Pavlović.

of the filmstrip with its sequence of images that alternate with interstitial non-images. Once the filmstrip is unspooled, illuminated, and projected at the appropriate speed, the interstitial non-images, usually black, slip from view. The result is a double disappearance, in which the "original" non-image of the camera is whirled out of sight as the film is projected onto a screen. As Mary Ann Doane (2002: 172) notes, almost forty percent of the running time of any celluloid-based film is invisible: "much of the movement or the time allegedly recorded by the camera is simply not there, lost in the interstices between frames" and lost – again, if differently – in the regulated rush of the projected filmstrip. The full and uninterrupted flow of reality recorded is therefore only apparent because the entire shebang is, as Doane (2002: 172) so beautifully puts it, "haunted by absence, by the lost time represented by the division between frames," a division that editing both redoubles and reorders.

"As a reinscription of the gap between film frames, editing potentially constitutes a persistent reminder of the abyss of darkness that subtends cinema" (Doane 2002: 185). Doane's existentially canny description, in which cinema is related to haunting absences and abyssal lacks, proves especially apt for Iván Zulueta, who is one of the most passionately celebrated and studied of Spanish "cult" filmmakers within his native land but whose work is little known outside it. In Zulueta's editorially capable hands, the play of division, disappearance, and loss that informs celluloid-based processes of recording, editing, and projection is deliberately courted in a welter of short experimental films throughout the 1970s that culminate, as it were, in his most memorable feature film: *Arrebato / Rapture*, shot in 1979, just a few momentous years after the death of the dictator Francisco Franco. Virtually unnoticed by the public at large when it premiered in 1980, *Arrebato* – which I shall be examining in a deliberately fractured and suspended manner – nonetheless captured the fancy of a number of film critics, professionals, and devotees, and has grown in stature to become an object of scrutiny and celebration that belies, even as it feeds upon, the film's relatively low-budget, previously marginalized status. A drug-driven, metacinematic tale of vampirism in which a Super 8 camera armed with an interval timer plays the part of Dracula, *Arrebato* was not only at odds with the lion's share of cinematic production in a country that was still coming to terms with nearly forty years of National-Catholic censorship, but was also subject to censorship of a more internationally urbane kind when the Cannes and Berlin film festivals refused to screen it on the grounds that its homoerotic and quasi-suicidal portrayal of the rituals of heroin consumption, central to its exploration of the artificial paradises of cinematic rapture, was too strong (Torres 2002: 19–20).

Distinguished by its amoral depiction of drugs, *Arrebato* is also characterized by its self-referential exposition of the mechanics and materials of filmmaking, showcasing almost everything from the camera lens, the filmstrip, and the frame to the Moviola, the projector, and the publicity poster (a genre in which Zulueta excelled as a graphic designer). At the elusive heart of *Arrebato*'s autobiographically inflected story of drugs and movies as interchangeable habits in need of fixes lie both a

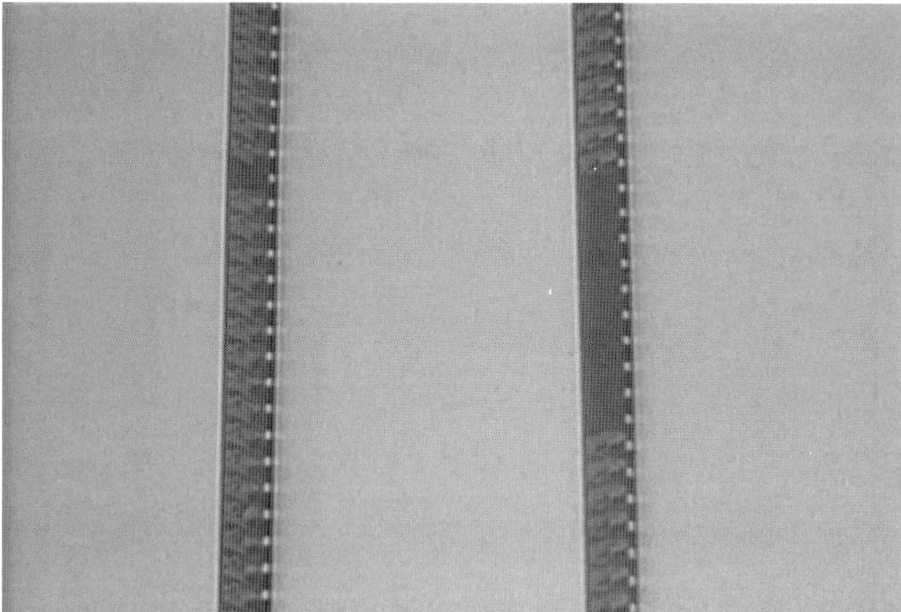

Figure 21.1 The growth of the red photogram (*Arrebato*, Iván Zulueta, 1980; prod. Nicolás Astiarraga PC).

delirious search for the precise pause in the stream of images – the verb "arrebatar" means, among other things, "to suspend or captivate the senses" – and a mysterious red photogram that expands over the filmstrip as the bodies filmed waste away and/or vanish (see Figure 21.1). The emphasis on filmstrips, frames, and pauses in *Arrebato* is such that "the invisible art" of editing is brought into view even as it is exposed as being bound to darkness and to what one of the protagonists calls, shortly before leaving his country house for the city (as did Dracula), "a thousand hidden rhythms." According to Augusto M. Torres (2005: 338), the film's executive producer, Zulueta, spent six or seven months editing the film but only one shooting it. Carlos Heredero (1989: 136), author of a lengthy monographic study, likewise underscores Zulueta's commitment to "segmentación sincopada" (syncopated segmentation), a phrase that recalls Luis Buñuel's understanding of montage, in which segmentation is explicitly likened to cellular creation: "lo que antes no era, ahora es" (what before was not, now is) (Buñuel 1982: 171). Far from adhering to famed professional editor Walter Murch's (2001: 25) assertion that "it is necessary to create a barrier, a cellular wall between shooting and editing," Zulueta moves between the two, prioritizing, if anything, the hands-on act of editing that appears, twice, at the opening of *Arrebato* and that undergirds the film's insistence on cuts, blinks, flickers, pauses, intervals, and disappearances.[1] Fernando de Felipe's (2005) felicitous summation of Zulueta's practice as "el abismo en el parpadeo" (the abyss in the blink of an eye) resonates, thus, with the idea of editing as a reinscription

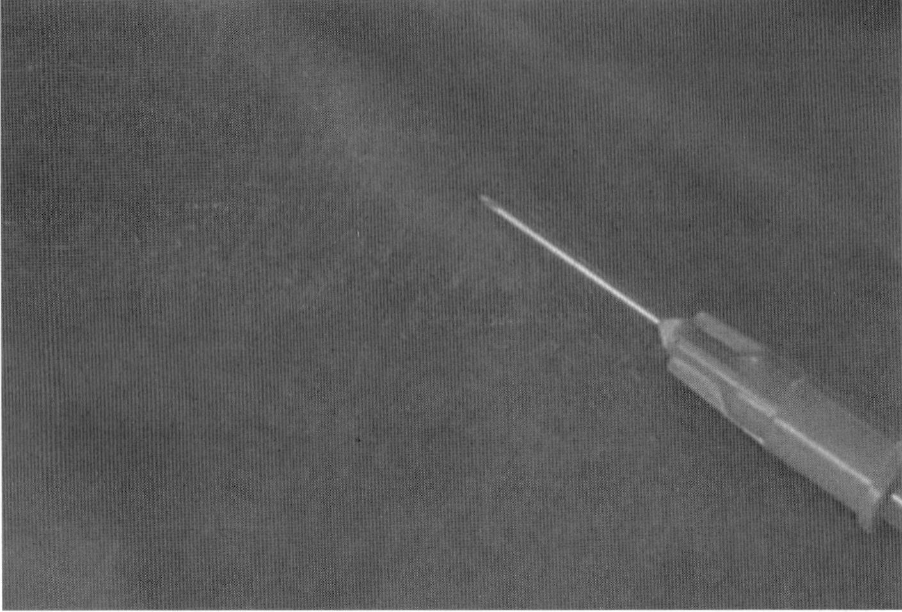

Figure 21.2 Piercing the skin (*Arrebato*, Iván Zulueta, 1980; prod. Nicolás Astiarraga PC).

of the interstices of the filmstrip and as a potential reminder of the loss that subtends cinema more generally.[2]

Filmstrips, the erstwhile material basis of editing, are intermittently present throughout *Arrebato*, realistically ensnaring and cutting one of the two filmmaking protagonists on his neck near the beginning – underscored in the published film script (Zulueta 2002: 30), the scene was apparently cut, along with nearly eighty minutes of the first working copy (Pérez Rubio 2005: 41), even though the two red marks on the character's neck remain visible in the final version – and fantastically engulfing and con-fusing both of them at the end in the single motile frame that remains visible in a filmstrip that has become otherwise entirely red. From two tiny red fleshly marks to one long red celluloid swath, *Arrebato* revives an etymological and isomorphic relation between skin and "pellicule," a Latinate word for a diaphanous tissue whose closest cognate, in Spanish, is "película," the word commonly used to designate a film in the cinematographic sense. The relationship between the natural covering of the body and the artificial strip coated with light-sensitive emulsion is even more imposing in Spanish, where the words for "skin" (*piel*) and "film" (*película*) remit to the same root. That film captures only the epidermis of corporeal phenomena (even when a body is pierced, as with a needle, or opened up, as in an autopsy) is a truism whose symbolic ramifications are well known: as the camera reproduces and immortalizes, it also arrests and dematerializes, proffering shells without souls (see Figure 21.2). It is thus not surprising that some of the most theoretically sophisticated critics of *Arrebato* profess a desire to stay with the surface, asserting, in contrast to the dark logic of vampire tales and the hermeneutic force of their own theorizations, that the film hides nothing, shows everything (Gómez Tarín 2001: 62; Cerdán and Fernández Labayen 2005: 281).

Now, although it undeniably brings many of its mechanisms to the proverbial surface of sight, *Arrebato* remains fraught with darkness and loss, with the *beneath* and *beyond* of chronological time that ecstasy and rapture alluringly promise. Figuratively charged though darkness and loss are, the editing process that is so crucial to Zulueta's film that it becomes narrative fodder has nevertheless come to be implicated in a more material loss: that of the filmstrip itself. Alberto Mira notes how *Arrebato*, as *film*, elicits a "yearning [that] audiences in the post domestic video era will fail to grasp to its full extent. Even in 1979 films were experiences firmly rooted in a present time which was lost after leaving the cinema only to be fondly remembered with all kinds of distortions" (2009: 162–3). The loss of a spectatorial experience in which darkened theaters, often inaccessible prints, and a lack of control over the flow of the images were all signal components dovetails with the loss of a directorial and editorial experience in which Moviolas and Steenbecks, filmstrips, and the physical cutting and joining of images were fundamental. The current tendency to experience movies in the privacy of one's home is adumbrated, however, in the incorporation of homemade Super 8 shorts and televised broadcasts of previous 35 mm features into *Arrebato*, whose vampiric tale of intersubjective relations between men is nourished by intermedial relations between machines. Accordingly, although most studies on Zulueta are understandably rife with auteurist comparisons, interfilmic references, and observations on the specificities of Spanish culture at a time of political transition, *Arrebato* also gestures to a transition of a more technological sort: from film to video and, albeit only virtually, from analog to digital.

Indeed, so attuned is *Arrebato* to the transitional and transformative varieties of cinematic production that a number of critics, most notably Vicente Benet (2005), Vicente Sánchez-Biosca (2005), and Santos Zunzunegui (2005), see it as allied to the "death" of (filmic) cinema and hence as gesturing, just possibly, to what Garret Stewart and others call "postfilmic cinema"; that is, cinema that has undergone the transition from photochemical impression to algorithmic computation and in which "intervals and interstices have been replaced by the flux and reflux of internal conversions" (Stewart 2007: 15). Benet, for whom *Arrebato* comprises nothing less than an allegory of the death of cinema, is especially intent on viewing the film not just retrospectively, in relation to the Spanish transition and the history of cinema, but also prospectively, as auguring a "transformación tecnológica digirida hacia otros horizontes que primero serán fundmentalmente electrónicos y después digitales" (technological transformation directed to other horizons that at first will be fundamentally electronic and then digital) (2005: 317). Here, too, the allegorical or figurative has material implications. After all, as D. N. Rodowick styles it, "the material basis of film is a chemically encoded process of entropy. This is one of many ways in which watching a film is literally a spectatorship of death" (2007:

Figure 21.3 The vampire in the filmstrip (*Arrebato*, Iván Zulueta, 1980; prod. Nicolás Astiarraga PC).

20). The figurative death of cinema hinges, in short, on the material disappearance of film in the form of a strip that erodes over time and occasionally bursts into flames, as does the vampire's coffin in the black-and-white neo-expressionist filmstrip near the beginning of *Arrebato* (see Figure 21.3).

With *Arrebato*, the disappearance *of* the filmstrip – and not just the disappearance *between* its frames – that marks the "afterlife" of celluloid-based films in an age of increasingly interactive digitalization has, as intimated, an uncannily prescient cast, figured in yet another disappearance: that of diegetic bodies *into* a single kinetic frame. In Stewart's suggestive phrase, "film appears before us bit by bit, but – unlike the physics of the digit – not all within a single composite image. Rather, [...] filmic imaging is strung out, rung by cellular rung, along the vertical spool of its own incremental passage" (2007: 11). Bit by bit, but perhaps also bite by bite, the "strung out" imaging of celluloid-based products is, in *Arrebato*, the stuff of vampiric, drug-induced figurations, as is the final fantasy of a single composite image in which the two protagonists come movingly together. It is here that *Arrebato* gestures to something more digital than analog: rather than a succession of photo-like images and interstitial non-images interrupted by a single mysterious red photogram that appears earlier in the film, by the end of the film the entire filmstrip within it has waxed red – save one lone frame that continues to move even though the projector is stopped. And it is here, moreover, that the film's insistence on the pause as a rapturous (a)temporal suspension – of which more later – is fantastically realized. A contradiction in terms, "fantastic realization" is nonetheless apposite to *Arrebato*'s ambivalent engagement of opposites, where it is less a question of everything being surface *or* depth, experimentation *or* narration, materiality *or* figuration than of an oscillating, flickering, promiscuous *in-between*.

Before *Arrebato* saw the light of day, Zulueta had honed his craft in the homiest of manners, manhandling film so that, to poach again from Stewart, "the strip, with the resulting activity of the track, [made] itself felt in, and against, the conveyed on-screen action" (2007: 9). Stewart's phrase, fitting for *Arrebato*, is especially so for the shorts that preceded it, notable among them *Kinkón* (1971), *Frank Stein* (1972), *Aquarium* (1975), *A Mal Gam A* (1976), *El mensaje es facial* / *The Message is Facial* (1976), and *Leo es pardo* / *Leo is Dark* (1976). As if in confirmation of Stan Brakhage's dictum, "realize the garden as you will – the growing is mostly underground" (2001: 18), Zulueta, who had come to know New York underground cinema during a visit to the city in 1964, returned to his native land filled with desire to go down a path already traced by such directors as Brakhage in *Window Water Baby Moving* (1959) and Andy Warhol in *Sleep* (1963). Before the underground experimentation of the 1970s, Zulueta had participated, however, in a number of commercial ventures, most importantly a television variety show called *Último grito* / *The Latest Craze* (1968–70) and, in 1969, his first feature film, *Un, dos, tres, al escondite inglés* / *One, Two, Three, Hide and Seek*, a decade before his second – and last – feature film, *Arrebato*. Taking its cues from Richard Lester's Beatles-driven romps, which the Francoist system barely tolerated, and setting its sights on the Eurovision song contest, *Un, dos, tres* offers a deliciously perverse incursion into consumer culture: a group of "alternative" pop musicians, who congregate in a record store called *Ugh!* in which no records are for sale, sets about murdering the official Spanish candidates for the contest – after, to be sure, each group has performed its respective ditty. The film, which on a formal level seems light years from Zulueta's experimental shorts, nonetheless conveys an irreverence toward Spain and the presumably enlightened and carefree Europe into which many Spaniards desired to lose themselves in order, supposedly, to find themselves anew.

The rhetoric of losing and finding oneself anew resonates with Zulueta's homemade experimental shorts, in which the poverty of his technical means and the censorial oppressiveness of the Spanish state issue in a plethora of fluid, fluctuating identities, claustrophobic interiors, mock-anguished expressions of bodily aggression and repulsion, and, especially in *A Mal Gam A*, images that veer into abstraction. The very title of *A Mal Gam A* makes visible a syllabic principle whose filmic counterpart is the division between the frames, thereby undercutting the meaning of the word "amalgam" (a blend, alloy, or emulsion), which is related, in turn, to the Greek word "malagma," meaning "emollient," a preparation that softens and soothes the skin. Given Zulueta's attention to the pellicule of film and given his fondness for images of amorphous – or polymorphous – substances from foaming seas to gurgling toilets, chewing-gum to silly putty, and swaying reeds to the twinkling of silver halides on photographic plates, it may not be entirely excessive to venture that *A Mal Gam A* suggests a Deleuzian "flow-cut," a "desiring machine" in which streams and circuits are arrested, broken apart, and fluidly rerouted: the word cut into its minimal syllables, the image into its minimal photographic units, and the insolubly fluid tension between them, suspension itself.

Excessive as the reference to desiring machines may be, it bears noting that excess is intrinsic to the rapturous states of becoming that propel *Arrebato*, the film for which Zulueta has attained "cult" status and thanks to which his experimental shorts have enjoyed a second life. "Ecstasy," or "rapture," entails a "standing outside" the self, a radical self-displacement, overcoming, and loss. That there may be something malignant and malicious in this ecstatic standing outside oneself is hinted at in the one syllable of *A Mal Gam A* that is a self-standing noun: *Mal*, which in Spanish conveys a sense both of sickness and of evil. That there may also be something cinematic here is borne out by the fact that cinema involves as its very condition of possibility a process of duplication and projection by which people and things, lights and shadows, are, in a very real – and yet eerily unreal – sense placed outside and beyond themselves. The fact that Zulueta plays the part of Jim Self not only supports Matt Losada's (2010: 6) claim that *A Mal Gam A* is the "most autobiographical of Zulueta's experimental films" but also saps it, inasmuch as "él mismo" – "himself" – is both *translated* and *deformed* as "Jim Self." In other words, Zulueta is arguably at his most autobiographical – and cinematic – when he displaces himself as someone, or something, not quite himself.

What comes into view is yet another tension, perhaps the most excessive and rapturous of all: the death drive and the pleasure principle, whose most poetic formulation continues to be the mystic's "I die because I do not die." That the mystic's adage rings true also for the vampire, the "living dead," is perhaps only one of its more unholy ironies. Whatever the case, in *A Mal Gam A*, as Losada observes: "the subjectivity of an enraptured Zulueta is linked through eyeline-matches to images defamiliarised by alterations in speed, repeated zooms and other manipulations, images that oscillate between the scatological and the sacred: images of toilets and flowing silly putty are juxtaposed with decayed religious iconography" (2010: 6). Had Losada followed the flow of the silly putty, a synthetically soft silicone polymer marketed as a plaything for children, he might have noted that it reappears throughout *Arrebato* as the constant companion of one of the two protagonists, the furtive, child-like amateur filmmaker Pedro P. (Will More) and, most strikingly, in the final scene in which Pedro, already absorbed into the world of visual machines, beckons to the other protagonist, José Sirgado (Eusebio Poncela), a disillusioned professional filmmaker, to join him. As José blindfolds himself, curls up in Pedro's bed, and awaits the final series of shots by which he too will be "disappeared" into the filmstrip, he clutches a crumpled white bed sheet, a kind of anticipatory shroud, while through his clinched fists oozes a mass of flesh-colored silly putty: as if he were losing his grip on both profilmic and diegetic reality and gradually dissolving into someone, something, else (see Figure 21.4).[3]

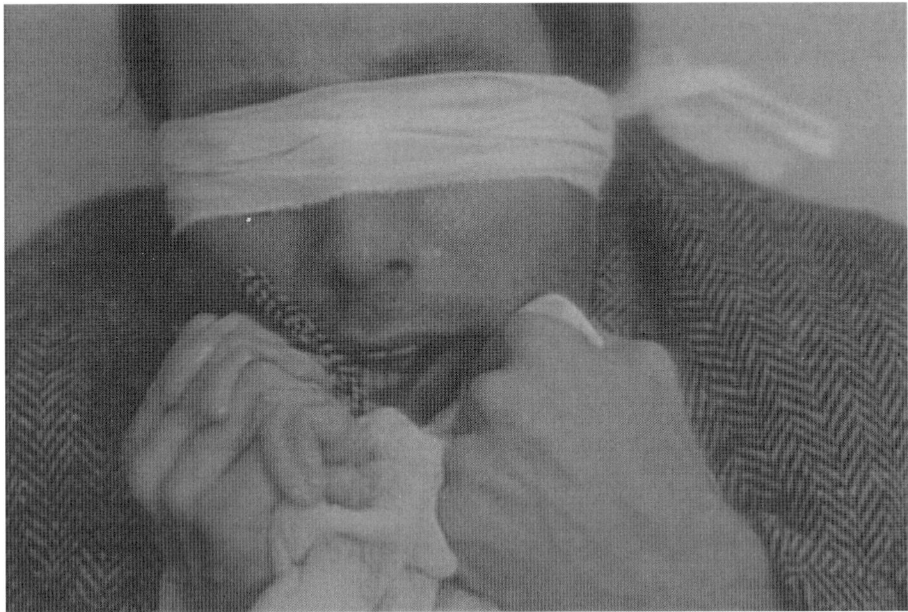

Figure 21.4 José (Eusebio Poncela) dissolving (*Arrebato*, Iván Zulueta, 1980; prod. Nicolás Astiarraga PC).

The image of flowing flesh gives greater heft to the back-and-forth dissolves between Pedro and José (reminiscent, as some critics have noted, of Ingmar Bergman's subtly vampiric *Persona*, 1966), in which the face of one man is superimposed onto the face of another. The flow-cut of flesh and film is also on display in *Aquarium*, a Super 8 short that features the same pallid, lanky actor (Will More) who will later play the part of the obsessive and rapturous home-moviemaker in *Arrebato*. *Aquarium* includes a brief sequence in which More, in the confines of Zulueta's apartment in the Edificio de España, at the time one of the few "skyscrapers" in the Spanish capital, vomits up some sardines while holding a telephone in his hand. The image of More's body heaving in gastric convulsion is intercut with a close-up of a woman who, as if looking at herself in a mirror, cracks a partial smile, removes her glasses, and daubs her chin, a gesture that More rather prissily performs after vomiting up the sardines into the unfolded pages of a newspaper. Arising from the couch, More, as if echoing the act of vomiting, throws the contents of the sardine-soaked newspaper up and out of a window of the high-rise. What the spectator next sees are sardines spread out on asphalt as a cane, wielded by the same woman who had appeared before, shunts them about. The camera then closes in on the woman's face, now upturned, and then, by way of a jagged dissolve, to the upper reaches of the building as time-lapsed clouds appear to "scrape" it. The quality of the image is poor and grainy; the sound absent; the interstices of the frames jarringly visible; and the filmed bodies, in and out of the space of the director's home, anything but stably domesticated.

Many of the details in *Aquarium* are caught up, however, in a decidedly less personal circuit: not just that of the New York underground but also that of the European avant-garde. As Heredero, Alberte Pagán, and others have noted, the cane prodding at sardines is a reworking of the cane prodding at a severed hand that appears as a "found object" after a series of overlapping dissolves – a cupped and punctured palm swarming with ants, a hairy underarm, a sea urchin – in Buñuel and Dalí's *Un chien andalou* (1929). There are other winks to Buñuel in other of Zulueta's films: for instance, in *Leo es pardo*, an androgynous woman strives to defend herself from a doppelgänger aggressor by retreating into a corner, a stance repeatedly assumed in *Un chien andalou*.[4] In yet another confusion of corporeal identities, the doppelgänger aggressor, wearing a leopard-skin print dress (a camouflage motif that also appears in *A Mal Gam A*), seems to stare at her "other" self – the same actress, Maribel Godínez, plays both parts – from behind a set of oversized sunglasses as she spits up, or devours in reverse, a piece of fruit. Zulueta's recourse to filming in reverse in this and other films brings into play yet another avant-garde master, Dziga Vertov (1984: 131), who called reverse motion the "negative of time." Filming in reverse is only one of the techniques that Vertov celebrated in the form of the kinetic, mechanical "eye" of the camera: "Kino-eye makes use of every possible kind of shooting technique: acceleration, microscopy, reverse action, animation, camera movement, the use of the most unexpected foreshortenings – all these we consider to be not trick effects but normal methods to be fully used" (Vertov 1984: 88). Zulueta, for whom Vertov is as fruitful a model as Buñuel and Brakhage, clearly concurs.

One amateur and the other professional, the protagonists of *Arrebato* are both men with movie cameras. The designation is not incidental. Vertov's *Man with a Movie Camera* (1929), which Lev Manovich has called "a true orgy of cinematography" and "a database of new interface operations" (2001: xxviii, xxx), attempts to realize the Kino-eye objectives of the conquest of time and space (Vertov 1984: 87–8) that are most tantalizingly at play in the final scene of *Arrebato*. And yet, long before that scene, whose capacity to captivate is the effect of a confluence of experimentation and narration, Zulueta mines other "normal methods" advocated by Vertov for abnormal effect, most insistently reverse motion's ostensible opposite: acceleration. Zulueta's most acute exercises in acceleration – and appropriation – can be found in two other shorts, *Frank Stein* and *Kinkón*, which rework two classic horror films from the 1930s, *The Bride of Frankenstein* (James Whale, 1935) and *King Kong* (Ernest B. Shoedsack and Merian C. Cooper, 1933). In both cases, Zulueta shoots the films directly from television and then accelerates and condenses them to only a few minutes each (*Aquarium* also includes shots of *The Bride of Frankenstein* on television). The upshot is a kinetic flickering and blurring of films past, their verbal titles distorted no less than their visual contents. As with the syllabic division of *A Mal Gam A*, the spooling cathode rays of the television recall the intervals between the filmic photogram and serve as reminders that *Frank Stein* and *Kinkón* have been *doubly* mediated, recycled, and reanimated, like the blood that courses through the veins of vampires.

Importantly, the films that Zulueta reworks, and replays, as experimental are commercial horror ventures, similar to the more modern *Count Dracula* (Jesús Franco, 1970), whose shooting the more resolutely experimental Pere Portabella took as the material for *Vampir-Cuadecuc* (1969–70) and *Umbracle* (1971–2), in which high-contrast black-and-white film stock and large segments of silence conjure up the glimmering origins of cinema and comment on the long vampiric night of Francoism. Despite his brushes with the agents of Francoism who confiscated and "disappeared" a number of his experimental shorts (Heredero 1989: 133–67), Zulueta's recycling of previous cinematic material is more disenchanted, politically speaking, than Portabella's, whose leftist commitment remains legible even when his films appear most opaque. Apolitical as well as amoral (which is perhaps to say political and moral *otherwise*), many of Zulueta's films, *Arrebato* among them, evince a de-eroticized depletion and an agoraphobic weariness with the new, so different from Vertov's enchanted enthusiasm for tracking the novelty of urban exteriors. Although Alberte Pagán (2005: 136) adduces Vertov's masterpiece to argue that *Arrebato*'s reliance on plot devices, such as the vampiric personification of the camera, deprives it of experimental value (as if time had stood still between late 1920s Moscow and late 1970s Madrid), it is possible to view, and valorize, *Arrebato* as effecting a wily transposition of experimentation into narrative by which experimentation, long the province of intellectual elites, is made to "stand outside itself" and is brought confusingly into contact with its commercially abjected other, the B-movie horror genre that José cultivates.

Such a transposition is of a piece with the transfusions, transformations, and transgressions that run throughout stories of vampires and other bastard hybrids such as Frankenstein's monster or the wolf man, the subject of José's previous film in *Arrebato*. But transposition is also of a piece with a generalized recycling or retrofitting in which pre-existing images, objects, and ideas, their aura all but lost, are found anew. In *Arrebato*, these "found objects," so dear to the avant-garde, include both an accelerated sample of *Go West Young Man* (Henry Hathaway, 1936), which is playing on the television when Pedro and José first see each other reflected on its screen, and an unspecified number of travelogues by Zulueta's friend and collaborator Jaime Chávarri – coauthor of the screenplay for *Un, dos, tres* and celebrated director of the documentary *El desencanto / The Disenchantment* (1976) – which play the part of Pedro's home movies (Torres 2002: 18–19). Pedro's movies are thus doubly homey, their uncanny charge heightened in the process. Projected onto a screen with a Super 8 camera and then filmed with a 35 mm one (Torres 2002: 18–19), Chávarri's home movies are at the recycled core of *Arrebato* and, as such, are critical to Pedro's frenzied search for the elusive "pause." As an interval, the pause offers perhaps the most compelling tie to Vertov, whose "theory of intervals" Zunzunegui perceptively brings into play with Pedro's filmmaking practice within Zulueta's film (2005: 328). According to Vertov (1984: 8), "*Intervals* (the transitions from one movement to another) are the material, the elements of the art of movement, and by no means the movements themselves. It is they (the intervals) which draw the movement to kinetic resolution." Despite the synthetic ring of the phrase, "kinetic resolution," like "fantastic realization," is something of a contradiction in terms, the quietude generally associated with resolution being the effect, in *Arrebato*, of a movement that continues – to the very end.

In *Arrebato*, the end is prefigured from the very beginning in the close-up of the filmstrip that Pedro pieces together from fragments hanging taped to a window and in the black-and-white filmstrip that José edits with the combative assistance of a professional editor, a filmstrip whose frames depict a female vampire who issues from a coffin and looks directly, defiantly, invitingly at the camera. The look prompts the professional editor to declare the shot to be worthless, but José, the disenchanted director, begs to differ, calling out "para, para, para" (stop, stop, stop) at the very moment that the shot, which the editor would leave behind and discard, appears on screen. The first moment of dramatic tension in *Arrebato* revolves, that is, around the voraciously unsettling look of both the vampire and the camera and the emotionally charged question as to where to cut the film and bring it to a stop. Although José's "para" (stop) may not be the same as Pedro's "pausa" (pause), it nonetheless shadows it forth as a problem of timing, whose chronological dimension has been personified, most strikingly by Goya, as an old man who feeds on the flesh of others, not unlike a vampire. It is in the scene in the editing room, moreover, that José, sporting vampire teeth and the previously mentioned red cut on his neck, comically announces that it is not that he likes the cinema but rather that the cinema likes him (the Spanish "gustar," which also means "to taste," reinforces the voracious cast of the statement). The cinema that comes to like him to the point of devouring him is not, however, the commercial cinema that is on display as he drives down Madrid's Gran Via after leaving the studio but rather the errant and erratic home movies of his friend and possible lover, Pedro.[5]

Although Pedro has already briefly appeared in the very first scene, his presence and relationship to José have yet to be "fleshed out." Rather, another body appears as José arrives home from the studio and the Gran Via: that of his drug-drowsy, half-naked, on-and-off girlfriend Ana (Cecilia Roth). Voluptuous as Ana's flesh and pouty as her painted lips surely are, it is instead a mysterious package from Pedro containing Super 8 footage, a video cassette, and a key that captures José's attention and fires his desire. All three main characters – José, Ana, and Pedro – partake of heroin, though in the case of Pedro his drug, as we soon learn via an extensive flashback, is not so much heroin as the Super 8 movies that he films at his secluded country house. Before the flashback, though, there is a painstakingly close depiction of the ritual of heroin consumption, after which José, flying high but moving slowly, begins to listen to the cassette and, later, to see the film. Filling the frame, the cassette is the material anchor of what Michel Chion (1994), drawing on the musical theories of Pierre Schaeffer, calls an "acousmatic" sound; that is to say, a sound that is heard but whose source remains obscured. Its source, as the opening scene makes clear, is Pedro, but for José it is a mechanical object that he activates with a touch of a finger and through which he reactivates a disembodied voice. The voice is raspy, barely a whisper, and, though diegetically tethered to both Pedro and the recorder, it is, tellingly enough, the voice of Zulueta himself (or Jim Self) who dubs what pass for Pedro's recorded utterances. The recurrent voiceover – thus rendered spectrally authorial and its provenance thereby vertiginously complicated – proceeds to urge José to look at, devour, and digest the filmic material in the package before going to Pedro's tiny, bare-bones flat in Madrid for the final installment.

The injunction to devour and digest amplifies, obviously enough, the vampiric imagery that has already flitted across the screen, but it also alters it: rather than the blood-drenched mouth of the female vampire on the filmstrip in the editing room, the encounter that the voice announces is toothless, the sprockets of the camera and projector ultimately proving more seductive than any bloody kiss. It is surely no accident that Pedro, hardly a leading man, is never more seductive than when mediated, for, although José had twice met him in Pedro's country home, it is only after listening to the tape and seeing the film, which captures the disappearance of Pedro's cousin Marta by the camera, that José experiences an apparently uncontrollable urge to go to him, join him. Pedro is a sinister, yet at times quite humorous, parody of Peter Pan, a creature who shudders in rapture at the click of the camera's shutter and who surrounds himself with comic books, music boxes, miniature theaters, red-eyed mechanical dolls, and other now quaintly antique playthings of childhood. The convulsive bouts of cinematic ecstasy that Pedro experiences every time he replays what he has filmed – and that neuropsychologists have related to the stroboscopic effects of filmic flicker – indicate that the rapture that will bind these two men together, Pedro and José, is of an unsettlingly familiar, even infantile sort, a mode of excess that relies on a regress to the sense of the marvelous that most "normal" adults have lost but that most "normal" children practice daily. In fact, the only moment in *Arrebato* in which José smiles in rapt fascination at his former lover Ana is when she dolls it up as Betty Boop, prancing in the light of a projector (see Figure 21.5).

And yet, the regress to childhood, implicit in the case of José, and the refusal to leave childhood, explicit in the case of Pedro, is anything but sweet and reassuring (though it is at times quite "funny"). For, what comes to bind the two men together is not merely their passion for cinema – a passion that Pedro reignites in José by way of his Méliès-like investment in the animating possibilities of inanimate objects – but also, and more intricately, their passion for the temporal pause or interval between instants, which is all but inseparable from the spatial gap between photograms. Fascinated by Pedro's passion for a practice that had become tedious for him, José, who also gives Pedro a particularly gooey form of silly putty, presents him with yet another gift, one made to the measure of his obsession with the pause: a "temporizador," which in English is both a "trimmer"

Figure 21.5 A nostalgic projection: Cecilia Roth camps it up as Betty Boop (*Arrebato*, Iván Zulueta, 1980; prod. Nicolás Astiarraga PC).

and a "timer," a chronometric device that allows Pedro to measure time, cut it up, move and manipulate it to his making. Like the cassette player and the Moviola, the timer – a Canon interval timer, to be precise – is presented in extreme close-up, cradled in the palm of Pedro's avid hand. It is this ever-so-timely gift that seals the relationship between the two men, a relationship that Torres (2002: 20) unhesitatingly describes as "homosexual" but that might best be rendered as "queer," in the sense of a twisting, bending, or crossing over and into the alternative "world" of celluloid itself. For it is ultimately *to* the filmstrip, not to the bed, that Pedro, already "at home" in the one lone frame that remains on the now entirely red filmstrip, beckons José to come by submitting himself, blindfolded and clench-fisted, to the rapid time-released fire of the Canon. And it is ultimately *in* the filmstrip that the two men might be seen – and, of course, not seen – as coming together.

There is, undoubtedly, something residually avant-garde in this rapturously queer overcoming of sequential time – one moment, one frame, after another – in favor of an encounter in a single, flickeringly framed space of a filmstrip that, if rerun through a projector at "normal" speed, might well be lost in the blink of an eye. For his part, Ivan Zulueta, after a lengthy reclusion in his family home in San Sebastian, a prolonged, perhaps half-hearted struggle with addiction, and sporadic, perhaps half-hearted attempts to make a "comeback," died in 2009. He lives on, like everyone who has been caught in the eye of a camera, in the never-never land of cinema, whose once prolific pauses, interstices, intervals, and luminous traces are themselves, increasingly, the stuff of dreams past.

Notes

1 In *Arrebato*, the professional director and editor are two separate individuals who argue, amicably, about editing; their relationship, however, disappears after the opening scene and is quickly replaced by a more disconcerting relationship between the professional filmmaker and an amateur one.

2 One of the last films Zulueta presented in public is a 16 mm short entitled *Párpados / Eyelids*, made in 1989 for the Spanish television program *Delirios de amor / Deliriums of Love*.

3 Like a mystic, bound to mystery, José closes and conceals his eyes in order, it seems, to experience an inner vision – another, paradoxical, way of "seeing" and of being.

4 *Leo es pardo* plays on the Spanish word for "leopard" as well as on the phrase "de noche todos los gatos son pardos," which literally means "by night all cats are grey" but that suggests an often morally charged inability to discern differences, a con-fusion of identities.

5 In his drive along the Gran Via, José sees the latest cinematic offerings to have invaded Spain (*Superman, The Deer Hunter, Oliver's Story, L'umanoide, Phantasm*, all from 1978 and 1979) announced alongside older ones (*Bambi* and *Quo Vadis*, from 1942 and 1951 respectively). The scene suggests that, try as he might, José, as a Spanish director, has little if any place in such an internationally market-driven world.

References

Benet, V. J. (2005) La materia del instante. In: Cueto, R. (ed.) *Arrebato... 25 años después*. Valencia: Ediciones de la Filmoteca, pp. 301–18.

Brakhage, S. (2001) The Camera Eye. In: *Essential Brakhage: Selected Writings on Filmmaking by Stan Brakhage*. Kingston: McPherson, pp. 14–23.

Buñuel, L. (1982) "Découpage" o segmentación cinegráfica. In: *Obra literaria*. Zaragoza: Heraldo de Aragón, pp. 171–4.

Cerdán, J. and Fernández Labayen, M. (2005) Ucro-topías: Tiempos transmodernos (acercamiento a las visiblidades de una película superficial). In: Cueto, R. (ed.) *Arrebato... 25 años después*. Valencia: Ediciones de la Filmoteca, pp. 277–300.

Chion, M. (1994) *Audio-Vision: Sound on Screen*. New York: Columbia University Press.

De Felipe, F. (2005) El abismo en el parpadeo. In: Cueto, R. (ed.) *Arrebato... 25 años después*. Valencia: Ediciones de la Filmoteca, pp. 195–218.

Doane, M. A. (2002) *The Emergence of Cinematic Time: Modernity, Contingency, the Archive*. Cambridge, MA: Harvard University Press.

Gómez Tarín, F. J. (2001) *Guía para ver y analizar "Arrebato."* Valencia: Nau Llibres / Octaedro.

Heredero, C. (1989) *Iván Zulueta: La vanguardia frente al espejo*. Alcalá de Henares: Festival de Cine de Alcalá de Henares.

Losada, M. (2010) Iván Zulueta's Cinephilia of Ecstasy and Experiment. *Senses of Cinema*. Online at: www.sensesofcinema.com/2010/feature-articles/ivan-zulueta (accessed July 11, 2011).

Manovich, L. (2001) *The Language of New Media*. Cambridge, MA: MIT Press.

Mira, A. (2009) The Dark Heart of the Movida: Vampire Fantasies in Iván Zulueta's *Arrebato*. *Arizona Journal of Hispanic Cultural Studies* 13: 155–69.

Mulvey, L. (2006) *Death 24× a Second: Stillness and the Moving Image*. London: Reaktion Books.

Murch, W. (2001) *In the Blink of an Eye: A Perspective on Film Editing*, 2nd edn. Los Angeles: Silman-James Press.

Pagán, A. (2005) Residuos experimentales en *Arrebato*. In: Cueto, R. (ed.) *Arrebato… 25 años después*. Valencia: Ediciones de la Filmoteca, pp. 113–39.

Pérez Rubio, P. (2005) Escrituras para la democracia: Reforma pactada vs. ruptura radical. In: Cueto, R. (ed.) *Arrebato… 25 años después*. Valencia: Ediciones de la Filmoteca, pp. 19–43.

Rodowick, D. N. (2007) *The Virtual Life of Film*. Cambridge, MA: Harvard University Press.

Sánchez-Biosca, V. (2005) *Arrebato* / *Rapture*: Iván Zulueta, Spain, 1980. In: Mira, A. (ed.) *The Cinema of Spain and Portugal*. London: Wallflower Press, pp. 169–77.

Stewart, G. (2007) *Framed Time: Toward a Postfilmic Cinema*. Chicago: University of Chicago Press.

Stoker, B. (1998 [1897]) *Dracula*. Oxford: Oxford University Press.

Torres, A. M. (2002) Mi personal *Arrebato*. In: Zulueta, I. *Arrebato: Guión cinematográfico*. Madrid: Ocho y Medio, pp. 7–21.

Torres, A. M. (2005) *Arrebato*. In: Cueto, R. (ed.) *Arrebato… 25 años después*. Valencia: Ediciones de la Filmoteca, pp. 333–42.

Vertov, D. (1984) *Eye: The Writings of Dziga Vertov*. Berkeley: University of California Press.

Zulueta, I. (2002) *Arrebato: Guión cinematográfico*. Madrid: Ocho y Medio.

Zunzunegui, S. (2005) Y los fantasmas vinieron a su encuentro. In: Cueto, R. (ed.) *Arrebato… 25 años después*. Valencia: Ediciones de la Filmoteca, pp. 319–30.

Further Reading

Aguilar, C. (1997) Arrebato. In: Pérez Perucha, J. (ed.) *Antología crítica del cine español, 1906–1995*. Madrid: Cátedra/Filmoteca Española.

Cueto, R. (ed.) (2005) *Arrebato … 25 años después*. Valencia: Ediciones de la Filmoteca.

Sánchez-Biosca, V. (1994) El pastiche y su límite en el discurso audiovisual español de los ochenta. *Revista Canadiense de Estudios Hispánicos* 18 (3): 469–78.

Tranche, R. R. (1995) Cine español (1975–1992): Otras prácticas, otras escrituras. *Revista Canadiense de Estudios Hispánicos* 20 (1): 143–50.

Index

Page numbers in *italics* signify images.

A Companion to Spanish Cinema, First Edition. Edited by Jo Labanyi and Tatjana Pavlović.